3 EDITION

SPECIAL EDUCATION

in CONTEMPORARY SOCIETY

This book is dedicated with love and appreciation to my family.

—RMG
April 2008

3^{EDITION}

SPECIAL EDUCATION
in CONTEMPORARY SOCIETY

An Introduction to Exceptionality

RICHARD M. GARGIULO
University of Alabama at Birmingham

Los Angeles • London • New Delhi • Singapore

For information:

 SAGE Publications, Inc.
2455 Teller Road
Thousand Oaks, California 91320
E-mail: order@sagepub.com

SAGE Publications Ltd.
1 Oliver's Yard
55 City Road
London EC1Y 1SP
United Kingdom

SAGE Publications India Pvt. Ltd.
B 1/I 1 Mohan Cooperative Industrial Area
Mathura Road, New Delhi 110 044
India

SAGE Publications Asia-Pacific Pte. Ltd.
33 Pekin Street #02-01
Far East Square
Singapore 048763

Printed in Canada

Library of Congress Cataloging-in-Publication Data

Gargiulo, Richard M.
Special education in contemporary society : an introduction to exceptionality/Richard M. Gargiulo.—3rd ed.
    p. cm.
Includes bibliographical references and index.
ISBN 978-1-4129-6317-6 (pbk.)
   1. Special education—United States. I. Title.

LC3981.G37 2009
371.9—dc22   2008022446

This book is printed on acid-free paper.

08   09   10   11   12   10 9 8 7 6 5 4 3 2 1

Acquisitions Editor:	Steve Wainwright
Associate Editor:	Deya Saoud
Editorial Assistant:	Julie McNall
Developmental Editor:	Elise Caffee
Production Editor:	Laureen A. Shea
Interior Designer:	Ravi Balasuriya
Typesetter:	C&M Digitals (P) Ltd.
Proofreader:	Jenifer Kooiman
Indexer:	Diggs Publication Services
Cover Designer:	Candice Harman
Marketing Manager:	Christy Guilbault

About the Author

I have always wanted to be a teacher. I guess I am a rarity in that I never changed my undergraduate major nor left the field of education. Teaching must be in my blood. I grew up in Staten Island, New York, in the shadows of Willowbrook State School, a very large residential facility serving individuals with developmental disabilities. As I recall, my initial exposure to people with disabilities probably occurred when I was about 10 or 12 years of age and encountered some of the residents from Willowbrook enjoying the park that was adjacent to their campus. This experience made a huge impression on me and, in some unknown way, most likely instilled within me a desire to work with people with disabilities.

I left New York City in 1965 and headed west—all the way to western Nebraska where I began my undergraduate education at Hiram Scott College in Scottsbluff. Three years later I was teaching fourth graders in the Milwaukee public schools while working toward my master's degree in mental retardation at the University of Wisconsin–Milwaukee. At the conclusion of my first year of teaching I was asked to teach a class of young children with intellectual disabilities. I jumped at the opportunity and for the next three years essentially became an early childhood special educator. It was at this point in my career that I decided to earn my doctorate. I resigned my teaching position and moved to Madison, where I pursued a Ph.D. in the areas of human learning, child development, and behavioral disabilities. Upon receiving my degree I accepted a faculty position in the Department of Special Education at Bowling Green State University (Ohio), where for the next eight years I was a teacher educator. In 1982 I moved to Birmingham, Alabama, and joined the faculty of the University of Alabama at Birmingham, where I currently serve as a professor in the Department of Leadership, Special Education, and Foundations.

I have enjoyed a rich and rewarding professional career spanning more than three decades. During the course of this journey I have had the privilege of twice serving as President of the Alabama Federation, Council for Exceptional Children, and also as President of the Division of International Special Education and Services (DISES), Council for Exceptional Children. I have lectured abroad extensively and was a Fulbright Scholar to the Czech Republic in 1991. I mentioned earlier that teaching has always been my passion. In 1999 I was fortunate to receive UAB's President's Award for Excellence in Teaching. In 2007 I received the Jasper Harvey award from the Alabama Council for Exceptional Children in recognition of being named the outstanding teacher educator in the state.

With a background in both educational psychology and special education my research has appeared in a wide variety of professional journals including *Child Development, Journal* of *Educational Research, Journal of Learning Disabilities, American Journal of Mental Deficiency, Childhood Education, Journal of Visual Impairment and Blindness, British Journal of Developmental Psychology, Journal of Special Education, Early Childhood Education Journal, International Journal of Clinical Neuropsychology,* and the *International Journal of Special Education,* among others.

In addition to the present text, I have authored or coauthored six other books, ranging in topics from counseling parents of children with disabilities, to child abuse, early childhood education, and my most recent one, young children with special needs.

Brief Contents

Detailed Contents

PART I. Foundations of Special Education

PART II. A Study of Individuals with Special Needs

7. Individuals with Attention Deficit Hyperactivity Disorder 243

8. Individuals with Emotional or Behavioral Disorders 275

9. Individuals with Autism Spectrum Disorders 325

Special Features

Making Inclusion Work

Suggestions for the Classroom

Preface

Special Education in Contemporary Society is first and foremost a textbook about people—individuals who, in many ways, are very much just like you. Yet these individuals happen to be recognized as exceptional—either as someone with a disability or someone with unique gifts and talents. Second, this book serves as a comprehensive introduction to the dynamic field of special education and the children and young adults who benefit from receiving a special education. My intention in writing Special Education in Contemporary Society was to provide you with a readable, research-based book that also stresses classroom application. By blending theory with practice, my aim was to provide teachers-in-training and practicing professionals with the knowledge, skills, attitudes, and beliefs that are so crucial to constructing learning environments that allow all students to reach their potential. I also wanted to portray the "human" side of special education. The field of special education is much more than meetings, forms, legal issues, or specific instructional strategies; it is about children and their families—their frustrations and fears, but perhaps more important, it is also about their accomplishments and triumphs. As a father of four daughters, I have traveled this rocky road. Each of my girls is recognized as exceptional: three are gifted and one has a disability. To me, special education is real. I confront it on a daily basis—it is my passion. I hope that by studying this book you too will develop an appreciation for and an understanding of the children whose lives you will touch.

Audience

Special Education in Contemporary Society was written for two primary audiences. First are those individuals preparing to become teachers, either general educators or special educators. Because meeting the needs of students with exceptionalities is often a shared responsibility, this book is also appropriate for professionals who work with individuals with special needs. Physical therapists, school psychologists, orientation and mobility specialists, and speech-language pathologists are only a few of the individuals who share in the responsibility of providing an appropriate education.

Organization of the Text

The first four chapters constitute Part I and focus on broad topics affecting all individuals with an exceptionality; these chapters are foundational for the remainder of the book. Chapter 1 introduces the field of special education, providing an overview of important terms, the prevalence of children and young adults with disabilities, and a framework for understanding exceptionality. An overview of important litigation and legislation, the identification and assessment of individual differences, the development of meaningful individualized instructional programs, and the issue of where students with exceptionalities are to be served are addressed in Chapter 2. In Chapter 3 we examine cultural and linguistic diversity and its relationship to exceptionality. The final chapter of Part I looks at issues confronting the parents and families of individuals with special needs.

Part II consists of ten chapters that thoroughly examine particular categories of exceptionality using a life-span approach. We will talk about intellectual disabilities; learning disabilities; attention deficit hyperactivity disorder; emotional and behavioral disorders; autism spectrum disorders; speech and language impairments; hearing impairments; visual impairments; and physical disabilities, health disabilities, and related low-incidence disabilities; we conclude by looking at individuals who are gifted and talented. Despite the diversity of these topics, each chapter follows a fairly consistent format. You will learn definitions, historical information, prevalence, causes, characteristics, assessment techniques, educational considerations, services for young children as well as adults, family issues, diversity, the role of technology, and current trends and controversies. Each chapter in Part II begins with a vignette offering a personal perspective on the exceptionality you will be studying. These stories should remind you that you are learning about real people who confront a myriad of issues that most individuals will never have to deal with.

Key Features of the Text

In order to make this textbook meaningful, practical, and also enjoyable to read, we have incorporated several distinct features. These learning tools include the following:

- Chapter-opening vignettes in the categorical chapters, primarily written by parents of children with disabilities, that offer personal stories on the exceptionality studied in a specific chapter. Through these vignettes, students gain a firsthand, vivid account of these parents, their fears and frustrations, their accomplishments and triumphs, and the issues they face on a daily basis.
- Instructional strategies, tips, techniques, and other ideas can be found throughout the text in boxes identified as "Suggestions for the Classroom."
- "FYI" features contain relevant information that adds depth and insight to particular discussion topics.
- "First Person" features add a human touch to the information students are learning. These stories, written by or about individuals with exceptionalities, provide an up close and personal encounter with children, adults, and families.
- Special and general educators offer candid perspectives and practical advice about providing services to students with special needs in inclusive settings in the "Making Inclusion Work" features.
- Each chapter concludes with study questions designed to help you focus on key chapter content and gauge your understanding of the material. A series of learning activities bring the content to life. Many of these suggested activities ask you to engage in a wide variety of meaningful and worthwhile tasks. Additionally, you will find a list of professional organizations and associations that you may wish to contact for additional information about a topic of particular interest.

New to This Edition

You are probably aware that the first and second editions were published by Thomson Learning (now Cengage). I'm very pleased that SAGE will publish the third edition and that it will be a key title on their growing list of special education textbooks. In addition to its key hallmarks, the new edition will incorporate the following new features and content:

- "Effective Instructional Practices" boxes in the "Educational Considerations" section of each chapter of Part II. This feature includes targeted teaching strategies and suggestions.
- New content on deaf-blindness in Chapter 13: Individuals with Physical Disabilities, Health Disabilities, and Related Low-Incidence Disabilities and refined attention to students with physical and health disabilities.
- New coverage of Response to Intervention in Chapter 6: Individuals with Learning Disabilities.
- CEC, Praxis II, and INTASC standards in the appendices, with integration grids that tie the CEC and INTASC standards into chapter content. Each chapter ends with two "Reflecting on Standards" exercises tied to the CEC knowledge and skill standards.

Supplemental Materials

Additional ancillary materials further support and enhance the learning goals of the third edition of *Special Education in Contemporary Society: An Introduction to Exceptionality*. These ancillary materials include the following:

STUDENT STUDY SITE http://www.sagepub.com/gargiulo3estudy

This Web-based student study site provides a variety of additional resources to build on students' understanding of the book content and extend their learning beyond the classroom. Students will have access to a sample Individualized Education Program and an Individualized Family Service Plan, in addition to the following features for each chapter:

- Chapter quizzes with 25 multiple-choice and true/false questions
- Key term flashcards
- Media links
- Full-text SAGE journal articles and discussion questions
- Additional Web resources and Internet activities

INSTRUCTOR'S RESOURCES ON CD-ROM The new Instructor's Resources on CD-ROM provide one integrated source for all instructor materials, including the following key components for each chapter:

- A PowerPoint presentation
- A lecture outline
- Classroom activities
- Discussion questions

- Web resources
- Suggested answers to end-of-chapter study questions
- A test bank available both in Word format and in Brownstone's Diploma Test Bank software for test creation and customization. Specific question types are as follows:
  a. 35 multiple-choice questions
  b. 10 true/false questions
  c. 10 short-answer questions
  d. 5 essay questions

VIDEOS To promote student discussion and learning in the classroom, adopters can receive videos on key topics, such as RTI, Co-Teaching, and Differentiated Instruction. For more information, or to request a copy of the Instructor's Resources on CD-ROM or the video DVD, contact Customer Care at (800) 818-7243.

Acknowledgments

Writing a textbook is a team effort, and this one is no exception. I owe a huge debt of gratitude to several friends and colleagues who shared my vision for this book and were also gracious enough to contribute their talents and expertise by writing chapters. I wish to publicly thank them for their hard work, dedicated effort, and patience with my compulsive behavior and attention to detail.

- Lou Anne Worthington, University of Alabama at Birmingham, "Individuals with Emotional or Behavioral Disorders"
- Karen B. Dahle, University of Alabama at Birmingham, "Individuals with Autism Spectrum Disorders"
- Betty Nelson, University of Alabama at Birmingham, "Individuals with Hearing Impairments"
- Carol Allison and Mary Jean Sanspree, University of Alabama at Birmingham, "Individuals with Visual Impairments"
- Kathy W. Heller, Georgia State University, "Individuals with Physical Disabilities, Health Disabilities, and Related Low-Incidence Disabilities"
- Julia L. Roberts, Western Kentucky University, "Individuals Who Are Gifted and Talented"

I am especially grateful to the many individuals who reviewed the third edition of this book. Their guidance and professional expertise, eye for accuracy, and thoughtful suggestions contributed immensely to making this edition of *Special Education in Contemporary Society* a market leader. I applaud and deeply appreciate the generous assistance of the following individuals: J'Anne Affeld, Northern Arizona University; Mark Alter, New York University; Michele Augustin, Washington University in St. Louis; Emiliano C. Ayala, Sonoma State University; Pam Baker, George Mason University; Andrew Beigel, Keuka College; Kristin Bewick, Wilkes University; Cheryl Camenzuli, Molloy College; Domenico Cavaiuolo, East Stroudsburg University; Walter Cegellka, St. Thomas University; Patricia Morris Clark, University of Maine at Augusta; Jo Beth DeSoto, Wayland Baptist University; Beverly Doyle, Creighton University; Teresa Gardner, Jacksonville State University; Heather Garrison, East Stroudsburg University; Annette Gorton, Miles Community College; Janice Grskovic, Indiana University Northwest; Robert Harrington, University of Kansas; Thienhuong Hoang, California State Polytechnic University, Pomona; Jack Hourcade, Boise State University; Sheila Dove Jones, Bloomsburg University of Pennsylvania; Juanita Kasper, Edinboro University of Pennsylvania; Donna Kearns, University of Central Oklahoma; Craig Kennedy, Vanderbilt University; Ava Kleinmann, Western New England College; Michelle LaRocque, Florida Atlantic University; Marcel Lebrun, Plymouth State University; DeAnn Lechtenberger, Texas

Tech University; Diane K. Mann, Edinboro University of Pennsylvania; Maria L. Manning, James Madison University; Nancy Marchand-Martella, Eastern Washington University; Teresa Oettinger Montani, Fairleigh Dickinson University; Rita Mulholland, The Richard Stockton College of New Jersey; Charolette Myles-Nixon, University of Central Oklahoma; Kimberely Fletcher Nettleton, Morehead State University; Ashley A. Northam, Chemeketa Community College; Holly Pae, University of South Carolina Upstate; Lee R. Pearce, Black Hills State University; Nicole Phillips, Daemen College and Frontier Central School District; Shaila Rao, Western Michigan University; Saleem `A Rasheed, Indiana University Northwest; Bruce A. Shields, Daemen College; Dale Smith, Alvernia College; Angela Snyder, Virginia Commonwealth University; Terry Spigner, University of Central Oklahoma; David W. Steitz, Nazareth College of Rochester; Suzanne Swift, Eastern New Mexico University; Ron Tinsley, Richard Stockton College of New Jersey; Sheila Marie Trzcinka, Indiana University Northwest; Tandra Tyler-Wood, University of North Texas; Linda B. Walker, Kent State University; Ronald P. Weitzner, Cleveland State University; Julia Wilkins, St. Cloud State University; Denise Winsor, University of Nevada, Las Vegas; Penelope Wong, Centre College; Ann K. Yehle, University of Wisconsin–Madison; and Cheryl Zaccagnini, Shippensburg University.

I would also like to thank those who reviewed the first and second editions, including Gary Stephen Allison, Mary Barbera, Jeanne Bauwens, Nettye Brazil, George Calhoun, Christine Fitch, Harold C. Griffin, Edward Helmstetter, Jack Hourcade, Paul McKnab, Maurice Miller, William Morrison, Joe Nolan, Dennis Nulman, Richard K. Simmons, Donald Stauffer, Donald J. Stedman, Linda Wheeler-Griffin, Lisa Altemueller, Martha A. Cocchiarella, Steven A. Crites, Steven Daley, Richard Dickson, Joyce Anderson Downing, Mary Bailey Estes, Richard W. Fee, Lisa M. Lauer, Richard L. Luftig, Michael R. Mayton, Breeda McGrath, Margaret T. McLane, Charolette Myles-Nixon, Ruth Nash-Thompson, Jerry D. Neal, Richard C. Nowell, John Palladino, William Thomas Southern, Marcee M. Steele, Shannon Stuart, Shirley E. Thompson, Sheri Trent, Robert J. Walden, Kathleen Waldron-Soler, Donna Wandry, Gail D. Zahn, and Victoria Townsend Zascavage.

I had the privilege of working with an outstanding and very talented team of professionals at Sage Publications, who took my jumbled ideas, poor sentence structure, and sometimes inaccurate references and turned them into a superb and scholarly book. Thank you for your support, enthusiasm, and confidence in me.

I will always be grateful for the encouragement, creative vision, professionalism, and gentle spirit of my editor, Steve Wainwright. Steve's enthusiasm for this project and his editorial competency are clearly evident throughout this book. A huge debt of gratitude is also due to Elise Caffee, developmental editor. Elise always made me feel as though no other book was more important than mine. Her insightful suggestions, attention to the smallest of details, and "no problem" attitude along with her pleasant demeanor made my job so much easier. Julie McNall served as my primary contact person throughout the evolution of this book. She helped me to maintain critical deadlines, answered countless questions, calmly dealt with my compulsiveness, and saw to it that this textbook actually made it to print. Jenifer Kooiman is a copy editor/proofreader par excellence. Thank you, Jenifer, for helping to produce such a reader-friendly book.

So many other individuals, many of whom labored behind the scenes, also contributed to the development of a book of which I am very proud to be the author. I deeply appreciate the dedicated efforts of those who created the supplemental materials for the Instructor's Resources CD, including Ron Tinsley, Richard Stockton College of New Jersey, who created the classroom activities and discussion questions; Heather Garrison, East Stroudsburg

University, who created the PowerPoint slides and lecture outlines; Laura E. Pierce, J. L. Gibson, Robert C. Pennington, Melinda Jones Ault, Ann Katherine Griffen, and Donald M. Stenhoff of the University of Kentucky, who created the test bank; and Teresa Gardner, Jacksonville State University, who created the sample syllabi and suggested answers for the study questions. Also critical were the efforts of those who worked on the student study site, including Terry Spigner and Charolette Myles-Nixon of the University of Central Oklahoma.

One other group of professionals whose contributions add a very practical perspective to this book are the educators who willingly shared their experiences and insights about working in inclusive settings: Susan Brennan, Catherine Davis, Erin de Haven, Astrid Freeman, Tonya Perry, Sarah Reynolds, Teresea Teaff, and Jennifer J. Tumlin. Thank you for sharing your expertise with the readers.

I would be remiss if I did not honor and praise those individuals who contributed to the First Person features and the chapter-opening vignettes. A very special thank-you for telling your story. The ability of each and every one of you to poignantly share an aspect of your lives added immensely to the "human side" of this text—a goal that I hope I achieved.

Finally, a very special acknowledgment is reserved for my family, who survived my 3:30 A.M. wake-up calls; struggled with my attempts at balancing the roles of husband, father, and author; and also understood why this book was personally so very important to me. Thank you. I love you dearly.

PART I

Foundations of Special Education

CHAPTER 1

Special Education in Context

People, Concepts, and Perspectives

We are all different. It is what makes us unique and interesting human beings. Some differences are obvious, such as our height, the color of our hair, or the size of our nose. Other features are not so readily discernible, such as our reading ability or political affiliation. Of course, some characteristics are more important than others. Greater significance is generally attached to intellectual ability than to shoe size. Fortunately, appreciation of individual differences is one of the cornerstones of contemporary American society.

Although most people would like to be thought of as "normal" or "typical" (however defined), for millions of children and young adults this is not possible. They have been identified and labeled by schools, social service agencies, and other organizations as exceptional, thus requiring special educational services. This textbook is about these individuals who are exceptional.

You are about to embark on the study of a vibrant and rapidly changing field. Special education is an evolving profession with a long and rich heritage. The past thirty years in particular have been witness to remarkable events and changes. It is truly an exciting time to study human exceptionality. You will be challenged as you learn about laws and litigation affecting students with special needs, causes of disability, assessment techniques, and instructional strategies, to mention only a few of the topics we will present. But perhaps more important than any of these issues is our goal to help you develop an understanding and appreciation for a person with special needs. We suspect that you will discover, as we have, that individuals with disabilities are more like their typically developing peers than they are different. People with disabilities and those without disabilities share many similarities. In fact, we believe that special education could rightly be considered the study of similarities as well as differences.

Finally, we have adopted a people-first perspective when talking about individuals with disabilities. We have deliberately chosen to focus on the person, not the disability or specific impairment. Thus, instead of describing a child as a "retarded student," we say a "pupil with mental retardation" or "a student with cognitive impairments." This style reflects more than just a change in word order; it reflects an attitude and a belief in the dignity and potential of people with disabilities. The children and adults whom you will learn about are first and foremost people.

Definitions and Terminology

Teachers work with many different types of pupils. Let's take a look at some of the children in the fifth-grade class of Daniel Thompson, a first-year teacher. As in many other classrooms across the United States, most of his students are considered to be educationally typical; yet five youngsters exhibit special learning needs. Eleven-year-old Victoria, for instance, is a delightful young girl with a bubbly personality who is popular with most of her classmates. She has been blind since birth, however, as a result of a birth defect. Miguel is shy and timid. He doesn't voluntarily interact with many of his classmates. This is his first year at Jefferson Elementary. Miguel's family only recently moved into the community from their previous home in Mexico. Mr. Thompson tells us that one boy is particularly disliked by the majority of his classmates. Jerome is verbally abusive, prone to temper tantrums, and on several occasions has been involved in fights on the playground, in the lunchroom, and even in Mr. Thompson's classroom despite the fact that his teacher is a former college football player. Mr. Thompson suspects that Jerome, who lives with his mother in a public housing apartment, might be a member of a local gang. Stephanie is teased by most of her peers. Although many of her classmates secretly admire her, Stephanie is occasionally called "a nerd," "a dork," or "Einstein." Despite this friendly teasing, Stephanie is always willing to help other students with their assignments and is sought after as a partner for group learning activities. The final student with special learning needs is Robert. Robert is also teased by his fellow pupils, but for reasons opposite to Stephanie. Robert was in a serious automobile accident when he was in kindergarten. He was identified as having cognitive delays in the second grade. Sometimes his classmates call him "retard" or "dumbo" because he asks silly questions, doesn't follow class rules, and on occasion makes animal noises that distract others. Yet Robert is an exceptional athlete. Everyone wants him on their team during gym class.

As future educators, you may have several questions about some of the students in Mr. Thompson's classroom:

- Why are these pupils in a general education classroom?
- Will I have students like this in my class? I'm going to be a high school biology teacher.
- Are these children called disabled, exceptional, or handicapped?
- What does *special education* mean?
- How will I know if some of my students have special learning needs?
- How can I help these pupils?

One of our goals in writing this textbook is to answer these questions as well as address other concerns you may have. Providing satisfactory answers to these queries is not an easy task. Even among special educators, confusion, controversy, and honest disagreement exist about certain issues. As you continue to read and learn, acquire knowledge and skill, and gain experience with individuals with disabilities, we hope you will develop your own personal views and meaningful answers.

Exceptional Children

Both general and special educators will frequently refer to their students as **exceptional children.** This inclusive term generally refers to individuals who differ from societal or community standards of normalcy. These differences may be due to significant physical, sensory, cognitive, or behavioral characteristics. Many of these children may require educational programs customized to their unique needs. For instance, a youngster with superior intellectual ability may require services for students identified as gifted; a child with a visual impairment may require textbooks in large print or Braille. However, we need to make an important point. Just because a pupil is identified as exceptional does not automatically mean that he or she will require a special education. In some instances, the student's educational needs can be met in the general education classroom by altering the curriculum and/or instructional strategies.

Children with disabilities are first and foremost children.

We must remember that exceptionality is always relative to the social or cultural context in which it exists. As an illustration, the concept of normalcy, which forms an important part of our definition of exceptionality, depends on the reference group (society, peers, family) as well as the specific circumstances. Characteristics or behaviors that might be viewed as atypical or abnormal by a middle-aged school administrator might be considered fairly typical by a group of high school students. Normalcy is a relative concept that is interpreted or judged by others according to their values, attitudes, and perceptions. These variables, along with other factors such as the culture's interpretation of a person's actions, all help to shape our understanding of what it is to be normal. Is it normal

- To use profanity in the classroom?
- For adolescent males to wear earrings or shave their head?
- To run a mile in less than four minutes?
- To study while listening to the stereo?
- To always be late for a date?
- To stare at the floor when reprimanded by a teacher?
- To be disrespectful to authority figures?
- To wear overly large, yet stylish, clothes?

The answer, of course, is that it all depends.

Disability versus Handicap

On many occasions, professionals, as well as the general public, will use the terms *disability* and *handicap* interchangeably. This is incorrect. These terms, contrary to popular opinion, are not synonymous but have distinct meanings. When talking about a child with a **disability,** teachers are referring to an inability or a reduced capacity to perform a task in a specific way. A disability is a limitation imposed on an individual by a loss or reduction of functioning, such as the paralysis of leg muscles, the absence of an arm, or the loss of sight. It can also refer to problems in learning. Stated another way, a disability might be thought of as an incapacity to perform as other children do because of some impairment in sensory, physical, cognitive, or other areas of functioning. These limitations only become disabilities when they interfere with a person's attainment of his or her educational, social, or vocational potential.

The term **handicap** refers to the impact or consequence of a disability, not the condition itself. In other words, when we talk about handicaps, we mean the problems or difficulties that a person with a disability encounters as he or she attempts to function and interact with the environment. We would like to extend this definition and suggest that a handicap is more than just an environmental limitation; it also can reflect attitudinal limitations imposed on the person with the disability by people without disabilities.

Individuals with disabilities often encounter various forms of discrimination in their daily lives, which frequently limits their full participation in society. As a result, some would suggest that these citizens are "marginalized and excluded from mainstream society" (Kitchin, 1998, p. 343). Sadly, in some ways, this is an accurate portrayal of contemporary life in America despite the ongoing efforts of activists and the disability rights movement, which seeks to end discrimination on the basis of disabilities. In fact, the term **handicapism** was coined more than three decades ago to describe the unequal and differential treatment experienced by those with a disability (Bogdan & Biklen, 1977).

A disability may or may not be a handicap, depending on specific circumstances and how the individual adapts and adjusts. An example should help clarify the differences between these two concepts. Laura, a ninth grader who is mathematically precocious, uses a wheelchair because of a diving accident. Her inability to walk is not a problem in her calculus class. Architectural barriers at her school, however, do pose difficulties for her. She cannot access the water fountain, visit the computer lab on the second floor, or use the bathroom independently. When describing Laura in these situations, we would be correct in calling her handicapped. It is important that professionals separate the disability from the handicap.

Gargiulo and Kilgo (2005) remind us that an individual with a disability is first and foremost a person, a student more similar to than different from his or her typically developing classmates. Just because a pupil is identified as having a disability should never prevent us from realizing just how typical he or she is in many other ways. As teachers, we must focus on the child not the impairment, separate the ability from the disability, and see the person's strengths rather than weaknesses. The accompanying First Person feature provides an example of this thinking. Also see Suggestions for the Classroom (page 8) when writing about or discussing individuals with disabilities.

Developmentally Delayed and At-Risk

Before we can answer the question "What is special education?" we have two more terms to consider: *developmentally delayed* and *at-risk*. These labels are incorporated in federal legislation (PL 99-457 and PL 108-446, discussed in Chapter 2) and are usually used when referring to infants and preschoolers with problems in development, learning, or other areas of functioning. Although these terms are incorporated in our national laws, Congress failed to define them, leaving this responsibility to the individual states. As you can imagine, a great deal of diversity can be found in the various interpretations, and no one definition is necessarily better than another. The result is the identification of a very heterogeneous group of youngsters.

Each state has developed specific criteria and measurement procedures for ascertaining what constitutes a **developmental delay.** Many states have chosen to define a developmental delay quantitatively, using a youngster's performance on standardized developmental assessments. In one state, a child might be described as being delayed if her performance on a standardized test is at least 25 percent below the mean for children of similar chronological age in one or more developmental areas such as motor, language, or cognitive ability. In another state, the determination is made when a preschooler's score on an assessment instrument is two or more standard deviations below the mean for youngsters of the same

First Person

Perceptions and Impressions

As a woman in my early 40s with cerebral palsy, I can readily reflect on how I am perceived by those who are not disabled. I was born with cerebral palsy, which affects my motor skills. I contend that it is much easier to be born with a disability than to acquire one later in life—I don't know what it is like to be "normal."

I am very blessed in being more independent than I ever dreamed would be possible! I drive an unadapted car, work part-time for a law firm, and live alone with help from a wonderful outside support team. I'm active in my church and in community affairs, serving on the board of the Independent Living Center as well as other activities. I'm a member of a local United Cerebral Palsy sports team. As you can see, not much grass grows under my feet!

Throughout my life, I have encountered many and varied reactions to my disability. Some people see me as a person who happens to be disabled. It is wonderful to be around them. They accept me as "Elizabeth." Yes, my speech is, at times, difficult to understand. Yes, I'm in constant motion. But these people see me first and can look beyond my disability, many times forgetting it. I am able to be myself!

When I do need assistance, all I have to do is ask. I have a strong family pushing me to be as independent as possible. I'm grateful to my stepfather, who said "You can do it!" My mother, afraid I might fall, was hesitant but supportive. My siblings have been great encouragers. I have many friends who are able to see beyond my disability.

I have also met people who have not been around individuals with physical disabilities. I can easily spot those who are uncomfortable around me. Sometimes, after being around me for a while, they may get used to me and then feel quite comfortable. In fact, when people ask me to say something again, rather than nodding their heads pretending to understand me, it shows that they care enough about what I said to get it right.

From those who feel uncomfortable around me, I usually get one of two reactions: "Oh, you poor thing!" or "You're such an inspiration—you're a saint to have overcome cerebral palsy!" I realize people mean well, but I see right through their insecurities. Think about some of their comments. I'm not a "thing," I'm an individual. I have the same thoughts, dreams, and feelings as anyone else.

Many times I am perceived as being retarded, even though I have a college degree. When I'm in a restaurant, my friend may be asked, "What does she want?" One day I was getting into the driver's seat of my car and a lady inquired, "Are you going to drive that car?" I kept quiet but I thought, "No, it will drive itself!" Recently, while flying home from Salt Lake City, the flight attendant asked my friend if I understood how the oxygen worked. I chuckled to myself. I have been flying for over thirty years! Furthermore, my former roommate had lived with an oxygen tank for three years, and we were constantly checking the flow level. (In defense of airlines, I must say that I have been treated with great respect.)

For those who say I am an inspiration, I can respond in one of two ways. I can take the comment as a sincere compliment and genuinely say, "Thank you." On the other hand, I can see it as an off-the-cuff remark. Those who say that I inspire them may be thinking, "I'm glad I'm not like her" or "Boy, she goes through so much to be here." As I stated earlier, I do things differently, and it takes me longer. But I have learned to be patient and the importance of a sense of humor. I am very grateful to have accomplished as much as I have.

SOURCE: E. Ray, personal communication.

chronological age. Each approach has its advantages and disadvantages. What is really important, however, is that the pupil be identified and receive the appropriate services (Gargiulo & Kilgo, 2005).

The use of the broad term *developmentally delayed* is also in keeping with contemporary thinking regarding the identification of young children with disabilities. Because of the

Suggestions for the Classroom

Suggestions for Communicating about Individuals with Disabilities

As a teacher, you are in a unique position to help shape and mold the attitudes and opinions of your students, their parents, and your colleagues about individuals with disabilities. Please consider the following points when writing about or discussing people with disabilities:

☑ **Do not focus on a disability** unless it is crucial to a story. Avoid tear-jerking human interest stories about incurable diseases, congenital impairments, or severe injury. Focus instead on issues that affect the quality of life for those same individuals, such as accessible transportation, housing, affordable health care, employment opportunities, and discrimination.

☑ **Do not portray successful people with disabilities as superhuman.** Even though the public may admire superachievers, portraying people with disabilities as superstars raises false expectations that all people with disabilities should achieve at this level.

☑ **Do not sensationalize a disability** by saying "afflicted with," "crippled with," "suffers from," or "victim of." Instead, say "person who has multiple sclerosis" or "man who had polio."

☑ **Do not use generic labels** for disability groups, such as "the retarded" or "the deaf." Emphasize people, not labels. Say "people with mental retardation" or "people who are deaf."

☑ **Put people first,** not their disability. Say "woman with arthritis," "children who are deaf," or "people with disabilities." This puts the focus on the individual, not the particular functional limitation. Because of editorial pressures to be succinct, we know it is not always possible to put people first. If the portrayal is positive and accurate, consider the following variations: "disabled citizens," "nondisabled people," "wheelchair user," "deaf girl," and "paralyzed child." "Crippled," "deformed," "suffers from," "victim of," "the retarded," and "infirm" are never acceptable under any circumstances.

☑ **Emphasize abilities,** not limitations. For example, say "uses a wheelchair/braces" or "walks with crutches," rather than "confined to a wheelchair," "wheelchair-bound," or "is crippled." Similarly, do not use emotional descriptors such as "unfortunate" or "pitiful."

☑ **Avoid euphemisms** in describing disabilities. Some blind advocates dislike "partially sighted" because it implies avoiding acceptance of blindness. Terms such as "handicapable," "mentally different," "physically inconvenienced," and "physically challenged" are considered condescending. They reinforce the idea that disabilities cannot be dealt with upfront.

☑ **Do not imply disease** when discussing disabilities that result from a prior disease episode. People who had polio and experience aftereffects years later have a "postpolio disability." They are not currently experiencing the disease. Do not imply disease with people whose disability has resulted from anatomical or physiological damage (such as a person with spina bifida or cerebral palsy). Reference to disease associated with a disability is acceptable only with chronic diseases, such as arthritis, Parkinson's disease, or multiple sclerosis. People with disabilities should never be referred to as "patients" or "cases" unless their relationship with their doctor is under discussion.

☑ **Show people with disabilities as active** participants in society. Portraying persons with disabilities interacting with nondisabled people in social and work environments helps break down barriers and open lines of communication.

SOURCE: Developed by the Research and Training Center on Independent Living, University of Kansas, Lawrence.

detrimental effects of early labeling, the Individuals with Disabilities Education Act (PL 101-476), commonly referred to as IDEA, permits states to use the term *developmentally delayed* when discussing young children with disabilities. In fact, PL 105-17, the 1997 reauthorization of this law, allows the use of this term, at the discretion of the state and local education agency, for children ages 3 through 9. We believe, as other professionals do, that the use of a specific disability label for young children is of questionable value. Many early childhood special education programs offer services without categorizing children on the basis of a disability. We believe this approach is correct.

When talking about children who are **at-risk,** professionals generally mean individuals who, although not yet identified as having a disability, have a high probability of manifesting a disability because of harmful biological, environmental, or genetic conditions. Environmental and biological factors often work together to increase the likelihood of a child's exhibiting disabilities or developmental delays. Exposure to adverse circumstances *may* lead to future difficulties and delays in learning and development, but it is not guaranteed that such problems will present themselves. Many children are exposed to a wide range of risks, yet fail to evidence developmental problems. Possible risk conditions include low birth weight, exposure to toxins, child abuse or neglect, oxygen deprivation, and extreme poverty, as well as genetic disorders such as Down syndrome or PKU (phenylketonuria).

Special Education

When a student is identified as being exceptional, a special education is sometimes necessary. Recall that just because the student has a disability does *not* mean that a special education is automatically required. A special education is appropriate only when a pupil's needs are such that he or she cannot be accommodated in a general education program. Simply stated, a **special education** is a customized instructional program designed to meet the unique needs of an individual learner. It may necessitate the use of specialized materials, equipment, services, and/or teaching strategies. For example, an adolescent with a visual impairment may require books with larger print; a pupil with a physical disability may need specially designed chairs and work tables; a student with a learning disability may need extra time to complete an exam. In yet another instance, a young adult with cognitive impairments may benefit from a cooperative teaching arrangement involving one or more general educators along with a special education teacher. Special education is but one component of a complex service delivery system crafted to assist the individual in reaching his or her full potential.

A special education is not limited to a specific location. Contemporary thinking requires that services should be provided in the most natural or normalized environment appropriate for the particular student. Such settings might include the local Head Start program for preschoolers with disabilities, a self-contained classroom in the neighborhood school for children with hearing impairments, or a special high school for students who are academically gifted or talented. Many times a special education can be delivered in a general education classroom.

Finally, if a special education is to be truly beneficial and meet the unique needs of students, their teachers must collaborate with professionals from other disciplines who provide **related services.** Speech-language pathologists, social workers, and occupational therapists are only a few of the many professionals who complement the work of general and special educators. Related services are an integral part of a student's special education; they allow the learner to obtain benefit from their special education.

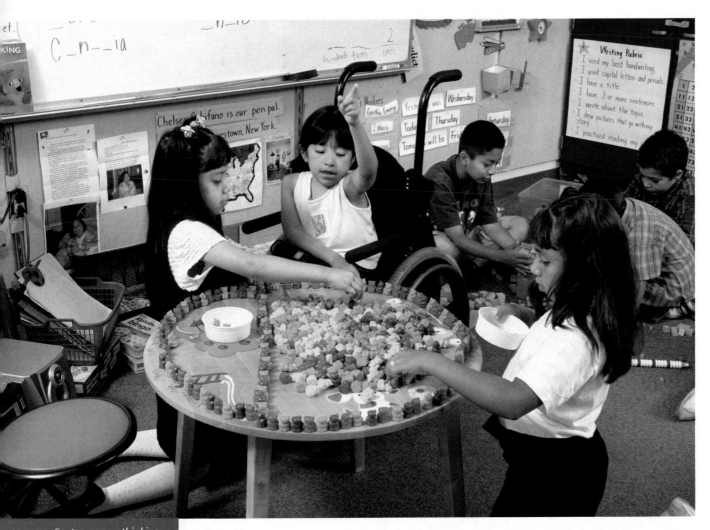

Contemporary thinking suggests that students with disabilities should be educated in the most normalized environment.

Before leaving this discussion on definitions and terminology, we believe it is important to reiterate a point we made earlier. Individuals with disabilities are more like their typical peers than they are different. Always remember to see the person, not the disability, and to focus on what people can do rather than what they can't do. It is our hope that as you learn about people with disabilities, you will develop a greater understanding of them, and from this understanding will come greater acceptance.

Categories and Labels

Earlier we defined a person with exceptionalities as someone who differs from a community's standard of normalcy. Students identified as exceptional may require a special education and/or related services. Many of these pupils are grouped or categorized according to specific disability categories. A **category** is nothing more than a label assigned to individuals who share common characteristics and features. Most states, in addition to the federal government, identify individuals receiving special education services according to discrete categories of exceptionality. Public Law (PL) 108-446 (the Individuals with Disabilities Education Improvement Act of 2004) identifies the following thirteen categories of disability:

- Autism
- Deaf-blindness
- Developmental delay
- Emotional disturbance
- Hearing impairments including deafness
- Mental retardation
- Multiple disabilities
- Orthopedic impairments
- Other health impairments
- Specific learning disabilities
- Speech or language impairments
- Traumatic brain injury
- Visual impairments including blindness

The federal government's interpretation of these various disabilities is presented in Appendix A. Individual states frequently use these federal definitions to construct their own standards and policies as to who is eligible to receive a special education.

Notably absent from the preceding list are individuals described as gifted or talented. These students are correctly viewed as exceptional, although they are not considered individuals with disabilities; nevertheless, most states recognize the unique abilities of these pupils and provide a special education.

In the following chapters, we will explore and examine the many dimensions and educational significance of each of these categories. It is important to remember, however, that although students may be categorized as belonging to a particular group of individuals, each one is a unique person with varying needs and abilities.

The entire issue of categorizing, or labeling, individuals with disabilities has been the subject of controversy. Labeling, of course, is an almost inescapable fact of life. How would you label yourself? Do you consider yourself a Democrat or Republican, are you overweight or thin, Christian or non-Christian, liberal or conservative? Depending on the context, some labels may be considered either positive or negative. Labels may be permanent, such as "cerebral palsy," or temporary, such as "college sophomore." Regardless, labels are powerful, biasing, and frequently filled with expectations about how people should behave and act.

Labels, whether formally imposed by psychologists or educators or casually applied by peers, are capable of stigmatizing and, in certain instances, penalizing children. Remember your earlier school days? Did you call some of your classmates "retard," "four-eyes," "fatso," "geek," or "nerd"? Were these labels truly valid? Did they give a complete and accurate picture of the person, or did the teasing and taunting focus only on a single characteristic? The labels we attach to people and the names we call them can significantly influence how individuals view themselves and how others in the environment relate to them.

For more than twenty years, investigators have been researching the effects of labels on children with disabilities and their teachers; unfortunately, the evidence is not clear-cut, and it is difficult to draw consistent conclusions (MacMillan, 1982; Smith, Neisworth, & Hunt, 1983; Ysseldyke, Algozzine, & Thurlow, 1992). The information gleaned from a variety of studies is frequently inconclusive, contradictory, and subject to methodological flaws (MacMillan). Kliewer and Biklen (1996) perhaps best capture the current state of affairs when they note that labeling or categorizing certain youngsters is a demeaning process frequently

Table 1.1	The Pros and Cons of Labeling Individuals with Special Needs
Advantages	**Disadvantages**
<ul><li>Labels serve as a means for funding and administering education programs.</li><li>Teacher certification programs and the credentialing process are frequently developed around specific disability categories (e.g., mental retardation, hearing impairment).</li><li>Labels allow professionals to communicate efficiently in a meaningful fashion.</li><li>Research efforts frequently focus on specific diagnostic categories.</li><li>Labels establish an individual's eligibility for services.</li><li>Treatments, instruction, and support services are differentially provided on the basis of a label—e.g., sign language for a student who is deaf, an accelerated or enriched curriculum for pupils who are gifted and talented.</li><li>Labels heighten the visibility of the unique needs of persons with disabilities.</li><li>Labels serve as a basis for counting the number of individuals with disabilities and thus assist governments, schools, agencies, and other organizations in planning for the delivery of needed services.</li><li>Advocacy and special interest groups, such as the Autism Society of America or the National Federation for the Blind, typically have an interest in assisting particular groups of citizens with disabling conditions.</li></ul>	<ul><li>Labels can be stigmatizing and may lead to stereotyping.</li><li>Labeling has the potential of focusing attention on limitations and what a person cannot do instead of on the individual's capabilities and strengths.</li><li>Labels can sometimes be used as an excuse or reason for delivering ineffective instruction; e.g., "Marvin can't learn his multiplication facts because he is mentally retarded."</li><li>Labels can contribute to a diminished self-concept, lower expectations, and poor self-esteem.</li><li>Labels are typically inadequate for instructional purposes; they do not accurately reflect the educational or therapeutic needs of the individual student.</li><li>Labeling can lead to reduced opportunities for normalized experiences in school and community life.</li><li>A label can give the false impression of the permanence of a disability; some labels evaporate upon leaving the school environment.</li></ul>

contributing to stigmatization and leading to social and educational isolation; on the other hand, a label may result in a pupil's receiving extraordinary services and support.

Despite the advantages of labeling children (see Table 1.1), we, like many of our colleagues in the field of special education, are not ardent supporters of the labeling process. We find that labeling too often promotes stereotyping and discrimination and may be a contributing factor to exclusionary practices in the educational and social arenas. Hobbs (1975) commented, many years ago, that labeling erects artificial boundaries between children while masking their individual differences. Reynolds and his colleagues (Reynolds, Wang, & Walberg, 1987), who strongly oppose labeling pupils with special needs, astutely observe that "the boundaries of the categories [mental retardation is a good illustration] have shifted so markedly in response to legal, economic, and political forces as to make diagnosis largely meaningless" (p. 396). Some professionals (Cook, 2001; Lipsky & Gartner, 1996; Stainback, Stainback, & Ayres, 1996) are of the opinion that labeling actually perpetuates a flawed system of identifying and classifying students in need of special educational services.

One of our biggest concerns is that the labels applied to children often lack educational relevance. Affixing a label to a child, even if accurate, is not a guarantee of better services. Rarely does a label provide instructional guidance or suggest effective management tactics. We are of the opinion that the delivery of instruction and services should be matched to the needs of the child rather than provided on the basis of the student's label. This thinking has led to calls for **noncategorical** programs constructed around student needs and common instructional requirements instead of categories of exceptionality. These programs focus on the similar instructional needs of the pupils rather than the etiology of the disability. Although noncategorical programs are gaining in popularity, it is still frequently necessary to classify students on the basis of the severity of their impairment—for example, mild/moderate or severe/profound.

Prevalence of Children and Young Adults with Disabilities

How many children and adolescents are identified as exceptional and have special needs? This is, as we will shortly see, not an easy question to answer. We begin by clarifying two key terms frequently encountered when describing the number of individuals with disabilities.

Definitions and Difficulties

Statisticians and researchers often talk about *incidence* and *prevalence*. Technically speaking, **incidence** refers to a rate of inception, or the number of *new* instances of a disability occurring within a given time frame, usually a year. As an illustration, it would be possible to calculate the number of infants born with Down syndrome between January 1 and December 31, 2008, in a particular state. This figure would typically be expressed as a percentage of the total number of babies born within the prescribed period of time; for example, 20 infants with Down syndrome out of 15,000 births would yield an incidence rate of .133 percent. **Prevalence** refers to the *total* number of individuals with a particular disability currently existing in the population at a given time. Prevalence is expressed as a percentage of the population exhibiting this specific exceptionality—for instance, the percentage of pupils with learning disabilities enrolled in special education programs during the current school year. If the prevalence of learning disabilities is estimated to be 5 percent of the school-age population, then we can reasonably expect about 50 children out of every 1,000 students to evidence a learning disability. Throughout this text, we will report prevalence figures for each area of exceptionality that we study. Of course, establishing accurate estimates of prevalence is based on our ability to gather specific information about the number of individuals with disabilities across the United States. Obviously, this is not an easy job. Fortunately, the federal government has assumed this responsibility. Each year the Department of Education issues a report (*Annual Report to Congress on the Implementation of the Individuals with Disabilities Education Act*) based on data supplied by the various states.

Efforts at gathering meaningful prevalence figures, which tend to vary from state to state, are frequently hindered by several issues such as:

- The accurate identification and assessment of children and adolescents with special needs (estimates are only as valid as the criteria and evaluation procedures used)
- Variations across states in the definition of disabilities
- Changing rules and regulations affecting special education (for example, who is eligible to receive a special education)
- The time-bound nature of some disabilities (a youngster recognized as disabled in the primary grades may not be considered so later on)

In summary, reliable prevalence data are difficult to obtain, and we recommend that the figures be interpreted cautiously.

Number of Children and Young Adults Served

More than 6.1 million U.S. students (6,109,569) between the ages of 6 and 21 were receiving a special education during the 2005–2006 school year (U.S. Department of Education, 2007). The number of students in each of the thirteen disability categories recognized by

Table 1.2	Number of Students Ages 6–21 Receiving a Special Education during School Year 2005–2006	
Disability	**Number**	**Percent of Total**
Specific learning disabilities	2,780,218	45.50
Speech or language impairments	1,157,215	18.94
Mental retardation	545,492	8.92
Emotional disturbance	472,384	7.73
Multiple disabilities	133,914	2.19
Hearing impairments	72,387	1.18
Orthopedic impairments	63,127	1.03
Other health impairments	561,028	9.18
Visual impairments	25,996	.42
Autism	193,637	3.16
Deaf-blindness	1,592	.02
Traumatic brain injury	23,509	.38
Developmental delay	79,070	1.29
Total	6,109,569	100.00

NOTE: Table based on data from the 50 states, Puerto Rico, the District of Columbia, and outlying areas.

SOURCE: U.S. Department of Education. (2007). *IDEA Data.* Available at https://www.ideadata.org/PartBReport.asp

the federal government is recorded in Table 1.2. Learning disabilities account for nearly half of all pupils with disabilities (45.50%); students with dual sensory impairments (deaf-blindness) represent the smallest category of exceptionality (.02%).

The growth in the number of students (ages 3–21) receiving a special education since the inception of PL 94-142 (now IDEA) in 1975 has been phenomenal. Each year the states report a continuously increasing number of individuals enrolled in special education programs. Since the 1976–1977 school year, the number of pupils being provided a special education has increased by an astonishing 95 percent (3,485,088 versus 6,813,656). This remarkable growth is portrayed in Figure 1.1.

While the growth of special education over the past decades has truly been noteworthy, some areas of disability have grown faster than others. For instance, the population of students identified as learning disabled has grown dramatically since the inauguration of PL 94-142. In 1976, learning disabilities accounted for approximately 25 percent of the total population of students with disabilities; today, slightly less than half of all individuals enrolled in special education have learning disabilities. Figure 1.2 depicts the changes in distribution for select categories of exceptionality.

With the passage of PL 99-457 (the Education of the Handicapped Act Amendments of 1986, currently referred to as IDEA), services for infants, toddlers, and preschoolers with special needs have significantly increased. This first major amendment to PL 94-142 was enacted because more than half the states did not require special education services for preschoolers with disabilities (Koppelman, 1986). PL 99-457 remedied this situation by mandating that youngsters between 3 and 5 years of age receive the same educational

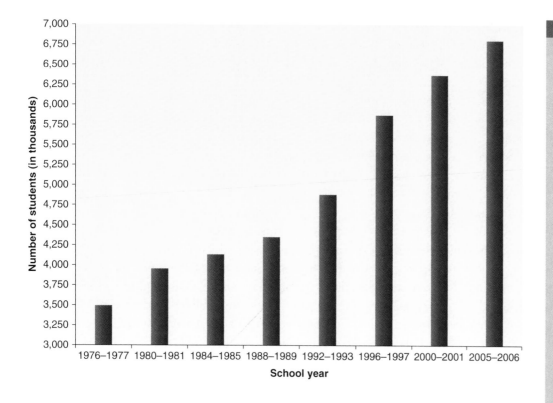

Figure 1.1

Growth in Number of Students Ages 3–21 Served in Special Education Programs in Select School Years: 1976–2005

Note: Figure based on data from the 50 states, Puerto Rico, the District of Columbia, and outlying areas.

Source: U.S. Department of Education. (1992–2002). *Annual Reports to Congress on the Implementation of the Individuals with Disabilities Education Act.* Washington, DC: U.S. Government Printing Office.

U.S. Department of Education. (2007). *IDEA Data.* Available at https://www.ideadata.org/PartBReport.asp

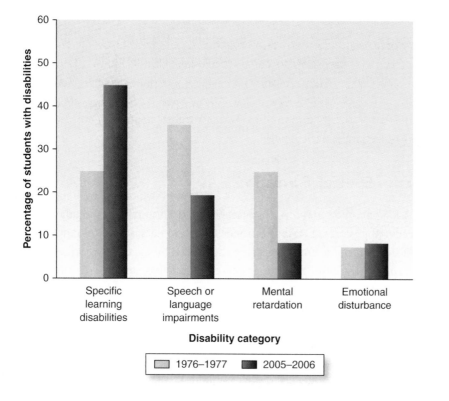

Figure 1.2

Changes in the Distribution of Students with Disabilities: 1976–1977 vs. 2005–2006

Note: Information based on children ages 6–21 served under IDEA.

Source: U.S. Department of Education. (1992). *Fourteenth Annual Report to Congress on the Implementation of the Individuals with Disabilities Education Act.* Washington, DC: U.S. Government Printing Office.

U.S. Department of Education. (2007). *IDEA Data.* Available at https://www.ideadata.org/PartBReport.asp

services and legal protections as their school-age counterparts, or else states would risk the loss of significant federal financial support. Full compliance with this mandate was finally achieved during the 1992–1993 school year. During the 2005–2006 school year, almost 704,000 preschoolers with special needs were receiving services under Part B of IDEA (U.S. Department of Education, 2007). By way of comparison, approximately 399,000 youngsters were served during the 1990–1991 school year (U.S. Department of Education, 1992). This growth translates into a 76 percent increase in the number of preschoolers receiving a special education.

Infants and toddlers with disabilities—that is, youngsters from birth through age 2— also benefited from PL 99-457. Part C of IDEA, which addresses this population, does *not* require that early intervention services be provided. Instead, states were encouraged, via financial incentives, to develop comprehensive and coordinated programs for these youngsters and their families. All states have met this challenge, and almost 298,000 infants and toddlers were the recipients of services as of the fall of 2005 (U.S. Department of Education, 2007).

You may have noticed that, throughout this discussion, we have failed to present any data concerning individuals who are gifted and talented. This was not an oversight. Federal legislation does *not* require that the states provide a special education for these students. Unfortunately, not all states mandate a special education for children identified as gifted and talented. As of the 2002–2003 school year, more than 3 million children and young adults were identified as gifted and talented and receiving a special education (U.S. Department of Education, 2002). If these students were included in the overall federal calculation of pupils with exceptionalities, this group of learners would rank as the largest.

A Brief History of the Development of Special Education

The history of special education can perhaps best be characterized as one of evolving or changing perceptions and attitudes about individuals with disabilities. Generally speaking, at any given time, the programs, resources, and practices that affect citizens with disabilities are a reflection of the current social climate. As people's ideas and beliefs about exceptionality change, so do services and opportunities. A transformation in attitude is frequently a prerequisite to a change in the delivery of services.

Pioneers of Special Education

The foundation of contemporary U.S. societal attitudes toward individuals with disabilities can be traced to the efforts of various European philosophers, advocates, and humanitarians. These dedicated reformers and pioneering thinkers were catalysts for change. Educational historians typically trace the beginnings of special education to the late eighteenth and early nineteenth centuries.

One of the earliest documented attempts at providing a special education were the efforts of the French physician Jean Marc-Gaspard Itard (1775–1838) at educating 12-year-old Victor, the so-called "wild boy of Aveyron." According to folklore, Victor was discovered by a group of hunters in a forest near the town of Aveyron. When found, he was unclothed, without language, ran but did not walk, and exhibited animal-like behavior (Lane, 1979). Itard, an authority on diseases of the ear and teaching youngsters with hearing impairments, endeavored in 1799 to "civilize" Victor. He attempted to teach Victor through a sensory training program and what today would be called behavior modification. Because this adolescent failed to fully develop language after five years of dedicated and painstaking instruction, and only mastered basic social and self-help skills, Itard considered his efforts a failure. Yet he successfully demonstrated that learning was possible even for an individual described by his contemporaries as a hopeless and incurable idiot. The title "Father of Special Education" is rightly bestowed on Itard because of his groundbreaking work 200 years ago.

Another influential pioneer was Itard's student Edouard Seguin (1812–1880). He developed instructional programs for youngsters whom many of his fellow professionals believed to be incapable of learning. Like his mentor Itard, Seguin was convinced of the importance of sensorimotor activities as an aid to learning. His methodology was based on a comprehensive assessment of the student's strengths and weaknesses coupled with a carefully constructed plan of sensorimotor exercises designed to remediate specific disabilities. Seguin also realized the value of early education; he is considered one of the first early interventionists. Seguin's ideas and theories, which he described in his book *Idiocy and Its Treatment by the Physiological Method,* provided a basis for Maria Montessori's later work with the urban poor and children with mental retardation.

The work of Itard, Seguin, and other innovators of their time helped to establish a foundation for many contemporary practices in special education. Examples of these contributions include individualized instruction, the use of positive reinforcement techniques, and a belief in the capability of all children to learn.

The Europe of the 1800s was a vibrant and exciting place, filled with idealism and fresh ideas about equality and freedom. It also gave birth to new concepts and approaches to educating individuals with disabilities, which eventually found their way to North America. In 1848, for example, Seguin immigrated to the United States, where in later years he helped to establish an organization that was the forerunner to the American Association on Mental Retardation. An American, the Reverend Thomas Hopkins Gallaudet (1787–1851) traveled to Europe, where he studied the latest techniques and innovations for teaching children who were deaf. Upon his return, he was instrumental in helping to establish the American Asylum for the Education of the Deaf and Dumb in Hartford, Connecticut. This facility, founded in 1817, was the first residential school in the United States and is currently known as the American School for the Deaf. Gallaudet University, a liberal arts college devoted to the education of students with hearing impairments, is named in honor of his contributions.

Table 1.3 summarizes the work of some of the progressive European and American thinkers and activists whose ideas and convictions have significantly influenced the development of special education in the United States.

The Establishment of Institutions

By the middle of the nineteenth century, several institutions—commonly referred to as asylums, or sometimes as "schools"—were established to benefit citizens with disabilities. These facilities provided primarily protective care and management rather than treatment and education (Gargiulo & Kilgo, 2005). Typically, these early efforts were established by enlightened individuals working in concert with concerned professionals. They were frequently supported financially by wealthy benefactors and philanthropists rather than state governments. Some states, however, mainly in the Northeast, began to support the development of institutions by the middle of the nineteenth century. Such efforts were seen as an indication of the state's progressive stature. At this time, there was no federal aid for individuals with disabilities.

By the end of the nineteenth century, residential institutions for persons with disabilities were a well-established part of the American social fabric. Initially established to provide training and some form of education in a protective and lifelong environment, they gradually

Table 1.3	Pioneering Contributors to the Development of Special Education
The Individuals	**Their Ideas**
Jacob Rodrigues Pereine 1715–1780	Introduced the idea that persons who were deaf could be taught to communicate. Developed an early form of sign language. Provided inspiration and encouragement for the work of Itard and Seguin.
Phillippe Pinel 1745–1826	A reform-minded French physician who was concerned with the humanitarian treatment of individuals with mental illness. Advocated releasing institutionalized patients from their chains. Pioneered the field of occupational therapy. Served as Itard's mentor.
Jean Marc-Gaspard Itard 1775–1838	A French doctor who secured lasting fame because of his systematic efforts to educate an adolescent thought to be severely mentally retarded. Recognized the importance of sensory stimulation.
Thomas Gallaudet 1787–1851	Taught children with hearing impairments to communicate through a system of manual signs and symbols. Established the first institution in the United States.
Samuel Gridley Howe 1801–1876	An American physician and educator accorded international fame because of his success in teaching individuals with visual and hearing impairments. Founded the first residential facility for the blind and was instrumental in inaugurating institutional care for children with mental retardation.
Dorothea Lynde Dix 1802–1887	A contemporary of S. G. Howe, Dix was one of the first Americans to champion better and more humane treatment of the mentally ill. Instigated the establishment of several institutions for individuals with mental disorders.
Louis Braille 1809–1852	A French educator, himself blind, who developed a tactile system of reading and writing for people who were blind. His system, based on a cell of six embossed dots, is still used today. This standardized code is known as Standard English Braille.
Edouard Seguin 1812–1880	A pupil of Itard, Seguin was a French physician responsible for developing teaching methods for children with mental retardation. His training emphasized sensorimotor activities. After immigrating to the United States, he helped to found an organization that was the forerunner of the American Association on Mental Retardation.
Francis Galton 1822–1911	Scientist concerned with individual differences. As a result of studying eminent persons, he believed that genius is solely the result of heredity. Those with superior abilities are born not made.
Alexander Graham Bell 1847–1922	Pioneering advocate of educating children with disabilities in public schools. As a teacher of students with hearing impairments, Bell promoted the use of residual hearing and developing the speaking skills of students who are deaf.
Alfred Binet 1857–1911	A French psychologist who constructed the first standardized developmental assessment scale capable of quantifying intelligence. The original purpose of this test was to identify students who might profit from a special education and not to classify individuals on the basis of ability. Also originated the concept of mental age with his student Theodore Simon.
Maria Montessori 1870–1952	Achieved worldwide recognition for her pioneering work with young children and youngsters with mental retardation. First female to earn a medical degree in Italy. Expert in early childhood education. Demonstrated that children are capable of learning at a very early age when surrounded with manipulative materials in a rich and stimulating environment. Believed that children learn best by direct sensory experience.
Lewis Terman 1877–1956	An American educator and psychologist who revised Binet's original assessment instrument. The result was the publication of the Stanford-Binet Scale of Intelligence in 1916. Terman developed the notion of intelligence quotient, or IQ. Also famous for lifelong study of gifted individuals. Considered the grandfather of gifted education.

deteriorated in the early decades of the twentieth century for a variety of reasons, including overcrowding and a lack of fiscal resources. The mission of institutions also changed from training to custodial care and isolation. The early optimism that had initially characterized the emerging field of special education was replaced by prejudice, unwarranted scientific views, and fears, slowly eroding these institutions into gloomy warehouses for the forgotten and neglected (Meisels & Shonkoff, 2000).

At one time education was a privilege, not a right.

Special Education in the Public Schools

It was not until the second half of the nineteenth century and the early years of the twentieth century that special education classes began to appear in public schools. Services for children with exceptionalities began sporadically and slowly, serving only a very small number of individuals who needed services. Of course, during this era, even children without disabilities did not routinely attend school. An education at this time was a luxury; it was one of the benefits of being born into an affluent family. Many children, some as young as 5 or 6, were expected to contribute to their family's financial security by laboring in factories or working on farms. Being able to attend school was truly a privilege. It is against this backdrop that the first special education classes in public schools were established. Examples of these efforts are listed in Table 1.4.

The very first special education classrooms were **self-contained;** students were typically grouped together and segregated from the other pupils. The majority of their school day was spent with their teacher in a classroom isolated from the daily activities of the school. In some instances, even lunch and recess provided no opportunity for interacting with typical classmates. This type of arrangement characterized many special education classrooms for the next fifty years or so.

Table 1.4	The Development of Public School Classes for Children with Disabilities	
Year	**City**	**Disability Served**
1869	Boston, MA	Deaf
1878	Cleveland, OH	Behavioral disorders
1896	Providence, RI	Mental retardation
1898	New York, NY	Slow learners
1899	Chicago, IL	Physical impairments
1900	Chicago, IL	Blind
1901	Worcester, MA	Gifted
1908	New York, NY	Speech impairment

After World War II, the stage was set for the rapid expansion of special education. Litigation, legislation, and leadership at the federal level, coupled with political activism and parental advocacy, helped to fuel the movement. Significant benefits for children with exceptionalities resulted from these efforts. In 1948, only about 12 percent of children with disabilities were receiving an education appropriate to their needs (Ballard, Ramirez, & Weintraub, 1982). From 1947 to 1972, the number of pupils enrolled in special education programs increased an astonishing 716 percent, compared with an 82 percent increase in total public school enrollment (Dunn, 1973).

Beginning in the mid-1970s and continuing to the present time, children with disabilities have secured the right to receive a free and appropriate public education provided in the most normalized setting. An education for these students is no longer a privilege; it is a right guaranteed by both federal and state laws and reinforced by judicial interpretation. We will talk about some of these laws and court cases in the next chapter. Special education over the past thirty years can perhaps best be seen as a gradual movement from isolation to participation, one of steady and progressive inclusion. (See the accompanying FYI feature.)

Professionals Who Work with Individuals with Exceptionalities

It is very common for teachers to work with professionals from other disciplines. A special education may require the expertise of other individuals outside the field of education. Recall our earlier definition of a special education, which incorporates this idea and the concept of related services. IDEA, in fact, mandates that educational assessments of a student's strengths and needs be multidisciplinary and that related services be provided to meet the unique requirements of each learner. Examples of related services include

- Physical therapy
- Audiology
- Transportation
- Speech and language
- Psychology

FYI...

A Timeline of Key Dates in the History of Special Education in the United States

1817 Rev. Thomas Hopkins Gallaudet becomes principal of the American Asylum for the Education of the Deaf and Dumb, the first residential school in the United States.

1831 Samuel Gridley Howe establishes the New England Asylum for the Blind.

1834 Louis Braille publishes the Braille code.

1839 First teacher training program opens in Massachusetts.

1848 Samuel Gridley Howe establishes the Massachusetts School for Idiotic and Feeble Minded Children.

1848 Dorothea Dix calls attention to the shocking conditions of American asylums and prisons.

1869 First public school class for children with hearing impairments opens in Boston.

1876 Edouard Seguin helps to organize the first professional association concerned with disabilities (mental retardation), predecessor to today's American Association on Mental Retardation.

1897 National Education Association establishes a section for teachers of children with disabilities.

1898 Elizabeth Farrell, later to become the first president of the Council for Exceptional Children, begins a program for "backwards" or "slow learning" children in New York City.

1904 The Vineland Training School in New Jersey inaugurates training programs for teachers of students with mental retardation.

1916 Louis Terman publishes the Stanford-Binet Scale of Intelligence.

1920 Teachers College, Columbia University, begins training program for teachers of pupils who are gifted.

1922 Organization that later would become the Council for Exceptional Children (CEC) is founded in New York City.

1928 Seeing Eye dogs for the blind are introduced in the United States.

1936 First compulsory law for testing the hearing of school-age children is enacted in New York.

1949 United Cerebral Palsy (UCP) association is founded.

1950 Association for Retarded Children (ARC) is founded (known today as the Association for Retarded Citizens, or simply the Arc).

1953 National Association for Gifted is founded.

1963 Association for Children with Learning Disabilities (forerunner to Learning Disabilities Association of America) is organized.

1972 Wolf Wolfensberger introduces the concept of normalization, initially coined by Bengt Nirge of Sweden, to the United States.

1973 Public Law 93-112, the Vocational Rehabilitation Act of 1973, is enacted; Section 504 prohibits discrimination against individuals with disabilities.

1975 Education for All Handicapped Children Act (PL 94-142) is passed; landmark legislation ensures, among other provisions, a free and appropriate public education for all children with disabilities.

1986 Education of the Handicapped Act Amendments of 1986 (PL 99-457) is enacted; mandates a special education for preschoolers with disabilities and incentives for providing early intervention services to infants and toddlers.

1990 Americans with Disabilities Act (PL 101-336) becomes law; prohibits discrimination on the basis of disability.

1990 PL 101-476, the Individuals with Disabilities Education Act (commonly known as IDEA) is passed; among other provisions, emphasizes transition planning for adolescents with disabilities.

1997 Individuals with Disabilities Education Act (PL 105-17) is reauthorized, providing a major retooling and expansion of services for students with disabilities and their families.

2001 No Child Left Behind Act of 2001 (PL 107-110) is enacted; a major educational reform effort focusing on academic achievement of students and qualifications of teachers.

2004 Individuals with Disabilities Education Improvement Act of 2004 (PL 108-446) is passed; aligns IDEA legislation with provisions of the No Child Left Behind Act; modifies the individualized education program (IEP) process in addition to changes affecting school discipline, due process, and evaluation of students with disabilities.

SOURCE: Information partially based on data from the 75th Anniversary Issue, *Teaching Exceptional Children, 29*(5), 1997, pp. 5–49.

- Recreational therapy
- Orientation and mobility
- Interpreting services
- Occupational therapy
- Nutrition
- Medical
- Social work
- Vocational education
- Rehabilitation counseling
- Parent counseling
- School nurse services

Related services are neither complete nor exhaustive, and additional services—such as assistive technology devices or interpreters for pupils with hearing impairments—may be required if a student is to receive benefit from a special education. The issue of what constitutes a related service, however, has generated some controversy among educators and school administrators. Disagreements are also common as to what kinds of services should be provided by the public schools and which services are rightfully the responsibilities of the child's parent(s).

There is a growing recognition of the importance of professionals' working together regardless of the different disciplines they may represent. No one discipline or profession possesses all of the resources or clinical skills needed to construct the appropriate interventions and educational programs for children and young adults with disabilities, a large number of whom have complex needs. Although the idea of professionals' working together in a cooperative fashion has been part of special education since the enactment of PL 94-142 some thirty years ago, we have not always been successful in implementing this idea. Obstacles range from poor interpersonal dynamics, to concerns about professional turf, to the lack of planning time, to the absence of administrative support for this concept. However, we find that professionals are increasingly working together. Professional cooperation and partnership are the key to delivering services in an efficient and integrated manner. "Serving students with disabilities in inclusive settings depends greatly on effective collaboration among professionals" (Hobbs & Westling, 1998, p. 14). McLean, Wolery, and Bailey (2004) identify several reasons why collaboration is beneficial:

- Incorrect placement recommendations are likely to be reduced.
- There is a greater likelihood that assessments will be nondiscriminatory.
- More appropriate educational plans and goals are likely to result from professional teaming.

Collaboration is *how* people work together; it is a style of interaction that professionals choose to use in order to accomplish a shared goal (Friend & Cook, 2007). For collaboration to be effective, however, service providers must exhibit a high degree of cooperation, trust, and mutual respect and must share the decision-making process. Additional key attributes necessary for meaningful collaboration include voluntary participation and parity in the relationship, along with shared goals, accountability, and resources (Friend & Cook). A good example of the beneficial outcomes of these collaborative efforts can be found in the development of a student's **individualized education program**, or **IEP**, which necessitates a collaborative team process involving parents, teachers, and professionals.

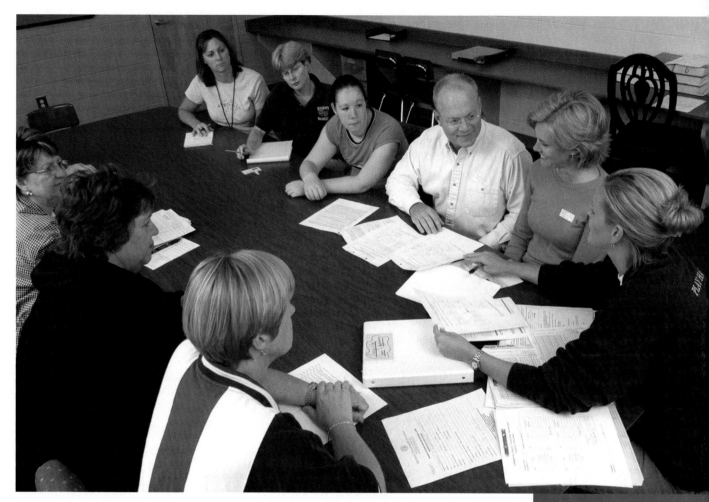

Effective programming for students with disabilities requires meaningful involvement of teachers, parents, and related service providers.

Several models are available for building partnerships among related services personnel, general education teachers, and special educators. We have chosen to examine two different approaches: consultative services and service delivery teams.

Consultative Services

A growing number of school districts are developing strategies for assisting general educators in serving children with disabilities. This effort is part of a larger movement aimed at making the neighborhood school and general education classroom more inclusive. One effective support technique is to provide assistance to general educators through consultative services. **Consultation** is a focused, problem-solving process in which one individual offers expertise and assistance to another. The intent of this activity is to modify teaching tactics and/or the learning environment in order to accommodate the needs of the individual student with disabilities. Instructional planning and responsibility thus become a shared duty among various professionals. Assistance to the general education teacher may come from a special educator, the school psychologist, a physical therapist, or any other related services provider. A vision specialist, for example, may provide suggestions on how to use various pieces of mobility equipment needed by a student who is visually impaired; a school psychologist or behavior management specialist may offer suggestions for dealing with the aggressive, acting-out behaviors of a middle school student with emotional problems. Hourcade and Bauwens (2003) refer to this type of aid as indirect consultation. In other instances, services are rendered directly to the student by professionals other than the classroom teacher. In this situation, specific areas of weakness or deficit are the target of remediation. Interventions are increasingly being provided by related services personnel in the general education classroom. The general educator also typically receives instructional tips on how to carry out the remediation efforts in the absence of the service provider.

We should also point out that consultative services are equally valuable for special educators. The diverse needs of pupils with disabilities frequently require that special education teachers seek programming suggestions and other types of assistance from various related services personnel. It should be obvious that no one discipline or professional possesses all of the answers. The complex demands of today's classrooms dictate that professionals work together in a cooperative fashion.

According to Pugach and Johnson (2002), consultative services are an appropriate and beneficial strategy, a means whereby all school personnel can collaboratively interact as part of their commitment to serving *all* children. Meaningful collaborative consultation requires mutual support, respect, flexibility, and a sharing of expertise. No one professional should consider himself or herself more of an expert than others. Each of the parties involved can learn and benefit from the others' expertise; of course, the ultimate beneficiary is the student. We believe that the keys to developing effective collaborative practices are good interpersonal skills coupled with professional competency and a willingness to assist in meeting the needs of all children.

Service Delivery Teams

Another way that professionals can work together is to construct a team. Special education teachers seldom work completely alone. Even those who teach in a self-contained classroom function, in some way, as part of a team (Crutchfield, 1997). According to Maddux (1988), a team consists of a group of individuals whose purpose and function are derived from a common philosophy and shared goals. Obviously, educational teams will differ in their membership; yet individual professionals, who typically represent various disciplines, appreciate their interdependence and sense of common ownership of their objective.

Besides having members from different fields, teams will also differ according to their structure and function. Such teams are often used in evaluating, planning, and delivering services to individuals with disabilities, especially infants and toddlers. The three most common approaches identified in the professional literature (McDonnell, Hardman, & McDonnell, 2003; McGoningel, Woodruff, & Roszmann-Millican, 1994) are multidisciplinary, interdisciplinary, and transdisciplinary teams. These approaches are interrelated and, according to Giangreco, York, and Rainforth (1989), represent a historical evolution of teamwork. This evolutionary process can be portrayed as concentric circles, with each model retaining some of the attributes of its predecessor. Figure 1.3 illustrates these various configurations.

MULTIDISCIPLINARY TEAMS The concept of a **multidisciplinary** team was originally mandated in PL 94-142 and was recently reiterated in the 2004 reauthorization of IDEA (PL 108-446). This approach utilizes the expertise of professionals from several disciplines, each of whom usually performs his or her assessments, interventions, and other tasks independent of the others. Individuals contribute according to their own specialty area with little regard for the actions of other professionals. There is a high degree of professional autonomy and minimal integration. A team exists only in the sense that each

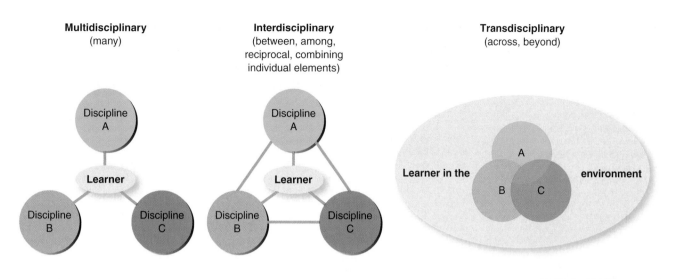

Figure 1.3

Multidisciplinary, Interdisciplinary, and Transdisciplinary Team Models

Source: M. Giangreco, J. York, and B. Rainforth, "Providing Related Services to Learners with Severe Handicaps in Educational Settings: Pursuing the Least Restrictive Option," *Pediatric Physical Therapy, 1*(2), 1989, p. 57.

person shares a common goal. There is very little coordination or collaboration across discipline areas. Friend and Cook (2007) characterize this model as a patchwork quilt whereby different, and sometimes contrasting, information is integrated but not necessarily with a unified outcome.

Parents of children with disabilities typically meet with each team member individually. They are generally passive recipients of information about their son or daughter. Because information flows to them from several sources, some parents may have difficulty synthesizing all of the data and recommendations from the various experts. Gargiulo and Kilgo (2005) do not consider the multidisciplinary model to be especially "family friendly."

INTERDISCIPLINARY TEAMS The **interdisciplinary** team model evolved from dissatisfaction with the fragmented services and lack of communication typically associated with the multidisciplinary team model (McCormick, 2003). In this model of teaming, team members perform their evaluations independently, but program development and instructional recommendations are the result of information sharing and joint planning. Significant cooperation among the team members leads to an integrated plan of services and a holistic view of the student's strengths and needs. Greater communication, coordination, and collaboration are the distinctive trademarks of this model. Direct services such as physical therapy, however, are usually provided in isolation from one another. Families typically meet with the entire team or its representative; in many cases, a special educator performs this role.

TRANSDISCIPLINARY TEAMS The **transdisciplinary** approach to providing services builds upon the strengths of the interdisciplinary model. In this model, team members are committed to working collaboratively across individual discipline lines. The transdisciplinary model is distinguished by two additional and related features: role sharing and a primary therapist. Professionals from various disciplines conduct their initial evaluations and assessments, but they relinquish their role (role release) as service providers by teaching their skills to other team members, one of whom will serve as the primary interventionist. This person is regarded as the team leader. For many children and adolescents with special needs, this role is usually filled by an educator. This individual relies heavily on the support and consultation provided by his or her professional peers. Discipline-specific interventions are still available, although they occur less frequently.

Figure 1.4
Characteristics of Teaming Models

Source: From *Young Children with Special Needs: An Introduction to Early Childhood Special Education*, 2nd ed., by R. M. Gargiulo and J. L. Kilgo. Copyright © 2005. Reprinted with permission of Delmar, a division of Thomson Learning.

Multidisciplinary teams   **Interdisciplinary teams**   **Transdisciplinary teams**

Least collaborative	Most collaborative
Least cooperative	Most cooperative
Least coordinated	Most coordinated
Least integrative	Most integrative

"The primary purpose of this approach," according to Bruder (1994), "is to pool and integrate the expertise of team members so that more efficient and comprehensive assessment and intervention services may be provided" (p. 61). The aim of the transdisciplinary model is to avoid compartmentalization and fragmentation of services. It attempts to provide a more coordinated and unified approach to assessment and service delivery. Members of a transdisciplinary team see parents as full-fledged members of the group with a strong voice in the team's recommendations and decisions.

Figure 1.4 illustrates some of the characteristics of each team model as viewed by Gargiulo and Kilgo (2005).

Cooperative Teaching

Cooperative teaching, or co-teaching as it is sometimes called, is an increasingly popular approach for achieving inclusion (Murawski & Dieker, 2004; Scruggs, Mastropieri, & McDuffie, 2007). With this strategy, general education teachers and special educators work together in a cooperative manner; each professional shares in the planning and delivery of instruction to a heterogeneous group of students. Hourcade and Bauwens (2003, p. 41) define **cooperative teaching** as

> direct collaboration in which a general educator and one or more support service providers voluntarily agree to work together in a co-active and coordinated fashion in the general education classroom. These educators, who possess distinct and complementary sets of skills, share roles, resources, and responsibilities in a sustained effort while working toward the common goal of school success for all students.

The aim of cooperative teaching is to create options for learning and to provide support to *all* students in the general education classroom by combining the content expertise of the general educator with the pedagogical skills of the special educator (Smith, Polloway, Patton, & Dowdy, 2008). Cooperative teaching can be implemented in several different ways. These arrangements, as identified by Friend and Cook (2007), typically occur for set periods of time each day or on certain days of the week. Some of the more common instructional models for co-teaching are depicted in Figure 1.5. The particular strategy chosen often depends on the needs and characteristics of the pupils, curricular demands, amount of professional experience, and teacher preference, as well as such practical matters as the amount of space available. Many experienced educators use a variety of arrangements depending on their specific circumstances.

One Teach, One Observe

In this version of cooperative teaching, one teacher presents the instruction to the entire class while the second educator circulates, gathering information (data) on a specific pupil,

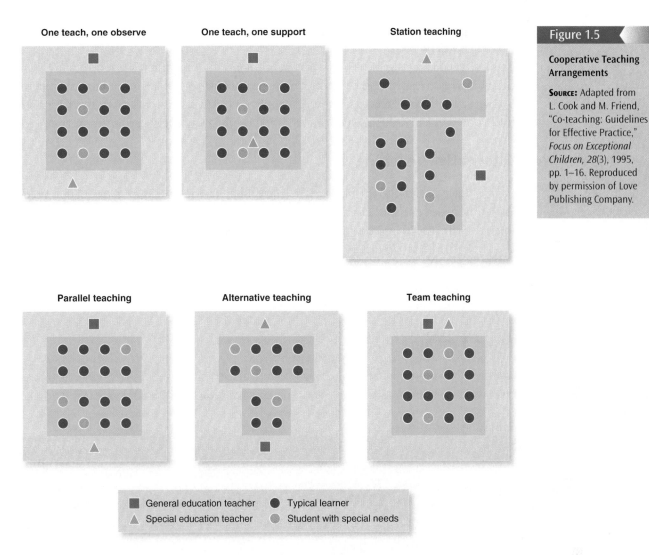

Figure 1.5

Cooperative Teaching Arrangements

SOURCE: Adapted from L. Cook and M. Friend, "Co-teaching: Guidelines for Effective Practice," *Focus on Exceptional Children, 28*(3), 1995, pp. 1–16. Reproduced by permission of Love Publishing Company.

a small group of students, or targeted behaviors across the whole class such as productive use of free time. Although this model requires a minimal amount of joint planning, it is very important that teachers periodically exchange roles to avoid one professional from being perceived as the "assistant teacher."

One Teach, One Support

Both individuals are present, but one teacher takes the instructional lead while the other provides support and assistance to the students. It is important that one professional (usually the special educator) is not always expected to function as the assistant; rotating roles can help to alleviate this potential problem.

Station Teaching

In this type of cooperative teaching, the lesson is divided into two or more segments and presented in different locations in the classroom. One teacher presents one portion of the lesson while the other teacher provides a different portion. Then the groups rotate, and the teachers repeat their information to new groups of pupils. Depending on the class, a third station can be established where students work independently or with a "learning buddy" to review material. Station teaching is effective at all grade levels.

Parallel Teaching

This instructional arrangement lowers the teacher/pupil ratio. Instruction is planned jointly but is delivered by each teacher to one-half of a heterogeneous group of learners. Coordination of efforts is crucial. This format lends itself to drill-and-practice activities or projects that require close teacher supervision. As with station teaching, noise and activity levels may pose problems.

Alternative Teaching

Some students benefit from small group instruction; alternative teaching meets that need. With this model, one teacher provides instruction to the larger group while the other teacher interacts with a small group of pupils. Although commonly used for remediation purposes, alternative teaching is equally appropriate for enrichment activities and in-depth study. Teachers need to be cautious, however, that children with disabilities are not exclusively and routinely assigned to the small group; all members of the class should participate periodically in the functions of the smaller group.

Team Teaching

In this type of cooperative teaching, both teachers share the instructional activities equally. Each teacher, for example, may take turns leading a discussion about the causes

Today's classrooms serve all children.

of World War II, or one teacher may talk about multiplication of fractions while the co-teacher gives several examples illustrating this concept. This form of cooperative teaching, sometimes called interactive teaching (Walther-Thomas, Korinek, McLaughlin, & Williams, 2000), requires a significant amount of professional trust and a high level of commitment.

Cooperative teaching should not be viewed as a panacea for meeting the multiple challenges frequently encountered when serving students with disabilities in general education classrooms; it is, however, one mechanism for facilitating successful inclusion. According to researchers (Rice, Drame, Owens, & Frattura, 2007; Scruggs et al., 2007), some of the key ingredients required for successful cooperative teaching include

- Voluntary participation
- Adequate planning time
- Mutual respect
- Administrative support
- Flexibility and creativity
- Personal and professional compatibility
- Shared instructional philosophy

Teachers also need to openly address potential obstacles, such as workload and time management, if co-teaching is to be successful (Smith et al., 2008).

To ensure that co-teaching is efficient and effective, Reinhiller (1996) recommends that teachers address the following five questions:

- Why do we want to co-teach?
- How will we know whether our goals are being met?
- How will we communicate and document the collaboration?
- How will we share responsibility for the instruction of all students?
- How will we gain support from others? (p. 46)

Keefe, Moore, and Duff (2004) offer the following guidelines for creating and maintaining a successful co-teaching experience:

- *Know yourself*—recognize your strengths and weaknesses; acknowledge preconceived notions about teaching in an inclusive setting.
- *Know your partner*—foster a friendship; accept each other's idiosyncrasies; appreciate differences in teaching styles.
- *Know your students*—discover the students' interests, listen to their dreams; embrace acceptance.
- *Know your "stuff"*—share information and responsibility; jointly create IEPs; be knowledgeable about classroom routines.

Like Murawski and Dieker (2004), we believe that in the final analysis the key question that must be answered is, "Is what we are doing good for the both of us and good for our students?"

Advantages and disadvantages of cooperative teaching are summarized in Table 1.5. An award-winning teacher's recommendations for facilitating successful co-teaching experiences are offered in Table 1.6.

Table 1.5	Advantages and Disadvantages of Cooperative Teaching Arrangements	
Instructional Model	**Advantages**	**Disadvantages**
Team Teaching	• Provides systematic observation/data collection • Promotes role/content sharing • Facilitates individual assistance • Models appropriate academic, social, and help-seeking behaviors • Teaches question asking • Provides clarification (e.g., concepts, rules, vocabulary)	• May be job sharing, not learning enriching • Requires considerable planning • Requires modeling and role-playing skills • Becomes easy to "typecast" specialist with this role
Station Teaching	• Provides active learning format • Increases small-group attention • Encourages cooperation and independence • Allows strategic grouping • Increases response rate	• Requires considerable planning and preparation • Increases noise level • Requires group and independent work skills • Is difficult to monitor
Parallel Teaching	• Provides effective review format • Encourages student responses • Reduces pupil/teacher ratio for group instruction or review	• Hard to achieve equal depth of content coverage • May be difficult to coordinate • Requires monitoring of partner pacing • Increases noise level • Encourages some teacher–student competition
Alternative Teaching	• Facilitates enrichment opportunities • Offers absent students "catch up" time • Keeps individuals and class on pace • Offers time to develop missing skills	• May select same low-achieving students for help • Creates segregated learning environments • Is difficult to coordinate • May single out students

SOURCE: From Walther-Thomas, Chris, Lori Korinek, Virginia L. McLaughlin & Brenda Toler Williams, *Collaboration for Inclusive Education: Developing Successful Programs,* 1/e. Published by Allyn and Bacon, Boston, MA. Copyright © 2000 by Pearson Education. Reprinted by permission of the publisher.

Universal Design for Learning

In today's climate of high-stakes testing and calls for greater student and teacher accountability, full access to the general education curriculum for students with disabilities is receiving growing attention. One way of ensuring access to, along with participation and progress in, the general education curriculum, as required by PL 108-446, is via the concept of universal design. Originally an idea found in the field of architectural studies, **universal design for learning** can be simply stated as "the design of instructional materials and activities that allows the learning goals to be achievable by individuals with wide differences in their abilities to see, hear, speak, move, read, write, understand English, attend, organize, engage, and remember" (Orkwis & McLane, 1998, p. 9). Universal design allows education professionals the flexibility necessary to design curriculum, instruction, and evaluation procedures capable of meeting the needs of *all* students (Hitchcock, Meyer, Rose, & Jackson, 2002). Universal design for learning is accomplished by means of flexible curricular materials and activities that offer alternatives to pupils with widely varying abilities and backgrounds. These adaptations are built into the instructional design rather than added on later as an afterthought. Universal design for learning provides equal access to learning, not

Table 1.6	Recommendations for Successful Co-teaching
For working with children with disabilities:	**For working with general education teachers:**
• When you construct your plan, think about how you can make it visual, auditory, tactile, and kinesthetic. You'll have a better chance of meeting different learning styles. • Think about what is the most important thing all students need to learn and then think about how you can break the task into smaller parts for some students and make it more challenging for students who are ready to move ahead. • Be keenly aware of student strengths, and plan to find a way for each student to be successful academically every day. • Working with a peer/buddy is often a helpful strategy. • Mix up your groups now and then. A student may need a different group for reading than for math. Try not to "label" anyone. • Children with disabilities (many children actually) need very clear, precise directions. Pair auditory with visual directions if possible. Students with more severe impairments may need to see objects. • It may be helpful to only give one direction at a time. This doesn't mean the pace has to be slow. In fact, a fast pace is often quite effective. Using signals (for example, for getting attention, transitions) can also be very helpful. • Be consistent. • Notice students being "good"—offer verbal praise or perhaps a small positive note. • Have high expectations for *all* children.	• Find teachers who welcome your students and whom you enjoy working with if possible. It is helpful to find co-teachers who have different strengths so you can complement each other. • Faithfully plan ahead with these teachers—at least a week ahead. • Be willing to do more than your share at first if necessary to get a solid footing for the year. It will pay off. • Keep communication open and frequent. Use positive language with each other as much as possible. Brainstorm solutions to challenges together, and try different solutions. • Document the work you do with students. Help with assessment as much as possible. • Attend open houses, parent conferences, and other similar meetings so the parents view you as part of the classroom community. • Look for the good in the teacher(s) and students, and tell them when you see a "best practice." • If you don't know the answer to something, ask. If you don't know some of the content very well, study. Find out who does something well, and observe him/her if it is a skill you need to work on. • When you say you will do something, be sure you follow through.

Source: D. Metcalf, H. B. Sugg Elementary School, Farmville, NC. The Council for Exceptional Children (CEC) 2004 Clarissa Hug Teacher of the Year.

simply equal access to information. It assumes that there is no one method of presentation or expression, which provides equal access for all learners. Learning activities and materials are purposely designed to allow for flexibility and offer various ways to learn (Scott, McGuire, & Shaw, 2003). Table 1.7 presents some of the many different ways in which a teacher could present a lesson.

Universal design for learning is envisioned as an instructional resource, a vehicle for diversifying instruction in order to deliver the general education curriculum to each pupil. UDL does not remove academic challenges; it removes barriers to access. Simply stated, universal design for learning is just good teaching (Ohio State University Partnership Grant, 2006).

According to Wehmeyer, Lance, and Bashinski (2002), "universally designed curriculum takes into account individual student interests and preferences and individualizes representation, presentation, and response aspects of the curriculum delivery accordingly" (p. 230). It offers the opportunity for creating a curriculum that is sufficiently flexible to meet the needs of all learners. Universal design provides a range of options for accessing, using, and engaging learning materials—explicitly acknowledging that no one option will work for all students (Hitchcock et al., 2002). Some of the beneficiaries of this strategy include, for example, individuals who speak English as a second language, pupils with disabilities, and students whose preferred learning style is inconsistent with the teacher's teaching style (Ohio State University Partnership Grant, 2006). Three essential elements of universal design for learning are summarized in Figure 1.6.

Table 1.7		Multiple Methods of Presenting Instructional Content		
Auditory	**Visual**	**Tactile/Kinesthetic**	**Affective**	**Technology**
Lecture	Video clips	Field trip	Small group work	Digitized video PalmPilot Video conferencing
Discussion	Sign language Speech reading	Sign language Gestures	Cross-age tutoring Peer-mediated instruction	Electronic discussion boards Online chat rooms
Song	Watch a play	Drawing	Role play	
Read aloud	Books	Braille books		Tape recorder iPod
Questioning	Graph, table, chart Slide show Transparency White board	Demonstration Role play Dance Games Manipulatives Build an object		Spreadsheet PowerPoint Overhead data projector

NOTE: Not an exhaustive list; some methods may fit more than one category.

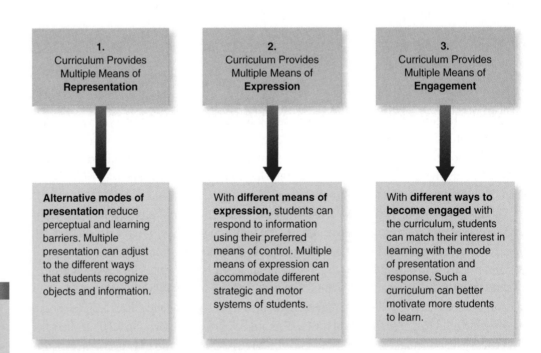

1. Curriculum Provides Multiple Means of **Representation**	2. Curriculum Provides Multiple Means of **Expression**	3. Curriculum Provides Multiple Means of **Engagement**
Alternative modes of presentation reduce perceptual and learning barriers. Multiple presentation can adjust to the different ways that students recognize objects and information.	With **different means of expression,** students can respond to information using their preferred means of control. Multiple means of expression can accommodate different strategic and motor systems of students.	With **different ways to become engaged** with the curriculum, students can match their interest in learning with the mode of presentation and response. Such a curriculum can better motivate more students to learn.

Figure 1.6	

Three Essential Qualities of Universal Design for Learning

SOURCE: Adapted from R. Orkwis and K. McLane, *A Curriculum Every Student Can Use: Design Principles For Student Access*, 1998. ERIC Document ED 423 654. p. 11.

Digital format is the most flexible means for presenting curricular materials:

- **Transformable** (easily changed from one medium of presentation to another)
- **Transportable** (customized for individual needs)
- **Recordable** ("learns" and "remembers" user patterns, tracks progress, and identifies areas of difficulty and strength)

Exceptionality across the Life Span

When we talk about special education, most people envision services for children of school age; yet the field embraces a wider range of individuals than students between the ages of 6 and 18. In recent years, professionals have begun to focus their attention on two distinct populations: infants/toddlers and preschoolers with special needs, and students with disabilities at the secondary level who are about to embark into adulthood. Meeting the needs of pupils at both ends of the spectrum presents a myriad of challenges for educators as well as related services personnel; however, professionals have a mandate to serve individuals across the life span.

Our purpose at this point is only to introduce some of the concepts and thinking about these two age groups. In later chapters, we will explore more fully many of the issues specific to young children with special needs as well as services for adults with disabilities.

Infants/Toddlers and Preschoolers with Special Needs

Prior to PL 94-142, services for infants, toddlers, and preschoolers with disabilities or delays were virtually unheard of. In many instances, parents had to seek out assistance on their own; public schools did not routinely offer early intervention or other supports. As we noted earlier in this chapter, even with the enactment of the Education for All Handicapped Children Act, more than half the states did not provide a special education for preschoolers with special needs. Today, professionals realize the importance and value of intervening in the lives of young children. Providing services to our youngest citizens with disabilities or delays has become a national priority. Presently, more than 1 million children from birth to age 5 receive some form of intervention or special education (U.S. Department of Education, 2007).

The Education of the Handicapped Act Amendments of 1986 (PL 99-457) is largely responsible for the rapid development of services for youngsters with disabilities or delays and those children who are at risk for future problems in learning and development. PL 99-457 is concerned with the family of the youngster with special needs as well as the child. This law clearly promotes parent–professional collaboration and partnerships. Parents are empowered to become decision makers with regard to programs and services for their son or daughter. We can see this emphasis in the **individualized family service plan**, or **IFSP** as it is commonly known. Similar to an IEP for older students with disabilities, the IFSP is much more family focused and reflective of the family's resources, priorities, and concerns. (Both of these documents will be fully discussed in Chapter 2.)

When professionals talk about providing services to very young children with disabilities or special needs, a distinction is generally made between two frequently used terms: *early intervention* and *early childhood special education*. **Early intervention** is typically used, according to Gargiulo and Kilgo (2005), to

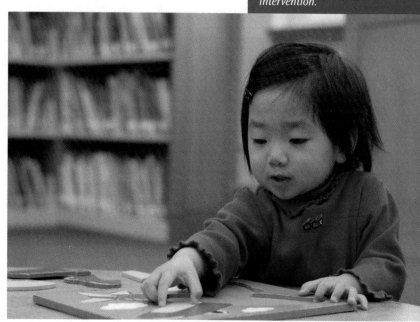

Young children with special needs greatly benefit from early intervention.

refer to the delivery of a coordinated and comprehensive package of specialized services to infants and toddlers (birth through age 2) with developmental delays or at-risk conditions and their families. **Early childhood special education** is used to describe the provision of customized services uniquely crafted to meet the individual needs of youngsters with disabilities between 3 and 5 years of age.

Early intervention represents a consortium of services, not just educational assistance but also health care, social services, family supports, and other benefits. The aim of early intervention is to affect positively the overall development of the child—his or her social, emotional, physical, and intellectual well-being. We believe that incorporating a "whole child" approach is necessary because all of these elements are interrelated and dependent on one another (Zigler, 2000).

Adolescents and Young Adults with Disabilities

Preparing our nation's young people for lives as independent adults has long been a goal of American secondary education. This objective typically includes the skills necessary for securing employment, pursuing postsecondary educational opportunities, participating in the community, living independently, and engaging in social/recreational activities, to mention only a few of the many facets of this multidimensional concept. Most young adults make this passage, or **transition,** from one phase of their life to the next without significant difficulty. Unfortunately, this statement is not necessarily true for many secondary students with disabilities. Full participation in adult life is a goal that is unattainable for a large number of citizens with disabilities. Consider the implications of the following facts gathered from various national surveys:

- Only 35 percent of adults with disabilities are employed on a full- or part-time basis, compared to 78 percent of adults without disabilities (Harris & Associates, 2004).
- Approximately one out of five adults with disabilities has less than a high school education; by way of comparison, only 11 percent of adults without disabilities lack a high school diploma (Harris & Associates, 2004).
- Only 55 percent of youths with disabilities are competitively employed after secondary school (National Longitudinal Transition Study 2, 2005).
- Three times as many individuals with disabilities live in poverty (incomes below $15,000) as compared to adults without disabilities (Harris & Associates, 2004).
- Approximately 21 percent of students with disabilities exit school by dropping out (U.S. Department of Education, 2006).
- About one out of three adults with disabilities is very satisfied with life in general compared to 61 percent of adults without disabilities (Harris & Associates, 2004).

The picture that the preceding data paint is rather bleak. This profile, according to one transition expert (Wehman, 1992), is unconscionable and unacceptable. What do these statistics say about the job professionals are doing in preparing adolescents with disabilities for the adult world? Can we do better? Obviously, we need to. It is abundantly clear that a large percentage of young people with disabilities have difficulty in making a smooth transition from adolescence to adulthood and from high school to adult life in their community. With more than 373,000 students with disabilities exiting the educational system annually (U.S. Department of Education, 2006), what happens to them after they leave is a crucial question confronting professionals and parents alike. This issue of transition has become one of the dominant themes in contemporary special education. Rarely has one topic, Wehman observes, captured the attention of the field for such a sustained period of time—more than two decades. Transitioning from high school to the many dimensions of independent adulthood has become a national educational priority.

TRANSITION DEFINED Several different definitions or interpretations of transition can be found in the professional literature. One of the earliest definitions was offered by Madeleine Will (1984), Assistant Secretary of Education, Office of Special Education and Rehabilitative Services (OSERS). Will viewed transition as

> a period that includes high school, the point of graduation, additional postsecondary education or adult services, and the initial years in employment. Transition is a bridge between the security and structure offered by the school and the opportunities and risks of adult life. . . . The transition from school to work and adult life requires sound preparation in the secondary school, adequate support at the point of school leaving, and secure opportunities and services, if needed, in adult situations. (p. 3)

According to Will, three levels of services are involved in providing for an individual to move successfully from school to adult employment. The top level, "no special services," refers to those generic services available to any citizen within the community, even if special accommodations may be necessary. An example of this form of support might be educational opportunities at a local community college or accessing state employment services. The middle rung of this model, "time-limited services," involves specialized, short-term services that are typically necessary because of a disability. Vocational rehabilitation services best illustrates this level of the model. "Ongoing services" constitutes the third level of this early model. This type of ongoing employment support system was not widely available in the early 1980s. However, it represented an integral component of Will's paradigm, and these services were promoted through federally funded demonstration projects (Halpern, 1992).

Commonly referred to as the "bridges model," Will's proposal sparked almost immediate debate and controversy from professionals who considered the OSERS interpretation of transition too restrictive or narrow (Brown, Albright, Rogan et al., 1988; Clark & Knowlton, 1988; Halpern, 1985). Adult adjustment, they argued, must be viewed as more than just employment. We agree with this point of view. Halpern, for example, believes it is wrong to focus exclusively on employment. Instead, he proposes that the primary goal of transition should be community adjustment, which includes "a person's residential environment and the adequacy of his or her social and interpersonal network. These two dimensions are viewed as being no less important than employment" (1985, p. 480). Thus, living successfully in the community should be the ultimate goal of transition. Halpern's reconfiguration of the OSERS model is portrayed in Figure 1.7.

Today, transition is viewed in much broader terms than Will originally proposed. This concept presently includes many different aspects of adult adjustment and participation in community life. The research evidence supports this expanded approach. Investigators (Hughes, Eisenman,

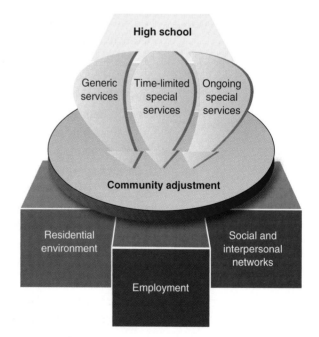

Figure 1.7

Halpern's Model of Transition Goals

SOURCE: A. Halpern, "Transition: A Look at the Foundations," *Exceptional Children,* 51(6), 1985, p. 481. Copyright © 1985 by The Council for Exceptional Children. Reprinted with permission.

Hwang, Kim, Killian, & Scott, 1997) have linked the roles of employment, personal competence, independent living, social interaction, and community adjustment to the successful passage from school to adult life for secondary special education students.

FEDERAL DEFINITION OF TRANSITION SERVICES PL 108-446 (IDEA) stipulates that each student with a disability is to receive **transition services,** which are defined as a coordinated set of activities for a student with a disability that

A. is designed within a results-oriented process, focused on improving the academic and functional achievement of the child with a disability to facilitate the child's movement from school to post-school activities, including post-secondary education, vocational training, integrated employment (including supported employment), continuing and adult education, adult services, independent living, or community participation;

B. is based upon the child's needs, taking into account the child's strengths, preferences, and interests; and

C. includes instruction, related services, community experiences, the development of employment and other post-school adult living objectives, and when appropriate, acquisition of daily living skills and functional vocational evaluation. [20 U.S.C. 1401 (34)]

INDIVIDUALIZED TRANSITION PLAN To ensure that the mandate for transition services is met, IDEA 2004 requires that each student, beginning no later than age 16 (and annually thereafter), have an **individualized transition plan (ITP)** incorporated into their IEP. This document, which complements the adolescent's IEP, must include postsecondary goals as well as a statement of the linkages and/or responsibilities that various agencies such as employment services, vocational rehabilitation, and the school system will assume in order to move the individual smoothly from school to living and working in the community. The ITP must also include a statement of transition service needs and courses of study that are intended to enhance the student's postschool success. Simply stated, an ITP is an annually updated instrument of coordination and cooperation. It is a working document that identifies the range of services, resources, supports, and activities that each student may require during the transition process.

TRANSITION CHALLENGES We conclude this introduction to transitioning adolescents from school to adult life by briefly examining two related areas of concern for professionals. The first issue is how to create a curriculum that prepares students to participate fully in all aspects of community life. Such a curriculum would need to address not only educational needs but also work behaviors, independent living skills, and recreational and leisure time activities. Traditional secondary curriculum, which typically emphasizes remedial academics, is often inadequate for preparing students for life after school (Berryman, 1993). As educators, we must increase the relevance of the curriculum. If we are to prepare students for successful postschool adjustment, then secondary programming for students with disabilities should reflect the basic functions of adult life—work, personal management, and leisure. The goal, according to McDonnell et al. (2003), is to link curricular content to the demands of living and working in the community as an independent adult. If we are to meet this challenge, our instructional strategies must change. Accompanying this shift from remedial academics to functional skills is the requirement that instruction occur in community-based settings—that is, in the natural environment where the skills are to be exhibited (Halpern, 1992). Research evidence (Hughes et al., 1997) supports the value and benefit of teaching skills in the actual environment in which they are to be performed.

The issue of curricular redesign must be balanced, however, by the increasing number of calls for greater emphasis on academic excellence. Thus, the second challenge for professionals is how to respond to the demands for higher standards while still preparing students for life after high school.

Beginning in the mid-1980s, various national reports strongly criticized the American educational system (Goodlad, 1984; National Commission on Excellence in Education, 1983). Major areas of concern included the declining academic achievement of U.S. students in comparison to youths from other industrialized nations, adult illiteracy, dropout rates, and readiness for school. These concerns were initially addressed in 1989 by the nation's governors, meeting at the first-ever Education Summit. Several broad national goals emerged from this historic conference, establishing a blueprint for educational progress. In March 1994, Congress enacted Goals 2000: Educate America Act (PL 103-227), which translated these reform efforts into law. Similarly, in 2001, Congress reauthorized the Elementary and Secondary Education Act, popularly known as the No Child Left Behind Act of 2001 (PL 107-110). This legislation (to be discussed in Chapter 2) reflects President George W. Bush's

Preparing young adults with disabilities to enter the workforce is an important role for schools.

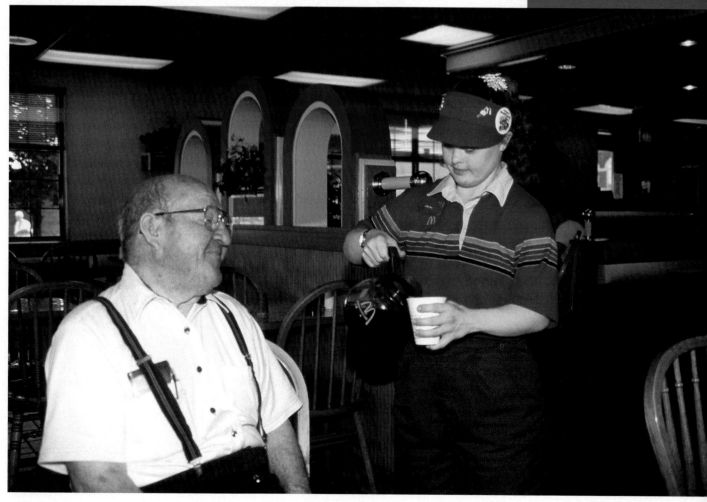

commitment to educational reform and greater accountability. This ambitious law requires that eventually all pupils, including those in special education, be expected to demonstrate proficiency in reading and mathematics, with science eventually being included.

Consequently, one question now confronting educators, parents, and even students is, What is an appropriate curriculum for students with disabilities at the secondary level, given this climate of tougher academic standards and greater educational accountability? Should the curriculum reflect an academic emphasis, should it focus on preparation for adult life, or is it possible to merge these two potentially conflicting points of view? Obviously, these are difficult questions, with no easy solution. What is best for one student may not be appropriate for another. Transition programs must be customized to the individual needs and desired outcomes of each young adult.

We believe an argument can be made that transitioning is for *all* students, not just those with disabilities. Transitioning, Wehman (1992) reasons, must be part of the overall educational reform movement. Many students, with and without disabilities, will require support and assistance as they cross the bridge from school to adult life in the community. Our job as educators is to make this journey as successful as possible for each and every one of our pupils.

Chapter in Review

Definitions and Terminology

- **Exceptional children** are individuals who resemble other children in many ways but differ from societal standards of normalcy. These differences may be due to physical, sensory, cognitive, or behavioral characteristics.

- When educators talk about a student with a **disability,** they are referring to an inability or incapacity to perform a particular task or activity in a specific way because of sensory, physical, cognitive, or other forms of impairment.

- The term **handicap** should be restricted to describing the consequence or impact of the disability on the person, not the condition itself.

- A **special education** can be defined as a customized instructional program designed to meet the unique needs of the pupil. A special education may include the use of specialized materials, equipment, services, or instructional strategies.

Categories and Labels

- The Individuals with Disabilities Education Improvement Act (PL 108-446) identifies thirteen disability categories.

- Empirical investigations fail to provide clear-cut answers to questions about the effects of labels on children and young adults with disabilities.

Prevalence of Children and Young Adults with Disabilities

- At the present time, more than 6.1 million students between the ages of 6 and 21 are receiving a special education. Of this total, about half are individuals with learning disabilities.

- Collectively, states are providing a special education to more than 7.1 million individuals from birth through age 21.

A Brief History of the Development of Special Education

- Historically speaking, the foundation of contemporary societal attitudes can be traced to the contributions of various reform-minded eighteenth- and nineteenth-century European educators, philosophers, and humanitarians.

- By the middle of the nineteenth century, several specialized institutions were established in the United States.

- It was not until the latter part of the nineteenth century and early years of the twentieth century that special education classes began to appear in public schools.

Professionals Who Work with Individuals with Exceptionalities

- Educators frequently work with a variety of other professionals representing several distinct disciplines. These individuals provide a wide variety of **related services,** ranging from occupational therapy to therapeutic recreation to psychological services and even transportation to and from school.

- Providing consultative services to both general and special educators is one way that school districts are attempting to meet the increasingly complex demands of serving students with disabilities.

- The three teaming models most frequently mentioned in the professional literature are **multidisciplinary, interdisciplinary,** and **transdisciplinary teams.**

Cooperative Teaching

- **Cooperative teaching,** or co-teaching as it is sometimes called, is an increasingly popular approach for facilitating successful inclusion.

- Cooperative teaching is an instructional strategy designed to provide support to all students in the general education classroom.

- Teachers can choose from multiple models of cooperative teaching depending on their specific circumstances.

Universal Design for Learning

- **Universal design for learning** is an instructional resource designed to meet the needs of all students; it provides equal access to learning.

- Universal design for learning allows for multiple means of representation, expression, and engagement.

Exceptionality across the Life Span

- Thirty years ago, services for children with disabilities younger than age 6 were virtually unheard of. Today, however, over 1 million children younger than 6 receive some type of intervention or special education.

- Over the past two decades, the issue of **transition** has become one of the dominant themes in contemporary special education.

- Every high school student who is enrolled in a special education program is to have an **individualized transition plan (ITP)** as part of his or her **individualized education program,** or IEP.

Study Questions

1. How is the concept of normalcy related to the definition of children identified as exceptional?

2. Differentiate between the terms *disability* and *handicap.* Provide specific examples for each term.

3. What is a special education?

4. Name the thirteen categories of exceptionality presently recognized by the federal government.

5. Compare and contrast arguments for and against the practice of labeling pupils according to their disability.

6. How are the terms *prevalence* and *incidence* used when discussing individuals with disabilities?

7. Identify contributing factors to the growth of the field of special education.

8. Why do you think the federal government has not mandated special education for students who are gifted and talented?

9. What role did Europeans play in the development of special education in the United States?

10. What are related services, and why are they important for the delivery of a special education?

11. List the characteristics that distinguish multidisciplinary, interdisciplinary, and transdisciplinary educational teams. What are the advantages and disadvantages of each teaming model?

12. How can cooperative teaching benefit students with and without disabilities?

13. Explain how universal design for learning benefits all students.

14. Why is transitioning important for students with disabilities at the secondary level?

15. What challenges do professionals face as they prepare adolescents to move from school to adult life in the community?

Key Terms

exceptional children
disability
handicap
handicapism
developmental delay
at-risk
special education

related services
category
noncategorical
incidence
prevalence
self-contained
collaboration

individualized education
program (IEP)
consultation
multidisciplinary
interdisciplinary
transdisciplinary
cooperative teaching

universal design for learning
individualized family service plan (IFSP)
early intervention
early childhood special education
transition
transition services
individualized transition plan (ITP)

Learning Activities

1. Keep a journal for at least four weeks in which you record how individuals with disabilities are represented in newspapers, magazines, television commercials, and other media outlets. Are they portrayed as someone to be pitied, or as a superhero? Is "people-first" language used? Do your examples perpetuate stereotyping, or are they realistic representations of persons with disabilities? In what context was the individual shown? What conclusions might a layperson draw about people with disabilities?

2. Visit an elementary school and a high school in your community. Talk to several special educators at each location. Find out how students with disabilities are served. What related services do these pupils receive? Ask each teacher to define the term *special education*. How are regular and special educators collaborating to provide an appropriate education for each learner? What strategies and activities are secondary teachers incorporating to prepare their students for life after graduation?

3. Obtain prevalence figures for students enrolled in special education programs in your state. How do these data compare to national figures? Identify possible reasons for any discrepancies. Do the figures suggest any trends in enrollment? Which category of exceptionality is growing the fastest?

4. Interview a veteran special educator (someone who has been teaching since the late 1970s). Ask this person how the field of special education has changed over the past decades. In what ways are things still the same? What issues and challenges does this teacher confront in his or her career? What is this person's vision of the future of special education?

5. Contact the office of disability support at your college or university. What types of services do they provide to students with disabilities? Volunteer to serve in this program.

Reflecting on Standards

The following exercises are designed to help you learn to apply the Council for Exceptional Children (CEC) standards to your teaching practice. Each of the reflection exercises below correlates with a knowledge or skill within the CEC standards. For the full text of each of the related CEC standards, please refer to the standards integration grid located in Appendix B.

1. Focus on Instructional Strategies (*CEC Content Standard #4 CC4S1*)

Reflect on what you have learned about co-teaching in this chapter. If you were to have a student with special needs in your class, which of these models (team teaching, station teaching, parallel teaching, alternative teaching) would you want to integrate into your teaching? What would be the advantages and disadvantages to you and your class in incorporating these strategies?

2. Focus on Collaboration (*CEC Content Standard #10 CC10K2*)

Reflect on what you have learned in this chapter about the importance of building partnerships to create students' individualized education programs. What collaborative skills do you have that will benefit you in this type of team work? What skills do you need to improve upon?

Technology Resources

Visit the Web-based SAGE Study Site at **http://www.sagepub.com/gargiulo3estudy** for these additional learning tools:

- Chapter quizzes
- Key term flashcards
- Media links

- Full-text SAGE journal articles
- Internet activities
- Additional Web resources

CHAPTER 2

Policies, Practices, and Programs

M any of the policies, procedures, and practices that are common in special education today have resulted from the interaction of a variety of forces, situations, and events. One example is the role that litigation and legislation have played in the development of the field. Coupled with this activity was the gradual realization by professionals that many of our earlier educational customs and methods were ineffective in meeting the needs of individuals with disabilities and their families. Several currently accepted practices, such as nondiscriminatory assessment, placement in a least restrictive environment, and meaningful parent involvement, reflect this correction in thinking.

The purpose of this chapter is to review a variety of contributions that have helped to shape contemporary special education. Besides the impact of national legislation and the courts, we will examine the identification and assessment of individual differences, instructional programming, and models of service delivery.

Litigation and Legislation Affecting Special Education

Over the past several decades, the field of special education has been gradually transformed and restructured, largely as a result of judicial action and legislative enactments. These two forces have been powerful tools in securing many of the benefits and rights presently enjoyed by more than 6.8 million pupils with disabilities.

Securing the opportunity for an education has been a slowly evolving process for students with disabilities. What is today seen as a fundamental right for these children was, at one time, viewed strictly as a privilege. Excluding students with disabilities from attending school was a routine practice of local boards of education in the 1890s and early 1900s. In 1893, local school officials in Cambridge, Massachusetts, denied an education to one individual because this student was thought to be too "weak minded" to profit from instruction. In 1919, in Antigo, Wisconsin, a student of normal intelligence but with a type of paralysis attended school through the fifth grade but was subsequently suspended because "his physical appearance nauseated teachers and other students, his disability required an undue amount of his teacher's time, and he had a negative impact on the discipline and progress of the school" (Osborne, 1996, p. 4). In both instances, state supreme courts upheld the decisions of the school boards. Today, these actions would be seen as clear violations of the pupils' rights and a flagrant disregard for the equal protection clause of the Fourteenth Amendment to the U.S. Constitution. Still, almost four decades passed before students with disabilities had a legal means for acquiring educational rights.

In the 1954 landmark school desegregation case, *Brown v. Board of Education of Topeka* (347 U.S. 483), the U.S. Supreme Court reasoned that it was unlawful to discriminate against a group of individuals for arbitrary reasons. The Court specifically ruled that separate schools for black and white students were inherently unequal, contrary to the Fourteenth Amendment, and thus unconstitutional. Furthermore, education was characterized as a fundamental function of government that should be afforded to all citizens on an equal basis. Though primarily recognized as striking down racial segregation, the thinking articulated in *Brown* had major implications for children with disabilities. Much of contemporary litigation and legislation affecting special education is legally, as well as morally, grounded in the precedents established by *Brown*.

The movement to secure equal educational opportunity for children with disabilities was also aided by the U.S. civil rights movement of the 1960s. As Americans attempted to deal with issues of discrimination, inequality, and other social ills, advocates for individuals with disabilities also pushed for equal rights. Parental activism was ignited. Lawsuits were filed and legislation enacted primarily as a result of the untiring, vocal, collaborative efforts of parents and politically powerful advocacy groups. The success of these tactics was felt at the local, state, and eventually, national level.

It is exceedingly difficult to say which came first, litigation or legislation. Both of these forces have played major roles in the development of state and federal policy concerning special education. They enjoy a unique and almost symbiotic relationship—one of mutual interdependence. Litigation frequently leads to legislation, which in turn spawns additional judicial action as the courts interpret and clarify the law, which often leads to further legislation (see Figure 2.1). Regardless of the progression, much of special education today has a legal foundation.

Key Judicial Decisions

Since the 1960s and early 1970s, a plethora of state and federal court decisions have helped to shape and define a wide range of issues affecting contemporary special education policies and procedures. Although a thorough review of this litigation is beyond the scope of this chapter, Table 2.1 summarizes, in chronological order, some of the landmark cases affecting the field of special education. Several of the judicial remedies emanating from these lawsuits serve as cornerstones for both federal and state legislative enactments focusing on students with disabilities. Furthermore, many of today's accepted practices in special education, such as nondiscriminatory assessments and due process procedures, can trace their roots to various court decisions.

Individuals with Disabilities Education Act: 1975–1997

Federal legislative intervention in the lives of persons with disabilities is of relatively recent origin. Before the late 1950s and early 1960s, little federal attention was paid to citizens with special needs. When legislation was enacted, it primarily assisted specific groups of individuals, such as those who were deaf or mentally retarded. The past thirty years, however, have witnessed a flurry of legislative activity that has aided the growth of special education and provided educational benefits and other opportunities and rights to children

Litigation
Mills v. Board of Education
(1972)

Legislation
IDEA (PL 94-142)

Litigation
Smith v. Robinson
(1984)

Legislation
Handicapped Children's
Protection Act
(PL 99-372)

Figure 2.1

An Example of the Interrelationship between Litigation and Legislation

Source: Adapted from *The Law and Special Education*, 2nd ed., by M. L. Yell, © 2006, p.15. Reprinted by permission of Pearson Education, Inc., Upper Saddle River, NJ.

(Text continues on page 48)

Table 2.1		A Synopsis of Selected Court Cases Influencing Special Education	
Case	**Year**	**Issue**	**Judicial Decision**
Brown v. Board of Education of Topeka, Kansas	1954	Educational segregation	Segregation of students by race ruled unconstitutional; children deprived of equal educational opportunity. Effectively ended "separate but equal" schools for white and black pupils. Used as a precedent for arguing that children with disabilities cannot be excluded from a public education.
Hobson v. Hansen	1967	Classifying students	Ability grouping or "tracking" of students on the basis of nationally normed tests, which were found to be biased, held to be unconstitutional. Tracking systems discriminated against poor and minority children, thus denying them an equal educational opportunity. Equal protection clause of Fourteenth Amendment violated.
Diana v. State Board of Education	1970	Class placement	Linguistically different students must be tested in their primary language as well as English. Students cannot be placed in special education classes on the basis of IQ tests that are culturally biased. Verbal test items to be revised so as to reflect students' cultural heritage. Group-administered IQ tests cannot be used to place children in programs for individuals with mental retardation.
Pennsylvania Association for Retarded Children v. Commonwealth of Pennsylvania	1972	Right to education	State must guarantee a free public education to all children with mental retardation ages 6–21 regardless of degree of impairment or associated disabilities. Students to be placed in the most integrated environment. Definition of education expanded. Case established the right of parents to participate in educational decisions affecting their children. State to engage in extensive efforts to locate and serve ("child-find") all students with mental retardation. Preschool services to be provided to youngsters with mental retardation if local school district serves preschoolers who are not retarded.
Mills v. Board of Education, District of Columbia	1972	Right to education	Extended the Pennsylvania decision to include all children with disabilities. Specifically established the constitutional right of children with exceptionalities to a public education regardless of their functional level. Students have a right to a "constructive education" matched to their needs, including specialized instruction. Presumed absence of fiscal resources is not a valid reason for failing to provide appropriate educational services to students with disabilities. Elaborate due process safeguards established to protect the rights of the child, including parental notification of pending initial evaluation, reassignment, or planned termination of special services.
Larry P. v. Riles	1972, 1979	Class placement	A landmark case parallel to the *Diana* suit. African American students could not be placed in classes for children with mild mental retardation solely on the basis of intellectual assessments found to be culturally and racially biased. The court instructed school officials to develop an assessment process that would not discriminate against minority children. Failure to comply with this order resulted in a 1979 ruling that completely prohibited the use of IQ tests for placing African American students in classes for children with mild mental retardation. Ruling applies only to the state of California.
Wyatt v. Stickney	1972	Right to treatment	Individuals with mental retardation residing in a state institution have a right to appropriate treatment. Absence of meaningful education reduces opportunity for habilitation and thus may be considered unlawful detention. State mandated to ensure a therapeutic environment for residential population.

(Continued)

Table 2.1			A Synopsis of Selected Court Cases Influencing Special Education (Continued)
Case	**Year**	**Issue**	**Judicial Decision**
Stuart v. Nappi	1978	Expulsion from school	Expulsion of a pupil with disabilities for disciplinary reasons without due process was disallowed. Expulsion was considered a change in placement and a denial of the opportunity for an appropriate education. School authorities, however, can temporarily suspend students with disabilities who are disruptive.
Armstrong v. Klein	1980	Extended school year	State's refusal to pay for schooling in excess of 180 days for pupils with severe disabilities is a violation of their rights to an appropriate education as required by PL 94-142. The court found that some children with disabilities will regress significantly during summer recess and have longer recoupment periods; thus, they are denied an appropriate education if not provided with a year-round education.
Tatro v. State of Texas	1980	Related services	U.S. Supreme Court held that catheterization qualified as a related service under PL 94-142. Catheterization was not considered an exempted medical procedure, as it could be performed by a health care aide or school nurse. Court further stipulated that only those services that allow a student to benefit from a special education qualify as related services.
Board of Education addressed of the Hendrick Hudson Central School District v. Rowley	1982	Appropriate education	First U.S. Supreme Court interpretation of PL 94-142. Court addressed the issue of what constitutes an "appropriate" education for a student with hearing impairments making satisfactory educational progress. Supreme Court ruled that an appropriate education does not necessarily mean an education that will allow for the maximum possible achievement; rather, students must be given a reasonable opportunity to learn. Parents' request for a sign language interpreter, therefore, was denied. An appropriate education is not synonymous with an optimal educational experience.
Smith v. Robinson	1984	Recovery of attorney fees	U.S. Supreme Court ruled that parents cannot be reimbursed for legal expenses under PL 94-142. Issue subsequently addressed by Congress, which enacted PL 99-372 permitting such payment. Court also stipulated that claims cannot be filed simultaneously under PL 94-142 and Section 504 of PL 93-112; when available, IDEA is to be the exclusive avenue.
Honig v. Doe	1988	Exclusion from school	Children with special needs whose behavior is a direct result of their disability cannot be expelled from school for misbehavior. If behavior leading to expulsion is not a consequence of the exceptionality, pupil may be expelled. Short-term suspension from school not interpreted as a change in pupil's individualized education program (IEP).
Daniel R.R. v. State Board of Education	1989	Class placement	Fifth Circuit Court of Appeals held that a segregated class was an appropriate placement for a student with Down syndrome. Preference for integrated placement viewed as secondary to the need for an appropriate education. Court established a two-prong test for determining compliance with the least restrictive environment (LRE) mandate for students with severe disabilities. First, it must be determined if a pupil can make satisfactory progress and achieve educational benefit in the general education classroom through curriculum modification and the use of supplementary aids and services. Second, it must be determined whether the pupil has been integrated to the maximum extent appropriate.

Table 2.1		A Synopsis of Selected Court Cases Influencing Special Education (Continued)	
Case	**Year**	**Issue**	**Judicial Decision**
			Successful compliance with both parts fulfills a school's obligation under federal law. Ruling affects LRE cases in Louisiana, Texas, and Mississippi, but has become a benchmark decision for other jurisdictions as well.
Timothy W. v. Rochester (New Hampshire) School District	1989	Right to education	Reaffirmation of the principle of zero-reject education. First Circuit Court of Appeals established entitlement to a free and appropriate public education regardless of the severity of the child's disability. IDEA interpreted to mean all students; pupil need not demonstrate an ability to benefit from a special education. Education defined broadly to include instruction in functional skills.
Carter v. Florence County School District Four	1991	IEP goals, private school costs	Fourth Circuit Court of Appeals held that an IEP goal of four months' progress in reading during the school year was insufficient to allow the pupil to achieve academic progress. Absence of meaningful growth seen as evidence of an inappropriate IEP and thus failure to provide an appropriate education. Case was eventually heard on a related issue by the U.S. Supreme Court in 1993 (*Florence County School District Four v. Carter*). The Court ruled that, because of the school district's failure to comply with IDEA, the student's parents were eligible to receive reimbursement for unilaterally enrolling their daughter in a nonaccredited private residential school as long as the school was providing an appropriate education.
Oberti v. Board of Education of the Borough of Clementon School District	1992	Least restrictive environment	Placement in a general education classroom with supplementary aids and services must be offered to a student with disabilities prior to considering more segregated placements. Pupil cannot be excluded from a general education classroom solely because curriculum, services, or other practices would require modification. A decision to exclude a learner from the general education classroom necessitates justification and documentation. Clear judicial preference for educational integration established.
Agostini v. Felton	1997	Provision of services	U.S. Supreme Court reversed a long-standing ruling banning the delivery of publicly funded educational services to students enrolled in private schools. Interpreted to mean that special educators can now provide services to children in parochial schools.
Cedar Rapids Community School District v. Garret F.	1999	Related services	U.S. Supreme Court expanded and clarified the concept of related services. Affirmed that intensive and continuous school health care services necessary for a student to attend school, if not performed by a physician, qualify as related services.
Schaffer v. Weast	2005	Burden of proof	A U.S. Supreme Court ruling addressing the issue of whether the parent(s) or school district bears the burden of proof in a due process hearing. The specific question before the Court was whether the parent(s), acting on behalf of their son or daughter, must prove that their child's individualized education program (IEP) is inappropriate or whether the school district must prove that the IEP is appropriate. The court ruled that the burden of proof is placed upon the party seeking relief.

Source: Adapted from R. Gargiulo and J. Kilgo, *Young Children with Special Needs: An Introduction to Early Childhood Special Education*, 2nd ed. (Clifton Park, NY: Delmar, 2005), pp. 31–34.

and adults with disabilities. Between 1827 and 1975, a total of 175 federal laws addressing individuals with disabilities were enacted; 61 of these laws were passed between March 1970 and March 1975 (Weintraub, Abeson, Ballard, & LaVor, 1976).

Given the multitude of public laws[1] affecting special education, we will focus on landmark legislation. We will examine four significant pieces of legislation that have dramatically affected the educational opportunities of infants, toddlers, preschoolers, school-age children, and young adults with disabilities. Our initial review will focus on PL 94-142, the Education for All Handicapped Children Act, or as it is now called, the Individuals with Disabilities Education Act (IDEA). This change in legislative titles resulted from the enactment on October 30, 1990, of PL 101-476, which will be reviewed later.

PUBLIC LAW 94-142 The Individuals with Disabilities Education Act is viewed as a "Bill of Rights" for children with exceptionalities and their families; it is the culmination of many years of dedicated effort by both parents and professionals. Like many other special educators, we consider this law to be one of the most important, if not the most important, pieces of federal legislation ever enacted on behalf of children with special needs. PL 94-142 may rightfully be thought of as the legislative heart of special education.

The purpose of this bill, which was signed into law by President Gerald Ford on November 29, 1975, is

> to assure that all handicapped children have available to them . . . a free appropriate public education which emphasizes special education and related services designed to meet their unique needs, to assure that the rights of handicapped children and their parents or guardians are protected, to assist States and localities to provide for the education of all handicapped children, and to assess and assure the effectiveness of efforts to educate handicapped children. [Section 601(c)]

In pursuing these four purposes, this legislation incorporates six major components and guarantees that have forever changed the landscape of education across the United States. Despite legislative and court challenges over the past three decades, the following principles have endured to the present day:

- **A free appropriate public education (FAPE).** All children, regardless of the severity of their disability (a "zero reject" philosophy), must be provided an education appropriate to their unique needs at no cost to the parent(s)/guardian(s). Included in this principle is the concept of related services, which requires that children receive, for example, occupational therapy as well as other services as necessary in order to benefit from special education.
- **The least restrictive environment (LRE).** Children with disabilities are to be educated, to the maximum extent appropriate, with students without disabilities. Placements must be consistent with the pupil's educational needs.
- **An individualized education program (IEP).** This document, developed in conjunction with the parent(s)/guardian(s), is an individually tailored statement describing an educational plan for each learner with exceptionalities. The IEP, which will be fully discussed later in this chapter, is required to address (1) the present level of academic

---

1. National legislation, or public laws (PL), are codified according to a standardized format. Legislation is thus designated by the number of the session of Congress that enacted the law followed by the number of the particular bill. PL 94-142, for example, was enacted by the 94th session of Congress and was the 142nd piece of legislation passed.

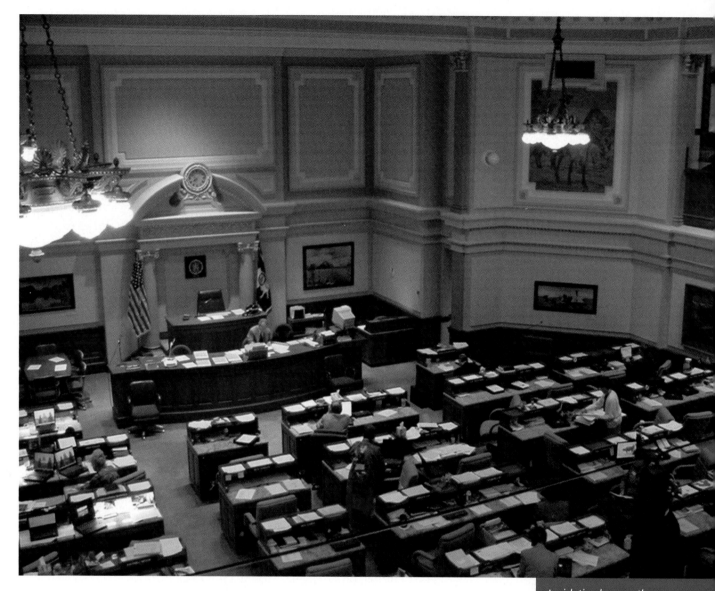

Legislation has greatly benefited individuals with disabilities and their families.

functioning (commonly referred to by school personnel as present level of performance); (2) annual goals and accompanying instructional objectives; (3) educational services to be provided; (4) the degree to which the pupil will be able to participate in general education programs; (5) plans for initiating services and length of service delivery; and (6) an annual evaluation procedure specifying objective criteria to determine if instructional objectives are being met. Many teachers and school administrators refer to this as progress monitoring.

- **Procedural due process.** The Act affords parent(s)/guardian(s) several safeguards as it pertains to their child's education. Briefly, parent(s)/guardian(s) have the right to confidentiality of records; to examine all records; to obtain an independent evaluation; to receive written notification (in parents' native language) of proposed changes to their child's educational classification or placement; and the right to an impartial hearing whenever disagreements arise regarding educational plans for their son/daughter. Furthermore, the student's parent(s)/guardian(s) have the right to representation by legal counsel.

- **Nondiscriminatory assessment.** Prior to placement, a child must be evaluated by a multidisciplinary team in all areas of suspected disability by tests that are neither racially, culturally, nor linguistically biased. Students are to receive several types of assessments, administered by trained personnel; a single evaluation procedure is not permitted for either planning or placement purposes.

- **Parental participation.** PL 94-142 mandates meaningful parent involvement. Sometimes referred to as the "Parent's Law," this legislation requires that parents participate fully in the decision-making process that affects their child's education.

Congress indicated its desire by September 1, 1980, to provide a free appropriate public education for all eligible children ages 3 through 21. The law, however, did not require services to preschool children with disabilities. Because many states were not providing preschool services to typical children, an education for young children with special needs, in most instances, was not mandated. Although this legislation failed to require an education for younger children, it clearly focused attention on the preschool population and recognized the value of early education.

PL 94-142 did contain some benefits for children under school age. It offered small financial grants (Preschool Incentive Grants) to the individual states as an incentive to serve young children with disabilities. It also carried a mandate for schools to identify and evaluate children from birth through age 21 suspected of evidencing a disability. Finally, PL 94-142 moved from a census count to a child count of the actual number of individuals with disabilities being served. The intent was to encourage the states to locate and serve children with disabilities.

Providing a special education to millions of students with disabilities is a very expensive proposition. Congress realized that many school districts would not have sufficient funds to provide the needed services without additional financial support from the federal government. It was the intent of Congress to pay 40 percent of the excess cost of educating pupils enrolled in special education programs. Unfortunately, federal support never achieved this level; over the years, actual appropriations have typically remained closer to 9–10 percent ("Congress Passes IDEA," 1997; U.S. Department of Education, 2002). Thus, the bulk of the costs for educating children with special needs falls on the financial shoulders of state governments and local school districts. Annual costs for educating a student in special education are approximately twice the expenditure for a student enrolled in general education (Center for Special Education Finance, 2004). Of course, the costs vary tremendously depending on the nature and severity of the student's disability.

PUBLIC LAW 99-457 (1986 AMENDMENTS TO PL 94-142) In October 1986, Congress passed one of the most comprehensive pieces of legislation affecting young children with special needs and their families—PL 99-457. This law changed both the scope and intent of services provided to preschoolers with special needs and formulated a national policy for infants and toddlers at risk for and with identified disabilities.

As noted earlier, IDEA gave the states financial incentives to provide an education and related services to preschool children with disabilities. This was a permissive or voluntary element of the Act, not a mandated requirement. Trohanis (1989) reported congressional data indicating that less than 80 percent of the estimated 330,000 youngsters with disabilities ages 3 to 5 were being served. An estimated 70,000 preschoolers were, therefore, unserved. PL 99-457, the Education of the Handicapped Act Amendments of 1986, was enacted to remedy this situation.

Simply stated, this law is a downward extension of PL 94-142, including all its rights and protections. This legislation does not require that preschoolers be identified with a specific disability label. It does demand that, as of the 1991–1992 school year, all preschoolers with special needs, ages 3 through 5 inclusive, are to receive a free and appropriate public education. This element of the law is a mandated requirement; states will lose significant amounts of federal preschool funding if they fail to comply. The goal of this legislation was finally accomplished in the 1992–1993 school year, when all states had mandates in place establishing a free and appropriate public education for all children with disabilities ages 3 through 5.

Title I of PL 99-457 created the Handicapped Infants and Toddlers Program (Part H), a new provision aimed at children from birth through age 2 with developmental delays or disabilities. This component of the legislation is voluntary; states are not compelled to comply. This part of the statute creates a discretionary program that assists states in implementing a statewide, comprehensive, coordinated, multidisciplinary,

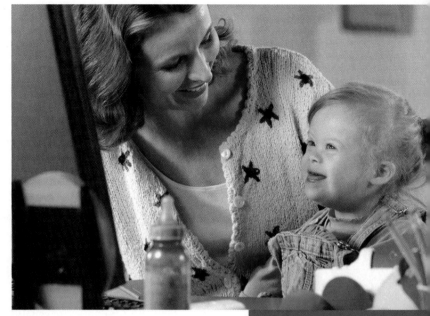

Many young children with developmental delays or disabilities have benefited from early intervention.

interagency program of services for very young children and their families who are experiencing developmental delays or who evidence a physical or mental condition that has a high probability of resulting in a delay, such as cerebral palsy or Down syndrome. (At the state's discretion, youngsters who are at risk for future delays may also be served.) As of September 30, 1994, all states had plans in place for the full implementation of Part H (U.S. Department of Education, 1995).

Eligible children and their families must receive a multidisciplinary assessment conducted by qualified professionals and a written individualized family service plan, or IFSP. An IFSP must be reviewed every six months (or sooner if necessary) to assess its continued appropriateness. The law requires that each infant or toddler be reevaluated annually. Regulations further stipulate that an IFSP must be developed within 45 days after a referral for services is made.

PL 99-457 is the product of a decade of hard work by parents, professionals, advocates, and legislators. It represents an opportunity to intervene and effect meaningful change in the lives of our nation's youngest and most vulnerable children.

PUBLIC LAW 101-476 (1990 AMENDMENTS TO PL 94-142) Arguably, one of the most important changes contained in this legislation was the renaming of PL 94-142 as the Individuals with Disabilities Education Act (IDEA). "Children" was replaced with the term "individuals" and "handicapped" became "with disabilities." This phrase signifies a change in attitude to a more appropriate person-first point of view. We now realize that an individual's disability is but one aspect of his or her personhood.

Congress also recognized the importance of preparing adolescents for a productive life after they exit from public school. These amendments required that each student have, no later than age 16, an individual transition plan (ITP) as part of his/her IEP. This plan allows for a coordinated set of activities and interagency linkages designed to promote the student's movement to postschool functions such as independent living, vocational training, and additional educational experiences.

PL 101-476 also expanded the scope of the related services provision by adding two services: social work and rehabilitation counseling. Another element of this legislation was the identification of autism and traumatic brain injury as distinct disability categories. Previously, these disabilities had been subsumed under other disability labels. Lastly, Congress repealed states' immunity from lawsuits for violating IDEA. This part of the Act allows parents and others to sue a state in federal court for noncompliance with the provisions of the law.

PUBLIC LAW 105-17 (1997 AMENDMENTS TO IDEA) After more than two years of intense and sometimes difficult negotiations, Congress was finally able to pass a comprehensive revision to IDEA. The IDEA Act Amendments of 1997 was overwhelmingly supported by both houses of the 105th Congress and was signed into law by President Bill Clinton on June 4, 1997.

This law restructures IDEA into four parts, revises some definitions, and revamps several key components, ranging from funding to disciplining students with disabilities to how IEPs are to be developed. Here are some of the more significant changes:

- Students with disabilities who bring weapons to school, possess or use illegal drugs, or pose a serious threat of injury to other pupils or themselves may be removed from their current placement only after a due process hearing and for no more than 45 days. Students who are suspended or expelled are still entitled to receive a free and appropriate public education in accordance with their IEP.
- Pupils with disabilities who exhibit less serious infractions of school conduct may be disciplined in ways similar to children without disabilities (including a change in placement) provided that the misbehavior was not a manifestation of the student's disability.
- IEPs are now required to state how the student with disabilities will be involved with and progress in the general education curriculum. Other provisions stipulate that transition planning will begin at age 14 instead of age 16, regular educators will become part of the IEP team, benchmarks and measurable annual goals will be emphasized, and the assistive technology needs of each learner must be considered by the IEP team.
- Orientation and mobility services for children with visual impairments are now included in the definition of related services.
- The present mandate of comprehensive triennial reevaluation of pupils with disabilities is lifted if school authorities and the student's parents both agree that this process is unnecessary.
- A new section on mediation requires states to offer mediation services to help resolve disputes as an alternative to using more costly and lengthy due process hearings. Parental participation is voluntary, and parents still retain their right to a due process hearing.
- The category of developmental delay may now be used when describing children ages 3 through 9. The use of this term is at the discretion of the state and local education agency.
- Initial evaluations and reevaluations are not restricted to the use of formal, standardized tests. A variety of assessment tools and strategies are to be used in an effort to gather relevant functional and developmental information. Curriculum-based tests, portfolio reviews, parental input, and the observations of teachers and related service providers may be considered in determining whether or not the student has a disability and in developing the content of the IEP. A student may not be considered eligible for a special education if educational difficulties are primarily the result of limited proficiency in English or lack of adequate instruction in math and/or reading.
- A new mechanism for distributing federal monies will occur once the appropriations reach a threshold of $4.9 billion. Upon attaining this level, states and local school systems will receive additional funding based on 85 percent of the population of children ages 3 to 21 and 15 percent of the number of children ages 3 through 21 who are in poverty. This switch to a census-based formula instead of the current

enrollment-driven formula resulted from a concern that some schools were overidentifying students to receive additional funding. No state would receive less than the amount of support it received in the year before activation of this new scheme.

- The reauthorization of IDEA requires schools to establish performance goals for students with disabilities in an effort to assess their academic progress. Additionally, these youngsters are to be included in statewide and districtwide assessment programs or given alternative assessments that meet their unique needs.

Civil Rights Legislation

Section 504 of the Rehabilitation Act of 1973

The four pieces of legislation that we just examined are representative special education laws. PL 93-112, the Rehabilitation Act of 1973, however, is a *civil rights* law. Section 504 of this enactment was the first public law specifically aimed at protecting children and adults against discrimination due to a disability. It said that no individual can be excluded, solely because of his or her disability, from participating in or benefiting from any program or activity receiving federal financial assistance, which includes schools (*CEC Today,* 1997).

Unlike IDEA, this Act employs a functional rather than a categorical model for determining a disability. According to this law, individuals are eligible for services if they:

1. have a physical or mental impairment which substantially limits one or more life activities;
2. have a record of such impairment; or
3. are regarded as having such an impairment by others.

"Major life activities" are broadly defined and include, for example, walking, seeing, hearing, working, and learning.

To fulfill the requirements of Section 504, schools must make "reasonable accommodations" for pupils with disabilities so that they can participate in educational programs provided to other students. Reasonable accommodations might include modifications of the general education program, the assignment of an aide, a behavior management plan, or the provision of special study areas (Smith, 2002; Smith & Patton, 1998). Students may also receive related services such as occupational or physical therapy even if they are not receiving a special education through IDEA.

Because the protections afforded by this law are so broad, an individual who is ineligible for a special education under IDEA may qualify for special assistance or accommodations under Section 504. An adolescent with attention deficit hyperactivity disorder (ADHD) or a student with severe allergies, for example, would be eligible for services via Section 504 although unlikely eligible to receive services under IDEA (*CEC Today,* 1997). All students who are eligible for a special education and related services under IDEA are also eligible for accommodations under Section 504; the converse, however, is *not* true.

Similar to IDEA, there is a mandate contained within Section 504 to educate pupils with special needs with their typical peers to the maximum extent possible. In addition, schools are required to develop an accommodation plan (commonly called a "504 plan") customized to meet the unique needs of the individual. This document should include a statement of the pupil's strengths and weaknesses, a list of necessary accommodations, and the individual(s)

Table 2.2	A Comparison of Key Features of IDEA and Section 504	
Provision	**IDEA**	**Section 504**
Purpose	Provides a free and appropriate public education to children and youth with specific disabilities.	Prohibits discrimination on the basis of a person's disability in all programs receiving federal funds.
Ages Covered	Individuals 3–21 years old.	No age restriction.
Definition of Disability	Twelve disabilities defined according to federal regulations plus state/local definition of *developmentally delayed*.	Broader interpretation of a disability than found in IDEA—a person with a physical or mental impairment that substantially limits a major life activity; has a record of such impairment; or is regarded as having such an impairment.
Funding	States receive some federal dollars for excess cost of educating students with disabilities.	Because this is a civil rights law, no additional funding is provided.
Planning Documents	Individualized education program (IEP).	Accommodation plan (commonly referred to as a "504 plan").
Assessment Provisions	A comprehensive, nondiscriminatory eligibility evaluation in all areas of suspected disability conducted by a multidisciplinary team; reevaluations every 3 years unless waived.	Eligibility determination requires nondiscriminatory assessment procedures; requires reevaluation prior to a "significant change" in placement.
Due Process	Extensive rights and protections afforded to student and parents.	Affords parents impartial hearing, right to inspect records, and representation by counsel. Additional protections at discretion of local school district.
Coordination	No provision.	School district required to identify a 504 coordinator.
Enforcement	U.S. Department of Education, Office of Special Education Programs.	Office for Civil Rights, U.S. Department of Education.

responsible for ensuring implementation. The purpose of this plan is to enable the student to receive a free, appropriate public education (Smith, 2002).

Finally, unlike IDEA, which offers protections for students only between the ages of 3 and 21, Section 504 covers the individual's life span. See Table 2.2 for a comparison of some of the key provisions of IDEA and Section 504.

PUBLIC LAW 101-336 (AMERICANS WITH DISABILITIES ACT) Probably the most significant civil rights legislation affecting individuals with disabilities, the Americans with Disabilities Act (ADA) was signed into law on July 26, 1990, by President George H. W. Bush, who stated, "Today, America welcomes into the mainstream of life all people with disabilities. Let the shameful wall of exclusion finally come tumbling down." This far-reaching enactment, which parallels Section 504 of PL 93-112, forbids discrimination against persons with disabilities in both the public and private sectors. Its purpose, according to Turnbull (1993), is to "provide clear, strong, consistent, and enforceable standards prohibiting discrimination against individuals with disabilities without respect for their age, nature or extent of disability" (p. 23).

The ADA goes far beyond traditional thinking of who is disabled and embraces, for instance, people with AIDS, individuals who have successfully completed a substance abuse program, and persons with cosmetic disfigurements. In fact, any person with an impairment that substantially limits a major life activity is covered by this legislation. It extends protections and guarantees of civil rights in such diverse arenas as private sector employment, transportation, telecommunications, public and privately owned accommodations, and the services of local and state government.

Examples of the impact of this landmark legislation include the following:

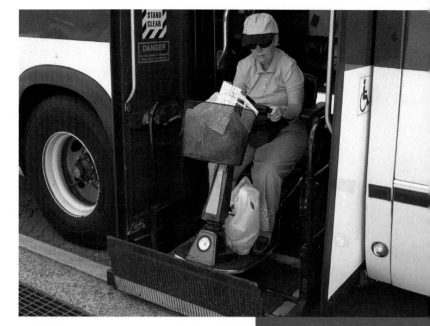

- Employers of fifteen or more workers must make "reasonable accommodations" so that an otherwise qualified individual with a disability is not discriminated against. Accommodations might include a Braille computer keyboard for a worker who is visually impaired or wider doorways to allow easy access for an employee who uses a wheelchair. Furthermore, hiring, termination, and promotion practices may not discriminate against an applicant or employee who has a disability.

The Americans with Disabilities Act requires that mass transit systems be accessible to citizens with disabilities.

- Mass transit systems, such as buses, trains, and subways, must be accessible to citizens with disabilities.
- Hotels, fast-food restaurants, theaters, hospitals, early childhood centers, banks, dentists' offices, retail stores, and the like may not discriminate against individuals with disabilities. These facilities must be accessible, or alternative means for providing services must be available.
- Companies that provide telephone service must offer relay services to individuals with hearing or speech impairments.

Think what this legislation means for the field of special education in general, and specifically for adolescents with disabilities as they prepare to leave high school and transition to the world of adults as independent citizens able to participate fully in all aspects of community life. Thanks to this enactment, the future of the almost 51 million Americans with disabilities is definitely brighter and more secure.

Educational Reform: Standards-Based Education

Over the past two decades, there has been a growing movement toward greater educational accountability, with accompanying calls for educational reform or restructuring resulting in enhanced academic excellence. (See, for example, President Clinton's Goals 2000: Educate America Act of 1994 [PL 103-227].) As a result of this trend, many states initiated challenging academic standards and more stringent graduation requirements for their students, while several professional organizations published performance indicators in various content areas, such as mathematics, language arts, and science. Likewise, many state departments of education are moving toward performance-based standards when establishing teacher licensure/certification requirements, thus linking student success with teacher qualifications. The overall focus of this movement, fueled by various political, social, and economic forces, was a concern over the learning outcomes of our students. It is equally concerned with establishing educational equity among all learners.

Educational standards, which are "general statements of what students should know or be able to do as a result of their public school education" (Nolet & McLaughlin, 2005, p. 5), are important for a couple of reasons. First, "they are intended," according to Nolet and McLaughlin, "to create equity across schools and classrooms in that they define what all teachers should teach and ... [they] also define the content that will be assessed and for which schools will be held accountable" (p. 5). Recent federal legislation embraces this thinking. The importance attached to standards-driven reform is clearly evident in the No Child Left Behind Act of 2001.

No Child Left Behind Act of 2001

In 2001 Congress reauthorized the Elementary and Secondary Education Act, popularly known as the No Child Left Behind Act of 2001 (PL 107-110). This legislation reflects President Bush's commitment to educational reform and accountability. A brief synopsis of this ambitious law reveals that eventually all pupils, including those in special education, are expected to demonstrate proficiency in mathematics and reading, with science eventually being included. Annual testing of children in grades three through eight is required, with students in grades ten through twelve assessed at least once. Schools are expected to show adequate yearly progress toward the goal of 100 percent proficiency by 2014. (A small percentage of students may be excused from participating in state- and districtwide achievement tests if their IEP provides for their exemption.) Because this law is concerned with the achievement of *all* students, test scores must be disaggregated according to the pupil's disability, socioeconomic status, race, ethnicity, and English language proficiency. The anticipated benefit of this requirement is that assessment results will directly translate into instructional accommodations, further aligning special education and general education into a unified delivery system responsible for serving all learners (Salend, 2008).

Schools that experience difficulty attaining the goal of adequate yearly progress will be provided technical and financial assistance. If a school fails to demonstrate adequate yearly progress for three consecutive years, the local school district is required to offer supplemental instructional services such as tutoring, after-school classes, and summer programs (Council for Exceptional Children, 2003). Parents of children in "failing" schools will be given the opportunity to transfer their children to other schools, including private and parochial schools.

In addition to stressing student educational accomplishment, other aspects of this law require that the public as well as parents be informed of individual school performance in addition to the qualifications of teachers. All elementary and secondary school teachers were expected to be "highly qualified" by the end of the 2005–2006 school year according to state criteria. Rigorous standards are also being imposed on teacher aides.

What are the implications of this law for general as well as special educators? How competently will students with special needs perform in this age of educational reform and standards-based education? Obviously, PL 107-110 emphasizes academic achievement as measured by student performance on standardized tests. The expectation seems to be that effective instructional strategies can compensate for a student's disability. The enactment of this law has ushered in an era of what is now commonly referred to as "high-stakes testing." Greater emphasis will most likely be placed on ensuring that pupils in special education are exposed to the general education curriculum. One can also anticipate that greater attention will be focused on aligning IEP goals with the content standards of the general education curriculum (Council for Exceptional Children, 2003). Finally, how colleges and universities prepare future teachers will also likely undergo significant change in an effort to ensure that graduates are highly qualified professionals.

Individuals with Disabilities Education Improvement Act of 2004

On November 19, 2004, Congress passed legislation reauthorizing the Individuals with Disabilities Education Act. The new version of this law is called the Individuals with Disabilities Education Improvement Act of 2004, commonly referred to as IDEA 2004. President George W. Bush signed this bill (PL 108-446) into law on December 3, 2004. Many of the provisions of this legislation became effective on July 1, 2005; some elements of the law became effective, however, on the date the President signed the bill. The impact of this legislation will unfold over the coming years. It is safe to say that IDEA 2004 will significantly affect the professional lives of both general education teachers and special educators. Parents of children with disabilities will also encounter new roles and responsibilities as a result of this law.

> The Individuals with Disabilities Education Improvement Act of 2004 (IDEA) [has] increased the focus of special education from simply ensuring access to education to improving the educational performance of students with disabilities and aligning special education services with the larger national school improvement efforts that include standards, assessments, and accountability [i.e., greater conformity with the No Child Left Behind Act]. (Nolet & McLaughlin, 2005, pp. 2–3)

In the following sections, you will find highlights of some of the significant issues addressed in this historic document.

INDIVIDUALIZED EDUCATION PROGRAM (IEP) PROCESS

- Short-term objectives and benchmarks will no longer be required except for those pupils who are evaluated via alternate assessments aligned to alternate achievement standards.
- IEPs must now include a statement of the student's present levels of academic achievement and functional performance.
- Assessment of the progress that a student is making toward meeting both academic and functional annual goals, which must be written in measurable terms, is still required. Reference, however, to the current requirement of reporting to the "extent to which progress is sufficient to enable the child to achieve goals by the end of the year" is eliminated. IEPs will now need to describe how the individual's progress toward achieving annual goals will be measured and when these progress reports will be made.
- A new provision of the legislation allows for members of the IEP team to be excused from participating in all or part of the meeting if the parents and school district agree that attendance is not necessary because the individual's area of curriculum or related service is not being reviewed or modified. The team member will be required, however, to submit written input into the development of the IEP prior to the meeting.
- PL 108-446 allows for alternatives to physical IEP meetings such as video conferencing and conference telephone calls.
- Once an IEP is established, IDEA 2004 will allow for changes to be made via a written plan to modify the document without convening the entire team and redrafting the whole IEP.
- The new legislation deletes references to transition services beginning at age 14. Now, transition services are to begin no later than the first IEP in effect when the student turns 16 (and updated annually). It also establishes a new requirement for postsecondary goals pertaining to appropriate education, training, employment, and independent living skills.
- School districts will be allowed, with parental consent, to develop comprehensive multiyear IEPs (not to exceed 3 years).
- The U.S. Department of Education is charged with developing and disseminating model IEP forms and model IFSP forms.

Special educators are required to be highly qualified.

IDENTIFYING STUDENTS WITH SPECIFIC LEARNING DISABILITIES Under IDEA 1997, when identifying an individual for a possible learning disability, educators typically looked to see if the student exhibited a severe discrepancy between achievement and intellectual ability. IDEA 2004 removed this discrepancy provision. School districts will now be able, if they so choose, to use a process that determines whether the pupil responds to empirically validated, scientifically based interventions—a procedure known as response to intervention (treatment). Under the new guidelines, rather than comparing IQ with performance on standardized achievement tests, general education teachers can offer intensive programs of instructional interventions. If the child fails to make adequate progress, a learning disability is assumed to be present, and additional assessment is warranted. (This concept will be discussed further in Chapter 6.)

HIGHLY QUALIFIED SPECIAL EDUCATION TEACHERS The language contained in IDEA 2004 concerning who is considered a "highly qualified" special educator is complementary to the standards promulgated in the No Child Left Behind Act (NCLB) of 2001, PL 107-110.

- All special education teachers must hold at least a bachelor's degree and be fully certified or licensed in the field of special education to be deemed highly qualified. Special educators employed as of July 1, 2005, were required to meet this standard.
- Special educators who teach core subjects in elementary schools can obtain highly qualified status by passing their state's licensing or certification exam.
- Teachers of middle- or high-school–aged students with significant cognitive deficits— that is, pupils whose progress will be assessed via alternate achievement standards— may be considered highly qualified if they meet the NCLB standards for *elementary* school teachers. The effective date of this provision was December 3, 2004.
- Currently employed special educators who teach multiple core academic subjects exclusively to students with disabilities may be designated highly qualified after successfully passing "a single, high-objective uniform state standard of evaluation" (HOUSSE), which addresses multiple subjects.

- A special education teacher who is new to the field but already deemed highly qualified in a single core academic area (such as science, reading, language arts, mathematics, foreign languages, or history) may become highly qualified by successfully completing the HOUSSE requirement for the remaining subjects taught. This requirement must be fulfilled within two years of the teacher's hire date. This provision, like the preceding one, became effective on December 3, 2004.
- This legislation does not address "highly qualified" requirements for early childhood special educators.

DISCIPLINE

- PL 108-446 stipulates that when a student is removed from the current educational setting for more than ten days, the pupil is to continue to receive those services that enable him or her to participate in the general education curriculum and to ensure progress toward meeting his or her IEP goals.
- IDEA 1997 allowed school authorities to unilaterally remove a student to an interim alternative educational setting (IAES) for up to 45 days for offenses involving weapons or drugs. IDEA 2004 now permits school officials to remove any pupil (including those with and without disabilities) to an IAES for up to 45 days for inflicting "serious bodily injury."
- Removal to an IAES will now be for 45 *school* days rather than 45 calendar days.
- Behavior resulting in disciplinary action still requires a manifestation review; however, language requiring the IEP team to consider whether the pupil's disability impaired the ability to control his or her behavior or comprehend the consequences of his or her actions has been eliminated. IEP teams will now need to ask only two questions:
  1. Did the disability cause or have a direct and substantial relationship to the offense?
  2. Was the violation a direct result of the school's failure to implement the IEP?
- IDEA 2004 modifies the "stay put" provision enacted during an appeals process. When either the local education agency (LEA) or parent requests an appeal of a manifestation determination or placement decision, the pupil is required to remain in the current IAES until a decision is rendered by the hearing officer or until the time period for the disciplinary violation concludes. A hearing must be held within 20 school days of the date of the appeal.

DUE PROCESS

- Parents will encounter a two-year statute of limitations for filing a due process complaint from the time they knew or should have known that a violation occurred. Alleged violations might involve identification, assessment, or placement issues or the failure to provide an appropriate education.
- A mandatory "resolution session" is now required prior to proceeding with a due process hearing. (The parents and school district may waive this requirement and directly proceed to mediation.) School districts must convene a meeting with the parents and IEP team members within 15 days of receiving a due process complaint. If the complaint is not satisfactorily resolved within 30 days of the filing date, the due process hearing may proceed.
- Under provisions of IDEA 1997, parents who prevailed in due process hearings and/or court cases could seek attorney's fees from the school district. IDEA 2004 now permits school districts to seek attorney's fees from the parents' attorney (or the parents themselves) if the due process complaint or lawsuit is deemed frivolous, unreasonable, or without foundation or the attorney continues to litigate despite these circumstances.

Reasonable attorney fees can also be awarded by the court if the complaint or lawsuit was filed for an improper purpose such as to harass, cause unnecessary delay, or needlessly increase the cost of litigation.

EVALUATION OF STUDENTS

- School districts will be required to determine the eligibility of a student to receive a special education and the educational needs of the child within a time frame of 60 calendar days. (This provision does not apply if the state has already established a timeline for accomplishing this task.) The 60-day rule commences upon receipt of parental permission for evaluation.

- Reevaluation of eligibility for a special education may not occur more than once per year (unless agreed to by the school district and parent), and it must occur at least once every three years unless the parent and school district agree that such a reevaluation is unnecessary.

- IDEA 2004 modifies the provision pertaining to native language and preferred mode of communication. New language in the bill requires that evaluations are to be "provided and administered in the language and form most likely to yield accurate information on what the child knows and can do academically, developmentally, and functionally, unless it is not feasible to so provide or administer."

- School districts are not allowed to seek dispute resolution when parents refuse to give their consent for special education services. If parents refuse to give consent, then the school district is not responsible for providing a free and appropriate public education.

ASSESSMENT PARTICIPATION

- PL 108-446 requires that *all* students participate in all state- and districtwide assessments (including those required under the No Child Left Behind Act, PL 107-110), with accommodations or alternative assessments, if necessary, as stipulated in the pupil's IEP. States are permitted to assess up to 1 percent of students (generally those pupils with significant cognitive deficits) with alternative assessments aligned with alternative achievement standards. This cap represents approximately 9 percent of all students with disabilities. IDEA 2004 further requires that assessments adhere to the principles of universal design when feasible.

The coming years will be ones of exciting opportunities and challenges as the entire educational community responds to the mandates of PL 107-110 and PL 108-446. These laws, like PL 94-142 more than thirty years ago, will dramatically change the educational landscape for both general education and special education.

Identification and Assessment of Individual Differences

One of the distinguishing characteristics of our field is the individuality and uniqueness of the students we serve. There is considerable wisdom in the maxim "No two children are alike." Experienced educators will quickly tell you that even though students may share a common disability label, such as learning disabled or visually impaired, that is where the similarity ends. These pupils are likely to be as different as day and night. Of course, the individuality of our students, both typical and atypical, has the potential for creating significant instructional and/or management concerns for the classroom teacher. Recall from Chapter 1 the types of youngsters enrolled in Mr. Thompson's fifth-grade classroom. Today's schools are serving an increasingly diverse student population. At the same time, there is greater cooperation and more shared responsibility between general and special educators as they collectively plan appropriate educational experiences for all learners.

When teachers talk about the individuality of their students, they often refer to **interindividual differences.** These differences are what distinguish each student from his or her classmates. Interindividual differences are differences *between* pupils. Examples might include distinctions based on height, reading ability, athletic prowess, or intellectual competency. Some interindividual differences are more obvious and of greater educational significance than others.

Interindividual differences are frequently the reason for entry into special education programs. One child might be significantly above (or below) average in intellectual ability; another might exhibit a significant degree of hearing loss. Categorization and placement decision making by school personnel revolve around interindividual differences. Stated another way, school authorities identify, label, and subsequently place a student in an instructional program on the basis of the student's interindividual differences.

However, not all pupils in a given program are alike. Children also exhibit **intraindividual differences**—a unique pattern of strengths and weaknesses. Intraindividual differences are differences *within* the child. Instead of looking at how students compare with their peers, teachers focus on the individual's abilities and limitations. We should point out that this is a characteristic of all pupils, not just those enrolled in special education programs. For example, Victoria, who is the best artist in her eighth-grade class, is equally well known for her inability to sing. One of her classmates, Melinda, has a learning disability. Her reading ability is almost three years below grade level; yet she consistently earns very high grades in math.

Intraindividual differences are obviously of importance to teachers. A student's IEP (individualized education program) reflects this concern. Assessment data, derived from a variety of sources, typically profile a pupil's strengths and needs. This information is then used in crafting a customized instructional plan tailored to meet the unique needs of the learner.

Referral and Assessment for Special Education

"Evaluation [assessment] is the gateway to special education but referral charts the course to the evaluation process" (Turnbull, Turnbull, Erwin, & Soodak, 2006, p. 232). Litigation, IDEA requirements, and today's best practices serve as our road map as we travel along the evaluation pathway to providing appropriate educational experiences for students with disabilities. This journey from referral to assessment to the development of an IEP and eventual placement in the most appropriate environment is a comprehensive process incorporating many different phases. Figure 2.2 illustrates this process. In the following sections, we examine several of the key elements involved in developing individualized program plans.

Prereferral

Although evaluation may be the gateway to special education, a great deal of activity occurs prior to a student's ever taking the first test. Careful scrutiny of our model reveals an intervention strategy known as **prereferral intervention,** which occurs prior to initiating a referral for possible special education services. The purpose of this strategy is to reduce

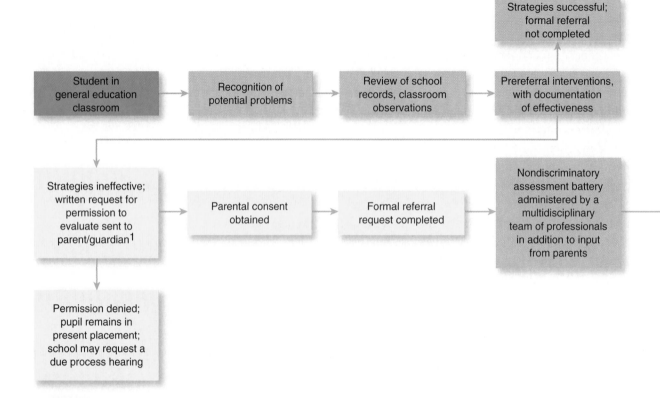

A Procedural Decision-Making Model for the Delivery of Special Education Services

1. IDEA does not mandate parental consent for referral but does require consent for evaluation.

2. Eligibility determination must occur within 60 days of referral.

3. If parents refuse consent for a special education, school district is not responsible for providing a free and appropriate public education.

4. IEP must be developed within 30 days of eligibility determination.

*Mandatory resolution session required prior to a due process hearing.

unwarranted referrals while providing individualized assistance to the student without the benefit of a special education. Although not mandated by IDEA, prereferral interventions have become increasingly common over the past two decades. In fact, IDEA 2004 permits the use of federal dollars to support these activities. Well over half of the states either require or recommend the use of this tactic with individuals suspected of having a disability (Buck, Polloway, Smith-Thomas, & Cook, 2003).

Prereferral interventions are preemptive by design. They call for collaboration between general educators and other professionals for the express purpose of developing creative, alternative instructional and/or management strategies designed to accommodate the particular needs of the learner. This process results in shared responsibility and joint decision making among general and special educators, related service providers, administrators, and other school personnel, all of whom possess specific expertise; the pupil's parents typically do not participate in this early phase. The child's success or failure in school no longer depends exclusively on the pedagogical skills of the general educator; rather, it is now the responsibility of the school-based **intervention assistance team** (also commonly known as teacher-assistance teams, instructional support teams, or child study teams) (Buck et al., 2003).

As beneficial as this strategy often is, it is not always successful. Detailed documentation of these intervention efforts provide a strong justification for the initiation of a formal referral.

Referral

A **referral** is the first step in a long journey toward receiving a special education. As we have just seen, a referral may start as a result of unsuccessful prereferral interventions, or it may be the outcome of **child-find** efforts (IDEA-mandated screening and identification of individuals suspected of needing special education).

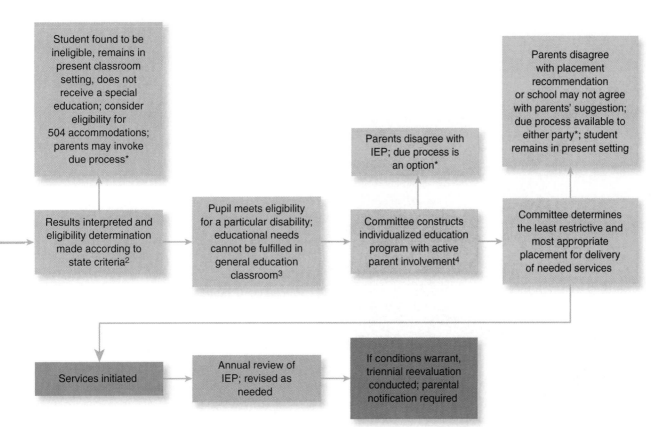

Simply stated, a referral is a written request to evaluate a student to determine whether the child has a disability. Typically, a referral begins with a general educator; it may also be initiated by a school administrator, related services provider, concerned parent, or other individual. Referrals typically arise from a concern about the child's academic achievement and/or social/behavioral problems. In some instances, a referral may be initiated because of a pupil's cultural or linguistic background; it may even be the result of problems caused by inappropriate teacher expectations or poor instructional strategies. Thus, the reasons for the referral may not always lie within the student. This is one reason why prereferral intervention strategies are so important. Only about 75 percent of the referrals for special education services actually result in placement; the remaining children are found ineligible (Ysseldyke, 2001).

Referral forms vary in their format. Generally, in addition to student demographic information, a referral must contain detailed reasons as to why the request is being made. Teachers must clearly describe the pupil's academic and/or social performance. Documentation typically accompanies the referral and may include test scores, checklists, behavioral observation data, and actual samples of the student's work. Teachers need to paint as complete a picture as possible of their concern(s), as well as their efforts to rectify the situation.

In most schools, the information that has been gathered is then reviewed by a committee, often known as the child study committee, special services team, or other such name. The composition of this group of professionals varies but typically includes an administrator, school psychologist, and experienced teachers. Other personnel may also be involved, depending on the nature of the referral. It is the job of this committee to review the available information and decide whether further assessment is warranted. If the team decides to proceed, a written request for permission to evaluate is sent to the child's parent(s). School

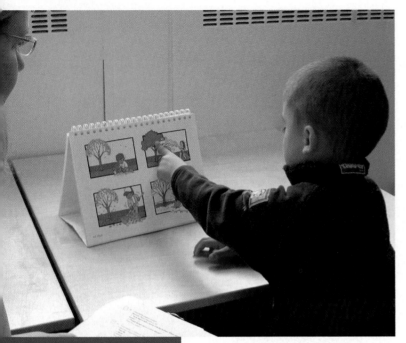

Assessments can be conducted at a young age and must be individualized and comprehensive.

authorities *must* obtain permission of the parent/guardian before proceeding with a formal evaluation. Interestingly, IDEA does not require parental consent for referrals. We believe, however, that it is wise to notify parents that a referral is being initiated, explain the reasons for the referral, and solicit their input and cooperation in the referral process.

Assessment

The first step in determining whether a student has a disability, and is in need of a special education, is securing the consent of the child's parent(s)/guardian(s) for the evaluation. As noted previously, this step is mandated by IDEA as part of the procedural safeguards protecting the legal rights of parent(s)/guardian(s). Under the provisions of IDEA, school officials must notify the pupil's parent(s)/guardian(s), in their native language, of the school's intent to evaluate (or refusal to evaluate) the student and the rationale for this decision; they must explain the assessment process and alternatives available to the parent/guardian, such as the right to an independent evaluation of their son or daughter. Many schools automatically send parent(s)/guardian(s) a statement of their legal rights when initial permission to evaluate is sought.

Assessment, according to McLean, Wolery, and Bailey (2004), "is a generic term that refers to the process of gathering information for the purpose of making decisions" (p. 13). Educational assessment can rightly be thought of as an information-gathering and decision-making process.

One of the goals of the assessment process is to obtain a complete profile of the student's strengths and needs. By law (IDEA), this requires the use of a **multidisciplinary team** of professionals, of which one member must be a teacher. In practice, some school districts are fulfilling this mission by establishing inter- and transdisciplinary assessment teams. Regardless of the model adopted by the school district, the team is responsible for developing an individualized and comprehensive assessment package that evaluates broad developmental domains (cognitive, academic achievement) as well as the specific areas of concern noted on the referral, such as social/emotional problems or suspected visual impairments.

Successful accomplishment of this task dictates the use of both formal and informal assessment tools. Once again, IDEA is very clear about this issue: No one procedure may be used as the sole basis of evaluation; a multitude of tests is required. IDEA regulations further require that the evaluations be presented in the pupil's native language or, when necessary, via other modes of communication such as sign language or Braille for students who are sensory impaired. Additionally, the selection and administration of the assessment battery must accurately reflect the child's aptitude and achievement and not penalize the student because of his or her impairment in sensory, manual, or speaking skills. The accompanying FYI feature describes some accommodations that may be needed for accurate assessment.

School psychologists, educational diagnosticians, and other professionals responsible for evaluating the student have a wide variety of assessment instruments at their disposal. Evaluators attempt to gauge both inter- and intraindividual differences by using both

FYI...

Assessment Accommodations

In order to accurately portray a pupil's abilities and needs, assessment accommodations are sometimes necessary. Accommodations are changes in how students access and demonstrate learning without changing the standards they are working toward. Accommodations must be individualized; not all pupils require them, nor do students with the same disability require the same type of accommodations. The need for accommodations may change over time; some individuals may require fewer accommodations while in other situations additional support is required. Listed below are examples of accommodations that IEP teams may find beneficial.

Presentation accommodations let students access assignments, tests, and activities in ways other than reading standard print. Students with print disabilities (inability to visually decode standard print because of a physical, sensory, or cognitive disability) may require a combination of these accommodations:

- Visual: large print, magnification devices, sign language, visual cues
- Tactile: Braille, Nemeth code, tactile graphics
- Auditory: human reader, audiotape or CD, audio amplification device
- Visual and auditory: screen reader, videotape, descriptive video, talking materials

Response accommodations allow students to complete assignments, tests, and activities in different ways or solve or organize problems using an assistive device or organizer. Response accommodations include:

- Different ways to complete assignments, tests, and activities: expressing responses to a scribe through speech, sign language, pointing, or an assistive communication device; typing on or speaking to a word processor, Brailler, or tape recorder; writing in a test booklet instead of on an answer sheet
- Materials or devices to solve or organize responses: calculation devices; spelling and grammar assistive devices; visual or graphic organizers

Timing and scheduling accommodations give students the time and breaks they need to complete assignments, tests, and activities and may change the time of day, day of the week, or number of days over which an activity takes place. These include:

- Extended time
- Multiple or frequent breaks
- Changing the testing schedule or order of subtests
- Dividing long-term assignments

Setting accommodations change the location in which a student receives instruction or the conditions of the setting. Students may be allowed to sit in a different location than the majority of students to:

- Reduce distractions
- Receive accommodations
- Increase physical access
- Use special equipment

Source: Adapted from S. Thompson, "Choosing and Using Accommodations on Assessments," *CEC Today, 10*(6), 2004, pp. 12, 18.

norm- and criterion-referenced assessments. Simply stated, **norm-referenced** tests are standardized tests and are linked to interindividual differences. Norm-referenced tests compare a pupil's performance with that of a representative sample of children, providing the evaluator with an indication of the pupil's performance relative to other individuals of similar

Table 2.3	Emerging Sources of Assessment Information
Source	**Description**
Naturalistic observation	Documentation of qualitative as well as quantitative aspects of youngster's behavior in natural environment. Information may be recorded formally (rating scales, observational recording systems) or informally (anecdotal records, audio recordings). Data can be used to support or refute information gathered from other sources.
Interviews	Information obtained from significant individuals in student's life—parents, teachers, older siblings, or the pupil him/herself. Interviews are a planned and purposeful activity whose purpose is to gain insight or perspective on specific areas of interest, such as the child's background or possible reasons for behavioral problems. Format may be formal (interviewer follows a predetermined set of questions) or informal (interview proceeds according to the individual's responses). Data may be gathered orally or in writing.
Work samples	Evidence of a pupil's actual classroom performance, typically focused on particular skill development. Sometimes referred to as a permanent product. Spelling tests, arithmetic fact sheets, and handwriting samples are examples of this information source. Work samples are especially useful when planning instructional intervention and modification. Requires teacher to think diagnostically and look, for example, at error patterns or clarity of directions.
Portfolios	A type of authentic assessment, portfolios are an outgrowth of the familiar work folder concept. They include a wide range of examples of a student's emerging abilities and accomplishments over time. Qualitative and quantitative indicators of performance might include writing samples, audio/video recordings, worksheets, drawings, photographs, or other forms of evidence. Useful for student self-assessment.

chronological age. Data are typically presented in terms of percentile ranks, stanines, or grade equivalent scores. Data gleaned from norm-referenced tests provide limited instructional information. In contrast, **criterion-referenced** tests are associated with intraindividual differences and can provide data that are useful for instructional planning. In this type of assessment procedure, a student's performance on a task is compared to a particular level of mastery. The criterion level is typically established by the classroom teacher. Criterion-referenced assessments are especially helpful, according to Hoy and Gregg (1994), "in determining which skills in the curriculum the student has mastered and which skills require further instruction" (p. 56). Teachers are concerned with the individual's pattern of strengths and needs rather than how the student compares with his or her classmates.

As mentioned earlier, evaluators must put together a complete educational portrait of the student's abilities. This frequently requires multiple sources of information, which typically include standardized tests, work samples, and observational data, among other forms of input. Table 2.3 summarizes some of the types of assessments increasingly being used by evaluation specialists to complement data derived from norm-referenced tests.

Instructional Programming and Appropriate Placement

When properly conducted, educational assessments lead to the development of meaningful IEPs and IFSPs. Measurable annual goals (and short-term objectives/benchmarks for pupils evaluated via alternate assessments) are crafted based upon data gleaned from these evaluations. But first, the multidisciplinary team must determine whether the student is eligible to receive special education services according to specific state criteria. Eligibility standards differ from state to state, but most are framed around IDEA criteria.

If team members, working in concert with the child's parent(s), determine that the student fails to qualify for a special education, we suggest developing intervention strategies and recommendations for accommodations to address the referral concerns. We believe this is necessary because the pupil will remain in his or her present placement—the general education classroom. Additionally, the team may wish to consider the pupil for a 504 accommodation plan if the student is eligible for such services. Parent(s)/guardian(s) must be sent written notification summarizing the evaluation and stating why their son or daughter is ineligible to receive a special education. If, however, it is determined that the pupil is eligible for a special education, the multidisciplinary team is then confronted with two monumental tasks: constructing the IEP/IFSP and determining the most appropriate placement for the student.

Designing Individualized Instructional Programs

According to IDEA, each student identified by a multidisciplinary child study team as disabled and in need of special education must have an individualized program plan of specially designed instruction that addresses the unique needs of the child, and in the case of infants and toddlers, the needs of the family as well. IEPs and IFSPs are guides to the design and delivery of customized services and instruction. They also serve as vehicles for collaboration and cooperation between parents and professionals as they jointly devise appropriate educational experiences.

Individualized Education Program

An individualized education program (IEP) is part of an overall strategy designed to deliver services appropriate to the individual needs of pupils ages 3 and older. By the time we reach the IEP stage, the appropriate permissions have been gathered, assessments have been conducted, and a disability determination has been made. We are now at the point where the IEP is to be developed, followed by placement in the most appropriate and least restrictive setting. Bateman and Linden (1998) make a very important point about *when* the IEP is to be developed. They believe that IEPs are often written at the wrong time. Legally, the IEP is to be developed within 30 days following the evaluation and determination of the child's disability, but *before* a placement recommendation is formulated. Placement in the least restrictive and most normalized setting is based on a completed IEP, not the other way around. An IEP should not be limited by placement options or the availability of services. We believe it is best to see the IEP as a management tool or planning vehicle that ensures that children with disabilities receive an individualized education appropriate to their unique needs. This focus is in concert with both the intent and spirit of IDEA.

For an in-depth example of an IEP, visit the SAGE Study Site at www.sagepub.com/gargiulo3estudy.

IEPs are written by a team. At a minimum, participation must include a parent/guardian; the child's teachers, including a general education teacher and a special educator; a representative from the school district; and an individual able to interpret the instructional implications of the evaluation. When appropriate, the student, as well as other professionals who possess pertinent information or whose expertise is desired, may participate at the discretion of the parent or school. Parents have a legal right to participate meaningfully in this planning and decision-making process; they serve as the child's advocate. Although IDEA mandates a collaborative role for parents, it does not stipulate the degree or extent of their participation.

FYI . . .

Elements of a Meaningful IEP

Current Performance. A statement of the student's present levels of educational and functional performance, including how the pupil's disability affects his or her involvement and progress in the general education curriculum, or, for preschoolers, how the disability affects participation in age-appropriate activities.

Goals. A statement of measurable annual goals (both functional and academic) that address the student's involvement and progress in the general education curriculum as well as the student's other education needs; short-term objectives or benchmarks are required for pupils who take alternate assessments aligned to alternate achievement standards.

Special Education and Related Services. A statement of special education, related services, and supplementary aids and services (based on peer-reviewed research) to be provided, including program modifications or supports necessary for the student to advance toward attainment of annual goals, to be involved and progress in the general education curriculum, extracurricular activities, and nonacademic activities, and to be educated and participate in activities with other children both with and without disabilities.

Participation with Typical Students. An explanation of the extent, if any, to which the student will *not* participate in the general education classroom.

Participation in State- and Districtwide Assessments. A statement of any individual modifications needed for the student to participate in a state- or districtwide assessment; if a student will not participate, a statement of why the assessment is inappropriate and how the pupil will be assessed.

Dates and Places. Projected date for initiation of services; expected location, duration, and frequency of such services.

Transition Services. Beginning at age 16, a statement of needed transition services identifying measurable postschool goals (training, education, employment, and, if appropriate, independent living skills), including a statement of interagency linkages and/or responsibilities.

Measuring Progress. A statement of how progress toward annual goals will be measured and how a student's parents (or guardians) will be regularly informed of such progress.

Age of Majority. Information provided at least one year before reaching the age of majority regarding transferral of rights to the student upon reaching the age of majority.

IEPs will vary greatly in their format and degree of specificity. Government regulations do not specify the level of detail considered appropriate, nor do they stipulate how the IEP is to be constructed—only that it be a written document. What is specified are the components (see the accompanying FYI feature).

As stated previously, an IEP is, in essence, a management tool that stipulates *who* will be involved in providing a special education, *what* services will be offered, *where* they will be delivered, and for *how long*. In addition, an IEP gauges *how successfully* goals have been met. Although the IEP does contain a measure of accountability, it is not a legally binding contract; schools are not liable if goals are not achieved. Schools are liable, however, if they do not provide the services stipulated in the IEP. IEPs are to be reviewed annually, although parents may request an earlier review. A complete reevaluation of the pupil's eligibility for special education must occur every three years. PL 108-446 waives this requirement, however, if both the parents and school officials agree that such a review is not necessary.

IEPs are not meant to be so detailed or complete that they serve as the entire instructional agenda, nor are they intended to prescribe curriculum (Goodman & Bond, 1993). They do have to be individualized, however, and address the unique learning and/or behavioral requirements of the student. It is for this reason that we find fault with the growing reliance on computer-generated goals and objectives. Although computer-managed IEPs may serve as a useful logistical tool, like Bateman and Linden (1998), we have grave doubts as to the educational relevancy of this procedure and question its legality. We hope teachers will use this resource only as a starting point for designing customized and individually tailored plans.

One of the challenges confronting the IEP team is ensuring that students have access to the general education curriculum as stipulated in both the 1997 and 2004 reauthorizations of IDEA. But what is the general education curriculum? In most instances, it is the curriculum that typical learners are exposed to, which is often established by individual state boards of education. The IEP must address how the pupil's disability affects his or her involvement in and ability to progress in the general education curriculum. The underlying assumption seems to be that even if a child is receiving a special education, he or she should engage the general education curriculum. Documentation is required if the team believes that this curriculum is inappropriate for a particular student.

IDEA 2004 requires the IEP team to develop measurable annual goals while also emphasizing exposure to the general education curriculum. Goal statements are purposely broad. Their

Parents play a crucial role in developing their child's individualized education program.

Suggestions for the Classroom

Suggested Individualized Education Program Meeting Agenda

☑ Welcome and introduction of participants and their respective roles

☑ Statement of purpose

☑ Review of previous year's IEP (except for initial placement) and accomplishments

☑ Discussion of student's present level of performance and progress:
  – Assessment information
  – Strengths and emerging areas

☑ Consideration of specific needs:
  – Instructional modifications and accommodations
  – Participation in state- and districtwide assessments
  – Related services
  – Assistive technology needs
  – Transition goals
  – Behavior intervention plan
  – Language needs for student with limited English proficiency
  – Braille instruction for student who is visually impaired

☑ Development of annual goals (and benchmarks if appropriate)

☑ Recommendations and justification for placement in least restrictive environment

☑ Closing comments, securing of signatures

☑ Copies of IEP to all team members

intent is to provide long-range direction to a student's educational program, not to define exact instructional tasks. Based on the pupil's current level of performance, goals are "written to reflect what a student needs in order to become involved in and to make progress in the general education curriculum" (Yell, 2006, p. 293). They represent reasonable projections or estimates of what the pupil should be able to accomplish within the academic year. They also answer the question, "What should the student be doing?" Annual goals can reflect academic functioning, social behavior, adaptive behavior, or life skills. Regardless of their emphasis, goal statements should be positive, student-oriented, and relevant (Polloway, Patton, & Serna, 2008).

Measurable annual goals should include the following five components:

- The student . . . (the who)
- Will do what . . . (the behavior)
- To what level or degree . . . (the criterion)
- Under what conditions . . . (the conditions)
- In what length of time . . . (the time frame)

Quality IEPs largely depend on having well-written and appropriate goals (and objectives) that address the unique needs of the individual. IEPs are the primary means of ensuring that a specially designed educational program is provided. The accompanying Suggestions for the Classroom provides a sample agenda for an IEP team meeting.

Individualized Family Service Plan

The individualized family service plan (IFSP) is the driving force behind the delivery of early intervention services to infants and toddlers who are at risk or disabled. The IFSP was originally conceived to focus on children younger than age 3, but recent changes in thinking now allow this document to be used with preschoolers who require a special education. This change was initiated by the federal government in an effort to minimize the differences between early intervention and preschool special education services; the government is now encouraging states to establish "seamless systems" designed to serve youngsters from birth through age 5 (U.S. Department of Education, 1993). As a result of this policy decision, states now have the authority to use IFSPs for preschoolers with special needs until the child's sixth birthday.

> For an in-depth example of an IFSP, visit the SAGE Study Site at www. sagepub.com/gargiulo3estudy.

Like an IEP, the IFSP is developed by a team consisting of professionals and the child's parents as key members. In addition, parents may invite other family members to participate, as well as an advocate. Typically, the service coordinator who has been working with the family, the professionals involved in the assessment of the youngster, and the service providers constitute the remainder of the group charged with the responsibility of writing the IFSP. The elements required for an IFSP, as stipulated in PL 108-446, are summarized in Table 2.4.

The IFSP was intentionally designed to preserve the family's role as primary caregiver. Well-constructed IFSPs, which are reviewed every six months, fully support the family and encourage their active and meaningful involvement. This thinking is in keeping with an empowerment model (Dunst & Trivette, 1989) that views families as capable (with occasional assistance) of helping themselves. It allows parents to retain their decision-making role, establish goals, and assess their own needs. It is also in keeping with our support of an ecological perspective (Bronfenbrenner, 1979), which argues that one cannot look at a child without considering the various systems and spheres of influence that provide support—in this instance, the infant's or toddler's family and community.

Information obtained from the assessment of the family and data about the infant's or toddler's developmental status are used to generate outcome statements or goals for the child and his or her family. Practitioners are increasingly emphasizing real-life or authentic goals for children with special needs (Pretti–Frontczak & Bricker, 2004). These goals, which are based on the priorities and concerns of the family, are reflected in the IFSP's required outcome statements. Interventionists no longer teach skills in isolation; rather, goals are developed that are relevant to the daily activities of the youngsters and their families. These statements need to be practical and functional, reflecting real-life situations occurring in the natural environment.

Service Delivery Options: Where a Special Education Is Provided

Now that the IEP/IFSP team has decided *what* will be taught, it must decide *where* special education services will be provided. The issue of appropriate placement of children with disabilities has generated considerable controversy and debate. In fact, it has been a point of contention among special educators for almost forty years. IDEA mandates that services be provided to students in the least restrictive setting—or, as Henry and Flynt (1990) call it, the most productive environment. The question confronting the team is, What is the most appropriate placement to achieve the goals (outcomes) of the IEP (IFSP)? The chosen setting must allow the pupil to reach his or her IEP (IFSP) goals and work toward his or her potential.

Table 2.4	Comparable Components of an IEP and IFSP
Individualized Education Program	**Individualized Family Service Plan**
A statement of the child's present levels of academic achievement and functional performance, including involvement and progress in the general education curriculum	A statement of the infant's or toddler's present levels of physical, cognitive, communication, social/emotional, and adaptive development
No comparable feature	A statement of the family's resources, priorities, and concerns
A statement of measurable annual goals, including benchmarks or short-term instructional objectives for children who take alternate assessments aligned to alternate achievement standards	A statement of measurable results or outcomes expected to be achieved for the infant or toddler and the family
A statement indicating progress toward annual goals and a mechanism for regularly informing parents/guardians of such progress	Criteria, procedures, and timelines used to determine the degree to which progress toward achieving the outcomes or results is being made
A statement of specific special education and related services and supplementary aids and services, based on peer-reviewed research, to be provided and any program modifications	A statement of specific early intervention services, based on peer-reviewed research, necessary to meet the unique needs of the infant or toddler and the family
An explanation of the extent to which the child will not participate in general education programs	A statement of the natural environments in which early intervention services will appropriately be provided, or justification if not provided
Modifications needed to participate in state- or districtwide assessments	No comparable feature
The projected date for initiation of services and the anticipated duration, frequency, and location of services	The projected date for initiation of services and the anticipated duration of services
No comparable feature	The name of the service coordinator
At age 16, a statement of transition services needed including courses of study in addition to measurable postsecondary goals	The steps to be taken to support the child's transition to other services at age 3

Source: Adapted from Individuals with Disabilities Education Improvement Act of 2004, Title 20 U.S. Code (U.S.C.) 1400 *et seq*, Part B Section 614 (d) (1) (A), and Part C Section 636 (d).

It is at this point in our decision-making model that school authorities, in collaboration with the child's parent(s)/guardian(s), attempt to reach agreement about where the student will be served. The principle guiding this decision is known as the **least restrictive environment (LRE).** This is a relative concept; it must be determined individually for each pupil. We interpret this principle to mean that students with disabilities should be educated in a setting that most closely approximates the general education classroom *and* still meets the unique needs of the individual. As we will see shortly, for a growing number of students, this setting is the general education classroom. The concept of LRE calls for maximum opportunity for meaningful involvement and participation with classmates who are nondisabled. One of its inherent difficulties is the required balancing of maximum integration with the delivery of an appropriate education.

Educational Placements

The federal government annually monitors the different settings in which pupils with disabilities receive a special education. Figure 2.3 illustrates the percentage of students in each of the six environments recognized by the U.S. Department of Education. Table 2.5 describes these six settings.

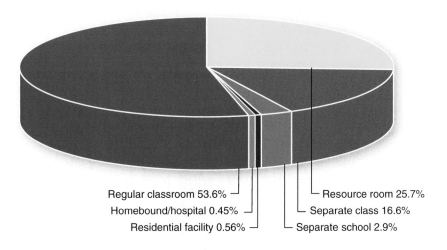

Figure 2.3

Percentage of Children with Disabilities Served in Various Educational Settings

Note: Data are for students ages 6–21 enrolled in special education during the 2005–2006 school year. Data as of fall 2005, updated July 2006.

Separate schools include both public and private facilities; residential settings include both public and private facilities.

Information based on data from the 50 states, the District of Columbia, Puerto Rico, and outlying areas.

Source: U.S. Department of Education. (2007). *IDEA data.* Available at https://www.ideadata.org/PartBReport.asp

Regular classroom 53.6%
Homebound/hospital 0.45%
Residential facility 0.56%
Resource room 25.7%
Separate class 16.6%
Separate school 2.9%

A Cascade of Service Delivery Options

As we have just seen, the federal government recognizes that no one educational setting is appropriate for meeting the needs of all children with disabilities. Effective delivery of a special education requires an array or continuum of placement possibilities customized to the individual requirements of each pupil. The concept of a continuum of educational services has been part of the fabric of American special education for almost four decades. Reynolds (1962) originally described the concept of a range of placement options in 1962. His thinking was later elaborated on and expanded by Deno (1970), who constructed a model offering a "cascade" or continuum of settings. A traditional view of service delivery options is portrayed in Figure 2.4.

Table 2.5	Definitions of Educational Settings Serving School-Age Students with Disabilities
Regular Class	Students who receive the majority of their education in a regular classroom and receive special education and related services outside the regular classroom for less than 21% of the school day. This placement option also includes individuals who are provided with specialized instruction or services within the regular classroom setting.
Resource Room	Students who receive special education and related services outside the regular classroom for at least 21% but less than 60% of the school day. Students are "pulled out" of the regular classroom and receive specialized instruction or services in a separate classroom for limited periods of time. Services may be individualized or offered in small groups. A common placement option for children with less severe disabilities.
Separate Class	Students who receive special education and related services outside the regular class for more than 60% of the school day. Commonly known as a self-contained classroom wherein pupils, usually those with more severe disabilities, receive full-time instruction or, in a modified version, participate in nonacademic aspects of school activities. Classroom is located in regular school building.
Separate School	Students who receive special education and related services in a public or private separate day school for students with disabilities, at public expense, for more than 50% of the school day.
Residential Facility	Students who receive a special education in a public or private residential facility, at public expense, 24 hours a day.
Homebound/Hospital	Students placed in and receiving a special education in a hospital or homebound program.

Source: Adapted from U.S. Department of Education. (2000). *Twenty-second Annual Report to Congress on the Implementation of the Individuals with Disabilities Education Act* (Washington, DC: U.S. Government Printing Office), p. II-14.

Figure 2.4

A Traditional View of Service Delivery Options

Source: Adapted from S. Graves, R. Gargiulo, and L. Sluder, *Young Children: An Introduction to Early Childhood Education* (St. Paul, MN: West, 1996), p. 398.

In this model, the general education classroom is viewed as the most normalized or typical setting; consequently, the greatest number of students are served in this environment. This placement would be considered the least restrictive option. Deviation from the general education classroom should occur only when it is educationally necessary for the pupil to receive an appropriate education. Each higher level depicted in Figure 2.4 represents a progressively more restrictive setting. Movement up the hierarchy generally leads to the delivery of more intensive services to children with more severe disabilities, who are fewer in number. However, intensive supports are now being provided in general education classrooms with increasing frequency. Environments at the upper levels are considered to be the most restrictive and least normalized; yet, as we will see shortly, they may be the most appropriate placement for a particular individual.

As originally conceived, the natural flow of this cascade of service delivery options would be in a downward movement from more restrictive settings to those viewed as least restrictive, such as the general education classroom with or without support services. Contemporary thinking, however, suggests that pupils should begin in the general education classroom and ascend the model, reaching a level that meets their unique needs. A key feature of this model, too often overlooked, is that a particular placement is only temporary; flexibility or freedom of movement is what makes this model work. The settings must be envisioned as fluid rather than rigid. As the needs of the pupil change, so should the environment; this is why there is an array of service delivery possibilities. In our opinion, there is no one best educational placement for each and every student with disabilities.

A Contemporary Challenge

At the present time, the field of special education is confronting the challenge of calls for greater inclusion of individuals with disabilities into all aspects of society, especially educational programs. Simply stated, some advocates for people with disabilities (and some parents as well) dismiss the long-standing concept of a continuum of service delivery possibilities and argue that *all* pupils with disabilities, regardless of the type or severity of their impairment, should be educated in general education classrooms at neighborhood schools. They argue further that students should be served on the basis of their chronological age rather than academic ability or mental age. This is truly an explosive proposal. The debate surrounding this issue is an emotionally charged one with great potential for polarizing the field of special education as other professionals, advocates, and parents argue fervently against this thinking. According to Gargiulo and Kilgo (2005), supporters of this movement see it as the next great revolution in special education, whereas opponents consider it the start of a return to the "dark ages" of special education—the era before PL 94-142. We suspect that the truth lies somewhere between these two extremes.

The intensity of this debate is fueled by several factors, one of which is the inconsistent use of terminology. As frequently happens in arguments, people are often saying the same thing but using different words. Therefore, we offer the following interpretations of key terms frequently encountered in describing this movement.

MAINSTREAMING The first potentially confusing term is **mainstreaming**, which first appeared on the educational scene more than thirty years ago. It evolved from an argument put forth by Dunn (1968), who, in a classic essay, questioned the pedagogical wisdom of serving children with mild mental retardation in self-contained classrooms, which was then common practice. Other professionals soon joined with Dunn in his call for a more integrated service delivery model, resulting in the beginning of a movement away from isolated special classes as the placement of choice.

We define mainstreaming—or, in contemporary language, integration—as the social and instructional integration of students with disabilities into educational programs whose primary purpose is to serve typically developing individuals. It represents a common interpretation of

Federal law stipulates that, to the maximum extent appropriate, pupils with disabilities are to be educated with their typical classmates.

the principle of educating children with disabilities in the least restrictive environment (LRE). Interestingly, the term *mainstreaming* itself never appears in any piece of federal legislation.

Parents no longer have to prove that their son or daughter should be mainstreamed; rather, schools must justify their position to exclude. They must prove that they have made a good-faith effort at integration or present strong evidence that an inclusionary setting is unsatisfactory (Osborne & DiMattia, 1995; Yell, 1995). PL 108-446 currently supports this thinking.

Mainstreaming must provide the student with an appropriate education based on the unique needs of the child. It is our opinion that policy makers never envisioned that mainstreaming would be interpreted to mean that *all* children with special needs must be placed in integrated placements; to do so would mean abandoning the idea of determining the most appropriate placement for a particular child. IDEA clearly stipulates that, to the maximum extent appropriate, children with disabilities are to be educated with their typical peers. We interpret this provision to mean that, for some individuals, an integrated or mainstream setting, even with supplementary aids and services, might be an inappropriate placement in light of the child's unique characteristics. A least restrictive environment does not automatically mean placement with typical learners. As educators, we need to make the distinction between appropriateness and restrictiveness.

LEAST RESTRICTIVE ENVIRONMENT (LRE) Least restrictive environment (LRE) is a legal term often interpreted to say individuals with disabilities are to be educated in environments as close as possible to the general education classroom setting. An LRE is not a place but a concept.

Determination of the LRE is made individually for each child. An appropriate placement for one student could quite easily be inappropriate for another. The LRE is based on the pupil's educational needs, not on his or her disability. It applies equally to children of school age and to preschoolers. Even infants and toddlers with disabilities are required by law (PL 102-119) to have services delivered in normalized settings.

Inherent within the mandate of providing a special education and/or related services within the LRE is the notion of a continuum of service delivery possibilities. Figure 2.4 (page 74) reflects varying degrees of restrictiveness, or amount of available contact with typical learners. Being only with children with disabilities is considered restrictive; placement with peers without disabilities is viewed as least restrictive. As we ascend the continuum, the environments provide fewer and fewer opportunities for interaction with typically developing agemates—hence the perception of greater restrictiveness. Despite a strong preference for association with students who are typical, this desire must be balanced by the requirement of providing an education appropriate to the unique needs of the individual. Consequently, an integrative environment may not always be the most appropriate placement option. Each situation must be individually assessed and decided on a case-by-case basis. The educational setting must meet the needs of the learner. The philosophy of the LRE guides rather than prescribes decision making (Meyen, 1995).

We recognize, as do many other special educators, that maximum integration with typically developing children is highly desirable and should be one of our major goals. The question is when, where, with whom, and to what extent are individuals with disabilities to be integrated.

REGULAR EDUCATION INITIATIVE (REI) The third concept that requires our attention is the **regular education initiative,** or as it is commonly called,

REI. REI is an important link in the evolution of the full inclusion movement. The term was introduced in 1986 by former Assistant Secretary of Education (Office of Special Education and Rehabilitative Services) Madeleine Will, who questioned the legitimacy of special education as a separate system of education and called for a restructuring of the relationship between general (regular) and special education. She endorsed the idea of shared responsibility—a partnership between general and special education resulting in a coordinated delivery system (Will, 1986b). Will recommended that general educators assume greater responsibility for students with disabilities. She envisioned a meaningful partnership whereby general and special educators would "cooperatively assess the educational needs of students with learning problems and cooperatively develop effective educational strategies for meeting those needs" (Will, 1986a, p. 415). Will (1986b) also believes that educators must "visualize a system that will bring the program to the child rather than one that brings the child to the program" (p. 21). As special educators, most of us can embrace this idea. Few professionals would dispute that the delivery of special education services would be significantly enhanced if there were greater coordination, cooperation, and collaboration between general and special educators.

FULL INCLUSION We see the movement toward **full inclusion** as an extension of REI and earlier thinking about where children with disabilities should be educated. Full

Full inclusion results in students with disabilities being seen as full-fledged members of the general education classroom.

| Segregated programs (if available) | → | Least restrictive environment | → | Regular education initiative | → | Full inclusion | → | ??? |
| Late 1960s to early 1970s | | Late 1970s | | Late 1980s | | Early to mid-1990s | | Early twenty-first century |

Figure 2.5

The Evolution of Placement Options for Children with Disabilities

Source: R. Gargiulo and J. Kilgo, *Young Children with Special Needs: An Introduction to Early Childhood Special Education,* 2nd ed. (Clifton Park, NY: Delmar, 2005), p. 165.

inclusion represents the latest trend in meeting the requirement of providing an education in the least restrictive environment (Bennett, DeLuca, & Bruns, 1997). Fox and Ysseldyke (1997) consider full inclusion as a further attempt at operationalizing the concept of LRE. Figure 2.5 illustrates the evolution of this thought process.

Full inclusion is a potentially explosive issue, with vocal supporters as well as detractors. It has emerged as one of the most controversial and complex subjects in the field of special education. As with other controversial topics, an agreed upon definition is difficult to develop. We offer the following succinct interpretation: Full inclusion is a belief that *all* children with disabilities should be taught exclusively (with appropriate supports) in general education class-rooms at neighborhood schools—that is, in the same school and age-/grade-appropriate class-rooms they would attend if they were not disabled. Successful implementation will require new thinking about curriculum design along with increased collaboration between general and special educators (Stainback & Stainback, 1992). Recall that Will (1986b) originally proposed this type of partnership in her regular education initiative.

Although the trend in judicial interpretations is toward inclusionary placement (Osborne & DiMattia, 1995), the LRE mandate does not require that all pupils be educated in general education classrooms or in their neighborhood schools. The framers of IDEA never pictured, according to Kauffman (1995), that the general education classroom located in the neighborhood school would be the least restrictive setting for all pupils. In fact, policy makers believed that a cascade of placement options would be required in order to provide an appropriate education for students with disabilities.

Advocates of full inclusion (Kennedy & Horn, 2004; Peterson & Hittie, 2003; Sailor, 2002; Stainback & Stainback, 1996) argue that the present pullout system of serving students with special needs is ineffective. They contend that "the diagnostic and instructional models, practices, and tools associated with the EHA [PL 94-142] and mainstreaming are fundamentally flawed, particularly for students considered to have mild to moderate disabilities" (Skrtic, 1995, p. 625). Children are labeled and stigmatized, their programming is frequently fragmented, and general educators often assume little or no ownership for students in special education (a "your" kids versus "my" kids attitude). Placement in a general education classroom, with a working partnership between special education teachers and general educators, would result in a better education for all pupils, not just those with special needs, and would occur within the context of the least restrictive environment.

When correctly instituted, full inclusion is characterized by its virtual invisibility. Students with disabilities are not segregated but dispersed into classrooms they would normally attend if they were not disabled. They are seen as full-fledged members of, not merely visitors to, the general education classroom. Special educators provide an array of services and supports in the general education classroom alongside their general education colleagues, often using strategies such as cooperative teaching in an effort to meet the needs of the pupils. Table 2.6 summarizes the key components of most models of full inclusion.

Full inclusion is definitely a controversial topic; even professional organizations have opposing viewpoints. For instance, the Association for Persons with Severe Handicaps (TASH)

Table 2.6	Key Elements of Full Inclusion Models
"Home school" attendance	Defined as the local school the child would attend if not disabled.
Natural proportion at the school site	The percentage of children with special needs enrolled in a particular school is in proportion to the percentage of pupils with exceptionalities in the entire school district; in general education classes, this would mean approximately two to three students with disabilities.
Zero rejection	All students are accepted at the local school, including those with severe impairments; pupils are not screened out or grouped separately because of their disability.
Age-/grade-appropriate placement	A full inclusion model calls for serving children with special needs in general education classrooms according to their chronological age rather than basing services on the child's academic ability or mental age.
Site-based management or coordination	Recent trends in school organizational reform suggest a movement away from central office administration for special education programs to one where the building principal (or other administrator) plays a large role in planning and administering programs for all children in the school.
Use of cooperative learning and peer instructional models	Instructional practices that involve children learning in a cooperative manner rather than in a competitive fashion and use students to assist in the instruction of classmates with disabilities can be effective strategies for integrating exceptional learners in the general education classroom.

Sources: W. Sailor, M. Gerry, and W. Wilson, "Policy Implications for Emergent Full Inclusion Models for the Education of Students with Disabilities," in W. Wang, H. Wolberg, and M. Reynolds (Eds.), *Handbook of Special Education,* Vol. 4 (New York: Pergamon Press, 1991), pp. 175–193; S. Stainback and W. Stainback, "Schools as Inclusive Communities," in W. Stainback and S. Stainback (Eds.), *Controversial Issues Confronting Special Education: Divergent Perspectives* (Boston: Allyn and Bacon, 1992), pp. 29–43.

has issued a statement fully supporting inclusion, which they consider to be a national moral imperative. However, the desirability of full inclusion is questioned in some professional circles. The Council for Learning Disabilities, for example, endorses the continuation of service delivery options. The Council for Exceptional Children (CEC), the premier professional organization in the field of special education, has also taken a stand on this issue. Their policy statement on full inclusion, adopted in 1993, reads as follows:

The Council for Exceptional Children (CEC) believes that all children, youth, and young adults with disabilities are entitled to a free and appropriate education and/or services that lead to an adult life characterized by satisfying relations with others, independent living, productive engagement in the community, and participation in society at large. To achieve such outcomes, there must exist for all children, youth, and young adults with disabilities a rich variety of early intervention, educational, and vocational program options with experiences. Access to these programs and experiences should be based on individual educational need and desired outcomes. Furthermore, students and their families or guardians, as members of the planning team, may recommend the placement, curriculum option, and the exit document to be pursued.

CEC believes that a continuum of services must be available for all children, youth, and young adults. CEC also believes that the concept of inclusion is a meaningful goal to be pursued in our schools and communities. In addition, CEC believes children, youth, and young adults with disabilities should be served whenever possible in general education classrooms in inclusive neighborhood schools and community settings. Such settings should be strengthened and supported by an infusion of specially trained personnel and other appropriate supportive practices according to the individual needs of the child. (Council for Exceptional Children, 1994, pp. 5–6)

The argument, as we see it, is not about *what* is taught or the kinds of services to be provided to students with disabilities, but *where* services are to be provided. We ought to be primarily concerned with how best to achieve the desired educational outcomes appropriate to the needs of the individual learner, rather than with the specific setting in which this occurs. Finally, there is one perplexing issue that still must be resolved. If we have accurately portrayed and interpreted full inclusion, then we believe it represents a radical departure from the concept of a cascade of placement options and, therefore, may well be a violation of current federal law. We suspect that, unfortunately, the resolution of this debate will rest with the courts.

Chapter in Review

Litigation and Legislation Affecting Special Education

- National and state laws, along with their subsequent interpretation by the courts, have certainly helped to shape and define contemporary special education policy and procedures.

Civil Rights Legislation

- Section 504 of PL 93-112 is the first federal law specifically aimed at protecting children and adults against discrimination due to a disability.

- The Americans with Disabilities Act (PL 101-336), which parallels Section 504 of PL 93-112, forbids discrimination against individuals with disabilities in both the public and private sectors of society.

Educational Reform: Standards-Based Education

- The No Child Left Behind Act is an example of federal legislation that focuses on educational accountability. All students, including those with a disability, are expected to demonstrate proficiency in key academic subjects.

- The reauthorization of the Individuals with Disabilities Education Act in 2004 (PL 108-446) aligns this legislation with some of the provisions of the No Child Left Behind Act. In addition, substantial changes occurred in the following areas of the law: the IEP process, the identification of an individual for a possible learning disability, teacher qualifications, student discipline, due process procedures, the evaluation of pupils, and participation of individuals with disabilities in state- and districtwide assessments.

Identification and Assessment of Individual Differences

- **Interindividual differences** are those characteristics that distinguish each student from his or her classmates. Interindividual differences might include distinctions based on height, intelligence, or gross motor skills.

- **Intraindividual differences** are differences within a particular student—that child's unique profile of strengths and weaknesses.

Referral and Assessment for Special Education

- When properly conducted, **educational assessments** lead to the development of meaningful IEPs (individualized education programs) and IFSPs (individualized family service plans).

- **Multidisciplinary teams** use **norm-** and **criterion-referenced tests** to determine if a student is eligible to receive a special education and/or related services.

Designing Individualized Instructional Programs

- An **individualized education program (IEP)** is essentially a management tool that stipulates who will be involved in providing a special education, what services and instruction will be provided, where they will be delivered, and for how long. In addition, the IEP is designed to gauge whether or not goals are successfully achieved.

- The **individualized family service plan (IFSP)** is the driving force behind the delivery of early intervention services to infants and toddlers and their families.

- The IFSP is family focused and is designed to preserve the parent's role of primary caregiver and principal decision maker. It must address the concerns and priorities of the family while also acknowledging the resources and strengths of the family.

Service Delivery Options: Where a Special Education Is Provided

- According to the principle of **least restrictive environment (LRE)**, services are to be provided in the setting that most closely approximates the general education classroom while still meeting the unique needs and requirements of the learner.

- **Mainstreaming** represents a popular interpretation of the principle of LRE.

- Implicit in the mandate of LRE is the notion of a continuum or **cascade of service delivery** options—a hierarchy of educational environments that allows for customized placement possibilities based on the needs of the individual pupil.

- **Full inclusion** seeks to place all students with disabilities, regardless of the type or severity of their impairment, in age-/grade-appropriate classrooms at neighborhood schools.

- The concept of full inclusion evolved from the **regular education initiative**, which sought a shared responsibility or partnership between general and special educators resulting in greater collaboration and cooperation in meeting the needs of pupils with disabilities.

Study Questions

1. How have litigation and legislation influenced the field of special education?

2. What is the significance of the following cases?
   - *Brown v. Board of Education*
   - *Pennsylvania Association for Retarded Children v. Commonwealth of Pennsylvania*
   - *Larry P. v. Riles*
   - *Board of Education v. Rowley*
   - *Daniel R.R. v. State Board of Education*

3. Name and describe the six major components and guarantees contained in PL 94-142.

4. What was the purpose of the Americans with Disabilities Act? List four areas where this law affects the lives of individuals who are disabled.

5. How did PL 108-446 modify PL 105-17?

6. Distinguish between interindividual and intraindividual differences.

7. How do prereferral interventions benefit the student suspected of requiring a special education?

8. How do norm-referenced and criterion-referenced tests differ?

9. List the key elements required of a meaningful IEP. Who is responsible for developing this document?

10. Compare the provisions and purpose of an IFSP with those of an IEP.

11. Define the following terms: mainstreaming, least restrictive environment, and regular education initiative. How are these terms related to the mandate of providing services in the LRE?

12. Distinguish between a cascade of services delivery model and the philosophy of full inclusion. What do you see as the advantages and disadvantages of full inclusion?

Key Terms

interindividual differences	intervention assistance team	norm-referenced	mainstreaming
intraindividual differences	child-find	criterion-referenced	regular education initiative (REI)
prereferral intervention	assessment	least restrictive	full inclusion
referral	multidisciplinary team	environment (LRE)	

Learning Activities

1. Interview an administrator of special education programs for your local school district. Find out how court decisions and legislative requirements have affected the delivery of special education services. Here are some suggested topics for discussion:
   - How has special education changed over the past several years as a result of judicial and legislative mandates?
   - What does the school district do to protect the rights of the students, involve parents, ensure due process, and assess in a nondiscriminatory manner?
   - How is the school district meeting the requirement of educating pupils with disabilities in the least restrictive environment?
   - What are the perceived advantages and disadvantages of IDEA at the local level?

2. Obtain a copy of your state's special education law. How do the requirements and provisions of the law compare with IDEA?

3. Obtain samples of several IEPs and IFSPs from different school districts in your vicinity. In what ways do the forms differ? How are they the same? Do they fulfill the requirements of the law as outlined in your textbook?

4. Visit several elementary and high schools in your area. What service delivery options are available for students with disabilities? Are children with different exceptionalities served in similar settings? Ask the teachers what they believe are the advantages and disadvantages of their particular environment.

Reflecting on Standards

The following exercises are designed to help you learn to apply the Council for Exceptional Children (CEC) standards to your teaching practice. Each of the reflection exercises below correlates with a knowledge or skill within the CEC standards. For the full text of each of the related CEC standards, please refer to the standards integration grid located in Appendix B.

1. Focus on Foundations (CEC Content Standard #1 CC1K4)

Reflect on what you have learned in this chapter about the rights of individuals with disabilities. What measures would you take in your classroom to make sure that your students were educated in the least restrictive environment possible?

2. Focus on Development and Characteristics of Learners (CEC Content Standard #2 CC2K6)

Reflect on what you have learned in this chapter about understanding the uniqueness of each of your students. Pair up with another student and assess his/her intraindividual differences (unique patterns of strengths and weaknesses). If you were to create an individualized education plan for this "student," what unique needs would he/she have?

Technology Resources

Visit the Web-based SAGE Study Site at **http://www.sagepub.com/gargiulo3estudy** for these additional learning tools:

- Chapter quizzes
- Key term flashcards
- Media links

- Full-text SAGE journal articles
- Internet activities
- Additional Web resources

Cultural and Linguistic Diversity and Exceptionality

The United States is an enormously diverse and pluralistic society—an amalgamation of different races, languages, folkways, religious beliefs, traditions, values, and even foods and music. As a nation, we greatly benefit from this cultural mixture; it is a defining characteristic of the United States and one of its great strengths. Perhaps nowhere else is this diversity more noticeable than in our schools.

Although in many instances we value and celebrate the richness of American diversity, all too often cultural differences result in prejudice and stereotypes as well as outright discrimination and unequal opportunities. Unfortunately, this statement is a valid characterization of some U.S. schools. In the opinion of various business leaders, policy makers, and educators, the educational environment encountered by many students from culturally and linguistically diverse backgrounds is inadequate, damaging, and openly hostile (Quality Education for Minorities Project, 1990). In some of our public schools, children from minority groups are seen as less than capable and/or difficult to teach. To our way of thinking, this situation is unacceptable and inexcusable. As educators working in increasingly cultural diverse environments, we need to model respect for and sensitivity to the cultural and linguistic characteristics represented by our students and their families.

The goal of this chapter is to examine the link between cultural and linguistic diversity and exceptionality. We will explore the historical patterns of American reaction to and acceptance of people from other lands. We will discuss issues of multicultural and bilingual education and consider the multitude of challenges confronting teachers who work with students with special needs from culturally and linguistically diverse backgrounds (see the accompanying FYI feature).

Cultural Diversity: The Changing Face of a Nation

The United States is made up of people from many different lands; in fact, only about 1.5 percent of Americans are native (U.S. Census Bureau, 2005). A vast number of Americans are descended from the millions of immigrants who entered the United States through Ellis Island, located in lower New York Harbor, in the latter part of the nineteenth and the early

FYI . . .

Cultural and Linguistic Diversity Quiz

True or False?

1. Many teachers have little or no training in working with children from diverse cultural and linguistic backgrounds.

2. Multicultural education is for all students.

3. Cultural differences have little effect on the way students learn.

4. Immigrants are in the United States to stay. The best thing teachers can do is to help them assimilate.

5. Young children don't really notice differences, so why make a big deal of multicultural education? It is better to be color-blind.

6. Schools in which there are no minority groups don't need a multicultural perspective.

7. The great majority of general and special education teachers in the United States come from the dominant culture.

8. Older students from diverse backgrounds are more at risk for educational failure than are younger children.

9. Most of the concepts of multicultural education are simply too difficult for children with disabilities.

10. A school should reflect and sanction the range of languages and dialects spoken by the students.

11. Multicultural education is a total curricular and instructional approach.

12. Children from minority groups are overrepresented in special education and underrepresented in programs for the gifted and talented.

Answer Key

1. True	4. False	7. True	10. True
2. True	5. False	8. True	11. True
3. False	6. False	9. False	12. True

Source: Adapted from M. Winzer and K. Mazurek, *Special Education in Multicultural Contexts* (Upper Saddle River, NJ: Prentice Hall, 1998), pp. 8, 45, 168.

decades of the twentieth century. Immigration to the United States has continued since then, but the countries of origin have shifted from Europe to Latin America and Asia (Lustig & Koestner, 2006). More than 1 million people immigrate to the United States annually. In 1990, the foreign-born population of the United States was nearly 20 percent (19.7%), more than double the percentage in 1960 (Winzer & Mazurek, 1998).

What are the implications of the following estimates and projections for our schools and classroom practices?

- By the year 2020, students of color are projected to make up almost half of all school-age youth (Gollnick & Chinn, 2009).
- By the year 2050, the U.S. population is projected to be 53 percent Anglo, 24 percent Latino, 13 percent black, 9 percent Asian, and 1 percent Native American (Chinn, 2002).
- About one in five residents, or approximately 19 percent of the U.S. population over the age of 5, speaks a language other than English at home (U.S. Census Bureau, 2007).
- At the present time, children of color make up the majority of students in several states and many urban areas, including Detroit, Los Angeles, Atlanta, Miami, Baltimore, New York, Chicago, Birmingham, and Houston (Lustig & Koestner, 2006; National Center for Education Statistics, 2007).

- Despite increasing cultural and linguistic diversity in our schools, almost 90 percent of general and special education teachers are white (Boyer & Mainzer, 2003).
- Minority children are disproportionally represented in special education programs. Enrollment patterns suggest, for instance, an overrepresentation of African Americans in classes for students with mental retardation or behavior disorders. Asian Americans are underrepresented in those programs but overrepresented in programs for individuals who are gifted and talented (Gollnick & Chinn, 2009; U.S. Department of Education, 2006).

The reasons for these changing demographics are many and varied. They include shifting immigration patterns and varying birthrates among women of various ethnic groups as well as other factors.

It is abundantly clear that the ethnic makeup of the United States is changing. It is equally obvious that this diversity will be reflected in our schools. Classrooms in the coming years will evidence even greater diversity than we find today. Teachers will most likely encounter families whose beliefs and practices vary significantly in important ways from those of mainstream American families. The challenge confronting educators and other professionals is how best to meet the needs of this changing and expanding population of learners.

Cultural Diversity in the Teaching Profession

As the number of students from culturally and linguistically diverse backgrounds continues to grow, the diversity of our teaching workforce has failed to keep pace with this expansion. At the present time, there is a notable absence of racial diversity among educators; teachers do not reflect the diversity of students they teach (Tyler, Yzquierdo, Lopez-Reyna, & Flippin, 2004). Slightly more than 83 percent of teachers are white, about 8 percent are African American, and approximately 8 percent are Hispanic or of other racial/ethnic groups (National Center for Education Statistics, 2006). Some 40 percent of our schools have no teachers of color on their staffs (National Collaborative on Diversity in the Teaching Force, 2004). A similar pattern is evident when examining special educators. About 84 percent of the members of the workforce are white, 11 percent are African American, and a scant 5 percent consider themselves Hispanic (Boyer & Mainzer, 2003). Overall, this situation is not expected to improve; in fact, it is projected that the teaching profession will become increasingly homogenous in the coming years (National Education Association, 2004).

We do not wish to imply or suggest that students who are culturally and linguistically diverse should be taught exclusively by teachers from traditionally underrepresented groups. There is little empirical evidence to suggest that children "of color learn better when taught by teachers of color" (Ladson-Billings, 1994, p. 26). Such a proposal would be neither feasible nor desirable and, according to Voltz (1998), would be counter to the goal of achieving greater diversity in the teaching force.

Schools in the United States are grounded in white, middle-class values, a culture that may hold little meaning for vast numbers of children who are poor and/or from ethnically or culturally diverse backgrounds (Benner, 1998). Still, most teachers, regardless of their own cultural and ethnic heritage, belong to the middle class and subscribe to the values of this group. Teachers from minority groups play a critical role in the education of all children, but especially for pupils from minority populations. In addition to serving as role models, these professionals often act as "cultural translators" and "cultural mediators" (Smith, Smith-Davis, Clarke, & Mims, 2000) for these students, helping them function successfully in the dominant culture.

From Assimilation to Cultural Pluralism

Issues of multiculturalism and bilingualism have challenged educators for almost a century. In the early decades of the twentieth century, one aim of schools was to assimilate children of immigrants into American culture as quickly as possible. There was a widely held belief that public education could unite the population and instill the ideals of American society in diverse groups of people. The goal of this assimilation or homogenizing process was to "Americanize" vast numbers of new citizens. They were expected to abandon their native languages, cultural heritage, beliefs, and practices. In their place would emerge a common American culture—"*E pluribus unum*" ("Out of many, one")—with an allegiance to the "American way of doing things." Metaphorically speaking, the United States was seen as a huge **melting pot**—a cauldron into which diverse people were dumped to melt away their differences, thus creating a citizenry who were very much alike (Tiedt & Tiedt, 2005).

For a variety of political and social reasons, Americans in the 1960s slowly began to question the wisdom of a melting pot theory as the country struggled with issues of civil rights and equal opportunity. Schools were no longer seen as the primary vehicle for homogenizing new citizens; instead, a student's ethnic heritage was to be valued and prized. Interest in cultural pluralism and multicultural education was ignited. As a result, a new set of metaphors evolved to counter the philosophy of America as a melting pot. The United States is now likened to a patchwork quilt, a floral bouquet, or a salad.

The notion of the United States as a melting pot society has gradually given way to **cultural pluralism** wherein cultural and ethnic differences are appreciated and respected. Cultural pluralism does *not* require cultural groups to relinquish or abandon their cultural heritage. Schools now value the richness that diversity brings to the classroom; diversity is seen as a strength rather than a weakness.

Terminology of Cultural Differences

Educators and other professionals in the field of education are confronted with a barrage of labels and terms used to describe the education of children from different cultural backgrounds. Sometimes this terminology contributes to inaccurate generalizations, stereotyping, and incorrect assumptions about certain individuals or groups of people. In some instances, it is even difficult to know how to correctly describe the youngsters themselves. Do we, for example, refer to some children as black or African American? Is it more appropriate to identify a student as Hispanic or Latino, and how about pupils from Asian cultures? Also, what is the difference between bilingual education and multicultural education? As you can see, the topic of cultural and linguistic diversity can easily become a source of confusion and controversy. Perhaps it is best to begin our discussion of key terminology by arriving at an understanding of what we mean by culture.

CULTURE We define **culture** as the attitudes, values, belief systems, norms, and traditions shared by a particular group of people that collectively form their heritage. A culture is transmitted in various ways from one generation to another. It is typically reflected in language, religion, dress, diet, social customs, and other aspects of a particular lifestyle (Gargiulo & Kilgo, 2005). Siccone (1995) points out that culture also includes the way particular groups of people interpret the world; it provides individuals with a frame of reference or perspective for attaching meaning to specific events or situations, such as the value and purpose of education or the birth of a child with a disability.

Zirpoli (1995) reminds professionals to guard against generalizing and stereotyping when working with pupils from various cultural groups. Even within specific groups, each person is unique, even though they may share distinctively similar group characteristics. Two students from the same racial group will most likely perform quite differently in the classroom regardless of their shared cultural heritage.

MULTICULTURALISM We live in a multicultural society; yet **multiculturalism** is a confusing and poorly understood concept (Janzen, 1994). In its most basic interpretation, multiculturalism refers to more than one culture. It acknowledges basic commonalities among groups of people while appreciating their differences. Implicit within the concept of multiculturalism is the belief that an individual can function within more than one culture. Multiculturalism also provides us with a foundation for understanding multicultural education.

MULTICULTURAL EDUCATION **Multicultural education** is an ambiguous and somewhat controversial concept. Sleeter and Grant (2006) characterize multicultural education as an umbrella concept involving issues of race, language, social class, and culture as well as disability and gender. Gollnick and Chinn (2009) portray multicultural education as an educational strategy wherein the cultural background of each pupil is valued, viewed positively, and used to develop effective instruction.

The clientele of U.S. schools is rapidly changing.

BILINGUAL EDUCATION A term frequently associated with multicultural education is **bilingual education,** an equally controversial and somewhat confusing concept. The two are not synonymous, however. Multicultural education can be infused throughout the curriculum without the benefit of bilingual education. Simply defined, bilingual education is an educational strategy whereby students whose first language is not English are instructed primarily through their native language while developing their competency and proficiency in English. Teachers initially use the language that the child knows best (Baca & Baca, 2004a). Once a satisfactory command of English is achieved, it becomes the medium of instruction.

Describing Diversity

U.S. society is an amalgamation of many different cultures. The U.S. government, however, officially recognizes only five distinct racial groups. The federal government uses this classification scheme when reporting, for example, Head Start enrollment, poverty figures, high school graduation rates, and other such statistics. The Office for Civil Rights within the U.S. Department of Education (1987) identifies citizens as follows:

- **American Indian or Alaskan Native.** A person having origins in any of the original peoples of North America and who maintains cultural identification through tribal affiliation or community recognition.
- **Asian or Pacific Islander.** A person having origins in any of the original peoples of the Far East, Southeast Asia, the Pacific Islands, or the Indian subcontinent. This area includes, for example, China, India, Japan, Korea, the Philippine Islands, and Samoa.
- **Hispanic.** A person of Mexican, Puerto Rican, Cuban, Central or South American, or other Spanish culture or origin regardless of race.
- **Black** (not of Hispanic origin). A person having origins in any of the black racial groups of Africa.
- **White** (not of Hispanic origin). A person having descended from any of the original peoples of Europe, North Africa, or the Middle East. (p. 37)

We should point out that the preceding descriptions are arbitrary and represent umbrella terms (Harry, 1992b). This terminology camouflages immense cultural and racial variability while obscuring the richness of individual cultures. Regardless of how specific groups of people are described, the diversity and variation within each group are tremendous. Various cultural groups are anything but homogenous; differences are likely to be found in language, ethnicity, social class, home country, and a host of other dimensions. It is important for teachers to acknowledge and respect this heterogeneity. They must also guard against perpetuating ethnic and racial stereotypes. Educators frequently fail to use qualifiers such as "some," "many," or "most" when discussing various cultural groups. This insensitivity to individuality can easily result in students' receiving an erroneous, oversimplified, and possibly stereotypical impression of a particular racial group (Ryan, 1993).

Teachers must also guard against assuming that the behaviors, beliefs, and actions of their particular cultural group are the correct or only way of doing something. Such assumptions reflect **ethnocentrism**—viewing one's own cultural group characteristics as superior or correct and the ways of other groups as inferior or peculiar.

Multicultural Education, Bilingual Education, and Student Diversity

By now it should be apparent that multicultural education is closely intertwined with issues of student diversity. Because the clientele of American schools is rapidly changing, there has been much debate and controversy over how best to educate children with culturally and linguistically diverse backgrounds. It is axiomatic that all students are different and not all people learn in the same way; this is especially true for students who are culturally and linguistically diverse. It would be foolish for teachers to expect children (or adults, for that matter) to leave their values, traditions, beliefs, and even their language at the schoolhouse door. Effective teachers are sensitive to the cultural heritage of each learner and attempt to provide educational experiences that are culturally relevant and culturally appropriate.

Multicultural Education: Concepts and Characteristics

Embedded within the concept of multicultural education is a belief that all students, regardless of their race, ethnicity, culture, and other characteristics such as social class or disability, should experience equal educational opportunities. Although no single recipe can accommodate all the facets of multicultural education, there are certain common ingredients. Figure 3.1 portrays six goals of multicultural education, as synthesized by Winzer and Mazurek (1998). These aims are broad and overlapping, supporting their contention that multicultural education is an orientation and not a specific pedagogical technique.

Throughout this chapter, we have stressed the multicultural nature of U.S. society. At the heart of this society is a core national culture, identified as the **macroculture,** which represents a shared culture. Traits such as individualism, independence, competitiveness, and ambition are characteristic of the American macroculture (Gollnick & Chinn, 2009), along with values such as equality and fair play. Within this larger culture are several distinct subcultures, or **microcultures,** which, while sharing attributes of the macroculture, maintain their own distinct values, norms, and behaviors. The United States is composed of many different microcultures, as illustrated in Figure 3.2. According to Banks (2007), the various microcultures to which a person belongs are interrelated and interact with one another to collectively influence the individual's behavior. Membership in a particular group does not define a person's behavior, but it does make certain types of behavior more likely.

Differences between the various microcultures and the macroculture are frequently a source of conflict and misunderstanding. A major goal of multicultural education, therefore, is for pupils to acquire the knowledge, attitudes, and skills needed to function effectively in each cultural

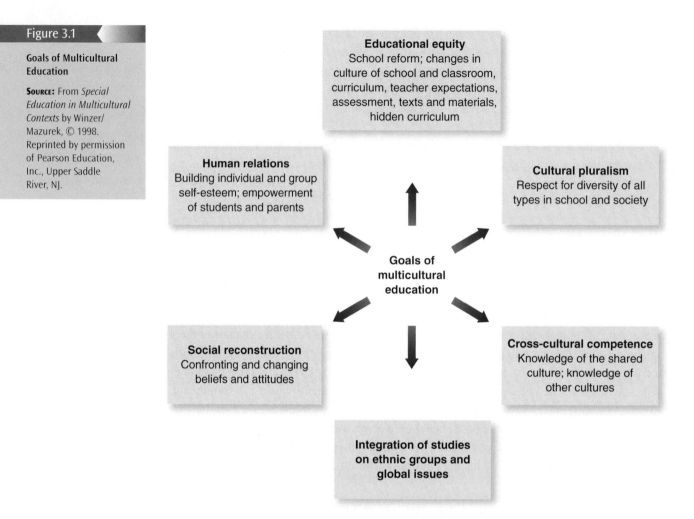

Figure 3.1

Goals of Multicultural Education

Source: From *Special Education in Multicultural Contexts* by Winzer/Mazurek, © 1998. Reprinted by permission of Pearson Education, Inc., Upper Saddle River, NJ.

Educational equity
School reform; changes in culture of school and classroom, curriculum, teacher expectations, assessment, texts and materials, hidden curriculum

Human relations
Building individual and group self-esteem; empowerment of students and parents

Cultural pluralism
Respect for diversity of all types in school and society

Goals of multicultural education

Social reconstruction
Confronting and changing beliefs and attitudes

Cross-cultural competence
Knowledge of the shared culture; knowledge of other cultures

Integration of studies on ethnic groups and global issues

setting (Banks, 2007). Banks argues that students in contemporary society should be able to function in their own as well as other microcultures, the macroculture, and the global community.

Bilingual Education: Concepts and Characteristics

As noted previously, multicultural education and bilingual education are not the same thing. Multicultural education can exist independently of bilingual education, but bilingual education cannot exist without multicultural education because it emphasizes the student's culture as well as language. As we have seen, approximately one out of five Americans, or almost 20 percent of the population, speaks a language other than English. The U.S. government estimates that there are more than 10 million school-age children whose primary language is not English (National Center for Education Statistics, 2007). Yet controversy and debate continue over how best to meet the needs of these students. In many school districts, bilingual education provides one possible answer. Not everyone, however, agrees with this strategy. Thirty states have enacted legislation or passed constitutional amendments establishing English as the "official" language of their state (Crawford, 2004; U.S. English, 2008), and five states actually prohibit bilingual education in their schools (Baca & Baca, 2004b).

Students whose first language is not English represent a very heterogeneous group of individuals. Their competency in their primary language as well as in English may vary greatly. Some of these pupils may be identified as **limited English proficient (LEP)**, the term incorporated in IDEA 2004. Other professionals, however, prefer the label *English*

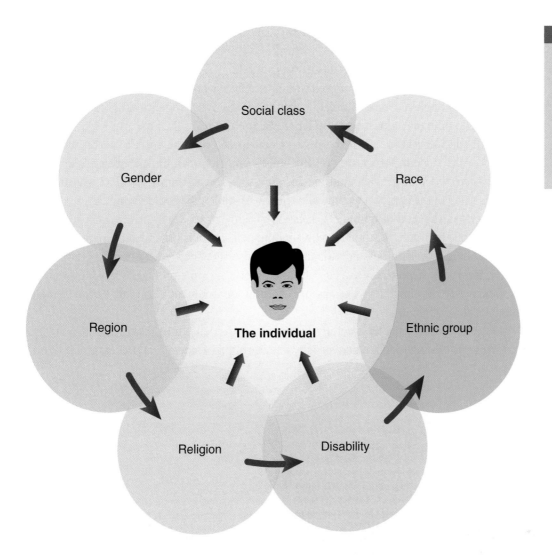

Figure 3.2

Influence of Microcultures on an Individual's Behavior

Source: Adapted from J. Banks, *Cultural Diversity and Education*, 5th ed. (Needham Heights, MA: Allyn and Bacon, 2006), p. 77.

language learners. The term *limited English proficient* refers to a reduced or diminished fluency in reading, writing, or speaking English. Typically, these students are unable to profit fully from instruction provided in English. Limited English proficiency is not a disparaging label. "It does not equate with lack of capacity or an inherent limitation," Winzer and Mazurek (1998) write, "but it is synonymous with the reality of children who speak another language and are not yet adept in English" (p. 51).

The primary purpose of bilingual education programs is to provide assistance to students with limited proficiency in English so that they can "function effectively in both their native language and English. . . . The student's native language and culture are taught concurrently with English and the dominant culture" (Gollnick & Chinn, 2006, p. 299). The result is that the pupil becomes bilingual and bicultural in the process. Similarly, Baca and Baca (2004a), authorities in the field of bilingual education, see the primary mission of bilingual education as providing instruction to pupils using the language they know best and then reinforcing this information through English, while also promoting cognitive as well as affective development and cultural enrichment. Although it is not explicitly stated, we believe that one of the principal goals of bilingual education is to provide increased educational opportunities for students whose native language is not English. It is interesting to note that, contrary to popular belief, the original aim of bilingual education was not to advocate bilingualism but rather to promote the acquisition of English language skills. Bilingual education was thought to be the quickest way for a non-English-speaking person to become literate in English (Janzen, 1994).

The research evidence on the effectiveness of bilingual education strongly suggests that bilingual education is the most appropriate approach for working with students with limited proficiency in English. Greater academic gains and improved language skills can be directly attributed to bilingual education (Winzer & Mazurek, 1998). Of course, the key to effective bilingual education is to match the instructional strategy to the specific needs and background of the student. Depending on the child's proficiency in his or her native language and English, different instructional models are used. The accompanying FYI feature summarizes some of the approaches typically used with students who are bilingual.

Experts in the field of bilingual education disagree as to which pedagogical strategy is most effective for teaching students who are bilingual. There is general agreement, however, that the more opportunities individuals have to use their newly acquired language skills with classmates, friends, family members, and others, the more proficient they will become. In comparison to classroom settings, the natural environment seems to better facilitate language development.

Educators must consider carefully when they transition students with limited English proficiency to all-English classrooms. Many of these pupils' academic failures appear to be due

FYI . . .

Instructional Options for Students Who Are Bilingual

Approach	Strategies
1. Transitional programs	Students are instructed in academic content areas via their native language only until they are sufficiently competent in English, then transition to all-English classes. Primary goal of this program is to move students as quickly as possible to English-only classes. Many students exit after two to three years of instruction. Most common instructional model; bilingual education legislation favors this approach.
2. Maintenance (developmental) programs	Strong native language emphasis. Pupils maintain proficiency in first language while receiving instruction in English. A long-term approach with less emphasis on leaving program. Solid academic foundation is stressed.
3. Enrichment programs	Typically used with monolingual children, who are introduced to new language and culture.
4. Immersion programs	English language is the exclusive medium of instruction; first language and culture are not incorporated. A "sink or swim" philosophy.
5. English as a second language (ESL) programs	Not a true form of bilingual education. Children typically receive instruction in English outside the regular classroom. Goal is to quickly develop English proficiency in bilingual students. Exclusive emphasis on English for teaching and learning; native language not used in instruction. An assimilationist model with multiple variations.
6. Sheltered English	Students receive instruction in academic subjects exclusively in English; no effort is made to maintain or develop proficiency in first language. English instruction is continually monitored and modified to ensure pupil's comprehension. Simultaneous exposure to English language and subject content matter.

to transitioning too quickly. Conversational fluency typically develops in children with LEP after approximately two years of instruction. Teachers, therefore, assume that pupils are ready to move because they appear to be proficient in English. However, according to investigators (Salend & Salinas, 2003; Zelasko & Antunez, 2000), the deeper and more complex language skills needed for academic success require an additional five to seven years of instruction. Movement to a monolingual English class setting should occur only if the teacher is certain that the student possesses the requisite language skills to compete in an academic environment.

Bilingual Special Education: Concepts and Characteristics

Students who are culturally and linguistically diverse *and* disabled present significant challenges for educators. How do we meet the needs of this growing population of pupils, which is estimated at approximately 530,000 (Baca, Baca, & de Valenzuela, 2004)? What is the most normalized environment for students experiencing "double jeopardy"—that is, linguistic differences and disability? Which area should teachers primarily focus on—the problems posed by the disability or the lack of English proficiency? These questions have no easy answers. One frequently mentioned solution is to place these pupils in classrooms with a special educator who is bilingual. In the majority of instances, however, this is not a feasible solution because of a severe shortage of qualified personnel (Deshler & Rodriguez-Walling, 2004). What these students truly need is an instructional model known as **bilingual special education.** Baca et al. define this concept as "the use of the home language and the home culture along with English in an individually designed program of special instruction for the student in an inclusive environment. Bilingual special education considers the child's language and culture as foundations upon which an appropriate education may be built" (p. 18). The main goal of these efforts is to assist the pupil in reaching his or her maximum potential. The student's primary language and culture are the vehicles for accomplishing this task.

One of the critical issues confronting professionals is how to merge two different programs, bilingual education and special education, into one cogent paradigm. The integration of these two programs requires a focus not only on the acquisition of English language proficiency but also the construction of individualized educational interventions. The goal is the development of both academic as well as English language skills, which often requires a team approach. Meaningful instruction for pupils who are culturally and linguistically diverse and disabled entails a coordinated effort involving general educators, special education teachers, and bilingual educators (Gollnick & Chinn, 2009; Salend & Salinas, 2003).

Attempts at providing a special education to pupils with LEP have frequently encountered a number of problems, including challenges obtaining an accurate diagnosis coupled with assessment difficulties which often lead to an inappropriate placement. These issues are intricately interrelated and complementary and must be considered within a broader content. Most educators, according to Winzer and Mazurek (1998), recognize that disability and cultural and linguistic differences are related phenomena that play a significant role in a student's learning and development. Cultural and linguistic characteristics frequently coexist and interact with disability-related factors. Consider if you will Ramón, a 9-year-old boy identified as mentally retarded and with limited English proficiency, whose parents are migrant workers. His family of six has an income below the federal poverty line. Ramón's special education program must address the interaction of these confounding variables. Winzer and Mazurek caution teachers to remember that pupils with LEP do not give up their right to bilingual education when found to be eligible for special education services. Too often, however, these students fall between the cracks of both programs.

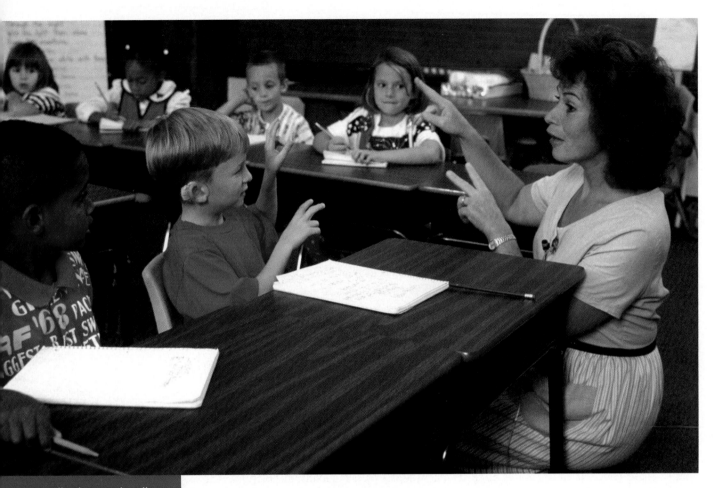

Pupils who are culturally and linguistically diverse and disabled present unique challenges for teachers.

If special education services are to be truly inclusive and meet the unique requirements of learners who are culturally and linguistically diverse, then special educators must focus their attention on the following four areas identified by Garcia and Malkin (1993, p. 52):

1. Information about the language characteristics of learners with disabilities who are bilingual or have limited English proficiency that will assist in the development of a language use plan
2. Information about cultural factors that influence educational planning and services
3. Characteristics of instructional strategies and materials that are culturally and linguistically appropriate
4. Characteristics of a learning environment that promotes success for all students

PL 108-446 also speaks to the issue of appropriate programming for these children. A student *cannot* be considered eligible for special education services under this law if their educational difficulties are primarily the result of limited proficiency in English or poor instruction.

Disproportional Representation of Minority Students in Special Education Programs

The disproportionate presence of pupils from minority groups in special education programs has been a pressing and volatile concern of educators for more than three decades

(Coutinho & Oswald, 2000). The fact that greater numbers of children from minority groups are placed in special education programs than would be anticipated based on their proportion of the general school population is commonly referred to as **overrepresentation.** At the same time, there is a long-standing pattern of **underrepresentation** (fewer students in a particular category than one might expect based on their numbers in the school population) of African Americans, Native Americans, and Hispanics in programs for children and youth who are gifted and talented (Borland, 2004; Clark, 2008; Gollnick & Chinn, 2009). Asian American children and Pacific Islanders are typically underrepresented in special education classes and overrepresented in classes for the gifted and talented (Chinn & Hughes, 1987; Donovan & Cross, 2002; U.S. Department of Education, 2006).

The fact that a disproportionate number of students from minority groups are enrolled in special education classrooms is a stinging indictment of the efficacy of the professional practices of special educators and a challenge to the concept of honoring diversity— presumably the cornerstone of our field (Artiles & Trent, 1994). At the heart of the discussion about disproportional representation is the issue of inappropriate placement in special education programs. The primary concern is with false positives—when a pupil from a cultural or linguistic minority is identified as disabled when, in fact, he or she is *not* disabled and is therefore inappropriately placed in a class for students with disabilities. To ignore the gifts and talents of children from diverse backgrounds is equally damaging and denies them the opportunity to reach their full potential (Artiles & Zamora-Durán, 1997). Many complex factors and circumstances influence student placement; however, for those racially and ethnically diverse students who are misclassified and inappropriately placed or denied access to appropriate services, the outcomes are often serious and enduring (U.S. Department of Education, 1997).

It should be noted that the problem of overrepresentation does not occur across all categories of disabilities. The disproportionate presence of students from minority groups occurs only in those disability categories in which professional judgment and opinion play a role in the decision-making process, such as mild mental retardation and behavior disorders. Overrepresentation is not a problem in disability areas that have a clear biological basis. For instance, sensory or motor impairments and severe and profound mental retardation do not yield dramatically different proportions than one would anticipate on the basis of the ethnic composition of the general school population (MacMillan & Reschly, 1998).

Office for Civil Rights Survey Data

The Office for Civil Rights (OCR) within the Department of Education has been concerned about over- and underrepresentation of minorities in special education programs since its creation in 1965. Beginning in 1968, OCR has conducted biennial surveys of representative school districts across the United States in which enrollment patterns of children in special education classes are analyzed. Generally speaking, information gleaned from these surveys portrays "persistent patterns of minority students being disproportionately represented in special education programs and classes relative to their enrollment in the general school population" (U.S. Department of Education, 1997, p. I-42).

The classic Chinn and Hughes (1987) analysis of OCR reports for school years 1978, 1980, 1982, and 1984 reveals that the number of African American children in classes for students with mild mental retardation was approximately twice as large as one would expect on the basis of their percentage of total school population. A similar pattern was found for the disability areas of behavior disorders and moderate mental retardation. The representation of African American children in programs for learners who are gifted and talented, however, was disproportionately low. Native American students also had disproportionately high representation in classes for students with learning disabilities and disproportionately low representation in programs for the gifted and talented. In contrast, almost twice as many Asian and Pacific Islander children were attending classes for pupils identified as gifted and talented as would be expected on the basis of their proportion of total school enrollment; in almost every other category, this group was underrepresented. White students, too, were consistently underrepresented in classes for students with mild and moderate mental retardation and overrepresented in classes for gifted and talented youth. The representation of Hispanic youngsters was disproportionately low across all categories of exceptionality.

The 1998–1999 school year was the first time that the states were required to report the race and ethnicity of students with disabilities served under IDEA. Table 3.1 presents recent information on the percentage and number of students receiving a special education in representative disability categories according to race. Although black students represent only about 20 percent of the total enrollment in special education programs, approximately 33 percent of the pupils in classes for students with mental retardation are African American. Interestingly, fewer black children are enrolled in programs for pupils with hearing impairments than one might expect based on their contribution to the total special education population. Additional representative comparisons can be found in the table.

Table 3.1		Number and Percentage of Students Ages 6–21 Receiving a Special Education in Select Disability Categories					
Disability		**American Indian/ Alaskan Native**	**Asian/Pacific Islander**	**Black**	**Hispanic**	**White**	**Total**
Specific Learning Disabilities	N	47,701	49,604	553,065	606,737	1,523,111	2,780,218
	%	1.72	1.78	19.89	21.82	54.78	
Speech or Language Impairments	N	15,243	35,345	177,309	206,765	722,553	1,157,215
	%	1.32	3.05	15.32	17.87	62.44	
Mental Retardation	N	6,709	11,055	179,819	81,801	266,108	545,492
	%	1.23	2.03	32.96	15.00	48.78	
Emotional Disturbance	N	7,172	5,450	135,796	51,637	272,329	472,384
	%	1.52	1.15	28.75	10.93	57.65	
Hearing Impairments	N	930	3,595	11,687	16,458	39,717	72,387
	%	1.28	4.97	16.15	22.74	54.87	
Traumatic Brain Injury	N	338	583	3,999	3,050	15,539	23,509
	%	1.44	2.48	17.01	12.97	66.10	
All Disabilities	N	91,789	133,228	1,245,087	1,088,933	3,550,532	6,109,569
	%	1.50	2.18	20.38	17.82	58.11	

Note: Information is for the 2005–2006 school year, updated July 17, 2006.

Based on data from the 50 states, Puerto Rico, the District of Columbia, and outlying areas.

Due to rounding, percentages do not always add to 100 percent.

Source: U.S. Department of Education, Office of Special Education Programs, "Children with Disabilities Receiving Special Education Under Part B of the Individuals with Disabilities Education Act." Available at http://www.ideadata.org

The entire issue of representational discrepancies is subject to debate and controversy. Harry (1992a), for instance, does not believe that placement rates in special education programs for Native American and Hispanic students are suggestive of overrepresentation when examined nationally. At the individual state and local level, however, a different picture emerges. Like Benner (1998), she argues that placement statistics must be examined cautiously and kept in perspective. In the opinion of Benner and Harry, the larger the enrollment of pupils from minority groups within a school district, the greater their representation will be in special education classrooms. This is to be expected. Furthermore, the larger the education program, the greater the likelihood of disproportionate representation. Harry sees this phenomenon as a classic "chicken-and-egg" question. "While large numbers of minority children may lead to a perceived need for more special education programs, it may also be that the greater availability of programs encourages increased placement of minority children" (p. 66).

These precautionary observations notwithstanding, the misclassification and/or inappropriate placement of minority students in special education programs frequently leads to stigmatization and lower expectations. This is especially true when a pupil is removed from the general education setting and consequently denied access to the general education curriculum, which often results in limited postsecondary educational and employment opportunities. In some school systems, the disproportionate representation of these students also results in significant racial separation.

Factors Contributing to Over- and Underrepresentation

A myriad of explanations have been put forth to explain the problem of over- and underrepresentation of culturally diverse students in some categories of special education. No one explanation fully accounts for this situation; the various reasons are complex and frequently intertwined. Patton (1998), for example, describes the problem as rooted in socioeconomic, sociocultural, and sociopolitical forces.

The overrepresentation of children of color is perhaps best understood as a relationship between family socioeconomic status and disability rather than between disability and minority group status per se. Individuals from minority groups typically populate urban centers and tend to be poor. Poverty and ethnicity are inextricably interwoven variables in American society (Donovan & Cross, 2002; MacMillan & Reschly, 1998). Report after report and survey after survey routinely indicate an overrepresentation of minority groups living in poverty. According to the Children's Defense Fund (2005), approximately 13 million children, or nearly one out of every five youngsters, lives in poverty.

Poverty often means limited access to health care (especially prenatal care), poor nutrition, and adverse living conditions. All of these variables increase the probability of a child being at risk for learning and developmental difficulties. Cultural and language differences only exacerbate the student's vulnerability, increasing the likelihood of educational failure and his or her need for special education services (Gargiulo & Kilgo, 2005).

The evidence strongly suggests that socioeconomic status rather than ethnicity is one of the primary reasons that students from racially and ethnically diverse populations encounter persistent academic problems in the public schools (MacMillan & Reschly, 1998). Poverty, however, is not the only culprit contributing to the disproportional representation of minorities in some special education programs. Faulty identification procedures, ineffective prereferral strategies, test bias,

> **Key Facts about America's Children**
>
> - 1 in 3 is born to unmarried parents
> - 1 in 5 under age 3 is poor
> - 1 in 8 has no health insurance
> - 1 in 8 never graduates from high school
> - 1 in 7 lives in a family receiving food stamps
> - 1 in 12 has a disability
>
> **Source:** *Key Facts About American Children,* Children's Defense Fund, August 2004. Available at http://www.childrensdefense.org/

Poverty and ethnicity are inextricably interwoven aspects of American society.

and inappropriate assessment techniques may also account for some of the overrepresentation. The lack of standardized tests appropriate for use with students who have limited English proficiency is another contributing factor (Coutinho & Oswald, 2000; Voltz, 1998). Although, as Winzer and Mazurek (1998) point out, biased and discriminatory assessment instruments do play a role, these factors alone are insufficient to account for the misplacement and disproportionate representation of pupils from minority groups in special education classes. Other relevant variables include teacher bias, different behavioral and academic performance standards for students from minority populations, and incongruity or discrepancy between the child's home culture and school expectations. For example, behaviors considered adaptive in a student's home, such as nonassertiveness and cooperation, may conflict with expectations in the classroom, where independence and competition are valued.

Incongruity may also exist in instructional methodology. Research has demonstrated that children from minority groups learn differently than white youngsters. African American pupils, for example, tend to be **field dependent/sensitive** (relational, global) learners who approach learning intuitively rather than analytically and logically (Ford, 1998). These students perform better in social settings like those found in cooperative learning environments and group work (Gollnick & Chinn, 2009). In contrast, white students and Asian/Pacific Islanders are typically **field independent** (detail-oriented and analytically inclined) learners who thrive in competitive settings where achievement and individual accomplishment are prized.

White teachers, as a whole, are typically field independent, whereas educators from minority populations are more likely to be field dependent. The lack of congruency between the cognitive style of many culturally diverse students and that of their teachers is another possible reason for disproportional representation. Teachers often perceive pupils with cognitive styles different from their own in negative ways. This, of course, exacerbates the student's learning problems. This incongruity frequently causes teachers to overlook a youngster's strengths and abilities and increases the likelihood of a referral for special education services. By the same token, a teacher may fail to recognize the attributes of the brightest pupils and thus be less likely to refer them to programs for students with special gifts and talents.

The reasons for the underrepresentation of certain groups in programs for the gifted and talented are as varied as the explanations for overrepresentation in other programs. Benner (1998) suggests that relevant factors include the politics of race and social class, attitudinal bias, and pressure from peers not to excel academically. Ford (1998) cites problems related to screening and identification, low teacher expectations and negative perceptions of minority pupils, and a lack of teacher training in the area of gifted education.

Consequences of Disproportional Representation

The over- and underenrollment of racial and ethnic minorities in some special education programs often leads to unequal educational opportunities. In many instances, removal from the general education classroom and assignment to a special education classroom results in an inferior and ineffective educational experience for these children (Donovan & Cross, 2002). The educational experiences of racially, ethnically, and culturally diverse pupils often put them at risk for underachievement and dropping out of school. In comparison to their white peers, students from ethnically and racially diverse backgrounds drop out of school at a much higher rate. In the 2004 school year, the dropout rate for Hispanic youth (23.8%) was almost three and a half times the rate for white pupils (6.8%). About 12 percent of African American students leave school before completing their education (National Center for Education Statistics, 2006). Adolescents who fail to graduate are more likely to be unemployed and constitute a disproportionate percentage of the incarcerated population (U.S. Department of Education, 1997).

The disproportionately high representation of racial and ethnic minorities as well as culturally and linguistically diverse students in some special education classrooms is a problem that has plagued educators for more than thirty years. Unfortunately, the debate over disproportionate representation, inappropriate placement, and misclassification of minority pupils is far from being resolved. However, advocates, policy makers, researchers, educators, and parents have moved beyond the mere condemnation of this long-standing and complex problem to seek solutions. Yet solutions to the issue of greater educational opportunity and quality of education remain elusive. A multifaceted, broad-based attack is necessary. Attention needs to be focused on the identification and referral process, assessment bias, instructional factors, and teacher attitudes, as well as environmental factors impinging on the student and the interrelationships among these variables.

Issues in Assessing Students from Culturally and Linguistically Diverse Groups

With the number of pupils from culturally and linguistically diverse backgrounds expected to grow to 24 million by the year 2010 (roughly equivalent to 40% of the projected school-age

Table 3.2	Assessment Outcomes for Culturally and Linguistically Diverse Students

- An accurate appraisal of a child's level and mode of functioning within the context of the child's cultural experiences

- A focus on a child's strengths and abilities as a basis for the development of new skills

- Identification of a child's specific educational needs, including both first and second language acquisition

- Literacy and basic level skills evaluation, especially for students who lack educational experiences

- Identification of emotional difficulties

- Generation of data that may be used for placement decisions and the formulation of an individual education program, if necessary

Source: M. Winzer and K. Mazurek, *Special Education in Multicultural Contexts* (Upper Saddle River, NJ: Prentice Hall, 1998), pp. 177–178.

population), teachers can expect to encounter an especially challenging and difficult task—accurately assessing children from diverse cultures for disabilities (*CEC Today*, 1997). The appropriate assessment of all students has been a long-standing concern among special educators, but it is an especially critical issue for youngsters from minority populations. Assessment is the primary vehicle through which access to services is determined and progress is evaluated, using variety of formal and informal means. We consider assessment to be a dynamic, multifaceted, multipurpose decision-making process whose primary goal is to evaluate the academic and behavioral progress of a student. Table 3.2 identifies some of the outcomes of this process for children from diverse cultural backgrounds.

Assessment of students from culturally and linguistically diverse backgrounds is both controversial and problematic (Utley & Obiakor, 2001). Because of the inherent difficulties, assessment of these learners has been characterized as "random chaos" (Figueroa, 1989). The absence of best practice guidelines for evaluating language minority and culturally diverse pupils results in a complicated and confusing assignment for teachers and other service providers.

Inappropriate assessment measures and evaluation procedures are thought to be one of the primary reasons for the disproportionate representation of culturally and linguistically diverse students in various special education programs. Concerns focus mainly on the use of standardized testing with this population, especially standardized tests of intelligence. Recall from Chapter 2 that the *Larry P.* and *Diana* lawsuits centered around claims that IQ tests were inherently unfair to students from minority groups and thus resulted in the misidentification and inaccurate labeling of these pupils, resulting in an inappropriate education.

Standardized testing has frequently been criticized for its failure to consider the cultural and experiential background of culturally and linguistically diverse students. A disregard for the life experiences of these students results in an unfair evaluation and a depressed portrayal of their ability. Remember, not all children approach a testing situation with homogenous backgrounds or a reservoir of similar life experiences. "A student who has no experience with an item presented on a test or has experienced it differently is apt to answer the question incorrectly" (*CEC Today*, 1997, p. 9). For instance, a 10-year-old from Hawaii, a state where there are no snakes, may have difficulty answering a question about rattlesnakes, whereas a youngster from New Mexico is very likely to be familiar with this creature. Likewise, an adolescent from rural Alabama who is asked about ice fishing is much less likely to answer the question correctly than his cousin from northern Wisconsin. Gollnick and Chinn (2009) believe that the use of standardized tests with children from minority groups measures only their degree of cultural assimilation, not their intelligence.

Assessment Challenges

There are several roadblocks to the goal of achieving meaningful and valid assessments of students who are culturally and linguistically diverse. Foremost is the lack of measurement tools that provide an accurate assessment of these students' abilities. Many standardized tests are simply not available in languages other than English or in appropriate dialects. Coupled with this problem is the issue of bias in the assessment process. All tests are biased to some degree; it is an unavoidable artifact of psychometric evaluation. Yet some of these unwanted influences are of greater concern than others. As a result of bias, test scores are frequently rendered suspect and may not reflect an accurate appraisal of the student's ability or skill. Linn and Miller (2005) note that bias may involve extrinsic variables, such as the child's response style or the value attached to competitive behavior in the pupil's culture. Intrinsic bias factors are difficulties with the instruments themselves, such as culturally bound test items (recall our rattlesnake example) or normative sampling issues. Bias can also come from several other sources, some of which are external to the child and others internal, such as issues of test validity and reliability when tests are translated, a lack of test-taking skills such as performing under time constraints, motivation, and appropriate response selection strategies, in addition to the obvious concern of linguistic bias when the student's primary language is not English. Individually and collectively, these sources of bias often result in incorrect assumptions about a student's abilities and may lead, in turn, to an inappropriate educational placement.

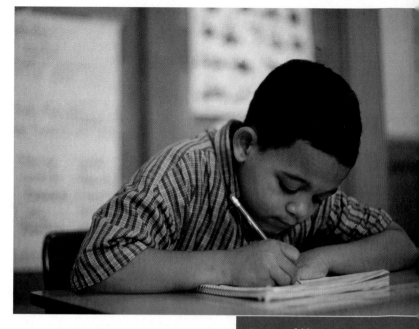

Because of bias, test scores may be suspect and may not reflect an accurate appraisal of a child's disability.

Assessment Safeguards

Professionals are fully aware of the importance of obtaining an accurate profile of an individual's strengths and weaknesses. To accomplish this goal and to minimize potential for abuses in the assessment process, PL 94-142 and its subsequent amendments contain several procedural safeguards. Realizing that nonbiased evaluations are crucial to special education, the framers of IDEA mandated **nondiscriminatory testing.** School districts are required to adopt

> procedures to assure that testing and evaluation materials and procedures utilized for the evaluation and placement of children with disabilities will be selected and administered so as not to be racially or culturally discriminatory. Such materials or procedures shall be provided and administered in the child's native language or mode of communication, unless it is clearly not feasible to do so, and no single procedure shall be the sole criterion for determining an appropriate educational program for a child. (20 U.S.C. Section 1412 [5] [C])

In addition, students are to be assessed by trained personnel who are part of a multi-disciplinary team that is responsible for the evaluation. Written communications with the pupil's parents are to be provided in the parents' native language.

Assessment Innovations

Professionals have long recognized that bias is a very real threat to the assessment process, especially for persons from culturally and linguistically diverse groups. Concern about this problem has resulted in efforts at minimizing test bias. Although a completely nonbiased or culture-fair assessment is unlikely, initial attempts at reducing bias focused on the instruments themselves. Many tests were revised in an effort to reduce the number of culturally specific test items (content bias) and the reliance on culturally specific language. Tests were also renormed, or restandardized, to reflect the growing diversity of American schoolchildren. Even the testing environment and the race of the examiner and his or her interactions with the student have come under scrutiny.

The primary purpose of these modifications has been to obtain a more accurate picture of a student's abilities, especially for pupils from culturally and linguistically diverse populations. The search for solutions to the problem of test bias has resulted in the development of pluralistic assessment techniques that are meant to be sensitive to the cultural and linguistic characteristics of children from minority groups. One example of this effort is the Kaufman Assessment Battery for Children (K-ABC) II designed by Kaufman and Kaufman (2004).

The K-ABC is used to assess children between 3 and 18 years of age. This instrument was normed on groups of white, Hispanic, African American, Native American, and Asian American children in addition to a population of individuals with disabilities. The K-ABC minimizes a student's verbal skills and abilities, thus enhancing its usefulness with children with limited English proficiency. A Spanish version is also available.

Concern about test bias has also resulted in an expanded understanding of the concept of intelligence. IQ tests have traditionally looked at intelligence in a somewhat narrow and restricted fashion, limiting the performance of many students. For instance, success in the classroom often depends on linguistic intelligence, an area in which many students from culturally and linguistically diverse backgrounds are deficient. Gardner (1983, 1993), however, argues for the concept of **multiple intelligences.** According to his theory, problem solving involves eight different, though somewhat related and interactive, intelligences:

- verbal/linguistic
- musical/rhythmic
- bodily/kinesthetic
- interpersonal
- logical/mathematical
- visual/spatial
- intrapersonal
- naturalist

His ideas have gained widespread acceptance among practitioners but, unfortunately, have received little attention from publishers of standardized tests (de Valenzuela & Baca, 2004). We believe that Gardner's theory has considerable merit. As educators, we need to stop thinking about how smart a student is and start asking, "*How* is the child smart?"

Contemporary Assessment Strategies

Many school districts are searching for better ways of assessing the growing population of students who are culturally and linguistically diverse. One particularly promising practice is the movement toward more authentic, performance-based assessment strategies such as **portfolio assessment** (Friend & Bursuck, 2006). This innovation could possibly help in resolving the problem of the over- and underrepresentation of language and ethnic minorities in some special education programs. This alternative assessment model is a relatively new idea for educators, although architects and graphic artists have been demonstrating their skills and competencies via work products for years.

Portfolio assessment is uniquely intriguing because it emphasizes the instructional environment and focuses on student performance and the outcomes of learning (McLoughlin & Lewis, 2005). Unlike infrequent or one-time standardized testing, performance-based assessment relies on the pupil's learning experiences and evaluates meaningful, real-world tasks using multiple performance indicators such as writing samples, speeches, artwork, videotapes, and work samples gathered over time and collected in a portfolio. Authentic assessments are relevant and culturally responsive assessments.

Portfolios are able to document, in a tangible way, a student's developmental progress. They can pinpoint areas of strength and weakness, thus facilitating instructional intervention. It is our opinion that portfolio assessment has great potential for meeting the needs of students who are culturally and linguistically diverse, especially those with disabilities. Information gleaned from portfolios typically results in more numerous, more specific, and more detailed recommendations and judgments about a child than does information derived from traditional, standardized testing (Linn & Miller, 2005).

Portfolio assessment, of course, is not the complete solution to eliminating bias in the assessment of culturally and linguistically diverse children. Several questions and concerns about this performance-based measure remain unanswered. Does portfolio assessment result in a fairer and more accurate portrayal of students from minority groups? Do portfolio data generate decisions about these students that differ from those formulated around the results of traditional testing? What is the basis for our standards or benchmarks? Do teachers use individual standards, or are comparisons based on districtwide, statewide, or even national performance indicators? The answers to these and other questions await further research evidence.

We believe that portfolio assessment should be an integral component of the assessment process. It represents an exciting alternative to assessing learning and the funds of student knowledge.

Assessment Recommendations

Accurately assessing students from culturally and linguistically diverse backgrounds presents many challenges for professionals. Issues of language, test bias, and other such matters are of real concern because they affect assessment results, which in turn affect educational decision making. Completely fair and nonbiased assessments may not be possible, but professionals can at least minimize those variables that may influence performance outcomes. The recommendations (*CEC Today*, 1997; Ortiz & Yates, 1988) in the accompanying Suggestions for the Classroom represent attempts at achieving authentic data and ensuring fairer, more accurate appraisals of culturally and linguistically diverse pupils and those with limited English proficiency.

Educational Programming for Students with Exceptionalities Who Are Culturally and Linguistically Diverse

Providing specific instructional strategies and tactics for students with disabilities who are culturally and linguistically diverse (and even pupils who are nondisabled) is an arduous, if not

Suggestions for the Classroom

Recommendations for Assessing Culturally and Linguistically Diverse Pupils

☑ Assessment of an individual's language competency in both English and his or her native language should be completed before administering other tests.

☑ In order to be eligible for a special education, a student must exhibit a disability when evaluated in his or her native language.

☑ Schools should incorporate ecological assessments that include not only multiple evaluation tools familiar to the examiner but also information gathered from the child's teachers, parents, and the student.

☑ Evaluators should use evaluation techniques that are as unbiased as possible. For example, a bilingual professional, not an interpreter, should administer the test.

☑ If a bilingual professional is unavailable, an interpreter may be used if he or she is first trained in assessment principles and terminology.

☑ Parents and other stakeholders should be involved when developing alternative assessments.

impossible, task. We can, however, offer some general suggestions for enhancing instructional effectiveness. Earlier we noted that effective teachers are sensitive to the cultural heritage of each student and attempt to provide educational experiences that are culturally relevant and appropriate. This is critically important. Our instructional practices must be culturally affirming, sensitive, and responsive. The pupil's cultural background should be seen as an instructional resource (Garcia & Ortiz, 2006). A meaningful educational program must incorporate the individual's language and culture. The degree to which this integration occurs is a valid gauge of academic success.

A pupil's life experiences can be the building blocks or foundation for developing a curriculum that is authentic and culturally relevant. Programs and services for children who are culturally and linguistically diverse and exceptional should be crafted around the principles and purposes of multicultural education in an effort to create a supportive climate for learning (Gollnick & Chinn, 2009). Additionally, Hoover and Collier (2004) suggest that the instructional strategies identified in the IEP "should exhibit culturally appropriate cues and reinforcements as well as culturally appropriate motivation and relevance" (p. 285). While attention to instructional strategies is crucial, effective programs for culturally and linguistically diverse students with exceptionalities must also consider the content (needed academic skills and knowledge), the instructional environment, student behaviors, and how these elements reciprocally interact and are influenced by the pupil's linguistic and cultural heritage (Hoover & Patton, 2005). Meaningful IEPs for pupils with disabilities who also exhibit cultural and/or linguistic diversity should reflect goals and instructional strategies that are appropriate to the student's disability while also reflecting his or her language status.

Attainment of IEP goals depends, in part, on establishing a supportive learning environment. One way of enhancing the context in which teaching and learning occur is through the careful selection and evaluation of instructional materials. Materials that reflect the sociocultural, linguistic, and experiential backgrounds of the students increase the likelihood that

Suggestions for the Classroom

Guidelines for Selecting and Evaluating Instructional Materials

☑ Are the perspectives and contributions of people from diverse cultural and linguistic groups—both men and women, as well as people with disabilities—included in the curriculum?

☑ Are there activities in the curriculum that will assist students in analyzing the various forms of the mass media for ethnocentrism, sexism, "handicapism," and stereotyping?

☑ Are men and women, diverse cultural/racial groups, and people with varying abilities shown in both active and passive roles?

☑ Are men and women, diverse cultural/racial groups, and people with disabilities shown in positions of power (i.e., the materials do not rely on the mainstream culture's character to achieve goals)?

☑ Do the materials identify strengths possessed by so-called "underachieving" diverse populations? Do they diminish the attention given to deficits, to reinforce positive behaviors that are desired and valued?

☑ Are members of diverse racial/cultural groups, men and women, and people with disabilities shown engaged in a broad range of social and professional activities?

☑ Are members of a particular culture or group depicted as having a range of physical features (e.g., hair color, hair texture, variations in facial characteristics and body build)?

☑ Do the materials represent historical events from the perspectives of the various groups involved or solely from the male, middle-class, and/or Western European perspective?

☑ Are the materials free of ethnocentric or sexist language patterns that may make implications about persons or groups based solely on their culture, race, gender, or disability?

☑ Will students from different ethnic and cultural backgrounds find the materials personally meaningful to their life experiences?

☑ Are a wide variety of culturally different examples, situations, scenarios, and anecdotes used throughout the curriculum design to illustrate major intellectual concepts and principles?

☑ Are culturally diverse content, examples, and experiences comparable in kind, significance, magnitude, and function to those selected from mainstream culture?

SOURCE: S. Garcia and D. Malkin, "Toward Defining Programs and Services for Culturally and Linguistically Diverse Learners in Special Education," *Teaching Exceptional Children, 26*(1), 1993, p. 55.

children will respond to them in a positive manner (Gollnick & Chinn, 2009). The accompanying Suggestions for the Classroom feature presents several guidelines that educators should consider when evaluating materials for their classroom.

Effectively instructing students with exceptionalities who are also culturally and linguistically diverse requires that teachers provide experiences that are culturally appropriate and pertinent. Instructional success with children from diverse populations depends largely on the teacher's ability to construct meaningful pedagogical bridges that cross over different cultural systems (Garcia & Ortiz, 2006). "When instruction and learning are compatible with a child's culture and when minority students' language and culture are incorporated into the school program, more effective learning takes place" (Winzer & Mazurek, 1998, p. vii).

Chapter in Review

Cultural Diversity: The Changing Face of a Nation

- Although the population of culturally and linguistically diverse students continues to grow, the diversity of the teaching workforce has failed to keep pace. About 80 percent of U.S. teachers are white, and it is projected that the teaching profession will become increasingly homogeneous over the next few years.

- The task of assimilating or "Americanizing" the children of immigrants was metaphorically described as a **melting pot,** whereby the various languages, beliefs, and customs of immigrants were melted away and replaced with a common American culture.

- In the latter part of the twentieth century, interest in **cultural pluralism** and multicultural education was sparked. U.S. society is now characterized metaphorically as a floral bouquet or patchwork quilt; cultural and ethnic differences are valued and respected.

Multicultural Education, Bilingual Education, and Student Diversity

- **Multicultural education** addresses issues of race, language, social class, and culture as well as disability and gender.

- **Bilingual education** is an educational strategy whereby students whose first language is not English are instructed primarily through their native language while developing competency and proficiency in English.

- **Limited English proficient** is a term used to describe individuals with a reduced fluency in reading, writing, or speaking English.

- **Bilingual special education** services embrace the use of the pupil's primary language and culture coupled with an individually tailored program of special instruction.

Disproportional Representation of Minority Students in Special Education Programs

- Historically, greater numbers of children from minority groups have been placed in special education classrooms than would be anticipated based on their proportion of the school population. This situation is commonly referred to as **overrepresentation. Underrepresentation** in certain programs, or fewer students than one would anticipate based on their numbers in the school population, is also a problem.

- The overrepresentation of children of color is perhaps best understood as a relationship between socioeconomic status and disability rather than between minority group membership and disability.

- Test bias, teacher expectations and bias, and incongruity in instructional methodology and cognitive styles may also account for this phenomenon.

Issues in Assessing Students from Culturally and Linguistically Diverse Groups

- Some of the barriers to achieving meaningful and valid assessments of students from culturally and linguistically diverse backgrounds are the lack of appropriate measurement tools and bias in the assessment process.

- Federal law requires that professionals use **nondiscriminatory testing** practices when evaluating pupils for possible special education placement.

- Some professionals have expanded their understanding of the notion of intelligence and argue for the concept of **multiple intelligences.**

- Another attempt at meaningful assessment of students from culturally and linguistically diverse backgrounds is a movement toward authentic, performance-based assessment techniques such as **portfolio assessment.**

Educational Programming for Students with Exceptionalities Who Are Culturally and Linguistically Diverse

- The child's cultural and linguistic heritage must be reflected in his or her IEP if instructional strategies are to be effective. The instructional materials should also mirror the sociocultural, linguistic, and experiential backgrounds of the students.

Study Questions

1. What do the terms *culture* and *cultural diversity* mean to you?

2. At one time, the United States was described as a melting pot. Why? Metaphorically speaking, American society is now characterized as a floral bouquet or patchwork quilt. What factors contributed to this change in thinking?

3. Define the following terms: cultural pluralism, multicultural education, and bilingual education.

4. Why is bilingual education a controversial topic?

5. Compare and contrast the various instructional models used with students who are bilingual.

6. Explain why pupils from minority groups experience disproportional representation in some special education programs.

7. What are the consequences of disproportional representation?

8. Why is the assessment of culturally and linguistically diverse students perceived to be problematic? How might these difficulties be corrected?

9. Define portfolio assessment. Identify the advantages of this strategy for evaluating the performance of children who are culturally and linguistically diverse.

Key Terms

melting pot	bilingual education	bilingual special education	nondiscriminatory testing
cultural pluralism	ethnocentrism	overrepresentation	multiple intelligences
culture	macroculture	underrepresentation	portfolio assessment
multiculturalism	microcultures	field dependent/sensitive	
multicultural education	limited English proficient (LEP)	field independent	

Learning Activities

1. Talk to a school psychologist, educational diagnostician, or other assessment specialist about strategies and procedures used when evaluating students from a culturally or linguistically diverse background. What types of modifications, if any, do they use? Do they have any concerns about the validity of the assessment process? What is their opinion about alternative assessments such as portfolios?

2. Visit several different schools in your area. Interview administrators or teachers about services available for pupils from culturally and linguistically diverse groups. Is there a problem of over- and underrepresentation in special education classes? What types of modifications are available to meet the needs of these pupils? How are parents and other family members involved in the school? Is multicultural education reflected in the school environment?

3. Attend various functions sponsored by ethnic groups in your community. Activities may include musical programs, art exhibitions, festivals, religious celebrations, school functions, and other ceremonies. How did you feel about participating in these activities? What did you learn as a result of your involvement? Were your personal viewpoints and stereotypes challenged as a result of this experience?

Reflecting on Standards

The following exercises are designed to help you learn to apply the Council for Exceptional Children (CEC) standards to your teaching practice. Each of the reflection exercises below correlates with a knowledge or skill within the CEC standards. For the full text of each of the related CEC standards, please refer to the standards integration grid located in Appendix B.

1. Focus on Learning Environments and Social Interactions (*CEC Content Standard #5 CC5S1*)

Reflect on your own culture and how you interact with people of other cultures. In what ways would you share your cultural background with your students? What strategies would you use to help your students appreciate their own cultural background and value the cultural diversity of others?

2. Focus on Professional and Ethical Practice (*CEC Content Standard #9 CC9K1*)

Reflect on what personal cultural biases you have. How might these biases affect your teaching? If possible, find an assessment to help you understand what hidden cultural biases you might have. Talk to colleagues, family, and friends to try and understand what biases you have that might hinder your teaching.

 ## Technology Resources

Visit the Web-based SAGE Study Site at **http://www.sagepub.com/gargiulo3estudy** for these additional learning tools:

- Chapter quizzes
- Key term flashcards
- Media links

- Full-text SAGE journal articles
- Internet activities
- Additional Web resources

CHAPTER 4

Parents, Families, and Exceptionality

T he family is our most fundamental social institution, the cornerstone of our society. It is also the primary arena in which an individual, whether disabled or not, is socialized, educated, and exposed to the beliefs and values of his or her culture. This crucial responsibility is generally assumed by the youngster's parents, who serve as principal caregivers and the child's first teachers. In this chapter, when we refer to a parent, we mean any adult who fulfills these essential caregiving duties and responsibilities for a particular child.

Being a parent of a child with a disability is not a role most parents willingly choose for themselves. Generally speaking, few individuals ever ask to be a parent of a person with special needs, nor are most parents ever fully prepared for this tremendous responsibility. Parenting a child with a disability can be a difficult, demanding, and confusing job; yet we believe it is a role that can also be filled with joy, triumphs, and satisfaction.

Although exceptionality can certainly change the ecology of the family and the interactions that occur within it, the role of the family, and of the parents in particular, remains essentially the same. Stated another way, although each family is unique, in the majority of instances professionals are primarily working with just another family—not a family that is dysfunctional. We believe it is important for teachers and other service providers to focus on the strengths and the resources of the family and not concentrate solely on the challenges and stresses that are sometimes experienced by families with a child who has a disability.

The purpose of this chapter is to more fully explore the issue of parent–professional partnerships and to examine the interactive relationship of exceptionality and its impact on the family. We have adopted a family systems approach to guide us on our journey. We will also explore the topic of cultural and linguistic diversity as it pertains to families and exceptionality. We conclude with suggestions for facilitating parent–professional partnerships.

Parent–Professional Relationships: Changing Roles

Many teachers believe that parental involvement is crucial to the success of the educational experience, especially for children with disabilities. Parents are a valuable resource

Role and Function of Parents	Approximate Era*
Parents as the cause of the child's disability (eugenics movement)	1880 to 1950s
Parents as founders of parent organizations and associations	1930s to 1950s
Parents as developers of educational and service programs	1950s to 1960s
Parents as recipients of professionals' decisions	1950s to 1970s
Parents as teachers of their children	Late 1960s to mid/late 1980s
Parents as political advocates	1970s to the present
Parents as educational decision makers	Mid-1970s to the present
Families as collaborators	Mid-1980s to the present

Figure 4.1

A Timeline of the Changing Roles of Parents of Children with Disabilities

*Eras do not represent discrete time periods; roles frequently overlap.

Source: Adapted from A. Turnbull, R. Turnbull, E. Erwin, and L. Soodak, *Families, Professionals, and Exceptionality,* 5th ed. (Upper Saddle River, NJ: Pearson Education, 2006), pp.102–110.

for professionals; in comparison to teachers and other service providers, parents typically have a greater investment in their children, not only of time but also emotion. Generally, no one else will know the child as well as the parents do; their experiences predate and exceed those of the professional. Yet only recently have professionals realized the value of parents and sought to establish collaborative relationships with them.

The history of parent–professional relationships is generally one of gloomy and counterproductive activities on the part of professionals (Gallagher, Beckman, & Cross, 1983). Today, parents are seen as collaborators and equal partners with professionals, but this was not always the case. The contemporary role of parents and families in alliance with professionals has been an evolving one. Turnbull, Turnbull, Erwin, and Soodak (2006) recently outlined the major roles that parents and families have played over time (see Figure 4.1). They characterize these shifting roles and responsibilities as a pendulum swinging back and forth across several dimensions:

- From viewing parents as part of the child's problem to viewing them as collaborators in addressing the challenges of exceptionality
- From insisting on passive roles for parents to expecting active and collaborating roles for families
- From viewing families as a mother–child dyad to recognizing the preferences and needs of all members of a family
- From responding to family needs in a general way to individualizing for the family as a whole and for each member of the family. (p. 14)

Not only have the roles of parents and families shifted, but relationships between parents and professionals have also changed over the years. We believe it is possible to describe three distinct periods in the history of parent–professional relationships:

1. Antagonistic and adversarial
2. Working partnerships
3. Parent empowerment and family-centered relationships

Antagonistic and Adversarial Relationships

The **eugenics movement** represents an early and dismal period in the history of parent–professional relationships. This campaign sought to improve the quality of humankind through selective breeding. It resulted in laws forbidding marriage between individuals with mental retardation and led to calls for their sterilization. The goal of the eugenicists was to reduce the number of "unfit" parents and thus, according to their faulty logic, the number of inferior offspring (Turnbull et al., 2006).

Although the eugenics movement gradually lost influence by the middle of the twentieth century, it provided the foundation for later thinking that parents were the cause of their child's disability. Perhaps nowhere else was this belief more prominent than in the work of Bettelheim (1950, 1967), who saw parents, especially mothers, as the primary reason that their son or daughter was autistic. Bettelheim coined the term *refrigerator moms*, viewing these mothers as cold, detached, uncaring, and rigid. He even went so far as to advocate that these youngsters be taken away from their natural parents and institutionalized so that they could receive loving and competent care.

This time period (mid-1940s to early 1970s) was characterized by professional dominance (Freidson, 1970). Professionals frequently adopted an attitude of superiority and were clearly seen as being in control. They were the exclusive source of knowledge and expertise. Doctors, teachers, psychologists, and other service providers automatically assumed that the parents would defer to their judgment and passively submit to their recommendations, advice, and suggestions. It is easy to see how this climate laid the groundwork for less than positive relationships. As a result of their treatment by professionals, parents often became angry, confused, frustrated, and distrustful. This "mishandling" by professionals (Roos, 1978) led many parents to become aggressive activists and advocates for change.

In all fairness, however, part of the reason for less than positive relationships may reside with the parents. In some situations, Gargiulo (1985) writes,

> part of the blame for less than positive interaction falls squarely on the shoulders of the parents. In some instances, parents have condemned the professional for not recognizing the disability sooner and occasionally have even accused the professional of causing the handicap [disability]. Some parents have inhibited the growth of the relationship with professionals by withdrawing. They have judged professionals to be insensitive, offensive, and incapable of understanding their situation because professionals themselves are rarely parents of an exceptional person. (p. 6)

Consequently, the actions and attitudes of both professionals and parents resulted in establishing barriers and an unfavorable atmosphere for working together.

Building Working Relationships

For the better part of the twentieth century, the families of children with disabilities had to contend with schools, and on occasion with professionals, that were at best apathetic to their needs and the needs of their children (Berry & Hardman, 1998). This situation dramatically improved with the enactment of PL 94-142 in 1975. IDEA, as it is presently known, requires that parents participate fully in education decisions affecting their son or daughter. Today, parents no longer speak of privileges; instead, they talk of rights.

IDEA ushered in a new era of parent–professional relationships. The status of parents has changed from that of passive recipients of services and advice to that of active participants—educational decision makers. These new roles and responsibilities for parents and families include active involvement in the identification and assessment process, program planning, and evaluation, as well as input on placement decisions. These roles are coupled with extensive due process and procedural safeguards. It is easy to see how PL 94-142 has come to be designated the "Parents' Law" (Gargiulo & Kilgo, 2005).

Table 4.1 illustrates how the attitudes and services of professionals have evolved over the past few decades. Notice the contemporary emphasis on families instead of just parents across each of the six areas.

Table 4.1	Changing Perspectives of Professionals toward Families with a Child with a Disability	
Issue	**Traditional Attitude**	**Contemporary Attitude**
1. "Vision"	Parents' greatest need (to which professional counseling and advice is geared) is to accept the burden of raising their child and to become realistic about his or her limitations and the fact that disability necessarily results in second-class citizenship.	Families need to be encouraged to dream about what they want for themselves and their son or daughter with a disability, and they need assistance in making those dreams come true. These dreams and future plans should lead to expectations that all members of the family are entitled to full citizenship. Vision replaces despair.
2. Support and assistance	Parents' difficulties in coping with the child are largely psychological or psychiatric in nature, and the proper interventions are psychiatric or psychological counseling.	Families can benefit from one another. One benefit that almost all families need is the emotional resiliency and information that other families have acquired about life with disabilities.
3. Socialization	Mothers need respite to alleviate the stress and burden of caring for their child.	Families need the child with disabilities to have friends and integrated recreational opportunities in order to respond to the child's needs for socialization, affection, and identity.
4. Hope for the future	Mothers need clinical information about disability.	Families need information about and inspiration from people with a disability who are successfully integrated into community life.
5. Instructional emphasis	Mothers need training related to skill development and behavior management so they can be "follow-through" teachers for their child and implement home-based lesson plans.	Families need encouragement and ways to ensure that the child has a functional education taught in natural environments. This encouragement and help should assist families to enlist the support of the natural helpers in those environments (e.g., family, friends, store clerks, bus drivers, scout leaders).
6. Social support	Many families are financially unable to meet their child's needs and should seek out-of-home placement.	Many families need new policies to provide, for example, direct subsidies and new tax credits to help meet the financial demands associated with disability in the home and family setting.

Source: Adapted from A. Gartner, D. Lipsky, and A. Turnbull, *Supporting Families with a Child with a Disability* (Baltimore: Paul H. Brookes, 1991), pp. 202–204.

The building of positive school–home partnerships requires that the family be viewed as a key partner in the education of the student with a disability. Parents are beneficial allies with professionals. Successful school experiences require the involvement of parents. Despite the importance of active and meaningful involvement, however, Turnbull et al. (2006) observe that many parents participate only passively in the educational decision-making process. These noted special educators speculate that some parents may not have the motivation to assume a more active role or may lack the requisite knowledge and skills to become active participants. In the vast number of cases, however, it is a lack of empowerment that limits or restricts their role as educational decision makers. It is this state of affairs that has led to the third stage of parent–professional interaction: parent empowerment and family-centered services. The current emphasis is now on families as collaborators with professionals.

Parent Empowerment and Family-Centered Relationships

The implementation of PL 99-457 and PL 101-476 signaled a change in the status of parent–professional relationships. With these enactments came the idea that families, not parents, should be the focal point of professionals' attention. One of the reasons for this shift was the evolving recognition that partnerships should not be limited exclusively to biological parents but can and should include other immediate and extended family members (Turnbull et al., 2006). Many professionals now operate under the assumption that the family serves as the primary decision maker in regard to setting goals and establishing priorities for the student with a disability. This change, of course, vastly extends the concept of parental involvement and significantly redefines the role of the special educator. Professionals no longer provide suggestions and services to families; rather, they work collaboratively with families, acting as coordinators and facilitators of service delivery (Blue-Banning, Summers, Frankland, Nelson, & Beegle, 2004).

The contemporary emphasis on building family–professional partnerships implies that families are full and equal partners with professionals. It also strongly suggests a collaborative relationship. Collaboration involves the sharing of information and resources as well as expertise and a commitment to jointly reaching decisions. Implicit within the concept of collaboration is an ethic of mutual respect and shared responsibility. For professionals, collaboration also means that they no longer have power *over* families but rather achieve power *with* families. Families and professionals thus find themselves linked together in a mutually supportive and empowering alliance.

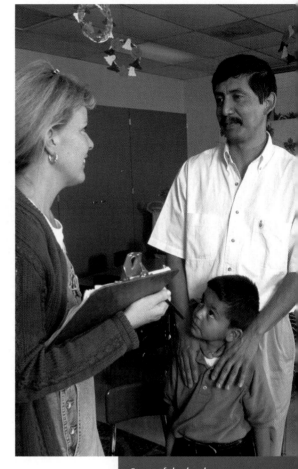

Successful school experiences require the meaningful involvement of parents.

The idea of a collaborative partnership between home and school is in concert with the theorizing of Bronfenbrenner (1977, 1979), who argued that an individual cannot be viewed in isolation but only as part of a larger social system. Professionals must have an appreciation of the social context in which the student develops and the interactions that occur among and between the various settings and individuals. Thus, we find that home, school, and community interact reciprocally and the actions of parents, siblings, grandparents, teachers, and other professionals all influence one another. How a family relates to the other social systems is crucial to the overall functioning of the family. Finally, Bronfenbrenner's ecological thinking provides a foundation for family systems theory, which views the family as a social system. In this interactive system, whatever happens to one member affects the rest. We now turn our attention to examining this contemporary approach of working with families.

A Family Systems Approach

The fundamental belief underlying a **family systems model** is that a family is an interrelated social system with unique characteristics and needs. It operates as an interactive and interdependent unit. Events and experiences that affect a particular family member

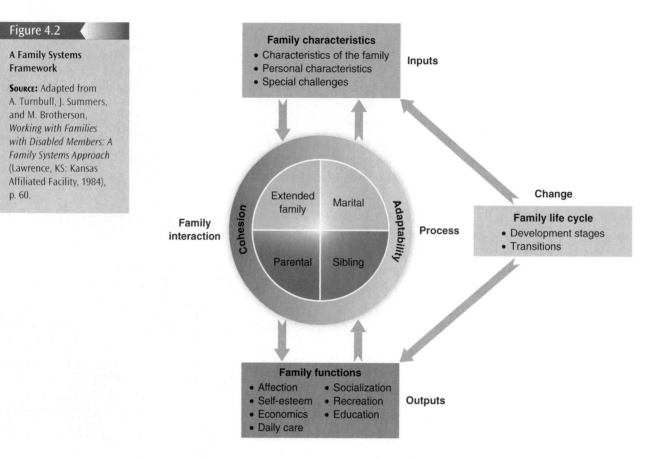

Figure 4.2

A Family Systems Framework

Source: Adapted from A. Turnbull, J. Summers, and M. Brotherson, *Working with Families with Disabled Members: A Family Systems Approach* (Lawrence, KS: Kansas Affiliated Facility, 1984), p. 60.

also affect the other members of the family. Because of this relationship, teachers and other service providers consider the entire family constellation as the appropriate focal point for professionals' attention.

Turnbull et al. (2006) have incorporated this thinking into a framework for applying family systems concepts to the study of families that have a child who is disabled. Their model (see Figure 4.2) contains four key elements, all of which are interrelated:

- Family characteristics
- Family interaction
- Family functions
- Family life cycle

Family characteristics are those features that make the family unique. "Inputs" include family size and form, cultural background, socioeconomic status, and geographic location. Additionally, each member's health status (both physical and mental), individual coping style, and the nature and severity of the disability are included as personal characteristics. A final component includes special challenges facing the family, such as poverty, substance abuse, and parents who themselves may have a disability. Collectively, these variables provide each family with its own unique identity, influence interactional patterns among the members, and determine how the family responds to the individual's exceptionality. It is easy to understand how a large family living in poverty in a rural location might differ in adaptation from an affluent suburban family with an only child who is disabled.

Family interactions comprise the relationships and interactions among and between the various family subsystems. How a particular family interacts depends in part on their degree of cohesion and adaptability. These two factors affect the quality of interactions and can only be interpreted in light of the family's cultural heritage.

Simply defined, **cohesion** refers to the degree of freedom and independence experienced by each member of the family. Cohesion occurs along a continuum, with some families being overly cohesive. In this situation, the development of an individual's autonomy and independence may be impeded. Such families are viewed as being overly protective. Other families may have a low degree of cohesiveness. In this situa-

A family can be viewed as an interrelated social system, each with its own unique characteristics.

tion, families are depicted as being underinvolved and the person with the disability fails to receive needed support. Well-functioning families aim to achieve a balance in cohesiveness.

Adaptability can be defined as the family's ability to change in response to a crisis or stressful event (Olson, 1988). Like cohesiveness, adaptability occurs along a continuum and is influenced by the family's cultural background. When a stressful event occurs, rigid families respond according to prescribed roles and responsibilities. They are unable to adapt to the demands of the new situation. This behavior places the family at risk for becoming isolated and dysfunctional (Seligman & Darling, 2007). For example, the introduction into a family of a youngster with multiple disabilities would very likely require some form of accommodation. Yet in a rigid family, with a clear hierarchy of power, the child care responsibilities would almost always fall on the mother. Such duties, according to the father's perception, are exclusively "woman's work"; therefore, he has no obligation to assist. On the other hand, it is impossible to predict how a chaotic family would respond to this situation. Chaotic families are characterized by constant change and instability. There is often no family leader, and the few existing rules are often altered, creating significant confusion (Turnbull et al., 2006). The key for most families is to maintain a balance between the extremes of high and low adaptability.

Family functions are the seven interrelated activities listed in Figure 4.2, all of which are necessary to fulfill the individual and collective needs of the family:

- **Affection**—emotional commitments and display of affection
- **Self-esteem**—personal identity and self-worth, recognition of positive contributions
- **Economics**—production and utilization of family income
- **Daily care**—day-to-day survival needs (food, shelter, health care)
- **Socialization**—developing social skills, establishing interpersonal relationships
- **Recreation**—leisure time activities for both family and individuals
- **Education**—involvement in educational activities, career choices

Turnbull et al. (2006) identify these nonprioritized functions as "outputs" and remind us that it is impossible to discuss family functions without regard to the other three main dimensions of their framework. These tasks and activities are common to all families, but they are likely to be affected by the presence of a member with a disability (Berry & Hardman, 1998). The effect may be positive, negative, or neutral.

Individual families will establish their own priorities for each of these functions. In one family, meeting the daily needs of food and shelter is of utmost importance; another family may emphasize recreation and leisure. Berry and Hardman (1998) note that some families may require assistance in several areas, others in only a few. Also, the amount of help from professionals will vary depending on specific circumstances.

Family life cycle is an important component of the Turnbull et al. (2006) framework. It refers to the developmental changes that occur in most families over time. These changes, though fairly predictable, may alter the structure of the family and in turn affect relationships, functions, and interactions.

The movement from one stage to another and the accompanying adjustment period are characterized as **transitions.** Transitions can be particularly stressful events for families, but especially for families with a member who is disabled. For many families, it is a time of challenge and uncertainty as to what the next stage holds for the family and the individual. For instance, when a toddler transitions from an early intervention program to Head Start or when a young adult leaves high school and secures employment, these events can be times of heightened anxiety and significant stress. Not all families successfully negotiate life cycle changes.

Life cycle functions, according to Seligman and Darling (2007), are highly age related. As a family moves through its life cycle, its priorities shift as the family encounters new situations. Turnbull et al. (2006) have identified four major life cycle stages and the accompanying issues that the parents and siblings of a child with a disability may encounter along the family's journey. Table 4.2 describes some of the developmental issues that an individual with an exceptionality presents to his or her family. We caution you, however, that how any particular family responds to a member with a disability is unique.

The Effects of a Child's Disability on Parents and the Family

It is important for teachers and other professionals to realize that the identification of an individual as disabled affects the entire family constellation and produces a wide range of reactions, responses, and feelings. In some cases, the awareness comes shortly after the birth of the baby; in others, it may occur during the preschool years as a result of illness or accident; many times, parents are told that their son or daughter has a disability upon entering school.

The effect on the family of a child with a disability mainly involves perceptions and feelings that are highly subjective and personalized for each family member. How a mother responds will most likely differ from the response of her father-in-law, and an older sibling will very likely have a different point of view. Likewise, exceptionality is frequently interpreted differently by different families, even if the type of disability (such as blindness or mental retardation) is the same. In some families, having a child with a disability is perceived as a tragedy; in others, it may be viewed as a crisis but one that can be managed; in still others, it is merely one more factor to be considered in a daily struggle to survive.

Table 4.2	Potential Family Life Cycle Issues	
Stage	**Parental Issues**	**Sibling Issues**
Early Childhood (Birth–Age 5)	• Obtaining an accurate diagnosis • Informing siblings and relatives • Locating services • Seeking to find meaning in the exceptionality • Clarifying a personal ideology to guide decisions • Addressing issues of stigma • Identifying positive contributions of exceptionality • Setting great expectations	• Less parental time and energy for sibling needs • Feelings of jealousy over less attention • Fears associated with misunderstandings of exceptionality
School Age (Ages 5–12)	• Establishing routines to carry out family functions • Adjusting emotionally to educational implications • Clarifying issues of mainstreaming [inclusion] vs. special class placement • Participating in IEP conferences • Locating community resources • Arranging for extracurricular activities	• Division of responsibility for any physical care needs • Oldest female sibling may be at risk • Limited family resources for recreation and leisure • Informing friends and teachers • Possible concern about younger sibling surpassing older • Issues of "mainstreaming" into same school • Need for basic information on exceptionality
Adolescence (Ages 12–21)	• Adjusting emotionally to possible chronicity of exceptionality • Identifying issues of emerging sexuality • Addressing possible peer isolation and rejection • Planning for career/vocational development • Arranging for leisure time activities • Dealing with physical and emotional changes of puberty • Planning for postsecondary education	• Overidentification with sibling • Greater understanding of differences in people • Influence of exceptionality on career choice • Dealing with possible stigma and embarrassment • Participation in sibling training programs • Opportunity for sibling support groups
Adulthood (Ages 21+)	• Planning for possible need for guardianship • Addressing the need for appropriate adult implications of dependency • Addressing the need for socialization opportunities outside the family for individuals with exceptionality • Initiating career choice or vocational program	• Possible issues of responsibility for financial support • Addressing concerns regarding genetic implications • Introducing new in-laws to exceptionality • Need for information on career/living options • Clarifying role of sibling advocacy • Possible issues of guardianship

Source: Adapted from A. Turnbull and H. Turnbull, *Families, Professionals, and Exceptionality: A Special Partnership*, 2nd ed. (Columbus, OH: Merrill, 1990), pp. 134–135.

Stages of Parental Reaction to Disability

A number of writers in the field have adopted a **stage theory** approach to describing parental reactions to the diagnosis of a disability (Bauer & Shea, 2003; Cook, Klein, & Tessier, 2008; Lambie, 2000). This popular interpretation suggests that many parents pass through a series of reactive stages to the news of their child's disability. Although no two families will respond identically, researchers have identified common stages that many families exhibit as they adjust to a member with a disability (Cook et al.).

Of course, it is impossible to predict how families, and parents in particular, will respond to a disability. Most stage theory models are constructed around the premise that families

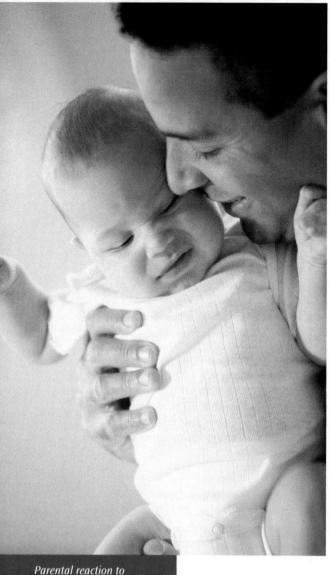

Parental reaction to the news of a disability typically results in a wide range of emotions.

experience a grief or mourning cycle much like the developmental stages of reaction to the death of a loved one (Kubler-Ross, 1969). Some models are more elaborate than others, but most identify three distinct stages or phases of parental reaction. The classic work of Gargiulo (1985) provides a good example. Before examining this model, we should point out that the stage theory approach has been criticized as being unduly negative, overly rigid, and lacking in empirical evidence (Blacher, 1984). However, the writings of many parents of children with disabilities eloquently and poignantly attest to the validity of this approach.

According to Gargiulo's (1985) model (see Figure 4.3), parental reaction to a disability includes three stages and encompasses a wide variety of feelings and reactions. His model is a generic one because parents of children with different disabilities frequently experience common feelings and react in similar fashion. Reactions differ more in degree than in kind. Gargiulo stresses the uniqueness and variability of the response pattern. He also emphasizes flexibility because of each family's unique situation and that feelings and emotions are likely to recur over the family life cycle. The order of parental response is not predictable, nor does movement completely depend on successful resolution of an earlier feeling. Gargiulo explains,

> It should be noted that not all parents follow a sequential pattern of reaction according to a predetermined timetable. The stages should be viewed as fluid, with parents passing forward and backward as their individual adjustment process allows. Some individuals may never progress beyond hurt and anger; others may not experience denial; still others accept and adjust rather quickly to their child's abilities and disabilities. Also both parents do not necessarily go through these stages together. Each parent will react in his or her own unique way. (p. 21)

Figure 4.3 suggests the diverse emotional pattern that some parents experience. The initial response is often one of *shock* and disbelief; parents are poorly prepared, in most

Figure 4.3

A Stage Model of Parental Reaction to Disability

Source: R. Gargiulo, *Working with Parents of Exceptional Children: A Guide for Professionals* (Boston: Houghton Mifflin, 1985), pp. 22–30.

Primary phase
Shock
Denial
Grief and depression

Secondary phase
Ambivalence
Guilt
Anger
Shame and embarrassment

Tertiary phase
Bargaining
Adaptation and reorganization
Acceptance and adjustment

Time

instances, for the news of their child's disability. Parents will sometimes evidence *denial* as a form of escape from the reality of the disability. The primary phase is also characterized by *grief,* as parents mourn the loss of their "ideal child" or "perfect baby." Depression and withdrawal are common consequences of the grieving process.

These initial reactions are followed by a secondary phase distinguished by what Blacher (1984) calls a period of emotional disorganization. It would not be uncommon during this stage for parents to vacillate between periods of total dedication and self-sacrifice (a martyr's posture) and rejection (in terms of affection and/or physical needs). Gargiulo (1985) identifies these behaviors as indicating *ambivalence.* One of the most common and difficult feelings for parents to deal with is *guilt*—that somehow they may have contributed to their son or daughter's disability. Guilt generally follows an "if only" thought pattern: "If only I didn't have that drink while I was pregnant," "If only we had gone to the hospital sooner," "If only I kept the medicine cabinet locked." During this stage, *overcompensation* is common, as parents attempt to "make it up" to the child. This represents an effort to appease the parent's feelings of guilt. Equally common is a display of *anger* and hostility, frequently followed by the question "Why me?" for which no satisfactory answer exists. Finally, *shame and embarrassment* are also typical consequences that parents may experience as a result of having a child who is disabled. Some parents are fearful of how family, friends, and society in general will react to their son or daughter, and social withdrawal is not unusual. A parent's self-esteem may also be threatened. One parent writes:

I felt I was a nobody. Any credits of self-worth that I could give myself from any of my personal endeavors meant nothing. Graduating from college and a first-rate medical school, surviving an internship, practicing medicine and having two beautiful sons and a good marriage counted for nil. All I knew at this point was that I was the mother of an abnormal and most likely retarded child. (Ziskin, 1978, p. 75)

Bargaining commences the tertiary phase, as parents seek to "strike a deal" with God, science, or anyone they believe might be able to help their child. Rarely seen by outsiders, it represents one of the final steps in a parent's ongoing process of adjustment. A period of *adaptation and reorganization* also occurs, as parents become increasingly comfortable with their situation and gain confidence in their parenting abilities. In Gargiulo's model, as in many others, *acceptance and adjustment* are seen as the eventual goal that most parents aim for. Acceptance is characterized as a state of mind whereby a deliberate effort is made to recognize, understand, and resolve problems. Parents also discover that acceptance involves not only accepting their son or daughter but also accepting themselves and acknowledging their strengths and weaknesses. Related to acceptance is the concept of adjustment, which implies both positive and forward-moving action. Adjustment is a gradual and, in some instances, a difficult and lifelong process that demands a realignment of goals and ambitions. For many parents, it is an ongoing struggle.

Gargiulo (1985) and, more recently, Berry and Hardman (1998) believe that the preceding reactions and feelings are legitimate, automatic, understandable, and perfectly normal. Parents have a right to exhibit these emotions and to express their feelings. They are natural and necessary for adjustment. They do not represent reflections of pathology or maladjustment.

Knowledge of these stages and patterns of reaction can facilitate professionals' understanding of parental behavior and assist them in providing appropriate support when necessary. Sensitive and caring support from professionals can be very important for parents because typical sources of support, such as friends and other family members, may not be available (Berry & Hardman, 1998). Researchers believe that a family's adaptation to disability is closely linked to the level of support received from other family members as well as community resources (D'Asaro, 1998). The availability and quality of social support is crucial to a family's ability to cope with and adjust to a child with a disability (Santelli, Turnbull, Marquis, & Lerner, 1997).

Disability and the Family

A family systems approach and the theorizing of Bronfenbrenner (1977, 1979) suggest that the entire family constellation is altered and affected in various ways by the presence of a child with an exceptionality. Contemporary thinking about families of children with disabilities has evolved from a dyadic focus on mother–child interactions to one that explores family dynamics within an ecological framework. Because we consider a family to be an interdependent and interactive social system, when a situation arises such as a child's disability, this issue must be viewed and can only be fully understood within the context of the family unit. As one sibling of a child with a disability notes:

> All of the members of my family are disabled. But most people recognize only the disability of my deaf sister. They do not realize that the disability of one member affects the entire family. Parents realize this to some extent because they themselves are affected—their attitude, their priorities, their lifestyles. But sometimes they become so involved with the problems directly related to their disabled child that they lose sight of the effect upon the other children. (Hayden, 1974, p. 26)

There is no easy way to answer the question "How does a child with a disability affect his or her family?" How one family copes and adapts to a member's disability will most likely be radically different from how another family does. Much depends on individual family factors such as the parents' marital integration, religious beliefs and values, financial resources, cultural heritage, and external support system. Additionally, child characteristics such as gender and the severity of the impairment also mediate the family's adaptation. In our view, all of these variables interact and commingle to produce overall family adaptation.

Marital Relationships

Being a parent of a child with a disability may contribute to marital tension and stress in some families. The research literature on divorce in families of children with disabilities is limited, however, and the findings are frequently contradictory. In some instances, divorce and marital difficulties are common adjustment problems (Banks, 2003; Hodapp & Krasner, 1995); in other situations, marriages are strengthened (Scorgie & Sobsey, 2000; Scorgie, Wilgosh, & McDonald, 1998). Investigators have also found no difference in divorce rates between families with and without children with disabilities (Seligman & Darling, 2007; Turnbull et al., 2006). Although being a parent of a child with disabilities may result in significantly greater stress for both mothers and fathers (Olsson & Hwang, 2001), it would be false to conclude that marital deterioration is an automatic consequence. It is simply unclear why some marriages remain intact and others disintegrate. We suspect that the answer lies in the mixture of parent and child characteristics interacting with specific ecological factors.

Mothers of Children with Disabilities

In many American households, women are primarily responsible for the raising of children, although more men are currently assuming greater child-rearing responsibilities. Still, in many families, mothers are particularly vulnerable to the stresses, strains, and added difficulties engendered by a child with a disability (Trachtenberg, Batshaw, & Batshaw, 2007). In some circumstances, these problems may be immediate, such as when a baby is born with Down syndrome or multiple disabilities; in other instances, mothers may encounter added stress when a disability is recognized after a son or daughter enters school. New roles, responsibilities, and routines for mothers are not uncommon when a youngster has a disability. The dynamics of the entire family relationship may also change.

A sense of feeling overwhelmed, concern about family finances, physical—and, in some instances, mental—exhaustion, impaired relationships with other family members, and the impact on employment are just some of the issues confronting mothers when their child has a disability. Of course, the type and severity of the disability, the time of its onset, and access to support systems often mediate the situation. Having a supportive husband or partner is crucial to helping mothers successfully cope with the stresses of raising their son or daughter with a disability (Power, 2004). In some communities, support groups and **respite care** provide a valuable source of relief for mothers as well as other family members.

Fathers of Children with Disabilities

Fathers are beginning to receive more attention from professionals, who are becoming increasingly cognizant of the needs of fathers and urging their active involvement in intervention programs for children with disabilities (Flynn & Wilson, 1998; Rump, 2002; Young & Roopnarine, 1994).

When researchers investigate the effect of a child with disabilities on fathers and mothers, discrepant findings are not unusual. Lamb and Meyer (1991) and, more recently, Trachtenberg et al. (2007), found, for example, that fathers and mothers react differently to the news of their child's disability. Fathers, in general, are less emotional in their reaction, tend to focus on the long-term consequences, and seem to be more affected by the visibility of the disability. Mothers are more expressive in their responses and are worried about the day-to-day burdens of child care.

The father's attitude toward his son or daughter who is disabled is very likely to influence the attitude of other family members (Flynn & Wilson, 1998; Seligman & Darling, 2007). A disability diagnosis can also affect how a father evaluates his family life, which can subsequently influence the perceptions of the entire family. These conclusions are in line with our family systems approach to understanding the effect of a disability. (See the accompanying First Person feature.)

Siblings of Children with Disabilities

Is having a sibling with a disability a positive or negative experience? The safest answer to this intriguing question is, "It depends." The research evidence provides conflicting findings. The impact of a brother or sister with special needs seems to be mediated by a number of variables; and of course, their needs can only be considered within the context of the entire family constellation. Siblings are likely to exhibit a wide range of adaptive responses that are affected by parental attitudes and expectations, family socioeconomic status, the severity and type of impairment, family size, sibling gender and age spacing, child-rearing

First Person

Daydreams

More than once during the last twelve years since our daughter, Kristina, was born with cerebral palsy I have daydreamed wistfully about what she might have been like if only . . .

Would she run fast and jump high? Would she enjoy reading as much as her mom and I? Would she love to climb trees like her dad, or make crafts like her mom? How much different would she look, would her face change, how might she look if she could sit or stand straight? Would her voice be different? Would she like the same things she likes now: cards, telephones, swimming, speed? Would she have done well in school? Would she enjoy math or English? What kinds of friends would she have made? How would I have responded to her first boyfriend? What kind of nickname might she have been given? Could she have performed a solo in a choir or played an instrument? How would she look riding a bike or rollerblading down the hill? Would she like tennis? Would she have gotten the same thrill with horses as her grandmother?

At first, I daydreamed out of self-pity; later I felt ashamed but now I have grown to view it as an occasionally pleasant diversion. I realize now, it is only human nature to wonder and second guess about choices made and paths not taken. Once our lives have irrevocably gone in one direction, many look back and wonder what it might be like to live in another place or time, do another job, or live another life. It's harmless, it's healthy.

I guess I stopped feeling ashamed of my daydreams when I realized that I couldn't be happier than I am right now. I have a wonderful wife, three willful and happy children, and many things that others daydream about. Despite human nature, down deep I do not want anything around me to change. While I might like to try on a different job much like I might like to try on a different style of clothes, I know it wouldn't be me. In the same way, I might like to meet a different Kristina, but she wouldn't have the same infectious laugh, the same genuine feelings, or the same love of life. I wouldn't like the impostor much and I know I couldn't love her. I've been blessed with the perfect one, and I could never have imagined anything better.

SOURCE: J. Cox, "Daydreams," *Our Young Children, 1*(1), 1997, p. 17.

practices, cultural heritage, and the availability of support systems (Gargiulo & Kilgo, 2005; Seligman & Darling, 2007). We must not forget, of course, that while a child with a disability affects his or her typical brother or sister, these siblings are also influencing, in both positive and negative ways, the sibling with an exceptionality.

Over the years, several investigators (Gallagher, Powell, & Rhodes, 2006; Lobato, Faust, & Spirito, 1988; Mason, Kruse, Farabaugh, Gershberg, & Kohler, 2000) have reported adverse outcomes in sibships involving an individual who is disabled. Some of the frequently mentioned deleterious effects include depression or social withdrawal and anxiety, as well as lower self-esteem and poor peer relationships. In addition, excessive child care requirements placed on older siblings often result in feelings of anger and resentment (McHugh, 2003). Some brothers/sisters exhibit "survivor's guilt" due to the absence of illness or disability in their own lives (Russell, Russell, & Russell, 2003). Younger siblings who are typical are sometimes concerned about becoming disabled or ill themselves; they worry about "catching it" (Rolland, 1994). Finally, when siblings lack adequate information about their brother's or sister's disability, they often become confused and concerned about their own identity (Seligman & Darling, 2007).

It would be totally incorrect, however, to portray sibships with a brother or sister with disabilities as having exclusively negative outcomes. The research literature also provides a more optimistic outlook. As an example, Grossman's (1972) classic retrospective investigation of siblings of children with mental retardation notes such benefits as greater tolerance toward others, increased compassion, and higher levels of empathy and altruism as a result of growing up with a brother or sister with a disability. Siblings typically exhibit a myriad of feelings toward a brother or sister with special needs. The accompanying First Person feature (page 129) vividly captures some of these emotions. Table 4.3 gives examples of some of the reactions and feelings sustained by brothers and sisters of children with disabilities.

Siblings can sometimes benefit from support groups or workshops such as Sibshops (Meyer & Vadasy, 1994) where brothers and sisters of siblings with special needs can share feelings and obtain peer support as well as information within a recreational environment. One valuable resource for siblings is the Sibling Support Project,[1] a national organization that focuses on the concerns of brothers and sisters of individuals with special needs.

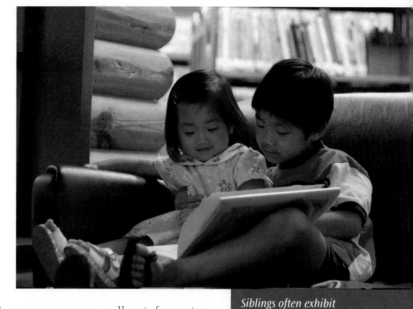

Siblings often exhibit a myriad of feelings toward a brother or sister with special needs.

Grandparents of Children with Disabilities

Professionals are becoming increasingly aware of the important role that grandparents play in contemporary family life. They are significant members of many family constellations. When a child with a disability enters the family unit, grandparents are affected just as parents and siblings are.

Just as parents exhibit a wide range of emotional responses to the news that their son or daughter has a disability, grandparents are not immune to feelings of grief, shock, depression, anger, and so forth (Trachtenberg et al., 2007). They, too, often go through stages of acceptance. Grandparents also experience a dual hurt: They are concerned and anxious not only about their grandchild but also about their own child, whom they may perceive as chronically burdened (Seligman, Goodwin, Paschal, Applegate, & Lehman, 1997).

How grandparents respond to a grandchild with a disability can be an additional stressor for the child's parents or a source of strength and support. Grandparents, in the words of Gearheart, Mullen, and Gearheart (1993), can be "the glue that holds the family constellation together" (p. 493). They are capable of greatly contributing to the overall functioning and well-being of the family. Their contributions can range from serving as alternative caregivers, to providing sources of community support, to assisting in the daily chores of shopping or running errands, but perhaps the greatest area of assistance is providing emotional support (Seligman & Darling, 2007).

As we have just seen, a person with a disability affects his or her family in many ways—some positive and others negative. It is refreshing, however, to see researchers and other professionals acknowledging the positive aspects that a child with a disability has on family life. No longer is a disability exclusively thought to be a burden for the family. "There has been a growing recognition," Glidden and Floyd (1997) write, "of the rewards and benefits involved in rearing children with disabilities" (p. 250). It is primarily a matter of perspective.

---

1. For additional information see http://www.siblingsupport.org/

Table 4.3	Emotional Responses of Children toward Siblings with a Disability
Resentment	Perhaps the most common reaction experienced by typical siblings is resentment. It is a natural by-product of being angry about having a brother or sister with a disability. Resentment may develop because the child with special needs may require a disproportionate amount of the parents' attention. This sibling may also prohibit the family from participating in certain experiences or excursions. Special treatments and/or therapy may contribute to family financial hardship. Older siblings may resent having to babysit, or having social constraints placed upon them by their younger brother or sister who is disabled.
Jealousy	Resentment can easily develop into jealousy, especially if the typical sibling perceives that he or she has lost "favor" with the parents. The brother or sister with a disability may become a rival or competitor for the parents' attention and affection. Often the typical sibling will engage in behaviors designed to secure parental attention, such as having academic or behavioral problems in school, telling lies, or exhibiting unusual mischievousness.
Hostility	From feelings of jealousy often comes hostility, which is a perfectly natural reaction. Unlike objective adults, children are subjective and consider events in terms of how they are personally affected. They may view their brother or sister with special needs, rather than the disability, as the source of all their problems. Therefore, feelings of hostility are usually aimed toward their sibling. These feelings may manifest themselves in physical aggression or verbal harassment and ridicule. In some instances, hostility is directed toward the parents through acts of disobedience or impertinence.
Guilt	Siblings without disabilities frequently evidence feelings of guilt; however, these reactions differ from the parents'. Their guilt may stem from the negative feelings they have about their brother or sister, or it may be a consequence of having mistreated their sibling. Furthermore, when viewing their sibling who has an impairment, some children experience guilt because of their own good fortune to be thought of as typical.
Grief	Siblings frequently grieve for their brother or sister who is disabled. Their grief is often a reflection of their parents' sorrow. They grieve not for what they have lost, but for what will possibly be denied to their sibling.
Fear	Typical siblings may also experience fear. They may be fearful of acquiring a disability or of their own future children being disabled. A further worry is that someday they may have to assume total responsibility for the care of their sibling.
Shame and embarrassment	Shame and embarrassment are common emotional responses of typical siblings. A child may be ashamed of his brother or sister who is mentally retarded, embarrassed to have friends visit, or embarrassed to be seen in public with his or her sibling.
Rejection	In some families, siblings who are typical may reject their brother or sister with a disability. They may reject the reality of the impairment. More commonly, however, rejection is shown by withholding affection or ignoring the sibling's existence.

Source: Adapted from R. Gargiulo, *Working with Parents of Exceptional Children: A Guide for Professionals* (Boston: Houghton Mifflin, 1985), pp. 51–52.

Working with Families Who Are Culturally and Linguistically Diverse

As we discovered in Chapter 3, teachers are working with a growing population of pupils who are culturally and linguistically diverse, of which a disproportionate number are enrolled in special education programs. Effective teachers are sensitive to the needs of these children as well as the needs of their parents and extended family members. If the cultural and linguistic heritage of the parents is not respected, then the development of optimal relationships will likely be undermined (Voltz, 1995).

Many of the strategies and programs, however, that are designed to solicit parental involvement have been devised primarily to serve middle- and upper-income English-speaking families from the macroculture (Kalyanpur & Harry, 1999; Lynch & Hanson, 2004). Thus, it is highly probable that families from culturally and linguistically diverse backgrounds will fail to

First Person

The Other Children

I first remember having a sense of special responsibility for my deaf sister when I was 3. It was my duty to keep her out of danger and mischief—a seemingly normal responsibility for an older sister. But the responsibility has at times felt unbearably heavy. As a 2-year-old, Mindy was not only typically rambunctious, she lived in a bizarre and often dangerous world all her own—separated from the rest of us by her deafness and her inability to communicate. It was a world of fascinating objects to handle, of races with Mother, Daddy, and big sister—a world, even, of nocturnal romps in the street while the rest of the family slept. And once, it was a world of pretty colored pills in the bathroom medicine cabinet.

"Second Mother" to Mindy

When Daddy spent a year in Korea, I became Mother's sole helper. My role as a second mother to Mindy held some prestige and much responsibility. It took away from play time with children my own age. And, just as a mother serves as an example for her children, I was expected to be an exceptionally "good" little girl. The high standards my mother set for my behavior, though, had not only to do with my setting an example; her reasons were also practical. Mindy's impetuous behavior left her with little patience, energy, or time to put up with shenanigans from me.

As I got older, problems resulting from my having a deaf sister increased. My mother began to attend college, and the new pressures and demands caused her to be demanding and dependent upon me. I did not understand why I would be severely chastised for the same behavior that Mindy, who embodied the behavior problems of three children, "couldn't help." My friends' parents seemed less critical of their children than my parents were of me. Mother and Daddy "expected more" from me, but it seemed to me that they gave me less.

The responsibility I felt for Mindy was tremendous. One year, when my "baby-sitting" duties involved periodic checking on my sister, Mindy wandered away between checks. After a thorough but fruitless search of the neighborhood, my mother hysterically told me that if anything happened to Mindy I would be to blame. I felt terrified and guilty. I was 7.

Competition and Rivalry

Mindy's achievements always met with animated enthusiasm from our parents. In contrast, it seemed, Mother and Daddy's response to my accomplishments were on the pat-on-the-back level. I was expected to perform well in every circumstance. I wanted my parents to be enthusiastic about my accomplishments too. I didn't want to have to beg for praise. I didn't want to be taken for granted. I wanted to be noticed.

Babysitter and Manager

When I was not baby-sitting, there was my role of "fetch and carry"—sometimes literally. Mindy's deafness prevented my parents from calling to her so I was appointed official messenger. "Go tell Mindy to come to dinner." "Go tell Mindy to come inside." "Go tell Mindy to clean up her room." At first I probably gloried a bit in my "authority."

But that soon grew stale. I was expected to stop whatever I was doing and bear some message to Mindy. And I discovered that like the royal messengers of old, bearers of orders or bad tidings are not cordially received. In retaliation against the inconvenience and hostile receptions, I made a point of being as bossy in my deliveries as possible—which resulted in acute mutual aggravation.

Love and Respect

In my junior year of high school, Mindy and I began to grow close as sisters. Our increased maturity and the circumstances of our father's being away in Vietnam caused us to turn to one another for companionship and comfort. In the process, we began to discover one another as individuals. We took time to understand our mutual antagonisms and to forgive each other a little. Mindy now understands that as a child my responsibility for her was immense and often intolerable, and that she thoughtlessly made it more difficult for me. She has forgiven me for the hurt and resentment caused her. Differences between us will always exist, but Mindy and I now understand and respect each other's needs without resentment.

The impact a disabled child has upon the other children in a family is tremendous—in both a positive and negative sense. Parents must not expect sainthood from their "other children." Most likely many years will pass before their nondisabled children fully understand why their sister or brother "couldn't help it," why they were expected to be model children, why attention from their parents was rationed, and why their parents sometimes seemed unduly critical and impatient. Until the "other children" do understand, their reactions may be "thoughtless" or "unfair." Before love can replace misunderstanding and intolerance, resentment must be recognized and accepted as a legitimate and even inevitable part of the struggle of growing up together.

SOURCE: V. Hayden, "The Other Children," *Exceptional Parent, 4*, 1974, pp. 26–29.

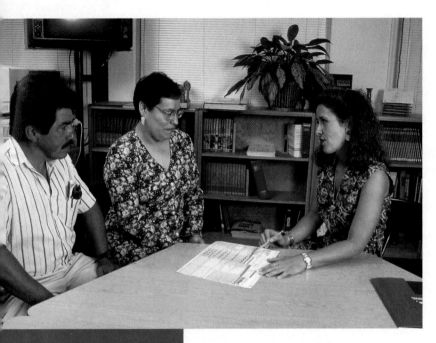

Teachers must exhibit cultural sensitivity when working with families whose cultural or linguistic heritage is different from theirs.

appreciate and respond to strategies designed to support home–school partnerships and enhance their role in the special education process.

Some of the roadblocks or obstacles that may impede the full and meaningful involvement of caregivers from outside the mainstream American culture include the parents' limited English proficiency, their previous negative experiences with schools, an unfamiliarity with their rights and responsibilities, a deference to teachers and other professionals as the decision makers ("teacher knows best"), and in some instances, a lack of trust in the educational system (Matuszny, Banda, & Coleman, 2007; Parette & Petch-Hogan, 2000; Voltz, 1998). Establishing meaningful collaborative relationships with families from culturally and linguistically diverse backgrounds also requires that professionals respect the family's interpretation of the disability and its origin; their child-rearing beliefs, medical practices, and traditions; the family's structure and decision-making style; and their religious views and preferred manner of communication (Gargiulo & Kilgo, 2005). The best intentions of teachers can easily be misinterpreted if they fail to consider the family's value system and cultural traditions. For example, a Hispanic American family may be uncomfortable with and reluctant to agree to a recommendation that they consider placement in a group home for their daughter with mental retardation. To the transition specialist, this may appear to be a perfectly reasonable and appropriate suggestion. However, unlike Anglo-Americans, who generally emphasize accomplishment, independence, and self-reliance, Hispanic Americans are more likely to value interdependence, cooperation, and familial cohesiveness. Because of these differences in values and beliefs, this recommendation will likely be inappropriate for this particular family.

It is very important that teachers exhibit cultural sensitivity when working with families with a cultural or linguistic heritage different from their own. **Cultural sensitivity** implies an awareness of, respect for, and appreciation of the many factors that influence and shape the values, priorities, and perspectives of both individuals and families (Hanson, 2004a). Educators need to be knowledgeable about different values, social customs, and traditions so that they can respond effectively to the needs of all their pupils while concurrently building partnerships with the students' families. By becoming informed about and sensitive to cultural differences, teachers are in a position to empower parents and create equitable relationships (Sileo, Sileo, & Prater, 1996). We offer the following note of caution, however: Building effective alliances with families from different cultural groups demands that professionals refrain from generalizing about families. Although similarities may exist among families, such as a shared heritage or common language, assuming that a family will behave in a certain way simply because of membership in a particular group often leads to stereotyping, which only hinders the development of meaningful home–school partnerships. Remember, just as each student is unique, so is each family. Although families are influenced by their cultural background, they should not be defined by it. No list of ideas or suggestions can guarantee that services will be provided in a culturally sensitive fashion, but the accompanying Suggestions for the Classroom feature offers recommendations for building meaningful relationships with families of culturally or linguistically diverse children.

Suggestions for the Classroom

Recommendations for Providing Families with Culturally Sensitive Services

☑ Provide information using the family's desired language and preferred means of communication—written notes, telephone calls, informal meetings, or even audiotapes.

☑ When appropriate, recognize that extended family members often play a key role in a child's educational development. Give deference to key decision makers in the family.

☑ Use culturally competent interpreters who are not only familiar with the language but also knowledgeable about educational issues and the special education process.

☑ Seek cultural informants from the local community who can assist teachers in understanding culturally relevant variables such as nonverbal communication patterns, child-rearing strategies, gender roles, academic expectations, medical practices, and specific folkways that might affect the family's relationships with professionals.

☑ Attend social events and other functions held in the local community.

☑ With the help of other parents or volunteers, develop a survival vocabulary of key words and phrases in the family's native language.

☑ Address parents and other caregivers as "Mr.," "Ms.," or "Mrs.," rather than using first names. Formality and respect are essential, especially when speaking with older members of the family.

☑ In arranging meetings, be sensitive to possible barriers such as time conflicts, transportation difficulties, and child care issues.

☑ Conduct meetings, if necessary, in family-friendly settings such as local community centers or houses of worship.

☑ Invite community volunteers to serve as cultural liaisons between the school and the pupil's family.

Sources: Graves, Gargiulo, & Sluder, 1996; Linan-Thompson & Jean, 1997; Misra, 1994; Parette & Petch-Hogan, 2000; Salend & Taylor, 1993.

Cultural Reactions to Disability

A family's cultural heritage shapes its reaction to and interpretation of disabilities. Because a disability is a socially and culturally constructed phenomenon (Linan-Thompson & Jean, 1997), families from culturally diverse backgrounds may have differing perspectives on the meaning of exceptionality. These alternative views can easily affect the evaluation process, educational planning, life goals, and our attempts at establishing collaborative relationships (Turnbull et al., 2006).

A disability should always be considered within its cultural context. Each culture defines what it considers to be deviant as well as normal. "Aspects of human variance that are perceived as disabling conditions in one culture may not be perceived as such in another" (Voltz, 1998, p. 66). Harry's (1995) research with families who are culturally diverse seems to suggest that a disability is defined by the child's ability to function in the home environment coupled with the family's expectations for the child's future. Differences in interpretation can pose problems for professionals. For instance, some parents may not consider their child's variance to be severe enough to warrant the label "disabled." Harry (1992) relates an account of a grandmother living in Puerto Rico whose daughter was labeled mentally retarded; the process repeated itself with her granddaughter. This grandmother questions the wisdom involved in the identification of her granddaughter:

> Now they're saying the same thing about my granddaughter, but she has nothing wrong with her mind either. She behaves well and she speaks clearly in both Spanish and English. Why do they say she's retarded?
>
> Americans say that the word handicap means a lot of things, it doesn't just mean that a person is crazy. But for us, Puerto Ricans, we still understand this word as "crazy." For me, a person who is handicapped is a person who is not of sound mind, or has problems in speech, or some problem of their hands or legs. But my children have nothing like that, thanks to God and the Virgin! (p. 147)

Just as the notion of disability is determined by society, the etiology or cause of a disability is also a reflection of a family's cultural reference. Different cultures perceive the cause of disability differently. Generally speaking, in the United States, we believe that the cause of a disability can be identified and treated scientifically (Hanson, 2004b). Families from different cultures may express a belief in fate, spiritual reasons, violation of social taboos, or intergenerational reprisals as possible causes for the child's disability (Hanson, Lynch, & Wayman, 1990). At the risk of stereotyping, some Hispanic American families may attribute a youngster's disability to "God's will." In Asian American families, a disability is thought to bring overwhelming shame upon the family, especially if the child is male; the etiology of the disability may be seen as punishment or retribution for past sins (Misra, 1994). Many Native American cultures have no word for *disability* (Robinson-Zañartu, 1996). In these families a child with a disability is viewed as resulting from "prenatal choice" and is typically accepted and integrated into the community, fulfilling roles commensurate with his or her abilities (Stewart, 1977).

Different meanings of disability and its etiology can be a source of tension between professionals and families from diverse cultural backgrounds. Alternative perspectives on disability and its meaning can easily affect the type of services and interventions a family is willing to ask for and accept, their degree of involvement in educational planning, and attempts at establishing partnerships. We are in complete agreement with Salend and Taylor (1993), who urge educators to be cognizant of and sensitive to parents' belief systems and to adjust our services and practices as needed.

Suggestions for Facilitating Family and Professional Partnerships

What ingredients are needed to establish a meaningful and effective alliance between professionals and families with children who are disabled? The answer to this question has commanded a great deal of attention. We believe that an awareness of and sensitivity to the needs of the family are essential prerequisites for establishing cooperative relationships. These relationships must be built around trust, mutual understanding, and respect. Perl (1995) suggests that interactions between parents and professionals can be facilitated when professionals are able to establish an atmosphere of genuine caring. The traits of honesty, empathy, and genuineness are also crucial to working effectively with families. Additionally, professionals must engage in **active listening**, which requires that service providers listen to parents and other significant persons and caregivers with understanding. Those who seek to establish meaningful partnerships with families must focus on the feelings and attitudes that accompany the words. They must be constantly aware of both verbal and nonverbal messages and their emotional significance. Listening demands the use of both the head and the heart.

As schools and other agencies continue to reach out to families and seek to build partnerships, it seems appropriate that the concept of *parent* involvement be broadened in favor of the term *family* involvement. In contemporary American life, many primary caregivers are adults other than the youngster's biological parents; grandparents, older siblings, foster parents, and extended family members often fill this vital role. The involvement of families can have a beneficial effect on many different dimensions of school life, including:

- pupil achievement;
- student's educational aspirations;
- the length of time individuals stay in school;
- teachers' perceived efficacy of their teaching abilities;
- teachers' perceptions of caregiver effectiveness; and
- caregivers' ratings of schools. (Matuszny et al., 2007)

Today, parent (family) participation in the educational decision-making process is a right, not a privilege. Professionals can facilitate meaningful partnerships with families by their actions and attitudes. Being supportive of families and their unique circumstances, demonstrating concern and empathy, and acknowledging one's own limitations can go a long way toward building lasting partnerships with a student's family. Carefully consider the following statements. Do you think that caregivers would appreciate hearing these remarks from a professional?

- It's not your fault. You are not powerful enough to have caused the kinds of problems your child has.
- What do you need for yourself?
- I think your son could be a success story for our agency.
- I value your input.
- Under the circumstances, you are doing the best you can do. Frankly, I don't know what I would do or how I would be able to carry on.
- If you were a perfect parent, your son would still be in this condition.
- I agree with you.
- Your child has made progress and I know he can do more, so we will continue to work with him.
- Why are you taking all of the blame? It takes two to make or break a relationship.
- I don't know. I can't tell you what's wrong with your child or what caused the problem.
- Your child knows right from wrong. She knows most of society's values and that's because you taught them to her.
- There is a lot of love in your family.
- You know, it's okay to take care of yourself too.
- I don't know. I have to give that serious thought.
- I believe in your instincts. You're the expert on your child.

- You're being too hard on yourself.
- Our agency will take your case.
- Thanks so much for your participation in the group [parent support group]. Your intelligence and your calm reasonableness are important influences in the group. (*Family Support Bulletin*, 1991, p. 20)

We also believe that effective alliances with caregivers of children with special needs require that service providers attend to the following suggestions developed by Gargiulo and Graves (1991):

1. **Explain terminology.** Many parents [caregivers] have no previous experience with exceptionality. This may be their first exposure to a disability label. The parents' [caregivers'] conceptualization of cerebral palsy or mental retardation is most likely very different from that of the professional.
2. **Acknowledge feelings.** Parents [caregivers] will frequently exhibit negative feelings when confronted with the news that their son or daughter is disabled. Professionals need to send a message that it is okay to have these feelings. They need to be acknowledged and then understood.
3. **Use a two-step process when initially informing parents [caregivers] that their child requires special educational services.** After sharing diagnostic information, it is strongly suggested that professionals allow parents [caregivers] time to comprehend and absorb what they have been told. The parents' [caregivers'] affective concerns must be dealt with before proceeding with matters such as intervention recommendations, treatment regimens and strategies, or duration of services. These issues should be addressed in a follow-up interview as the parents' [caregivers'] emotional state permits.
4. **Keep parents [caregivers] informed.** Use a variety of two-way communication techniques. Be as positive as possible when discussing a child's performance. Demonstrate respect, concern, and a sincere desire to cooperate.
5. **Be accountable.** If you agree to assume certain responsibilities or gather information for the parents [caregivers], be certain to follow through. Accountability demonstrates to the parents [caregivers] that they can depend on you. Trust, consistency, and dependability significantly increase the chances for an effective relationship. (p. 178)

Remember, being a parent of a child with disabilities is not a role that most parents freely choose for themselves. Yet it is within professionals' power to help make this a beneficial experience while promoting the development and effective functioning of the entire family unit.

Special attention is sometimes required when working with parents of students from culturally and linguistically diverse backgrounds. Like many other parents, these families are often an untapped resource for educators. As we have seen, effective involvement of these families in the educational lives of their children requires that teachers be sensitive to the cultural norms, values, and beliefs held by the family.

Chapter in Review

Parent–Professional Relationships: Changing Roles

- Three distinct periods characterize the history of parent–professional relationships: (1) antagonistic and adversarial; (2) working partnership; (3) parent empowerment and family-centered relationships.

- The passage of IDEA changed the status of parents from passive recipients of services to active participants and allies with professionals.

- The focal point of professionals' attention is now the child's family rather than just the parents. The family is seen as the primary decision maker.

A Family Systems Approach

- A **family systems model** considers the family to be an interactive and interdependent unit; whatever affects one family member has repercussions for the other members of the unit.

- The Turnbull family system model contains four interrelated components: **family characteristics, family interactions, family functions,** and **family life cycle.**

Stages of Parental Reaction to Disability

- A **stage theory** model for explaining parental reactions to the diagnosis of a disability is constructed around the premise that parents experience a grief cycle similar to the stages of reaction to the death of a loved one.

Disability and the Family

- The entire family constellation is affected by the presence of a child with a disability. The various subsystems and individual family members are uniquely impacted. No two families are likely to deal with an exceptionality in quite the same way.

Working with Families Who Are Culturally and Linguistically Diverse

- If the values, traditions, and beliefs of caregivers from culturally and linguistically diverse backgrounds are not addressed, then the development of optimal relationships will very likely be hindered.

- Teachers must exhibit **culturally sensitive** behavior when working with families whose backgrounds differ from their own.

Suggestions for Facilitating Family and Professional Partnerships

- In order to establish meaningful and effective alliances with families with children who are disabled, it is recommended that professionals create partnerships built around the principles of honesty, trust, and respect.

- Service providers must be genuine and exhibit a caring attitude, using **active listening** when communicating with family members and other significant adults.

Study Questions

1. How has the relationship between parents and professionals changed over the years? What circumstances have aided this process?

2. What was the purpose of the eugenics movement, and how did it affect relationships between professionals and parents?

3. Why do professionals currently believe that efforts should be directed toward working with families of children with special needs instead of just parents?

4. Define the term *collaboration* as it pertains to professionals and parents.

5. What is the rationale behind a family systems model?

6. Identify the four key components of the Turnbull family systems framework. Explain the characteristics of each of these elements.

7. How does the concept of cohesion differ from adaptability in the Turnbull model?

8. What are the stages of emotional response that many parents go through when informed that their child has a disability? Give examples of the types of behavior typically exhibited at each stage.

9. What cautions does Gargiulo stress when applying a stage theory model to parents of children with disabilities?

10. In what ways might a child with a disability affect his or her family?

11. What does the research literature suggest about the impact of childhood disability on marital relationships, mothers, fathers, siblings, and grandparents of children with special needs?

12. Name five emotional responses typically exhibited by siblings of children with disabilities.

13. Why is an awareness of and sensitivity to cultural and linguistic differences important for professionals when working with families of children with disabilities?

14. Describe what you believe to be key personal characteristics of professionals who work with families of individuals with disabilities.

Key Terms

eugenics movement
family systems model
family characteristics
family interactions

cohesion
adaptability
family functions

family life cycle
transitions
stage theory

respite care
cultural sensitivity
active listening

Learning Activities

1. Talk to family members of a person with a disability. Learn how the family adapted to the person's exceptionality and how the family as a whole and individual members were or still are affected by the disability. Be certain to ask sensitive questions and ensure confidentiality.

2. Attend a support group meeting for family members of a person with a disability. What kinds of information were presented, and how was it delivered? In your opinion, did those in attendance benefit from the experience?

3. Develop a list of resources and supports in your community aimed at assisting individuals with disabilities and their families. Share your list with your classmates. Examples of resources and supports might include recreational opportunities, religious programs, support groups, respite care, local chapters of national

parent/advocacy groups, and health care professionals who work with people with disabilities.

4. Discuss with two general educators and two special education teachers the strategies and techniques they use to establish parent–professional partnerships. What activities seem to be most effective for ensuring meaningful participation? How do these professionals ensure the involvement of parents from culturally and linguistically diverse backgrounds?

5. Volunteer to work for an organization that provides respite care for families of children with disabilities. Keep a journal about your experiences.

6. Interview parents or other family members from diverse cultural backgrounds as a means of learning about their perspectives on disabilities and the educational system, as well as any culturally specific behaviors and values such as child-rearing practices and communication styles.

Reflecting on Standards

The following exercises are designed to help you learn to apply the Council for Exceptional Children (CEC) standards to your teaching practice. Each of the reflection exercises below correlates with a knowledge or skill within the CEC standards. For the full text of each of the related CEC standards, please refer to the standards integration grid located in Appendix B.

1. Focus on Professional and Ethical Practice (*CEC Content Standard #9 CC9S6*)

Reflect on a time when you have negatively stereotyped someone because of their culture, language, religion, gender, disability, socioeconomic status, or social orientation. How might stereotyping a student or their family negatively affect your teaching? What strategies might you want to put in place in your classroom to avoid stereotyping?

2. Focus on Collaboration (*CEC Content Standard #10 CC10S3*)

Reflect on the various ways your family was involved in your education. What are the advantages to fostering meaningful partnerships with your students' families? How will you want to involve families in your classroom?

 Technology Resources

Visit the Web-based SAGE Study Site at **http://www.sagepub.com/gargiulo3estudy** for these additional learning tools:

- Chapter quizzes
- Key term flashcards
- Media links
- Full-text SAGE journal articles
- Internet activities
- Additional Web resources

PART II

A Study of Individuals with Special Needs

It is not enough to give the handicapped life. They must be given a life worth living.

—Helen Keller (1880–1968)

CHAPTER 5

Individuals with Mental Retardation or Intellectual Disabilities

Lauren

Our daughter, Lauren, is an extraordinary child. But she is certainly not an easy child. Sometimes people use the word "exceptional" to describe a child like Lauren who has Down syndrome.

Jason and I were married when we were both thirty-three and were ready to have children. I was pregnant with Lauren by the time we celebrated our first anniversary. The delivery of our baby was long and difficult, with some concerns about an irregular heartbeat and a possible emergency C-section. Finally, she was born on a Monday afternoon around 5:00 P.M. As exhausted as I felt, I was excitedly anticipating holding my new baby. I noticed a nurse looking at the baby and whispering into the doctor's ear. My doctor looked at me and said, "We think the baby has Down's," as they passed Lauren to me. I was stunned for a moment and then asked, "Is it a boy or a girl?" I was only allowed to see my baby girl very briefly, before my husband and the nurse took her to the special care nursery. It was not the moment of joy we had been expecting at the birth of our child. Instead, we were both shocked and divided into our own private worlds of grief.

Even though I was familiar with Down syndrome (due to my training as a special educator), I suddenly felt like I knew nothing. I wanted to be able to hold Lauren because I felt it would help me to make a connection with her. Nothing about her delivery had gone the way we expected and then I realized that in all the conversations we had before she was born, not one time had we discussed or considered the possibility of a birth defect or any problems.

Lauren's health was a critical issue as I began an endless series of doctor visits with her, making sure to check each possible health complication associated with Down syndrome. Our pediatrician saw Lauren frequently and guided us through the process step by step. Lauren had a very mild heart defect, but it did not require surgery or even medication. Her hearing and vision were normal, except for nystagmus—Lauren's eyes waver from side to side constantly as if she were reading. The ophthalmologist told us this would never go away but it would become less obvious and improve with time. We talked with a geneticist who explained the characteristics of Down syndrome, and we met with a developmental pediatrician who assessed Lauren's development. We were grateful for their help and recommendations.

Soon after Lauren was home I began to call agencies in the area that assisted parents of children with special needs. We were directed to a federally funded agency that provides assistance to parents of developmentally delayed children from birth to 3 years of age. At 6 weeks old Lauren was the focus of a group assessment conducted in our home by a team of professionals including a speech therapist, occupational therapist, physical therapist, special education teacher, and a service coordinator to assist with all the paperwork. Lauren was lying on the floor, the center of our attention. She was already smiling and holding her head up. We all identified goals for us to work on and set up regular visits by her teacher and therapist. I felt more confident that I was taking the right steps to help Lauren develop to her full potential. It seems incredible how many people were involved in our lives during those early years.

I will always remember Lauren learning to walk; it's one of my favorite memories. She has to work so hard to do things that can be so easy for other children. Our physical therapist would visit us once a month. She advised us not to encourage Lauren to walk because she was developing upper body strength by crawling. So that kind of relieved us of one more concern. By 13 or 14 months Lauren did start walking. And she loved it. You could see it in her facial expression just how exciting it must have felt; she was so proud of herself. I can still see her walking across the yard. She would take a few steps, fall down, and get up over and over again. You could hear her laughing the whole time. Lauren is certainly not a timid child; she does the things she enjoys with enthusiasm.

Because of Lauren's excellent motor development we expected her other milestones would continue to be close to a typical progression. Unfortunately, Lauren's speech progress was very slow. She said her first word around 15 months, which was "ba" for ball. She really didn't refer to Jason or me with any words, even though she was making the sounds "mama" and "dada." We insisted she begin receiving speech therapy at 2 years old. Everything I read told me that children with Down syndrome have trouble developing language, and I was seeing it firsthand.

Currently I am enrolled in a sign language class because Lauren communicates better with signs and visual prompts. I am looking forward to the day she and I can have our first conversation. She communicates in any way that she is able, which is a combination of words, signs, and gestures. She and I deal with many frustrating moments struggling to understand each other. It may take some time, but I cannot wait to hear her express her thoughts and feelings to me with words.

Lauren is now in elementary school, where she participates in an inclusion class for most of the school day and attends a resource class for direct speech instruction and some academics for about one hour a day. We love having her included with her typical peers in a general education classroom.

Lauren's progress is exciting to witness. When we went to a local restaurant for lunch recently, the hostess looked at her and said, "How are you?" and Lauren looked at her and clearly responded "Good" with the sign. She loves greetings and will ask others, "How are you?" This is a welcome change from that awkward feeling you have as a parent when you feel as though you have to "talk" for your child.

Lauren's behavior is the biggest obstacle for our family. The days when we could scoop her up and move on as we managed to calm her down are over. She currently weighs 80 pounds, and she is next to impossible to move when she decides she isn't going anywhere. Transitions are difficult for her, and flexibility isn't Lauren's style. Although it is helpful to have a routine to structure her day, it just isn't realistic to always follow routines, especially on weekends.

We feel fortunate that we have neighbors, teachers, friends, and family that accept and celebrate Lauren's accomplishments with us. They don't mind singing "Happy Birthday" and blowing out the candles just because there is a cake, even when it isn't anyone's birthday. My dream is for Lauren to form lasting friendships with peers, develop her own personal interests, and achieve her academic potential. I believe meeting these goals will help Lauren live a full and meaningful life.

—*D. Shipman*

M ental retardation is a powerful term. It is also an emotionally laden label, one that conjures up various images of people with mental retardation. What do you think of when someone says "mental retardation"? Do you immediately think of the character from the movie *Radio* or *I Am Sam*? Maybe you recall meeting a young girl with Down syndrome when you volunteered to help during last year's Special Olympics, or perhaps you recollect how you felt when a group of adults with intellectual disabilities sat by you in a restaurant. Often our images of individuals with mental retardation are based on stereotypes resulting from limited contact and exposure. Consequently, many of us are susceptible to inaccuracies, misconceptions, and erroneous beliefs about this population. As a result, people who are mentally retarded frequently encounter prejudice, ignorance, and in some instances, outright discrimination simply because society has identified them as being "different." Yet despite the diversity represented by this group, we firmly believe that children and adults with mental retardation are first and foremost people who are more like their nonretarded counterparts than they are different. In fact, very few ever fit the images and stereotypes commonly portrayed by the media.

The goal of this chapter is to examine basic issues and concepts necessary for understanding the field of mental retardation and individuals identified as such. In this chapter, we will look at historical foundations, evolving definitions and classification models, causes of mental retardation, characteristics of persons with mental retardation, contemporary educational practices, and trends in service delivery along with related concepts. We have adopted a life-span perspective for exploring the concept of mental retardation. This chapter, and those that follow, will therefore address topics and issues pertaining to infancy through adulthood.

Defining Mental Retardation or Intellectual Disabilities: An Evolving Process

Mental retardation is a complex and multifaceted concept. Mental retardation has been studied by psychologists, sociologists, educators, physicians, and many other professionals. This multidisciplinary interest in and investigation of mental retardation, while beneficial, has significantly contributed to problems of conceptual and definitional clarity (Drew & Hardman, 2007). Yet, by its very nature, intellectual disabilities cannot be studied independently of other disciplines. We fully agree with Drew and his colleague that there is considerable merit in a multidisciplinary approach; however, we must not lose sight of what should be our central focus, the individual with mental retardation.

1961 AAMR Definition

The American Association on Mental Retardation (AAMR)[1] has been a tremendous help in advancing our understanding of the concept of mental retardation. Founded in 1876, AAMR's sixth definition appeared in 1961 and was widely adopted. This slightly revised version of a 1959 manual on terminology and classification describes mental retardation as "subaverage general intellectual functioning which originates during the developmental period and is associated with impairments in adaptive behavior" (Heber, 1961, p. 3). Let us analyze the meaning of these phrases. "Subaverage general intellectual functioning" is defined as an intelligence quotient (IQ) greater than one **standard deviation** (SD) (a statistic describing variance from the mean or average score of a particular group) below the mean for a given age group. In 1961, this was interpreted to be an IQ below 85 or 84 depending on which standardized IQ test was used. The "developmental period" extended from birth to approximately age 16. The criterion of "impairment in adaptive behavior" is a critical and unique aspect of this definition. The inclusion of this factor establishes dual criteria for identifying someone as mentally retarded (Scheerenberger, 1987).

Adaptive behavior, which Heber first introduced, refers to an individual's ability to meet the social requirements of his or her community that are appropriate for his or her chronological age; it is an indication of independence and social competency. Thus, according to Heber's definition, a person with an IQ of 79 who did not exhibit significant impairment in adaptive behavior would *not* be identified as mentally retarded. (See Figure 5.1.)

The association's definition, though widely used, was not without its critics. Professional concern focused on the lack of appropriate assessment instruments for measuring adaptive behavior as well as a belief that the definition was overly inclusive—almost 16 percent of the population could have an IQ within the range thought to indicate mental retardation. These concerns and others led to a revised definition in 1973.

Intellectual functioning

	Low	High
Adaptive behavior Low	Mentally retarded	Not mentally retarded
High	Not mentally retarded	Not mentally retarded

Figure 5.1

Relationship between Intellectual Functioning and Adaptive Behavior

NOTE: Classification of an individual as mentally retarded requires both low intellectual functioning and deficits in adaptive behavior.

1973 AAMR Definition

Herbert Grossman chaired a committee charged with revising the 1961 AAMR definition. Grossman's (1973) definition viewed mental retardation as "significantly subaverage general intellectual functioning existing concurrently with deficits in adaptive behavior, and manifested during the developmental period" (p. 11). Though paralleling its predecessor, the Grossman definition is conceptually distinct. First, the 1973 definition refers to *significantly* subaverage intellectual ability. Operationally, intellectual disability was psychometrically redefined as performance at least two standard deviations below the mean. This more conservative approach considered the upper IQ limit to be 70 or 68 (again, depending on whether the Stanford-Binet Intelligence Scale [SD = 16 points] or Wechsler Intelligence Scale for Children [SD = 15 points] was used). Statistically speaking, this represents the lower 2.27 percent of the population instead of the approximately 16 percent included in the Heber definition. (See Figure 5.2.) Adopting this standard eliminated the classification of "borderline" mental retardation incorporated in Heber's conceptual scheme.

---

1. In 1987, the American Association on Mental Deficiency (AAMD) changed its name to the American Association on Mental Retardation. In January 2007 the Association changed its name again. It is now known as the American Association on Intellectual and Developmental Disabilities (AAIDD), which is consistent with European and Canadian terminology. The U.S. Department of Education, however, still retains the term *mental retardation*. We have chosen to use both terms interchangeably.

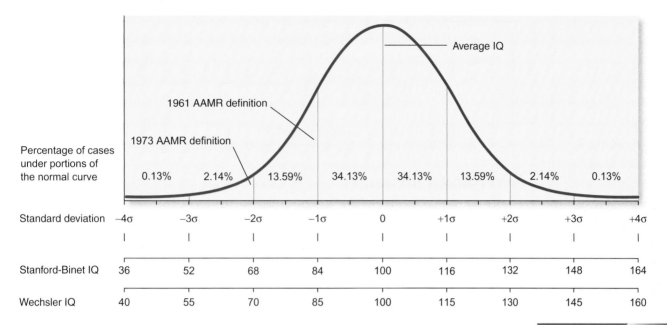

	-4σ	-3σ	-2σ	-1σ	0	+1σ	+2σ	+3σ	+4σ

Figure 5.2

The Normal Curve: A Theoretical Distribution of Intelligence

Note: The 1961 AAMR definition defines mental retardation as an IQ lower than 85 (84) on a standardized measure of intelligence. The 1973 AAMR definition defines mental retardation as an IQ lower than 70 (68). Later versions allow for professional judgment when considering intellectual performance.

The Grossman definition also sought to clarify the relationship between adaptive behavior and intellectual functioning. The 1973 definition attempted to focus greater attention on adaptive behavior and described it as the ability of an individual to meet "the standards of personal independence and social responsibility expected of his [her] age and cultural group" (Grossman, 1973, p. 11). Adaptive behavior was to be considered within the context of the person's age and sociocultural group. Grossman's work attempted to strengthen the link between IQ and adaptive behavior in an effort to reduce the number of pupils identified as mentally retarded solely on the basis of their IQ. The 1973 definition also extended the concept of the developmental period to age 18 to more accurately reflect when most people complete their education.

Although the 1973 Grossman definition, incorporated into IDEA 2004 (PL 108-446), represented a conceptual advancement over the work of Heber, shortcomings remained. As an illustration, many educators were concerned that lowering of the IQ threshold to 68 (70) would deny special education services to many students who otherwise would have been eligible for placement in programs serving individuals with mild mental retardation. It was feared that these children would be misclassified and inappropriately placed and thus "drown in the mainstream" (Scheerenberger, 1987). MacMillan (1989) echoed this concern. He characterized these students as "residing in a no-man's land," roughly equivalent to an educational demilitarized zone, ineligible for special education services. Once again, AAMR revised its definition of intellectual disabilities to achieve greater clarity and a contemporary focus.

1983 AAMR Definition

In 1983, the AAMR published yet another revision to its manual on terminology and classification. Once again, Grossman led the organization's efforts. This eighth edition, mirroring its 1973 predecessor, describes mental retardation as "significantly subaverage general intellectual functioning resulting in or associated with concurrent impairments in adaptive behavior and manifested during the developmental period" (Grossman, 1983, p. 1).

Though very similar in wording to the 1973 definition, this version contains some important changes. The 1983 Grossman edition suggests using a range of 70–75 when describing the upper limits of intellectual performance on a standardized measure of intelligence rather than a strict cutoff of 70. An IQ score of 70 is intended only as a guideline. Flexibility is the key to understanding the operation of this definition. The clinical judgment of the professional plays an important role when making a diagnosis of mental retardation.

The 1983 AAMR definition was generally well accepted by the professional community. Like all definitions, however, it was time-bound. As our knowledge base and ideas about intellectual disabilities change, so do our definitions. In 1992, AAMR issued yet another version of its thinking about mental retardation.

1992 AAMR Definition

In May 1992 Ruth Luckasson and her colleagues (Luckasson et al., 1992) crafted a new definition of mental retardation, which was published in *Mental Retardation: Definition, Classification, and Systems of Supports*. According to this manual,

> *Mental retardation* refers to substantial limitations in present functioning. It is characterized by significantly subaverage intellectual functioning, existing concurrently with related limitations in two or more of the following applicable adaptive skill areas: communication, self-care, home living, social skills, community use, self-direction, health and safety, functional academics, leisure, and work. Mental retardation manifests before age 18. (p. 5)

Application of this definition requires careful consideration of the following four essential assumptions:

1. Valid assessment considers cultural and linguistic diversity as well as differences in communication and behavioral factors.
2. The existence of limitations in adaptive skills occurs within the context of community environments typical of the individual's age peers and is indexed to the person's individualized needs for supports.
3. Specific adaptive limitations often coexist with strengths in other adaptive skills or other personal capabilities.
4. With appropriate supports over a sustained period, the life functioning of the person with mental retardation will generally improve. (Luckasson et al., 1992, p. 5)

The 1992 AAMR definition is a highly functional definition. It portrays mental retardation as a relationship among three key elements: the individual, the environment, and the type of support required for maximum functioning in various settings. It essentially reflects the "fit" between the person's capabilities and the structure and expectations of the environment. This ninth version also represents a conceptual shift away from viewing mental retardation as an inherent trait to a perspective that considers the person's present level of functioning and the supports needed to improve it. The interaction among the individual, the environment, and support is depicted in Figure 5.3. The framers of the 1992 definition selected an equilateral triangle to represent their thinking because it shows the equality among the three elements.

The 1992 AAMR description of mental retardation stresses functioning in one's community rather than just focusing on the clinical aspect of the individual such as IQ or adaptive behavior (Smith, Polloway, Patton, & Dowdy, 2008). This definition is an optimist one; it assumes that a person's performance will improve over time when appropriate supports are provided. Though certainly a unique portrayal of mental retardation, this definition, like its predecessors, retains an emphasis on intellectual performance coupled with impairments in adaptive skills.

The 1992 version of the AAMR definition of intellectual disabilities has proven to be fairly controversial, and not all professionals in the field are embracing it (Conyers, Martin, Martin, & Yu, 2002; Polloway, Smith, Chamberlain, Denning, & Smith, 1999), possibly because it represents a paradigm shift from a deficiency-based model of mental retardation to a support-based model. The purpose of this definition, according to Reiss (1994), a member of the committee that crafted it, is to encourage people to change their thinking about mental retardation and to serve as a cornerstone for contemporary public policy. It remains to be seen whether this objective is accomplished and if the 1992 version is incorporated into federal and state statutes. Research (Conyers et al.; Denning, Chamberlain, & Polloway, 2000) suggests that this reformulated description of mental retardation is having minimal influence on changing guidelines used by individual states for identifying students with mental retardation. Currently, forty-three states still follow the federal (IDEA) definition of mental retardation (Müller & Markowitz, 2004). Recall that this definition mirrors the 1973 Grossman definition of mental retardation.

Questions and concerns raised in various professional circles about the 1992 definition have led to yet another interpretation of mental retardation. In 2002 AAMR offered its latest effort at describing intellectual disabilities.

Figure 5.3

General Structure of the 1992 AAMR Definition of Mental Retardation

Source: *Mental Retardation: Definition, Classification, and Systems of Supports*, 9th ed. (Washington, DC: American Association on Mental Retardation, 1992), p. 10. Reprinted with permission.

2002 AAMR Definition

The 2002 AAMR definition (Luckasson et al., 2002) represents the most recent attempt in an evolving understanding of mental retardation. The purpose of the tenth edition was to "create a contemporary system of diagnosis, classification, and systems of support for the disability currently known as mental retardation" (Luckasson et al., p. xii).

The current AAMR definition states that

mental retardation is a disability characterized by significant limitations both in intellectual functioning and in adaptive behavior as expressed in conceptual, social, and practical adaptive skills. This disability originates before age 18. (Luckasson et al., 2002, p. 1)

Accompanying this description are five assumptions considered essential when applying this definition:

- Limitations in present functioning must be considered within the context of community environments typical of the individual's age, peers, and culture.
- Valid assessment considers cultural and linguistic diversity as well as differences in communication and sensory, motor, and behavioral factors.
- Within an individual, limitations often coexist with strengths.
- An important purpose of describing limitations is to develop a profile of needed supports.
- With appropriate personalized supports over a sustained period, the life functioning of the person with mental retardation will generally improve. (Luckasson et al., 2002, p. 1)

Like the ninth edition developed ten years earlier, the 2002 AAMR definition retains a positive perspective toward individuals with intellectual disabilities while continuing to acknowledge the significance of adaptive behavior and systems of support. It also preserves the idea that mental retardation is a "*function* of the relationship among individual functioning, supports, and contexts" (Wehmeyer, 2003, p. 276). This newest conceptualization of mental retardation, while not flawless, represents a logical step in the continuing challenge of advancing our understanding of the concept of mental retardation. Unfortunately, Wehmeyer anticipates that this definition will largely be greeted with silence, if not outright ambivalence, by special educators.

Assessing Intellectual Ability and Adaptive Behavior

The constructs of *intelligence* and *adaptive behavior* play key roles in our understanding of the concept of mental retardation. Yet both of these terms are somewhat difficult to define and assess. For the sake of clarity we will discuss each concept separately; but remember they are intricately interrelated and provide the foundation for contemporary thinking about intellectual disabilities.

Intellectual Ability

The question of what constitutes intelligence and how to describe it has challenged educators, psychologists, and thinkers throughout the years. Even today there is disagreement among professionals as to the meaning of this term and the best way of measuring intelligence. Intelligence is perhaps best thought of as a construct or theoretical abstraction; it is not a visible entity but rather a human trait whose existence is inferred based on a person's performance on certain types of cognitive tasks. Because no one has ever seen intelligence but only deduced its presence, professionals have come to the realization that they are "attempting to explain one of the most complex and elusive components of human functioning" (Beirne-Smith, Patton, & Kim, 2006, p. 95).

These difficulties notwithstanding, a great amount of effort has been expended on trying to accurately assess intellectual functioning. The most common way of determining an individual's cognitive ability is through an IQ or intelligence test. Two of the more widely used individually administered IQ measures are the Wechsler Intelligence Scale for Children, 4th Edition, or WISC-IV (Wechsler, 2003), and the fifth edition of the original work of Binet and Simon from the early twentieth century, the Stanford-Binet Intelligence Scale (Roid, 2003). As noted in Chapter 3, some psychologists and psychometrists rely on the Kaufman Assessment Battery for Children (Kaufman & Kaufman, 2004), especially when evaluating youngsters from culturally and linguistically diverse backgrounds.

Data gleaned from the WISC-IV, the Stanford-Binet V, and similar measures are thought to represent a sample of an individual's intellectual skills and abilities. These data are usually summarized as an IQ score. Originally an IQ was defined as a ratio between the person's mental age (MA or developmental level) and chronological age (CA) multiplied by 100. For instance, a student whose chronological age is 10 but performs on an IQ test like a typical 5-year-old would have an IQ of 50; if accompanied by deficits in adaptive behavior, this individual would very likely be identified as mentally retarded. Today, deviation IQs or standard scores have replaced intelligence quotients in most professional circles. A standard score is nothing more than an expression of how far a particular raw score deviates from a specific reference point such as the test mean. Standard scores are often expressed as standard deviations.

If large numbers of people were assessed with an IQ test, their performance would reflect a distribution of scores represented as a bell-shaped curve, or normal curve (see Figure 5.2). In this theoretical statistical distribution, an average IQ score is designated as 100 (representing equivalence between MA and CA). Most people cluster around the center of the curve, with fewer individuals at the extremes of the distribution. Variance from the mean or average score occurs in a predictable fashion and is referred to in terms of standard deviations. One standard deviation (SD) on both the Stanford-Binet V and the WISC-IV is equivalent to 15 IQ points. Both tests have a mean IQ of 100.

Although IQ testing is very common in schools, the issue of assessing someone's intelligence, especially if a special education placement may result, is somewhat controversial. Cautionary flags and reasons for concern tend to focus on these issues:

- **Potential for cultural bias.** Intellectual assessments are often criticized because of their highly verbal nature and reflection of middle-class Anglo standards.
- **Stability of IQ.** An IQ test only reports a person's performance at a particular point in time; intelligence is not static but capable of changing, and in some cases, the change can be significant.
- **Overemphasis on IQ scores.** An IQ score is not the sole indicator of an individual's ability, nor is it a measure of the person's worth; yet IQ is often stressed at the expense of other factors such as motivation or adaptive skills.

Persons with intellectual disabilities can be taught how to live independently.

Despite the various criticisms and concerns, IQ testing does a good job of predicting how well a student will do in school—in other words, his or her potential for academic success. Still, educators should not overly rely on a single IQ score as a predictor of performance in the classroom; an IQ score should only be one piece of the diagnostic puzzle. With increasing frequency, professionals are looking at alternative or supplemental indicators of performance and are gathering information using a holistic approach, including work samples, parent/teacher interviews, behavior checklists, and classroom observation. Collectively, these sources of data can provide a more realistic and valid picture of the child's performance and potential.

Adaptive Behavior

The notion of adaptive behavior was first introduced in the 1973 AAMR definition of mental retardation. It was retained in the 1983 description of mental retardation and is the underpinning of the latest AAMR definition. Adaptive behavior is seen as "the degree to which, and the efficiency with which, the individual meets the standards of maturation, learning, personal independence, and/or social responsibility that are expected for his or her age level and cultural group" (Grossman, 1983, p. 11). In continuing this thinking, the 2002 AAMR definition describes adaptive behavior as "the collection of conceptual, social, and practical skills that have been learned by people in order to function in their everyday society" (Luckasson et al., 2002, p. 73). Stated another way, it is how well a person copes with the everyday demands and requirements of his or her environment. The idea of context is important for understanding the concept of adaptive behavior. Because behavior is strongly influenced by cultural factors, age and situation appropriateness must always be considered within the setting in which it occurs. For example, a teenage girl who uses her fingers while eating might be viewed as exhibiting inappropriate behavior; however, this behavior is only maladaptive when considered within the context of Western cultures.

Both the 1992 and 2002 AAMR definitions, like earlier formulations, stress adaptive behavior, but now it is more clearly articulated. In earlier versions, adaptive behavior was described globally; in the Luckasson et al. (2002) configuration, it is seen as significant limitations in the expression or performance of conceptual, social, and practical adaptive skills. Table 5.1 illustrates these three areas and provides examples of the skills.

It is not always easy to assess adaptive behavior. It is usually measured by direct observation, structured interviews, or standardized scales. Informants may include parents, teachers, caregivers, or other professionals. One of the more widely used instruments for assessing adaptive behavior is the AAMR Adaptive Behavior Scale—School (Lambert, Nihira, & Leland, 1993), which provides a comprehensive assessment of an individual's competency over a wide range of behaviors. The school version assesses performance in the areas of personal responsibility and daily living skills, along with social adaptation and maladaptive behavior. Another form is available for evaluating individuals with mental retardation who reside in community and residential settings: the AAMR Adaptive Behavior Scale—Residential and Community (Nihira, Leland, & Lambert, 1993). Like its companion scale, this instrument is norm referenced and individually administered and contains two main sections: personal independence and social adaptation.

Classification of Individuals with Mental Retardation or Intellectual Disabilities

A classification system is a convenient way for differentiating among individuals who share a common characteristic—in this instance, mental retardation. Of course, we must remember that there is a great degree of variability among this population despite the fact that they share a common label. Because intellectual disabilities exist along a continuum, there

Table 5.1	2002 AAMR Adaptive Skill Areas
Skill Area	**Examples of Behavior**
Conceptual	• Language (receptive and expressive) • Reading and writing • Money concepts • Self-direction
Social	• Interpersonal • Responsibility • Self-esteem • Gullibility (likelihood of being tricked or manipulated) • Naiveté • Follows rules • Obeys laws • Avoids victimization

Practical	• Activities of daily living:
	  – Eating
	  – Transfer/mobility
	  – Toileting
	  – Dressing
	• Instrumental activities of daily living:
	  – Meal preparation
	  – Housekeeping
	  – Transportation
	  – Taking medication
	  – Money management
	  – Telephone use
	• Occupational skills
	• Maintains safe environments

SOURCE: Adapted from *Mental Retardation: Definition, Classification, and Systems of Support*, 10th ed. (Washington, DC: American Association on Mental Retardation, 2002), p. 42.

have been numerous proposals on how to classify people with this disability. Many years ago, Gelof (1963) reported the existence of almost two dozen classification schemes. Like definitions of mental retardation, classification models tend to vary according to a particular focus. We will examine several systems—some vintage ones along with the most contemporary thinking in this area. Types of classification systems include grouping individuals with intellectual disabilities according to etiology or cause of the disability, severity of the condition, and educational expectations. Finally, the current strategy classifies on the basis of levels of support.

An Etiological Perspective

Traditionally, individuals with intellectual disabilities have been classified based on known or presumed medical/biological causes. This etiological orientation assumes that mental retardation is a consequence of a disease process or biological defect. Examples include mental retardation that is due to infections such as rubella (German measles) or maternal syphilis, chromosomal abnormalities such as Down syndrome, or metabolic disorders such

Table 5.2	Classification of Mental Retardation According to Measured Intelligence	
Classification Level	**Measured IQ**	**SD below Mean**
Mild retardation	55–70	2 to 3
Moderate retardation	40–55	3 to 4
Severe retardation	25–40	4 to 5
Profound retardation	Under 25	More than 5

NOTE: IQ scores are approximate.
SD = standard deviation.

as phenylketonuria (PKU). (These examples and others will be more fully explored in a later section of this chapter.) Although useful for physicians and other health care workers, this classification scheme has limited applicability for nonmedical practitioners.

Intellectual Deficits

A long-standing and popular classification scheme among psychologists and educators is one based on the severity of intellectual impairment as determined by an IQ test. This model is one of the most widely cited in the professional literature and, until recently, reflected the position of the AAMR dating back to the 1973 Grossman definition of mental retardation. According to this system, deficits in intellectual functioning and related impairments in adaptive behavior result in individuals' being classified into one of four levels of mental retardation—mild, moderate, severe, or profound—with mild representing the highest level of performance for persons thought to be mentally retarded and profound the lowest. Intellectual competency is often the primary variable used in constructing these discriminations; Table 5.2 presents the IQ ranges typically used.

An Educational Perspective

Another classification system popular with educators since the 1960s is to classify students with intellectual disabilities on the basis of expected or anticipated educational accomplishments. Generally speaking, special education teachers classified children into two groups: **educable mentally retarded** (EMR) or **trainable mentally retarded** (TMR). These designations are roughly equivalent to the AAMR labels of mild and moderate mental retardation, with IQs ranging from about 50–55 to 70–75 and 35–40 to 50–55, respectively. (Before the enactment of PL 94-142, public schools rarely served individuals with IQs less than 35; therefore, these youngsters were not labeled according to this system.) As you might expect, the term *educable* implies that a youngster has some, albeit limited, academic potential; *trainable* implies that a child is incapable of learning but possibly could be trained in nonacademic areas. Over the years, professionals have learned that these prognostic labels, which represent an "educability quotient," are inaccurate and present a false dichotomy; we affirm that all children are capable of learning when presented with the appropriate circumstances. The notion of presumed academic achievement has slowly fallen out of favor in professional circles. These terms are currently considered pejorative and tend to perpetuate stereotypical and prejudicial attitudes.

Levels of Support

In 1992, the AAMR (Luckasson et al., 1992), in a dramatic and controversial maneuver, shifted from a classification model based on severity of intellectual impairment to one based on the type and extent of needed supports. This scheme, retained in the 2002 definition (Luckasson et al., 2002), classifies individuals with mental retardation according to the **level of support**—intermittent, limited, extensive, or pervasive—needed to effectively function across adaptive skill areas in various natural settings, rather than according to the person's deficits. In fact, AAMR recommends abandoning references to the severity of retardation. Table 5.3 describes the four classification levels currently endorsed by the AAMR.

The aim of this approach is to explain an individual's functional (rather than intellectual) limitations in terms of the amount of support he or she requires to achieve optimal growth and development at home, school, the workplace, and other community settings (Beirne-Smith et al., 2006). This model, which represents more than a mere substitution for the previous AAMR IQ-based classification scheme, extends the concept of support beyond the intensity of needed support to include the type of support system required. **Natural supports** typically include family members, friends, teachers, and coworkers. **Formal supports** are usually thought of as government-funded social programs like Social Security payments or health care programs, habilitation services, and even the advocacy efforts of groups like the Council for Exceptional Children or The Arc, a national organization on mental retardation. It is probably too early to tell how professionals, school systems, and other groups will respond to this new way of thinking about classifying people with intellectual disabilities.

Table 5.3	Classification of Mental Retardation According to Intensities of Support	
Support Level	**Description**	**Examples**
Intermittent	Supports on an as-needed or episodic basis. Person does not always need the support(s), or person needs short-term supports during life-span transitions. When provided, intermittent supports may be of high or low intensity.	• Loss of employment • Acute medical crisis
Limited	Supports characterized by consistency over time, time-limited but not intermittent; may require fewer staff and less cost than more intense levels of support.	• Job training • Transitioning from school to adult status
Extensive	Supports characterized by regular involvement (e.g., daily) in at least some environments (such as work or home) and not time-limited.	• Ongoing home living assistance
Pervasive	Supports characterized by their constancy and high intensity; provided across all environments, potential life-sustaining nature. Pervasive supports typically involve more staff and intrusiveness than extensive or time-limited supports.	• Chronic medical situation

Source: Adapted from *Mental Retardation: Definition, Classification, and Systems of Supports*, 10th ed. (Washington, DC: American Association on Mental Retardation, 2002), p. 152.

A Brief History of the Field

It is generally believed that individuals thought to be mentally retarded have been present in all societies throughout the ages. Historically speaking, the field of mental retardation resembles an ever-changing mosaic influenced by the sociopolitical and economic climate of the times. Attitudes toward and understanding of mental retardation have also affected the treatment of people with mental retardation. Mental retardation is a field that is continually evolving—from the ignorance of antiquity to the highly scientific and legal foundations of the late twentieth century. Along this pathway, people with intellectual disabilities have had to endure and battle myths, fear, superstition, attempts at extermination, and educational and social segregation before arriving at today's policy of normalization and inclusion.

Early Civilizations

Early written records from the era of the Greek and Roman empires make reference to citizens who were most likely mentally retarded. In some instances, these accounts date back to almost 1550 B.C. (Lindman & McIntyre, 1961). In many ways, the Greek and Roman societies were highly advanced and civilized, but the treatment of infants with disabilities would be judged cruel and barbaric by today's standards. Scheerenberger's (1983) detailed account of the history of mental retardation reveals, for example, that in the city-state of Sparta, which placed a premium on physical strength and intellectual ability, eugenics and infanticide were common, everyday occurrences. Only the brightest and strongest of citizens were encouraged to have children. Newborns were examined by a council of inspectors, and babies thought to be defective or inferior were thrown from a cliff to die on the rocks below.

The early days of the Roman Republic mirrored the practices of the Greeks. Deformed infants were routinely allowed to perish—but only during the first eight days of life. Fathers held complete control over their children and could do whatever they wished, including selling or killing them. This doctrine of *patria potestas* is unparalleled in any other society.

The Middle Ages

From the fall of the Roman Empire in A.D. 476 to the beginning of the Renaissance in the 1300s, religion became a dominant social force, heralding a period of more humane treatment of individuals with disabilities. Churches established monasteries and asylums as sanctuaries for persons with intellectual disabilities. Children with mental retardation were often called *les enfants du bon dieu* ("the children of God"). Infanticide was rarely practiced because the largely agrarian societies required many workers in the fields. In some instances, individuals thought to be mentally retarded found their way into castles where, though protected and shown favor, they served as buffoons and court jesters entertaining the nobility (Gargiulo, 1985). King Henry II of England enacted a policy in the twelfth century, *de praerogative regis* ("of the king's prerogative"), whereby "natural fools" became the king's wards (Drew & Hardman, 2007).

At the same time, it was an era in which fear and superstition ran rampant. People with mental retardation were frequently thought to be "filled with Satan" and to possess demonic powers, which often led to torture and death for practicing witchcraft. It was not uncommon for individuals with intellectual disabilities to be sent to prison and kept in chains because they were perceived to be a danger to society and their behavior unalterable.

Early Optimism

The beginning of the "modern" period in the history of mental retardation traces its roots to the early nineteenth century. It was during this period that the groundbreaking work of Jean-Marc Itard (1774–1838) occurred. Recall from Chapter 1 that his pioneering efforts with Victor, the so-called *homme sauvage* or "wild man," earned him the title Father of Special Education. His systematic attempts at educating Victor, whom he believed to be a victim of social/educational deprivation, signals the start of the notion that individuals with mental retardation are capable of learning—however limited it may be.

Edouard Seguin (1812–1880) was inspired by the work of his mentor, Itard. Based on his religious convictions, Seguin advocated fervently for the education of children with intellectual disabilities. In 1837, Seguin established the first school in Paris for the education of children with mental retardation. Because of the political turmoil in France in the mid-1800s, Seguin emigrated in 1848 to the United States, where he played a principal role in helping to establish residential facilities for persons with mental retardation in several states. In 1876, the Association of Medical Officers of American Institutions for Idiotic and Feeble-Minded Persons was established, with Seguin as its first president. This association was the forerunner of AAMR, now known as AAIDD, the American Association on Intellectual and Developmental Disabilities.

Protection and Pessimism

The late nineteenth and early twentieth centuries witnessed the development of large, geographically isolated institutions for the mentally retarded. The focus of these facilities changed as the invigorating optimism characteristic of the early 1800s generally gave way to disillusionment, fear, and pessimism (Morrison & Polloway, 1995). Institutions were overcrowded and understaffed. Their mission shifted from one of education and rehabilitation, as espoused by Seguin and others, to a new custodial role. Caring concern was slowly replaced by an unjustified concern with protecting society from individuals with intellectual disabilities.

One of the unfortunate consequences of this shift in societal attitude was that institutions became permanent residences for people with mental retardation; thus, they were no longer prepared for their eventual return to society (Drew & Hardman, 2007). Education and training functions virtually disappeared, and only the most rudimentary care was provided. Over time, these institutions deteriorated, becoming warehouses for society's unwanted citizens. Living conditions were harsh and often deplorable. This situation was poignantly captured by Blatt and Kaplan (1966) in their classic photographic essay on institutional life, *Christmas in Purgatory.*

Beginning in the 1960s, a highly visible call for more humane and normalized living arrangements for people with intellectual disabilities was issued. Initiated in Sweden by Nirje (1969), the principle of **normalization** emphasizes "making available to the mentally retarded patterns and conditions of everyday life which are as close as possible to the norms and patterns of the mainstream of society" (p. 181). In the United States, the idea that persons with mental retardation have a right to culturally normative experiences was championed by Wolfensberger (1972). This concept, coupled with a renaissance of societal concern for the mentally retarded, helped to facilitate a movement, beginning in the 1970s, toward **deinstitutionalization** and more community-based services for individuals who are mentally retarded. Today, legislative as well as legal action has resulted in more normalized lifestyles and greater access to all aspects of society for our fellow citizens with intellectual disabilities.

The Emergence of Public Education for Students with Mental Retardation

Although institutions were firmly established as part of the American social fabric in the late 1800s, public education for children with mental retardation was virtually nonexistent. The first public school class for "slow learning" youngsters was formed in Providence, Rhode Island, at the very end of the nineteenth century. Recall that these programs were largely segregated or self-contained classes and would remain so for the better part of the twentieth century. Classes for higher-functioning pupils with intellectual disabilities began to grow, in part as a result of the popularizing of IQ testing. Scheerenberger (1983) reports that by 1930, sixteen states had enacted either mandatory or permissive legislation regarding special classes for children with mental retardation. By 1952, forty-six of the forty-eight states provided an education to children with mental retardation. Youngsters with severe or profound mental retardation, however, were largely excluded from public education.

The 1960s and 1970s marked the beginning of an era of national concern for the rights of individuals, a focus that continues today. People with intellectual disabilities would benefit from this attention. Aided by the actions of President Kennedy, who had a sister with mental retardation, enlightened social policies, new educational programs, and a national research agenda were all forthcoming. At the same time, advances in the field of psychology and education demonstrated that, to some degree, all individuals with mental retardation are capable of learning. Professionals also began a movement toward less restrictive and more integrated educational placements for students with mental retardation—an emphasis with a very contemporary flavor. But perhaps the principal legacy of this era, which is foundational to today's educational programming, is a greater acceptance of persons with mental retardation and their right, as fellow citizens, to live their lives in the most normalized fashion.

Prevalence of Mental Retardation or Intellectual Disabilities

How many people in the United States are intellectually disabled? Although this may seem a relatively straightforward and factual question, in reality, it is somewhat difficult to answer. According to data from the U.S. Department of Education (2007), 545,492 children between the ages of 6 and 21 were identified as mentally retarded and receiving a special education during the 2005–2006 school year. These students represent approximately 9 percent of all pupils with disabilities and about 1 percent of the total school-age population. Although a figure of approximately 545,000 may seem large, over the years the number of students

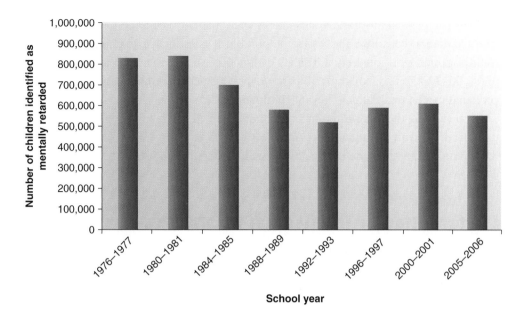

Figure 5.4

Changes in the Approximate Number of Children Classified as Mentally Retarded in Representative Years

NOTE: Enrollment figures represent children ages 6–21 served under Part B and Chapter 1.

SOURCE: Various U.S. Department of Education Annual Reports to Congress on the Implementation of IDEA.

classified as mentally retarded has decreased significantly. Since the enactment of PL 94-142 in 1975, almost 275,000 fewer pupils are being served in classes for individuals with mental retardation, representing a decrease of about 34 percent. Figure 5.4 documents this dramatic reduction.

The federal government, for the first time since the 1987–1988 school year, is now requiring states to report the number of preschoolers receiving a special education according to their disability label. This requirement represents a shift away from allowing states to use the term *developmentally delayed* when reporting preschoolers with disabilities. According to the U.S. Department of Education (2007), more than 22,700 preschoolers are recognized as being mentally retarded. This figure represents 3.2 percent of all youngsters with a disability.

There are several reasons for this downward shift in the number of school-age children classified as intellectually disabled. Prevention and early intervention efforts have certainly played a role in decreasing the number of children identified as mentally retarded. Other plausible explanations include changes in the definition of mental retardation, the impact of litigation (for example, *Diana v. State Board of Education* [1970]; *Larry P.* [1972]), changes in referral tactics, and the placement of higher-functioning students with intellectual disabilities into programs for pupils with learning disabilities. But perhaps the most compelling reason for the gradual reduction in the number of children classified as mentally retarded is a growing reluctance on the part of professionals to identify (or misidentify) youngsters as mildly mentally retarded, especially if they are from minority groups (Beirne-Smith et al., 2006; Oswald, Coutinho, Best, & Nguyen, 2001).

For many years, the federal government estimated the prevalence of intellectual disabilities in the general population to be about 3 percent. According to the President's Committee for People with Intellectual Disabilities (2007), approximately 7 to 8 million people in the United States have mental retardation, a figure that has not substantially changed in several decades. Mental retardation directly affects one out of ten American families. Researchers, however, have serious questions about the accuracy of the 3 percent prevalence figure. Most contemporary thinking suggests a prevalence figure closer to 1 percent of the general population (Beirne-Smith et al., 2006).

Within the population of individuals considered mentally retarded, persons with mild mental retardation constitute the largest proportion. It is estimated that approximately 90 percent of people with intellectual disabilities function, to use a familiar term, at the mild level (IQ 50–70/75). The remaining 10 percent are classified as exhibiting moderate, severe, or profound mental retardation (Drew & Hardman, 2007).

As you can see, the answer to our original question, "How many people are intellectually disabled?" is truly a difficult one. An objective answer to this query depends on many variables, suggesting that a definitive answer will likely remain elusive.

Etiology of Mental Retardation or Intellectual Disabilities

Determining the cause, or **etiology,** of mental retardation is a difficult process. An individual may be mentally retarded for a multitude of reasons, and often the cause is unknown. In fact, in only about half of all cases of intellectual disabilities can a specific cause be cited (Beirne-Smith et al., 2006). Generally speaking, the less severe the retardation, the greater is the likelihood that a particular cause cannot be determined.

Although scientists and other researchers are unable to determine the etiology of mental retardation in every instance, we do know a great deal about what causes mental retardation or is at least implicated as a possible etiological factor. Investigators have designed several different schemes or models for classifying known and/or suspected causes of intellectual disabilities. For the purpose of this discussion, we have adopted the AAMR (Luckasson et al., 2002) format for categorizing etiological factors typically associated with mental retardation. The 2002 AAMR model designates three main sources of possible causes of mental retardation, based on the time of onset: **prenatal** (occurring before birth), **perinatal** (occurring around the time of birth), and **postnatal** (occurring after birth). Table 5.4 identifies some of the variables that often lead to intellectual disabilities.

Prenatal Contributions

Even a quick glance at Table 5.4 suggests that many different factors, of various origins, contribute to the possibility that a developing fetus may be at risk for mental retardation. In some instances, mental retardation will be an inescapable fact; in other cases, it is highly probable. Fortunately, researchers are making great strides in the areas of detection and prevention of certain types of intellectual disabilities.

CHROMOSOMAL ABNORMALITIES **Down syndrome,** the most common and perhaps best-known genetic disorder, was first described by Dr. John Langdon Down in 1866; however, it was not until 1959 that Down syndrome was linked to a chromosomal abnormality (Lejune, Gautier, & Turpin, 1959). Most people have forty-six chromosomes arranged in twenty-three pairs; people with Down syndrome have forty-seven. Chromosomes are rod- or threadlike bodies that carry the genes that provide the blueprint or building blocks for development. About 5 percent of all people with mental retardation have Down syndrome (Beirne-Smith et al., 2006). The most common type of Down syndrome, accounting for approximately 90 percent of cases, is known as trisomy 21. In this instance, an extra chromosome becomes attached to the twenty-first pair, with the result that there are three (tri) chromosomes at this particular site.

Table 5.4		Possible Causes of Mental Retardation			
Prenatal Factors	**Examples**	**Perinatal Factors**	**Examples**	**Postnatal Factors**	**Examples**
Chromosomal abnormalities	• Down syndrome • Fragile X syndrome • Turner syndrome	Gestational disorders	• Low birth weight • Prematurity	Infections and intoxicants	• Lead poisoning • Encephalitis • Meningitis • Reye's syndrome
Metabolic and nutritional disorders	• Phenylketonuria • Tay-Sachs disease • Galactosemia • Prader-Willi syndrome	Neonatal complications	• Hypoxia • Birth trauma • Seizures • Respiratory distress • Breech delivery • Prolonged delivery	Environmental factors	• Child abuse/ neglect • Head trauma • Malnutrition • Environmental deprivation
Maternal infections	• Rubella • Syphilis • HIV (AIDS) • Cytomegalovirus • Rh incompatability • Toxoplasmosis			Brain damage	• Neurofibromatosis • Tuberous sclerosis
Environmental conditions	• Fetal alcohol syndrome • Illicit drug use				
Unknown influences	• Anencephaly • Hydrocephalus • Microcephaly				

Scientists are uncertain as to exactly what causes Down syndrome. Thyroid problems, drugs, and exposure to radiation are all suspected, but there appears to be a strong link between maternal age and Down syndrome. It is estimated that at age 25, the incidence of Down syndrome is about 1 out of 1,250 births; at age 30, 1 in 1,000 births; at age 35, 1 in 400 births; at age 40, 1 in 100 births; and for women at age 45, the risk is about 1 out of 20 (March of Dimes, 2007; Roizen, 2007). It is important to note that age itself does not cause Down syndrome, only that there is a strong correlation. Down syndrome affects all racial and socioeconomic groups equally.

Down syndrome most often results in mild to moderate mental retardation. In some instances, however, individuals may be severely retarded, and in others, near normal intelligence is possible. Besides intellectual disabilities, this chromosomal aberration frequently results in other health concerns such as heart defects, hearing loss, intestinal malformations, vision problems, and an increased risk for thyroid difficulties and leukemia (March of Dimes, 2007).

People with Down syndrome have distinctive physical characteristics. Among the most commonly observed features are an upper slant of the eyes, short stature, flat nose, somewhat smaller ears and nose, an enlarged and sometimes protruding tongue, short fingers, reduced muscle tone, and a single crease (Simian crease) across the palm of the hand (people without Down syndrome have parallel lines). Most individuals with Down syndrome will exhibit some, but not all, of these identifying characteristics.

Down syndrome most often results in mild to moderate mental retardation.

Life expectancies for people with Down syndrome have increased dramatically. In the 1920s and 1930s, the life span for a child with Down syndrome was generally less than 10 years; today, thanks to advances in medicine and health care, large numbers of individuals with Down syndrome are living well into their mid-50s (March of Dimes, 2007). With advancing chronological age, however, Bush and Beail (2004) note that these people face a greater risk for developing Alzheimer's disease.

Fragile X syndrome is one of the more recently identified conditions linked to mental retardation. This syndrome affects approximately 1 in 4,000 males (Mazzocco, 2000) and at least half as many females (Crawford, Acuna, & Sherman, 2001), making it one of the leading inherited causes of mental retardation (Taylor, Richards, & Brady, 2005). Because of the involvement of the X chromosome, this condition, which is caused by an abnormal or defective gene, predominantly affects males, although females can be carriers of the gene that causes it.

Individuals who have this disorder have a deficiency in the structure of the X chromosome of the twenty-third pair. Under a microscope, one of the "arms" of the X chromosome appears pinched or weakened and thus fragile. Females, who have two X chromosomes, are less susceptible to the defective gene; males, who have one X and one Y chromosome, are substantially at risk.

Typical characteristics associated with this syndrome include cognitive deficits of varying degrees, a long narrow face, large ears, prominent forehead, and large head circumference. At puberty, enlarged testicles are present (Meyer, 2007). Behaviorally, individuals with Fragile X syndrome typically exhibit attention disorders, self-stimulatory behaviors, and speech and language problems. Meyer reports that about one-third of girls with this disorder have mild mental retardation or learning disabilities. The Fragile X syndrome also appears to be associated with other disabilities such as autism and disorders of attention (Beirne-Smith et al., 2006).

METABOLIC AND NUTRITIONAL DISORDERS Phenylketonuria, more commonly known by its acronym, **PKU,** is an example of an inborn error of metabolism. It is a recessive trait, meaning that both parents have to be carriers of the defective gene. When this occurs, there is a 25 percent chance that the infant will be born with PKU. There is an equal probability, however, that the baby will be healthy (and a 50 percent chance it will be an asymptomatic carrier). PKU appears in about 1 out of every 10,000 to 15,000 births and is most common among Northern European ethnic groups.

PKU affects the way an infant's body processes or metabolizes protein. Affected babies lack the liver enzyme needed to process phenylalanine, which is common in many high-protein foods such as milk. As a result of this deficiency, phenylalanine accumulates in the bloodstream and becomes toxic. This metabolic malfunction, if not promptly treated, leads to brain damage and mental retardation, which is often severe.

Elevated levels of phenylalanine can be detected in the blood and urine of newborns within the first few days of life. All states now routinely screen for this disorder, although it is not a mandatory procedure in all instances. If unusually high levels of phenylalanine are found, the infant is placed on a special diet, reducing the intake of protein. Researchers have found that if dietary restrictions are introduced within the first three weeks of life, the devastating consequences of PKU are significantly minimized and normal developmental milestones are usually achieved (Channon, German, Cassina, & Lee, 2004). It is unclear, however, how long the dietary restrictions must be maintained. As individuals with PKU get older, dietary control becomes more difficult. Of particular concern are women of childbearing age who have PKU. The metabolic imbalances within these women can cause serious consequences to the developing fetus. In more than 90 percent of these pregnancies, babies are born with mental retardation and heart defects, and they are usually of low birth weight. However, returning to an individualized, restricted diet prior to pregnancy and maintaining it throughout pregnancy usually results in a healthy baby (March of Dimes, 2004). Awareness of this concern has resulted in warning labels on many popular food items such as diet soft drinks and some low-fat foods ("Caution: product contains phenylalanine").

Galactosemia is another example of an inborn error of metabolism. In this disorder, infants are unable to process galactose, a form of sugar, typically found in milk and other food products. Manifestation of this condition in newborns typically includes jaundice, liver damage, heightened susceptibility to infections, failure to thrive, vomiting, and cataracts, along with impaired intellectual functioning (Drew & Hardman, 2007). If galactosemia is detected early, a milk-free diet can be started, which substantially reduces the potential for problems and delays.

MATERNAL INFECTIONS Viruses and infections often cause intellectual disabilities and a host of other problems. While pregnant, a woman and her developing child are very susceptible to a wide variety of potentially damaging infections. Exposure during the first trimester of pregnancy usually results in severe consequences. **Rubella** (German measles) is a good example of this type of infection. This mild but highly contagious illness has been linked to mental retardation, vision and hearing defects, heart problems, and low birth weight. Rubella is one of the leading causes of multiple impairments in children. With the introduction of a rubella vaccine in 1969, instances of rubella-related disabilities have substantially decreased.

Sexually transmitted diseases such as gonorrhea and **syphilis** are capable of crossing the placenta and attacking the central nervous system of the developing fetus. In contrast to rubella, the risk to the unborn child is greater at the later stages of fetal development.

Acquired immune deficiency syndrome (**AIDS**), which is attributed to the human immunodeficiency virus (HIV), is another probable cause of mental retardation and other developmental delays. Generally transmitted via unprotected sexual intercourse with an infected person or the sharing of hypodermic needles, the HIV virus crosses the placenta and affects the central nervous system while also damaging the immune system, leaving the fetus substantially at risk for opportunistic infections. Pediatric AIDS is suspected of being a leading infectious cause of intellectual disabilities. At the same time, HIV is the single most preventable cause of infectious mental retardation.

Maternal–fetal **Rh incompatibility,** although technically not an infection, is another potential cause of mental retardation. At one time, this disease was a leading cause of mental retardation, affecting approximately 20,000 infants annually. Since 1968, there has been a dramatic reduction in the number of cases of Rh disease, thanks to the development of a treatment that usually prevents its occurrence (March of Dimes, 2001). Simply stated, Rh disease is a blood group incompatibility between a mother and her unborn child. This discrepancy is the result of the Rh factor, a protein found on the surface of red blood cells. Rh-positive blood contains this protein; Rh-negative blood cells do not (Beirne-Smith et al., 2006).

Rh incompatibility often leads to serious consequences such as intellectual disabilities, cerebral palsy, epilepsy, and other neonatal complications. The problem arises when an Rh-negative mother carries an Rh-positive baby, which causes her to produce antibodies against any future Rh-positive fetus. For this reason, Rh-negative women today generally receive an injection of Rh immune globulin within 72 hours of delivering an Rh-positive baby. In the vast majority of cases, this procedure prevents the production of antibodies, thus preventing problems in any future pregnancies.

Toxoplasmosis is a further example of maternal infection that typically poses grave risks to an unborn child. Toxoplasmosis is contracted through exposure to cat fecal matter; it is also present in undercooked or raw meat and raw eggs. If the mother is exposed to this parasitic infection during pregnancy, especially in the third trimester, it is very likely that fetal infection will occur. Infected infants may be born with intellectual disabilities, cerebral palsy, damaged retinas leading to blindness, microcephaly (unusually small head), enlarged liver and spleen, jaundice, and other very serious complications. Antibiotics seem to provide some defense for both mother and child.

Our final illustration of maternal infections is **cytomegalovirus** (CMV), an especially common virus that is part of the herpes group. Most women have been exposed to this virus at some time in their lives and thus develop immunity. If initial exposure occurs during pregnancy, however, the fetus may be severely affected. CMV often leads to brain damage and thus mental retardation, blindness, and hearing impairments.

ENVIRONMENTAL CONTRIBUTIONS Many unsafe maternal behaviors—among them, smoking, illicit drug use (for example, cocaine, heroin), and the consumption of alcohol before and during pregnancy—have been linked to impaired fetal development. The use of alcohol, in particular, has captured the attention of scientists and researchers for many years. In 1973, the term **fetal alcohol syndrome,** or FAS, was first coined (Jones, Smith, Ulleland, & Streissguth, 1973). Currently, FAS is one of the leading causes of mental retardation in the United States (Davidson & Myers, 2007). Each year approximately 40,000 babies are born with some degree of alcohol-associated damage or defect (March of Dimes, 2005).

Alcohol can damage the central nervous system of the unborn child, and brain damage is not uncommon. FAS is characterized by a variety of physical deformities, including facial abnormalities, heart defects, low birth weight, and motor dysfunctions. In addition to mild to moderate intellectual disabilities, attention disorders and behavioral problems are usually present. Less severe and more subtle forms of alcohol-related damage are recognized as **fetal alcohol effect** (FAE). The effects of excessive alcohol consumption last a lifetime; yet this condition is entirely preventable.

UNKNOWN INFLUENCES Several types of cranial malformations are the result of unknown prenatal factors. **Anencephaly** is but one illustration. In this condition, a large portion or the entire brain fails to develop properly, with devastating consequences for the infant. A more common condition is **microcephaly,** characterized by an unusually small head and severe retardation. **Hydrocephalus** is a disorder associated with the interference or blockage of the flow of cerebrospinal fluid, resulting in an accumulation of excess fluid that typically leads to an enlarged cranial cavity and potentially damaging compression on the brain. Doctors can surgically implant shunts that remove the excess fluid, thereby minimizing the pressure on the infant's brain and consequently the severe effects of this condition.

Perinatal Conditions

GESTATIONAL DISORDERS The two most common problems associated with gestational disorders are **low birth weight** and **premature birth.** Prematurity is generally defined as a birth that occurs prior to 37 weeks of gestation. Low birth weight is defined as less than 5 pounds, 5 ounces (2500 grams), and very low birth weight as less than 3 pounds, 5 ounces (1500 grams). In the majority of instances, but not all, low birth weight infants are premature. Not all babies with gestational disorders will have a disability or encounter future difficulties in school. However, some of these children may develop subtle learning problems, some may be mentally retarded, and still others may have sensory and motor impairments.

NEONATAL COMPLICATIONS Complications surrounding the birth process may cause intellectual disabilities and other developmental delays. One common example is **anoxia** (oxygen deprivation) or **hypoxia** (insufficient oxygen). Anoxia may occur because of damage to the umbilical cord or as a result of a prolonged and difficult delivery. Obstetrical or **birth trauma,** such as the improper use of forceps, may cause excessive pressure on the skull, which in turn may damage a portion of the infant's brain. A **breech presentation** is another illustration of a neonatal problem. In a breech delivery, the infant exits the birth canal buttocks first instead of the more typical headfirst presentation. This fetal delivery position raises concerns about the possibility of damage to the umbilical cord and a heightened threat of injury to the baby's head because of the greater intensity and frequency of uterine contractions later in the birth process. Worries about the infant's skull also arise when a **precipitous birth** (one lasting less than two hours) occurs. The gentle molding of the skull may not take place during a precipitous birth, thus increasing the risk of tissue damage and intellectual disabilities (Drew & Hardman, 2007).

Postnatal Factors

INFECTIONS AND INTOXICANTS Lead and mercury are two examples of environmental toxins that can cause mental retardation. **Lead poisoning** is a serious public health problem. Because of its highly toxic nature, lead is no longer used in the manufacturing of gasoline or paint. But even though it is no longer commercially available, some youngsters are still at risk for lead poisoning. Children who live in older homes or apartments may ingest lead by eating peeling paint chips containing lead. Lead poisoning can cause seizures, brain damage, and disorders of the central nervous system.

Infections represent another source of concern for young children. **Meningitis,** a viral infection, causes damage to the covering of the brain known as the meninges. Meningitis

Complications surrounding the birth process may cause mental retardation and other developmental delays.

may result from complications associated with typical childhood diseases such as mumps, measles, or chicken pox. Because it is capable of causing brain damage, mental retardation is a distinct possibility. Equally devastating is **encephalitis,** which is an inflammation of the brain tissue. Encephalitis may cause damage to the central nervous system and can result from complications of infections typically associated with childhood such as mumps or measles.

ENVIRONMENTAL FACTORS A wide variety of environmental or psychosocial influences are often associated with intellectual disabilities, especially instances of mild mental retardation. Debilitating factors may include nutritional problems, adverse living conditions, inadequate health care, and a lack of early cognitive stimulation. Many of these factors are associated with lower socioeconomic status. Child abuse and neglect along with head trauma resulting from automobile accidents or play-related injuries are also potential contributing factors. Of course, not all children exposed to these traumatic postnatal situations become intellectually disabled. These illustrations only represent evidence correlated with, but not necessary causes of, mental retardation. It is perhaps best to think of these variables as interacting risk factors, with some children being more vulnerable than others. Fortunately, most children exposed to these unfavorable circumstances develop normally.

Although a large portion of mental retardation is attributed to environmental factors, contemporary thinking suggests that mental retardation associated with psychosocial influences is the result of *interaction* between environmental and genetic or biological contributions. Stated another way, a youngster's genetic endowment provides a range of intellectual opportunity that is then mediated by the environment to which that individual is exposed.

As you can see, the question "What causes intellectual disabilities?" is indeed a difficult one to answer. Many variables must be considered, and in many cases, we just don't know why a particular child is retarded. Perhaps the more intriguing question to ask is, "Can we prevent mental retardation?"

Prevention of Mental Retardation or Intellectual Disabilities

Prevention of mental retardation has been a goal of scientists, medical researchers, and a host of other professionals for several decades. In many instances, unfortunately, the cause of mental retardation is still unknown. Let us focus our attention, however, on the accomplishments. Each year, thanks to advances in medical research, we prevent approximately:

- 250 cases of intellectual disabilities due to PKU because of newborn screening and dietary intervention;
- 1,000 cases of mental retardation due to congenital hypothyroidism, also as a result of newborn screening and the use of thyroid hormone replacement therapy;
- 1,000 cases of mental retardation by using Rh immune globulin (Rhogam) to prevent Rh disease and severe jaundice;
- 5,000–7,000 cases of intellectual disabilities caused by Hib meningitis by using the Hib vaccine; and
- 4,000 cases of mental retardation resulting from measles, largely due to vaccination efforts and greater public awareness. (Alexander, 1998);

Other examples of successful preventive efforts include the removal of lead, a highly toxic substance, from gasoline and paint. Additionally, legislation mandating the use of car seats or seat belts and encouraging children to wear bicycle helmets has helped to reduce the incidence of head trauma as a possible cause of mental retardation. Obviously, the more we know about the etiology of intellectual disabilities, the better our chances are of preventing it.

Researchers typically identify three levels of prevention: primary, secondary, and tertiary. According to Graham and Scott (1988), **primary prevention** refers to eliminating the problem before its onset or occurrence; **secondary prevention** aims at minimizing or eliminating a potential risk factor; and **tertiary prevention** seeks to limit the adverse consequences of an existing problem while maximizing a person's potential. From a different perspective, Luckasson et al. (1992) write that

> primary prevention efforts are directed toward the parents of the person with mental retardation or the person who might otherwise develop a condition which would result in mental retardation. Secondary prevention efforts are directed toward the person who is born with a condition that might otherwise result in mental retardation. Tertiary prevention efforts are directed toward the person who has mental retardation. (p. 72)

An example of primary prevention would be heightening the awareness of pregnant women about the potential dangers of smoking and alcohol use while pregnant. Good prenatal health care, prevention of child abuse, and genetic counseling prior to conception also illustrate primary prevention tactics. After a child is conceived, the fetus can be analyzed for genetic or chromosomal abnormalities through medical procedures known as **amniocentesis, chorionic villus sampling** (CVS), and a noninvasive test, **ultrasound.** These three tests are all viewed as primary prevention measures.

Chorionic villus sampling is a diagnostic procedure usually performed at about ten to twelve weeks of gestation. With this procedure, which has only been available since 1983, chorionic tissue or placenta material is sampled for chromosomal or genetic birth defects. Although CVS is slightly more risky than amniocentesis, detection of defects occurs earlier in fetal development.

In the vast majority of instances, these prenatal biochemical analyses do not reveal the presence of a disorder or defect. When the results are positive, however, and indicate that the fetus has, for example, Down syndrome, parents are confronted with a decision as to whether to terminate the pregnancy (called an elective or **therapeutic abortion**) or to begin planning and preparation for an infant who will most likely be disabled. These are very difficult and often painful decisions involving a variety of moral and ethical dilemmas.

Finally, ultrasound is a mapping or imaging of the fetus accomplished by a procedure much like sonar. This test can be done anytime during the pregnancy and without risk to the baby. Ultrasound is useful for detecting hydrocephalus, defects in the development of limbs, and in some cases, central nervous system defects such as **spina bifida.**

The screenings of newborns for PKU and galactosemia shortly after birth are representative of secondary prevention. PKU screening, which has been available since 1957, is a relatively inexpensive test that allows health care professionals to establish dietary controls and thus halt the effects of this inherited genetic disorder. Surgical implantation of a shunt to remove excess fluid around the brain in instances of hydrocephalus also illustrates secondary prevention efforts.

Tertiary prevention strategies are aimed at maximizing the quality of life for a person with mental retardation. Early intervention for a toddler with Down syndrome, inclusive education programs for school-age children with mental retardation, and comprehensive community-based services for adults with intellectual disabilities are examples of tertiary efforts across the life span.

Research holds the key to new opportunities for preventing various types of mental retardation. Two promising areas are fetal treatments, involving in utero intervention for certain defects, and gene therapy, which is designed to correct genetic flaws. Only time will tell how successful we will be in preventing some forms of mental retardation.

Characteristics of Individuals with Mental Retardation or Intellectual Disabilities

When discussing characteristics common to people with mental retardation, it is important to remember that although, as a group, they may exhibit a particular feature, not all individuals identified as mentally retarded will share this characteristic. Persons with intellectual disabilities are an especially heterogeneous population; interindividual differences are considerable. Many factors influence individual behavior and functioning—among them, chronological age, the severity and etiology of the disability, and educational opportunities. We caution you to remember that the following descriptions represent generalizations and are only useful for framing this discussion. Finally, in several ways, individuals with mental retardation are more like their nonretarded counterparts than they are different, sharing many of the same social, emotional, and physical needs.

Learning Characteristics

The most common defining characteristic of someone identified as intellectually disabled is impaired cognitive functioning which, you may recall, can vary greatly. Investigators are typically not concerned with the person's intellectual ability per se but rather with the impact that lower IQ has on the individual's ability to learn, acquire concepts, process information, and apply knowledge in various settings such as school and community. Scientists do not yet fully understand the complexity of the learning process in human beings. Learning is a difficult concept to define—in many ways, it is unique to the individual—and is composed of many interrelated cognitive processes. Learning, then, is not a unitary variable. We have chosen, therefore, to briefly examine several of the characteristics that researchers believe influence learning.

Some students with intellectual disabilities experience difficulty learning because they fail to attend to the relevant attributes of the task.

ATTENTION Attention, which is a multidimensional concept, plays a key role in learning. Many of the learning difficulties of individuals with mental retardation are thought to be due to attentional deficits. Before learning a task, a person must be able to attend to its relevant attributes. Tomporowski and Tinsley (1997) theorize that individuals who are mentally retarded experience difficulty focusing their attention, maintaining it, and selectively attending to relevant stimuli. They also have less attention to allocate. It may well be that children with intellectual disabilities perform poorly on certain learning tasks because they do not know how to attend to the relevant aspects or dimensions of the problem.

MEMORY Memory, which is an important component of learning, is often impaired in children with mental retardation. Generally speaking, the more severe the retardation, the greater are the deficits in memory (Drew & Hardman, 2007). Early investigators researching memory processes of individuals with mental retardation frequently distinguished between short-term memory (STM)—data recalled after a few seconds or hours—and long-term memory (LTM), the retrieval of information days or months later. Early experiments suggested that persons who are intellectually disabled experience difficulty with STM learning tasks (recalling directions in sequence) (Ellis, 1963); however, when LTM is assessed (recalling their telephone number or address), individuals with mental retardation perform comparably with their nonretarded peers (Belmont, 1966). Unfortunately, many of these early investigative efforts were plagued by methodological flaws, making interpretation of the results difficult. Contemporary researchers have shifted their attention away from an LTM versus STM model to one that considers memory as an important component of an information processing model.

Researchers have identified several factors that may contribute to the memory difficulties of persons with intellectual disabilities. Among them are problems attending to relevant stimuli (Westling & Fox, 2004); inefficient rehearsal strategies; and an inability to generalize skills to novel settings or tasks (Tomporowski & Tinsley, 1997).

ACADEMIC PERFORMANCE As you might anticipate, students with mental retardation encounter difficulties in their academic work. Generally, this deficiency is seen across all subject areas, but reading appears to be the weakest area, especially reading comprehension (Katims, 2000). Pupils identified as mentally retarded are also deficient in arithmetic, but their performance is more in line with their mental age (Drew & Hardman, 2007). Remember, just because a student is not academically successful does not mean that he or she cannot excel in other school endeavors such as athletics or the arts.

MOTIVATION Despite its importance for understanding individuals who are intellectually disabled, motivational factors have not received the attention they deserve (Morrison & Polloway, 1995). Yet these variables are crucial for understanding the discrepancy that often exists between an individual's performance and his or her actual ability. It is not unusual for children with mental retardation to approach a learning situation with heightened anxiety. A history of failure in earlier encounters contributes to this generalized feeling of apprehension; consequently, pupils seem to be less goal oriented and lacking in motivation.

Past experiences with failure typically lead individuals with intellectual disabilities to exhibit an **external locus of control**; that is, they are likely to believe that the consequences or outcomes of their behavior are the result of circumstances and events beyond their personal control, rather than their own efforts. Repeated episodes of failure also give rise to a related concept, **learned helplessness** (Seligman, 1992)—the perception that no matter how much effort they put forth, failure is inevitable. ("No matter how hard I try, I won't be successful!") This expectancy of failure frequently causes students with mental retardation to stop trying, even when the task is one they are capable of completing. Educators sometimes refer to this behavior as the "pencil down syndrome."

Accumulated experiences with failure also result in a style of learning and problem solving characterized as **outer-directedness,** or a loss of confidence and trust in one's own abilities and solutions and a reliance on others for cues and guidance (Bybee & Zigler, 1998). While not solely limited to individuals with intellectual disabilities, this overreliance on others contributes to a lack of motivation and increased dependence. Once again, the origin of this behavior can be traced to the debilitating effects of repeated failure.

GENERALIZATION It is not unusual for individuals with mental retardation to experience difficulty in transferring or **generalizing** knowledge acquired in one context to new or different settings. In a large number of instances, learning in someone who is mentally retarded is situation specific; that is, once a particular skill or behavior is mastered, the individual has difficulty duplicating the skill when confronted with novel circumstances—different cues, different people, or different environments (Langone, Clees, Oxford, Malone, & Ross, 1995). Therefore, teachers must plan for generalization; typically it does not occur automatically. Generalization of responses can be facilitated, for example, by using concrete materials rather than abstract representations; by providing instruction in various settings where the strategies or skill will typically be used; by incorporating a variety of examples and materials; or by simply informing the pupils of the multiple applications that are possible.

LANGUAGE DEVELOPMENT Speech and language development are closely related to cognitive functioning. In fact, speech and language difficulties are more common among individuals with mental retardation than in their nonretarded counterparts (Warren & Yoder, 1997). Given the association between intellectual ability and speech and language, it is not surprising that students with intellectual disabilities experience a great deal of difficulty with academic tasks, such as reading, that require verbal and language competency.

Speech disorders are common among individuals with mental retardation. These may include errors of articulation such as additions or distortions, fluency disorders (stuttering), and voice disorders such as hypernasal speech or concerns about loudness. In fact, researchers have found that speech and language difficulties are a fairly common secondary disability among students with intellectual disabilities (Beirne-Smith et al., 2006).

Despite the prevalence of speech disorders, language problems are receiving increased attention from professionals because deficits in this arena are highly debilitating. There is a strong correlation between intellectual ability and language development—the higher the IQ, the less pervasive the language disorder. Although children with mental retardation, especially those with higher IQs, acquire language in the same fashion as their nonretarded peers, development occurs more slowly, their vocabulary is more limited, and grammatical structure and sentence complexity are often impaired (Morrison & Polloway, 1995). Yet language is crucial for the independent functioning of the individual with intellectual disabilities. Deficits in this area represent one of the greatest obstacles hindering the integration of people with mental retardation into the mainstream of society (Owens, 2002).

Social and Behavioral Characteristics

The ability to get along with other people is an important skill; and it is just as significant for individuals who are mentally retarded as it is for those who are nonretarded. In fact, in some situations, social adeptness or proficiency may be as important, if not more important, than intellectual ability. In the area of employment, for example, when workers with intellectual disabilities experience difficulty on the job, it is frequently due to problems of social interactions with coworkers and supervisors rather than job performance per se (Butterworth & Strauch, 1994).

Individuals with intellectual delays often exhibit poor interpersonal skills and socially inappropriate or immature behavior; as a result, they frequently encounter rejection by peers and classmates. It is not unusual for individuals with mental retardation to lack the social competency necessary to establish and maintain friendships with coworkers and others (Chadsey-Rusch, 1992). Greenspan and Love (1997) note that the success or failure of students with intellectual disabilities who are placed in general education classrooms is often determined by their social skills. This lack of social ability can pose significant difficulties as increasing numbers of individuals with mental retardation are seizing the opportunity to participate in more normalized environments. Direct social skill instruction is one way of enhancing the social development of persons who are mentally retarded. Behavior modification techniques can reduce inappropriate social behaviors while establishing more desirable and acceptable behaviors. The modeling of the appropriate behavior of classmates is another way that students with intellectual disabilities can acquire more socially attractive behaviors, which in turn can lead to greater peer acceptance.

Educational Considerations

Educators and other professionals no longer consider students with mental retardation to be uneducable. Children who are retarded are capable of learning. To be successful, however, they require an instructional program that is individualized to meet their unique needs. Additionally, the instruction provided to these learners must be comprehensive and functional, equipping them, to the maximum extent possible, with the experiences they need to live and work in their respective communities, both now and in the future. As with other pupils, our goal as teachers should be one of developing independence and self-sufficiency. Obviously, for this population of children, this objective dictates that an education be interpreted broadly and not construed solely as academic learning. As we explore the issue of educational opportunities for individuals who are mentally retarded, you will discover that the concepts of individualization and appropriateness are of paramount importance.

In this part of the chapter, we will explore the various educational options available to children who are intellectually disabled and where these services are delivered. Our focus here is on school-age individuals; preschool and adult programming will be addressed in later sections.

Where Are Students with Mental Retardation or Intellectual Disabilities Educated?

Despite the contemporary trend toward educating children with disabilities in more normalized settings, pupils with mental retardation are more than three times as likely as other students with exceptionalities to be educated in a separate class. Only 16.6 percent of all individuals with disabilities were educated in self-contained classrooms during the 2005–2006 school year, but 50 percent of youngsters with mental retardation were placed in this environment (U.S. Department of Education, 2007). Historically speaking, this administrative arrangement has characterized the delivery of educational services to pupils who are intellectually disabled. Over the years, the U.S. Department of Education has chronicled this national trend. In 1991, for example, they found that only about 6 percent of students identified as mentally retarded were educated in the general education classroom, with an additional 22 percent being served in a resource room. A separate classroom was the placement of choice for more than half (59%) of these pupils, and 10 percent were receiving services in a separate school. A 1995 Department of Education survey found a similar, albeit improving, placement pattern. Approximately 7 percent of students with intellectual disabilities were assigned to the general education classroom, and some 27 percent attended a resource room. Thus, about one-third of the youngsters with mental retardation spent at least part of their educational day in the general education classroom, but more than 57 percent of these students received services in a self-contained classroom and 8 percent attended a separate school. More recent national data (see Figure 5.5) reflect greater opportunities for participation in more normalized placements, but in the eyes of many authorities and advocates, much still needs to be done toward having children with mental retardation educated in less restrictive settings.

Educational Programming Options

Generally speaking, educational programming for pupils who are intellectually disabled reflects a marriage of various emphasis areas or focal points. Among these concentrations

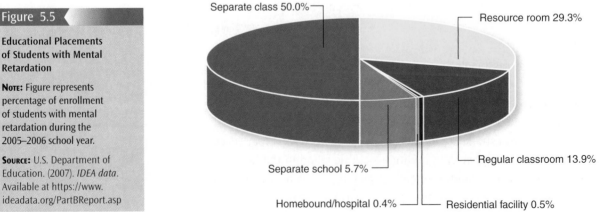

Figure 5.5

Educational Placements of Students with Mental Retardation

Note: Figure represents percentage of enrollment of students with mental retardation during the 2005–2006 school year.

Source: U.S. Department of Education. (2007). *IDEA data*. Available at https://www.ideadata.org/PartBReport.asp

Separate class 50.0%

Resource room 29.3%

Regular classroom 13.9%

Separate school 5.7%

Homebound/hospital 0.4%

Residential facility 0.5%

are functional academic skills, vocational training, community living, and self-help skills, along with a growing emphasis on exposure to the general education curriculum. Of course, the individual needs of the student must dictate how a specific educational program is constructed. Remember, children with mental retardation represent an especially heterogeneous population of learners with a wide range of skills and abilities. The curriculum designed for these pupils must be individualized, functional, and comprehensive (Beirne-Smith et al., 2006). In addition, instructional programming for the intellectually disabled must be forward looking, giving due consideration to these students' current needs and future life goals.

We cannot stress enough the importance of individually crafted instructional programs. A "one size fits all" approach for instructing individuals with intellectual disabilities is inappropriate. Effective curriculum must not only be individualized, emphasizing academic as well as adaptive skills; it must also be comprehensive (Drew & Hardman, 2007). A comprehensive curriculum for learners with cognitive limitations (Polloway, Patton, & Serna, 2008) should, among other things,

- be responsive to the needs of the individual student at the current time;
- provide maximum interaction with nondisabled peers and access to the general education curriculum, while also attending to specific curricular needs missing in the general education curriculum;
- be based on a realistic assessment of adult outcomes; and
- be sensitive to diploma requirements and graduation goals.

FUNCTIONAL CURRICULUM A **functional curriculum** is one that instructs pupils in the life skills they require for successful daily living and prepares them for those situations and environments they will encounter upon leaving school. In a functional curriculum, academic skills are applied to everyday, practical life situations—for example, making change, following directions in a cookbook, reading washing instructions, or completing a job application. Known as **functional academics**, these skills are often the core of instructional programs for some individuals with mild or moderate mental retardation. Additionally, these students are exposed to curriculum content focusing on personal hygiene, independent living skills, community resources, and other issues that, collectively, are designed to enhance their current and future independence and successful adjustment (Johnson, 2005).

Several approaches are available for teaching functional academics. Two of the most commonly used strategies are functional, generalized skills useful for life routines and embedded academic skills appropriate to specific life situations. In some situations, however, it may be necessary to simply bypass academic instruction (Browder & Snell, 2000). Browder and Snell recommend that the IEP team consider the following six factors when selecting an instructional approach:

1. The student's preferences
2. The parent's preferences
3. The student's chronological age or number of years left in school
4. The student's current and future settings
5. The student's rate of learning academic skills
6. The student's other skill needs (p. 500)

A functional curriculum may be appropriate for some students with mental retardation.

Table 5.5 provides an example of the application of these instructional options.

A functional curriculum is concerned with the application of skills to real-life situations. This requires that instruction occur as much as possible in natural settings, using actual items rather than mere representations in simulated settings. This instructional technique, known as **community-based instruction,** is most appropriate for individuals with mental retardation. This strategy eliminates many of the difficulties that pupils with intellectual disabilities have when attempting to transfer and generalize skills learned in the classroom to other settings in which the skill is to be used. Simulated experiences, though useful, are often ineffective with this population. For example, reading a menu or shopping for groceries can easily be simulated in the classroom; however, it is generally more effective when these particular skills occur *in vivo,* or in the actual environment. Research suggests that students with mental retardation learn more efficiently and retain more if skill instruction occurs in a natural setting (Browder & Snell, 2000; Wehmeyer & Sailor, 2004).

Variations of a functional curriculum are also appropriate for individuals identified as moderately mentally retarded and, in some cases, for students considered severely retarded. As with their higher-functioning counterparts, areas of emphasis—or domains, as they are sometimes called—are individualized based on the current and future needs of the student. Typical domains include self-help skills, socialization, communication, and vocational

Table 5.5	Approaches for Teaching Functional Academics	
Academic Approach	**Learning Outcomes**	**Examples**
Functional, generalized skills usable across life routines	Student will learn some pivotal skills (e.g., useful word and number recognition and counting) and use them in home, school, and community activities.	Sharon is mastering generalized counting skills. She can count dollars to make a purchase, objects to do simple addition in math class, and ingredients when cooking with her mother. She not only learns sight words related to daily activities, such as following her schedule, but also learns high-frequency words that she uses in reading and other academic subjects.
Embedded academic skills usable in specific life routines	Student will acquire an academic response as part of a daily life routine (e.g., use money to buy school lunch; use time and word schedule to organize day).	Juan has a sight word vocabulary of five words. He uses each of these words in a specific way. For example, he finds his name on a set of job cards at his work site. He can select a sweatshirt that has the name of his school to wear on school spirit day.
Adaptations to bypass academic skills	Student will learn to use adaptations that avoid the need for an academic skill (e.g., money envelopes, bus passes).	Because it is difficult for Lauren to count money, her teacher helps her use a predetermined amount of money to make purchases (e.g., a dollar for a soda).

Source: Adapted from M. Snell and F. Brown, *Instruction of Students with Severe Disabilities*, 5th ed. (Upper Saddle River, NJ: Prentice Hall, 2000), p. 498.

training, along with using community resources and exposure to very basic or "survival" academics. An example of this last domain might include functional or environmental reading of survival words and phrases such as *danger, exit, on, off, gentlemen, detour, fire escape, don't walk, keep out, beware of dog,* and other key protective vocabulary. Equally useful are career and vocational terms identified by Schilit and Caldwell (1980). Their list of 100 important terms includes words such as *boss, wages, tools, break,* and *first aid.* Arithmetic concepts might stress quantitative concepts such as big/little or more/less, telling time, learning telephone numbers and addresses, calendar activities, money recognition, and other types of functional numerical concepts. As noted previously, instruction should occur in the community using natural settings to maximize the meaningfulness and relevancy of the instruction and to allow for the integration of skills from other domains (Browder & Snell, 2000). An illustration of this type of activity would be a trip to a local grocery store, where several different functional skills could be practiced. The goal of these activities, and others like them, is to decrease the students' dependence on others and to enhance their ability to live and work independently in their community.

STANDARDS-BASED CURRICULUM In some instances, a functional curriculum approach may not be appropriate. The needs of some individuals with intellectual disabilities may best be served by exposure to both traditional academic subjects—in other words, the general education curriculum—and life skills, depending on the needs of the student and the wishes of the parents. As children get older and progress through school, however, there is often a sense of urgency to incorporate a life skills curriculum in preparation for adulthood (Hickson, Blackman, & Reis, 1995). Yet one perplexing challenge confronting both general and special educators is how to blend or integrate the standards-based general education curriculum with a life skills curriculum (Hoover & Patton, 2004).

In many ways a functional curriculum runs counter to the basic tenets of the philosophy of full inclusion with its emphasis on age- and grade-appropriate placement. Does this philosophy mean that a student with intellectual disabilities should enroll, for example, in a geometry or foreign language class? In some instances, the answer might be yes; in other cases, this would be an inappropriate recommendation. We believe that all students with mental retardation should be integrated, to the maximum extent possible, in classrooms and activities with their same-age peers who are not disabled. The general education classroom, however, is not necessarily the appropriate learning environment for all pupils who are mentally retarded. Some pupils will achieve greater educational benefit from instruction in settings outside of school. The key to an appropriate education for students with intellectual disabilities is individualization. Just as all students in the general education classroom do not learn the same material, pupils who are mentally retarded must have their instructional program developed around their unique characteristics and specific educational requirements.

Instructional Methodology

Once a decision is made about *what* to teach, educators are then confronted with the question of *how* best to instruct their students. These important issues are interrelated. Decisions that professionals make about what and how to teach pupils who are mentally retarded are crucial for the students' success in school (Beirne-Smith et al., 2006). Here we will briefly examine representative instructional strategies that have proven effective with individuals who are intellectually disabled. But first we offer some general instructional suggestions (Christenson, Ysseldyke, & Thurlow, 1989) that have been shown to positively affect children's learning and performance in the classroom. (See the accompanying Suggestions for the Classroom.)

Suggestions for the Classroom

Characteristics of Effective Teachers

☑ Effective special educators have high expectations for their students; they *expect* their pupils to learn and succeed. Effective teachers establish realistic goals, monitor progress carefully and frequently, provide feedback, and reward successes.

☑ Skilled instructors individualize their instruction to meet the unique needs of each child, teaching the child *how* to learn as well as what to learn. Students are actively engaged and participate in the learning process. Teachers explicitly communicate why a particular skill or concept is important, when it is to be used, and how it should be applied. New learning is anchored to previously learned material. Lessons are well planned and carefully conceived so as to enhance student achievement. Positive academic outcomes are the result of instructional clarity.

☑ Effective teachers involve all children and interact frequently with them. Their teaching tactics are many and varied, designed to maintain pupil attention and elicit correct responses. Student performance is evaluated frequently, using multiple procedures. Data are used to assess student understanding of the material and to plan future lessons.

Instructional methodologies and accommodations that are often used with pupils who are mentally retarded are the same ones that make learning successful for *all* students (Friend & Bursuck, 2006). Friend and Bursuck believe that general educators are capable of reasonably accommodating in their classrooms most students with special needs, including pupils with intellectual disabilities. To accomplish this goal, they recommend the following seven steps, which they call INCLUDE:

- **I**dentify classroom environmental, curricular, and instructional demands.
- **N**ote student learning strengths and needs.
- **C**heck for potential areas of student success.
- **L**ook for potential problem areas.
- **U**se information gathered to brainstorm instructional adaptations.
- **D**ecide which adaptations to implement.
- **E**valuate student progress. (p. 148)

This generic model is applicable to a variety of classroom settings. It is based on the assumption that student performance is a result of the interaction between the learner's characteristics and the instructional environment. By skillfully analyzing the student's learning needs and the requirements of the classroom, teachers are often able to maximize student success and accomplishment.

Similarly, Smith and his colleagues (2008) recommend that teachers consider the following teaching and learning adaptations, which are designed to improve learning outcomes for students with mental retardation:

- Ensure attention to relevant task demands.
- Teach ways to learn content while teaching content itself.
- Focus on content that is meaningful to the students, to promote learning as well as to facilitate application.
- Provide training that crosses multiple learning and environmental contexts.
- Offer opportunities for active involvement in the learning process. (p. 233)

In our opinion, these suggestions are applicable to *all* pupils, not just individuals with intellectual disabilities.

TASK ANALYSIS We begin with an approach known as **task analysis,** which is often identified with a functional or life skills curriculum. A functional curriculum is a highly individualized, individually referenced model (Hickson et al., 1995) in which the teacher crafts each pupil's curriculum based on the skills and abilities that are part of the student's repertoire. In task analysis, which is part of a behavioral approach to instruction, a complex behavior or task is broken down and sequenced into its component parts (Alberto & Troutman, 2006). Task analysis, according to Alberto and Troutman, is the foundation for teaching complex functional and vocational skills to individuals with disabilities.

Alberto and Troutman (2006) offer working guidelines that define the basic steps for conducting a task analysis:

- Define target behavior or task.
- Identify the prerequisite skills for learning the task: "What does the student need to know?"

- Identify needed materials to perform the task.
- Observe a competent person performing the task, and list the steps necessary for successful task completion in sequential order.

We believe that an additional component is necessary. Teachers must take steps to ensure that the student is capable of generalizing the particular skill to other settings. Recall that this is part of the reasoning for teaching functional skills in their natural setting.

Researchers have used task analysis to teach a wide variety of daily living and vocational skills to individuals with varying degrees of cognitive impairment. Examples of these successful efforts include teaching food preparation skills to elementary students with moderate to severe mental retardation (Fiscus, Schuster, Morse, & Collins, 2002); teaching functional counting skills to young children with moderate to severe mental retardation (Xin & Holmdal, 2003); and teaching laundry skills to high school students with moderate mental retardation (Taylor, Collins, Schuster, & Kleinert, 2002).

COOPERATIVE LEARNING Cooperative learning is another instructional intervention that educators frequently employ, especially when teaching pupils with intellectual disabilities in inclusive or integrated settings. This strategy is growing in popularity and is considered a promising instructional approach (McMaster & Fuchs, 2002). Unlike most of today's classrooms, which tend to emphasize competition among students, cooperative learning encourages pupils with varying strengths and abilities to work together toward achieving a common goal. **Cooperative learning** can be defined as an instructional technique in which small, heterogeneous groups of learners are actively involved in jointly accomplishing an activity or assignment. The teacher structures the task in such a fashion that each pupil significantly contributes to the completion of the activity according to his or her ability. Although recognition and rewards are based on group performance, the success of each individual directly affects the accomplishments of their classmates (Johnson, Johnson, & Holubec, 1998).

Cooperative learning, which can take many different forms, can be used with any subject area; however, it requires careful planning and consideration of the needs and abilities of each team member. Pupils with disabilities may require special preparation and support in order to allow for their maximum participation and benefit (Johnson et al., 1998). Teachers, for instance, may have to review certain social skills with their students who are mentally retarded. One of the keys to successfully involving students with cognitive delays in the general education setting is providing the necessary and appropriate supports.

Cooperative learning has been shown to increase the opportunities for students with disabilities to experience success in school (Lewis & Doorlag, 2006). Cooperative learning benefits all pupils, contributes significantly to student achievement, enhances the self-esteem of individuals with special needs, and increases the acceptance and understanding of children with disabilities (Smith et al., 2008).

Cooperative learning is a popular instructional strategy for teaching pupils with mental retardation in inclusive settings.

EFFECTIVE INSTRUCTIONAL PRACTICES   Teaching Pupils with Intellectual Disabilities

Steps to Good Teaching

Students with intellectual disabilities, like other pupils, typically respond to well-planned instructional strategies. The following mnemonic (CLOCS-RAM) identifies eight steps that are characteristic of good teaching.

C = Clarity	The student must know exactly what to do (i.e., have no doubt about what is expected).
L = Level	The student must be able to do the task with a high degree of accuracy (i.e., be able to get at least 80 percent correct), but the task must be challenging (i.e., the student should not easily get 100 percent correct repeatedly).
O = Opportunities	The student must have frequent opportunities to respond (i.e., be actively engaged in the task a high percentage of the time).
C = Consequences	The student must receive a meaningful reward for correct performance (i.e., the consequences of correct performance must be frequent and perceived as desirable by the student).
S = Sequence	The tasks must be presented in logical sequence so that the student gets the big idea (i.e., steps must be presented and learned so that the knowledge or skill is built on a logical progression or framework of ideas, which is a systematic curriculum).
R = Relevance	The task must be relevant to the student's life and, if possible, the student understands how and why it is useful (i.e., the teacher attempts to help the student see why the task is important in the culture).
A = Application	The teacher helps the student learn how to learn and remember by teaching memory and learning strategies and applying knowledge and skills to everyday problems (i.e., teaches generalizations, not just isolated skills, and honors the student's culture).
M = Monitoring	The teacher continuously monitors student progress and always knows and can show what the student has mastered and the student's place or level in a curriculum or sequence of tasks.

Source: J. Kauffman, M. Mostert, S. Trent, and P. Pullen, *Managing Classroom Behavior*, 4th ed. (Boston: Allyn and Bacon, 2006), p. 17.

SCAFFOLDING Our final example is a teaching strategy called **scaffolding.** This technique is especially applicable to students with mental retardation, who are often characterized as "inactive" or "passive" learners. The aim of this approach is to help pupils become independent, proficient problem solvers. Scaffolding is a cognitive approach to instruction. In this teacher-directed strategy, various forms of support are provided to students as they initially engage in learning a new task or skill. As the student becomes increasingly competent, the supports or "scaffolds" are gradually removed. This instructional method begins with what the pupil already knows and attempts to connect new information with previously learned material. New information is presented in a logical sequence, building on the student's knowledge base. Pupils are then given the opportunity to apply and practice what they have learned. Suggestions for using this instructional technique can be found in the accompanying Suggestions for the Classroom (page 180).

These three examples are by no means the only instructional models appropriate for students with intellectual disabilities. Other approaches, such as direct instruction and learning strategies (discussed in Chapter 6), are also useful.

Making Inclusion Work

As an eighth-grade English Language Arts teacher with eleven years of teaching experience, I find teaching to be a new adventure every day.

I strive to enhance the learning opportunities for all of my students. Many of my current students are struggling writers, as identified by teachers from previous years. Keeping these students involved, interested, and yearning to learn, but at the same time making sure that every child is challenged and thriving can sometimes be a difficult task. But I have asked for this setting because I want to rise to the occasion and see my students succeed.

Inclusive Education Experience

Working in an inclusive classroom takes careful planning. First, I make sure that I know my students' abilities and weaknesses. I make the classroom inclusive of all learners, which builds a positive community. I have had students in my regular English classes who are visually impaired, students who are in wheelchairs, students who are self-contained in another teacher's room except for reading class. I have come to understand the importance of community and peer support. The teacher in any classroom, but especially the inclusive classroom, becomes the coach or facilitator of learning. Since the children come to school at multiple levels of learning, the teacher must meet the student where he or she is in the learning process and build from that point.

The challenge lies in assisting each child at his/her level and moving him/her along in the learning process. With one teacher and a class of twenty-five learners, moving around the class to help every child is difficult. The student/teacher ratio is high in the regular education class. Another challenge is keeping up with the paperwork that informs the teacher of the accommodations or modifications in the child's IEP. Third, a child who is too challenged or is not challenged enough can become frustrated, which may lead to other disruptive classroom issues. Finally, having all of the students involved in learning at the same time with material that everyone can understand is a challenge. Some students may feel comfortable reading lower-level books while others need more advanced materials. As their teacher, I am responsible for teaching them all.

I am constantly working on resolutions for my dilemmas, however, and I come closer to my answers every day. I rely on my colleagues for ideas that work in their classes. We have an idea exchange at team meetings as we discuss pedagogy and students. I learn from reading professional articles and books. I have always individualized my instruction, but I have learned to do it more effectively.

Strategies for Inclusive Classrooms

Collaboration with special education teachers is a must. They have teaching tips that work well with all students.

- Accommodate instruction and assignments as needed to ensure success for all students, not just those with IEPs; however, only modify assignments for those students who have IEPs. Simple accommodations include providing a word bank for vocabulary quizzes, a study guide before a test, rubrics before a project, a copy of class notes, a book on audiotape, and the use of a computer. Testing or quizzing accommodations include reading a quiz or test aloud to a student, allowing the student to read the quiz or test aloud, explaining directions or language, reducing the number of choices but covering the same objectives, extending the time permitted, allowing the student to dictate his or her answers, allowing mistakes to be corrected for extra points, or allowing a test to be retaken for an average of both scores.

- Understand the importance of presentation. Type assignment directions, activity sheets, quizzes, and tests in a larger font size such as 14 point to make the print easier to read. Be sure the print is clear and legible for the student. Allow students to use a note card to read line-by-line multiple-choice answers separately. Allow for white space around directions so the students will not confuse the directions with the actual test or quiz questions.

- Teach students that organization is pertinent to learning success. Allow a peer to help a student organize his or her notebook. Often a student has difficulty studying because he or she lacks the organizational skills needed to prepare for tests or quizzes.

- Realize that students are often embarrassed to ask for help during class. Periodically monitor students' progress throughout class by individually inquiring with each student about his or her progress. Be available before and after school for study sessions and in between classes for additional assistance.

- Make sure students are on-task by walking around their desks and prompting them to return to the task at hand if they are not working diligently.

- Elicit the aid of parents in a three-way partnership among student, parents, and teacher. Communicate the progress of the student through the student's daily assignment agenda. For example, have the student record any special assignments or daily homework in an agenda. This teaches the student the responsibility of finding out the daily requirements expected of him or her. As a teacher, read the student's agenda and clarify any mistakes or omissions the student may have made, record any newly earned grades, and comment on the student's progress. At night, parents also check the student's agenda and communicate any questions or comments by writing in the student's agenda for the teachers to read the following day.

Working with Parents and Families

Parents want to be informed. When a student does not do well on an assignment or seems to fall behind in class, contact the parents via e-mail, phone, note, or in person to inform them of their child's progress or any concerns. Parents also enjoy seeing samples of their child's classwork. For instance, sending home a portfolio during each grading period gives parents an opportunity to see growth in writing skills or progress in reading comprehension. A commentary sheet requesting parents and child to analyze the enclosed work is an excellent means of feedback for teachers. This process of commenting on favorite pieces of writing and selecting a writing piece for publication in a contest or school literary magazine also causes the child to reflect on his or her improvements.

Hosting parent seminars as a team of teachers once a semester on topics such as "Boosting Your Child's Study Habits," "Interpreting SAT-9 Scores" with the emphasis on building on strengths and improving weaknesses, and "Improving Reading Comprehension with Reading Strategies" provides an avenue for improving students' learning with the collaboration of students, parents, and teachers. Parents often desire to help their child at home but are not always equipped with the necessary tools to do so. Through parent seminars, parents learn strategies they can use at home to reinforce the learning that takes place at school. Parents learn of these seminars and other events through team newsletters that are distributed with report cards or progress reports during each grading period.

Each effort at communication through phone calls, notes, person-to-person contact, or e-mail is recorded in my communication log, including the name of the person with whom I spoke, the means of communication, time and date, and a brief description of the conversation. This helps me to remember the conversation's details in case I need to follow up with the student and parent in the future.

Advice for Making Inclusion and Collaboration Work

My advice to new teachers working in inclusive settings would be to learn as much as possible not only about a special-needs student's academic performance and needs but also about the individual. Sometimes just knowing about a student's personal interests can be a catalyst to help him or her improve learning. Learn about the student's academic performance and needs by talking with the special education teacher and reviewing last year's report card, standardized test scores, and portfolio. Learn about the student's personal interests by having the student complete a reading and writing questionnaire, participate in book talks or reading/writing conferences, and observe the student interacting with other students. Use the knowledge that you have gained to improve students' learning progress.

Knowing a child's learning styles, weakness, and strengths allows you to approach the child's difficulties and challenges with new insight. This also shows the student that you care about him or her as an individual and not just as a member of a class. Finally, do not be afraid to continue to elicit the help of parents, special education teachers, other team teachers, counselors, administrators, and other education professionals who work directly with the child. Sharing ideas and collaborating with others will greatly benefit all involved.

—Tonya Perry
Berry Middle School, Hoover, Alabama
Eighth grade, Language Arts
Alabama State Teacher of the Year 2001
One of the four national finalists:
National Teacher of the Year 2001

Suggestions for the Classroom

Using Scaffolding in the Classroom

☑ **Introduce the concept.** List all of the steps in the strategy using concrete illustrations. Teacher then models the strategy.

☑ **Regulate difficulty during guided practice.** Strategy is presented one step at a time using simplified situations. Pupils are guided through the process with the teacher providing assistance.

☑ **Provide varying contexts for student practice.** Students initially practice the strategy using authentic problems under the guidance of their teacher. Pupils eventually conduct practice sessions in small group settings.

☑ **Provide feedback.** Instructor provides constructive feedback. Evaluative checklists are available so students can self-evaluate their performance.

☑ **Increase student responsibility.** Students are required to use the strategies independently. As pupils become increasingly proficient, supports are gradually decreased. Teacher evaluates for student mastery.

☑ **Provide independent practice.** Students are provided with extensive opportunities for practice and apply the steps to novel situations. (Friend & Bursuck, 2006)

Services for Young Children with Mental Retardation or Intellectual Disabilities

The importance of early intervention for young children identified as, or suspected of being, mentally retarded cannot be overestimated. Early intervention can be defined as the services and supports rendered to children younger than age 5 with disabilities, or those who evidence risk factors, and their families. Early intervention represents a consortium of services—not just educational assistance but also health care, social services, family supports, and other benefits. The aim of early intervention is to affect positively the overall development of the child—his or her social, emotional, physical, and intellectual well-being. Thanks to the work of social scientists from various disciplines, federally funded research projects, and the impact of legislation such as PL 99-457 (The Education of the Handicapped Act Amendments of 1986), significant advancements have occurred in this arena. As a result, the quality of life for countless youngsters with intellectual disabilities and other impairments has been improved.

Hickson et al. (1995) describe two main goals of early intervention for young children with mental retardation. The focus of these efforts varies, depending on the severity of the impairment. For preschoolers considered to have moderate or greater degrees of retardation, the main emphasis is on furthering their development by reducing delays in reaching significant developmental and cognitive milestones such as walking or talking. (Similar programs that focus on infants with mental retardation, such as babies with Down syndrome, are frequently identified as **infant stimulation** programs.) Some youngsters may also profit from programs that stress functional objectives centered around activities of daily living.

Children thought to be mildly mentally retarded and those considered to be at risk will benefit from programs whose chief aim is to prepare these young students for successful academic experiences upon entering school. These experts go on to state that the primary objectives of early intervention for young children with less severe mental retardation are (1) "to minimize and, if possible, reverse the impact of delays or deficits in normal cognitive development on later school performance; and (2) to support family efforts to achieve desired intellectual, vocational, and social outcomes" (p. 223). The second goal, in our opinion, would seem to be appropriate for all individuals with intellectual disabilities regardless of their age or severity of impairment.

To these two laudable goals we would like to add a third objective: prevention of mental retardation. You may remember that in Chapter 1 we reviewed the benefits of early intervention for young children who were at increased risk of delayed development and possibly mental retardation due to environmental factors such as poverty and related conditions. Gargiulo and Kilgo (2005) identify these children as being **environmentally at-risk.** Other intervention programs target different audiences. Children who are at risk or highly vulnerable for cognitive impairments include youngsters with **established risk**—that is, children with a diagnosed medical disorder of known etiology and a predictable outcome or prognosis, such as Down syndrome or Fragile X syndrome. In other cases, infants, toddlers, and preschoolers who are **biologically at-risk** for intellectual delays and deficits because of low birth weight, prematurity, fetal alcohol syndrome, or HIV infection often profit from their involvement with early intervention activities.

It is important to keep in mind that early intervention programs for youngsters with intellectual disabilities, regardless of the severity of cognitive impairment, are not designed as "anti–mental retardation vaccinations"; rather, they are a first step in a comprehensive, coordinated, and ongoing effort aimed at enhancing the child's potential in all areas of development. Combating the deleterious effects of mental retardation will require a coordinated effort among parents, professionals, advocates, and government officials (Hickson et al., 1995).

Today, many early intervention programs are structured around a concept known as **family-centered early intervention.** Although the needs of young children with disabilities are an important intervention focus, early interventionists and other service providers are becoming increasingly aware that the needs of youngsters are often inseparable from those of their family. Young children with special needs frequently require a constellation of services based not only on their specific needs but also on the differential needs of the family unit. Family-centered early intervention embraces a positive view of the youngster's family; professionals now talk about enabling and empowering families rather than viewing the child and his or her family as having deficits that necessitate intervention to "fix" the problem. This movement away from a deficit model reflects contemporary thinking (Gargiulo & Kilgo, 2005).

An emphasis on family-centered early intervention characterizes many early childhood special education programs, but it is important to remember that the delivery of services is customized to meet the unique needs of the child as well as the family. Besides the importance attached to individualization, effective programs are comprehensive, normalized, and outcome based, and provide for interaction between disabled and nondisabled youngsters. These benchmarks are appropriate regardless of the curriculum orientation adopted. Typical approaches include a developmental model based largely on the theorizing of Jean Piaget; an operant or behavioral approach consistent with the work of B. F. Skinner; the Montessori method; and a functional curriculum representing a hybrid of the first two approaches. Beirne-Smith et al. (2006) note that no one approach has been shown to be clearly superior to the others and stress that "curriculum should be chosen based on the individual needs of the child and the family" (p. 340).

Transition into Adulthood

Adolescence is a time of transition and, for individuals with mental retardation, one that is often difficult and stressful. Edgar (1988) characterizes this period of movement from student to independent adulthood as one of "floundering." For many young adults with intellectual disabilities, this journey is not a successful one. Becoming a productive, self-sufficient, and independent adult frequently remains an elusive goal.

Despite the approaching thirty-fifth anniversary of IDEA, according to Drew and Hardman (2007), the graduates of special education programs do not yet participate fully in the economic and social mainstream of their communities. Today, unfortunately, many individuals with mental retardation are either underemployed or remain unemployed (Harris & Associates, 2004). Besides employment difficulties, researchers have found that for many citizens with mental retardation, independent living is an objective not yet attained (Krauss, Seltzer, Gordan, & Friedman, 1996). The preceding evidence suggests that professionals must do a better job of planning timely transitioning experiences for adolescents with intellectual disabilities if they are to reach their full potential as adults.

Transition planning is a shared responsibility of educators and other school personnel, adult service providers from the community, family members, and perhaps most important, the student. It is a comprehensive and collaborative activity focusing on adult outcomes that are responsive to the adolescent's goals and vision for adulthood (Sitlington & Clark, 2006). Thoma (1999) believes that meaningful transition planning requires that adult team members listen to and respect the desires and preferences of the student for his or her own adult lifestyle. You may also remember that transition services are mandated by federal law.

Successful adjustment as an independent adult requires careful planning commencing long before graduation from high school. Public Law 108-446, which recently reauthorized IDEA, requires that transition services begin no later than the first IEP in effect when the student turns 16 (and updated annually). This legislation also established a new requirement for postsecondary goals pertaining to appropriate education, training, employment, and independent living skills.

In earlier chapters, we have reviewed the requirements for effective transition planning and the key elements of an individualized transition plan or ITP. Here we focus on the area that is probably preeminent in transition planning for adolescents with mental retardation: employment.

For most individuals, with or without intellectual disabilities, work is an important part of daily life. Work is often used as a gauge of social status, financial success, and personal fulfillment, and is a vehicle for opportunities to participate in one's community. Oftentimes uninformed persons believe that persons with mental retardation are incapable of obtaining and holding a job. This is simply not true, even though employment rates for adults with mental retardation are dismal—especially for young women who are mentally retarded (Harris & Associates, 2004). Generally speaking, with appropriate training, individuals with mental retardation are able to secure and maintain meaningful and gainful employment. Persons who are intellectually disabled make good employees. In those cases where they are unsuccessful on the job, it is frequently due not to their skill level or job performance but to a lack of interpersonal and social behaviors appropriate to the workplace (Butterworth & Strauch, 1994).

Training is often the key to successful employment, and it begins during the transition period. Historically speaking, early job training programs centered around a model known as a **sheltered workshop.** At one time this was a very popular training option, particularly for individuals with moderate or severe retardation, who typically require long-term and intense support. Sheltered workshops are generally large facilities that provide job training in a segregated environment. Clients, as the workers are called, typically work on contract jobs that are often repetitive in nature and require low skill level—for instance, sorting "junk mail" inserts. Typically, these jobs are of short duration and offer the clients minimal job training. Placement in a sheltered workshop may, in some cases, be transitional to obtaining employment in the community, but it is more likely to be a permanent position.

In recent years, sheltered workshops have come under fire. Critics (Kregel, 2001; Murphy, Rogan, Handley, Kincaid, & Royce-Davis, 2002) have focused their attention on the low wages paid to workers, the segregated work setting, the absence of meaningful training, and the failure to move clients into competitive employment. This dissatisfaction, coupled with the contemporary movement toward more integrated and normalized experiences for individuals with mental retardation, has given rise to the notion of **supported competitive employment.** In this model, which has proven effective in preparing adolescents for employment in community settings, an individual with intellectual disabilities is placed on a competitive job site alongside other workers who are not disabled. A **job coach** or employment specialist provides on-the-job assistance and support to the worker with retardation. This person's role is to train the adolescent with mental retardation on the specific job requirements and then, hopefully, to decrease support services as the employee becomes more proficient. Job coaches are also usually responsible for locating the job and matching the needs of the employer to the abilities of the student (worker).

The use of a supported competitive employment model has grown significantly over the past decade; it has been shown to be a cost-effective strategy with benefits accruing to both employer and employee (Beirne-Smith et al., 2006). Researchers have found that individuals with intellectual disabilities who are trained using this approach tend to function better in competitive employment settings than persons who only have experience in sheltered workshops (McDonnell, Hardman, & McDonnell, 2003), in addition to reporting higher job satisfaction (Test, Carver, Evers, Haddad, & Person, 2000). Employment opportunities typically range from entry level custodial or food service positions to jobs in various high technology industries.

Although this model is in keeping with contemporary thinking regarding self-determination (discussed in the next section of this chapter), supportive competitive employment has its limitations. Some of the drawbacks include excessive dependence on the job coach, disruption of the work environment by the presence of the job coach, and differential performance when the job coach is on-site (Simmons & Whaley, 2008). These disadvantages have contributed to the idea of using coworkers as natural supports (Mank, Cioffi, & Yovanoff, 2003). These individuals typically function as mentors and friends, offering valuable assistance and encouragement as needed to workers with intellectual disabilities.

For many young adults with mental retardation, competitive employment is a realistic goal. By providing

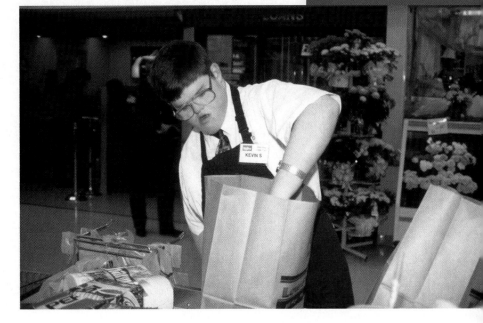

Many adults with mental retardation are capable of working successfully in the community.

early and carefully crafted transitioning experiences, schools can maximize the probability that students who are mentally retarded will have successful postschool adjustment, not only in the area of employment but in other domains as well.

Adults with Mental Retardation or Intellectual Disabilities

Over the past several years, professionals and advocates alike have devoted increased attention to the needs of adults who are mentally retarded. For some of these individuals, successful adjustment to the community is an appropriate and achievable objective. For all intents and purposes, they are no different from most other adults without disabilities, although at times they may require (as others sometimes do) support and assistance from family members, friends, coworkers, or social service agencies. Here we will focus on the community adjustment of adults with intellectual disabilities who require more intense and ongoing support.

Earlier in this chapter, we introduced the principle of normalization, defined as "making available to the mentally retarded patterns and conditions of everyday life which are as close as possible to the norms and patterns of the mainstream of society" (Nirje, 1969, p. 181). The principle of normalization attempts "to establish and/or maintain personal behaviors which are as culturally normative as possible" (Wolfensberger, 1972, p. 28). The overarching philosophy is that individuals with mental retardation (and other disabilities)

Persons with mental retardation are seeking greater control over their lives and fuller participation in all aspects of society.

should be integrated, to the greatest extent possible, in all aspects of daily life such as employment, recreation, living arrangements, and other areas of community life.

The principle of normalization has given rise to the belief that individuals with intellectual disabilities, especially those with more severe cognitive impairments, have a right to make their own choices and decisions in life and to become as independent as possible—in short, to have some degree of personal control over their own lives. These decisions may be as simple as what to watch on television, what time to go to bed, or which dress to wear, or they may involve more profound choices such as where to live and with whom. This decision-making capacity is often referred to as **self-determination** or, to use AAMR [AAIDD] terminology, self-direction. Although self-determination is a critical adaptive skill, educators should bear in mind that self-determination reflects North American and Western European ideals and beliefs; other cultures may not value independence and personal decision making as highly as European Americans. Teachers, therefore, are strongly encouraged to consider the cultural preferences and heritage of their pupils when formulating instructional strategies for developing skills in self-determination (Turnbull, Turnbull, Erwin, & Soodak, 2006).

Because free choice is typically a restricted activity for large numbers of adults with mental retardation, **self-advocacy** is gaining in both popularity and importance. People with intellectual disabilities are encouraged, via self-help groups, to speak out on issues of personal importance such as living arrangements and personal relationships. The purpose of self-advocacy is for individuals with mental retardation to gain greater personal control over their lives and to foster their own independence. Self-advocacy empowers people and helps them to assertively state their needs, wants, and desires.

Of course, successfully adjusting to life in one's community requires more than skills in self-determination and self-advocacy; it is also predicated on acceptance and support from the general public. Several other variables besides community acceptance that are likely to influence success in community living are illustrated in Figure 5.6.

Figure 5.6

Variables Affecting Successful Community Living of Adults with Intellectual Disabilities

Source: Adapted from M. Beirne-Smith, J. Patton, and S. Kim, *Mental Retardation*, 7th ed. (Upper Saddle River, NJ: Pearson Education, 2006).

Family Issues

A child with mental retardation (or any other disability) typically elicits a wide range of emotional responses, which can vary from anger and denial to awareness and acceptance. Additionally, parents may worry about financial obligations, educational concerns, the impact of the disability on siblings, long-term care requirements, and a host of other fears. These families often require understanding, assistance, and support. The importance of a natural support network, which may include coworkers, neighbors, friends, aunts and uncles, and other family members, should not be underestimated (McDonnell et al., 2003). For many parents of children with disabilities, these individuals, and not professionals, serve as the "first line of defense" in dealing with a child who is recognized as being mentally retarded. Other parents of youngsters with Down syndrome, for example, can often provide sensitive assistance and serve as a valuable resource on community services for infants with special needs. Long-term and mutually sustaining relationships are frequently established between parents of children with intellectual disabilities because of this common connection. Support is necessary because a child with mental retardation may significantly affect the structure, function, and overall development of the entire family constellation (Gargiulo & Kilgo, 2005). In this case, valuable assistance is available from The Arc, a national organization on intellectual disabilities, which offers information and support not only to parents but also to siblings and other family members such as grandparents.

It is impossible to predict how a family will respond to a child with mental retardation. This term means different things to different families. As a society, we must value all families and should not overlook the potential benefits that an individual with intellectual disabilities brings to his or her family. See the accompanying First Person feature written by a young adult with Down syndrome.

Issues of Diversity

A long-standing concern exists among special educators about the misclassification and/or inappropriate placement of students from minority backgrounds in special education programs. All too often, diversity is incorrectly linked with disability. It is indeed unfortunate that children from minority groups are frequently seen as deviant or disabled.

The issue of cultural diversity is intricately interwoven into the fabric of American special education. It is related to discussions of identification, psychoeducational assessment, etiology, educational placement, and intervention. The overrepresentation of children of color is particularly relevant to a discussion on mental retardation. The U.S. Department of Education (2006) reports, for example, that African American youth constitute 15 percent of the public school population, yet about one out of every three pupils in classes for the mentally retarded are from this group (U.S. Department of Education, 2007). Drew and Hardman (2007) observe that individuals are often misdiagnosed as mentally retarded when, in fact, their behavior is more a reflection of cultural differences than an indication of reduced or impaired functioning.

We know that the overrepresentation of minorities in special education classes, especially programs for children with intellectual disabilities, is a multifaceted problem. Contributing factors range from culturally biased assessment instruments to the insidious role of poverty to teacher bias and expectation. The challenge that continually confronts educators and other professionals is how to combat this problem. The answer to this perplexing issue has eluded special educators for much too long.

First Person

Meredith—In Her Own Words

What can you tell us about yourself and your family?

I am Meredith, age 22, and I live with my parents in Alabama. I have a younger brother named Zach. One of my favorite childhood memories is dressing up at Halloween. Zach was Captain Hook and I was Peter Pan, and another time he was a cowboy and I was an Indian. We also had fun at Christmas, which is my favorite holiday to celebrate. My family has many traditions I enjoy. One is getting an ornament each year to remind us of our interests, like my Barbie Doll collection, and my two former dogs, Scamper and Misha.

What do you like to do in your free time?

For fun, I go out with my boyfriend, Matthew, or my girlfriends. Matthew and I usually go out to dinner and a movie. We take turns having dinner at each other's house and we love watching the Three Stooges videos. I'm also involved with People First, a self-advocacy group for people with disabilities. I am the chaplain and open the meeting with words of encouragement about having a positive attitude. At church I help out in the fourth-grade Religious Education classroom. I also volunteer for the North Shelby County Library and Alabama Wildlife Rehabilitation Center.

What can you tell us about your experience at school?

I graduated from Oak Mountain High School. During high school, I was nominated for the Homecoming Court, and was voted Best Choral Student. I really enjoyed high school because it had a great atmosphere and I had many friends. My favorite subjects were Government, Choir, and Environmental Science. I also liked our pep rallies and football games. My least favorite subject was Math. My best high school memory is getting to be in the Macy's Thanksgiving Day parade. We walked 3 miles singing and dancing in New York City where it was very cold. Some of the challenges were trying to be smart and independent. While in high school I joined the Special Olympics Rhythmic Gymnastics Team and I still compete today. I also am on a Special Olympics bowling team.

What can you tell us about your work background?

During my senior year, I started to get work experience. I got to work at a video store, a card shop, restaurant, and Jefferson State Community College. My first real job was at a department store where I helped organize and fold clothes. I don't have a job right now, but am working with my job coach to find one. I'd like to work in an office or clothing store.

What do you see yourself doing in the future?

My dream for the future is to have a job, live in my own place, and maybe one day get married. My grandmother, who was very sweet, is my role model. She was a very strong woman and never complained even though she had diabetes for over fifty years. She always encouraged me to be healthy and take care of myself.

What is one thing you want people to remember about you?

I would like people to know that I love my life.

A Final Word

When our daughter, Meredith, was born with Down syndrome, we faced numerous medical, social, and educational challenges. We had no way of knowing that very soon we would become partners with doctors, speech, physical, and occupational therapists, early interventionists, teachers, job coaches, and other advocates who value the rights and dignity of individuals with disabilities. This partnership has created lasting bonds of friendship, changed attitudes, strengthened inclusive educational practices, and allowed Meredith to achieve many goals.

Meredith's literary abilities have far exceeded our earliest expectations. She is an excellent reader with incredible spelling and comprehension skills. Her passion for learning and wanting to educate herself is remarkable. Meredith is a delightful, self-confident young woman with a sense of humor, knows no prejudice, and loves unconditionally. Meredith is an extraordinary person trying to live an ordinary life and we are blessed to be her parents.

Technology and Individuals with Mental Retardation or Intellectual Disabilities

Technology holds significant promise for improving the quality of life for individuals with mental retardation. It also has great potential for assisting teachers in providing a high-quality and appropriate education to students with disabilities, including those who are intellectually disabled. Lewis and Doorlag (2006) note that there are two types of technology to consider when talking about pupils with disabilities: instructional technology and assistive technology. **Instructional technology** is any device that supports the teaching/learning process, such as computers or televisions. **Assistive technology** is technology that is specially designed to assist persons with disabilities. Assistive technology is defined in federal law.

Clearly, students with mental retardation can benefit from the application of technology in the classroom. Thanks to the reauthorization of IDEA, technology is a viable mechanism for expanding access to the general education curriculum. Increasingly, technology is being recommended to assist pupils with cognitive impairments achieve in more challenging curriculums. Table 5.6 illustrates how various types of technology may benefit students with intellectual disabilities as well as other pupils.

Table 5.6	Application of Technology to Students with Intellectual Disabilities	
	Application	**Purposes**
Reading Tools	Text and screen reading programs	Translate a variety of text-based documents to speech.
	Scan-and-speak programs and tools	Translate printed information into digital text that can be read by text-to-speech functions.
	Tools for organizing content area information	Help students organize a variety of information to facilitate comprehension and to aid studying for tests and other evaluations.
Writing Tools	Word processors	Support the writing process by easing the logistical burdens of creating and, in many cases, reading text to facilitate editing and revising.
	Spell checkers and electronic writing supports	Support students' writing by providing feedback about accurate spelling and by providing information such as synonyms, definitions, and translations from one language to another.
	Word prediction software	Supports those who have difficulty typing or spelling by predicting a user's words and offering a selection of possible words from which to choose.
	Prompted writing tools	Scaffold the writing process by offering directions, cues, guidance, or pictures that can prompt users' background knowledge, guide them in various types of writing, and promote revision.
	Speech recognition programs	Permit users to dictate their compositions by transcribing their dictation into written text.

Source: Adapted from C. Okolo, "Technology and Individuals with Mild Disabilities," In J. Lindsey (Ed.), *Technology and Exceptional Individuals*, 4th ed. (Austin, TX: Pro-Ed, 2008), p. 329.

Trends, Issues, and Controversies

As we conclude this chapter, we hope that you have gained an understanding of and appreciation for the many complex and often related issues surrounding the subject of intellectual disabilities. Topics such as amniocentesis and the accompanying question of abortion, test bias and the overrepresentation of minorities in programs for the mentally retarded, concerns about appropriate placements, and thoughts about the quality of life of persons with mental retardation are only some of the many issues that have captured the attention of parents, educators, policy makers, advocates, legislators, and a host of other concerned individuals.

Like others, we too are concerned about where we have been, where we are today, and what the future holds for the field of intellectual disabilities. Understanding the present state of affairs is often beneficial when contemplating where we might be headed. In fact, the past is often seen as a prologue to the future. With this in mind, we must point out that although individuals who are mentally retarded will most likely benefit from advances in technology, medical breakthroughs, new legislation, and a host of other beneficial developments, attitudinal change is frequently the precursor to a change in the delivery of services and the recognition of the rights of our fellow citizens with disabilities.

Attempting to anticipate where the field of intellectual disabilities is going is perhaps best left to the futurist or the clairvoyant. This disclaimer notwithstanding, our vision of the future includes the following:

- More community-based activities will be available across several domains, including employment, education, and residential options.
- There will be a growing emphasis on the application of assistive technology to meet the needs of the person with mental retardation; to varying degrees, individuals with intellectual disabilities will join the information age.
- Quality of life and normalization across the life span will become increasingly prominent national advocacy issues.
- Human services providers as well as communities will be confronted with a growing geriatric population with intellectual disabilities.
- Biomedical research and well-designed psychosocial interventions will lead to a reduction in the number of people identified as mentally retarded.
- More inclusive educational placements will be the norm for students with significant cognitive impairments, requiring intensive supports.
- Greater attention will be paid across all age groups to fostering self-advocacy and self-determination, as persons with intellectual disabilities seek greater control over their lives and fuller participation in all aspects of society.

Overall, we foresee significant improvement in the coming years in both the quality and quantity of programs and services for persons who are mentally retarded.

Chapter in Review

Defining Mental Retardation or Intellectual Disabilities: An Evolving Process

- Contemporary practice considers mental retardation to be the result of interactions among the person, the environment, and those supports required to maximize the individual's performance in particular settings or environments.

Assessing Intellectual Ability and Adaptive Behavior

- **Intelligence** is a theoretical construct whose existence can only be inferred on the basis of a person's performance on certain types of cognitive tests that only represent a sample of the person's intellectual skills and abilities.

Classification of Individuals with Mental Retardation or Intellectual Disabilities

- Some models group persons with intellectual disabilities according to the **etiology** or cause of the disability; others label persons according to the severity of their cognitive impairment, such as mildly or severely mentally retarded.

- Educators sometimes label students with mental retardation as **educable mentally retarded** (EMR) or **trainable mentally retarded** (TMR).

- The 2002 AAMR definition classifies individuals with mental retardation on the basis of the extent or **levels of support** they require to function effectively across adaptive skill areas in various natural settings, such as home, school, or job.

Prevalence of Mental Retardation or Intellectual Disabilities

- Currently, approximately 9 percent of all students with disabilities are recognized as being mentally retarded, or about 1 percent of the total school-age population.

- The vast majority of persons with intellectual disabilities have an IQ between 50 and 70–75.

Etiology of Mental Retardation or Intellectual Disabilities

- One way of categorizing etiological factors is on the basis of time of onset: before birth (**prenatal**), around the time of birth (**perinatal**), or after birth (**postnatal**).

Characteristics of Individuals with Mental Retardation or Intellectual Disabilities

- Common behaviors of persons with mental retardation include **attention deficits**, or difficulty focusing and attending to relevant stimuli, and **memory problems**.

- Past experiences with failure frequently lead individuals who are intellectually disabled to doubt their own abilities and thus exhibit an **external locus of control**.

- Recurring episodes of failure also give rise to learned helplessness. These accumulated instances of failure frequently result in a loss of confidence and trust in one's own problem-solving abilities and a reliance on others for direction and guidance. This behavior is identified as **outer-directedness**.

- Individuals with intellectual impairments also often exhibit poor interpersonal skills and socially inappropriate or immature behaviors.

Educational Considerations

- Students who are mentally retarded are more than three times as likely as other children with disabilities to be educated in a self-contained classroom.

- Many students with intellectual disabilities are exposed to a **functional curriculum**, whose goal is to equip these children with the skills they require for successful daily living both now and in the future.

- Best practice dictates that instruction occurs as much as possible in natural settings rather than simulated environments. This instructional concept is known as **community-based instruction**.

- **Task analysis** is frequently used with persons who are mentally retarded.

- **Cooperative learning** is another instructional intervention that educators often employ. This strategy is especially useful when teaching pupils with intellectual disabilities in inclusive or integrated classrooms.

- **Scaffolding**, which is a cognitive approach to instruction, is a teacher-directed strategy in which various forms of support are provided to students as they engage in learning a new task or skill.

Adults with Mental Retardation or Intellectual Disabilities

- The principle of **normalization** currently guides the delivery of services to individuals with intellectual disabilities. This notion suggests that persons who are mentally retarded should have a lifestyle that is as culturally normative as possible.

- The principle of normalization has also given rise to the belief that those who are mentally retarded should have a right to make their own choices and decisions about various aspects of their lives. This decision-making capacity is often referred to as **self-determination.**

Technology and Individuals with Mental Retardation or Intellectual Disabilities

- **Instructional technology** is any piece of equipment that facilitates the teaching/learning process.

- **Assistive technology** is any apparatus or equipment that is used to enhance or maintain the functional capabilities of individuals with mental retardation and other disabilities.

Study Questions

1. How has the definition of mental retardation changed over the past several decades?

2. Identify the three key elements of the 1992 AAMR definition of mental retardation. How are they conceptually interrelated?

3. Why is the assessment of intelligence such a controversial issue?

4. What is adaptive behavior, and how is it assessed?

5. List four different strategies for classifying individuals with intellectual disabilities.

6. How have society's view and understanding of persons who are intellectually disabled changed over the centuries?

7. What factors have contributed to the gradual reduction in the number of individuals classified as mentally retarded?

8. Mental retardation is often the result of various etiological factors. List seven possible causes of intellectual disabilities. Give an example of each.

9. How do learned helplessness, outer-directedness, and generalizing affect learning in students with mental retardation?

10. Define the term *functional academics*. How are functional academics related to the concept of community-based instruction?

11. What is cooperative learning, and why is it a popular instructional technique?

12. List and describe the necessary steps for effectively using scaffolding with students with intellectual disabilities.

13. How has family-centered early intervention influenced programming activities for young children with mental retardation?

14. Distinguish between a sheltered workshop for adults with mental retardation and the contemporary practice of supported competitive employment.

15. What is assistive technology, and how might it benefit individuals who are intellectually disabled?

Key Terms

standard deviation	deinstitutionalization	galactosemia	fetal alcohol effect
adaptive behavior	etiology	rubella	anencephaly
educable mentally retarded	prenatal	syphilis	microcephaly
trainable mentally retarded	perinatal	AIDS	hydrocephalus
level of support	postnatal	Rh incompatibility	low birth weight
natural supports	Down syndrome	toxoplasmosis	premature birth
formal supports	Fragile X syndrome	cytomegalovirus	anoxia
normalization	phenylketonuria (PKU)	fetal alcohol syndrome	hypoxia

birth trauma	chorionic villus sampling	functional academics	family-centered early intervention
breech presentation	ultrasound	community-based instruction	sheltered workshop
precipitous birth	therapeutic abortion	task analysis	supported competitive employment
lead poisoning	spina bifida	cooperative learning	
meningitis	external locus of control	scaffolding	job coach
encephalitis	learned helplessness	infant stimulation	self-determination
primary prevention	outer-directedness	environmentally at-risk	self-advocacy
secondary prevention	generalizing	established risk	instructional technology
tertiary prevention	functional curriculum	biologically at-risk	assistive technology
amniocentesis			

Learning Activities

1. Make arrangements to visit classrooms serving students with intellectual disabilities. What differences did you observe between elementary and secondary programs? Did the instructional program differ for students with severe or profound cognitive impairments in comparison to pupils with mild or moderate mental retardation? What pedagogical techniques or teaching strategies did the teachers use? How did the other children interact with and relate to their classmates with mental retardation? Was a particular curriculum incorporated? What was your overall impression of the program; what specific features stood out?

2. Visit several businesses in your community that employ individuals with intellectual disabilities. Interview the employer or supervisor. Find out how successful these individuals have been. What type of training do workers with mental retardation require? How have customers and/or coworkers accepted these individuals? Why did the company hire someone who is mentally retarded (financial reasons, corporate policy, public relations)? Are they good employees? Have the workers with intellectual disabilities posed any special challenges or problems for the employer?

3. Visit various residential facilities in your area that serve individuals with mental retardation. Interview the caregivers. Discover what the daily routine is like for individuals with mental retardation. Do the various facilities allow for different degrees of independence and decision making on the part of the residents?

What is your opinion of the quality of life of these individuals? How has the community accepted their neighbors with intellectual disabilities? What supports and services are made available to the residents? Do the individuals with mental retardation participate in the life of the community—attend special events and festivities; utilize community recreational facilities such as parks, museums, or the zoo; make purchases in local shops?

4. Involve yourself with various community agencies and organizations that focus on individuals with mental retardation. Attend a meeting of The Arc or a parent support group. Volunteer to work at the Special Olympics, become a Best Buddy, or assist in programs offering respite care to parents of children with intellectual disabilities.

5. Prepare a multimedia presentation for your class on an aspect of mental retardation that personally interests you. Here are some possible topics:
   • Assistive technology
   • Prenatal diagnostic screening
   • Supported competitive employment
   • Group homes
   • Causes and prevention of intellectual disabilities
   • Overrepresentation of minorities in classes for the mentally retarded
   • Assessment of intelligence
   • Early intervention

Reflecting on Standards

The following exercises are designed to help you learn to apply the Council for Exceptional Children (CEC) standards to your teaching practice. Each of the reflection exercises below correlates with a knowledge or skill within the CEC standards. For the full text of each of the related CEC standards, please refer to the standards integration grid located in Appendix B.

1. **Focus on Individual Learning Differences** (*CEC Content Standard #3 CC3K1*)

   Reflect on an individual with mental retardation or intellectual disabilities that you have known. How has that individual made an impact on his or her family,

friends, teachers, and/or community? What struggles did that individual have as a result of their differences? What did you learn from this person about individuals with disabilities?

2. **Focus on Instructional Planning** (*CEC Content Standard #7 CC7S7*)

   Reflect on what you have learned in this chapter about students with mental retardation or intellectual disabilities. If you were to have a student with Down syndrome in your class, how would you need to modify your teaching to integrate affective, social, and life skills within your day-to-day curriculum?

Organizations Concerned with Mental Retardation or Intellectual Disabilities

The Arc (formerly the Association for Retarded Citizens of the United States)

1010 Wayne Avenue
Silver Spring, MD 20910
(301) 565-3842
URL: http://thearc.org/

American Association on Intellectual and Developmental Disabilities

444 N. Capitol Street N.W., Suite 846
Washington, DC 20001
(800) 424-3688 (toll-free, outside of DC)
(202) 387-1968
URL: http://www.aamr.org

National Down Syndrome Congress

1370 Center Drive, Suite 102
Atlanta, GA 30338
(800) 232-6372 (toll-free); (770) 604-9500
URL: http://www.ndsccenter.org/

National Down Syndrome Society

666 Broadway, Suite 810
New York, NY 10012
(800) 221-4602 (toll-free); (212) 460-9330
(212) 979-2873 (fax)
URL: http://ndss.org

Technology Resources

Visit the Web-based SAGE Study Site at http://www.sagepub.com/gargiulo3estudy for these additional learning tools:

- Chapter quizzes
- Key term flashcards
- Media links

- Full-text SAGE journal articles
- Internet activities
- Additional Web resources

CHAPTER 6

Individuals with Learning Disabilities

What's a Mother to Do?

"What's a mother to do?" I moped silently. I knew that there was something slightly wrong. Was Ryan just lazy? His seventh-grade teachers had just told us so in the parent conference. As I painfully replayed the conference in my mind, I reflected on my son's school experiences.

Ryan had a very successful elementary school experience up until the fifth grade. In fifth grade things got a bit more difficult. His disorganization and his lack of ability to do written work began to destroy his confidence and academic success. Grades dropped from mostly A's to C's and D's. Ryan's teacher and his classmates loved him; but he failed at least one subject each grading period—usually a different one each time. He never brought assignments home, frequently did the wrong homework—if he did it at all—and forgot to turn in finished homework. His teacher said that he had trouble getting his books, pen, and paper out at the beginning of class. She said that he was, therefore, behind before he even got started. His fifth-grade penmanship looked like that of a much younger child. He could not spell. His backpack was a mess of wadded up papers. We all thought Ryan was just a typical boy. Neither we nor the teachers ever mentioned the possibility of a learning disability.

Then we were in middle school. Ryan was still one of the most popular kids in the class—sociable, handsome, and clearly the class "stud," but his grades were gradually deteriorating. We asked for a parent–teacher conference. At the conference, my husband and I were attacked by his team of teachers. They seemed to think we were bad parents. "Why don't you make Ryan do his work?" they asked.

Ryan's seventh-grade test scores clearly showed a large discrepancy. Spelling was at the third-grade level while all other skills were at or above a twelfth-grade level. His reading comprehension was excellent, vocabulary was extensive; yet he did not read for pleasure. He passed most classes with only average grades. His teachers told us he was lazy. Once again, not one teacher mentioned the possibility of a learning disability.

I did not know what to do with this smart yet obviously learning-disabled child. I finally asked for help when our son was in the eighth grade. I agree that being classified as a special education student gives a child a certain unfavorable stigma; but I did not know any other way to help my child. Ryan somehow survived middle school, thanks largely to the efforts of his special education teacher.

That summer we moved to a larger city about two hours away. As a family, we decided not to seek special education services for Ryan as he began his freshman year in high school. We did not want him to carry the stigma of special education into this new environment. His grades always ranged from A's to F's. I had to constantly help him with his written work. He composed very well, but sometimes I had to type as he "wrote" his work orally. He had to go to summer school every summer to keep up, but somehow managed to pass almost all of his classes and eventually graduate.

After a few years of successful employment Ryan was ready for college. He began by taking a history class at a nearby university and, with Mom's help on all papers, made a B in that class. He joined a fraternity. It was great fun. In the fall, he took a full load and quickly landed on academic probation. At that point I started looking for help from the university, only to find out that he could not get financial help until he got off academic probation. Ryan was still ambivalent about letting his professors know that he had a learning disability and would not ask the office of Disability Support Services to contact his professors. So, again, he was in school depending on his mother to be his personal "special education" resource. He is now a third-semester freshman. He composes beautifully, but we are still writing orally while I or his girlfriend types his papers. He forgets to go to class sometimes and usually runs late to his part-time job or the pool where he coaches swim teams. His notebooks and his car are full of school supplies, athletic equipment, and miscellaneous stuff that is wildly disorganized.

I want my child to get a college degree and not have to work night shifts in the retail world for the rest of his life. We are now borrowing money to send him to school, hoping that he will pass every class, and worrying what will happen with his health insurance when he turns 24 and our policy no longer covers him. The financial burden is killing us, and I'm still in a quandary. What's a mother to do?

—*Anonymous*

Persons with learning disabilities are a very heterogeneous group. We will learn about children and adults who typically have normal intelligence but, for some reason, fail to learn as easily and efficiently as their classmates and peers. The idea that some individuals might possess a hidden or invisible disability is of relatively recent origin. The notion of learning disabilities is slightly more than four decades old, but it has quickly grown and today represents the largest category of children and youth enrolled in special education.

The study of learning disabilities involves professionals from many different disciplines. Our knowledge base about this perplexing field has been greatly enriched by the contributions of investigators and practitioners from psychology, medicine, speech and language, and education, as well as other disciplines. Despite this solid multidisciplinary foundation, individuals with learning disabilities are often an enigma to their parents, teachers, and researchers, and the field itself has generated significant controversy, confusion, and debate.

In reality, most individuals have imperfections and, to some degree, experience difficulty in learning, but in some instances these problems are more pronounced than in others. For large numbers of people, these learning difficulties are chronic and will persist throughout life. It would be wrong to assume, however, that these individuals are incapable of accomplishments and a life of quality. Some of the most distinguished individuals and brightest minds the world has ever known had extreme difficulty in learning and could easily be considered learning disabled. These eminent people include Leonardo da Vinci, Auguste Rodin, Albert Einstein, Thomas Edison, Woodrow Wilson, Winston Churchill, and Ernest Hemingway. Other noted personalities include Walt Disney, George Patton, Nelson Rockefeller, Tom Cruise, and Bruce Jenner (Lerner & Kline, 2006; Smith, Polloway, Patton, & Dowdy, 2008). By all accounts, the preceding individuals are very successful persons; but they are exceptions. The vast majority of children and adults with learning disabilities will be frequently misunderstood and experience ongoing challenges and frustrations in their daily lives.

In this chapter, we will explore several issues and attempt to answer a number of questions related to learning disabilities. What is a learning disability? How many individuals are thought to be learning disabled? Can we cure it? What instructional strategies work best for students who are learning disabled? How do professionals determine if someone has a learning disability? Of course, there are many other questions about this puzzling field of study, and some for which we do not have complete answers. We begin our exploration of learning disabilities by examining various definitions.

Defining Learning Disabilities

Students with learning disabilities have always been in our classrooms, but professionals have often failed to identify these pupils and recognize their special needs. These children have been known by a variety of confusing and sometimes controversial labels, including neurologically impaired, perceptually disordered, dyslexic, slow learner, remedial reader, and hyperactive. More than thirty-five years ago, Cruickshank (1972) published a list of some forty terms used to describe students known today as learning disabled. Deiner's (1993) more recent analysis found more than ninety terms used in the professional literature to characterize individuals with learning disabilities. It is easy to see why controversy and confusion surround this population of learners. Part of the problem is the many different disciplines involved in serving these students. Based on their professional training, physicians, speech-language pathologists, educators, and psychologists each describe persons with learning disabilities in their own unique way. Over the years, however, the various terms have been consolidated into the concept now known as learning disabilities. Today, this term enjoys wide acceptance among educators and the general public.

Defining the term *learning disability* has proven to be problematic. At one time, Vaughn and Hodges (1973) identified thirty-eight different definitions. Hammill (1990) notes that eleven definitions have enjoyed varying degrees of official status in the field. Defining what a learning disability is has thus been an evolving process over the past forty years.

The term *learning disabilities* was initially used by Samuel Kirk in 1963 at a meeting of parents and professionals concerned about children with various learning difficulties. His proposed label was enthusiastically received and helped to unite the participants into an organization known as the Association for Children with Learning Disabilities, the forerunner of today's Learning Disabilities Association. Although the term was coined in 1963, Kirk had defined the concept a year earlier. His definition of **learning disabilities** was

a retardation, disorder, or delayed development in one or more of the processes of speech, language, reading, writing, arithmetic, or other school subject resulting from a psychological handicap caused by a possible cerebral dysfunction and/or emotional or behavioral disturbances. It is not the result of mental retardation, sensory deprivation, or cultural and instructional factors. (Kirk, 1962, p. 263)

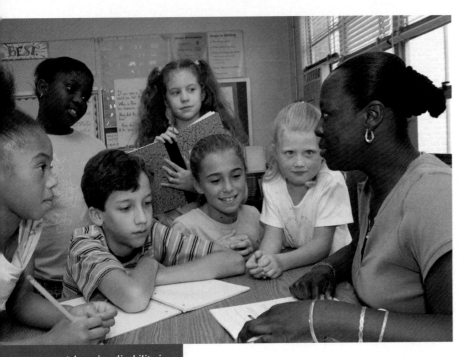

A learning disability is an umbrella concept covering a wide range of difficulties.

As you will see, elements of this definition, which is an umbrella concept encompassing a multitude of educational "sins," appear in many of the later definitions of learning disabilities, including subaverage academic performance, processing disorders, and the exclusion of certain etiological possibilities.

National Advisory Committee on Handicapped Children

In the late 1960s, Congress was considering the funding of various programs that would benefit individuals with learning disabilities. As part of this process, the U.S. Office of Education was requested to craft a definition of learning disabilities. A committee was established with Kirk as its chair. Their discussions resulted in the following definition, which was subsequently incorporated in the Specific Learning Disabilities Act of 1969 (PL 91-230):

> Children with special (specific) learning disabilities exhibit a disorder in one or more of the basic psychological processes involved in understanding or in using spoken and written language. These may be manifested in disorders of listening, thinking, talking, reading, writing, spelling or arithmetic. They include conditions which have been referred to as perceptual handicaps, brain injury, minimal brain dysfunction, dyslexia, developmental aphasia, etc. They do not include learning problems that are due primarily to visual, hearing, or motor handicaps, to mental retardation, emotional disturbance, or to environmental disadvantage. (U.S. Office of Education, 1968, p. 34)

It is not surprising, given the fact that Kirk spearheaded this task force, that there is a high degree of similarity between Kirk's initial description and the committee's definition. Nonetheless, three differences are evident:

1. An emphasis on children
2. The addition of thinking disorders as an example of learning disabilities
3. The addition of emotional disturbance as an exclusionary etiological contribution (Hammill, 1990)

This definition proved to be immensely popular and was later, with slight modifications, incorporated in PL 94-142. In fact, by 1975 more than thirty states were using some version of the committee's definition as their state definition of learning disabilities (Mercer, Forgnone, & Wolking, 1976).

Federal Definition of Learning Disabilities

After the Education for All Handicapped Children Act was enacted in 1975, the U.S. Office of Education spent two years developing the accompanying rules and regulations for identifying and defining individuals with learning disabilities. The following official federal definition of learning disabilities was published in the *Federal Register* in December 1977:

> "Specific learning disability" means a disorder in one or more of the basic psychological processes involved in understanding or in using language, spoken or written, which may manifest itself in an imperfect ability to listen, speak, read, write, spell, or to do mathematical calculations. The term includes such conditions as perceptual handicaps, brain injury, minimal brain dysfunction, dyslexia, and developmental aphasia. The term does not include children who have learning disabilities which are primarily the result of visual, hearing, or motor handicaps, or mental retardation, or emotional disturbance, or of environmental, cultural, or economic disadvantage. (U.S. Office of Education, 1977, p. 65083)

This definition was retained in the Individuals with Disabilities Education Act (PL 101-476), commonly called IDEA, and is incorporated, with a few word changes, in both the 1997 and 2004 reauthorizations of IDEA (PL 105-17, PL 108-446).

In the same issue of the *Federal Register,* the U.S. Office of Education issued the regulations and operational guidelines that were to be used by professionals as the criteria for identifying pupils suspected of being learning disabled. These regulations required that

(a) A team may determine that a child has a specific learning disability if:
  (1) The child does not achieve commensurate with his or her age and ability levels in one or more of the areas listed in paragraph (a) (2) of this section, when provided with learning experiences appropriate for the child's age and ability levels; and
  (2) The team finds that a child has a severe discrepancy between achievement and intellectual ability in one or more of the following areas:
    i. Oral expression;
    ii. Listening comprehension;
    iii. Written expression;
    iv. Basic reading skill;
    v. Reading comprehension;
    vi. Mathematics calculation; or
    vii. Mathematics reasoning. (U.S. Office of Education, 1977, p. 65083)

This definition of learning disabilities and its accompanying regulations describe a syndrome rather than a particular student. Like the other definitions we have examined, the federal interpretation is useful for classifying children but provides little information on how to instruct these pupils.

The IDEA definition contains two key elements worthy of additional attention. One central component is the idea of a **discrepancy** between the student's academic performance and his or her estimated or assumed ability or potential. This discrepancy would not be anticipated on the basis of the pupil's overall intellectual ability—generally average to above average IQ. This discrepancy factor is considered by many professionals to be the *sine qua non* of the definition of learning disabilities. It explains how, for instance, a 10-year-old with above average intelligence reads at a level a year or more below expectations for his chronological age. Generally speaking, in most instances, a discrepancy of two years or more below expected performance levels in one academic area is necessary for a designation of learning disabilities. Unfortunately, the federal government failed to stipulate what was meant by "a severe discrepancy." Early on, they attempted to quantify the notion of a discrepancy by offering several formulas, but their efforts only led to criticism and confusion (Council for Learning Disabilities, 1986; Reynolds, 1992). Thus, the rules and regulations were published without a method for quantifying a severe discrepancy.

You may recall from Chapter 2 that IDEA 2004 removed this discrepancy provision. While PL 108-446 does not prohibit the use of a discrepancy approach for identifying pupils suspected of being learning disabled (Cortiella, 2006), it does give educators another way of discovering whether a student has a learning disability. School districts will now be able, if they so choose, to use a process that determines if the pupil responds to empirically validated, scientifically based interventions—a procedure known as **response to intervention,** or RTI. We will have much more to say about this new way of thinking later in this chapter.

The 1977 federal interpretation also specifies that a learning disability cannot be due primarily to sensory impairments, mental retardation, emotional problems, or environmental, cultural, or economic disadvantage. This language has come to be known as the **exclusionary clause.** This concept has generated considerable concern in some circles because it seems to suggest that students with other impairments cannot be considered learning disabled as well. Mercer and Pullen (2005), however, believe that the word *primarily* suggests that a learning disability can coexist with other exceptionalities. We believe that what is important is that professionals recognize that a youngster is experiencing learning difficulties, regardless of their etiology, and thus is in need of some form of intervention.

Association for Children with Learning Disabilities

The federal definition of learning disabilities has had its share of criticism and accompanying controversy. As a result, in 1986 the Association for Children with Learning Disabilities (now known as the Learning Disabilities Association of America) proposed a definition that incorporates several key elements not found in the IDEA definition. This substitute definition stresses the lifelong aspect of learning disabilities, addresses issues of socialization and self-esteem, eliminates the exclusionary language, and suggests that adaptive behaviors (daily living skills) may also be compromised by this disability. This group's definition is as follows:

> Specific Learning Disabilities is a chronic condition of presumed neurological origin which selectively interferes with the development, integration, and/or demonstration of verbal and/or nonverbal abilities. Specific Learning Disabilities exists as a distinct handicapping condition and varies in its manifestations and in degree of severity. Throughout life, the condition can affect self-esteem, education, vocation, socialization, and/or daily living activities. (Association for Children with Learning Disabilities, 1986, p. 15)

The Continuing Debate

After reading all of these definitions, you may believe that the field of learning disabilities is in a continual state of confusion and raucous debate over what a learning disability is. You may be partly correct. Some of the confusion is due to the different theoretical orientations of professionals working in the field. Remember, this is a multidisciplinary field that embraces sometimes competing viewpoints as to the very nature of the construct and its etiology. As noted earlier, it is perhaps best to envision learning disabilities as a family or syndrome of disabilities affecting a wide range of academic and/or behavioral performance. The key elements of the various definitions are summarized in Table 6.1.

Table 6.1	Common Components of Definitions of Learning Disabilities

- Intellectual functioning within normal range

- Significant gap or discrepancy between a student's assumed potential and actual achievement

- Inference that learning disabilities are not primarily caused by other disabilities or extrinsic factors

- Difficulty in learning in one or more academic areas

- Presumption of central nervous system dysfunction

A Brief History of the Field

Learning disabilities is an evolving and ever-changing field. Over the years, it has been influenced and significantly shaped by eminent individuals, various movements, governmental policies, research findings, and theoretical debates and has benefited from the activities of various advocacy/interest groups. The collective outcome of these sometimes competing efforts has been the present-day concept of learning disabilities.

The origins of the field of learning disabilities are international, multicultural, and multidisciplinary (Hallahan, Kauffman, & Lloyd, 1999). In fact, according to Hallahan et al., over the past century seven different groups and professions have been involved, in varying degrees, in influencing the growth of the field. Their estimation of the relative level of involvement of these groups is illustrated in Figure 6.1.

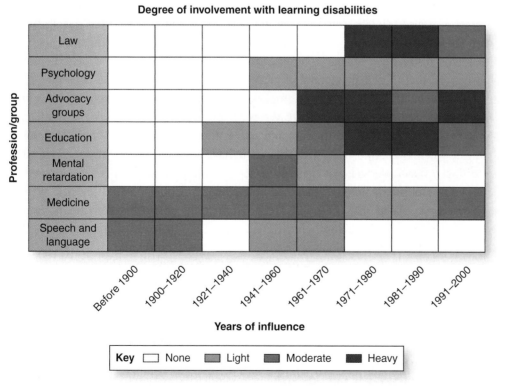

Figure 6.1	

Professions/Groups Contributing to the Development of the Field of Learning Disabilities

Note: Intensity of shading corresponds to amount of involvement, with darkest shading indicating highest involvement level.

Source: Adapted from D. Hallahan, J. Kauffman, and J. Lloyd, *Introduction to Learning Disabilities*, 2nd ed. (Boston: Allyn and Bacon, 1999), p. 4.

Figure 6.2

Phases in the Development of the Field of Learning Disabilities

Source: Adapted from J. Lerner and F. Kline, *Learning Disabilities and Related Disorders*, 10th ed. (Boston: Houghton Mifflin, 2006), p. 25.

Lerner and Kline (2006) divide the development of the field into four distinct historical periods spanning almost 200 years. These phases, illustrated in Figure 6.2, are discussed in the following sections.

Foundation Phase

Although the modern-day concept of learning disabilities traces its origin to an address given by Samuel Kirk in 1963, the roots of this concept lie in the studies of brain functions conducted in the nineteenth and early twentieth centuries. Neurologists and other physicians of this era were interested in detecting which areas of the brain control specific activities such as speech or reading. By investigating adults with brain damage, these early pioneers were able to identify regions of the brain that appeared to be associated with particular cognitive impairments such as aphasia (inability to speak). James Hinshelwood, for example, was a Scottish medical researcher who was intrigued by a young boy's inability to learn to read. Despite apparently normal intelligence and vision, this child exhibited a severe reading disability that Hinshelwood called "word blindness." He attributed this problem to a defect in a specific area of the boy's brain.

These pioneering efforts paved the way for later scientists such as Kurt Goldstein, a physician who studied soldiers suffering from traumatic brain injuries acquired during World War I. He noticed that many of these young men exhibited perceptual impairments; they were highly distractible, unable to attend to relevant stimuli, and overly meticulous. He hypothesized that these behavioral and perceptual impairments were the consequence of damage to the brain. Goldstein's theorizing was later expanded on by Alfred Strauss, a neuropsychiatrist, and his colleague Heniz Werner, a developmental psychologist. Both men fled Nazi Germany and joined the research staff at the Wayne County Training School in Michigan, where they studied children thought to have brain injury and mental retardation. Interestingly, they observed that these students exhibited characteristics similar to those identified by Goldstein, although they had not suffered any obvious head injuries. Werner and Strauss speculated that the pupils' retardation could be attributed to brain damage resulting from nongenetic factors. They developed a list of behavioral characteristics that distinguished between individuals with and without brain injury and suggested instructional tactics that could benefit students with learning disabilities.

Transition Phase

Beginning in the 1930s, teachers, reading specialists, psychologists, and others began to apply the scientific research evidence to children with learning problems. During this period, various individuals from different professional backgrounds played key roles in developing assessment instruments and remediation strategies designed to ameliorate academic difficulties (Lerner, 2003). Among the important theorists and contributions of this period are the following:

- Samuel Orton, a specialist in neurology, hypothesized that language disorders in children were due to the absence of cerebral dominance. He also devoted considerable energy to working with pupils with severe reading disorders, whom he called dyslexic. He speculated that their reading difficulties were due to neurological problems. The Orton Dyslexia Society is named in honor of his contributions in this area.
- Grace Fernald, an educator who worked at the laboratory school at the University of California, Los Angeles, established a clinic for children who were experiencing significant learning difficulties despite their normal intellect. Over the years, she perfected various remedial reading and spelling programs. One of her tactics was a visual-auditory-kinesthetic-tactile (VAKT) approach to learning. This technique is the foundation of today's multisensory approach to instruction.
- Newell Kephart, a colleague of Strauss at the Wayne County Training School, pioneered a perceptual-motor development theory of learning. He advocated movement and physical exercises, among other corrective activities, as a means of remediating learning problems, which he attributed to deficiencies in perceptual-motor integration.
- Marianne Frostig was another early worker in the field of learning disabilities. She believed that a youngster's academic difficulties, especially poor reading, were a consequence of poorly developed visual perceptual skills. Assessment and remediation efforts, therefore, centered on specific aspects of visual perception. Frostig constructed her Developmental Test of Visual Perception as a means of pinpointing areas of weakness. Deficits were remediated by means of specially prepared exercises in hopes of improving visual perceptual abilities and thus the student's performance in reading. Her approach, like Kephart's, remained popular for many years but eventually fell out of favor among professionals for lack of empirical evidence documenting its effectiveness.

Integration Phase

In the latter part of the twentieth century, learning disabilities became an established disability area in schools across the United States (Lerner & Kline, 2006). As mentioned earlier, it was Samuel Kirk who initially popularized the term *learning disabilities*. This new term was welcomed by parents whose children had previously been identified as neurologically impaired, perceptually handicapped, brain damaged, and other pejorative labels. When schools elected to serve these students, many of whom were experiencing significant academic difficulties, they were often incorrectly placed in classes for pupils with mental retardation or, in some instances, in settings for children with emotional problems; others received services from remedial reading specialists. Some pupils were denied help because school authorities were unable to classify them using the then current disabilities categories necessary for placement in a special education program.

The integration era witnessed the enactment of PL 91-230, the Specific Learning Disabilities Act of 1969, soon followed by the landmark "Bill of Rights" for children with disabilities, PL 94-142, now referred to as IDEA. Other milestones included the establishment of the Association for Children with Learning Disabilities in 1964, followed four years later by the birth of the Division for Children with Learning Disabilities (DCLD) as part of the Council for Exceptional Children (CEC). In 1982, a group of DCLD members withdrew from CEC over policy issues and created an independent association also concerned about individuals with learning disabilities, the Council for Learning Disabilities. Also in 1982, other former DCLD members began a new division under the auspices of CEC, the Division for Learning Disabilities.

The Current Phase

It is hard to pinpoint the end of the integration phase and the beginning of the current phase. Beginning in the last decades of the twentieth century, however, the field of learning disabilities has been affected by several, sometimes controversial, forces. Some special educators believe that the field is embarking on a period of turbulent transition (Hallahan & Mercer, 2002). Mercer and Pullen (2005) predict that the field will be buffeted by a variety of social, political, economic, and professional forces. The question is, How will the field respond to these challenges? Some of the emerging challenges or issues identified by Lerner and Kline (2006) include concerns about the movement toward full inclusion, how best to serve culturally and linguistically diverse learners, the impact of computer technology, and the increasing attention devoted to youngsters with attention deficit disorders, along with issues of high-stakes assessment and several other matters. Many of these topics will be addressed elsewhere in this chapter.

Prevalence of Learning Disabilities

It is difficult to ascertain the percentage of students with learning disabilities because of variations used in determining eligibility for services. Current estimates range from 1 to 30 percent of the school population (Lerner & Kline, 2006). Recent statistics compiled by the federal government suggest that approximately 2.78 million pupils ages 6 to 21 are identified as learning disabled (U.S. Department of Education, 2007). Thus, learning disabilities is by far the largest category of special education, accounting for slightly less than one-half (45.5%) of all individuals receiving services in the 2005–2006 school year.

The growth of the field of learning disabilities is nothing short of phenomenal. During the 1976–1977 school year, the initial year of federal reporting, the number of pupils identified as learning disabled was slightly less than 800,000; over the next twenty-nine years, this figure gradually increased to well over 2.7 million youngsters, an increase of approximately 250 percent.

This dramatic increase is obviously cause for concern. Critics assert that the number has grown because the concept itself is ill defined (Hallahan, Lloyd, Kauffman, Weiss, & Martinez, 2005), and because it is extremely difficult to distinguish between underachieving pupils and those diagnosed as learning disabled (Kavale, 2002). However, not all professionals are convinced that the growth is unwarranted. Several valid reasons could account for the spiraling growth rate. According to Lerner and Kline (2006), the rapid increase is an artifact of (1) greater public awareness of the disability, resulting in more referrals for services; (2) improved diagnostic and assessment procedures; and (3) higher social acceptance of the label and less accompanying stigma.

The number of pupils identified as learning disabled varies by age. The number of children receiving services increases steadily between the ages of 6 and 9 (from approximately

28,000 to about 203,000), which is not too surprising considering the increasing academic demands of the elementary school curriculum. The bulk of students served (41%), however, are between the ages of 10 and 13, with a sharp decrease observed for individuals between 16 and 21 years of age (U.S. Department of Education, 2006). The downward trend during the later teen years may be due to a significant dropout problem among adolescents who are learning disabled.

Finally, the federal government now counts preschoolers with learning disabilities. The U.S. Department of Education (2007) reports in excess of 12,000 toddlers with learning disabilities. This number represents 1.7 percent of all preschoolers with a disability.

Etiology of Learning Disabilities

Despite intense research activity over the years, pinpointing the precise cause or causes of learning disabilities has remained an elusive goal. In fact, researchers have been unable to offer much in the way of concrete evidence as to the etiology of learning disabilities (Hallahan et al., 2005). Many of the proposed causal factors remain largely speculative. In the vast majority of instances, the cause of a person's learning disability remains unknown. Just as there are many different types of learning disabilities, there appear to be multiple etiological possibilities. We should point out that the cause of an individual's learning difficulties is often of little educational relevance. In other words, knowing why a particular pupil is learning disabled does not necessarily translate into effective instructional strategies and practices. Nonetheless, investigators posit four basic categories for explaining the etiology of learning disabilities: acquired trauma, genetic/hereditary influences, biochemical abnormalities, and environmental possibilities (Mercer & Pullen, 2005).

Neurological dysfunction is suspected as a cause of some learning disabilities.

Acquired Trauma

The medical literature uses the term *acquired trauma* when describing injury or damage to the central nervous system (CNS) that originates outside the person and results in learning disorders. Depending on when the damage occurs, the trauma is identified as prenatal (before birth), perinatal (during birth), or postnatal (after birth). These traumas, according to Mercer and Pullen (2005), have been linked to learning problems in children.

One example of an acquired trauma that may manifest itself pre-, peri-, or postnatally is **brain injury.** Historically speaking, professionals have long presumed CNS dysfunction as a probable cause of learning disabilities (Hallahan & Mercer, 2002), and for some students this is a valid assumption. Spivak (1986) estimates that as many as 20 percent of children identified as learning disabled have had a prior brain injury. (Of course, this also means that eight out of ten youngsters do not evidence brain damage.) The belief that injury to the CNS is a likely cause of learning disabilities is common in some professional circles. Advances in neuroimaging techniques such as magnetic resonance imaging (MRI), computed tomography (CT), and other computerized neurological measures have allowed researchers, in some instances, to establish the importance of neurological dysfunction as a cause of learning disabilities. In the majority of cases, however, there is no definitive evidence of brain damage. In the absence of clear clinical evidence, it is perhaps best to view these data as speculative and inferential. For this reason, professionals, especially physicians, often use terms such as *assumed brain injury* and *presumed CNS dysfunction* when talking about learning disabilities.

Brain injury is certainly one type of acquired trauma that can occur before, during, and after birth, but a number of other factors have also been implicated as possible causes of learning disabilities:

PRENATAL CAUSES

- Smoking
- Illicit drugs
- Use of alcohol

PERINATAL CAUSES

- Prolonged and difficult delivery
- Anoxia
- Prematurity/low birth weight
- Trauma caused by medical instruments such as forceps

POSTNATAL CAUSES

- Strokes
- Concussions
- Meningitis/encephalitis
- High fever
- Head injury resulting from falls or accidents (Mercer & Pullen, 2005)

Genetic/Hereditary Influences

Do learning disabilities "run" in families? Researchers investigating this question believe that some learning problems are indeed inherited. Over the years, a fairly strong link has been established between heredity and some types of learning disabilities (Galaburda, 2005; Plomin & Kovas, 2005). Raskind (2001) notes, for instance, that reading and spelling deficits are substantially inherited. **Familiality studies,** which examine the tendency of certain conditions to occur in a single family, suggest that reading difficulties (Pennington, 1990) and certain types of speech and language impairments (Lewis, 1992) are family related. Familiality does not clearly prove heritability, however; learning problems may occur in certain families for environmental reasons, such as child-rearing practices. We recommend, therefore, that the findings of familiality studies be interpreted cautiously.

Although it is difficult to control for the effect of environmental influences on learning, **heritability studies** enable investigators to more clearly answer the question, "Are learning disabilities inherited?" In this investigative technique, scientists compare the school performance of monozygotic twins (identical twins, developing from the same egg with identical genetic characteristics) with that of dizygotic twins (fraternal twins, developing from two different eggs with different genetic makeup). The research evidence generally supports the hypothesis that certain types of learning problems, including reading disabilities, are more common among identical twins than fraternal twins (Reynolds et al., 1996; Wood & Grigorenko, 2001).

Biochemical Abnormalities

In some youngsters, biochemical conditions are suspected of causing learning disabilities. Over the years, several different theories have enjoyed varying degrees of popularity among parents and professionals. In the mid-1970s, Feingold (1975, 1976) championed the view that allergic reactions to certain artificial colorings, flavorings, and additives contained in many food products contribute to children's learning problems and hyperactive behavior. He recommends that parents restrict the consumption of foods containing natural salicylates, including apples, oranges, and some types of berries; ban products containing artificial colors and flavors; and limit the intake of certain other products such as toothpaste and compounds containing aspirin. The scientific community, however, has found little support for Feingold's theory (Kavale & Forness, 1983).

Another popular theory of this era was megavitamin therapy, whose chief advocate was psychiatrist Alan Cott. Cott (1972) theorizes that learning disabilities can be caused by the inability of a person's blood to synthesize a normal amount of vitamins. In an effort to treat learning disabilities, large daily doses of certain vitamins are recommended to counteract the suspected vitamin deficiency. Again, scientific research (Arnold, Christopher, Huestis, & Smeltzer, 1978) has failed to substantiate the benefit of this treatment.

We suspect that, in some instances, an individual's biochemical makeup may affect his or her learning and behavior. The current research evidence, however, cannot definitively support this hypothesis.

Environmental Possibilities

Another school of thought attributes the etiology of learning disabilities to a host of environmental factors such as low socioeconomic status, malnutrition, lack of access to health care, and other variables that may contribute to neurological dysfunction (Hallahan et al., 2005). Although the IDEA definition and others specifically exclude these conditions as etiological possibilities, many educators believe that these risk factors indirectly contribute to the learning and behavioral difficulties of some pupils.

Another variable implicated as causing learning disabilities is the quality of instruction that students receive. Simply stated, some children are identified as learning disabled as a result of poor teaching. Engelmann (1977) estimates that the vast majority of students labeled learning disabled "have been seriously mistaught. Learning disabilities are made, not born" (p. 47). Recently, during a visit to a foreign country, your author was told by a veteran special educator of a slogan in her country that speaks directly to this issue: "There are no bad students, only poor teachers." Lovitt (1978) also contends that learning disabilities may result from poor teachers and inadequate instruction. While implying that the quality of the learning environment contributes to learning disabilities, researchers also note that learning problems can often be remediated by exposure to individualized and high-quality instructional practices.

Characteristics of Individuals with Learning Disabilities

There is probably no such entity as a "typical" person with learning disabilities; no two students possess the identical profile of strengths and weaknesses. The concept of learning disabilities covers an extremely wide range of characteristics. One pupil may have deficits in just one area while another exhibits deficits in several areas; yet both will be labeled learning disabled. Some children will experience cognitive difficulties, others may have problems with motor skills, and still others may exhibit social deficits.

Over the years, parents, educators, and other professionals have identified a wide variety of characteristics associated with learning disabilities. One of the earliest profiles, developed by Clements (1966), includes the following ten frequently cited attributes:

- Hyperactivity
- Perceptual-motor impairments
- Emotional lability
- Coordination problems
- Disorders of attention
- Impulsivity
- Disorders of memory and thinking
- Academic difficulties
- Language deficits
- Equivocal neurological signs

Parents of children with learning disabilities (Ariel, 1992) have described many of the same behaviors. Lerner and Kline's (2006) recent list includes the following learning and behavioral characteristics of individuals with learning disabilities:

- Disorders of attention
- Poor motor abilities
- Psychological process deficits and information-processing problems
- Lack of cognitive strategies needed for efficient learning
- Oral language difficulties
- Reading difficulties
- Written language problems
- Quantitative disorders
- Social skills deficits

Not all students with learning disabilities will exhibit these characteristics, and many pupils who demonstrate these same behaviors are quite successful in the classroom. It is often the frequency, intensity, and duration of the behaviors that lead to problems in school and elsewhere. Furthermore, in some instances, the characteristics are contradictory. One youngster, for example, is rambunctious and "always on the go" (hyperactive) while a classmate who is also learning disabled may be overly lethargic and inactive (hypoactive). The way deficits are manifested also varies according to grade level. A language disorder may exhibit itself as delayed speech in a preschooler, as a reading problem in the elementary grades, and as a writing difficulty at the secondary level (Lerner & Kline, 2006).

Gender differences also play a role in the recognition of learning disabilities. Boys are four times as likely as girls to be identified as learning disabled. Lerner and Kline (2006) synthesize several lines of research suggesting that, in actuality, there are not fewer girls with learning disabilities, but girls are not as readily identified—perhaps because of differences in the kinds of disabilities they exhibit. These experts note that "boys tend to exhibit more physical aggression and loss of control . . . [while] girls with learning disabilities tend to have more cognitive, language, and social problems, and to have severe academic achievement deficits in reading and math" (p. 17).

Learning disabilities encompass a broad range of characteristics beyond those associated primarily with academic problems. Mercer and Pullen (2005), for instance, believe that cognitive and social/emotional factors are also key elements (see Figure 6.3). Common cognitive disorders include deficits in attention, metacognition, memory, and perception. Social and emotional difficulties include hyperactive behaviors, low self-esteem, and learned helplessness.

In the past, professionals concerned with learning disabilities have typically focused on the elementary school-age child; in recent years, however, the field has adopted a life span approach. We now realize that learning disabilities may manifest themselves at different stages of life and that problems present themselves in different ways depending on the age of the individual (Lerner & Kline, 2006).

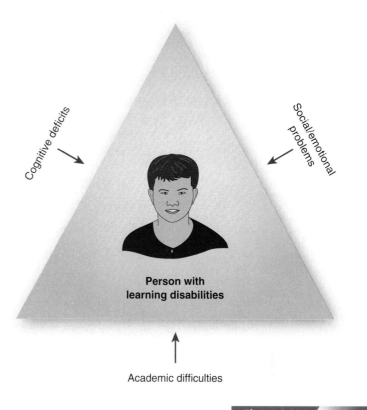

Figure 6.3

Broad Characteristics Associated with Learning Disabilities

Learning Characteristics

Most professionals agree that the primary characteristics of students with learning disabilities are deficits in academic performance. A learning disability does not exist without impairments in academic achievement. These deficits may involve several different categories of school performance.

READING Well over half of all students identified as learning disabled exhibit problems with reading (Bender, 2008; Lerner & Kline, 2006). The difficulties experienced by these youngsters are as varied as the children themselves. Some pupils have trouble with reading comprehension; others evidence word recognition errors; still others lack word analysis skills or are deficient in oral reading. Table 6.2 lists several areas of reading difficulty common among students with learning disabilities. Deficits in reading are thought to be a primary reason for failure in school; they also contribute to a loss of self-esteem and self-confidence (Polloway, Patton, & Serna, 2008).

One term frequently heard when discussing reading problems is **dyslexia.** Simply stated, dyslexia is a type of reading disorder in which the student fails to recognize and comprehend written words—a severe impairment in the ability to read. It is generally thought that this problem results from difficulties with **phonological awareness**—a lack of understanding of the rules that govern the correspondence between specific sounds and certain letters that make up words (Lyon, Shaywitz, & Shaywitz, 2003; Raskind, 2001). In other words, letter-sound recognition is impaired.

MATHEMATICS Researchers estimate that about one out of every four pupils with learning disabilities receives assistance because of difficulties with mathematics (Lerner & Kline, 2006). Students who experience this problem are unique; not all children exhibit the same deficiency or impairment. In some instances, pupils may have difficulty with computational skills, word problems, spatial relationships, or writing numbers and copying

Table 6.2	Common Reading Problems of Students with Learning Disabilities	
	Problem Areas	**Observations**
Reading Habits	Tension movements	Frowning, fidgeting, using a high-pitched voice, lip biting
	Insecurity	Refusing to read, crying, attempting to distract the teacher
	Loses place	Losing place frequently (often associated with repetitions)
	Lateral head movements	Jerking head
	Holds material close	Deviating extremely (from 15 to 18 inches)
Word Recognition Errors	Omissions	Omitting a word (e.g., *Tom saw [a] cat*)
	Insertions	Inserting words (e.g., *The dog ran [fast] after the cat*)
	Substitutions	Substituting one word for another (e.g., *The house ~~horse~~ was big*)
	Reversals	Reversing letters in a word (e.g., *no* for *on*, *was* for *saw*)
	Mispronunciations	Mispronouncing words (e.g., *mister for miser*)
	Transpositions	Reading words in the wrong order (e.g., *She away ran* for *She ran away*)
	Unknown words	Hesitating for 5 seconds at words they cannot pronounce
	Slow, choppy reading	Not recognizing words quickly enough (20 to 30 words per minute)
Comprehension Errors	Cannot recall basic facts	Unable to answer specific questions about a passage (e.g., *What was the dog's name?*)
	Cannot recall sequence	Unable to tell sequence of the story that was read
	Cannot recall main theme	Unable to recall the main topic of the story
Miscellaneous Symptoms	Word-by-word reading	Reading in a choppy, halting, and laborious manner (no attempt to group words into thought units)
	Strained, high-pitched voice	Reading in a pitch higher than conversational tone
	Inadequate phrasing	Inappropriately grouping words (e.g., *The dog ran into [pause] the woods*)
	Ignored or misinterpreted punctuation	Running together phrases, clauses, or sentences

Source: C. Mercer and P. Pullen, *Students with Learning Disabilities,* 6th ed. (Upper Saddle River, NJ: Prentice Hall, 2005), p. 195. Reprinted by permission of Pearson Education, Inc., Upper Saddle River, NJ.

shapes. Other classmates may have problems with telling time, understanding fractions and decimals, or measuring. Problems that begin in elementary school generally continue through high school and may have debilitating consequences in adulthood.

WRITTEN LANGUAGE Many individuals with learning disabilities exhibit deficits in written language, including spelling, handwriting, and composition (Hallahan et al., 2005). Researchers (Jennings, Caldwell, & Lerner, 2006) speculate that a link exists between these areas of deficiency and a person's reading ability. The association between reading and writing impairments should not be too surprising, as both may arise from a lack of phonological awareness.

Poor penmanship may be due to the absence of the requisite fine motor skills needed for legible handwriting and/or a lack of understanding of spatial relationships (for example,

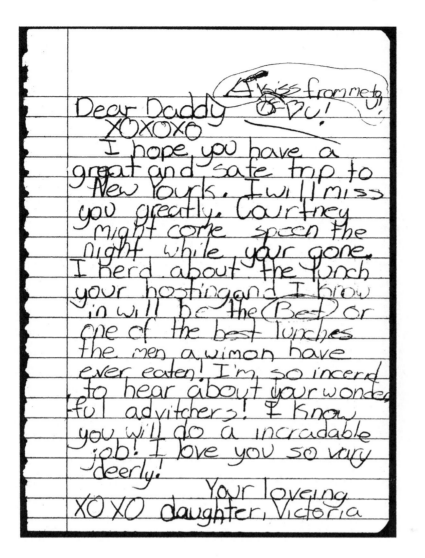

Figure 6.4

Writing Sample of a 10-Year-Old Girl

*Dear Daddy
A kiss from me to you!*

XOXOXO

I hope you have a great and safe trip to New York. I will miss you greatly. Courtney might come spend the night while you are gone. I heard about the lunch you are hosting and I know it will be the best or one of the best lunches the men and women have ever eaten! I'm so interested to hear about your wonderful adventures! I know you will do a incredible job! I love you so very dearly.

XOXO

Your loving daughter, Victoria

up, down, bottom), which may contribute to difficulties with letter formation and spacing between words and sentences (see Figure 6.4).

Children's writing changes as they mature. According to Hallahan et al. (1999), the focus of a youngster's writing "shifts from (1) the process of writing (handwriting and spelling) to (2) the written product (having written something) to (3) communication with readers (getting across one's message)" (p. 396). Early on, pupils focus on becoming competent in mastering the mechanical aspects of composition—spelling and handwriting; in later grades, they learn to organize and present their ideas in a lucid and logical fashion. Children who are learning disabled, however, lag behind their nondisabled peers. Investigators have observed that individuals with learning disabilities use less complex sentence structure, incorporate fewer ideas, produce poorly organized paragraphs, and write less complex stories (Hallahan et al., 2005).

Spelling is another problem area for students with learning disabilities. They may omit certain letters or add incorrect ones. Auditory memory and discrimination difficulties are thought to be part of the reason for their problem.

SPOKEN LANGUAGE Persons with learning disabilities frequently experience difficulties with oral expression—a problem that can affect both academic performance and

Reading difficulties are very common among students with learning disabilities.

social interactions. Problems with appropriate word choice, understanding complex sentence structures, and responding to questions are not uncommon. Specific mechanical deficits may involve syntax (rule systems that determine how words are organized into sentences), semantics (word meanings), and phonology (sound formation and blending of sounds to form words). One aspect of oral expression that is receiving increased attention is **pragmatics**—the functional use of language in social situations. Researchers note that children with learning disabilities sometimes experience communication problems in social settings (Pearl & Donahue, 2004). Participating in conversations with friends can be especially troublesome for someone who is learning disabled. The ebb and flow that is characteristic of conversations may elude them, and nonverbal language clues may also be overlooked. In short, many individuals with learning disabilities are not good conversationalists.

MEMORY It is well documented that children and adolescents with learning disabilities have significant difficulties remembering both academic and nonacademic information, such as doctor appointments, homework assignments, multiplication facts, directions, and telephone numbers. Teachers frequently comment that, with these students, it seems to be "in one ear and out the other," which can be highly aggravating for teachers as well as parents.

Research evidence suggests that students with learning disabilities have problems with short-term memory as well as working memory (Swanson & Sachse-Lee, 2001). **Short-term memory** tasks typically involve the recall, in correct order, of either aurally or visually presented information (such as lists of digits or pictures) shortly after hearing or seeing the items several times. **Working memory** requires that an individual retain information while simultaneously engaging in another cognitive activity. Working memory is involved, for example, when we try to remember a person's address while also listening to directions on how to arrive there (Swanson, 1999).

Students with learning disabilities, in contrast to their typical peers, apparently do not spontaneously use effective learning strategies (such as rehearsal or categorizing of items) as an aid in recall. Deficits in memory, particularly working memory, often translate into difficulties in the classroom. Success with reading and math seems to depend more on working memory than on short-term memory (*CEC Today*, 2003). Working memory also appears to be crucial for word recognition and reading comprehension (Ashbaker & Swanson, 1996).

METACOGNITION It is not unusual for persons with learning disabilities to exhibit deficits in **metacognition**—the ability to evaluate and monitor one's own performance. Students who are learning disabled often lack an awareness of their own thinking process (Butler, 1998). Metacognitive skills typically consist of several key components: (1) a recognition of task requirements—that is, the strategies and resources needed to perform effectively; (2) implementation of the appropriate process; and (3) monitoring, evaluating, and adjusting one's performance to ensure successful task completion (Butler). Competency as a learner requires that students exhibit these metacognitive skills.

The reading problems of some children with learning disabilities may be due to deficiencies in metacognition. Reading comprehension difficulties, for example, may be due to deficits in the following skills:

- **Clarifying the purpose(s) of reading:** Pupils do not adjust their reading styles to accommodate the difficulty of the text.
- **Focusing attention on important goals:** Youngsters with reading problems experience difficulty in selecting the main ideas of a paragraph.
- **Monitoring one's level of comprehension:** Inefficient readers do not recognize that they are failing to understand what they are reading.
- **Rereading and scanning ahead:** Children with learning disabilities do not go back and reread portions of previously read text, nor do they scan upcoming material as an aid to comprehension.
- **Consulting external sources:** Ineffective readers do not utilize external sources like dictionaries and encyclopedias. (Hallahan et al., 2005)

Fortunately, as you will learn later, metacognitive skills can be taught.

Many individuals with learning disabilities believe that no matter how hard they try, they will still fail.

ATTRIBUTIONS What individuals believe about what contributes to their success or failure on a task is known as *attribution.* Many students with learning disabilities attribute success not to their own efforts but to situations or events beyond their control, such as luck. These pupils are identified as being outwardly directed.

Chronic difficulties with academic assignments often lead children with learning disabilities to anticipate failure; success is seen as an unattainable goal no matter how hard they try. Youngsters who maintain this attitude frequently give up and will not even attempt to complete the task. Seligman (1992) identifies this outlook as **learned helplessness.** Loss of self-esteem and a lack of motivation are common consequences of this phenomenon.

Because of their propensity for academic failure, individuals with learning disabilities tend to become passive or inactive learners. They are not actively involved or engaged in their own learning and often fail to demonstrate initiative in the learning process. When confronted with a task, persons with learning disabilities use less effective strategies; they have a deficiency in strategic learning behavior (Deshler, Ellis, & Lenz, 1996). Swanson (1989) calls these pupils "actively inefficient learners." In some cases, attributions can be altered through the use of various reinforcement and motivational strategies that attempt to demonstrate to the pupil the link between his or her own efforts and success (Fulk, 1996; Sexton, Harris, & Graham, 1998).

Social and Emotional Problems

Research suggests that some students with learning disabilities, in comparison to their typical peers, have lower self-esteem (Pearl & Donahue, 2004; Vaughn, Sinagub, & Kim, 2004) and a poor self-concept, most likely due to frustration with their learning difficulties (Mercer & Pullen,

2005). Teachers perceive pupils with learning disabilities to be significantly lower in social competency and school adjustment than their classmates (Tur-Kaspa & Bryan, 1995). Investigators are now beginning to realize that deficits in social skills are a common characteristic among many, but not all, individuals with learning disabilities (Kavale & Mostert, 2004; Wiener, 2004). Many of these students are deficient in social cognition; they are inept at understanding and interpreting social cues and social situations, which can easily lead to impaired interpersonal relationships. The social-emotional difficulties of persons with learning disabilities may be the result of social imperceptiveness—a lack of skill in detecting subtle affective cues. Students with learning disabilities often experience rejection by nondisabled peers and have difficulty making friends, possibly because they misinterpret the feelings and emotions of others (Lerner & Kline, 2006).

Attention Problems and Hyperactivity

Individuals who are learning disabled frequently experience difficulty attending to tasks, and some exhibit excess movement and activity, or hyperactive behavior. It is not unusual for educators to mention these characteristics when describing students with learning disabilities. Teachers note that some pupils have difficulty staying on task and completing assignments, following directions, or focusing their attention for a sustained period of time—they are easily distracted. In other instances, children are perceived to be overly active and fidgety, racing from one thing to another as if driven. Problems with inattention, distractibility, and hyperactivity can easily impair and impede an individual's successful performance in the classroom, at home, and in social situations.

The term usually heard when discussing this condition is **attention deficit hyperactivity disorder (ADHD),** typical in the language of medical professionals and psychologists. This label is derived from the *Diagnostic and Statistical Manual of Mental Disorders—Text Revision,* revised in 2000 by the American Psychiatric Association and commonly referred to as DSM-IV-TR. Although hyperactivity and attention disorders are fairly common among persons with learning disabilities, with estimates ranging from about 10 to 40 and possibly 70 percent of children with learning disabilities displaying characteristics of ADHD (Bender, 2008; Forness & Kavale, 2002; Kube, Peterson, & Palmer, 2002), the terms are *not* synonymous—not all students with learning disabilities have ADHD, and vice versa. The exact relationship between learning disabilities and ADHD is not fully understood, but scientists and researchers are now beginning to unravel this complex phenomenon.

Assessment of Learning Disabilities

Federal law dictates that individuals being considered for possible placement in a program for children with learning disabilities receive a multidisciplinary evaluation that is conducted by a team of professionals in a nondiscriminatory fashion. Recall that this evaluation process will only occur if the recommended prereferral strategies have proven ineffective. IDEA requires, among other regulations, that

- Tests are administered by trained individuals.
- Tests are reliable and valid and appropriate for the purpose for which they are being used.

- Tests are neither racially nor culturally discriminatory.
- Tests are administered in the student's native language or preferred means of communication.
- No single measure is used as the basis for determining a pupil's eligibility.

Once the evaluation is completed, the team determines the youngster's eligibility for placement in a learning disabilities program in light of their state's definition of learning disabilities and federal guidelines.

Assessment Decisions

At the heart of assessing a student for possible placement in a program for individuals with learning disabilities is determining whether the student exhibits a severe discrepancy between estimated or perceived ability and actual educational achievement. This discrepancy is typically established by comparing a student's performance on a standardized achievement test with a measure of cognitive abilities or intelligence. Frequently used measures of intellectual performance (mentioned in Chapter 5) include the Wechsler Intelligence Scale for Children (4th edition), the Stanford-Binet Intelligence Scale (5th edition), and the more recently developed Kaufman Assessment Battery for Children. A wide variety of achievement tests are available to educational diagnosticians. Comprehensive batteries designed to measure overall academic achievement include the well-known Iowa Test of Basic Skills, the Stanford Achievement Test, and the Wechsler Individual Achievement Test. Many other achievement tests assess a student's abilities in content areas such as math, reading, and language arts. Several states use the concept of a severe discrepancy to identify individuals with learning disabilities.

A variety of complicated mathematical formulas are used to arrive at a discrepancy score. Unfortunately, there is no nationally agreed upon mechanism for determining a discrepancy; different states use different formulas and even different tests in an effort to quantify the gap between potential and performance. As a result, a child identified as learning disabled in one state may be ineligible for services if the family relocates to another state.

Researchers, parents, and practitioners alike are now questioning the educational validity of identifying youngsters as learning disabled solely on the basis of a discrepancy formula and are calling for the use of alternative strategies such as relying on professionals' clinical judgment and experience in addition to assessing discrepancies among various cognitive and academic skills (Lerner & Kline, 2006).

RESPONSE TO INTERVENTION Recently, with the reauthorization of IDEA 2004, some of these concerns were addressed. States and local school districts now have the *option* of choosing between the achievement-ability discrepancy model or making eligibility decisions on the basis of how a pupil responds to scientific, research-based educational interventions. This strategy is commonly referred to as response to intervention (RTI) or response to treatment.

There is no formal definition of RTI, nor is there one model or strategy that is widely accepted by researchers or educators (Bradley, Danielson, & Doolittle, 2007; Cortiella, 2006). Generally speaking, RTI is a procedure whereby a pupil is exposed to increasing levels of instructional intervention with ongoing **progress monitoring.** Essentially, RTI

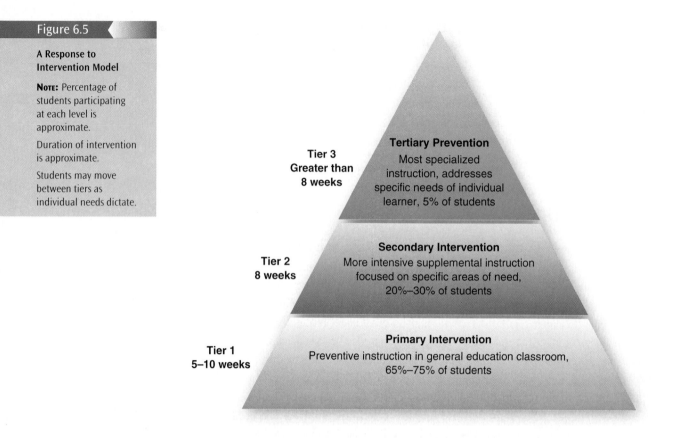

Figure 6.5

A Response to Intervention Model

NOTE: Percentage of students participating at each level is approximate.

Duration of intervention is approximate.

Students may move between tiers as individual needs dictate.

Tier 3
Greater than 8 weeks

Tertiary Prevention
Most specialized instruction, addresses specific needs of individual learner, 5% of students

Tier 2
8 weeks

Secondary Intervention
More intensive supplemental instruction focused on specific areas of need, 20%–30% of students

Tier 1
5–10 weeks

Primary Intervention
Preventive instruction in general education classroom, 65%–75% of students

is an instructional and dynamic assessment process based on rigorous scientific research (Kame'enui, 2007) and is typically portrayed as a multitiered model of prevention generally consisting of three levels. One such conceptualization is illustrated in Figure 6.5. This configuration is thought to best serve the early intervention and identification aims of RTI (Fuchs & Fuchs, 2005).

The student initially receives research-based instruction in the general education classroom. If the child fails to demonstrate "responsiveness" after receiving increasingly individualized and intensive instruction, a learning disability is presumed to be present and a referral for special education services is usually initiated. Using reading instruction as an example, Table 6.3 highlights the differences, according to one RTI model, between primary, secondary, and tertiary interventions.

The RTI model represents a significant conceptual shift in thinking from a "wait to fail" approach to one that emphasizes early identification and possible prevention (Bradley et al., 2007). This approach to determining whether a pupil has a learning disability eliminates poor or inadequate teaching as a possible reason for low achievement. It also places greater instructional responsibility on the shoulders of general educators.

While most of the early attention of RTI has focused on its application to reading, several benefits are recognized. Some of the advantages include a reduction in the number of inappropriate referrals for special education, interventions linked to ongoing assessment, greater collaboration between general and special educators, a reduction in the number of students recognized as having a learning disability, and less stigma placed on the learner (Klingner & Edwards, 2006; Marston, Muyskens, Lau, & Canter, 2003; Speece, Case, & Molloy, 2003).

Although support for this process is growing in some educational circles, the research evidence is limited, and some professionals still adhere to the traditional discrepancy model

Table 6.3	A Response to Intervention Model: Tiers of Instruction		
	Tier 1 (Primary)	**Tier 2 (Secondary)**	**Tier 3 (Tertiary)**
Definition	Reading instruction and programs, including ongoing professional development and benchmark assessments (3 times per year)	Instructional intervention employed to supplement, enhance, and support Tier 1; takes place in small groups	Individualized reading instruction extended beyond the time allocated for Tier 1; groups of 1–3 students
Focus	All students	Students identified with reading difficulties who have not responded to Tier 1 efforts	Students with marked difficulties in reading or reading disabilities who have not responded adequately to Tier 1 and Tier 2 efforts
Program	Scientifically based reading instruction and curriculum emphasizing the critical elements	Specialized, scientifically based reading instruction and curriculum emphasizing the critical elements	Sustained, intensive, scientifically based reading instruction and curriculum highly responsive to students' needs
Instruction	Sufficient opportunities to practice throughout the school day	• Additional attention, focus, support • Additional opportunities to practice embedded throughout the day • Preteach, review skills; frequent opportunities to practice skills	Carefully designed and implemented, explicit, systematic instruction
Interventionist	General education teacher	Personnel determined by the school (classroom teacher, specialized reading teacher, other trained personnel)	Personnel determined by the school (e.g., specialized reading teacher, special education teacher)
Setting	General education classroom	Appropriate setting designated by the school	Appropriate setting designated by the school
Grouping	Flexible grouping	Homogeneous small-group instruction (e.g., 1:4, 1:5)	Homogeneous small-group instruction (1:2, 1:3)
Time	Minimum of 90 minutes per day	20–30 minutes per day in addition to Tier 1	50-minute sessions (or longer) per day depending upon appropriateness of Tier 1
Assessment	Benchmark assessments at beginning, middle, and end of academic year	Progress monitoring twice a month on target skill to ensure adequate progress and learning	Progress monitoring at least twice a month on target skill to ensure adequate progress and learning

Source: Adapted from S. Vaughn and G. Roberts, "Secondary Interventions in Reading," *Teaching Exceptional Children, 39*(5), 2007, p. 41. Copyright © 2007. Reprinted with permission by the Council of Exceptional Children.

(Kavale, Holdnack, & Mostert, 2005). Many educators view RTI as a "promising practice" while acknowledging that several issues need to be addressed, for instance:

- Its application to other content areas such as mathematics;
- How responsiveness to intervention is determined;
- What the most effective duration of intervention is; and
- How many tiers or levels of intervention are required before a student is identified as learning disabled (Fuchs, Mock, Morgan, & Young, 2003; Stecker, 2007; Vaughn & Fuchs, 2003).

We suspect that these and other issues will be successfully resolved in the coming years. It will be interesting to see how local school districts respond to the RTI option for identifying pupils suspected of having a learning disability.

Assessment Strategies

Traditionally, standardized tests have played a major role in the evaluation of students thought to be learning disabled. These instruments are also known as **norm-referenced assessments** because an individual's performance is compared to a normative group of peers (for example, all sixth graders in their state or a national sample of sixth graders) who have taken the same test. Standardized assessment requires rigid adherence to directions for administering, scoring, and interpreting the results. Teachers and psychologists rely heavily on standardized tests when assessing for learning disabilities. Norm-referenced tests provide a great deal of statistical information, allowing professionals to *compare* a particular student's performance with that of other pupils in the normative group. **Criterion-referenced assessments,** on the other hand, *describe* a youngster's performance. Criterion-referenced tests measure a student's abilities against a predetermined criterion or mastery level. In other words, the child's performance is compared with a standard expectation (100% knowledge of multiplication facts), not with the performance of others. Criterion-referenced tests, also commonly called teacher-made tests, offer a means of educational accountability, in that a teacher can demonstrate that a student has learned specific skills. It is a bit more difficult to show improvement in terms of percentile rankings or even grade-level scores (Lerner & Kline, 2006).

Although standardized testing is a useful component of a nondiscriminatory evaluation and provides meaningful information for identification purposes, norm-referenced tests are weak in providing instructional direction. Teacher-made tests are perhaps better suited for guiding instruction. One of the chief benefits of criterion-referenced tests is that they can help in instructional planning and decision making and in monitoring progress toward educational goals. Individualized educational programs (IEPs) are often constructed around data gleaned from various types of criterion-referenced tests.

Assessment strategies should always fit the question we are asking about a particular student. Professionals must also pay careful attention to the purpose of the assessment and how the data will be used (Aiken, 2006).

CURRICULUM-BASED ASSESSMENT   One frequently voiced concern about standardized testing is that the test items do not necessarily reflect or represent the content of the curriculum that a student has been exposed to. **Curriculum-based assessment** (CBA), on the other hand, is a form of criterion-referenced assessment in which test items are based on objectives found in the local school curriculum. In this model, a pupil's performance, usually in the areas of math and reading, is evaluated several times a week with test items mirroring the daily instructional tasks. The student's performance is then charted or graphed so that his or her progress toward specific educational goals is easily recognized. The frequent and systematic sampling of a child's performance provides teachers with evidence of the effectiveness of their teaching tactics and may suggest the need for changes in instructional strategies. According to Lerner (2003), CBA is widely used in special education and is most useful for students with learning disabilities because it reinforces the important link between assessment and instruction.

PORTFOLIO ASSESSMENT   Disillusionment with traditional testing has contributed, in some educational circles, to a movement toward alternative assessment procedures. One form of alternative assessment is **authentic assessment,** which is believed to paint a more accurate or genuine picture of what a pupil can and cannot accomplish in real-life situations such as in the classroom or at home. An example of an authentic procedure is **portfolio assessment.** A portfolio is a collection of samples of a student's best work gathered over a period of time (Taylor, 2006). According to Paulson, Paulson, and Meyer (1991), "a portfolio is a purposeful collection of student work that exhibits the student's effort, progress, and achievements in one or more areas" (p. 60). Mercer and Pullen (2005) see portfolio assessment as an attempt to improve the evaluation process and enhance instructional decision making.

One of the critical issues in portfolio assessment is knowing what to include in the portfolio and how to evaluate the person's efforts. A portfolio should have a specific purpose; without direction, it can easily become a mere collection of products.

A wide variety of student-generated products can be included in a portfolio. The teacher must first consider the goals of the instructional program and then select samples to match its intent. Using goals from the child's IEP is one strategy the teacher may wish to employ in determining what to include (Lerner & Kline, 2006). Examples of the diverse work products that might be part of a portfolio include audio recordings of oral reading samples, summaries of science experiments, poems, art projects, book reports, excerpts from journals, weekly quizzes, and math worksheets. Because portfolios reflect student progress, Salend (1998) recommends that they be used during parent–teacher conferences.

Educational Considerations

As noted elsewhere, individuals with learning disabilities are an especially heterogeneous population whose disabilities range from mild to severe. These students require a diversity of educational interventions and teaching strategies designed to meet their unique academic, social, and behavioral needs.

Where Are Students with Learning Disabilities Educated?

The educational placement of children with special needs is currently one of the most controversial issues in the field of special education, and children with learning disabilities are not immune to this debate. Where students receive instruction can significantly affect their attitude, achievement, and social development (Mercer & Pullen, 2005).

From a historical perspective, the resource room has been one of the most common service delivery models for serving children with learning disabilities. Since the mid-1990s, however, there has been a subtle shift away from this option—most likely reflecting the trend toward more inclusive programs. For example, during the 1992–1993 school year, more than half (54%) of all pupils identified as learning disabled received instruction in a resource room (U.S. Department of Education, 1994). In this model, students leave the regular classroom on a regularly scheduled basis and travel to another classroom where they receive individualized instruction from a special educator. At the conclusion of their assigned time, students return to the general education classroom. More recent statistics indicate, however, that the regular classroom is currently the more popular placement. During the 2005–2006 school year, over half of all youngsters with learning disabilities received services in the regular classroom, and almost 35 percent were assigned to a resource room (U.S. Department of Education, 2007). This means that about nine out of every ten individuals with learning disabilities spend some, most, or all of their school day in a regular classroom (see Figure 6.6).

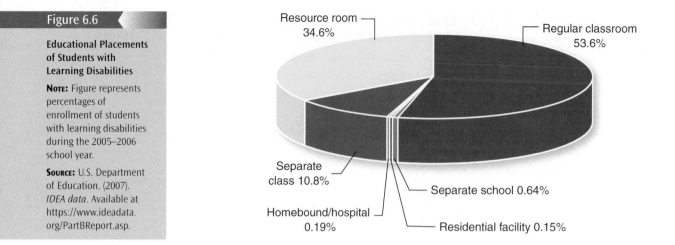

Figure 6.6

Educational Placements of Students with Learning Disabilities

NOTE: Figure represents percentages of enrollment of students with learning disabilities during the 2005–2006 school year.

SOURCE: U.S. Department of Education. (2007). *IDEA data*. Available at https://www.ideadata.org/PartBReport.asp.

Resource room 34.6%

Regular classroom 53.6%

Separate class 10.8%

Separate school 0.64%

Homebound/hospital 0.19%

Residential facility 0.15%

Researchers and others, however, argue against full inclusion as the placement option for *all* pupils with learning disabilities (Klingner, Vaughn, Hughes, Schumm, & Elbaum, 1998; National Joint Committee on Learning Disabilities, 2003; Swanson, 2000; Vaughn, Elbaum, & Boardman, 2001). The environment that is most appropriate for individuals with learning disabilities is the setting that is most enabling; inclusion must be done on a responsible basis and meet the unique needs of each child.

An individualized placement recommendation can only occur if there is a continuum of options from which to choose. Federal legislation does not require that pupils with learning disabilities be served only in the regular classroom. Legal scholars (Bateman & Linden, 1998; Osborne, 1997; Yell, 2006) note that the principle of least restrictive environment does not allow educators to presume that a single educational setting is appropriate for all youngsters with a particular type of disability. Such a notion would clearly be at odds with current federal law (Gargiulo & Kilgo, 2005). The contemporary controversy surrounding the question of where to educate pupils with special needs is a good example of where one size does not fit all; placing all students with learning disabilities in the general education classroom essentially ignores and disregards the concept of individualized planning (Crockett & Kauffman, 2001). Like Mercer and Pullen (2005), we are of the opinion that issues of placement must be evaluated on a case-by-case basis and decided based on the needs of the student rather than being directed by trends or philosophies that are insensitive to the uniqueness and individuality of each learner.

Instructional Approaches

There is no one "best" or "correct" way to teach individuals with learning disabilities. Just as we saw with the issue of educational placement, no single size or approach fits all. Individualization is the key to meeting the instructional needs of pupils with learning disabilities. Teachers often find that a wide variety of accommodations and modifications are necessary if the student is to experience success in the classroom. Some children will need additional time for testing or ask that a learning task be broken into smaller and more manageable segments; other pupils may require the privacy provided by a study carrel; some youngsters may need assistance in developing effective learning strategies; still others will benefit from additional drill and practice. What works for one student will not necessarily be appropriate for another.

✓ EFFECTIVE INSTRUCTIONAL PRACTICES | Teaching Reading

Phonic Analysis

Many students with learning disabilities experience difficulty with reading. A skill deficit often encountered is phonic analysis. Phonic analysis is a vital component of early reading instruction. Students must establish a strong understanding of letter-sound combinations and correspondence. They must also be able to recognize word parts. The following teaching strategies can help struggling readers learn to decode using phonic analysis skills.

- **Instructional content:** Teach letter-sound correspondence in a logical order. Most useful initially are the consonants *b, c, d, f, g, h, k, l, m, n, p, r, s,* and *t,* and the vowels. Present continuous letter sounds (e.g., *s* and /*sss*/, *m* and /mmm/, *n* and /nnn/) before stop letter sounds (*p* and /p/, *k* and /k/). Select letters that represent sounds found in decodable text that students will read.
- **Instructional content:** Introduce the most common sounds of the letters first. Lowercase letters should be taught before uppercase ones.
- **Instructional content:** Teach the letter combinations that most frequently occur in text.
- **Instructional content:** Avoid teaching letter-sound correspondence and letter combinations that sound similar and may confuse students. For instance, /m/ and /n/ and /sh/ and /ch/ should not be taught together. Letter combinations with the same sound, such as /ir/ and /ur/ and /ee/ and /ea/ can be taught at the same time.
- **Instructional content:** Teach phonograms containing letter-sound correspondences that have been introduced. Phonograms or rimes (which are parts of a word to which consonants or blends are added to make a word) such as *ap, at, ip, it, un,* and *et* paired with initial consonants or onsets provide opportunities to segment and blend sounds to make words. These words should be featured in the decodable text that students will read.
- **Instructional delivery:** Teach students to blend the letter sounds together in a seamless fashion. For instance, students should be taught to say *mmmaaannn* rather than separating the sounds /m/ /a/ /n/.
- **Instructional materials:** Have students read decodable texts—texts that contain words with the sounds and patterns you have previously taught and students have mastered.
- **Connections to spelling:** Have students spell the words so that their phonics instruction can be reinforced. Spelling and reading are closely related skills. Here are some examples of ways to make connections to spelling:
  - Introduce letter-sound correspondences for spelling as they are being introduced and taught in reading.
  - Have students sort words into spelling patterns.
  - Have students identify words from their text with patterns that match what they are learning in phonics.

Source: D. Bryant, D. Smith, and B. Bryant, *Teaching Students with Special Needs* (Boston: Allyn and Bacon, 2008). pp. 404–405.

In this section, we look at some of the various pedagogical strategies for teaching students with learning disabilities. Educators have a broad array of instructional approaches and strategies at their disposal, some of them more effective than others. We recommend that teachers select their instructional tactics only after carefully considering the research evidence. The field of learning disabilities has a history of "hopping on the bandwagon" and vigorously advocating a particular instructional approach or strategy; unfortunately, in some cases, these procedures were lacking in empirical support. One example was the allegiance of many teachers to perceptual motor training, which was eventually shown to be ineffective (Hammill & Larsen, 1974; Kavale, 1990). Professionals must validate the effectiveness of their interventions.

We have chosen to examine three broad approaches to teaching academic skills: cognitive training, direct instruction, and learning strategies. Keep in mind that there is no "silver bullet" or magic formula for teaching students with learning disabilities; in most instances, it is a matter of matching the needs of the student to a particular instructional model.

COGNITIVE TRAINING Cognitive training is an umbrella approach covering a variety of educational procedures. It seeks to manipulate or modify a student's underlying thought patterns to effect observable changes in performance. Proponents of this approach believe that what occurs internally in the learner during the learning process is just as important as what happens externally. The pupil is seen as the critical agent in determining how information is processed—that is, identified, interpreted, organized, and utilized (Mercer & Pullen, 2005). Self-instruction and the use of mnemonic strategies are two instructional techniques frequently associated with cognitive training.

Developed by Meichenbaum (1977; Meichenbaum & Goodman, 1971), **self-instruction** is a strategy whereby students initially talk to themselves out loud while performing a task—children verbalize instructions necessary to complete the activity and then verbally reward themselves for success. Self-instruction makes the pupil aware of the various steps used in problem solving and then gradually brings these strategies under covert verbal control. According to Hallahan et al. (2005) and Lerner and Kline (2006), the following six steps are typically used during cognitive training:

1. Student observes the teacher perform a task while verbalizing aloud.
   a. Questions about the activity
   b. Instructions on how to perform the task
   c. A self-evaluation of performance
2. Pupil performs the task with teacher providing verbal directions.
3. Child performs the activity while verbalizing aloud.
4. Student performs the task while whispering instructions.
5. Pupil performs the activity while using covert or inner speech.
6. Child monitors and self-evaluates own performance (for example, "I did a good job" or "I need to work faster").

The goal of cognitive training, considered by some authorities to be a form of cognitive behavior modification, is not only to modify the pupil's behavior but also to increase the learner's awareness of the behavior and the thinking process affiliated with it (Lerner & Kline, 2006). Cognitive training has proven to be a beneficial strategy for remediating a wide variety of academic difficulties typically encountered by individuals with learning disabilities (Hallahan et al., 2005). Table 6.4 provides a list of suggestions for teachers on using cognitive training strategies.

Mnemonic strategies are tools for helping students recall facts and relationships. Teachers frequently help their students transform abstract material into a more concrete form by constructing personally meaningful representations of the information—that is, a picture or pattern of letters. For example, one trick frequently used by beginning music students to help recall the treble staff is the saying "**E**very **g**ood **b**oy **d**oes **f**ine," which represents the notes e, g, b, d, and f.

DIRECT INSTRUCTION Unlike cognitive training with its emphasis on the uniqueness of each learner, **Direct Instruction (DI)** focuses on the characteristics or components of the task or concept to be learned. The aim of DI is to produce gains in specific academic skills without worrying about possible processing deficits. "The key principle in Direct Instruction," Gersten, Carnine, and Woodward (1987) write, "is deceptively simple. For all students to learn, both the curriculum materials and teacher presentation of these materials must be clear and unambiguous" (pp. 48–49).

Based on the pioneering work of Bereiter and Engelmann (1966) in the 1960s, DI represents a highly organized instructional approach. Proponents of this model emphasize controlling the

Table 6.4	Principles of Effective Cognitive Training Programs
Teach a few strategies at a time	Rather than bombard children with a number of strategies all at once, teach them just a few. In this way, there is a better chance that the students can learn the strategies in a comprehensive and not a superficial fashion.
Teach self-monitoring	It is helpful if students keep track of their own progress. When checking their own work, if they find an error, they should be encouraged to try to correct it on their own.
Teach them when and where to use the strategies	Many students with learning disabilities have problems with the metacognitive skill of knowing when and where they can use strategies that teachers have taught. Teachers must give them this information as well as extensive experience in using the strategies in a variety of settings.
Maintain the students' motivation	Students need to know that the strategies work. Teachers can help motivation by consistently pointing out the benefits of the strategies, explaining how they work, and charting students' progress.
Teach in context	Students should learn cognitive techniques as an integrated part of the curriculum. Rather than using cognitive training in an isolated manner, teachers should teach students to employ cognitive strategies during academic lessons.
Don't neglect a nonstrategic knowledge base	Sometimes those who use cognitive training become such avid proponents of it that they forget the importance of factual knowledge. The more facts children know about history, science, math, English, and so forth, the less they will need to rely on strategies.
Engage in direct teaching	Because the emphasis in cognitive training is on encouraging students to take more initiative in their own learning, teachers may feel that they are less necessary than is actually the case. Cognitive training does not give license to back off from directly teaching students. Students' reliance on teachers should gradually fade. In the early stages, teachers need to be directly in control of supervising the students' use of the cognitive strategies.
Regard cognitive training as long term	Because cognitive training often results in immediate improvement, there may be a temptation to view it as a panacea or a quick fix. To maintain improvements and have them generalize to other settings, however, students need extensive practice in applying the strategies they have learned.

Source: Adapted from D. Hallahan, J. Lloyd, J. Kauffman, M. Weiss, and E. Martinez, *Learning Disabilities,* 3rd ed. (Needham Heights, MA: Allyn and Bacon, 2005), p. 239. Reprinted with permission.

details of instruction so as to actively engage students' involvement in learning. Drill and practice are stressed. DI lessons, which are teacher-directed, are precisely scripted, fast paced, and typically presented to small groups of children, usually five to ten. Teachers lead their students using a "script" or precisely worded lesson in an effort to ensure consistency and quality of instruction. Teachers elicit student response via hand signals or cues (such as clapping or snapping the fingers), which results in choral or unison responding by the group. This technique is designed to maintain the pupils' attention. Correct answers are immediately praised, and incorrect responses receive corrective feedback.

According to Friend and Bursuck (2006), DI consists of six key components:

1. An explicit step-by-step strategy
2. Development of mastery at each step in the process
3. Strategy (or process) corrections for student errors
4. Gradual fading from teacher-directed activities toward independent work
5. Use of adequate, systematic practice with a range of examples
6. Cumulative review of newly learned concepts (pp. 173, 176)

Learning strategies help pupils become more actively engaged in their own learning.

The effectiveness of this skills training instructional model is well documented. Students exposed to DI methods demonstrate significant gains in academic learning (Marchand-Martella, Slocum, & Martella, 2004; Vaughn & Linan-Thompson, 2003; Walker, Shippen, Alberto, Houchins, & Cihak, 2005). Several different types of commercial programs based on DI teaching principles are available in the areas of reading, language, mathematics, social studies, and science.

LEARNING STRATEGIES Some authorities believe it is not enough to teach specific academic skills to pupils with learning disabilities. These students tend to be inefficient learners because they often lack systematic strategies and plans for remembering, monitoring, and directing their own learning. In contrast to proficient learners, individuals with learning disabilities haven't learned the "tricks of the trade"—the secrets to being a successful student (Lerner & Kline, 2006). A **learning strategies** approach to instruction focuses on teaching students *how* to learn—how to become a more purposeful and efficient learner.

Unlike other instructional methodologies, which focus on learning a particular task or academic content, learning strategies are seen as the "techniques, principles, or rules that facilitate the acquisition, manipulation, integration, storage, and retrieval of information across situations and settings" (Alley & Deshler, 1979, p. 13). In other words, learning strategies are the tools that individuals use to help themselves learn and recall new material. The goal of this approach is to help students become more actively engaged and involved in their own learning.

Learning strategies are skills for learning. Probably the most widely used model for teaching these skills, which has evolved after years of research, is the Strategies Intervention Model (SIM) developed by scholars at the University of Kansas (Deshler et al., 1996; Lenz, Ellis, & Scanlon, 1996). Recently renamed the Strategic Instruction Model, this approach is one of the field's most comprehensive models for providing strategy instruction. It can, according to one authority, "be used to teach virtually any strategic intervention" (Sturomski, 1997, p. 7).

Most often used with adolescents who are learning disabled, the SIM can be applied to all areas of curriculum typically encountered by middle school and high school students. This pedagogical technique emphasizes the cognitive aspects of learning rather than focusing on mastering specific subject content (Lenz & Deshler, 2004).

Success has been demonstrated across a wide range of academic areas, including essay writing, study skills, reading comprehension, math problems, and science (Bender, 2008). A learning strategies approach is especially relevant for today's classroom. As more emphasis is placed on exposure to the general education curriculum, this model can assist students in meeting this demand. With its emphasis on mastering cognitive strategies and empowering the student, a learning strategies model is a natural complement to the general classroom curriculum.

Suggestions for the Classroom

Suggestions for Teaching Students with Learning Disabilities

☑ Capitalize on the student's strengths.

☑ Provide high structure and clear expectations.

☑ Use short sentences and a simple vocabulary.

☑ Provide opportunities for success in a supportive atmosphere to help build self-esteem.

☑ Allow flexibility in classroom procedures (for example, allowing the use of tape recorders for note taking and test taking when students have trouble with written language).

☑ Make use of self-correcting materials that provide immediate feedback without embarrassment.

☑ Use computers for drill and practice and teaching word processing.

☑ Provide positive reinforcement of appropriate social skills at school and home.

SOURCE: National Dissemination Center for Children with Disabilities, *Fact Sheet No. 7: Learning disabilities* (Washington, DC: Author, 1998, 2004).

We believe, as others do, that no one instructional approach can meet the vast and complex needs of all individuals with learning disabilities. Teachers need to have an array of interventions at their disposal. Success in the classroom often depends, in part, on the match between learner characteristics and the teaching techniques used.

The accompanying Suggestions for the Classroom feature offers instructional recommendations that have been found to be effective with some students who are learning disabled.

Services for Young Children with Learning Disabilities

Determining whether a young child is learning disabled, or at risk for learning disabilities, is a difficult task. Many professionals believe that the earlier we identify a child, the sooner intervention can be initiated; of course, prevention is always preferable to remediation. Yet the notion of a preschool child having a learning disability is controversial. Testing at this age is mainly for purposes of prediction, not identification. The challenge confronting educators is determining which factors are truly indicative of future learning difficulties and which are simply manifestations of variation in growth and development. It is not uncommon for professionals to talk about a young child's being at risk for problems in learning and development. Because of their exposure to adverse circumstances, some youngsters experience greater vulnerability and have a heightened potential for future problems in the classroom. Factors that *may* place a child at risk (Gargiulo & Kilgo, 2005; National Joint Committee on Learning Disabilities, 2006), include

- Maternal alcohol and drug abuse
- Home environment lacking adequate stimulation
- Chronic poverty
- Oxygen deprivation

Making Inclusion Work

My training in the field of special education began many years ago in South America where it was common practice to teach children with disabilities in self-contained classrooms. After transferring to the United States and earning a degree in Special Education, the range of possibilities for educating children with disabilities was a welcomed change. Starting out as a resource room teacher and eventually becoming an inclusion specialist has been an interesting and rewarding educational experience.

Inclusive Education Experience

Evolving into an inclusion teacher from a resource room teacher has definitely been an interesting journey. In the beginning it was challenging, although I welcomed the opportunity to serve my students in their least restrictive environment. It was difficult, however, for some general education teachers. This was especially true of the veteran teachers who did not understand the purpose of having students with disabilities in their classroom as well as having another educator in "their room." When the time came to implement the accommodations stated in the students' IEP, some teachers had difficulty understanding the need for the accommodations. A few made comments relating to the fact that the

children should be able to do the work if they were being served in the regular classroom, while others alluded to the fairness to the other children. Working through this process was trying at times. This was especially true when working with students with learning disabilities—mainly because their disability is not readily obvious. Often, general educators could not figure out why these children were not performing like the rest of the class. Many times these children were labeled lazy or they were simply misunderstood. It took the general education teachers some time to appreciate the benefits of inclusion for *all* students in the class. It took some convincing and collaboratively working with them on a daily basis to make it successful.

Through the years I have seen tremendous changes toward the acceptance of children with disabilities. General educators have become more knowledgeable about pupils with disabilities thanks, in part, to working collaboratively with special educators. Working together as a team has proven to be the most productive and effective way to teach students with special needs.

Strategies for Inclusive Classrooms

The support of the school administration is the backbone of any solid inclusion program. It takes a great

- Accidents and head trauma
- Inadequate maternal and infant nutrition
- Prematurity
- Rh incompatibility
- Low birth weight
- Prolonged or unusual delivery

Remember, these factors do not guarantee that problems will arise; they only set the stage. Many young children are subject to a wide variety of risks yet never evidence any problems in school (Gargiulo & Kilgo, 2005).

A related controversy is the application of the "learning disability" label to preschoolers. The regulations accompanying the current federal definition of learning disabilities considers deficits in academic performance and a discrepancy between a child's ability and academic achievement when identifying a pupil as learning disabled. How appropriate is this deal of time to effectively plan for students in an inclusive class. I would say this is one of the most important aspects of an inclusion model. It is crucial that the general education teacher has time to meet and plan with the special education teacher. It is important to communicate openly about students' needs. It is necessary to evaluate the effectiveness of the various instructional strategies used in the classroom and to be sure that the needs of all learners are being met. It is vitally important that related service providers, paraprofessionals, and other individuals working with the student be informed of their progress or the problems that sometimes arise.

Successful Collaboration

Successful collaboration entails a wide variety of options. In my opinion, one of the most important things that the special educator can do is to earn the trust of the teacher(s) they work with on a daily basis. When there is trust in the relationship, collaboration will naturally fall into place. It is important that the special educator and general education teacher share responsibilities for *all* students. Together they plan and implement strategies that will not only benefit students with IEPs, but all children in the class. Each teacher brings his or her own strengths, skills, and knowledge to the classroom in an effort to serve all students. It is important that if problems ever develop, both the special educator and general education teacher support each other and work together in problem solving.

Working with Parents and Families

Parent and family involvement is crucial. Parents' input during the development of the individualized education program is extremely important since they work with the child on a daily basis outside of school. It is necessary that they share their concerns with the team in order to better serve their son or daughter. Parents need to become 'educators' and help their child continue the learning process at home. Additionally, it is important that parents communicate openly with their child's teachers and provide feedback. Together parents and school personnel can provide an effective inclusive environment that meets the unique needs of the child.

Advice for Making Inclusion and Collaboration Work

Making inclusion and collaboration work entails a wide array of strategies. It is not an easy task and takes hours of planning to successfully implement, but the results are worth it. Yet, even when school personnel and parents have their hearts in the right place, difficulties may arise that make the process extremely frustrating. This is when all concerned need to focus on the common goal of what is best for the child. Administrative support, teachers working together for the good of all children, and active parent involvement often results in a successful inclusive environment benefiting all students.

—Astrid Freeman
Oak Mountain Middle School
Shelby County (Alabama) Schools

label when most preschoolers have not been exposed to academic work? Academic tasks are typically not introduced until the first grade, although a growing number of kindergartens and some preschools are stressing preacademic skills. Fuchs et al. (2007) describe the use of a discrepancy approach for identifying a learning disability in young children as a "wait and fail" method for ascertaining who may be eligible for special educational services. We believe that the needs of the young child are best served when professionals focus on the antecedents of learning disabilities. These precursors are often noted by simply observing the child engage in a variety of age-appropriate tasks such as cutting and coloring, imaginary play, or various gross motor activities such as running, hopping, or skipping. Table 6.5 identifies some of these warning signs. These indicators are simply that—warnings; they do *not* mean that learning problems will automatically appear later on.

There is a growing reluctance among some educators to label young children as having a learning disability. Instead, the more generic, and less stigmatizing, noncategorical label "developmentally delayed" is finding increasing favor in some professional circles.

Table 6.5	Common Characteristics of Preschoolers at Risk for Being Identified as Learning Disabled

"He knocks into building blocks, bumps into doors, falls out of his chair, and crashes into his playmates."	• Inability to negotiate his body through his environment • Poor depth perception • Sitting in double-jointed fashion • Toe walking • Lurches while walking
"She's so smart yet has the attention span of a flea—she flits from one thing to another, and sometimes speaks like a broken record."	• Distractibility • Short attention span • Impulsiveness (impulsivity) • Hyperactivity • Preservation (doing the same thing over in the same way)
"She can talk about topiary trees, but she can't pull up her zipper or draw a circle, and hates putting toys and puzzles together."	• Poor motor coordination • Difficulty coordinating hand–eye maneuvers • Clumsiness
"He understands everything I say to him, but he does not express himself well like his brother and sister."	• Delayed speech • Uses sounds/words out of sequence: aminals, Home I ran • Limited vocabulary • Inappropriate use of words • Disorganized phrases
"He looks at everything but doesn't seem to see anything in particular. His hands seem to see better than his eyes."	• Difficulty focusing • Problems distinguishing shapes and color • Difficulty remembering what he sees • Problems remembering the order of things he sees • Difficulty making sense of what he sees
"She's four years old but acts much younger."	• Immature behavior/appearance • Immature speech • Immature coordination/movement • Immature choice and use of toys
"Her eyes look at me so intently, and she listens. But it just doesn't seem to get through."	• Problems understanding what she hears • Difficulty remembering what she hears • Problems remembering sequences of sounds • Difficulty following simple directions • Overreaction to noise • Does not enjoy being read to aloud
"He overreacts or underreacts to everything—it's like his emotion thermostat is malfunctioning."	• Indiscriminate or catastrophic reactions • Laughing one moment, crying the next • Very low or very high threshold of pain • Dislike of being touched or cuddled • No reaction or overreaction to being touched
"He never seems to be 'put together' right, and yet I spend so much more time and energy helping him than I do the other kids."	• Disorganized movement • Disorganized language • Disorganized appearance

Source: *Learning Disabilities Fact Sheet—Early Childhood.* Learning Disabilities Association of America. Available at http://www.paec.org/david/ese/early.pdf.

The reauthorization of IDEA in 1997 (PL 105-17) allowed states to use this descriptor for children ages 3 through 9 who require a special education and related services. Unfortunately, there is no federal definition of this term; each state is responsible for determining what the label means. The absence of federal guidance has resulted in significant variations in definition. Some states use various quantitative descriptions and others use a variety of qualitative approaches when deciding if a youngster is developmentally delayed. Despite this drawback, this label suggests a developmental status and not a disability category, which hopefully will result in more inclusive models of service delivery (Gargiulo & Kilgo, 2005).

When preschoolers are found to be in need of a special education, teachers can choose from among several different curriculum models, including a developmental/cognitive model, a behavioral model, and a functional curriculum approach. We will briefly describe the major tenets of these models, drawing upon the work of Gargiulo and Kilgo (2005).

The **developmental/cognitive model** is based on the theorizing of Piaget, who sees cognitive development as resulting from maturation coupled with the youngster's active interaction and involvement with the environment. Instructional activities are designed according to Piaget's stages of cognitive development with an emphasis on stimulating a pupil's cognitive abilities (language, memory, concept formation).

A **behavioral curriculum model** is based on learning principles derived from behavioral psychology—particularly reinforcement theory. Curricula based on a behavioral approach emphasize direct instruction following a precise and highly structured sequence of instructional activities.

The **functional curriculum** approach stresses behaviors that have immediate relevance for students as they confront the demands of their natural environment. Developmental age is of less importance than the individual's proficiency in acquiring age-appropriate skills. Rather than emphasizing developmental sequences or preacademic skills, this model is oriented toward activities of daily living. Functional, age-appropriate skills needed in various natural settings are task-analyzed into a sequence of observable and measurable subskills. Learning to perform these skills enables youngsters with disabilities to function with greater independence while also increasing their chances of being successfully included in normalized settings.

Teachers who work with young children rarely adhere strictly to one particular model. Rather, they use a combination of approaches, selecting strategies that are most appropriate for meeting the needs of their students.

Transition into Adulthood

Adolescence is a difficult period for many young persons, but especially for students with learning disabilities. These individuals frequently have a history of failure at academic tasks, a diminished self-concept, a lack of motivation, and some degree of social ineptness. The daily demands encountered in high school often make it extremely difficult for adolescents with learning disabilities to succeed. Mercer and Pullen (2005) identify some of the many challenges confronting these pupils:

- Gaining information from lectures and written materials
- Working independently with little feedback
- Demonstrating knowledge through tests
- Interacting appropriately
- Exhibiting motivation and sustained effort

Adolescence can be an especially difficult time for students with learning disabilities.

Only recently have professionals become cognizant of the unique requirements facing students with learning disabilities in secondary schools. For many years, educators incorrectly assumed that children with learning disabilities would simply "outgrow" them. As a result, adolescents with learning disabilities have received less attention than their younger counterparts. What professionals failed to realize is that problems with attention and memory, deficits in planning and organizing, and difficulties with problem solving often continue well into adolescence and beyond.

One of the purposes of an education is to prepare individuals to lead independent and productive lives as adults—to become contributing members of society. Unfortunately, our educational system has a less than stellar record of success with secondary students who are learning disabled. Recent statistics compiled by the U.S. Department of Education (2007) indicate that only 60 percent of students with learning disabilities graduate from high school, and almost 27 percent drop out of school. One can only conclude that our schools are failing to appropriately serve the vast number of these students.

One means of remedying this situation is through the development of a customized **transition plan.** PL 108-446 mandates that a transition plan be part of each adolescent's IEP. The purpose of this document is to develop goals and activities that are individually tailored to fulfill the student's postschool aspirations. Developing a meaningful ITP is a team effort requiring the active involvement of professionals, parents, and perhaps most important, the student—after all, it is his or her life goals that the document addresses. Transition planning typically focuses on several different streams or options, including vocational training, preparation for postsecondary educational opportunities, or various employment possibilities.

Careful transition planning is crucial for successful adjustment later in life. The secondary school curriculum must not only prepare adolescents with learning disabilities academically, but it should also focus on preparation for future challenges such as independent living, employment options, and postsecondary schooling. Additionally, we believe that transition plans, after considering the individual needs of the student, should also focus on self-determination, social skills, and assistance with understanding and adjusting to one's lifelong disability.

Adults with Learning Disabilities

The needs of adults with learning disabilities have traditionally received little attention; only recently have professionals begun to focus on this group. In many instances, however, a learning disability is a lifelong problem; many of the characteristics of learning disabilities persist into adulthood (Hudson, 2006; Silver, 2004). Adults with learning disabilities sometimes have great difficulty "finding their niche in the world" (Lerner & Kline, 2006, p. 297). A learning disability typically interferes with living independently, obtaining and maintaining

Table 6.6	Characteristics of Successful and Unsuccessful Adults with Learning Disabilities
Successful Adults	**Unsuccessful Adults**
• Maintain perseverance in dealing with life events • Develop coping strategies and know how to reduce stress • Maintain emotional stability • Have and use support systems • Demonstrate motivation and persistence • Pursue careers that maximize their strengths and minimize their weaknesses • Develop creative ways to compensate and problem-solve • Maintain a positive attitude toward learning	• Do not understand or accept their learning disability • Fail to take control of their lives • Maintain a sense of learned helplessness and fail to assume responsibility • Seek and promote dependent relationships • Exhibit a lack of drive and motivation • Fail to establish social support systems • Drop out of secondary school

Source: Adapted from C. Mercer, *Students with Learning Disabilities*, 5th ed. (Upper Saddle River, NJ: Prentice Hall, 1997), p. 400. Reprinted by permission of Pearson Education, Inc., Upper Saddle River, NJ.

employment, maintaining social relationships, and experiencing satisfaction with life in general (Tymchuk, Lakin, & Luckasson, 2001; Witte, Philips, & Kakela, 1998).

One should not necessarily paint a bleak picture for adults with learning disabilities. Many of these individuals achieve success and enjoy a life of quality. Successful adults establish goals, work hard, and exhibit a high degree of perseverance while also acknowledging their limitations (Raskind, Goldberg, Higgins, & Herman, 2002). Table 6.6 identifies some of the characteristics exhibited by successful and unsuccessful adults with learning disabilities.

Postsecondary educational opportunities are becoming increasingly common for adults with learning disabilities. Researchers estimate that about 13 percent of students with learning disabilities are enrolled in four-year colleges or universities; an additional 24 percent attend two-year institutions such as community colleges while 15 percent are enrolled in vocational/technical schools (Wagner, Newman, Cameto, Garza, & Levine, 2005). These figures may appear small, but they represent a dramatic increase in the number of college-bound students with learning disabilities. Although this growth is laudable, many students with learning disabilities do not fully consider postsecondary options (Mull, Sitlington, & Alper, 2001). Section 504 of PL 93-112 prohibits discrimination against individuals with disabilities and requires institutions to offer reasonable accommodations to students with learning disabilities (and other impairments). Hallahan et al. (2005) offer several examples of accommodations appropriate for students with learning disabilities:

ADJUSTMENT IN COURSE REQUIREMENTS AND EVALUATION

- Giving extra time on exams
- Allowing students to take exams in a distraction-free room
- Allowing students to take exams in a different format (for example, substituting an oral exam for a written one)

MODIFICATIONS IN PROGRAM REQUIREMENTS

- Waiving or substituting certain requirements (for example, a foreign language)
- Allowing students to take a lighter academic load

AUXILIARY AID

- Providing tape recordings of textbooks
- Providing access to a Kurzweil Reading Machine (a computer that scans text and converts it into auditory output)
- Recruiting and assigning volunteer note-takers for lectures (p. 180)

Success in college obviously requires more than just course accommodations. Students must exhibit appropriate social skills, learn time management and organization skills, and develop self-discipline, effective study habits, and perhaps most important, self-advocacy. Most institutions have an office of disability support services that provides students with disabilities with an array of special services designed to meet their unique requirements and enhance their chances of earning a degree. See the FYI feature for a related discussion provided by students with learning disabilities who are successfully attending college.

Family Issues

A learning disability is a family affair; it affects not only the individual but, in many instances, parents, siblings, grandparents, and extended family members. Parents pay a heavy emotional toll as they deal, on a daily basis, with their son's or daughter's learning and behavioral difficulties. Yet most families of children with learning disabilities are not dysfunctional but well adjusted (Dyson, 1996).

Brothers and sisters of an individual with learning disabilities may also be affected by their sibling's disability. Feelings of embarrassment, anger, and resentment are not unusual. Although in some families siblings are adversely affected, in others brothers and sisters adjust well and seem to positively benefit from their relationships (Dyson, 1996). Positive sibling adjustment appears to be associated with parental acceptance of the child with a disability.

In keeping with the idea that parents are crucial to the well-being and adjustment of the family, Lerner and Kline (2006) offer the following recommendations for parents:

- Become an informed consumer—educate yourself about learning disabilities.
- Be an assertive advocate—protect your child's legal rights while also seeking appropriate programs in the community as well as schools.
- Be firm yet empathetic in managing the child's behavior.
- Devote time and attention to other family members.
- Make a life for yourself.

A potentially rich resource for individuals with learning disabilities and their parents is the Internet. We urge caution, however, as the accuracy of information on the Internet cannot always be guaranteed.

Issues of Diversity

Currently, approximately one out of every three U.S. students is African American, Hispanic, or Asian American (U.S. Department of Education, 2006). Researchers believe that by the

FYI...

Young Adults with Learning Disabilities Speak Out: The Truth about Having a Learning Disability

Having a learning disability leads to serious psychological, emotional, and social consequences, according to the testimony of several students with learning disabilities who are successfully enrolled in college. The students' remarks made note of the fact that their success was due largely to their acceptance of their disability and an acknowledgment that life would be harder for them than for their nondisabled counterparts.

The Emotional Impact

Students said having a learning disability causes extreme damage to their self-esteem. The cumulative effects of the disability include behavior problems, anger, depression, job failure, and poor interpersonal relationships. In some cases, the students even cited their disability as contributing to drug, alcohol, and sexual abuse as well as suicidal tendencies.

The students vividly remember school experiences that reinforced their negative self-concept, such as teachers making them feel they were bad because they had difficulty understanding concepts, being called lazy or careless, having their skills underestimated, rarely being asked to think, and having their faults emphasized while their areas of success were ignored.

Coming to Grips with Having a Learning Disability

For students with learning disabilities to succeed, they must accept their learning problem, said the students. In this process, the students went through different stages. First may be denial. Then they must learn how to understand their own problem. At this point, students may feel "blessed and cursed" by their disability. From there, they must realize that while their disability is only a part of who they are, it will be a force they must accept and deal with on many levels, including socially and academically. Then, they must accept that many facets of life will be more difficult for them than others; therefore, they must develop coping strategies. Finally, students with disabilities must learn to lead a balanced life, recommended the students.

What Teachers Can Do to Help

Teachers play a vital role in helping students with disabilities, said the students. They pleaded with teachers to understand their learning and emotional problems and to care. They said "bad" teaching lives a long time, dashing hopes and dreams as well as demeaning their self-esteem in small cumulative steps. Having a good attitude toward students with learning problems is important, as is having high expectations of those students. They asked that teachers not let them get out of work they can do but help them find alternate ways to do the work.

Additionally, the students said it would be helpful if teachers or counselors would tell them what their life will be like with a learning disability, so they will know what is in store for them academically and socially. The students further recommended that school personnel help parents develop a realistic understanding of a learning disability. That way, the students will not have to fight with their parents to understand their difficulties or take the necessary steps to help them achieve their dreams.

Source: Adapted from *CEC Today, 5*(9), 1999, p. 10.

year 2020, students of color will represent approximately half of the entire school population in the United States (Gollnick & Chinn, 2009). Given immigration patterns and differential birth rates among various ethnic groups, demographers expect this trend to continue. Many of these children live in poverty in large urban centers. Poverty can have a deleterious effect on school performance. In fact, some educational researchers believe that the vast majority

Table 6.7	Students Ages 6–21 with Learning Disabilities, by Race/Ethnicity	
Group	**Number of Students**	**Percentage of Students**
White	1,523,111	54.78
Black	553,065	19.89
Hispanic	606,737	21.82
American Indian/Alaskan Native	47,701	1.72
Asian/Pacific Islander	49,604	1.78
Total	2,780,218	100.00

Note: Data are for the 2005–2006 school year. Due to rounding, percentages do not add to 100 percent.

Source: U.S. Department of Education. (2007). *IDEA data.* Available at https://www.ideadata.org/PartBReport.asp

of individuals attending urban schools who are classified as learning disabled are not truly learning disabled; rather, they are students whose performance in the classroom is adversely affected by the ravages of poverty (Blair & Scott, 2002).

Teachers are confronted with significant challenges in their attempts to meet the educational needs of these pupils, especially when these students have limited English proficiency. One major issue for professionals who work with culturally and linguistically diverse students is distinguishing between learning problems that may arise from cultural differences and those that are due to learning disabilities (Taylor & Leonard, 1999). It is crucial that teachers make every effort to differentiate between differences and disabilities; cultural and linguistic differences must not be interpreted as a disability.

More than 1.25 million culturally and linguistically diverse children have a learning disability (U.S. Department of Education, 2007). Data compiled by the federal government on culturally and linguistically diverse students who are learning disabled are presented in Table 6.7. Because of long-standing concerns about disproportionate representation of racial and ethnic minorities in special education, Congress now requires that states maintain records according to race and ethnicity for enrollment, educational placement, school exiting status, and discipline. This information will help Congress to monitor disproportionate representation and, if necessary, suggest corrective revisions to current policies, practices, and procedures. Of course, attention must also focus on the broader issues of child poverty and its effect on school performance.

Technology and Individuals with Learning Disabilities

With the enactment of PL 105-17 and continuing with IDEA 2004, educators are now required to consider the appropriateness of **assistive technology** as a tool or intervention for every student with an IEP. Assistive technology refers to any technological device, regardless of sophistication, that enables the user to increase, maintain, or improve his or her functional capabilities. Students with learning disabilities are increasingly using assistive technology to compensate for barriers to learning. In fact, some see technology acting as a "cognitive prosthesis" allowing individuals with learning disabilities to become more effective and efficient learners (Bryant & Bryant, 2003). Innovative ways of delivering instruction to pupils with learning disabilities include videodiscs, CD-ROMs, and of course, the Internet. Another common application is word processing, which Lerner and Kline (2006) characterize as a "boon for students with learning disabilities who have difficulties with handwriting, spelling, and written composition" (p. 38). The writing skills of individuals with learning disabilities benefit from the use of word processing programs. Revisions are easily accomplished, poor handwriting is no longer a concern, and spelling and grammar checks improve the quality of the written product (Graham, Harris, & Larsen, 2001; MacArthur, 2000).

Researchers (Bender, 2008) have found that the use of hypermedia (interactive computer programs that incorporate various media) enhances the mathematical problem-solving abilities of students with learning disabilities. Improved performance in spelling is another area where computer-assisted instruction has aided children with learning disabilities (Belson, 2003).

Trends, Issues, and Controversies

The field of learning disabilities abounds with issues and controversies. We have chosen to briefly examine two contemporary issues confronting the field: the inclusion movement and efforts at educational reform.

Challenges in Service Delivery: The Full Inclusion Movement

The subject of full inclusion for students with learning disabilities is certainly one of the most controversial issues confronting the field of learning disabilities today. Parents, policy makers, educators, and administrators alike continue to wrestle with the various emotionally charged dimensions of this topic. For some, according to Mercer (1997),

> the inclusion movement represents a reduction of essential instructional services to students with learning disabilities and a threat to the existing area of learning disabilities within the educational structure. To others, inclusion represents an opportunity for students with learning disabilities to function successfully in a community of diverse learners without the stigmatization of being segregated. (p. 64)

The issue of full inclusion is sometimes portrayed as one of equity—a belief that individuals with disabilities have a right to participate in normalized educational experiences and should not be excluded from this opportunity simply on the basis of their impairment(s). Some advocates (Peterson & Hittie, 2003) argue that students with learning disabilities *deserve* to be educated in the general education setting.

As we saw earlier in this chapter, the regular classroom is currently the most popular placement for serving students with learning disabilities. Advocates of full inclusion believe that full-time placement in the general education classroom will result in enhanced academic performance, greater acceptance by typical peers, and better coordination between regular and special educators. However, those who advocate maintaining a continuum of service

FYI . . .

A Reaction to Full Inclusion: A Reaffirmation of the Right of Students with Learning Disabilities to a Continuum of Services

The National Joint Committee on Learning Disabilities (NJCLD) supports many aspects of school reform. However, one aspect of school reform that the NJCLD cannot support is the idea that all students with learning disabilities must be served only in regular classrooms, frequently referred to as full inclusion. The NJCLD believes that full inclusion, when defined this way, violates the rights of parents and students with disabilities as mandated by the Individuals with Disabilities Education Act (IDEA).

Because each student with learning disabilities has unique needs, an individualized program must be tailored to meet those needs. For one student, the program may be provided in the regular classroom; yet for another student, the regular classroom may be an inappropriate placement. Therefore, the NJCLD supports the use of a continuum of services and rejects the arbitrary placement of all students in any one setting.

Source: National Joint Committee on Learning Disabilities. (2003). Retrieved August 29, 2007 from http://www.ldonline.org/about/partners/NJCLD.

delivery options point out that pupils with learning disabilities are often poorly served in general education settings (McLeskey, Hoppery, Williamson, & Rentz, 2004; Vaughn et al., 2001; Zigmond, 2003). Zigmond and others (Schumm, Moody, & Vaughn, 2000; Swanson, 2000) note that the research evidence fails to support the efficacy of full inclusion for students with learning disabilities, at least as it pertains to achievement outcomes. Concerns about a lack of individualization of instruction (Zigmond & Baker, 1996) and apprehension about the appropriateness of exclusive exposure to the general education curriculum (Kauffman, 1999; Martin, 2002) are among the reasons that some special educators do not fully embrace full inclusion. Many of the professional associations concerned with learning disabilities have adopted policy statements opposing full inclusion. The accompanying FYI feature presents one such position paper.

We believe that a balanced approach to this controversy is appropriate. With skillful planning, equitable allocation of resources, a clear delineation of responsibilities, and careful attention to what will be taught and how it will be evaluated, full inclusion is not only feasible but also beneficial for some students with learning disabilities (Hallahan et al., 2005). However, we strongly encourage educators and other professionals to keep in mind the principle of individualization, which is the benchmark of special education. One size (program) does not fit all; it is a matter of a "goodness of fit." This means that for some children with learning disabilities, full inclusion is appropriate, but others may be better served in a resource room or possibly a self-contained classroom. Perhaps as we enter the twenty-first century, our energy and attention should focus on improving the quality of our instructional practices for *all* learners, with an emphasis on the individual needs of the student and not the place or location that services are provided.

Educational Reform Movement

Over the past several years, a number of reports have sharply criticized the U.S. educational system, especially when achievement outcomes of U.S. pupils are compared with those of their European and Asian counterparts. These reports have led to calls for higher academic standards in the United States. One early by-product of this pursuit of educational excellence was the enactment in March 1994 of PL 103-227. Commonly referred to as the Goals 2000: Educate America Act, this law seeks, among other provisions, to raise academic standards and increase high school graduation rates.

Although many professionals laud the provisions of this legislation, it is notably silent as far as addressing students with disabilities. In fact, there is genuine concern in some educational circles that with more rigorous standards of academic competency and stringent evaluation requirements, students with disabilities, including learning disabilities, may be shortchanged in their drive toward obtaining a high school diploma. In response to the mandates contained in PL 103-227, several states have instituted higher graduation standards, and there is a growing national trend toward greater teacher accountability for student performance. (Recall, for example, the emphasis on accountability found in the No Child Left Behind Act, PL 107-110.) This push poses some interesting challenges for both general and special educators because many students with learning disabilities experience difficulty fulfilling current academic expectations, let alone the newer performance guidelines.

The impact of the Goals 2000: Educate America Act can be seen in the latest IDEA reauthorization. Possibly in reaction to Goals 2000, PL 105-17 contains several requirements that speak to the overall intent of the law. For instance, each pupil's IEP must now contain a statement that addresses the extent to which the student will be involved in and progress in the general education curriculum. IDEA 2004 maintains this requirement. An implication of this standard is that general educators will be held increasingly accountable for the performance of individuals with learning disabilities and other impairments. The 2004 version of IDEA also requires the inclusion of children with disabilities in state- and districtwide assessments (using appropriate accommodations) in an attempt to gauge their educational progress. Previously, these students were routinely excluded from testing programs most likely because their anticipated weak performance would reflect poorly on the school in ratings or rankings relative to other schools.

As we just mentioned, another chapter in the latest educational reform movement is the No Child Left Behind Act of 2001, which we initially examined in Chapter 2. Recall that all states are currently engaged in standards-based school reform efforts. Accountability is the buzzword as PL 107-110 stresses outcomes, as measured by academic achievement, for *all* learners, including pupils with disabilities. High-stakes testing is now commonplace for students, teachers, and administrators. Our concern, however, is with those individuals who fail to meet performance standards. Will we see an increase in referrals for special education services? Are we destined to have more children identified as learning disabled as schools continue to focus on high standards and accountability (Brooks, 2002)? Will IEP goals become more closely aligned with the content standards of the general education curriculum? Will students with learning disabilities simply drop out of school as a result of the growing emphasis on accountability and academic performance? Obviously, the No Child Left Behind Act has important implications for special education, especially for pupils recognized as learning disabled.

The current educational reform movement, with its clarion call for greater accountability and higher academic standards, will certainly affect students with learning disabilities. We anticipate that in the short term the quest for academic excellence will raise more questions than it answers; it is probably too early to assess the overall impact of these legislative endeavors. As the repercussions become clearer and researchers provide answers and suggestions for change, we believe that the vast majority of learners will see benefit from this movement.

Chapter in Review

Defining Learning Disabilities

- Persons with learning disabilities are a diverse group of individuals who, despite normal intelligence, fail to learn as easily and efficiently as their classmates and peers.

- The current IDEA definition contains two key concepts: (1) a **discrepancy** between the student's academic performance and his or her estimated or assumed ability or potential; and (2) the proviso that a learning disability cannot be due primarily to factors such as sensory impairments, mental retardation, emotional problems, or environmental, cultural, or economic disadvantage (the **exclusionary clause**).

Prevalence of Learning Disabilities

- Learning disabilities is the largest category within special education, accounting for slightly less than half of all individuals receiving services.

- Government figures indicate that about 2.78 million pupils are identified as learning disabled.

Etiology of Learning Disabilities

- In the vast majority of instances, the cause of a person's learning disability is unknown.

- Researchers offer four possible factors for explaining the etiology of learning disabilities: injury or damage to the central nervous system (CNS), heredity, biochemical abnormalities, and environmental factors.

Characteristics of Individuals with Learning Disabilities

- Persons with learning disabilities are a very heterogeneous population.

- The primary characteristics of students with learning disabilities are deficits in academic performance.

- Reading is the most common problem encountered by children identified as learning disabled.

- Some individuals who are learning disabled have difficulty attending to tasks, and some exhibit excess movement and activity or hyperactive behavior. This condition is often identified as **attention deficit hyperactivity disorder** (ADHD).

Assessment of Learning Disabilities

- State and local school districts now have the option of making eligiblity decisions on the basis of how a pupil responds to research-based educational interventions, a process known as response to intervention or RTI.

- Norm-referenced assessments *compare* an individual's performance to that of a normative group of peers.

- Criterion-referenced assessments provide educators with a *description* of the student's abilities, measured against a predetermined mastery level.

- Curriculum-based assessment is a type of criterion-referenced assessment.

Educational Considerations

- About nine out of every ten students with learning disabilities spend at least part of their day in the general education classroom.

- There is no one best or correct way to teach individuals with learning disabilities.

- Cognitive training is an approach concerned with the manipulation or modification of a student's underlying thought patterns; **self-instruction** and **mnemonic strategies** are examples of cognitive training.

- **Direct Instruction** (DI) focuses on analyzing the characteristics or components of the task to be learned and actively involving the student in the learning process.

- **Learning strategies** focus on teaching students *how* to learn by meaningfully involving them in the instructional process.

Study Questions

1. Developing a definition of learning disabilities has proven to be problematic. Describe three reasons why this process has been so challenging.

2. What are the main components of most definitions of learning disabilities?

3. Identify the four historical phases and their respective contributions to the development of the field of learning disabilities.

4. List four possible causes of learning disabilities. Give an example of each.

5. Identify and describe five learning and behavioral characteristics common to individuals with learning disabilities. In your opinion, which one of these deficits is most debilitating? Why?

6. What is RTI? Describe the intervention process typical of most RTI models.

7. Distinguish between norm-referenced and criterion-referenced assessments. What type of information does each test provide?

8. What is the current trend in educational placement of students with learning disabilities? Do you agree with this trend? Why or why not?

9. Identify the major components of the following instructional approaches used with students who are learning disabled: cognitive training, direct instruction, and learning strategies. What are the advantages and disadvantages of each approach?

10. Why is it difficult to determine if a preschooler is learning disabled?

11. What unique problems confront secondary students with learning disabilities? How can public schools help adolescents meet these challenges?

12. Describe the variables that contribute to the successful adjustment of adults with learning disabilities.

13. In what ways might an individual with learning disabilities affect his or her family?

14. Why is it difficult to distinguish between cultural/linguistic differences and a learning disability?

15. How can technology be used to benefit individuals with learning disabilities?

16. Describe two contemporary issues confronting the field of learning disabilities. How will these challenges affect programs for children and adolescents with learning disabilities?

Key Terms

learning disabilities
discrepancy
response to intervention
exclusionary clause
brain injury
familiality studies
heritability studies
dyslexia

phonological awareness
pragmatics
short-term memory
working memory
metacognition
learned helplessness
attention deficit hyperactivity
    disorder (ADHD)

progress monitoring
norm-referenced assessments
criterion-referenced assessments
curriculum-based assessment
authentic assessment
portfolio assessment
self-instruction
mnemonic strategies

Direct Instruction (DI)
learning strategies
developmental/cognitive model
behavioral curriculum model
functional curriculum
transition plan
assistive technology

Learning Activities

1. Obtain a copy of the definition of learning disabilities from your state department of education, and compare it with the IDEA definition. In what ways are these definitions similar and dissimilar? Pay particular attention to eligibility criteria. How would you improve your state's definition?

2. Interview a school psychologist or educational diagnostician and inquire about the assessment and identification procedures used to determine if a student is learning disabled. Ask about the strengths and weaknesses of the various assessment instruments. Do the evaluation procedures differ depending on the grade level of the pupil? How is a discrepancy between intelligence and achievement determined? What strategies does this professional use to gather information from parents and teachers? How are children from culturally and linguistically diverse backgrounds assessed?

3. Visit an elementary school, a middle school, and a high school in your community that serve individuals with learning disabilities. Observe in the classrooms, and interview the general educators and special educators who work with these students. What instructional approaches are used? How are the students evaluated? Does the delivery system vary according to grade level? How do the general and special educators work together? In your opinion, are the children with learning disabilities accepted by their classmates? Identify strengths and weaknesses of the learning disabilities program at each site. Would you want to be a teacher in these schools? Why or why not?

4. Interview a college student with learning disabilities. What types of supports and services does the college/university provide to students with learning disabilities?

What academic and/or social areas pose the greatest challenge for this individual? What learning strategies work best for him or her? Ask the person to identify areas of strength both in and out of school. Does the individual require accommodations in the workplace? If so, what types of modifications are necessary? Inquire about the person's postschool plans and the availability of support services in the community.

5. Attend a local chapter meeting of a sibling and/or parent group for individuals with learning disabilities. What issues and concerns were addressed at this meeting? Determine what types of services and supports are available in your community for individuals with learning disabilities across the life span. Ask siblings and/or parents about the challenges and rewards of living with a person with a learning disability.

Organizations Concerned with Learning Disabilities

Council for Learning Disabilities (CLD)
1184 Antioch Road
Box 405
Overland Park, KS 66210
(913) 491-1011

Division for Learning Disabilities,
Council for Exceptional Children
1110 North Glebe Road, Suite 300
Arlington, VA 22201-5704
(703) 620-3660

International Dyslexia Association
40 York Avenue
Fourth Floor
Baltimore, MD 21204
(410) 296-0232
(800) 222-3123

Learning Disabilities Association of America (LDA)
4156 Library Road
Pittsburgh, PA 15234
(412) 341-1515
(412) 341-8077

National Center for Learning Disabilities
381 Park Avenue S., Suite 1401
New York, NY 10016
(212) 545-7510
(888) 575-7373

Reflecting on Standards

The following exercises are designed to help you learn to apply the Council for Exceptional Children (CEC) standards to your teaching practice. Each of the reflection exercises below correlates with a knowledge or skill within the CEC standards. For the full text of each of the related CEC standards, please refer to the standards integration grid located in Appendix B.

1. Focus on Individual Learning Differences
(CEC Content Standard #3 CC3K1)

Reflect on a time when you weren't able to learn a skill or concept as quickly as you wanted to (for example, playing a sport or musical instrument or a particular

subject in school). How did you feel about yourself? How did people treat you? What did you learn from that experience that will help you as you work with individuals who have learning disabilities?

2. Focus on Instructional Planning
(CEC Content Standard #7 CC7K4)

Reflect on what you have learned in this chapter about students with learning disabilities. If you were to have a student with a learning disability in your general education class, how might you utilize technology to meet the various demands of your learning environment?

Technology Resources

Visit the Web-based SAGE Study Site at **http://www.sagepub.com/gargiulo3estudy** for these additional learning tools:

- Chapter quizzes
- Key term flashcards
- Media links

- Full-text SAGE journal articles
- Internet activities
- Additional Web resources

CHAPTER 7

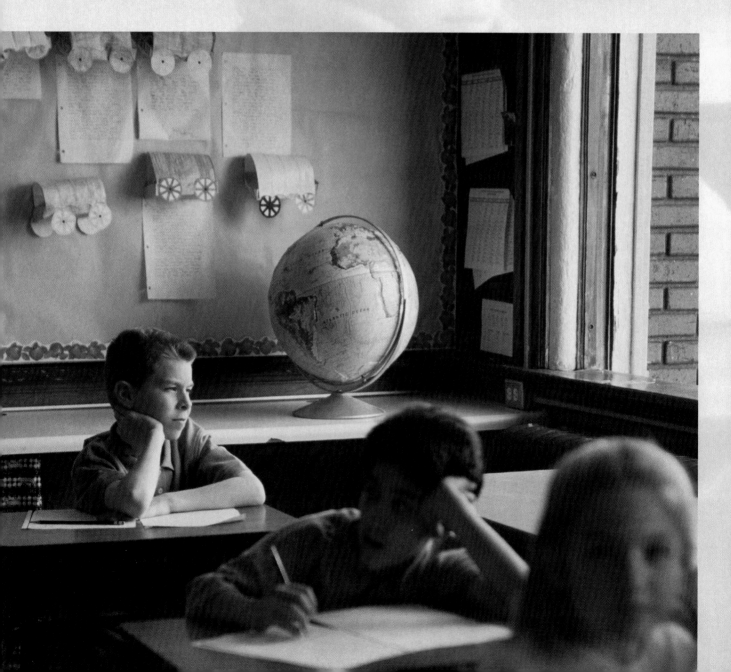

Individuals with Attention Deficit Hyperactivity Disorder

A "Buffer-Boy" with a Ph.D.

I am Rick Parsons. By title I am a professor of Counseling and Educational Psychology at West Chester University outside Philadelphia, Pennsylvania, a licensed psychologist with a practice in suburban Philly, and an author of more than 20 books and 50 professional articles. From a brief review of my professional accomplishments one might conclude that I have had a relatively successful career. I should also tell you that in my childhood I was a student with undiagnosed attention deficit hyperactivity disorder (ADHD).

I went to a Catholic grade school at a time when those with unique learning needs were neither recognized nor diagnosed, nor did they receive services. The idea of ADHD was not a mainstay in the early to late 1950s. Children who were easily distracted, impulsive, often engaging and annoying of classmates, and most often itchy or squirmy, were viewed as bad, out of control, or having strange diseases. The "treatment" of the day was most often of a punitive nature—detention, suspension, and even expulsion. Yet, I was one of the "lucky" ones. I was not suspended or expelled.

I can remember to this day the report cards. The grades were always mediocre, mostly 80s and a few 90s. The comments always pointed to how I could do better *if* I did my homework. There was always the direction that I needed to work on my *self-control* and *think before I acted*! You see I was, and still can be, a bit impulsive.

In the first few years of school I struggled with reading, being unable to really focus and attend. As a result, I was put in the slow reading group, believing I wasn't very bright. In later years, as we would stand for recitation or spelling bees, I would often become the object of the teacher's negative attention because of my talking in line, goofing around, and most often simply moving. At times I could be in constant motion—moving my hands, swaying back and forth, tapping and drumming with my fingers, moving to the distraction and sometimes entertainment of those near me, and almost always to the frustration of the teacher attempting to run the class.

Back then the teachers employed various "interventions." I was publicly reprimanded and sent to the principal. I had notes sent home to my parents, and I even was put in time-out. Time-out for me often took the form of simply being asked to sit in the back of the class, the very back; or if need be, I could take up temporary residence in the coat closet, and even once under the teacher's desk.

Yes, the experience was one in which the message was clear. There was something wrong with this boy. After all, he came from a nice family that was actively involved in the parish, he had an older sister and brother who were excellent students, and even he had his moments in which he would shine. But this child completely lacked self-control; he was a red "C" student.

The poor attention and impulsive behavior were not restricted to school nor bounded by the classroom. My parents had to deal with a 5-year-old who took a bus trip to the local town—just because. They parented me through years of behaviors such as climbing onto the rooftops of local stores, helping myself to penny candy, never watching where I was going or what I was doing and therefore constantly having accidents, breaking things, or simply appearing to be a klutz. The words "Pay attention," "Stand still," "Slow down," or "Watch what you're doing" became my mantra and the directive from most who knew me. And these messages took their toll.

Experience after experience had me doubt my educational abilities, my social acceptability, my emotional maturity, and even my fundamental goodness. That all changed when I met a wonderful nun, my seventh-grade teacher, Sister Mary. Without formal training in special education—simply having a respect for all of life and its uniqueness—Sister Mary helped me to understand that I wasn't bad, or immature, or ill; rather I just had a different way of learning and lots of energy to channel. It was during this seventh grade that "buffing" became more than a possible future career. Sister Mary structured my seat work so that as soon as I finished my work, and if I could wait patiently while she checked my work and assuming it was correct, I could exit the class and operate the buffing machine. Running the buffer became a way to release energy. Operating that machine became a statement of personal competence. The fact that running the buffer was contingent on successfully completing my work helped me to attend to my work, increase my success, and eventually believe in my academic abilities.

And even though today I can still easily be distracted by external stimuli, the unconditional guidance from teachers like Sister Mary has helped me accept that it's okay to be me—it's just a challenge.

—*Rick Parsons*

Attention deficit hyperactivity disorder (ADHD) is believed to affect about 3 to 5 percent of the school-age population (American Psychiatric Association, 2000; National Institute of Mental Health, 2006). Despite the relatively high estimate of prevalence, ADHD is not recognized as a separate disability category under the current IDEA legislation. However, youngsters who have ADHD may still be eligible for a special education. In response to the lobbying efforts of parents, professionals, and advocates, in 1991 the U.S. Department of Education issued a memorandum directed to state departments of education, stating that pupils with ADHD could receive a special education and related services under the disability category "other health impaired" (OHI). In fact, the regulations that accompany PL 108-446 specifically mention ADHD as a condition that renders an individual eligible for services under the rubric "other health impaired." Children with ADHD are also eligible for accommodations in general education classrooms under the protections of Section 504 of the Rehabilitation Act of 1973 (PL 93-112).

Because of the high degree of overlap or **comorbidity** among ADHD, learning disabilities, and emotional disorders (Brown, 2006; U.S. Department of Education, 2006b), and the academic and social difficulties frequently experienced by individuals with ADHD, we have chosen to explore this topic in greater detail in a separate chapter while acknowledging that ADHD is not identified by the federal government as a discrete disability category. We believe, however, it is important for educators and other professionals to be able to recognize these students and offer services, supports, and accommodations regardless of how they might (or might not) be labeled.

ADHD is frequently misunderstood; it is a disability plagued by misconceptions and myths. The behavior of individuals with ADHD is also often misinterpreted, with their actions being seen as indicators of laziness, disorganization, and even disrespect (Smith, Polloway, Patton, & Dowdy, 2008). Some people even question the legitimacy of this disability, believing that it has only been created to absolve parents (and teachers) of any responsibility for the child's conduct (Cohen, 2006).

The goal of this chapter is to examine several concepts and issues associated with ADHD. We will answer a variety of questions, such as "What is ADHD and what causes it?" "How can I help students with ADHD?" and "What role does medication play in the treatment of ADHD?" We begin our examination by defining the term *attention deficit hyperactivity disorder.*

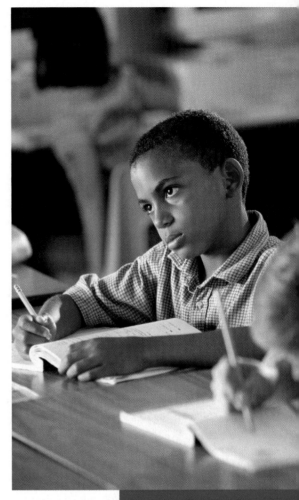

ADHD affects males more than females.

Defining Attention Deficit Hyperactivity Disorder

Because IDEA does not define ADHD, we use the definition put forth by the American Psychiatric Association (2000), which describes this condition as "a persistent pattern of inattention and/or hyperactive impulsivity that is more frequent and severe than is typically observed in individuals at a comparable level of development" (p. 85). This description, derived from the *Diagnostic and Statistical Manual—Text Revision,* commonly referred to as DSM-IV-TR, also contains criteria to assist professionals, mainly physicians, in determining whether a child has ADHD. These guidelines are listed in Table 7.1. In examining the table, you may recognize yourself (we are all forgetful at times and occasionally easily distracted); but in individuals with ADHD, it is the chronic nature of the characteristics and their duration that often lead to impaired functioning in activities of daily living.

The American Psychiatric Association (2000) definition recognizes three subtypes of ADHD based on the individual's unique profile of symptoms: (1) ADHD, predominantly inattentive type; (2) ADHD, predominantly hyperactive-impulsive type; and (3) ADHD, combined type. The vast majority of individuals with ADHD exhibit the combined type (Barkley, 2006).

Table 7.1	Diagnostic Criteria for Attention Deficit Hyperactivity Disorder

Six (or more) of the following symptoms of inattention and/or hyperactivity-impulsivity that have persisted for at least 6 months to a degree that is maladaptive and inconsistent with developmental level:

Inattention	• Often fails to give close attention to details or makes careless mistakes in schoolwork, work, or other activities • Often has difficulty sustaining attention in tasks or play activities • Often does not seem to listen when spoken to directly • Often does not follow through on instructions and fails to finish schoolwork, chores, or duties in the workplace (not due to oppositional behavior or failure to understand instructions) • Often has difficulty organizing tasks and activities • Often avoids, dislikes, or is reluctant to engage in tasks that require sustained mental effort (such as schoolwork or homework) • Often loses things necessary for tasks or activities (e.g., toys, school assignments, pencils, books, or tools) • Is often easily distracted by extraneous stimuli • Is often forgetful in daily activities
Hyperactivity	• Often fidgets with hands or feet or squirms in seat • Often leaves seat in classroom or in other situations in which remaining seated is expected • Often runs about or climbs excessively in situations in which it is inappropriate (in adolescents or adults, may be limited to subjective feelings of restlessness) • Often has difficulty playing or engaging in leisure activities quietly • Is often "on the go" or often acts as if "driven by a motor" • Often talks excessively
Impulsivity	• Often blurts out answers before questions have been completed • Often has difficulty awaiting turn • Often interrupts or intrudes on other (e.g., butts into conversations or games)

Also, some hyperactive-impulsive or inattentive symptoms were present before age 7.

The symptoms must be present in two or more settings (e.g., at school [or work] and at home).

Clear evidence of clinically significant impairment in social, academic, or occupational functioning must be demonstrated.

The symptoms do not occur exclusively during the course of a pervasive developmental disorder, schizophrenia, or other psychotic disorder and are not better accounted for by another mental disorder (e.g., mood disorder, anxiety disorder, dissociative disorder, or a personality disorder).

Source: Adapted from American Psychiatric Association, *Diagnostic and Statistical Manual of Mental Disorders—Text Revision* (Washington, DC: Author, 2000), pp. 92–93.

A Brief History of the Field

Individuals with attention deficit hyperactivity disorder have been recognized for more than 100 years. In 1902, George Still, a London physician, described a group of youngsters who had average or above intelligence yet were disobedient toward adults, acted impulsively, and exhibited inattention along with hyperactivity (Still, 1902). He identified these children as manifesting "defective moral conduct." Still speculated that there was a hereditary foundation to their condition and that these children had neurological impairments. In the late 1930s it was discovered that administering stimulant medication to individuals with characteristics similar to those described by Dr. Still decades earlier had a calming effect on their behavior (Bradley, 1937).

Our early understanding of persons with ADHD was also aided by the work of Heinz Werner and Alfred Strauss, who had worked with children with mental retardation in

Germany. These scientists, having left Germany and immigrated to the United States, observed that some institutionalized children with mental retardation exhibited behavior patterns of distractibility and hyperactivity not unlike those attributed to persons with brain injury. In a series of experiments comparing the performance of supposedly brain-injured children with mental retardation and youngsters who were mentally retarded but without brain injury, Werner and Strauss found that children with brain injury were more likely to focus on background objects rather than the target stimulus (Strauss & Werner, 1942; Werner & Strauss, 1941). Their "figure–ground" investigations, although methodically flawed, offered evidence of the detrimental effects that distractibility and hyperactivity can have on a child's cognitive performance. Youngsters who displayed high levels of distractibility and hyperactivity were commonly referred to as exhibiting the **Strauss syndrome.**

The work of Werner and Strauss was replicated several years later by Cruickshank and his colleagues. These investigators (Cruickshank, Bice, & Wallen, 1957) extended the earlier figure–ground research of Werner and Strauss to children with cerebral palsy. Conceptually, this was an important extension. The youngsters in the Werner and Strauss study were assumed to have brain damage, whereas the children in the Cruickshank experiment all had cerebral palsy—a disability characterized by motor impairments resulting from brain damage (see Chapter 13). Additionally, the individuals evaluated by Werner and Strauss were mentally retarded, but the Cruickshank et al. subjects primarily exhibited normal or near-normal intellectual ability. The finding of hyperactivity and inattention in children without mental retardation was important because it established a link between attentional difficulties and learning problems (Hallahan, Lloyd, Kauffman, Weiss, & Martinez, 2005).

Cruickshank extrapolated his findings into educational recommendations for students who today would likely be recognized as exhibiting ADHD. He called for reducing nonessential classroom stimuli, following a highly structured teacher-directed program, and enhancing the stimulus value of instructional materials (Cruickshank, Bentzen, Ratzeburg, & Tannhauser, 1961). Although these suggestions form the nucleus of many of today's interventions for pupils with ADHD, there is a lack of scientific support for their efficacy (Barkley, 2006).

In the 1950s and 1960s, **minimal brain injury** was the label typically used to describe individuals with distractible, impulsive, and/or hyperactive behavior but no discernible neurological abnormalities. Use of this term soon faded because professionals believed that the designation "minimal" depreciated the difficulties experienced by these individuals. Additionally, in many instances, there was insufficient neurological evidence that the brain tissue was actually damaged (Hallahan et al., 2005).

The 1960s were known as the "Golden Age of Hyperactivity" (Barkley, 1998). During this era the label **hyperactive child syndrome** came into vogue, replacing minimal brain injury as the term of choice. Professionals favored this description because it focused attention on observable behaviors rather than relying on speculative indicators of brain injury. Eventually, during the 1980s, the hyperactive child syndrome label lost its position of prominence as investigators focused their interest on the inattention component of ADHD as the major deficit exhibited by children with ADHD (Hallahan et al., 2005).

Prevalence of Attention Deficit Hyperactivity Disorder

As we noted earlier, ADHD is believed to affect approximately 3 to 5 percent of the school-age population (American Psychiatric Association, 2000; Barkley, 2006), or an estimated

Students with ADHD frequently exhibit other academic and behavioral difficulties.

2 million children (National Institute of Mental Health, 2006). According to Lerner and Kline (2006), ADHD represents one of the most common chronic conditions of childhood. It is obvious that the number of individuals with ADHD continues to grow, most likely because of greater awareness and improved diagnostic procedures.

Recall that ADHD is not one of the thirteen disability categories recognized by the federal government; these pupils may be served, however, under the label "other health impaired." Between the 1993–1994 school year and the 2005–2006 school year, the OHI category saw an increase of almost 478,000 students, or an astonishing 575 percent increase (U.S. Department of Education, 2006c; 2007). Of course, not all of the growth can be attributed to pupils with ADHD. We suspect, however, that individuals with ADHD are largely responsible for the dramatic growth of this category.

The research literature generally suggests that ADHD is more readily identified in males than females. This condition is diagnosed four to nine times more often in boys than in girls (U.S. Department of Education, 2006b). This statistic suggests the possibility of a gender bias in identification and diagnosis: Boys may be overidentified and girls underidentified. We believe that this situation exists because ADHD manifests itself differently in males and females. Boys are more likely to exhibit disruptive, hyperactive behavior, thus being more noticeable to teachers. Girls, on the other hand, are more likely to be withdrawn and exhibit inattention; consequently, they are less likely to be identified (Vaughn, Bos, & Schumm, 2007). Though gender bias may explain part of the discrepancy between males and females, scientific evidence points to actual biological differences as the primary contributing factor (Barkley, 2006).

Etiology of Attention Deficit Hyperactivity Disorder

The precise cause of attention deficit hyperactivity disorder is unknown. To date, no single etiological factor has been discovered, although researchers are exploring several possibilities including neurological foundations, hereditary contributions, and environmental conditions. As scientists learn more about ADHD, it is likely that multiple causes will be identified.

Neurological Dysfunction

Research suggests that neurological dysfunction plays a key role in individuals with ADHD. Anatomical differences and imbalances in brain chemistry are being closely examined as etiological possibilities (Moore et al., 2006; Salend & Rohena, 2003; Weyandt, 2005). In recent years, neuroscientists have been able to advance our understanding of the functioning of the human brain—particularly as it relates to individuals with ADHD. Aided by advances in neuroimaging technology, researchers are using scans of the brain such as computed tomography (CT) and magnetic resonance imaging (MRI) procedures, as well as other techniques, to learn about brain structure and activity. Several regions of the brain, specifically the frontal lobes, parts of the basal ganglia, and the cerebellum, appear to consistently exhibit abnormalities in persons with ADHD (Barkley, 2006; Brown, 2006; Castellanos et al., 2002). See Figure 7.1 for regions of the brain thought to be affected.

The prefrontal and frontal lobes, located in the far forward region of the brain, are responsible for control of **executive functions**—behaviors such as self-regulation, working memory, inner speech, and arousal levels, among other dimensions. The basal ganglia, consisting of several parts (caudate and globus pallidus), is responsible for control and coordination of motor behavior. The cerebellum is also involved in controlling motor behavior (Hallahan et al., 2005). Disorganization and inattention, frequently implicated with ADHD,

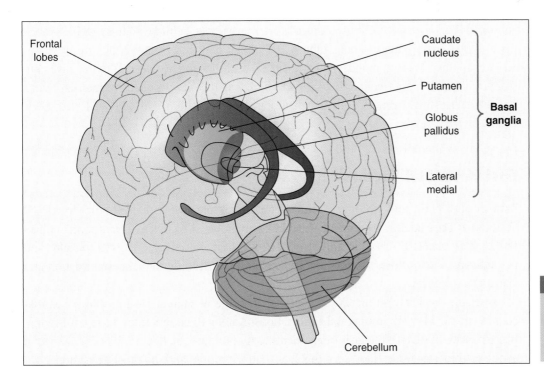

Figure 7.1

Areas of the Brain Suspected of Affecting Attention Deficit Hyperactivity Disorder

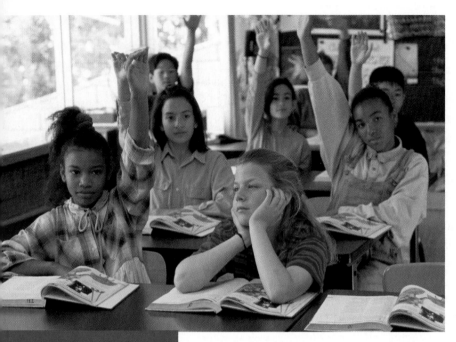

Pupils with ADHD are typically served in the general education classroom.

are believed to be associated with impairments in the prefrontal and frontal cortex, whereas hyperactive behavior is thought to be due to abnormalities in the cerebellum and/or basal ganglia (Solanto, 2002).

Scientists are also exploring the possibility of chemical abnormalities in the brain as a reason for ADHD. Although the neurological basis for ADHD is not fully comprehended, a deficiency or imbalance in one or more of the neurotransmitters in the brain is suspected. Simply stated, neurotransmitters are the chemicals that transport electrical impulses (messages) from one brain cell or neuron to another across tiny gaps known as the synaptic cleft. Current thinking suggests that ADHD results from a deficiency or dysfunction of the neurotransmitter dopamine in the regions of the brain that control activity and attention (Gupta, 2000; Mill et al., 2006). Although the precise nature of the defect is not known, investigators believe that the level of dopamine is too low in the frontal cortex, thereby interfering with aspects of executive functioning, and elevated in the basal ganglia region, contributing to impulsive and hyperactive behavior (Castellanos, 1997).

Hereditary Factors

There is strong evidence of the role of heredity in contributing to ADHD. Hereditary factors are believed to account for a large percentage of hyperactive-impulsive behavior (Daley, 2006). Approximately one out of three persons with ADHD also has relatives with this condition (Barkley, 2006). Family studies further reveal that a child who has ADHD is much more likely to have parents who exhibit ADHD (Levy, Hay, & Bennett, 2006). Additionally, researchers investigating monozygotic (identical) and dizygotic (fraternal) twins have consistently found a higher concordance of ADHD in identical twins than in fraternal twins, strongly suggesting a genetic link (Larsson, Larsson, & Lichtenstein, 2004; Martin, Levy, Pieka, & Hay, 2006).

Environmental Factors

Various pre-, peri-, and postnatal traumas are also implicated as contributing to ADHD (Barkley, 2006; National Institute of Mental Health, 2006). Examples of environmental factors include maternal smoking and alcohol abuse, lead poisoning, low birth weight, and prematurity. Many of these factors are also suspected as leading to mental retardation and learning disabilities.

Research (Hallahan et al., 2005; National Institute of Mental Health, 2006) has discounted many other environmental explanations. Among the popular myths regarding suspected causes of ADHD, but lacking in scientific support, are too much/too little sugar, food additives/coloring, yeast, fluorescent lighting, bad parenting, and too much television.

Characteristics of Individuals with Attention Deficit Hyperactivity Disorder

Characteristics of persons with attention deficit hyperactivity disorder vary considerably. This disorder generally manifests itself early in a child's life. In fact, some precursors have been noted in infancy (Barkley, 2000). It would not be uncommon for behaviors associated with ADHD to be exhibited as early as kindergarten or first grade (Vaughn et al., 2007). Though many young children are sometimes inattentive, fidgety, or somewhat impulsive, the developmental features that distinguish ADHD from typical patterns of behavior in young children include the following:

- Chronic over time
- Generally pervasive across situations
- Deviant from age-based standards
- Increased comorbidity with other learning and psychiatric disorders (Vaughn et al., p. 82)

ADHD presents itself in many different ways. In some students, inattention is the primary deficit. These pupils have difficulty concentrating on a specific task; they are forgetful and easily distracted. Students who exhibit hyperactive-impulsive disorder are constantly in motion; racing from one activity to another, they have difficulty sitting still or playing quietly. Individuals with a combined type of ADHD manifest aspects of both types. Table 7.2 provides examples of characteristics typical of students with ADHD. (See the accompanying First Person feature.)

Behavioral Inhibition and Executive Functioning

Contemporary thinking suggests that problems with **behavioral inhibition** are the primary characteristic of persons with ADHD (Barkley, 2006). Behavioral inhibition consists of three

Table 7.2	Representative Characteristics of Pupils with Attention Deficit Hyperactivity Disorder		
Inattention		**Hyperactivity**	**Impulsivity**
• Making careless mistakes		• Fidgeting	• Blurting answers before questions are completed
• Having difficulty sustaining attention		• Being unable to stay seated	• Having difficulty awaiting turn
• Seeming not to listen		• Moving excessively (restless)	• Interrupting/intruding upon others
• Failing to finish tasks		• Having difficulty engaging quietly in leisure activities	
• Having difficulty organizing		• Being "on the go"	
• Avoiding tasks requiring sustained attention		• Talking excessively	
• Losing things			
• Becoming easily distracted			
• Being forgetful			

SOURCE: Adapted from M. Wolraich and A. Baumgaertel, "The Practical Aspects of Diagnosing and Managing Children with Attention Deficit Hyperactivity Disorder," *Clinical Pediatrics*, 36(9), 1997, pp. 497–504.

First Person

Good Things Come in Small Packages

Like any expectant first-time mom, I was thrilled at the thought of becoming a parent. My joy, however, quickly turned to fear when I went into premature labor. My concerns were multiplied when I developed pulmonary edema and could barely breathe. The only thing that kept me sane was the constant, rhythmic heartbeat of my baby girl coming through loud and clear on the fetal monitor. My family knew how serious my condition was, but I was in a total fog—completely unaware that the doctor had addressed the possibility of my husband's having to choose between my life and that of our unborn child. Six days after entering the hospital, and four days after our life-threatening ordeal, our daughter Helen was born.

Five weeks premature and weighing only 4 lbs. 12 oz., she made a feisty entrance into the world. My husband and I were able to take her home just two days later. With the exception of developing jaundice, she had no health problems whatsoever. Developmental milestones such as rolling over, sitting alone, and pulling up were reached well within normal limits. She even took her first step on her first birthday. Although she was tiny, we had no concerns for her physical development.

Helen's intellectual and emotional growth initially appeared right on track as well; sometimes she was even ahead of the norm. She talked at a very young age. She used simple but complete sentences by the time she was 18 months old and could carry on a decent conversation by age 2.

When the time came for her to start kindergarten, we had some reservations about her beginning school; but at the time, her starting public school was the best option for our family. Helen was one of the youngest children in her class and was definitely the smallest. Our first hint of trouble came during this year. She struggled with reading and math, but her teacher had no worries about her moving on to first grade. She saw no problem that a little maturity couldn't fix.

Helen made great strides in first grade but still struggled. Approximately one month before the year was over, the light seemed to turn on—she got it!! Her teacher lamented the fact that she could not keep her another six weeks. Much as in kindergarten, my husband and I discussed the possibility of either having her tested for a learning disability or repeating the grade, but her teacher believed she would be fine.

Second grade was a repeat of first. No problems at the beginning of the school year, then increasing struggles as the year progressed, and of course the "eureka" moment near the end of the year. As in both kindergarten and first grade, Helen's teacher strongly recommended against holding her back, citing the social stigma of repeating while crediting many of her problems to her immaturity. Yet again, a referral for special education was discouraged.

In was not until third grade that we had a major turning point. The work was becoming more difficult, and her frustration was growing. The final straw came one evening when, after a long and confusing homework session, Helen put her head down on the table and began to cry. When I asked her what was wrong, she began to sob uncontrollably, then threw herself into my arms and

elements that affect the ability to (1) withhold a planned response; (2) interrupt a response that has already been initiated; and (3) protect an ongoing activity from competing or distracting stimuli (Barkley; Lawrence et al., 2002). Problems with behavioral inhibition can lead to a variety of difficulties in the classroom. According to Hallahan et al. (2005), students may have trouble, for example, waiting their turn, resisting distractions, delaying immediate gratification, or interrupting a faulty line of thinking.

Barkley (2006) and Brown (2006) both note that individuals with ADHD also often have difficulty with executive functions. Recall from our earlier discussion of the etiology of ADHD that executive functions involve a number of self-directed behaviors such as pleaded with me, "Mommy, why can't I learn like every-body else?" I honestly don't remember what I told her. All I could really think of was getting to school the next day to talk with her teacher. Thus began the long saga of figuring out exactly where the problems were and how we would address them.

After multiple tests to determine her eligibility for special education, all the assessments indicated "normal" results. But thank goodness the principal, counselor, and her teacher saw past the scores and into the eyes and heart of a little girl who was quickly losing any belief in herself. We hired a tutor, made modifications in the classroom, and Helen took more diagnostic tests—still nothing that would qualify her for services under special education. About two-thirds of the way through the school year, Helen's pediatrician diagnosed her with ADHD; thus, she was eligible to receive a special education under the label Other Health Impaired. She began taking Ritalin, and we saw a gradual improvement in her schoolwork.

The improvement we saw did not come without a price. Helen was very angry with her father and me when she realized why she was taking medication every day. She was truly terrified of not having any friends if they found out she had ADHD.

About halfway through fourth grade, we decided to try the extended release form of her medication. We did this in hopes that she would not feel as though she was being "watched" by her classmates when she had to go take medicine in the middle of the day, and also to help with her homework in the late afternoon and early evening. Unfortunately, coming off the medication in the evening turned into a "crash and burn" event most nights. Helen even began to have suicidal ideation and one night did not eat dinner because, as she put it, she "could control herself" (in reference to living or dying).

We of course changed medications, and the emotional outbursts tapered off. The remainder of fourth and fifth grade was an up-and-down roller coaster, ending with yet another twist in the ride. Helen's younger sister was identified as gifted, thus creating a new set of struggles with self-confidence and self-esteem.

Currently, as a seventh grader (but the size of a third grader), she is developing new friends and her own sense of style and self. Academics continue to be a daily struggle. She tends to get lost in lengthy operations and has a great deal of trouble focusing attention and identifying perti-nent information. Helen has a tremendous problem with spelling and grammar. She also has trouble transferring and assimilating knowledge from one situation to another. Helen is very rules oriented and desperately needs struc-ture, but she cannot provide that structure for herself. She tends to vacillate from overly focused to airhead. At times, Helen appears almost belligerent—she is unable to "shift gears" as circumstances change. We frequently see this with her schoolwork. She continues to make the same mistakes over and over again because of her unwillingness (inability) to adopt a different strategy—because, in her eyes, her way is the correct way.

Her father and I continue to try to instill the idea of effort being more important than grades, but she holds herself to a higher standard. I am not sure what the next eight to ten years hold. Helen is a very hard worker, but at this point in time a four-year college degree may or may not be in her future. Our biggest concern is that she find something she enjoys and that she can excel in. Our goal is not for her to make the honor roll or be rich, but for Helen to be a self-confident and fulfilled young woman.

—Anonymous

self-regulation, working memory, inner speech, and arousal levels, among other dimensions. Impaired executive functioning in children with ADHD affects a wide range of performance. Difficulty following rules or directions, forgetfulness, and a lack of emotional control are just a few of the ways that students are affected.

Social and Emotional Issues

Social problems and emotional difficulties are not uncommon among individuals with ADHD. Children with ADHD often experience difficulty making friends and maintaining appropriate relationships with peers (Chronis, Jones, & Raggi, 2006; Olmeda, Thomas, & Davis, 2003). Diminished self-confidence, low self-esteem, and feelings of social isolation/rejection are fairly typical in some individuals with ADHD (Friend & Bursuck, 2006). In some instances, in their attempts to be popular and gain friends, students with ADHD, because of their impaired impulse control, actually wind up aggravating peers and further ostracizing themselves from the very individuals with whom they are attempting to establish relationships.

Persons with ADHD may manifest a wide variety of emotional difficulties. Some individuals may exhibit aggression and antisocial behaviors; in others, withdrawn behavior, depression, and anxiety disorders are typical (Brown, 2006; National Institute of Mental Health, 2006). A majority of parents of children with recognized emotional disorders report that their child also exhibits ADHD (U.S. Department of Education, 2006b).

Comorbidity

Students with ADHD frequently have other academic and behavioral difficulties. Learning disabilities, for example, are very common among individuals with ADHD (Bender, 2008; Pierce, 2003). In an interesting distinction, Silver (1990) observes that a learning disability affects the brain's *ability* to learn whereas ADHD interferes with a person's *availability* to learn. On the other hand, pupils who are gifted and talented (see Chapter 14) are also frequently recognized as having ADHD. Some of these students, in fact, exhibit intense curiosity, creativity, and concentration (Dodson, 2002; Honos-Webb, 2005). Additionally, researchers have found that children with ADHD have coexisting psychiatric disorders at a much higher rate than their peers without ADHD (U.S. Department of Education, 2006b). Unfortunately, at the present time, investigators are unable to fully explain the reasons for the high degree of overlap between ADHD and other impairments.

Assessment of Attention Deficit Hyperactivity Disorder

Identifying pupils with attention deficit hyperactivity is not always easy, although many teachers will say "You know it when you see it." Valid and reliable assessment of ADHD is difficult; there is no single, definitive medical or psychological test that clearly distinguishes these children from others. Identifying a child as having ADHD is a multidimensional process. Typical strategies for assessing this condition involve direct observation of the youngster and the use of behavior rating scales and other types of observation instruments completed by parents, teachers, and other professionals. Teachers, in particular, represent a valuable source of information about the child as they are involved with this student in a variety of academic and social situations (Weyandt, 2001).

Assessment and diagnosis of ADHD is a multifaceted endeavor involving the gathering of specific medical, behavioral, and educational data (U.S. Department of Education, 2006a). The intent of these efforts is to glean as much useful information as possible in order to accurately assess the child's condition.

Medical Evaluation

Generally speaking, a medical evaluation is designed to rule out medical conditions that might be contributing to the pupil's hyperactivity and/or inattention. Examples of these conditions include epilepsy, thyroid problems, or brain tumors (Hallahan et al., 2005; National Institute of Mental Health, 2006). Knowledge of a child's health status can also assist the health care professional in deciding which type of medication to prescribe, should that be a treatment option.

Professionals confronted with making a diagnosis of ADHD can also seek guidance from guidelines disseminated by the American Academy of Pediatrics (2000). Their recommendations, crafted around DSM-IV-TR criteria, include the following six recommendations:

- In a child 6 to 12 years old who presents with inattention, hyperactivity, impulsivity, academic underachievement, or behavior problems, primary care clinicians should initiate an evaluation for ADHD.
- The diagnosis of ADHD requires that a child meet Diagnostic and Statistical Manual of Mental Disorders, Fourth Edition criteria.
- The assessment of ADHD requires evidence directly obtained from parents or caregivers regarding core symptoms of ADHD in various settings, the age of onset, duration of symptoms, and degree of functional impairment.
- The assessment of ADHD requires evidence directly obtained from the classroom teacher (or other school professional) regarding core symptoms of ADHD, duration of symptoms, degree of functional impairment, and coexisting conditions.
- Evaluation of the child with ADHD should include assessment for coexisting conditions.
- Other diagnostic tests are not routinely required to establish a diagnosis of ADHD. (pp. 1158–1170)

An interesting phenomenon is sometimes observed during the clinical interview. In novel and structured situations, such as a physician's office, it is not unusual for the child to be symptom free of characteristics typically associated with ADHD—much to the bewilderment of their parents or caregivers. This phenomenon, recognized many years ago, is commonly referred to as the **doctor's office effect** (Cantwell, 1979).

Behavioral/Educational Evaluation

Rating scales provide another important source of information about the student suspected of having ADHD. Evaluation of the child's performance in the classroom and his or her behavior at home will assist professionals in establishing a complete picture of the pupil's condition and ensure that the data are as accurate as possible. Although behavioral rating scales can accurately distinguish between children with and without ADHD (U.S. Department of Education, 2006a), their usefulness and accuracy are largely dependent upon raters' knowledge of the individual and their perception of his or her behavior. Despite the standardized nature of these instruments, bias is a real concern.

One example of a reliable and valid assessment measure is the ADHD Rating Scale—IV (DuPaul, Power, Anastopoulos, & Reid, 1998). Similar to other rating indices, informants rate an individual's performance using a Likert scale ("never or rarely," "sometimes," "often," or "very often"). The Conners' Teachers Rating Scale—Revised (Conners, 1997) is another representative example of a commonly used standardized rating scale. This instrument allows the evaluator to rate a variety of ADHD characteristics on the basis of how closely the statement portrays the student. Some assessment instruments primarily assess symptoms of ADHD; other scales are multidimensional. Table 7.3 shows sample test items from one such measure. This instrument, which is typically completed by teachers, evaluates the impact of ADHD on cognitive processes, social/emotional behaviors, and impulsivity/hyperactivity.

Table 7.3	Sample Test Items from the "Strengths and Limitations Inventory: School Version"				
		Never Observed	Sometimes Observed	Often Observed	Very Often Observed
Attention/ Impulsivity/ Hyperactivity	Exhibits excessive nonpurposeful movement (can't sit still, stay in seat).				
	Does not stay on task for appropriate periods of time.				
	Verbally or physically interrupts conversations or activities.				
	Does not pay attention to most important stimuli.				
Reasoning/ Processing	Makes poor decisions.				
	Makes frequent errors.				
	Has difficulty getting started.				
Memory	Has difficulty repeating information recently heard.				
	Has difficulty following multiple directions.				
	Memory deficits impact daily activities.				
Executive Function	Has difficulty planning/organizing activities.				
	Has difficulty attending to several stimuli at once.				
	Has difficulty monitoring own performance throughout activity (self-monitoring).				
	Has difficulty independently adjusting behavior (self-regulation).				
Interpersonal Skills	Has difficulty accepting constructive criticism.				
	Exhibits signs of poor self-confidence.				
Emotional Maturity	Inappropriate emotion for situation.				
	Displays temper outbursts.				
	Does not follow classroom or workplace "rules."				

Source: C. Dowdy, J. Patton, T. Smith, and E. Polloway, *Attention Deficit/Hyperactivity Disorder in the Classroom* (Austin, TX: Pro-Ed, 1998), pp. 112–113.

Educational Considerations

How does a teacher assist the student who exhibits attention deficit hyperactivity disorder? With an estimated 2 million school-age children exhibiting this disorder (National Institute of Mental Health, 2006), this is an important issue for many classroom teachers and parents. Most pupils with ADHD experience significant difficulty in school, where attention and impulse control are prerequisites for success. Most children with ADHD respond to a structured and predictable learning environment where rules and expectations are clearly stated and understood, consequences are predetermined, and reinforcement is delivered immediately (National Dissemination Center for Children with Disabilities, 2004). Of course, environmental modifications alone are not the key to success. Educational researchers believe that **multimodal interventions,** or concurrent treatments, are generally more effective for individuals with ADHD than any one particular strategy (Brown, 2006; dos Reis, Owens, Puccia, & Leaf, 2004; Evans et al., 2006; MTA Cooperative Group, 1999a, 1999b). Instructional adaptations, behavioral interventions, home–school communication, medication, and counseling represent some of the available intervention options for individuals with ADHD. We have chosen to highlight four of these treatment approaches, including a concluding examination of the role of medication in the treatment of ADHD. But first we look at the issue of the educational setting that is most appropriate for pupils with ADHD.

Where Are Students with Attention Deficit Hyperactivity Disorder Educated?

Because the federal government does not recognize attention deficit hyperactivity disorder as a discrete disability, information usually provided by the U.S. Department of Education on the educational settings in which these pupils are served is unavailable. Individuals with ADHD who qualify for a special education are eligible for services under the category of "other health impaired." It is not possible, however, to distinguish which students in this group have ADHD.

Given our current educational climate of emphasizing inclusionary placement for individuals with disabilities, it is safe to assume that large numbers of students with ADHD receive services in the general education classroom. Mercer and Pullen (2005) offer support for this assumption, citing evidence that the majority of students with ADHD are appropriately served in the general education classroom. Sometimes this placement involves general education teachers and special educators working together as a collaborative team. Of course, the most appropriate setting for a student with ADHD must be decided on a case-by-case basis.

Recall that not all students with ADHD qualify for special education services under IDEA (PL 108-446). These individuals will most likely receive accommodations in the general education classroom through the protections afforded them under Section 504 of PL 93-112. See the accompanying Suggestions for the Classroom feature for a list of accommodations appropriate for designing 504 plans (and IEPs too).

Teachers who are successful in working with children with ADHD, regardless of the educational setting in which they are served, typically incorporate a three-pronged strategy. They begin by identifying the unique needs of the child. For example, the teacher determines how, when, and why the pupil is inattentive, impulsive, and hyperactive. The teacher then selects different educational practices associated with academic instruction, behavioral interventions, and classroom accommodations that are appropriate to meet the child's needs. Finally, the teacher combines these practices into an IEP or other individualized plan and integrates this program with educational activities provided to other students. The three steps, which summarize this strategy, are as follows:

- Evaluate the child's individual needs and strengths.
- Select appropriate instructional practices.
- Integrate practices within the IEP if the student is receiving a special education.

"Because no two children with ADHD are alike, it is important to keep in mind that no single educational program, practice, or setting will be best for all children" (U.S. Department of Education, 2006b, p. 4).

We will now examine several different treatment approaches typically used to meet the unique needs of students with ADHD.

Suggestions for the Classroom

Accommodations Help Students with Attention Deficit Hyperactivity Disorder

Children and youth with attention deficit hyperactivity disorder (ADHD) often have serious problems in school. Inattention, impulsiveness, hyperactivity, disorganization, and other difficulties can lead to unfinished assignments, careless errors, and behavior that is disruptive to oneself and others. Through the implementation of relatively simple and straightforward accommodations to the classroom environment or teaching style, teachers can adapt to the strengths and weaknesses of students with ADHD. Small changes in how a teacher approaches the student with ADHD or in what the teacher expects can turn a losing year into a winning one for the child. Examples of accommodations that teachers can make to adapt to the needs of students with ADHD are grouped below according to areas of difficulty.

Inattention

- ☑ Seat student in quiet area.
- ☑ Require fewer correct responses for grade.
- ☑ Seat student near good role model.
- ☑ Reduce amount of homework.
- ☑ Seat student near "study buddy."
- ☑ Instruct student in self-monitoring using cueing.
- ☑ Increase distance between desks.
- ☑ Pair written instructions with oral instructions.
- ☑ Allow extra time to complete assigned work.
- ☑ Provide peer assistance in note taking.
- ☑ Shorten assignments or work periods to coincide with span of attention; use timer.
- ☑ Give clear, concise instructions.
- ☑ Break long assignments into smaller parts so student can see end of work.
- ☑ Seek to involve student in lesson presentation.
- ☑ Assist student in setting short-term goals.
- ☑ Cue student to stay on task—i.e., private signal.
- ☑ Give assignments one at a time to avoid work overload.

Impulsiveness

- ☑ Ignore minor inappropriate behavior.
- ☑ Acknowledge positive behavior of nearby students.
- ☑ Increase immediacy of rewards and consequences.
- ☑ Seat student near role model or near teacher.
- ☑ Use time-out procedure for misbehavior.
- ☑ Set up behavior contract.

☑ Supervise closely during transition times.

☑ Instruct student in self-monitoring of behavior—i.e., hand raising, calling out.

☑ Use "prudent" reprimands for misbehavior (i.e., avoid lecturing or criticism).

☑ Call on only when hand is raised in appropriate manner.

☑ Attend to positive behavior with compliments, etc.

☑ Praise when hand raised to answer question.

Motor Activity

☑ Allow student to stand at times while working.

☑ Supervise closely during transition times.

☑ Provide opportunity for "seat breaks"—i.e., run errands, etc.

☑ Remind student to check over work product if performance is rushed and careless.

☑ Provide short breaks between assignments.

☑ Give extra time to complete tasks (especially for students with slow motor tempo).

Academic Skills

☑ If reading is weak: Provide additional reading time; use "previewing" strategies; select text with less on a page; shorten amount of required reading; avoid oral reading.

☑ If written language is weak: Accept nonwritten forms for reports (i.e., displays, oral reports); accept use of typewriter, word processor, tape recorder; do not assign large quantity of written work; test with multiple-choice or fill-in questions.

☑ If oral expression is weak: Accept all oral responses; substitute a display for an oral report; encourage student to tell about new ideas or experiences; pick topics easy for student to talk about.

☑ If math is weak: Allow use of calculator; use graph paper to space numbers; provide additional math time; provide immediate corrective feedback and instruction via modeling of the correct computational procedure.

Organization Planning

☑ Ask for parental help in encouraging organization.

☑ Allow student to have extra set of books at home.

☑ Provide organization rules.

☑ Give assignments one at a time.

☑ Encourage student to have notebook with dividers and folders for work.

☑ Assist student in setting short-term goals.

☑ Provide student with homework assignment book.

☑ Do not penalize for poor handwriting if visual-motor defects are present.

☑ Supervise writing down of homework assignments.

☑ Encourage learning of keyboarding skills.

☑ Send daily/weekly progress reports home.

☑ Allow student to tape-record assignments or homework.

☑ Regularly check desk and notebook for neatness; encourage neatness rather than penalize sloppiness.

Compliance

☑ Praise compliant behavior.

☑ Supervise student closely during transition times.

☑ Provide immediate feedback.

☑ Seat student near teacher.

☑ Ignore minor misbehavior.

☑ Set up behavior contract.

☑ Use teacher attention to reinforce positive behavior.

☑ Implement classroom behavior management system.

☑ Use "prudent" reprimands for misbehavior (i.e., avoid lecturing or criticism).

☑ Instruct student in self-monitoring of behavior.

☑ Acknowledge positive behavior of nearby students.

Mood

☑ Provide reassurance and encouragement.

☑ Make time to talk alone with student.

☑ Frequently compliment positive behavior and work product.

☑ Encourage social interactions with classmates if student is withdrawn or excessively shy.

☑ Speak softly in nonthreatening manner if student shows nervousness.

☑ Reinforce frequently when signs of frustration are noticed.

☑ Review instructions when giving new assignments to make sure student comprehends directions.

☑ Look for signs of stress build-up and provide encouragement or reduced workload to alleviate pressure and avoid temper outburst.

☑ Look for opportunities for student to display leadership role in class.

☑ Spend more time talking to students who seem pent up or display anger easily.

☑ Conference frequently with parents to learn about student's interests and achievements outside of school.

☑ Provide brief training in anger control: encourage student to walk away; use calming strategies; tell nearby adult if getting angry.

☑ Send positive notes home.

Socialization

☑ Praise appropriate behavior.

☑ Encourage cooperative learning tasks with other students.

☑ Monitor social interactions.

☑ Provide small group social skills training.

☑ Set up social behavior goals with student and implement a reward program.

☑ Praise student frequently.

☑ Prompt appropriate social behavior either verbally or with private signal.

☑ Assign special responsibilities to student in presence of peer group so others observe student in a positive light.

—Harvey C. Parker

Source: A.D.D. Warehouse, 304 Northwest 70th Avenue, Plantation, FL 33317; (800) 233-9273. Available online at http://www.addwarehouse.com

Functional Behavioral Assessment

Behavioral strategies are an effective intervention technique for students with ADHD. One example of this approach is the use of **functional behavioral assessment.** A functional behavioral assessment focuses on determining the purpose or function that a particular behavior serves. This process entails, according to Alberto and Troutman (2006), "detailed observation, analysis, and manipulation of objects and events in a student's environment to determine what is occasioning and maintaining the [inappropriate] behaviors" (p. 62). Once this analysis is completed, the goal is to construct interventions that modify the antecedent or triggering behaviors and/or the consequences that are reinforcing and maintaining the undesirable performances.

Self-Regulation/Monitoring

Self-regulation is a behavioral self-control strategy drawn from the early work of Glynn, Thomas, and Shee (1973) on self-monitoring. It is a highly recommended intervention strategy for students with ADHD (Daly & Ranalli, 2003; Reis, 2002; Weiss & Illes, 2006). "Self-regulation requires students to stop, think about what they are doing, compare their behavior to a criterion, record the results of their comparison, and receive reinforcement for their behavior if it meets the criterion" (Johnson & Johnson, 1999, p. 6). Self-monitoring includes all of the preceding steps with the exception of dispensing reinforcement. Self-regulation techniques can be used across all grade levels and are appropriate for youngsters served in special education settings and general education classrooms alike.

Self-regulation is a common intervention strategy used with students with ADHD.

Self-regulatory strategies are frequently used to modify common classroom behaviors such as working independently, staying on task, completing assignments, or remaining at one's desk. Five sequential steps form the basis of self-regulation, which should focus on a positive target behavior (Johnson & Johnson, 1999). After the teacher determines the student's current level of performance, the student follows these steps:

1. **Self-observation**—looking at one's own behavior, given a predetermined criterion
2. **Self-assessment**—deciding if the behavior has occurred, through some form of self-questioning activity
3. **Self-recording**—recording the decision made during self-assessment on a private recording form
4. **Self-determination of reinforcement**—setting a criterion for success, and selecting a reinforcer from a menu of reinforcers
5. **Self-administration of reinforcement**—administering a reinforcer to oneself

Before allowing students to follow these steps independently, it is recommended that teachers teach self-reinforcement strategies by first demonstrating the necessary steps through modeling or guided practice. Self-monitoring of behavior has been shown to increase academic productivity and on-task behavior of students in both elementary and secondary classrooms (Hallahan et al., 2005).

✓ EFFECTIVE INSTRUCTIONAL PRACTICES   Managing Students with ADHD

Classwide interventions are time-efficient strategies for managing students with ADHD without singling out or stigmatizing the child. They also have the advantage of benefiting *all* pupils, not just the pupil with ADHD. Classwide interventions can have a positive effect on the academic and behavioral difficulties frequently associated with ADHD. Some of these instructional options are listed below.

	Intervention	Key Features	Pros	Cons	Behavior Outcomes	Academic Outcomes
Behavioral	Contingency Management	Positively state rules Clear expectations and guidelines Identify reinforcers and punishers	Effective Flexible Adaptive Engaging, fun	Requires consistency to be effective Setup time	↓ Hyperactivity, inattentive, disruptive behavior ↑ Compliance, time on task	↑ Work accuracy and completion
	Therapy Balls	Replacing child's seat with a gym ball	Effective Socially valid Simple to implement	Costly ($$) May not be practical for whole class	↑ In-seat behavior	↑ Written work
	Self-Monitoring	Identify target behavior Explicitly teach rating scale Decisions on when and how to monitor the behavior	Teaches autonomy and responsibility One-to-one teacher attention Inexpensive	Setup time Gradual shift toward positive behavior	↑ Time on task ↓ Inattentive and inappropriate behaviors	
	Peer Monitoring	Outline appropriate and inappropriate behaviors Practice system before use Clear guidelines and rules	Focus on prosocial behaviors Use of peers to improve behavior	Requires vigilance and practice to prevent peer rejection	↓ Talking out	

Home–School Collaboration

Home–school collaboration is essential for all pupils, but especially for those with ADHD; it is an important ingredient for promoting their success at school (Jones & Teach, 2006). As illustrated in Figure 7.2 (page 264), this partnership must be "ongoing, reciprocal, mutually respectful, and student centered" (Bos, Nahmias, & Urban, 1999, p. 4).

Parents have played a key role in their children's education ever since the enactment of PL 94-142 in 1975. Their involvement has recently been expanded, however, as part of IDEA 2004 (PL 108-446), and input from parents is now solicited during prereferral and eligibility

Behavioral (continued)	Instructional Choice	Teacher-developed menu of assignments or tasks Student choice of task	Simple to implement Inexpensive	Preparation Possible student expectancy	↓ Behavior problems	↑ Academic engagement
Academic	Classwide Peer Tutoring	Pair students together Alternate tutor–learner roles Provides immediate corrective feedback	Teacher can monitor whole class Peer attention Immediate feedback Self-selected pace Inexpensive	Setup time Initial training period	↑ Time on task ↓ Disruptive behavior	↑ Performance in math, reading, and spelling
	Instructional Modification	Altering the assignment	Personalized to target students' needs	Time consuming Challenging to find adequate modifications	↓ Disruptive behavior ↑ Task engagement	↑ Performance in reading and writing
	Computer-Assisted Instruction	Use of computer programs to supplement instruction Align with curriculum	Provides additional instruction Fun, engaging Builds fluency	Expensive Need computer access Some programs may not be appropriate	↑ Time on task	↑ Math performance

Note: ↑ indicates increase, ↓ indicates decrease.

Source: Adapted from J. Harlacher, N. Roberts, and K. Merrell, "Classwide Interventions for Students with ADHD," *Teaching Exceptional Children*, 39(2), 2006, pp. 6–12.

meetings as well as when planning positive behavioral interventions. Bos et al. (1999) note that home–school collaboration can be used in many areas of school life, but it is especially appropriate for students with ADHD when parents and teachers communicate about monitoring medication effects, completing homework assignments, establishing goals and rewards, assessing intervention effectiveness, and developing behavior management plans. The communication techniques themselves can range from simple (daily checklists or rating scales) to more sophisticated strategies such as weekly journals or traveling notebooks (communication folders). What is important is not the method used but that consistent and meaningful communication occur. Parents and teachers should use whatever strategies work best for them.

Figure 7.2

Components of Effective Home–School Collaboration

Source: C. Bos, M. Nahmias, and M. Urban, "Targeting Home–School Collaboration for Students with ADHD," *Teaching Exceptional Children, 31*(6), 1999, p. 4.

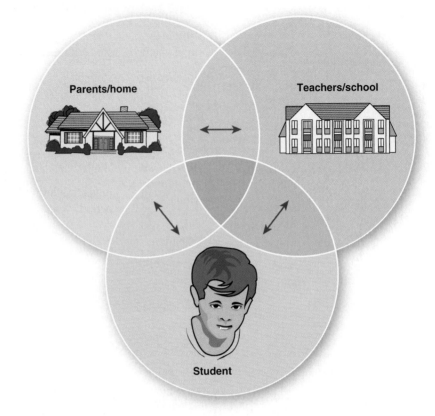

Instructional Modification

As noted earlier, environmental modifications are often crucial if the student with ADHD is to succeed in the classroom. Instructional adaptations coupled with modifications of the learning environment are powerful tools that can help the pupil sustain attention while cultivating a climate that fosters learning and encourages the child to control his or her behavior. The following list of adaptations may benefit the individual with ADHD, regardless of educational placement.

As noted earlier in this chapter, even if a student is ineligible for a special education, general educators are required, under Section 504 of PL 93-112, to accommodate individual differences and learning styles of children who exhibit an impairment (such as ADHD) that substantially limits a major life activity such as learning. Lerner and Lowenthal (1993) offer the following suggestions for teachers:

1. Place the youngster in the least distracting location in the class. This may be in front of the class, away from doors, windows, air conditioners, heaters, and high-traffic areas. It may be necessary for the child to face a blank wall or be in a study carrel to enable the child to focus attention.

2. Surround the student with good role models, preferably peers that the child views as significant others. Encourage peer tutoring and cooperative learning.

3. Maintain a low pupil–teacher ratio whenever possible through the use of aides and volunteers.

4. Avoid unnecessary changes in schedules and monitor transitions because the child with ADHD often has difficulty coping with changes. When unavoidable disruptions

do occur, prepare the student as much as possible by explaining the situation and what behaviors are appropriate.

5. Maintain eye contact with the student when giving verbal instructions. Make directions clear, concise, and simple. Repeat instructions as needed in a calm voice.

6. Combine visual and tactile cues with verbal instructions since, generally, multiple modalities of instruction will be more effective in maintaining attention and increasing learning.

7. Make lists that help the student organize tasks. Have the student check them off when they are finished. Students should complete study guides when listening to presentations.

8. Adapt worksheets so that there is less material on each page.

9. Break assignments into small chunks. Provide immediate feedback on each assignment. Allow extra time if needed for the student to finish the assignment.

10. Ensure that the student has recorded homework assignments each day before leaving school. If necessary, set up a home–school program in which the parents help the child organize and complete the homework.

11. If the child has difficulty staying in one place at school, alternate sitting with standing and activities that require moving around during the day.

12. Provide activities that require active participation such as talking through problems or acting out the steps.

13. Use learning aids such as computers, calculators, tape recorders, and programmed learning materials. They help to structure learning and maintain interest and motivation.

14. Provide the student opportunities to demonstrate strengths at school. Set up times in which the student can assist peers. (pp. 4–5)

Medication

Many professionals believe that medication, particularly **psychostimulants,** can play an important role in the treatment of ADHD. It is our opinion that the use of medication should always be in conjunction with educational and behavioral interventions; medication represents only one part of a total treatment package and should not be seen as a panacea for dealing with ADHD. In fact, instructional and environmental accommodations should always be the first intervention tactic used to assist pupils with ADHD (U.S. Department of Education, 2006a; 2006b). Although medication may play a vital role in treating ADHD, teachers should never recommend to parents that their son or daughter needs to be on medication. Only the child's health care professional can make such a determination. Interestingly, despite the importance of medication in helping children with ADHD, few educators are knowledgeable about ADHD and the use of stimulant medication (Snider, Busch, & Arrowood, 2003).

The most popular stimulant medication is Ritalin, with Cylert, Dexedrine, and Adderall also commonly prescribed. See Table 7.4 for an overview of these and other medications. (See the accompanying FYI feature on page 267 on the myths and misunderstandings surrounding Ritalin.) It is estimated that 70 to 80 percent of children with ADHD respond favorably to medication (American Academy of Pediatrics, 2000; Miranda, Jarque, & Tarraga, 2006). Researchers attribute the effectiveness of stimulant medication to the drug's ability to activate or enhance particular aspects of neurological functioning. By increasing the arousal level of the central nervous system (CNS), these drugs enable individuals with ADHD to concentrate better, to control their impulsivity and distractibility, and to increase their attention span (Barkley, 2006).

Table 7.4	Examples of Psychostimulant Medication Typically Used in Treating Attention Deficit Hyperactivity Disorder				
Brand Name	Generic Name	Approved Age of Use	Onset of Effectiveness	Duration of Effectiveness	Comments
Ritalin	Methylphenidate	6 and older	Less than 30 minutes	Approximately 4 hours	Most frequently prescribed. Excellent safety record.
Dexedrine	Dextroamphetamine	3	Less than 30 minutes	Approximately 4 hours	Must be administered frequently. Excellent safety record.
Cylert	Pemoline	6	Approximately 2–4 weeks	Approximately 6–8 hours	Safety concerns. One daily dose.
Adderall	Dextroamphetamine sulfate	3	Approximately 30 minutes	Approximately 8 hours	Requires only one daily dose.
Concerta	Methylphenidate HCL	6	Approximately 30 minutes	Approximately 8–12 hours	One daily dose. Minimal side effects.
Strattera	Atomoxetine HCL	6 and older	Usually within 24 hours; therapeutic level reached in 3–4 weeks	Upwards of 12 hours	Typically one daily dose. Only medication clinically proven effective for adults with ADHD.

SOURCE: Adapted from J. Lerner and F. Kline, *Learning Disabilities and Related Disorders*, 10th ed. (Boston: Houghton Mifflin, 2006), p. 204.

Stimulant medication plays an important role in the treatment of ADHD.

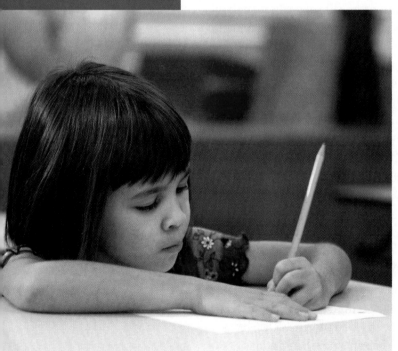

An analysis of the chemical and neurological effects on the CNS of stimulant medication is beyond the scope of this discussion; simply stated, scientists believe that psychostimulants operate by increasing the production of dopamine, a chemical neurotransmitter, which in turn activates the executive functioning capabilities of the brain—areas involved in organizing, planning, and attention (Solanto, 2002; U.S. Department of Education, 2006a).

After reviewing scientific evidence, the National Institute of Mental Health (2006) concluded that stimulant drugs are quite safe when taken as directed and at normal prescription dosages. In the vast majority of youngsters who take psychostimulants for ADHD, significant improvement in behavior is observed (Barkley, 2006). Greater benefits are generally found, however, for behavioral outcomes in comparison to academic performance (DuPaul, 2006; Northup, Gulley, Edwards, & Fountain, 2001). The student is less distractible and exhibits greater attention to task, but psychostimulants do not make the child smarter nor necessarily result in improved academic achievement.

Medical management of ADHD is not without its drawbacks and critics. It has also been shown to be ineffective for about 25 to 30 percent of individuals who take psychostimulants (Barkley, 2006; Gresham, 2002). Many side effects are associated with the use of psychostimulants; some of the more common ones are listed in Table 7.5 (page 268).

FYI...

Myths and Misunderstandings: The Ritalin Quiz

After the following statements, circle T (true) if you agree or F (false) if you do not agree.

		True	False
1.	Children should stop taking Ritalin when they reach their teenage years.	T	F
2.	Children build up a tolerance to Ritalin.	T	F
3.	Taking Ritalin will lead to drug abuse later in the child's life.	T	F
4.	Children can become addicted to Ritalin.	T	F
5.	Ritalin will stop children from growing.	T	F
6.	When children reach their teenage years, Ritalin no longer controls aggression and impulsiveness but does cause the child to act out.	T	F
7.	Ritalin causes children to lose their appetite.	T	F
8.	Children taking Ritalin may have a hard time falling asleep.	T	F
9.	Ritalin can cause some children to become more hyperactive.	T	F
10.	Children taking Ritalin complain about their head hurting (headaches).	T	F
11.	Children taking Ritalin complain about their belly hurting (stomachaches).	T	F
12.	When children take Ritalin, it dulls their personality.	T	F
13.	Ritalin builds up in the child's bloodstream.	T	F
14.	Ritalin can cause some children to tic (uncontrolled muscle movement).	T	F
15.	Ritalin can cause children to have seizures.	T	F
16.	Ritalin can cause a child's heart to beat much faster.	T	F
17.	Ritalin can cause depression in some children.	T	F

Answers:

1. F	4. F	7. T	10. T	13. F	16. F
2. T or F	5. F	8. T	11. T	14. T	17. F
3. F	6. F	9. T	12. F	15. F	

Source: C. Pancheri and M. Prater, "What Teachers and Parents Should Know about Ritalin," *Teaching Exceptional Children*, *31*(4), 1999, p. 21.

Partly as a result of concerns about the side effects associated with the use of psychostimulants, a new nonstimulant medication, Strattera (atomoxetine HCL) became available in January 2003. This drug, typically administered once daily, affects the action of the neurotransmitter norepinephrine. It is probably too early, however, to assess the effectiveness of Strattera as compared to Ritalin or other psychostimulants in controlling ADHD (Hallahan et al., 2005) or to make definitive statements about its long-term use.

Table 7.5	Side Effects Typically Associated with Psychostimulants
• Insomnia	• Weight loss
• Irritability	• Decreased appetite
• Abdominal pain	• Depression
• Nausea	• Drowsiness
• Headaches	

Source: S. Kollins, R. Barkley, and G. DuPaul, "Use and Management of Medications for Children Diagnosed with Attention Deficit Hyperactivity Disorder (ADHD)," *Focus on Exceptional Children, 33*(5), 2001, pp. 1–23; National Institute of Mental Health, "*Attention Deficit Hyperactivity Disorder,*" 2006, available at http://www.nimh.nih.gov/health/publications/adhd/summary.shtml

A **rebound effect** is sometimes observed in children using psychostimulants. As the effects of the medication gradually wear off, typically in the late afternoon or early evening, their behavior significantly deteriorates—they temporarily display greater impulsivity, distractibility, and hyperactivity than what was previously observed (Lerner & Kline, 2006).

Home–school communication is vitally important for monitoring medication effectiveness. Once a child is placed on medication, school personnel are often asked to provide feedback regarding the student's behavior, academic performance, and social adjustment, as well as any side effects from the medication. Information gleaned from both parents and teachers is useful to the physician in determining the overall effectiveness of the medication regime. Because teachers cannot contact a youngster's physician without parental permission, communication between teachers and caregivers is essential. Parent–teacher communication can take many forms—telephone calls, notes, or having teachers complete checklists and rating scales.

We encourage schools to establish written policies regarding the administration and storage of any medication given to pupils by school personnel. We also recommend that any adult who administers medication to a child complete a daily medication log; at a minimum, this log should include the medication name, dosage, time, and signature of the person administering the drug. Finally, parents and teachers need to be careful that they do not send a message to the student that medication is a substitute for self-responsibility and self-initiative; nor does the use of psychostimulants absolve the parents and teachers of their responsibilities for dealing with individuals with ADHD (Hallahan et al., 2005).

Finally, we should point out that not all professionals and parents are in favor of using psychostimulants. Some individuals are fearful that prescribing Ritalin (or other medications) will lead to the illicit use of drugs in later years. Fortunately, this is a misconception. It is true that teenagers with ADHD exhibit a higher incidence of drug abuse when compared to adolescents without ADHD, but there is no scientific evidence that this is the result of using Ritalin (Barkley, 2006). Research, in fact, suggests that just the opposite is true. Individuals taking Ritalin as children are less likely to use illicit drugs as teenagers (Wilens, Faraone, Biederman, & Gunawardene, 2003).

Adolescents and Adults with Attention Deficit Hyperactivity Disorder

Attention deficit hyperactivity disorder is, in most instances, a lifelong struggle, despite the popular misconception that youngsters "outgrow it" as they mature. This certainly is not true for vast numbers of individuals who continue to exhibit symptoms well into adolescence and adulthood (Barkley, Fischer, Smallish, & Fletcher, 2002; Kessler et al., 2006). Approximately eight out of ten children with ADHD will continue to display symptoms in adolescence (Barkley, 2006). Although the signs may become more subtle (see Table 7.6), academic difficulties persist and impaired social skills remain common (Friend & Bursuck, 2006). More than one-third of adolescents with ADHD eventually drop out of school (Barkley, 2000).

When one considers the preceding facts, the prognosis for adults with ADHD is not overly promising in most cases. Well over half of individuals who experience ADHD in childhood will continue to be challenged by symptoms of impulsivity, inattention, and hyperactivity as adults (Barkley, 2006; National Institute of Mental Health, 2006). Only an estimated 20 to 35 percent of youngsters with ADHD will be unimpaired as adults (Smith et al., 2008).

Because professionals wrongly assumed that ADHD was primarily a childhood disorder, little attention was paid to this condition in adults. Only in recent years has ADHD in adolescents and adults become an area of interest for physicians, researchers, and others.

As noted previously, there is no definitive medical or psychological test to determine ADHD; this statement is equally valid for adults with ADHD. What is often quite revealing and most helpful to clinicians is the individual's personal history (see the chapter opener). Although subjective in interpretation, it does provide professionals with a starting point for recognizing this condition.

As adults, persons with ADHD exhibit a variety of characteristics including:

- Feelings of restlessness
- Difficulty in engaging in quiet, sedentary activities
- Frequent shifts from one uncompleted activity to another
- Frequent interrupting or intruding on others
- Avoidance of tasks that allow for little spontaneous movement
- Relationship difficulties
- Anger management difficulties
- Frequent changes in employment (Weyandt, 2001, p. 17)

These symptoms have the potential for significantly affecting a wide range of life activities, including employment opportunities and marital relations.

Table 7.6	Representative Characteristics of Attention Deficit Hyperactivity Disorder in Adolescents	
• Excessive talking		• Academic failure
• Restlessness		• Impaired social relationships
• Antisocial behavior		• Difficulty maintaining employment
• Low self-concept/self-esteem		• Difficulty following through on tasks
• Inattentiveness		• Alcohol and drug abuse
• Impulsiveness		• Difficulty following instructions
• Depression		• At risk for school suspension, dropping out

Source: R. Barkley, *Attention-Deficit Hyperactivity Disorder: A Handbook for Diagnosis and Treatment*, 3rd ed. (New York, Guilford, 2006).

Educational/Vocational Outcomes

It is not unusual for individuals with ADHD to experience employment difficulties. Barkley (1999–2000) notes that adults with ADHD are more likely than those without ADHD to be fired, and they also change jobs three times more often than peers without ADHD. At age 35, more than one-third of adults with ADHD are self-employed (Smith et al., 2008). When one considers the characteristics of adults with ADHD, this is not too surprising. Successful employment for adults with ADHD often depends on a "goodness of fit"—that is, matching the job requirements with the individual's unique profile of symptoms. It would probably be unwise to encourage an adult who is impulsive and has difficulty maintaining attention to task to seek a career as an accountant or proofreader.

Educationally, young adults with ADHD are less likely than those without ADHD to graduate from college (Murphy, Barkley, & Bush, 2002). This finding points out the need for supportive services and accommodations for these individuals. Postsecondary institutions are legally required (Section 504 of PL 93-112 and the Americans with Disabilities Act, PL 101-336) to provide special services for their students with ADHD (and other disabilities), but students need to self-advocate and inform school officials of their requirements.

Marital Relations

Marital relations (and interpersonal relationships in general) sometimes suffer from the debilitating consequences of ADHD. Spouses frequently voice concern and frustration about their husband's or wife's behavior. Poor listening, messiness, unfinished household chores, forgetfulness, and saying things without thinking are just some of the typical difficulties confronting couples.

Obviously, ADHD can significantly affect a marriage and the entire family constellation. Some of these issues may be resolved through counseling sessions, medication, and/or household environmental modifications, such as establishing a daily "to do" list or dividing household chores into small, manageable segments. Couples can usually develop effective strategies for dealing with ADHD when they engage in open and honest communication while maintaining a sense of humor.

Issues of Diversity

Attention deficit hyperactivity disorder affects people of all ages, social class, races, and cultures (Imperio, 2003; Weyandt, 2001). When ADHD coexists with cultural and linguistic diversity, it can, according to Smith et al. (2008), present a special set of challenges to teachers. Recall from Chapter 3 that teachers must be sensitive to the values, customs, and heritage of students from culturally and linguistically diverse backgrounds. This statement is especially valid when talking about pupils who exhibit ADHD.

One area of particular concern for professionals is the identification of ADHD in individuals from culturally and linguistically diverse backgrounds. Some are fearful that ethnic and cultural factors may lead to the overdiagnosis of ADHD in some groups (Williams, Lerner, Wigal, & Swanson, 1995), especially African American boys. Because this disorder is frequently identified by means of behavior rating scales, which rely on the subjective opinions of the evaluators, the issue of bias may arise. This concern is especially troublesome when the rater's background differs from that of the student. Differences have been found in how teachers evaluate for ADHD in European American versus African American youngsters. African American boys, for example, were thought to exhibit the most severe symptoms of ADHD, and European American girls were seen as manifesting the least severe symptoms (Reid et al., 2000). In another investigation, both African American males and females were evaluated much higher on rating scales assessing ADHD than were European American children (Reid, Casat, Norton, Anastopoulos, & Temple, 2001).

The question then arises, Are these authentic group differences (which likely reflect normative behaviors) or an indicator of rater bias? Unfortunately, this issue remains unresolved and awaits further research.

Chapter in Review

Defining Attention Deficit Hyperactivity Disorder

- **Attention deficit hyperactivity disorder** (ADHD) is not recognized as a discrete disability under current IDEA legislation.

- Students with ADHD may receive a special education, if eligible, under the category of "other health impaired."

- The American Psychiatric Association definition considers inattention, impulsivity, and hyperactivity to be key components of this condition.

Etiology of Attention Deficit Hyperactivity Disorder

- Neurological dysfunction, heredity, and environmental factors are suspected of causing ADHD.

Characteristics of Individuals with Attention Deficit Hyperactivity Disorder

- ADHD presents itself in many different ways. Problems with **behavioral inhibition** are seen as one of the primary characteristics of persons with ADHD.

- **Executive functions** are often impaired in individuals with ADHD.

- Students with ADHD frequently experience other academic, social, and behavioral problems. This overlap is called **comorbidity**.

Assessment of Attention Deficit Hyperactivity Disorder

- The assessment and diagnosis of ADHD is a multifaceted endeavor typically involving a medical evaluation and input from parents and teachers via behavioral rating scales.

Educational Considerations

- It is generally believed that most students with ADHD receive services in the general education classroom.

- **Multimodal interventions,** or concurrent treatments, are generally more effective for individuals with ADHD than any one particular strategy.

- Behavioral interventions, instructional adaptations, home–school collaboration, and the use of medication are some of the intervention options available to students with ADHD.

- **Psychostimulants** should only be used in conjunction with behavioral and educational interventions.

Adolescents and Adults with Attention Deficit Hyperactivity Disorder

- In most instances, ADHD is a lifelong condition.

Study Questions

1. Do you think attention deficit hyperactivity disorder (ADHD) should be recognized as a separate disability category according to IDEA? Support your position.

2. What are the three subtypes of ADHD? List three symptoms typical of each subtype.

3. Identify three possible causes of ADHD. Give an example of each.

4. Give five examples of characteristics typical of children and adolescents with ADHD.

5. Why do you think pupils with ADHD frequently exhibit other academic and behavioral difficulties?

6. How is ADHD diagnosed? What role do parents and teachers play in the diagnostic process?

7. What role does medication play in the treatment of ADHD? Why is this approach controversial? Describe three other intervention options for students with ADHD.

8. ADHD is usually a lifelong condition. In what ways might this disorder affect the lives of adults with ADHD?

9. Why are some professionals concerned about the identification of ADHD in students from culturally and linguistically diverse backgrounds?

Key Terms

comorbidity
Strauss syndrome
minimal brain injury

hyperactive child syndrome
executive functions
behavioral inhibition

doctor's office effect
multimodal interventions
functional behavioral assessment

self-regulation
psychostimulants
rebound effect

Learning Activities

1. Observe students with ADHD in both elementary and secondary classrooms. Ask their teachers what accommodations they typically provide to these pupils. Discover if there are particular instructional strategies that these educators prefer.

2. Interview two adults with ADHD. Learn how this condition has affected their lives. What kinds of

strategies have these individuals developed for dealing with their disorder?

3. Attend a local chapter meeting of CHADD (Children and Adults with Attention-Deficit/Hyperactivity Disorder). What issues and concerns were addressed at this meeting? What resources are available in your community for persons with ADHD across the life span?

Organizations Concerned with Attention Deficit Hyperactivity Disorder

CHADD (Children and Adults with Attention-Deficit/Hyperactivity Disorder)
8181 Professional Place, Suite 150
Landover, MD 20785
(301) 306-7070
(800) 233-4050

A.D.D. Warehouse
300 N.W. 70th Avenue, Suite 102
Plantation, FL 33317
(954) 792-8100
(800) 233-9273

Attention Deficit Information Network
475 Hillside Avenue
Needham Heights, MA 02194
(781) 455-9895

Attention Deficit Disorder Association (ADDA)
15000 Commerce Parkway
Suite C
Mount Laurel, NJ 08054
(856) 439-9099

Reflecting on Standards

The following exercises are designed to help you learn to apply the Council for Exceptional Children (CEC) standards to your teaching practice. Each of the reflection exercises below correlates with a knowledge or skill within the CEC standards. For the full text of each of the related CEC standards, please refer to the standards integration grid located in Appendix B.

1. Focus on Instructional Strategies (*CEC Content Standard #4 CC4S5*)

Reflect on what you have learned about self-regulation and monitoring in this chapter. If you were to have a student in your class who needed to learn new techniques for self-regulation, what might be some self-reinforcement strategies you could teach him or her? What types of reinforcement do you think would be effective?

2. Focus on Learning Environment and Social Interactions (*CEC Content Standard #5 CC5S5*)

Reflect on what you have learned in this chapter about students with ADHD. If you were to have a student in your class who got distracted easily by his or her peers, how might you modify your student's learning environment?

Technology Resources

Visit the Web-based SAGE Study Site at **http://www.sagepub.com/gargiulo3estudy** for these additional learning tools:

- Chapter quizzes
- Key term flashcards
- Media links

- Full-text SAGE journal articles
- Internet activities
- Additional Web resources

CHAPTER 8

Individuals with Emotional or Behavioral Disorders

Mike

Mike was a happy baby who was constantly moving. Not running all over the place, but he would rock when he played or sat or rode in a car. He even rocked himself to sleep on his hands and knees as a baby in his crib. Mike appeared to be very bright and very verbal. He could converse better than most children his age. The problem we had was that he couldn't sit still.

By the time he was in kindergarten, he was diagnosed with ADHD. He was prescribed Ritalin and then Clonidine was added because he had such emotional mood swings. His kindergarten teacher was wonderful about communicating with us and working with him. I don't know how we'd have managed without her. I felt she had his best interest at heart in all that she did and she treated him with love and kindness, but Mike was held back in kindergarten due to his immaturity. The school convinced us it would be the best thing for him. Yet, I had no idea how devastating this would be for Mike's self-esteem.

During his second year of kindergarten, he began having thoughts he couldn't control. His teacher called us because he told her he was having thoughts of killing his brother with a knife and said he would never do that, but couldn't stop thinking about it. This was the beginning of his obsessive thoughts. During the next two to three years of school, Mike developed frequent outbursts of anger that were incredible to see in a child so small. He would fly into a rage over the least thing, rant and rave loudly, occasionally throw things, and then suddenly be as calm as a kitten. He frequently blamed all of his problems on the fact that he "failed" kindergarten and was stupid. His schoolwork began to suffer drastically. Mike's obsessive thoughts included burning down the house, killing his beloved cat, and a fear that someone was going to break into the house and kill him.

By the third grade, Mike was exhibiting eye twitches, grunts, sniffing, and throat clearing. He would pull his hair when he became frustrated, and when he couldn't do his schoolwork, he hit himself or bit his arms. He occasionally came home with teeth prints on his forearm or other forms of self-injurious

Written by Lou Anne Worthington, University of Alabama at Birmingham, and Richard M. Gargiulo behavior. He began to show signs of depression and we decided it was time to switch from his pediatrician to a specialist. While these behaviors seem bizarre, they weren't frequent at first and only gradually got to the point that they were interfering with his life. Then they seemed to go from occasional to constant in the space of a couple of weeks. He had frequent headaches, stomachaches, and vomiting episodes and he began picking at his fingers and lips until they bled. We saw a pediatric neurologist who diagnosed him with Tourette's syndrome, OCD, ADHD, and depression. He was placed on new medicines and in spite of (or because of) them, we saw a whirlwind of worsening behaviors. He began crouching on the floor in church, in the car, and under his desk at school. He was very upset that he wasn't normal like everyone else. It was heartbreaking to see your child go through these things and not be able to "make it go away." Although my faith had been my mainstay in all that we went through, it was put to the test the day we drove home with Mike crouching on the floorboard and crying. He looked up and said, "If God really loves me, why did He make me this way? Why do I have to have all these problems?"

Mike's grades worsened and so did his relationships with classmates. He began to come home telling me that kids made fun of him for clearing his throat and other behaviors. He got into frequent arguments with classmates and sometimes told me about things that they had said or done to him which proved to be untrue. He seemed to believe the stories that he told. He usually held in his outbursts at school, but began to come apart as soon as I picked him up at school. His teacher was wonderfully patient with him and tried everything imaginable. She gave him tests orally, which helped, and allowed him to run an errand to calm him down or wake him up as the situation warranted (he began to sleep to escape when he felt stressed out).

His home life worsened. He began to cry easily when he had anger outbursts and sometimes he said he wanted to kill himself. He also said he wanted to kill me a time or two and stormed off listing horrifyingly descriptive ways he would do this under his breath. I remember thinking that if he were a little older, I would be afraid for my safety.

Within a few weeks of starting yet another round of medications for depression/OCD, hallucinations, and ADHD, we began to see improvement. It took a year to get somewhat back on track; his grades were still awful but he felt better, and that was all I cared about at that point. We finished the fourth grade somehow and changed schools for the fifth grade.

When Mike went to junior high, we had to fight for everything we got in his IEP meetings. We got him in special education under the umbrella of "other health impaired." We also fought for and got resource room services for the subjects we felt he needed. Gradually we were able to pull him from the resource classes and put him back into general education classes. By the end of the eighth grade he was in all regular classes, but we held our breath each time report cards came out.

Mike is now nearing the end of the tenth grade and I look back with amazement at how far he/we have come. He is enrolled in all regular classes now and on the general diploma track. After years of hounding and consequences for lost/undone homework, he is managing his grades with almost no intervention from us and has earned mostly A's and B's (with an occasional C in algebra or English). He is happy now, and although he is almost 17, he rarely asks to go out or do things with friends. We are working on getting him to drive, but he has been hesitant and a little fearful.

When I look back, I think that what has helped Mike the most is the right combination of medications and caring, dedicated teachers who went the extra mile. We don't know what the future holds for Mike, but we will face it with him as it comes and we'll all be the stronger for it in the long run.

—*Anonymous*

The education of children and youth with emotional and behavioral disorders has long been a subject of controversy. As the chapter opener demonstrates, many individuals struggle to effectively address the needs of these children in home, school, and community settings. The child in this feature, Mike, has a history of behavioral problems, including aggressive behavior, that have been of concern to his mother and school officials for many years. These concerns are legitimate, as we all want our children to reach their full potential. Mike, however, was fortunate in that he had access to appropriate educational, medical, and psychological services. Too many children and youth with emotional and behavioral disorders do not have access to early and appropriate interventions (Kauffman, 2005). Without effective interventions, these individuals may not experience positive outcomes. Left untreated, students with emotional or behavioral disorders are at high risk for experiencing negative long-term outcomes, including academic failure, school dropout, incarceration, and under- or unemployment (Nelson, Babyak, Gonzalez, & Benner, 2003; Quinn, Rutherford, Leone, Osher, & Poirer, 2005).

This chapter focuses on students with problematic behaviors. It would be a mistake, however, to assume that all children and youth with emotional or behavioral disorders exhibit acting-out, aggressive behaviors. In fact, students with these disabilities represent an extremely heterogeneous group exhibiting a wide range of behaviors, including those related to such debilitating disorders as schizophrenia, depression, anxiety, and conduct disorders. Despite this heterogeneity, however, they share at least three experiences in common. First, their behaviors are almost always upsetting and troubling to those who teach, live, and work with them. Second, they are often blamed for their disability by those around them, who do not recognize that they are disabled and believe they are capable of changing their behavior if they so desire. Finally, these students encounter ostracism and isolation because of the stigma associated with individuals considered to be **mentally ill**—a generic term used by many professionals outside the field of special education for individuals with emotional or behavioral disorders. In fact, the reactions of those who encounter students with emotional or behavioral disorders are often more debilitating than the disability itself. Indications are that, as we begin a new millennium, we will be better able to help students like Mike through a more coordinated system of care that encompasses many human service agencies, including education.

Defining Emotional or Behavioral Disorders

There is no universally accepted definition of **emotional or behavioral disorders** (Cullinan, 2007; Webber & Plotts, 2008). Disagreements among professionals stem from many factors, including a diversity of theoretical models (for example, psychodynamic, biophysical, behavioral); the fact that all children and youth behave inappropriately at different times and in different situations; the difficulty of measuring emotions and behavior; and the variance across cultures in terms of what is acceptable and unacceptable behavior. Similarly, the terms we use to describe this population are many and diverse: emotionally disturbed, behaviorally disordered, emotionally conflicted, socially handicapped, personally impaired, socially impaired, and many others. This diversity of definitions and terms is compounded by the marked variability in people's definitions of "normal" behavior. We each view behavior through personal lenses that reflect our own standards, values, and beliefs. What appears to you as abnormal behavior may appear to another person as within the range of normal human behavior (Rosenberg, Wilson, Maheady, & Sindelar, 2004; Webber & Plotts).

Four Dimensions of Behavior

At least four dimensions of behavior are common to most definitions of emotional or behavioral disorders: (1) the frequency (or rate) at which the behavior occurs; (2) the intensity of the behavior; (3) the duration of the behavior; and (4) the age-appropriateness of the behavior (Coleman & Webber, 2002; Wicks-Nelson & Israel, 2006). Frequency of behavior indicates how often a behavior occurs. For example, many students talk out in class from time to time; however, the student who talks out thirty times during a class period may be engaging in atypical behavior. Intensity refers to the severity of behavior. Temper tantrums, for example, can range from whining that is irritating to others to more serious acts of physical aggression. Duration refers to the length of time a behavior occurs. For example, out-of-seat behavior can range from relatively brief (and mildly problematic) episodes to substantially longer periods that create major disruptions in classroom learning. Finally, age-appropriateness must be considered. For example, sexual acting-out behavior among adolescents may be disturbing to many adults, but it is a fairly common, if problematic, behavior at this age. At the preschool and early elementary levels, however, sexual acting-out behavior is of much greater concern. It is important for teachers to remember that behavior viewed as problematic at one developmental level may be fairly typical or common at another age (Wicks-Nelson & Israel).

Disturbed and Disturbing Behavior

In 1981, James Kauffman, a noted authority in the field of emotional or behavioral disorders, made a critical distinction between *disturbed* behavior and *disturbing* behavior. He noted that some behaviors are inappropriate in some instances and not in others, simply because of differences in setting expectations. For example, the use of profanity may be within the range of acceptable behavior to a group of adolescents out "cruising" on a Saturday night, but most teachers would find such language unacceptable in the classroom. Likewise, drinking alcohol during adolescence is relatively common and is highly influenced by one's peers. This behavior, while disturbing to many adults, may not constitute disordered behavior. According to Kauffman, these behaviors are *disturbing* because they occur in a certain place and time and in the presence of certain individuals. In contrast, *disturbed* behavior occurs in many settings, is habitual, and is part of the individual's behavior pattern. For example, stealing, if it occurs in many settings over a long period of time, may be indicative of disordered behavior.

Transient Nature of Problematic Behavior

The transient nature of problematic behavior has been the focus of research for many years. For example, a landmark study by Rubin and Balow (1971) found that more than 50 percent of all school-age children were perceived by their teachers to have behavior problems at some point during their elementary years. In this same study, 7.5 percent of school-age children were consistently perceived by their teachers to exhibit problematic behavior. These findings suggest that it is common for children and youth (as well as adults) to have periods in their lives that are characterized by conflict, crisis, depression, stress, and ineffective decision making. These difficult periods may occur at vulnerable points in an individual's life—for example, when a family member or friend has died. The resulting acting-out behavior, though disturbing, may be transient and may disappear altogether after sufficient time to grieve has elapsed (Newcomer, 2003).

Typical and Atypical Behavior

Some children with emotional or behavioral disorders exhibit unusual, or qualitatively different, behaviors—behaviors that are not typical at *any* age. For example, children and youth with **Tourette's syndrome** exhibit peculiar behaviors such as uncontrollable motor movements (tics) and inappropriate vocalizations such as barking, profanity, or other socially inappropriate comments that are not developmentally typical at any age. These atypical behaviors are considered by some professionals to be disordered or disturbed.

Variability in Cultural and Social Standards of Behavior

Kauffman (2005) notes that only a few behaviors are universally recognized as abnormal in every cultural group and across all social strata. Examples of behaviors that appear to deviate from nearly all cultural norms are muteness, serious self-injury, eating one's feces, and murder. In contrast, the majority of behaviors considered to be disordered are labeled as such because they violate standards that are specific to an individual's culture and social milieu. Hitting others, swearing, sexual behavior, and physical aggression are but a few of the behaviors in which normative standards vary markedly across cultures.

Federal Definition

The Individuals with Disabilities Education Improvement Act (IDEA), or PL 108-446, uses the term **emotional disturbance** to describe the population referred to in this chapter as those with emotional or behavioral disorders. The federal definition of emotional disturbance, modeled after one proposed by Eli Bower (1960), is as follows:

Excluding students thought to be socially maladjusted from the IDEA definition of emotional disturbance is controversial.

> The term means a condition exhibiting one or more of the following characteristics over a long period of time and to a marked degree that adversely affects a child's educational performance:
>
> - An inability to learn that cannot be explained by intellectual, sensory, or health factors.
> - An inability to build or maintain satisfactory interpersonal relationships with peers and teachers.
> - Inappropriate types of behavior or feelings under normal circumstances.
> - A general pervasive mood of unhappiness or depression.
> - A tendency to develop physical symptoms or fears associated with personal or school problems.
>
> The term includes schizophrenia. The term does not apply to children who are socially maladjusted, unless it is determined that they have an emotional disturbance. [July 1, 2006. 34 C.F.R. § 300.7(c)(4)]

Since the passage of Public Law 94-142 in the mid-1970s, only two changes have been made to this definition: (1) Autism, originally included in this category, became a separate disability category in 1990. (2) Prior to 1997, the term used was *serious emotional disturbance.*

In contrast to the current federal definition, Bower's (1960, 1981) definition did *not* exclude students considered to be **socially maladjusted.** Rather, Bower intended for the five components of the definition to be indicators of social maladjustment (Bower, 1982). Although there is much professional disagreement regarding the definition of social maladjustment, the following one is typical:

> [Students who are socially maladjusted] are those whose social, not emotional, behaviors inhibit meaningful normative growth and development. Specifically, they disregard or defy authority, refuse to meet minimal standards of conduct required in regular schools relating to society's normative expectations. . . . They are chronic social offenders. (Raiser & Van Nagel, 1980, p. 519)

Social maladjustment is often equated with **conduct disorders,** one of the most common psychiatric disorders among children and youth, and there have been many attempts to exclude these children and youth from special education and related services (Jensen, 2005). In your classroom, you may have a difficult time understanding why these students may not qualify for special education and related services, as you will probably perceive them as being very disabled by their behavior. You will not be alone in this perception. The Council for Children with Behavioral Disorders (CCBD) and others have been most vocal and active in advocating for the inclusion of students with conduct disorders in the federal definition (Council for Children with Behavioral Disorders, 1990; Forness & Kavale, 2000).

Subsequent research has supported neither the five criteria nor the "socially maladjusted" exclusionary clause in the current federal definition (Cullinan, 2007). Many have argued that this definition is not sufficient for identifying the full range of emotional or behavioral disorders found among children and youth (Newcomer, 2003). Other criticisms have targeted the ambiguity of such terms as "a long period of time," "to a marked degree," "inability to learn," and "pervasive" (Forness & Kavale, 2000; Kerr & Nelson, 2006). The phrase "adversely affects a child's educational performance" has been criticized because at times it has been narrowly interpreted to mean only academic performance and not performance related to critical behavioral, social, and vocational skills. Rosenberg et al. (2004) criticize the phrase "inability to learn" because it may give the impression that children and youth with emotional or behavioral disorders do not have the capacity to learn—a conclusion that is simply untrue.

Contemporary Terminology and Definitions

In 1990, more than thirty special education advocacy and professional organizations began to collaborate with professionals in mental health fields in an attempt to establish a more workable and functional definition. This group of professionals, known as the Mental Health and Special Education Coalition, has been most active in advocating for changes in the federal definition (Forness & Kavale, 2000). One of its recommendations was to change the term *serious emotional disturbance* to *emotional or behavioral disorder.* The latter term is generally accepted in the field today because it (1) has greater utility, (2) is more representative of the students who experience problems with their emotions, their behavior, or both, and (3) is less stigmatizing than *emotional disturbance.*

The definition proposed by this coalition is as follows:

The term *emotional or behavioral disorder* means a disability that is

- characterized by behavioral or emotional responses in school programs so different from appropriate age, cultural, or ethnic norms that the responses adversely affect educational performance, including academic, social, vocational, and personal skills;
- more than a temporary, expected response to stressful events in the environment;
- consistently exhibited in two different settings, at least one of which is school-related; and
- unresponsive to direct intervention applied in general education, or the condition of the child is such that general education interventions would be insufficient.

The term includes such a disability that co-exists with other disabilities.

The term includes a schizophrenic disorder, affective disorder, anxiety disorder, or other sustained disorder of conduct or adjustment, affecting a child if the disorder affects educational performance as described [above]. (McIntyre & Forness, 1996, p. 5)

Despite the many advantages of this proposed definition, little progress has been made to date toward incorporating it into federal law. Opponents have argued that it would result in an enormous influx of students with behavioral problems, severely straining the financial resources of federal and state governments (Webber & Plotts, 2008). Recent research, however, suggests this may not be the case, and many special educators support the integration of this definition into federal legislation (Forness & Kavale, 2000).

Classification of Individuals with Emotional or Behavioral Disorders

The term *emotional or behavioral disorders* encompasses a wide range of disorders. When a student is given this broad label, educators know very little about the specific nature or characteristics of the student's disability. To provide greater clarity and specificity, educators and mental health professionals have attempted to classify the many different types of emotional or behavioral disorders. Thus, for example, if a student is identified as having a conduct disorder, educators can anticipate that the student's behavior will be characterized by acting-out, aggressive, and rule-violating behavior. This pattern can be distinguished from schizophrenia, which is characterized by disturbances in thought processes, hallucinations, and bizarre behavior.

Two widely used classification systems are pertinent to the field of education. **Clinically derived classification systems** have been developed by psychiatrists and mental health professionals to describe childhood, adolescent, and adult mental disorders. The most widely used psychiatric, or clinically derived, classification system in the United States is the *Diagnostic and Statistical Manual of Mental Disorders, Fourth Edition, Text Revision* (DSM-IV-TR), which was revised by the American Psychiatric Association (APA) in 2000. **Statistically derived classification systems** are developed using sophisticated statistical techniques to analyze the patterns or "dimensions" of behaviors that characterize children and youth with emotional or behavioral disorders.

Clinically Derived Classification Systems

In general, there are no "tests" available to medical professionals to diagnosis emotional or behavioral disorders among children and youth. For many years, psychiatrists and other mental health professionals have relied on clinically derived classification systems, such as the DSM-IV-TR, to assist them in making psychiatric diagnoses. These systems group behaviors into diagnostic categories and provide criteria useful for making diagnoses. Clinically derived systems also include descriptions of symptoms, indicators of severity, prevalence estimates, and information about variations of disorders. To make a diagnosis, psychiatrists and other mental health professionals may observe an individual's behavior over time and across different settings and then compare these behaviors to diagnostic criteria provided in a classification system.

Although such systems in the past have focused primarily on adult disorders, in recent years they have increasingly included disorders found among children (House, 2002; Wicks-Nelson & Israel, 2006), including attention deficit hyperactivity disorder, conduct disorder, pervasive developmental disorders, schizophrenia, anxiety disorders, depressive disorders, mood disorders, psychoactive substance abuse disorders, dissociative disorders, and adjustment disorders. A psychiatric diagnosis does not mean, however, that a child will qualify for special education and related services (Forness, Walker, & Kavale, 2003). Although many students with psychiatric diagnoses are eligible for special education, such eligibility is independent of, and uses criteria different from, those criteria found in a clinically derived classification system (Kauffman, 2005).

Statistically Derived Classification Systems

Some researchers use sophisticated statistical techniques to establish categories, "dimensions," or patterns of disordered behavior that appear to be common among children and youth with emotional or behavioral disorders. Using these methods, researchers have been able to develop normative standards across a variety of dimensions to assist in making important decisions, such as eligibility for special education and related services.

Two global dimensions that have been consistently identified are **externalizing disorders** and **internalizing disorders** (Achenbach & Edelbrock, 1978, 1983). Externalizing disorders, sometimes referred to as "undercontrolled" disorders, are characterized by aggressiveness, tempter tantrums, acting out, and noncompliant behaviors. Externalizing disorders are disturbing to others and generally result in considerable disruption in the classroom. In contrast, internalizing disorders, sometimes referred to as "overcontrolled" disorders, are characterized by social withdrawal, depression, and anxiety. Children and youth with internalizing disorders are far less likely to be identified by their teachers and families because they do not create the "chaos" that often characterizes children and youth with externalizing disorders. These internalizing disorders, however, are equally serious; if left untreated, they can lead to a variety of negative long-term outcomes, including suicide (U.S. Department of Education, 2000). In general, males tend to be at more risk for developing externalizing disorders, whereas females appear to be at greater risk for developing internalizing disorders (Webber & Plotts, 2008). However, when females with externalizing disorders are identified, their problems may be more severe than their male counterparts (Nelson et al., 2003).

Other dimensions have also emerged from statistically derived procedures. Perhaps the best-known dimensions are those reported by Quay and Peterson (1996), reflected in the six scales of their Revised Behavior Problem Checklist (see Table 8.1). This behavioral rating scale is used by many educators to identify children and youth with emotional or behavioral disorders.

Some interesting findings in current research suggest that children and youth with emotional or behavioral disorders rarely exhibit problems along only one dimension. Rather, they

Table 8.1	Quay and Peterson's Dimensions of Problem Behaviors
Conduct Disorder	This dimension is characterized by physical aggression, difficulty controlling anger, open disobedience, and oppositionality.
Socialized Aggression	This dimension includes behaviors similar to conduct disorders except that children and youth display these behaviors in the company of others. Behaviors include stealing and substance abuse in the company of others, truancy from school, gang membership, stealing, and lying.
Attention Problems/ Immaturity	This dimension is often associated with attention deficit disorder. It includes behaviors such as short attention span, diminished concentration, distractibility, and impulsivity, as well as behaviors such as passivity, undependability, and childishness.
Anxiety/Withdrawal	This dimension is related to internalizing disorders. It includes behaviors related to poor self-confidence and self-esteem, hypersensitivity to criticism and rejection, generalized fearfulness and anxiety, and reluctance to try new behaviors because of fear of failure.
Psychotic Behavior	This dimension includes psychotic symptoms such as speech disturbance, bizarre ideation, delusions, and impaired reality testing.
Motor Tension Excess	This dimension is characterized by overactivity, including restlessness, tension, and "jumpiness."

Source: Adapted from H. Quay and D. Peterson, *Manual for the Revised Behavior Problem Checklist* (Odessa, FL: Psychological Assessment Resources, 1996), p. 1. Reproduced by special permission of the publisher, Psychological Assessment Resources, Inc., 16204 North Florida Avenue, Lutz, Florida 33549, from the *Revised Behavior Problem Checklist* by Herbert Quay, Ph.D. Copyright 1983, 1996 by PAR, Inc. Further reproduction is prohibited without permission of PAR, Inc.

often have elevated levels along two or more dimensions (Forness, 2003). In fact, researchers (Forness, Kavale, & Davanzo, 2002; Nelson et al., 2003) note that the co-occurrence of disorders may be the norm rather than the exception. For example, a student may have both a conduct disorder and attention problems. The fact that disorders often co-occur means that the students in your classroom will often present very complex behaviors, frequently requiring multifaceted interventions designed to address a wide range of behaviors.

A Brief History of the Field

The inclusion of students with emotional or behavioral disorders in public schools is a relatively recent phenomenon. Throughout history, the nature of this disability has frequently resulted in stigma and ostracism by society in general, and exclusion from education in particular. Even today, as we have seen, there is debate and controversy regarding whether or not these students should be educated in our public schools.

The historical roots of the field of emotional or behavioral disorders are intertwined with the history of other fields of study—most notably, mental retardation, psychiatry, and psychology (Kauffman, 2005). Not until 1886 was a legal distinction made between "insanity" and "feeblemindedness" (Hayman, 1939). This distinction was an important one, as it marked the separation of emotional or behavioral disorders from mental retardation. Differentiating the history of emotional or behavioral disorders from that of mental retardation before that time is difficult. Because this common history has been detailed in the chapter on mental retardation, this historical review begins with the twentieth century. Unless otherwise noted, the historical account that follows is based on a synthesis of several substantive resources: Despert (1965), Kauffman, Lewis (1974), Rie (1971), and Safford and Safford (1996).

The Mental Hygiene Movement

In 1909, Ellen Key published *The Century of the Child*, a most prophetic work in that much progress was made in educating and treating children and youth with emotional or behavioral disorders during the twentieth century. The first teacher training program in special education appeared in Michigan in 1914, and school psychology as a specialized field began to emerge.

Many other events of the first two decades of the century helped promote more effective treatment of individuals with "emotional disturbance," a term that first began to be used around 1910. In 1908, Clifford Beers published *A Mind That Found Itself*, in which he described his nervous breakdown and subsequent maltreatment in a mental hospital. This book profoundly influenced public opinion, and Beers collaborated with two prominent leaders in mental health, Adolph Meyer and William James, to establish the National Committee for Mental Hygiene in 1909. The founding of this committee began the mental hygiene movement, which focused on efforts such as detection, prevention, and rehabilitation in the schools.

The mental hygiene movement was greatly influenced by Sigmund Freud's work on infant sexuality and psychosocial development. Because of Freud's emphasis on early childhood experiences, children and youth became a major focus of study and research. Freud's work formed the foundation for many of the first attempts to formally educate children and youth with emotional or behavioral disorders during the first several decades of the twentieth century. Psychiatrist William Healy and psychologist Grace Fernald, founders of the Juvenile Psychopathic Institute in Chicago in 1909, used Freudian or psychodynamic methods. Similarly, the National Committee on Mental Hygiene established several children's clinics in the United States, each of which adopted Freudian theory as its treatment approach.

Near the end of this period, a very different body of research began to emerge, one that would profoundly influence special educators throughout the remainder of the twentieth century. John Watson introduced behaviorism to North America in his 1913 essay *Psychology as a Behaviorist Views It*.

Early Research on Emotional or Behavioral Disorders

In the 1920s and 1930s, numerous longitudinal studies were undertaken on child development. This knowledge base led to the development of more effective educational programs for children and youth with emotional or behavioral disorders. Additionally, several prominent organizations were formed in the 1920s, including the American Orthopsychiatric Association and the Council for Exceptional Children. The first psychiatric hospital was founded in Rhode Island in 1931, and schools that specialized in the treatment of children and youth with emotional or behavioral disorders, especially those with psychotic disorders, were established. For example, Loretta Bender began her pioneering work with children with schizophrenia at her school located at the Bellevue Psychiatric Clinic in New York City in 1934. Bellevue School subsequently became a fertile training ground for many future leaders in the field of special education. In 1935, Leo Kanner published *Child Psychiatry*, the first textbook on child psychiatry published in the United States. Finally, in the 1930s, Dr. Karl Menninger's work stressed the importance of addressing the "total environment" when treating individuals with emotional or behavioral disorders, and his work greatly influenced psychiatry in the coming decades.

The Birth of a Specialized Field of Study

The years 1940–1960 marked the birth of special education for children and youth with emotional or behavioral disorders as a specialized field of study. Many experimental educational programs were established at this time. In the 1940s, the state of New York opened a number of schools for youths considered to be emotionally disturbed. Also in the 1940s, Fritz Redl and David Wineman established the Pioneer House for delinquent and disturbed youth in Detroit. These educators pioneered the "Life-Space Interview," a technique that influenced subsequent generations of special educators.

The Depression and World War II hampered funding for research and education for children and youth with emotional or behavioral disorders. At the same time, however, these world events brought to the United States several Europeans who would become leaders in special education. In the field of emotional or behavioral disorders, perhaps the most notable of these individuals was Bruno Bettelheim, who became a prominent leader in educational methods based on psychoanalytic theory. Although experimental programs for educating children and youth with emotional or behavioral disorders were developed from 1940 to 1960, many children and youth with emotional or behavioral disorders were still being denied a public education.

The Emergence of Conceptual Models

In the 1960s, research on classroom programs, practices, and curricula for children and youth with emotional or behavioral disorders appeared in the professional literature for the first time. These publications presented a variety of conceptual models that had evolved during the preceding decades, many of which remain prominent in special education programs today. The emergence of these models, representing various theoretical approaches with differing assumptions and strategies, was one of the most significant developments in the field. (See Table 8.2 for a brief description of some of these models.) Educators now had a variety of approaches to use with pupils who exhibited emotional or behavioral disorders. As Kauffman (2005) points out, practitioners are seldom guided exclusively by a single model; in many instances, teachers incorporate a number of different viewpoints in their work.

Besides the emergence of these conceptual models, several other important events occurred between 1960 and 1980. Substantial progress was made in the identification and assessment of students with emotional or behavioral disorders. Specifically, the works of Bower (1960) and Quay and Peterson (1975) provided assessment tools for identifying this population of students and also increased our understanding of the nature of emotional and behavioral disorders. In 1964, the Council for Children with Behavioral Disorders (CCBD) was formed, creating one of the world's largest professional organizations in this field of study. Public funding was generated to prepare teachers to work with children with emotional or behavioral disorders in 1963 through the enactment of PL 88-164. Finally, the passage of PL 94-142 in 1975 led to the formal inclusion of these students in public education for the first time.

Prevalence of Emotional or Behavioral Disorders

How prevalent are emotional and behavioral disorders among school-age children and youth? The answer to this question is not a simple one; prevalence estimates for this population vary

Table 8.2	Conceptual Models of Emotional or Behavioral Disorders
Model	**Approach**
Behavioral	Based on the work of B. F. Skinner and other behavioral psychologists, this model assumes that behavior is a function of environmental events. Maladaptive behaviors are thought to be learned and maintained by the environment. Seeks to establish a replicable cause–effect relationship. Uses systematic observations and data collection procedures. Behavior can be modified by changing antecedent or consequent events. Frank Hewett's "engineered" classroom, described in his book *The Emotionally Disturbed Child in the Classroom* (1968), was constructed around a behavioral approach.
Psychodynamic	Based on the thinking of Sigmund Freud and his followers, this model proposes that disturbed behaviors are symptomatic of underlying conflict between hypothetical mental functions (id, ego, superego) that are in dynamic interaction. Unconscious motivation for behavior must be understood in order for intervention to be successful. Individual psychotherapy for the student (and sometimes the parents) is frequently used to uncover deep-rooted problems typically originating in the child's past. A permissive classroom environment and an accepting teacher are also called for.
Psychoeducational	Like the psychoanalytic model, this approach emphasizes unconscious motivations and underlying conflicts, but it is balanced by the realistic demands of functioning at home, school, and the community. Teachers attempt to gain an understanding of the child's unconscious motivation for problem behaviors through therapeutic conversations (life space interviews) and try to help the student gain insight and acquire self-control through planning and reflection. *Conflict in the Classroom* (1965) by Nicholas Long, William Morse, and Ruth Newman offers a perspective on the psychoeducational model.
Ecological	This model attributes behavioral problems to the student's interactions in the family, at school, and in the community. Problematic behavior results from a lack of a "goodness of fit" between the student and the particular social milieu. Intervention attempts to alter the social settings and the transactions occurring therein. Project Re-ED, a residential treatment program established by Nicholas Hobbs in 1961, is an example of this approach.
Humanistic	This model, arising from the social-political movement of the 1960s and 1970s, stresses self-direction, self-fulfillment, and self-evaluation. Pupils are encouraged to be free and open. It is assumed that children are capable of generating their own solutions to their problems when provided with a caring and supportive environment where teachers are nonauthoritarian.
Biogenic	Underlying this model is a belief that emotional or behavioral disorders, such as depression or hyperaggression, are the result of physiological flaws. Treatments, therefore, may consist of drug therapy, biofeedback, dietary management, or even surgery. The Feingold diet, popular in the 1970s as a treatment for hyperactivity, is an example of this model.

Source: J. M. Kauffman, *Characteristics of Emotional and Behavioral Disorders of Children and Youth*, 8th ed., © 2005. Adapted with permission of Pearson Education, Inc., Upper Saddle River, NJ.

widely. Among the reasons for this variance are conflicting definitions and a lack of consensus on what constitutes acceptable behavior.

From a historical perspective, the percentage of public school students receiving special education under this category grew from 0.5 percent in the mid-1970s to 1.0 percent in the mid-1980s. Since that time, however, growth in this category, unlike many other IDEA disability categories, has been negligible or even negative (Kauffman, 2005). The number of students being served under this category is far less than the original federal estimate of 2 percent (U.S. Department of Education, 1980). Moreover, this estimate is considered extremely conservative by many professionals in the field (Cullinan, 2007). Students with emotional or behavior disorders are considered to be the most underidentified of all IDEA disability categories (Landrum, Katsiyannis, & Archwamety, 2004).

The U.S. Department of Education (2007) reports that during the 2005–2006 school year, 472,384 students ages 6–21 were receiving a special education and related services because of an emotional disturbance. This number represents 7.7 percent of the total number of students served in special education, making this the fifth largest disability category for students in this age range.

At the preschool level, the U.S. Department of Education (2007) reports that only 5,789 children ages 3–5 were identified as emotionally disturbed during the 2005–2006 school year. This low level of identification may be due to at least two factors. First, because there is an emphasis on noncategorical labeling at the preschool level and early elementary grades, many students who ultimately are identified as emotionally disturbed may be labeled "developmentally delayed" during the early childhood years. Second, school personnel may be hesitant to identify a youngster as emotionally disturbed during the early childhood years (Cullinan, 2007).

Although less than 1 percent of the school-age population currently receives special education services for emotional or behavioral disorders (U.S. Department of Education, 2006), credible studies in the United States indicate that at least 3 percent to 6 percent of children and youth exhibit serious and persistent problems (Blanchard, Gurka, & Blackman, 2006). Numerous reasons have been offered for the underidentification of students with emotional or behavioral disorders. One major reason is the marked variability across states in identifying pupils with emotional or behavioral disorders (Kauffman, 2005). The range of students receiving a special education varies from a low of .10 percent in Arkansas to a high of 1.52 percent in Vermont (U.S. Department of Education). Recall that IDEA allows states to adopt their own definitions, provided that state definitions identify an equivalent group of students. In fact, state definitions vary so widely that identification may be more a function of where an individual lives than of any other factor. Kauffman believes that social policy and economic factors also play critical roles in underidentification.

Etiology of Emotional or Behavioral Disorders

Our understanding of the causes of emotional or behavioral disorders has increased substantially in recent years. A major milestone was the publication in 1999 of a national report, *Mental Health: A Report of the Surgeon General* (Satcher, 1999). For the first time in history, the country's most prominent health care leader, the surgeon general, recognized that addressing the needs of both children and adults with mental illness is a pressing national concern.

This report describes the current research regarding many of the risk factors associated with mental disorders of childhood. These risk factors often interact in a synergetic fashion; as the number of risk factors increases, so do the chances of negative outcomes such as emotional or behavioral disorders.

Biological Risk Factors

Although most professionals agree that the development of emotional or behavioral disorders is due to both biological and environmental factors, there has been increased consensus that biological factors are particularly influential in the etiology of several disorders. These emotional or behavioral disorders can be the result of either genetic influences or biological insults. Disorders that most likely have a genetic influence include autism, bipolar disorder, schizophrenia, social phobia, obsessive-compulsive disorder, and Tourette's syndrome. Biological insults such as injury, infection, lead poisoning, poor nutrition, or exposure to toxins (including intrauterine exposure to alcohol, illicit drugs, or cigarette smoke) may also influence the development of emotional or behavioral disorders.

Numerous studies suggest that infant temperament (that is, an infant born with a "difficult" temperament) may precede the development of emotional or behavioral disorders (Coleman & Webber, 2002; Crockenberg & Leerkes, 2005; Shaw, Gilliom, & Giovannelli, 2005). Despite the early research in this area, more recent studies indicate that "difficult" infant temperament can be mediated to some extent by the environment.

Research indicates that as many as 50 percent of students with emotional or behavioral disorders have additional disabilities (National Institute of Mental Health, 2006a). For example, some students with conduct disorders are also depressed; in fact, these children often have a family history of depression (National Institute of Mental Health, 2006b). Parental depression also increases the risk of children and youth developing anxiety disorders, conduct disorder, and alcohol dependency.

Suicide among depressed children and youth is a major concern in our society. Studies suggest that more than 90 percent of children and adolescents who have committed suicide had an apparent, though not identified, emotional or behavioral disorder before their deaths. Table 8.3 lists some of the warning signs of an impending suicide. As an educator, you need to be especially alert to these warning signs and be sure to report them to parents, counselors, administrators, and other appropriate professionals.

Psychosocial Risk Factors

Research suggests that conduct disorders have both biological and environmental components, with substantial psychosocial risk factors involved in their development. Environmental

Table 8.3	Behavioral Suicide Warning Signs
Behavior	**Manifestations**
Quiet, withdrawn, few friends	Often not recognized because the individual is not noticed and makes no obvious trouble.
Changes in behavior	Personality changes—e.g., from friendliness to withdrawal, lack of communication, and sad and expressionless appearance, or from a quiet demeanor to acting out and troublemaking.
Increased failure or role strain	Often pervasive in school, work, home, friends, and love relationships, but often manifested clearly in school pressures for young people.
Recent family changes	Illness, job loss, increased consumption of alcohol, poor health, etc.
Recent loss of a family member	Death, divorce, separation, or someone leaving home.
Feelings of despair and hopelessness*	Shows itself in many forms, from changes in posture and behavior to verbal expression of such feelings.
Symptomatic acts	Taking unnecessary risks, becoming involved in drinking and drug abuse, becoming inappropriately aggressive or submissive, giving away possessions.
Communication*	Such statements as "Life is not worth living," "I'm finished," "Might as well be dead," or "I wish I were dead."
Presence of a plan*	Storing up medication, buying a gun.

*To be viewed with heightened concern.
Source: Adapted from the Crisis Center, *Ten Behavioral Suicide Warning Signs* (Birmingham, AL: n.d.).

factors such as parental discord, a parent's mental illness or criminal behavior, overcrowding in the home, and large family size may result in conditions conducive to the development of conduct disorders—especially if the child or youth does not have a loving, nurturing relationship with at least one parent. Other risk factors include early maternal rejection and family neglect and abuse.

Poverty has been shown to be a significant risk factor for the development of emotional or behavioral disorders, as it often translates into increased family stress, poor health care, underachievement, and other negative outcomes (Barr & Parrett, 2001). The United States has one of the highest poverty rates of all developed countries, and although emotional and behavioral disorders occur among all socioeconomic classes, children who live in poverty may be at especially high risk.

One important finding in recent years is that biological and environmental factors often are not mutually independent influences in the development of emotional or behavioral disorders; that is, one may directly influence the other. For example, attention deficit hyperactive disorder may have biological origins, but the difficult behaviors of these children and youth often influence and change their relationships with significant others in their lives (Wicks-Nelson & Israel, 2006). In these exchanges, coercive interactions may occur, thus creating a negative environment that may worsen the condition. Consider, for example, the following scenario:

Jesse, a fourth grader with attention deficit hyperactivity disorder, genuinely dislikes completing his math worksheets. During this time, he often talks out, gets out of his seat, and is noncompliant and disrespectful to his teacher to avoid completing these tasks. His noncompliant and disruptive behavior often escalates to the point that he is sent to the office. Consequently, Jesse is negatively reinforced as his avoidance behavior is reinforced. Additionally, his teacher may be negatively reinforced if he or she views Jesse's noncompliant and disrespectful behavior as aversive. This means that both individuals are more likely in the future to engage in the same behavior, creating a coercive cycle that strengthens the behaviors of both Jesse and his teacher.

As a teacher, you need to be aware of the coercive nature of these interactions and how you may be able to disrupt coercive cycles. By understanding that the function of Jesse's behavior is escape or avoidance, you can respond to him in more productive ways. For example, you could reinforce Jesse's on-task behavior and not engage in exchanges that allow him to escape or avoid his assignments. Additionally, you have the power to change the nature of the assignment (worksheets) to one that is less aversive for him (for example, allowing him to use drill-and-practice software).

The role of **child maltreatment** in the development of a number of emotional or behavioral disorders is well established (Kauffman, 2005). Child maltreatment has been associated with such problems as depression, conduct disorder,

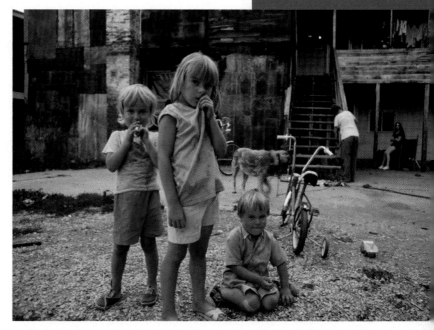

Children who live in poverty may be at especially high risk for developing emotional or behavioral disorders.

Table 8.4	Four Main Types of Child Maltreatment

- **Physical abuse** is characterized by the infliction of physical injury as a result of punching, beating, kicking, biting, burning, shaking, or otherwise harming a child. The parent or caretaker may not have intended to hurt the child; rather, the injury may have resulted from overdiscipline or physical punishment.

- **Child neglect** is characterized by failure to provide for the child's basic needs. Neglect can be physical, educational, or emotional.

  - **Physical neglect** includes refusal or delay in seeking health care, abandonment, expulsion from the home or refusal to allow a runaway to return home, and inadequate supervision.

  - **Educational neglect** includes the allowance of chronic truancy, failure to enroll a child of mandatory school age in school, and failure to attend to a special educational need.

  - **Emotional neglect** includes such actions as marked inattention to the child's need for affection, refusal or failure to provide needed psychological care, spousal abuse in the child's presence, and permission of drug or alcohol use by the child.

  This assessment of child neglect requires consideration of cultural values and standards of care as well as recognition that the failure to provide the necessities of life may be related to poverty.

- **Sexual abuse** includes fondling a child's genitals, intercourse, incest, rape, sodomy, exhibitionism, and commercial exploitation through prostitution or the production of pornographic materials. Many experts believe that sexual abuse is the most underreported of child maltreatment because of the "conspiracy of silence" that so often characterizes these cases.

- **Emotional abuse (psychological abuse/verbal abuse/mental injury)** includes acts of omission by the parents or other caregivers that have caused, or could have caused, serious behavioral, cognitive, emotional, or mental disorders. In some cases of emotional abuse, the acts of parents or other caregivers alone, without any harm evident in the child's behavior or condition, are sufficient to warrant Child Protective Services intervention.

Source: Based on 42 U. S. C. § 1506(g). *Child Abuse Prevention and Treatment Act*. Public Law 104-235, 1996.

posttraumatic stress disorder, delinquency, and attention deficit hyperactivity disorder. Child maltreatment includes neglect, physical abuse, sexual abuse, and emotional abuse; Table 8.4 describes these four main types of child maltreatment. As a teacher, your role is critical in identifying and reporting your suspicions of child maltreatment to law enforcement and social service agencies.

Prevention of Emotional or Behavioral Disorders

How do we prevent the onset of emotional or behavioral disorders? How do we minimize the risk of negative long-term outcomes for those students who do develop these disorders? This section will describe two bodies of research focusing on the prevention of emotional and behavioral disorders among children and youth.

Research on Resiliency

How do we explain the fact that some children and youth, despite the most adverse circumstances, do not develop emotional or behavioral disorders? How is it that these resilient individuals become healthy, well-adjusted adults? Janas (2002) and Milstein and Henry (2000) identified four attributes of resilient children. First, resilient children appear to be socially competent; they are adept at establishing and maintaining positive relationships with both peers and adults. Second, resilient children have excellent problem-solving skills; they seek resources and help from others. Third, resilient children are autonomous; they have a strong identity and are able to act independently. Finally, resilient children develop clear goals and high aspirations; they see their futures as hopeful and bright.

What are the implications of this research for you as an educator? Resilient adults often report that, as children, they established a close, loving relationship with a supportive adult; many times, these adults were their teachers. Just one loving, caring relationship with an adult can foster resiliency in a student who is at risk for developing emotional or behavioral disorders, and thus possibly help prevent negative long-term outcomes.

Research on Positive Behavioral Support

Educators have many approaches at their disposal for responding to students who exhibit problematic behavior in the classroom. The traditional school response has been punishment, which includes reactive responses such as reprimands, corporal punishment, suspension, and expulsion (Johns, Mather, & McGrath, 2003). The behaviors of children with emotional or behavioral disorders are often so chronic and intense that they are at high risk for receiving significant amounts of punishment. However, research suggests that punishment methods (1) are generally ineffective over time; (2) may serve as a reward for students; (3) may serve as models of coercive and/or aggressive behavior for students; (4) do not teach students more appropriate behavior; (5) do not consider environmental factors that may contribute to problematic behavior; and (6) do not examine why the problematic behavior occurs (Beach Center on Families and Disabilities, 1999; Ruef, Higgins, Glaeser, & Patnode, 1998).

Although corporal punishment has been banned in many states, a significant number of students still receive corporal punishment, despite research that indicates it is ineffective as a preventive strategy and has a negative impact on the social, psychological, and educational development of children and youth (Robinson, Funk, Beth, & Bush, 2005).

An alternative strategy for responding to problematic behavior is **positive behavioral support.** This is a schoolwide approach designed to prevent problem behaviors before they occur and, when they do occur, to intervene early to prevent them from escalating further. The idea is to respond *proactively* rather than *reactively* (Scheuermann & Hall, 2008). Positive behavioral support is defined as "the application of positive behavioral interventions and systems to achieve socially important behavior change" (Sugai et al., 1999, p. 6). Such schoolwide approaches have been shown to be effective in preventing problematic behaviors (Leedy, Bates, & Safran, 2004; Luiselli, Putnam, & Sunderland, 2002; Scott, Payne, & Jolivette, 2003).

A positive behavioral support model is designed to address the complexity of problematic behaviors through such efforts as promoting academic achievement, involving the family, emphasizing positive, nurturing relationships between students and staff, and identifying problematic behaviors *before* they become chronic and/or severe. This approach recognizes that problematic behaviors are often the result of both student and environmental variables (Scheuermann & Hall, 2008). PL 108-446 requires IEP team members to consider using positive behavioral supports when addressing behaviors that impede the learning of a student with a disability and/or the learning of others.

The focus of the positive behavioral support model is prevention. The prevention model depicted in Figure 8.1 identifies three critical levels of prevention. The goal of the schoolwide intervention team at the **primary prevention** level is to reduce the number of new cases of problem behavior. Examples of such prevention efforts include schoolwide social skills training programs, clearly identified and implemented incentives for positive behavior (such as giving points, tied to identified reinforcers, for following school and classroom rules), and manipulation of environmental factors that may be contributing to problematic behavior (such as a lack of sufficient adult supervision on the playground). The **secondary prevention level** is designed to minimize the possibility that students at high risk will engage in misbehavior. Examples of approaches at this level include targeting groups of students with common concerns, such as those who have experienced significant losses (death of a parent or sibling, parental divorce) and those who need more intensive instruction in specific areas (social skills, academic tutoring). The third and most intensive level of prevention is **tertiary prevention,** which includes interventions designed for individual student behavior. Examples of this level of prevention include the development and implementation of a token economy, individual counseling, and individually tailored self-monitoring programs. The purpose of tertiary prevention is to provide appropriate supports and interventions for students with chronic and intensive problem behaviors, thereby assisting them to engage in more appropriate and productive behaviors.

Characteristics of Children and Youth with Emotional or Behavioral Disorders

Children and youth with emotional or behavioral disorders are, as we have seen, an extremely heterogeneous population; consequently, the characteristics they display in the classroom are highly diverse. Not every student with emotional or behavioral disorders will exhibit all of the characteristics described here; rather, each student will be unique in terms of both strengths and needs.

Figure 8.1

Levels of Prevention

Source: Adapted from G. Sugai, R. H. Horner, G. Dunlap, M. Hieneman, T. J. Lewis, C. M. Nelson, T. Scott, C. Liaupsin, W. Sailor, A. P. Turnbull, R. Turnbull III, D. Wickham, M. Ruef, and B. Wilcox, *Applying Positive Behavior Support and Functional Assessment in Schools* (Washington, DC: Office of Special Education Programs, Center on Positive Behavioral Interventions and Supports, 1999), p. 11.

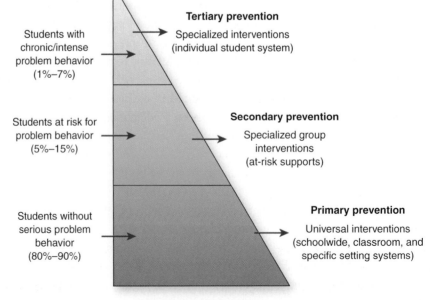

Students with chronic/intense problem behavior (1%–7%)

Tertiary prevention
Specialized interventions (individual student system)

Students at risk for problem behavior (5%–15%)

Secondary prevention
Specialized group interventions (at-risk supports)

Students without serious problem behavior (80%–90%)

Primary prevention
Universal interventions (schoolwide, classroom, and specific setting systems)

Total student enrollment

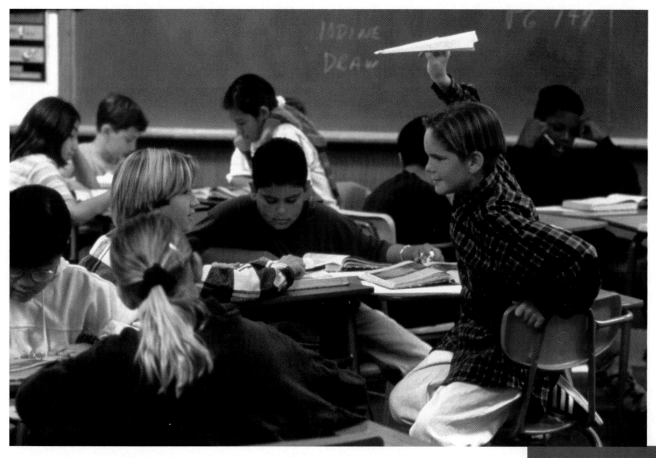

Children and youth with emotional or behavioral disorders are an especially heterogeneous population.

Learning Characteristics

Although intellectually, students with emotional or behavioral disorders may include individuals who are gifted and those who are mentally retarded, a consistent finding of research has been that pupils with emotional or behavioral disorders typically score in the low-average range on measures of intelligence (Vaughn, Levy, Coleman, & Bos, 2002).

A major concern is the chronic school failure, despite average intellectual ability, experienced by many of these students (Lane, 2003; Nelson, Benner, Lane, & Smith, 2004). Wagner and Davis (2006) report that students with emotional or behavioral disorders fare much worse than average in terms of grades, grade retention, high school graduation rates, dropout rates, and absenteeism. In fact, students with emotional or behavioral disorders are retained at twice the rate of other students with disabilities (Nelson et al., 2003). It is uncertain whether students with emotional or behavioral disorders experience academic difficulty because of a lack of motivation or maladaptive behaviors, especially those associated with externalizing disorders; regardless, these pupils are at very high risk for school failure (Nelson et al., 2003).

Social Characteristics

Perhaps the most salient characteristic of students with emotional or behavioral disorders is their difficulty building and maintaining satisfactory relationships with peers and adults as evidenced by the high number of pupils identified with externalizing disorders (Nelson et al., 2003). Many of these children, especially those exhibiting aggressive behavior, experience rejection by both peers and adults (Dunlap et al., 2006). Moreover, it appears that the presence of aggressive behavior is a major predictor of future delinquency and incarceration, particularly if it appears in early childhood. Follow-up studies of adolescents with emotional or behavioral disorders suggest extraordinarily high rates of incarceration for this population—representing almost half of all incarcerated youth with disabilities (Quinn et al., 2005).

Language/Communication Characteristics

Studies in the last decade yield some interesting findings regarding the language and communication characteristics of students with emotional or behavioral disorders. Deficits in the area of pragmatics (the social use of language) appear to be relatively common (Hooper, Roberts, Zeisel, & Poe, 2003; Rinaldi, 2003; Rogers-Adkinson & Hooper, 2003). Studies suggest that students with emotional or behavioral disorders use fewer words per sentence, have difficulty staying on a topic, and use language that is inappropriate to social conversation (Nelson, Benner, & Rogers-Adkinson, 2003; Rogers-Adkinson, 2003).

Assessing Students with Emotional or Behavioral Disorders

As an educator, you will encounter many challenging student behaviors, including inattention, disruptiveness, verbal and physical outbursts, lack of organizational skills, and poor social and interpersonal skills (Dunlap et al., 2006). These challenging behaviors will often perplex you, and you may have difficulty differentiating behaviors that are "disturbing" from those that are "disturbed." Your ability to make this distinction is critical, however, if students with emotional or behavioral disorders are to be identified and appropriately served in a timely manner. Some students, particularly those with pervasive developmental disorders and schizophrenia, will be relatively easy for you to identify. Likewise, the acting-out, rule-violating behaviors of children and youth with conduct disorders are hard to overlook because their behaviors result in considerable havoc and disturbance in the classroom. Students with other types of emotional or behavioral disorders, however, may exhibit behaviors that are much more difficult to judge. For example, because the behaviors of very young children change so quickly, you may find it difficult to determine whether their problematic behaviors are developmentally appropriate or indicative of emotional or behavioral disorders. Children's behavior is notoriously variable; problem behaviors are often inconsistent and can change dramatically over time. Finally, you may overlook the behaviors of students who are depressed or anxious because these behaviors typically do not disrupt the learning process in your classroom. Your ability to identify and express your concerns to appropriate school personnel regarding the problematic behaviors represents an important first step in the assessment process.

Assessment Strategies

The assessment of children and youth with emotional or behavioral disorders is a complex process that necessitates a multimethod, multisource approach. Assessment strategies must include a variety of methods or instruments (for example, rating scales, interviews, observations) and a variety of sources or informants (the student, teachers, parents, peers). Such an approach is essential because of the transient nature of behavior, normal developmental variations, and variability in cultural and social standards of behavior. Table 8.5 provides

Table 8.5	Common Assessment Strategies Used to Evaluate Students with Emotional or Behavioral Disorders	
Strategy	**Description/Purpose**	**Advantages and Disadvantages**
Interviews with student, parents, and teachers	**Description:** Lists of specific questions presented by an interviewer to elicit responses from an informant. **Purpose:** To provide a picture of the student's presenting problems as perceived by the informant; provide information about the environmental context in which the problem behavior is occurring; provide important developmental, historical information about the student. Results are used to formulate assessment questions and subsequent assessment strategies.	**Advantages:** Can guide assessment process and address concerns of all those involved with the student, as well as the student. **Disadvantages:** Reliability and validity are difficult to establish; informants may provide inaccurate information; interviewer bias may occur.
Examination of student records	**Description:** Inspection of cumulative records, disciplinary history, and other records of school achievement/performance. **Purpose:** To provide documentation that problems have existed over time and give some indication of whether the student's behavior may be affecting learning.	**Advantages:** Provides information on whether other factors (e.g., excessive absences, frequent school changes) may explain the behavior; documents behavior over time; addresses impact on learning. **Disadvantages:** Records may be incomplete or inaccurate.
Parent, teacher, and student rating scales	**Description:** Typically comprised of items that an informant rates in terms of severity (e.g., mild, moderate, severe) or frequency of occurrence (e.g., never, seldom, often). **Purpose:** Rating scales may be formal or informal. Formal rating scales are often used to determine eligibility, as they provide normative comparisons regarding children's behavior. Informal scales serve many purposes, such as identification of particular points in the day when problematic behavior occurs.	**Advantages:** Allow for normative comparisons that enable school personnel to make decisions regarding eligibility; enable educators to assess the student across informants (e.g., parents, teacher, students); are easy, quick, and inexpensive. **Disadvantages:** Possible rater bias and subjectivity. Also, many rating scales adopt a deficit-based, as opposed to a strength-based, assessment approach.
Observations in natural settings	**Description:** Anecdotal observations are narrative recordings (i.e., a written, running record) of student behavior; they are often used to identify the possible functions or purposes of student's behavior. Systematic observations reflect quantified accounts of student's behavior (e.g., how many times and for how long a student is out of seat). **Purpose:** To provide a picture of the student's spontaneous behavior in everyday settings; provide a systematic record of the student's behavior that can be used for intervention; provide verification of teacher and parent reports about the child's behavior.	**Advantages:** Provide an objective, quantifiable assessment of observable behavior; allow for a functional assessment of the student within the context of the natural environment (most systematic observations are sensitive to intervention effects). **Disadvantages:** Can be time-consuming; may not be representative or reflect behavior typical of the student; most lack normative data; may not be sensitive to variations in classroom normative standards.
Medical evaluations	**Description:** Psychiatric and other medical evaluations designed to diagnose emotional or behavioral disorders and/or other medical problems. **Purpose:** To rule in or out emotional or behavioral disorders and/or other medical conditions; may include identification of appropriate medical interventions, such as medication.	**Advantages:** Help ensure that a student's behavior is not the result of a medical condition unrelated to an emotional or behavioral disorder (e.g., allergic reaction, infection). **Disadvantages:** May not have much value in terms of educational interventions; are expensive and can be time-consuming.

(Continued)

Table 8.5	Common Assessment Strategies Used to Evaluate Students with Emotional or Behavioral Disorders (Continued)	
Strategy	**Description/Purpose**	**Advantages and Disadvantages**
Standardized, norm-referenced assessments of intelligence, academics, and other areas of concern	**Description:** Measures of intelligence, academics (reading, math, writing), communication, motor skills, etc. **Purpose:** To rule in or out other areas of suspected disability; to provide normative comparisons of student abilities and performance; to assist in eligibility determination.	**Advantages:** Provide objective and normative comparisons of student abilities and performance levels; assist with eligibility decision making. **Disadvantages:** May not provide relevant information for intervention purposes; typically provide global, nonspecific information about student's abilities and performance levels.
Functional behavioral assessment	**Description:** Incorporates a variety of techniques and strategies to identify the causes (functions) of behavior; focus is on identifying biological, social, affective, and environmental factors that trigger and maintain the problematic behavior. **Purpose:** By determining the function of the behavior, interventions can be developed and implemented by manipulating antecedents to, and consequences following, the problematic behavior; designed to teach student more appropriate, alternative behavior and to prevent the behavior from occurring by providing positive behavioral supports.	**Advantages:** Is directly tied to intervention; helps teach the student more positive and appropriate behavior; serves as the foundation for positive behavior support; identifies environmental and other factors that may be contributing to the problematic behavior; provides a method for ongoing monitoring of the student's behavioral progress. **Disadvantages:** Requires considerable teacher training and can be time-consuming; may not always address important factors such as distorted cognitions and thought patterns and other non-directly observable variables that contribute to problematic behavior.
Other informal assessment strategies such as examination of work samples, criterion-referenced tests, and curriculum-based assessment	**Description:** Include error analysis, analysis of instructional and curriculum variables that need to be considered when planning curriculum and instruction. **Purpose:** To identify specific strengths and needs of the student within the context of the general education (or independence) curriculum.	**Advantages:** Are directly tied to curriculum and instruction; provide considerable guidance for IEP development and implementation; provide a method for ongoing monitoring of the student's academic progress. **Disadvantages:** May be time-consuming and require teacher training.

an overview of some of the strategies commonly used to assess students with emotional or behavioral disorders. Each of these strategies serves a distinct purpose in the assessment process, and each has its own unique advantages and disadvantages. Data from these strategies are typically aggregated throughout the phases to obtain a complete picture of the student's strengths and presenting learning and behavioral difficulties.

Recent Trends in Assessment of Students with Emotional or Behavioral Disorders

In recent years, three initiatives have strengthened the assessment process as it relates to students with emotional or behavioral disorders: person-centered planning, strength-based assessment, and functional behavioral assessment.

In **person-centered planning** (Wacker & Berg, 2002) the IEP team, including the parents (and at times, the student), begins the IEP development process by creating a "vision" for the student's future. Typically, this vision includes an analysis of the student's strengths, preferences, and needs. By collaboratively articulating this vision *before* developing an IEP, the team seeks to address the student's long-term goals and aspirations in the IEP. Person-centered planning forces IEP team members to look beyond the "next year" and to consider long-term solutions and interventions that will successfully address the "vision" for the student.

Strength-based assessment is a reaction against the deficit orientation or model of traditional assessment approaches (Epstein, Rudolph, & Epstein, 2000). For example, behavior rating scales, which are commonly used throughout the assessment process, often include only items that identify behavioral deficits; they do not address the student's behavioral strengths. Epstein (2002) defines strength-based assessment as

> the measurement of the emotional and behavioral skills, competencies, and characteristics that create a sense of personal accomplishment; contribute to satisfying relationships with family members, peers, and adults; enhance one's ability to deal with adversity and stress; and promote one's personal, social, and academic development. (p. 3)

Functional behavioral assessment acknowledges that students engage in inappropriate behavior for many reasons. Stea and Ristic (2006) identify several factors that influence or may trigger a student's misbehavior. These precursors or antecedents to problematic behaviors may include physiological factors such as illness, allergies, medication side effects, or fatigue; classroom environmental factors such as seating arrangements, noise levels, or disruptions; or curriculum and instructional factors, such as assignments that are too difficult, tedious and laborious assignments, or unclear expectations. By identifying the antecedents to a student's problematic behavior, the teacher can then take a preventive or proactive approach to intervention. For example, by knowing that assignments are too difficult for a student, the teacher can provide appropriate adaptations to facilitate the student's success and prevent acting-out behavior from ever occurring.

The consequences that follow a student's behavior are also important factors to consider when choosing appropriate interventions for children and youth with emotional or behavioral disorders. A student who finds work too difficult, for example, may act out in an effort to avoid or escape the task. If the student is successful in avoiding the task, he or she is reinforced for this acting-out behavior. Examples of consequences that may increase the likelihood of continued misbehavior include sensory stimulation, avoidance/escape, and attention. As a teacher, you need to be aware of your own possible role in the maintenance or escalation of a student's misbehavior. The consequences that follow a student's misbehavior may inadvertently reinforce the very behaviors you want to decrease.

Functional behavioral assessment has historically been used with individuals with severe developmental disorders such as autism spectrum disorders or severe mental retardation (Safran & Oswald, 2003; Scott et al., 2004). It is now, due to PL 108-446, a required component of the assessment process for students with disabilities who present behavioral challenges.

A functional behavior assessment examines the circumstances surrounding the occurrence and/or nonoccurence of the challenging behavior, seeking to identify variables and events that are consistently present in those situations. The student's behavior during these times is examined to determine the function of the challenging behavior and to identify which variables might be maintaining it (Lane, Weisenbach, Phillips, & Wehby, 2007; McConnell, Cox, Thomas, & Hilvitz, 2001). By understanding and manipulating the variables that precede and follow misbehavior, educators and parents can design interventions that will assist them in developing and implementing positive behavior supports for students. In fact, a functional behavioral assessment is considered to be a cornerstone or foundation of positive behavior supports (Chandler & Dalquist, 2006; Umbreit, Ferro, Liaupsin, & Lane, 2007).

Identification of antecedents and consequences is directly tied to the development of a **behavioral intervention plan,** required by PL 108-446 for students with disabilities who exhibit problematic behaviors in school. In developing this plan, the IEP team must consider the use of positive behavioral interventions, strategies, and supports to address the problematic behaviors. In effect, the IEP team must develop a proactive plan of intervention. This approach contrasts with more traditional approaches to student discipline, which are primarily reactive and punitive in nature.

Educational Considerations

Children and youth with emotional or behavioral disorders present unique challenges in terms of educational placement and programming. Interventions for students with emotional or behavioral disorders can be divided into three broad categories: physical environment interventions, academic and instructional interventions, and behavioral and cognitive-behavioral interventions. These categories represent an array of interventions reflecting various conceptual and theoretical models and include a range of primary, secondary, and tertiary intervention approaches.

Where Are Students with Emotional or Behavioral Disorders Educated?

In passing the 2004 Amendments to IDEA, Congress voiced its preference that students with disabilities be educated in general educational environments. Clearly, this preference has not been implemented for students with emotional or behavioral disorders, who represent one of the most segregated groups of all students with disabilities. Currently, a majority of students with emotional or behavioral disorders receive a special education and related services in environments that segregate them from their nondisabled peers for all or part of the school day (U.S. Department of Education, 2007). During the 2005–2006 school year, only one in three students with emotional or behavioral disorders was receiving a special education in the general education classroom (see Figure 8.2). Relative to other students with disabilities, children and youth with emotional or behavioral disorders are more likely to be educated in separate schools, residential settings, and home/hospital settings.

Figure 8.2

Educational Placements for Students with Emotional or Behavioral Disorders

Note: Figure represents percentage of enrollment of students with emotional or behavioral disorders during the 2005–2006 school year.

Source: U.S. Department of Education. (2007). *IDEA data.* Available at https://www.ideadata.org/PartBReport.asp

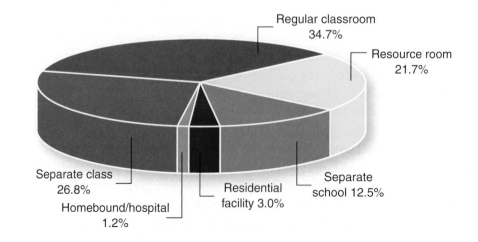

Regular classroom 34.7%
Resource room 21.7%
Separate class 26.8%
Homebound/hospital 1.2%
Residential facility 3.0%
Separate school 12.5%

Many explanations have been offered for this pattern of restrictive placements. For example, various researchers have suggested:

- Students with emotional or behavioral disorders (and their teachers) often do not receive the supports they need to succeed in general education classroom environments (Logan & Stein, 2001).
- Educational placements are often determined by the availability of services, despite federal prohibition of this practice (Frey, 2002).
- Only those students with the more severe forms of emotional or behavioral disorders are identified; therefore, more restrictive placements may be necessary (Landrum et al., 2004).
- The problematic behaviors exhibited by some students with severe emotional or behavioral disorders make it particularly difficult to successfully include them in less restrictive placements (Nelson et al., 2003).

Physical Environment Interventions

A number of proactive interventions related to management of the physical environment are appropriate for use with students with emotional or behavioral disorders. Most of these interventions are at the primary level of prevention; that is, they are appropriate for all students, not just those with emotional or behavioral disorders.

Time management involves proactive interventions such as maximizing student engagement time, scheduling appropriately, and teaching time management skills. Because students with emotional or behavioral disorders experience considerable academic failure, teachers should endeavor to maximize the time spent in instruction and make every effort to keep their students on-task as much as possible. Because on-task behavior is incompatible with off-task and disruptive behavior, a teacher can do much to prevent misbehavior in his or her classroom through effective time management. Although there is much variation from classroom to classroom, research shows that as much as half the time allocated for instruction during the school day is lost to students' off-task behavior, interruptions, disruptive behavior, and lack of teacher preparation (Mastropieri & Scruggs, 2002). This means that you should make every effort to prepare for instruction in advance, minimize classroom interruptions, and interact substantively with students to keep them focused on-task. By creating and developing effective schedules, teachers can minimize the likelihood of disruptive behavior. For suggestions on effective scheduling, see the accompanying Suggestions for the Classroom.

Educators should also teach time management skills directly to students. Strategies include requiring students to maintain calendars on which they list their assignments and activities; helping students establish and prioritize goals for assignment completion; and allocating time during the school day to help students develop timelines and plan for completing assignments (Salend, 2008).

Closely related to time management is **transition management.** Transition times are those periods during the day when students are moving from one activity to another, such as changing classes, moving from one assignment to another, or beginning or ending the school day. Transitions create situations in which disruptive student behavior is increased. According to Polloway, Patton, and Serna (2008), teachers can minimize disruptive behavior during transition times by (1) giving students specific directions about how to move from one activity to another; (2) establishing, teaching, and having students rehearse transition routines; and (3) rewarding students for making orderly and smooth transitions.

Suggestions for the Classroom

Suggestions for Effective Scheduling

☑ Place class schedule in a prominent location.

☑ Intersperse more challenging tasks with less difficult ones.

☑ Alternate lecture, discussion, and movement types of activities.

☑ Adjust the length of activities and/or the schedule to meet the attentional, developmental, and ability level of students.

☑ Review and discuss the schedule frequently with students.

☑ Inform students in advance of any schedule changes.

☑ Schedule routine opening and closing activities each day.

SOURCES: Based on E. Polloway, J. Patton, and L. Serna, *Strategies for Teaching Learners with Special Needs,* 9th ed. (Upper Saddle River, NJ: Pearson Education, 2008); S. Salend, *Creating Inclusive Classrooms,* 6th ed. (Upper Saddle River, NJ: Pearson Education, 2008).

Teachers can also use cues or signals to help students make transitions successfully, thereby minimizing disruptions. Examples include verbal cues, physical cues (light blinking, buzzer sounding, hand gestures), and creative dismissal cues ("All students with green eyes may line up for lunch."). Examples of two cueing systems (one picture cue and one physical cue) are shown in Figure 8.3. These systems, if taught and routinely used with students, may assist teachers in helping students to settle down quickly and get started on the next activity or assignment.

Proximity and movement management includes making sure that high-traffic areas are free from congestion, developing clear procedures for the use of classroom space and equipment, and ensuring sufficient separation of students to minimize inappropriate behavior (Salend, 2008). Gunter, Shores, Jack, Rasmussen, and Flowers (1995) suggest that teachers can use both proximity and movement to facilitate desired student behavior by

- placing the desks of disruptive students near the teacher's desk or main work area;
- interacting briefly and frequently with students;
- providing praise, reprimands, and consequences when in close physical proximity to students.

Classroom arrangement includes the physical layout of the classroom as well as classroom décor. Physical layout includes student seating and grouping arrangements; location of materials, equipment, and personal items; removal of tempting or dangerous items; and location of the teacher's desk. The following suggestions have been made regarding seating and grouping arrangements:

- Students should be seated in locations that provide teachers with easy visual and physical access at all times (Salend, 2008).
- Savage (1999) recommends using rows for direct instruction, circular patterns for discussions, and clustered arrangements for group work.

Activity wheel

Discussion
quiet, hands up

Working hard alone
quiet, in seats

Free play
inside voices

Helping allowed
soft talk

Give me five

Figure 8.3

Examples of Cueing Systems

Source: C. Webster-Stratton, *How to Promote Children's Social and Emotional Competence* (Thousand Oaks, CA: Sage, 1999), pp. 56, 149. Copyright © 1999 by Sage Publications, Inc. Reprinted by permission of Sage Publications, Inc.

- Place disruptive students in the "action zone" in the classroom. The action zone consists of seats across the front of the classroom and down the center. Research reviewed by Savage (1999) suggests that students seated in the action zone attend more to tasks, participate more, have higher levels of achievement, and demonstrate more positive attitudes.
- Disruptive students should be seated near the teacher to allow for proximity control and frequent monitoring.

Teachers can also minimize the likelihood of disruptive behavior by removing items that are physically tempting, distracting, or dangerous. The location of the teacher's desk may influence student behavior. The teacher's desk should have a barrier-free view of all students and be positioned to allow the teacher to move quickly if a situation necessitates (Salend, 2008).

For students who need a quiet, distraction-free place to study, the use of study carrels may be helpful. If study carrels are used, teachers should make sure their use is continuously monitored and be cautious not to overuse them as they may isolate or stigmatize students if used excessively (Salend, 2008).

Classroom ambience, according to Di Giulio (2000), refers to the feeling one gets on entering a classroom. Some classrooms, when you enter them, just seem to have a sense of orderliness and pleasantness in terms of lighting, sound, visual appeal, temperature, and odor. As reported by Savage, studies indicate that attractive classrooms influence students' behavior in positive ways. In contrast, unattractive classrooms have been associated with student reports of headaches, fatigue, and discomfort and with increased instances of teacher control statements and student conflicts. The implications of this research are that teachers should endeavor to make their classroom environments as attractive as possible.

Making Inclusion Work

Think back if you will, and try to pinpoint the moment that you knew you wanted to be a teacher. For me, that moment came while standing on the tarmac of the outdoor basketball court in third grade. Each day, a very fair blonde girl just my age arrived by yellow school bus. She came to our school each day only for recess. She was nearly blind and stood on the court each day, staring at the sun and waving her hand in front of her eyes. I was saddened as to why she would not talk to me or play like the other kids. I told my mother that I wanted to learn more about this girl and what was wrong with her. She had a form of autism and despite my efforts, I was unable to form a friendship with her. Teachers and students just left her alone and I knew she must feel alone.

There are few things I remember about third grade except a very fair teacher, a teacher who yelled at me one time, and the girl I wanted so desperately to befriend. For those very reasons, I decided and declared during the middle of that year that I wanted to be a teacher—a teacher who would be fair and could help students with disabilities. Certainly, I would not be a teacher who yelled. It was important to me that all students felt included in everything about school. I felt so strongly that I never changed my mind or career path in twenty-plus years.

One of the benefits of spending many years in special education has been the opportunity to vicariously ride the swinging pendulum regarding the inclusion of students with special needs. As a teacher, counselor, and coordinator, all in the field of special education,

I have seen and experienced the continuum of inclusion from the worst of times to what I consider the beginning of the best of times. What a great opportunity we have to grant each and every student the right to success they so desperately desire and deserve.

My very first job, some twenty-two years ago, was teaching students with emotional/behavioral disorders (E/BD) attending a separate special education school. Fourteen students, eleven boys and three girls, were brought by bus to our county school and somewhat thrown together in a self-contained classroom. The students' ages ranged from 14 through 21 and, although they were diagnosed as having E/BD, the disabilities and needs varied greatly. As a first-year teacher, survival was my objective, not teaching anyone to read or divide. Unfortunately, it was a terrifying, difficult year. As a teacher, I did not have the training or support needed to properly meet the needs of the students in my classroom. Students already typically deficient in social skills and academics were given scant opportunity for practice or success. In addition, there were virtually no positive peer role models within the classroom. I was discouraged because I knew we were letting these students down by separating them from the rest of the children. Needless to say, progress was minimal.

Fast-forward twenty-two years. I thankfully work in a society with an educational and legal system that now recognizes the benefits and need for inclusion of all students. It is a pleasure and honor to work with

Academic and Instructional Interventions

Positive behavioral supports include providing effective academic content and instruction to students with emotional and behavioral disorders (Scheuermann & Hall, 2008). Although there has been much research on effective social-emotional behavioral interventions for students with emotional or behavioral disorders, the research on effective academic curriculum and instructional practices for these students has been limited.

The paucity of research on academic and instructional interventions is unfortunate given the high rates of academic failure experienced by these students. One significant way in which educators can help to minimize these negative long-term outcomes is through the provision of a sound academic program. There is a strong correlation between poor academic students and teachers preparing the way for meaningful inclusion of students. Not only do I get to work as a counselor and behavior interventionist with many students who have special needs, but I also teach at the university level, training preservice general education and special education teachers. Whether I am in a public school or university classroom, I seize the occasion to champion the benefits of inclusion for students and teachers alike.

A predominant concern teachers have shared with me over the years is that they are willing to welcome most children with special needs into their classrooms if they are told how to include the students and what to do! The exception, however, is usually students with E/BD. The majority of these students want to be in a safe environment and they crave structure, consistency, and predictability. An attitude geared toward welcoming any student into a safe learning environment is half of the formula for successful inclusion. Students will know if they are welcome in your classroom. They will likely feel welcomed and safe if you are clear about your expectations, are consistent, and are well prepared. Avoid assuming the worst and that students "can't." Assume they "can" with careful planning and preparation. Say what you mean and always mean what you say—follow through.

Preparation is so very important and may include modification of the curriculum, teaching styles, and classroom management procedures and practices. Does this mean you must change everything you do for one student? Absolutely not. It does mean that having students with special needs in your classroom should give you cause to reflect on your personal teaching style, strategies, tolerance levels, expectations, procedures, and behavior management style. Reflection on your practices as a teacher will shed light on your readiness to include all students, and you will be well on your way to making preparations for special-needs students.

Although this may all sound a bit overwhelming, the best news is that you are not alone. Collaboration may very well be the biggest key to successful inclusion. You will have access to a host of wisdom, knowledge, and experience from the professionals with whom you work. Take advantage. Be proactive with teachers and parents and learn as much about each student as possible. Access the special educators in your building and seek their knowledge regarding the special needs of your students. You may need to take the first step and ask for help. The special educator in your building may be hesitant as well, for fear of stepping on your turf. It is also important to establish your own relationship with the parents and well worth the effort to do so before the need arises to discuss a problem. Time spent getting to know each student personally is possibly the best investment. Once you know what interests a student, meaningful engagement in academics is more likely and building of relationships will be easier. Collaborating and preplanning for the arrival of a student with special needs may mean the difference between success and failure for everyone. A favorite quote of mine comes from a third-grade student included for the very first time. After his first day in a general education class, I inquired how his day went and he responded, "Good. I got to be a real person today."

—Teresa (Tracy) Teaff
Arlington Independent
School District, Arlington, Texas
Behavior Interventionist, Programs
for Emotional/Behavioral Disorders

achievement and juvenile delinquency (Allen-DeBoer, Malmgren, & Glass, 2006). The hope is that if educators can design academic programs that strengthen the achievement levels of this population, delinquency rates will decrease. Academic achievement may serve as a critical protective or preventive factor for students with emotional or behavioral disorders.

Several researchers (Barton-Arwood, Wehby, & Falk, 2005; Lane et al., 2007) recommend a primary focus on academic interventions rather than social-emotional-behavioral interventions. Effective academic interventions may result not only in higher academic achievement but also in improved behavior (Nelson et al., 2004; Wehby, Falk, Barton-Arwood, Lane, & Cooley, 2003). Research suggests, however, that interventions that focus solely on improving behavior are not always accompanied by simultaneous improvement in academics. It is difficult for a student to be academically successful while simultaneously engaging

Attractive classrooms influence students' behavior in positive ways.

in inappropriate behavior. To be effective, academic intervention must address two areas of concern: academic curriculum and instructional delivery. Academic curriculum includes the instructional programs or materials used by classroom teachers to teach specific content; instructional delivery refers to teaching skills or strategies that exist independently of instructional materials (Stein & Davis, 2000).

ACADEMIC CURRICULUM In many respects, the academic curriculum for students with emotional or behavioral disorders mirrors that of students without disabilities. This population varies widely, however, in achievement and ability levels, and educators must adapt or modify the curriculum accordingly. PL 108-446 mandates that, to the maximum extent appropriate, students with disabilities have access to the general education curriculum. For students with emotional or behavioral disorders, this may necessitate appropriate supports and curriculum modifications. By incorporating students' interests into the curriculum, educators can enhance both the behavior and the academic engagement of these students. Thus, teachers should endeavor to design a curriculum that is both relevant and motivating for students with emotional and behavioral disorders.

INSTRUCTIONAL DELIVERY One important finding from research on students with emotional or behavioral disorders is that student–teacher instructional interactions are often very low, particularly when students are aggressive (Wehby, Symons, Canale, & Go, 1998). As a teacher, you must make an effort to engage often and substantively when providing instruction to students with emotional or behavioral disorders.

What limited research is available suggests that students with emotional or behavioral disorders benefit from certain teaching strategies (Scheuermann & Hall, 2008). Five strategies are discussed briefly here: effective instructional cycles, teaching mnemonics, self-monitoring strategies, curriculum-based measurement, and content enhancements.

Components of an **effective instructional cycle** include

- Beginning each lesson with a statement of goals
- Beginning each lesson with a review of previous, prerequisite learning
- Presenting new material in small steps, with student practice following each step
- Providing active and sufficient practice for all students
- Asking many questions, checking frequently for student understanding, and obtaining responses from all students
- Providing systematic feedback and corrections to students
- Providing explicit instruction and practice for seatwork activities and, when necessary, actively monitoring students during these activities
- Continuing to provide practice until students are independent and confident (Rosenshine & Stevens, 1986)

Mnemonic strategies are tools for helping students recall facts and relationships. Mnemonic strategies have been found to be extremely effective in promoting academic achievement among students with disabilities, including those with emotional or behavioral disorders (Scruggs & Mastropieri, 2000). There are many different types of mnemonic strategies; a few of these are illustrated in Figure 8.4.

Self-monitoring strategies, such as assignment checklists and self-monitoring checklists, can be used to assist students with emotional or behavioral disorders. These strategies help students by providing the cues necessary to complete a task successfully. You may want to incorporate these strategies for all your students, not just those with emotional or behavioral disorders. See Figure 8.5 for an example of an academic self-monitoring checklist.

Curriculum-based measurement (CBM), according to Deno (1998), "is a standardized set of observational procedures for repeatedly measuring growth in core reading, writing, and arithmetic skills" (p. 12). By incorporating curriculum-based measurement into instructional delivery efforts, teachers can ensure that there is a close match between the content being presented and students' levels of achievement.

Content enhancements include graphic organizers, content diagrams, semantic maps, advance organizers, guided notes, and study guides. Content enhancements help students understand major concepts, ideas, and vocabulary in a manner that is conducive to knowledge acquisition, organization, and retrieval. These enhancements make explicit the content to be learned, link concepts together, and help students link new content to previously learned content.

Behavioral and Cognitive-Behavioral Interventions

Researchers (Cooper, Heron, & Heward, 2007) have identified two broad-based intervention approaches that have substantial support: behavior modification and cognitive-behavior modification. These two intervention approaches share many common features, including positive reinforcement, ongoing monitoring, and contingency management. There is one

Figure 8.4

Examples of Mnemonic Strategies

Source: Adapted from M. A. Mastropieri and T. E. Scruggs, *Teaching Students Ways to Remember: Strategies for Learning Mnemonically* (Cambridge, MA: Brookline Books, 1990).

The Keyword Method
To help a student remember that the word "barrister" is another word for lawyer . . .

Your Honor, my client is INNOCENT!

The Keyword Method
To help students remember that insects have six legs . . .

Look at the insects on these sticks!

The STICKS remind you that insects have SIX legs.

Reconstructive Elaborations
To help students remember that early bridges often rotted and washed away . . .

Dang! These old bridges are no good!

Letter Strategies
Letter strategies include both **acronyms** and **acrostics**. Acronyms create new words by combining the first letters of a list or series of words. For example, the acronym HOMES is tied to the Great Lakes:

H = Huron
O = Ontario
M = Michigan
E = Erie
S = Superior

Acrostics are similar to acronyms, but they consist of sentences. The first letter of each sentence represents a different word, a strategy that can be useful when information must be remembered in sequence. For example, "My very educated mother just served us nine pizzas," to remember the names of the planets (Mercury, Venus, Earth, Mars, etc.).

Figure 8.5

Example of an Academic Self-Monitoring Checklist

Source: M. E. McConnell, "Self-Monitoring, Cueing, Recording, and Managing: Teaching Students to Manage Their Own Behavior," *Teaching Exceptional Children, 32*(2), 1999, p. 18.

Name _____ Date _____

Assignment checklist

1. Is my name on the paper?   Yes ____ No ____
2. Do all sentences begin with a capital letter?   Yes ____ No ____
3. Do all my sentences end with the correct punctuation?   Yes ____ No ____
4. Did I answer all of the questions?   Yes ____ No ____
5. Do I need extra help?   Yes ____ No ____
6. Do I need more time?   Yes ____ No ____
7. Do I understand the assignment?   Yes ____ No ____
8. Did I finish all of my work?   Yes ____ No ____
9. Did I follow teacher directions?   Yes ____ No ____
10. Did I turn in my assignment?   Yes ____ No ____

primary difference, however. Whereas strict behavioral approaches rely on *external* sources of behavioral control (in school settings, this external source of control is often teacher-mediated), cognitive-behavioral approaches seek to promote students' *internal* control or self-regulatory behavior (that is, these strategies are self-mediated or self-managed) (Gumpel & David, 2000; Janney & Snell, 2000).

Both behavioral and cognitive-behavioral interventions range from primary to tertiary levels of prevention. These interventions can also be placed on a continuum in terms of their intrusiveness and restrictiveness. The intervention ladder pictured in Figure 8.6 suggests that most students will respond to mildly intrusive and restrictive interventions and only a few will require more intensive and restrictive interventions. Teachers should attempt less intensive and restrictive interventions first and proceed to the next level only if these interventions are unsuccessful.

One example of a mildly intrusive intervention strategy is classroom rules and routines. Students may misbehave because they do not understand the behavior expected of them. For example, a student may not understand that talking out is inappropriate during teacher-led presentations but may be permitted during cooperative learning activities. Teachers can do much to prevent misbehavior in their classrooms by making their expectations clear. This means that teachers should pay particular attention to the establishment and consistent enforcement of classroom rules and routines. Classroom rules provide structure for acceptable and

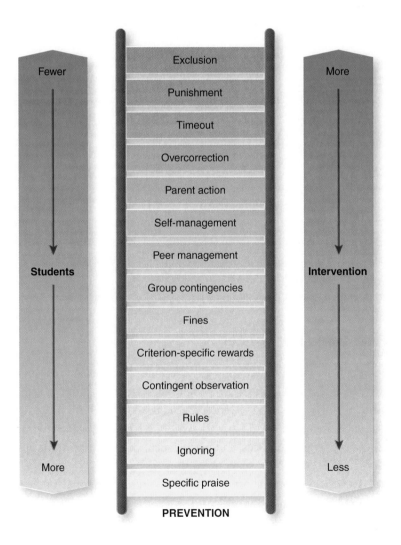

Figure 8.6

A Ladder of Intervention Strategies

Source: Adapted from D. D. Smith and D. M. Rivera, *Effective Discipline,* 2nd ed. (Austin, TX: Psycho-Educational Services, 2001), p. 17. Reprinted with permission.

Suggestions for the Classroom

Guidelines for Establishing Classroom Rules

☑ Keep the wording of rules simple and clear.

☑ Select the fewest possible number of rules (3–6).

☑ Use different rules for different situations.

☑ Rules should be stated behaviorally, and they should be enforceable.

☑ Rules should be stated positively.

☑ Rules should be reasonable.

☑ Specify consequences for both rule adherence and rule infraction, and provide consequences consistently.

☑ Give examples and nonexamples of each rule.

☑ Discuss the need for rules in the classroom.

☑ Check for student understanding of rules.

☑ Review rules regularly.

☑ Post the rules in a prominent location in the room.

☑ Obtain written commitments from students that they will follow the rules.

SOURCES: Based on P. Burden, *Powerful Classroom Management Strategies* (Thousand Oaks, CA: Corwin, 2000); M. Kerr and C. Nelson, *Strategies for Managing Behavior Problems in the Classroom*, 6th ed. (Upper Saddle River, NJ: Pearson Education, 2006).

unacceptable student behaviors (Vaughn, Bos, & Schumm, 2007); for guidelines on establishing classroom rules, see the Suggestions for the Classroom. Classroom routines are those procedures that occur periodically throughout the school day—for example, sharpening pencils, class dismissal, turning in assignments, or making up work during absences—that allow the classroom to run smoothly and effectively. In addition, the Effective Instructional Practices feature provides some tips for managing behavioral issues in the classroom.

Special Programmatic Concerns

The behaviors characteristic of students with emotional or behavioral disorders, such as aggression, disruptiveness, and suicidal behavior, necessitate that careful thought be given to the development and implementation of appropriate education programs. Four areas of special programmatic concern are social skills training, interpersonal problem solving and conflict resolution, provision of related services, and management of behavioral crises at school.

SOCIAL SKILLS TRAINING The majority of students with emotional or behavioral disorders have difficulty interacting successfully with their peers, teachers, and parents. Although social skills training is used frequently, research on its effectiveness has resulted

✓ EFFECTIVE INSTRUCTIONAL PRACTICES | Behavioral Principles

Principles for Strengthening (or Increasing) Existing Behavior

Response increment principles include the following:

Principle 1: Positive Reinforcement Principle

Provide positive reinforcement immediately after desired behavior occurs.

Example: Praise the child following task completion.

Principle 2: Premack Principle (First you work, then you play.)

Allow the child to engage in a favored activity immediately following the occurrence of the desired behavior.

Example: Completion of a disliked math assignment prior to completing a favored activity such as putting a puzzle together.

Principle 3: Contingency Contracting Principle

Specify in writing the desired behavior and the positive consequences that will follow if the child engages in the desired behavior.

Example: Allow the child to listen to preferred music following the observance of the desired behavior.

Principles for Developing New Behavior

Response acquisition principles include the following:

Principle 1: Successive Approximations Principle

Reward successive steps to the desired behavior.

Example: For problematic off-task behavior, first reward the child for staying on task for 5 minutes, then 10 minutes, then 15 minutes, and so on.

Principle 2: Modeling Principle

Allow the child to observe a prestigious person engaging in the desired behavior.

Example: For problematic handwriting behavior, have a peer demonstrate the correct letter formation and have the student model the formation.

Principle 3: Cueing Principle

To teach a child to engage in a particular behavior at certain time, provide a cue or prompt just before the desired behavior is expected.

Example: Teacher and child mutually develop a signal to cue the child to begin a task.

Principle 4: Discrimination Principle

To teach a child to engage in a specific behavior under one set of circumstances but not another, help the child only when his or her behavior is appropriate to the cue.

Example: Reinforce the use of an "inside" voice when the child is in the classroom but not on the playground.

Principles for Decreasing or Extinguishing Undesired Behavior

Response decrement principles include the following:

Principle 1: Extinction

Arrange conditions so that the child receives no reinforcement following the undesired behavior.

Example: Ignoring talking-out behavior.

Principle 2: Reinforcement of Incompatible Behavior

Reinforce an alternative or desired behavior that is inconsistent with the undesired behavior.

Example: Reinforce on-task behavior to decrease the child's out-of-seat behavior.

Principle 3: Response Cost

Arrange conditions so that something the child considers reinforcing is taken away when the undesired behavior occurs.

Example: Taking away television privileges when a child hits another child.

in inconclusive findings (Maag, 2006). Social skills training can occur at any level of prevention—primary, secondary, and tertiary—and some professionals have called for the implementation of primary (schoolwide) social skills training programs and the infusion of social skills instruction into the curriculum (Forgan & Gonzalez-DeHass, 2004; Lane et al., 2003).

Social skills training often uses direct instruction to teach students appropriate social behaviors. It assumes that behavioral problems in the classroom reflect social skill problems and that social skills are learned behaviors that, consequently, can be taught (Lane et al., 2003). Social skills training attempts to increase students' social competence. The end goal is to increase students' social acceptance, friendship-making skills, and ability to participate successfully in school and community events and activities.

The importance of teaching social skills to students with emotional or behavioral disorders cannot be overstated, as adequate social skills are critical precursors to academic instruction. Unless children have the basic social skills—asking for assistance, following directions, adhering to classroom rules, routines, and procedures—attempts to teach academics to these students will be largely unsuccessful. Research on social skills training has yielded mixed results; at best, it has resulted in modest gains (Gresham, Sugai, & Horner, 2001; Leffert & Siperstein, 2003; Maag, 2006). Most of the concerns regarding this approach have centered around the generalization and maintenance of social skills. Although a student may be able to demonstrate a specific social skill during a role-playing situation, that same skill may not be demonstrated in more natural settings such as the classroom or playground.

INTERPERSONAL PROBLEM SOLVING AND CONFLICT RESOLUTION   Closely related to social skills training is the teaching of interpersonal problem solving and conflict resolution. **Interpersonal problem solving** focuses on teaching students the "thinking" skills necessary to avoid and resolve interpersonal conflicts, resist peer pressure, and cope with their emotions and stress. Students are taught to identify their problems, consider and select from a range of alternative solutions, and evaluate the results of their selection. One example of interpersonal problem solving is the FAST strategy, developed by Vaughn and Lancelotta (1990):

> **F** = **F**reeze and Think! What is the problem?
> **A** = **A**lternatives? What are my possible solutions?
> **S** = **S**olution evaluation. Choose the best solution. Is it safe? Is it fair?
> **T** = **T**ry it! Slowly and carefully. Does it work?

Strategies such as this one can be taught to both large and small groups, as well as to individual students. Students are taught to go through the steps of problem solving, such as those detailed in the FAST strategy, whenever they encounter a problem or conflict.

Conflict resolution programs are similar to problem solving approaches. However, conflict resolution programs are designed to teach not only problem-solving skills but skills related to negotiation and mediation.

PROVISION OF RELATED SERVICES   The 2004 Amendments to IDEA require that related services be provided to help students with disabilities benefit from special education services. Two of these related services, counseling and school health services, are particularly applicable to students with emotional or behavioral disorders.

Counseling services are essential for many students with emotional or behavioral disorders. Research shows, however, that students with emotional or behavioral disorders seldom receive counseling services, and when these services are provided, they may be of poor quality (Etscheidt, 2002).

School health services often take the form of medication administration and monitoring. For many students with emotional or behavioral disorders, psychopharmacological interventions have proven to be very successful in improving academic and social functioning (Forness et al., 2003). Teachers, therefore, need to be well versed in the use of medication and its effects (Haslam & Valletutti, 2004; Kline, Silver, & Russell, 2001) and also be able to collaborate effectively with families and physicians (Forness, 2003).

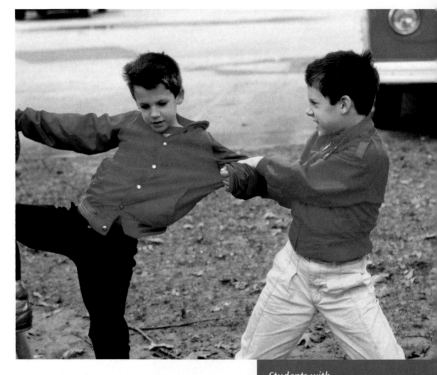

Students with emotional or behavioral disorders often have difficulty interacting appropriately with peers.

MANAGEMENT OF BEHAVIORAL CRISES AT SCHOOL Although students who become violent at school often are not identified as having emotional or behavioral disorders, some students with this type of disability will, at times, become physically aggressive toward themselves or others. Some students with emotional or behavioral disorders may engage in self-injurious behavior or self-destructive acts; others may become so angry that they physically attack others.

In recent years, **crisis prevention and management programs** have been implemented to teach educators how to effectively and proactively address students' violent, aggressive, and/or self-injurious behaviors. Crisis management programs typically are preventive and proactive in orientation; educators are taught verbal mediation strategies to defuse acting-out behavior before it reaches the point of a physical crisis. If these verbal mediation strategies are unsuccessful, educators are taught to use physical restraint and employ safety techniques to protect the welfare of both the acting-out student and those around him or her.

School-based interventions alone are insufficient for meeting the many complex needs and challenges of students with emotional or behavioral disorders (Forness, 2003). To adequately address their needs will take the concentrated, sustained, and collaborative efforts of multiple social service agencies and families. Research suggests that the most effective interventions for students with emotional or behavioral disorders are comprehensive, broad-based, and enduring (National Dissemination Center for Children and Youth with Disabilities, 2003).

Services for Young Children with Emotional or Behavioral Disorders

A growing body of research suggests a clear developmental pattern of emotional or behavioral disorders that typically begins at a very early age and appears to persist throughout adolescence and adulthood (Dunlap et al., 2006; Forness, 2003). Infants and toddlers who are born with a "difficult temperament"—those who are frequently irritable, display

Emotional or behavioral disorders that develop at an early age are likely to persist throughout adolescence and adulthood.

irregular patterns of sleeping and eating, and are highly emotional—may be at especially high risk for progressing to more acting-out aggressive behaviors, even before they reach their elementary years. Although many believe that very young children who exhibit these antisocial behaviors will outgrow them, research suggests that this is often not the case. In fact, early antisocial behavior appears to be a particularly potent precursor or antecedent to such negative long-term outcomes as dropping out, delinquency, violence, and drug abuse in adolescence and adulthood (Dunlap et al.). Moffitt (1994) describes this developmental pattern of problematic behavior as "life course persistent"—the earlier children demonstrate emotional or behavioral problems, the more likely these problems are to continue in adolescence and adulthood.

These research results provide potent arguments for early and effective intervention efforts (New Freedom Commission on Mental Health, 2003). Early intervention is a critical first step in providing comprehensive, intense, and sustained intervention for children and youth with emotional or behavioral disorders (Jones, Dohrn, & Dunn, 2004; Nelson et al., 2003). Although early intervention services are clearly beneficial, both in preventing emotional or behavioral disorders from developing and in minimizing their impact once they do develop, these important services are often lacking for several reasons. Dunlap et al. (2006) note a pervasive lack of resources for early intervention services except for those young children with the most severe forms of emotional or behavioral disorders. In addition, some teachers are hesitant to identify very young children with problematic behaviors, although research suggests that educators are capable of successfully identifying youngsters who are at risk for antisocial behavior (Lane, 2003). Several early intervention programs that do exist, however, have much research support in terms of effectiveness. For example, First Steps to Success (Beard & Sugai, 2004; Walker et al., 1997) is a comprehensive and collaborative school–home early intervention program designed for at-risk kindergartners who exhibit emerging antisocial behavior. Programs such as this one, that involve the concerted efforts of teachers, parents, and peers, can be most effective with very young children who exhibit early-onset antisocial behavior (Hocutt, McKinney, & Montague, 2002).

Transition into Adulthood

Throughout this chapter, much emphasis has been placed on the negative long-term outcomes experienced by children and youth with emotional or behavioral disorders. Numerous studies indicate that the presence of emotional or behavioral disorders is a very accurate predictor of school failure, delinquency, adult psychiatric problems, and substance abuse (Lane, Little, Redding-Rhodes, Phillips, & Welsh, 2007). Youth with externalizing problems, such as conduct disorders, are at very high risk for psychiatric hospitalization, incarceration, and under- and unemployment (Wagner, Cameto, & Newman, 2003). Youth with internalizing disorders, such as anxiety and depression, are at heightened risk for negative long-term outcomes as well.

A particularly alarming statistic is that approximately 45 percent of students with emotional or behavioral disorders leave school before graduation—the highest dropout rate among all categories of students with disabilities (Wagner, Newman, Cameto, Garza, & Levine, 2005).

An equally disturbing finding is that the majority of students with emotional or behavioral disorders are not identified and served until their adolescent years. In stark contrast to students in other disability categories, who are identified and served at much earlier ages, the U.S. Department of Education (2006) reports that almost two-thirds of all students receiving special education and related services because of emotional or behavioral disorders are adolescents. During the 2002–2003 school year, the peak age for placement of these students was 15 years of age. Clearly, educators need to work more aggressively to identify and serve this population at earlier ages and to implement effective dropout prevention and transition programs.

Relative to students with other types of disabilities, there is a conspicuous absence of research on effective transition programming for adolescents with emotional or behavioral disorders (Corbett, Clark, & Blank, 2002). This lack of research, coupled with the dismal findings on long-term outcomes for students with emotional or behavioral disorders, emphasizes the need for effective vocational training for students with emotional or behavioral disorders (U.S. Department of Education, 2003).

To plan effectively for the transition of adolescents with emotional or behavioral disorders from school to adulthood, educators need to understand that these students have a developmental disability that will require intervention throughout their life span. This means that transition planning needs to be comprehensive and broad-based. Transition services need to go well beyond just preparing these students for employment. Rather, there is a need to view transition in terms of postsecondary educational opportunities, independent living choices, and community participation in addition to vocational possibilities. Middle school and secondary school educators need to provide instruction in such diverse areas as personal management, personal health, leisure skills, citizenship, and social skills (Sabornie & deBettencourt, 2004). Effective transition planning includes vocational training, parental and student involvement, interagency collaboration, paid work experience, follow-up employment services, community-based instruction, and community-referenced curriculum.

One promising approach is a **wraparound plan,** which should begin in the elementary years and continue throughout the secondary years and adulthood. *Wraparound* refers to an approach that "wraps" services and supports around the student and his or her family. This network of coordinated interagency services is provided in natural school, home, and community environments (Anderson & Matthews, 2001; Kutash, Duchnowski, Sumi, Rudo, & Harris, 2002). Such a plan allows for the coordinated involvement of multiple agencies to facilitate the successful transition from school to adulthood for adolescents with emotional or behavioral disorders. Such wraparound plans may be essential for adolescents because many do not have access to the many critical services offered in their communities.

Adults with Emotional or Behavioral Disorders

Once a student with emotional or behavioral disorders leaves secondary education and enters postsecondary education or employment, the protections offered by IDEA no longer apply. Two other legislative acts protect these young adults in the areas of education and employment: Section 504 of the Rehabilitation Act of 1973 (PL 93-112) and the Americans with Disabilities Act (ADA) (PL 101-336). Both Section 504 and the ADA guarantee individuals with disabilities "equal access" to postsecondary programs if they are "otherwise qualified." This does not mean that individuals with disabilities are automatically guaranteed access to postsecondary institutions; they must meet the admission criteria for the

Postsecondary institutions cannot deny admission simply because a student has a disability.

institution to which they apply. It does mean that postsecondary institutions cannot deny admission simply because the individual has a disability. If an individual with a disability is admitted to a federally funded postsecondary institution, he or she is entitled to "reasonable accommodations." These accommodations might include extended time on assignments, texts on audiotapes, and peer tutoring.

Postsecondary program options for students with emotional or behavioral disorders include vocational and technical programs, trade schools, adult education programs, two-year community colleges, and four-year colleges and universities. Given the alarming drop-out rates among students with emotional or behavioral disorders, however, many of these students never enter, much less complete, postsecondary programs that will prepare them for meaningful careers (Walker, Ramsey, & Gresham, 2004; Zigmond, 2006).

Employment training is available to many young adults with emotional or behavioral disorders through vocational rehabilitation services. Educators should not assume, however, that all students with emotional or behavioral disorders will receive these services. Vocational rehabilitation is an eligibility program, not an entitlement program, and eligibility criteria differ from those in IDEA. For young adults who do qualify for vocational rehabilitation services, an Individualized Written Rehabilitation Program is developed and implemented. This plan addresses areas such as basic skill development, communication skills, and specific on-the-job skills.

For those students pursuing postsecondary education, preparation must begin early in their secondary years. Areas of instruction that will need to be addressed include time management skills, organizational skills, study skills, and self-advocacy. Another important area is helping students learn about the types of support services they may need during their years in higher education, such as writing centers, counseling services, tutoring, and instructional supports. Learning how to advocate for these services and apply for disability services in higher education settings are critical skills that should be incorporated into an individual transition plan early during a student's secondary years.

Family-Centered Interventions

Some professionals, including educators, blame parents for the behavioral problems exhibited by children and youth with emotional or behavioral disorders. This "blaming" often creates a major barrier to working effectively and collaboratively with families (Jensen, 2005). Rather than blaming parents, effective programs for children and youth with emotional or behavioral disorders seek to involve parents or caretakers, along with teachers and other professionals from the community, in providing interventions and services that meet the needs of the student and the family (Kutash et al., 2002). Many of these programs incorporate a **family-centered approach.** This approach recognizes the central role that the family plays in the lives of individuals and focuses on the strengths and capabilities of the family unit (Allen & Petr, 1997).

Raising a child with emotional or behavioral disorders is extraordinarily difficult and often highly stressful for the family. The child's disability may affect family finances, put a strain on marital and sibling relationships, create a need for respite care, and disrupt family routines and schedules (Collins, 2003). Another common stressor is the isolation that caretakers often experience because of the negative reactions of others to the child's behaviors (Taylor-Richardson, Heflinger, & Brown, 2006). These negative reactions from extended family members, neighbors, teachers, and others can be emotionally and physically draining. As an educator, you need to interact positively with parents as much as possible and be careful that your communications with parents are not primarily negative.

One strategy for increasing positive (and two-way) communication with parents is the development of a school–home communication system. Such a system, illustrated in Figure 8.7, fosters positive and constructive communication regarding a child's progress both at home and at school. These systems enable educators and parents to address behaviors of mutual concern and to implement interventions consistently in both environments.

Issues of Diversity

An issue of continued and often heated controversy has been the overrepresentation of African American students, particularly males, in special education programs for students with emotional or behavioral disorders (Coutinho, Oswald, Best, & Forness, 2002; DeValenzuela,

Date _____   **Missy's School–Home Daily Report**

Teacher's signature _____

____ Yes   ____ No   Completed assignments
____ Yes   ____ No   Followed teacher's directions
____ Yes   ____ No   Handed in completed homework
____ Yes   ____ No   Followed classroom rules
____ Yes   ____ No   Interacted well with peers

Teacher's comments:

Parent's signature _____

____ Yes   ____ No   Completed chores
____ Yes   ____ No   Followed parent's directions
____ Yes   ____ No   Completed homework
____ Yes   ____ No   Followed home rules
____ Yes   ____ No   Interacted well with siblings

Parent's comments:

Missy's self-evaluation
How did I do?

Totals ____ Yes   ____ No

Missy's comments:

____ My day was great! (more than 8 "Yes")
____ My day was okay. (6–8 "Yes")
____ Today was not so great. (below 6 "Yes")

Figure 8.7

School–Home Daily Report

Copeland, Qi, & Park, 2006). Additionally, once identified, these pupils are more likely to be taught in more restrictive, segregated environments (Skiba, Poloni-Staudinger, Gallini, Simmons, & Feggins-Azziz, 2006). Some explanations for overrepresentation focus on culturally insensitive and inappropriate assessment practices (Taylor, Gunter, & Slate, 2001). An "overreliance" on standardized, norm-referenced tests may place African Americans at particularly high risk for placement in programs for students with emotional or behavioral disorders. In recent years, comprehensive models have been developed that support the success of students from culturally and linguistically diverse backgrounds. For example, the Comprehensive Support Model (Obiakor, Utley, Smith & Harris-Obiakor, 2002) requires that educators plan for the success of these pupils by analyzing various contextual factors such as government, schools, communities, and families.

In contrast to the overrepresentation of African Americans, relatively little has been written about the underrepresentation of female students in these programs. What research does exist indicates that girls are seldom referred, identified, or placed in special education programs for students with emotional or behavioral disorders (Nelson et al., 2003). One suggested explanation is that girls are much more likely to exhibit internalizing disorders such as depression or anxiety, whereas boys are more likely to display externalizing behaviors such as aggression (Cullinan, Evans, Epstein, & Ryser, 2003). Because internalizing disorders are not typically disruptive to the learning process, educators may not see the behaviors of these students (most often girls) as of serious concern and hence not refer them for special education. This means that when girls are identified, they may experience more severe problems and require more intensive intervention (Nelson et al., 2003). A related explanation is possible referral bias. Girls may be socialized to be more passive and withdrawn than boys; consequently, educators may expect girls to exhibit more "internalizing" types of behavior (Wicks-Nelson & Israel, 2006).

Technology and Individuals with Emotional or Behavioral Disorders

Numerous "low-tech" aids are available to assist educators in recording and documenting students' behavior (see Table 8.6). Another recent and exciting use of technology has been the videotaping of students' behavior and subsequent engagement of students in self-evaluating their behaviors. This strategy has shown much promise in helping students engage in more appropriate behavior in the classroom. Technology has also been integrated into behavior intervention plans as an effective reinforcer for appropriate student behavior. Students often find computers inherently reinforcing, and educators and families can capitalize on this by incorporating the use of computers into their intervention plans (White, Palmer, & Huffman, 2003).

Trends, Issues, and Controversies

Throughout this chapter, much attention has been paid to the very poor outcomes experienced by children and youth with emotional or behavioral disorders. Although the outcomes for this population are generally dismal, we begin the twenty-first century with proven strategies and practices that can greatly improve these outcomes. Professionals now have available an arsenal of primary, secondary, and tertiary intervention strategies. Despite these advances, however, many barriers remain to appropriate service provision, including (1) chronic teacher shortages, coupled with high teacher attrition rates; (2) public policy and societal attitudes that work to limit services; and (3) a lack of interagency collaboration across education and community service agencies.

Table 8.6	Using Technology with Students with Emotional or Behavioral Disorders
Examples of "Low" and "High" Technology	**Applications of Technology**
Wrist counters, golf counters, beads-in-pocket	Recording student performance—for example, task completion or in-seat behavior. Minimal disruption of teaching/learning process.
Videotaping	Applicable to diverse situations such as aggressive/disruptive behavior, social skills deficits, and attention problems. Most effective when utilized with self-management strategies and viewing demonstrations of appropriate student behavior.
Internet access	Useful as a reinforcer for exhibiting appropriate behavior; can be incorporated into a behavior intervention plan. Student has access only to approved sites.
Computer software	Learning games and instructional software programs can be used, for example, to increase on-task behavior and enhance academic learning. Also applicable as a reinforcer.

Teacher Shortages

One major barrier is the chronic shortage of qualified educators to teach students with emotional or behavioral disorders (Boe & Cook, 2006). Given the stressful challenges these students bring to school, many educators do not find job satisfaction when working with this population (Jones et al., 2004). Consequently, the recruitment and retention of teachers is very difficult, and special education teacher shortages are common throughout the United States (U.S. Department of Education, 2002). When teachers are recruited, those who work with students with emotional or behavioral disorders have the highest attrition rate of all special educators (Jones et al.). Teacher shortages combined with high attrition mean that school systems are often forced to hire under- and unqualified teachers to fill vacancies (*CEC Today*, 2001). Thus, there is an urgent need to recruit and retain well-qualified and committed teachers.

Public Policy and Societal Attitudes

Another major barrier involves political pressures, social policy, and societal attitudes regarding children and youth with emotional or behavioral disorders. Public policies, such as zero tolerance, often result in compromised service provision to students with emotional or behavioral disorders. The common societal attitude that children and youth with emotional or behavioral disorders are "throwaway" children who don't belong in public schools can be debilitating and destructive to efforts to provide appropriate services. Reconciling these policies and attitudes is an ongoing and formidable challenge, with no easy solutions.

Lack of Interagency Collaboration

"Passing the buck" is a major barrier to effective service provision. Some educators believe that it is the responsibility of other agencies to "fix the problem" of children and youth with emotional or behavioral disorders; conversely, personnel in these "other" agencies may believe that service provision is the responsibility of education because it is mandated by IDEA. Service agencies, such as mental health and social work, often are not mandated to provide services to the same extent and degree as education (Kutash et al., 2002; Warger, 2002). If the needs of students with emotional or behavioral disorders are to be met, schools and service agencies must stop this vicious cycle of passing the buck and take joint responsibility for improving the outcomes for these children.

Creating Systems of Care

Only a minority of students with emotional or behavioral disorders receive any of the mental health or social services that they and their families so desperately need, and in most instances, mental health services are provided by the schools, not mental health service agencies (Kutash et al., 2002). Even when services are available, they are usually fragmented and divorced from one another, with little or no effort to integrate and streamline efforts.

The challenge of coordinating and integrating services across a variety of agencies has recently been addressed by several federal initiatives, using a **systems of care model** (Anderson & Matthews, 2001). A system of care is defined as an integrated, community-based system that addresses the multiple domains of challenges encountered by children and youth with emotional or behavioral disorders and their families (Kutash et al., 2002).

A systems of care model necessitates that everyone involved in serving the child (including family members, educators, and agency providers from the fields of mental health, social services, juvenile justice, health services, and others) work together to provide an individually tailored and coordinated system of care for the student (Hocutt et al., 2002). Multiple agency involvement, wraparound planning, family empowerment and support, and individualized care are cardinal characteristics of this model (Duckworth et al., 2001; Kutash et al., 2002).

Chapter in Review

Defining Emotional or Behavioral Disorders

- There is no universally accepted definition of emotional or behavioral disorders.

- Terms used to describe individuals with emotional or behavioral disorders are very diversified and compounded by the variability in our understanding of what constitutes "normal" behavior.

- The current IDEA definition of **emotional disturbance** is controversial.

Classification of Individuals with Emotional or Behavioral Disorders

- **Clinically** and **statistically derived classification systems** are frequently used to classify the many different types of emotional or behavioral disorders.

- **Externalizing disorders** are sometimes referred to as "undercontrolled" behaviors, and **internalizing disorders** are sometimes referred to as "overcontrolled" behaviors.

Prevalence of Emotional or Behavioral Disorders

- Students with emotional or behavioral disorders represent an underidentified population. Currently, less than 1 percent of all pupils in public schools are recognized as having emotional or behavioral disorders.

Etiology of Emotional or Behavioral Disorders

- Most professionals believe that the development of emotional or behavioral disorders is related to both biological and psychosocial risk factors.

Prevention of Emotional or Behavioral Disorders

- **Positive behavioral support** is a schoolwide approach designed to prevent problem behaviors from occurring and, if they do occur, to intervene early to prevent escalation. It represents a proactive rather than reactive approach to dealing with problematic behaviors.

Characteristics of Children and Youth with Emotional or Behavioral Disorders

- Research indicates that pupils with emotional or behavioral disorders typically score in the low-average range on measures of intelligence.

- Perhaps the most salient characteristics of students with emotional or behavioral disorders is their difficulty in building and maintaining satisfactory relationships with peers and adults.

Assessing Students with Emotional or Behavioral Disorders

- **Person-centered planning, strength-based assessment, and functional behavioral assessment** are representative of the contemporary trends in assessment of pupils with emotional or behavioral disorders.

- A **behavioral intervention plan** is mandated by PL 108-446 for those individuals who exhibit problematic behaviors in school.

Educational Considerations

- Students with emotional or behavioral disorders are the most likely of all pupils with disabilities to be educated in self-contained classrooms or in programs outside the public school system.

- Effective management of the physical environment includes proactively addressing such areas as **time management, transition management, proximity and movement management, classroom management, and classroom ambience.**

- **Mnemonic** and **self-monitoring strategies, curriculum-based measurement,** and **content enhancements** are examples of effective academic and instructional strategies designed to assist students with emotional or behavioral disorders to access the general education curriculum.

- At the classroom level, educators can tap an array of interventions including **social skills training, interpersonal problem solving and conflict resolution,** and **crisis prevention and management programs.**

Transition into Adulthood

- Students with emotional or behavioral disorders have the highest dropout rate among all categories of pupils with disabilities.

- To improve the outcomes for both adolescents and adults with emotional or behavioral disorders, recent research suggests that **wraparound planning** and **systems of care** are necessary. These approaches incorporate a **family-centered approach** designed to actively involve the student and his or her family in planning integrated services.

Study Questions

1. Explain why each of the following factors should be taken into consideration when defining emotional or behavioral disorders:
   a. dimensions of behavior (frequency, intensity, duration, age-appropriateness)
   b. "disturbed" versus "disturbing" behavior
   c. transient nature of problematic behavior
   d. "typical" versus "atypical" behavior
   e. variability in cultural and social standards of behavior

2. Why is the federal definition of emotional disturbance controversial? How does this definition differ from the one proposed by the Mental Health and Special Education Coalition? Discuss the pros and cons of each definition.

3. Compare and contrast clinically and statistically derived classification systems. Give examples of each.

4. Define externalizing and internalizing disorders. Give an example of behaviors reflecting each of these two dimensions.

5. Describe the various conceptual models in the field of emotional or behavioral disorders.

6. List four causes of, and risk factors associated with, emotional or behavioral disorders.

7. How does a positive behavioral support model differ from traditional disciplinary methods?

8. What are some of the significant learning, social, and language/communication characteristics of children and youth with emotional or behavioral disorders?

9. List five strategies that are typically used to assess students with emotional or behavioral disorders.

10. What is a functional behavioral assessment?

11. Describe how you would use the following intervention strategies with students with emotional or behavioral disorders: social skills training; interpersonal problem solving and conflict resolution; counseling and school health services; crisis prevention and management programs.

12. How can a teacher manipulate the physical environment to assist students with and without emotional or behavioral disorders?

13. List five academic and instructional interventions that are effective with pupils with emotional or behavioral disorders.

14. Provide an argument for providing early intervention services for students who have, or who are at risk for developing, emotional or behavioral disorders.

15. What does research say about the long-term outcomes for students with emotional or behavioral disorders?

16. What issues need to be considered when planning for the transition of adolescents with emotional or behavioral disorders?

17. Why is disproportionate representation an issue for students with emotional or behavioral disorders?

18. Define the terms *wraparound planning* and *systems of care*.

Key Terms

mentally ill	externalizing disorders	time management	content enhancements
emotional or behavioral disorders	internalizing disorders	transition management	social skills training
	child maltreatment	proximity and movement management	interpersonal problem solving
Tourette's syndrome	positive behavioral support		
emotional disturbance	primary prevention	classroom arrangement	conflict resolution
socially maladjusted	secondary prevention	classroom ambience	crisis prevention and management programs
conduct disorders	tertiary prevention	effective instructional cycle	
clinically derived classification systems	person-centered planning	mnemonic strategies	wraparound plan
	strength-based assessment	self-monitoring strategies	family-centered approach
statistically derived classification systems	functional behavioral assessment	curriculum-based measurement	systems of care model
	behavioral intervention plan		

Learning Activities

1. Break into small groups to debate whether or not Mike is "socially maladjusted" as defined by the current federal definition of emotional disturbance.

2. Visit a local mental health center and interview a counselor, psychologist, or social worker. Determine the extent to which this mental health center has created linkages with the public schools.

3. Work with a group to develop a presentation on promoting resiliency among children and youth.

4. Visit a local school. Investigate the extent to which a positive behavioral support model is being implemented. Identify ways in which such a model might be integrated into the school at the primary, secondary, and tertiary levels of prevention.

5. Interview a special educator who teaches students with emotional or behavioral disorders. Ask him or her to describe the types of assessment strategies typically used with this population in the school setting.

6. Prepare a class presentation on one of the following:
   a. conduct disorder
   b. schizophrenia
   c. obsessive-compulsive disorders
   d. depression and/or suicide

Organizations Concerned with Emotional or Behavioral Disorders

Council for Children with Behavioral Disorders (CCBD), Council for Exceptional Children
1110 N. Glebe Road
Suite 300
Arlington, VA 22201-5704
(703) 620-3660

Federation of Families for Children's Mental Health
9605 Medical Center Drive
Suite 280
Rockville, MD 20850
(240) 403-1901

Mental Health America
2000 N. Beauregard Street
Sixth Floor
Alexandria, VA 22311
(703) 684-7722

American Psychological Association
750 First Street N.E.
Washington, DC 20002-4242
(800) 374-2721

American Psychiatric Association
1000 Wilson Boulevard
Suite 1825
Arlington, VA 22209-3901
(703) 907-7300

Reflecting on Standards

The following exercises are designed to help you learn to apply the Council for Exceptional Children (CEC) standards to your teaching practice. Each of the reflection exercises below correlates with a knowledge or skill within the CEC standards. For the full text of each of the related CEC standards, please refer to the standards integration grid located in Appendix B.

1. Focus on Learning Environments and Social Interactions (*CEC Content Standard #5 CC5S10*)

Reflect on what you have learned about behavior management in this book thus far. Based on what you have learned, how would you establish your classroom rules? What kinds of rules do you think are important to have in your class? How do you plan to assess which classroom rules are best suited for your particular students?

2. Focus on Instructional Planning (*CEC Content Standard #7 CC7S12*)

Reflect on a teacher you have had who used his/her instructional time in class effectively. Why was he/she effective? How did he/she schedule the instructional time in class to make things flow well? What steps do you plan to take in your instructional planning to make sure to use instructional time wisely?

Technology Resources

Visit the Web-based SAGE Study Site at **http://www.sagepub.com/gargiulo3estudy** for these additional learning tools:

- Chapter quizzes
- Key term flashcards
- Media links

- Full-text SAGE journal articles
- Internet activities
- Additional Web resources

CHAPTER 9

Individuals with Autism Spectrum Disorders

Autism from a Personal Perspective: A True Story of Beating the Odds and Winning

I would like to begin by dedicating my story to my parents, who never gave up, and to the loving memory of my grandmother, who would become a very instrumental person in my life. May her legacy live on through my words and testimony.

When I was 18 months old, a military psychiatrist diagnosed me with early childhood autism. My parents and I were living in Germany while my dad was serving in the army. My parents were told that the military could not provide any treatment or intervention, but if they found a program that I could benefit from that was located near a military base, the army would take care of relocating us. We came back to Anniston (Alabama), which is my hometown, and we lived with my grandmother for a few months until we knew what to do and where we were going. My first symptoms started with being nonverbal, rocking, sound sensitivity, and resistance to change.

However, I had some special abilities such as drawing, and I loved music. I'm also visually impaired, which has bothered me since birth but never had anything to do with autism. This was a disability I already had before. I got my first pair of glasses after I turned a year old. I no longer drive right now because of my extreme low vision. I currently use public transportation services to get around town. After coming home from Germany, my mother started taking me to see some doctors, which did little good. Some would say, "Well, he's just a baby going through some phases and he'll come out of it soon." Well, that wasn't enough for my mother. She knew there was something more wrong with me, and nobody was listening yet. I still wasn't talking yet, and I kept to myself a lot. My grandmother took this pretty hard because the last time she saw me, I was only a few months old. Now I was already walking and playing.

I have a favorite story that I would like to share. The story is about how my grandmother got me to speak my first words. This would be a pioneering example of how important early intervention is to children with disabilities. Every night when she would put me to bed, she would look at me and say,

Written by Karen Bowen Dahle, University of Alabama at Birmingham

"Say mama, say mama" at me. She would do this every night until one night I looked up at her and I said, "Mama" back to grandma. That was how I finally began talking. This was the greatest joy that my grandmother ever had, and that's how my silence was broken. I was 3 years old at the time, and this was just the beginning. After having no luck with the doctors on trying to learn more about my situation, my mother took me to the mental health center in Anniston and met with a social worker. After meeting with this person, my mother learned about the Autism Society of Alabama, and then she learned about the TEACCH program at the University of North Carolina located in Chapel Hill. We tried a few programs while living in Anniston and had no success. These programs were only experimental at the time. I recall one scenario where they had me do a task and when I didn't cooperate or understand, I got squirted with a water gun for punishment. There was another scenario where I was held down in a chair and I would be kickin' and screamin' because I didn't like the feeling of being restrained. None of these scenarios was working or providing any results, and it all seemed to be set toward punishment rather than praise.

My parents decided to move to North Carolina and have me enrolled in the TEACCH program. We moved to Fayetteville, and my father got reassigned to Fort Bragg Military Reservation. They also put me into a preschool devoted to working with children with disabilities that had ties to the TEACCH program. This program was unique and in a class by itself. I really believe it was one of the only renowned programs in the whole country to provide a different approach to autism. I would go through three and a half years of various sessions with TEACCH to help improve my language, communication, and social skills. The major emphasis was to train my parents on how to work with me and have a better understanding of autism. TEACCH stands for Treatment and Education of Autistic and related Communication handicapped CHildren. They would give my parents a variety of tasks to perform with me at home because they felt the home was a better environment to learn in rather than sending me away to an institution. We would travel to the TEACCH center once a month for progress reports and meetings, and get new home assignments. The TEACCH center was a two-hour drive from Fayetteville and is located outside of the Raleigh area. There were also times where my therapists came and worked with me in our house. They would conduct behavioral observations and give ideas and suggestions.

This was a very coordinated program between my parents, teachers, therapists, and anyone involved with me. I would like to stress that TEACCH was not a cure for autism. But it did reduce the severity, and I made a lot of progress along the way. I believe what has helped me the most is the early diagnosis and early intervention. You really have to play your part and be supportive, which proved to be crucial in my overcoming autism. Everybody was in it together and it's like a team—that's what I remember most about the program.

After leaving TEACCH, it was recommended that I be put in special education classes when I got ready to enroll in school and I would remain there until I graduated. But I made a lot more progress than anticipated. Although I was in special education classes most of my life, I did participate in regular classes and after-school programs. My high school was very helpful and supportive in making it possible for me to be a part of any program offered by my school that I desired to be involved in. I played basketball and became team manager. I also took art and speech classes, which I enjoyed very much.

After graduating high school I got involved with Vocational Rehabilitation. I spent some time in Talladega, Alabama, at E. H. Gentry Technical Facility, which is affiliated with the Alabama Institute for the Blind and Deaf, to study electronics, and then I got a computer and taught myself how to use some of the Microsoft Office programs. My efforts led me to getting a job and moving to Birmingham to live on my own and have an independent life. I have lived successfully on my own for eight years.

I'm now currently employed with the Alabama Department of Rehabilitation Services (ADRS) as a telephone operator. I've been with the agency for seven years, and it's been a very exciting time for me, with many great opportunities to get involved in. For a long time, I didn't like to talk to others about my experiences with autism because I was afraid of the prejudices and negative reactions that people might have. When I began working with ADRS, I slowly began to share my experiences with my colleagues and those fears began to diminish. I realized there was a need for firsthand perspectives about autism. With the support and courage from my friends at ADRS and the Autism Society of Alabama, I have found my courage to speak to others and be a voice of hope to our community. I have already had some great opportunities come my way, and the best is yet to come.

I also own a disc jockey business. I play at weddings, private parties, school dances, and a variety of other entertainment functions. I've had a wonderful life, and I wouldn't change a thing. If I could do it over again, I would. Learning from these experiences has prepared me for many challenges that came later in my life, and it's kept me strong during these times. I would like to thank those who have helped and supported me through it all.

—Jerimie Goike

Although most people have heard the term **autism spectrum disorders,** their perceptions may be colored by television shows and movies. For example, did you see the movie *Rain Man* or *Mercury Rising*? In these two movies, individuals with autism spectrum disorders (commonly referred to as ASD) are portrayed as possessing very special recall and mathematical skills. You may believe that all individuals with ASD possess these unique abilities. This is a common misperception; only rarely do individuals with autism spectrum disorders actually demonstrate these special skills.

In contrast to the movies, many television shows portray individuals with ASD as locked into their own world, unable to communicate or to give or receive affection. Often, it is implied that if someone could just break through their autistic isolation, there would be a genius inside. In addition, individuals with ASD are often shown as being aggressive and/or self-injurious. These are all common myths about ASD. Most individuals with autism spectrum disorders learn to speak or communicate with sign language, picture symbols, and often, assistive technology. Although their deficits may impair the way they give and receive affection, even the most severely impaired individuals with autism spectrum disorders demonstrate and accept affection from the significant people in their lives. The belief that a genius exists inside each individual with ASD is fueled by the presence of unevenly developed skills. For example, a child may be able to read fluently but may not understand a word he or she has read.

What does ASD really look like? Although all individuals with autism spectrum disorders show characteristic deficits in communication and social skills, as well as restrictive behaviors and interests, each person is unique. A wide range of behavioral symptoms associated with autism spectrum disorders include hyperactivity, short attention span, impulsivity, aggressiveness, and self-injurious behaviors. The degree to which these symptoms are demonstrated, in combination with the intellectual capability of the individual, helps to define the person's strengths and weaknesses. It is the variability of these behaviors that has resulted in professionals referring to autism as a spectrum disorder with a range of mild to severe features (National Institute of Child Health and Human Development, 2005). Despite their deficits, individuals with autism spectrum disorders can lead productive lives and can be integral parts of their family, school, and community. Students with ASD benefit from educational interventions and can learn from the adults and peers around them. Individuals with autism spectrum disorders want friends, as do their typical peers, and learn from social opportunities and community inclusion. This chapter will explore these topics in more detail, beginning with the evolution of the disorder.

Defining Autism Spectrum Disorders: An Evolving Process

Autism spectrum disorders remains one of the least understood and most mysterious of the **pervasive developmental disorders.** Although an estimated 1 million to 1.5 million people in the United States today have autism spectrum disorders or a related developmental disorder (Autism Society of America, 2007), most people have never met an individual with ASD. Therefore, it may surprise you that the prevalence rate makes ASD the fastest growing developmental disability—more common than Down syndrome. The National Institute of Child Health and Development (2005) has published the following description of autism:

> Autism is a complex neurobiological disorder of development that lasts through a person's lifetime. People with autism have problems with social interaction and communication, so they may have trouble having a conversation with you, or they may not look at you in the eye. They sometimes have behaviors that they have to do or that they do over and over, like not being able to listen until their pencils are lined up or saying the same sentences again and again. They may flap their arms to tell you they are happy, or they might hurt themselves to tell you they are not. (p. 1)

Interestingly, it was not until 1943 that Leo Kanner identified the symptoms that characterize autism. Kanner (1943/1985) described eleven children with an "inability to relate themselves in the ordinary way to people and situations" (p. 41). Kanner used the term *autistic,* which means "to escape from reality," to describe this condition. Prior to Kanner's work, individuals with autism spectrum disorders were given many labels, including childhood schizophrenia, feebleminded, idiot, mentally retarded, and imbecile. Kanner believed that these children came "into the world with innate inability to form the usual, biologically affective contact with people, just as other children come into the world with innate physical or intellectual handicaps" (p. 50). In addition, Kanner described these children as having an excellent rote memory, delays in the acquisition of speech and language (including pronoun reversals, echolalia, and extreme literalness), and an anxiously obsessive desire for the maintenance of sameness.

The word *autistic* was borrowed from a term used to describe **schizophrenia** that means a withdrawal from relationships. Kanner (1943/1985) used the term to describe an "inability to relate to themselves," and noted that the disorder starts as an "extreme autistic aloneness that, whenever possible, disregards, ignores, shuts out anything that comes to the child from outside" (p. 41). Kanner differentiated autism from schizophrenia in three areas: an extreme aloneness from the very beginning of life, an attachment to objects, and a powerful desire for aloneness and sameness.

Despite Kanner's distinction between autism and schizophrenia, for many years children with autism were described in the literature as having childhood schizophrenia, early infantile autism, or childhood onset pervasive developmental disorder. It was hypothesized that many of these children would develop schizophrenia as adults, which clinicians now know is not true. The use of these terms added to the diagnostic confusion and lack of understanding regarding ASD.

A lot has changed in the field since 1943. Clinicians now have specific criteria that define autism, described in the most recent edition of the *Diagnostic and Statistical Manual of Mental Disorders—Text Revision* (DSM-IV-TR) (American Psychiatric Association, 2000). Despite the fact that families of children with autism spectrum disorders frequently experience chronic stress (Tunali & Powers, 2002), research has failed to support bad parenting as the cause of ASD. It is now accepted that ASD is a complex medical disorder in which genetic, environmental, and neurological causes are all implicated. Professionals have made many advances in treatment, which can positively affect the lives of individuals with autism spectrum disorders. However, researchers have still not found a cure.

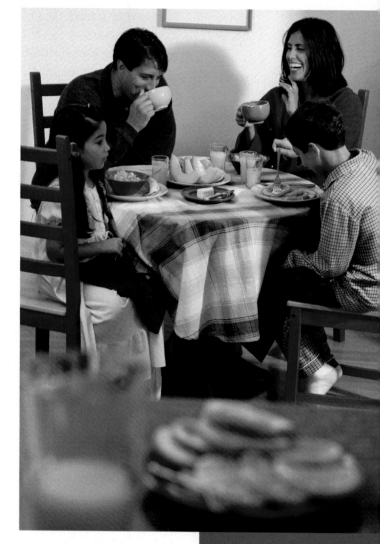

Professionals no longer believe that poor parenting causes autism spectrum disorders.

Classification of Individuals with Autism Spectrum Disorders

Classifying people by diagnostic categories can be unfortunate to the extent that it masks an individual's unique identity. Rather than homogeneous entities, diagnostic categories should be seen as guidelines for understanding the heterogeneity of individuals.

Following is a review of two of the diagnostic systems used most frequently to identify and classify ASD and other developmental disorders. These are the DSM-IV-TR (American Psychiatric Association, 2000) and the Individuals with Disabilities Education Improvement Act of 2004, PL 108-446.

Although medical tests cannot diagnose autism spectrum disorders, medical tests are helpful in ruling out specific disorders such as hearing and vision loss, and in diagnosing any associated neurological disorder such as epilepsy, Fragile X, or tuberous sclerosis. Because the characteristics and associated conditions of autism spectrum disorders vary so much, an individual should ideally be evaluated by a multidisciplinary committee that may include a neurologist, psychologist, developmental pediatrician, speech-language pathologist, and special education personnel (Dahle, 2003b).

As already mentioned, an accurate diagnosis is important in order for the individual to receive appropriate interventions and gain access to special educational services. These interventions must be customized for each student, taking into account his or her developmental status and their educational, behavioral, and psychosocial needs (Handleman & Harris, 2008; Myers & Johnson, 2007).

American Psychiatric Association and the Multiaxial System

The American Psychiatric Association (APA) periodically updates the diagnostic and statistical manual (DSM) that defines mental disorders and general medical conditions. Autism first appeared in the third edition of the DSM, published in 1977; before that time, the DSM did not recognize autism as a separate disorder. The Autism Society of America was instrumental in the inclusion of autism in the DSM-III and influenced the definition that was ultimately used (Freeman, 1999). Since 1980, autism has been included in the DSM as a pervasive developmental disorder to highlight the fact that autism is a developmental disorder of childhood, not a psychotic disorder like schizophrenia. As previously noted, individuals who fall under the pervasive developmental disorder category in the DSM-IV-TR exhibit common deficits, but differ in terms of severity. Describing an individual's condition using a **multiaxial system** allows for a more accurate presentation of the current symptoms, the associated conditions, and the severity of the disability.

Pervasive Developmental Disorders

Included in the diagnostic category of pervasive developmental disorders with autism are **Rett's disorder, childhood disintegrative disorder, Asperger syndrome,** and **pervasive developmental disorder, not otherwise specified** (PDD, NOS) (see Table 9.1).

Asperger Syndrome

In the past, individuals with "autisticlike" characteristics who were higher functioning than the typical person with ASD were not differentiated diagnostically from those with other pervasive developmental disorders. Yet, according to Klin, McPartland, and Volkmar (2005), Asperger syndrome differs from autism spectrum disorders and PDD-NOS on the basis of the pupil's ability to read at grade level (with or without comprehension) and their intellectual functioning. The distinction is not due to deficits in social-behavioral functioning or the use of pragmatic language. In fact, individuals with Asperger syndrome have no significant delay in language development (American Psychiatric Association, 2000). In contrast, motor clumsiness (Klin et al.; Williams, 2001) and sensory perceptual deficits (Dunn, Myles, & Orr, 2002) appear to be more common in individuals with Asperger syndrome.

Table 9.1	Pervasive Developmental Disorders				
	Autism	**Rett's Disorder**	**Childhood Disintegrative Disorder**	**Asperger Syndrome**	**PDD, NOS**
Age of onset	Prior to age 3	Between 5 and 48 months	After age 2 and before age 10	After age 3	Unknown
Male: female ratio	4–5 males: 1 female	Reported in females only	More common in males	More common in males	Unknown
Prevalence	2–5 per 10,000	1 in 10,000	Rare, less common than autism	Limited, but more common in males	Unknown
Communication deficits	Yes	Yes	Yes	Normal language development	May be reported
Socialization deficits	Yes	Often social interaction develops later	Yes	Yes	Yes
Repetitive and restrictive behavior	Yes	Stereotypical hand-wringing or hand washing	Yes	Yes	May be reported
Mental retardation	75% moderate to severe retardation	Severe or profound retardation	Severe mental retardation	Not typical	Retardation may or may not be present
Regression in bowel or bladder control, play, or motor skills	No	Yes	Yes	No	Not reported
Seizures	25% in adolescence	Increased frequency of EEG abnormalities and seizures	Increased frequency of EEG abnormalities and seizures	Not reported	Not reported

Note: EEG = electroencephalogram.
Source: *Diagnostic and Statistical Manual—Text Revision* (Washington, DC: American Psychiatric Association, 2000), pp. 70–84, 830.

Many times, individuals with Asperger syndrome are diagnosed later in life due to a lack of understanding of the early warning signs. Given the benefits of early intervention, it is essential for early childhood educators and special education teachers to be aware of the possible indicators of Asperger syndrome (Laramie, 2001). The presence of a cluster of these characteristics over a period of time should result in a formal referral for special education services (Dahle & Gargiulo, 2003). If found eligible for services, students with Asperger syndrome may qualify for eligibility through a multitude of classifications because Asperger syndrome is not a distinct educational category identified by IDEA 2004. Regardless of the eligibility category, most young children with Asperger syndrome will be educated in the general classroom (Gargiulo & Kilgo, 2005).

Individuals with Disabilities Education Act

Autism is one of the specific categories defined in IDEA. The 2004 amendments define autism as a

> developmental disability significantly affecting verbal and nonverbal communication and social interaction, usually evident before age 3, that adversely affects a child's educational performance. Other characteristics often associated with autism are engagement in repetitive activities and stereotyped movements, resistance to environmental change or change in daily routines, and unusual responses to sensory experiences. The term does not apply if a child's educational performance is adversely affected primarily because the child has an emotional disturbance as defined below.
>
> A child who manifests the characteristics of "autism" after age 3 could be diagnosed as having "autism" if the criteria in the preceding paragraph are satisfied. (34 CFR §300.7 (c))

The IEP committee makes a determination of a child's eligibility for special education and related services based on educational assessments, medical tests, observations, and other evaluations. Placement in the autism category depends on specific state standards.

Other Considerations for Classification

Regardless of the classification system used, autism spectrum disorders are generally described as mild, moderate, or severe depending on the cognitive and functioning level of the individual. Emerging research suggests that individuals within the spectrum may exhibit a full range of cognitive development (Edelson, 2006; Freeman & Van Dyke, 2006).

About 10 percent of individuals with ASD have special skills in areas such as mathematical calculations, memory feats, artistic and musical abilities, and reading. These individuals were originally described as "idiot savants," from the French term meaning "unlearned skill." Dr. Bernard Rimland introduced the term **autistic savant** to describe someone with these skills (Edelson, 2000). Many individuals with ASD possess unique skills such as strong visual-spatial abilities, nonverbal problem-solving skills or exceptional auditory memories that may enhance their performance in the areas of communication, academics, or behavior (National Research Council, 2001). Another example of a savant skill was shown in the popular movie *Mercury Rising,* where an individual with autism spectrum disorders demonstrated unusual skills in the area of memory and code-breaking. In comparison to these autistic savants, only 1 percent of the general population and individuals with intellectual disabilities possess these skills (Edelson).

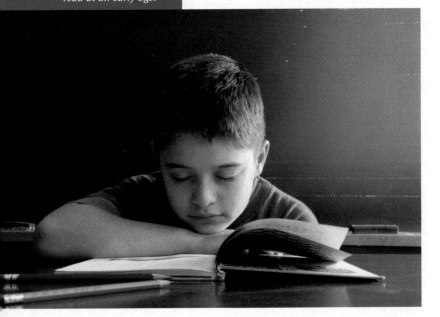

Some young children with autism spectrum disorders are able to read at an early age.

Associated Conditions

Multiple medical and psychiatric conditions associated with autism spectrum disorders include

- attention deficit hyperactivity disorder (ADHD)
- obsessive-compulsive disorder (OCD)
- tic disorders
- affective disorders
- anxiety disorders
- sleep disorders (Tsai, 2007)

Individuals with ASD also have a higher risk for seizures, which supports the theories of brain involvement (Tsai, 2007). Although researchers generally agree that autism spectrum disorders are associated with other medical conditions, there is confusion about the extent and nature of coexisting neurobiological influences (Rutter, 1994).

A Brief History of the Field[1]

The field of autism has continued to grow since Kanner (1943/1985) identified the first eleven children with autism. You will read about some of the early researchers in the field and early theories on the causation of autism. In addition, the evolution of the understanding of the biological causes of autism will be introduced through the work of current researchers.

Psychogenic Theories

Following Kanner's initial research on autism, many researchers focused on inappropriate or bad parenting as a cause of autism. Rank (1949) blamed "bad mothering" and emphasized deviant maternal characteristics. These theories, known as **psychogenic theories** of autism, were embraced by Freudian therapists. They believed that if certain basic psychological bonds were not established between parent and child, the child would not be able to establish relationships with others and would fail to progress. Individual psychotherapy was recommended for the child and the parents. In *The Empty Fortress: Infantile Autism and the Birth of Self* (1967), Bruno Bettelheim observed that during infancy parents direct extremely negative feelings specifically and only to the child who becomes autistic. Bettleheim's book added further blame to the parents of the individual with autism, particularly the mother.

In 1985, Bernard Rimland disputed these psychogenic theories of autism. An advocate for families with children with autism and the father of an individual with autism, Rimland reacted to the idea that parents, particularly mothers, were judged to be guilty of causing their child's autism based on a hypothesis that had not been proved. Rimland set forth nine points as evidence for the biological origins of autism that are still considered valid today. Nevertheless, the controversy over the causes of autism did not stop with Rimland's work. It was the continued research on the biological causes of autism and the advocacy of the Autism Society of America (formerly the National Society for Autistic Children founded by Bernard Rimland) that eventually quieted the psychogenic theories of causation.

---

1. We have chosen to use the term *autism* in this section of the chapter because it was the terminology of choice in earlier decades.

Organic Theories

In the 1940s and 1950s, Loretta Bender and other researchers suggested that autism may be organically based and that the mother's behavior was a reaction to the child's condition (Rutter, 1978). The high incidence of seizures in the autistic population, documented in the 1960s, continues to support an organic framework for autism (Volkmar & Nelson, 1990). Finally, the biological basis of autism was no longer in question because of its association with mental retardation (Volkmar & Pauls, 2003).

Behavioral Theories

Fester was one of the first behavioral psychologists to propose that autism was environmentally determined (LaVigna, 1985). Behavioral psychologists such as Fester believed that the child with autism was not conditioned properly by his or her parents. Fester and those who followed provided the foundation for what is known today as **applied behavior analysis (ABA).** The work of Ivar Lovaas (1993) grew out of Fester's work in behavior modification. A major impetus of Lovaas's work initially was in the area of self-injurious behavior. At first, Lovaas used forms of punishment, such as shock, to reduce self-injurious behaviors. Later, Lovaas learned that individuals with autism adapted to these forms of punishment, which did not reduce the self-injurious behaviors. Today, Lovaas no longer uses physical punishment to decrease self-injurious behaviors, although the command "no" and timeout are used with parental permission (Johnson, 1994).

Prevalence of Autism Spectrum Disorders

Autism spectrum disorder is the fastest growing developmental disability (Autism Society of America, 2007). The DSM-IV-TR (American Psychiatric Association, 2000) cites a conservative range of 2 to 5 cases per 10,000, as compared to the Autism Society of America, which cites a rate of 1 in every 150 individuals. The National Institute of Mental Health (2007) estimates a rate of 2 to 6 instances of ASD per 1,000 individuals. This projection suggests a rate of 1 in 500 to 1 in 150 children with autism spectrum disorders. The risk for ASD is four times higher in males than females (Hyman & Towbin, 2007). Regardless of the data sources, the number of persons with ASD is on the rise.

Recent statistics compiled by the U.S. government indicate that approximately 194,000 pupils ages 6–21 were identified as having autism in the 2005–2006 school year (U.S. Department of Education, 2007). Data about individuals with autism were first reported in the 1991–1992 school year. Since that time, the number of pupils receiving a special education because of autism and related pervasive developmental disorders has increased about 1800 percent (U.S. Department of Education, 2006).

There are currently almost 30,300 preschoolers identified with autism as their primary disability. This number represents 4.3 percent of all youngsters with a disability (U.S. Department of Education, 2007).

The National Institutes of Health has declared autism as a national health problem because of the number of individuals with autism that are being identified and the associated financial costs of dealing with this disability (Italia, 2007). The reported incidence of autism spectrum disorders and autisticlike behaviors is on the rise for several reasons. First, clinicians are evaluating and diagnosing individuals more accurately, including individuals with milder forms of the disability that would have gone undiagnosed previously. Second, as a result of advances in medicine, more babies are surviving that would have died fifty years ago when Kanner first brought autism to the attention of clinicians. Third, special education legislation has mandated early intervention and specialized services, bringing more individuals with ASD to the attention of the public schools. In addition, IDEA added a separate category for autism; individuals that were previously labeled as mentally retarded, learning disabled, or emotionally disturbed are now being properly identified as having autism. Finally, the different diagnostic criteria that were used to identify autism until the publication of the DSM-III in 1977 may also account for the increasing prevalence data.

Etiology of Autism Spectrum Disorders

The etiology of autism spectrum disorders is complex; in most cases, the underlying pathologic mechanisms are unknown. Autism spectrum disorders are heterogeneous disorders, often diagnosed retrospectively based on the existence or absence of specific characteristics. Current thinking suggests that autism spectrum disorders are of neurological or biological origin. While the precise means are unknown, and it is likely that there is no single cause, genetic contributions along with abnormal brain chemistry and development are the primary suspected factors (Courchesne, 2004; National Institute of Mental Health, 2007; Santos, Coelho, & Maciel, 2006).

The evidence for a genetic contribution to autism spectrum disorders is incontrovertible, although the exact mode of transmission is still hypothesized (Ronald et al., 2006; Volkmar & Pauls, 2003). Family studies as well as studies of twins clearly support an underlying genetic vulnerability to ASD (Hyman & Towbin, 2007; Korvatska, Van de Water, Anders, & Gershwin, 2002). In a small percentage of instances, autism spectrum disorders are caused by medical conditions such as Fragile X syndrome and tuberous sclerosis (Hyman & Towbin).

Neuroimaging studies implicate structural abnormalities of the brain in individuals with ASD (Polleux & Lauder, 2004; Volkmar & Pauls, 2003). Anomalies of the cerebellum, cerebral cortex, and brain stem are just some of the regions being investigated (Akshoomoff, Pierce, & Courchesne, 2002; Haist, Adamo, Westerfield, Courchesne, & Townsend, 2005; Trottier, Srivastava, & Walker, 1999). Figure 9.1 illustrates major brain structures implicated in ASD.

Neurochemical research is focusing on neurotransmitters such as serotonin, dopamine, and epinephrine and their role in causing autism spectrum disorders (National Institute of Mental Health, 2007; Trottier et al., 1999).

Finally, a great deal of recent attention has focused on a link between vaccinating for measles, mumps, and rubella (MMR) and ASD. Empirical research does not support a causal relationship between this vaccine and the development of autism spectrum disorders (Hyman & Towbin, 2007; National Institute of Mental Health, 2007; Smeeth et al., 2004).

Scientists currently believe that autism spectrum disorders are behavioral syndromes with multiple biological etiologies (Rutter, 2005); no one variable is likely to cause ASD.

Characteristics of Individuals with Autism Spectrum Disorders

Table 9.2 (page 337) presents the DSM-IV-TR criteria for autism (American Psychiatric Association, 2000). A diagnosis of autism requires evidence that six of the twelve symptoms are present, including at least two symptoms in the social skill category and at least one symptom in each of the remaining areas.

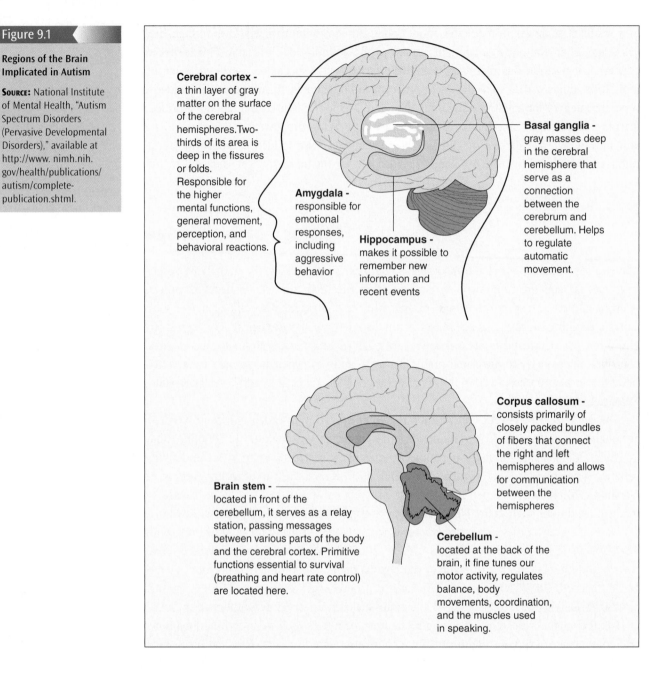

Figure 9.1

Regions of the Brain Implicated in Autism

Source: National Institute of Mental Health, "Autism Spectrum Disorders (Pervasive Developmental Disorders)," available at http://www. nimh.nih. gov/health/publications/ autism/complete-publication.shtml.

Theory of Mind

The **theory of mind** is a cognitive hypothesis that seeks to explain the inability of the individual with autism spectrum disorders to realize that other people have their own unique points of view about the world. Specifically, many individuals with ASD do not understand that others may have different thoughts, plans, and perspectives from their own (Myers & Johnson, 2007). Typically developing children appear to acquire this skill by age 4 (Astington & Barricult, 2001). Jon Paul Bovee, an adult with autism, explains how he views the theory of mind in the accompanying First Person feature.

Social Interaction Symptoms

The symptoms in the social interaction category are marked impairment in the use of multiple nonverbal behaviors (eye-to-eye gaze, facial expression, body postures and gestures),

Table 9.2	Diagnostic Criteria for Autism

A. A total of six (or more) items from (1), (2), and (3) with at least two from (1) and one each from (2) and (3):

  1. qualitative impairment in social interaction, as manifested by at least two of the following:

    a. marked impairment in the use of multiple nonverbal behaviors such as eye-to-eye gaze, facial expression, body postures, and gestures to regulate social interaction

    b. failure to develop peer relationships appropriate to developmental level

    c. a lack of spontaneous seeking to share enjoyment, interests, or achievements with other people (e.g., by a lack of showing, bringing, or pointing out objects of interest)

    d. lack of social or emotional reciprocity

  2. qualitative impairment in communication as manifested by at least one of the following:

    a. delay in or total lack of the development of spoken language (not accompanied by an attempt to compensate through alternative modes of communication such as gesture or mime)

    b. in individuals with adequate speech, marked impairment in the ability to initiate or sustain a conversation with others

    c. stereotyped and repetitive use of language or idiosyncratic language

    d. lack of varied, spontaneous make-believe play or social imitative play appropriate to developmental level

  3. restrictive repetitive and stereotyped patterns of behavior, interests, and activities as manifested by at least one of the following:

    a. encompassing preoccupation with one or more stereotyped and restricted patterns of interest that is abnormal either in intensity or focus

    b. apparently inflexible adherence to specific, nonfunctional routines or rituals

    c. stereotyped and repetitive motor mannerisms (e.g. hand or finger flapping or twisting, or complex whole-body movements)

    d. persistent preoccupation with parts of objects

B. Delays or abnormal functioning in at least one of the following areas, with onset prior to age 3 years: (1) social interaction, (2) language as used in social communication, or symbolic or imaginative play.

C. The disturbance is not better accounted for by Rett's Disorder or Childhood Disintegrative Disorder.

Source: *Diagnostic and Statistical Manual—Text Revision* (Washington, DC: American Psychiatric Association, 2000), p. 75.

First Person

Think about Thinking

People with autism do not think about setting up a theory about how we think. I think how I think, and I know that I think differently from other persons without autism. But, I do not theorize the differences between the way I think and the way that someone without autism thinks. That is not something that a person with autism would do. It is not that some of us are not capable of doing that, it is just that this would not fit the kind of thinking that people with autism would do. Theory of Mind has its validity and makes good points of what is noticeable but it needs to be fleshed out by people with autism and our thinking, experiences, and the way of life. This way, the way people with autism think will be thought of as being just as valid as the thoughts of people who do not have autism. I have autism and will always be influenced in my thinking by my experiences. I could not think any differently than I do. To assume that I would [sic] be like asking a person without autism to try to think exactly like me, to walk in my shoes. That kind of thinking would be of the utmost ubsurdity [sic].

Source: J. Bovee, "My Experiences with Autism and How It Relates to 'Theory of Mind': Part 2," *Advocate*, *32*(6), 1999, pp. 20–21.

failure to develop age-appropriate peer relationships, lack of spontaneous seeking to share interests and achievements with others, and lack of social or emotional reciprocity (see Table 9.2). Often the individual with ASD does not point or show objects of interest to others, shows little or no expressed pleasure in interaction, and lacks coordinated gaze. This person rarely or never directs appropriate facial expressions to others and does not show interest in an object or activity even when reference to the object is accompanied by pointing, facial cues, or name calling.

These symptoms are devastating to individuals with autism spectrum disorders. Carter, Davis, Klin, and Volkmar (2005) note that even the highest-functioning individuals often experience significant difficulties in developing friendships and relating to others. Individuals with ASD also have problems with social exchanges. They may fail to take social norms or the listener's feelings into account. They may rely exclusively on limited conversational strategies or stereotyped expressions, elaborating on some idiosyncratic interest or echoing a previous statement. For example, an individual with ASD may tell someone she smells whenever the person wears a particular perfume to work. Another individual may only talk to you if you talk about his favorite topic—pizza! The individual shows relatively little interest in others unless he or she needs help or responds to questions; there is little or no reciprocal social communication. An individual with these deficits will not ask you how you are feeling or seem to notice if there has been a change in mood. Social impairments in persons with autism spectrum disorders significantly affect their involvement with others in educational, vocational, and social settings (National Education Association, 2006).

A lack of appropriate social skills is a common problem among individuals with autism spectrum disorders.

Communication Symptoms

A lack of speech has long been considered a hallmark of autism spectrum disorders. In individuals with ASD who do speak, "their speech may not be functional or fluent and may lack communicative intent" (Johnson & Myers, 2007, p. 1192). Typical communication deficits include a delay in spoken language development, marked impairment in conversational skills, stereotyped and repetitive use of language, and a lack of spontaneous age-appropriate make-believe or social imitative play in addition to echolalia, or "parroting" the speech of others (American Psychiatric Association, 2000; Johnson & Myers).

The speech of individuals with ASD is clearly abnormal in rhythm, has an odd intonation or inappropriate pitch, and may sound toneless or mechanical. Deficits in the pragmatic or social use of language are also common (Volkmar & Pauls, 2003). Approximately 25 to 30 percent of youngsters with autism spectrum disorders begin to use words and then suddenly cease to speak, often between 15 and 24 months of age (Johnson & Myers, 2007).

The development of speech by age 5 or 6 is viewed as a positive sign for a good outcome (Nordin & Gillberg, 1998). Some of the early prespeech deficits that may facilitate an early diagnosis and thus early intervention include

- lack of recognition of mother's (or father's or consistent caregiver's) voice;
- disregard for vocalizations (e.g., lack of response to name), yet keen awareness of environmental sounds;
- delayed onset of babbling past 9 months of age;
- decreased or absent use of prespeech gestures (waving, pointing, showing);
- lack of expressions such as "oh oh" or "huh";
- lack of interest or response of any kind to neutral statements (e.g., "Oh no, it's raining again!"). (Johnson & Myers, 2007, p. 1192)

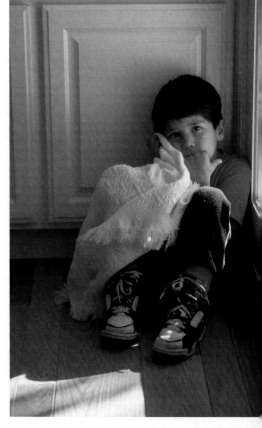

Many individuals with autism spectrum disorders engage in stereotypical and repetitive behaviors.

Repetitive and Restrictive Behaviors

Repetitive and restrictive behaviors (see Table 9.2) include preoccupation with at least one stereotyped and restricted pattern of interest to an abnormal degree, inflexible adherence to nonfunctional rituals or routines, stereotyped and repetitive motor mannerisms, and preoccupation with parts of objects. Individuals with ASD may

- play with toys in the same manner
- be rigid about routines or object placements
- eat few foods or only foods with a certain texture
- smell food
- be insensitive to pain
- be unaware of danger
- show unusual attachment to inanimate objects
- exhibit repeated body movements (hand flapping, rocking, finger licking)

Many professionals are now considering whether these actions represent a distinct diagnostic category or are manifestations of coexisting psychiatric disorders such as attention deficit hyperactivity disorder or obsessive-compulsive disorder (Johnson & Myers, 2007; Tsai, 2007). If so, this may explain why some individuals receive various diagnoses prior to being identified as having autism spectrum disorder.

Other Characteristics

In addition to the three primary characteristics of autism spectrum disorders, symptoms that can co-occur include problems with concentration, attention, and activity level; anxiety disorders; affective or mood disorders; and learning difficulties. These behaviors are briefly summarized in Table 9.3.

Assessment of Autism Spectrum Disorders

The assessment of an individual with autism spectrum disorders is confounded by the fact that the very behaviors necessary for proper testing—the ability to sit still, pay attention, follow directions, and respond verbally—are often difficult for the individual with ASD. Some professionals believe that these deficits render persons with ASD untestable, and generally disregard the results of formal cognitive and achievement tests. However, most researchers believe that intellectual assessments and achievement tests can be administered effectively and used in planning programs for individuals with ASD. Behavioral assessments and rating scales can generate additional information about the individual with autism spectrum disorders, without the problems associated with a formal testing situation.

Intellectual Assessment

One of the common myths about autism spectrum disorders is that inside each child is a genius. This myth may have arisen because of the uneven nature of their skills, often

Table 9.3	Associated Characteristics of Individuals with Autism Spectrum Disorders
Areas of Concern	**Behaviors**
Concentration and Attention	• Hyperactivity • Short attention span • Impulsivity
Anxiety Disorders	• Self-injurious behaviors • Excessive scratching or rubbing • Limiting diet to a few foods • Eating nonedible items (pica) • Obsessive-compulsive disorders
Affective Disorders	• Abnormalities of mood or affect (giggling or crying for no apparent reason) • Sleeping problems (difficulties falling asleep, frequent awakening, early morning awakening) • Bed-wetting • Depression, suicidal ideation
Learning Difficulties	• Uneven achievement • Impaired executive functioning • Poor reading comprehension • Inadequate receptive/expressive language skills

FYI . . .

Examples of "Splinter Skills"

John noticed the sequence of numbers as he turned the pages of books (usually cookbooks illustrated with colored photographs of food). Soon he was writing the numbers on walls or on a chalkboard. From the car speedometer, he learned how to count by tens. From the binding on a set of books, he learned Roman numerals.

Numbers meant so much to him that if one was missing from the pages of a book it caused him to cry, but he resolved his unhappiness by writing in the number by hand. In instances where a publisher had inserted pages of illustrations in a book without numbering them in sequence with the pages of the text, John wrote numbers in by hand and then renumbered the pages of the text to keep the sequence correct.

If page 1 was preceded by unnumbered introductory pages, he numbered backwards into the numbers below zero. If lowercase Roman numerals were used in the introductory pages of a book, he would write in negative Roman numerals, numbering backward until he came to the front cover.

All this was before he learned to talk . . .

Barry amazed people because at 7 months he was echoing sounds from the TV set. By the time he was a year-and-a-half old, he could recite from memory substantial passages from phonograph records, and he knew his ABCs. Barry's accomplishments of rote memory were not matched by conceptual understanding, however. It took years of work when he was a school-age child to learn the meaning of such concepts as up and down and above and below. It wasn't until he was past the age of 8 that he began to be able to speak his own thoughts. Developing that ability was a long, slow process. The realization that the image in photos and in the mirror was himself did not come until he was more than 10 years old.

Source: B. Sposato, *A Little about Autism and Some People Who Are Autistic* (Nebraska Chapter of the National Society for Children and Adults with Autism, 1986), pp. 1–3.

referred to as "splinter" skills (see the accompanying FYI feature). Despite these unusual abilities, many individuals with ASD exhibit significant cognitive deficits (Bowler, 2006; Hyman & Towbin, 2007; Shea & Mesibov, 2005). The exact prevalence, however, of intellectual disabilities in persons with autism spectrum disorders is somewhat controversial (Edelson, 2006).

For all individuals with ASD, we know that the severity of the symptoms affects the individual's overall level of functioning, particularly in the areas of language and social skills. What is most important is not the individual's IQ, but his or her ability to function independently in society. Nevertheless, intellectual assessments are important components in determining an individual's eligibility for special education services, in making psychiatric diagnoses, and often in placement for group homes or vocational settings. Therefore, tests measuring intellectual ability as well as checklists assessing adaptive levels of functioning are typically administered as part of an overall assessment battery.

Screening and Diagnosis

There is no specific test to diagnose autism spectrum disorders. Physicians look for behavioral symptoms to make a diagnosis. These symptoms may be noticeable within the first few months of life, or they may appear any time prior to age 3. In some instances, it is not unusual to find characteristics being recognized later primarily because they were likely confused with the symptoms of other disorders.

In the past decade, researchers have identified several characteristics that are helpful in making an early diagnosis of ASD. It has been shown that a diagnosis of autism spectrum disorders at age two is reliable, valid, and stable (Lord et al., 2006).

The diagnosis of ASD should include two steps. The first step is a developmental screening (a brief assessment designed to identify youngsters who should receive a more thorough evaluation) and surveillance (a process whereby healthcare professionals monitor children who may have a developmental disability). It is recommended that screening tests be given to *all* children during their 9-, 18-, 24-, or 30-month well-child visits. Additional screening is warranted if the youngster is at high risk (for example, has a sibling or parent with ASD) or presents characteristics suggestive of autism spectrum disorders.

The second step in the diagnostic process is a comprehensive evaluation by a team of professionals. Typical evaluations include clinical and educational observations, caregiver interviews, developmental histories, psychological testing, speech-language assessments, and possibly one or more diagnostic scales. Because ASD is a complex disorder, neurological and genetic testing may be appropriate.

Many instruments have been developed for assessment of autism spectrum disorders, yet no single tool should be used for diagnosing ASD. Diagnostic instruments typically rely on caregivers' descriptions of the child's development as well as direct observation of the individual in both structured and unstructured situations. The "gold standards" of diagnostic assessments include the Autism Diagnostic Observation Schedule (ADOS) (Lord et al., 1989) and the Autism Diagnostic Interview—Revised (ADI-R) (Lord, Rutter, & Le Couteur, 1994). The ADOS is a focused interaction with the individual with ASD, which is balanced by parental concerns as reflected in the ADI-R interview. The findings offer a description of the characteristics of the individual and the consistency of the symptoms with the features identified by the American Psychiatric Association (1994). (See Table 9.2.)

SCREENING FOR ASPERGER SYNDROME Until recently, screening instruments often did not identify children with mild ASD, such as those youngsters with more functional adaptive skills, intellectual flexibility, or Asperger syndrome. Today, however, the Autism Spectrum Screening Questionnaire (Ehlers, Gillberg, & Wing, 1999) and the Childhood Asperger Syndrome Test (Williams et al., 2005) provide a reliable means for identifying school-age children with Asperger syndrome or milder forms of ASD. These two tools focus on social and behavioral impairments in children without significant language delays.

Educational Considerations

Where Are Individuals with Autism Spectrum Disorders Educated?

During the 2005–2006 school year, about four out of every ten (39.8%) school-age students with ASD received services in a self-contained classroom; almost one-third (31.2%) were assigned to the general education classroom (U.S. Department of Education, 2007). Figure 9.2 profiles where pupils with autism spectrum disorders receive a special education. It is interesting to note that nearly twice as many individuals with ASD are educated in a resource room as compared to students receiving services in a separate school.

Separate class
39.8%

Regular classroom
31.2%

Homebound/hospital
0.45%

Resource room 18.2%

Residential facility 0.73%

Separate
school 9.5%

Figure 9.2

Educational Placement of Students with Autism Spectrum Disorders

Note: Figure represents percentages of enrollment of students with autism during the 2005–2006 school year.

Source: U.S. Department of Education. (2007). *IDEA data.* Available at https://www.ideadata.org/PartBReport.asp.

Instructional Approaches

Individuals with autism spectrum disorders are a very heterogeneous population. These students typically require a diversity of educational interventions and teaching strategies. It is well documented that effective instructional approaches are structured, predictable, and geared to the person's level of functioning (Autism Society of America, 2007). Most individuals with ASD demonstrate appropriate behaviors in structured rather than in unstructured situations, and special education programs with more structure are generally associated with better outcomes.

Generally speaking, the most effective programs for pupils with autism spectrum disorders are those that begin early, are intensive, and are multidisciplinary (Hume, Bellini, & Pratt, 2005; Hyman & Towbin, 2007). Many of these programs incorporate evidence-based practices, use principles of applied behavior analysis, or rely on structured teaching methodologies. Surprisingly, there is a paucity of research identifying best practice interventions (Autism Society of America, 2007; National Research Council, 2001).

Although no one instructional approach is effective with all students with autism spectrum disorders (Autism Society of America, 2007; Smith, Polloway, Patton, & Dowdy, 2008), an emphasis on developing functional communication abilities and appropriate social skills is characteristic of most approaches. For other pupils with ASD, their individualized educational programs might focus on self-help skills along with functional academics. In most instances, the various instructional interventions aim to maximize the individual's independence and future integration in the community. Refer to the Suggestions for the Classroom feature for additional tips for teaching high-functioning students with autism spectrum disorders.

Among the various instructional approaches available to teachers, applied behavior analysis (ABA) is widely accepted as an effective strategy (National Institute of Mental Health, 2007). Applied behavior analysis is based on the premise that responses that are reinforced are more likely to occur again than are responses that are ignored (Alberto & Troutman, 2006). Therefore, learning can be shaped by reinforcement. ABA programs are intensive, structured teaching programs that use a variety of behavior modification techniques. ABA provided the foundation for the early successful work of Lovaas (1987) with preschoolers with autism spectrum disorders.

An example of another long-standing and successful instructional intervention is Project TEACCH (Treatment and Education of Autistic and related Communication-handicapped Children). This model involves the use of structured teaching and collaboration between caregivers and teachers. Project TEACCH emphasizes predictability, organization of the physical environment, and visually structured activities (Mesibov, Shea, & Schopler, 2005).

Regardless of the approach used, effective instructional programs for pupils with autism spectrum disorders build on the child's strengths while also focusing on the child's areas of interest.

(*Text continues on page 348*)

Suggestions for the Classroom

Tips for Teaching High-Functioning Individuals with Autism Spectrum Disorders

☑ **Avoid abstract ideas whenever possible.** Individuals with autism spectrum disorders frequently have problems with abstract and conceptual thinking. While some students may eventually acquire a few abstract skills, others never will. When abstract concepts must be used, use visual cues, such as gestures or written words, to augment the abstract ideas.

☑ **Avoid speech students might misinterpret.** Most high-functioning people with autism spectrum disorders use and interpret speech literally. Until you know the capabilities of the individual, it is recommended that you avoid
  - Idioms (save your breath, jump the gun, second thoughts, etc.)
  - Double meanings (most jokes have double meanings)
  - Sarcasm, such as saying, "Great!" after someone has just spilled a soft drink all over the table
  - Nicknames

☑ **Break down tasks.** If a pupil doesn't appear capable of learning a task, break it down into smaller steps, or present the task in several different ways (e.g., visually, verbally, or physically).

☑ **Assist students with organizational skills.** Individuals with autism spectrum disorders often have difficulty with organizational skills, regardless of their intelligence and/or age. Even a "straight A" student with autism spectrum disorders who has a photographic memory can sometimes be incapable of remembering to bring a pencil to class or remembering a deadline for an assignment. In such cases, assistance should be provided in the least intrusive way possible. Strategies could include putting a picture of a pencil on the cover of the student's notebook or reminders at the end of the day of assignments that are to be completed at home. Always praise the pupil when she remembers something she has previously forgotten.

☑ **Prepare students for change.** It is important to prepare the student for all unexpected changes, such as an assembly, a substitute teacher, rescheduling of classes, and so forth. Use a written or visual schedule to prepare for change.

☑ **Make adjustments for auditory and visual distractions.** Be aware that normal levels of auditory and visual input can be perceived by individuals with autism spectrum disorders as too much or too little. For example, the hum of fluorescent lighting is extremely distracting for some people with autism spectrum disorders. Consider environmental changes, such as removing some of the visual clutter from the room, or seating changes if the student seems distracted or upset by his or her classroom environment.

☑ **Facilitate group work.** If a class activity involves pairing off or choosing partners, draw numbers or use some other arbitrary means of pairing. You could also ask a class leader whether he or she would agree to choose the individual with autism spectrum disorders as a partner. This should be arranged prior to pairing. The pupil with autism spectrum disorders is most often the individual left with no partner. This is unfortunate because this student could benefit most from having a partner.

☑ Most importantly, be positive, be creative, and, most of all, be flexible!

SOURCE: Adapted from S. Moreno, "Tips for Teaching High-Functioning People with Autism." Available at http://maapservices.org/Tips_For_Teaching.asp. Used by permission.

✔ EFFECTIVE INSTRUCTIONAL PRACTICES | Social Stories

Students with autism spectrum disorders typically experience difficulty interpreting social situations. These individuals are frequently unable to accurately assess and respond to various social, behavioral, and environmental cues. Social stories represent a relatively recent and increasingly popular strategy for ameliorating these deficits and, in turn, enhancing the social skills of students with autism spectrum disorders. This intervention technique is also particularly helpful in facilitating the integration of pupils with ASD in inclusive learning environments.

A social story is an individually designed story aimed at increasing the individual's awareness and understanding of social situations and the perspectives of others while teaching appropriate responses and self-management techniques.

Researchers have identified the basic steps necessary for developing a social story:

1. Target a specific problematic social situation
2. Identify salient features of context and setting
3. Share this information with the individual and others

The following is an example of a social story that is designed to explain to a student when it is appropriate to run at school:

Running

I like to run. It is fun to go fast.
It is okay to run when I am playing outside.
I can run when I am on the playground.
I can run during P.E.
It is not okay to run when I am inside, especially at school.
Running in the hallways is not safe.
Teachers worry that someone may get hurt if I run into them.
When people are inside, they walk.
I will try to walk in the hallways and only run when I am outside on the playground.

Writing a Social Story

Begin by observing the student in the situation you hope to address. Let the pupil's perspective tell you which aspects of the situation should be the focus of the story. Include those things that usually occur in the social situation, but also consider possible variations.

There are three types of sentences used in writing social stories:

- *Descriptive* sentences objectively define where a situation occurs, who is involved, what that person is doing, and why.
- *Perspective* sentences describe the reactions and feelings of others in a given situation.
- *Directive* sentences are positively stated, individualized statements of desired responses. They may begin with "I can try . . ." or "I will work on . . . ." Try to avoid sentences starting with "Do not." In the above example, the final sentence is the directive sentence.

A social story needs to have three to five descriptive and perspective sentences for each directive sentence. Avoid using too many directive sentences. They will be lost without adequate contextualization.

Presenting a Social Story

Customize the language and the presentation to students' abilities. Young children and nonreaders will need pictures to accompany the story. The pictures need to be very simple and very specific. Delete extraneous details and backgrounds. These children will also require larger fonts and less information on each page. A storybook is a good idea. For older pupils and readers, the story can be presented on one page. Alternatively, each sentence can be mounted on black construction paper and bound in book format.

Present the story in a calm, stress-free environment. Be consistent. Present the story once each day, preferably right before the particular event. Once the story is mastered and the individual has incorporated it into his or her social repertoire, slowly decrease its use.

The empirical evidence on the effectiveness of social stories is growing. The support to date, however, does not yet warrant the label validated or evidence-based practice.

Source: Adapted from F. Sansosti, K. Powell-Smith, and D. Kincaid, "A Research Synthesis of Social Story Interventions for Children with Autism Spectrum Disorders," *Focus on Autism and Other Developmental Disorders, 19*(4), 2004, pp. 194–204. "Social Stories," Center for Autism and Related Disabilities, University of Florida. Retrieved January 15, 2008 from http://www.card.ufl.edu/socialstories.htm

Making Inclusion Work

Working with children with autism spectrum disorders is often like riding a roller coaster without a seat belt—you never know what will be around the next corner or if the next bump will dump you out of the car. I have found that no two children and no two days are the same where ASD is involved. The needs of our children change on a daily, sometimes hourly, basis. Striving to meet these needs (sensory, anxiety, and food based) and provide an education is a full-time job. In my classroom there are five adults and ten children ages 5–11. Most of the children are included in the general education setting for some part of their day. Next year four of our kindergartners and I will take on the challenge of full inclusion for the first time in our county.

Inclusive Education Experience

I find the most difficult challenge facing my students is a fear of autism spectrum disorders. Most general education teachers have no experience with ASD; their only reference is the movie *Rain Man*. Many teachers will refuse to work with my students simply because of their label. To dispel this fear I arrange for my students to meet with their general education teachers in the week before school starts. This gives the teacher and the child a chance to check each other out. The teachers can see that this student is just a kid, a little odd sometimes, but nothing scary. This also gives the students a chance to see their new room and new teacher before the chaos of the first day. It gives them a reference point to start the year.

When I begin a year with a new teacher, I provide him or her with information about ASD, samples of the child's work, appropriate modifications, and the student's present level of performance. Then we meet over lunch or a snack during the week before school starts and discuss the student. Once teachers put a face to the child's name they tend to be less afraid of the "autism" part of the experience.

Currently all of my students receive constant support in the general education setting (an aide or myself), and this seems to help the general education teachers feel more comfortable. Sometimes students will need to leave the room because of behavioral outbursts or breakdowns. Many teachers outside of special education do not feel qualified to handle these situations. I try to model the appropriate responses and encourage the other teachers to ask me questions. Prior to the school year I make emergency plans with the IEP team for each child. During our planning sessions I tell everyone that no one should attempt to restrain a child if they have not been trained. I take responsibility in most emergency situations.

When providing students with sensory strategies in the general education setting, I take into account how distracting the item will be. Sensory strategies should be discussed prior to implementation. General education teachers might not understand the importance of an item and take it away because it is a toy or the child is fidgeting. Strategies used within the general education setting should be discrete and small. Sometimes it is necessary to go in and explain the importance of a sensory item to the other students in the classroom. I have found that doing this eliminates the "I want what he has" battles.

I also provide an inservice for teachers in our county on autism spectrum disorders. This is a great way to reach a wider audience and help teachers who are not in my school. Offering experiences like this helps teachers become more comfortable with the disability. I encourage all of the teachers I work with to attend and was happy to have several general education teachers from other schools participate. Providing learning experiences like this is a good way to bridge the gap between general and special education.

My students will be in the school system for at least 12 years. Their needs and cognitive skills will change over time; some of our boys will be in general education classes with no support by the time they reach the fifth grade. Part of my job as a special educator is to educate my colleagues about the disorder. If we are to advocate for the rights of our students, we have to educate the general population. Autism spectrum disorders are nothing to be afraid of.

Strategies for Inclusive Classrooms

- Bring models of modifications and accommodations to planning sessions—for example, a visual schedule, a test with a word bank. It is more effective to be able to show someone what you are suggesting.
- Provide brief articles about ASD to those teachers who are interested in learning more about the disability.
- Make sure fidgets and other small sensory items meet the students' needs without disrupting the rest of the class.
- Let other students try out the sensory items you bring in.
- Meet with the general education teachers as much as possible and let them know they can ask you to help prepare general lessons as well as modified lessons.
- Constantly assess the success of your students in the general education setting.
- Data are extremely important. Carry a clipboard or sticky notes. You should be able to back up any statement you make about your students.
- Provide social skills training for the students outside the general education setting. It may embarrass students to have social skills lessons with their peers. Sometimes it is better to practice the lesson outside the room and then bring it into the classroom.
- It is imperative to share the responsibilities of the classroom for inclusion to work. The students need to be a shared responsibility; there should be no "my" students and "your" students. Let the teacher know that you are there for all students.

Working with Parents and Families

In the field of autism spectrum disorders, working with the parents is essential to success. I often go on home visits with the younger students. This way I can model the responses to certain outbursts or inappropriate behavior. I have also gone to restaurants and grocery stores with the families to model behaviors. I have found that it is more successful to model than to just tell a parent what to do.

It is also important for the parents to become familiar with the general education teacher and classroom. In an inclusive program the parents should feel comfortable talking to the general education teacher as well as the special education teacher. When the special education teacher serves as a go-between (with parents and other teachers), communication breaks down. Parent–teacher conferences should be held with all the members of the team and not just one teacher. It is important to have the parents support each other. We started a parent support group this year. This provided the parents with someone other than me to turn to with questions and problems. I began it at the beginning of school and then a parent took over. Parents need to talk to each other and compare experiences; having a child with such an intense disability can sometimes make parents feel isolated and helpless.

Special education teachers should familiarize themselves with the local resources for parents and families. Social services, food banks, and local agencies can be excellent resources. However, many families are too overwhelmed and do not know where to look for outside help.

Advice for Making Inclusion and Collaboration Work

My advice would be to always remember that kids are kids. A disability is only part of a child, and while it may shape most of their world, they are still kids. They still need love and support. You as the teacher need to know how to provide these things to your students and still encourage academic growth. Learn about the disability as much as possible, but learn everything about the kids.

—Sarah Reynolds
Leslie Fox Keyser
Elementary School, Warren County, VA
Kindergarten–fifth grade, children with autism

Services for Young Children with Autism Spectrum Disorders

There is no known cure for autism spectrum disorders, but developmentally appropriate educational programming in the early years can play a significant role in enhancing functioning in later life (Hume et al., 2005; Harris, Handleman, & Jenett, 2005). Identifying and diagnosing ASD early can provide access to appropriate services that result in a better prognosis (Autism Society of America, 2007). In addition to receiving appropriate services, another goal of early intervention services is to decrease the need for restrictive placements in the future (Gargiulo & Kilgo, 2005).

Early Intervention Services

Federal law mandates services for young children with disabilities, including evaluation, assessment, and treatment. Early intervention services, tailored to the individual's needs, typically include a structured educational and behavioral approach with related and specialized services. These related and specialized services, delivered through a collaboration of agency delivery providers, may include

- assistive technology and services
- school nursing services
- parent counseling and training
- nutrition services
- artistic and cultural programs—art, music, and dance therapy
- occupational therapy
- speech and language therapy

Early intervention for a child with autism spectrum disorders begins with the development of an individualized family service plan (IFSP), which typically addresses needs in the areas of social skills, functional skills (dressing, toilet training, self-feeding), communication, and behavior modification (Autism Society of America, 2000). No one program is applicable to all children with ASD; the strengths and needs of each child must be considered in the development of a specific educational plan.

Communication Deficits and Safety Issues

Many preschool children with autism spectrum disorders lack even the most basic communication skills. They may not come when they are called, may not recognize their name, may have no idea of the notion of carrying out an activity upon either verbal or nonverbal request, and may have no concept of "First you do this, and then this happens." Safety also becomes an issue, as preschool children with ASD are able to run, open doors, and climb, but do not come when called, understand "no," or comprehend the possible dangers of busy streets or getting lost. On the other hand, very young children with autism spectrum disorders can be carried, cuddled, and cajoled in ways that would not be appropriate for an older child.

Curriculum Issues

In planning for preschool children versus older children with ASD, the curriculum is usually less well defined. Even structured teaching needs special adaptation at the preschool level because of the behaviors that are targeted. Behavioral models provide useful starting points for establishing control of young children's attention and reducing interfering behaviors. However, it is important to teach both communication and social skills as part of the overall program. Classroom adaptations for preschoolers with autism spectrum disorders are an important component for ensuring academic success (Dahle, 2003a).

Preschool Programs

Multiple types of programs are available for preschool children with autism spectrum disorders. We believe, like Myers and Johnson (2007), that a healthy skepticism is called for in evaluating intervention programs, especially those that promise to ameliorate the symptoms of ASD. Substantial research continues to support behavioral treatment as producing long-lasting and significant gains for many young children with autism spectrum disorders (Myers & Johnson). The National Academy of Sciences (2002), in addition to the American Academy of Pediatrics (2001), recommends a minimum of 25 hours every week of educational services.

Transition into Adulthood

As adolescents with autism spectrum disorders grow into adults, they face the same developmental, psychological, social, and sexual issues as their nondisabled peers. However, their ability to deal with these issues is confounded by their unresolved communication, behavior, and social deficits. While adolescents with ASD may show a greater interest in other people, many still lack the most fundamental skills to form friendships. Unfortunately, as their interest in others increases, their opportunities for structured social interactions decreases as they transition from educational programs. Opportunities to participate in community programs are often limited by the individual's lack of leisure and recreational skills, the limited availability of programs, and by the lack of appropriate structure in the available programs.

IDEA 2004 requires that school personnel assist the family with planning for transition from school beginning at age 16. (See the accompanying FYI feature). It is important that both families and school personnel begin the transition planning as early as possible to address the myriad problems that confront adolescents with autism spectrum disorders.

Transition planning is a process that includes the individual, the family, and community agencies. These coordinated activities must be based on the individual's needs, taking into account the student's preferences and interests. Activities may include instruction in daily living skills, exposure to community experiences, the development of objectives for employment, and functional vocational evaluation. Interagency collaboration is vital to the transition plan to ensure that the family has both knowledge and access to the services offered in their community.

FYI...

Transition Planning: Questions to Address

When thinking about transition from high school, sometimes it is helpful to start the process with a list of questions to act as a springboard for discussion. Below is a list of questions composed by a mother whose son has autism spectrum disorders. Some parents like to hold family meetings with siblings and the individual with ASD so that they can all share in the planning. You may want to share this list with the parents you work with to help them start planning for their child's transition.

- What does your child like to do?
- What can your child do?
- What does your child need to explore?
- What does your child need to learn to reach his or her goals?
- What about college (four year, community), vocational education, or adult education?
- How about getting a job (competitive or supportive)?
- Where can your child go to find employment and training services?
- What transportation will your child use?
- Where will your child live?
- How will your child make ends meet?
- Where will your child get health insurance?

Many people think of adulthood in terms of getting a job and living in a particular area, but having friends and a sense of belonging in a community are also important. To address these areas, a few additional questions have been added:

- What about friendship? Are supports needed to encourage friendships?
- Do people in the community know your son or daughter?
- Are supports needed to structure time for recreation? Exercise?
- Does your child have any special interests that others may share as a hobby?
- Can you explore avenues for socializing such as religious affiliation or volunteer work?

It is also important that the transition process involves taking action. After identifying areas of interests and setting goals, one must take some active steps to meet those goals. For example, a student with autism spectrum disorders with particularly sharp computer skills is dismissed from school early a few days a week to work with an aide at a data processing office. This position was acquired through the vocational rehabilitation office and they continue to provide needed support. Before beginning this job, the student was taught appropriate office social skills and important office procedures such as using a time clock.

Another student who prefers to be outdoors is more suited to work with a community clean-up project than in an office. Again, this emphasizes the need to develop a plan tailored to each individual's skills and preferences. Many professionals and families believe that three or four different experiences can be helpful in assessing a student's desires and capabilities while he is still in high school. The bottom line for all students is to prepare them for their lives after high school, whether that involves employment or further education.

Source: Adapted from Autism Society of America, *Thinking About Transition*. (2007). Available at http://www.autism-society.org/site/PageServer?pagename=about_lwa_highschool

Adults with Autism Spectrum Disorders

The majority of individuals with autism spectrum disorders are not able to either live or work independently as adults. Although symptoms may decrease with age, adults with ASD continue to manifest socially or psychiatrically inappropriate behaviors throughout life, along with markedly restricted interests and activities (Nordin & Gillberg, 1998). About one-third of adults with autism spectrum disorders are able to achieve some degree of partial independence (American Psychiatric Association, 2000). Included in this group are adults whose deficits are so mild that their disorder may go undetected and unreported until adulthood.

For those individuals who are not able to live independently, families—and the individual, if capable—have many decisions to make, ranging from day treatment programs to residential care placements to employment options. Residential care may include traditional institutional and group home settings, as well as supervised apartment living. As adults with autism spectrum disorders age, their families often become unable to care for them, particularly if aggressive or self-injurious behaviors are present. Parents also worry about their adult child's future when the family is no longer there to provide care. The most common residential and employment options are reviewed here.

Some adults with autism spectrum disorders live in group homes located in residential neighborhoods.

Supervised Group and Apartment Living

Some adults with autism spectrum disorders are able to live independently with support services from community agencies. Services usually involve helping problem-solve issues such as money management, medication management, transportation, and assisting individuals in interacting within their communities.

Supervised group homes are usually located in a residential setting. The homes are staffed with trained professionals who assist the residents based on their individual level of need. Typically, residents participate in sheltered workshops, supported employment, or day treatment programs. In the evenings, staff members assist residents with their personal care, housekeeping, and meal preparation, and implement behavior management programs.

A supervised apartment may be the choice for an individual who would prefer to live with fewer people but still requires some supervision and assistance. A staff person usually checks on the resident intermittently and provides agreed-upon services. These resources and supports may include

- home helpers to assist with household duties
- case managers to help locate and coordinate various services
- financial assistance to help with extra costs such as medical services
- adaptive equipment, counseling, or necessary home modifications

Adult Foster Care

Adult foster care is another option for individuals with autism spectrum disorders. Sometimes the person with ASD puts so many demands on the family that living at home is no longer a feasible option. In foster care, the individual lives permanently in another home with the members of that family. The family may or may not receive specialized training in caring for an adult with autism spectrum disorders. The families that agree to foster care receive government funding to assist in the care of the individual.

Residential Services

Existing residential services for adults with autism spectrum disorders vary in size, location, and source of funding. Institutions may be managed by the state or by privately funded agencies. Some parents are vehemently opposed to institutions and believe that they should be closed; other parents fight to maintain these facilities as options for care. Most service options have been designed for individuals with disabilities other than ASD and may have trouble accommodating all but the highest-functioning individual with autism spectrum disorders (Sullivan, 2005). The need for specially trained staff, the availability of appropriate programming (occupational therapy, speech-language services, recreational and leisure services), and access to psychological, psychiatric, and medical care are all issues families must address when looking for the "right" or "best" residential placement.

Employment Options

Two common types of employment for the adult with ASD who cannot work independently are sheltered workshops and supported employment. Sheltered workshops are supervised, structured settings that provide training in specific job skills. Typically, businesses contract with a sheltered workshop to complete a particular task in a contracted length of time. Sheltered workshops have many disadvantages, including low wages, minimal vocational training, and a lack of interaction with typical peers (Gerhardt & Holmes, 2005). These researchers also note that workshops frequently tend to be a final placement for adults with autism spectrum disorders rather than a step toward a less restrictive employment setting.

In a supported employment model, the person with autism spectrum disorders works at a job in the community alongside typical coworkers. Intensive training, assistance, and support is provided by a **job coach**. As the individual with ASD gains competency at the job, support is gradually faded. A job coach may supervise one individual for all or part of the day on the job site. In addition to on-site training, a job coach can assist with transportation, train coworkers who are nondisabled, and act as a liaison with family members and employers. Over the years, an increasing number of individuals with autism spectrum disorders have secured employment in the general workplace as a result of supported employment initiatives (Gerhardt & Holmes, 2005).

Family Issues

The family of an individual with autism spectrum disorders experiences lifelong issues in caring for their child. From the beginning, family members are aware that something is different with their child as compared to his or her peers. Frequently, parents are told that their child will "grow out of it." Usually, by the time the family receives a diagnosis of ASD, they have spent years dealing with various professionals and searching on their own for the cause of their child's disability. Confusion, frustration, and anger are all part of their everyday existence. The diagnosis is probably the first and most important step in the family's quest to deal with their child's disability. Understanding the diagnosis lets the family know there is a name for their child's condition that is recognized by professionals as a treatable disorder and should help alleviate any guilt they may have from feeling that they have caused their child's disability (Marcus, Kunce, & Schopler, 2005).

Following the diagnosis, the family's journey continues as they try to determine the most appropriate educational placement, intervention, and adjunctive therapies for their child. Programs that promise to eliminate symptoms or offer a "cure" for their child's condition may confuse parents. Parents often receive conflicting recommendations from professionals, which leads them to question whether they are doing the right thing for their child. As many treatments are not reimbursable by insurance, some families have placed themselves in financial distress in order to try new therapies in hope of a "cure."

Mothers are typically the primary caregivers for children with autism spectrum disorders, although fathers are often helpful with specific tasks. Not surprisingly, the presence of a child with ASD exerts a pervasive and stressful effect on the family, and directly and indirectly affects many aspects of their life (Marcus et al., 2005; Seligman & Darling, 2007). Many families report that with advancing age, their child becomes more difficult to deal with, particularly if there are behavior management problems.

Many parents are in a constant struggle with the demands placed on their nondisabled children and the parents' need of assistance from them. It is important that siblings understand the diagnosis of ASD on a developmentally appropriate level. As the child grows, information needs to be presented and discussed with them rather than relying on a "one-shot" explanation. Otherwise, misunderstandings are bound to occur. As parents age, siblings need to understand what plans have been made for the individual with ASD and what, if any, is their responsibility (Gallagher, Powell, & Rhodes, 2006). According to Marcus et al. (2005), research on siblings of children with autism spectrum disorders is limited and has produced mixed results. Some findings suggest that siblings show no major effects, but other findings have shown that siblings of children with ASD develop more adjustment problems. Sibling support groups are a popular method for supporting siblings and giving them information about the disability as needed. These support groups encourage the siblings of individuals with autism spectrum disorders to express their feelings and to ask questions about ASD.

Issues of Diversity

According to the Autism Society of America (2007), the disorder knows no racial, ethnic, or social boundaries. ASD occurs in all parts of the world, in all races and societies, and in all types of families. As we saw earlier, no social or psychological characteristics of parents or families have proven to be associated with autism spectrum disorders.

Technology and Individuals with Autism Spectrum Disorders

As described in Chapter 2, IDEA mandates the use of assistive technology, when appropriate, to enable an individual with disabilities to benefit from a special education. In the case of autism spectrum disorders, both low-tech and high-tech devices can be used to facilitate and improve communication. However, we still do not know much about the effectiveness of these technologies with individuals with ASD. Most of the research on the use of assistive technology with individuals with autism spectrum disorders has focused on speech-generating devices such as **augmentative or alternative communication** (AAC) options including v**oice output communication aids (VOCAs)** and a myriad of low-tech devices, including most visual symbols.

High-Tech Devices

VOCAs are electronic devices that can be programmed to produce synthetic speech. These devices can be as simple as programming "yes" or "no" response keys or as complex as producing multiple words, sentences, and social comments. An overlay with pictures or icons enables the child to choose what he or she would like to say or respond to by pressing the appropriate response. Some of these devices require little training on the part of the user; however, most users are dependent on a communication partner to change the overlays for them when the topic changes because it is often beyond the physical abilities of the user. The efficacy of these devices with individuals with ASD has received little attention in the literature (Blishak & Schlosser, 2003), although there is some evidence that nonverbal individuals with autism spectrum disorders "benefit from exposure to high-tech AAC devices" (Paul & Sutherland, 2005, p. 956).

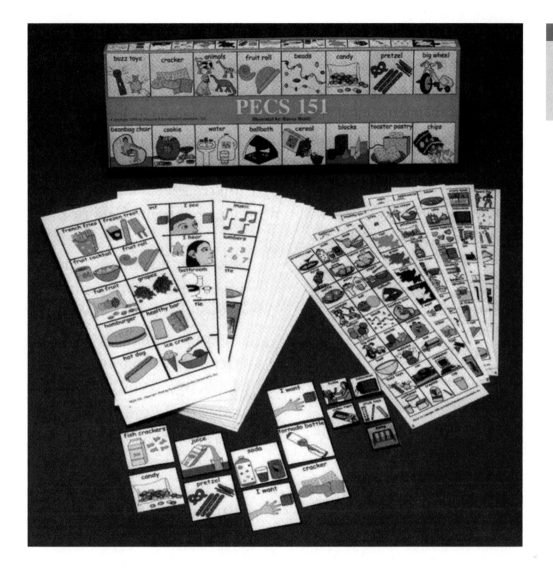

Figure 9.3

Picture Communication Aids

Source: Courtesy Pyramid Educational Products, Inc.

Low-Tech Devices

Visual strategies involve the use of pictures and sign language to communicate. In most picture exchange programs, the individual hands the instructor a picture of what he or she wants or needs as a form of communication. Bondy and Frost (1998) have pioneered a system known as the Picture Exchange Communication System (PECS), illustrated in Figure 9.3. Pictures can be grouped together by topic, such as how to get dressed or how to wash your hands, or arranged as a discussion board. An advantage of pictures is the reduction of auditory instruction and a reliance on the visual strengths of individuals with autism spectrum disorders. PECS has been shown to spontaneously generalize to different settings for children with ASD (Kravits, Kamps, Kemmerer, & Potucck, 2002), to increase spontaneous communication skills, and to improve social interactions and decrease problem behaviors (Charlop-Christy, Carpenter, Le, LeBlanc, & Kellet, 2002). In addition to the empirical evidence, anecdotal reports also support the effectiveness of PECS with children with autism spectrum disorders (Paul & Sutherland, 2005).

Research suggests that that introduction of AAC systems to nonverbal children with autism spectrum disorders does not interfere with the acquisition of speech (Myers & Johnson, 2007; Paul & Sutherland, 2005); in fact, there is some evidence that it may actually stimulate the development of speech (Millar, Light, & Schlosser, 2006).

Trends, Issues, and Controversies

Parents of individuals with autism spectrum disorders are exposed to a variety of treatments that promise dramatic improvement or "cures" for their child. With so many possible causes of ASD, there are likely as many possible treatments that may help the family in caring for their child. Unfortunately, research has not advanced to the point that the cause can always be matched to an appropriate treatment. Families often rely on anecdotal reports of treatments rather than waiting for the research to support the claims of improvement. Who can blame them? As long as the treatment does not harm the child, some families do not believe they can wait for science to catch up and miss an opportunity that could make a difference in the life of their child. Many parents stay up-to-date on treatment methodologies and current debates using the Internet. Unfortunately, these parents frequently "become susceptible to the promotions of specific therapies that usually have little to offer other than hope" (Marcus et al., 2005, p. 1058).

In the language of the ASD community, unproven techniques and therapies fall under the heading of complementary and alternative medicine (CAM) (Myers & Johnson, 2007). A multitude of treatment options, both biological and nonbiological, are considered CAM therapies, including, for example, dietary and vitamin treatments, hormone injections, facilitated communication, music therapy, and auditory integration training, along with optometric training. While case reports and anecdotal evidence lend credence to the popularity of these interventions, the scientific literature, which requires the use of a randomized, double-blind, placebo-controlled study, does not support these treatments (Hyman & Towbin, 2007). What is regrettably lacking in the field of autism spectrum disorders are "large-scale, rigorously designed, replicated intervention studies that compare the major autism intervention approaches" (Marcus et al., 2005, p. 1059). Until this evidence is available, parents and professionals alike need to carefully evaluate treatment options for individuals with autism spectrum disorders. Families should be especially cautious of a treatment strategy or intervention if they encounter the following claims or situations:

- treatments that are based on overly simple scientific theories;
- therapies that claim to be effective for multiple, unrelated conditions or symptoms;
- claims that children will respond dramatically and some will be cured;
- use of case reports or anecdotal data rather than carefully designed studies to support claims for treatment;
- lack of peer-reviewed references or denial of the need for controlled studies; or
- treatments that are said to have no potential or reported adverse effects. (Myers & Johnson, 2007, p. 1173)

Chapter in Review

Defining Autism Spectrum Disorders: An Evolving Process

- The field of **autism spectrum disorders** and pervasive developmental disorders is still relatively new, with the first clinical description of ASD appearing in the literature in 1943.

- Autism spectrum disorders was not described as a separate clinical category until 1977.

Classification of Individuals with Autism Spectrum Disorders

- The most current DSM-IV-TR includes autism as one of five distinct disorders in a category called **pervasive developmental disorders.**

- Individuals with **Asperger syndrome** are now recognized by professionals as distinctly different from persons with high-functioning autism.

- The IDEA included autism as a separate diagnostic category in 1990. The definition of autism in IDEA 2004 is fairly consistent with the description in the DSM-IV-TR.

Prevalence of Autism Spectrum Disorders

- According to the federal government, more than 224,000 pupils ages 3–21 were identified as having autism during the 2005–2006 school year.

- Prevalence rates vary considerably.

Etiology of Autism Spectrum Disorders

- We do not know the cause of autism, and we do not know how to prevent it.

- Current research is looking for biological markers; in general, any injury to the neurological system is suspect. This includes genetic contributions and structural abnormalities of the brain.

Characteristics of Individuals with Autism Spectrum Disorders

- Three cardinal characteristics define autism spectrum disorders: (1) social interaction deficits, (2) communication deficits, and (3) repetitive and restricted interests by age 3.

- Additional symptoms frequently reported in individuals with ASD include problems with concentration and attention, anxiety disorders, affective disorders, and learning difficulties.

Assessment of Autism Spectrum Disorders

- A good clinician will evaluate the presence of ASD symptoms using several diagnostic observation scales and inventories.

- Functional assessments of individuals with autism spectrum disorders helps to identify emerging skills. It is not uncommon to find that an individual with autism spectrum disorders has **splinter skills** because of the uneven nature of their cognitive development.

Educational Considerations

- Almost 40 percent of all school-age students with autism spectrum disorders currently receive services in a self-contained classroom.

- Structured educational approaches are consistently identified as the most appropriate for individuals with ASD. Behavior modification strategies are often used to achieve this structure.

Services for Young Children with Autism Spectrum Disorders

- Early educational intervention makes a positive difference in the life of an individual with autism spectrum disorders.

- The major focus of most early intervention programs is to address the communication deficits and behavioral problems of very young children.

Study Questions

1. Describe the DSM-IV-TR system and compare it to the IDEA classification system.

2. Name and describe the other pervasive developmental disorders (excluding ASD).

3. Prior to the acknowledgment of the genetic and neurological causes of autism spectrum disorders, what were the prevailing theories and treatments?

4. Why is the prevalence of ASD increasing?

5. List three possible causes of autism spectrum disorders.

6. What does the term *autistic savant* mean?

7. Name the three cardinal characteristics of ASD.

8. Detail the characteristics of the most common interventions used to educate individuals with autism spectrum disorders.

9. What are the key issues related to transitioning into adulthood for individuals with ASD?

10. Describe the issues that families typically have to deal with when they have a child with autism spectrum disorders.

11. How can technology be used with individuals with ASD?

12. What is complementary and alternative medicine? Describe the type of research that is needed to rigorously evaluate treatment options for individuals with autism spectrum disorders.

Key Terms

autism spectrum disorders
pervasive developmental
    disorders
schizophrenia
multiaxial system
Rett's disorder

childhood disintegrative
    disorder
Asperger syndrome
pervasive developmental
    disorder, not otherwise
    specified (PDD, NOS)

autistic savant
psychogenic theories
applied behavior analysis (ABA)
theory of mind
job coach

augmentative or alternative
    communication (AAC)
voice output communication
    aid (VOCA)

Learning Activities

1. If possible, observe a student with autism spectrum disorders in a special education setting and in an inclusive setting. What are the advantages and disadvantages of both educational settings? What kinds of educational interventions did you observe? What kind of educational environment would you want if this were your child or sibling?

2. Consider participating in a local support group for individuals with autism spectrum disorders and listen to the families' concerns and needs. Is there something you or your friends could do to help, such as providing respite care? Have you ever considered extending your friendship to an adult with ASD? Contact an organization in your area and offer to be a friend to an adult with autism spectrum disorders.

Organizations Concerned with Autism Spectrum Disorders

Autism Society of America
7910 Woodmont Avenue, Suite 300
Bethesda, MD 20814-3067
(800) 3AUTISM
(301) 657-0881
http://www.autism-society.org

Autism Speaks
2 Park Avenue
11th Floor
New York, NY 10016
(212) 252-8584
http://www.autismspeaks.org

Indiana Resource Center for Autism (IRCA)
Indiana Institute on Disability and Community
Indiana University
2853 E. Tenth Street
Bloomington, IN 47408-2696
(812) 855-6508
http://www.iidc.indiana.edu/~irca/Welcomez.html

Kennedy Krieger Institute
707 N. Broadway
Baltimore, MD 21205
(443) 923-9200
http://www.kennedykrieger.org/

Ohio Center for Autism and Low Incidence
5220 N. High Street
Columbus, OH 43214
(866) 886-2254
http://www.ocali.org

Reflecting on Standards

The following exercises are designed to help you learn to apply the Council for Exceptional Children (CEC) standards to your teaching practice. Each of the reflection exercises below correlates with a knowledge or skill within the CEC standards. For the full text of each of the related CEC standards, please refer to the standards integration grid located in Appendix B.

1. Focus on Learning Environments and Social Interactions (*CEC Content Standard #5 CC5S4*)

Reflect on what you have learned about the social interaction difficulties individuals with autism spectrum disorders sometimes have. If you were to have a student with autism spectrum disorders in your class, how might you encourage him/her to participate in group and one-on-one interactions with other students? How might you modify assignments to allow positive social interaction?

2. Focus on Instructional Planning (*CEC Content Standard #7 CC7S7*)

Reflect on what you have learned about inclusion of students with autism spectrum disorders in a general education classroom. If you were to teach at a school where students with autism spectrum disorders received services in a self-contained special education classroom, how might you coordinate with the special education teacher to involve his/her students in your classroom? How might you be able to involve students with autism spectrum disorders to help them learn affective, social, and life skills while working with other general education students?

Technology Resources

Visit the Web-based SAGE Study Site at **http://www.sagepub.com/gargiulo3estudy** for these additional learning tools:

- Chapter quizzes
- Key term flashcards
- Media links

- Full-text SAGE journal articles
- Internet activities
- Additional Web resources

CHAPTER 10

Individuals with Speech and Language Impairments

A Parent's Story

Adam's life started with my pregnancy. It was a normal pregnancy with no complications. I had a caesarian section when Adam was a week overdue. He weighed 9½ pounds, a very healthy baby. Adam reached all of his developmental milestones at normal times. He crawled at 6 months, walked at 10 months, and said his first word at 12 months. His speech and language continued to develop at a normal pace.

When it was time to eat solid foods, we had a problem. Adam had a strong gag reflex and did not seem to want to eat any foods that were not pureed. I came to the conclusion that he was not just picky. In addition, Adam drooled a great deal until he turned 3. I knew this was a lot longer than normal. I talked to the pediatrician about the eating and drooling. He said it was probably from teething and told me to keep introducing foods, eventually he will eat them.

When Adam was about 2 years old, I noticed that he could not pronounce n, t, d, l, and s correctly. I knew that l and s were not supposed to be mastered until the age of 4. I just thought he would master these by the time he was 4.

My husband, Rick, and I started to notice a great deal of frustration in Adam, who was now 3. What was the cause of it? We did not know and assumed it was age related. He did not seem to understand punishment. We would ask him why he was on his "thinking bench," and he could never answer. He would get more upset and answer something inappropriate. We would go to the pool during the summer. Adam would ask at least ten times, "Where are we going?" I would answer and could tell he just did not understand. I would try to rephrase and sometimes this would help. Adam did not seem to understand simple directions, question words (Why? How?), sequencing, verb tense, and common language concepts. All of these things were very subtle, and other people did not notice. He was not acquiring language concepts that children learn without formal teaching, and his pronunciation was not getting better.

In the fall, Adam started preschool. At this time I was starting to put some of the pieces together and had some concerns. In October I had a teacher conference and told the teacher of my concerns

Original chapter contribution by Linda McCormick, University of Hawaii and asked her if she noticed anything. She did. I told her I felt like he would hear me but not understand what I said. She noticed that he did not understand "yes" and "no" questions and when asked simple things that she knew he knew, he would say "I don't know." He was still a very picky eater but would try a few new things and only eat a very small bite. The teacher recommended that we have him screened by the speech pathologist who was coming to the school in a few weeks.

Adam went to the speech and language screening, and we waited for the results. The speech pathologist sent home a brief report that gave his results and called us that night to discuss them. I remember it vividly, even that it was raining that night. She told me he had scored very low, in the 1 percent range for some of the tests, matter-of-factly telling me he needed to be evaluated fully and would possibly need to go to a special school. I was floored! I wish my husband had been on the phone with me to hear it for himself; I knew there were going to be many questions that I did not ask or have an answer for. I wondered how this could be so severe and me be that blind to the severity. I knew something was wrong, but I did not realize that it was this bad.

Adam was scheduled at a facility known in town for being on the cutting edge and recommended on the school list of places for referral. Rick and I both went to the evaluation and met with the speech pathologist afterward. She was very kind and supportive, giving us books to read and scheduling his therapy. Adam was diagnosed with a mild to moderate language disorder, mild articulation difficulty, and low facial muscle tone. I felt very overwhelmed. What do we do now? How can I help? Does this mean he will have to struggle his whole life? How can I manage this? Rick was upset as well, but in a different way. He was defensive. He asked if Adam was stupid, and would he go to college? We were both dealing with fear and sadness that something was wrong with our child. After we talked more to each other and learned more about what was wrong, things settled down. The overall experience with the first speech pathologist was terrible and the second time was very supportive.

Adam is now 4 and has made great progress. He has matured socially, improved his speech and language skills, and goes to occupational therapy as well. Rick and I both incorporate therapy into everyday happenings. I feel like this is just a part of my everyday normal life and not a big problem. I primarily take Adam to therapy. Rick takes him sometimes as well. It has been important for both of us, as parents, to stay involved with his therapy.

I still wonder about the future and how this will affect Adam. I have to put that aside and do the best that I can now, hoping for the best later. Adam likes to go to therapy and is much less frustrated. Because he was diagnosed and started therapy at such a young age, his future will be bright.

—Lori Smith

Although Adam's mother does not mention an IEP, Adam may have been one of the more than 330,000 preschoolers who received services in the speech and language impairment category under IDEA in the 2005–2006 school year (U.S. Department of Education, 2007). Services for young children like Adam will be described later in this chapter.

The main focus of this chapter is on students who demonstrate communication difficulties that are not the result of or directly associated with another disability. The disability category under which these children are served is *speech and language impairments*. The communication difficulties of children who have a primary disability other than speech and language impairment are noted but not discussed as they are addressed in other chapters. First, we will introduce the discussion of speech and language delays and disorders with a review of the nature of speech, language, and communication.

The Nature of Speech, Language, and Communication

Of all the singular gifts bestowed on humans, the acquisition and use of language is undoubtedly the most miraculous. Most people give little thought to this remarkable achievement that begins in the womb. Even before they are out of diapers, most children have a vocabulary of 50 words or more and by age 2, they are producing short but intelligible sentences. Three-year-olds are chatty and engaging as they begin to acquire the rules for tense and number, often overextending them to produce amusing statements like "I seed two mouses in the picture." At this age they are also discovering that words have different meanings depending on how you string them together. By kindergarten, most children have an impressive vocabulary, typically in excess of 2,000 words. Table 10.1 shows the amazing accomplishments of language learning and the activities that parents typically use to facilitate these accomplishments. When attainment of any of the milestones shown in Table 10.1 is delayed or there is a disturbance in one or more of the components necessary for communication, the child is at risk for a language disorder.

It is important to begin by differentiating the concepts *speech, language,* and *communication* so that you can be as precise as possible when you talk about speech and language impairments with other professionals. You are familiar with the three terms, but you may have used then interchangeably, and they have very distinct meanings. **Speech** is the expression of language with sounds—essentially the oral modality for language. Compared to other ways of conveying ideas and intentions (for example, manual signing, writing, gesturing), speech is probably the most difficult. Humans are not the only species to produce sounds, but we are the only species with a vocal tract that permits production of the variety and complexity of sounds required for speech. Speech production depends on precise physiological and neuromuscular coordination of (1) respiration (the act of breathing); (2) phonation (production of sound by the larynx and vocal fold); and (3) articulation (use of the lips, tongue, teeth, and hard and soft palates to form speech sounds). Speech is considerably more than a motor behavior. It is willed, planned, and programmed by the central nervous system—the brain, spinal cord, and peripheral nervous system.

Language is a "rule-based method of communication involving the comprehension and use of signs and symbols by which ideas are represented" (Bryant, Smith, & Bryant, 2008, p. 56). In many ways language can be thought of as a code. It is a code in the sense that it is not a direct representation of the world but, rather, something with which to represent ideas and concepts about the world. What does it mean to *know* a language? It means that you are able to apply the basic units and the complex rules governing relationships among sounds, words, sentences, meaning, and use of the language.

Language contains five major interrelated yet distinct elements (see Figure 10.1, page 366)—phonology, morphology, semantics, syntax, and pragmatics—that are present at both the receptive and expressive levels. These components, according to Owens (2006), represent the basic rule systems found in language. *Form* incorporates syntax, morphology, and phonology or the elements that connect sounds or symbols with meaning. *Content* encompasses the meaning of words and sentences (semantics), while *use* addresses the social aspects of language or pragmatics.

Developmental Milestones for Acquiring Speech and Language

Children's development is mapped using a chart of developmental milestones. These milestones are behaviors that ...time, forming the building blocks for growth and continued learning. Some of the categories within which these ...are seen include:

- Cognition—thinking, reasoning, problem solving, understanding
- Language—expressive and receptive abilities
- Motor coordination—gross/fine motor, jumping, hopping, throwing/catching, drawing, stacking
- Social interaction—initiating peer contact, group play
- Self-help—dressing, eating, washing

	Milestones in Language Development	Activities to Encourage Your Child's Language
By Age 1	• Recognizes name • Says 2–3 words besides "mama" and "dada" • Imitates familiar words • Understands simple instructions • Recognizes words as symbols for objects: car—points to garage, cat—meows	• Respond to your child's coos, gurgles, and babbling • Talk to your child as you care for him or her throughout the day • Read colorful books to your child every day • Tell nursery rhymes and sing songs • Teach your child the names of everyday items and familiar people • Take your child with you to new places and situations • Play simple games with your child such as "peek-a-boo" and "pat-a-cake"
Between 1 and 2 Years of Age	• Understands "no" • Uses 10 to 20 words, including names • Combines two words such as "daddy bye-bye" • Waves good-bye and plays pat-a-cake • Makes the "sounds" of familiar animals • Gives a toy when asked • Uses words such as "more" to make wants known • Points to his or her toes, eyes, and nose • Brings object from another room when asked	• Reward and encourage early efforts at saying new words • Talk to your baby about everything you're doing while you're with him or her • Talk simply, clearly, and slowly to your child • Talk about new situations before you go, while you're there, and again when you are home • Look at your child when he or she talks to you • Describe what your child is doing, feeling, hearing • Let your child listen to children's records and tapes • Praise your child's efforts to communicate
Between 2 and 3 Years of Age	• Identifies body parts • Carries on "conversation" with self and dolls • Asks "What's that?" and "Where's my?" • Uses two-word negative phrases such as "no want" • Forms some plurals by adding "s": book, books • Has a 450-word vocabulary • Gives first name, holds up fingers to tell age • Combines nouns and verbs: "mommy go" • Understands simple time concepts: "last night," "tomorrow" • Refers to self as "me" rather than by name	• Repeat new words over and over • Help your child listen and follow instructions by playing games: "Pick up the ball," "Touch Daddy's nose" • Take your child on trips and talk about what you see before, during, and after the trip • Let your child tell you answers to simple questions • Read books every day, perhaps as part of the bedtime routine • Listen attentively as your child talks to you • Describe what you are doing, planning, thinking

Table 10.1	Developmental Milestones for Acquiring Speech and Language (Continued)	
	Milestones in Language Development	**Activities to Encourage Your Child's Language**
Between 2 and 3 Years of Age (Continued)	• Tries to get adult attention: "Watch me" • Likes to hear same story repeated • May say "no" when means "yes" • Talks to other children as well as adults • Solves problems by talking instead of hitting or crying • Answers "where" questions • Names common pictures and things • Uses short sentences like "Me want more" or "Me want cookie," matches 3–4 colors, knows big and little	• Have the child deliver simple messages for you ("Mommy needs you, Daddy") • Carry on conversations with the child, preferably when the two of you have some quiet time together • Ask questions to get your child to think and talk • Show the child you understand what he or she says by answering, smiling, and nodding your head • Expand what the child says. If he or she says, "more juice," you say, "Adam wants more juice."
Between 3 and 4 Years of Age	• Can tell a story • Has sentence length of 4–5 words • Has a vocabulary of nearly 1,000 words • Names at least one color • Understands "yesterday," "summer," "lunchtime," "tonight," "little/big" • Begins to obey requests like "Put the block under the chair" • Knows his or her last name, name of street on which he/she lives, and several nursery rhymes	• Talk about how objects are the same or different • Help your child to tell stories using books and pictures • Let your child play with other children • Read longer stories to your child • Pay attention to your child when he or she is talking • Talk about places you've been or will be going
Between 4 and 5 Years of Age	• Has sentence length of 4–5 words • Uses past tense correctly • Has a vocabulary of nearly 1,500 words • Points to colors red, blue, yellow, and green • Identifies triangles, circles, and squares • Understands "in the morning," "next," "noontime" • Can speak of imaginary conditions such as "I hope" • Asks many questions, asks "who?" and "why?"	• Help your child sort objects and things (examples: things you eat, animals) • Teach your child how to use the telephone • Let your child help you plan activities such as what you will make for Thanksgiving dinner • Continue talking with him about his interests • Read longer stories to her • Let him tell and make up stories for you • Show your pleasure when she comes to talk with you
Between 5 and 6 Years of Age	• Has a sentence length of 5–6 words • Has a vocabulary of around 2,000 words • Defines objects by their use (you eat with a fork) and can tell what objects are made of • Knows spatial relations like "on top," "behind," "far," and "near" • Knows her address • Identifies a penny, nickel, and dime • Knows common opposites like "big/little" • Understands "same" and "different" • Counts ten objects • Asks questions for information • Distinguishes left and right hand • Uses all types of sentences—for example, "Let's go to the store after we eat"	• Praise your child when she talks about her feelings, thoughts, hopes, and fears • Comment on what you did or how you think your child feels • Sing songs, rhymes with your child • Continue to read longer stories • Talk with him as you would an adult • Look at family photos and talk to him about your family history • Listen to her when she talks to you

Source: http://www.ldonline.org/ld_indepth/speech-language/lda_milestones.html. *Speech and Language Milestone Chart.* 1999.

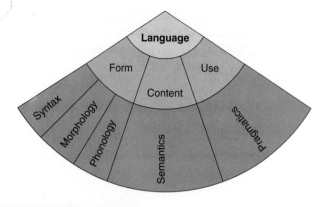

Figure 10.1

Basic Components of Language

Source: From R. Owens, *Language Development: An Introduction*, 6th ed. (Boston: Allyn and Bacon). Copyright © 2005 by Pearson Education. Reprinted by permission of the publisher.

The **phonology** of language includes the sounds that are characteristic of that language, the rules governing their distribution and sequencing, and the stress and intonation patterns that accompany sounds. The **morphology** of a language includes the rules governing how words are formed from meaningful units called morphemes. At the most basic level, **semantics** is the linguistic realization of what the speaker knows about the world—what people talk about. Semantics is concerned with relationships (1) between words and meanings, (2) between words, (3) between word meanings and sentence meanings, and (4) between linguistic meaning and nonlinguistic reality. The **syntax** of language contains rules for how to string words together to form phrases and sentences, what sentences are acceptable, and how to transform sentences into other sentences. Knowledge of the syntax of a language allows a speaker to generate an infinite number of new sentences and recognize sentences that are not grammatically acceptable. The major concern in **pragmatics** is the effectiveness of language in achieving desired functions in social situations. Attitudes, personal history, the setting, the topic of conversation, and the details of the preceding discourse are among the social and contextual factors that determine how speakers cast their sentences (and how listeners interpret them). Table 10.2 summarizes these five components of language. You may want to refer back to this table when you are reading about specific disorders later in this chapter.

Communication is the exchange of ideas, information, thoughts, and feelings. It does not necessarily require speech or language. Examples of nonlinguistic communication behaviors are gestures, posture, eye contact, facial expression, and head and body movement. Nonlinguistic communication modes may be used as the only method of communication, or

Table 10.2	Components of Language		
Component	**Definition**	**Receptive Level**	**Expressive Level**
Phonology	The sounds characteristic of a language, rules governing their distribution and sequencing, and the stress and intonation patterns that accompany sounds	Discrimination of speech sounds	Articulation of speech sounds
Morphology	The rules governing how words are formed from the basic element of meaning	Understanding of the grammatical structure of words	Use of grammar in words
Semantics	The linguistic realization of what the speaker knows about the world—the meanings of words and sentences	Understanding of word meanings and word relationships	Use of word meanings and word relationships
Syntax	Rules for how to string words together to form phrases and sentences—the relationships among the elements of a sentence	Understanding of phrases and sentences	Use of grammar in phrases and sentences
Pragmatics	The social effectiveness of language in achieving desired functions—rules related to the use of language in social contexts	Understanding of social and contextual cues	Use of language to affect others

Source: Adapted from L. McCormick, "Introduction to Language Acquisition," in L. McCormick, D. F. Loeb, and R. L. Schiefelbusch (Eds.), *Supporting Children with Communication Difficulties in Inclusive Settings*, 2nd ed. (Boston: Allyn and Bacon, 2003).

they may be used in conjunction with linguistically encoded methods. The communication process begins when a person has an idea or intention and wants to share it. The idea or intention is formulated into a message and then expressed to another person or persons. The other person receives the message and reacts to or acknowledges it. In any communication there is always a potential for message distortion because of the many possible message modalities and the many possible connotations and perceptions of the communication partners.

Defining Speech and Language Impairments

Speech and/or language impairments are problems in communication and related areas such as oral motor function. Delays and disorders may range from so subtle that they have little or no impact on daily living and socialization to the inability to produce speech or to understand and use language. Fortunately, only a very small percentage of children are at the most extreme level of severity. However, because of the importance of language and communication skills in a child's life (or, for that matter, in anyone's life), even mild to moderate disorders or disturbances can have a profound effect on all aspects of life, sometimes isolating children from their peers and their educational environments.

Severe communication and language disabilities are most likely to occur secondary to pervasive cognitive, neurological, or physical disabilities. Table 10.3 provides an overview of language difficulties that are secondary to learning disabilities, autism spectrum disorders, mental retardation, and traumatic brain injury. These communication difficulties are described in more depth in the respective chapters that address these disability categories.

The Individuals with Disabilities Education Improvement Act (PL 108-446) label for students with communication difficulties is "speech and language impairment." Children are eligible for services in this category if they have "a communication disorder such as stuttering, impaired articulation, a language impairment or a voice impairment, which adversely affect a child's educational performance" (Sec. 300.7 [c] [11]). IDEA includes speech and language disorders under both special education and related services.

The American Speech-Language-Hearing Association (1993) defines a communication disorder as "an impairment in the ability to receive, send, process, and comprehend concepts or verbal, nonverbal, and graphic symbols systems. A communication disorder may be evident in the processes of hearing, language, and/or speech" (p. 40).

Classifying Speech and Language Impairments

Speech Disorders

Speech is the most common and the most complex mode for expression of language. It requires coordination of the neuromusculature of the breathing and voice-producing mechanisms, as well as integrity of the mouth or oral cavity. Figure 10.2 (page 369) shows the organs used in speech production.

Simply stated, a speech impairment is present when the individual's speech deviates to such a degree that it interferes with communication, attracts unfavorable attention, and adversely affects the listeners, speaker, or both (Bernthal & Bankson, 2004). There are three basic types of speech impairments: articulation disorders, fluency disorders, and

Table 10.3	Language Difficulties Secondary to Other Disabilities	
	Phonology	**Morphology/Syntax**
Learning Disabilities	• Delayed acquisition of sounds • Inferior perception and/or production of complex sounds • Inefficient use of phonological codes in short-term memory • Impaired sensitivity to sounds	• Shorter and less elaborate sentences • Failure to encode all relevant information in sentences • Difficulties with negative and passive constructions, relative clauses, contractions, and adjectival forms • Confusion of articles (a, an, the) • Difficulty with verb tense, plurality, possession, and pronouns • Delayed acquisition of morphological rules • Difficulty with rules for auxiliaries, modals, prepositions, conjunctions, and other grammatical markers
Autism Spectrum Disorders	• Difficulties with expressive prosody (e.g., fluctuations in vocal intensity, monotonous pitch, tonal contrasts inconsistent with meanings)	• Confusions of pronominal forms (e.g., gender confusion [he for she or it], case substitution [him for he], first- and second-person singular forms [you for I or me]) • Less complex sentences than peers
Mental Retardation	• Delayed development of phonological rules • Problems with speech production	• Production of shorter, less complex sentences with fewer subject elaborations or relative clauses • Delayed morpheme development • Delayed development of syntax
Traumatic Brain Injury	• Sound substitutions and omissions • Slurred speech • Difficulties with speech prosody (pitch, loudness, rate, and rhythm)	• Deficits in syntactic comprehension • Fragmented, irrelevant, and lengthy utterances • Mutism immediately after the injury, followed by telegraphic production
	Semantics	**Pragmatics**
Learning Disabilities	• Word-finding and definitional problems • Restricted word meanings (too literal and concrete) • Difficulty with multiple word meanings • Excessive use of nonspecific terms and indefinite reference • Difficulty comprehending certain conjunctions (but, or, if, then, either)	• Difficulty with questions and requests for clarification • Difficulty initiating and maintaining conversation • Difficulty with relational terms (comparative, spatial, temporal)
Autism Spectrum Disorders	• Word-finding problems • Inappropriate answers to questions	• Limited range of communicative functions • Difficulty initiating and maintaining conversation • Few gestures • Failure to make eye contact prior to or during communicative interactions • Preference to follow rather than lead in a conversation • Failure to engage communication partners at a level that requires sharing
Mental Retardation	• Use of more concrete word meanings • Slower rate of vocabulary acquisition	• Difficulty with speech-act development • Difficulty with referential communication • Difficulty initiating and maintaining a conversation • Difficulty repairing communication breakdowns
Traumatic Brain Injury	• Small, restricted vocabulary • Word-finding problems	• Difficulty with organization and expression of complex ideas • Socially inappropriate and off-topic comments • Less use of the naming function

Source: Adapted from L. McCormick & D. F. Loeb, "Characteristics of Students with Language and Communication Difficulties," in L. McCormick, D. F. Loeb, and R. L. Schiefelbusch (Eds.), *Supporting Children with Communication Difficulties in Inclusive Settings,* 2nd ed. (Boston: Allyn and Bacon, 2003).

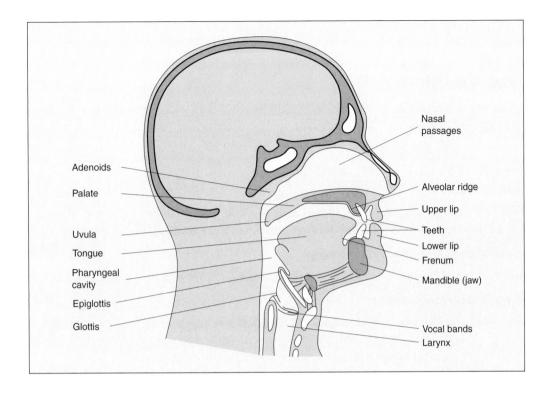

Figure 10.2

Organs Typically Used in
the Production of Speech

voice disorders. One of the most prevalent of all speech problems is **articulation disorders** (Owens, Metz, & Haas, 2007). Articulation disorders are errors in the production of speech sounds. They include **omissions** (*han* for *hand*), **substitutions** (*wabbit* for *rabbit*), **distortions** (*shlip* for *sip*), and **additions** (*footsball* for *football*). These errors may be related to anatomical or physiological limitations in the skeletal, muscular, or neuromuscular support for speech production, or to other factors (for example, cerebral palsy, hearing loss). A child has a severe articulation disorder if pronunciation is so poor that his/her speech is unintelligible most of the time to family members, teachers, and peers. A phonological disorder is different from an articulation disorder. A child has a phonological disorder if he/she has the ability to produce a given sound and does so correctly in some instances but fails to produce the sound correctly at other times. It is important for speech-language pathologists to discriminate the two because intervention goals and strategies are very different (Owens et al.). The focus of therapy for articulation disorders is acquisition of the correct speech sound(s), generalization of the sound(s) to different settings, and maintenance over time. The focus of therapy for phonological disorders is to help the child identify the error pattern(s) and gradually produce more linguistically appropriate sound patterns. For additional information on articulation disorders, see the accompanying FYI feature.

Fluency disorders are difficulties with the rhythm and timing of speech. A fluency disorder is basically "an interruption in the flow of speaking characterized by atypical rate, rhythm, and repetitions in sounds, syllables, words, and phrases. This may be accompanied by excessive tension, struggle behavior, and secondary mannerisms" (American Speech-Language-Hearing Association, 1993, p. 40). **Stuttering** is the most familiar fluency disorder. It is marked by rapid-fire repetitions of consonant or vowel sounds especially at the beginning of words, prolongations, hesitations, interjections, and complete verbal blocks (Ramig & Shames, 2006). Developmental stuttering typically begins between the ages of 2 and 6. Stuttering is situational in that it appears to be related to the setting or circumstances of speech. A child is more likely to stutter when talking with people he considers important (parents, teachers) and when called upon to speak before a group of people (for example, in front of the class). There appears to

FYI...

Questions and Answers about Articulation Problems

Q. Will a child outgrow a functional articulation problem?

A. A child's overall speech pattern will usually become more understandable as he or she matures, but some children will need direct training to eliminate all articulation errors. The exact speech pattern of the individual child will determine the answer to this question.

Q. Do children learn all sounds at once?

A. Sounds are learned in an orderly sequence. Some sounds, such as *p, m,* and *b,* are learned as early as 3 years of age. Other sounds, such as *s, r,* and *l,* often are not completely mastered until the early school years.

Q. At what age should a child be producing all sounds correctly?

A. Children should make all the sounds of English by 8 years of age. Many children learn these sounds much earlier.

Q. How can I help a child pronounce words correctly?

A. By setting a good example. Don't interrupt or constantly correct the child. Don't let anyone tease or mock (including friends or relatives). Instead, present a good model. Use the misarticulated word correctly with emphasis. If the child says, "That's a big wabbit," you say, "Yes, that is a big rabbit. A big white rabbit. Would you like to have a rabbit?"

Q. Can an adult with an articulation problem be helped?

A. Most articulation problems can be helped regardless of a person's age, but the longer the problem persists, the harder it is to change. Some problems, such as those relating to nerve impulses to the muscles of articulation (dysarthria), are particularly difficult and generally require a longer period of help than a functional disorder. Other conditions that may influence progress in a child or adult include hearing ability, condition of the oral structures such as the teeth, frequency of help obtained, motivation, intelligence, and cooperation.

Q. Who can help?

A. Contact a speech-language pathologist if you are concerned about speech. A speech-language pathologist is a professional trained at the master's or doctoral level to evaluate and help the child or adult with an articulation problem as well as other speech and/or language disorders. The speech-language pathologist can advise whether professional help is indicated and how to arrange for assistance. The speech-language pathologist can also give you guidance or provide services to help prevent or eliminate a problem. Early help is especially important for more severe problems.

Q. Is it important to correct an articulation problem?

A. When you consider the possible impact an articulation problem may have on one's social, emotional, educational, and/or vocational status, the answer becomes obvious. Our speech is an important part of us. The quality of our lives is affected by the adequacy of our speech.

Source: Adapted from American Speech-Language-Hearing Association, *Answers and Questions about Articulation Problems* (Rockville, MD: n.d.).

be no single cause of stuttering, and no apparent link to psychological or organic incidents. Stuttering, however, is more common in males than in females. Investigators also note that a child has a greater likelihood of stuttering if he or she is a twin (Ramig & Shames).

No single therapy method is most effective for stuttering. As they mature, children can learn to manage their stuttering by deliberately prolonging certain sounds or by speaking slowly to get through a "block." Sometimes the problem disappears without treatment. In many instances, children who stutter seem to recover or outgrow the condition without formal intervention (Owens et al., 2007). See the accompanying FYI feature for frequently asked questions and answers about stuttering.

FYI . . .

Questions and Answers about Stuttering

Q. What is stuttering?

A. Stuttering is the condition in which the flow of speech is broken by abnormal stoppages (no sound), repetitions (st-st-stuttering), or prolongations (ssssstuttering) of sounds and syllables. There may also be unusual facial and body movements associated with the effort to speak.

Q. Aren't all people nonfluent to some extent?

A. Yes. Almost all children go through a stage of frequent nonfluency in early speech development. Adults may interject syllables ("uh") and occasionally repeat words, phrases, and sounds, but these nonfluencies are accepted as normal and usually are not a cause for concern.

Q. Does stammering mean the same thing as stuttering?

A. Most people use the terms interchangeably.

Q. What causes stuttering?

A. We still do not know what causes stuttering. It may have different causes in different people, or it may occur only when a combination of factors comes together. It is also possible that what causes stuttering is different from what makes it continue or get worse. Possible influences include incoordination of the speech muscles; rate of language development; the way parents and others talk to the child; and other forms of communication and life stress.

Q. Is stuttering caused by emotional or psychological problems?

A. Children who stutter are no more likely to have psychological problems than children who do not stutter. There is no evidence that emotional trauma causes stuttering.

Q. At what age is stuttering likely to appear?

A. Stuttering typically begins between 2 and 5 years of age, but occasionally begins in a school-age child and, more rarely, in an adult.

Q. If I think my child is beginning to stutter, should I wait or seek help?

A. You should seek a professional evaluation. Most children outgrow their nonfluency, but others will not. The problem of stuttering may be prevented from developing if treated early enough.

Q. Once stuttering has developed, can it be treated?

A. Yes, there are a variety of successful approaches for treating both children and adults.

Q. Can stuttering be "cured"?

A. Stuttering is not a disease. Rather than think in terms of an absolute "cure" for stuttering, the goal should be to progress toward improved fluency and success in communicating.

Q. What should I do when I hear a child speaking nonfluently?

A. Children may be unaware that they are speaking nonfluently. Do not call attention to the nonfluent speech pattern or allow others to do so.

Do not say, "Stop and start over," "Think before you talk," "Talk slower," or "Cat got your tongue?" Listen patiently and carefully to what the child is saying, and do not focus on how it is being said.

Q. What should I do when I hear an adult stuttering?

A. Adults who stutter need the same patience and attention to their ideas as speakers who don't stutter. Don't look away, and don't hurry them or fill in words. This attempt to help can create anxiety and self-consciousness and make the problem worse.

Source: Adapted from American Speech-Language-Hearing Association, *Answers and Questions about Stuttering* (Rockville, MD: n.d.).

Individuals who stutter may also be clutterers. **Cluttering** is a related fluency disorder characterized by excessively fast and jerky speech. Like stuttering, cluttering interferes with the flow of a person's speech. It seems to result from disorganized speech planning, talking too fast or in spurts, or simply being unsure what one wants to say. Speech may initially be clear; then it gradually increases in speed, shifts to an irregular rhythm, and becomes mumbled. Symptoms of cluttering may include reading and writing disorders, word repetitions, short attention span, and grammatical errors. A difference between stutterers and clutterers is that the stutterer is usually very aware of his or her fluency problem, whereas the clutterer may seem oblivious to the problem. Speech-language pathologists typically collaborate with special education teachers who have expertise in learning disabilities and behavior disorders when working with children who demonstrate cluttering.

Voice disorders are problems with the quality or use of one's voice that result from disorders of the larynx. They are characterized by "the abnormal production and/or absences of vocal quality, pitch, loudness, resonance, and/or duration, which is inappropriate for an individual's age and/or sex" (American Speech-Language-Hearing Association, 1993, p. 40). Speech may be excessively hoarse, or lack appropriate inflection. Voice disorders may be caused by temporary conditions such as colds or allergies, chemically induced irritation, or vocally demanding activities, or more permanent abnormalities such as vocal nodules. Although voice disorders are more common in adults than in children, there are cases in which a child's voice is difficult to understand or unpleasant. The two types of voice disorders are phonation disorders and resonance disorders. The characteristics of a **phonation** disorder are breathiness, hoarseness, huskiness, and straining. In severe cases, the individual may not have any voice at all.

A **resonance** disorder may be characterized by **hypernasality** (too many sounds coming through the air passages of the nose) or **hyponasality** (too little resonance of the nasal passages). Hypernasality is often a result of cleft palate. Too much air passes through the nasal cavities during production of sounds, giving the speaker a distinctive "twang." Because the flow of air through the nostrils is impeded, the speaker with hyponasality sounds as if his nose is clamped or she has a cold.

Language Disorders

How well children understand and use language affects not only their ability to learn to read and write but also the perceptions of peers, family members, teachers, and society at large. When a child starts school, the perception of his or her language skills becomes particularly influential (DeThorne & Watkins, 2001). When children's communication skills do not match others' expectations, children are likely to be perceived negatively and may consequently experience less academic and social success. Speech-language pathologists and teachers have two responsibilities: (1) to address children's specific language difficulties, and (2) to minimize the social impact of particular speech-language characteristics by promoting understanding of and acceptance of language difficulties in the classroom.

Recall the components of language as reviewed above in Table 10.2. Each of these five components of language (phonology, morphology, semantics, syntax, pragmatics) has rules that must be mastered if the child is to have language competence. Language disorders occur when there is delay or difficulties with mastery in one or more of these areas.

A **phonological disorder** is defined as abnormal organization of the phonologic system or a significant deficit in speech production or perception. A developmental phonological disorder is the difficulty of organizing speech sounds into patterns. A child with a phonological disorder may be described as hard to understand or as not saying the sounds right—the child is likely to have difficulty decoding spoken language and may make substitutions for sounds. A child has a phonological disorder (as opposed to an articulation disorder) if he/she has the ability to produce a given sound and does so correctly in some instances but fails to produce the sound correctly at other times. Unlike articulation disorders, a phonological disorder reveals a pattern of responses and is therefore a rule-based phenomenon. Assessment for these children focuses on determining which sounds the child can produce, the contexts of correct and incorrect sound production, and the child's use or overuse of phonological processes.

Apraxia of speech is a neurological phonologic disorder that results from impairment of the capacity to select, program, or execute the positioning of the speech muscles to produce speech sounds. The speech mechanisms are operating, but the child cannot get them to operate properly—when the child wants to speak, he/she has difficulty planning what to say and the motor movements to use. The weakened or slowed processes affect speech prosody, stress intonation, and rhythm. The speech of these children is characterized by groping attempts to articulate sounds correctly. There are frequent speech-sound substitutions and omissions with sound-sequencing difficulties and distortions and obvious struggle to retrieve desired sounds and patterns.

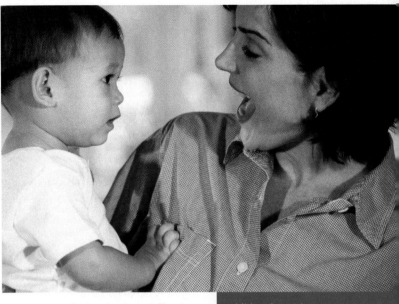

Children learn the rules of language by listening and imitating what they hear.

Disorders involving morphology involve difficulties with morphological inflections. Morphological inflections (also called grammatical morphemes) are inflections on nouns, verbs and adjectives that signal different kinds of meanings. For example, when you add the morphological inflection –s to dog, this signals plurality. Children with a **morphological disorder** have problems learning and using morphological rules. They use fewer grammatical morphemes and produce more grammatical errors than same-age peers.

Semantic disorders are characterized by poor vocabulary development, inappropriate use of word meanings, and/or inability to comprehend word meanings. Most evident are problems with word finding, the ability to generate a specific word that is evoked by a situation, stimulus, sentence, context, or conversation. Children with semantic difficulties also demonstrate restrictions in word meanings, difficulties with multiple word meanings, excessive use of nonspecific terms (for example, *thing, stuff*) and indefinite references (for example, *that* and *there*), and difficulties with comprehension of conjunctions and relational terms.

Children with **syntactical deficits** have difficulty acquiring the rules that govern word order and other aspects of grammar such as subject–verb agreement. They have problems processing sentences, even relatively simple ones, and they typically produce shorter and less elaborated sentences with fewer cohesive conjunctions than their peers. Most evident is their inability to organize and express complex ideas.

Children with **pragmatic difficulties** have problems understanding and using language in different social contexts. They do not understand how to infer their listeners' needs, so they do not know what and how much information they need to provide in an interaction. Other weaknesses include lack of understanding of the rules for (1) when and how to make eye contact; (2) how close it is permissible to stand when talking to someone; (3) when to request clarification of information; (4) how to interpret direct and indirect requests; and (5) how to introduce topics.

Table 10.4 presents indicators of a possible language impairment. These behaviors might suggest the need for an evaluation by a speech-language pathologist.

Table 10.4	Behaviors Indicative of a Possible Language Impairment in Children

Child mispronounces sounds and words.

Child omits word endings, such as plural –s and past-tense –ed.

Child omits small unemphasized words, such as auxiliary verbs or prepositions.

Child uses an immature vocabulary, overuses empty words, such as *one* and *thing,* or seems to have difficulty recalling or finding the right word.

Child has difficulty comprehending new words and concepts.

Child's sentence structure seems immature or overreliant on forms, such as subject-verb-object. It's unoriginal, dull.

Child's question and/or negative sentence style is immature.

Child has difficulty with one of the following:
- Verb tensing
- Pronouns
- Word order
- Articles
- Irregular verbs
- Irregular plurals
- Auxiliary verbs
- Prepositions
- Conjunctions

Child has difficulty relating sequential events.

Child has difficulty following directions.

Child's questions are often inaccurate or vague.

Child's questions are often poorly formed.

Child has difficulty answering questions.

Child's comments are often off-topic or inappropriate for the conversation.

There are long pauses between a remark and the child's reply or between successive remarks by the child. It's as if the child is searching for a response or is confused.

Child appears to be attending to communication but remembers little of what is said.

Child has difficulty using language socially for the following purposes:
- Request needs
- Greet
- Respond/reply
- Relate events
- Pretend/imagine
- Request information
- Share ideas, feelings
- Entertain
- Protest
- Gain attention
- Clarify
- Reason

Child has difficulty interpreting the following:
- Figurative language
- Emotions
- Humor
- Body language
- Gestures

Child does not alter production for different audiences and locations.

Child does not seem to consider the effect of language on the listener.

Child often has verbal misunderstandings with others.

Child has difficulty with reading and writing.

Child's language skills seem to be much lower than other areas, such as mechanical, artistic, or social skills.

Source: From R. Owens. *Language Disorders: A Functional Approach to Assessment and Intervention,* 4th ed. (Boston: Allyn and Bacon). Copyright © 2004 by Pearson Education. Reprinted by permission of the publisher.

Central Auditory Processing Disorder (CAPD)

Defining **central auditory processing disorder (CAPD)** presents some difficulty because it has been the center of considerable controversy in the field of language disorders. Most authorities agree, however, that it is a problem in the processing of sound, not attributed to hearing loss or intellectual capacity. Simply stated, central auditory processing involves how we use and interpret auditory information. CAPD occurs when the ear and the brain do not work together as smoothly as they should. CAPD varies in degree from mild to severe. It may be the primary or secondary disorder, and involves aspects of listening skills necessary for language development. In children with CAPD, these deficits are not the result of peripheral hearing loss; hearing is usually normal. These children demonstrate problems with auditory figure–ground (difficulty attending to a speaker when there is noise in the background), auditory memory, auditory discrimination (hearing the difference between similar sounds or words), auditory attention (maintaining listening focus), and auditory cohesion (for example, drawing inferences from conversations, understanding riddles, comprehending verbal math problems).

The causes of CAPD are varied and can include head trauma, lead poisoning, possibly chronic ear infections, and unknown reasons. Some neurophysiological basis for this disorder is likely. Because there are many different possibilities—even combinations of causes—each child has to be assessed on an individual basis.

Historical Perspectives

For many years, individuals with speech and language impairments and other disabilities were referred to as "handicapped," the origin of the word referring to the image and practice of individuals with disabilities begging on streets with a cap in hand to catch donations. The work of Itard, referenced in Chapter 5, is considered classic early speech and language research. There was great fascination and curiosity regarding the "Wild Boy's" development of fundamental speech sounds and gradual use of these sounds in language for communication of his wants and needs. Early language deprivation, like that experienced by Victor, is one of the many etiologies identified for speech and language disorders.

Van Riper and Emerick (1996) have classified historic reactions toward individuals with disabilities into three categories:

- **Rejection**—being thrown from mountain peaks in ancient Sparta
- **Objects of pity**—frequently used within the context of religious practices throughout the ages
- **A rewarding source of humor**—"Balbus Blaesus," an individual who stuttered and was caged and displayed on the Appian Way along with other individuals with disabilities

Although contemporary society has moved forward in the treatment of individuals with disabilities, these early reactions persist. Consider your own reactions to persons with speech and language impairments.

- **Rejection.** How many friends did you have in school with significant speech and language disorders? How many individuals with speech and language impairments were class leaders or had parts in school plays? How many of these individuals dated?
- **Objects of pity.** What happened when it was time to read aloud in class? How did you feel when those students were asked to present projects in class and had difficulty

with the speech and language aspects of their presentation? Were you uncomfortable? Did you feel sorry for them? Did they give oral presentations?

- **A rewarding source of humor.** Have you ever laughed at jokes or imitations of these individuals behind their backs? Have you laughed at the "humor" created by the speech and language disorders of cartoon characters such as Tweety Bird, Sylvester, Elmer Fudd, Porky Pig, and Donald Duck? Would it be funny to you if you had the same speech and language impairment as one of these cartoon characters? How would you feel as you watched everyone around you laugh at the cartoon?

Educational programming and intervention for students with speech and language impairments have been available since the early twentieth century. In 1910, the Chicago public schools hired the first "speech correction teachers." Until the 1950s, school-based speech-language pathologists had many titles, including *speech correctionists, speech specialists,* or *speech teachers.* Van Hattum (1969) credits a growing understanding of language development and skills in the identification and remediation of language disorders for the change to the term *speech therapist.* Students typically worked with speech therapists in large groups, primarily at the elementary school level.

As the profession continued to expand, and professionals in the field of speech and language disorders practiced in a wider variety of settings, specialists generally adopted a medical/clinical model, leading to the presently used term, *speech-language pathologist.* Today speech-language pathologists work in a wide variety of settings, including rehabilitation centers, nursing care facilities, health departments, and of course, public and private schools. General and special education teachers work most frequently with school-based speech-language pathologists.

Prevalence of Speech and Language Impairments

Communication disorders, which include speech and language impairments, are a high-incidence disability. According to the U.S. Department of Education (2007), approximately 20 percent of children receiving special education services are receiving services for speech and language impairments. This estimate does not include children who receive services for speech and language impairments that are secondary to other conditions such as deafness. It is estimated that one in ten persons in the United States has a speech and language disorder of one type or another (National Dissemination Center for Children with Disabilities, 2004). During the 2005–2006 school year, a total of 1,157,215 students ages 6–21 were identified as having speech and language impairments (U.S. Department of Education, 2007).

Youngsters with speech and language disorders represent almost half of preschoolers receiving a special education. Approximately 47 percent of all 3-, 4-, and 5-year-olds with a disability exhibit speech and language impairments. The U.S. Department of Education (2007) reports over 330,000 preschoolers in this category.

Etiology of Speech and Language Impairments

The etiologies, or causes, of speech and language impairments can be broadly subdivided in several different ways. One way is to classify them into **functional** versus **organic** etiologies.

Functional etiologies, such as environmental stress, have no obvious physical basis. Organic etiologies, such as cleft palate, can be linked to a physiological deficit.

Additionally, impairments may be classified as congenital, developmental, or acquired. Congenital disorders are those existing at birth; developmental disorders emerge during the preschool years. Acquired disorders are usually the result of injury, disease, or environmental insult; they most frequently result in childhood **aphasia,** which is a loss or impairment of language functions. Causative factors for developmental disorders are largely unknown, but may involve brain dysfunction, or can be secondary to hearing loss or autism. Such factors have important implications for prognosis and service delivery. Speech and language impairments can also be classified by age of onset, severity, and behavioral characteristics of the disorder (symptoms).

The etiologies of communicative disorders are frequently complex. Although most children evaluated within the context of the educational system have functional communication disorders, familiarity with causative factors of organic disorders is nonetheless important for educators. Etiologies may include congenital malformations, prenatal injury, tumors, and problems with the nervous or muscular systems, the brain, or the speech mechanism itself. Exposure to teratogens, including X-rays, viruses, drugs, and environmental toxins, can also cause congenital disorders. During the first six to twelve weeks of embryonic life, many organs are being formed. Any agent capable of damaging one organ may affect various systems developing simultaneously. A prime example of such an agent is maternal rubella (German measles). When contracted during the first trimester of pregnancy, this teratogen is capable of causing multiple and concurrent congenital problems such as cardiac defects, cataracts, mental retardation, microcephaly, short stature, hearing loss, and a variety of concurrent speech and language pathologies (Bell, 2007).

Communication problems that result from disease or traumatic insult after birth are acquired disorders. Traumatic brain injury following a motor vehicle accident is an example of an acquired disorder that frequently has negative implications for speech and language abilities. Meningitis, a disease resulting in inflammation of brain tissue, is a relatively common pediatric disorder. Complications of meningitis can result in hearing loss and associated communication deficit. Speech and language problems resulting from such an illness would represent an acquired communication disorder.

Articulation, voice quality, and fluency can be influenced by abnormalities in respiration (airflow in and out of the lungs), phonation (sound produced by the larynx), and vocal resonance (vibration within the vocal tract). Such disorders vary in degree and can occur in isolation, in combination with each other, or in conjunction with other language pathologies. Normal neurophysiology, as well as skeletal and muscular support for respiration and phonation, are necessary for speech skills to develop properly. The clinical entities presenting structural hazards to articulation include lips, teeth, limited tongue mobility (lingual frenulum), **cleft lip,** and/or **cleft palate,** as well as a number of syndromes frequently characterized by craniofacial malformation. Hearing loss, mental retardation, learning disabilities, and emotional disturbance are also commonly associated with communicative disorders and have implications for language as well as speech development.

Prevention of Speech and Language Impairments

It is difficult to assign differential responsibility to hereditary versus environmental factors (nature versus nurture) when language is disordered. Because linguistic skills are so closely linked to academic performance, determinants of language abilities are of interest to all educators.

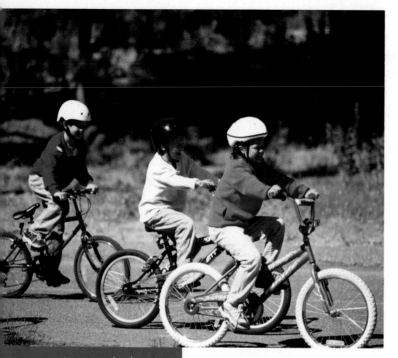

Language develops within the context of social relationships.

Any risk factor or disability that affects a child's cognitive, motor, and/or social development is also very likely to affect that child's language development; yet attempts to determine specific etiology are often not very productive. From the standpoint of prevention, however, it is useful to keep in mind the factors necessary for normal language acquisition. Four sets of variables seem to have a profound influence on language learning: (1) biological preparation; (2) successful nurturance; (3) sensorimotor experiences; and (4) linguistic experiences (McCormick, 2003a). The strongest evidence for the contention that language is a biologically determined capability comes from the fact that all cultures have language and all humans learn to talk (unless limited by sensory, neuromuscular, or cognitive impairment). As discussed earlier in this chapter, infants arrive in this world prepared to understand and use language. Their biological preparation includes neuromotor capabilities, an impressive supply of attentional and perceptual abilities, and a strong desire to interact with others. Successful nurturance requires a nurturing environment in which responsive adults carefully mediate the introduction of new stimuli. The dynamic regulation of stimuli is evident in caregiving rituals such as feeding and diapering, joint action routines (for example, peek-a-boo), and a variety of other daily interactions. Adults use these exchanges to help infants learn the rules of turn taking, the meaning of particular gestures, imitation of sounds and gestures, and mutuality. Sensorimotor experiences are the means through which infants construct their understanding of the world by acting on it, both physically and mentally (Piaget, 1952). These experiences make it possible for infants to progress, in less than two short years, from being totally reflexive and largely immobile to becoming planful thinkers who can move about independently and communicate their intentions. Finally, linguistic experiences (called child-directed speech) undoubtedly plays an important role in language learning. Caregivers facilitate language learning by continuously adjusting the phonologic, semantic, syntactic, and pragmatic characteristics of their speech when they address infants. If any one or some combination of these factors is lacking or deficient, the child is at risk for language delay and/or disorders.

Language is possibly the most complex human behavior. Yet despite significant differences in child-rearing practices across cultures, almost all normal children develop native language at about the same chronological age. Most children appear to learn their language system in a matter of a few years without formal instruction. However, development of mature language skills requires an environment that provides substantial communicative interaction. In virtually every known culture, language develops within the context of social relationships—primarily the parent or caretaker relationship. Research suggests that variability in such relationships may account for at least some differences in linguistic skills.

Months of rich social and communicative exchange precede actual production or expression of language by the child. During infancy and early childhood, caregivers respond to nonlinguistic communications, decode linguistic attempts, and provide adequate models for and shaping of the expressions of language. When these interactions fail to occur, the child is at risk for **developmental language delay.** Delayed language means that a child is slow to develop adequate vocabulary and grammar, or language age does not correspond to the child's chronological age. Refer back to Table 10.1, which lists some normal developmental milestones in speech and language, along with activities related to normal speech and language development. Awareness of basic developmental guidelines is of the utmost importance for professionals involved in the educational arena for the very young child, as communication disorders linked to developmental delays are less amenable to modification with increasing age.

For those families with one or more children having a congenital organic deficit identified as the primary cause of a communication disorder, genetic counseling is important. Genetic counseling provides not only medical and genetic information, but counseling and support for the family as well. Such counseling, when properly done, can assist parents in making informed reproductive choices as well as uncovering risks for associated medical problems. Indications for referral for genetic evaluation are very broad. A positive family history or distinct physical features suggestive of syndromic involvement are certainly indications for referral. In many instances, no specific cause for the communication disorder can be established. Nevertheless, medical follow-up by a qualified geneticist is advisable, as subsequent changes in medical status may reveal etiology or a possible link to a syndrome.

Characteristics of Speech and Language Impairments

Language, as well as its associated pathologies, can be broadly categorized into two basic types: **receptive language,** or the ability to understand what is meant by spoken communication, and **expressive language,** which involves production of language that is understood by and meaningful to others (Friend & Bursuck, 2006). Children with language disorders have difficulty expressing thoughts or understanding what is said. Expressive language skills and possible areas of deficit include grammar, syntax, fluency, vocabulary, and repetition. Receptive language deficits address response, abstraction, retention, and recall issues. A student who is unable to follow directions efficiently in the classroom may have a receptive language disorder; the child who cannot communicate clearly because of poor grammar, insufficient vocabulary, or production problems such as an articulation disorder suffers from an expressive language disorder.

Children with language impairments frequently struggle in the classroom as well as at home and in other community settings. Some of the difficulties (Bos & Vaughn, 2006) you may observe in children with expressive language disorders include

- limited vocabulary;
- incorrect grammar or syntax;
- excessive repetition of information;
- difficulty in formulating questions.

Youngsters with receptive language problems typically have difficulty

- following oral directions;
- understanding humor or figurative language;
- comprehending compound and complex sentences;
- responding to questions appropriately.

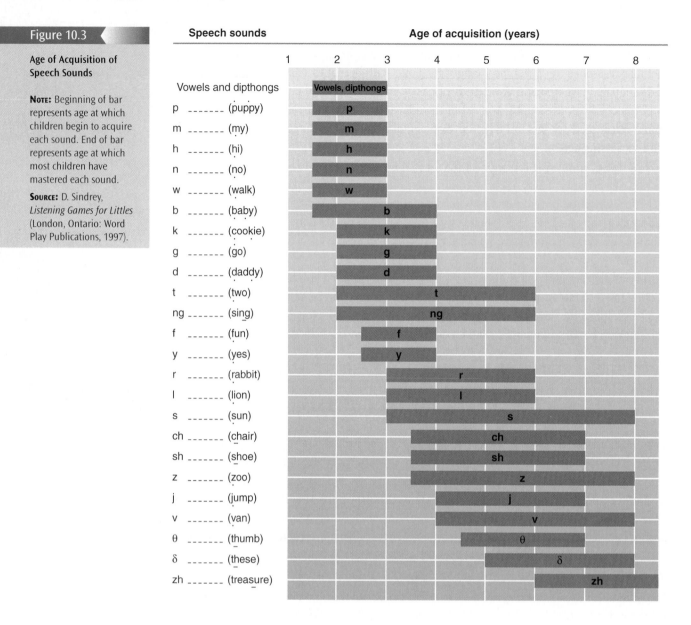

Figure 10.3

Age of Acquisition of Speech Sounds

Note: Beginning of bar represents age at which children begin to acquire each sound. End of bar represents age at which most children have mastered each sound.

Source: D. Sindrey, *Listening Games for Littles* (London, Ontario: Word Play Publications, 1997).

Speech sounds — **Age of acquisition (years)**

Vowels and dipthongs
p ------- (puppy)
m ------- (my)
h ------- (hi)
n ------- (no)
w ------- (walk)
b ------- (baby)
k ------- (cookie)
g ------- (go)
d ------- (daddy)
t ------- (two)
ng ------- (sing)
f ------- (fun)
y ------- (yes)
r ------- (rabbit)
l ------- (lion)
s ------- (sun)
ch ------- (chair)
sh ------- (shoe)
z ------- (zoo)
j ------- (jump)
v ------- (van)
θ ------- (thumb)
δ ------- (these)
zh ------- (treasure)

How do young children learn language? The answer to this question still eludes researchers, and conflicting theories abound. Beginning before age 2 and largely completed before age 4, most children acquire intelligible speech and possess a basis for development of adult grammar (McCormick, 2003a). However, there is substantial variability in the normal development of speech and language in children. For example, the age of mastery of various speech sounds may vary by as much as three years. By age 8, however, virtually all speech sounds in the child's native language should be correctly produced (see Figure 10.3).

Assessing Speech and Language Impairments

Assessment is an important step in the habilitation and management of communication disorders. The purpose of assessing the child in whom language or speech problems is suspected should be to gain insight into his or her functional abilities, limitations, and perceived needs. A wide range of assessment tools, both formal and informal, are available to assess language and speech. Some of these tools are also available in Spanish. Most of these evaluation procedures are conducted by a speech-language pathologist within the educational system or in private practice.

One of the most important tools in the assessment process for speech and language impairments is the case history. Amassing identifying information such as gender, age, natural or adoptive parents, and pertinent family status information is helpful. The initial family interview is of paramount importance to the assessment and rehabilitative effort, and sets the tone for future interactions between professionals and families. Asking parents of young children questions such as "What issues have prompted you to have your child evaluated?" or "What would be most helpful for me to know about your child?" can aid in determining parental concerns. **Family-directed assessment** focuses on information that families choose to provide regarding needs, concerns, resources, and priorities. This type of assessment is useful for infants, toddlers, and preschool-age youngsters. In this procedure, families participate in the assessment process by identifying strengths and needs and are empowered in the process of determining which support services are most necessary.

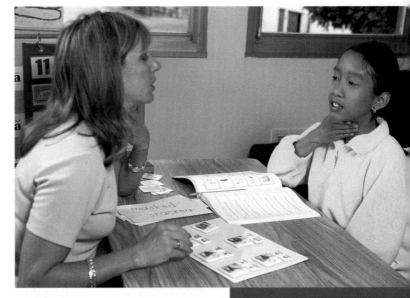

Assessment is an important first step in the habilitation and management of communication disorders.

Central auditory processing ability and language performance are difficult to evaluate as separate entities. Evaluation often necessitates a team approach involving teachers, speech-language pathologists, audiologists, neurologists, physicians, and learning disabilities specialists. Children with CAPD process auditory input in a way that is slow and inaccurate, and they work harder to interpret what they hear than their classmates do. These children are at risk for noticeable listening difficulties in many classroom situations. For example, spelling tests and note taking are activities often adversely affected by CAPD. Behavioral characteristics of children exhibiting signs of CAPD may also mimic those with learning disabilities (LD), attention deficit hyperactivity disorder (ADHD), or dyslexia.

Effective assessment should be holistic, including both formal and informal measures. Information relative to the child's hearing, motor skills, oral and respiratory mechanisms, general physical condition, educational records, and social and developmental histories must be amassed and reviewed. In addition to physical, educational, and communicative ability, consideration of the child's psychological and social status, as well as family dynamics, will affect decisions regarding effective intervention strategies. IDEA 2004 mandates that information provided by parents be included in the assessment process. While testing is important, asking questions, gathering information, observing, and directly interacting with the child also yield critical insights. This type of informal assessment requires input from the child's family members, caregivers, and significant others. Open-ended questions, such as "What concerns prompted you to seek evaluation of your child?" allow professionals to explore various social, cultural, and family issues that need to be considered in designing meaningful and individualized approaches to remediation. Awareness of these issues and their relationship to the communication difficulties provides a framework for effective treatment.

Observing the child's general appearance may also identify significant but subtle physical anomalies consistent with some congenital abnormalities that impair the communication process. Such markers might include low-set ears and peculiarities of the head, jaw, teeth, and tongue and should also be noted during the initial interview.

A speech assessment evaluates articulation, voice, and fluency abilities of the child. The articulation test is a formal evaluation procedure designed to identify sounds or phonemes that are not produced correctly in light of the student's age. The Goldman-Fristoe Test of Articulation-2 (Goldman & Fristoe, 2000) is a commonly used measure of articulation. When determining accuracy of production, test items evaluate various consonants in initial, middle, and final positions (for the sound /t/, for example, position varies in the words *two, platter, cat*).

The professional who seeks to assess language pathology faces a formidable task, however, in determining what constitutes "normalcy" for language. Evaluating children in our culturally diverse society is particularly difficult. Care must be taken that normative data account for individual and cultural differences that affect language acquisition. How can we effectively distinguish speech and language pathology in the midst of cultural diversity? Educational professionals must observe the child's speech production and compare its quality and content to that of the child's own peers. Informal measures, such as conversational sampling of speech, often provide more useful information than do formal assessment tools. Educators are encouraged to use such informal evaluation methods to enhance the evaluation process. Obtaining a **language sample** from a very young child is sometimes impossible because the child does not have speech that is sufficiently developed to provide such a sample. In this case, **prelinguistic** communicative behaviors can be used; these are frequently obtained by parent interview as well as by direct observation. A variety of scales and checklists have been designed for this purpose. The BRIGANCE® Diagnostic Inventory of Early Development II (Brigance, 2004) is an excellent example of a criterion-referenced assessment that can be used in this way.

Any comprehensive assessment of linguistic ability will require a variety of assessment measures that consider developmental level, maturity, gender, ethnicity, and cultural background (Cohen & Spenciner, 2007). On the basis of such findings, management objectives can be designed for the child and his or her family. Results of assessment may provide a baseline for pre- and postintervention comparisons, as well as indicating a need for referral to various other professional disciplines. Well-designed and -implemented evaluation techniques help determine whether linguistic competence is outside the range of normalcy, as well as clarify what communication problems are amenable to change, how much improvement can be expected, the need for a range of professional services, and variables that will influence treatment outcomes.

Assessing communication disorders, as described by Cohen and Spenciner (2007), involves six steps. First, the child must be *screened* to determine if there is a possibility of communicative disability. Next, a *referral* is made to professionals who will conduct the needed assessments. Third, *eligibility* is reviewed to determine the existence of disability, consider the need for related services, and indicate the child's strengths and weaknesses. In an effort to link instructional services with assessment, *program planning* then takes place. During this stage, locations and types of services are explored, classroom environments are assessed, and preliminary instructional design begins. Once instruction is under way, student progress, the pace of instruction, and indications for instructional modification are addressed via *program monitoring*. Finally, *program evaluation* determines whether IEP and program goals have been met as well as the overall effectiveness of treatment strategies.

Families with children who have speech and language impairments, like all families, have complicated dynamics. When a problem affects one member of the family, other members are affected as well. Family strength and needs assessments should be routinely used. The task of assisting families in creating or maintaining adequate and adaptive resources for dealing with any type of communication disorder is complex and challenging. Effective assessment and management of children with language impairments requires not only a working knowledge of communication disorders, their causes, and habilitation strategies, but an understanding and appreciation of families and their struggle in this adaptive process.

Educational Considerations

Educational planning for children with speech and language impairments involves many factors. Planning concepts that need to be considered in the classroom setting include seating arrangements, reducing distractions in the physical environment, and interactive techniques to enhance the teaching/learning process. The accompanying Suggestions for the Classroom feature outlines some educational and treatment approaches that can be used by parents, general and special education teachers, and therapists for children with central auditory processing disorders. These suggestions are valid for many other speech and language disorders discussed in this chapter and provide a good beginning when planning.

Where Are Students with Speech and Language Impairments Served?

The majority of children with speech and language impairments are served in the regular or general classroom setting. Figure 10.4 graphically represents the educational placements typically used with pupils who have a speech or language impairment.

Services for Young Children with Speech and Language Impairments

The very young linguistically disordered child represents a unique population. As knowledge regarding pediatric speech and language pathologies continues to expand, it has been noted repeatedly that there are time-locked "critical periods" for acquisition of communication skills. These windows of opportunity for language learning have historically been the subject of much study and debate. Is there an optimal time frame for providing intervention for communication disorders? Is there a point at which such intervention is really too late to be effective? Research indicates that for virtually all communication deficiencies, the younger the child, the more positive the outlook for remediation strategies.

Figure 10.4

Educational Placement of Students with Speech and Language Impairments

NOTE: This figure represents the percentages of enrollment of students with speech and language disorders during the 2005–2006 school year.

Other placements include separate schools, residential facilities, and homebound/hospital settings.

SOURCE: U.S. Department of Education. (2007). *IDEA data*. Available at https://www.ideadata.org/PartBReport.asp.

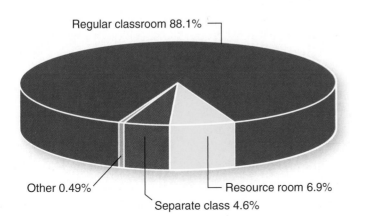

Regular classroom 88.1%

Other 0.49%

Separate class 4.6%

Resource room 6.9%

Suggestions for the Classroom

Educational and Treatment Approaches for Central Auditory Processing Problems

One approach focuses on training certain auditory and listening skills, such as auditory discrimination (for example, telling the difference between *peas* and *bees*), localization of sound, sequencing sounds, or identifying a target sound in a noisy background. Training these skills in isolation, however, may not help a child understand complex language, such as a teacher's instructions. Therefore, another approach concentrates on teaching more functional language skills (vocabulary, grammar, conversational skills) and uses strategies (visual aids, repeating directions) to facilitate the processing of language.

Changes at home and in the classroom can also help a child with central auditory processing problems.

☑ **Seating:** To help the child focus and maintain attention, select seating that is away from auditory and visual distractions. A seat close to the teacher and the blackboard and away from the window and the door may be helpful.

☑ **Setting:** Reduce external visual and auditory distractions. A large display of posters or cluttered bulletin boards can be distracting. A study carrel in the room may help. Ear plugs may be useful to block distracting noise from a heater or air conditioner, the pencil sharpener, or talking in the hallway. Check with an audiologist to find out if ear plugs are appropriate and which kind to use. Placing mats and cloth poster boards on classroom walls has been shown to decrease the reverberation of noise. A structured classroom setting may be more beneficial than an open classroom situation.

To improve the listening environment, an audiologist may recommend the use of a device that transmits the teacher's voice directly to the student's ear while blocking out background noise. The audiologist can provide recommendations on the potential benefit of available options based on the child's individual needs.

Speaking:

☑ Gain the child's attention before giving directions.

☑ Speak slowly and clearly, but do not overexaggerate speech.

☑ Use simple, brief directions.

☑ Give directions in a logical, time-ordered sequence. Use words that make the sequence clear, such as *first, next, finally.*

☑ Use visual aids and write instructions to supplement spoken information.

☑ Emphasize key words when speaking or writing, especially when presenting new information. Pre-instructions with emphasis on the main ideas to be presented may also be effective.

☑ Use gestures that clarify information.

☑ Vary loudness to increase attention.

☑ Check comprehension by asking the child questions or asking for a brief summary after key ideas have been presented.

☑ Paraphrase instructions and information in shorter and simpler sentences rather than just repeating them.

☑ Encourage the child to ask questions for further clarification.

☑ Make instructional transitions clear.

☑ Review previously learned material.

☑ Recognize periods of fatigue and give breaks as necessary.

☑ Avoid showing frustration when the child misunderstands a message.

☑ Avoid asking the child to listen and write at the same time. For children with severe central auditory processing problems, ask a buddy to take notes, or ask the teacher to provide notes. Tape-recording classes is another effective strategy.

Central auditory processing problems can affect learning, particularly in areas such as spelling and reading. It is important to identify problems early and help the child acquire adaptive strategies to compensate. If your student is a "poor" listener, frequently misunderstands speech, and has difficulty following directions, direct his or her parents to consult an audiologist or speech-language pathologist to determine if a problem exists.

SOURCE: Adapted from American Speech-Language-Hearing Association. *Processing Problems in Children* (Rockville, MD: n.d.).

✓ EFFECTIVE INSTRUCTIONAL PRACTICES   Teaching Language Skills

The teacher's use of effective teaching strategies will help students with language difficulties gain the concepts and content that they need for success in content area classes. Key strategies that can be used in teaching language concepts or patterns include the following:

- Gear the activities to the student's interests and cognitive level.
- Get the student's attention before engaging in communication activities.
- Bombard the student with the concept or skill frequently throughout the day in a functional manner.
- When speaking, place stress on the target concept or language pattern.
- Pause between phrases or sentences so that the student has time to process the new concept or language pattern.
- Decrease the rate of presentation when first introducing the concept or language pattern.
- When introducing a new concept or language pattern, use familiar, concrete vocabulary and simple sentence patterns.
- If possible, present the new concept or language pattern by using more than one input mode (e.g., auditory, visual, kinesthetic). Gestures and facial expressions that are paired with a specific language pattern often assist students in understanding the form. For example, giving a look of puzzlement or wonder when asking a question can serve as a cue to the students.
- Pair written symbols with oral language. For instance, demonstrating morphological endings such as *s* (plurals) and *ed* (past tense) can be done in writing. The students can then be cued to listen for what they see.

SOURCE: C. Bos and S. Vaughn, *Strategies for Teaching Students with Learning and Behavior Problems,* 6th ed. (Boston: Allyn and Bacon, 2006). p. 84.

The sooner early intervention begins for a youngster with communication disorders, the more promising the outcomes.

Early intervention to address communication problems in the preschool child affords a unique opportunity for successful outcomes.

To provide effective intervention for preschoolers, we must first be able to identify them. Early identification should include evaluation and treatment for young children and their families. Those at risk for having a delay in speech, language, or hearing need to be screened early and at regular intervals. Children identified as high risk include those from neonatal intensive care units, children with chronic ear infections, those with known genetic defects, and children with fetal alcohol syndrome, neurological defects, or delayed language.

Public Law 99-457 mandates that speech-language pathologists evaluate and treat children between the ages of 3 and 5. All states currently serve youngsters from birth to 5 years of age. When providing services to infants and toddlers, assessment of the family—its strengths, needs, and interaction patterns—is as important as the evaluation of the child. Because the structure of the American family is changing, caregivers other than parents may be involved in treatment strategies. Many of the newly developed rating scales, which specifically analyze communication-promoting behaviors between a child and his or her caregiver, reflect the importance of this relationship. This type of observation is a valuable tool in quantifying strengths and weaknesses in daily communicative interactions—for example, the level of vocabulary used with the child, the number of attempts to engage the child in communication, the quality of voice animation and body language, responses to the child's attempts to communicate, and imitation of the child's efforts—and planning appropriate remediation strategies.

Evaluation of language skills in the preschool child should always include such measures as adaptive behavior scales, parent interviews, and informal language sampling. More formal assessment tools for examining language in very young children are increasing in number. Many of these tests are developmental scales that look at language as part of the assessment process.

Young children with speech and language impairments (whether as a primary or secondary disability) generally thrive in general education preschool settings. These settings provide daily interactions with peer models and exposure to a rich variety of experiences. Children have the opportunity to observe, learn, and practice age-appropriate social, communication, and cognitive skills. The single most essential element of language intervention in these settings is arranging the environment (McCormick, 2003b). Environmental arrangement entails selection and use of materials, arrangement of the physical space, and the provision of structure to activities.

Adolescents and Adults with Speech and Language Impairments

Transitioning from the educational world to the adult workplace presents a special challenge for professionals involved with adolescents with communication problems. This period of rapid change from childhood to adulthood involves social, emotional, psychological, and cognitive variables. Searching for one's own identity, coping with issues of sexuality, striving for independence, group loyalty, and identification are complex issues that are compounded by communication disorders. Working effectively with the adolescent population requires tremendous understanding and empathy from the educational professional. The intense desire of the adolescent to be like others can retard well-intentioned diagnostic and rehabilitative efforts.

Family Issues

It is imperative that professionals understand and have some empathy for the emotional and family history dilemmas invariably associated with the families of children with communication disorders. Luterman (2002) describes the medical model of assessment as "diagnosis by committee." In this model, parents are confronted by an array of professional "experts" delivering reports filled with technical jargon, much of which is neither understood nor retained. Indeed, many parents of communicatively impaired children describe the initial assessment of their child as very unpleasant or upsetting. Contemporary medical and educational models for assessment and treatment of speech and language impairments are largely child centered in their approach. Ignoring the needs of the family, they fail to address the concerns of those who are most significantly affected by the impairment.

Appropriately designed family-centered intervention is based only in part on formal assessment. The value of any assessment procedure is only as good as the counseling that accompanies it. Allowing parents to "tell their story," share concerns, and "be the expert" regarding their child is essential to empower them as partners in the habilitation process. Including parents and family members as active participants in both assessment and habilitation encourages involvement from those most intimately involved with the child, increasing effectiveness in treating communication disorders. Ideally, parents then emerge as actual partners in the rehabilitative process.

The hour or two a week that a child with a speech or language impairment might spend with a speech-language pathologist is infinitesimal compared to the time spent with other adults (parent, teachers) and peers. The speech-language pathologist attempts to learn as much as possible about the child's activities in various environments so that all of the child's communication partners can be involved in the intervention process. For instance, the speech-language pathologist works with family members to develop a better understanding of the child's needs and how best to facilitate interaction and communication. Specifically, the speech-language pathologist collaborates with family members to help them learn how to keep conversations with the child focused on the present, reduce distractions during conversations, slow the rate and decrease the complexity of language directed to the child, and maximize nonlinguistic cues.

Issues of Diversity

The United States is currently experiencing near record immigration. More than 14 million individuals immigrated to the United States in the 1990s, and just as many new arrivals are predicted for this decade. One result of this influx of new citizens is that one in five U.S. children has a parent who is an immigrant (Urban Institute, 2007). This most likely means that vast numbers of children who do not speak standard American English as their first language will be in need of help with one aspect of language or another.

How families interact with their children and the prelinguistic skills that develop from these interactions vary considerably across cultures (Johnson & Wong, 2002). Observations of non-Western cultural groups make it clear that the large literature on child-directed talk primarily describes Western parent–child interaction patterns. When working with children from culturally and linguistically diverse populations, the speech-language pathologist may draw teaching materials directly from the children's homes and communities, capitalizing on whatever communication skills they have, regardless of whether they are verbal or nonverbal, in English or another language.

Over the past several decades, the descriptor for individuals who are second-language learners has changed. The term *limited English proficient (LEP)*, which was popular in the 1990s, has been replaced, in some educational circles, by *potentially English proficient (PEP)* (Quinones-Eatman, 2001). The former term seemed to emphasize what the child does not know rather than the positive aspects of bilingualism. IDEA 2004, however, still uses the term *limited English proficient.*

The lack of reliable and valid tests makes it extremely difficult to identify bilingual children with speech and language impairments. There is always the issue of whether speech and language variations are due to a disorder or to the child's development in the second language (Bunce, 2003). Too often PEP children are mistakenly placed in special education classes based on their scores on tests normed on English-speaking students. Many are misdiagnosed and labeled as having mental retardation, learning disabilities, or speech and language impairments.

Intervention for PEP children who have language impairments depends on age, severity of the disability, attitude and goals of the family, resources and available social interactions, and vocational expectations (Bunce, 2003). Most intervention programs incorporate a variety of techniques similar to those used with monolingual children with language impairments, combined with techniques for second-language learners. The former focus on the different components of language—pragmatics, semantics, morphology, syntax, and phonology. Additional techniques for second-language learners include (1) teaching vocabulary and syntax in the context of ongoing activities, (2) allowing time for comprehension to develop before insisting on production, (3) using predictable books, (4) using peer buddies, and (5) incorporating parents and other family members as teaching partners.

Technology and Individuals with Speech and Language Impairments

Symbols, aids, strategies, and techniques used to enhance the communication process are commonly known as **augmentative or alternative communication (AAC).** This includes sign language and various communication boards, both low-tech and high-tech devices, that are used by individuals with impaired oral motor skills.

Kangas and Lloyd (2006) define an augmentative communication strategy as one that aids, enhances, or supplements the individual's residual speech skills. On the other hand, alternative communication completely supplants typical communication, such as a device with computerized speech output. The use of AAC systems and devices has been shown to be of significant benefit to pupils with communication challenges (Millar, Light, & Schlosser, 2006). These devices provide a means for children with speech and language impairments to interact and communicate with family members, teachers, friends, classmates, and other individuals (Kangas & Lloyd).

Technology has opened a world of opportunity for children who are nonverbal to access and use alternative and augmentative communication devices. Under IDEA, these devices are classified as assistive technology. Children who may benefit from AAC include children with autism spectrum disorders who are nonverbal, children with cerebral palsy, and students who are mentally retarded. The most basic AAC devices can be nonelectronic or electronic. Most beginners use a form of nonelectronic AAC called communication boards. This low-tech device usually starts with a limited number of choices (two to four). Choices can be represented by real items, pictures of items, or symbols for items (printed words or Bliss symbols, for example). Having children express a choice regarding foods or activities (concrete choices that can be implemented immediately) are typical beginning activities. As the AAC user makes gains in his or her ability and desire to express concrete preferences and connects the use of the communication board to the desired response, the communication board options grow in the number of possible selections. The use of high-tech electronic AAC devices begins in the same way. The added feature is that the AAC selections can include voice capabilities. Some of the most basic electronic AAC devices (for example, Cheap Talk) can be fitted for as few as one or as many as eight selections per template used. DynaVox, another popular AAC device for school-age children, can be programmed for as few as two selections and expanded over time to handle all of the communication needs of an adult. To date, the most sophisticated system available is the Liberator. Stephen Hawking, Nobel prize winner and author of *Theory of the Black Hole,* has used a Liberator for communication because of the effects of amyotrophic lateral sclerosis (ALS) on his oral motor function.

Electronic communication boards are an example of an alternative or augmentative communication device.

Most advanced high-tech AAC devices have voice selection capabilities. This allows the user to have a voice of the same gender and age range as herself or himself. For children with significant motor challenges, many electronic AAC devices are now made single-switch accessible.

Although the history of AAC spans only a little more than four decades, the sum of its accomplishments is impressive. In the early 1970s, there were fewer than a dozen published reports of hearing individuals with severe communication disability using manual signs, communication boards, or modified typewriters to augment or replace speech. Today there are hundreds of books, chapters, periodicals, and newsletters devoted exclusively to AAC information and research reports. Most university personnel preparation programs now have at least one AAC course, and there is a professional organization (International Society for Augmentative and Alternative Communication) for people interested in the AAC field that publishes a quarterly journal (*Augmentative and Alternative Communication*).

Trends, Issues, and Controversies

Speech and language impairments represent a *high-incidence disability*—an impairment that has far-reaching and pervasive effects. Advances in the areas of early intervention, genetic research, and enhanced assistive technology continue to improve the prognosis for those with speech and language disorders. As research data confirm the merits of early intervention for children with communication disorders, particularly language disorders, medical and educational professionals have become increasingly aware of the urgent need for early and accurate diagnosis and timely, well-designed provision of services.

Both medical and educational assessment techniques are the subject of ongoing review and modification. With the advent of sophisticated neurodiagnostic procedures such as brain mapping, the base of knowledge regarding the causes of many speech and language impairments is expanding rapidly. More effective management strategies will surely follow the acquisition of such understanding. As the human genome project unlocks the complexities of the genetic code, the incidence of syndromes and disorders with a hereditary component may be reduced as medical intervention concurrently becomes more effective.

Cultural diversity, dialects, and nonstandard English have come to the forefront in political and educational arenas because of their implications for linguistic performance. Common tools for assessing speech and language ability will continue to be reviewed for their adequacy in measuring linguistic skills of populations that are increasingly multicultural.

Controversy certainly persists regarding the etiologies of various speech and language disorders, such as CAPD and stuttering. With increased understanding of the underlying neurophysiological basis of such problems, educational management strategies for these and other disorders continue to improve. Digital technology has certainly enlarged the array of electronic devices that increase message redundancy or offer viable alternatives to conventional methods of communication. Such assistive technology provides avenues for communication that did not previously exist.

Inclusion of family members as partners in remediation efforts is currently viewed as best practice. Particularly for the young children, parental attitude toward and involvement in the intervention process is crucial (Guralnick, Connor, Neville, & Hammond, 2002).

Rapid technological change is a hallmark of contemporary society. Biomedical innovations and increasingly sophisticated interventions and assessment strategies should encourage individuals and families dealing with speech and language impairments and hold promise for continued progress for those professionals who endeavor to assist them.

Chapter in Review

The Nature of Speech, Language, and Communication

- **Speech** is the expression of language with sounds—essentially, the oral modality for language.

- **Language** is a code whereby ideas about the world are represented through a conventional system of arbitrary signals for communication.

- Language has five components—**phonology, morphology, semantics, syntax,** and **pragmatics**—that are present at both the receptive and expressive levels.

- **Communication** is the exchange of ideas, information, thoughts, and feelings. It does not necessarily require speech or language.

Defining Speech and Language Impairments

- The most common speech problem is an **articulation disorder**, which includes substitutions, omissions, distortions, and additions.

- Stuttering and cluttering are examples of **fluency disorders.**

- **Voice disorders** are associated with the larynx. Phonation and resonance are illustrations of this disorder.

- **Apraxia** of speech involves both speech and language disorders. It results from the inability to position speech muscles necessary to produce speech sounds.

- **Central auditory processing disorder (CAPD)** is a problem in the processing of sound not attributed to hearing loss or intellectual ability.

Prevalence of Speech and Language Impairments

- About 20 percent of children receiving special education services are receiving services for speech and language impairments.

Etiology of Speech and Language Impairments

- Speech and language problems can result from **functional** (without an obvious physical basis) or **organic** (associated physiological deficit) etiologies.

- Disorders may be congenital or the result of an acquired insult.

- **Aphasia** is the loss or impairment of language functions.

Characteristics of Speech and Language Impairments

- The ability to understand what is meant by spoken communication is known as **receptive language**; the production of language that is understood by and meaningful to others is identified as **expressive language.**

Assessing Speech and Language Impairments

- Identifying speech and language impairments frequently involves collaborative teams using formal and informal performance measures.

Educational Considerations

- The vast majority (almost 90 percent) of pupils with speech or language impairments receive services in the general education classroom.

Technology and Individuals with Speech and Language Impairments

- **Augmentative or alternative communication** (AAC) devices include symbols, aids, strategies, and techniques used as a supplement or alternative to oral language. Sign language and communication boards, both manual and electronic, are two examples of these devices.

Study Questions

1. What are the two main categories of communication disorder?

2. How does IDEA define speech and language impairments?

3. List the three broad categories of speech disorders, and give an example of each.

4. Define language, and explain how it is different from speech.

5. List several factors that cause or contribute to voice disorders.

6. At what age should a child be pronouncing all sounds correctly? What course of action should be taken if he or she is not?

7. List the five rules that must be learned for successful language acquisition to occur.

8. Define central auditory processing disorder. What types of intervention strategies are most effective with this population?

9. Describe the evolution of the role of the speech-language pathologist during the twentieth century.

10. How does a developmental disorder differ from one that is acquired?

11. How has family-centered early intervention influenced remediation strategies for young children with speech and language impairments?

12. List an age-appropriate developmental milestone for a child 2 to 3 years of age.

13. Define expressive and receptive language.

14. Describe an effective informal measure of communication skills for the young child.

15. What difficulties are inherent to assessment of speech and language skills in a culturally diverse population?

16. Define AAC, and describe its use by children with speech and language impairments.

Key Terms

speech	distortions	disorder	cleft lip
language	additions	apraxia of speech	cleft palate
phonology	fluency disorders	morphological disorder	developmental language
morphology	stuttering	semantic disorder	delay
semantics	cluttering	syntactical deficits	receptive language
syntax	voice disorders	pragmatic difficulties	expressive language
pragmatics	phonation	central auditory processing	family-directed assessment
communication	resonance	disorder (CAPD)	language sample
articulation disorders	hypernasality	functional	prelinguistic
omissions	hyponasality	organic	augmentative or alternative
substitutions	phonological	aphasia	communication (AAC)

Learning Activities

1. Visit an educational setting serving students with speech and language impairments. How was the students' classroom performance affected by their communication difficulty? How were their social interactions with other students and teachers affected? Were any special teaching techniques used or classroom modifications made to enhance their performance? Was therapy given outside of the general education classroom? Was this arrangement positive or negative? How did intervention differ for older children? What was your overall impression of the services provided?

2. Visit a clinic or hospital in your community providing services to persons with speech and/or language impairments. Interview the speech-language pathologist. What types of disorders are served? Are there special challenges in assessment techniques? What types of intervention strategies are used? What interaction does this professional have with the community at large? With area schools? Is there a team approach in use? Is there a family-centered remediation model for implementing therapy?

3. Prepare a resource book for your class that describes common types of speech and language impairments and their characteristics. Include appropriate assessment, referral, and remediation strategies. Provide information on causes and prevention, assistive technology, need for early intervention, and classroom strategies. Provide some Web sites of interest for each disorder.

4. Compile a list of local agencies (public and private), medical facilities, civic groups, and educational settings that provide services to persons with speech and language impairments. Be sure to include contact information as well as a brief description of services provided.

5. Visit a local preschool program for children at risk for language delay. Interview a staff member. Find out how young children are screened for speech and language problems, and describe the process. Volunteer to help with screenings if possible. What types of language stimulation activities are used? How are families included in this process? What is your opinion regarding the effectiveness of the program?

Organizations Concerned with Speech and Language Impairments

Alliance for Technology Access
1304 Southpoint Boulevard, Suite 240
Petaluma, CA 94954
(707) 778-3011

American Speech-Language-Hearing Association (ASHA)
10801 Rockville Pike
Rockville, MD 20852
(301) 897-5700; (V/TT) (800) 638-8255

Cleft Palate Foundation
1504 E. Franklin Street, Suite 1022
Chapel Hill, NC 27514
(919) 933-9044

Division for Communicative Disabilities and Deafness (DCDD)
Council for Exceptional Children
1110 N. Glebe Road
Suite 300
Arlington, VA 22201-5704
(703) 620-3660

National Craniofacial Association
P.O. Box 11082
Chattanooga, TN 37401
(800) 332-2373

National Easter Seals Society
230 W. Monroe Street, Suite 1800
Chicago, IL 60606-4802
(312) 726-6200

National Dissemination Center for Children with Disabilities
P.O. Box 1492
Washington, DC 20013-1492
(800) 695-0285 (Voice/TTY)

Reflecting on Standards

The following exercises are designed to help you learn to apply the Council for Exceptional Children (CEC) standards to your teaching practice. Each of the reflection exercises below correlates with a knowledge or skill within the CEC standards. For the full text of each of the related CEC standards, please refer to the standards integration grid located in Appendix B.

1. Focus on Foundations (*CEC Content Standard #1 CC1K5*)

Reflect on what you have learned about how students with speech and language impairments are diagnosed. If you had a student in your class with a culturally or linguistically diverse background who exhibited signs of speech or language impairments, what kinds of issues might you have in defining and identifying if he/she had exceptional learning needs? How might you need to work with families and school personnel to make sure to address the student's learning needs?

2. Focus on Individual Learning Differences (*CEC Content Standard #3 CC3K1*)

Reflect on what you have learned about students with speech and language impairments. If you were to have a student in your class who needed to daily meet with a speech-language pathologist, how might you support the student's attendance at therapy? How do you think the student might feel about standing out from his/her peers? How might his/her exceptional learning needs affect his/her relationships with peers? What can you, as a teacher, do to help alleviate any discomfort for the student?

Technology Resources

Visit the Web-based SAGE Study Site at **http://www.sagepub.com/gargiulo3estudy** for these additional learning tools:

- Chapter quizzes
- Key term flashcards
- Media links
- Full-text SAGE journal articles
- Internet activities
- Additional Web resources

CHAPTER 11

Individuals with Hearing Impairments

A Parent's Story

We didn't think we would ever have a child. We were married for eleven years before the magic day. Christine is our little miracle child. Preparing for parenthood was lots of fun. We decorated a nursery, went shopping for furniture and clothes, and set up a college fund. Baby showers and teas were an exciting end to an uneventful pregnancy. My pregnancy was normal with no complications. The delivery was induced since my blood pressure was rising at the end. I had natural childbirth. She was beautiful . . . two eyes, one nose, one mouth, ten fingers, ten toes, and all in the right places. All the early checkups were routine, no problems.

I didn't start to worry until Christine was about 6 months of age. My pediatrician listened to my concerns. At an office visit, Christine was playing with the paper on the exam table when the doctor came in. He clapped his hands loudly. I almost jumped out of my skin, but our little girl never knew he was in the room. He examined her ears and found nothing wrong. He sent us to an ENT [ear, nose, and throat specialist].

The first ENT said that there must be fluid behind her eardrums, so we got tubes. That didn't seem to make any difference. That ENT sent us to another ENT. The second ENT told me I was a hypochondriac and there was nothing wrong with my child. Finally, we were sent to another ENT, who diagnosed Christine as being hearing impaired, but because of her age, he was not sure of the severity. Let the grieving begin . . . no one plans on having a child with a disability. All our hopes and dreams popped like a balloon. What were we going to do? Where do we find help?

We started reading and calling, talking to everyone. Christine got her first set of hearing aids before her first birthday, but they were not strong enough. Each time we got bigger and more powerful hearing aids. At age 1, she was finally diagnosed as profoundly hearing impaired. We wanted her to talk. We wanted her to be independent. I didn't want to send her to a special school, isolated from society.

We started Auditory Verbal Therapy. We made it a part of our daily life. It was once told to us that Auditory Verbal Therapy was living your life but narrating everything you see and do. After about six months with the most powerful hearing aids made, we didn't see any or very much progress.

Written by Betty Nelson, University of Alabama at Birmingham

Being in the medical profession, we started reading and talking to people about cochlear implants. That would be the next step. We talked to several surgeons in Georgia, Texas, Tennessee, and here at home in Alabama. Christine was implanted at 2 years 4 months of age and the implant was turned on the first of November. It was a frightening time for all of us. She was our little miracle child, and we had waited so very long for her. Christine and our lives began again after her implant was stimulated. It worked!!!!!! The first month was very hard on all of us, with lots of tears from us all. It was a new world with sound. She was turning to her name within two weeks. We worked with her every day, all waking hours. We sang, talked, and babbled.

Christine was enrolled in a church preschool with normal hearing kids. We pushed her out there, but we were always right behind her all the way. Currently, Christine is in a mainstreamed elementary school with a sound field system in the classroom. She gets some help from a teacher of the hearing impaired when she needs it. We are there to help with anything she might not understand and to reinforce what is taught in the classroom. She is making straight A's so far. Christine enjoys dancing competitively. We don't know how she does it.

If you were to sit and talk to her today, you would never know she had a disability. She has beautiful speech with great inflections in her voice. We were at a company party, there were a lot of people we didn't know and who didn't know us. The kids were all swimming in the lake. I overheard one little boy ask his mother why Christine didn't talk to him, she did earlier that day. I interrupted and asked the little boy if she had her back to him while he was talking. We told him she was deaf and could not hear him without her processor on. All the other parents were astonished. "But she talks so well, she doesn't sound deaf or sign," people said. We had to tell them all about cochlear implants and what a huge change it made in our life. Christine sounds like any other normal hearing child. That made us feel great. Strangers couldn't tell she was hearing impaired.

If we can tell anyone about cochlear implants, it would be to say that it was the best thing that happened to us. It is worth looking into and doing. It is a lot of hard work. As a family, we have dedicated many hours and money to the rehabilitation of Christine.

We are very grateful for having a child like her. She is a joy to be with and watching her now . . . all the hard work we have done early on has paid off. Granted, she will never have normal hearing and has to work harder than anyone in her classes, but we wouldn't change a thing. She is a great example of what a cochlear implant at an early age can do for someone.

—*Kitty McBride*

For most people, hearing is an automatic process. The ability to hear allows individuals to gain information about themselves and the world around them through development of communication skills and identification of environmental auditory clues. Language, the central communication skill in humans, is learned by interacting with the environment and associating stimuli in numerous ways (Allen & Cowdery, 2009). Typically, an individual's language is refined and speech is developed through a series of activities: observing, listening, understanding, imitating others, hearing oneself, and comparing and perfecting speech and language components of the communication process. Parts of these activities and the development of language and speech may be difficult for individuals with hearing impairments.

Definitions and Concepts in the Field of Hearing Impairment

Hearing impairment is a general term used to describe disordered hearing. We should point out that the use of this term is offensive to some individuals who are deaf and hard of hearing because the word *impairment* implies a deficiency. Although we acknowledge this viewpoint, the label *hearing impairment* is preferred by the federal government when describing this disability category. We have chosen to be consistent with the terminology used by the U.S. Department of Education.

Hearing sensitivity loss refers to a specific aspect of hearing impairment, and is ordinarily described as ranging in severity from mild to profound. The term **deaf** is often overused and misunderstood, and may be applied inappropriately to describe a wide variety of hearing loss. It can be defined as referring to those for whom the sense of hearing is nonfunctional for the ordinary purposes of life. The federal definition (PL 108-446) describes deafness as a hearing loss that adversely affects educational performance and is so severe that the child is impaired in processing linguistic information (communication) through hearing, with or without amplification (hearing aids). Deafness precludes successful processing of linguistic information through audition, with or without a hearing aid (Kuder, 2008). The term *Deaf,* used with a capital D, refers to those individuals who want to be identified with Deaf culture. It is inappropriate and misleading to use the term *deaf* in reference to any hearing loss that is mild or moderate in degree.

Persons who are hearing impaired but possess enough **residual hearing** (remaining usable hearing) to hear and understand speech may be described as **hard of hearing.** Hard of hearing individuals are those in whom the sense of hearing, although defective, is functional either with or without a hearing aid. For these persons, the use of a hearing aid is frequently necessary or desirable to enhance residual hearing (Kuder, 2008).

A **minimal hearing loss (MHL),** although not currently classified as a hearing impairment, is gaining significant attention. Persons with MHL have difficulty hearing spoken language at a distance or in the presence of background noise. Both of these conditions are present in classrooms and can significantly affect the ability of a child with MHL to learn language and succeed academically (Kaderavek & Pakulski, 2002; Kuder, 2008). The extent to which persons with hearing impairment have difficulty in developing speech and language, as well as the degree of auditory communication difficulty they experience, is heavily influenced by the degree of hearing loss.

The Anatomy of the Auditory System

The ear is divided into four connected sections: the **outer ear** (also known as the auricle), the **middle ear,** the **inner ear,** and the **central auditory nervous system** (see Figure 11.1). The outer ear functions to protect the middle ear, direct sound into the ear canal, and enhance sound localization. In addition, the outer ear serves to enhance the intensity of sounds in the mid-frequency range where the sound spectrum of speech is located.

Sound waves enter the outer ear and travel through the ear canal to the **tympanic membrane** (eardrum), causing a vibrating action. The tympanic membrane is attached to one of three of the smallest bones in the body, the **malleus** (hammer), through which the sound vibrations are transmitted to the second and third of the smallest bones, the **incus** (anvil) and the **stapes** (stirrup). These three bone structures form the **ossicular chain,** a bridge of bones across which sound vibrations travel to the inner ear. Together with the tympanic

Figure 11.1

A Cross Section of the Human Ear

Source: Redrawn from J. Northern, *Hearing Disorders,* 3rd ed. (Boston: Allyn and Bacon, 1996), p. 16.

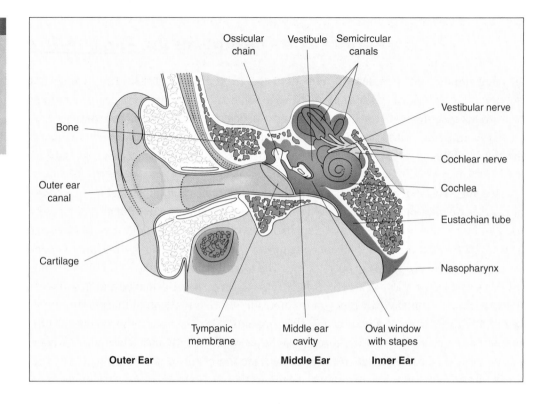

membrane, the ossicles convert airborne sound waves into mechanical (vibratory) energy and transfer this to the inner ear.

The footplate of the stapes, the smallest of the three middle ear bones, fits into the **oval window,** an opening into the inner ear. The vibratory motion of the stapes footplate in the oval window transmits mechanical energy to fluid-filled channels within the snail-like structure of the **cochlea** (inner ear). The cochlea houses the end organ of hearing, called the **organ of Corti.** Waves set up in the cochlear fluid, the result of vibratory energy from the tympanic membrane and ossicular chain, stimulate nearly 20,000 tiny hair cells in the organ of Corti arrayed along the length of the cochlea. This mechanical energy is transformed into electrical nerve impulses. The hair cells near the oval window respond to high-frequency energy, and those in the middle and at the apex of the cochlea to low-frequency energy. The resultant nerve impulses course through the auditory nervous system pathways to the auditory cortex, located in the temporal lobe of the brain, for message decoding (Herer, Knightly, & Steinberg, 2007).

Classifications of Hearing Loss

The classification or type of hearing loss refers primarily to the site of disorder in the auditory system causing the hearing impairment. A **conductive hearing loss** is caused by a blockage or barrier to the transmission of sound through the outer or middle ear. It is referred to as a conductive loss because sound is not conducted normally through the mechanical sound-conducting mechanisms in the disordered outer or middle ear (Stach, 1998). As a result, sounds are soft or attenuated in some way for the listener, but clearly heard when loud enough. Common causes of a conductive loss include inflammation, infection of the middle ear (**otitis media**), objects in the ear, or malformations of the outer or middle ear. Typically, a conductive loss can be reversed by medical or surgical intervention.

A **sensorineural hearing loss** is caused by disorders of the inner ear (cochlea), the auditory nerve that transmits impulses to the brain, or both. In this type of hearing loss, there is not only a loss of hearing sensitivity, but sounds are usually distorted to the listener and speech often is not heard clearly. This type of hearing loss may be congenital or may occur as a result of accident, illness, or disease. Although a small percentage of sensorineural hearing losses can be medically or surgically treated, most cannot be and are permanent in nature (Bess & Humes, 2003).

A **mixed hearing loss** is a combination of both a conductive and a sensorineural loss. In many cases, the conductive portion of the hearing loss may respond to medical or surgical treatment. Typically, however, the listener continues to experience the effects of the residual sensorineural impairment and may be a candidate for a hearing aid (Bess & Humes, 2003).

A **central hearing disorder** is one resulting from disorder or dysfunction in the central auditory nervous system between the brainstem and the auditory cortex in the brain. A hearing loss may or may not accompany this type of hearing impairment. The listener with this impairment may be able to hear, but not make sense of or understand speech. Additional problems, such as short- and long-term auditory memory and reading comprehension disability (Salvia, Ysseldyke, & Bolt, 2007), may also be present. This impairment may be referred to as a central auditory processing disorder, as described in Chapter 10 (Stach, 1998).

A similar type of hearing loss is **auditory neuropathy/auditory dys-synchrony.** In this type of hearing loss, the cochlea is functioning normally but there is an absence of neural function. A relatively recent area of research, auditory neuropathy/auditory dys-synchrony is estimated to be present in 1 of every 10 children with a hearing impairment and 3 of every 1,000 high-risk neonates. The effect of this type of loss is highly variable, and its eventual outcome is unpredictable (Scott, 2003).

A final, much less common type of hearing loss is **functional or nonorganic hearing loss.** Persons with this disorder typically demonstrate a loss of hearing that is inconsistent with **audiometric test** findings (Roeser, Valente, & Hosford-Dunn, 2007). In most cases, some organic hearing loss actually exists in these persons, but they may exaggerate the loss at the time of the audiometric evaluation. In some cases, test results show no organic hearing loss at all, although the individual may claim a hearing deficit.

Persons with hearing loss caused by a disorder in the brain or auditory nerve can be expected to have more difficulty processing sound and developing speech and language than those with hearing impairments caused by readily treatable factors such as ear infection. The type and degree of hearing loss often have significant implications for treatment and education.

Degree of Hearing Loss

The severity of auditory and speech communication disorders is often directly related to the degree or severity of hearing loss. Although there are individual differences in the effects associated with a given degree of hearing loss, listeners with mild hearing impairments generally experience less difficulty in auditory communication interactions than persons with a severe or profound degree of hearing loss. Persons with no hearing at all in one ear but normal hearing in the other experience some specific hearing deficits, but do not lose half of their hearing.

Measurement of Hearing Impairment

An **audiologist** is an independent professional who holds certification and/or licensure and provides evaluation, rehabilitation, and prevention services to persons with hearing

Accurate assessment of a hearing loss is important for determining its impact on communication.

impairments. Audiologists are the primary specialists in evaluating hearing loss and determining the extent to which that loss constitutes an impairment and disability. Typically, the assessment of hearing begins with the goal of accurately measuring hearing threshold levels. If a hearing loss exists, the audiologist uses test and measurement procedures to determine the extent of the deficit, the impact on communication function, whether the hearing loss can be treated medically or surgically, or whether the use of hearing aids or other amplification systems is indicated.

Auditory threshold measures obtained by the audiologist during a hearing evaluation are plotted on a graph called an **audiogram** (see Figure 11.2). The horizontal axis of an audiogram is divided into octave intervals corresponding to the principal test frequencies of interest during the evaluation. The **frequency** of a particular sound is a measure of the rate at which the sound source vibrates and is measured in **hertz (Hz),** so named in honor of a German scientist. The frequency of sounds can be precisely measured electronically. Pitch is the psychological correlate of frequency and cannot be measured as precisely because it is perceived differently from one person to the next. But in general, as the frequency of a sound increases, a listener perceives the sound as having increased in pitch. The audiogram typically displays a range of frequencies from about 250 Hz to 8,000 Hz. Most sounds important to human beings fall between 125 and 8,000 Hz, with most of the energy in human speech concentrated in the range of 500 to 3,000 Hz (Berk, 2006).

The vertical axis of the audiogram displays hearing threshold levels (HTLs) in increments of 10 **decibels (dB),** with 0 dB at the top (representing no hearing loss). As the hearing loss increases, the hearing thresholds are plotted lower down on the audiogram. Decibels are units of sound pressure. Sound pressure is a physical measure that can be precisely determined. It is associated with the psychological sensation of loudness, which is not perceived identically by all persons. In general, as sound pressure in decibels increases, the sensation of loudness increases. Human speech normally ranges between 40 and 60 dB sound pressure level; any sound above 130 dB sound pressure level, such as large electrical turbines (145 dB), can be extremely painful and damaging (Bess & Humes, 2003). Table 11.1 (page 402) presents the decibel levels of everyday sounds from our environment.

During the basic hearing evaluation process, **pure-tone audiometry** is conducted through earphones or other means to obtain an audiogram. Stimuli are delivered to the listener until a test signal of a particular frequency is barely audible 50 percent of the time. It is then presented to the person being evaluated, and a hearing threshold level for that signal can be plotted on the audiogram. This is a convenient and well-accepted measurement technique permitting an efficient determination of hearing threshold levels across the frequency range most important for hearing and understanding speech and environmental sounds. Ordinarily, pure-tone audiometry will be conducted in two modes, air conduction and bone conduction. **Air-conduction audiometry** is carried out with earphones or speakers and reflects hearing thresholds measured through the outer, middle, and inner ears. In contrast,

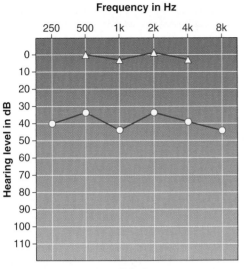

Panel A

An audiogram demonstrating that when the outer or middle ear is not functioning normally, resulting in a conductive hearing loss, the intensity of the air-conducted signals must be raised before threshold is reached while the bone-conduction thresholds remain normal.

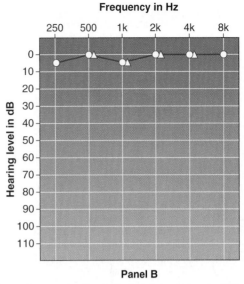

Panel B

An audiogram showing that when the outer and middle ear are functioning normally, air-conduction and bone-conduction thresholds are the same.

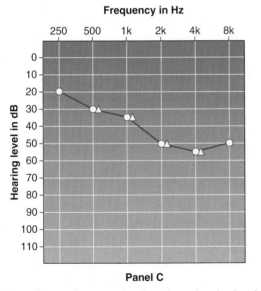

Panel C

An audiogram demonstrating that when a hearing loss is of cochlear origin, resulting in a sensorineural hearing loss, both air- and bone-conduction thresholds are affected similarly.

Panel D

Audiogram showing a mixed hearing loss.

○ Air conduction   △ Bone conduction

Figure 11.2

Audiograms Demonstrating Types of Hearing Loss

Source: Adapted from B. Stach, *Clinical Audiology: An Introduction* (San Diego, CA: Singular Publishing Group, 1998), pp. 79–80, 98.

bone-conduction audiometry is carried out with a small vibrator placed on the forehead or on the bone behind the ear, stimulating the inner ear directly. This reflects hearing sensitivity as measured primarily from the inner ear, not from the conductive mechanism in the outer and middle ears. A comparison of air- and bone-conduction hearing threshold levels forms the basis of determining the type of hearing loss present.

Table 11.1	Decibel Levels of Common Environmental Sounds

Noise levels are measured in decibels (dB). The higher the decibel level, the louder the noise. Sounds louder than 80 decibels are considered potentially hazardous. The noise chart below gives an idea of average decibel levels for everyday sounds around you.

Painful	• 150 dB = rock music peak • 140 dB = firearms, air raid siren, jet engine • 130 dB = jackhammer • 120 dB = jet plane take-off, amplified rock music at 4–6 ft., car stereo, band practice
Extremely Loud	• 110 dB = rock music, model airplane • 106 dB = timpani and bass drum rolls • 100 dB = snowmobile, chain saw, pneumatic drill • 90 dB = lawnmower, shop tools, truck traffic, subway
Very Loud	• 80 dB = alarm clock, busy street • 70 dB = busy traffic, vacuum cleaner • 60 dB = conversation, dishwasher
Moderate	• 50 dB = moderate rainfall • 40 dB = quiet room
Faint	• 30 dB = whisper, quiet library

Source: Adapted from the American Speech-Language-Hearing Association. Available at http://www.asha.org/public/hearing/disorders/noise.htm.

For example, Panel A in Figure 11.2 shows a conductive hearing loss. When the audiogram is examined closely, the bone-conduction hearing threshold levels (HTLs) can be seen to be clustered around the 0 dB level, suggesting no hearing loss for these stimuli. On the other hand, O's, representing air-conduction HTLs for the right ear, cluster around the 40 dB hearing level. These results suggest that, when the inner ear is stimulated directly by bone conduction, hearing thresholds are normal. However, when the test stimuli are delivered through the ear canal, a 40 dB hearing loss is present. This leads the audiologist to suspect the presence of some conductive disorder affecting the outer or middle ear transmission system that may be causing the hearing loss. Panel B in Figure 11.2 illustrates normal right ear hearing threshold levels. It can be seen that both triangles (bone conduction) and O's (air conduction) cluster around the 0-to-10 dB range at each test frequency, suggesting no hearing loss. Panel C displays findings for an individual with similar bone- and air-conduction deficits, indicating mild to moderate sensorineural hearing loss. Panel D shows findings for a person with dissimilar bone-conduction and air-conduction losses in the right ear, referred to as a mixed loss in hearing.

Other Types of Hearing Assessment

Often, a hearing screening is the initial point at which hearing loss is suspected, and more sophisticated audiological procedures may be required. The American Speech-Language-Hearing Association (ASHA) has developed guidelines for hearing screening (1993). ASHA suggests that the process involve (1) a case history; (2) visual inspection of the outer ear, ear canal, and eardrum; (3) pure-tone audiologic hearing screening; and (4) tympanometry screening. It is important to note that hearing screening aims to determine only whether a hearing loss may be present, not the degree or type of hearing impairment.

Audiologists are trained to conduct hearing screening programs in hospital newborn nurseries, in schools, and for adults. Some school systems employ audiologists, and hearing screening programs may fall within their purview. However, in most school settings, it is the speech-language pathologist who is best equipped to conduct hearing screening, refer students who are suspected of having a hearing loss for further audiologic evaluation, and make recommendations for school placement. Audiologic assessment is an essential component in the determination of a hearing loss and its impact on communication. However, a thorough assessment battery, including assessment of cognitive functioning, speech and language skills, social-emotional adjustment, and academic achievement, is required for appropriate school placement (Simeonsson & Rosenthal, 2001).

Special assessments are often used when evaluating the hearing of young children or students with special needs.

Hearing is a complex hierarchy of functions, the assessment of which requires highly sophisticated instrumentation and procedures in a clinical setting. Furthermore, test procedures appropriate for cooperative adults are not useful with young and many special needs children. For example, **play audiometry** is often used with children who are difficult to test or unable to follow simple commands. In this procedure, the child is conditioned to respond to sounds in specific ways in order to determine the hearing threshold levels. **Speech audiometry** measures an individual's **speech recognition threshold (SRT)**, as well as that person's speech recognition ability in various listening conditions. Other types of auditory system assessment include electrophysiological measures of auditory function from the inner ear through the auditory brainstem to the cortex of the brain **(auditory evoked potentials)**. **Evoked otoacoustic emissions** from the inner ear can be measured with sensitive microphones to examine functions in the inner ear far beyond the understanding of scientists in the past. To detect possible problems in the middle ear, **acoustic immittance** measures are used, placing a small probe in the ear to measure the transmission of sound through the eardrum and ossicular chain (American Speech-Language-Hearing Association, 2007a). Using all of these procedures, audiologists have opened new windows into mechanisms to evaluate human hearing, leading to better assessment and remediation for those with hearing impairments.

Age of Onset

The effects of hearing impairment depend significantly on the age at which the impairment occurs. **Prelingual** hearing impairment refers to disordered hearing present at birth or occurring before the development of speech and language. **Postlingual** impairment describes an auditory deficit acquired after the acquisition of speech and language (Berk, 2006). The age at which the hearing loss occurs is critical because normal language development is very much dependent on an intact auditory system.

Not surprisingly, postlingually deaf children generally develop better speech, language, reading, and writing skills than prelingually deafened youngsters. Currently, great importance is placed on the early identification of hearing impairment in neonates and infants so that early intervention can reduce the effects of the hearing impairment on these skills, as well as on other areas such as social/cognitive development and academic achievement (Gallagher, Easterbrooks, & Malone, 2006).

The American Speech-Language-Hearing Association (ASHA) (2004; 2007b) estimates that 1 in every 22 infants born in the United States has some type of hearing loss, with 1 in every 1,000 infants exhibiting a severe or profound hearing loss. Hearing loss is the most common congenital disorder in newborns. Forty states, the District of Columbia, and Puerto Rico currently have legislation that requires universal hearing screening for newborns. It is estimated that with this legislation, currently 95 percent of all newborns born in hospitals receive screening ("Early Hearing Campaign Honored," 2007).

A Brief History of the Field

The history of education of the hearing impaired is complex and controversial. Hearing impairments have probably existed in the North American region since the early settlement of this area by diverse Native American populations. Despite occasional references to provision of educational services for individuals with hearing impairments, however, there is no evidence of any organized program development until the nineteenth century (Moores, 2001).

In 1817, the first school in the United States for students with significant hearing impairments, the American Asylum for the Education of the Deaf and Dumb, was established in Hartford, Connecticut. This institution was begun through the efforts of a young divinity student named Thomas Hopkins Gallaudet. The name of the school was eventually changed to the American School for the Deaf (ASD), and the student population broadened to include individuals with hearing impairment from other states (Moores, 2001).

During this time period in France, a number of schools for the hearing impaired were experimenting with l'Epée's methods of communication, which were primarily manual. Gallaudet visited these schools and was greatly influenced by the work of l'Epée. In an effort to establish effective systems of **manual communication** in the United States, Gallaudet brought Laurent Clerc, a deaf Frenchman and well-known educator of the hearing impaired, to the United States. However, other American deaf educators went to Europe and were impressed by the **oral approaches** and philosophies. Of special interest were those methods that discouraged the use of any form of manual communication or sign language (Van Hasselt, Strain, & Hersen, 1988).

Many parents of children with significant hearing impairments assumed that living and learning with other individuals with similar problems was best for their children, and early formal education efforts were centered primarily in residential schools. Residential schools at this time were selective and would not serve all students with significant hearing impairments, especially those from minority groups or those with other significant disabilities. Day schools gained popularity partly because of these restrictive policies.

In 1864, Abraham Lincoln signed legislation establishing the nation's first college for the hearing impaired, known today as Gallaudet University. However, the debate over which method (oral or manual) was more appropriate for the instruction and communication of individuals with significant hearing impairments was now in full force. The two central figures in this debate were Thomas Gallaudet's son Edward, a renowned legal scholar, and Alexander Graham Bell, known to most as the inventor of the telephone and audiometer, who was an internationally recognized educator of the deaf. Bell's position centered on the issue of segregation in policy and practice. He believed that the manual philosophy,

The issue of what constitutes the least restrictive environment for students with hearing impairments is controversial.

particularly in residential schools, as well as the use of sign language, fostered segregation of individuals with significant hearing impairments from the mainstream of society. Bell proposed a number of radical pieces of legislation that would (1) eliminate residential schools, (2) ban the use of manual communication in any form, (3) legislate that no adult with a significant hearing impairment could become a teacher of the deaf, and (4) forbid two adults with significant hearing impairments to marry. Interestingly, for many years the oral approach was more widely accepted than the manual position.

Edward Gallaudet strongly opposed these positions from both a moral and a methodological point of view. He believed that those who used the manual method (1) could learn when expectations were appropriately high, (2) would not feel isolated from society, (3) could and would participate in general life activities, and (4) would benefit socially by having friends with common interests (Moores, 2001). Eventually, Gallaudet's position gained support in Congress through appropriations to establish teacher preparation programs emphasizing the manual approach.

In the 1970s, **total communication** (TC)—combining a number of sensory modalities with manual and oral communication—was adopted by many professionals as the best approach to working with individuals with significant hearing impairments. Those who argued for TC criticized the practice of keeping many children with hearing impairments in oral programs until 9 or 10 years of age, especially those who had limited early success, because critical periods for attaining the basic linguistic principles were potentially missed. Those who argued against TC expressed concern that it would be difficult to emphasize all methods of communication and do justice to all. They further argued that the manual method would be the primary avenue of communication because it was significantly quicker and easier to learn. The debate continues today, indicated by the fact that Gallaudet University publishes a journal with a total communication orientation (*American Annals for the Deaf*), and the A. G. Bell Association publishes one with an oral orientation (*Volta Review*). Both journals are world renowned for their quality of content and research articles.

The educational placement options available for hearing impaired children today are a result of historical, political, and cultural forces. Since the 1980s, there has been a significant increase in the visibility of cultural advocacy groups for individuals who are hearing impaired. The "deaf rights" movement, embraced by many residential schools and deaf communities, increasingly polarized proponents of various methodologies. Advanced medical interventions such as gene therapy and cochlear implantation were not initially embraced by many culturally deaf adults, further complicating the cultural controversy. Educators today struggle to determine what constitutes the least restrictive environment (LRE) within the public school arena for children with significant hearing impairment. Although a number of educational placement options are available to facilitate LRE, parents as well as professionals frequently find themselves drawing legal and educational battle lines simply trying to *define* what constitutes such an environment.

The 1997 amendments to IDEA (PL 105-17) introduced a requirement to consider the communication needs of children with hearing impairments when making educational placement decisions. IDEA 2004 continues this stipulation. Communication-rich environments are an essential element in the education of children who are deaf and hard of hearing (Katz & Schery, 2006). What might be the LRE for many other children with disabilities may not be the LRE for a student with a hearing impairment because of the child's unique communication needs. Are there peers at the recommended placement site who can communicate with the child? Does the teacher have adequate skills in the communication mode typically used by the child? Does the teacher possess the skills necessary to meet the unique instructional needs of a student with hearing impairments? There are many questions regarding the implementation of the LRE requirement to consider—especially the communication needs of the pupil. Unfortunately, personnel responsible for making placement recommendations frequently do not have an adequate understanding of the educational needs of children who are deaf or hard of hearing (Easterbrooks & Baker, 2001; Katz & Schery).

Prevalence of Hearing Impairment

Investigators estimate that hearing loss affects nearly 28 million people. Further, 1 in every 22 infants born in the United States has some degree of hearing impairment, and 1 in every 1,000 infants has a severe or profound hearing impairment (Herer et al., 2007).

Figure 11.3 shows the prevalence of hearing loss by age group in the United States. It is easily seen that prevalence of hearing loss increases as people age; persons above 65 years of age are about eight times more likely to have a hearing impairment than young adults in the 18–34 age category.

According to the U.S. Department of Education (2007), 72,387 students between the ages of 6 and 21 were defined as having a hearing impairment and receiving special

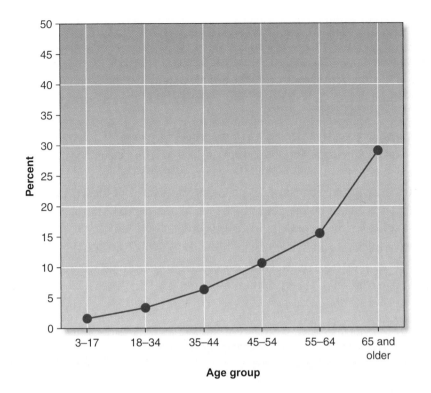

Figure 11.3

Estimate of the Prevalence of Hearing Impairment by Age Group

Source: National Center for Health Statistics. (1994). *National Health Survey Interview*, Series 10, No. 188. Available at http:/www.cdc.gov/nchs/data/series/sr_10/sr10_188.pdf

education services during the 2005–2006 school year. These students represent 1.1 percent of all pupils with disabilities and 0.11 percent of the total school-age population. At the same time, almost 7,800 preschoolers were receiving a special education because of a hearing impairment. This figure represents 1.1 percent of all preschoolers with a disability (U.S. Department of Education, 2006).

Etiology of Hearing Impairment

Causes of hearing loss can be classified in several ways. For example, hearing losses may be congenital (occurring before birth) or acquired (occurring after birth). Hearing losses occurring around the time of birth are generally considered to be congenital, whether or not the loss was actually documented at that time. Further, hearing losses may be classified as genetic or nongenetic. Genetic or hereditary factors are one of the leading causes of hearing impairments in children (Schirmer, 2001). It has been estimated that in approximately one-third of all persons with hearing loss greater than about 55 dB, the origin of the loss is hereditary (Toriello, Reardon, & Gorlin, 2004). **Adventitious (acquired) hearing losses** of this magnitude constitute roughly another third of all cases, and unknown factors are responsible for the remaining third. The etiology of hearing loss is an important variable in determining immediate and long-range educational strategies.

Genetic/Hereditary Factors

Genetic causes are thought to account for more than 150 different types of deafness (Bess & Humes, 2003). Researchers estimate that about one-half of all congenital deafness is the result of genetic factors (Petersen & Willems, 2006). Of the several known modes of genetic inheritance, three mechanisms are most important. **Autosomal dominant** inheritance is characterized by expression of a trait (hearing loss) even if the gene for it is carried on only one chromosome of a matched pair. Conditions such as Waardenburg syndrome (multicolored iris, white forelock, sensorineural hearing loss) and dominant progressive hearing loss (a sensorineural hearing loss that progresses over a period of years) are examples of autosomal dominantly inherited hearing losses.

In **autosomal recessive** inheritance, both genes of a pair must carry the characteristic in order for it to be expressed. Usher's syndrome (bilateral sensorineural hearing loss and visual defects due to retinitis pigmentosa) is an example of autosomal recessive inheritance.

The third major mechanism of genetic transmission is **X-linked** inheritance. In the X-linked recessive form of this transmission mode, the parents are apparently normal and the altered gene is associated with the X chromosomes of the male offspring. Most X-linked recessive hearing losses are sensorineural in type (Toriello et al., 2004).

Table 11.2 summarizes some of the disorders, both genetic and acquired, associated with hearing loss in children.

Table 11.2	Disorders Associated with Hearing Loss in Children
Cytomegalovirus (CMV)	• Most common congenital viral infection causing hearing loss today, occurring in 1 in 1,000 live births • Contracted in utero or postnatally from the mother • Can result in sensorineural hearing loss as well as CNS, cardiac, optic, and growth abnormalities • Symptoms may not be apparent at birth, with onset about 18 months of age • Progresses rapidly during the first year
Down Syndrome	• Congenital chromosomal abnormality (trisomy 21) • Frequently have low-set small ears, external canal stenosis, middle ear deformities, and facial nerve abnormalities • 30% of these children have sensorineural hearing loss • Most have poor Eustachian tube function, resulting in chronic middle ear disease with associated conductive fluctuant hearing loss
Meningitis	• Neonatal infection, can be viral or bacterial • Most common cause of acquired sensorineural hearing loss • Hearing loss can range from mild to profound, and may be progressive • Symptoms may include headache, neck stiffness, photophobia, and suppurative otitis media
Ototoxicity	• Can be caused by a wide variety of strong antibiotics such as aminoglycosides (gentamicin, kanamycin, etc.), chemotherapeutic agents such as cisplatin, or loop diuretics • Can also result from exposure to various chemical agents in the environment • Characterized by a progressive high-frequency sensorineural hearing loss following such exposure
Usher's Syndrome	• Autosomal recessive • Occurs in 6%–12% of congenitally deaf children, and 3 in 100,000 of the general population • Involves retinitis pigmentosa and progressive moderate to severe sensorineural hearing loss • Can vary greatly in age of onset, severity, and progression
Waardenburg Syndrome	• Autosomal hereditary dominant • 20% have white forelock, 99% have increased distance between the eyes, 45% have two differently colored eyes (typically one brown and one blue) • Depigmentation of the skin and eyebrows that meet over the bridge of the nose are also common features of this syndrome • 50% have mild to severe sensorineural hearing loss, which can be unilateral or bilateral and is progressive

Infections

Many infectious agents that cause hearing loss are well documented; they can occur prenatally (before birth), at or around the time of birth (perinatally), or later in life (postnatally). During the mid-1960s, a rubella (German measles) outbreak caused an inordinate number of infants to be born with a hearing impairment. During that time span, approximately 10 percent of all congenital deafness was attributed to this disease, with half of these cases involving a severe sensorineural hearing loss. Fortunately, with the development of rubella vaccines, the incidence of this disease has dramatically decreased.

Common perinatal infections that may result in hearing impairment include cytomegalovirus (CMV), hepatitis B virus, and syphilis. Today, CMV infection is the leading viral cause of sensorineural hearing loss in children (Picard, 2004; Stach, 1998). Most children do not show clinical signs of the infection at birth but begin to demonstrate progressive evidence of it in the early years of life.

Measles and mumps viruses are examples of viral infections that can cause sensorineural hearing loss later in life, but for which there are now preventive vaccines. Hearing losses due to these viruses were all but completely eliminated, but failure to inoculate all children against these diseases has put them on the rise again and raised the risk of increased incidence of associated hearing loss.

Many nonviral infections can cause significant hearing loss. Bacterial meningitis can cause severe bilateral sensorineural hearing loss. Although viral meningitis can also cause hearing loss, most instances of hearing loss due to meningitis result from the bacterial form.

Otitis media is one of the leading causes of mild to moderate conductive hearing loss in children (Gallaudet Research Institute, 2005). It is the most common reason for visits to physicians for children under age 6 (Schirmer, 2001). Fluid accumulation in the middle ear resulting from this disease typically causes a 15 to 40 dB conductive hearing loss and, if not treated, can lead to sensorineural impairment. Otitis media is most often treated by administering antibiotics or, in some instances, through placement of tubes in the ears.

Developmental Abnormalities

Some congenital causes of hearing loss involve abnormal development of outer or inner ear structure. **Atresia** (a narrowing or closure of the external ear canal and/or malformation of the middle ear) is a developmental disorder that affects the fetus early in pregnancy and results in malformation of the outer and/or middle ears. This frequently results in a conductive hearing loss that may or may not be treated successfully with surgical intervention.

Environmental/Traumatic Factors

Low birth weight, and its associated conditions, and asphyxia (breathing difficulties) are causes of serious hearing loss that frequently occur at birth or shortly thereafter. Both factors can result in conditions that actually cause hearing loss by traumatizing the ear. Some prescription drugs (including antibiotic medications) are known to be toxic to the inner ear, and the resulting hearing loss can occur prenatally when drugs are administered to the mother or during medical treatment later in life. The resulting hearing loss is typically sensorineural in type and permanent once damage is done. Intense noise, head injuries involving fractures of the skull, and dramatic pressure changes in the middle ear are all examples of traumatic causes of damage to the ear and hearing loss.

Hearing impairment has a wide range of causes, many of which have important implications for treatment and educational intervention to minimize the effects of hearing loss on children and adults.

Characteristics of Individuals with Hearing Impairments

Variations in etiology, onset, degree, and type of hearing loss, as well as family and educational situations, result in a widely diverse hearing impaired population. However, children and adults with hearing disabilities characteristically experience significant issues with regard to social and intellectual development, speech and language, and educational achievement.

Intelligence

Over the past twenty years, reviews of the research on the intellectual characteristics of children with a hearing impairment have suggested that the distribution of intelligence or IQ scores for these individuals is similar to that of their hearing counterparts (Simeonsson & Rosenthal, 2001). Findings suggest that intellectual development for people with a hearing impairment is more a function of language development than cognitive ability. Any difficulties in performance appear to be closely associated with speaking, reading, and writing the English language, but are not related to level of intelligence (Marschark, 2006).

Speech and Language

Speech and language skills are the areas of development most severely affected for those with a hearing impairment, particularly for children who are born deaf. The majority of deaf children have a very difficult time learning to use speech (McLean, Wolery, & Bailey, 2004). Numerous papers published within the past fifty years on speech skills of children with a hearing loss suggest that the effects of a hearing loss on English language development vary considerably (Berk, 2006). For individuals who experience mild to moderate hearing losses, the effect may be minimal. Even for those with a prelingual moderate loss, effective communication skills are possible because the voiced sounds of conversational speech remain audible. Although the person with this type of hearing loss cannot hear unvoiced sounds and distant speech, language delays can be reduced or prevented by early diagnosis, the use of advanced technologies, and treatment. Thus, a vast majority of these individuals are able to use speech as the primary mode for English language acquisition.

For the individual with profound congenital deafness, most loud speech is inaudible, even with the use of the most sophisticated hearing aids. These individuals are unable to receive information through speech unless they have learned to speechread (lipread). Sounds produced by the individual who is deaf are often difficult to understand. Children who are deaf exhibit significant articulation, voice quality, and tone discrimination problems. Researchers have found that, even as early as 8 months of age, babies who are deaf appear to babble less than their hearing peers (Allen & Cowdery, 2009). This has been attributed to the fact that deaf infants do not experience the same auditory feedback from babbling as their hearing counterparts and therefore are not as motivated to continue the activity.

In 1990, the U.S. Food and Drug Administration approved cochlear implants for children between the ages of 2 and 17. Implants are now used at an even earlier age. Research indicates that the optimal age to implant a youngster is 10–15 months. New debates surround the potential benefit of early bilateral implantation. Early research indicates that pediatric implant users are receiving substantial benefit that will be evident in their development of speech and language (Berg, Ip, Hurst, & Herb, 2007).

Social Development

Social-emotional development in young children with hearing impairments shows the same developmental patterns as in those without a hearing loss with regard to preschool friendships and ethnic, age, and gender peer preferences. Social-emotional development, however, also depends heavily on the ability to use communication skills. A hearing loss modifies one's capacity to receive and process auditory stimuli; thus, the individual who is deaf or hard of hearing receives reduced auditory information and/or information that is distorted. As a result, there appear to be some differences in the way young deaf children play as compared to their hearing counterparts.

Young deaf children typically have less language interaction during play and appear to prefer groups of two rather than larger group sizes. These patterns may be attributed to the difficulty of dividing their attention, which is so visual in its nature, and their poorer knowledge of language appropriate to play situations. They also engage in less pretend play, possibly because language deficits impede their ability to script elaborate imaginary situations. Deaf children spend less time in cooperative peer play when they are with other deaf children; even though they are interested in and initiate the interaction, they frequently get no response from their play partner because of language deficits. When deaf and hearing children attempt to play but do not share a common communication system—both relying on oral skills or both relying on sign skills—they demonstrate little interest in playing together or sustaining a friendship (Lederberg, 1993; Marschark, 2006). This suggests a need to develop communication skills within the hearing peer group and among all teachers if children placed in inclusive classroom settings are to avoid social isolation. The poem "Deaf Donald" by Shel Silverstein is a poignant example of what may happen without such support (see Figure 11.4).

Social and emotional development depend, in part, on a person's ability to communicate.

There is an increasing awareness and acceptance of children with disabilities by their peer group. This is recognized and promoted by toy manufacturers as more "awareness" products become available on the open market. Mattel has assisted in awareness of hearing impairments through the introduction of the "Sign Language Barbie," which is distributed through Toys "R" Us (see Figure 11.5, page 413).

As children with a hearing impairment grow and mature, their capacity for receiving and using language hinders their overall social-emotional growth (developing friendships). Reviews of the literature on social and psychological development in adolescents who are deaf have suggested distinct differences from their hearing peers in such areas as maturity, awareness of social mores and attitudes, and social interactions (Marschark, 2007). The need for social interaction may tend to further isolate these individuals from the mainstream, as they seek and form social and professional relationships with others with hearing impairments. The Internet is providing more opportunity

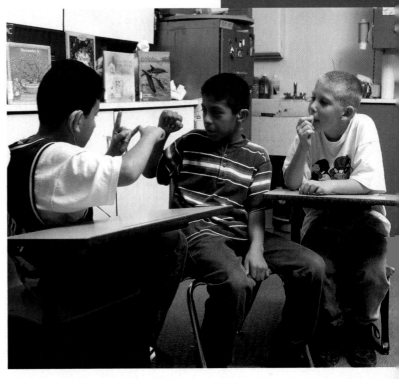

DEAF DONALD

Deaf Donald met Talkie Sue

But was all he could do.

And Sue said, "Donald, I sure do like you."

But was all he could do.

And Sue asked Donald, "Do you like me too?"

But was all he could do.

"Good-bye then, Donald, I'm leaving you."

But was all he did do.

And she left forever so she never knew

That means I love you.

Figure 11.4

"Deaf Donald" by
Shel Silverstein

Source: Copyright © 1981
by Evil Eye Music, Inc.
Used by permission of
HarperCollins Publishers.

for interaction within the hearing impaired peer group through the use of chatrooms.

Educational Achievement

The educational achievement of students with hearing impairments may be significantly delayed in comparison to that of their hearing peers. Students who are deaf or have a partial hearing impairment have considerable difficulty succeeding in an educational system that depends primarily on the spoken word and written language to transmit knowledge. Low achievement is characteristic of students who are deaf (Geers, 2006); they average three to four years below their age-appropriate grade levels. Even students with mild to moderate losses achieve below expectations based on their performance on tests of cognitive ability (Williams & Finnegan, 2003).

Reading is the academic area most negatively affected for students with a hearing impairment. Any hearing loss, whether mild or profound, appears to have detrimental effects on reading performance. Research suggests that pupils who are hearing impaired read at approximately a third- to fourth-grade level (Gallaudet Research Institute, 2007; Kuntze, 1998; Traxler, 2000). Consequently, many of these individuals will encounter difficulty reading a typical newspaper.

Although researchers report slight variations in educational achievement scores, there is no question that high-stakes testing is of great concern for this group of children. The difficulty the majority of students with hearing impairments across the country experience taking high school exit exams and the fact that most of them do not pass these tests are issues of profound concern among educators (Johnson, 2003).

Assessment of Individuals with Hearing Impairments

The primary objective of an assessment of individuals with a hearing impairment is to put together an accurate picture of cognitive, communicative, and personal characteristics

(Simeonsson & Rosenthal, 2001). This information is central to designing individualized instructional plans and other experiential activities to promote development.

Cognitive Assessment

It is crucial that the intellectual assessment of students with hearing impairments use measures that do *not* rely primarily on verbal abilities as indicators of cognitive functioning. There are several nonverbal assessment options considered appropriate for individuals with hearing impairments. This includes the nonverbal portion of the Kaufman Assessment Battery for Children (Kaufman & Kaufman, 2004) and the performance section of the Wechsler Intelligence Scale for Children (Fourth Edition) (Wechsler, 2003). Because of the nonverbal nature of these instruments, however, they have limited predictive validity in relation to achievement that requires verbal skills (Schum, 2004). As a result, their usefulness has yet to be determined in functional educational practice.

The two most widely used measures of academic achievement with this population are the Stanford Achievement Test (SAT) (Psychological Corporation, 2002) and individual state annual assessments. The psychometric qualities of the SAT include excellent data representing diverse performance levels of individuals with hearing impairments (Luckner & Bowen, 2006).

Communication Assessment

The most serious negative aspect of a hearing impairment is its effect on language and speech development. Inadequate auditory stimulation during early development almost always leads to marked problems in language acquisition and speech production (Allen & Cowdery, 2009). Language assessment with this population should examine both receptive and expressive communication skills, including (1) form of language, (2) content of language, and (3) use of language. However, most language assessments do not assess all these areas. In most cases, several different assessment tools and techniques (such as language sampling) are needed to accurately determine the individual's language abilities (Simeonsson & Rosenthal, 2001).

Speech assessment with this population should include a battery of tools designed to ascertain the individual's articulation, pitch, loudness, quality, and rate. Analysis of these speech functions will provide a basis for designing speech therapy objectives as part of the individualized educational program (IEP) for the student with a hearing impairment.

Personal/Social/Behavioral Assessment

A number of measures of personal, social, and behavioral functioning are being used with individuals with hearing impairments. The assessment of personal/social characteristics with this population is very challenging given the language content of most of the measures in this area, which are designed to be completed by a rater in response to items in the domains of social adjustment, self-image, and emotional adjustment. Sattler (2006) stresses caution when inferring development in these areas. Individuals with a hearing impairment may respond atypically to a personality measure, not because they exhibit aberrant social-emotional development, but as a result of their linguistic difficulties.

Figure 11.5

Sign Language Barbie

NOTE: Now a teacher of American Sign Language (ASL), this Barbie comes with several teaching tools designed to introduce kids to the language. Use the plastic chalkboard and sign display to make ASL sentences with reusable stickers—included are stickers and cards for more than 50 different word signs. On the back of the box is a diagram of the complete ASL alphabet so kids can learn how to fingerspell words as well. Barbie herself is dressed in a suitably preppy but chic outfit that includes a blue twin sweater set and a multicolored plaid skirt. Her right hand is shaped in the sign for "I love you."

BARBIE is a trademark owned by and used under license from Mattel, Inc. ©2002 Mattel, Inc. All Rights Reserved.

Educational Considerations

One method of classifying hearing impairment is by degree. Hearing loss can range from mild to profound based on the level of intensity required (measured in decibels, or dB) at various frequencies (described in hertz, or Hz) to establish hearing threshold. This classification system is directly related to the individual's ability to hear and comprehend speech. Factors such as these, as well as whether the hearing loss is pre- or postlingual, fluctuant or stable, clearly have significant educational implications. (See Table 11.3.)

Table 11.3	Impact of Hearing Loss on Students		
Degree of Hearing Loss	**Possible Psychosocial Impact of Hearing Loss**	**Effect of Hearing Loss on Speech and Language**	**Potential Educational Needs and Programs**
Minimal (borderline) 16–25 dB HL	May be unaware of subtle conversational cues, causing child to be viewed as inappropriate or awkward. May miss portions of fast-paced peer interactions, which could begin to have an impact on socialization and self-concept. May exhibit immature behavior. Child may be more fatigued than classmates because of greater listening effort.	May have difficulty hearing faint or distant speech. At 15 dB student can miss up to 10% of speech when teacher is at a distance greater than 3 feet and when the classroom is noisy, especially in the elementary grades when verbal instruction predominates.	May benefit from a hearing aid or personal FM system, depending on loss configuration. Would benefit from soundfield amplification if classroom is noisy and/or reverberant. Favorable seating. May need attention to vocabulary or speech, especially with recurrent otitis media history. Appropriate medical management necessary for conductive losses. Teacher requires inservice on impact of hearing on language development and learning.
Mild 26–40 dB HL	Barriers beginning to build, with negative impact on self-esteem as child is accused of "hearing when he or she wants to," "daydreaming," or "not paying attention." Child begins to lose ability for selective hearing and has increasing difficulty suppressing background noise, which makes the learning environment stressful. Child is more fatigued than classmates because of listening effort needed.	At 30 dB can miss 25%–40% of speech. The degree of difficulty experienced in school will depend upon the noise level in the classroom, distance from the teacher, and the configuration of the hearing loss. Without amplification, the child with 35–40 dB loss may miss at least 50% of class discussions, especially when voices are faint or speaker is not in line of vision. Will miss consonants, especially when a high-frequency hearing loss is present.	Will benefit from a hearing aid and use of a personal FM or soundfield FM system in the classroom. Needs favorable seating and lighting. Refer to special education for language evaluation and educational follow-up. Needs auditory skill building. May need attention to vocabulary and language development, articulation or speech reading, and/or special support in reading. May need help with self-esteem. Teacher inservice required.
Moderate 41–55 dB HL	Communication is often significantly affected, and socialization with peers with normal hearing becomes increasingly difficult. With full-time use of hearing aids/FM systems, child may be judged as a less competent learner. There is an increasing impact on self-esteem.	Understands conversational speech at a distance of 3–5 feet (face-to-face) only if structure and vocabulary controlled. Without amplification, the amount of speech missed can be 50% to 75% with 40 dB loss and 80% to 100% with 50 dB loss. Is likely to have delayed or defective syntax, limited vocabulary, imperfect speech production, and an atonal voice quality.	Refer to special education for language evaluation and for educational follow-up. Amplification is essential (hearing aids and FM system). Special education support may be needed, especially for primary-age children. Attention to oral language development, reading, and written language. Auditory skill development and speech therapy usually needed. Teacher inservice required.

Table 11.3	Impact of Hearing Loss on Students (Continued)		
Degree of Hearing Loss	**Possible Psychosocial Impact of Hearing Loss**	**Effect of Hearing Loss on Speech and Language**	**Potential Educational Needs and Programs**
Moderate to severe 56–70 dB HL	Full-time use of hearing aids/FM systems may result in child's being judged by both peers and adults as a less competent learner, resulting in poorer self-concept and diminished social maturity, and contributing to sense of rejection. Inservice to address these attitudes may be helpful.	Without amplification, conversation must be very loud to be understood. A 55 dB loss can cause child to miss up to 100% of speech information. Will have marked difficulty in school situations requiring verbal communication in both one-to-one and group situations. Delayed language, syntax, reduced speech intelligibility, and atonal voice quality likely.	Full-time use of amplification is essential. Will need resource teacher or special class depending on magnitude of language delay. May require special help in all language skills, language-based academic subjects, vocabulary, grammar, and pragmatics, as well as reading and writing. Probably needs assistance to expand experiential language base. Inservice of general educators required.
Severe 71–90 dB HL	Child may prefer other children with hearing impairments as friends and playmates. This may further isolate the child from the mainstream; however, these peer relationships may foster improved self-concept and a sense of cultural identity.	Without amplification, may hear loud voices about 1 foot from ear. When amplified optimally, children with hearing ability of 90 dB or better should be able to identify environmental sounds and detect all the sounds of speech. If loss is of prelingual onset, oral language and speech may not develop spontaneously or will be severely delayed. If hearing loss is of recent onset, speech is likely to deteriorate with quality becoming atonal.	May need full-time special aural/oral program with emphasis on all auditory language skills, speech reading, concept development, and speech. As loss approaches 80–90 dB, may benefit from a total communication approach, especially in the early language learning years. Individual hearing aid/personal FM system essential. Need to monitor effectiveness of communication modality. Participation in regular classes as much as possible. Inservice of general educators essential.
Profound 91 dB HL or more	Depending on auditory/oral competence, peer use of sign language, parental attitude, and other factors, child may or may not increasingly prefer association with the Deaf culture.	Aware of vibrations more than tonal pattern. Many rely on vision rather than hearing as primary avenue for communication and learning. Detection of speech sounds dependent upon loss configuration and use of amplification. Speech and language will not develop spontaneously and are likely to deteriorate rapidly if hearing loss is of recent onset.	May need special program for children who are deaf, with emphasis on all language skills and academic areas. Program needs specialized supervision and comprehensive support services. Early use of amplification likely to help if part of an intensive training program. May be cochlear implant or vibrotactile aid candidate. Requires continual appraisal of needs in regard to communication and learning mode. Part-time in general education classes as much as benefits student.

Source: Adapted from K. Anderson, "Hearing Conservation in the Public Schools Revisited," *Seminars in Hearing, 12*(4), 1991, pp. 361–363.

Individuals with a mild hearing loss may encounter difficulty hearing in a noisy classroom setting or distinguishing distant sounds; however, their speech discrimination ability is often within normal limits. Appropriate accommodations for such a student may include preferential seating, possible use of a hearing aid or personal FM system, greater redundancy in the instructional model, and increased collaboration with parents to facilitate learning.

The individual with a moderate hearing loss—depending on type, degree, and age of onset—may experience significant delays in speech and language. Articulation deficits, reduced vocabulary, difficulty mastering various grammatical and syntactical concepts, and poor voice quality are common problems. Hearing aid use coupled with personal FM systems is necessary for such students, in addition to the rehabilitative strategies cited previously.

A severe or profound hearing loss, again depending on the type, degree, and age of onset, may severely impede speech and language development. Individuals with severe to profound losses frequently have poor auditory discrimination, which often limits the effectiveness of conventional amplification devices. A team approach to remediation should be used, which involves substantial interaction with the child's managing audiologist to ensure accuracy of diagnostic information as well as appropriateness of amplification. Students with this degree of hearing loss will need significant accommodation in the educational environment to be successful, including intense visual language reinforcement for the instruction of grammar and syntax. See the accompanying Suggestions for the Classroom on teaching students with hearing impairments.

Where Are Students with Hearing Impairments Served?

Under the contemporary philosophy of providing individualized instruction in the least restrictive environment (LRE), individuals with a hearing impairment can receive their education in a number of settings, generally classified into two broad categories: (1) regular public school programs and (2) special school programs. Family preference for educational placement may be influenced by such factors as the degree of loss, age of onset, mode of communication, presence of other disabilities, and available resources. (See the accompanying First Person Feature on page 419.)

Figure 11.6 shows the various educational environments attended by children with hearing impairments during the 2005–2006 school year. More than 85 percent of children with hearing impairments attend public schools. This is a dramatic shift from the historical educational placement of residential education. Before 1975, when PL 94-142 was enacted, about 80 percent of students with hearing impairments were served in special schools, typically state residential schools for the deaf.

Figure 11.6

Educational Placement of Children with Hearing Impairments

Note: Figure represents percentages of enrollment of students with hearing impairments during the 2005–2006 school year.

Source: U.S. Department of Education. (2007). *IDEA data.* Available at https://www.ideadata.org/PartBReport.asp.

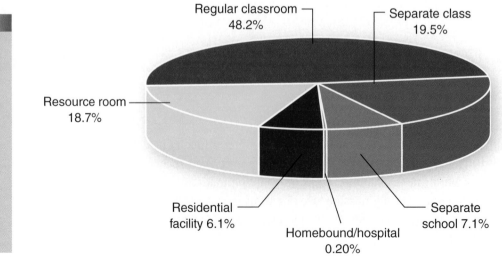

Regular classroom 48.2%
Separate class 19.5%
Resource room 18.7%
Residential facility 6.1%
Homebound/hospital 0.20%
Separate school 7.1%

Suggestions for the Classroom

Suggestions for Teaching Students with Hearing Impairments

Suggestion #1: Promote acceptance of your students: Your student will benefit from a classroom where he/she feels accepted and where modifications are made without undue attention.

How to Do It

☑ Welcome the student to your class. Your positive attitude will help other students accept him/her.

☑ Discuss your student's hearing loss with him/her; let him/her know you are willing to help.

☑ As appropriate, have your student, the audiologist, or another person explain the student's hearing loss to your entire class.

☑ Make modifications seem as natural as possible so the student is not singled out.

☑ Accept your student as an individual; be aware of his/her assets as well as his/her limitations.

☑ Encourage your student's special abilities or interests.

Suggestion #2: Be sure hearing aids and other amplification devices are used when recommended: This will enable your student to use his/her hearing maximally.

How to Do It

☑ Realize that hearing aids make sounds louder, but not necessarily clearer. Hearing aids don't make hearing normal.

☑ Be sure your student's hearing aids or other devices are checked daily to see that they are working properly.

☑ Encourage the student to care for his/her hearing aid(s) by putting it on, telling you when it is not functioning properly, etc.

☑ Be sure your student always has a spare battery at school.

☑ Know who to contact if your student's device is not working properly.

Suggestion #3: Provide preferential seating: Appropriate seating will enhance your student's ability to hear and understand what is said in the classroom.

How to Do It

☑ Seat near where you typically teach. It will be helpful if your student is at one side of the classroom so he/she can easily turn and follow classroom dialogue.

☑ Seat where your student can easily watch your face without straining to look straight up. Typically the second or third row is best.

☑ Seat away from noise sources, including hallways, radiators, pencil sharpeners, etc.

☑ Seat where light is on your face and not in your student's eyes.

☑ If there is a better ear, place it toward the classroom.

☑ Allow your student to move to other seats when necessary for demonstrations, classroom discussions, or other activities.

Suggestion #4: Increase visual information: Your student will use lipreading and other visual information to supplement what he/she hears.

How to Do It

☑ Remember that your student needs to see your face in order to lipread!
  - Try to stay in one place while talking to the class so your student does not have to lipread a "moving target."

    – Avoid talking while writing on the chalkboard.

    – Avoid putting your hands, papers, or books in front of your face when talking.

    – Avoid talking with your face turned downward while reading.

    – Keep the light on your face, not at your back. Avoid standing in front of windows where the glare will make it difficult to see your face.

☑ Use visual aids, such as pictures and diagrams, when possible.

☑ Demonstrate what you want the student to understand when possible. Use natural gestures, such as pointing to objects being discussed, to help clarify what you say.

☑ Use the chalkboard—write assignments, new vocabulary words, key words, etc., on it.

Suggestion #5: Minimize classroom noise: Even a small amount of noise will make it very difficult for your student to hear and understand what is said.

How to Do It

☑ Seat your student away from noisy parts of your classroom.

☑ Wait until your class is quiet before talking to them.

Suggestion #6: Modify teaching procedures: Modifications will allow your student to benefit from your instruction and will decrease the need for repetition.

How to Do It

☑ Be sure your student is watching and listening when you are talking to him/her.

☑ Be sure your student understands what is said by having him/her repeat information or answer questions.

☑ Rephrase, rather than repeat, questions and instructions if your student has not understood them.

☑ Write key words, new words, new topics, etc., on the chalkboard.

☑ Repeat or rephrase things said by other students during classroom discussions.

☑ Introduce new vocabulary to the student in advance. The speech-language pathologist or parents may be able to help with this.

☑ Use a "buddy" to alert your student to listen and to be sure your student has understood all information correctly.

Suggestion #7: Have realistic expectations: This will help your student succeed in your classroom.

How to Do It

☑ Remember that your student cannot understand everything all of the time, no matter how hard he/she tries. Encourage him/her to ask for repetition.

☑ Be patient when student asks for repetition.

☑ Give breaks from listening when necessary. Your student may fatigue easily because he/she is straining to listen and understand.

☑ Expect student to follow classroom routine. Do not spoil or pamper your student.

☑ Expect your student to accept the same responsibilities for considerate behavior, homework, and dependability as you require of other students in your classroom.

☑ Ask the student to repeat if you can't understand him/her. Your student's speech may be distorted because he/she does not hear sounds clearly. Work with the speech-language pathologist to help your student improve his/her speech as much as possible.

☑ Be alert for fluctuations of hearing due to middle ear problems.

☑ Request support from the audiologist, the speech-language pathologist, or others when you feel uncertain about your student and what is best for him/her.

SOURCE: Adapted from C. Johnson, P. Benson, and J. Seaton, *Educational Audiology Handbook* (San Diego: Singular, 1997), pp. 370–371.

First Person

Mindy

My experience growing up as a person who is deaf has been enriching. I have a successful career thanks to supportive parents who always treated me like a typical child. During my difficult times, they supported me wholeheartedly. Some parents of children who are deaf tend to be overprotective, but not my parents. They encouraged me to make my own decisions. I do not think that I would be as successful as I am today without them.

After my parents found out that I was deaf, they enrolled me in a preschool where I learned Cued Speech. A new teacher arrived and told my parents that Signing Exact English (SEE) would be more useful and social than Cued Speech. My parents then enrolled in sign language classes so that they could communicate with me.

In elementary school I was in a self-contained room with other students who were deaf and a teacher who used SEE. I loved that environment. At the time that I was about to enter the sixth grade, I was faced with a decision. Did I want to attend the Alabama School for the Deaf or an integrated middle school? I do not remember how I decided, but I chose the local middle school. I was in culture shock. My classroom was full of 30 hearing students. I was the only student who was deaf in the entire grade. (There were a few other students who were deaf, but they were in different grades.) I had to rely on my interpreter for everything, so I became shyer and less outgoing than I was in elementary school. Many of my classmates learned to sign or fingerspell, but I still missed so much information vital to socialization. I remember walking through the hallways and my interpreter would walk with me and tell me all kinds of gossip she heard. I was shocked; I had no idea what the students were talking about. As I entered high school, I became very unhappy. I noticed that high school students were more into cliques. I felt as though I did not belong.

At a summer camp for children who are deaf, a camp counselor told me about the Model Secondary School for the Deaf (MSSD) at Gallaudet University in Washington, DC. I was interested, so I mentioned it to my parents. Of course, they said I was too young to be so far away. Yet the thought of attending this school stayed with me. I wrote a letter to Gallaudet asking for information about the school. They sent me a colorful, fancy brochure, and I was impressed. I brought it up once again with my parents, but they shrugged it off. I filled out the application anyway and asked them to sign the papers just in case.

I think my parents thought that I would change my mind if things got serious. When MSSD called my parents to come for an intake interview, they kept asking me if I really wanted to do this. I was determined as ever to go. We made the trip to MSSD, and I fell in love with the school immediately. Once again, however, I was in culture shock because I was not aware of the Deaf culture. The students made fun of my clothes, my makeup, and my use of SEE. I was bewildered by all of this. I eventually learned American Sign Language, which was the language of choice. A friend once charged me a penny every time I signed using SEE. I loved the social aspects of being at MSSD. Unlike my middle school, I was able to be involved in any activity that I wished. I was viewed as the "deaf" girl at my middle school, but at MSSD, I was looked at as "Usher Syndrome" girl.

I am currently a school counselor at a school for the deaf, where I have worked for the past eight years. I have had to face many obstacles as I moved to a town where I knew no one. I chose to face my challenges rather than staying home and believing that things would not work out for me. I still face challenges now as a person who is deaf-blind. I am not completely blind yet, but my vision is slowly deteriorating. I have learned how to use grade one Braille, and I am currently learning grade two. I have also completed orientation and mobility training so that I can become somewhat independent in challenging areas such as heavy traffic. I have learned everything possible in order to be independent in case I lose my sight completely.

In the summer of 2006 I had a cochlear implant because of concerns about my safety in the future. I will need to depend upon environmental sounds if and when I lose my vision. I now enjoy hearing the birds sing and water running. When the audiologist turned on my cochlear implant, it was the strangest sensation. The first sounds I heard were my husband's voice and that of the audiologist. Then I entered the bathroom. I did not realize that bathrooms were so noisy! Funny, I always thought that bathrooms were silent. After I got home, I noticed that flushing toilets even had a sound, so I was incredulous of that. I had never heard those sounds until I received my implant. It was one of the best decisions I ever made for myself.

I know I will face additional challenges as my vision deteriorates, but I have a wonderful support system consisting of my husband, family, and friends. I am confident that I will be able to overcome whatever obstacles come my way.

PUBLIC SCHOOL PROGRAMS Public school programs include inclusive classroom settings, resource rooms, self-contained classrooms, and itinerant services. The overall goal of these settings is to include the student to the greatest extent possible in the educational/social processes in which all other children, with and without disabilities, participate. Since the implementation of IDEA, the vast majority of students who are deaf or hard of hearing are attending neighborhood schools with their hearing peers.

SPECIAL SCHOOL PROGRAMS Special school programs include public and private residential and/or day schools with specifically prepared teachers and dormitory facilities for students when appropriate. The overall goal of these programs is to provide a positive learning environment, a sense of belonging, personal identification, and acceptance of hearing impairment (Scheetz, 2001). Residential schools also typically accept day and commuting students. As mentioned previously, these types of schools have experienced a dramatic decline in enrollment since the mid-1970s. This shift has caused great concern among deaf adults because residential schools have long been the support foundation in the establishment of Deaf culture.

Instructional Interventions

METHODS OF COMMUNICATION Communication implies a transfer (exchange) of knowledge, ideas, opinions, and feelings; it involves encoding and decoding messages. The basic foundation for communication is language, which is often defined as a system of rules governing sounds, words, meaning, and use. When a child is born with a hearing impairment, depending on the severity of the hearing problem, normal language acquisition is disrupted. Other means of communication are viable alternatives to spoken language. Sign language, in one of its multiple forms, and **fingerspelling** using the manual alphabet (see Figure 11.7) are examples of such alternatives. See Table 11.4 (page 422) for a description of the three sign language systems that are most commonly used. Other methods of instruction include oral, auditory verbal, cued speech, total communication, and the Rochester Method (fingerspelling). For educators of the deaf and the Deaf culture, which method of communication to use is at the root of the current philosophical debate.

Within the placement options previously described, three different approaches to communication may be used: (1) an auditory-oral approach, (2) total communication (TC), or (3) a bilingual-bicultural (bi-bi) approach. See Table 11.5 (page 422) for a description of these approaches. A survey of deaf and hard of hearing educational programs in a 39-state sample found that more than two-thirds of the programs used total communication (Meadows-Orlans, Mertens, Sass-Lehrer, & Scott-Olson, 1997). The majority of public school programs using TC employ a form of Signed English for the sign language component. Many residential programs and postsecondary programs for the deaf endorse the bi-bi approach, which uses American Sign Language (ASL). There are few data suggesting that one instructional approach is significantly better than another.

AUDIOLOGISTS Audiologists have served hearing impaired students within the context of educational settings for many years. The relatively high incidence of hearing impairment coupled with the explosive increase in rehabilitative technology for these students surely

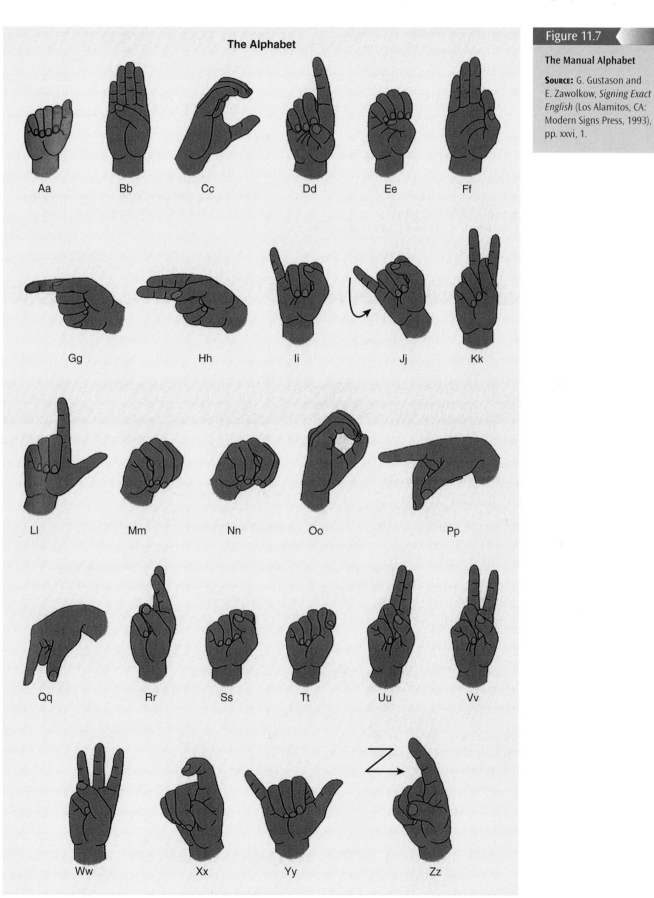

The Alphabet

Figure 11.7

The Manual Alphabet

Source: G. Gustason and E. Zawolkow, *Signing Exact English* (Los Alamitos, CA: Modern Signs Press, 1993), pp. xxvi, 1.

Table 11.4	Sign Language Systems	
Sign System	**Description**	**Advantages/Disadvantages**
American Sign Language (ASL)	• Considered the natural language of the deaf • Has a unique syntax system, not a word-by-word interpretation • System most frequently used by interpreters in public settings (churches, concerts, ceremonies, etc.)	• Unique syntax could make transition to English more challenging
Signing Exact English	• Most like spoken English • Close match to ASL • Uses English word order • System most commonly used in public schools	• Can be understood by ASL users • English word order should make the transition to English less challenging
Signed English	• Uses ASL signs in English word order patterns	• Even closer match to ASL but with the advantage of English word order

SOURCE: Adapted from S. Kuder, *Teaching Students with Language and Communication Disabilities,* 3rd ed. (Boston: Allyn and Bacon, 2008), p. 235.

Table 11.5	Educational Approaches Used When Working with Students with Hearing Impairments		
	Basic Position	**Objective**	**Method of Communication**
Bilingual-Bicultural	Considers American Sign Language (ASL) to be the natural language of the Deaf culture and urges recognition of ASL as the primary language choice with English considered a second language	To provide a foundation in the use of ASL with its unique vocabulary and syntax rules; ESL instruction provided for English vocabulary and syntax rules	ASL (American Sign Language)
Total Communication	Supports the belief that simultaneous use of multiple communication techniques enhances an individual's ability to communicate, comprehend, and learn	To provide a multifaceted approach to communication to facilitate whichever method(s) work(s) best for each individual	Combination of sign language (accepts the use of any of the sign language systems), fingerspelling, and speechreading
Auditory-Oral	Supports the belief that children with hearing impairments can develop listening/receptive language and oral language expression (English) skills; emphasizes use of residual hearing (the level of hearing an individual possesses), amplification (hearing aids, auditory training, etc.), and speech/language training	To facilitate the development of spoken (oral) English	Spoken (oral) English

warrants their inclusion as an educational team member. Using a collaborative approach to the education of hearing impaired students, audiologists frequently provide support to classroom teachers and aides, speech pathologists, teachers of the hearing impaired, special educators, reading specialists, resource teachers, and interpreters. The American Speech-Language-Hearing

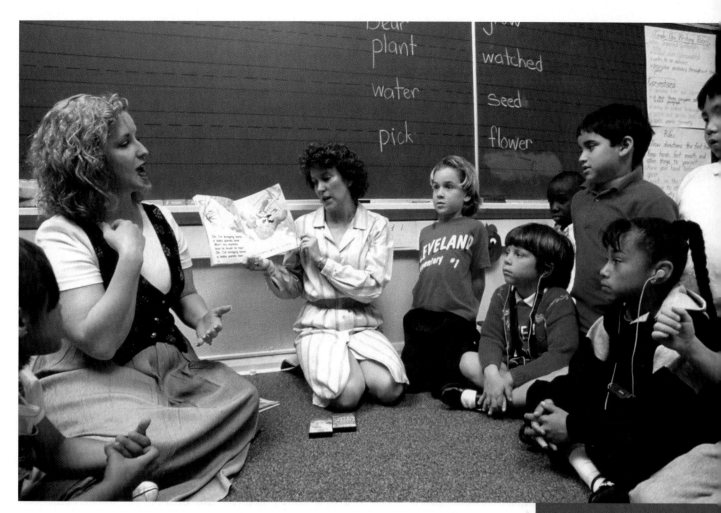

Today, the majority of students with hearing impairments attend public schools.

Association (ASHA) recommends in its *Guidelines for Audiology Services in the Schools* (1993) that there be at least 1 audiologist for every 12,000 students in a school system. Current statistics indicate high variability in the number of educational audiologists state to state, with the overall number of such professionals significantly below ASHA's 1993 recommendation (Johnson & Danhauer, 1999).

INTERPRETERS When an **interpreter** is used, three people are involved in the communication experience: the interpreter, the person who is deaf or hard of hearing, and the hearing person. The primary role of the educational interpreter is to relay to the student anything that is said in class by employing communication processes such as repetition, sign language, fingerspelling, body language, and verbal expressions. Many sign language systems (such as ASL, Signed English, or Signing Exact English) may be used, depending on the preferred communication mode or need of the individual with a hearing impairment. An **oral interpreter** may be used for cochlear implant users or individuals with a great deal of residual hearing. Oral interpreters use clear enunciation, slightly slower speech, and expressive mouth and facial movements to improve the visibility of the spoken message. In conjunction with the communication process, an interpreter may also use **transliteration.** For example, the interpreter may change the exact wording of the hearing person's communication in order to help the individual with a hearing impairment to better understand

Interpreters play a very important role in the education of students with hearing impairments.

the context of the message. However, the interpreter is never a contributing member in the communication exchange.

Educational interpreters play diverse roles at all grade levels. They may assist students in the classroom, tutor individual students, assist regular and special educators in classroom activities, or interpret lectures. As increasing numbers of individuals with a hearing impairment choose to attend regular schools, the demand for interpreters is growing. A critical shortage of qualified interpreters exists in many educational settings, especially in rural areas. There is also a nationwide shortage of qualified interpreter preparation programs.

Services for Young Children with Hearing Impairments

Early intervention for the child with a hearing impairment is grounded in the same basic concepts as early intervention and early childhood special education programs for those with other disabilities (birth through age 5). Screening programs designed to detect hearing loss in school-age populations have existed for years. However, for those children born with

✓ EFFECTIVE INSTRUCTIONAL PRACTICES — Promoting Language Development in Young Children with Hearing Impairments

- *Speak using an ordinary tone/volume.* Make sure the student's attention is focused on the speaker. Talk naturally and clearly and use simple phrases or simple but complete sentences, depending on the pupil's language level. Do not shout or exaggerate words or slow down your speech unnaturally. Highlighting lips with lipstick can assist a young child in following speech. A mustache or long hair obscuring the face can cause loss of visual information.

- *Clarify idioms.* Explain idioms in context (e.g., explain "It's raining cats and dogs" when you have used the expression after dashing inside during a cloud burst). This prevents misunderstandings and enriches the child's language.

- *Check with the student to ensure comprehension.* Sometimes asking "Tell me what I just said" provides information about how much a child understands. However, many children with a hearing loss have difficulty articulating their responses. Therefore, you may need to observe the child's actions for a short period to check for understanding. A perplexed look or doing nothing may indicate lack of understanding, and you will need to find additional, preferably visual, methods for getting the message across.

- *Institute a buddy system to facilitate a child's understanding of directions and curriculum content.* Many times children understand another child better than they do an adult, so have a child's buddy explain the information again after you have finished. Furthermore, attentive peer modeling of both speech and behavior is an excellent resource for the child with hearing deficits.

- *Show real-life pictures when reading or talking about a topic, and use simple signs, point, or have an example of the object you're explaining.* Pupils with a hearing loss need visual information to learn. Acting out experience-based language lessons or stories is helpful. Using environmental labels around the classroom can start such children on the road to learning language through print.

- *Provide language boards or books for children who have difficulty producing intelligible speech or manual signs.* Try providing a flannel board with pictures, words, or other graphic symbols to help communicate information such as available interest centers or answers to routine questions. The child can point to the board to indicate a response or choice. Preteach key vocabulary words from a story that will be read to the class, or send the book home with the child beforehand so that the words can be introduced by the family (and reinforced afterward).

Source: Adapted from L. Katz and T. Schery, "Including Children with Hearing Loss in Early Childhood Programs," *Young Children, 61*(1), 2006, p. 94.

a hearing impairment, identification and intervention as early as possible is critical. There is an obvious relationship between expressive and receptive communication skills and the hearing mechanism that facilitates such skills, which begin long before a child's first words are ever spoken. Because more children are being identified at an earlier age, the emphasis of many early intervention programs has changed in order to meet the needs of younger children with hearing impairments, many of whom will receive cochlear implants.

Failure to identify and provide appropriate services for children who are hearing impaired has a profoundly negative impact on the development of language and speech, as well as educational achievement. Only about 50 percent of infants with hearing loss are identified using a **high-risk register** (Johnson, Benson, & Seaton, 2001). With the use of sophisticated diagnostic technology, universal newborn screening programs designed to identify hearing loss in infants have increased in number and scope. States that have legislated universal newborn screening programs, however, have encountered substantial difficulty with family compliance for follow-up testing. Because of this limitation, providing timely services to families of hearing impaired infants has been difficult. Early intervention programs provide families with information on language development, communication skills, the use of

Making Inclusion Work

My name is Catherine Davis and I have been a teacher of the deaf and hard of hearing in the Blue Valley School District in Overland Park, Kansas, for four years. The first year I worked as an itinerant deaf education teacher serving six schools. Then I was lucky enough to get to start a center-based resource room program in a brand new elementary school. There I teach preschool through fifth-grade students whose IEP teams have decided that due to the educational impact of their hearing loss—often accompanied by additional disabilities such as ADHD, cognitive, motor, and/or vision—they would be best served in this program rather than in their neighborhood school. My students spend the majority of their day in the general education classroom but come to me for academic support as well as auditory training, speech reading, and sign language instruction.

I grew up in a small Midwestern town where there was not a lot of diversity. One boy in my high school was deaf and I watched the other kids tease him, thinking he couldn't understand what they were saying because he couldn't hear them. He could. I decided to become his friend, learned to sign, and eventually started tutoring him. Thus, my love of teaching, combined with an interest in deafness and signing, began. After graduating from high school in 1992, I attended an interpreter-training program at the University of Kansas. Seeking to utilize my skills and have an adventure at the same time, I set out for Homer, Alaska, where I accepted a job interpreting for two Native Alaskan students. Miles from home, I encountered beauty and adventure, but also a challenge for which I was definitely unprepared. The two students with whom I worked had multiple disabilities and needed significant support. Unfortunately, the itinerant teacher was not always there to provide this support. Even though I loved Alaska and my job, this experience solidified my desire to teach and I knew I needed more training. So after a year I returned to Kansas. I completed a B.S. in Elementary Education and an M.S. in Deaf Education, and I am now in my final year of my Ph.D. in Special Education with a focus on Deaf Education.

Inclusive Education Experience

The group of kids that I currently work with is truly representative of the type of caseload that a future teacher of the deaf can expect to have. They are as different as they could be. I have one first grader who has a cochlear implant and communicates solely through sign language and another first-grade student who is hard of hearing, wears hearing aids, and uses an FM system. She is oral but learning to sign. A second-grade student has multiple disabilities including ADHD, aphasia, and vision loss. She wears hearing aids and an FM system, and uses both verbal and sign language. The fifth grader I teach has a severe hearing loss, wears hearing aids, uses an FM system, and also has multiple disabilities including motor, cognitive, and vision impairments. Her predominant mode of communication is oral.

At the beginning of every year I do an inservice for the entire staff in order to provide suggestions for working with students with a hearing loss. I also go into the general education classrooms and do lessons with all of the students explaining hearing loss, sign language, and Deaf culture as well. Often these lessons occur only with the classroom teacher or the special education teachers. However, I believe the whole school needs to be educated to really ensure that my students are fully included. I find that the more people know, the less apprehensive they are to interact with these kids. I let them try on hearing aids, listen to an

FM system, watch a video on cochlear implants, learn some sign language, and even try to take a spelling test by reading lips to simulate what it might be like for students with a hearing loss.

Strategies for Inclusive Classrooms

Because of the diverse student needs, I am required to be versatile in my communication style. My philosophy on communication modality is not to have one! Instead, I go forward based on where the student is when he or she enters my program. At any given time, I use an eclectic combination of anything that works—sign, voice, gestures, drawing pictures, writing, acting—whatever it takes. In addition to working with the student at his/her level, it is critical to develop a good working relationship with the family.

One of the first things that I tell classroom teachers who are going to have a student who is deaf or hard of hearing in their classroom is that most accommodations are pretty simple. They shouldn't be scared! First of all, students with a hearing loss should be given priority seating so they will have a better opportunity to hear as well as have visual access to the teacher's mouth for lipreading or see their interpreter if they use one. I also tell teachers that anytime they can make their teaching more visual they should do so. This can be accomplished by writing new vocabulary on the board or accompanying it with a picture, or by using visual schedules. The students will have a much easier time following along with these visual cues added. If the child uses sign language, one of the best ways for the teacher and student to learn is to make it a part of the lesson for all students. I worked with a kindergarten teacher last year who really embraced this concept. She often invited me into her classroom to do lessons with her class. Eventually she and the interpreter took over the teaching. Anytime her class learned a new sight word, they paired it with the sign. She said that using this extra modality really accelerated the child's learning. A preschool teacher I worked with two years ago used sign language so much, and also encouraged her kids to sign, that a visiting parent had to ask which one of the students was deaf!

Our school music teacher is another good example of someone with whom I collaborate often. The school put on a musical last year, and the whole student body learned to sign the songs. The parent of one of my students came to my room the next day to thank me; she was nearly in tears. She said that she never thought that she would see her child up on a stage singing and signing with everyone else, just like one of the other kids. Obviously, this kind of integration and collaboration benefits not only the student who is deaf, but everyone involved.

Another thing I do is to encourage teachers to be good advocates for their students. This often takes sustained determination to educate others about the child's needs. Although the many meetings and abundance of paperwork that this can require can seem overwhelming at times, the results are worth it. Teachers also need to teach the children with hearing loss to be good advocates for themselves. Fostering independence in students with disabilities is a component that is sometimes overlooked. In order for them to have a quality life within their educational setting, and also outside of school, students need to know how to request an interpreter, manage their audiological equipment, and educate people about their hearing loss.

The reality is that hearing loss is a low-incidence disability. In my experiences in rural settings, both in Kansas and Alaska, I have seen how isolating it can be for the student to be the only one, or one of few who are deaf or hard of hearing in their school. Therefore, it is especially important to me that I do everything I can to make sure the students I work with are included as much as possible. By being flexible and adaptable both in my teaching and in my communication style, by collaborating with staff, students, and parents, and by being a good advocate for my students and encouraging them to be good advocates for themselves, I find that my students are very successful in an inclusive setting.

—Catherine Davis
Liberty View Elementary School,
Overland Park, Kansas
Teacher of the Deaf and Hard of Hearing

residual hearing, amplification, self-help, and social-emotional development for children with hearing loss. These programs are usually not child centered in design, but place strong emphasis on parent and family instruction and involvement. Meeting the needs of each individual family requires unique design of interventional strategies.

As previously mentioned, the vast majority of hearing impaired infants have normally hearing parents. Whether a deaf child is born to deaf or hearing parents may influence social, educational, and cultural issues that the family unit faces. For example, many hearing parents of children who are severely impaired probably do not know or use sign language. They may be unaware of cultural issues related to the deaf community, and how such issues might relate to their own child's education options. Some research indicates that deaf parents are more likely to view hearing impaired children in a positive way, which may result in greater normalization of the parent–child relationship (Katz & Schery, 2006; Maxon, Brackett, & van den Berg, 1991). Allen and Cowdery (2009) suggest that early intervention programs should focus on helping the child with a hearing impairment develop within the structure of his or her family, just as a child with normal hearing develops within this context.

Transition and Individuals with Hearing Impairments

The process of transition, enabling the person with a hearing impairment to make a comfortable and positive change from one environment to another, requires systematic planning and evaluation. IDEA mandates individual transition plans (ITPs) for children with disabilities age 16 and older in public schools. It also requires ongoing modification to remain current and sensitive to the needs of these individuals and their families. As previously discussed, many students with severe to profound hearing impairments lag behind their peers in personal/social/behavioral maturity, which affects the structure of transition planning.

Stress is often associated with changes, and transition can be especially difficult for the family as well as the pupil. Families learning to adjust to the new challenges of having an adolescent or young adult who is deaf or hard of hearing are often assisted by teachers, counselors, or other specialists. Family life plays a key role in the transition process for deaf adolescents. Many times, the audiologist, social worker, speech-language pathologist, and special education teacher assist the family in gathering the information needed to make the initial educational placement and communication training decisions.

The Laurent Clerc National Deaf Education Center, located at Gallaudet University, provides excellent information families and teachers can use to promote transition and independence.

Legislation facilitating transition as a national priority for the hearing impaired began with the passage of PL 89-36 in 1968, which established the National Technical Institute for the Deaf (NTID) at the Rochester Institute of Technology, and Section 504 of the Rehabilitation Act of 1973 (PL 93-112), which mandated that institutions of higher education provide accessible facilities and support services for individuals with disabilities. In addition, Congress currently funds six postsecondary programs for the deaf and hard of hearing: Gallaudet University, NTID, and Regional Postsecondary Education Programs for the Deaf located at California State University at Northridge, St. Paul Technical College, Seattle Central Community College, and the University of Tennessee Center on Deafness.

Transition into a new educational or vocational environment involves a variety of community professionals and services. Itinerant teachers of the hearing impaired, in concert with the cooperation and coordination of the special education and general education teacher, the interpreter, and other support personnel, may assist in meeting the challenges of transitioning between special and general education programs or postsecondary educational and/or vocational programs.

The transition for many individuals with a hearing impairment also involves personal, social, and community adjustments. The new experiences are enlarged not only by communication difficulties but also by the diverse literacy skills needed in the new environment. Transition to postsecondary education, vocational training, and/or employment can be eased by career counseling and coursework centered on vocational skills and independent living, as outlined in the student's ITP. For students desiring a college degree, in addition to stressing academic achievement, a successful college preparatory training program involves instruction regarding dorm life, responsible social behavior, and problem-solving strategies for coping with the multitude of problems that college students who have hearing impairments are likely to encounter (King, De Caro, Karchmer, & Cole, 2001).

Services for Adults with Hearing Impairments

Adult support services often provide a vital link between the hearing impaired and the hearing world (Scheetz, 2001). These diverse services may be used to enhance public knowledge regarding deafness, facilitate communication, or aid in the transfer of information.

Two basic types of mandated services are offered statewide for adults who are deaf or hard of hearing. The first is a State Commission or Office on Deafness, whose services include advocacy, information gathering and dissemination, referral to appropriate agencies, interpreting services, and job placement and development.

The second type of service is offered through each state's vocational rehabilitation service. A coordinator of rehabilitation services for the deaf and hard of hearing provides vocational evaluation, job placement, and counseling, often in conjunction with the transition plan while the student is still in high school. State rehabilitation offices can also help students preparing to enter postsecondary academic environments. Under the Americans with Disabilities Act, colleges and universities are required to provide qualified sign language interpreters and other auxiliary aids needed to ensure effective communication opportunities for the deaf and hard of hearing student population, even if these services are not provided by the state vocational rehabilitation system.

For more than 120 years, the National Association for the Deaf (NAD) has been actively involved in obtaining the basic rights under the U.S. Constitution for individuals with hearing impairments. Additionally, NAD provides political advocacy at the state and federal levels and promotes issues important to the deaf population. NAD also publishes books on a wide range of topics and issues related to hearing impairment (Moores, 2001).

Another significant organization promoting the integration of the hearing impaired population into mainstream society is the Alexander Graham Bell (AGB) Association. The philosophy of the AGB Association is based on the improvement of oral speech communication. The AGB Association serves as a clearinghouse of materials and information concerning oral teaching methods, technology, and related topics. See the end of this chapter for a detailed listing of organizations and agencies that have been established to provide services for the hearing impaired.

Another popular adult resource is Self-Help for Hard of Hearing People (SHHH). SHHH provides advocacy, information, and assistance to hard of hearing individuals. Extremely active, this organization has more than 250 local chapters nationwide.

Family Issues

Family dynamics can be severely disrupted when a child is born with a significant hearing impairment. Parental, sibling, and grandparenting roles are often dramatically altered by such an event. Because the effects of hearing impairment are so pervasive, particularly with regard to communication, accepting and "normalizing" the child's disability can be quite difficult. The expected or fantasized child does not arrive, and the family experiences an initial state of emotional shock and disbelief. The level of impact on the family may vary, but for most families such an event can create a crisis atmosphere of considerable magnitude.

Family Reaction

Approximately 90 percent of all children with hearing impairments have hearing parents (Picard, 2004). After the initial emotional states of shock and disbelief, stresses on the family can increase as individual members come to understand that communicating with the child who is hearing impaired is different and likely always will be. From these initial reactions, parents go through different stages of grieving such as uncertainty, frustration, denial, depression, and anxiety (Ulrich & Bauer, 2003). They may initially blame their spouse, fate, or the professional community, or even misdirect anger and frustration toward themselves. Parents may have difficulty accepting assistance or recommendations from professionals, extended family, and friends. Some may become overprotective of the child and turn their attention away from other family members. Others may withdraw, finding isolation easier than coping with the child care demands placed upon them (Meadows-Orlans, 1995).

Perhaps the greatest factor in positive resolution of such emotionally charged issues is acceptance of the hearing impairment. Achieving genuine acceptance of any disability is, for most families, an ongoing process. Stages of this process are not necessarily completed independently and in successive order, just as achieving a measure of acceptance does not prevent certain situations from reopening old emotional wounds. Grieving and uncertainty may emerge time and again during the child's development, but will be less severe as the family's coping mechanisms improve. The stages of grieving that follow the birth of a baby with a hearing loss are healthy expressions of normal emotional reactions. The process of working through such feelings should not be hurried; it allows the family members opportunities to recognize and acknowledge change in their lives, as well as time to formulate positive strategies for accommodating the child with the hearing impairment. In this process, the development of positive relationships is individually and collectively encouraged (Meadows-Orlans, 1995). Parental support groups provide a very effective arena for expressing concerns, offering support and encouragement, and formulating effective parenting strategies.

Siblings and Grandparents

Siblings and grandparents are not immune from the emotional issues that accompany the birth of a hearing impaired child. There is little formal research that examines the

Individuals with Visual Impairments

Carrie

The series of whistles sounds. She steps onto the starting block and bends into position as the official instructs. The beep of the starter propels the swimmers into the water. It is a good start. She and Jennifer surface at the same time, just short of Beth. Steadily Jennifer pulls ahead. C'mon, Carrie, you can do it! I think to myself. Jennifer's lead widens. I turn my head; I can't watch. She's worked so hard to not succeed now. At the turn, she flips just as Jennifer starts back for the last 50 meters. It's now or four more years. Suddenly she begins to narrow the margin. Is it too little too late? Maybe. I begin to yell (and others around me). Please, dear God! She's doing it! Oh, no, the flags. It's so close. Yes, she does it! She out-touches Jennifer by hundredths of a second. But the clock does not register. Quickly the judges check the computers. Yes, she really did it! She doesn't know. Frantically I send word by a friend. When she hears the news, she stops in disbelief, then her right arm shoots straight up with joy.

She came through again. I don't know why I'm surprised. She has done it time and time again. That's just Carrie. All of her life she has amazed me as well as others she has encountered. While second place does not sound like much of an accomplishment, it is to a disabled child. Perhaps disabled is not the right word.

Carrie, now 22, was born with oculocutaneous albinism. As with all disabilities, this has a complex definition. For Carrie, it means she has no pigment in her eyes, skin, or hair, she is extremely sensitive to light, she has nystagmus, and she is legally blind. She has also had some other physical problems along the way, but has developed into an outstanding young lady earning her place on the United States Paralympic Team.

The road to victory has not been easy, and sometimes Carrie did not choose the easy route. Even as a small child many people saw the special qualities in Carrie and encouraged and guided her. Others have been unable to see beyond her shortcomings. The key to her success has been her strength of character to focus on her abilities, not her disabilities. Her favorite saying is "I may not have eyesight, but I have vision."

Written by Carol Allison and Mary Jean Sanspree, University of Alabama at Birmingham

Her academic life has definitely had its ups and downs. Her level of success and happiness seems to have been determined by her attitude, which is closely related to the attitude of her teachers and her classmates. The more creative and open the atmosphere, the more Carrie has achieved. Quite often the more creative teachers found ways to minimize her visual limitations and maximize her intellectual and creative abilities.

Swimming is not her only accomplishment. She is a college senior majoring in Liberal Arts with a concentration in Visual Arts. She is an award winner not only in the disabled world, but also in the "real world." Of all her talents, gifts, awards, recognition, and more, the one I am most proud of is the Right Stuff Award that she received at Space Camp in Huntsville, Alabama. This award is presented each camp session to one female and one male who have demonstrated outstanding leadership and personal effort. This shows me that she has developed into the kind of person who will contribute to society in a positive manner.

—*Jane Willoughby*

NOTE: For additional coverage of Carrie, check out the First Person box on page 468, written in her own words about her experience with her visual impairment.

Visual impairment is a term that describes people who cannot see well even with correction. Throughout history, *blindness* has been used as a term to mean that something is not understood, such as "I was blind to that idea" or the aged person is "old and blind." How many times do we use the stereotypes of the blind beggar on the street corner and the blind person groping for mobility in the environment? The stigma associated with loss of vision affects encounters with others, who may assume that the person is dependent on others for everything.

Famous success stories about persons who are blind include those of Helen Keller and Mary Ingalls. Helen Keller and her teacher, Annie Sullivan, pursued their lifelong journey from Tuscumbia, Alabama, to Perkins Institute for the Blind (now known as Perkins School for the Blind), to Radcliffe College, and then to employment with the American Foundation for the Blind. Keller helped develop schools for the blind all over the world (Lash, 1980).

Mary Ingalls was a student at Iowa College for the Blind (now Iowa Braille and Sight Saving School) in 1881. Her scholastic endeavors were made famous through Laura Ingalls Wilder's *Little House on the Prairie*, which later became a television series. Laura's portrayal of the determination of her sister Mary and their family to continue her education after she lost her vision at age 14 showed the world the success a person who is blind can achieve.

Movies about persons with visual impairments and publicity about musicians and athletes who are visually impaired have helped to change the image of persons with visual impairments. Braille in elevators, voice output on computers, and access to restaurant hosts who read the menu reflect a recognition that the person with vision loss is competent with only a visual acuity difference. Such changes allow independence in the everyday world with only a few accommodations.

The goal of this chapter is to provide an understanding of the visual process, vision loss, the effects of vision loss on school performance and vocation, and the roles of the family and community. Historical foundations, classifications of vision loss, educational practices, and technological interventions are presented for you to examine how the general educational curriculum may be adapted for the student with a visual impairment.

Defining Visual Impairments

Visual impairment including blindness is defined in the Individuals with Disabilities Education Improvement Act (IDEA) (PL 108-446) as an impairment in vision that, even with correction, adversely affects an individual's educational performance. The term includes both partial sight and blindness. Educational services for students with visual impairments are determined by variations of the definition specified in IDEA. This definition encompasses students with a wide range of visual impairments, who may vary significantly in their visual abilities. One student may have no functional vision and must learn through tactual means; another may be able to read and write print with modifications such as enlarged print; still others may use a combination of both Braille and print. An appropriate learning medium for each student must be determined by the student's ability to use each of these means or a combination of both.

Visual impairments may include a reduction of **visual acuity** (the ability to visually perceive details) of near or distant vision or a restriction in the field of vision. In other words, acuity affects how well a child sees materials presented up close or how accurately the child can see work presented on chalkboards or maps across the room. An impairment involving the **visual field** refers to the amount of vision a student has in the quadrant regions to the right, left, up, and down while gazing straight ahead. Students may exhibit unusual head turning or positioning in order to view materials with the portion of the visual field that is functional. Students with a **field loss,** or a restriction to the visual field, must be taught to use auditory cues for safety purposes on the playground, in the classroom, and in other environments.

Other areas of consideration in understanding a student's visual abilities include the age of the student at the time of the vision loss, the severity and stability of the eye condition, and whether the condition is the result of hereditary or congenital conditions. This information is usually obtained through a medical or clinically based assessment by an optometrist or ophthalmologist and does not necessarily include how the person functions in various settings throughout the school, home, or community.

Understanding the definitions of visual impairments is critical for the educational team in developing an appropriate educational program. Over the years, the term **legally blind** has been used as a federal definition of blindness. This definition involves using a **Snellen chart,** which is a clinical measurement of the true amount of distance vision an individual has under certain conditions. Legal blindness is a visual acuity of 20/200 or less in the better eye with correction or a visual field that is no greater than 20 degrees. In this definition, 20 feet is the distance at which visual acuity is measured. The 200 in this definition indicates the distance (200 feet) a person with normal vision would be able to identify the largest symbol on the eye chart. The second part of the definition refers to field restriction, which involves the amount of vision a person has to view objects peripherally. The legal definition is considered in education, but by itself has little value in planning a functional educational program for students with visual impairments.

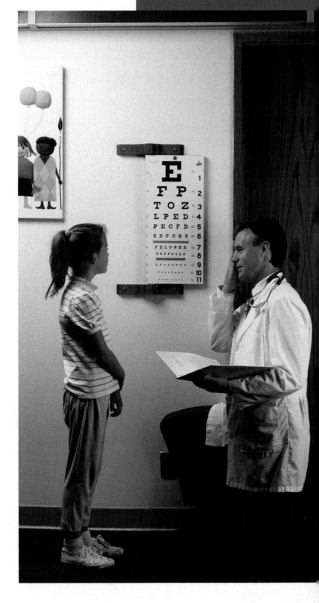

Legal blindness is visual acuity of 20/200 or less in the better eye after correction or a visual field that is no greater than 20 degrees.

Individuals identified as **blind** use tactile and auditory abilities as the primary channels of learning. They may have some minimal light or form perception or be totally without sight. Braille or other tactile media are commonly the preferred literacy channel. Orientation and mobility training is required for all students who are blind.

Individuals are considered **functionally blind** when the primary channel of learning is through tactile or auditory means. They may use limited vision to obtain additional information about the environment. These individuals usually use Braille as the **primary literacy medium** (most frequently used method of reading) and require orientation and mobility training.

A person is described as having **low vision** when the visual impairment interferes with the ability to perform daily activities. The primary channel of learning is through visual means with the use of prescription and nonprescription devices. The literacy medium varies with each individual according to the use of the remaining vision and the use of low vision devices. Orientation and mobility training is required for students to learn to use **residual vision** (usable vision).

Persons with deaf-blindness have limited vision and hearing that interfere with visual and auditory tasks. Individuals who are **deaf-blind** learn tactually. Braille and sign language are the preferred literacy and communication media. A sign language interpreter and orientation and mobility training are required for persons with deaf-blindness.

The Eye and How It Works

The human eye is the organ that gives us the sense of sight, allowing us to learn more about the surrounding world than we do with any of the other four senses. We use our eyes in almost every activity we perform, whether reading, working, watching television, writing a letter, or driving a car. The eye allows us to see and interpret the shapes, colors, and dimensions of objects by processing the light. Light enters the eye first through the clear **cornea** and then through the circular opening in the **iris** called the **pupil.** Next the light is converged by the crystalline **lens.** The light progresses through the gelatinous **vitreous humor** to a clear focus on the **retina,** the central area of which is the **macula.** In the retina, light impulses are changed into electrical signals and sent along the **optic nerve** to the occipital (posterior) lobe of the brain, which interprets these electrical signals as visual images.

If the incoming light from a faraway object focuses before it gets to the back of the eye, that eye's refractive error is called **myopia** (nearsightedness). If incoming light has not focused by the time it reaches the back of the eye, that eye's refractive error is **hyperopia** (farsightedness).

In the case of **astigmatism,** one or more surfaces of the cornea or lens (the eye structures that focus incoming light) are not spherical (shaped like the side of a basketball) but cylindrical (shaped like the side of a football). As a result, there is no distinct point of focus inside the eye but, rather, a smeared or spread-out focus. Astigmatism is the most common refractive error.

The eyeball, which measures approximately one inch in diameter, is set in a protective cone-shaped cavity in the skull called the **orbit** or socket. The orbit is surrounded by layers of soft, fatty tissue that protect the eye and enable it to turn easily. Three pairs of muscles regulate the motion of each eye.

Figure 12.1 shows the anatomy of the human eye; Table 12.1 presents key terminology associated with the functioning of the eye.

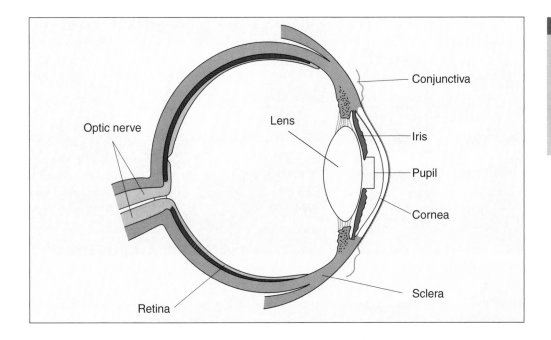

Figure 12.1

Schematic of the Eye

Source: National Eye Institute. (2007). *Photograph and Image Catalog: Normal eye anatomy NEA05.* Available at http://www.nei.nih.gov.

Table 12.1	Terminology Describing Eye Functioning
Aqueous humor	A clear, watery fluid that fills the front part of the eye between the cornea, lens, and iris.
Choroid	The middle layer of the eyeball, which contains veins and arteries that furnish nourishment to the eye, especially the retina.
Conjunctiva	A mucous membrane that lines the eyelids and covers the front part of the eyeball.
Cornea	The transparent outer portion of the eyeball that transmits light to the retina.
Iris	The colored, circular part of the eye in front of the lens. It controls the size of the pupil.
Lens	The transparent disc in the middle of the eye behind the pupil that brings rays of light into focus on the retina.
Optic nerve	The important nerve that carries messages from the retina to the brain.
Pupil	The circular opening at the center of the iris that controls the amount of light allowed into the eye.
Retina	The inner layer of the eye containing light-sensitive cells that connect with the brain through the optic nerve.
Sclera	The white part of the eye; a tough coating that, along with the cornea, forms the external protective coat of the eye.
Vitreous body	A colorless mass of soft, gelatinlike material that fills the eyeball behind the lens.

Classification of Visual Impairments

Children are eligible for special education services according to the amount of vision loss and how that vision loss affects educational performance. The most common visual impairments affecting the school-age child include **cataracts, glaucoma, optic nerve atrophy,** myopia, **albinism,** eye injury, cortical visual impairment, and **retinopathy of prematurity (ROP).** Examples of how children see with different eye diseases are shown in Figure 12.2.

Some visual impairments are secondary to systematic diseases such as diabetes, cancer, muscular dystrophy, and arthritis. A list of these visual impairments and their characteristics can be found in Table 12.2 (page 453).

(a)

Normal vision

(b)

Glaucoma

(c)

Age-related macular degeneration

(d)

Cataract

(e)

Diabetic retinopathy

Figure 12.2

Examples of Eye Diseases

Source: National Eye Institute. (2007). *Photograph and Image Catalog: Eye disease simulation.* Available at http://www.nei.nih.gov.

A Brief History of Visual Impairments

Education for and changes of attitudes toward persons with visual impairments were of great interest to Diderot (1749), who wrote to King Louis of France a philosophical work called *Letter on the Blind for the Use of Those Who See*. Diderot had contact with two people who were blind: Nicholas Saunderson, a mathematics professor, and Maria Theresia von

Table 12.2	Common Visual Impairments of School-Age Students	
Condition	**Cause**	**Characteristics**
Ocular albinism	Total or partial absence of pigment, hereditary condition	Nystagmus, light sensitivity, decreased visual acuity
Congenital cataracts	Congenital anomaly, infection, severe malnutrition, systemic disease, or trauma	Blurred vision, nystagmus
Congenital glaucoma	Increased pressure of the eye	Excessive tearing, cloudy lens, pain, restricted visual fields
Optic atrophy	Degeneration of the optic nerve, may be congenital or hereditary	Loss of central vision, color vision, and reduced visual acuity
Myopia	Elongation of the eye	Extreme nearsightedness, decreased visual acuity
Eye injury	Trauma	Poor visual acuity or blindness resulting from injury
Retinopathy of prematurity (ROP)	Prematurity and low birth weight	Loss of peripheral vision; total blindness may occur

Paradis, a Viennese pianist and music teacher. Diderot was one of the early champions of the visually impaired and believed that persons who were blind could lead normal lives.

In 1784, Valentin Haüy established the Institut des Jeunes Aveugles in Paris. This institution for blind youth was the first school for the education of children with vision loss. Haüy used Roman letters to teach students who were blind. His students, however, were using night writing codes within the school. In the 1800s, one of Haüy's students, Louis Braille, developed an embossed communication system so he could write to his friends in a simpler manner than using raised letters (Scholl, Mulholland, & Lonergan, 1986). His system of embossed dots was not accepted by educators until later, but his system of **Braille** dots remains today as the literacy code accepted throughout the world.

The first schools for the blind in the United States were financially supported through the school in Paris. These schools are currently known as the Perkins School for the Blind in Boston, established in 1829; the New York Institute for the Blind, incorporated in 1831; and the Overbrook School for the Blind in Philadelphia, opened in 1833. These residential schools, modeled after the Institut des Jeunes Aveugles in Paris, were the brainchild of Samuel Gridley Howe, who had visited European schools to learn how to provide education for the blind in the United States (Scholl et al., 1986).

Residential programs were designed to prepare students with visual impairments for daily living skills and menial jobs. Students were expected to function within a sheltered environment and go into life as a member of a separate society that was labeled as "helpless" or dependent. The schools were a type of experiment to see if students with disabilities could learn community skills and function as participating citizens instead of dependents of society.

In the early 1900s, children with visual impairments were served by various agencies such as hospitals, children's services for rehabilitation, and residential schools; there were no laws mandating services. Children were often recruited to attend residential schools where they would learn vocational skills so they could become active members of the community (Best, 1919). In the 1950s and 1960s, vision professionals endorsed "sight-saving" classes located in public schools that "saved" children's remaining vision by not allowing them to use their residual vision. Children were blindfolded and taught to read and write tactually.

In the 1950s and 1960s, parents and educators also saw a need for an array of school placement options for students with visual impairments (American Foundation for the Blind, 1993). Focusing on individual rights, this movement was related to the civil rights movement, the development of Project Head Start, and the growing needs of young children who were born with visual impairments during the baby boom following World War II (Lang, 1992). Residential and public school options developed to meet the educational needs of the child and his/her rights within the community.

In the 1970s, professionals accepted the theory that vision should be stimulated and children taught to more efficiently and effectively use remaining vision. Natalie Barraga (1973) shared the opinion that children could learn to use vision that was left and that this use would get better with practice. The training of residual vision was known as **visual efficiency.** The child was taught to use spectacles, magnifiers, and any other assistive devices to improve the use of any remaining vision. The theory that visual skills can be learned is still discussed today.

At this time, children with visual impairments were attending both residential and public schools; however, laws such as PL 94-142 required school districts to identify and serve children with visual impairments in the local community. Many of these students were placed in the general education classroom with assistance provided by vision specialists serving as consultants. Vocational training was not emphasized because integration of children with visual impairment allowed access to the general education curriculum. Since the 1990s, IDEA has combined a number of laws to require that students with visual impairments receive specialized vision services from infancy through young adulthood.

Prevalence of Visual Impairments

How many children with visual impairments can you expect to be in your school district or residential school? IDEA defines a child as eligible for special education services when the nature of the visual impairment interferes with the student's participating in the general education curriculum. Although visual impairments are relatively rare among children and youth, specialists must be used for intervention within the school program.

It is estimated that 2.8 percent of school-age children in the United States experience a vision loss significant enough to require specialized support in the educational program (National Eye Institute, 2004). The U.S. Department of Education (2007) reports that approximately 26,000 children ages 6–21 were receiving services in the 2005–2006 school year because of a visual impairment. When compared to the total number of school-age children who are receiving a special education, students with visual impairments make up only 0.4 percent of pupils with a disability. Visual impairment, therefore, is one of the least prevalent disabilities. Recent data from the U.S. Department of Education indicates that slightly more than 3,400 preschoolers were receiving a special education in the 2005–2006 school year because of visual impairments. This group of youngsters represents 0.5 percent of all preschoolers with a disability.

A significant number of children with visual impairment also have concomitant developmental or physical disabilities. Vision loss may be associated with cerebral palsy, muscular dystrophy, injuries, arthritis, or some other childhood disease. As a result of improvements in neonatology and advanced medical procedures, this population continues to increase. Students in this category are often reported to the U.S. Department of Education in other disability areas, with the visual impairment recognized as a secondary disability.

The Vision Process and Etiology of Visual Impairments

In working with students with visual impairments, it is important to understand what can happen when the parts of the visual system do not perform as they should. Here we review some of the causes of visual impairments and how they can affect the student's functional vision.

Light enters the eye through the cornea (see Figure 12.1), which is the clear, transparent covering at the front of the eye. The cornea is curved in shape and serves as a strong protective structure for the inner parts of the eye. It assists in focusing the optical image that will reach the brain. If the cornea is damaged through trauma or disease and attention is not given to the disturbance, then the inner area may become infected, which can result in permanent visual impairment and even total blindness.

As light passes through the cornea, it goes into an area called the anterior chamber, which is filled with aqueous fluid. This fluid helps bring nutrients to and remove waste from the back surface of the cornea. It also helps maintain the shape of the eye. The major disease that occurs in the aqueous humor is glaucoma, which can result in a loss of visual acuity as well as a loss in the visual field. Students with glaucoma often have headaches and require frequent periods of rest. Students may also need medication to treat this disease. Student health care plans should include this information.

The next section of the eye that light must travel through is the iris. The iris is the colored, circular muscle of the eye that controls the amount of light that comes into the eye by regulating the size of the pupil. The pupil is the opening in the iris where light enters the eye. If the iris is malformed, the function of light control will be interrupted and the child can become **photophobic** (sensitive to light). Students may require sunglasses or other optical devices to reduce the amount of light reaching the retina. Close work may result in fatigue and blurring. Mobility training should be provided, if required, to work with depth perception in moving about the environment. Teachers should be aware of children with abnormalities to the iris and refer them for further medical attention.

The lens is a colorless, transparent oval structure suspended behind the iris. The function of the lens is to filter and bend the light rays before they reach the back part of the eye. Cataracts are lenses that are opaque or cloudy as a result of trauma or age. Children with congenital cataracts often have the cataracts removed. If needed, this should be done as early as possible to allow for normal vision development. In the absence of the lens, the eye will appear flat **(aphakic)** and light will not be filtered appropriately. The child will be photophobic and may complain of serious glare problems. Depending on the location of the cataract, a child's color vision may also be distorted. Squinting, caused by a lack of visual stimulation and resulting in reduced visual acuity, can be a characteristic of a child with cataracts. Low illumination may be preferred. Additional time may be required to move from one activity to another to accommodate lighting needs. Cataracts may also be associated with Down syndrome, Marfan syndrome, and rubella.

Behind the lens, light must travel through a clear liquid gel (vitreous body). This thick fluid serves as a filter for light and helps maintain the shape of the eye. If the lens becomes infected and cloudy, the light rays to the back of the eye will be distorted, resulting in reduced visual acuity. In diabetes, this part of the eye often contains particles or tissue from vascular bleeding, which can distort vision, affecting peripheral vision as well as central visual acuity. The child sees blurry and distorted images and has difficulty reading and observing objects at a distance.

After the light goes through the vitreous fluid, it reaches the retina. The retina, located in the innermost part of the eye, contains layers of light-sensitive nerve cells. It is very thin and has an intricate vascular system. This is the area where the light is sent to the optic nerve for transmission to the brain. Most retina disorders result in blurred vision. Unlike other eye diseases associated with pain, the retina has no pain fibers or other physical characteristics such as red and inflamed eyes. The purpose of the retina is to receive the light image and send it to the brain through the optic nerve. The optic nerve carries the light messages (electrical signals) to the brain, where they are interpreted as visual images known as sight.

Rods and cones are photoreceptive cells found in the retina. **Rod cells,** located mainly in the peripheral areas, are extremely light sensitive. Responsible for shape and motion, they function best in reduced illumination. Rod cells are not responsive to color. **Cone cells** are located mainly in the central area of the retina. Color is defined in the cone cells. Only special cones are found in the macula area, which is the area of best central vision, and the fovea area, which is the area of most acute vision. **Macular degeneration** is a common eye disease in adults, but it may also occur in young people. This disease involves damage to the central part of the retina cones, affecting central vision, photophobia, and color vision.

If a child has retinopathy of prematurity (ROP), vascular growth has been interrupted by premature birth. The veins and arteries begin to grow in an unorganized manner causing bundles, which pull together and detach the retina. The child first loses peripheral vision and then the whole field of vision unless surgical intervention is immediate. Spotty vision, retinal scarring, field loss, and glaucoma may also be present. Training in early intervention and sensory stimulation are areas of concern.

According to the Texas School for the Blind (2007), other retinal diseases include the following:

- **Retinitis pigmentosa** is a hereditary condition involving gradual degeneration of the retina, which can result in night blindness, photophobia, and eventually loss of macular vision.
- Toxoplasmosis is a severe infection transmitted through contact with domestic animals such as cats or chickens. Lesions on the retina can reduce visual acuity and field vision. Squinting is an observable characteristic of children with toxoplasmosis.
- Albinism is a congenital condition characterized by a lack of pigment (skin, hair, or eyes). If the eyes are the only area affected, it is called ocular albinism. These children may be extremely photophobic and sensitive to glare, both in the classroom and outdoors. They may have high refractive problems, but the visual fields are usually normal. Fatigue may become a factor in close work.
- **Coloboma** is a congenital condition that results in a teardrop shape of the pupil, iris, lens, retina, choroid, or optic nerve. Field of vision may be affected, problems with glare may also be present, and problems with depth perception may occur.
- Optic nerve atrophy is caused by a variety of diseases. Early treatment can prevent a loss of visual acuity. Without treatment, optic atrophy can result in low visual acuity to total blindness.

Prevention of Visual Impairments

Most visual impairments are genetic in source, but others can be prevented or controlled. Prenatal care can prevent eye problems secondary to sexually transmitted diseases, prematurity, or known hereditary problems. Screening of babies in the hospital nursery, youngsters in the preschool setting, and older students on a regular basis can help detect and prevent eye diseases that cause visual impairments.

Eye safety is a preventive measure against eye injuries that can hinder visual acuity and even cause blindness. Ocular trauma can affect the orbit, the eyelids, and other structures of the eye, and immediate intervention is necessary. Some trauma causes infections, changes in the appearance of the eye, and even blindness.

Early Detection

Vision screening is a necessary beginning to eye care, although such screening does not replace a professional eye examination. Vision problems affect 1 in 20 preschoolers and 1 in 4 school-age children (Prevent Blindness America, 2007a). Early screening and diagnosis can detect the prognosis for visual impairments. Screenings and eye examinations should take place shortly after birth, at 6 months of age, before entering school, and periodically throughout the school years.

Eye Safety

Many types of eye injuries can be prevented.

Eye injuries are common. They can range from a mild abrasion with bleeding in the front of the eye to retinal detachment, penetration of the eye, or actual rupture of the globe (eyeball). Some injuries heal without loss of vision; others result in the loss of the eye. At least 90 percent of all eye injuries to children can be prevented by understanding the dangers, identifying and correcting hazards, and using greater care when supervising children (Prevent Blindness America, 2007b). Some of the most frequent causes of eye injuries are

- Misuse of toys or altering toys
- Falls involving home furnishings and fixtures such as beds, stairs, tables, and toys
- Misuse of everyday objects, such as home repair and yard care products, personal use items, kitchen utensils, silverware, pens, and pencils
- Accidental exposure to harmful household and cleaning products, such as detergents, paints, pesticides, glues, and adhesives
- Automobile accidents (a leading cause of eye injuries to young children)
- Fireworks, which may cause injury to the user and bystanders alike (Kuhn et al., 2000)

Characteristics of Individuals with Visual Impairments

Visual impairment affects the type of experiences the child has, ability to travel within the environment, and actual involvement in the immediate and secondary communities. These factors will be affected differently depending on the amount of vision loss. The child with low vision has experiences that are different from the child who is legally blind or totally blind. The Optometric Extension Program Foundation (2007) has developed a checklist of observable characteristics of vision difficulties in children to assist teachers in making reliable observations of children's visual behavior (see Table 12.3).

Table 12.3	Behavioral Characteristics in Vision Function Problems
Unusual turning of the head, body, or eye
Holding reading material extremely close to the face
Excessive rubbing of the eye
Watery eyes
Eye fatigue
Frequent eye pain
Frequent headaches
Squints or shades the eye to view objects
Constantly having difficulty in keeping up when reading and writing
Using markers such as pencils and fingers when reading
Difficulty copying from the board or transparencies
Confusion in writing letters and numbers appropriately
"Clumsy" movement from one environment to another
Poor posture in both standing and sitting
Reluctance to participate in social and physical activities
Poor grades
Difficulty with color identification or color coordination
Sensory perceptual coordination
Misaligns columns when writing math problems
Requires additional time to complete a task
Fails to make eye contact when talking to people
Behavior problems

Source: Optometric Extension Program Foundation, *Educator's Guide to Classroom Vision Problems.* Available at http://www.healthy.net/oep/educate.htm.

Because the eye serves as the primary sensory input for most individuals, it becomes extremely important for those working with school-age children to be aware of the visual abilities necessary for maximum academic achievement:

- Clear visual acuity at both near and distance
- Ability to fixate at all distances and in all planes
- Binocular coordination
- Development of color preferences
- Central and peripheral visual abilities
- Visual perceptual imagery

Social and Emotional Development

The everyday experiences of children who have visual impairments are affected because they do not respond visually to people in the environment. Maintaining eye contact during speech, smiling at someone in a friendly manner, and reaching out to touch someone nearby are not innate skills for the child who cannot see details in the immediate surroundings. For the child with visual impairment, knowledge about body parts, eating skills, age-appropriate behavior, clothing, and other social skills are not learned by viewing others in the family or community. Socially appropriate behaviors must be intentionally taught to the person with a visual impairment so that other people will be at ease during communication.

Social behaviors affect the emotional development of the child with a visual impairment. The child must feel accepted by peers and others in the community. If the eye contact or verbal communication is not appropriate for the age of the child, adults and children may tend to leave the child out of social events or talk for the child.

The child with a visual impairment should also talk about emotions and how to project those emotions in the sighted world. Often the child with a visual impairment is lonely and needs structure to integrate into community activities. The child may feel isolated and have low self-esteem because he or she appears to be on the fringe of events within the family or community. Physical communication within social interactions, such as touching people appropriately, affects the social and emotional facets of the child. It is necessary to address feelings and emotions so that the child with a visual impairment can know what emotions are and how others detect emotional changes in their faces or body language.

A child who has low vision will display more visual and tactual skills in the social situation. The appropriate responses shown because of paired visual and tactile experiences will often make the child with low vision appear to have less of a vision loss than is really present. However, the child with low vision may have optical devices, enlarged materials, mobility devices, and technology for reading and writing with print. This may cause frustration for the child because of the complexity of the devices and materials needed to obtain information visually and auditorily.

The child who is legally blind will retrieve information tactually and auditorily, with minimal use of vision for tasks where large objects or light affect mobility decisions. Many parents notice that the young child does not turn his/her head toward the person talking and seems to grope for toys on the floor, hold onto the wall, or sit alone rather than explore the room. The child will also concentrate on items within the immediate environment, talk out when it is not appropriate, and ask questions to maintain voice contact with people in the room. The child who is legally blind will travel with a cane and will read and write with magnification, Braille, or both, according to reading speed, comprehension, and preference.

The child who is totally blind, with no light perception or possibly with prosthetic eyes, will depend on tactual and auditory skills for all information. The child will often not react to any visual cues, will usually sit in one place until someone guides him or her to another setting, and will be dependent on others for stimulation within the immediate environment. The child will use a cane to travel and will use the hands for locating and describing objects. The child will use Braille reading and writing for literacy and will have to use listening skills for learning new ideas.

Vocational Skills

Children with visual impairments begin vocational skills training at an early age if early intervention is provided or a preschool class is available. Children learn about dressing,

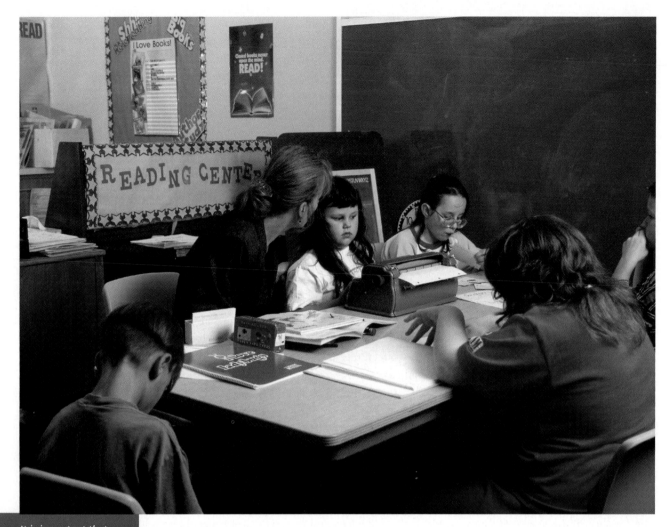

It is important that children with visual impairments feel accepted by their classmates.

eating, cooking, telling time, and using calendars for scheduling events in daily life. As the child progresses through school, a specialized curriculum may be introduced to teach about earning money, having a job, and traveling within the community.

Entering the world of work is an issue for vocational development. The student must know how to bathe, dress, prepare a meal, and plan the travel details to get to a job. After arriving at the workplace, the student must learn the building layout and the location of necessary sites such as the main office, restroom, lunchroom, and other important places within the company. Job duties and responsibilities must be explained so that job tasks can be completed successfully. Ethical behavior within the workplace must be learned before the first day of work. Ways to communicate with people within the work setting is also an educational issue.

The child with visual impairments faces quality-of-life issues that may differ from those faced by persons with other disabilities. The amount of vision loss, the intervention strategies, and the quality of life should all be taken into account. Independence begins in the early years and continues throughout life, affecting the quality of life at work, at home, and in the community. Vocational skills are a part of the preschool plan, the educational program, and the transition to adulthood so that age-appropriate skills are learned and used for independence.

Assessment of Students with Visual Impairments

Public Law 108-446 assures that all students with disabilities will have available a free appropriate public education. A comprehensive assessment is required to determine eligibility for special education services and to develop an educational program that provides for the individual needs of each pupil. In developing an educational program for children with visual impairments, the assessment process must comply with the equivalent guidelines for other areas of exceptionality while also diagnosing and determining the unique needs and abilities of students with visual impairments.

Some children may be identified at birth as having a visual impairment through routine medical examinations, but many others are not identified until later. Parents or caregivers may notice unusual developmental behaviors caused by a vision loss. Some children may be diagnosed with a visual impairment following an accident or childhood illness. Other children may be identified through preschool or kindergarten vision screening programs.

A screening for visual acuity is often provided at school or in the physician's office. The acuity chart most often used for testing and reporting vision loss is the Snellen chart (see Figure 12.3). An example of a distance loss on the Snellen chart is 20/70, meaning that the person has to be 20 feet away from the chart to see what the normal eye can see from 70 feet. This chart is a 20-foot distance test; other tests are given for near vision and other vision problems.

Any student identified with a suspected vision problem should be referred to a licensed ophthalmologist or optometrist for further evaluation, including a medical examination and report. The information in this report should include etiology, medical history and diagnosis, ocular health, visual abilities, recommended low vision devices, and a reevaluation date. This information may be provided to the educational system through a written ocular report (see Figure 12.4).

Interpretation of these data for the educational team should be by a trained and certified teacher of the visually impaired. This information is crucial to the development of an appropriate educational experience. If conditions warrant, further assessment should be obtained and considered by the multidisciplinary team.

In addition to a medical examination, a clinical low vision evaluation is also necessary to determine if a student could benefit from other optical or nonoptical low vision devices. The low vision examination involves acuity tests, visual field testing for peripheral or central vision loss, and an interview with the individual to see what he or she would like to do for work, school, or leisure activities. A personal prescription for low vision devices, technology, or referrals to community agencies is part of the low vision plan. If low vision devices cannot assist the student with reading, writing, or distant viewing, then auditory and tactual prescriptions are recommended as pre-Braille or listening skill practice. The student's vision teacher can attend this evaluation and bring materials relevant to the scheduled daily activities. Examples of educational materials pertinent to the student with visual impairments are reading texts, daily writing journals, workbooks, maps, or charts.

Figure 12.3

Snellen Chart

Source: National Eye Institute. (2007). *Photograph and Image Catalog: Eye charts EC01.* Available at http://www.nei.nih.gov.

Report from Eye Physician				
This report is to be used in educational planning.				
Student name:	John Doe		Age:	10 years
Date of examination:	November 4, 2008		Physician name:	David Seebetter, MD
Visual acuity without Rx	Near: 20/350	Far: 20/400		
Visual acuity with Rx	Near: 20/200	Far: 20/400		
Current Rx:	Spectacles for protection only. UV sunglasses recommended.			
Diagnosis/etiology:	Affects:			
Retinopathy of prematurity	Central vision _____		Peripheral vision __X__	
Prognosis:	Vision has been stable for the past year; return visit in one year for follow-up examination.			
Medication:	None			
Other treatment:	None			
Low vision devices:	Near: Handheld magnifier—8x magnification; closed circuit TV			
	Far: Monocular telescope			
Technology needed:	Closed circuit TV, speech reader on computer, radio reading service, slow-speed tape recorder, talking watch, talking calculator			
Print size:	Large print _____			
	Closed circuit TV/size print __X__	Self-adjust		
	Bold line paper __X__			
Braille	Braille __X__	Braille should be considered for speed of reading and comprehension.		
	Books on tape __X__			
Classroom modifications	Lighting _____			
	Seating preference __X__	Near teacher or class activity; special table for Brailler, CCTV		

Figure 12.4

Ocular Report

Functional Vision Evaluation

Each child's ability to use vision is unique, and the ability to use what vision the child has (visual efficiency) may be improved through specific programs of instruction. An important element in planning an educational program for children with visual impairments is assessment of a student's present **functional vision.** In other words, an assessment is needed to see how well each student uses vision to complete a specific task.

Because of the role that vision plays in the overall development of each child, a functional vision evaluation must be performed before all other educational evaluations. This is to ensure that each child will have access to the materials and equipment needed to participate and perform to the best of that student's abilities. Under the supervision of a teacher of students with visual impairments, each pupil must be observed in a variety of environments that occur throughout the student's daily routine. This observation must include the student performing various tasks that require both near and distant visual abilities. Observations should encompass both individual and group activities, including oral and silent reading groups, desk work, and board work. The functional vision evaluation should also include travel within the school environment—playground, restroom, music room, lunchroom, and physical education sites—as well as accessing modes of transportation. The evaluation should also include samples of the student's work and reports of activities in the home and community.

The functional vision evaluation is a collaborative effort of the educational team for purposes of program planning. Specific recommendations, accommodations, modifications, and intervention strategies for the student in all environments can be based on a comprehensive evaluation. The team approach to the functional evaluation can provide a continuum of appropriate strategies in the educational and community settings.

Learning Media

Another important component in the assessment process is to determine the most effective learning and literacy media. **Literacy medium** refers to sensory channels and is based on the student's preferred method of reading and writing—print, Braille, or both. Regardless of the level of vision a student has or whether the pupil has an additional disability, a learning medium assessment must be conducted to determine the student's preferred mode of learning and literacy (Pugh & Erin, 1999).

Learning media include the materials and methods a student uses in conjunction with the sensory channels in the process of learning. Visual learning media include pictures, videos, imitation, and demonstration. Tactual learning media include models, real objects, and physical prompting. Auditory learning media include verbal communication, taped information, and environmental sounds (Levack, 1994). A hearing evaluation is required as a part of the auditory media determination.

Determination of print size is important so that the child with a visual impairment can readily use low vision devices prescribed for reading, writing, and leisure activities. A vision specialist can inform the child and family about specific low vision devices, where to use them, and what size print is required for each device. The standard print sizes recommended range from 6 point, the size used in telephone directories, to 24 point, used in large print texts.

Braille as a literacy medium is used together with print and auditory input if the child has any residual vision. This enables the student to read print for survival skills, and to sign documents. An individual who is totally blind will use Braille and listening skills for input. Braille is addressed in the IEP, so that the child with a visual impairment will have ongoing consideration of Braille as a reading medium.

Braille consists of patterns of six possible dots arranged in two columns of three (see Figure 12.5). The combination of dots indicates a certain letter of the alphabet. Each language has a Braille code that matches the letters in the alphabet of that language. American Braille has two "grades." In **grade one Braille,** each letter of a word is spelled out using the Braille letter corresponding to the print letter. This is the first level taught, so that all of the alphabet is learned. **Grade two Braille** is made up of contractions representing parts of words or whole words, similar to print shorthand. The primers begin with words contracted so that the child learns the spelling of the word with grade one and the whole word in a sentence with grade two. Many elevators and signs use grade two, because that is the standard for Braille readers. Examples of grade one and grade two Braille are presented in Figure 12.6 (page 465).

Braille is usually the reading medium for choice for pupils who are totally blind.

Figure 12.5

Braille Card

Source: American Printing House for the Blind, Inc., Louisville, KY.

**Braille Alphabet and Numbers
Used by the Blind**

Close your eyes and read this with your fingers.

The Braille system is comprised of signs formed by the use of all the possible combinations of 6 dots numbered and arranged thus:

$$1 \bullet \bullet 4$$
$$2 \bullet \bullet 5$$
$$3 \bullet \bullet 6$$

Letters are capitalized by prefixing dot 6. The first ten letters preceded by the number sign represent numbers. Punctuation marks are formed in the lower part of the cell.

In addition to ordinary print the Braille system provides for the writing of foreign languages, musical scores, mathematical and chemical notations, and other technical matter.

This is

Educational Assessment and Program Planning

Appropriate assessment strategies are a prerequisite to effective teaching. Assessments can provide critical information on the ways in which various visual impairments can affect learning and the need for instructional adaptations. Many students with visual impairments have the same educational goals as other pupils and can often be successfully included in the general education classroom. In planning an educational program for a student with visual impairments, other assessments must also be considered. However, educational assessments must be modified for accessibility, either with larger print, Braille, oral presentation,

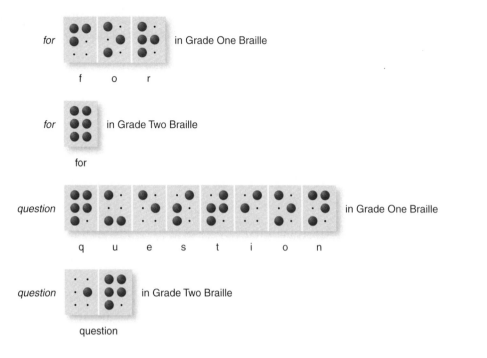

Figure 12.6

Examples of Braille

or omission of items that test visual skills. The evaluation must measure the skills of the student using the modifications with which the student is familiar so that the results will paint a picture of academic functioning level.

Students who have a visual impairment also have unique educational needs and should be evaluated in these areas to determine the appropriate educational placement and program. These skills "form the foundation for all instructional planning for students who are blind or have low vision, including those individuals who have additional disabilities" (Lewis & Russo, 1998, p. 43). Such evaluations include

- Basic academic skills
- Learning and literacy media
- Verbal and nonverbal communication skills
- Social interaction skills
- Visual efficiency skills
- Orientation and mobility skills
- Independent living skills
- Career/vocational skills
- Use of assistive technology

Eligibility Determination

Recall that to determine eligibility for special education because of a disability, the IEP team must base its decision on data from multiple sources. A functional vision evaluation and a learning media assessment should be part of the initial evaluation for individuals with visual impairments. However, a student with a visual disorder may not be eligible for or need specialized services if the disorder has no adverse effect on the student's educational progress.

Table 12.4	Assessment Modifications for Students with Visual Impairments
Proctor for Braille transcription (recording or transfer scores)	
Large print materials and tests	
Oral presentation of materials (reader assistance for texts and other materials)	
Assistive technology	
Extended time limits (1.5 or twice the time is usually recognized for low vision and blind)	
Small or individual group assessment	
Preferred seating	
Shorter periods of testing with rest breaks between sessions	

Instructional planning requires a comprehensive assessment to establish current levels of performance. Using the information from multiple assessments, the IEP team determines the student's current levels of performance and develops an individualized educational program. In keeping with the requirements of IDEA, parents and students are informed and involved in all areas of the planning process.

The success of the IEP depends on selecting and using appropriate instruments that address issues or concerns relevant to the needs of the student with a visual impairment. This process may be completed by having appropriately trained personnel use both formal and informal assessment instruments. Few formal instruments are available, however, because children with visual impairments are so diverse in age, background, and environmental influences, as well as in levels of visual abilities. Numerous factors, such as acuity, color blindness, age of onset, field vision restrictions, and other disabilities, affect a child's visual ability. Given the unique needs and diversity of these students, trained teachers of the visually impaired must be involved in the assessment process and the interpretation of test results.

Students with visual impairments are not usually included in standardized testing; however, they should participate with needed modifications or accommodations (see Table 12.4). Although the validity and reliability of the assessment may be compromised if too many modifications are made, instructional planning, including pupil and program evaluation, can be enhanced. In reporting test results, any modification or accommodations that were made should be recorded.

Many students with visual impairments are able to participate in testing programs when appropriate modifications are made.

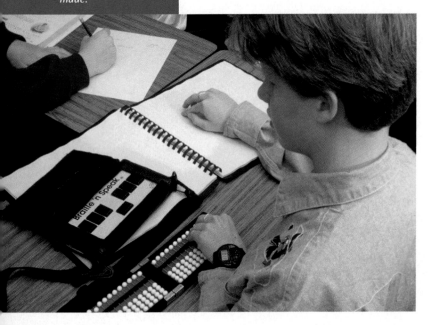

Many states require all students to participate in statewide testing programs, developed with specific guidelines and scores, to progress to the next grade or academic level. IDEA requires the IEP team to determine a student's participation in state and districtwide assessment programs. The team must verify that the student is in need of modifications in order to participate, or if the student will not participate, the team must state why the assessment is not appropriate and what alternate assessments will be used.

Educational Considerations

Students with visual impairments require an educational plan to prepare for independent and productive lives. Educational goals delineate the needs of the child and the family. Appropriate accommodations allow for acquisition of information through incidental learning, observation and imitation, and social behavior.

Where Are Students with Visual Impairments Educated?

The passage of IDEA and policy statements from professional organizations and agencies all reinforce the principle that in order to meet the unique needs of children with sensory impairments and help them become responsible and independent members of a fully integrated society, we must offer a full continuum of services. According to the U.S. Department of Education (2007), over half of all students with visual impairments received services in the general education classroom during the 2005–2006 school year. Approximately one out of five pupils with visual impairments was assigned to a resource room, and only about 6 percent were placed in a residential facility (see Figure 12.7). The IEP team should determine the educational setting that is most appropriate for each student, keeping in mind current levels of academic, psychosocial, physical, and vocational functioning and the materials and instructional techniques that are successful with that child. See the accompanying First Person feature.

Instructional Considerations

Instructional goals for most students with visual impairment include communication skills, social competency, employability, and independence, in addition to academic progress (American Foundation for the Blind, 1993). The IEP team must decide how these goals will be accomplished. Often an array of low vision devices will be required, depending on the needs of the student. The team will have to decide whether the child requires materials to be read, enlarged, or put into Braille and whether low vision devices or technology such as an abacus or a talking calculator will be used.

The vision-related needs of the pupil should be supported within the general education curriculum wherever appropriate. The need for direct, specialized services also varies throughout the child's education, depending on the goals of the educational program and the way in which these goals are met in the classroom. Table 12.5 (page 471) describes some types of equipment that can be used to meet the needs of students with visual impairments in the general education classroom.

Individuals who are visually impaired should acquire compensatory skills and experiential learning by accessing the expanded core curriculum (Huebner, Merk-Adam,

Figure 12.7

Educational Placements of Students with Visual Impairments

Note: Figure represents percentages of enrollment of students with visual impairments during the 2005–2006 school year.

Source: U.S. Department of Education. (2007). *IDEA data.* Available at https://www.ideadata.org/PartBReport.asp.

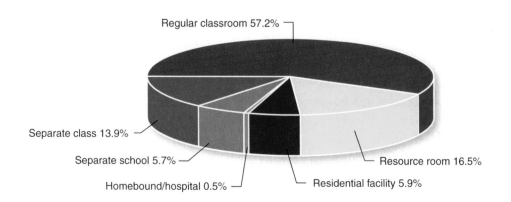

Regular classroom 57.2%
Separate class 13.9%
Separate school 5.7%
Homebound/hospital 0.5%
Residential facility 5.9%
Resource room 16.5%

First Person

The Face of "Different"

It was a bright sunny day outside. The kids were going out to play, but a few of us were staying inside. I started to draw after staring at a friend's face. It was just a line with some curves. "That's different," remarked a classmate. "Wow, that's really good," said Mr. Tom. "Thank you," I replied.

At that point, I realized that I was good at something and at the same time realized that there was something "different" about me. I was drawing someone's face as if it were a silhouette. It was different from my classmates' drawings. These words of encouragement and approval would have seemed small to most, but to a 6-year-old it was awesome. I was just drawing what I saw. How could that have been different from anyone else, or even that good?

I was born with oculocutaneous albinism, which is the lack of pigment in the eyes, the skin, and the hair. A common side effect is a visual impairment, but this varies in severity from one person to another. The idea of being visually impaired and able to draw astounded Mr. Tom. He was surprised by my ability to depict how I saw the world. I enjoyed arts and crafts time during elementary school and still amazed many teachers by this talent. It was as if I was redefining their perception of my abilities.

In second grade there was a test to see how many addition problems we could solve correctly in two minutes. The teacher remarked that I would need extra time. Full of embarrassment, I wanted to prove her wrong. And I did. The same type of situation occurred in middle school. The challenge was reading maps for geography class. The maps were small with many black lines. "How is she going to do this with a visual impairment?" many remarked.

I could see shapes and color. So I colored them in and then labeled them as I studied. It made things more difficult and was a different approach, but it worked. The test came back with a 97 and I was excited.

There were many times that I needed to take a different approach in my study tactics. I was more successful in class with teachers who were open-minded or who accentuated my strengths and minimized my weaknesses. My senior year in high school I read the book *Dr. Jekyll and Mr. Hyde* by Robert Louis Stevenson. Reading a novel was difficult because it took me longer to read than most students. I would feel discouraged and defeated, therefore losing motivation in the class. My teacher asked me to draw or paint how I envisioned the main characters, Dr. Jekyll and Mr. Hyde. The two characters are really one person but with a different look and contrasting personalities. She was pleased by the end result and distributed the grade on the ability to envision the description rather than the test alone.

There is not a map or a face that can guide and show a teacher how to educate a student with a visual impairment. I learned by doing and trying things by myself and with others. I was not the face of "different" as a child. Different is not a face to identify or a point to relate to, different is the line with curves between two points. Different is the process in which children as individuals learn, create, grow, and therefore succeed. It is the path and our attitude that depict our face. "We are all 'different,' and I thank you!"

—Carrie Willoughby

Stryker, & Wolffe, 2004). The expanded core curriculum is the body of knowledge and skills that are needed by pupils with visual impairments because of their unique disability-specific needs. Students who are visually impaired need the expanded core curriculum in addition to the core academic curriculum found in general education. The expanded core curriculum should be used as a framework for assessing pupils, planning individual goals, and providing instruction. The expanded core curriculum typically includes the following:

- Compensatory skills
- Orientation and mobility

✔ EFFECTIVE INSTRUCTIONAL PRACTICES | Accommodations for Students with Visual Impairments

Communication and accessibility are keys to providing an environment in which the student with visual impairments can realize his or her academic potential. Accommodations should provide the pupil with the ability to fully participate in the classroom as well as reduce the effects of the visual impairment.

Instructional Area	Accommodations
Reading	• Consult with the VI teacher on any optical devices the student may need to read printed materials. • Allow extra time for low-vision readers, as they may experience eye fatigue. • Provide reading materials to the VI teacher in advance to be enlarged, scanned, Brailled, or recorded on tape. • Textbooks and books commonly used in educational settings are available on recorded tapes through Recordings for the Blind and Dyslexic (www.rfd.org). Students must be registered before ordering texts. • Recreational books in recorded or Braille format can be ordered through the Library for the Blind and Physically Handicapped (www.lcweb.log.gov/nls/). This is a free service, but users must be registered before ordering. • Many local library systems have popular books available on audiotape.
Writing	• Some pupils with low vision need dark, bold, or raised lined paper for writing assignments. • Some individuals will need to use a typewriter or a computer for completing written assignments. • Braille readers may Braille their assignments and ask the VI teacher to transcribe it into print. • Some Braille readers use an electronic Braille note taker such as Braille 'n Speak for written assignments. The assignment is inputted in Braille and then translated into a print copy for the classroom teacher.
Note-taking	• Students with visual impairments may take notes on their Brailler, electronic note taker, or computer or may use a cassette recorder. • Any notes written on the board should be spoken aloud for the pupil who is visually impaired. • Students with visual impairments should be seated as close to an object or display as possible. • Keep information in a visually simple and organized format for all students with visual perceptual difficulties. • Use high-contrast writing tools when using an overhead, chalkboard, or dry-erase board. • Use of a Smart Board attached to the student's or classroom computer can provide the individual with an accessible version of the notes. • Use of a Smart Board with text conversion software allows the student to access the electronic version of the notes with a screen reading or voice output program.

Source: Adapted from L. Schrenko, *Visual Impairment* (Georgia Department of Education, February 2002). Available at http://www.glc.k12.ga.us/passwd/trc/ttools/attach/accomm/visimp.doc.

- Social skills
- Independent living skills
- Recreation and leisure skills
- Career education
- Assistive technology
- Visual efficiency skills
- Self-determination

Making Inclusion Work

During the spring of my senior year as an undergraduate student in elementary education, I was required to complete a 24-hour practicum for a special education course. The site I chose was the North Dakota School for the Blind. After my experiences at the school, I realized that I was very interested in working with children who were blind and visually impaired. This led me to search for graduate programs in the field of blindness. I was fortunate enough to locate the vision program at the University of Alabama at Birmingham. From my first day in the program, I had the opportunity to work with children of varying degrees of visual impairment, as well as additional disabilities. After completing my graduate work, I worked as an itinerant teacher for the visually impaired in southwestern Iowa for four years and went on to become the state consultant for children with deaf-blindness in Iowa. Currently, I am a doctoral student at Iowa State University and working as a teacher for the visually impaired with Heartland Area Education Agency in the Des Moines area.

Inclusive Education Experience

Working with children with visual impairments and multiple disabilities is definitely challenging, yet very rewarding. This is especially true when working with general education teachers in inclusive settings. You have to have a starting point that everyone can agree upon, including acceptance of the child with special needs as a full member of the general education class and an understanding that the general education teacher is that child's full-time teacher—not the five other service providers that also work with the child once a week. If the IEP team can come to such an agreement, then everything else seems to fall into place. For example, it may be that a teacher of the visually impaired works with the general education teacher to adapt lessons by creating tactile materials, story boxes, or even working with the entire class by teaching a class lesson.

One of my more memorable teaching experiences was collaborating with a first-year teacher who was working with a kindergartener, Andrew, who had multiple disabilities, including deaf-blindness. I taught a cooking lesson to the class once a month, in order to model interacting with Andrew for the other children and adults in the classroom. This worked well for the kindergarten teacher because it incorporated math, reading, and social skills. It was a wonderful opportunity, however, for the other children to see that Andrew could be an active and important member of the class, as they worked in small groups to get to know Andrew. By the end of the school year, the children were able to tell the adults what Andrew liked and disliked. The students also knew how to interact with Andrew so that he could respond to them with facial expressions and vocalizations.

Overall, as a teacher of the visually impaired, being able to work with the kindergarten class took extra time and preparation on my part. However, classrooms today are changing, as are the instructional expectations of both general education and special education teachers. It takes teamwork and collaboration to make programs work for children with special needs and to give them the best possible start to being active and contributing members of their community.

—Susan A. Brennan
Heartland Area Education Agency,
Johnston, Iowa
Teacher of the Visually Impaired

Table 12.5	Examples of Core and Expanded Curriculum-Specific Equipment
Academics	• Magnifiers, glasses, closed circuit television, Braille, bookstands, videotapes, scanners, optical character recognition system • Word processing programs, slate and stylus, electronic spell checkers, bold line writing paper, embossed writing paper, signature writing guides • Abacus, scientific calculator, talking clock, Braille/print protractors and rulers, embossed and bold line grid pattern sheets, spreadsheet software • Tactile globes, relief maps, Braille and large print maps, tactile anatomy atlas, speech output devices such as thermometers and environmental controls
Leisure Time and Recreational Activities	• Adapted games, large print books, radio reading services, beeper balls, buzzers, wheelchair adapted for basketball and tennis play, lifts for swimming pools, adapted snow and water skiing equipment, descriptive video
Daily Living and Self-Help	• Walkers, feeding adaptations, Braille labels, voice-activated switches, button switches, large print telephone buttons, automatic thermostats, Braille calendars, electronic address books and calendars, magnifiers for hand sewing and sewing machines, electronic mobility devices, lifts for automobiles and chairs

The expanded core curriculum essentially creates a parallel curriculum of disability-specific skills supplementary to the general education curriculum. The academic curriculum must be modified to meet the individual needs of each student, so that progress is based on skill level and successful completion of expectations in each subject area. Specialized areas of the regular curriculum, such as art, music, and home economics, are also considered appropriate for pupils with visual impairments. Modifications and accommodations of lessons can often be achieved through the use of visual, auditory, or tactual experiences.

Adaptations of materials and the environment may be necessary to enable students who are visually impaired to participate in the educational program and derive maximum benefit from the experience (see Table 12.6). Adaptations may vary according to individual needs, which should be assessed before making special provisions available to the student.

Students with visual impairments require instruction in **orientation and mobility,** which is a related service according to IDEA. Orientation is being aware of where you are, where you are going, and the route to get there. Mobility is moving from place to place. A child must be able to put the orientation and mobility together to travel independently. Orientation and mobility training includes sensory training, concept development, and motor development. A certified orientation and mobility specialist can evaluate the child's functional level and prescribe specific training. See the accompanying Suggestions for the Classroom (page 473) for orientation and mobility tips for the general educator.

A child must be empowered to negotiate the environment skillfully and confidently. Opportunities for exploration must be provided for good posture, good health, and flexible muscles. With confident movement, the child can achieve good self-esteem and master independent travel within the community.

Young Children with Visual Impairments

The focus in early childhood education is not only on visual and auditory tasks, but also on the whole realm of developmental skills that must be taught, with modifications, to the child

Table 12.6	Environmental Adaptations for Students with Visual Impairments			
	Lighting	**Color and Contrast**	**Size and Distance**	**Time**
What to observe	• Variety of lighting situations • Lighting at different times of day • Low vision devices used	• Contrast between object and background • Color contrast • Tactile tasks such as locker for books	• Placement and size of objects at near • Placement and size of objects at far	• Time for completion of visual discrimination during tasks
What to use	• Light sensitivity: shades, visors, tinted spectacles • Low light: lamp or illuminated low vision device • Room obstructions: preferential seating, furniture placement • Glare: Nonglare surface on areas such as chalkboards, computer screens, desktop, paper, maps, globes	• Bold line paper • Black print on white background • Dark markers • One-sided writing on paper • Dark placemat for contrast during eating • Floor contrast for mobility ease • Tactile markings for outline discrimination • Contrast to define borders on walls • Lock and key is preferred over combination locker	• Enlarged materials • Preferred seating • Electronic devices • Magnification • Optical character recognition • Adjustment of desks, tables, and chairs • Additional storage space for Braille, large print books, low vision devices near each workstation	• Verbal cues for actions in classroom • Increased time for task completion • Calling student by name • Announcements when entering or leaving room • Encourage participation in demonstrations • Opportunity to observe materials prior to lesson • Authentic manipulative objects • Schedule instructional time in early part of day • Convenient use and storage of materials
Desired results	• Better posture • Greater concentration • Less fatigue	• Better visual efficiency • Less fatigue • Safer travel	• Ease of viewing • Appropriate adaptations for specific vision loss	• Less fatigue • Inclusion in class activities • Time efficiency

with visual impairments. These basic readiness skills should be integrated for age-appropriate cognitive development:

- Sensory development
- Gross motor development
- Fine motor development
- Social development
- Receptive language development
- Expressive language development
- Self-help development

The early intervention team can assist the family with activities that stimulate each of the developmental areas. Children are referred through state child-find activities, physicians, and other agencies to early intervention services, which are available for children from birth to age 3. Services are provided according to the youngster's IFSP (individualized family service plan), with the child receiving services prescribed by the specialists involved on the team. The specialists who work with the child and family act as consultants, and some may provide direct services. Intervention may be offered in the youngster's home or an early childhood education program in the community.

Suggestions for the Classroom

Orientation and Mobility Tips

☑ Eliminate unnecessary obstacles; inform student of changes in room arrangement or of any temporary obstacles.

☑ Keep doors completely closed or completely open to eliminate the possibility of the student's running into a partially open door.

☑ Allow the student to travel with a companion to frequently used rooms such as the library, school office, restroom, and gym. Discuss routes with turns and landmarks.

☑ Allow student to move about freely until the room and route are familiar.

☑ Encourage sighted guide for fire drills, field trips, assemblies, and seating in rooms that ordinarily have no assigned seats.

☑ Encourage independent travel in the familiar settings at school.

Source: Adapted from R. Craig and C. Howard, "Visual Impairment," in M. Hardman, M. Egan, and D. Landau (Eds.), *What Will We Do in the Morning?* (Dubuque, IA: W. C. Brown, 1981), p. 191.

At age 3, the child should transition to an early childhood class for youngsters with vision loss. A well-designed transition plan includes planning with the school administrators, general educators, parents or other caregivers, and related services personnel in support of the move to school. The service coordinator and vision specialist should also have input into the construction of the IEP. This will assure that the receiving teacher knows about the child's progress and goals for the future. Age-related needs that should be addressed by the team when designing a transition plan include travel, low vision devices, educational activities, and leisure activities. Other services that family and school officials should consider include

- Adaptive technology services
- Transcription services
- Access to an equipment resource center
- Activities of daily living
- Community education
- Reader services
- Orientation and mobility
- Low vision examination

Transition into Adulthood

IDEA mandates that the individualized education program include a transition plan for college preparation or vocational training. A full range of options and support services for appropriate placement in the least restrictive environment should be available (American Foundation for the Blind, 1993). Student interests, family involvement in future education, and appropriate placement location and program are integral parts of the transition plan.

The goals for adolescents and young adults include vocation selection, continuing education, travel skills, low vision devices, reading material, community resources, family education, and independence on the job. The wide spectrum of individual needs quickly defines the goals with regard to job training, technical school education, or college entrance. A transition plan for each student must be designed no later than age 16.

Planning transition of a student into higher education or vocational programs involves assessing the individual's level of functioning. The transition team, including the family, must be familiar with and prepared to respond to the adolescent's strengths and needs with respect to functional domains such as cognitive, social, and daily living skills. Professionals, in conjunction with the adolescent and his or her family, also need to identify the specific community resources needed to assist the young adult in preparing for life after school. This mapping for the future should include information about postsecondary educational opportunities as well as vocational, recreational, and independent living options (American Foundation for the Blind, 2007).

If the adolescent is exiting the public school system, the school and family can help the student prepare to enter the adult world through transition planning as mandated by IDEA. Planning should be based on the adolescent's needs, taking into consideration his or her strengths, preferences, and interests. Orientation and mobility, social adjustment, and activities of daily living skills may also need to be addressed.

Vocational training is an important component of transitional planning for adolescents who are visually impaired.

The goal of transition to adulthood is success in the community. Success is measured by the young adult, the family, and the employer. Continuous observation of a student's performance is an integral part of educational and vocational training. These observations and reported skills or behaviors enable a college and career habilitation plan to be designed and regularly updated.

Adults with Visual Impairments

Adults with visual impairments are often isolated from peers in the community. Some of the specific needs of adults with visual impairments are transportation, low vision evaluation and prescription, technology support, social opportunities, and orientation and mobility training. Without leisure and work support, successful integration into the community becomes difficult. Adults should have access to radio reading services, auditory books, low vision devices, leisure activities, and other community support. Adults who have a vision loss late in life are often dramatically affected. In some instances, loss of self-esteem, depression, and loneliness are typical consequences. Community information and referral systems, however, can make a difference for the adult with a visual impairment.

The adult who has a vision loss will often need job training accommodations, transportation to the workplace, and possibly housing near the job site. The accommodations should be individualized, match the job description and responsibilities, and be appropriate for a person with a vision loss. Some job descriptions specify the visual acuity needed for the job, and some include options for vision loss adaptations.

An individual with a vision loss that occurs in adulthood usually has job skills that were learned prior to the loss. In this case, the individual can assist the employer with reasonable adaptations to the work area. If the job requires good vision, the worker may have to compete for another job within the agency or in the community. Sometimes the person with a visual impairment will need to obtain job training through the state vocational rehabilitation services.

The adult with vision loss should be independent within the workplace unless the setting is a sheltered workshop or another specialized work environment. Independence can be achieved through training with low vision devices, job coaching to help find areas of the job where modifications must be made, and reasonable changes to the workstation to accommodate the person with a vision loss.

Family Issues

Families of persons with visual impairments face issues that are directly related to the independence of the family member with a vision loss. If a child is born with a visual impairment, the parents and other family members confront issues at every developmental age level. The family of the infant and toddler must address the nature of the visual impairment, the services available for the family, and the educational needs of the youngster during the early developmental years. As the child enters school, the family often becomes a partner in educational planning and the primary source of leisure activities. As the child begins to participate in school and interact with classmates, the family role often changes to that of an advocate supporting the needs of children with visual impairment.

If a person loses vision in adolescence, issues related to the teen years begin the family advocacy process. Secondary special educators and families frequently work together on independent living, postsecondary education, employment options, and linkages with adult services. Issues such as accepting that a person will not obtain a driver's license and may encounter difficulty with employment, dating, or entry to postsecondary education are typical concerns of most families. If the person with a vision loss is an adult, issues of employment, mobility, independence, and community living are some of the areas of concern.

The family is the core community for the person with vision loss and frequently assumes an advocacy role. Advocacy for persons with visual impairment is provided through parent organizations, service agencies, and professional organizations. According to the Council for Exceptional Children (1996), special education has a heritage of advocacy. Professionals as well as families work together as a voice for persons with special needs. Families and persons with visual impairments advocate for educational and vocational needs and help to implement needed legislation.

Parent and professional organizations, support groups, and advocacy groups can provide information about local and national resources for families. The benefit of parent groups is that families within a community join hands to learn from and offer support to one another. These support groups also serve as a resource for educators, rehabilitation professionals, employers, and legislators on issues affecting persons with visual impairments.

Issues of Diversity

In planning the educational program for the student with visual impairments, the team must have an appreciation and understanding of cultural diversity. Certain cultures may have a greater susceptibility to eye diseases such as glaucoma or diabetes; others may have diets that cause eye disease specific to vitamin deficiency. Children from low socioeconomic communities tend to have less access to medical intervention. Eye care may be difficult to obtain, and issues of cost or availability may prevent follow-up on medications.

A diversity of backgrounds often means a diversity of skills. Diversity issues for children with visual impairments are multifaceted because of the many eye diseases, different ages of onset, and the accommodations that are needed for the student to succeed. Educational plans should address cultural and linguistic differences and how the family and school personnel can work together to achieve the goals for the child. Diversity issues must be recognized prior to assessments and evaluations so that eligibility and placement will be appropriate for the child.

Language difference may present problems in assessment and placement, as well as in program progress. Ongoing family and school communication may become a problem if the language barrier is not considered in each aspect of the educational plan. Cultures and customs may create barriers for educational planning in social skills and in orientation and mobility. In some cultures, conversation is face to face, and it is considered impolite to walk while conversing. This could be a problem for the child and the family when learning orientation and mobility.

Integration of skills such as Braille into the home may be difficult if the family does not understand the reasons for or mechanism of certain activities. On the other hand, if the parents also have a visual impairment, they may require Braille or large print for written documents and may also need translation into the family's native language. Either situation must be addressed as a diversity issue demanding sensitivity and cooperation of all parties who have an interest in the child.

Technology and Individuals with Visual Impairments

Advances in technology have provided opportunities for students with visual impairments to participate in educational programs on a level with sighted peers. After determining the individual needs of the pupil with a visual impairment, the educational team must consider the array of specialized materials and equipment that allow the student full participation in the least restrictive environment. Identification and use of these resources can make a notable difference in the educational program and future of the student with a visual impairment.

The American Printing House for the Blind in Louisville, Kentucky, is a valuable resource for special media, tools, and materials needed for an educational program. The American Foundation for the Blind has many publications on technology for consumers with visual impairments. Recordings for the Blind and Dyslexic is a national educational library for people with print disabilities, including blindness and visual impairments. It provides taped textbooks along with reference and professional materials for people who cannot read standard print because of a disability.

Legal Aspects

The 1997 and 2004 IDEA amendments strengthened the assistive technology requirements for students with visual impairments. Assistive technology devices and services have long been incorporated within the concepts of special education, related services, and supplemental devices and services. PL 108-446 requires the IEP team to consider the provision of assistive technology devices and services in the development of the student's IEP. Under IDEA, Braille instruction is required unless the IEP team determines that it is not appropriate after evaluation of the student's reading and writing skills, needs, and appropriate reading and writing media.

Emphasis on technology in schools has made computers and assistive technology devices available to all children in educational programs. From simple computers to communication devices and environmental controls, technology offers students with disabilities the tools to succeed in school, to compete at work, and to achieve independence. A child who is blind or visually impaired can read books from simple devices that enlarge printed words on a screen or by using computers to convert text into enhanced image display, Braille, synthetic speech, or optical character recognition.

Technology and Literacy

Technology has the potential to equalize opportunity and enhance the functioning of students with visual impairments. Technology plays an integral role in learning and all aspects of daily living, from literacy to mobility to independent living. Students with visual impairments must have technology prescribed so that specialized equipment and devices are accessible in daily activities. Today, many children and young adults are learning to use various forms of technology regardless of the level of visual impairment. See Table 12.7 for ways that persons who are visually impaired can access and interact with computers.

Table 12.7	Accessibility for Individuals with Visual Impairment	
Method of Access	**Device**	**Description**
Screen Magnification	ZoomText inLARGE	Software to enlarge print on computer screen
Video Magnifiers	Closed Circuit Television (CCTV)	Hardware used to project magnified images onto video monitor
Synthetic Speech	JAWS Window-Eyes	Screen reading software that allows text to be converted to speech
Braille Writer	Perkins Brailler	A machine with keys corresponding to each six dots of the Braille code to create all characters of the code
Braille Embosser	Mountbatten Brailler	Electronic Braille embosser that translates text from Braille keyboard to a printer
Braille Translators	Duxbury Braille Translator	A software program that takes a computerized text file and converts and formats the document properly for printing
Optical Character Recognition (OCR)	Kurzwell Reader Open Book	A system that provides the capacity to scan printed text, have it spoken in synthetic speech, or saved to a computer file
Global Positioning Satellite (GPS) System	Trekker	(Hardware) An orientation tool system that determines position such as intersections and allows one to plan and follow routes by communicating with satellites in earth's orbit
	BrailleNote GPS	(Software) A mobility system that allows the user to generate or understand and develop routes throughout the environment

Literacy is an essential component of any student's educational program, including students with vision impairments. According to Koenig (1992), literacy can be demonstrated in four ways:

- When an individual is successful in communicating through writing
- When an individual is successful in communicating with a desired audience
- When an individual can successfully apply reading and writing skills
- When an individual is successful in reading and writing at different levels throughout the life span

Technology plays a vital role in the lives of students who are visually impaired.

Each student needs to have the opportunity to access information according to his or her unique requirements. Accessing and correctly using appropriate technology is a developmental process that should result in providing these students the ability to become as independent as their sighted peers. With appropriate assessment and training in technology, students who are blind or visually impaired can compete successfully in educational programs. To do so, however, students who are visually impaired must have access to equivalent tools at the same time as their sighted peers. They must have access to a wide variety and large quantity of reading materials. They should have immediate access to research, expanded note-taking skills, and access

Table 12.8	Technology Tools and Skills for Students with Visual Impairments
Adaptive Hardware	• Refreshable Braille displays • Screen enlargement peripherals • Speech synthesizers • Printers • Braille embosser • Electronic note-takers • Voice output devices • Braille input/output devices
Adaptive Software	• Braille translation software • Screen readers • Screen enlargement software • Speech recognition software
Use of Adapted Output Systems	• Enhanced image systems • Synthesized speech systems • Refreshable Braille displays • Use of Braille printers
Use of Adapted Input Systems	• Braille input devices • Use of voice recognition systems • Use of optical character recognition (OCR) systems

Source: J. Gense and M. Gense, "Using Assistive Technology for Learners Who Are Blind or Visually Impaired," in Pennsylvania College of Optometry (Eds.), *Increasing Literacy Levels: Final Report* (Starkville: Mississippi State University Rehabilitation Research & Training Center on Blindness and Low Vision, 1997).

to an ongoing telecommunication system. Besides the general technology tools and skills for all students, additional items that may be needed by students who are blind or visually impaired are listed in Table 12.8.

In most public and residential schools, competence with computers and other types of technology for communication and literacy are accepted as prerequisite skills for the academic curriculum. Because computer technology must often be adapted for students with visual impairments, a computer proficiency requirement is frequently a part of an individualized education program. A vision specialist assists with classroom modifications and training while the general education curriculum is implemented. The vision specialist also needs to be knowledgeable about changing technology necessary to ensure meaningful participation in the general education classroom (Goodman & Wittenstein, 2003).

Based on diagnostic information about the student's desires and needs in the classroom and community, an individualized technology plan can be designed for each student. To ensure that the individualized plan is thorough and up to date, an assistive technology team should develop a blueprint for the student's program (Griffin, Williams, Davis, & Engleman, 2002). Team members typically include the following persons:

- Student
- Parent or primary caregiver
- General education teacher
- Vision teacher
- Technology specialist

Table 12.9	Technology Accommodations for Students with Visual Impairments	
Skill: Reading Class—Book Reports	**Benchmark**	**Accommodations**
Student will read a book on the class book list and write a book report.	A written report incorporating the required format will be submitted to the teacher by the assigned date.	1. Book on tape 2. Braille book 3. Computer 4. Screen reader 5. Braille printer 6. Print printer

- Orientation and mobility specialist
- Occupational therapist
- Physical therapist
- Rehabilitation specialist
- Eye care professional
- Product vendors

School programs include standards for general student progress, minimum competencies, and benchmarks for measuring competency. Learners who are visually impaired should be required to meet the same standards, but with adaptive hardware and software appropriate to each student. An example of a school technology plan with adaptations for a student with visual impairments is shown in Table 12.9.

Trends, Issues, and Controversies

Trends, issues, and controversies directly affecting children with visual impairments include teacher shortages, access to certified orientation and mobility specialists, numbers of students assigned to teachers of the visually impaired, reading and literacy media assessment, and vocational training. Issues and trends, as well as controversies, are addressed by professional groups such as the Council for Exceptional Children Division on Visual Impairments, the Association for Education and Rehabilitation of the Blind and Visually Impaired, the National Association of State Directors of Special Education, and the American Foundation for the Blind. Consumer groups such as the National Federation of the Blind and the American Council of the Blind address issues from the perspective of the person with a visual impairment. These groups work to address these issues with the U.S. Department of Education, special educators, university faculty, and local and state directors of special education.

The profound teacher shortage in the field of visual impairment is an issue affecting all school districts in the United States. Few colleges and universities have the necessary resources to prepare teachers in a profession with a relatively small number of public and residential school students (Council for Exceptional Children, 2000). Currently, only about 250 new teachers of the visually impaired graduate college each year, thus contributing to the shortage of these professionals (Ferrell, 2007). Many of these individuals work in large urban school districts. Rural parts of the United States, with smaller school districts and fewer students with visual impairments, often lack certified teachers.

Just as there is a shortage of teachers of the visually impaired, there is also a shortage of orientation and mobility specialists. IDEA requires mobility evaluation and education for children with special needs. With only a small number of universities training orientation and mobility professionals, the need for these specialists by public and residential schools continues to grow. As a result, these services are often lacking, especially in rural areas. Since orientation and mobility instructors are not usually educators, they are hired in the same category as related service personnel and are costly for school districts. They often serve all students with visual impairments in the district, whereas the teacher of the visually impaired has a lighter caseload to teach. The suggested caseload for a teacher is six students to one teacher (Pugh & Erin, 1999).

The caseload of teachers of the visually impaired as well as orientation and mobility specialists continues to grow because of the shortage of qualified professionals. Larger caseloads affect the number of hours available to fulfill the IEP for each child. When a teacher has more than twenty students, distributed in general education classrooms at several different schools, time for travel and planning detracts from actual class time with the students. A reduction in class caseloads would enable teachers to fulfill IEP goals with more stable outcomes.

Prescriptions for reading and literacy media require a team approach based on the physician's and the teacher's educational recommendations. Reading media assessment is necessary to determine the appropriate low vision devices, enlargements, technology, or Braille use for each student. Some students need large print; others may require magnification or Braille; still others use books on tape. IDEA requires that the use of Braille be assessed in each student's IEP. Appropriate assessments of reading and writing media needs are limited. Teachers often use observations, work samples, and physician suggestions to validate media needs because functional levels are important for daily needs. With few certified teachers, it is difficult to provide this assessment for all students who are visually impaired.

Issues of transition center around evaluation and prognosis, vocational preparation, and how outcomes will be measured. Independence of students as they move into higher education or vocational training is a responsibility of the school and family and is often a problem with transition into the community. Because so many jobs require vision to complete the task, job training and higher education choices are sometimes difficult to select and implement. School representatives and families must construct a life plan with the student so that the benchmarks for success are attainable and reasonable and provide a meaningful and independent life of quality. Issues of community support also affect the successful outcomes of transition plans.

Chapter in Review

Defining Visual Impairments

- The educational definition of **visual impairment** is vision impairment that, even with correction, adversely affects an individual's educational performance.

- Visual impairment includes both **partial sight** and blindness.

The Eye and How It Works

- Light enters the eye first through the clear, transparent area in front of the eye known as the **cornea** and passes through the other structures to the **retina**.

- In the retina, light impulses are changed into electrical signals and travel along the **optic nerve** and back to the occipital lobe of the brain, which interprets the electrical signals as visual images.

Classification of Visual Impairments

- The most common visual impairments affecting school-age children are **cataracts, glaucoma, optic nerve atrophy, myopia, albinism, eye injury**, and **retinopathy of prematurity (ROP)**.

Prevalence of Visual Impairments

- Visual impairment is one of the least prevalent disabilities, accounting for only 0.4 percent of pupils with a disability who are receiving a special education.

The Vision Process and Etiology of Visual Impairments

- If the cornea is damaged through trauma or disease, then the inner area may become infected, which could result in permanent visual impairment.

- Glaucoma is the major disease that occurs in the aqueous humor. This may result in a loss of visual acuity as well as a loss in the visual field.

- If the iris is malformed, the function of light control will be interrupted and the child can become **photophobic** (sensitive to light).

- Cataracts are lenses that are opaque or cloudy due to trauma or age. Children with congenital cataracts often have the cataracts removed.

- **Macular degeneration** is a common eye disease in adults, but it may also occur in young people.

- **Rods** and **cones** are photoreceptive cells found in the retina.

- If a youngster has retinopathy of prematurity (ROP), vascular growth has been interrupted by premature birth.

- **Retinitis pigmentosa** is a hereditary condition involving gradual degeneration of the retina.

Prevention of Visual Impairments

- Most visual impairments are genetic in origin, but others such as injury can be prevented.

Assessment of Students with Visual Impairments

- The acuity chart that is most often used for testing and reporting vision loss is the **Snellen chart.**

- An important first step in planning an educational program for a child with visual impairments is to assess the pupil's present **functional vision.**

- Another important component in the assessment process is to determine the most effective **learning** and **literacy media.**

- **Braille** is used as a literacy medium along with print and auditory input if the child has any residual vision.

Educational Considerations

- Almost six out of ten pupils with visual impairments are served in the general education classroom.

- Many students with visual impairments have the same education goals as other pupils.

- Instructional goals for most students with visual impairment include communication skills, social competency, employability, and independence, in addition to academic progress.

- Students with visual impairments may also require instruction in **orientation and mobility.**

Technology and Individuals with Visual Impairments

- With appropriate assessment and training in technology, students who are blind or visually impaired can compete successfully in educational programs.

- Technology plays an integral role in learning and all aspects of daily living, from literacy to mobility to independent living.

Study Questions

1. What is the legal definition of blindness? How does it differ from the IDEA definition?

2. What does the Snellen chart assess? What does 20/200 mean?

3. Describe how the eye functions.

4. Define the terms *myopia, hyperopia,* and *astigmatism.*

5. List five eye problems common to school-age children.

6. Why is early detection of vision problems important?

7. Describe the social and emotional characteristics of persons with visual impairments.

8. What is functional vision, and how is it evaluated?

9. Define the term *learning media.* Give three examples of different forms of learning media.

10. In what two educational settings do the majority of students with a visual impairment receive a special education?

11. What are some common educational accommodations that a student with visual impairments may require?

12. List five signs of possible vision problems in children.

13. Identify three critical issues that must be addressed if an adolescent is to successfully transition to postsecondary education or enter the workforce.

14. Besides cultural differences, what diversity issue must be addressed for parents who are also visually impaired?

15. Identify five technology accommodations that can be provided in high school for a student who is legally blind.

16. Discuss the shortage of orientation and mobility specialists and how a child's educational plan is affected by a shortage of personnel.

Key Terms

visual impairment	cornea	cataracts	macular degeneration
visual acuity	iris	glaucoma	retinitis pigmentosa
visual field	pupil	optic nerve atrophy	coloboma
field loss	lens	albinism	vision screening
legally blind	vitreous humor	retinopathy of	functional vision
Snellen chart	retina	prematurity (ROP)	literacy medium
blind	macula	Braille	learning media
functionally blind	optic nerve	visual efficiency	grade one Braille
primary literacy medium	myopia	photophobic	grade two Braille
low vision	hyperopia	aphakic	orientation and mobility
residual vision	astigmatism	rod cells	
deaf-blind	orbit	cone cells	

Learning Activities

1. Spend a day traveling with an itinerant teacher of the visually impaired. Describe the types of instruction this professional provided for one or two of the pupils. What IEP goals were addressed? How was technology used to adapt the general education curriculum? How did classmates relate to the child with a visual impairment? What type of assistance did the vision specialist offer to the general educator? What problems or difficulties, if any, did you observe? Write a summary of your experience and share it with your classmates.

2. Search the Internet for information about the following three educational tools: an electronic Brailler, screen readers, and optical character recognition systems. Develop IEP goals and accompanying benchmarks for a secondary student who is legally blind and preparing to transition to a community college. How will this equipment be used to assist the adolescent in adapting to the general education curriculum? What individuals should be involved in planning the transition experience?

3. Interview an adult with a visual impairment. Find out about the type and age of onset of the vision loss. Ask about personal and family reactions to the loss of vision. What type of low vision devices or technology does this individual use on a daily basis? If possible, identify any adjustment concerns about independence, mobility, vocational and career issues, community involvement, and personal relationships. Share your impressions of this interview with your fellow students.

4. Travel with an orientation and mobility specialist and observe the training of a person with a visual impairment. What type of equipment was used? What travel techniques were addressed during the lesson? How did the orientation and mobility specialist evaluate the individual? Ask if you can use the various devices. How did it feel to navigate about the environment while simulating a visual impairment?

Organizations Concerned with Visual Impairments

American Council for the Blind
1155 15th Street N.W., Suite 1004
Washington, DC 20005
(800) 424-8666

American Foundation for the Blind
11 Penn Plaza, Suite 300
New York, NY 10001
(800) 232-5463

American Printing House for the Blind
1839 Frankfort Avenue
P.O. Box 6085
Louisville, KY 40206-0085
(800) 223-1839

Helen Keller National Art Show
CEC Division on Visual Impairments
c/o Low Vision
924 S. 18th Street
Birmingham, AL 35294
(205) 934-6723

National Federation of the Blind
1800 Johnson Street
Baltimore, MD 21230
(410) 659-9314

National Dissemination Center for Children with Disabilities
P.O. Box 1492
Washington, DC 20013-1492
(800) 695-0285

The National Braille Press
88 St. Stephen Street
Boston, MA 02115
(888) 965-8965

Recording for the Blind and Dyslexic
20 Roszel Road
Princeton, NJ 08540
(866) 732-3585

The Seeing Eye, Inc.
P.O. Box 375
Morristown, NJ 07963-0375
(973) 539-4425

Descriptive Video Services
125 Western Avenue
Boston, MA 02134
(617) 300-3600

Blind Outdoor Leisure Development
P.O. Box M
Aspen, CO 81612
(970) 923-0578

National Park Service
U.S. Department of the Interior
Office on Accessibility
1849 C Street N.W.
Washington, DC 20240

U.S. Association of Blind Athletes
33 N. Institute Street
Colorado Springs, CO 80903
(719) 630-0422
(719) 630-0616 (fax)

The National Library Service for the Blind and Physically Handicapped
Publications and Media Section
Library of Congress
Washington, DC 20542
(888) 657-7323

Seedlings
Braille Books for Children
P.O. Box 51924
Livonia, MI 48151-5924
(734) 427-8552

Reflecting on Standards

The following exercises are designed to help you learn to apply the Council for Exceptional Children (CEC) standards to your teaching practice. Each of the reflection exercises below correlates with a knowledge or skill within the CEC standards. For the full text of each of the related CEC standards, please refer to the standards integration grid located in Appendix B.

1. Focus on Instructional Strategies (*CEC Content Standard #4 CC4S3*)

Reflect on what you have learned about accommodations needed for students with visual impairments. If you were developing a reading program for your class and you had a student in your class with a visual impairment, in what ways might you modify your instruction to take into account all of your students' learning needs? How might you need to integrate assistive technology into your instruction?

2. Focus on Learning Environments and Social Interactions (*CEC Content Standard #5 CC5S9*)

Reflect on what you have learned about students with visual impairments. If you were to have a student in your class with a visual impairment, how might you help him/her develop increased independence? How might you modify your classroom or your teaching strategies to create an environment where a student with visual impairments would feel comfortable? How might your other students assist you in creating this type of environment?

Technology Resources

Visit the Web-based SAGE Study Site at **http://www.sagepub.com/gargiulo3estudy** for these additional learning tools:

- Chapter quizzes
- Key term flashcards
- Media links
- Full-text SAGE journal articles
- Internet activities
- Additional Web resources

CHAPTER 13

Individuals with Physical Disabilities, Health Disabilities, and Related Low-Incidence Disabilities

Natalie's Story

Natalie is an amazing young lady who has exceeded most of the expectations of those who made assumptions based on her "labels" and therefore had lowered expectations for her. Fortunately, she did not live down to their expectations!! Natalie has cerebral palsy (severe spastic quadriplegic and athetoid) with poor head and trunk control and only some limited use of her left hand/arm. She has undetermined visual acuity; a questionable degree of mental retardation; used to have seizures of varying types; and has a G-tube for most of her nutrition/caloric intake. She has had braces, splints, eye patching, and numerous surgeries (including spinal fusion).

Although Natalie is nonverbal, she can make approximately 30 words/sounds (that mean 150–200 different things depending on the context or situation), and she uses an electronic augmentative communication device. Using a combination of two to four symbols, she can say approximately 1,500 sentences, 300 words, and 100 names!

Natalie was our third of three girls. She born in 1975, five to six weeks premature. She was bluish-gray at birth, indicating a lack of oxygen, and had facial bruising indicating a traumatic birth (face presentation). So she had the three leading causes of cerebral palsy going against her! She was diagnosed at 6½ months. She started therapy at 8½ months. At 6½ years, Natalie was given her first psychological test, which indicated an IQ of 65. Natalie was to be educated as if she had potential for normal intelligence, and she started school in an academically based class for students with orthopedic impairments.

Our family had to move, and it was then "determined" that Natalie would be placed in a self-contained, center-based class for students with severe mental retardation because all of the therapies were conveniently located there. I, of course, objected. We were told that she wouldn't really "fit" into the orthopedically impaired program as those kids were more "advanced." (Please note

Written by Kathryn Wolff Heller, Georgia State University, and Richard M. Gargiulo that the terms "convenient" and "fit into" seem in direct contradiction to what is stated for an IEP (*Individualized* Education Program.)

From 1985 to 1987, we were fortunate to have a teacher who, despite the label of severe mental retardation, knew Natalie had capabilities and academic potential. This teacher's philosophy was that if Natalie was having a problem with something, it was not that Natalie couldn't learn it, but more likely she just needed to change her approach. She worked with sight words and numbers and picture boards that increased in complexity as Natalie became proficient using them. As Natalie's skills developed, we started our search for the "right" augmentative communication device. After a yearlong assessment we found the ideal augmentative communication device for Natalie, a Touch Talker. Within six months, I had programmed two-thirds of what is currently in her device. People began to see Natalie in a totally different way, and recognize her intelligence and humor and emotions, and lots of frustrations. They began to relate to her in a totally different way . . . all because she could finally communicate!

Natalie's label changed, and she was moved from the severe mental retardation class into a moderate mental retardation class in a public middle school. We tried again for placement in an orthopedic impairments class, and were again denied.

Finally, she was placed into an orthopedically impaired class her last year of middle school. It was probably her best year for academic learning, as she worked one-on-one on her individual goals, but also was part of group learning. She thrived in the group setting, and quite often had to be reprimanded for answering other students' questions!

Unfortunately, inclusion in high school, with the opportunity to go into general education classes, did not work for Natalie—it came too late. We tried, but it's a little hard to start with high school curriculum when you haven't had the basics! She was, for the most part, in a self-contained orthopedically impaired class for her last seven years. Her teacher involved peer tutors in much of Natalie's program, which was very motivating for Natalie and gave her the opportunity to make friends. It was kind of like bringing inclusion to Natalie. They definitely were a benefit to her, both socially and academically.

Transition planning for Natalie was a challenge because of the severity of Natalie's disabilities and the lack of experience with this type of student. We stressed the need to develop assertiveness, as Natalie—like so many folks with disabilities—was too often passive in situations that were not to her liking, but there was no such program. We encouraged goals based on our vision for Natalie's future, which was living and working in the community with supports.

Through school, she did participate in community-based vocational training, and worked in several locations. Although these were not jobs that she could actually do independently, they did offer an opportunity to work on her communication and mobility goals. And she brought an awareness to those stores—and the community that frequented them—of the possibility that a person with severe disabilities could work, wanted to work, and was excited about it!

One of our proudest moments was when Natalie received a standing ovation as she graduated from high school, and there have been many proud moments since. Natalie has had two paying jobs. She lives in her own home with a roommate and a live-in care provider. She is working on understanding and accepting more independence each day. She has given many presentations to community groups and is an active advocate for people who can't speak for themselves.

Through the years, Natalie has been blessed by many wonderful teachers, aides, therapists, and specialists who gave so much of themselves for her benefit. I hope that they will someday realize the impact that each one of them has had, individually and collectively, on Natalie and—through her—on the community as a whole. Natalie is an inspiration, and a wonderful example of what can be!

—*Beth Tumlin*

S tudents who have physical or health disabilities comprise one of the most diverse categories of learners in special education because of the wide range of diseases and disorders included in this category. Pupils with physical disabilities may range from those with severe physical conditions resulting in an inability to talk, walk, point, or make any purposeful movement to those students with only some difficulty walking or an unseen skeletal abnormality. Individuals with health disabilities may range from those with severe health problems forcing them to stay home to those with a hidden disability, such as a tumor. In addition, there are several **low-incidence disabilities** that can also include physical or health disabilities, such as traumatic brain injury, deaf-blindness, and multiple disabilities. The term *low incidence* generally refers to a disability that occurs infrequently. In fact, children who exhibit the three impairments listed above account for only about 2.5 percent of all pupils receiving a special education (U.S. Department of Education, 2007). What places all of these students together in this chapter is that they frequently share some dimension or aspect of physical or health impairments.

Many individuals with physical or health disabilities are capable of living independent and productive lives.

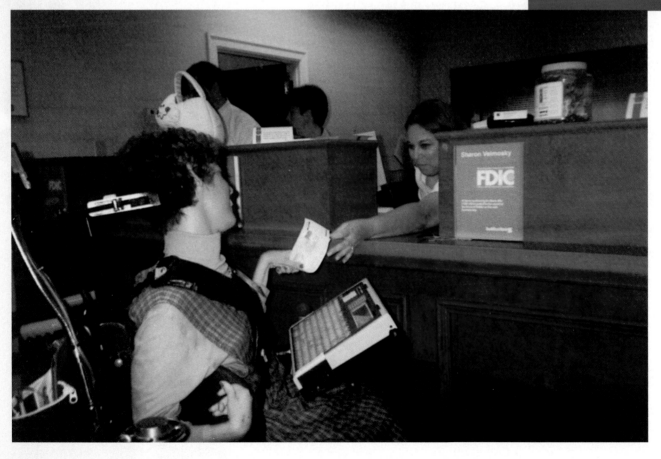

At the beginning of this chapter, we read about Natalie, whose story is typical of many individuals who have a severe physical disability. Natalie has one of the most common physical disabilities (cerebral palsy) that occurs in schoolchildren. In her case, she also has a health disability (epilepsy). She has faced several challenges in her education, such as appropriate assessment, correct educational placement, selection of appropriate curriculum, and use of specialized strategies for teaching and adapting academics for a student who is essentially unable to speak. She uses several types of **assistive technology,** such as an **augmentative communication** device and a power wheelchair. Although she encountered problems regarding her placement and lack of inclusion, she has achieved successes in terms of acquired skills and transition to paid employment.

This chapter will examine what it means for a student to have a physical, health, or related low-incidence disability. Definitions will be given, along with a history of the field, data on the prevalence of these disabilities, and some of their causes. A sampling of some of the most common types of physical, health, and related low-incidence disabilities will be explored. A model will be presented explaining how school performance is affected by a physical, health, or related low-incidence disability, along with strategies to address these students' needs. Many other areas will also be reviewed, including services for young children, transition, adult issues, family issues, diversity, technology, and current issues in the field of physical and health disabilities. We begin by defining physical, health, and related low-incidence disabilities as they are addressed in education.

Defining Physical Disabilities, Health Disabilities, and Related Low-Incidence Disabilities

Many students have various physical or health conditions, but only those with physical or health disabilities that interfere with their educational performance require special education services. According to the Individuals with Disabilities Education Improvement Act of 2004 (IDEA; PL 108-446), students with physical impairments may qualify for special education services under three possible categories: **orthopedic impairments, multiple disabilities,** and **traumatic brain injury.** Students with health disabilities may qualify under the IDEA category of **other health impairments.** Children with the loss of both vision and hearing receive services under the label **deaf-blind.**

The federal definition of orthopedic impairments provides examples of impairments resulting from congenital anomalies (irregularities or defects present at birth), diseases, or other causes (see Table 13.1). In our chapter opener, Natalie was classified under this definition of orthopedic impairments and received special education services because of the impact of her cerebral palsy on her school functioning. Although Natalie had other impairments (seizures), she could be accommodated under the educational program in orthopedic impairments.

When students have two or more primary disabilities that cannot be accommodated by one special education program, they may be classified as having multiple disabilities. For example, a child who has a severe physical impairment and is deaf may be classified as having a multiple disability; this pupil may require services from a teacher certified to teach students with orthopedic impairments and another teacher certified to teach students who are deaf/hard of hearing. Many possible combinations of disabilities can fall under the category of multiple disabilities, but because a physical or health disability is often involved, this category is addressed in this chapter.

Table 13.1	Federal Definitions Pertaining to Physical or Health Disabilities and Deaf-Blindness

Deaf-blindness means concomitant hearing and visual impairment, the combination of which causes such severe communication and other developmental and educational needs that students cannot be accommodated in special education programs solely for children with deafness or children with blindness.

Multiple disabilities means concomitant impairments (such as mental retardation–blindness, mental retardation–orthopedic impairment, etc.), the combination of which causes such severe educational needs that students cannot be accommodated in special education programs solely for one of the impairments. The term does not include deaf-blindness.

Orthopedic impairment means a severe orthopedic impairment that adversely affects a child's educational performance. The term includes impairments caused by congenital anomaly (e.g., clubfoot, absence of some member, etc.), impairments caused by disease (e.g., poliomyelitis, bone tuberculosis, etc.), and impairments from other causes (e.g., cerebral palsy, amputations, and fractures or burns that cause contractures).

Other health impairment means having limited strength, vitality, or alertness, including a heightened alertness to environmental stimuli, that results in limited alertness with respect to the education environment that

   i.   Is due to chronic or acute health problems such as asthma, attention deficit disorder or attention deficit hyperactivity disorder, diabetes, epilepsy, a heart condition, hemophilia, lead poisoning, leukemia, nephritis, rheumatic fever, and sickle cell anemia; and

   ii.   Adversely affects a child's educational performance.

Traumatic brain injury means an acquired injury to the brain caused by an external physical force, resulting in total or partial functional disability or psychosocial impairment, or both, that adversely affects educational performance. The term applies to open or closed head injuries resulting in impairments in one or more areas, such as cognition; language; memory; attention; reasoning; abstract thinking; judgment; problem-solving; sensory, perceptual, and motor abilities; psychosocial behavior; physical functions; information processing; and speech. The term does not apply to brain injuries that are congenital or degenerative, or to brain injuries induced by birth trauma.

Source: 34 C. F. R. § 300.7 (c) Public Law 108-446.

Children who have an acquired brain injury as a result of external force, such as from a car accident, may be served under the category of traumatic brain injury. Traumatic brain injury may result in impairments in several different areas, including physical disabilities, sensory impairments, cognitive abnormalities, language abnormalities, and behavioral disorders. This category does not include individuals who have brain injury that occurred before or during birth or that was acquired as a result of a degenerative disease.

Students with "other health impairments" have limited alertness to the educational environment because of health problems that limit strength, vitality, or alertness. This health impairment may be chronic (persisting over a long period of time) or acute (having a short and usually severe course). The federal definition in Table 13.1 gives several examples of health impairments, including asthma, heart conditions, diabetes, and attention deficit hyperactivity disorder. This is only a partial listing of all of the possible conditions that may be included in this disability area.

Pupils who have visual or hearing impairments of such magnitude that they cannot be appropriately accommodated in a special education program for children with deafness or blindness are identified as deaf-blind. Most of us could not imagine what it would be like to be without the use of both our hearing and our eyesight. We gather so much information about our surroundings through these two senses. The loss of both hearing and vision represents one of the most challenging of all disability categories. It would be wrong to assume, however, that students classified as deaf-blind are completely unable to see or hear—the term is not absolute. In reality, many children classified as deaf-blind experience a broad range of perceptions. Some pupils may be completely blind but only partially deaf, while in other instances a youngster might be partially sighted but have a severe hearing loss. Fortunately, a majority of these individuals possess some degree of functional hearing and vision (Miles, 2005). Only a very few pupils classified as deaf-blind are profoundly deaf *and* totally blind (Alabama Institute for Deaf and Blind, 2007).

The challenges facing this group of children are sometimes formidable and often include severe communication deficits, impaired mobility, and diminished social skills. Mental retardation and physical impairments are often present in individuals who are deaf-blind (National Consortium on Deaf-Blindness, 2007). For pupils who are profoundly deaf and totally blind, their experience with and knowledge of the world is very narrow, often extending only as far as their fingertips can reach (Miles, 2005). Helen Keller said, "Blindness separates a person from things, but deafness separates him from people." Helping a child who is deaf-blind relate to the world is a tremendous undertaking, a responsibility that frequently falls to teachers, family members, and other professionals.

A Brief History of the Field

Physical and health disabilities have existed throughout history, and reactions to individuals who have this type of disability have varied across civilizations, cultures, and individual beliefs. Reactions have ranged from abandonment and extermination to providing educational, social, and medical treatment. A brief historical review of the treatment of individuals with physical or health disabilities will help to provide an understanding of present-day practices.

Early History

In ancient civilizations, individuals with physical or health impairments did not often live long. A lack of sophisticated medical treatment made it impossible to treat many of these impairments. Many cultures did not value individuals who were viewed as being incapable of contributing to group survival. Infants were often abandoned to die. Individuals who later developed injury or illness were often ostracized and forced to leave the group. However, some artifacts do indicate that some attempts were made to heal the effects of illness and disability in ancient times. For example, primitive skulls have been found with holes cut into them; evidence suggests that people were trying to cure epilepsy by cutting a hole through the skull to let "evil spirits out" (Temkin, 1971).

During the Middle Ages, religious influence typically resulted in more humanitarian care. Individuals with disabilities were often viewed as "children of God" and received protection from the Church. However, in some instances, individuals with disabilities (such as seizure disorders) were perceived as witches or possessed by evil spirits and were burned at the stake (Gargiulo, 1985).

In the 1800s, physicians and researchers showed an increased interest in physical disabilities and studied individuals with disabilities to find effective treatments. For example, in the 1860s, Dr. William Little described several cases and treatments of what is now referred to as cerebral palsy (because of his pioneering efforts, the disorder was initially named Little disease). At about this time, the first schools were opened for individuals with physical disabilities, in the form of residential institutions.

The first institution in the United States for children with physical disabilities was the Industrial School for Crippled and Deformed Children in Boston, established in 1890

(Eberle, 1922). This and other institutions were well intended, and provided a centralized place that could house needed equipment and provide specialized treatment and training. However, over the years, many institutions degenerated into providing only custodial services. Residential institutions often became places to "protect" society from "undesirables" (Macmilan & Hendrick, 1993). This practice of separating individuals with disabilities from society has been questioned in modern society, with the recognition that persons with physical and health impairments can contribute positively to society and should be allowed to do so.

Emergence of Public Education

It was not until the 1900s that public schools for "crippled children" were established (La Vor, 1976), first in Chicago and then in New York, Cleveland, and Philadelphia. These schools permitted expensive equipment to be centrally located and enabled highly trained professionals to work with these children. However, this segregated setting did not allow students with physical disabilities to interact with students without disabilities in the educational environment. Unfortunately, students with physical disabilities were not always welcome in public school. In *Beattie v. State Board of Education* (1919), the courts ruled that students with physical disabilities could be excluded from school because they were said to have a "depressing and nauseating effect" on other students (Ysseldyke & Algozzine, 1982). Over time, the educational setting changed to allow the integration of students with physical and health disabilities into neighborhood schools and general education classes. The move to more integrated school placements took a combination of legislation, shift in ideology, and advances in medical and technological practices.

Prevalence of Physical Disabilities, Health Disabilities, and Related Low-Incidence Disabilities

Reported prevalence figures for physical and health disabilities vary widely, depending on the specific condition. For example, the United Cerebral Palsy Association (2007) reports that 764,000 children and adults in the United States have cerebral palsy and approximately 8,000 infants and 1,200–1,500 preschool-age children are diagnosed each year. Spina bifida is reported as occurring in approximately 1 out of every 1,000 newborns in the United States (Spina Bifida Association of America, 2004). The Epilepsy Foundation of America (2007) reports that approximately 45,000 children under the age of 15 develop epilepsy each year, and more than 3 million Americans are currently diagnosed with epilepsy. The American Lung Association (2007) estimates that more than 6.2 million children under the age of 18 have asthma. The estimated number of individuals diagnosed with AIDS in the United States is approximately 988,000, with 9,100 of these being children under the age of 13 (Centers for Disease Control and Prevention, 2007a).

Not every school-age child with a physical or health impairment requires special education services, because the condition may not have a negative impact on the student's academic performance. The U.S. Department of Education (2007) annually compiles information from each state on the number of school-age children receiving special education by disability category. During the 2005–2006 school year, in the area of physical and health disabilities, a total of 781,578 school-age children received services across the categories of orthopedic impairments (63,127 children), multiple disabilities (133,914 children), traumatic brain injury (23,509 children), and other health impairments (561,028 children). These four areas comprised approximately 13 percent of the students receiving a special education, with a range of .38 percent (traumatic brain injury) to 9.1 percent (other health impairments). Pupils with deaf-blindness (1,592 children) were reported as making up only .02 percent of all individuals receiving a special education. This figure, however, is thought to be underestimated because many children who are deaf-blind are placed in other categories (for example, multiple disabilities) when they have additional physical or intellectual impairments.

Etiology of Physical Disabilities, Health Disabilities, and Related Low-Incidence Disabilities

The etiology (or cause) of physical and health disabilities varies greatly according to the specific disease or disorder. Some of the most common etiologies resulting in physical and health disabilities are genetic and chromosomal defects, teratogenic causes, prematurity and complications of pregnancy, and acquired causes. In some cases, certain physical or health disabilities have multiple etiologies. For example, cerebral palsy can be caused by prenatal abnormalities, biochemical abnormalities, genetic causes, congenital infections, environmental toxins, prematurity-associated complications, or postnatal events (Griffin, Fitch, & Griffin, 2002; Heller & Tumlin-Garrett, 2009). On the other hand, the exact cause of some physical and health disabilities are unknown.

Chromosomal and Genetic Causes

Among the most common causes of physical and health disabilities are hereditary conditions resulting from defects in one or both parents' chromosomes or genes. Several genetic defects are believed to contribute to a range of physical and health disabilities, such as muscular dystrophy, sickle cell anemia, hemophilia, and cystic fibrosis (Heller, 2009b; Heller, Mezei, & Schwartzman, 2009). In some cases, infants may be born with several disabilities resulting from an inherited congenital syndrome (for example, Cockayne syndrome, which can result in mental retardation, dwarfism, deaf-blindness, unsteady gait, and tremors). In these examples, the inherited gene clearly causes the disease or disorder.

Although there are about sixty genetic causes of deaf-blindness (DB-Link, 2007), we have chosen only two illustrative syndromes. Our first example is **CHARGE Association** (syndrome), which represents a collection of physical irregularities present at birth. This syndrome is an extremely complex disorder typically involving extensive medical as well as physical challenges. CHARGE Association is a relatively rare disorder occurring in 1 out of every 9,000–10,000 births. In the vast majority of cases, there is no history of CHARGE syndrome or any other similar condition in the family (CHARGE Syndrome Foundation, 2007). CHARGE is an acronym that stands for

C = coloboma, a congenital condition resulting from an unusually shaped (teardrop) pupil and/or other abnormalities of the eye contributing to difficulties with depth perception, visual acuity, and sensitivity to light

H = heart defects, which may range from minor to life-threatening conditions

A = atresia, complications of the respiratory system

First Person

Virginia

As early as the fourth grade I became aware that I probably didn't see as well as others in the dark. But not being able to see at night just seemed like it should be normal.

However, in seventh grade, in anticipation of our Washington, D.C. school trip, I was a little worried about the whole not being able to see at night thing, so my mom and I went to talk to the school nurse who was also going on the trip. She checked my eyes and said that I just needed glasses (not that that had anything to do with not being able to see in the dark). My mom made an appointment with the eye doctor, and he also said that I needed glasses. My dad told the doctor that the main reason for the appointment was to find out why I couldn't see in the dark. He examined my eyes again and said that I would have to take some additional tests at Emory University.

The summer before eighth grade I discovered the real reason I couldn't see in the dark: I had Usher syndrome. I couldn't believe it, and I didn't want to believe it. I didn't want to lose a sense that was so very precious to me. I used my sight not only to get around but also, because of my hearing loss, for lipreading. At such a young age, I was worried about being "normal." For the next two years I was in a state of denial. I refused to talk about my condition, and if I was forced to talk about it, it only brought pain. How could I, a person who relied so heavily on sight to communicate, lose my vision? It just didn't seem fair, and I felt so alone. No one knew or understood what I was going through. Of course, I had my family and friends supporting me, but I still felt alone.

It wasn't until I was 15 that I began to accept my deaf-blindness. Now I'm OK with my disability. While I have learned to accept my vision as something that has shaped who I am today, I am in no way completely cured of all my emotional pain. No way! I still struggle with adjusting to the changes in my vision. I worry about completing college and what the future holds. There are some days when I get so frustrated that all I want to do is run away and scream. It's hard, but all I can do is take one day at a time and trust that God has an awesome plan for my life.

R = retarded physical growth; in some instances mental retardation is also present

G = genital abnormalities—incomplete or underdeveloped genitals, more common in males

E = ear defects, structural deformities in the outer, middle, or inner ear; hearing loss may range from mild to profound (Alabama Institute for Deaf and Blind, 2007; CHARGE Syndrome Foundation)

In order to make a diagnosis of CHARGE, four of the preceding six characteristics must be present. In addition, children who exhibit this syndrome frequently experience high levels of anxiety while also displaying compulsive behaviors (Silberman, Bruce, & Nelson, 2004).

Our second illustration is **Usher syndrome**. This inherited disorder is one of the leading causes of deaf-blindness after childhood. Approximately 1 in 20,000 individuals is born with this condition (Alabama Institute for Deaf and Blind, 2007). Usher syndrome results in congenital deafness, progressive vision loss (retinitis pigmentosa), and, in some children, mental retardation. Vision difficulties are typically noted in adolescence or early adulthood, eventually leading to night blindness and tunnel vision. Hearing loss is evidenced in both ears and is usually in the moderate (45–55 dB) to severe (71–90 dB) range. Significant balance difficulties are also associated with this syndrome. (See the accompanying First Person feature.)

Nationally, approximately 3 percent of students exhibit deaf-blindness as a result of Usher syndrome (Gallaudet Research Institute, 2005). Interestingly, in parts of south Louisiana the Acadian French (Cajuns) have a much higher prevalence rate. In fact, some 30 percent of the deaf population in three parishes (counties) exhibit Usher syndrome, while an estimated 15 to 20 percent of the students enrolled in the Louisiana School for the Deaf have this disorder (Melancon, 2000). This phenomenon is most likely the consequence of years of intermarriage in this close-knit ethnic community.

Finally, some 17 percent of children who are deaf-blind evidence this disability at birth or within the first five years of life. The overwhelming majority of students with deaf-blindness, however, are adventitiously deaf-blind, that is, they are born with both vision and hearing but lose some or all of these senses as a result of illness or injury (Miles, 2005; National Consortium on Deaf-Blindness, 2007). How deaf-blindness impacts a child's development depends on several key variables, including age of onset, the degree and type of hearing and vision loss, the stability of each sensory loss, and, perhaps most important, the educational interventions provided (Alabama Institute for Deaf and Blind, 2007).

Teratogenic Causes

Many physical and health disabilities are caused by teratogenic agents that affect the developing fetus. **Teratogens** are outside causes, such as infections, drugs, chemicals, or environmental agents, that can produce fetal abnormalities.

Certain congenital infections can result in severe multiple disabilities in the unborn child. Infections are acquired by the mother and then passed on to the developing fetus. Several prenatal infections that may result in severe birth defects are referred to by the acronym STORCH—syphilis, toxoplasmosis, other, rubella, cytomegalovirus, and herpes. The effects of these infections on the fetus can vary from no adverse effect to severe disabilities or death. A baby who contracts one of these infections during gestation may be born with cerebral palsy, blindness, deafness, mental retardation, and several other abnormalities, including heart defects, kidney defects, brain abnormalities, and deaf-blindness (Best & Heller, 2009b).

The fetus is also at risk of developing physical and health disabilities when exposed to certain drugs, chemicals, or environmental agents. Maternal abuse of alcohol, for example, has been linked to a range of physical, cognitive, and behavioral abnormalities that can result in lifelong damage (Merrick, Merrick, Morad, & Kandel, 2006; Tsai, Floyd, Green, & Boyle, 2007). Serious fetal abnormalities can also occur as a result of prescription medications taken for maternal illness or disease (for example, certain antibiotics and seizure medications). Environmental toxins such as radiation have been linked to birth defects, as have dietary deficiencies. Certain maternal diseases, such as diabetes, have also been associated with a higher risk of fetal disability. Maternal trauma from falls or car accidents can cause bleeding in the fetus's brain, resulting in neurological impairments (Akman, 2000).

Prematurity and Complications of Pregnancy

Infants are usually born at approximately 40 weeks of gestation, weighing approximately 7½ pounds (Kliegman, Behrman, Jensen, & Stanton, 2007). An infant born before 37 weeks is considered premature.

Infants who are premature and born with very low birth weight (less than 1,500 grams) are at risk of having disabilities. These infants can develop neurological problems resulting in cerebral palsy, epilepsy, vision loss, hearing loss, deaf-blindness, and/or psychosis (Valcamonico et al., 2007). Cognitive functioning can be affected, resulting in mental retardation or learning disabilities, which can lead to future educational difficulties (Hille et al., 2007).

In some instances, babies that are born on time and with average weight encounter complications during the perinatal period. The most common cause of brain injury during the perinatal period is asphyxia—a decrease of oxygen in the blood. Among infants who survive an episode of asphyxia, several disabilities may occur such as cerebral palsy, epilepsy, and cognitive deficits (Rennie, Hagmann, & Robertson, 2007).

Acquired Causes

Many physical and health disabilities in addition to related low-incidence disabilities, are acquired after birth by infants, children, and adults. These acquired causes include trauma, child abuse, infections, environmental toxins, and disease. For example, deaf-blindness may be caused by meningitis. Traumatic brain injury is usually due to an acquired cause resulting from some type of trauma (for example, falls, accidents, child abuse). The extent of disability will depend on the cause and its severity.

Characteristics of Individuals with Physical Disabilities, Health Disabilities, and Related Low-Incidence Disabilities

The specific characteristics of an individual who has a physical or health disability will depend on the specific disease, its severity, and individual factors. Two individuals with identical diagnoses may be quite different in terms of their capabilities. Also, it is important to remember that students who have severe physical disabilities (even individuals who are unable to talk, walk, or feed themselves) may have normal or gifted intelligence. No one should judge a person's intellectual ability based on physical appearance.

A multitude of physical and health disabilities may be encountered at school. Each of them has differing characteristics, treatments, and prognoses. To illustrate the range of conditions included under physical and health disabilities, this section describes a number of sample conditions across the four IDEA categories of orthopedic impairments, multiple disabilities, traumatic brain injury, and other health impairments. Table 13.2 gives an outline of the categories, subcategories, and sample conditions that will be discussed. Characteristics of individuals with deaf-blindness will also be reviewed.

Characteristics of Students with Orthopedic Impairments

The IDEA category of orthopedic impairments contains a wide variety of disorders. These can be divided into three main areas: neuromotor impairments, degenerative diseases, and musculoskeletal disorders. Each of these areas has unique characteristics and contains many different disabilities. Following is a sampling of some of the most commonly found orthopedic impairments in the school-age population.

NEUROMOTOR IMPAIRMENTS A **neuromotor impairment** is an abnormality of, or damage to, the brain, spinal cord, or nerves that send impulses to the muscles of the body.

Table 13.2	**Examples of Physical and Health Disabilities**
Physical Disabilities	**Health Disabilities**
Orthopedic Impairment	Other Health Impairments

Neuromotor impairments
     • Cerebral palsy
     • Spina bifida
	Major health impairments
	     • Seizure disorders
	     • Asthma

Degenerative diseases
     • Muscular dystrophy
	Infectious diseases
	     • AIDS

Musculoskeletal disorders
     • Juvenile rheumatoid arthritis
     • Limb deficiency	

Multiple Disabilities*	
Physical disability plus another disability	
Traumatic Brain Injury*	
Physical disability resulting from traumatic brain injury	

NOTE: *Multiple disabilities and traumatic brain injury can occur without a physical disability being present. They only fall under the category of physical disabilities when a physical disability is present.

Neuromotor impairments often result in complex motor problems that can affect several body systems (for example, limited limb movement, loss of urinary control, loss of proper alignment of the spine). Individuals with neuromotor impairments have a higher incidence of additional impairments, especially when there has been brain involvement (for example, mental retardation, seizures, visual impairments). Two types of neuromotor impairments that fall under the IDEA category of orthopedic impairments are cerebral palsy and spina bifida.

1. **Cerebral Palsy Cerebral palsy** refers to several nonprogressive disorders of voluntary movement or posture that are caused by malfunction of or damage to the developing brain that occurs before or during birth or within the first few years of life (Beers, Porter, Jones, Kaplan, & Berkwits, 2006; Miller, 2005). This disorder is associated with many different etiologies, including teratogens (such as the STORCH infections), prematurity, complications of pregnancy (such as lack of oxygen), acquired causes, and certain genetic syndromes.

Individuals with cerebral palsy have abnormal, involuntary, and/or uncoordinated motor movements. The severity can range from mild to severe. Some mild forms of cerebral palsy may only be noticeable when the person runs and appears to move in an uncoordinated fashion. At the other extreme, individuals with severe forms of cerebral palsy are unable to make the motor movements necessary to walk, sit without support, feed themselves, chew food, pick up an object, or speak.

The four most common types of cerebral palsy are spastic, athetoid, ataxia, and mixed. **Spastic cerebral palsy** is characterized by very tight muscles occurring in one or more muscle groups. This tightness results in stiff, uncoordinated movements. In **athetoid cerebral palsy,** movements are contorted, abnormal, and purposeless. Individuals with **ataxic cerebral palsy,** or **ataxia,** have poor balance and equilibrium in addition to uncoordinated voluntary movement. **Mixed cerebral palsy** refers to a combination of types, such as spastic and athetoid, as in the case of Natalie described at the beginning of this chapter.

Cerebral palsy is also classified by which limbs (arms and legs) are affected. This classification system is also used for other types of motor disorders and paralysis. Some of the major classifications are **hemiplegia,** in which the left or right side of the body is involved; **diplegia,** in which the legs are more affected than the arms; **paraplegia,** in which only the legs are involved; and **quadriplegia,** in which all four limbs are involved (see Figure 13.1). Natalie's spastic cerebral palsy is the type in which all four limbs are severely involved. Hence, she is described as having severe spastic quadriplegic cerebral palsy, in addition to the athetoid form.

Although cerebral palsy is considered nonprogressive because the brain damage does not progress, further complications and additional disabilities may result. Many individuals develop contractures (shortening of the muscle) that further decrease motor movement and can result in deformity. Abnormal muscle tone can result in conditions such as curvature of the spine (scoliosis) and hip displacement. Abnormal oral reflexes may result in a need for a feeding tube (a tube going into the stomach through which nutritional liquids are given when the person is unable to eat sufficient amounts of food). Individuals with cerebral palsy have an increased incidence of other disorders, including epilepsy, visual impairments, and mental retardation (Heller & Tumlin-Garrett, 2009). However, intellectual ability can range from gifted to mental retardation, and accurate scores can be difficult to obtain.

At present, there is no cure for cerebral palsy. Cerebral palsy is often managed through medication (such as diazepam or baclofen) and/or surgery, which decrease the effects of tight muscles and deformity, although movement abnormalities still remain. Part of a student's treatment regime will also include the use of various braces or splints, known as **orthotics,** to help maintain alignment and decrease the development of **contractures** (shortened muscles that result in the inability to fully extend a joint, such as being unable to fully extend the arm at the elbow or completely straighten at the knees). New, experimental treatments are being continually tried in the hope of improving motor function (Liptak, 2005).

2. Spina Bifida During the first 28 days of pregnancy, special embryo cells form a closed tube that will become the brain and spinal cord. When this process is interrupted and the tube does not completely close, a congenital abnormality known as a neural tube defect occurs. When it occurs in the area of the spinal cord, a condition known as **spina**

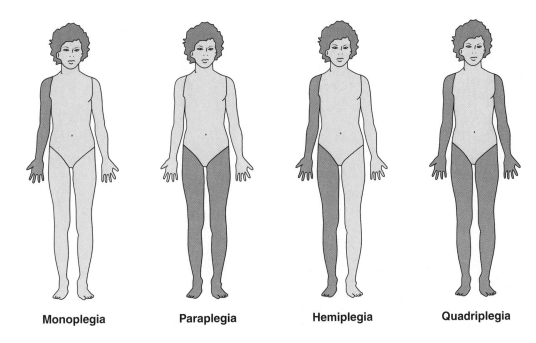

Monoplegia   **Paraplegia**   **Hemiplegia**   **Quadriplegia**

Figure 13.1

Topographical Classification of Cerebral Palsy

bifida results. In the most severe form, myelomeningocele spina bifida, the baby is born with a sac on its back and the spinal cord pouches out into the sack (see Figure 13.2). The spinal cord does not properly function at the point of the sac and below. Surgery will be performed to remove the sac when the infant is born, but the damage to the spinal cord cannot be reversed (Herring, 2002). However, research is being done to determine if the effects of spina bifida can be decreased by closing the defect with prenatal surgery during the second trimester (Management of Myelomeningocele Study, 2007).

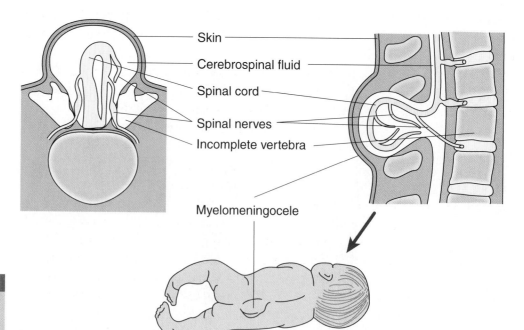

Figure 13.2

Normal Development of the Neural Tube, Normal Spine at Birth, and Spina Bifida

The characteristics of myelomeningocele spina bifida depend on the location of the defect. As with a spinal cord injury, there will be a lack of movement and sensation below the area of injury. Although the defect can occur anywhere along the spinal column, it typically occurs in the lower part of the spinal cord. Usually the student will have difficulty walking, but can do so with braces, crutches, or a walker. Some children will need a wheelchair for long distances, and others may only be able to get about using a wheelchair.

In addition, many students will need to catheterize themselves to empty their bladder. Also, a high incidence of latex allergies may require latex-free gloves and avoidance of latex products.

Students with spina bifida are at risk of hydrocephalus (a buildup of cerebral spinal fluid in the brain). To treat hydrocephalus, a shunt (small tube) is placed under the skin from the brain into the abdominal area to drain the excess fluid. It is important for teachers to know the signs and symptoms to look for should the shunt become blocked, such as headache, changes in vision, personality changes, deterioration in school performance, vomiting, and emotional disturbances (Mavinkurve, Bagley, Pradilla, & Jallo, 2005). If shunt failure is suspected, the teacher will need to notify the appropriate personnel immediately, and the child will usually require surgery to replace the shunt.

Many individuals with spina bifida and hydrocephalus are at risk for cognitive and learning impairments. The majority of students will fall into the low-average range of intelligence (Jacobs, Northam, & Anderson, 2001). There may also be learning problems because of deficits in such areas as attention, memory, recall, motor reaction times, visual-perceptual skills, and organizational skills (Heller, 2009c; Iddon, Morgan, Loveday, Sahakian, & Pickard, 2006). Some young children with spina bifida have also been found to have poor comprehension of abstract concepts and difficulty using language functionally within social situations (Vachha & Adams, 2003). Appropriate modifications and instructional strategies are needed to provide an appropriate education for these students.

DEGENERATIVE DISEASES The second group of disabilities within the category of orthopedic impairments is degenerative diseases that affect motor movement. Degenerative diseases are typically grouped separately because of their unique and poignant impact on individuals. The student with a degenerative disease will often need increasingly more complex adaptations and assistive technology to permit continued participation in school activities. Teachers are also confronted with emotional issues regarding the loss of capabilities, as well as issues of death and dying. One of the most common degenerative diseases found in the school population is **Duchenne muscular dystrophy.**

Muscular dystrophy includes a group of inherited diseases that are characterized by progressive muscle weakness from degeneration of the muscle fiber. When an infant is born with Duchenne muscular dystrophy, no disability is initially apparent. Usually by age 3, leg weakness begins to manifest in some problems walking and running; by age 5, walking may appear abnormal. Between ages 5 and 10, there is further weakness of the legs accompanied by arm weakness. Often around 10 or 12 years of age, the child can no longer walk and needs a wheelchair. Through the teenage years, muscle weakness continues; the child will no longer be able to push the wheelchair and will need an electric wheelchair. Over time, it will become increasingly difficult to move the arms or keep the head upright. As the muscles used for breathing weaken, most individuals will develop respiratory infections and die in their late teens or early 20s. It is important to note that only the muscles are degenerating, not the mind.

There is currently no effective treatment for Duchenne muscular dystrophy. The aim of treatment is to try to maintain functioning and help the person walk as long as possible.

Physical and occupational therapy are used in an effort to prevent deformity of the legs and arms and may include the use of braces and splints. Medications will be prescribed for a variety of problems, such as respiratory infections, and surgery may be performed to release contractures and prevent early deformity.

Issues of death and dying often come to the surface, and students may want to discuss their fears with a teacher. Teachers need to be good listeners and give these students a chance to discuss their feelings. Programs are also available for students with terminal illness to give them support during this difficult time.

Teachers need to be observant of the disease's progression and let the special educator know if problems are occurring. Often these problems indicate that the student's assistive technology needs to be changed. For example, a student who was using a pencil to write may need to change to a keyboard and then to a smaller adapted keyboard as motor movement is lost and fatigue increases. Teachers need to have a supportive attitude and provide appropriate modifications.

ORTHOPEDIC AND MUSCULOSKELETAL DISORDERS Students with orthopedic or musculoskeletal disorders greatly vary in the severity of their physical disability. Although some of these conditions can result in severe physical limitations, the person usually does not have cognitive, learning, perceptual, language, or sensory issues to the extent that is found in many neuromotor impairments. Two examples in this category are juvenile rheumatoid arthritis and limb deficiencies.

1. **Juvenile Rheumatoid Arthritis Juvenile rheumatoid arthritis (JRA)** is a chronic arthritic condition affecting the joints that occurs before 16 years of age. Although there are different types of JRA, symptoms typically include (1) joint stiffness after immobility, (2) pain with joint movement, (3) limitations in joint motion, and, in some children, (4) fever (Heller & Avant, 2009). Over time, this disease may go into remission, stabilize, or progress and cause permanent deformity of the joints. The disease may result in additional disabilities, such as contractures, and the systemic effect of the disease may result in visual impairments.

Treatment of JRA is primarily supportive, as there is currently no cure. Medications are often given to reduce joint inflammation, treat pain, control additional effects of the disease (such as vision problems), and help prevent contractures or deformities (Hsu, Lin, Yang, & Chiang, 2004). Students often need physical and occupational therapy.

As with any condition that involves pain, students' learning will be affected when pain is present. Fatigue and lack of stamina may also interfere with learning. Modifications are often made to address these issues. For example, sitting too long can actually be harmful and result in pain when getting up. The student may need to stand or move about periodically in class (such as to sharpen a pencil or go to the board). Students with JRA may need to leave class early to get to their next class and avoid jostling in the hallways. If significant joint deformity has occurred, assistive technology (such as an adapted keyboard) may also be needed.

2. **Limb Deficiency** A **limb deficiency** refers to any number of skeletal abnormalities in which an arm(s) and/or leg(s) is partially or totally missing. A student may be born missing an arm or leg or may lose a limb in an accident. Typically, individuals with limb deficiencies will be fitted with a prosthetic device (artificial limb). There are many different types of prosthetic devices with different levels of complexity. A student may have a leg prosthetic

Some students may use their feet for such tasks as accessing a communication device.

that allows walking and running or an artificial hand that permits grasping and writing. If the limb has been missing from birth, the child may have learned to do things using other limbs. For example, some students who are missing both arms can write and feed themselves with their feet. Some students may type with their feet. Whether a prosthetic device is used or not, many students will still require some modifications and may need specialized instruction in such areas as one-handed keyboarding.

Characteristics of Students with Multiple Disabilities

Multiple disabilities is an umbrella term under which various educational, rehabilitation, government, and advocacy groups include different combinations of disabilities. In IDEA, this category refers to persons with concomitant impairments whose needs cannot be met in a special education program designed solely for one of the impairments. Although there is no single definition, the term does imply two or more disabilities whose combination usually creates an interactional, multiplicative effect rather than just an additive one. Some examples include learners with

- intellectual disabilities and spina bifida
- deafness and AIDS
- behavior disorders and muscular dystrophy
- cerebral palsy and seizures
- learning disabilities and asthma

Depending on the type of multiple disabilities, cognitive functioning may vary from gifted to profound mental retardation. Usually there will be a need for modifications, assistive technology, and specialized teaching strategies.

Characteristics of Students with Traumatic Brain Injury

Traumatic brain injury refers to temporary or permanent injury to the brain from acquired causes such as car accidents, accidental falls, and gunshot wounds to the head; it does not include congenital or degenerative conditions or birth trauma. Approximately 5.3 million people in the United States have a disability as a result of a traumatic brain injury (Centers for Disease Control and Prevention, 2007b). Although a person can acquire a traumatic brain injury at any age, one of the highest rates is among teenagers and young adults from 15 to 24 years of age.

The effects of an injury will differ depending on the cause. A penetration injury, such as a bullet going through the brain, will result in certain specific effects. The effects of the injury are usually specific to the site of injury, with secondary effects occurring in other areas as a result of complications.

Traumatic brain injury can also be caused by car accidents and falls. This type of injury, known as an acceleration injury, results in diffuse damage throughout the brain. When the head hits the steering wheel of a car, for example, the brain (which is floating in cerebral spinal fluid) is thrown violently forward against the skull. This initial site of impact is referred to as "coup" (see Figure 13.3). The brain is then thrown backward and hits the back of the skull. This second site of impact is known as "contracoup." The brain continues to move back and forth, hitting against the skull, and suffering further damage against any sharp bony protrusions. Often the brain will be twisting as well, breaking and damaging nerve cells throughout. The result is diffuse damage across the brain. Complications such as hemorrhage (bleeding) and edema (swelling) often cause further damage to the brain.

The effects of a traumatic brain injury range from no ill effects to severe disability. Most head injuries are mild, with no abnormalities found on neurological exams, and the person

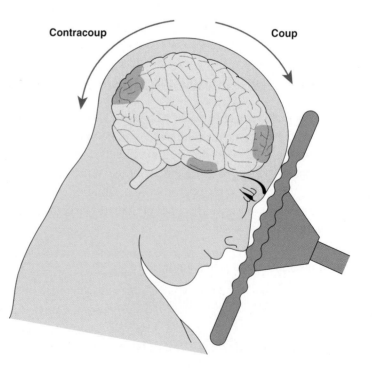

Figure 13.3 ◄

Traumatic Brain Injury

Source: Adapted from S. Grandinette and S. Best, "Traumatic Brain Injury," in K. W. Heller, P. E. Forney, P. A. Alberto, S. Best, and M. N. Schwartzman (Eds.), *Understanding Physical, Health, and Multiple Disabilities*, 2nd ed. (Upper Saddle River, NJ: Pearson Education, 2009), p. 122.

often does not require medical treatment. Even following a mild injury, however, problems such as headache, fatigue, distractibility, memory problems, and perceptual motor slowing can occur and persist for months, years, or permanently. These problems often go undetected until difficulties arise during classroom activities. In one case, a girl fell out of a window and was taken to the emergency room. Although she had no apparent damage, she failed the school year. In retrospect, the teacher and parent were able to trace the student's academic difficulties as beginning after the accident and realized that some cognitive deficits must have occurred.

Students with moderate and severe cases of traumatic head injury typically require hospital stays and rehabilitation services before reentering school. The person with a severe traumatic brain injury often enters the hospital in a coma and slowly regains some or most abilities. Typically, motor skills return first and higher-level cognitive skills last. Improvement can be a long process, with the most dramatic gains occurring over the first year but skills continuing to improve over about a five-year period.

Some individuals may fully recover from a traumatic brain injury, while others may have permanent disabilities. A traumatic brain injury has the potential for causing lifelong disabilities across physical, cognitive, social, behavioral, health, and sensory domains. In the area of physical disabilities, some individuals are left without the ability to walk or use their hands. However, the permanent physical disability is often more subtle, with decreased balance and speed in walking and decreased hand speed and dexterity (Kuhtz-Buschbeck et al., 2003). Although these may seem mild, they can interfere with participation in sports and activities requiring good hand control.

Cognitive deficits can remain after a severe traumatic brain injury. These can range from severe mental retardation to mild cognitive impairments. Individuals may have deficits in sustained attention, problem solving, shifting attention, planning, initiation, organization, and memory (Slomine et al., 2002). Impairments in these areas often result in learning problems and difficulty with setting goals, monitoring and evaluating performance, shifting strategies to address a problem, remaining focused over time, and remembering information. Teachers will need to use systematic instruction and specialized strategies to address these problems.

Impairments in social and behavioral functioning are common in individuals with traumatic brain injury. These may range from difficulty interacting with others to irritability and aggression (Alderman, 2003). Poor social interactions can occur when the injury has resulted in difficulty in reading social cues and monitoring social responses. Some individuals have personality changes with poorly controlled behavior in which they act on impulse, often with aggressive behavior (Slomine et al., 2002; Ylvisaker, Jacobs, & Feeney, 2003). These types of behaviors are often considered the most challenging to address in the classroom setting. A behavior management plan is usually constructed to provide guidelines on how to address the behavior problems.

During the reauthorization of IDEA in 1990, traumatic brain injury was added as a separate disability category, in part because of its unique and multiple characteristics that can interfere with learning and functioning. These students need to be constantly assessed, because skill levels do improve over time. For example, one student with a three-year-old severe traumatic brain injury was being taught to use pictures to communicate when suddenly she began to laugh at a misspelled word on a bulletin board. She had regained the ability to read most words without anyone realizing it. Unlike those with developmental disabilities, students with traumatic brain injury may be left with "splinter skills," meaning that they have some advanced skills but lack other simple ones. For example, one student with severe traumatic brain injury could identify any number, no matter how large, but had difficulty with the concept that 1 plus 1 equals 2. Teachers need to use various modifications and techniques to address the many problems that

Suggestions for the Classroom

Strategies That May Be Used with Students with Traumatic Brain Injury

Impairments	Strategies	Examples
Poor attention	Decrease distractions.	Move away extra pencils.
	Provide cues to attend.	Touch card that says "Listen."
	Limit amount of information.	Divide up information.
	Provide advance organizers.	Give list of important events.
Memory problems	Teach verbal rehearsal strategies.	Student repeats list of people.
	Teach use of visual imagery.	Student visualizes battle for history.
	Provide information in writing.	Give teacher's notes.
	Give a school schedule.	Put pictures by each subject.
	Repeat directions.	Repeat one direction at a time.
Decreased writing speed and accuracy	Give more time on tests.	Student takes test over two periods.
	Decrease assignment load.	Student writes two fewer papers.
	Have student type instead of writing by hand.	Student writes faster using keyboard.
Decreased stamina and endurance	Allow rest breaks.	Student rests for five minutes.
	Adjust school day.	Student comes for half day.
	Have peer carry books.	Friend helps with books.
Impulsive behavior	Encourage "thinking time."	Have student wait, then answer.
	Discuss rules each day.	Review rules.
	Redirect inappropriate behavior.	Tell student to sit, open book.
	Remove unnecessary material.	Book bags are placed at side of room.
	Role-play.	Practice different scenarios.

can occur in a student with a traumatic brain injury; some sample strategies are provided in the accompanying Suggestions for the Classroom. The special education teacher needs to work closely with the general education teacher in helping to use the most appropriate techniques.

Characteristics of Students with Other Health Impairments

Disabilities that fall under the IDEA category of other health impairments are often divided into two areas: major health impairments and infectious diseases. Students will not typically require special education services unless these conditions are severe. These impairments often result in more absences, fatigue, and decreased stamina.

MAJOR HEALTH IMPAIRMENTS Many major health impairments fall under the category of other health impairments. Some of these can be treated effectively; others have no cure. Many of them can give rise to emergency situations that need to be handled immediately, and some can result in death. Two of the most commonly occurring health impairments are seizure disorders and asthma.

1. **Seizure Disorders** A **seizure** is a sudden, temporary change in the normal functioning of the brain's electrical system as a result of excessive, uncontrolled electrical activity in the brain. A seizure may be due to a high fever, ingestion of certain drugs or poisons, certain metabolic disorders, or chemical imbalances. Seizures may also be the result of a prenatal or perinatal brain injury, head trauma, infections such as meningitis, congenital malformations, or unknown causes (Beers et al., 2006). A person has a seizure disorder, also known as **epilepsy,** when the seizures are recurrent. Often the reason for the seizure disorder is unknown.

Seizures are of many different types, depending on where in the brain the abnormal electrical activity occurs. Seizures may be characterized by altered consciousness, motor activity, sensory phenomena, inappropriate behaviors, or some combination of these. Three of the most commonly encountered seizure disorders are absence seizures, complex partial seizures, and tonic-clonic seizures.

An individual who has **absence seizures** (formerly known as *petit mal* seizures) will suddenly lose consciousness, stop moving, and stare straight ahead (or the eyes may roll upward). The person will not fall, but simply stop and appear trancelike. If the seizure occurs when the person is talking, the person will stop in midsentence and, when the seizure ends, continue the sentence as if nothing has happened. Typically, these seizures do not last more than 30 seconds, but they can occur several hundred times a day (Tovia, Goldberg-Stern, Shahar, & Kramer, 2005). Often the person is not aware of what has happened. When the seizure occurs during a teacher's lecture, the child often doesn't understand why the teacher is suddenly talking about something different. These seizures have been mistaken for daydreaming, but the student cannot be brought out of the seizure by touch or loud voices. Often it is the observant teacher who first detects that something is wrong with the student.

In a **complex partial seizure**, consciousness is impaired and the person usually exhibits a series of motor movements that may appear voluntary but are beyond the person's control. For example, some individuals having a complex partial seizure will appear dazed and engage in purposeless activity such as walking aimlessly, picking up objects, or picking at their clothes. Some individuals may start laughing, gesturing, or repeating a phrase. Whatever the person's particular pattern, the same pattern will usually be repeated with each seizure. In other words, if a child walks in a circle when having a complex partial seizure, then that is what his or her seizures are expected to look like each time one occurs.

Tonic-clonic seizures (formerly known as *grand mal* seizures) are typically what people think of when they hear that a person has a seizure disorder. This is a convulsive seizure in which the person loses consciousness and becomes very stiff. A person who is standing when the seizure occurs will drop to the floor and may sustain injuries from the fall. This stiffness is followed by a jerking phase in which the body makes rhythmic jerking motions that gradually decrease. During this phase, saliva may pool in the mouth and bubble at the lips. Breathing may become shallow or irregular. Usually there is a loss of bladder control. These seizures usually last between two and five minutes. After the seizure, the student may be slightly disoriented at first and not realize what has happened. The person is usually exhausted and will often sleep. There are many misconceptions of what to do when this type of seizure occurs. See the accompanying Suggestions for the Classroom for information on the steps to take when a tonic-clonic seizure occurs.

The most common treatment for seizures is medication. Other treatments may be used when the seizures are severe and cannot be controlled by medication, such as surgery on

Suggestions for the Classroom

Steps for Teachers to Take When a Tonic-Clonic Seizure Occurs

What to do

☑ Stay calm; note time of onset.

☑ Move furniture out of the way to prevent injury.

☑ Loosen shirt collar and put something soft under head.

☑ Turn student on his or her side to allow saliva to drain out of mouth.

☑ If seizure continues more than 5 minutes, or if multiple seizures occur one right after another, or if this is the first seizure, call for an ambulance.

☑ If seizure stops but the student is not breathing, give mouth-to-mouth resuscitation (this rarely occurs).

☑ After the seizure is over, reassure student.

☑ Allow student to rest.

What NOT to do

☑ Do not put anything in the mouth.

☑ Do not restrain movements.

☑ Do not give liquids immediately after seizure.

part of the brain, special diets, and electrical stimulation of the vagus nerve (Wilfogn, 2002). However, these treatments are not always effective and seizures may still occur.

It is important for teachers to know the steps to take when seizures happen. Often they will have a seizure information sheet to provide them with pertinent information. When a seizure occurs, teachers will often be asked to fill out a seizure report that describes what the seizure looked like, how long it lasted, and what treatment was given. The teacher will also need to be supportive of the child and try to minimize embarrassment (especially when there is a loss of bladder control). Often classmates will think seizures are contagious or their classmate is dead. It is important to help children understand that seizures are not contagious and to explain in simple terms what has happened.

2. **Asthma** Asthma is the most common pulmonary disease of childhood and is on the increase (American Lung Association, 2007). Children who have asthma breathe normally until they come in contact with a substance or situation that triggers an asthma attack, such as pollen, air pollution, a respiratory infection, or exercise. When an asthma attack is triggered, the person has difficulty breathing. Symptoms include shortness of breath, wheezing, coughing, and labored breathing.

Asthma is treated by avoiding triggers and taking medication. In some instances, triggers can be removed or reduced. For example, if being close to the classroom hamster triggers an attack, then the hamster should be removed or placed in a different location. If exercise is a trigger, the student may need some modifications in physical education class. Medication may be taken on a regular basis to decrease the possibility of an asthma attack. When an asthma attack occurs, the student often uses a prescribed inhaler (medication delivered in a spray form). It is important that the inhaler be used immediately if an attack occurs, so the inhaler needs to be readily accessible. If the student goes on a field trip, for example, the inhaler needs to go with him or her.

For most students, the asthma attack will stop once the inhaler is used. However, for some students, the inhaler will help but not stop the attack. It is very important that all school personnel know what steps to take should an asthma attack occur. Although it is rare for an asthma attack to be fatal, it is a possibility. If the student is experiencing severe respiratory problems, an ambulance should be called. When the asthma attack lasts for a long period of time (for example, several days), teachers will need to assist the student in completing missed work.

INFECTIOUS DISEASES Several infectious diseases fall under the heading of other health impairments. Some infectious diseases are readily transmittable (such as tuberculosis); others may pose no threat in the school environment (such as AIDS).

Acquired immune deficiency syndrome (AIDS) is one of the newest chronic illnesses of childhood. It is caused by the human immunodeficiency virus (HIV), which destroys the immune system, leaving the person open to serious, life-threatening diseases (such as pneumocystis carinii pneumonia). Transmission generally occurs in one of three ways: (1) having sex with an infected partner, (2) sharing contaminated needles during drug use, and (3) passing on the infection from mother to infant. It cannot be acquired through casual contact because it is only transmitted in blood, semen, vaginal secretions, and breast milk (Best & Heller, 2009a). Because it is not transmitted in saliva, even sharing toothbrushes or kissing will not transmit the infection.

Some students are born with the infection from an infected mother; adolescents may acquire the infection from sex with an infected partner or by sharing needles during drug use. Children born with the HIV virus may have developmental delays, motor problems, nervous system damage, and additional infections. Adolescents acquiring the disease may also develop life-threatening infections, nervous system abnormalities, and other impairments (such as visual impairments). Treatment consists of a combination of medications that may slow the disease's effect on the immune system. However, the disease is considered terminal in most cases.

Often children with AIDS will not initially need any modifications in the school setting. However, as the disease progresses, they will require some modifications because of fatigue and frequent absences. A supportive attitude should be in place, especially given the social stigma surrounding the disease. Misconceptions that students or teachers have should be dispelled with accurate information.

Characteristics of Students with Deaf-Blindness

Describing the characteristics of pupils with deaf-blindness is a difficult task. This is an extremely heterogeneous population varying tremendously in their needs, abilities, and educational requirements. Some consider deaf-blindness to be a spectrum disability (Brown & Bates, 2005) because of the enormous diversity exhibited by individuals who are deaf-blind.

As we stated at the beginning of this discussion, in addition to impaired hearing and vision, large numbers of students who are deaf and blind exhibit cognitive deficits (65%), physical impairments (58%), or complex health needs (41%) (National Consortium on Deaf-Blindness, 2007). Speech and language impairments are also typical of individuals who are deaf-blind.

Behavioral and social difficulties often accompany deaf-blindness. These deficits are frequently a result of the person's inability to understand language and effectively communicate with others (Miles, 2005). In addition to problems with communication, difficulties navigating the environment are also common. The restrictions and challenges represented by these two areas usually lead to feelings of isolation among children and adults who are deaf-blind.

Assessment of Physical Disabilities, Health Disabilities, and Related Low-Incidence Disabilities

In order to qualify for special education services, students with a physical or health disability need to have a thorough assessment. The assessment will determine whether they qualify for special education services, and which ones are needed. The assessment for initial eligibility typically involves a medical evaluation and a series of educational evaluations. Depending on the student's medical condition and school functioning, other assessments involving related services and assistive technology will need to be performed.

First and foremost, a student will need a medical evaluation by a licensed physician that provides a diagnosis of the student's physical or health condition. The medical evaluation will typically include important information such as medications, surgeries, special health care procedures, and special diet or activity restrictions. Any sensory deficits should also be noted.

Once a medical diagnosis confirms a physical or health disability, a determination needs to be made as to whether the disability negatively affects the student's educational performance. A comprehensive educational assessment (or for preschool children, a developmental assessment) will be performed to determine the effects of the physical or health disability. The precise educational assessment instruments will vary according to the student's age and abilities. Assessments will document deficits in areas such as preacademic functioning, academic functioning, adaptive behavior, motor development, language and communication skills, and social-emotional development.

A psychological evaluation may be given if there is a significant deficit in academic or cognitive functioning. However, it is often very difficult to evaluate cognitive functioning (possible mental retardation) when the student has severe physical disabilities and is unable to speak. This is especially the case when the student has not yet learned to use a communication device, or cannot do so reliably because of severe motor constraints. Psychological and educational misdiagnosis and misplacement do occur, as they did in the case of Natalie.

If the educational evaluations demonstrate that the student's physical or health disability is affecting his or her educational performance, a decision will be made as to which educational category the student qualifies for: orthopedic impairments, multiple disabilities, traumatic brain injury, or other health impairments. Additional assessments will be performed based on the medical and educational evaluations. If the physician orders physical or occupational therapy, for example, the student will need to have assessments in these areas. If the student qualifies for speech-language pathology services, assessments will occur in that area as well. If the student has a physical disability, an assistive technology assessment may be performed by the special education teacher in conjunction with the educational team, or the school system may have a specialist or team of specialists in that area. If the student requires specialized health care procedures, such as tube feeding, an individual health (or health care) plan will be developed, and the student will be assessed to determine if he or she can be taught to self-perform the procedure. Depending on the student's needs, other assessments may be performed to provide appropriate educational services to the student.

Assessment of Students with Deaf-Blindness

The low-incidence nature of deaf-blindness coupled with the scarcity of appropriate assessment instruments presents a unique set of challenges to teachers and other professionals (Silberman et al., 2004). Because children and adolescents with deaf-blindness evidence a wide range of unique needs, it is recommended that assessments be conducted by a transdisciplinary team across multiple environments, including school, home, and community settings (Engleman, Griffin, Griffin, & Maddox, 1999). Valid assessment of individuals with deaf-blindness dictates collaboration among family members and professionals. The goal is to obtain needed information that provides a representative portrait of the whole child without fragmenting the student's strengths and needs (Barraga & Erin, 2001). The key is to conduct multiple assessments over both time and contexts.

Unfortunately, norm-referenced assessments are of little value when assessing pupils with deaf-blindness. Criterion-referenced tests, developmental scales (frequently normed on children without disabilities), and informal observations often yield useful information. Even these assessment strategies, however, are not without their limitations (Engleman et al., 1999). Experts recommend that assessments focus on what the child *has* learned as well as what he or she *needs* to learn (Silberman et al., 2004). For young children with deaf-blindness developmental scales are often useful. The INSITE Developmental Checklist (Morgan, 1989) is one example of an assessment instrument appropriate for use with youngsters with dual sensory impairments and multiple disabilities. Older pupils are typically evaluated via tools that focus on desired outcomes of adulthood. The Functional Skills Screening Inventory (Becker, Schur, Paoletti-Schelp, & Hammer, 1983) is an example of an outcome-based assessment instrument appropriate for individuals age 8 through adulthood. Personal care, communication skills, work concepts, and community living are just some of the areas evaluated by this inventory.

Educational Considerations

Educational considerations for students with physical or health disabilities include the setting in which each student can receive an appropriate education, the impact of the physical or health disability on that student's school performance, and the best ways of meeting that student's needs in the educational setting. Each of these considerations will be discussed in turn.

Where Are Students with Physical or Health Disabilities Educated?

Students with physical and health disabilities are educated in a variety of settings. Settings can range from a regular classroom to a homebound/hospital setting, with several other settings in between (such as resource room, separate class, separate school, and residential facility). The appropriate setting is determined by the educational team, based on student assessments, educational goals, and planned interventions. For example, one student with cerebral palsy who is nonverbal may need special education services addressing reading and writing; this student may go to a resource room for the majority of the day to learn how to use an assistive technology device and receive specialized instruction. A second pupil with cerebral palsy may just need monitoring in regular education classes. A third student with cerebral palsy may be several grade levels behind across all areas; this individual may need to be in a separate class to meet his or her educational goals. Some children may have such severe health problems that homebound instruction is necessary; in this case, a teacher goes to the student's house to provide instruction.

Educational placement of students with physical and health disabilities varies greatly across the IDEA categories of orthopedic impairments, multiple disabilities, traumatic brain injury, other health impairments, and deaf-blindness (see Figure 13.4). The largest number of students with orthopedic impairments are educated in the regular classroom (49.3%), followed by a separate class (25.5%) and resource room (18.4%). This is not surprising, as most of this population does not have additional cognitive impairments. However, when the student's physical disability is severe, additional support is needed and may be provided in a resource room or separate class.

In contrast, the most common placement for students with multiple disabilities is a separate class (45.0%), followed by a separate school (20.0%), and then resource room (16.9%).

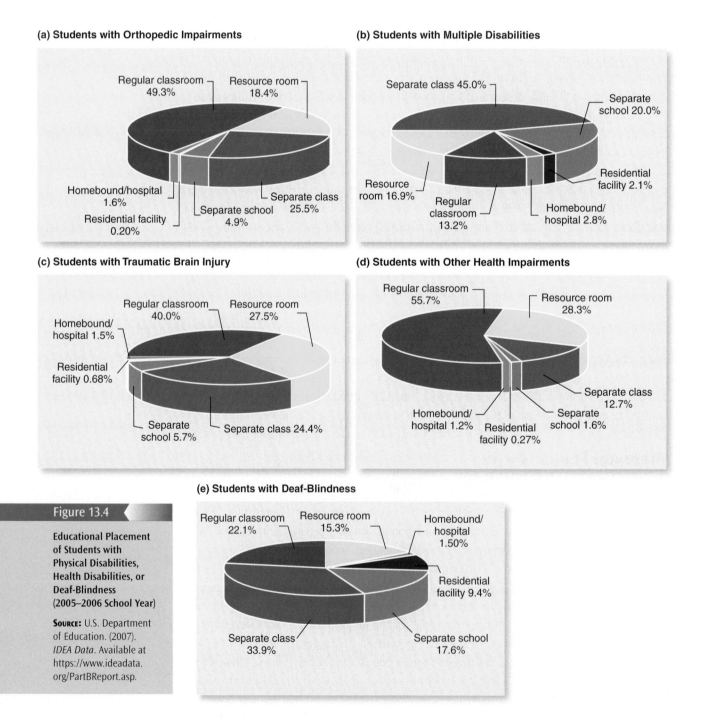

(a) Students with Orthopedic Impairments

(b) Students with Multiple Disabilities

(c) Students with Traumatic Brain Injury

(d) Students with Other Health Impairments

(e) Students with Deaf-Blindness

Figure 13.4

Educational Placement of Students with Physical Disabilities, Health Disabilities, or Deaf-Blindness (2005–2006 School Year)

Source: U.S. Department of Education. (2007). *IDEA Data.* Available at https://www.ideadata.org/PartBReport.asp.

Students with multiple disabilities often have severe physical disabilities with concomitant severe mental retardation. Although many states are trying to phase out separate schools, they remain part of the range of options available to students.

Students with traumatic brain injury vary greatly in the severity of injury and its effects on the individual. Four out of ten pupils with traumatic brain injury are served in the regular or general education classroom, with placement in a resource room (27.5%) or separate class (24.4%) about equally split. Functioning often improves during the first few years after injury, and the educational placement will typically change over a fairly short period of time.

Like pupils with orthopedic impairments, students with other health impairments are most likely to be educated in the regular classroom (55.7%). However, frequent absences, fatigue, inattention, pain, and other health-related factors often result in a need for placement in a resource room (28.3%) or separate class (12.7%).

At this time, individuals who are deaf-blind are often educated in more restrictive settings. Only about one out of five students (22.1%) is educated in the regular classroom, while approximately 50 percent of these pupils receive a special education in either a separate class (33.9%) or separate school (17.6%).

Impact on School Performance

Several variables affect school performance for a student with a physical or health disability according to the Physical and Health Disabilities Performance Model (Heller, 2009a). These variables can be divided into three major areas: type of disability, functional effects, and psychosocial and environmental factors (see Figure 13.5). Students with physical or health disabilities will typically have one or more problems in each of these major areas, and their interaction can negatively affect the students' school performance. A better understanding of these areas and how they affect each child's school performance will help the teacher and the educational team make appropriate decisions regarding educational objectives and necessary modifications.

TYPE OF DISABILITY The first major area to affect student performance is the type of disability. Pupils with orthopedic impairments, for example, will often have problems accessing materials while students with other health impairments are more likely to have problems of endurance and stamina. The severity of the specific disability will also be a factor. The teacher will need to be familiar with the student's specific disability, its severity, and its implications for academic performance.

FUNCTIONAL EFFECTS OF THE DISABILITY The second area that affects student performance is the functional effects of the disability on each particular student. As shown in Figure 13.5, this area is divided into seven categories: (1) atypical movements and motor abilities, (2) sensory loss, (3) communication impairments, (4) fatigue and lack of endurance, (5) health factors, (6) experiential deficits, and (7) cognitive impairments and processing issues (Heller, 2009a). The student's disability, its severity, and how it affects the particular student will determine which of these seven categories is a factor in affecting academic performance.

1. **Atypical Movements and Motor Abilities** The first category pertains to any atypical movements or limitations of movement of the limbs (arms and legs). A student whose disabilities limit the movement of arms, hands, and fingers may be unable to do school tasks involving writing or manipulating material without proper modifications. Even with modifications, performance may be affected. For example, a student who can only write using a computer with an adapted keyboard may only be able to write 15 words a minute and cannot write for long periods of time because of fatigue.

Figure 13.5

Physical and Health
Disabilities Performance
Model

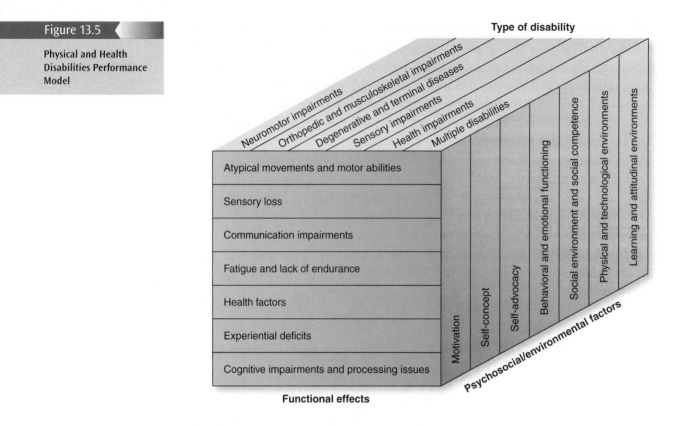

Functional effects

2. **Sensory Loss** Some physical disabilities will have a lack of sensation (for example, touch, temperature) affecting the arms or legs, which can subtly affect students' perception of items and certain concepts (for example, coldness of ice, smoothness of paper). In addition, there is an increased incidence of vision and hearing loss in many types of physical disabilities. Not being able to see an activity or hear what is being said will obviously impact student performance.

3. **Communication Impairments** When speaking is affected, students' performance can be severely affected. Questions may go unanswered, and teachers may have difficulty understanding students' responses. Students will typically use augmentative communication devices, but unless the students can spell, no augmentative communication device will have all the vocabulary needed to answer or ask questions. Also, it can take some time for students to learn to use their devices, during which time they will lose opportunities to communicate with others.

4. **Fatigue and Lack of Endurance** The fourth category of functional effects is fatigue and endurance. Some students with physical and health disabilities may experience fatigue and limited stamina, which affects their ability to concentrate and hence their school performance. In some instances, fatigue may be so severe that the child needs short rest breaks throughout the day, a rest period within the school day, or a shortened school day.

5. **Health Factors** The fifth category refers to various health issues associated with physical difficulties that can interfere with school performance. For example, some students may experience pain during the school day, such as a student with juvenile rheumatoid arthritis or a student with a poorly fitted artificial leg. A student who is experiencing pain or discomfort will be unable to attend fully to the lesson taught in class.

Other health factors include the side effects of medications (for example, fatigue from seizure medications) or absences and missed information ranging from a few seconds because of an absence seizure to days as a result of illness.

6. **Experiential Deficits** Some students with physical and health disabilities may lack experiences or concepts that are important to school performance. Students with severe physical disabilities may not have the same common experiences as their peers because of mobility or motor problems. For example, the pupil with physical disabilities may have never been to a movie theater, while in other instances a student may have an inaccurate concept because he or she is unable to manipulate an item (for example, believing that cotton balls are sticky). Teachers need to avoid making assumptions about the student's concepts or experiences. They need to assess the student's knowledge carefully and teach the missing information to the student.

7. **Cognitive Impairments and Processing Issues** The seventh category deals with learning issues. Students with physical and health disabilities often reach developmental milestones (such as sitting, standing, or walking) differently or more slowly than children without disabilities. Some children, such as those with cerebral palsy, have a higher incidence of mental retardation (Nehring, 2004). Some physical disabilities, such as spina bifida with hydrocephalus, are associated with problems in perception, motor planning, attention, memory, organization, impulsivity, hyperactivity, and sequencing (Lazzaretti & Pearson, 2004). Obviously, when these cognitive impairments and processing issues are present, performance will be affected. Various instructional strategies are needed to meet these students' learning needs.

PSYCHOSOCIAL AND ENVIRONMENTAL FACTORS The third major area that can affect school performance—the third dimension in Figure 13.5—consists of seven individual and environmental factors: (1) motivation, (2) self-concept, (3) self-advocacy, (4) behavioral and emotional functioning, (5) social environment and social competence, (6) physical and technological environments, and (7) learning and attitudinal environments (Heller, 2009a). Each of these is shaped by the student's personality, reaction to his or her disability, and the reactions of those in the student's environment.

1. **Motivation** How much a student is motivated in the school environment will typically affect performance. Although this varies across all students, there may be additional factors to consider for students with physical or health disabilities. For example, a student with Duchenne muscular dystrophy may become depressed over this terminal condition and not be as motivated to do schoolwork. In these instances, the student may need counseling and antidepressant therapy.

Lack of motivation may also be a product of others' reactions to the student. Sometimes teachers, peers, and parents do things for the student that the student is completely capable of doing, such as helping to feed the student or opening a door every time the student wheels up to it. This can result in **learned helplessness.** Learned helplessness is a lack of persistence at tasks that can be mastered. Students exhibiting learned helplessness have the capability to perform the particular task, but after repeated instances of others doing the task for him, the student waits for someone else to do the task for him rather than doing it himself. For example, if doors are always opened for the student using a wheelchair, he may passively wait for a door to be opened instead of learning to open it himself. It is critical to encourage students with physical or health disabilities to do everything they are capable of doing.

2. **Self-Concept** Children's self-concept can have an effect on performance. Self-concept refers to the general understanding and ideas we have about ourselves, and it is closely tied to self-esteem. As early as preschool, children with physical disabilities recognize they are different from others and can often associate the name of their disability with at least one of its effects (Dunn, McCartan, & Fuqua, 1988). Students with physical and health

impairments may feel like outsiders in everyday life; they may feel different, deprived, or unable to live like other children. Some children may feel guilt over their disability and feel they are a hindrance to other people. Students' reactions to their disability may result in feelings of isolation and unhappiness (Rydstrom, Englund, & Sandman, 1999). Some students may need assistance in learning to accept and cope with their disability. Teachers need to be alert for signs that a student may need this sort of help.

3. Self-Advocacy How well students are able to advocate for themselves can affect their performance. Students with disabilities should be taught from an early age what they need to succeed in the classroom and how to ask for it. Although the educational team and the special education teacher should assist the general education teacher in making modifications, some things can go unnoticed. For example, if the student with a physical disability is unable to move his head well and cannot see what is being written on the board, he should politely ask to be moved. Some children are shy, unwilling, or unable to ask for minor modifications. It is not unusual for children to sit through an entire class unable to see the board because of poor self-advocacy skills. Teachers should encourage students with physical or health impairments to inform them if something needs to be changed in order for them to access the material.

A lack of self-advocacy skills may not only result in missed learning and poorer school performance; it can be life-threatening. For example, a student with diabetes may need a snack; if it is forgotten and she says nothing, the result could be a life-threatening insulin reaction. Students need to learn about their particular disability, learn to tell others of their needs, and stand by what they know is correct.

4. Behavioral and Emotional Functioning Students may exhibit behavioral or emotional problems that interfere with school performance. Some students may have feelings of depression, anger, or hopelessness over their disability; a few individuals will have severe emotional and behavioral problems. It is important to be alert for these emotional problems, which can affect school performance. In some instances, behavior intervention programs or counseling will be needed.

5. Social Environment and Social Competence Some students may have delayed or maladaptive social functioning. Social interaction may be inhibited by the disability, as when the student lacks shared experiences because of severe physical disability or is unable to observe and model nonverbal interactions (eye contact, body position) because of a visual impairment (Sacks & Silberman, 2000). If students are unable to explain their disability, misconceptions and misunderstandings may lead to avoidance by peers. To help promote socialization, students need to be taught how to explain their disability to peers and be provided with social skills in addition to a positive social environment.

6. Physical and Technological Environments In order to optimize performance, environments need to be arranged so that pupils with physical and health disabilities can properly access them. The physical environment, including classrooms, needs to be arranged in such a way so as to allow the student to maneuver easily (for example, widened aisles to accommodate an individual in a wheelchair). In addition, appropriate assistive technology should be available and accessible so that the student can participate fully in classroom activities.

7. Learning and Attitudinal Environments Finally, performance may be affected by an ineffective learning environment or negative attitudes toward the student. An ineffective learning environment is the direct result of the way the teacher sets up the teaching/learning situation and interacts with the pupil. Students with physical and health impairments

Classrooms, and other environments, must be arranged so as to allow ease of access for students with physical and health disabilities.

typically need several modifications in order to learn. When teachers are not responsive to these students' needs, they will typically do poorly in class. Special education teachers need to work with general education teachers in a team effort to make the necessary modifications.

Meeting Educational Needs

Meeting the educational needs of students with physical or health disabilities requires several types of modifications. These will be discussed under four main headings: (1) physical/ health monitoring, (2) modifications and adaptations, (3) specialized instructional strategies, and (4) specialized expanded curriculum areas.

PHYSICAL/HEALTH MONITORING It is the responsibility of teachers and school officials to maintain a safe, healthy environment for their students (DPHD Critical Issues and Leadership Committee, 1999; Heller, Fredrick, Best, Dykes, & Cohen, 2000). Maintaining a safe, healthy environment includes having efficient evacuation plans, school emergency procedures, proper infection control procedures, and teachers trained in CPR and first aid.

Teachers must know what type of medical condition each student has, how to monitor the student's physical or health impairment for problems, and what to do if a problem occurs. For example, if a student has a generalized tonic-clonic seizure, the teacher should have a plan in place and be able to immediately assist the student. In this example, immediate action is needed. Some monitoring may be more subtle, such as picking up signs that the student with muscular dystrophy is deteriorating and may need further modifications.

MODIFICATIONS AND ADAPTATIONS Several modifications and adaptations may be needed to assure that students with physical or health impairments are getting what they need to succeed in school. Major areas of concern include environmental arrangement, communication, instructional and curricular modifications, modifications and assistive technology for specific content areas, class participation, assignments and classroom tests, and sensory and perceptual modifications.

Often the special education teacher completes a checklist of needed modifications for each student with a physical or health disability and then discusses it with the general education teacher and other school personnel. Using a checklist helps assure that a variety of modifications have been considered and that everyone is using the same modifications across environments.

1. Environmental Arrangements Several types of environmental modifications may be needed to accommodate a student with a physical or health impairment. Fatigue or endurance issues may necessitate a modified day, rest breaks, or classrooms in close proximity. A student with very severe health issues may need a homeroom near an exit for easy access to an ambulance. In the classroom, a student may need widened aisles for wheelchair access or preferential seating in order to see the teacher or the board. In some cases, the student will need a special chair or desk to accommodate physical limitations. A student with restricted or impaired arm movement may need classroom materials to be positioned in a certain location or stabilized so they do not roll around.

2. Communication Most students with physical and health disabilities will not need any adaptations in the area of communication. However, students with conditions such as severe cerebral palsy will often have speech that is not understandable. In our chapter opener, Natalie was able to communicate approximately 30 words or sounds that could mean about 150 to 200 different things depending on the context. Her use of an augmentative communication device opened up her world by allowing others to understand her.

It is very important that the teacher understand how the student communicates and how the teacher should present questions. Augmentative communication devices, for example, may range from a notebook with pictures to electronic devices with voice output, and may be used along with various sounds or words that the student can say. However, some students may not be able to use their communication device very reliably when they are still learning how to use it. The teacher may be instructed to ask questions giving answers in a multiple-choice format when calling on these students. For example, the teacher may ask the class, "On which mountain did the expedition take place?" Susan, a student with severe cerebral palsy, indicates she knows the answer. The teacher calls on her and asks, "Susan, is it (a) Mt. Rainier, (b) Annapurna, (c) Mt. St. Helens, or (d) Mt. Everest?" Upon hearing the correct one, Susan points to the "D" on her board to indicate her answer. The best way for communication to take place in the classroom setting will be discussed between the special and general education teachers and, once agreed upon, recorded on the modification checklist.

3. Instructional and Curricular Modifications Often students with physical and health disabilities will require instructional and curricular modifications. Modifications in this area may include providing a study outline, extra repetition, or more frequent feedback. Students with physical disabilities who have speech impairments are often behind in their reading and may require material at a lower grade level. This may involve providing outlines at a reading level that the student can understand or using alternate textbooks that are easier to follow. Sometimes individual instruction from a special education teacher will be needed. Materials may need to be altered for accessibility (such as a larger calculator with bigger keys), and the curriculum may need to be altered to address the student's educational needs. Some students may need help with organizational skills, and others may need two sets of books because they are not physically capable of carrying their books back and forth between home and school.

4. **Modifications and Assistive Technology for Specific Content Areas** Often students will require modifications or assistive technology to access different school subjects. For example, to make a computer accessible for writing, some students with cerebral palsy may need to use a larger keyboard with bigger keys to correctly select the one they want. A student with a spinal cord injury may access the keyboard by using a voice recognition program in which the words appear on the screen as the student speaks into a microphone. In Natalie's case, she needed to use her augmentative communication device as a keyboard that connected to the computer in order to write.

5. **Class Participation** Some modifications may be needed to allow a student with a physical or health disability to participate in class. It is important to determine how the student will gain the teacher's attention, especially if he is unable to raise his hand. Some students may need extra time to respond to a question in class because of motor difficulties using an augmentative communication system. Some teachers will patiently wait for the response. Others may elect to give the student some questions that will be asked the next day in class so the student can program his or her augmentative communication device with the answers. For some students, it is more appropriate to ask questions using a multiple-choice format, as described previously.

6. **Assignments and Tests** Some students will need assignments and tests modified because of fatigue and endurance issues—either because of a health problem or because of the physical effort involved in slowly completing an assignment or test. Assignments may need to be abbreviated or broken up into shorter segments, or students may need extra time to complete assignments and tests. A student may be offered alternate ways to complete an assignment or test, such as using a computer or telling the answers instead of writing them. Students may be unable to complete several essay questions because of the time and effort it takes to complete one question; a student with severe spastic quadriplegia cerebral palsy, for example, may take twenty minutes to type two sentences when using an alternate access mode for a computer. In these cases, the student may be given an alternate format such as multiple choice or short answer.

7. **Other Modifications** Some students may need modifications or assistance in the areas of mobility, bathrooming, and eating. If a party is given in class, the teacher needs to know if a student needs a special spoon or a special feeding technique. If a student needs to use the restroom, the teacher needs to know if the student cannot get onto the toilet without help. Advanced planning is necessary to determine what type of help a student needs and who will provide that help.

SPECIALIZED INSTRUCTIONAL STRATEGIES   Teachers need to know how to implement **specialized instructional strategies** for students with physical and health disabilities. Such strategies include using special techniques for teaching nonverbal students phonics, adapting assessment procedures, utilizing the student's reliable means of response, using alternative approaches for learning the writing process when alternate-access keyboarding is slow, and supporting chronically ill and terminally ill students. For example, when teaching students with severe speech and physical impairments to sound out a word, the special education teacher may use the Nonverbal Reading Approach (Heller, 2005a; Heller, Fredrick, Tumlin, & Brineman, 2002), which teaches the student who cannot talk to sound out the word using internal speech. Certain math algorithms that do not involve carrying a number may be advantageous for students using computers to write out their work (Heller, 2005b). The special

Making Inclusion Work

My inspiration and passion for teaching special education stems from a lifetime of experience: growing up with a sister with severe cerebral palsy who spent time in many different programs in the school system. I began my professional career teaching in a K–1 class for students with moderate, severe, and profound intellectual disabilities after graduating with a degree in Mental Retardation Education. After four years in that setting, I completed my master's degree in Orthopedic Impairments (OI) and have been teaching OI at the high school level ever since. Five out of my seven high school students are fully included in the general curriculum and are college or career bound. The other two students are partially included in the general elective curriculum. I am currently working on my PhD in Orthopedic Impairments and Assistive Technology.

Inclusive Education Experience

In most cases, I favor inclusive education for students whose primary disability is physical. It is much easier to justify making physical modifications and accommodations for access to the general curriculum than it is to justify removing students due to modification and accessibility difficulties. Many different models exist for including students, ranging from intermittent checkups with the teacher to random student observations to having full-time assistance from either the OI teacher or a paraprofessional. Using an inclusion model allows teachers to collaborate, problem-solve, and inspire each other creatively. It also exposes teachers and students to a variety of teaching and learning styles. Because of multiple needs in the classroom, information is often explained in a variety of ways, and information is often presented through different modalities. Many students shine when they are given access to experiences they have not had before because of their physical limitations. Classmates are given the opportunity to look past the students' physical limitations and see their capabilities. The benefits for all students in the inclusive environment are reciprocal.

I have often run into lowered expectations and skepticism about the OI students' abilities. This is when it is necessary to get into the classroom and prove students' capabilities. The negativity usually doesn't last long. Another problem arises when OI students in inclusive environments use assistive technology. Although AT often equalizes access, it can be tremendously frustrating as well. Some of the most common initial problems with inclusive OI are the general education teachers' fears of not being supported, not knowing how to interact or communicate with the student, or concerns over assistive technology use. Associated medical problems education teacher often uses these specialized approaches when teaching students with physical or health disabilities and will instruct other teachers regarding their use.

Teachers also need to know how to implement specialized strategies to prevent **communication breakdowns**. Often teachers and students who are using augmentative communication devices will have a communication breakdown—a misunderstanding or misinterpretation of what is being communicated. Heller and Bigge (2005) provide an example of a student (S) who was telling about a party at school, including the refreshments, activities, and people invited. The Boy Scout master (BSM) listened to the details and said, "You must have enjoyed that."

S: No.

BSM: You didn't?

S: No.

can be intimidating as well. One way to overcome these problems is through education, training, and modeling by the OI teacher.

Strategies for Inclusive Classrooms

A good schedule can make it or break it, so scheduling is first and foremost. Schedule your students to allow for the most support from you. This might mean manipulating everyone's schedule multiple times. It is imperative that the lines of communication between collaborating teachers are two-way. It is the responsibility of the special education teacher to communicate the specific needs of the students in the class to the general education teacher. It is not solely the general education teacher's responsibility to provide instruction. Here are some helpful hints:

Provide the general education teacher with IEP-driven modifications and strategies for success as well as emergency plans. Encourage the general education teacher to keep these strategies and plans in his/her gradebook or other high-use area for quick reference.

Discuss expectations of the student and each teacher or paraprofessional supporting the student before beginning collaborative teaching.

Successful Collaboration

Successful collaboration means that the teachers have developed a good, professional working relationship and that all students have been enriched by the collaborative activities. This begins with open communication and effective planning. The structure of the class typically comes from the classroom teacher, and modifications and individualization are provided by

the OI teacher in the class. It is important, however, for both teachers to be able to switch roles and interact with all students in the class.

Working with Parents and Families

I have had the unique advantage of being on both sides: family and school system. As difficult as it might be, encourage the family to plan for the future early. Along with the parents, define realistic expectations for the students and strive to meet them. Parents know their children better than anyone. Listen to them and be sensitive to their needs. Establish how you will communicate with the parents regarding timelines, grades, progress, and parent–teacher conferences.

Advice for Making Inclusion and Collaboration Work

Transitioning into teaching in the OI classroom can be overwhelming. Teachers are always multitasking, supporting multiple students with multiple disabilities across multiple subjects in the same classroom at the same time. Trying to keep up with the pace of regular education while trying to work in extended time, technology, individualization, and physical access can be a vast undertaking. The best advice is to stay organized and stay focused on the needs of the students and on providing the best education in the most productive and appropriate learning environment possible.

—Jennifer Tumlin
Wheeler High School, Marietta, Georgia
9th through 12th grades, Orthopedic Impairments

BSM: But you told me all about it. Did something bad happen?

S: No.

BSM: But you didn't enjoy it?

S: No.

BSM: Well, you did go, didn't you?

S: No.

BSM: You didn't! Why not? Were you somewhere else?

S: No.

BSM: Were you ill?

S: No.

BSM: I don't get it, then. (p. 272)

✓ **EFFECTIVE INSTRUCTIONAL PRACTICES** | **Teaching Students with Physical or Health Disabilities**

Recommended Classroom Adaptations

Students with physical and health disabilities often require adaptations to accommodate their specific disabilities. This can include adaptations to the environment, instructional materials, and teaching strategies. Some effective practices are as follows:

- Make classroom adaptations to accommodate students' mobility and seating needs (e.g., widened aisles for wheelchairs, sit near side of room to see board and access computer, special desk).
- Use and properly arrange adaptations and assistive technology as determined by the special education teacher and educational team to provide access to the learning environment (e.g., slant board and stabilization of material on desk, alternate keyboard, augmentative communication device, books and worksheets scanned into the computer).
- Assist students with physical disabilities to participate as much as possible in classroom activities requiring a motor response (e.g., bring needed items to student, help student manipulate materials, partner student with peer to assist each other with task).
- Use a variety of systematic instructional strategies that effectively address the student's individual learning needs (e.g., learning strategies, content enhancement strategies, antecedent prompts, response prompts).
- Use specialized instructional strategies specifically developed for students with physical disabilities as appropriate (e.g., teach students who are nonverbal to use internal speech to decode words as in the Nonverbal Reading Approach).
- Assist students who use augmentative forms of communication to learn to use their communication devices successfully across learning and social environments during the school day. Also, allow students to answer questions using their most reliable form of communication.
- Allow more time for student to respond, take tests, or hand in assignments when oral or written communication is affected by the disability.
- Modify assignments or tests to accommodate student's disability (e.g., reduce paper tasks, break up assignments into shorter segments, alternate test or assignment format).
- Maintain a safe, healthy environment by observing for health-related problems and knowing the steps to take should a problem occur (e.g., seizure, fatigue, medication side effects).

Source: Adapted from K. Heller and M. Coleman-Martin, "Classroom Adaptations for Students with Physical, Health, and Multiple Disabilities," in K. W. Heller, P. E. Forney, P. A. Alberto, S. Best, and M. N. Schwartzman (Eds.), *Understanding Physical, Health, and Multiple Disabilities*, 2nd ed. (Upper Saddle River, NJ: Pearson Education, 2009).

In this example, the student was trying to tell the Boy Scout master about a party that his class had planned, but that had not yet taken place. The Boy Scout master assumed that the party had already occurred.

Several strategies can be used to avoid a communication breakdown. The first is to be aware that you may be making an erroneous assumption that is leading to the breakdown. It is important to clarify or check each part of the information as it is being presented ("We are talking about a party?" "Yes." "At school?" "Yes." "That your class had?" "No.") Another strategy is to ask, "Am I missing something?" and then ask by categories, "Is it a person?" "A place?" "A feeling?" "A time?" and so on. It is also important to verify by asking, "Is that exactly right?" This will help assure that you are understanding the message correctly. It is equally important that the student have a way of saying, "You are not understanding my message" (Heller & Bigge, 2005).

SPECIALIZED EXPANDED CURRICULUM AREAS The IEP team will determine the appropriate goals for a student with a physical or health disability. In some cases, a student will be on a regular academic curriculum; in others, a student with mental retardation may be in a functional curriculum. In either case, students may also be taught additional curricular areas, referred to as *specialized expanded curriculum areas*. These areas often pertain to the technology they use, the adaptations they will need for independent living, and the health care they need because of their particular physical or health disability. For example, students may be taught to use their assistive technology and augmentative communication devices. Students who require health care procedures (such as tube feeding for nutrition) may be taught how to do the procedure themselves, along with other management issues related to the procedure (Heller & Tumlin, 2004). Independent living skills (such as cooking, cleaning, shopping, and dressing) often require adaptations, and students may be taught how to perform these tasks with the necessary modifications. Other possible specialized expanded curriculum areas include social skills, vocational skills, community skills, mobility skills, and leisure skills.

Meeting the Educational Needs of Students Who Are Deaf-Blind

Pupils who are deaf-blind frequently present a variety of instructional challenges for educators. The impact of the loss (or diminished capacity) of both vision and hearing result in significant educational needs. The consequences of this disability are much greater than simply adding up the effects of the individual sensory losses (Silberman et al., 2004). As a result, communication needs and navigation of the environment are typically the focus of attention for these students.

Individuals with deaf-blindness require highly individualized and specialized instruction, often on a one-to-one basis (Bowe, 2005). Direct teaching is also frequently required because, unlike other pupils (with and without disabilities), incidental learning is severely limited because of the loss of the distance senses of vision and hearing. Most students who are deaf-blind use their residual vision or hearing to learn. Those who totally lose vision and hearing (a minority of pupils) learn through the sense of touch, in which "their hands become their eyes" (Silberman et al., 2004, p. 506). Other senses such as taste and smell are also used to learn about the environment (Prickett & Welch, 1998).

Like other students, the education of pupils with deaf-blindness addresses all domains of learning. Communication/language, however, is typically the priority subject for these children. "Without the ability to communicate other curriculum areas become meaningless" (Engleman et al., 1999, p. 65). Information gleaned from both formal and informal assessments is often used to establish areas of instructional emphasis as well as suggest teaching strategies (Silberman et al., 2004).

COMMUNICATION Learning to communicate without the ability to hear is probably the most significant challenge that students with deaf-blindness will encounter. Yet it is also their greatest opportunity—for language opens the world to them (Alabama Institute for Deaf and Blind, 2007). Pupils who are deaf-blind vary tremendously in their communication abilities and consequently their educational needs. Recall that many of these children have some residual hearing and vision, and a few are capable of speech. In many instances, however, touch, gestures, and body movements are the primary form of communication, although some individuals will learn more complex forms of communication such as sign language. Conventional literacy skills often fail to develop in individuals with deaf-blindness, and language acquisition typically lags behind that of their peers (Engleman et al., 1999).

Because communication is critical to all activities at school, at home, and in the community, it is imperative that the pupil develop an effective and efficient system of communication. This may entail acquiring tactile means of receptive and expressive communication or developing the student's residual vision and hearing for purposes of communication. There are multiple forms of communication available to both teachers and parents. For instance, if vision is sufficient, some students who are deaf-blind will use the standard manual alphabet (see Figure 11.7, page 421). However, if the pupil's vision is inadequate, the alphabet can be traced in the palm of the individual's hand.

Some of the principal communication systems used with individuals who are deaf-blind include

- touch cues
- object symbols
- multiple versions of sign language
- Braille
- fingerspelling
- picture symbols
- large print
- Tadoma method of speechreading
- speechreading (Miles, 2005)

It is crucial that teachers, paraprofessionals, interpreters, **interveners**, and parents/family members incorporate as many of the communication systems as possible so that the child will have maximum access to the largest possible array of expressive and receptive modes of communication (Engleman et al., 1999). Table 13.3 presents additional information on some of these nonlinguistic communication forms.

As the student gains competency with nonverbal interactions, symbolic communication becomes a frequent adjunct to the student's system of communication. It is often beneficial to incorporate simple gestures or objects that serve as representations or symbols for various

Table 13.3	Representative Nonlinguistic Communication Systems
Intentional Behavior	Student is taught very deliberate actions to indicate a particular preference—an effort by the teacher to avoid confusing choice-making behavior from random movements.
Touch Cues	Minimal prompt used to convey information to a learner who is deaf-blind. Two taps on the shoulder, for example, tells the pupil to stand up.
Communication Shelves	This tactic helps bring a sense of order into the world of children with deaf-blindness. Placing items in a specific order on a shelf teaches the student that activities have a definite beginning and an end in addition to the concepts of time and sequence. Organizational skills are also aided.
Signals and Gestures	Body signs and other tactual cues indicating desired behaviors, such as reaching for or pushing away a particular object or pulling a person toward a desired location.
Sign Language	An alternative to spoken language. Multiple forms of this system are available, with American Sign Language (ASL) considered the natural language of persons who are deaf. (For additional information, revisit Chapter 11 on hearing impairments.)
Tadoma	In this mode of communication the individual places his or her thumb on the speaker's lips and his or her fingers along the jaw line, touching the speaker's cheek and throat while monitoring the particular movements and actions associated with speech.

Source: Adapted from M. Engleman, H. Griffin, L. Griffin, and J. Maddox, "A Teacher's Guide to Communicating with Students with Deaf-Blindness," *Teaching Exceptional Children, 31*(5), 1999, p. 69.

activities. For example, a spoon may indicate mealtime, a small rubber ball could represent recess, and a sweater might mean dismissal time. These representations help the pupil understand that one thing may represent another while also enabling the child to anticipate specific events. Reliable routines are particularly important to individuals who are deaf-blind. Consistency aids in reducing anxiety, helping the child feel secure, and increasing predictability. Unexpected or unanticipated events, such as the absence of a paraprofessional or a fire drill prior to lunch, need to be communicated as quickly as possible to minimize confusion and fearfulness (Engleman et al., 1999; Miles, 2005).

ORIENTATION AND MOBILITY Being able to safely and independently navigate the environment (at school, at home, and in the community) is another major area of emphasis for individuals who are deaf-blind. Mobility training becomes a significant instructional challenge for the orientation and mobility (O&M) specialist when the student exhibits a dual sensory impairment. In some instances, a lack of motivation to explore the world coupled with difficulty in establishing an effective means of communication are but two of the obstacles confronting this professional. Generally speaking, the earlier the instruction begins, the greater the likelihood that the pupil will be able to successfully move about with confidence and independence.

COLLABORATIVE EFFORTS It should be obvious from our discussion of these two key areas that multiple professionals are involved in the education of persons with deaf-blindness. It is not unusual to find vision teachers, O&M specialists, interpreters, physical and occupational therapists, and other professionals all working together to ensure that the individual needs of the pupil are fully met in an integrated and coordinated fashion. The needs of students with deaf-blindness far exceed the skills and knowledge of any one professional (Silberman et al., 2004). Collaboration, therefore, is imperative. Collaborative efforts also enhance the prospect of success in inclusive learning communities (Hudson, 1997).

Services for Young Children with Physical Disabilities, Health Disabilities, and Related Low-Incidence Disabilities

As with school-age children, young children with physical disabilities, health disabilities, and related low-incidence disabilities typically need a collaborative approach utilizing expertise from a variety of disciplines. Professional staff such as physical therapists, occupational therapists, speech-language pathologists, special education teachers, preschool teachers, adapted physical education teachers, nurses, and physicians, as well as families, may be involved in the education of the young child with physical or health disabilities. This team of individuals will determine the major goals and objectives for the young child, including a safe and healthy environment, motor development and positioning, communication development, concept development, and early academic and functional skills.

Maintaining a safe, healthy environment involves special considerations for the young child. Young children may not understand why they have certain restrictions (such as no sweets if they have diabetes) or the exact nature of their disability (what is happening when they have a seizure, and why). The teacher needs to understand what restrictions are necessary and help the young child comply with them. Also, some young children may have the misconception that they have a particular condition because they did something bad. The teacher should be alert for such misconceptions and notify the parents.

Children with physical disabilities, multiple disabilities, and deaf-blindness often show delays or little progress in motor development—rolling over, sitting, crawling, walking, reaching for items, grasping items—and may receive the services of a physical therapist and an occupational therapist. These professionals can provide positioning suggestions and equipment, mobility devices, adaptive toys, devices for daily living (such as adapted feeding utensils and toothbrushes), and orthotics (such as leg braces). They may suggest changes in the environment to eliminate architectural barriers as they seek to integrate therapy intervention strategies into the child's daily routines (Effgen, 2005). Teachers will often integrate some of the therapy goals and objectives into the preschool classroom.

When young children with physical disabilities have communication problems, one of the major emphases of early intervention is to promote communication. It is often difficult to determine if a child will be understandable using speech or if the child will require an augmentative communication system. To encourage communication and decrease frustration, augmentative communication may be combined with speech therapy, giving the child a means of communicating while also working on speech production.

Some parents may not want their child to use augmentative communication for fear that it will interfere with speech production and reduce their child's motivation to speak. Augmentative communication is never meant to replace speech, but to supplement it. There are no data to support the idea that AAC interferes with speech production; in fact, studies indicate that augmentative communication often increases speech production. A review of more than 100 studies indicated that at least 40 percent of children using augmentative communication increased their speech production (Silverman, 1995).

Because many young children with physical disabilities, health disabilities, and related low-incidence disabilities lack common experiences or the ability to manipulate common items, teachers will often need to work on concept development. Although concept development (for example, round versus square, colors) is typically addressed with the preschool child, even more basic concepts may need to be addressed with the child with a severe physical disability. Concepts such as "an orange is soft, not hard like a rock," or "a sponge can be squeezed" may need to be introduced. Failure to address these basic concepts can interfere with comprehension of material that will be addressed later in the school curriculum.

Children with physical disabilities, health disabilities, and related low-incidence disabilities will be participating in all or part of the preschool curriculum, and it is important that appropriate adaptations and modifications be in place. For coloring and drawing, for example, the child may need an adapted crayon or may begin using a simple drawing program on a computer. The special education teacher, with input from other members of the educational team, will assist in determining the appropriate modifications and assistive technology.

Transition into Adulthood

As students with physical disabilities, health disabilities, and related low-incidence disabilities transition into adulthood, they often face major decisions regarding college, employment, and independent living. Hopefully, these issues have been discussed for many years with preparations made well in advance to make a smooth transition from high school to the next environment. Through the help of transition planning, legislation, technological advances, and options for support, more opportunities now exist for individuals with physical and health disabilities than ever before.

With the passage of PL 101-476, each adolescent's IEP is required to include a **transition plan.** A transition plan identifies goals specific to that student aimed at meeting the student's needs after high school. Identification of transition needs and services is part of the planning process. Effective transition planning requires a joint effort among the family, student, school personnel, and adult service providers. Successful implementation of the transition plan will ideally result in a smooth transition to a good job/employment opportunity, a desirable residential placement, a positive socialization situation, and a high quality of life (Blacher, 2001).

Career preparation should occur throughout students' school years. Some students will be preparing to go on to vocational school, community college, or university before seeking employment. Others will seek employment after finishing high school. Individuals with disabilities may use one of several vocational education service delivery programs, including secondary vocational education, secondary special needs vocational education, postsecondary vocational and technical education, apprenticeship programs, and vocational rehabilitation programs (Sitlington & Clark, 2006).

Vocational education is important for some adolescents with physical or health disabilities.

Students who are able to go to college, and who decide to do so, may find it very stressful to leave familiar surroundings and supports. However, colleges and universities typically offer services for individuals with physical and health disabilities to assist them with accommodations and accessibility issues. Other modifications, such as modified test taking or assignment adjustments, will also be addressed through these college and university services for individuals with disabilities. It is important in the high school years that students learn to be self-advocates and learn how to find and use available resources to make the appropriate accommodations.

Technology has made more jobs than ever before accessible for individuals with physical and health disabilities. Many jobs today are computer based, and individuals with severe physical and health disabilities can often work in these fields by adapting the computer to meet their specific needs. Modifications may be quite simple, such as having the keyboard placed in a different position for easy access or using a software program that provides a keyboard on the screen to be accessed with a joystick. Many other job opportunities are possible with often minor modifications. A willingness to figure out what is necessary to make a job possible and following through with appropriate modifications is critical for success.

Some individuals with physical disabilities, health disabilities, and related low-incidence disabilities who are unable to work in competitive employment may benefit from **supported employment** or other employment models. In supported employment, the person with a disability works in the regular work setting and becomes a regular employee; however, training and continued support are necessary. A **job coach** (or job specialist) provides on-the-job assistance to the person with a disability. Often individuals who will benefit from this model have also received community-based vocational instruction during high school with a job coach. This previous training can help a student learn important job skills and also acquaints the student with a supported employment model.

It is difficult to predict the employment outlook for individuals with physical disabilities, health disabilities, or related low-incidence disabilities. When the physical or health disability is mild, it may not interfere with employment opportunities. However, students with mild physical or health disabilities may have inappropriate social behaviors or poor work habits that make finding and keeping a job difficult without further training. Students who have severe physical disabilities will be unable to do many physically demanding jobs, but if they have normal cognitive functioning, they may be able to perform intellectually based jobs with the use of assistive technology. However, students with severe physical disabilities still face major barriers to employability, such as mobility issues, difficulty communicating, bathroom assistance, and mealtime assistance (Bowe, 2000). These problems, among others, contribute to a significant underemployment rate for individuals with cerebral palsy and other severe physical disabilities (Clark & Bigge, 2005; Wehman, 2006) as well as those with deaf-blindness and multiple disabilities.

Adults with Physical Disabilities, Health Disabilities, and Related Low-Incidence Disabilities

Many adults with physical disabilities, health disabilities, and related low-incidence disabilities will make a positive transition into adulthood and be integrated into work and community environments. Their success will depend partly on community acceptance, as well as on the provision of necessary accommodations and support. With these kinds of disabilities, having appropriate medical and technological support will also be critical in assuring a high quality of life.

The impact of a physical or health disability in the adult years will vary greatly, depending on the specific impairment, its prognosis, and possible complications. Many individuals who have mild physical or health disabilities may experience only minor problems resulting from their disability. At the other extreme, individuals who have a terminal illness (Duchenne muscular dystrophy, AIDS, cystic fibrosis) may die in their early adult years, or not even survive to adulthood. Many other adults, such as those with cerebral palsy, may experience complications and multiple health issues, such as scoliosis (curvatures of the spine) and contractures, further limiting movement and mobility and resulting in pain. Multiple surgeries may be needed to address these types of musculoskeletal problems.

Some problems that occur in adults with physical disabilities can be prevented. A shocking lack of preventive medical care (general medical checkups, dental care) has been found among adults with cerebral palsy. As a result, adults with cerebral palsy are more susceptible to medical problems that could have been prevented or treated in their early stages. Providing preventive and appropriate medical care is key to adult health.

Family Issues

Families with children who have physical disabilities, health disabilities, or related low-incidence disabilities can be put under tremendous stress. Sources of stress include juggling the demands of the disability and ongoing medical treatment, dealing with uncertainties about the child's future health and independence, financial strains, lack of respite care, routine changes and disruptions, and overall exhaustion (Murphy, Christian, Caplin, &

Young, 2007). For example, the young woman in our chapter opener has been to more than seventy-three doctors, therapists, and rehabilitation engineers, involving countless appointments, medications, and treatments, as well as thirteen surgeries. This is not unusual for a family that has a child with a severe physical disability.

Stress can also result from the additional care and daily activities that may need to be performed for the child. Absences from school because of illness, surgeries, and medical treatments may add stress when one of the parents needs to stay home (or in the hospital) with the child. Day to day, the child may need help with such basic tasks as eating, toileting, and obtaining desired items. Some children will require regular medical treatments at home (such as respiratory physical therapy to decrease respiratory secretions) or at a clinic (such as dialysis).

Stress may be associated with the type of physical or health impairment as well as its prognosis. Higher stress has been found in parents of children with degenerative diseases such as Duchenne muscular dystrophy than in parents of children with chronic illness such as cystic fibrosis (Barakat & Kazak, 1999). Both of these conditions are terminal, so issues of death and dying also arise. Some debilitating disabilities require extensive family support. Some families will provide lifetime care for a child with a severe physical or health disability.

Despite the added stress, most families are able to manage the demands of having a child with a physical or health disability with the child being a valued, loved, and contributing member of the family. Many factors contribute to the family's coping ability, including support from concerned others, positive family appraisal, spiritual support, advocacy, positive social interactions, education and information, parental involvement that enhances a sense of control, and consistency in the medical care of the child (Lin, 2000; Turnbull, Turnbull, Erwin, & Soodak, 2006). Teachers can help families by being supportive, helping parents be an active part of the IEP team, and not being judgmental toward the parents.

Issues of Diversity

Physical disabilities, health disabilities, and related low-incidence disabilities occur in students from all backgrounds, cultures, and economic levels. Unlike other disabilities, such as mental retardation and learning disabilities, there are no questions regarding misclassification and culture bias in identification of a physical or health disability. However, misunderstanding can result from cultural differences in how the disability is viewed and miscommunication between parents and school.

Different families cope with illness and disability in diverse ways, and some are influenced by their particular culture. For example, some Hmong view epilepsy as a sign of distinction that could qualify them for the divine office of shaman (Fadiman, 1997). More often the cultural influences are subtler.

Misunderstandings can occur between the school and family as a result of cultural differences. In one study (Geenen, Powers, & Lopez-Vasquez, 2001), for example, culturally and linguistically diverse parents described themselves as being very involved in the transition process while school officials reported far less involvement. This discrepancy can be explained by these parents' heavy involvement in talking with their children about life after high school and caring for their disability, but lack of participation in the school-based transition process. Many of these families viewed transitioning a student into adulthood as a family and community responsibility rather than an educational one. Understanding and respecting cultural differences is important to providing positive educational experiences for the student.

Technology and Individuals with Physical Disabilities, Health Disabilities, and Related Low-Incidence Disabilities

Technology encountered in the school setting can be grouped into five major categories: technology productivity tools, information technology, instructional technology, medical technology, and assistive technology (Lindsey, 2008). Most students, whether they have disabilities or not, will use **technology productivity tools** (such as computers), **information technology** (such as the World Wide Web), and **instructional technology** (such as software programs teaching multiplication or map skills). In addition to these forms of technology, students with physical or health impairments will often require medical and assistive technology.

Many students with physical or health impairments require medical technology to sustain life and functionality. Medical technology devices can range from battery-powered artificial limbs that restore movement to individuals who have lost an arm or leg to pumps that deliver medication. Other examples of medical technology are inhalers and nebulizers for individuals with asthma, glucose monitoring devices and injection systems for individuals requiring insulin, ventilators for individuals who need additional support to breathe, and gastrostomy tubes and supporting equipment for delivery of nutrition. Teachers should be knowledgeable about their students' medical technology and know what to do should a problem arise.

Assistive technology has opened doors for students with physical or health disabilities. The Technology-Related Assistance to Individuals with Disabilities Act of 1988 defines *assistive technology* as "any item, piece of equipment, or product system, whether acquired commercially off the shelf, modified or customized, that is used to increase, maintain, or improve functional capabilities of individuals with disabilities." Thus, assistive technology can range from something as simple as a bent spoon used when eating to a sophisticated computer-based augmentative communication system. Assistive technology can be divided into low-tech and high-tech categories, according to the complexity of the device. Table 13.4 gives some examples of both categories across several different activities.

Table 13.4	Examples of Low-Tech and High-Tech Assistive Technology Solutions	
Activity	**Low-Technology**	**High-Technology**
Reading	• Book stand, nonslip mat • Turn pages with mouthstick or eraser tip of pencil • Ruler to help keep place on page	• Electric page turner • Software to scan book into computer to easily move through book, highlight material, or read text aloud
Writing	• Pencil with built-up grip • Wider spaced paper • Mouthstick with pencil attached	• Computer with alternate input (switch or voice recognition)
Math	• Counter • Abacus • Money cards	• Graphing calculators • Electronic worksheet program that can correctly position the cursor for regrouping
Eating	• Spoon with built-up handle • Hand splint to hold spoon • Adaptive cup • Scoop dish	• Electric feeder • Robotic arm
Leisure	• Card holder • Bigger baseball	• Sport wheelchair • Adapted bicycle • Computer games

Source: Adapted from M. Engleman, H. Griffin, L. Griffin, and J. Maddox, "A Teacher's Guide to Communicating with Students with Deaf-Blindness," *Teaching Exceptional Children, 31*(5), 1999, p. 69. Copyright © 1999 by the Council for Exceptional Children. Reprinted with permission.

Types of assistive technology commonly used by students with physical disabilities include computer assistive technology, augmentative communication, positioning and seating devices, mobility devices, assistive technology for daily living and environmental control, and assistive technology for recreation and leisure. These various types of assistive technology can greatly improve the students' functioning and be critical in providing access to school, home, community, and work environments.

Computer Assistive Technology

Students with physical or health disabilities use computers for communication, academic tasks, leisure, and socialization. Depending on the extent of the physical or health disability, a wide range of modifications can be made to the computer. These modifications typically fall into three categories: input modifications, processing aids, and output modifications (Alliance for Technology Access, 2004).

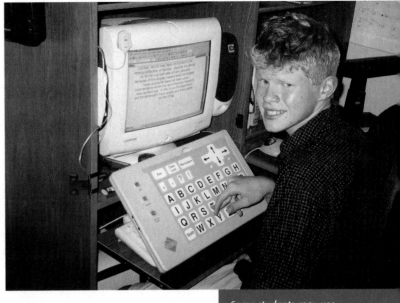

Some students may use an alternate keyboard to access a computer.

INPUT MODIFICATIONS Input devices provide information to the computer; standard input devices are the keyboard and mouse. For students with physical or health disabilities who have difficulty using these, a number of alternatives are available. Some students may need to activate the Accessibility Options available on most computers, such as the option to make keys not repeat when held down. Simple appliances may be placed over the standard keyboard to make it accessible. For example, some students drag their hand across the keyboard and need a keyguard (a plastic cover with holes for each key) to prevent accidentally pushing an unwanted key.

Students may use alternate keyboards that are larger, smaller, or differently configured than the standard keyboard in order to accommodate their physical impairment. Some students may use an on-screen keyboard; that is, the keyboard is displayed on the computer screen. A student may control the on-screen keyboard using any number of alternate input devices, such as a trackball, joystick, touchpad, touch monitor (directly touching the keyboard on the screen), or switch.

Some input devices do not use a keyboard at all. For example, voice recognition software enables a student to talk to the computer, which writes what is said.

PROCESSING AIDS Once a student has a way of inputting information into the computer, there may be a problem with the speed at which the student can type. Whether the student is using a standard keyboard, alternative keyboard, voice-recognition software, or typing by raising an eyebrow, input may be slow. Several processing aids can increase the speed at which information is typed. One of the most common processing aids is a **word prediction program.** As a student types the first letter, the computer displays a list of words commonly used by this user that start with the letter typed. If the word is displayed, the student can type the corresponding number instead of the entire word. If the word is not displayed, the on-screen list continues to change as more letters are typed.

OUTPUT MODIFICATIONS Computers commonly have two types of output: the screen monitor and the printer. However, students with physical or health disabilities may require additional modifications. Some students may need to use speech synthesizers that allow the computer to "read aloud" what is on the screen. Others may need a larger monitor or a software program that can magnify what is on the screen. Printers can also be modified to allow large size fonts.

Augmentative Communication

Another form of assistive technology is augmentative communication, also known as augmentative and alternative communication (AAC). Augmentative communication refers to the various forms of communication that are used as a supplement or alternative to oral language, including communication behaviors, gestures, sign language, picture symbols, alphabet, communication devices, and computers with synthetic speech (Miranda, 2005). Often students will use a combination of ways to communicate. The educational team will be involved in determining the most appropriate forms of augmentative communication for each individual student. (Refer to page 503 for a photo of an augmentative communication device.)

Learning to use augmentative communication is an essential part of a student's education when the student is unable to use speech effectively. Becoming proficient is critical in order to be able to make wants and needs known, communicate thoughts, participate in class activities, and socialize with others. Teachers play a vital role in teaching students to use their augmentative communication devices and supporting their use in all classroom activities. It is important that the teacher understand the forms of communication the student is using, and how they are used.

Positioning and Seating Devices

To provide access to activities, curriculum, and assistive devices, it is imperative that the student with a physical or health disability has proper positioning and seating. Position will always affect the quality and precision of a person's movement and ability to accomplish a task (Best, Reed, & Bigge, 2005). Proper positioning and seating are achieved through a wide range of special chairs and inserts that can go into a chair or wheelchair to achieve optimal positioning. Proper positioning not only helps the student move as efficiently as possible, but it can also reduce deformity and promote feelings of physical security. If students are unable to move themselves, their position may need to be changed frequently throughout the day to avoid any

Some students with cerebral palsy require the use of positioning equipment during the school day.

stiffness or pressure sores (skin breakdown from staying in one position for too long).

A student may use several different positioning devices throughout the day. Some devices may allow the student to sit a certain way, while other devices help the student lie on his or her side, stomach, or back. A prone stander may be used to support the student in a standing position. Such positioning devices may enable students to participate in activities they would not be able to do from a wheelchair, such as wash dishes at a sink while positioned in a prone stander. They can also increase muscle strength and movement, stimulate bone growth, improve circulation, and increase the movement of food through the gastrointestinal system. The physical therapist will determine the most therapeutic positions for the student and the types of devices to use to help the student achieve these positions.

Mobility Devices

Students with physical or health disabilities may use a wide range of mobility devices to move from one location to another. One of the most common devices is the wheelchair, either manual or power. Manual wheelchairs are pushed by the student (or someone else). Power wheelchairs have a motor that allows the wheelchair user to operate the chair by means of a joystick or other device. Self-operated wheelchairs can give their users tremendous independence.

Depending on the disability, a student may use the wheelchair all the time when moving about, or only when fatigued. Many people are surprised to see a student using a wheelchair one moment, then walking around the next. The type of chair and its frequency of use will depend on the student's disability.

Individuals with physical disabilities use many other types of mobility devices. Some may use a power-operated scooter instead of a traditional wheelchair. A student who can stand and walk with support may use a **walker.** Others who need even less support may use canes or crutches. Older individuals may drive cars that have been modified for their use. Whichever mobility device is used, the teacher should be familiar with it and know what type of support the student needs in order to use it.

Environmental Control and Assistive Technology for Daily Living

An **environmental control unit (ECU)** is a device that allows the user to control electric appliances, telephones, and other items that use electric outlets. The device may be a stand-alone unit (that can be mounted onto a wheelchair) or be purchased as a software package that can be used with a computer or some electronic augmentative communication devices. The electrical appliances are equipped with receivers. The user then chooses an appliance (such as the TV or a room light) and what the user wants it to do (such as turn on or off) from a list on the ECU, which sends a signal to the appliance. ECUs can help students with physical or health disabilities to manipulate their surroundings independently.

Many other types of assistive technologies are available to help with daily living. Personal care items such as modified toothbrushes and hairbrushes can help the individual with a physical disability who has restricted arm and hand motion or who cannot grasp well. These items may have elongated handles, built-up handles, or Velcro straps. Modified washcloths that fit over the hand like a mitt and Velcro around the wrist may also be used.

Modifications for eating and preparing food include special cutting boards with edges and safety knives, modified dishes with one side higher than the other to help with scooping, and modified cups to help with drinking. Students who are unable to move their arms may use a mechanical feeder that scoops food onto a spoon and brings the spoon up to the mouth with the touch of a switch.

Dressing aids include special sticks with hooks on the end that can be used to pull pants and zippers up or down and devices to help put on socks when the individual cannot reach to the floor. Modified clothing, such as garments with Velcro along the seams to go over braces, can also make dressing easier.

Assistive Technology for Play and Recreation

Numerous assistive technology devices are available for play and recreation. Children who cannot manipulate toys may have battery-operated toys they can activate by a switch.

Students with physical or health disabilities enjoy playing a variety of sports.

Switches may also be used to turn on and off radios or televisions. Computer games can often be accessed using joysticks or other input devices. Other types of recreational games, such as card games and board games, may require the use of a simple device to hold the cards, or a dice holder that can be knocked over to roll the dice.

Individuals with physical or health disabilities can also enjoy playing sports and engaging in physical activities. Some school systems have adapted sports teams, such as wheelchair basketball or wheelchair soccer, for students with physical disabilities. Many students with disabilities can participate in a wide variety of sports with minor modifications and assistive technology devices—for example, hitting a ball off a tee, allowing an extra swing at bat, or using a small adapted ramp that holds a bowling ball and allows the wheelchair user to push the ball down the ramp into the bowling lane. Individuals who like to exercise may be able to use adapted tricycles, bicycles, and mobility devices.

Trends, Issues, and Controversies

Three major issues in the field of physical disabilities, health disabilities, and related low-incidence disabilities are (1) assessing capabilities and needs of students with very severe physical disabilities; (2) provision of specialized technology, adaptations, and instructional strategies; and (3) selection of appropriate curriculum.

The first issue is appropriate assessment of students with severe physical disabilities in terms of cognitive functioning and evaluation of what the student has learned. When a young child cannot reliably move or speak, and is not yet using augmentative communication effectively, psychological testing can be of limited value or accuracy. We have come across twelve instances over the past decade in which young children with severe speech and physical impairments had been labeled as having severe mental retardation, but whose intelligence was later determined to range from mild retardation to gifted. In our chapter opener, Natalie's category changed multiple times, although her intellectual capabilities remained the same. Assessment difficulties are also present for students with multiple disabilities and deaf-blindness.

Because of this difficulty, two major areas need to be addressed: finding a reliable response and providing an appropriate curriculum. While these students are learning augmentative communication, it is essential to find some **reliable means of response**—that is, a consistent, reliable way for the student to answer questions. This could be looking at the answer (eye gazing), touching the answer, hitting a switch to indicate the answer, or having the teacher move a finger across answers until the student makes a noise indicating a selection. Typically, this means that questions must be presented in a multiple-choice format, at least until students have literacy skills and can type out their own responses. Having a reliable means of response makes it possible to assess what the student knows. Given the lack of experiences and inability to communicate thoughts and questions, intelligence testing may still not be accurate, even when the student has a reliable way to respond to the questions. However, it does give the teacher an accurate way of determining if the student has learned the material.

A second issue involves the provision of specialized technology, adaptations, and instructional strategies. Barriers to obtaining and using the necessary technology include funding issues, appropriate assessment, selection of devices, training to use the devices, and ongoing technical support.

The third area to consider is curriculum. Some students with physical or health disabilities will be on an academic curriculum; others will be on a more functional curriculum because of mental retardation. However, when the student has severe speech and physical impairments, it may not be obvious where the student is functioning. If the student is on a functional curriculum, more advanced skills should also be taught periodically to determine if the student can learn them. For example, if the student is only introduced to pictures for communication, how do we know that the student is not capable of learning words? This concern is best summed up by Natalie's mom (Tumlin, 2001), who points out:

> A non-verbal child cannot provide her own opportunities to prove more than what is expected. When placement is based strictly on test scores and/or assumptions, quite often our kids end up living *down* to expectations, are isolated from normal interactions and experiences, and learn inappropriate behaviors to be what is "normal."

Placing students in inappropriate curriculums or teaching them less than they are capable of learning may be due to **spread** (Kirshbaum, 2000)—the overgeneralization of a disability into unrelated areas, often resulting in stereotyping. For example, people may assume that someone who uses a wheelchair has a cognitive impairment, or may react to a person who is blind by talking more loudly. It is important to interact with individuals with disabilities based on what they demonstrate, rather than on unfounded assumptions.

Chapter in Review

Defining Physical Disabilities, Health Disabilities, and Related Low-Incidence Disabilities

- Students who have physical and health disabilities comprise one of the most diverse categories of students receiving special education services.

- Depending on their disability, they may come under one of four IDEA categories: **orthopedic impairments, multiple disabilities, traumatic brain injury, and other health impairments.**

- Individuals with the concomitant loss of both vision and hearing are referred to as **deaf-blind.**

Prevalence of Physical Disabilities, Health Disabilities, and Related Low-Incidence Disabilities

- Physical and health disabilities vary widely in reported prevalence figures.

- Pupils with deaf-blindness are representative of a low-incidence disability accounting for only .02 percent of all individuals receiving a special education.

- Children with physical or health disabilities and low-incidence disabilities comprise about 13 percent of the special education population.

Etiology of Physical Disabilities, Health Disabilities, and Related Low-Incidence Disabilities

- Physical disabilities, health disabilities, and related low-incidence disabilities have many causes. Some of the more common etiologies can be grouped under chromosomal and genetic causes, **teratogens**, prematurity and complications of pregnancy, and acquired causes.

Characteristics of Individuals with Physical Disabilities, Health Disabilities, and Related Low-Incidence Disabilities

- The characteristics of individuals with physical disabilities, health disabilities, and related low-incidence disabilities depend on the specific condition and its severity.

- Individuals with such neuromotor impairments as **cerebral palsy** and **spina bifida** have impaired motor movements and often have additional disabilities associated with their condition.

- Children with degenerative diseases, such as **Duchenne muscular dystrophy,** have progressive loss of control to move their bodies and die early in life.

- Students with orthopedic and musculoskeletal disorders, such as **juvenile rheumatoid arthritis** and **limb deficiencies,** can have severe physical limitations.

- Individuals with multiple disabilities have a combination of disabilities, often including a physical or health impairment.

- Pupils with traumatic brain injury may have deficits across cognitive, motor, physical, health, sensory, language, social, and behavioral domains.

- Major health impairments (such as **seizure disorders**) and infectious diseases (such as AIDS) can affect an individual's endurance and attention.

- Students with deaf-blindness are an especially heterogeneous group of learners varying tremendously in their needs, abilities, and educational requirements.

Educational Considerations

- Educational placement of students with physical disabilities, health disabilities, and related low-incidence disabilities varies greatly.

- Physical and health disabilities vary in their impact on school performance according to the type of disability involved, the **functional effects** of the disability, and the **psychosocial** and **environmental factors** surrounding the disability.

- Meeting the educational needs of students with physical disabilities, health disabilities, and related low-incidence disabilities involves monitoring, modifications and adaptations, and specialized instructional strategies.

Technology and Individuals with Physical Disabilities, Health Disabilities, and Related Low-Incidence Disabilities

- Prominent is the role of medical and assistive technology. Advances in medical technology have helped individuals lead healthier lives.

- Types of assistive technology used by individuals with physical disabilities, health disabilities, and related low-incidence disabilities include computer assistive technology, augmentative communication, positioning and seating devices, mobility devices, environmental control and daily living devices, and play and recreation devices.

Study Questions

1. Which IDEA categories include students with a physical or health disability, and how are they defined?

2. What are the major causes of physical disabilities, health disabilities, and deaf-blindness?

3. Explain the following conditions: cerebral palsy, spina bifida, traumatic brain injury, Duchenne muscular dystrophy, limb deficiency, seizure disorders, AIDS, and deaf-blindness.

4. Explain the steps you would take if a tonic-clonic seizure occurred in your classroom.

5. How does a physical disability, health impairment, or low-incidence disability affect school performance?

6. What does it mean to maintain a safe, healthy environment?

7. What types of modifications and adaptations may need to be used in the classroom? Include seven major areas in your discussion.

8. Identify five of the principal communication systems used with pupils who are deaf-blind.

9. Describe how communication breakdowns can occur when talking with an individual using an augmentative

communication device. Describe some techniques to prevent such breakdowns from occurring.

10. What are specialized instructional strategies and specialized expanded curriculum areas? Provide examples.

11. What are some stresses that occur in families that have a child with a physical or health impairment? How are these stresses different from those experienced by families with other types of disabilities?

12. What are the major types of assistive technology available to students with physical disabilities, health disabilities, or low-incidence disabilities?

13. What is augmentative communication? Does its use interfere with speech production?

14. What is "spread," and how may it affect a person with a physical or health disability?

Key Terms

low-incidence disabilities
assistive technology
augmentative communication
orthopedic impairments
multiple disabilities
traumatic brain injury
other health impairments
deaf-blind
teratogen
CHARGE association
Usher syndrome
neuromotor impairment
cerebral palsy
spastic cerebral palsy
athetoid cerebral palsy

ataxic cerebral palsy (ataxia)
mixed cerebral palsy
hemiplegia
diplegia
paraplegia
quadriplegia
orthotics
contractures
spina bifida
Duchenne muscular dystrophy
juvenile rheumatoid arthritis (JRA)
limb deficiency

seizure
epilepsy
absence seizure
complex partial seizure
tonic-clonic seizure
asthma
acquired immune deficiency syndrome (AIDS)
learned helplessness
specialized instructional strategies
communication breakdowns
interveners

transition plan
supported employment
job coach
technology productivity tools
information technology
instructional technology
word prediction program
walker
environmental control unit (ECU)
reliable means of response
spread

Learning Activities

1. Visit a Web site specializing in assistive technology (e.g., www.abledata.com or www.closingthegap.com). What types of assistive technology are provided on the site? Select five different assistive technology devices and describe their use, who they are for, their price, and your overall impression of the device.

2. Learn about your own state's disability definitions and special education certification categories. Does your state use the orthopedic impairments, traumatic brain injury, multiple disabilities, other health impairment and deaf-blind categories? How are they defined? What types of special education certification does your state provide, and is there specialized training in physical and health disabilities?

3. Visit a school and observe students with low-incidence disabilities. What types of modifications, adaptations, and assistive technologies are being used? What are the roles of the occupational therapist, physical therapist,

speech-language pathologist, nurse, special education teacher, general education teacher, student, and parents in determining modifications, adaptations, and selection of assistive technology?

4. Interview a high school student (or parent of a child) with a physical or health disability. Ask the student about his or her disability and its treatment. Ask the student what it is like to have the particular disability. Does he or she feel that it has interfered with school, activities, making friends? What does the student think that teachers need to know about the disability?

5. Contact local chapters of organizations involved with physical and health disabilities, such as the Epilepsy Foundation of America or the United Cerebral Palsy Association. Find out what services they provide. Obtain samples of literature they have for the public. Attend a support meeting to gain insight into some of the issues in that area.

Organizations Concerned with Physical Disabilities, Health Disabilities, or Related Low-Incidence Disabilities

Most physical disabilities, health impairments, and low-incidence disabilities are represented by their own separate organization or support group; only a small sample of organizations is listed here. The reader is encouraged to locate organizations dealing with a specific disability by searching the World Wide Web.

Brain Injury Association of America
1608 Spring Hill Road
Suite 110
Vienna, VA 22182
(800) 444-6443

Centers for Disease Control and Prevention
1600 Clifton Road N.E.
Atlanta, GA 30333
(800) 311-3435

Division for Physical and Health Disabilities, Council for Exceptional Children
1110 North Glebe Road, Suite 300
Arlington, VA 22201-5704
(703) 620-3660

Muscular Dystrophy Association
3300 E. Sunrise Drive
Tucson, AZ 85718
(800) 344-4863

National Organization for Rare Disorders (NORD)
P.O. Box 1968
Danbury, CT 06813
(800) 999-6673

United Cerebral Palsy Association
1660 L Street N.W., Suite 700
Washington, DC 20036-5602
(800) 872-5827

Reflecting on Standards

The following exercises are designed to help you learn to apply the Council for Exceptional Children (CEC) standards to your teaching practice. Each of the reflection exercises below correlates with a knowledge or skill within the CEC standards. For the full text of each of the related CEC standards, please refer to the standards integration grid located in Appendix B.

1. Focus on Learning Environments and Social Interactions (*CEC Content Standard #5 CC5S1*)

Reflect on someone you know who has a physical disability or a related low-incidence disability. How are they often misunderstood or treated by the general population? If you were to have a student in your class with a physical disability, or related low-incidence disability, how might you need to educate your general education students so that your classroom is a safe, equitable, positive, and supportive learning environment?

2. Focus on Communication (*CEC Content Standard #6 CC6S1*)

Reflect on what you have learned in this chapter about the educational needs of students with physical disabilities and related low-incidence disabilities. If you were to have a student with cerebral palsy in your class, what strategies might you need to implement to make sure communication with your student is clear? What assistive technologies might you need to implement?

Technology Resources

Visit the Web-based SAGE Study Site at **http://www.sagepub.com/gargiulo3estudy** for these additional learning tools:

- Chapter quizzes
- Key term flashcards
- Media links

- Full-text SAGE journal articles
- Internet activities
- Additional Web resources

CHAPTER 14

Individuals Who Are Gifted and Talented

It's All Up to the Parent

My mom still laughs about it—knowingly laughs at my naïveté, joyfully laughs with his possibilities. At 18 months, Jake (my firstborn and only born at the time) was splashing in the tub playing name that alphabet letter. Randomly I held up sponge letters as he giggled and shouted their names at me. But he misidentified the I as L. When I told Mom about it, she was thrilled! I, on the other hand, explained, "But he missed one." There was silence, then laughter on the phone.

I've learned so much in the six years since then. For example, I've learned that most 18-month-olds can't speak in full sentences, much less know all the letters by name. And I've learned that most 4-year-olds can't read. In spite of all the child development books on the market and in my personal library, I've learned that gifted children are virtually ignored. Their educational, social, and emotional needs are very different from other children's, so unless the book solely deals with the gifted, it's not very beneficial. And I guess the most important thing I've learned is that, right or wrong, it's usually all up to the parent.

Academically, I have found that very few teachers understand or even recognize the gifted child. This became painfully clear to me as day after day I had to drag my first grader, my Jake, out from behind the couch forcing him to go to school. I have found that I am the one responsible to make sure he is challenged in the classroom and at home. I vividly remember the meeting I had with his teachers, then his principal. I had researched, read numerous books, prepared sample lessons, and organized the cognitive test results from an independent psychologist. I walked a fine line between concerned parent who wants the best for her child and so offers resources and suggestions—and the pushy, domineering mother who knows best. Luckily for Jake, it worked beautifully. I met with open-minded, open-hearted professionals. He now has two very caring, understanding teachers from different grades individualizing instruction and challenging him. The couch is no longer an issue—this year.

The academic struggles Jake has battled in no way compare to the emotional issues we deal with almost daily. I see his confusion as people constantly expect more from him than other 7-year-olds because he is so bright. I see his frustration as he tries to explain some complicated make-believe

Written by Julia Link Roberts, Western Kentucky University

game to his age peers. I see his boredom as he brings home worksheets that force him to "practice" a math skill twenty times that he knew after three. I see his hurt as he worries about the sick and misfortunate. And I see his anger over things that aren't fair.

Oh, how I wish people understood! If administrators only knew that the best way to remove the learning ceiling is to cluster group by ability. If teachers only realized that gifted kids have very different academic and social needs. If they only knew how a little differentiation literally changes the life of a gifted child. (I well remember Jake's response to just the possibility of doing an independent project. He paced the floor rushing out his words about king cobras and books and where's the poster board! And I well remember the void of all expression when the teacher "didn't get around to it.") And if gifted kids only knew that there would be challenge, there would be intellectual peers who could share ideas, there would be teachers and principals who just plain understood.

But until that happens, it seems to be up to the parent. I am the one who discovers the opportunities—The Center for Gifted Studies, the Super Saturdays enrichment classes, the summer reading programs, the independent learning. I am the advocate passing on information to the school, gifting the teacher with the latest curriculum book, serving on the School Council. And I see changes. I see how much information opens eyes. And I've seen how opened eyes facilitate change. And I am beginning to get the feeling I'm not alone.

—Tracy Inman

S tereotypes of children who are gifted and talented are numerous, and many people believe that they represent the truth about gifted children. Some people think that a person is not gifted unless radically accelerated or that being gifted means having few or diminished social skills. Others gather their impressions about giftedness from one or a few individuals they have known or heard about, and then they generalize about people who are gifted based on this limited information. Many of the resulting stereotypes are just that—stereotypes; they are often inaccurate or misleading when applied to students who are gifted or talented and gifted individuals in general.

Some people say that every child is gifted; if they mean all children are special, then, of course, they are right. However, they are using a different meaning of *gifted* from the one used in this chapter to describe a category of exceptional children. Other people use the term *gifted* only in connection with the arts or athletics; we often read about the gifted tennis player or the gifted violinist. As the term is used in education, however, children who are **gifted and talented** have abilities and talents that can be demonstrated or have the potential for being developed at exceptional levels. These children have needs that differ in some degree from those of other children.

In this chapter, we examine the concept of giftedness, the characteristics of children and young people who are gifted and talented, and the special needs created by these characteristics. We will trace the historical development of the concept of giftedness; describe trends in support, and lack of support, for addressing the needs of gifted individuals; and elaborate on strategies that can be used in schools and in other settings to develop students' maximum potential. Finally, we will explore some current issues and challenges in identifying and providing services for children who are gifted and talented.

See the accompanying FYI feature for a preview of frequently asked questions about students who are gifted and their education.

FYI . . .

FAQ (Frequently Asked Questions) about Children and Youth Who Are Gifted and Talented

Q. Can all children become gifted?

A. From the data neurobiology is providing, it is evident that nearly all children are born with very complex and unique brain structures. Although each child is different, they all seem to have extraordinary potential. I believe that, if given the opportunity to develop optimally, most children could perform at the level we now call *gifted*, and it probably would be more natural for them to do so.

Q. Which is more important for the development of intelligence, heredity or environment?

A. Both are important, and current research recognizes that the interaction between them is complex and interdependent. At this time, few knowledgeable scientists even try to speak of one as being more important than the other.

Q. What is the biggest problem with labeling a child gifted? Would it be better to call children who are gifted by another word?

A. The word *gifted* does give an unfortunate connotation to the group of children who bear this label. People often think these children were given a gift; that is, they did nothing to earn their ability or talent. Americans tend to be suspicious of anyone who gets something for nothing. We think that people who didn't earn what they have probably do not deserve to have it, and certainly they should not have more. This line of thinking has been responsible for a lot of misunderstanding about gifted children. However, giving them a different label would still not solve the problems labeling causes. We have this label now, so perhaps the best we can do is to be sure everyone, including the child who is gifted, understands what we mean by it.

Q. Will grouping students who are gifted together result in "elitism"?

A. When this question is asked, "elitism" usually implies that the students who are gifted will become arrogant and snobbish and think they are better than other children. Research indicates that grouping gifted students together appropriately and flexibly in the areas in which they need advanced or accelerated work will not only result in their growth academically, but will give them a more realistic view of their abilities. Students who are always ahead of their classmates and do not have to study or are never challenged are in danger not only of becoming bored and dull, but of falsely assuming that they are superior to other students. Because they are never challenged, they do not learn good study skills and will have problems later as they try to pursue higher education. Arrogance can come either from unrealistic appraisal of their talent or from trying to cover up for the feeling of being different and not understanding why others continually reject them. In either case, flexible and appropriate grouping with intellectual peers will decrease that type of elitism, not increase it.

Q. Considering the focus on inclusion in the regular classroom, when is it appropriate to have special programs for students who are gifted?

A. When the material and the pacing used in the classroom are not allowing students to grow and learn, special provisions must be made. When there is no provision for students who are gifted to interact with intellectual peers, ways in which such groupings can occur must be planned. Research indicates that these are the minimum provisions that pupils who are gifted must have if they are to continue to develop and not regress, losing ability and motivation. For many students who are gifted, an appropriately individualized classroom can provide the differentiated materials and instruction needed. However, for children with gifts and talents whose pace and level of learning are significantly beyond their

(Continued)

(Continued)

classmates,' the least restrictive environment will *not* be the regular classroom. These students will need special classes and mentoring to grow and learn.

Q. Which is better for a gifted learner, acceleration or enrichment?

A. Pupils who are gifted need both acceleration and enrichment, and any gifted program should be designed to provide both. When to use each will depend on the student's needs.

Q. What is the difference between differentiation and individualization?

A. *Differentiation* for learners who are gifted is the preparation that is made for the curriculum to respond to their characteristic needs, such as allowing for a faster pace of learning and choosing themes and content that allow for more complex investigation. Individualization for children who are gifted is the process of adapting that curriculum to the needs and interests of a particular student. A program for gifted learners requires both to be really successful.

Q. Are most gifted children hyperactive?

A. Most children with gifts and talents have high levels of energy; they require less sleep, and they are very, very curious. These traits can look like hyperactivity, but there is a difference. The energy of a child who is gifted is focused, directed, and intense. The energy of a hyperactive child is diffuse, random, and sporadic. Gifted children can attend to an activity of their interest for long periods of time; hyperactive children cannot. The brighter the child, the more the energy may look excessive.

Q. Why do some teachers, principals, and other school personnel seem to have negative attitudes toward gifted students?

A. Unfortunately, studies show that this is too often true. Children who are gifted do not fit easily into the structure of most schools and classrooms. Because they can be two to four years ahead of the curriculum offered at any grade level, they make it very hard for a teacher of twenty to thirty other children to find appropriate curricular experiences for them. They often question and seek more information about ideas than the teacher is prepared to give. This can be seen as a challenge to the teacher's authority. They may refuse to do work that they consider boring or to repeat or practice lessons if they already understand the material. In a classroom where everyone is expected to do much the same work and cover the same material, this can be seen as a real problem. Pupils who are gifted can be demanding, challenging, intense, critical, oversensitive, highly verbal, and physically active, and they can devour material rapidly. None of these traits are problems in themselves, but they can present real problems for teachers who are not prepared to meet these needs. Some teachers do not know what to do with these youngsters and feel incompetent and threatened by them. For administrators, children who are gifted present needs for special services. This may be perceived as pressure on an already tight budget or cause special arrangements to be made that seem unnecessary. Fortunately, these attitudes often can be changed with inservice in gifted education.

Q. Do culturally diverse students require a separate curriculum?

A. If the instruction is individualized and the curriculum is differentiated, a separate curriculum is not necessary. What is important, however, is that the teacher and others involved in gifted programs in which cultural diversity exists hold positive attitudes toward cultural differences, that they be aware of cultural and ethnic history and traditions, that lots of resources related to diverse populations be made available, and that the program be flexible and responsive to each child's needs.

Source: Adapted from B. Clark, *Growing Up Gifted,* 7th ed., © 2008. Adapted by permission of Pearson Education, Inc., Upper Saddle River, NJ.

Defining Giftedness: Refining the Meaning

During the early twentieth century, the public equated giftedness with high intelligence. Terman (1925), for instance, considered individuals gifted if they had an IQ greater than 140—the top 1 percent of the population. The connection between high intelligence and giftedness remains with us today. However, this restrictive view of giftedness has been expanded to include other dimensions and categories.

The first national report on gifted education, known as the Marland Report, offered the following definition, specifying six categories of giftedness (Marland, 1972, p. 10):

> Gifted and talented children are those identified by professionally qualified persons who by virtue of outstanding abilities are capable of high performance. These are children who require differentiated educational programs and/or services beyond those normally provided by the regular school program in order to realize their contribution to self and society.
>
> Children capable of high performance include those with demonstrated achievement and/or potential ability in any of the following areas: (1) general intellectual ability, (2) specific academic aptitude, (3) creative or productive thinking, (4) leadership ability, (5) visual and performing arts, and (6) psychomotor ability.

Many states have essentially adopted this definition, with the exception of psychomotor ability. Although individuals do demonstrate giftedness in psychomotor ability, the category has been removed because the development of athletic ability is generously funded in other ways.

The second national report on gifted education, *National Excellence: A Case for Developing America's Talent* (Ross, 1993), uses the term *talent* rather than *gifted*: "Children and youth with outstanding talent perform or show the potential for performing at remarkably high levels of accomplishment when compared with others of their age, experience, or environment" (p. 3). Like the Marland Report, it notes that "outstanding talent" can be evidenced in general intellectual ability, specific academic ability, creative thinking, leadership ability, and/or the visual and performing arts. At the same time, it stresses that "outstanding talents are present in children and youth from all cultural groups, across all economic strata, and in all areas of human endeavor" (p. 3). The recommendations contained in *National Excellence* provide a blueprint for states to use in expanding their definitions of children who are gifted and talented.

Renzulli (1978, 1998) has proposed a "Three Ring" model of giftedness, represented visually as three intersecting circles (see Figure 14.1). Giftedness is defined as comprising three traits: creativity, above average intellectual abilities, and task commitment. The focus of this model is on endeavors and activities that demonstrate giftedness; some examples of these behavioral manifestations are listed in Table 14.1 (page 547).

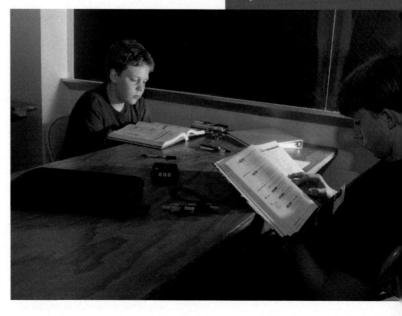

Giftedness manifests itself in many different ways.

Figure 14.1

Renzulli's "Three Ring" Definition of Giftedness

Source: Adapted from J. Renzulli, "What Makes Giftedness? Reexamining a Definition," *Phi Delta Kappan, 60,* 1978, p. 184.

Piirto (2007) provides a definition of giftedness that applies to school settings. In this context, the gifted population includes

> those individuals who, by way of learning characteristics such as superior memory, observational powers, curiosity, creativity, and the ability to learn school-related subject matters rapidly and accurately with a minimum of drill and repetition, have a right to an education that is differentiated according to these characteristics because all children have a right to be educated according to their needs. (p. 37)

These children can be observed early, and their education should be planned to address their needs from preschool through college. Piirto also presents a model of talent development (see Figure 14.2, page 548) "in circular (not linear) form to indicate that the giftedness construct is not lines and angles, but a sphere, a circle, which enfolds all kinds of talent" (p. 37).

As you can see, definitions of gifted have evolved from an exclusive focus on high intelligence to a range of categories and indicators of talent. Identifying giftedness and talent in specific categories highlights the need for services to be customized to the individual's area(s) of identified strength(s). Identifying areas of giftedness is essential in order to match services and learning opportunities to need. Fairness is not offering the same educational opportunities to all children of the same age; rather, it is providing learning opportunities matched with needs, interests, and abilities.

Some examples may help. Jimmy was outstanding in many areas. He was so good at science that teachers encouraged him to become a physician or a research scientist; he was such an outstanding writer that his English teachers thought he was bound to be a journalist; he was also a talented musician and could have pursued a career in music. Jimmy was

Table 14.1	Illustrations of Gifted Behavior as Portrayed by Renzulli's "Three Ring" Model
Above Average Ability (general)	• High levels of abstract thought • Adaptation to novel situations • Rapid and accurate retrieval of information
Above Average Ability (specific)	• Applications of general abilities to specific area of knowledge • Capacity to sort out relevant from irrelevant information • Capacity to acquire and use advanced knowledge and strategies while pursuing a problem
Task Commitment	• Capacity for high levels of interest, enthusiasm • Hard work and determination in a particular area • Self-confidence and drive to achieve • Ability to identify significant problems within an area of study • Setting high standards for one's work
Creativity	• Fluency, flexibility, and originality of thought • Open to new experiences and ideas • Curious • Willing to take risks • Sensitive to aesthetic characteristics

Source: J. Renzulli and S. Reis, *The Schoolwide Enrichment Model*, 2nd ed. (Mansfield Center, CT: Creative Learning Press, 1997), p. 9.

intellectually gifted, gifted in specific academic areas, and talented in the performing arts. Chin Lan was very talented in math and science and should have been identified as gifted in those specific academic areas; in other academic areas, she was ready for the academic challenges provided for others her age. Luis, who performed at grade level in academic subjects, was charismatic and had the ability to get others to do what he wanted; he was gifted in leadership and needed opportunities to develop his skills as a leader. Albert was very creative; his teachers saw his ideas as pushing the limits. Gifted in creative thinking, he was also academically talented in English and social studies. Sara was an outstanding musician and took advantage of opportunities to develop her musical talents. All of these students were recognized as gifted and/or talented, but each one was unique. Each pupil needed services to allow him or her to make continuous progress in his or her area of strength.

Following are some important features of giftedness and talent, as used in this chapter and applied in school settings:

- Each state establishes its own definition of children and young people who are gifted and talented. Although there are similarities, it is important to know the definition in the state where you live and/or work.
- In states in which gifted children constitute a category of exceptionality, laws governing exceptional children also apply to children and young people who are gifted and talented.
- Being specific about the area of giftedness will make it possible to offer appropriate services and educational opportunities to allow continuous progress to be made in each category of talent or giftedness. Being specific also facilitates communication as you describe a young person as being gifted in mathematics, gifted in leadership, or intellectually gifted.
- Using giftedness and talent interchangeably will allow concentration on the performance or potential for performance at levels that are exceptional in comparison with others of the same age, environment, or experience.
- Giftedness and talent will be found in children from all ethnic and racial groups and from all socioeconomic levels.

Figure 14.2

Piirto's Giftedness Construct

Source: J. Piirto, *Talented Children and Adults: Their Development and Education,* 3rd ed. (Waco, TX: Prufrock Press, 2007), p. 46. Reprinted with permission.

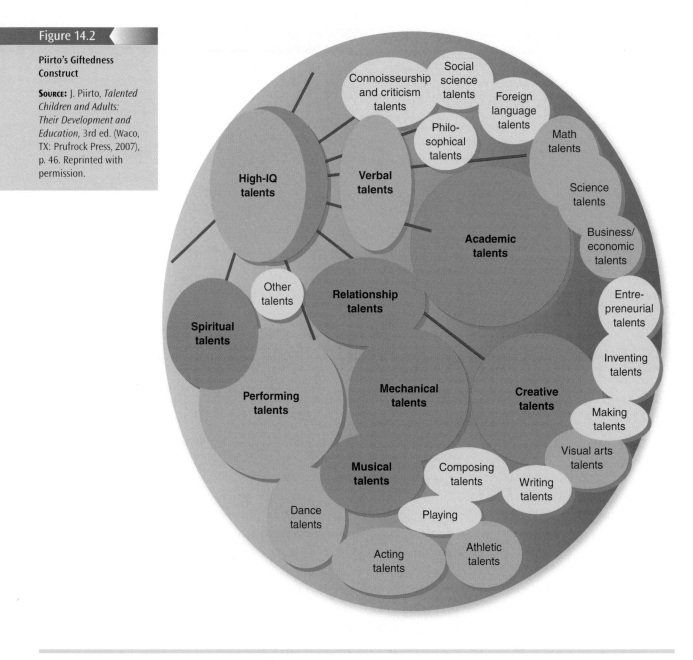

Assessing Giftedness and Talent

The goal of assessment is to enable educators and parents to address the strengths and needs of children who are gifted and talented in one or in several categories. A thorough assessment paints a picture of the child, including his/her characteristics, interests, and strengths. Each category of giftedness must be assessed in different ways, using both informal and formal measures. Multifactor assessment of a student's strengths may include such diverse informal measures as a portfolio of work samples, anecdotal records, checklists or rating scales of gifted characteristics, and evaluations by experts of a pupil's creative products or performance.

A specific example of an informal measure of giftedness is the "jot-down." Jot-down forms can be used to help teachers focus on behaviors that in combination indicate giftedness. Teachers observe characteristics and behaviors and "jot down" the names of pupils they see demonstrating the behavior described in the box on a jot-down sheet. (See Figure 14.3 for an example of a jot-down.) Using jot-down sheets enables educators to observe students in class and to gather information about students as they encounter new and challenging learning activities. Behaviors in the boxes on the jot-down sheets may be seen in all children; when observed in clusters, however, they may indicate a child who is gifted and talented intellectually, academically, creatively, in leadership, or in the visual or performing arts.

Checklists provide another way of assessing a pupil's gifts and talents. The Pfeiffer-Jarosewich Gifted Rating Scales (Pfeiffer & Jarosewich, 2003) for school-age children is one example of an assessment instrument that looks at the various dimensions of giftedness. Teachers evaluate students in the areas of intellectual ability, academic ability, creativity, the arts, and motivation as well as leadership abilities. Data gleaned from this rating scale can then be used with other sources of information to assist professionals in developing a picture of the student's strengths.

Teachers who are knowledgeable about the characteristics of children who are gifted become talent scouts as they document behaviors that are indicative of giftedness in various

Specific Academic Area Jot-Down

Brief description of observed activity _____

Check one: _____ Language arts
_____ Social studies
_____ Math
_____ Science   Grade _____

Date _____ / _____ / _____
Month Day Year
Teacher _____
School _____

1. As students show evidence of the following characteristics in comparison with age peers, jot their names down in the appropriate box(es).
2. When recommending students for gifted services, use this identification jot-down as a reminder of student performances in this specific academic area.

Sees connections.	Asks many probing questions.	Shares what he/she knows, which may be seen as answering "too often."	Provides many written/oral details.
Is widely read or likes to read about subject area.	Absorbs information quickly from limited exposure.	Has a large vocabulary in subject area.	Benefits from rapid rate of presentation.
Displays intensity for learning within subject area.	Requires little or no drill to grasp concepts.	Generates large number of ideas or solutions to problems.	Has knowledge about things age peers may not be aware of.
Prefers to work independently with little direction.	Displays leadership qualities within subject area.	Applies knowledge to unfamiliar situations.	Offers unusual or unique responses.

Figure 14.3

An Example of a Jot-Down Sheet

Source: Developed by L. Whaley and M. Evans, The Center for Gifted Studies, Western Kentucky University.

categories. It is important for educators to understand that giftedness comes in many different forms, each with recognized needs. The needs of students who are gifted and talented in each category arise from strengths rather than from deficits—strengths that make them children with exceptionalities when compared with age peers.

Obviously, the first step in addressing the needs of individuals who are gifted and talented is to have educators who are knowledgeable about their characteristics. Applying this knowledge allows teachers to recommend the pupil for additional informal and formal assessment and to make accommodations for the student in their curriculum. Parent and peer nominations are also useful in identifying students, and self-nomination is often a good predictor of leadership potential.

Tests of intellectual ability provide a formal measure of intellectual giftedness. No child can be fully represented by a number, but tests of intellectual ability can provide important information in identifying intellectual giftedness and planning appropriate modifications and services. Individual measures of intelligence such as the Wechsler Intelligence Scale for Children—Fourth Edition (Wechsler, 2003) or the fifth edition of the Stanford-Binet Intelligence Test (Roid, 2003) are preferred to group measures for their ability to present a more comprehensive assessment. Another critical consideration is to look for instruments that are not biased. Up-to-date information on assessment measures is vital to planning and implementing an identification process that is defensible. Once formal measures indicate intellectual giftedness, further assessment should be made to identify areas of the curriculum that need to be differentiated to allow the student to be challenged academically and intellectually.

Formal assessment of specific academic ability can best be made with instruments that remove the learning ceiling. **Off-level testing** (the use of measures intended for older children) is important in assessing giftedness in a specific academic area. Grade-level achievement tests have a low ceiling and do not allow a child to demonstrate what he/she knows in that content area. Examples of off-level testing are using the Woodcock-Johnson III Tests of Achievement (Woodcock, McGrew, & Mather, 2001) to measure a specific area of reading or mathematics or using the Scholastic Assessment Test (SAT), formerly known as the Scholastic Aptitude Test, with middle school students to ascertain the level of reasoning and achievement in mathematics or verbal ability. Giftedness in a content area can be assessed through academic work, but students who are not challenged will not produce high-level products. Students who are gifted in a specific academic area will usually demonstrate their high level of work when given opportunities to take part in designing the learning experience, allowing them to pursue an aspect of the content area of great interest. Pretesting each unit will allow assessment of achievement in a specific content area to be ongoing and to reflect the academic progress being made.

Creativity is defined in many ways—creative personality, creative products, creative thinking. Measures to assess creativity, therefore, must be chosen to match the kind of creativity that is being identified. Educators frequently assess creativity through creative products or tests of creative thinking. To assess products for creativity, it is wise to have scoring guides or rubrics available to students as they embark on creating the products. Tests by E. Paul Torrance (1966, 1998) and Frank Williams (1993) are frequently used to assess creative thinking skills.

Educators often equate leadership with elected positions. Being elected to office, however, is only one possible indicator of talent in leadership. Leadership talent is best identified by observing behaviors that suggest leadership potential. Students should have the opportunity to present a leadership portfolio, including evidence of leadership opportunities outside of school. Leadership may be shown in a specific academic area or in an area of the visual or performing arts. Self-nomination through a portfolio can be coupled with peer nomination.

Identifying leadership potential is important in order to match leadership opportunities with young people ready to develop their leadership skills.

Artists in the specific talent area are most appropriate to assess talent in the visual and performing arts. Experts in the visual and performing arts are prepared to recognize talent that is exceptional for a young person when compared with others the same age. Products, sometimes assembled in a portfolio, and performances provide the means for assessing talent in the arts. Of course, recognizing and identifying talent is important in order for schools to provide learning opportunities to develop the talent to the highest levels possible.

School districts should establish policies that reflect best practices in screening and assessment (Evans, 2001; Gubbins, 2006; Landrum, Callahan, & Shaklee, 2001; Landrum & Shaklee, 1998):

- Each district should have a written plan for nominating and identifying students for gifted services.
- The nominating process for gifted education services should be ongoing.
- Screening for services can occur at any point in the school year.
- Assessment should be made in the language in which the student is fluent.
- Nonbiased measures should be used, taking into consideration ethnicity, culture, developmental differences, gender, economic conditions, disabilities, and environmental influences.
- Multiple measures include self-nomination, parent and teacher nomination, product and performance assessment, portfolios, and test scores.
- The school district should have written procedures on informed consent, student retention, student reassessment, student exiting, and appeals procedures.

Teachers frequently assess creativity by evaluating the creative products of students.

Differences among Children Who Are Gifted and Talented

Although individuals who are gifted and talented share many characteristics, they also differ in a variety of ways. The differences among individuals in each category of giftedness are important to recognize, for they will indicate the type of instructional modifications needed for the students to make continuous progress. Assessment provides the data and information needed to understand the degree of giftedness. Off-level testing (using measures that allow for assessing beyond-grade-level performance) is necessary to remove the ceiling effect of grade-level assessment. Individuals who perform at or show the potential to perform at the very high end for any category of giftedness and talent are often referred to as highly or profoundly gifted or talented.

As one examines individuals in each category of giftedness, the degree of giftedness is most apparent among individuals who are gifted in intellectual ability. Certainly IQ is

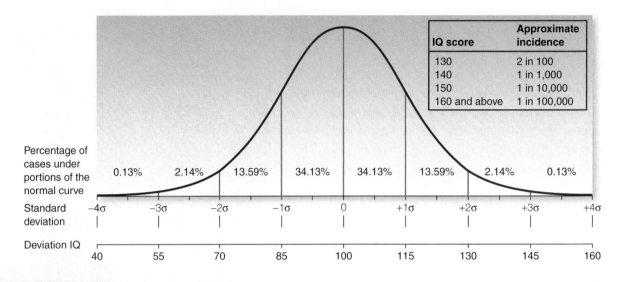

IQ score	Approximate incidence
130	2 in 100
140	1 in 1,000
150	1 in 10,000
160 and above	1 in 100,000

Percentage of cases under portions of the normal curve

0.13%   2.14%   13.59%   34.13%   34.13%   13.59%   2.14%   0.13%

Standard deviation   −4σ   −3σ   −2σ   −1σ   0   +1σ   +2σ   +3σ   +4σ

Deviation IQ   40   55   70   85   100   115   130   145   160

Figure 14.4

A Theoretical Distribution of Intelligence

Source: Boxed matter from G. Cartwright, C. Cartwright, and M. Ward, *Educating Special Learners,* 2nd ed. (Belmont, CA: Wadsworth, 1981), p. 191.

not the only indicator of a person who is intellectually gifted, but it is one criterion that should be considered. Looking at a normal curve, an IQ score that is two standard deviations above the mean may qualify a student for gifted services, but other young people will score three and four standard deviations above the mean (see Figure 14.4). Obviously these pupils are all significantly different from the average child, but they also differ significantly from each other. The specific characteristics of each student who is gifted become important when educators are matching instruction to the needs of the individual. A "one-size-fits-all" approach to service options for students who are gifted is inappropriate because it does not address needs or allow for continuous progress.

Exceptional levels of potential and performance can be found in all academic and talent categories. For example, many young people who are gifted mathematically need to work above grade level, but a few are able to work several grades above their age-mates. One young third grader successfully completed a year of algebra with eighth graders, scoring at the top of the class. A 13-year-old studied calculus on his own, then took the College Board Advanced Placement exam in calculus. He scored a 5 on the exam, the highest score possible on an AP exam, usually earning the student six hours of college credit in calculus. Few children of these ages, even those who are gifted in mathematics, could or should be working at these levels; however, for a small number of children, it is necessary. Providing such advanced study is essential in order to allow them to continue learning in their area of specific academic giftedness.

A Brief History of the Field of Gifted and Talented Education

The field of gifted and talented education in the United States has its roots in the late nineteenth century but grew and matured in the twentieth century. The twenty-first century brings both challenges and promise to the education of children who are gifted. The history of the field will be described through key events, individuals, and movements that have shaped the study of giftedness and the implementation of programming and services to address the needs of children and youth who are gifted and talented.

The First Half of the Twentieth Century: Pioneering the Field

The development of intelligence testing in the late nineteenth century and the early part of the twentieth century provided the means for the study of gifted individuals. The initial work on measuring intelligence was done by Alfred Binet in France; its purpose was not to measure high-end intelligence but rather to identify children and adults who might not benefit from schooling. William Stern, a German psychologist, developed the formula for the intelligence quotient, or IQ. With the ability to measure intelligence, cognitive science emerged as a field of study.

Lewis Terman (1925), known as the founder of gifted education, conducted a major longitudinal study of gifted children. The measure used to define giftedness was an IQ of 140 or higher. This study of 1,500 children, begun by Terman in the 1920s, continued for seventy years (beyond his lifetime by colleagues), following the children through their adult lives. The study provided information about the characteristics of gifted children and disproved widely held beliefs that gifted children were characterized by social and emotional peculiarities and that "early ripe" would lead to "early rot." Debunking the mythology about gifted individuals was a major contribution of this long-term study.

Another early pioneer in the field of gifted education was Leta S. Hollingworth, who began a longitudinal study of highly gifted children in 1916. Her study yielded information about the characteristics of this exceptional population. She wrote *Gifted Children: Their Nature and Nurture* (1926), the first comprehensive textbook on gifted education. Hollingworth also directed attention to the emotional needs of children who are gifted and believed that giftedness is influenced by both heredity and environment, a view still popular today. Hollingworth was one of the first to start classes for gifted children, believing that appropriate learning opportunities must be matched to students' needs and their readiness to learn.

The 1950s, 1960s, and 1970s: Establishing Foundations for the Field

Understanding intelligence as the g factor (general intelligence) is based on the belief that intelligence is a unitary trait. Founded on work begun in the 1950s, however, J. P. Guilford in 1967 published *The Nature of Human Intelligence*, in which he described multiple intelligences. Guilford's theory, the structure-of-the-intellect model, provides a theoretical foundation for the concept of intelligence. Guilford proposed a total of 120 different kinds of intelligences. His theory of multiple intelligences continues to have a tremendous impact on the understanding of children and youth who are gifted and talented.

The emergence of national organizations has fostered the development of the emerging field of gifted education. The National Association for Gifted Children (NAGC), started in 1954, now has affiliates in most states. The Association for the Gifted, a division of the Council for Exceptional Children, was established in 1958 and advocates for appropriate educational opportunities for gifted and talented children as a category of individuals who are exceptional. Parents and educators combine their efforts in these national organizations and their state affiliates to ensure that the needs of children who are gifted and talented are considered in the development of policies and legislation.

The next important impetus to gifted and talented education came in 1957 with the Russian launching of *Sputnik I*. This demonstration of Soviet progress in science and technology shook public confidence in the United States and initiated the space race. Suddenly, legislation sought to provide challenging learning opportunities for young people in mathematics

The field of gifted education has expanded its understanding of intelligence.

and science, with the goal of producing superior mathematicians and scientists. During international crises, gifted individuals often are considered valuable resources to be cultivated. During less tumultuous times, however, their value among the public diminishes, producing a roller-coaster effect.

In 1961, Virgil Ward coined the term *differential education* to describe a curriculum that would enable gifted students to learn at appropriate levels. In *Educating the Gifted: An Axiomatic Approach*, Ward set forth guidelines for writing such a curriculum. Although the curriculum does not need to be entirely different for academically talented students, it must be tied to their characteristics in order to enhance learning. It should be different in ways that encourage learning by young people who are ready to learn at more complex levels that would not be appealing to all students. By highlighting the need to design curriculum to address the needs of academically talented youth—a concept introduced decades earlier by Hollingworth—Ward's work provides a foundation for differentiating the curriculum in defensible ways.

The 1972 Marland Report, mentioned earlier, documented the lack of recognition of the needs of children who are gifted and talented. More than half the personnel in the schools surveyed responded that they had no gifted children in their districts, and twenty-one states reported no services for gifted students. This report, and materials appended to it, noted that the societal and personal costs of not providing services to this population of exceptional children are high. The Marland definition of giftedness (see page 545) broadened the view of giftedness from one based strictly on IQ to one encompassing six areas of outstanding or potentially outstanding performance.

The passage of Public Law 94-142, The Education for All Handicapped Children Act, in 1975 led to an increased interest in and awareness of individual differences and exceptionalities. PL 94-142, however, was a missed opportunity for gifted children, as there is no national mandate to serve them. Mandates to provide services for children and youth who are gifted or talented are the result of state rather than federal legislation.

The 1980s and 1990s: The Field Matures and Provides Focus for School Reform

Building on Guilford's multifaceted view of intelligence, Howard Gardner and Robert Sternberg advanced their own theories of multiple intelligences in the 1980s. Gardner (1983) originally identified seven intelligences—linguistic, logical-mathematical, spatial, bodily-kinesthetic, musical, interpersonal, and intrapersonal (see Table 14.2). Describing these intelligences as relatively independent of one another, he later added naturalistic as an eighth intelligence (Gardner, 1993). Sternberg (1985) presented a triarchic view of "successful intelligence," encompassing practical, creative, and executive intelligences. Using these models, the field of gifted education has expanded its understanding of intelligence while not abandoning IQ as a criterion for identifying intellectually gifted children.

A Nation at Risk (National Commission on Excellence in Education, 1983) described the state of education in U.S. schools as abysmal. The report made a connection between the education of children who are gifted and our country's future. This commission found that 50 percent of the school-age gifted population was not performing to full potential and that

Table 14.2	Gardner's Multiple Intelligences		
Intelligence	**Characteristics**	**Possible Career Choices**	**Examples**
Linguistic	Ability to use language effectively in written and oral expression; highly developed verbal skills; often think in words	Novelist, lecturer, lawyer, playwright	Ernest Hemingway, Martin Luther King, Jr.
Logical-mathematical	Ability to use calculation to assist with deductive and inductive reasoning; good at seeing patterns and relationships; think abstractly and conceptually; tend to be logical and systematic	Mathematician, physicist	Albert Einstein, Stephen Hawking
Spatial	Ability to manipulate spatial configurations; good at pattern recognition, sensitive to shape, form, and space; think in pictures or images	Architect, sculptor, interior decorator, engineer	I. M. Pei, Michelangelo
Bodily-kinesthetic	Ability to control and skillfully use one's body to perform a task or express feelings and ideas; able to communicate through body language; keen athletic ability	Dancer, athlete, surgeon	Mikhail Baryshnikov, Michael Jordan
Musical	Ability to discriminate pitch; sensitivity to rhythm, texture, and timbre; ability to hear themes; production of music through performance or composition	Musician, composer	Leonard Bernstein, Ludwig van Beethoven
Interpersonal	Ability to understand other individuals—their actions, moods, and motivations—and to act accordingly; sensitive to ideas and feelings of others, empathetic	Counselor, teacher, politician, salesperson	Carl Rogers, Nelson Mandela
Intrapersonal	Ability to understand one's own feelings, values, and motivations; self-reflective, inwardly motivated; insightful and self-disciplined	Therapist, religious leader	Sigmund Freud, Mother Theresa
Naturalist	Ability to understand interrelationships; capacity to discriminate and classify, recognizes patterns and characteristics; evidences a concern for the environment, sensitive to natural phenomena	Conservationist, forester	John Audubon, Charles Darwin

Source: Adapted from N. Colangelo and G. Davis (Eds.), *Handbook of Gifted Education,* 3rd ed. (Boston: Allyn and Bacon, 2003), p. 102. Adapted by permission.

mathematics and science were in deplorable condition in the schools. The message in this report percolated across the country and was responsible for a renewed interest in gifted education as well as in massive education reform that occurred nationally and state by state.

The Jacob K. Javits Gifted and Talented Students Education Act (PL 100-297) was passed in 1988. The Javits Act states that "gifted and talented students are a national resource vital to the future of the Nation and its security and well-being" [Sec. 8032 (a) (2)]. This legislation provided for the Office of Gifted and Talented Education, a national research center focusing on gifted children, and demonstration projects in gifted education. In 1993, *National Excellence: A Case for Developing America's Talent* (Ross, 1993), the second national report on gifted children, was issued by the Office of Educational Research and Improvement in the U.S. Department of Education. The National Research Center on the Gifted and Talented continues to generate research that is used by school, district, state, and national decision makers as they design and implement policy and enact legislation. The demonstration projects have focused on developing talents in areas with a large percentage of children who have been underrepresented in gifted services. The Javits legislation, reauthorized in 2001 as part of the No Child Left Behind Act (PL 107-110), was funded at $11.14 million in fiscal year 2004; it was expanded to include grants to individual states to build an infrastructure in gifted education. Congress approved an appropriation of approximately $7.6 million for the Javits Program in fiscal year 2008.

Academic standards have become increasingly important in the past decade. Standards have been established in content areas by several professional and learned societies representing various disciplines and for special educators by the Council for Exceptional Children and other accrediting agencies. The National Association for Gifted Children has promulgated programming standards in gifted education. In 1989, the National Council of Teachers of Mathematics (NCTM) issued the first content standards. Content standards have since been established in history, science, foreign language, the arts, geography, civics, and language arts. The focus on standards continues into the twenty-first century, as evidenced by the revised content standards in mathematics that NCTM released early in 2000. These curriculum standards have spurred interest in ensuring a significant content focus in school—a "must" for all children, including those who are gifted and talented.

The Twenty-First Century: Challenges and Promise Present

The No Child Left Behind Act (PL 107-110) places the focus on reaching proficiency at grade level. For children who are gifted, the goal of reaching proficiency is very limiting as their achievement is often at higher levels. When this is the case, reaching proficiency, in some instances, requires moving backward.

The standards movement continues to provide momentum to education. Professional organizations are continuing to focus on standards. Leaders in the National Association for Gifted Children and the Council for Exceptional Children are working together to craft a set of standards for both undergraduate and graduate students in gifted education.

Prevalence of Giftedness and Talent

Educators believe that approximately 3 to 5 percent of the school-age population is gifted (Clark, 2008). Of course, the number of students identified as gifted or talented depends on the definition of giftedness used by each state. Many pupils exhibit gifts and talents across several areas, and this overlapping results in much higher estimates of who is gifted or talented. Some professionals (Renzulli & Reis, 2003) believe that 10 to 15 percent of the school-age population can be thought of as gifted. The National Association for Gifted Children (2007) believes that approximately 3 million children are gifted and talented. This group represents about 6 percent of the school-age population. If this projection is accurate, then pupils considered gifted or talented could conceivably constitute the largest group of students with exceptionalities.

Etiology of Giftedness and Talent

What makes a child gifted and talented? No doubt giftedness results from a combination of genetic makeup and environmental stimulation. No one knows the precise role of genetics or of the environment, but it is clear that both genetic patterns and environmental stimulation play key roles in developing a child's potential to perform at exceptionally high levels. Understanding giftedness necessitates recognizing that the relationship between genes and a stimulating environment is complex. No longer is it acceptable to view intelligence as fixed at birth; rather, potential intelligence is created by a far more complex interplay between nature and nurture (Clark, 2008).

Neuroscience provides evidence of the vital role played by stimulation in increasing a child's capacity to learn. According to Clark (2008), "the development of intelligence is enhanced or inhibited by the interaction between the genetic pattern of an individual and the opportunities provided by the environment throughout the individual's lifespan" (p. 56). The brain changes physically and chemically when stimulated or challenged. Parents and educators, therefore, play significant roles in developing an optimum level of children's capacity to learn at high levels.

Characteristics of Individuals Who Are Gifted and Talented

Understanding the characteristics of children and young people who are gifted and talented can help educators and parents recognize behaviors that are indicative of giftedness (see Table 14.3). Many characteristics resemble the characteristics of all children; however, the degree and intensity of the characteristic provide clues that the child may be exceptional. For example, all children are curious, but children who are intellectually gifted and talented may ask so many probing questions that adults think they may be driven to distraction.

Interestingly, the very characteristics identified in Table 14.3 sometimes result in a phenomenon known as the "paradoxical negative effect" (Blackbourn, Patton, & Trainor, 2004). In this situation, behaviors displayed by students with gifts and talents may work to their detriment. For example, high verbal abilities may lead the student to dominate class discussion, self-confidence may be misinterpreted as arrogance, and a dislike for rules and routine may be perceived as a disruptive influence.

Children who are intellectually gifted and talented often perform childhood tasks on an advanced schedule. They may talk in sentences early, read before entering school, or think abstractly before age-mates. These children display exceptional memories and learn at a rapid pace. They are knowledgeable about things about which their age peers are not aware. They show a propensity for learning and, if allowed to learn about areas of interest at a challenging pace, may not distinguish work from play.

A second characteristic is exceptional talent in one or more specific academic areas. One child may be exceptional in mathematics but perform on grade level in language arts; another may be a gifted writer but not evidence the same level of talent in science. Children who are gifted in a specific academic area read widely and intently about that subject area, require little or no drill to grasp concepts, and have large vocabularies in that specific subject area. This intense interest may be viewed as being "single-minded" or may be seen as an opportunity to develop the interest and talent to an exceptional level. Such focus is an advantage when choosing a college major or, later, a career.

A third category of giftedness is creativity. All children are creative; however, some are exceptionally creative. These children have many unusual ideas and a strong imagination. They have a high level of energy that may get them in trouble. They may daydream and become easily bored with routine tasks. They have a high level of tolerance for ambiguity and are risk takers. Creative children view the world from their own vantage points. With appropriate experiences, they may be future entrepreneurs.

Leadership is another category or characteristic of giftedness. Others look to leaders when a decision needs to be made, and children who are gifted in leadership are sought after to lead activities, projects, and play. Leaders initiate activities and make plans to reach goals. They get others to work toward goals, which may be desirable or undesirable. Children who

Table 14.3	Representative Characteristics of Students Who Are Intellectually Gifted and Talented*
Academic/Learning Characteristics	• Ability to reason and think abstractly • Acquires information easily • Enjoys learning • Highly inquisitive • Demonstrates interest in a variety of areas/activities • Generalizes knowledge to novel settings • Intellectually curious • Highly motivated, persistent learner • Sees relationships among seemingly unrelated items, facts, and ideas • Early reader • Exhibits sustained attention and concentration • Excellent memory • Highly verbal • Generates elaborate and possibly nontraditional responses to questions • Good problem-solving skills • Conceptualizes and synthesizes information quickly
Social and Emotional Characteristics	• Works well independently • High energy level • Self-confident • Exhibits qualities of leadership • Relates well to older classmates, teachers, and adults • Sensitive and empathetic • Intrinsically motivated • Risk taker • Critical of self, strives for perfection • Concern for justice and idealism • Intense • Dislike of routine, rules, and regulations • Likely to have internal locus of control

*Attributes are examples only; not all individuals identified as intellectually gifted will exhibit these features.

Source: Adapted from B. Clark, *Growing Up Gifted,* 7th ed., © 2008. Adapted by permission of Pearson Education, Inc., Upper Saddle River, NJ.

are leaders may be seen as bossy. Children who display early leadership abilities have personal qualities that make them charismatic.

A final dimension of giftedness and talent focuses on the visual and performing arts. Some children may display exceptional talent in art, music, dance, and/or drama. They exhibit an intense interest in one or more of the visual and performing arts. They quickly grasp concepts in the talent area, demonstrate original work in that area, and perform at exceptional levels when compared with their age-mates.

Figure 14.5 summarizes characteristics of individuals who are gifted and talented on these five dimensions of giftedness. See the accompanying FYI feature (page 560).

Educational Considerations

Research suggests that most classroom teachers make no or only minor modifications to meet the unique needs of learners who are gifted (Archambault et al., 1993). Westberg and colleagues (Westberg, Archambault, Dobyns, & Salvin, 1993) observe that little attention is given to differentiating instruction, curricular practices, or grouping arrangements when teachers are confronted with pupils who are gifted. Ten years later Westberg and Daoust (2003) replicated the earlier study. The results showed that differentiation practices were no more likely to be found in the classrooms than they were a decade earlier. This situation is regrettable. Children who are gifted and talented need opportunities to work hard on challenging learning tasks. Instructional practices need to be modified in order to address the cognitive and social-emotional needs of students with unique talents and gifts.

Educators use a variety of instructional strategies to serve pupils who are gifted and talented. This eclectic approach reflects a contemporary trend of not endorsing any one model of instructional delivery (Gibson & Efinger, 2001), but rather providing instruction that best meets the needs of the individual learner. Here we review several different instructional strategies that can benefit pupils who are gifted and talented.

Differentiation

All children are not expected to wear the same size shoes because they are in the same grade. Likewise, parents and educators should expect tremendous differences in interests, needs, and abilities among children and youth of the same age. **Differentiation** of the curriculum is necessary in order to accommodate these differences and to provide a learning environment in which all children, including children who are gifted and talented, can thrive. "In differentiated classrooms, teachers begin where students are, not the front of a curriculum guide. They accept and build upon the premise that learners differ in important ways" (Tomlinson, 1999, p. 2).

All children deserve to make continuous progress. "For all children to make continuous progress, learning experiences must be differentiated to lift the learning ceiling. Differentiation allows each student who is ready to learn at a more complex level and at a faster pace to continue learning each day" (Roberts & Roberts, 2005, p. 179). Children need to learn challenging content and to develop cognitive skills throughout their school careers. Children who do not learn to tackle challenging learning tasks may never learn to do so. See the Suggestions for the Classroom feature (page 561) for an explanation of differentiated programming.

In order to make progress possible, the teacher must preassess what a student already knows. **Preassessment** is the key to ascertaining appropriate levels of instruction in each content area so that new learning can occur. In order to know what content and skills to preassess, the teacher must first have a well-planned unit of study, including content and skills recommended by local and state guidelines as well as by the national curriculum standards. Preassessment will then allow the teacher to differentiate learning experiences and keep the

---

Visual/performing arts

Outstanding in sense of spatial relationships
Unusual ability for expressing self, feelings, moods, etc., through art, dance, drama, music
Good motor coordination
Exhibits creative expression
Desire for producing "own product" (not content with mere copying)
Observant

Leadership

Assumes responsibility
High expectations for self and others
Fluent, concise self-expression
Foresees consequences and implications of decisions
Good judgment in decision making
Likes structure
Well-liked by peers
Self-confident
Organized

Creative thinking

Independent thinker
Exhibits original thinking in oral and written expression
Comes up with several solutions to a given problem
Possesses a sense of humor
Creates and invents
Challenged by creative tasks
Improvises often
Does not mind being different from the crowd

General intellectual ability

Formulates abstractions
Processes information in complex ways
Observant
Excited about new ideas
Enjoys hypothesizing
Learns rapidly
Uses a large vocabulary
Inquisitive
Self-starter

Specific academic ability

Good memorization ability
Advanced comprehension
Acquires basic-skills knowledge quickly
Widely read in special-interest area
High academic success in special-interest area
Pursues special interests with enthusiasm and vigor

Figure 14.5

Characteristics of Various Areas of Giftedness

Source: Copyrighted material from the National Association for Gifted Children (NAGC). This material may not be reprinted without permission of NAGC, Washington, DC, (202) 785-4268, www.nagc.org.

FYI . . .

Myths and Truths about Gifted Students

Common Myths about Gifted Students

- Gifted students are a homogeneous group, all high achievers.
- Gifted students do not need help. If they are really gifted, they can manage on their own.
- Gifted students have fewer problems than others because their intelligence and abilities somehow exempt them from the hassles of daily life.
- The future of a gifted student is assured; a world of opportunities lies before the student.
- Gifted students are self-directed; they know where they are heading.
- The social and emotional development of the gifted student is at the same level as his or her intellectual development.
- Gifted students are nerds and social isolates.
- The primary value of the gifted student lies in his or her brain power.
- The gifted student's family always prizes his or her abilities.
- Gifted students need to serve as examples to others, and they should always assume extra responsibility.
- Gifted students make everyone else smarter.
- Gifted students can accomplish anything they put their minds to; all they have to do is apply themselves.
- Gifted students are naturally creative and do not need encouragement.
- Gifted children are easy to raise and a welcome addition to any classroom.

Truths about Gifted Students

- Gifted students are often perfectionistic and idealistic. They may equate achievement and grades with self-esteem and self-worth, which sometimes leads to fear of failure and interferes with achievement.
- Gifted students may experience heightened sensitivity to their own expectations and those of others, resulting in guilt over achievements or grades perceived to be low.
- Gifted students are asynchronous. Their chronological age, social, physical, emotional, and intellectual development may all be at different levels. For example, a 5-year-old may be able to read and comprehend a third-grade book but may not be able to write legibly.
- Some gifted children are "mappers" (sequential learners), while others are "leapers" (spatial learners). Leapers may not know how they got a "right answer." Mappers may get lost in the steps leading to the right answer.
- Gifted students may be so far ahead of their chronological age mates that they know more than half the curriculum before the school year begins! Their boredom can result in low achievement and grades.
- Gifted children are problem solvers. They benefit from working on open-ended, interdisciplinary problems—for example, how to solve a shortage of community resources. Gifted students often refuse to work for grades alone.
- Gifted students often think abstractly and with such complexity that they may need help with concrete study and test-taking skills. They may not be able to select one answer in a multiple choice question because they see how all the answers might be correct.
- Gifted students who do well in school may define success as getting an "A" and failure as any grade less than an "A." By early adolescence they may be unwilling to try anything where they are not certain of guaranteed success.

Source: ERIC Clearinghouse on Disabilities and Gifted Education. Retrieved October 13, 2007 from http://eric.hoagiesgifted.org/fact/myths.html. Original source material: S. Berger, *College Planning for Gifted Students*, 2nd ed. (Reston, VA: Council for Exceptional Children, 1998), p. 16.

unit challenging for all students in the class. Without preassessing the students' knowledge and skills, teachers will assume that how well students do on the end-of-unit assessment is the result of their teaching; with preassessment, teachers will know what students knew as they began the unit.

Suggestions for the Classroom

Differentiated Programming: What It Is and What It Isn't

Differentiated programming and *differentiated instruction* are terms for what is really a simple educational concept—providing instruction that meets the differing needs of all students. Although the concept is simple, making it a reality in the classroom is complex. For the student who is gifted, it means the opportunity to advance as far as possible. For a slower learner, it means offering support for advancement at a pace that allows mastery. Other students have varying abilities, learning styles, interests, and needs, which also must be met. This is what differentiated programming attempts to do.

Differentiated instruction is

☑ Having high expectations for all students.

☑ Providing multiple assignments within units that are oriented toward students with different levels of achievement.

☑ Allowing students to choose, with teacher direction, ways to learn and how to demonstrate what they have learned.

☑ Permitting students to demonstrate mastery of material they already know and progress at their own pace through new material.

☑ Structuring class assignments so they require high levels of critical thinking but permit a range of responses.

☑ Assigning some activities geared to different learning styles, levels of thinking, levels of interest, and levels of achievement.

☑ Providing students with opportunities to have choices about what they learn.

☑ Flexible. Teachers may move students in and out of groups after assessing their instructional needs.

Differentiated instruction is not

☑ Individualization. It isn't a different lesson plan for each student each day.

☑ Giving all students the same work most of the time.

☑ Students spending significant amounts of time teaching material they have mastered to others who have not mastered it.

☑ Assigning more work at the same level to high-achieving students.

☑ All the time. Often, it is preferable for students to work as a whole class.

☑ Grouping students into cooperative learning groups that do not provide for individual accountability or do not focus on work that is new to all students.

☑ Using only the differences in student responses to the same class assignment to provide differentiation.

☑ Limited to acceleration. Teachers are encouraged to use a variety of strategies.

SOURCE: Susan Allan, unpublished manuscript.

Educators often use a variety of instructional strategies to meet the unique needs of pupils who are gifted and talented.

Instructional Strategies

CURRICULUM COMPACTING Curriculum compacting is a differentiation strategy that is often used in the general education classroom (Reis & Renzulli, 2005). Simply stated, **curriculum compacting** is an instructional procedure whereby the time spent on academic subjects is telescoped or reduced so as to allow the student(s) to make continuous progress. The first phase is to determine the goals and objectives of the regular curriculum. The second step in the process is to assess what the student or students already know before beginning to teach a unit of study. If the preassessment indicates that one or more pupils have already mastered the content or a major portion thereof, this student or cluster of students will have time to delve into more complex content and to develop different and perhaps more sophisticated products. Curriculum compacting is a strategy that responds well to the characteristics of children who are gifted and talented intellectually, in specific academic areas, or in the visual and performing arts. Language arts and mathematics are two content areas where curriculum compacting has been shown to be effective (Reis et al., 2003). See the accompanying First Person feature for teaching suggestions from an award-winning educator (page 564).

HIGHER-LEVEL THINKING AND PROBLEM SOLVING Leaders of business and industry have told educators for decades that it is very important for students to develop higher-level thinking and problem-solving skills. If all teachers combine higher-level thinking skills with significant content, all children will thrive. Children who are gifted and talented will be ready for higher-level thinking and problem solving before many of their age-mates. Services provided by a teacher of gifted pupils can complement the teaching of thinking by the general educator. A gifted resource teacher can provide opportunities for individual and team projects that require higher-level thinking.

FLEXIBLE GROUPING The one-room school is a well-known example of **flexible grouping.** A 9-year-old child could spell with 13-year-olds but do math with 7-year-olds, if those groupings matched his/her level of achievement. Preassessment provides a defensible rationale for grouping and regrouping children to allow for continuous progress. Grouping by interests, needs, and abilities can be used within a heterogeneous classroom, in a homogeneous classroom, or between classrooms or teams. Flexible grouping is necessary if all children, including those who are gifted and talented, are to thrive in a classroom and make continuous progress.

CLUSTER GROUPING **Cluster grouping** is the practice of placing five or more students who have similar needs and abilities with one teacher. For example, seven fourth-grade students who are gifted in mathematics are placed together in a classroom. The purpose of cluster grouping is twofold. First, from a practical standpoint, a teacher is far more likely to plan instruction to address the need for more advanced content and a faster pace of instruction with a cluster than with a single student. Second, others who have similar needs and interests provide an intellectual peer group as well as age-mates for the students in the cluster.

Cluster grouping has advantages for both students and teachers. For the students who are gifted and talented, the cluster arrangement promotes challenging cognitive and positive social-emotional development. For teachers, the cluster provides a group for which to plan rather than single students sprinkled among all of the teachers.

TIERED ASSIGNMENTS This instructional strategy allows the teacher to offer variations of the same lesson to children with differing levels of ability. As an example, if the class is reading *Charlotte's Web*, one group of students might be working on basic facts about the plot while tier two might be asked to write a story about one of the main characters. Pupils who are gifted and in tier three might be asked to write their own chapter from the point of view of one of the characters. **Tiered assignments** allow for individualization of instruction according to level of readiness.

PROBLEM-BASED LEARNING The application of critical thinking skills and the development of problem-solving abilities along with the acquisition of knowledge are some of the benefits associated with using **problem-based learning** in the classroom. In this model, students are confronted with authentic, real-world situations, such as global warming, that are "ill-structured problems." The pupils are asked to solve the problem, which typically has multiple solutions. Teachers function as tutors and facilitators as the children work through various solutions and scenarios and evaluate their responses. Sometimes teachers model effective problem-solving strategies by thinking out loud and questioning their own hypotheses and recommendations. Pupils are often highly motivated and very engaged in their own learning (Smith, Polloway, Patton, & Dowdy, 2008).

PACING INSTRUCTION Individuals who are gifted and talented learn at a faster pace in their area of talent or special interest than their age-mates. This faster pace provides the rationale for differentiation strategies. *Prisoners of Time* (National Education Commission on Time and Learning, 1994) reports, "Some students take three to six times longer than others to learn the same thing. . . . Under today's practices, high-ability students are forced to spend more time than they need on a curriculum developed for students of moderate ability. Many become bored, unmotivated, and frustrated. They become prisoners of time" (p. 15).

Because children who are gifted and talented often complete their work in a fraction of the time that it takes their age-mates, teachers often provide more work to keep them busy. This practice is contrary to the needs of those children who can complete the assignment rapidly. The need for accelerated pacing must be linked not with more work but with increasingly complex content and challenging learning experiences.

CREATIVITY Creativity is important for all children. According to Clark (2008), it is "a highly complex human ability that is beyond giftedness and can bring forth that which is new, diverse, advanced, complex, or previously unknown, so that humankind can experience growth in life as fuller, richer, and/or more meaningful" (p. 188). Developing creative thinking skills is an especially important element of services for children who are gifted and talented. E. Paul Torrance (1969) describes four skills that are essential for a creative thinker: originality, fluency, flexibility, and elaboration. Originality is the ability to produce novel ideas. Fluency involves the ability to generate many ideas, and flexibility is the ability to switch categories of

First Person

One Size Does Not Fit All

How might a classroom involved in the inclusion of gifted students look? Please take a glimpse into my Primary 1 (kindergarten) classroom, room 21, for a moment, for inclusion is what you will see.

All of the children are working in math centers. Brandy and Alison are using random number generators (dice) to create simple addition sentences. Once they have generated two numbers to write down, they add the numbers together for the sum, and as all good mathematicians do, they double-check their work. At the same time, Lane and Shelby are busy using the random number generators to do double-digit addition. They squeal when they realize that their sum actually took them above 100. Sam and Megan are well above the regular addition process. They have stepped into the world of multiplication. They are using the random number generators and teddy bear counters to create groups representing multiplication. The entire room is a buzz of mathematical vocabulary and a celebration of learning . . . music to any teacher's ears. My journey to inclusion of the gifted student within my classroom was a result of realizing that I was not meeting the needs of my students.

As a seventeen-year teaching veteran, I have taught grades kindergarten through sixth grade. Throughout those years, I have worn many hats. For a two-year period I was the Curriculum Coordinator for our building. I had the pleasant task of formally assessing students as a part of a verification process of our primary talent pool process. Bright-eyed primary students sat eagerly across from me amazing me with their high-ability thought processes. Each time a tiny student answered a question that was well above the typical/average level of learning for a primary student, I always asked, "Where did you learn about multiplication . . . square root . . . such difficult words to read?" The response was *always* the same: "My mom" or "My dad." I was always saddened to never hear, "My teacher." When I returned to the classroom, I became determined to be in on the fun of removing the ceiling of learning for my students. When one of my students amazes everyone by sharing something brilliant, I am hoping she/he will be able to share . . . "My teacher taught me that!"

As our children walk through the door of our classrooms we must ever be cognizant of the fact that *"One size does not fit all."* Every classroom, without exception, is a classroom of diverse learners. Through a variety of means, teachers have the ability to orchestrate a classroom so that all needs can and will be met. The most important information a teacher must know before reaching all children includes: What does *each* of my children know, what do they need to know, how are they able to apply what they have learned, and what kind of connection has each child made to his/her own world?

Before every thematic unit in our kindergarten classroom, the children help prepare a KWL (sometimes a KWHL) chart. *K* stands for "What do we know, or think we know, about this subject?" The *W* represents "What would we like to learn about this subject?" And the *L* is a follow-up for "What have we learned about this subject?" We also have a category for *H*, "How will we find out what we want to know?" The KWL chart is a good way

ideas. Elaboration is the ability to provide detail to ideas. All teachers should incorporate the teaching of creative thinking skills as an integral part of their curriculum.

Students who are gifted in creativity need opportunities to develop this talent in a risk-free learning environment (Piirto, 2007). They need to interact with creative adults, speculating on possibilities and examining the creative process as well as creative products. Pupils who are gifted thrive when given opportunities to combine their creativity with an interest in a content or talent area.

for me to get a pulse of the class's knowledge and interest concerning the content I plan to present. I am able to use the information from the children to divide them into interest groups or to determine if the content needs to be modified in any way for particular students. The KWL is simply one form of preassessment used in our classroom on a regular basis. As the teacher, I simply must know *what* my children know. If a student or group of students is already equipped with the information I want to teach and I "plow ahead" with that unit without adjustments, then I have committed a grave injustice to my students. I have asked them to be patient as I teach the other students. As adults we are outraged when we are asked to sit still and listen to something we already know forwards and backwards. Our children are the same. When we teach content that a child has mastered, we are asking her/him to run in one spot over and over, much like a cartoon character that never seems to get anywhere.

Children not only come to us at different levels, they learn at different paces. Once you know what the children know individually, you must monitor progress through formative assessments. If a child has mastered a concept, he/she should be able to move on. If a child knows how to do simple addition with 100% accuracy, he/she should not be put through the nightmarish experience of extra work in simple addition. That child is ready to move on, not run in place! Math is one area in which I enjoy using the compacting process. For that quick learner, once I find out where he/she is, we move forward. The result of the pretesting is a learning atmosphere such as I described earlier. The overall assessment process is simply described. The pretest is the map for instruction. The formative tests are the detours. The posttesting is the determination of how successful we are in finding the final destination.

Literacy in a classroom should be individualized as much as math. In my classroom each child has his/her own word ring and reading assignments made on a weekly basis. Monitoring the word ring and reading progress at school enables the children to make continuous progress no matter what the reading level of each child may be. I love encouraging the children to go home and "impress" their parents or some other grown-up at home. When discussion of what they are learning is encouraged, the children are more prone to make school-learning connections transfer to home-learning connections. Parents are certainly vital participants in their child's education. But as the teacher, you will be looked upon as the one who should set the pace. We should be ever mindful that the pace for a child means continuous learning.

Textbooks are wonderful resources for teachers, but they are certainly no substitute for allowing children to think for themselves. I love to have the children use questioning . . . questioning of everything. I especially enjoy setting the stage for learning with a variety of materials centered on certain content and then turning the children loose on creating their own questions. Creativity, problem solving, and real-world learning become the products of such an environment.

Imagine the absolute misery Einstein would feel today sitting in a typical primary classroom. Sitting through simple addition would be torture for him! Every classroom today has the potential of having an Einstein in it. We must make it our duty and responsibility to meet the needs of the Einsteins of the future.

—Patrice McCrary
Cumberland Trace Elementary School
Warren County, KY
2003 Kentucky Teacher of the Year
2006 All-USA Teacher Team

There is no one "correct" way to teach students who are gifted and talented. Teachers must skillfully match the needs of the pupil with the demands of the curriculum. Effective teaching of learners who are gifted and talented, as with other students, requires planning. It is a matter of constructing a "goodness of fit" between the individual's learning style and the specific content of the curriculum. As educators, our goal should be to develop each pupil's gifts and talents to their fullest degree. The accompanying Effective Instructional Practices feature offers suggestions for teaching students who are gifted (see page 570).

Making Inclusion Work

I am still somewhat of a rookie in the field of education. I taught eighth-grade language arts for three years. Although I loved that position and learned so much from it, I recently decided to take on a new challenge—the position of countywide gifted and talented teacher/coordinator. Throughout my career I have attended a wide variety of workshops related to teaching writing, reading across the curriculum, differentiated educational strategies, gender-based instruction, and gifted education. I have served as a model teacher for beginning teachers, and with my new position as gifted teacher/coordinator, I give workshops across the county about the selection process for children who are gifted and talented and strategies for differentiation and acceleration that can be used with all students. I work with four elementary schools and one high school, collaborating with teachers on service plans for students who are gifted and talented. Soon I will be teaching four days a week during which children in grades 3–8 who are gifted and talented from across the county will come to my classroom and work in a resource room setting.

Strategies for Inclusive Classrooms

Based on my teaching experience, I believe that the key to effective instruction centers on two key ingredients—relationships with students and the belief that *every* child has strengths. I set high expectations for all my students. When I plan units, I try to begin with some sort of preassessment to find out what my students already know about the content that I am about to present. Based on the results, I can then adjust my activities to fit the needs of each of my students. Various preassessments that I have used include the following:

- Brainstorming: Students list questions that they have pertaining to that topic.
- KW Charts: Students chart what they already know, what they want to know about a topic, and how they want to learn it.
- Anticipation Guides: Students are given a list of statements that relate to the concepts that will be covered during the unit. They read each statement, put a checkmark next to the ones with which they agree, engage in discussions about their answers, use the text and other materials for the chapter to either prove or disprove their answers, and finally review the statements and change them as necessary to make them true. The entire class debates the evidence that proves the statements and must come to consensus about each one.
- Most Difficult First: Students are presented with the most difficult vocabulary words from our list, and those who score 80 percent or better on a definition pretest are assigned another activity.

The beauty of each of these strategies is that each one can be used with any content area. Once I have diagnosed the situation, I can then decide which activities my students should complete.

I have found that cluster grouping is a highly effective strategy with students of all ability levels. In my opinion, the most positive outcome of this strategy is that the students who are gifted can excel to their fullest potential when presented with problem-solving activities, yet they don't feel burdened by the lack of motivation sometimes evidenced by their classmates. Additionally, those students who may lack academic confidence gain confidence in their abilities because they find that without someone else to carry the load, they can do it . . . and they usually do! It's a win/win situation for everyone.

Obviously, based on the repeated success of the differentiated projects, I would highly recommend them to all teachers at any grade level and ability level. In planning for these types of projects, I first reflect on the particular learning styles that exist in my classroom, choose a project type to fit each one, and then develop scoring criteria for each project choice. For example, for visual learners I might choose to include a poster option; for bodily/kinesthetic learners, I might choose a role play; for those who are verbally gifted, I might choose a newspaper article; and for those who are more intrapersonal in nature, I might choose creation of a Web page that requires individual work. Of course, with each new unit, I adjust the project choices accordingly because I don't want my students to become bored or accustomed to the same types of choices. I have never had a student complain about doing the projects—honestly! They much prefer them to tests, and so do I. In my opinion, these types of projects are true assessments of what students have learned because they tend to gravitate toward the choices that favor their own particular learning style, and consequently, they do well because they can show me what they know in the way that they know best. I have found that the products my students present to me provide me with an effective tool for building relationships with them because they have the freedom to demonstrate their understanding in a way that is completely unique to them.

Finally, my experience with independent studies has proven to be successful. I have found that allowing students to choose their topic to demonstrate a particular skill is very beneficial because they have the freedom to study something that is meaningful to them. Also, the types of products that they create will be specific to their own particular ability levels.

Successful Collaboration

My teaching experience has taught me one very important lesson . . . collaboration is crucial! Due to scheduling problems with planning time, our school cannot plan units by cross-curricular teams (including math, science, language arts, and social studies.) However, during my first three years of teaching, I was fortunate enough to work very closely with another language arts teacher who had the same philosophy about teaching and learning that I did. We both believed that all students can learn, and we both were passionate about offering them challenges that expanded their minds and were enjoyable and fostered creativity in the process. We collaborated daily and often fed off one another in our planning of units. Once we were comfortable with one another, we decided to approach the eighth-grade social studies teacher and plan some activities that extended the students' learning of social studies concepts while in language arts class. Perhaps our most successful language arts/social studies collaboration resulted when we planned to read the Revolutionary War novel *My Brother Sam Is Dead* as the students were studying the Revolutionary War. The students loved it, and so did we! As we read the novel, I actually called upon the students to clarify some questions I had periodically, based on what they had learned previously about the war. It's a very gratifying experience to see students begin to make connections from one subject to another. When they master this skill, they are truly demonstrating higher-level thinking skills. My heart smiled as I listened to both my students who are gifted or talented and those with lower ability rattle off war facts without even blinking. Again, setting high expectations for everyone in the room paid huge dividends because students of varying levels gained confidence in their academic abilities.

Working with Parents and Families

While collaboration with other teachers has been beneficial for me, close contact with parents and families is also important. In fact, in some cases, it has saved me. I have had several students who were obviously gifted, yet they were unmotivated and were underperforming academically. When I realized that these students were underachieving, my first inclination was to contact the parents to ask for suggestions concerning tapping into their child's interests. I realized that if I could tweak assignments to cater to their areas of interest, they would be much more likely to get involved and have an appropriate learning experience. The line of communication was beneficial both ways, however. Making parents aware of the situation also gave them the chance to ask me for suggestions about ways to inspire their children at home. Although I have had many students who rose to every occasion and performed to the absolute best of their ability, I have had just as many who were less than excited about school because of sheer boredom and complacency. Those individuals definitely require more work, but inspiring them is worth all of the effort—for the student, the parent, and the teacher.

Advice for Making Inclusion and Collaboration Work

When students who are gifted or talented are involved, open-mindedness and flexibility are critical in making inclusion and collaboration work. I believe that the key to success in these situations is to appreciate each student for what he or she can offer the class. It is the teacher's responsibility to know each student's strengths and needs and to continuously assess his or her progress in order to promote academic growth. Modifying activities to fit students' needs, regardless of their ability level, is critical in providing appropriate learning experiences. Although I have always respected my students with gifts and talents, I have tried very hard to let all of my other pupils know that I value them just as much and to convey the message that everyone can learn something from someone else. I believe this philosophy creates an atmosphere of community, and when everyone cares about and helps everyone else, it's a truly productive, magical learning environment.

—Erin DeHaven
Breckinridge County Middle School,
Breckinridge, KY
Gifted and Talented Teacher/Gifted Coordinator

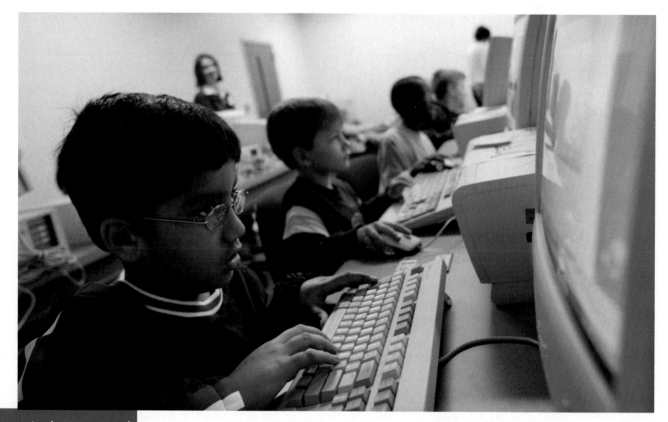

As educators, our goal should be to develop each child's gifts and talents to their fullest degree.

Service Delivery Options

Pupils with gifts and talents require exposure to a curriculum that is rigorous and intellectually challenging. These students need instruction that is more complex and abstract than that provided to their typical peers (Burns, Purcell, & Hertberg, 2006). In many instances, this necessitates programming options outside of the general education classroom. The general education classroom, as traditionally organized in terms of curriculum and instruction, is seen as inadequate for meeting the needs of pupils who are gifted and talented (Clark, 2008). Silverman (1995b) believes that too many children who are gifted are "languishing in the regular classroom" (p. 220) because they are exposed to a curriculum that is too simple and mastered long ago. The general education classroom is, in many cases, an exceedingly restrictive placement for pupils with special talents and gifts, rather than a least restrictive setting (Gallagher, 2003). As a result, many schools provide a range or continuum of service delivery options designed to meet the unique needs of students who are gifted. Figure 14.6 portrays an array of programming alternatives appropriate for gifted learners from elementary to high school.

GIFTED RESOURCE SERVICES Children identified in any area of giftedness or talent need some time with others who share their interests and abilities. Working with other children of similar abilities takes away the feeling that many children who are gifted have that they must hide their abilities in order to "fit in." This service is typically provided through a resource room or pull-out program. Such a program can be the highlight of the students'

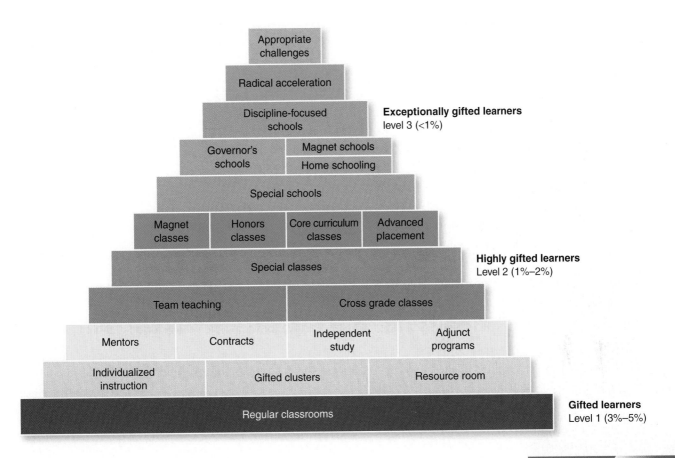

Appropriate challenges

Radical acceleration

Discipline-focused schools

Exceptionally gifted learners
level 3 (<1%)

Governor's schools

Magnet schools

Home schooling

Special schools

Magnet classes | Honors classes | Core curriculum classes | Advanced placement

Special classes

Highly gifted learners
Level 2 (1%–2%)

Team teaching | Cross grade classes

Mentors | Contracts | Independent study | Adjunct programs

Individualized instruction | Gifted clusters | Resource room

Regular classrooms

Gifted learners
Level 1 (3%–5%)

Figure 14.6

Levels of Programming Options for Gifted Learners

NOTE: All programs for gifted learners, regardless of how they are structured, must provide differentiation, flexible grouping, continuous progress, intellectual peer interaction, continuity, and teachers with specialized education.

SOURCE: Adapted from B. Clark, *Growing Up Gifted,* 7th ed. (Upper Saddle River, NJ: Pearson Education, 2008), p. 405. Reprinted by permission of Pearson Education.

day or week. It is important that classroom teachers see the time with the gifted resource teacher as an important service but not the only one needed by these children. Children who are gifted and talented are gifted all day, all week; they need ongoing instruction that will remove the learning ceiling and allow for continuous progress. Table 14.4 (page 571) lists some of the advantages and disadvantages of a resource room model.

ACCELERATION The child who is achieving above grade level and is ready to learn at increasingly advanced levels needs **acceleration.** Acceleration matches learning opportunities to the readiness of the student to learn at challenging levels. Researchers have found several beneficial outcomes for acceleration (Colangelo, Assouline, & Gross, 2004; Kulik, 2003). Among these positive outcomes are greater academic achievement, increased interest in school, and enhanced self-concept. Contrary to the worries of some parents and administrators, when properly implemented, acceleration does not contribute to social and emotional problems (Swiatek, 1993).

Acceleration may take several forms. Acceleration may focus on one content area, such as art or mathematics, or it may be a full-year acceleration known as grade skipping. It may also mean starting school at a younger age. Children who are reading when they come to school need to continue to improve their reading skills and to enhance their comprehension. Reading may be accelerated in the class with a cluster of children who are also early readers, or the child/children may join the first grade for the portion of the day devoted to reading. The skipping of a grade will usually be successful if the child wants to do it and if the receiving teacher wants the situation to work well. Acceleration includes taking high

✓ EFFECTIVE INSTRUCTIONAL PRACTICES — Differentiated Instruction

The goal of schools must be to create, support, and encourage lifelong learning. The most likely way to achieve that goal is differentiation, an instructional strategy that is a popular topic for educators to discuss but is less frequently implemented. Because all fourth or eighth graders, however, are not at the same level of achievement in any content area and their interests differ greatly, differentiation is very important. It is the strategy that is most likely to ensure continuous progress of all children, including those who are gifted and talented.

Effective instruction for learners with gifts and talents involves five steps:

Step 1. Preassess.

Once you have planned the unit of study, the starting point in planning differentiation must be to preassess.

Guiding Question: "Who already knows the content and can demonstrate the skills even before the unit of study begins?"

Step 2. Group children for instructional purposes.

Preassessment results provide information to help you decide which students can be clustered for instructional purposes for a particular unit of study. Grouping facilitates learning, providing the vehicle for differentiating learning experiences.

Guiding Question: "Which students are ready to learn the content at the same level and would benefit from being grouped for instruction?"

Step 3. Match learner experiences to the preassessment data (level of achievement, interests).

Differentiation does not just mean providing different learning experiences or offering choice; rather, differentiation is the intentional match of content (basic to complex), process (level of cognitive skill), and product (visual, written, oral, kinesthetic, and technological).

Guiding Question: "How can the learning experiences be shaped to match the preassessment results and to ensure intellectual stimulation?"

Step 4. Provide products (ways to demonstrate what has been learned) that will motivate and teach.

A variety of products can be used that will allow students to show what they have learned but in ways that will motivate them to learn.

Guiding Question: "What products will interest students and prepare them to build expertise for current and future use?"

Step 5. Reflect, reflect, reflect.

Learning experiences that remain isolated do not promote lifelong learning. If learning is to be ongoing, reflecting on what has been learned and what questions one wants to learn next is essential.

Guiding Question: "What questions will promote reflection and ongoing learning?"

school classes while in middle school or taking College Board Advanced Placement classes throughout high school. It may involve taking advanced courses on the Internet or by correspondence. It may also include early entrance into college.

Besides acceleration, teachers have several other techniques at their disposal for modifying the curriculum in an effort to meet the needs of students with gifts and talents. Examples of these strategies can be found in Table 14.5. A variety of strategies and service

Table 14.4	Advantages and Disadvantages: The Resource Room and Pull-out Models
Advantages	**Disadvantages**
1. Pull-out programs are relatively easy to set in motion.	1. Costs more as extra teachers have to be hired and special facilities provided.
2. The teacher in the regular classroom has more time to work with the other students.	2. The regular classroom teacher may get frustrated and feel that students leaving is a disruption to their educational plan.
3. Students who are left in classroom have a chance to shine.	3. Students in the regular classroom may feel resentful.
4. The teacher in the pull-out program can focus on critical and creative thinking because the teacher in the regular classroom focuses on the standard curriculum.	4. The academically talented students might have to make up work in the regular classroom while having more work in the pull-out classroom.
5. The differentiation of curriculum is separated from the classroom flow.	5. Curriculum may have no relationship to curriculum in the regular classroom.
6. Students receive special help in areas of strength.	6. Students are treated differently according to ability.
7. Teachers may feel as if they have "their" kids.	7. Teachers are isolated from the other teachers.
8. Students can have time with other students to discuss intellectual interests that may not be shared by students in the regular classroom.	8. Students may feel different from the rest of the students in their regular classroom.
9. Collaboration with other teachers is encouraged.	9. Students are academically talented all the time and not just during pull-out time.
10. Small groups of students can do special projects that would not be possible in the regular classroom.	10. Small groups of students may receive special privileges other students don't receive (e.g., access to computers, field trips).
11. Teachers of the talented can provide intensive instruction in areas of expertise (e.g., the arts, foreign language).	11. Turf issues with regular classroom teacher may arise (e.g., homework, lessons and assemblies missed).

Source: J. Pirto, *Talented Children and Adults,* 3rd ed. (Waco, TX: Prufrock, 2007), p. 87.

Table 14.5	Strategies for Addressing the Needs of Advanced Learners	
Types	**Focus of Opportunities**	**Examples**
Enrichment	Opportunities to learn above and beyond what is usually provided at a particular grade level	• In-depth study • Junior Great Books • Competitions • Problem-solving programs • Interdisciplinary seminars
Acceleration	Opportunities to learn at a pace that matches achievement and interest	• Subject acceleration • Early kindergarten entrance • Grade acceleration
Differentiation	Opportunities to have curriculum matched to levels of interest and achievement	• Tiered assignments based on content, process, and product
Grouping	Opportunities to learn with others at the same levels of interest and/or achievement	• Cluster grouping • Pull-out homogeneous classes • Magnet schools with a focus on math, science or the arts

options need to be in place in classrooms and schools to address the wide range of gifted learners' needs.

INDEPENDENT STUDY Independent study allows children of all ages to explore topics of interest and provides challenge if appropriate guidelines are established. These guidelines would include use of primary sources and resources that are matched to the child's level of reading and knowledge of the topic. This strategy enables the child to pose questions about topics of interest and to extend learning to related topics if he/she has demonstrated in a preassessment that he/she has mastered the core content. Independent study is a positive option for children, including those who are gifted and talented, only if they are taught to work independently. Because children are gifted does not mean that they have had the experiences that prepare them to take responsibility for their own learning. The skills needed to conduct primary research and to work independently must be taught. Once the young person refines these skills, independent study can provide alternate learning experiences that will allow the student to tap an area of interest and pursue it in depth.

HONORS AND ADVANCED PLACEMENT COURSES Honors and Advanced Placement classes are appropriate for young people who are ready to learn at advanced levels. Honors courses are offered to middle and high school students who are ready to work hard on advanced content. College Board Advanced Placement (AP) classes are available in approximately thirty different academic areas. Although the AP class is taken at the high school, a score of 3 or higher on the AP exam will earn three or more college credits at most institutions. AP classes may be taken by young people who demonstrate their readiness to learn at the college level no matter their year in school.

MENTORSHIPS "Most mentorships involving the gifted and talented are one-on-one, the relationship most supportive for providing specialized, individual attention to a protégé's development" (Clasen & Clasen, 2003, p. 255). The **mentor** and young person share an interest, making the relationship important to both parties. A mentor may be an older student or an adult with similar interests, a professional, or an artist.

Mentorships are important for young people when pursuing passionate interests and for exploring careers. Working with a mentor can open doors to opportunities. Some mentors will communicate via technology. Some may be in a university, a laboratory, or an office. Mentorships may be formal or informal. They may be set up for a specific period of time, or they may be ongoing. Successful mentorships allow serious learners opportunities to pursue ideas in depth.

SELF-CONTAINED CLASSES AND SPECIAL SCHOOLS Learning with others who share their interests and have similar abilities is essential for children and youth who are gifted and talented. A self-contained class of students who are intellectually gifted provides a learning environment in which many of them will thrive. Special schools are found in many urban school districts. These magnet programs for middle and high school students typically focus on math and science or the visual and performing arts. Several states sponsor residential high schools that are academies for mathematics and science and/or the visual and performing arts.

SUMMER AND SATURDAY PROGRAMS Summer and Saturday programs should challenge young people to learn at high levels and provide opportunities to get to know others who share their interests and have similar abilities. Such programs are offered at colleges and universities

First Person

Summer Programming

After much counting down, the long awaited end of the school year is finally here. The anxiously awaited three months of relaxation have arrived. For most gifted kids, this is a time for complete shutdown and withdrawal. They could spend hours sitting in the mind-numbing aura of a television or sleep for 12 hours a day. For some gifted kids, summer is recuperation from the harsh school year they just survived. But for others, myself included, summer is when the long anticipated summer camp takes place. Instead of shutting down and withdrawing, we are stimulated and placed in an environment where gifted kids have no problem "socializing." New information is absorbed, and the brain is kept awake and active. Things some gifted kids miss out on in the school year are presented in large quantities. Things like a caring mentor,

an inspiring role model, or just a decent learning environment. Self-esteem skyrockets, and gifted kids begin to understand themselves more, by being around others like them. For me, summer programs were life changing. I gained assertiveness, self-confidence, and self-respect. I learned that I was not alone in the world. I learned that there were many other kids going through the same things I did each school day. I found out that I did, in fact, have the potential to do many things that I never knew I could, such as be popular among my peers, be accepted as who I am, and be known as something more than just "the smart kid."

—Graham Oliver
Paducah, KY
Ninth Grade

as well as by some school districts. The academic content should take students beyond age-level expectations and content. National and state associations for gifted education can be a good source of information on summer and Saturday programs. The accompanying First Person feature offers one adolescent's perspective on a summer camp experience.

COMPETITIONS Competitions do not constitute gifted education, but they do provide motivation and challenge for some young people who are gifted and talented. Just as athletes have both individual and team sports, some competitions are for individuals, others for pairs of children, and still others for teams. Information about a few competitions can be obtained from the Web sites listed at the end of the chapter, but there are many other competitions targeting a variety of interests and academic areas. *Competitions for Talented Kids* (Karnes & Riley, 2005) provides important information about competitions.

Services for Young Children Who Are Gifted and Talented

The educational needs of young children with special gifts and talents have largely been overlooked (Piirto, 2007). Among the reasons are a lack of federal legislation guaranteeing these children an education, difficulties in identifying this unique population of learners, problems in constructing developmentally appropriate educational experiences, and an inconsistent commitment to serving the nation's brightest and best preschoolers.

Table 14.6	Characteristics of Young Talented Children

1. They are precocious, regardless of the talent area. Some may demonstrate precocious behaviors in several talent areas.

   a. Verbally talented children acquire vocabulary and speak in sentences earlier than age-mates. They can break letter codes and make abstract verbal connections.

   b. Mathematically talented children acquire numeration and number concepts sooner than age-mates.

   c. Musically talented children may often sing on key, demonstrate an interest in the piano or other musical instruments, and stop what they are doing to listen to music.

   d. Children talented in visual arts demonstrate artwork that is similar to that of older children.

   e. Kinesthetically or psychomotor-talented children demonstrate advanced motor ability.

   f. Spatially talented children may want to take things apart to see how they work, and demonstrate an understanding of mechanics that is advanced for their age.

   g. Children talented in the inter- and intrapersonal areas will demonstrate advanced understanding of social relationships, and demonstrate emotion about such things that age-mates will not perceive.

2. They have excellent memories.

3. They concentrate intensely on what interests them, for longer periods of time than age-mates.

4. Dyssynchrony [uneven development] is obvious, especially in high-IQ children.

5. Affective precocity may lead to the assumption of leadership roles and to preferring older companions for play.

Source: J. Piirto, *Talented Children and Adults,* 3rd ed. (Waco, TX: Prufrock Press, 2007), p. 225.

Early identification is essential to meeting the needs of these youngsters. Parents and other adult caregivers are especially astute at recognizing talents and gifts. More often than not, when parents suspect that their son or daughter is gifted, follow-up assessments support the parents' beliefs (Robinson, Shore, & Enersen, 2007). Table 14.6 lists some of the characteristics typical of young children who are talented.

Despite the early evidence of gifts and talents, children are frequently not identified until the third or fourth grade. In fact, professionals disagree about the appropriateness of early identification of young children with gifts and talents. Critics of early programming argue that young children are rushed through their childhood. Supporters feel that there is a moral imperative to identify these youngsters and offer them challenging and stimulating opportunities to develop their unique abilities and gifts (Smutny, Walker, & Meckstroth, 2007). One common proposal is early admission to kindergarten or first grade. Howley, Howley, and Pendarvis (1995) consider this suggestion to be pedagogically sound and essential to the development of the child's gifts. When making such a decision, however, parents and educators need to carefully consider the individual's physical and emotional maturity so that an appropriate educational experience can be designed. Preschoolers who evidence gifts in one area, such as artistic talent, may be quite average in their verbal skills and social ability. Parents and

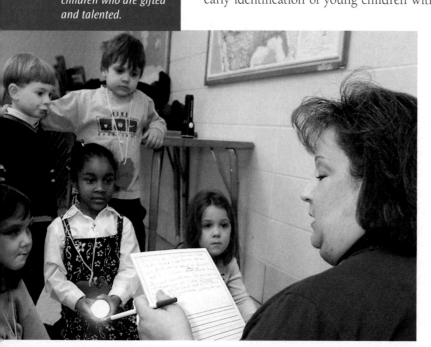

Early identification is crucial for meeting the needs of young children who are gifted and talented.

professionals must be sensitive to this variability and be careful not to develop unrealistic expectations of superiority in all areas of development.

Early school experiences for academically talented pupils must be both enriching and accelerated. The primary concern, however, should always be the child, with his/her special abilities second (Piirto, 2007). Play, which is the "work" of a child, must be a critical component of any curriculum. The curriculum must be balanced and address all areas of development while reflecting the interests of the child. Finger painting and block building are just as important as counting and matching rhyming words.

Adolescents and Adults Who Are Gifted and Talented

Adolescence is a time of awkwardness for most young people, and adolescents who are gifted and talented are no exception. At a time in life when differences can be a liability, adolescents with gifts and talents need opportunities to be with others who share their interests and have similar abilities in order to know that their needs, interests, passions, and characteristics are "normal" for them. Csikszentmihalyi, Rathunde, and Whalen (1997) conducted a longitudinal study of 200 talented teenagers. They found some definite differences between talented teenagers and other adolescents. They describe the talented teens as having "personality attributes well suited to the difficult struggle of establishing their mastery over a domain: a desire to achieve, persistence, and a curiosity and openness to experience" (p. 82). Although we know that stereotyping adolescents who are gifted as misfits is not supported by research, "it must be understood that there are unique stresses and dynamic issues associated with a person's giftedness" (Robinson et al., 2007, p. 15).

Early adolescence is a challenging time for all young people, and middle school students who are gifted often feel pressure to "fit in." Middle schoolers who are gifted in any of the categories need challenging opportunities to make continuous progress in their talent areas and to share high-level learning experiences with others who are equally interested in this area. In reality, a lack of appropriately challenging instruction frequently leads to apathy and disengagement from the teaching/learning process (Tomlinson, 1994). Girls of middle school age frequently learn to compete "with boys" or "for boys"; these choices can profoundly affect their later choices. By the time young people enter high school, they set their course of study by the choices they make, selecting or avoiding the most rigorous courses. They also begin to consider and make career choices. Early adolescence is often a particularly complicated and difficult time for students with gifts and talents.

One of the key questions confronting professionals is how best to meet the educational needs of young people who are gifted and talented. Educators disagree as to which pedagogical strategy is best. Among the instructional options available to adolescents and young adults are enrolling in Advanced Placement (AP) classes, high school honors classes, or Saturday programs; seeking early admission to college; and attending a **magnet high school** (a secondary school with a particular focus such as science, mathematics, or the performing arts). Despite the general availability of these services, a fairly large portion of high school dropouts (estimated between 10 and 20 percent) are gifted (Davis & Rimm, 2004). We can only speculate that these students are unfulfilled and not academically challenged. Perhaps the lack of support services, the absence of a caring mentor, and the need to be accepted by peers interact to contribute to this phenomenon. For those individuals with gifts and talents who pursue postsecondary education, many colleges and universities offer a variety of honors classes and other opportunities for accelerated and in-depth study and investigation.

One well-known outlet for adults who are gifted is MENSA. Primarily a social organization, this international group consists of individuals who have an IQ in the top 2 percent of the general population. MENSA has approximately 50,000 U.S. members who come from all walks of life but share one common trait—high intelligence (MENSA, 2007).

Family Issues

A synthesis of research evidence paints a picture of some of the characteristics of families who have children who are gifted (see Table 14.7). Families exert a powerful influence on any child, but especially on a child who is gifted (Subotnik, Kassan, Summers, & Wasser, 1993). If parents believe, Clark (2008) writes, that "their child has special ability, they will hold different expectancies [and] allow more opportunities to develop this ability" (pp. 65–66). Family support is vital if ability is to translate into achievement and accomplishment.

Parents play a critical role in their son's or daughter's classroom performance. In a classic study of 12,000 high school students over a four-year period, Steinberg (1996) found that parents and peers exerted the greatest influence on the young person's academic performance, greater than the teacher or the student's IQ score. Steinberg emphasizes the importance of parents' setting a priority on academic excellence.

Providing opportunities beyond school to develop talents or to further study in areas of interest can be expensive but critical to the student's future. Parents must understand

Table 14.7	Characteristics of Families of Children Who Are Gifted
Few children in family
Gifted child oldest or only child
Early stimulation and enrichment given to children, including reading to them, encouraging language development, and exposure to a variety of experiences (e.g., museums, exhibits, and visual and performing arts)
Parents older and better educated than typical parents
Parents show high energy and love of learning
Strong work ethic and valuing of achievement modeled by parents
Parents set clear standards that are flexible and fairly administered
Parents respect the rights and dignity of children
All members of the family are encouraged to develop to the highest level of their ability as individuals
Family relationships and parent–child interactions are healthy
Parents and children share work, learning, and play
Parents involved in school-related activities

Source: B. Clark, *Growing Up Gifted*, 6th ed. (Upper Saddle River, NJ: Prentice Hall, 2002), p. 152. Reprinted by permission.

how important it is for their children to find intellectual peers. It is well worth the time and resources that it takes to have the child who is interested in the violin play with a youth orchestra or the young person who is interested in any number of academic pursuits to drive to the nearest university to participate in a Saturday program. These experiences are often turning points that validate the need to work hard in order to achieve at high levels.

Parents may benefit from reading about children who are gifted and their needs. Parents can also benefit from joining state and national associations that advocate for gifted education. They need to know their legal rights and the regulations affecting gifted education in their state and local school system (Karnes, Stephens, & McHard, 2008). Parents need information about due process procedures if they believe that their child is not being provided appropriate services and is not being challenged to learn at appropriately high levels.

Issues of Diversity

Children who are gifted and talented come from all socioeconomic, racial, and ethnic groups. A concern among educators is to be certain that children from all backgrounds are afforded quality educational opportunities that allow for gifts and talents to emerge and to ensure that students from diverse backgrounds receive appropriate services to develop their talents to optimal levels. A challenge to teachers is to become talent developers so that all pupils are able to demonstrate their special talents and gifts. Despite the best efforts of professionals, three particular dimensions of diversity remain issues today: (1) gifted and talented students with disabilities; (2) girls who are gifted and talented; and (3) the assessment and identification of gifts and talents in pupils from culturally and linguistically diverse populations.

Students with Gifts and Talents and Disabilities

Only recently have educators devoted attention to individuals with gifts and talents who also have a disability. All too often, the gifts and talents of these students are overlooked and services are focused on the disability. It is tragic that people with disabilities are seldom thought of as possessing gifts and talents (Davis & Rimm, 2004)—most likely because of biases, prejudices, and stereotypic expectations that prevent us from seeing their strengths. Yet think, for example, of the following eminent individuals who, although disabled, are truly gifted and talented in their respective fields of endeavor: Stephen Hawking, theoretical physicist (amyotrophic lateral sclerosis [ALS], also known as Lou Gehrig's disease); Franklin D. Roosevelt, U.S. President (polio); Helen Keller, author and social activist (dual sensory impaired); and Ray Charles, musician (visually impaired). In each of these instances, their accomplishments overshadow their disability. Children who are gifted and disabled require programming aimed at remediating the deficit(s) caused by the disability and accommodations that minimize its impact, as well as opportunities that nurture and develop their gifts and talents to the fullest potential (Clark, 2008).

A student may have two (or more) disabilities. These **twice exceptional** learners often experience "double jeopardy." A child who is identified as gifted may also have a learning disability, a behavior disorder, a sensory impairment, a physical disability, or attention deficit hyperactivity disorder (ADHD). The challenge confronting professionals is to make a diagnosis that is appropriate. This can be a difficult task because one exceptionality may mask another or the characteristics of the two exceptionalities may be similar. For example, the pupil who has a learning disability but is intellectually gifted will likely perform at an average level, thereby camouflaging the need for gifted services as well as their need for services due to a learning disability. Another frequent problem is thinking that a child has ADHD when in actuality the child is gifted and exhibiting high energy and intense curiosity. "Gifted children with ADHD are usually labeled as underachieving or lazy long before they are ever labeled as ADHD" (Flint, 2001, p. 65). Knowing the characteristics of children who are gifted and talented in any category is the key to recognizing behaviors that reveal gifts and talents in children with and without other exceptionalities.

A great deal of attention is currently being directed to pupils who are gifted and talented and also learning disabled, a population that is frequently misunderstood. In many cases, these students are not receiving the services that would allow for the full expression of their potential. In too many instances, their disability masks their gifts and talents, or their giftedness allows them to compensate and achieve at or near grade level so their learning disability goes undetected; either way, these unique learners are not being appropriately served. Robinson et al. (2007) and King (2005) argue persuasively that these pupils require intervention specially tailored to their needs.

Children who are twice exceptional are sometimes referred to as *paradoxical learners*. Gifted students who are learning disabled exhibit characteristics such as distractibility, inattentiveness, and inefficient learning strategies while, at the same time, presenting patterns typical of students who are gifted. How can teachers best meet the needs of these children? Do we teach to their learning disability, their giftedness, or both? According to Weinfeld, Barnes-Robinson, Jeweler, and Shevitz (2005), students who have both gifts and learning disabilities require an intervention program that nurtures their gifts and talents while accommodating for learning weaknesses. Baum, Rizza, and Renzulli (2006) also recommend teaching to the gifts while providing strategies that compensate for the disability. Effective instructional programming for these pupils thus requires a blending of instructional practices, such as cognitive training coupled with differentiated programming or curriculum compacting.

Nielsen and Higgins (2005) identify four key elements that must be present for successful programming of students who are twice exceptional. According to these experts, these learners require

- a continuum of service delivery options ranging from the general education classroom to a self-contained classroom supported by related service professionals;
- a complex, integrated, and interdisciplinary curriculum because of their unique learning profiles;
- services and programs that address their social, emotional, and behavioral needs;
- instruction that targets their gifts and talents while simultaneously providing individualized special education supports.

Girls Who Are Gifted

Although it may seem a bit unusual to include females who are gifted in a section devoted to diversity, there is ample evidence that girls who are gifted are an underrepresented population and an untapped national resource. This inequity appears to be embedded in a complex and interwoven web of educational, social, and personal barriers including sex-role stereotyping, unequal educational opportunities, and personal as well as parental expectations (Reis, 2006; Rimm, 2002). Collectively, these barriers frequently become obstacles to achievement and advancement. Some of the characteristics of gifted females are presented in Table 14.8.

Table 14.8	A Profile of Gifted Females
Younger Gifted Girls	• Many gifted girls are superior physically, have more social knowledge, and are better adjusted than are average girls, although more highly gifted girls are not as likely to seem well adjusted. • Highly gifted girls are often second-born females. • Highly gifted girls have high academic achievement. • In their interests, gifted girls are more like gifted boys than they are like average girls. • Gifted girls are confident in their opinions and willing to argue for their point of view. • Gifted girls by age 10 express wishes and needs for self-esteem and are interested in fulfilling needs for self-esteem through school and club achievements, although highly gifted girls are often loners without much need for recognition. • Gifted girls are more strongly influenced by their mothers than are gifted boys. • Actual occupations of parents do not affect gifted girls' eventual career choices. • Gifted girls have high career goals, although highly gifted girls aspire to careers having moderate rather than high status.
Adolescent Females	• Gifted girls' IQ scores drop in adolescence, perhaps as they begin to perceive their own giftedness as undesirable. • Gifted girls are likely to continue to have higher academic achievement as measured by grade point average. • Gifted girls take less rigorous courses than gifted boys in high school. • Gifted girls maintain a high involvement in extracurricular and social activities during adolescence. • Highly gifted girls do very well academically in high school; however, they often do not receive recognition for their achievements. • Highly gifted girls attend less prestigious colleges than highly gifted boys, a choice that leads to lower-status careers.

Source: Adapted from B. Kerr, *Smart Girls Two*, Rev. ed. (Scottsdale, AZ: Gifted Psychology Press, Inc., 1997).

The education of girls with gifts and talents cannot be neglected. Giftedness in females must be nurtured. Reis (2006) offers the following recommendations for developing this talent pool in both girls and boys:

- Provide equal treatment in a non-stereotyped environment and, in particular, provide encouragement for advanced coursework.
- Reduce sexism and stereotyping in classrooms and establish equity in classroom interactions.
- Help gifted adolescents understand healthy competition.
- Group gifted students homogeneously in separate classes or in clusters within heterogeneous classrooms.
- Expose gifted adolescents to other gifted adults who can act as role models through direct and curricular experiences—field trips, guest speakers, seminars, books, videotapes, articles, and movies.
- Provide educational interventions compatible with cognitive development and styles of learning (independent study projects, small group learning opportunities, etc.)
- Use a variety of authentic assessment tools such as projects and learning centers in addition to tests. (pp. 104–105)

Silverman (1995a) suggests that to preserve giftedness in girls, schools should offer them intellectually challenging courses and assistance in selecting career paths commensurate

Table 14.9	Recommendations for Developing the Gifts and Talents of Female Students

Gifted and Talented Girls Should	Teachers Should	Parents, Teachers, and Counselors Should
• Have exposure to or personal contact with female role models and mentors who have successfully balanced career and family. • Participate in discussion groups and attend panel discussions in which gifted and talented girls and women discuss the external barriers they have encountered. • Pursue involvement in leadership roles and extracurricular activities. • Participate in sports, athletics, and multiple extracurricular activities in areas in which they have an interest. • Discuss issues related to gender and success such as family issues in supportive settings with other talented girls. • Participate in career counseling at an early age and be exposed to a wide variety of career options and talented women who pursue challenging careers in all areas.	• Provide equitable treatment in a nonstereotyped environment and, in particular, provide encouragement. • Reduce sexism in classrooms and create an avenue for girls to report and discuss examples of stereotyping in schools. • Help creative, talented females appreciate and understand healthy competition. • Group gifted females homogeneously in math/science or within cluster groups of high-ability students in heterogeneous groups. • Encourage creativity in girls. • Use problem solving in assignments and reduce the use of timed tests and timed assignments within class periods; rather, provide options for untimed work within a reasonable time frame. • Expose girls to other creative, gifted females through direct and curricular experiences—field trips, guest speakers, seminars, role models, books, videotapes, articles, movies. • Provide educational interventions compatible with cognitive development and styles of learning (i.e., independent study projects, small group learning opportunities, and so forth) and use a variety of authentic assessment tools such as projects and learning centers instead of just using tests. • Establish equity in classroom interactions. • Provide multiple opportunities for creative expression in multiple modalities.	• Form forces to advocate for programming and equal opportunities and to investigate opportunities for talented, creative girls. • Spotlight achievements of talented females in a variety of different areas; encourage girls and young women to become involved in as many different types of activities, travel opportunities, and clubs as possible. • Encourage girls to take advanced courses in all areas as well as courses in the arts and reinforce successes in these and all areas of endeavor; ensure equal representation of girls in advanced classes. • Encourage relationships with other creative girls who want to achieve. • Maintain options for talented, creative girls in specific groups such as self-contained classes, groups of girls within heterogeneous classes and in separate classes for gifted girls, science and math clubs, or support groups. • Consistently point out options for careers and encourage future choices but help girls focus on specific interests and planning for future academic choices, interests, and careers.

SOURCE: Adapted from S. Reis, "External Barriers Experienced by Gifted and Talented Girls and Women," *Gifted Child Today, 24*(4), 2001, pp. 33–34.

with their abilities. Additionally, girls who are gifted may require supplementary educational experiences in order to reach their potential (Noble, Subotnik, & Arnold, 1999). Instruction may be necessary to develop assertiveness, instill confidence, and enhance self-esteem. Exposure to female mentors who can offer girls personal and professional advice along with work experience is another common recommendation for fostering the talents and gifts of girls (Robinson et al., 2007). Table 14.9 offers additional suggestions and strategies for developing the gifts and talents of female students.

Identifying and Serving Children from Diverse Backgrounds

One contemporary challenge in the field of gifted education, as in other areas of exceptionality, is that of identifying and serving children from culturally diverse backgrounds and from all socio-economic groups. There is ample evidence that culturally diverse students are underrepresented in the pool of individuals identified as gifted (Clark, 2008; Davis & Rimm, 2004; Ford, Harris, Tyson, & Trotman, 2002). African American pupils, for example, constitute approximately 16 percent of public school enrollment, but only about 8 percent of those in programs for the gifted and talented (Ford, 1998). The Javits legislation mentioned earlier in this chapter emphasizes that children with special gifts and talents can be found throughout society; our job as teachers is to find and provide services for these children. "Culturally diverse children," Plummer (1995) writes, "have much talent, creativity, and intelligence. Manifestations of these characteristics may be different and thus require not only different tools for measuring these strengths, but also different eyes from which to see them" (p. 290).

In a classic investigation, Frasier and her colleagues (1995) identified ten core attributes of giftedness in African American, Native American, and Hispanic children. These characteristics include:

- communication skills
- imagination/creativity
- humor
- inquiry
- insight
- interests
- memory
- motivation
- problem solving
- reasoning

The process of identifying gifted children from culturally diverse backgrounds is sometimes described as finding "the light under the bushel basket" (Gallagher & Gallagher, 1994, p. 410). According to Gallagher and Gallagher, intellectual giftedness often resides within the individual; however, adverse environmental factors, such as poverty or language differences, can mask that gift—like placing a basket over a light. The task of educators is to find strategies that remove the basket and let the light shine forth.

Several factors are thought to contribute to the underrepresentation of culturally diverse learners in programs for gifted and talented pupils. Commonly mentioned variables include the deleterious consequences of poverty, test bias, faulty identification policies, conflicting cultural values, teacher attitudes and expectations, and rigid definitions of giftedness (Davis & Rimm, 2004; Ford, 1998; Robinson et al., 2007). To combat these forces, recommendations have included:

Students from culturally diverse backgrounds are significantly underrepresented in programs for children who are gifted and talented.

- Culturally sensitive identification practices
- Establishing support services (career counseling, mentors, role models)
- Greater community and family involvement
- Multimodal assessment practices, including alternative (nontraditional) strategies (such as peer ratings, portfolios, teacher nominations, and checklists)
- Early identification

Portfolio assessment was thought to be one way of tapping into diverse talent areas. Its alignment with Gardner's concept of multiple intelligences makes it an especially attractive option for assessing giftedness. Unfortunately, this strategy as well as other proposed solutions have not solved the problem of underrepresentation.

Appropriate educational opportunities must be in place to develop the talents of children from low-income backgrounds; otherwise, millions of high-ability children from challenging socioeconomic backgrounds will fail to stay in the upper quartile of achievement (Wyner, Bridgeland, & Diiulio, 2007). Special care must be taken to nurture their talents, encourage them to achieve at high levels, and pursue higher education opportunities. Wyner et al. are optimistic because a large number of children who fall in the upper quartile are from low-income backgrounds; however, it is discouraging that

> there are far fewer lower-income students achieving at the highest levels than there should be, they disproportionately fall out of the high-achieving group during elementary and high school, they rarely rise into the ranks of high achievers during these periods, and perhaps most disturbingly, far too few ever graduate from college or go on to graduate school. (p. i)

The challenge for educators in today's schools is to create learning environments that are intellectually stimulating and nurture the gifts and talents of all students so that it is just as attractive to be an outstanding student as it is to play on a championship team. See Table 14.10 for instructional suggestions designed to meet the unique needs of traditionally underrepresented groups of learners who are gifted and talented.

Technology and Individuals Who Are Gifted and Talented

Children and young adults with a passion for knowledge in areas of interest thrive when given access to technology. Access to mentors and colleagues who have similar interests increases exponentially through technology such as electronic mail and teleconferencing. Resources that have been difficult to obtain are readily available with high-tech possibilities. Virtual high schools and virtual universities offer access to courses previously unavailable in smaller

Table 14.10	Suggestions for Teaching Culturally Diverse Students Who Are Gifted
African American Gifted Children	• Use small groups for instruction, building trust and belonging. • Provide structure by use of contracting, clear goals, and individualization. • Provide mentors and role models. • Emphasize use of oral language, providing many opportunities for debate, discussion, and oral presentations. • Provide for visual learning experiences, manipulative materials, and active real-life experiences in learning.
Native American Gifted Children	• Use storytelling, metaphor, and myths as media for delivering information. • Develop personal and group goals relevant to those of the tribal community as well as the student. • Provide visual and spatial experience. • Teach from whole to details. • Explore and honor belief in collective tribal self as an alternative worldview. • Use intuitive ability in learning experiences.
Hispanic Gifted Children	• Use cooperative intellectual peer groups for learning and encouraging independent production. • Provide visual and kinesthetic learning experiences. • Provide extensive experience with both English and Spanish. • Use successful Hispanic Americans as mentors. • Include the family as part of the educational team.

Source: Adapted from B. Clark, *Growing Up Gifted,* 7th ed. (Upper Saddle River, NJ: Pearson Education, 2008), pp. 333–336.

or rural schools or those with limited advanced curriculum. The World Wide Web makes distance learning a viable mode for delivering advanced course content in just about any academic area. Students can also engage in problem-solving exercises and computer simulation activities, either individually or with peers in other states or regions of the world.

Technology has the potential to lessen the isolation experienced by young people who are gifted and talented but do not know others who share their interests and enthusiasm. Not only is technology useful for young people who are gifted and talented, they are often among the leaders who are changing the frontiers of technology. Connections are made, distances evaporate, and unlimited opportunities for learning become readily available with the use of technology.

Trends, Issues, and Controversies

A plethora of issues and controversies confronts educators and other professionals concerned about the education of children and youth who are gifted and talented. We hope to shed some light on a few of these contemporary topics.

Striving for World-Class Standards

In *National Excellence* (Ross, 1993), Secretary of Education Richard W. Riley states that the United States is facing a "quiet crisis in how we educate top students. Youngsters with gifts and talents that range from mathematical to musical are still not challenged to work to their full potential. Our neglect of these students makes it impossible for Americans to compete in a global economy demanding their skills" (p. iii).

PL 103-227, the Goals 2000: Educate America Act, predicted that students in the United States would be first in the world in mathematics and science by the year 2000. This goal of international eminence has not been attained. The need to focus on high standards and opportunities for children to learn at challenging levels continues. Top students are not served well when they score at the 99th percentile on standardized tests and earn all A's on their report cards without being challenged. The situation is regrettable when a student scores at the 95th percentile in the United States on a standardized test but is at the 50th percentile in Japan (Ross, 1993).

The Third International Mathematics and Science Study sounded another alarm. In comparison to high school students from 41 countries, the mathematics and science test scores for U.S. twelfth graders were among the lowest, including pupils enrolled in AP classes (National Center for Education Statistics, 1998). These achievement comparisons with students from other countries raise serious concerns about the need for more rigorous curriculum and increasingly challenging learning opportunities.

Assumptions are often made that children who are gifted and talented will learn in spite of all circumstances. On the contrary, students who are gifted are less likely to make a year's achievement gain than are other students (Sanders, 1998). The No Child Left Behind legislation provides little incentive for teachers to gear instruction to individuals who have already achieved proficiency (Neal & Schanzenbach, 2007). Because of the emphasis on proficiency, students who have already achieved proficiency or who are way beyond this level of accomplishment are not receiving the opportunities that allow them to make continuous progress. Unfortunately, the minimum competency requirements of No Child Left Behind have taken the instructional focus off of guiding our most talented students in recognizing, developing, and enriching their gifts. Because the student who is gifted can easily achieve minimum competency, it is imperative that we look at these children in terms of a growth model. Every pupil, in every classroom, should be experiencing gains; whether those gains are toward minimum proficiency or talent development is irrelevant (S. Burkhardt, February 16, 2007, personal communication).

The goal of school for all children, including children who are gifted and talented, is to make continuous progress. Consequently, it is unacceptable for "proficiency" to place a lid on expectations and on learning for any child who is already at proficiency or beyond.

Equity and Excellence

The issue of equity and excellence has often been distorted into a question of equity versus excellence. Equity allows each child to have his/her needs addressed; it is not doing the same thing for all students on the same time schedule. Each child deserves quality educational opportunities that will allow for continuous progress in academic and talent areas. Excellence involves the pursuit of personal excellence. High standards are critical for all children; however, all children will not be served well unless they are challenged. What will be challenging for each student depends on what he/she already knows and is able to do. All children need to be accepted for who they are and must be genuinely challenged if they are to reach their personal goals.

The "Lake Wobegon phenomenon" describes a situation in which every child is above average. Such a situation denies some children the opportunity to reach a level of personal excellence. It is often said that we need to see that all children achieve at the same high levels. The same comment would never be made about athletics. All students need opportunities to develop their gifts and talents, just as athletes are encouraged to do; but they will achieve different levels of personal excellence when afforded the same opportunities. Equity and excellence are equally important in a society that values moving forward in all fields of endeavor.

Full Inclusion

The general education classroom has become the "ideal" setting for many educators. For some students with exceptionalities, the general education classroom offers the best alternative; however, for children who are gifted and talented, the idea of full inclusion is often very restrictive. Results of a study by the National Research Center on the Gifted and Talented indicate that third- and fourth-grade teachers typically make only minor modifications in the regular curriculum to address the needs of students who are gifted (Archambault et al., 1993; Westburg & Daoust, 2003). Full inclusion offers challenges to teachers who understand that the needs of children who are gifted and talented cannot be met without differentiating the curriculum.

For young people who are gifted and talented, the least restrictive alternative is often a self-contained class or magnet school. Many states have established residential high schools for mathematics and science and/or the performing arts. Urban school districts across the country have magnet schools with a focus on math and science, the health sciences, and/or the performing arts. Children who are gifted and talented need to be with others who think as they do and who are ready to accept the intellectual challenge.

Services for Gifted Students Instead of the Gifted Program

The trend to move to services for children who are gifted rather than "the" gifted program is in tune with methods of identification that emphasize multiple measures. Children with gifts and talents in science need challenging instruction to allow for the continuous development of their scientific knowledge, skills, and interests. Likewise, children who are gifted in leadership need appropriate opportunities to develop their leadership skills to a higher level, and artistically gifted children need instruction that will provide for the honing of their artistic talents—talents that may differentiate them from other children in their age bracket.

A gifted program is limited in its potential for addressing student needs. Matching services to need (for gifted students, the need often is created by a strength) is key to developing our children's talents. One service may be similar to classes that have been known as the gifted program; however, it is only one service. Such a service offers advantages because the teacher has expertise and experience with students who have special talents, and the pupils benefit by associating with others who share their interests and have similar abilities. These classes offer opportunities to address the cognitive as well as the social-emotional needs of children who are gifted and talented.

Teachers who are specialists in specific content areas can offer other services. Who better to offer services to develop talent in mathematics than a teacher of math or in art than a teacher of art? The goal of each service is to focus on continuous progress, a concept that will allow children to be challenged beyond grade level. For all children, the learning ceiling must be removed, allowing them to learn what they are ready to learn, at a pace that will encourage them to maintain interest.

Talent Development

Children who are gifted and talented represent a relatively small part of a school's population, yet they constitute a group with special needs—needs created by their strengths. In spite of the fact that students who are gifted and talented do not appear needy, their needs are intense and must be addressed if they are to develop their talents to the fullest.

The development of top talent is essential if our communities, states, nation, and world are to thrive. Talent does not develop in a vacuum (see Figure 14.7). Schools that develop top talent have this as a conscious goal. They provide children with numerous, quality opportunities to find their talents and then opportunities to develop those talents.

Figure 14.7

Essential Components of a Plan for Talent Development Schools

Source: Used with permission of J. L. Roberts. Copyright © 2008.

Table 14.11	Essential Components of a Plan for Talent Development Schools
Opportunities	**Examples**
Celebrate a wide range of accomplishments/talents	• Announcements and newsletter articles • Assemblies • Banners, trophies, Hall of Fame • Press releases
Explore and find interests/passions	• Resources—books, people, and Internet • Field trips to museums, labs, science centers, concert halls, universities • Experts to talk about or demonstrate a talent area • Classes in Saturday or summer programs, specialized camps
Learn basic skills and foundational knowledge in artistic, academic, and athletic areas	• Special classes • Visits to talk with and observe experts • Equipment (e.g., labs, instruments, computer programs, etc.) • Resources that interest and challenge • Lessons
Refine skills in talent areas as advanced content is learned	• Access to scientists, artists, and other mentors • Specialized equipment • Time with others who share interests and are equally advanced • Instruction with specific feedback • Independent study with mentor
Create/produce in talent area	• Competitions, contents, recitals, exhibits • Mentors focused on scholarly or artistic production • Time devoted to talent area • Performance for peers in talent area • Publications

Source: Used with permission of J. L. Roberts. Copyright © 2008.

First, students need opportunities to discover interests or passions that can develop into top-level talents. They also need opportunities to work with teachers and mentors in their talent areas in addition to opportunities to refine their skills and expand their content knowledge. Finally, young people need opportunities to produce knowledge through research and publications and to perform in competitions, contests, recitals, and exhibitions. Celebrating a wide range of accomplishments and talents is important throughout the talent development process. Examples of talent development opportunities are presented in Table 14.11.

Opportunities are not really opportunities until a person knows about them. The focus of schools must be on developing the gifts and talents of students from all socioeconomic levels and all racial and ethnic backgrounds, as well as students with a range of gifts and talents, including pupils with disabilities. Schools need to celebrate artistic and academic talents in the same ways that they celebrate athletic talent. As Madame Morrible says in the musical *Wicked*, "Never apologize for talent! Talent is a gift! And that is my special talent, encouraging talent" (Cote, 2005, p. 56). Students need individuals to encourage the development of their talents. Children who are gifted and talented need teachers and mentors in the home, school, and community who will provide opportunities that will ensure that they enjoy learning on an ongoing basis and that they make continuous progress in their talent area. Children with gifts and talents will not make it on their own.

Chapter in Review

Defining Giftedness: Refining the Meaning

- Two national reports provide definitions of children who are gifted and talented; however, each state is responsible for establishing its own definition of giftedness. Generally speaking, definitions include high intellectual ability along with giftedness in specific academic areas, creativity, leadership, and/or the visual and performing arts.

Assessing Giftedness and Talent

- The assessment of gifts and talents necessitates multifactorial assessment of the student's strengths, using both formal and informal measures.

Prevalence of Giftedness and Talent

- Educators believe that approximately 3–5 percent of the school-age population is gifted. Some professionals estimate that 10–15 percent of school-age youth are gifted and talented.

Etiology of Giftedness and Talent

- The etiology or causes of giftedness are both genetic and environmental. The complex interaction of genetic patterns and environmental stimulation produces an individual with the capacity to learn or perform at exceptionally high levels in one or more areas of accomplishment.

Characteristics of Individuals Who Are Gifted and Talented

- The characteristics of children who are gifted and talented vary tremendously across the many dimensions of giftedness.

- The degree and intensity of characteristics are often the keys to understanding gifted behavior. Seldom, if ever, do children who are gifted and talented exhibit all of the cognitive and social-emotional characteristics associated with this exceptionality.

Educational Considerations

- The educational needs of pupils with gifts and talents are often best fulfilled via a variety of instructional strategies. Interventions must be planned to allow pupils to make continuous progress, even in areas in which they are advanced.

- Strategies to remove the learning ceiling include **differentiating the curriculum** and **curriculum compacting**.

- The curriculum must include learning experiences that combine complex content, high-level thinking and problem solving, and opportunities to think creatively. Other important accommodations addressing the needs of children who are gifted are **cluster grouping**, **cooperative learning activities**, and **problem-based learning**.

- A continuum of services is vital to ensure the development of talent to high levels.

- **Acceleration** is an appropriate option for many gifted children. **Independent study, mentors, honors** and **Advanced Placement** courses provide challenging learning experiences.

- **Self-contained classrooms** and **special schools** provide other venues for delivering services to gifted young people.

- **Summer and Saturday programming** are important options but should not be in lieu of services within the school setting.

Adolescents and Adults Who Are Gifted and Talented

- Adolescence can be an especially difficult time for students who are gifted and talented. Choosing between making continuous progress in their talent areas and remaining popular with their peers is one area of potential conflict.

Issues of Diversity

- Children who are gifted and talented come from all socioeconomic, racial, and ethnic groups.

- Professionals encounter three unique challenges when confronting issues of diversity: serving students with gifts and talents and a disability; meeting the needs of girls who are gifted and talented; and appropriately identifying and serving children with gifts and talents who happen to be culturally diverse.

Study Questions

1. How are children with gifts and talents identified?

2. Why is the assessment of giftedness an important and difficult process?

3. How have society's view and understanding of children with gifts and talents changed over time?

4. The etiology of giftedness is seen as the commingling or interaction of what variables?

5. Identify five characteristics typically associated with individuals considered gifted and talented. What implications do these characteristics have for their teachers?

6. Describe the various delivery models that are frequently used to meet the cognitive and social-emotional needs of children who are gifted and talented.

7. Define the following terms: curriculum differentiation, preassessment, curriculum compacting, flexible grouping, and pacing.

8. Distinguish between the concepts of acceleration and enrichment. How can they be used together?

9. List five early indicators of gifts and talents.

10. What challenges do families of children who are gifted and talented frequently encounter?

11. Why are some groups of children underrepresented in programs for students who are gifted and talented?

12. How can technology be used to enhance learning opportunities for students with gifts and talents?

13. Why do some educators believe that full inclusion is not the best option for students who are gifted and talented?

Key Terms

gifted and talented
off-level testing
creativity
differentiation

preassessment
curriculum
  compacting
flexible grouping

cluster grouping
tiered assignments
problem-based
  learning

acceleration
mentor
magnet high school
twice exceptional

Learning Activities

1. Write a statement about your philosophy of learning that could guide your teaching of students with gifts and talents.

2. Volunteer to assist with an academic competition, Saturday program, or summer program for children and youth who are gifted and talented. Keep a journal of your experiences. How do the children compare with their typical age-mates? What strengths did you observe among the participants? How do the children relate to and interact with their coaches and teachers? What are the advantages and benefits of these activities?

3. Interview two individuals of similar chronological age who are considered gifted and talented. Ask these persons to define what it means to be gifted. Have them describe their educational experiences, career goals, likes and dislikes, social relationships (including family

members), and other topics of interest to you. What similarities and differences did you observe between the two individuals? How do these persons differ from their typical age-mates?

4. Visit schools in your area that serve students with gifts and talents. What services are available for pupils who are gifted and talented? What differences did you observe between elementary and secondary programs? What instructional techniques did teachers use that were effective with students who are gifted and talented? How did the other pupils interact with their classmates who are gifted? What was your overall impression of the services—what specific features stood out? How are the individual needs of the students being addressed or ignored? Would you like to be a teacher of children who are gifted and talented? Why or why not?

5. What is the definition of children who are gifted and talented in your state? How does it compare with the definitions presented in this textbook?

6. Locate information about the advocacy organization in your state. What professional development opportunities does it offer? What information does it provide to teachers?

Organizations Concerned with Giftedness

The Council for Exceptional Children, The Association for the Gifted (CEC-TAG)
1110 N. Glebe Road
Suite 300
Arlington, VA 22201-5704
(703) 620-3660

National Association for Gifted Children (NAGC)
1707 L Street N.W., Suite 550
Washington, DC 20036
(202) 785-4268
E-mail: nagc@nagc.org

National Research Center on the Gifted and Talented
NEAG Center for Gifted Education and Talent
Development
2131 Hillside Road, Unit 3007
Storrs, CT 06269-3007
(860) 486-4626

Supporting Emotional Needs of the Gifted (SENG)
P.O. Box 488
Poughquag, NY 12570
(845) 797-5054

World Council for Gifted and Talented Children, Inc.
c/o University of Winnipeg
515 Portage Avenue
Winnipeg, Manitoba
Canada R3B 2E9
(204) 279-1421

Reflecting on Standards

The following exercises are designed to help you learn to apply the Council for Exceptional Children (CEC) standards to your teaching practice. Each of the reflection exercises below correlates with a knowledge or skill within the CEC standards. For the full text of each of the related CEC standards, please refer to the standards integration grid located in Appendix B.

1. Focus on Instructional Strategies (*CEC Content Standard #4 CC4S3*)

Reflect on what you have learned about students who are gifted and talented. If you had an individual who was gifted and talented in math, and well above the rest of your class, how might you use differentiated instruction to keep him/her challenged while still addressing the needs of the remainder of your pupils? What are some other instructional strategies you could incorporate in your class to meet his/her needs?

2. Focus on Learning Environments and Social Interactions (*CEC Content Standard #5 CC5K5*)

Reflect on what you have learned about the social needs of students who are gifted and talented. If you were to have a pupil in your class who was gifted and talented and often received instruction outside your classroom at a higher grade level, what difficulties might this individual have in developing social skills with his/her peers? How might you help encourage or facilitate social interactions when the student is in your classroom during the day?

Technology Resources

Visit the Web-based SAGE Study Site at **http://www.sagepub.com/gargiulo3estudy** for these additional learning tools:

- Chapter quizzes
- Key term flashcards
- Media links
- Full-text SAGE journal articles
- Internet activities
- Additional Web resources

Postscript

You may recall that in Chapter 1 you were introduced to some of the students in Daniel Thompson's fifth-grade class. Mr. Thompson's classroom was like most classrooms in the United States: the majority of the students were typical learners, but five individuals were thought to have special learning needs.

- Victoria, age 11, is a very popular student with a great personality who has been blind since birth.
- Miguel is very shy and timid and interacts minimally with his classmates. Miguel only recently moved into the community from his home in Mexico.
- Jerome is particularly disliked by his peers. He is verbally abusive, often has temper tantrums, and frequently fights with other children. Mr. Thompson suspects that he might be a member of a local gang.
- Stephanie endures friendly teasing from her classmates, who secretly admire her intellectual gifts and talents.
- Robert is an outstanding athlete. In the classroom, however, he asks silly questions, has difficulty following class rules, and occasionally makes animal noises, much to the displeasure of his classmates. Robert has cognitive delays as a result of an automobile accident.

Mr. Thompson wondered why these students were in his class and how he could help them. Hopefully, after studying the preceding chapters, listening to your instructor's presentations, and completing course assignments, along with critically reflecting on the content, you are now in a position to respond to the six questions originally posed in Chapter 1:

1. Why are these students in a general education classroom?
2. Will I have students like this in my class?
3. Are these children called disabled, exceptional, or handicapped?
4. What does special education mean?
5. How will I know if some of my students have special learning needs?
6. How can I help these students?

Teaching children and young adults with exceptionalities is a very challenging yet richly rewarding career. When you stand before your class as a dedicated, committed, and caring professional, you possess the power to make a difference in the lives of all your students. I congratulate you on choosing to become a member of a dynamic profession—teaching.

Good Luck!

Appendix A

Federal Definitions of Disabilities

Autism means a developmental disability significantly affecting verbal and nonverbal communication and social interaction, generally evident before age 3, that adversely affects a child's educational performance. Other characteristics often associated with autism are engagement in repetitive activities and stereotyped movements, resistance to environmental change or change in daily routines, and unusual responses to sensory experiences. The term does not apply if a child's educational performance is adversely affected primarily because the child has an emotional disturbance as defined below.

A child who manifests the characteristics of autism after age 3 could be diagnosed as having autism if the criteria in the preceding paragraph are satisfied.

Deaf-blindness means concomitant hearing and visual impairments, the combination of which causes such severe communication and other developmental and educational needs that they cannot be accommodated in special education programs solely for children with deafness or children with blindness.

Deafness means a hearing impairment that is so severe that the child is impaired in processing linguistic information through hearing, with or without amplification, that adversely affects a child's educational performance.

Emotional disturbance is defined as follows:

  i. The term means a condition exhibiting one or more of the following characteristics over a long period of time and to a marked degree that adversely affects a child's educational performance:
  A. An inability to learn that cannot be explained by intellectual, sensory, or health factors.
  B. An inability to build or maintain satisfactory interpersonal relationships with peers and teachers.
  C. Inappropriate types of behavior or feelings under normal circumstances.
  D. A general pervasive mood of unhappiness or depression.
  E. A tendency to develop physical symptoms or fears associated with personal or school problems.
  ii. The term includes schizophrenia. The term does not apply to children who are socially maladjusted, unless it is determined that they have an emotional disturbance.

Hearing impairment means an impairment in hearing, whether permanent or fluctuating, that adversely affects a child's educational performance but that is not included under the definition of deafness in this section.

Mental retardation means significantly subaverage general intellectual functioning, existing concurrently with deficits in adaptive behavior and manifested during the developmental period, that adversely affects a child's educational performance.

Multiple disabilities means concomitant impairments (such as mental retardation–blindness, mental retardation–orthopedic impairment, etc.), the combination of which causes such severe educational needs that they cannot be accommodated in special education programs solely for one of the impairments. The term does not include deaf-blindness.

Orthopedic impairment means a severe orthopedic impairment that adversely affects a child's educational performance. The term includes impairments caused by congenital anomaly (e.g., clubfoot, absence of some member, etc.), impairments caused by disease (e.g., poliomyelitis, bone tuberculosis, etc.), and impairments from other causes (e.g., cerebral palsy, amputations, and fractures or burns that cause contractures).

Other health impairment means having limited strength, vitality or alertness, including a heightened alertness to environmental stimuli, that results in limited alertness with respect to the educational environment, that

   i. is due to chronic or acute health problems such as asthma, attention deficit disorder or attention deficit hyperactivity disorder, diabetes, epilepsy, a heart condition, hemophilia, lead poisoning, leukemia, nephritis, rheumatic fever, and sickle cell anemia; and

  ii. adversely affects a child's educational performance.

Specific learning disability is defined as follows:

   i. *General.* The term means a disorder in one or more of the basic psychological processes involved in understanding or in using language, spoken or written, that may manifest itself in an imperfect ability to listen, think, speak, read, write, spell, or to do mathematical calculations, including conditions such as perceptual disabilities, brain injury, minimal brain dysfunction, dyslexia, and developmental aphasia.

  ii. *Disorders not included.* The term does not include learning problems that are primarily the result of visual, hearing, or motor disabilities, of mental retardation, of emotional disturbance, or of environmental, cultural, or economic disadvantage.

Speech or language impairment means a communication disorder, such as stuttering, impaired articulation, a language impairment, or a voice impairment, that adversely affects a child's educational performance.

Traumatic brain injury means an acquired injury to the brain caused by an external physical force, resulting in total or partial functional disability or psychosocial impairment or both, that adversely affects a child's educational performance. The term applies to open or closed head injuries resulting in impairments in one or more areas, such as cognition; language; memory; attention; reasoning; abstract thinking; judgment; problem-solving; sensory, perceptual, and motor abilities; psychosocial behavior; physical functions; information processing; and speech. The term does not apply to brain injuries that are congenital or degenerative, or to brain injuries induced by birth trauma.

Visual impairment including blindness means an impairment in vision that, even with correction, adversely affects a child's educational performance. The term includes both partial sight and blindness.

Source: Individuals with Disabilities Education Act, 34 CFR 300.7 (c). July 1, 2006.

Appendix B

Professional Standards

Council for Exceptional Children (CEC) Standards Correlated by Chapter

Knowledge and Skill Base for All Beginning Special Education Teachers: Common Core

STANDARD #1: FOUNDATIONS Special educators understand the field as an evolving and changing discipline based on philosophies, evidence-based principles and theories, relevant laws and policies, diverse and historical points of view, and human issues that have historically influenced and continue to influence the field of special education and the education and treatment of individuals with exceptional needs both in school and society. Special educators understand how these influence professional practice, including assessment, instructional planning, implementation, and program evaluation. Special educators understand how issues of human diversity can impact families, cultures, and schools, and how these complex human issues can interact with issues in the delivery of special education services. They understand the relationships of organizations of special education to the organizations and functions of schools, school systems, and other agencies. Special educators use this knowledge as a ground upon which to construct their own personal understandings and philosophies of special education.

Knowledge								Chapter							
		1	2	3	4	5	6	7	8	9	10	11	12	13	14
CC1K1	Models, theories, and philosophies that form the basis for special education practice.	•	•			•	•		•	•	•	•	•	•	•
CC1K2	Laws, policies, and ethical principles regarding behavior management planning and implementation.							•	•					•	
CC1K3	Relationship of special education to the organization and function of educational agencies.						•								
CC1K4	Rights and responsibilities of students, parents, teachers, and other professionals, and schools related to exceptional learning needs.		•								•	•	•	•	•
CC1K5	Issues in definition and identification of individuals with exceptional learning needs, including those from culturally and linguistically diverse backgrounds.	•		•		•	•	•	•	•	•	•	•	•	

Knowledge		Chapter													
		1	2	3	4	5	6	7	8	9	10	11	12	13	14
CC1K6	Issues, assurances and due process rights related to assessment, eligibility, and placement within a continuum of services.		•				•		•		•	•	•	•	•
CC1K7	Family systems and the role of families in the educational process.		•		•					•		•		•	•
CC1K8	Historical points of view and contribution of culturally diverse groups.	•		•		•	•	•	•	•	•	•	•		•
CC1K9	Impact of the dominant culture on shaping schools and the individuals who study and work in them.			•						•					
CC1K10	Potential impact of differences in values, languages, and customs that can exist between the home and school.			•								•			
Skills		1	2	3	4	5	6	7	8	9	10	11	12	13	14
CC1S1	Articulate personal philosophy of special education.														

STANDARD #2: DEVELOPMENT AND CHARACTERISTICS OF LEARNERS Special educators know and demonstrate respect for their students first as unique human beings. Special educators understand the similarities and differences in human development and the characteristics between and among individuals with and without exceptional learning needs (ELN).[1] Moreover, special educators understand how exceptional conditions can interact with the domains of human development and they use this knowledge to respond to the varying abilities and behaviors of individuals with ELN. Special educators understand how the experiences of individuals with ELN can impact families, as well as the individual's ability to learn, interact socially, and live as fulfilled contributing members of the community.

Knowledge		Chapter													
		1	2	3	4	5	6	7	8	9	10	11	12	13	14
CC2K1	Typical and atypical human growth and development.					•	•				•	•	•		•
CC2K2	Educational implications of characteristics of various exceptionalities.	•				•	•	•	•	•	•	•	•	•	•
CC2K3	Characteristics and effects of the cultural and environmental milieu of the individual with exceptional learning needs and the family.					•	•	•	•	•	•	•	•	•	•
CC2K4	Family systems and the role of families in supporting development.				•	•			•		•	•	•		•
CC2K5	Similarities and differences of individuals with and without exceptional learning needs.	•	•			•		•	•	•	•		•		•
CC2K6	Similarities and differences among individuals with exceptional learning needs.		•					•		•		•		•	•
CC2K7	Effects of various medications on individuals with exceptional learning needs.							•						•	•

---

1. "Individual with exceptional learning needs" is used throughout to include individuals with disabilities and individuals with exceptional gifts and talents.

STANDARD #3: INDIVIDUAL LEARNING DIFFERENCES Special educators understand the effects that an exceptional condition[2] can have on an individual's learning in school and throughout life. Special educators understand that the beliefs, traditions, and values across and within cultures can affect relationships among and between students, their families, and the school community. Moreover, special educators are active and resourceful in seeking to understand how primary language, culture, and familial backgrounds interact with the individual's exceptional condition to impact the individual's academic and social abilities, attitudes, values, interests, and career options. The understanding of these learning differences and their possible interactions provides the foundation upon which special educators individualize instruction to provide meaningful and challenging learning for individuals with ELN.

Knowledge		Chapter													
		1	2	3	4	5	6	7	8	9	10	11	12	13	14
CC3K1	Effects an exceptional condition(s) can have on an individual's life.	•				•	•	•	•	•	•	•	•	•	•
CC3K2	Impact of learners' academic and social abilities, attitudes, interests, and values on instruction and career development.					•	•	•	•	•		•	•	•	•
CC3K3	Variations in beliefs, traditions, and values across and within cultures and their effects on relationships among individuals with exceptional learning needs. Family, and schooling.			•	•					•					
CC3K4	Cultural perspectives influencing the relationships among families, schools, and communities as related to instruction.				•					•		•			
CC3K5	Differing ways of learning of individuals with exceptional learning needs including those from culturally diverse backgrounds and strategies for addressing these differences.				•		•			•					

STANDARD #4: INDIVIDUAL LEARNING DIFFERENCES Special educators possess a repertoire of evidence-based instructional strategies to individualize instruction for individuals with ELN. Special educators select, adapt, and use these instructional strategies to promote positive learning results in general and special curricula[3] and to appropriately modify learning environments for individuals with ELN. They enhance the learning of critical thinking, problem solving, and performance skills of individuals with ELN, and increase their self-awareness, self-management, self-control, self-reliance, and self-esteem. Moreover, special educators emphasize the development, maintenance, and generalization of knowledge and skills across environments, settings, and the life span.

Skills		Chapter													
		1	2	3	4	5	6	7	8	9	10	11	12	13	14
CC4S1	Use strategies to facilitate integration into various settings.	•				•			•	•		•		•	•
CC4S2	Teach individuals to use self-assessment, problem solving, and other cognitive strategies to meet their needs.						•	•	•	•		•			

2. "Exceptional Condition" is used throughout to include both single and coexisting conditions. These may be two or more disabling conditions or exceptional gifts or talents coexisting with one or more disabling conditions.

3. "Special Curricula" is used throughout to denote curricular areas not routinely emphasized or addressed in general curricula, e.g., social, communication, motor, independence, self-advocacy.

Skills		**Chapter**													
		1	2	3	4	5	6	7	8	9	10	11	12	13	14
CC4S3	Select, adapt, and use instructional strategies and materials according to characteristics of the individual with exceptional learning needs.					•	•	•	•	•			•	•	•
CC4S4	Use strategies to facilitate maintenance and generalization of skills across learning and environments.								•			•		•	•
CC4S5	Use procedures to increase the individual's self-awareness, self-management, self-control, self-reliance, and self-esteem.						•	•	•	•				•	•
CC4S6	Use strategies that promote successful transitions for individuals with exceptional learning needs.						•			•				•	•

STANDARD #5: LEARNING ENVIRONMENTS AND SOCIAL INTERACTIONS Special educators actively create learning environments for individuals with ELN that foster cultural understanding, safety and emotional well-being, positive social interactions, and active engagement of individuals with ELN. In addition, special educators foster environments in which diversity is valued and individuals are taught to live harmoniously and productively in a culturally diverse world. Special educators shape environments to encourage the independence, self-motivation, self-direction, personal empowerment, and self-advocacy of individuals with ELN. Special educators help their general education colleagues integrate individuals with ELN in regular environments and engage them in meaningful learning activities and interactions. Special educators use direct motivational and instructional interventions with individuals with ELN to teach them to respond effectively to current expectations. When necessary, special educators can safely intervene with individuals with ELN in crisis. Special educators coordinate all these efforts and provide guidance and direction to paraeducators and others, such as classroom volunteers and tutors.

Knowledge		**Chapter**													
		1	2	3	4	5	6	7	8	9	10	11	12	13	14
CC5K1	Demands of the learning environment.						•		•	•		•	•	•	•
CC5K2	Basic classroom management theories and strategies for individuals with exceptional learning needs.						•	•	•	•				•	
CC5K3	Effective management of teaching and learning.						•		•	•		•	•	•	•
CC5K4	Teacher attitudes and behaviors that influence behavior of individuals with exceptional learning needs.	•							•	•	•				•
CC5K5	Social skills needed for educational and other environments.								•	•	•	•	•	•	•
CC5K6	Strategies for crisis prevention and interventions.								•					•	
CC5K7	Strategies for preparing individuals to live harmoniously and productively in a culturally diverse world.			•						•		•			
CC5K8	Ways to create learning environments that allow individuals to retain and appreciate their own and each other's respective language and cultural heritage.			•									•		

(Continued)

(Continued)

Skills		Chapter													
		1	2	3	4	5	6	7	8	9	10	11	12	13	14
CC5S1	Create a safe, equitable, positive, and supportive learning environment in which diversities are valued.			•						•		•		•	•
CC5S2	Identify realistic expectations for personal and social behavior in various settings.														•
CC5S3	Identify supports needed for integration into various program placements.								•						•
CC5S4	Design learning environments that encourage active participation in individual and group activities.									•		•	•	•	•
CC5S5	Modify the learning environment to manage behavior.						•	•	•					•	•
CC5S6	Use performance data and information from all stakeholders to make or suggest modifications in learning environments.														
CC5S7	Establish and maintain rapport with individuals with and without exceptional learning needs.														
CC5S8	Teach self-advocacy.											•			
CC5S9	Create an environment that encourages self-advocacy and increased independence.											•	•		
CC5S10	Use effective and varied behavior management strategies.							•	•					•	
CC5S11	Use the least intensive behavior management strategy consistent with the needs of the individual with exceptional learning needs.								•						
CC5S12	Design and manage daily routines.								•						

STANDARD #6: COMMUNICATION Special educators understand typical and atypical language development and the ways in which exceptional conditions can interact with an individual's experience with and use of language. Special educators use individualized strategies to enhance language development and teach communication skills to individuals with ELN. Special educators are familiar with augmentative, alternative, and assistive technologies to support and enhance communication of individuals with exceptional needs. Special educators match their communication methods to an individual's language proficiency and cultural and linguistic differences. Special educators provide effective language models and they use communication strategies and resources to facilitate understanding of subject matter for individuals with ELN whose primary language is not English.

Knowledge		Chapter													
		1	2	3	4	5	6	7	8	9	10	11	12	13	14
CC6K1	Effects of cultural and linguistic differences on growth and development.			•							•	•			
CC6K2	Characteristics of one's own culture and use of language and the ways in which these can differ from other cultures and uses of language.										•	•			

Knowledge		Chapter													
		1	2	3	4	5	6	7	8	9	10	11	12	13	14
CC6K3	Ways of behaving and communicating among cultures that can lead to misinterpretation and misunderstanding.														
CC6K4	Augmentative and assistive communication strategies.					•					•	•		•	•
Skills		**1**	**2**	**3**	**4**	**5**	**6**	**7**	**8**	**9**	**10**	**11**	**12**	**13**	**14**
CC6S1	Use strategies to support and enhance communication skills of individuals with exceptional learning needs.										•	•		•	•
CC6S2	Use communication strategies and resources to facilitate understanding of subject matter for students whose primary language is not the dominant language.											•			

STANDARD #7: INSTRUCTIONAL PLANNING Individualized decision-making and instruction is at the center of special education practice. Special educators develop long-range individualized instructional plans anchored in both general and special curricula. In addition, special educators systematically translate these individualized plans into carefully selected shorter-range goals and objectives, taking into consideration an individual's abilities and needs, the learning environment, and a myriad of cultural and linguistic factors. Individualized instructional plans emphasize explicit modeling and efficient guided practice to assure acquisition and fluency through maintenance and generalization. Understanding of these factors as well as the implications of an individual's exceptional condition guides the special educator's selection, adaptation, and creation of materials and the use of powerful instructional variables. Instructional plans are modified based on ongoing analysis of the individual's learning progress. Moreover, special educators facilitate this instructional planning in a collaborative context including the individuals with exceptionalities, families, professional colleagues, and personnel from other agencies as appropriate. Special educators also develop a variety of individualized transition plans, such as transitions from preschool to elementary school and from secondary settings to a variety of postsecondary work and learning contexts. Special educators are comfortable using appropriate technologies to support instructional planning and individualized instruction.

Knowledge		Chapter													
		1	2	3	4	5	6	7	8	9	10	11	12	13	14
CC7K1	Theories and research that form the basis of curriculum development and instructional practice.					•	•			•			•	•	•
CC7K2	Scope and sequences of general and special curricula.									•					
CC7K3	National, state or provincial, and local curricula standards.														
CC7K4	Technology for planning and managing the teaching and learning environment.					•	•		•			•	•	•	•
Skills		**1**	**2**	**3**	**4**	**5**	**6**	**7**	**8**	**9**	**10**	**11**	**12**	**13**	**14**
CC7S1	Identify and prioritize areas of the general curriculum and accommodations for individuals with exceptional learning needs.									•				•	•

(Continued)

(Continued)

Skills		Chapter													
		1	2	3	4	5	6	7	8	9	10	11	12	13	14
CC7S2	Develop and implement comprehensive, longitudinal individualized programs in collaboration with team members		•												
CC7S3	Involve the individual and family in setting instructional goals and monitoring progress.											•			
CC7S4	Use functional assessments to develop intervention plans.								•					•	
CC7S5	Use task analysis.					•									
CC7S6	Sequence, implement, and evaluate individualized learning objectives.														
CC7S7	Integrate affective, social, and life skills with academic curricula.					•			•					•	•
CC7S8	Develop and select instructional content, resources, and strategies that respond to cultural, linguistic, and gender differences			•						•					
CC7S9	Incorporate and implement instructional and assistive technology into the educational program.											•			•
CC7S10	Prepare lesson plans.														
CC7S11	Prepare and organize materials to implement daily lesson plans.														
CC7S12	Use instructional time effectively.								•						
CC7S13	Make responsive adjustments to instruction based on continual observations.														
CC7S14	Prepare individuals to exhibit self-enhancing behavior in response to societal attitudes and actions.					•									

STANDARD #8: ASSESSMENT Assessment is integral to the decision-making and teaching of special educators, and special educators use multiple types of assessment information for a variety of educational decisions. Special educators use the results of assessments to help identify exceptional learning needs and to develop and implement individualized instructional programs, as well as to adjust instruction in response to ongoing learning progress. Special educators understand the legal policies and ethical principles of measurement and assessment related to referral, eligibility, program planning, instruction, and placement for individuals with ELN, including those from culturally and linguistically diverse backgrounds. Special educators understand measurement theory and practices for addressing issues of validity, reliability, norms, bias, and interpretation of assessment results. In addition, special educators understand the appropriate use and limitations of various types of assessments. Special educators collaborate with families and other colleagues to assure nonbiased, meaningful assessments and decision-making. Special educators conduct formal and informal assessments of behavior, learning, achievement, and environments to design learning experiences that support the growth and development of individuals with ELN. Special educators use assessment information to identify supports and adaptations required for individuals with ELN to access the general curriculum and to participate in school, system, and statewide assessment programs. Special educators regularly monitor the progress of individuals with ELN in general and special curricula. Special educators use appropriate technologies to support their assessments.

							Chapter								
Knowledge		1	2	3	4	5	6	7	8	9	10	11	12	13	14
CC8K1	Basic terminology used in assessment.		•			•	•		•	•			•		
CC8K2	Legal provisions and ethical principles regarding assessment of individuals.		•									•	•	•	•
CC8K3	Screening, prereferral, referral, and classification procedures.		•	•				•			•	•	•	•	•
CC8K4	Use and limitations of assessment.					•	•	•	•	•	•		•		•	•
Skills		1	2	3	4	5	6	7	8	9	10	11	12	13	14
CC8S1	Gather relevant background information.														
CC8S2	Administer nonbiased formal and informal assessment strategies.			•											
CC8S3	Use technology to conduct assessments.														
CC8S4	Develop or modify individualized assessment strategies.								•						
CC8S5	Interpret information from formal and informal assessments.														
CC8S6	Use assessment information in making eligibility program, and placement decisions for individuals with exceptional learning needs, including those from culturally and/or linguistically diverse backgrounds.			•											
CC8S7	Report assessment results to all stakeholders using effective communication skills.														
CC8S8	Evaluate instruction and monitor progress of individuals with exceptional learning needs.														
CC8S9	Develop or modify individualized assessment strategies.														
CC8S10	Create and maintain records.														

STANDARD #9: PROFESSIONAL AND ETHICAL PRACTICE Special educators are guided by the profession's ethical and professional practice standards. Special educators practice in multiple roles and complex situations across wide age and developmental ranges. Their practice requires ongoing attention to legal matters along with serious professional and ethical considerations. Special educators engage in professional activities and participate in learning communities that benefit individuals with ELN, their families, colleagues, and their own professional growth. Special educators view themselves as lifelong learners and regularly reflect on and adjust their practice. Special educators are aware of how their own and others' attitudes, behaviors, and ways of communicating can influence their practice. Special educators understand that culture and language can interact with exceptionalities, and are sensitive to the many aspects of diversity of individuals with ELN and their families. Special educators actively plan and engage in activities that foster their professional growth and keep them current with evidence-based best practices. Special educators know their own limits of practice and practice within them.

Knowledge		Chapter													
		1	2	3	4	5	6	7	8	9	10	11	12	13	14
CC9K1	Personal cultural biases and differences that affect one's teaching.														
CC9K2	Importance of the teacher serving as a model for individuals with exceptional learning needs.														
CC9K3	Continuum of lifelong professional development.			•											
CC9K4	Methods to remain current regarding research-validated practice.														
Skills		1	2	3	4	5	6	7	8	9	10	11	12	13	14
CC9S1	Practice within the CEC Code of Ethics and other standards of the profession.														
CC9S2	Uphold high standards of competence and integrity and exercise sound judgment in the practice of the professional.														
CC9S3	Act ethically in advocating for appropriate services.														
CC9S4	Conduct professional activities in compliance with applicable laws and policies.														
CC9S5	Demonstrate commitment to developing the highest education and quality-of-life potential of individuals with exceptional learning needs.														
CC9S6	Demonstrate sensitivity for the culture, language, religion, gender, disability, socio-economic status, and sexual orientation of individuals.				•										
CC9S7	Practice within one's skill limit and obtain assistance as needed.														
CC9S8	Use verbal, nonverbal, and written language effectively.														
CC9S9	Conduct self-evaluation of instruction.														
CC9S10	Access information on exceptionalities.														
CC9S11	Reflect on one's practice to improve instruction and guide professional growth.														
CC9S12	Engage in professional activities that benefit individuals with exceptional learning needs, their families, and one's colleagues.			•											

STANDARD #10: COLLABORATION Special educators routinely and effectively collaborate with families, other educators, related service providers, and personnel from community agencies in culturally responsive ways. This collaboration assures that the needs of individuals with ELN are addressed throughout schooling. Moreover, special educators embrace their special role as advocate for individuals with ELN. Special educators promote and advocate the learning and well-being of individuals with ELN across a wide range of settings and a range of different learning experiences. Special educators are viewed as specialists by a myriad of people who actively seek their collaboration to effectively include and teach individuals with ELN. Special educators are a resource to their colleagues in understanding the laws and policies relevant to individuals with ELN. Special educators use collaboration to facilitate the successful transitions of individuals with ELN across settings and services.

Knowledge		Chapter													
		1	2	3	4	5	6	7	8	9	10	11	12	13	14
CC10K1	Models and strategies of consultation and collaboration.	•			•			•			•				
CC10K2	Roles of individuals with exceptional learning needs, families, and school and community personnel in planning of an individualized program.	•								•	•	•	•	•	•
CC10K3	Concerns of families and individuals with exceptional learning needs and strategies to help address these concerns.				•									•	•
CC10K4	Culturally responsive factors that promote effective communication and collaboration with individuals and exceptional learning needs, families, school personnel, and community members.				•				•						
Skills		1	2	3	4	5	6	7	8	9	10	11	12	13	14
CC10S1															
CC10S2	Collaborate with families and others in assessment of individuals with exceptional learning needs.							•							
CC10S3	Foster respectful and beneficial relationships between families and professionals.				•										
CC10S4	Assist individuals with exceptional learning needs and their families in becoming active participants in the educational team.				•										
CC10S5	Plan and conduct collaborative conferences with individuals with exceptional learning needs and their families.				•										
CC10S6	Collaborate with school personnel and community members in integrating individuals with exceptional learning needs into various settings.														
CC10S7	Use group problem-solving skills to develop, implement, and evaluate collaborative activities.														
CC10S8	Model techniques and coach others in the use of instructional methods and accommodations.														
CC10S9	Communicate with school personnel about the characteristics and needs of individuals with exceptional learning needs.														
CC10S10	Communicate effectively with families of individuals with exceptional learning needs from diverse backgrounds.				•										
CC10S11	Observe, evaluate, and provide feedback to paraeducators.														

INTASC Standards Correlated by Chapter*

Interstate New Teacher Assessment and Support Consortium (INTASC) Standards for General and Special Education Teachers

PRINCIPLE 1 The teacher understands the central concepts, tools of inquiry, and structures of the discipline(s) he or she teaches and can create learning experiences that make these aspects of subject matter meaningful for students.

		Chapter												
		1	2	3	4	5	6	7	8	9	10	11	12	13
1.03	All teachers understand that students with disabilities may need accommodations, modifications, and/or adaptations to the general curriculum depending on their learning strengths and needs.	•				•	•	•	•	•	•	•	•	•
1.04	All teachers have knowledge of the major principles and parameters of federal disabilities legislation.		•	•		•	•	•	•	•	•	•	•	•
1.05	All teachers know about and can access resources to gain information about state, district, and school policies and procedures regarding special education, including those regarding referral, assessment, eligibility, and services for students with disabilities.		•			•	•	•	•	•		•	•	•

PRINCIPLE 2 The teacher understands how children learn and develop, and can provide learning opportunities that support the intellectual, social, and personal development of each learner. The teacher understands the central concepts, tools of inquiry, and structures of the discipline(s) he or she teaches and can create learning experiences that make these aspects of subject matter meaningful for students.

		Chapter												
		1	2	3	4	5	6	7	8	9	10	11	12	13
2.01	All General and Special Education Teachers have a sound understanding of physical, social, emotional, and cognitive development from birth through adulthood.	•				•	•	•	•	•	•	•	•	•
2.02	All teachers continually examine their assumptions about the learning and development of individual students with disabilities.		•			•	•	•	•	•	•	•	•	•
2.03	All teachers recognize that students with disabilities vary in their approaches to learning depending on factors such as the nature of their disability, their level of knowledge and functioning, and life experiences.	•		•		•	•	•	•	•	•	•	•	•
2.04	All teachers are knowledgeable about multiple theories of learning and research-based teaching practices that support learning.					•	•	•	•	•	•	•	•	•

*Chapter 14 not included because INTASC standards do not directly address students who are gifted and talented. For a complete list of INTASC standards, visit http://www.ccsso.org/content/pdfs/corestrd.pdf.

PRINCIPLE 3 The teacher understands how students differ in their approaches to learning and creates instructional opportunities that are adapted to diverse learners.

		Chapter												
		1	2	3	4	5	6	7	8	9	10	11	12	13
3.01	All General and Special Education Teachers build students' awareness, sensitivity, acceptance, and appreciation for students with disabilities who are members of their classrooms, schools, and communities.	•		•	•									
3.02	All teachers recognize that a specific disability does not dictate how an individual student will learn.	•	•			•	•	•	•	•	•	•	•	•
3.03	All teachers understand that a disability can be perceived differently across families, communities, and cultures based on differing values and belief systems.			•	•	•	•	•	•	•	•	•	•	•
3.04	All teachers understand and are sensitive to cultural, ethnic, gender, and linguistic differences that may be confused with or misinterpreted as manifestations of a disability.			•	•	•	•	•	•	•	•	•	•	•

PRINCIPLE 4 The teacher understands and uses a variety of instructional strategies to encourage students' development of critical thinking, problem solving, and performance skills.

		Chapter												
		1	2	3	4	5	6	7	8	9	10	11	12	13
4.01	All General and Special Education Teachers have shared responsibility for the education of students with disabilities including the implementation of instructional strategies to support the student's learning in the general and/or expanded curriculums.	•	•			•	•	•	•	•	•	•	•	•
4.02	All teachers understand how different learning theories and research contribute to effective instruction for students with disabilities.					•	•	•	•	•	•	•	•	•
4.03	All teachers use research-based practices including explicit instruction and planned maintenance and generalization to support initial learning and generalization of concepts and skills for students with disabilities.					•	•	•	•	•	•	•	•	•
4.04	All teachers understand that it is particularly important to provide multiple ways for students with disabilities to participate in learning activities.			•		•	•	•	•	•	•	•		•
4.05	All teachers provide a variety of ways for students with disabilities to demonstrate their learning.	•				•	•	•	•	•	•	•	•	•
4.06	All teachers adjust their instruction in response to information gathered from ongoing monitoring of performance and progress of students with disabilities.			•		•	•	•					•	•
4.07	All teachers use strategies that promote the independence, self-control, and self-advocacy of students with disabilities.					•	•	•	•	•	•	•	•	•
4.08	All teachers expect and support the use of assistive and instructional technologies to promote learning and independence of students with disabilities.					•	•	•	•	•	•	•	•	•

PRINCIPLE 5 The teacher uses an understanding of individual and group motivation and behavior to create a learning environment that encourages positive social interaction, active engagement in learning, and self-motivation.

		Chapter												
		1	2	3	4	5	6	7	8	9	10	11	12	13
5.01	All General and Special Education Teachers identify the interests and preferences of students with disabilities and use this information to design activities that encourage students with disabilities to make positive contributions to the learning community.		•							•				•
5.02	All teachers help students with disabilities develop positive strategies for coping with frustrations in the learning situation that may be associated with their disability.					•	•	•	•	•	•	•	•	•
5.03	All teachers take deliberate action to promote positive social relationships among students with disabilities and their age-appropriate peers in the learning community.					•	•	•	•	•	•	•	•	•
5.04	All teachers recognize factors and situations that are likely to promote (or diminish) intrinsic motivation, and create learning environments that encourage engagement and self-motivation of students with disabilities.								•	•	•		•	•
5.05	All teachers participate in the design and implementation of individual behavioral support plans and are proactive in responding to the needs of individual students with disabilities within the learning community.		•								•	•		•

PRINCIPLE 6 The teacher uses knowledge of effective verbal, nonverbal, and media communication technologies to foster active inquiry, collaboration, and supportive interaction in the classroom.

		Chapter												
		1	2	3	4	5	6	7	8	9	10	11	12	13
6.01	All General and Special Education Teachers have knowledge of the general types of communication strategies and assistive technologies that can be incorporated as a regular part of their instruction.		•			•	•	•		•	•	•	•	•
6.02	All teachers collaborate with speech/language pathologists and other language specialists to identify the language and communication skills that need to be developed in students with disabilities, and to work cooperatively to teach those skills across settings.									•	•	•		•
6.03	All teachers understand that linguistic background has an impact on language acquisition as well as communication content and style.			•		•	•	•	•	•	•	•	•	•
6.04	All teachers provide multiple opportunities to foster effective communication among students with disabilities and other members of the classroom as a means of building communication and language skills.										•	•	•	•
6.05	All teachers are sensitive to the verbal and nonverbal messages they may convey to students with disabilities through their interactions during instruction.									•	•	•	•	•

PRINCIPLE 7 The teacher plans instruction based on knowledge of subject matter, students, the community, and curriculum goals.

		Chapter												
		1	2	3	4	5	6	7	8	9	10	11	12	13
7.01	All General and Special Education Teachers contribute their expertise as members of a collaborative team to develop, monitor, and periodically revise individualized educational plans for students with disabilities.		•	•					•	•				•
7.02	All teachers plan ways to modify instruction, as needed, to facilitate positive learning results within the general curriculum for students with disabilities.	•	•			•	•	•	•	•		•	•	•
7.03	All teachers collaborate to plan instruction related to expanded curriculum in general education classrooms for students with disabilities who require such curriculum.		•			•	•	•	•	•		•	•	•
7.04	All teachers design the learning environment so that the individual needs of students with disabilities are accommodated.	•	•			•	•	•	•	•	•	•	•	•
7.05	All teachers monitor student progress and incorporate knowledge of student performance across settings into the instructional planning process, using information provided by parents and others in those settings.		•			•	•	•	•	•	•	•	•	•

PRINCIPLE 8 The teacher understands and uses formal and informal assessment strategies to evaluate and ensure the continuous intellectual, social, and physical development of the learner.

		Chapter												
		1	2	3	4	5	6	7	8	9	10	11	12	13
8.01	All General and Special Education Teachers understand the purposes, strengths, and limitations of formal and informal assessment approaches for making eligibility, placement, and instructional decisions for students with disabilities.		•	•					•	•	•	•	•	•
8.02	All teachers use a variety of assessment procedures to document students' learning, behavior, and growth within multiple environments appropriate to the student's age, interests, and learning.			•		•	•	•	•	•	•	•	•	•
8.03	All teachers collaborate with others to incorporate accommodations and alternate assessments into the ongoing assessment process of students with disabilities when appropriate.					•	•	•	•	•	•	•	•	•
8.04	All teachers engage all students, including students with disabilities, in assessing and understanding their own learning and behavior.						•	•	•	•	•	•	•	•
8.05	All teachers understand that students with disabilities are expected to participate in district and statewide assessments and that accommodations or alternate assessments may be required when appropriate.									•			•	•

PRINCIPLE 9 The teacher is a reflective practitioner who continually evaluates the effects of his/her choices and actions on others and who actively seeks out opportunities to grow professionally.

		Chapter												
		1	2	3	4	5	6	7	8	9	10	11	12	13
9.02	All teachers continually challenge their beliefs about how students with disabilities learn and how to teach them effectively.	•				•	•	•	•	•	•	•	•	•
9.03	All teachers actively seek out current information and research about how to educate the students with disabilities for whom they are responsible, including information that will help them understand the strengths and needs of students with disabilities as well as ways to more effectively promote their learning.					•	•	•	•	•	•	•	•	•
9.04	All teachers reflect on the potential interaction between a student's cultural experiences and their disability.			•	•	•	•	•	•	•		•	•	•

PRINCIPLE 10 The teacher fosters relationships with school colleagues, families, and agencies in the larger community to support students' learning and well-being.

		Chapter												
		1	2	3	4	5	6	7	8	9	10	11	12	13
10.01	All General and Special Education Teachers share instructional responsibility for students with disabilities and work to develop well-functioning collaborative teaching relationships.	•								•		•	•	•
10.02	All teachers understand the purposes of, and are effective members of, the different types of teams within the special education process (e.g., child study and teacher assistance teams, multidisciplinary teams that focus on identification and placement, IEP/IFSP teams).	•										•		•
10.04	All teachers accept families as full partners in planning appropriate instruction and services for students with disabilities, and provide meaningful opportunities for them to participate as partners in their children's instructional programs and in the life of the school.			•	•	•	•	•	•	•	•	•	•	•

SOURCE: The Interstate New Teacher Assessment and Support Consortium (INTASC) standards were developed by the Council of Chief State School Officers and member states. Copies may be downloaded from the Council's Web site at http://www.ccsso.org.

Council of Chief State School Officers. (1992). *Model standards for beginning teacher licensing, assessment, and development: A resource for state dialogue.* Washington, DC: Author. Retrieved June 3, 2008 from http://www.ccsso.org/content/pdfs/corestrd.pdf

PRAXIS™ Series of Professional Assessment for Beginning Teachers

Topics covered by the Praxis II® test, *Education of Exceptional Students: Core Content Knowledge* (0353), are shown here.

Descriptions of each of the content areas covered by the test are provided below. For each content area, the approximate percentage of examination questions pertaining to that area is shown. Not every subtopic in a given content area appears on any one form of the test, but every form of the test contains questions on a broad range of subtopics.

I. Understanding Exceptionalities (25%–30% of test questions)

- Human development and behavior as related to students with disabilities, including
  - social and emotional development and behavior
  - language development and behavior
  - cognition
  - physical development, including motor and sensory
- Characteristics of students with disabilities, including the influence of
  - cognitive factors
  - affective and social-adaptive factors, including cultural, linguistic, gender, and socioeconomic factors
  - genetic, medical, motor, sensory, and chronological age factors
- Basic concepts in special education, including
  - definitions of all major categories and specific disabilities, as well as the incidence and prevalence of various types of disabilities
  - the causation and prevention of disability
  - the nature of behaviors, including frequency, duration, intensity, and degrees of severity
  - the classification of students with disabilities; labeling of students; ADHD; the implications of the classification process for the persons classified, etc.
  - the influence of level of severity and presence of multiple exceptionalities on students with disabilities
- The influence of (an) exceptional condition(s) throughout an individual's life span

II. Legal and Societal Issues (15%–20% of test questions)

- Federal laws and legal issues related to special education, including
  - IDEA 2004
  - Section 504
  - Americans with Disabilities Act (ADA)
  - Important legal issues, such as those raised by the following cases: *Rowley* re: program appropriateness, *Tatro* re: related services, *Honig* re: discipline, *Oberti* re: inclusion
- The school's connections with the families, prospective and actual employers, and communities of students with disabilities; for example:
  - teacher advocacy for students and families, developing student self-advocacy
  - parent partnerships and roles

Source: PRAXIS materials from *The Praxis Series: Test at a Glance—Education of Exceptional Students: Core Content Knowledge*. Reprinted by permission of Educational Testing Service, the copyright owner.

Note: Permission to reprint PRAXIS materials does not constitute review or endorsement by Educational Testing Service of this publication as a whole or of any other testing information it may contain.

- public attitudes toward individuals with disabilities
- cultural and community influences on public attitudes toward individuals with disabilities
- interagency agreements
- cooperative nature of the transition planning process
- Historical movements/trends affecting the connections between special education and the larger society; for example:
  - deinstitutionalization and community-based placements
  - inclusion
  - application of technology
  - transition
  - advocacy
  - accountability and meeting educational standards

III. Delivery of Services to Students with Disabilities (50%–60% of test questions)

- Background knowledge, including
  - conceptual approaches underlying service delivery to students with disabilities, including cognitive, constructivist, psychodynamic, behavioral, sociological, ecological, therapeutic (speech/language, physical, and occupational), and medical approaches
  - placement and program issues such as early intervention; least restrictive environment; inclusion; role of Individualized Education Program (IEP) team; due process guidelines; categorical, noncategorical, and cross-categorical programs; continuum of educational and related services; related services and their integration into the classroom, including roles of other professionals; accommodations, including access to assistive technology; transition of students into and within special education placements; community-based training; post-school transitions
  - integrating best practices from multidisciplinary research and professional literature into the educational setting
- Curriculum and instruction and their implementation across the continuum of educational placements, including
  - the Individualized Family Service Plan (IFSP)/Individualized Education Program (IEP) process
  - Instructional development and implementation; for example: instructional activities, curricular materials and resources, working with classroom and support personnel, tutoring options
  - teaching strategies and methods; for example: modification of materials and equipment, learning centers, facilitated groups, study skills groups, self-management, cooperative learning, diagnostic-prescriptive method, modeling, skill drill, guided practice, concept generalization, learning strategy instruction, and Direct Instruction
  - instructional format and components; for example: small and large group instruction, facilitated group strategies, functional academics, general academics with focus on special education, ESL and limited English proficiency, language and literacy acquisition, self-care and daily living skills, prevocational and vocational skills
  - career development and transition issues as related to curriculum design and implementation for students with disabilities according to the criteria of ultimate functioning
  - technology for teaching and learning in special education settings; for example: integrating assistive technology into the classroom; computer-assisted instruction; augmentative and alternative communication; adaptive

Source: PRAXIS materials from *The Praxis Series: Test at a Glance—Education of Exceptional Students: Core Content Knowledge.* Reprinted by permission of Educational Testing Service, the copyright owner.

Note: Permission to reprint PRAXIS materials does not constitute review or endorsement by Educational Testing Service of this publication as a whole or of any other testing information it may contain.

access for microcomputers; positioning and power mobility for students with physical disabilities; accessing and using information technology; use of productivity tools; technology for sensory disabilities; and voice-activated, speech synthesis, speech-recognition, and word-prediction software

- Assessment, including
  - use of assessment for screening, diagnosis, placement, and the making of instructional decisions; for example: how to select and conduct nondiscriminatory and appropriate assessments; how to interpret standardized and specialized assessment results; how to use evaluation results effectively in development of an Individualized Family Service Plan (IFSP)/Individualized Education Program (IEP); how to prepare written reports and communicate findings
  - procedures and test materials, both formal and informal, typically used for prereferral, referral, eligibility, placement, and ongoing program monitoring
  - how to select, construct, conduct, and modify nondiscriminatory, developmentally and chronologically age-appropriate informal assessments, including teacher-made tests, curriculum-based assessment, and alternatives to norm-referenced testing (including observation, anecdotal records, error analysis, miscue analysis, self-evaluation questionnaires and interviews, journals and learning logs, portfolio assessment)
- Structuring and managing the learning environment, including
  - structuring the learning environment; for example: the physical-social environment for learning (expectations, rules, consequences, consistency, attitudes, lighting, acoustic characteristics, seating, access, safety provisions, and strategies for positive interactions); transitions between lessons and activities; grouping of students; integration of related services (occupational therapy, physical therapy, speech and language therapy)
  - classroom management techniques; for example: behavioral analysis (identification and definition of antecedents, target behavior, and consequent events); behavioral interventions; functional analysis; data gathering procedures (such as anecdotal data, frequency methods, and interval methods); self-management strategies and reinforcement; cognitive-behavioral interventions; social skills training; behavior management strategies
- Professional roles, including
  - specific roles and responsibilities of teachers; for example: teacher as a collaborator with other teachers, teacher educators, parents, community groups, and outside agencies; teacher as a multidisciplinary team member; maintaining effective and efficient documentation; selecting appropriate environments and services for students; critical evaluation and use of professional literature and organizations; reflecting on one's own teaching; teacher's role in a variety of teaching settings (self-contained classroom, resource room, itinerant, co-teacher in inclusion setting, etc.); and maintaining student confidentiality
  - influence of teacher attitudes, values, and behaviors on the learning of exceptional students
  - communicating with parents, guardians, and appropriate community collaborators; for example: directing parents and guardians to parent-educators or to other groups and resources; writing reports directly to parents; meeting with parents to discuss student concerns, progress, and IEPs; encouraging parent participation; reciprocal communication and training with other service providers

---

SOURCE: PRAXIS materials from *The Praxis Series: Test at a Glance—Education of Exceptional Students: Core Content Knowledge*. Reprinted by permission of Educational Testing Service, the copyright owner.

NOTE: Permission to reprint PRAXIS materials does not constitute review or endorsement by Educational Testing Service of this publication as a whole or of any other testing information it may contain.

Glossary

absence seizure A type of epileptic seizure lasting for a brief period of time whereby the individual loses consciousness and stops moving, formerly known as petit mal seizures.

acceleration An instructional strategy typically used with pupils who are gifted and talented; one approach is placing students in a grade level beyond their chronological age.

acoustic immittance A technical term for measurements of middle ear function.

acquired immune deficiency syndrome (AIDS) An infectious disease caused by HIV (human immunodeficiency virus) that destroys the immune system, leaving the person open to serious, life-threatening diseases.

active listening A type of listening in which a person is attentive to the feelings as well as the verbal message that is being communicated.

adaptability The ability of an individual or family to change in response to a crisis or stressful event.

adaptive behavior The ability of an individual to meet the standards of personal independence as well as social responsibility appropriate for his or her chronological age and cultural group.

additions An articulation disorder wherein the speaker inserts extra sounds in spoken words.

adventitious hearing loss Hearing loss that is acquired after birth, not inherited.

air-conduction audiometry A procedure for measuring hearing sensitivity at certain frequencies using pure tones presented to the listener through earphones or speakers.

albinism A hereditary condition with partial or total absence of pigment in the eye.

amniocentesis A diagnostic medical procedure performed to detect chromosomal and genetic abnormalities in a fetus.

amplified telephone A telephone containing a variable output control designed to increase volume for the listener.

anencephaly Cranial malformation; large part of the brain fails to develop.

anoxia Loss of or inadequate supply of oxygen associated with birth process and frequently resulting in brain damage.

aphakic Absence of the lens, causing light sensitivity and loss of visual acuity.

aphasia Loss or impairment of language functions.

applied behavior analysis Application of learning principles derived from operant conditioning; used to increase or decrease specific behaviors.

apraxia of speech Speech and language disorder comprised of both a speech disorder, caused by oral-motor difficulty, and a language disorder, characterized by the resultant limitations of expression.

articulation disorders Errors in the formation of individual sounds of speech.

Asperger syndrome A pervasive developmental disorder with severe and sustained impairments in social interaction and the development of restricted, repetitive patterns of behavior, interests, and activities.

Disorder causes clinically significant impairments in other important areas of functioning.

assessment The process of gathering information and identifying a student's strengths and needs through a variety of instruments and products; data used in making decisions.

assistive listening devices Devices such as FM or sound field systems that improve the clarity of what is heard by an individual with hearing impairments by reducing background noise levels.

assistive technology Any item, piece of equipment, or product system that increases, maintains, or improves functional capabilities of individuals with disabilities.

asthma A lung disease with acute attacks of shortness of breath and wheezing.

astigmatism One or more surfaces of the cornea or lens are cylindrical, not spherical, resulting in distorted vision.

ataxic cerebral palsy A type of cerebral palsy that is characterized by poor balance and equilibrium in addition to uncoordinated voluntary movement.

athetoid cerebral palsy A type of cerebral palsy in which movements are contorted, abnormal, and purposeless.

atresia The absence or closure of the ear canal; can be congenital or acquired from injury or disease.

at-risk An infant or child who has a high probability of exhibiting delays in development or developing a disability.

attention deficit hyperactivity disorder (ADHD) A disorder characterized by symptoms of inattention, hyperactivity, and/or impulsivity. Frequently observed in individuals with learning disabilities.

auditory neuropathy/auditory dyssynchrony A hearing loss in which the cochlea is functioning normally but with loss of neural function.

audiogram A graphic representation of audiometric findings showing hearing thresholds as a function of frequency.

audiologist A professional who studies the science of hearing, including anatomy, function, and disorders, and provides education and treatment for those with hearing loss.

audiometric test A test designed to measure auditory sensitivity and determine the nature and severity of any loss of hearing.

auditory evoked potentials Neural impulses produced from within the auditory system in response to stimulation of the auditory pathway and recorded as bioelectric events using a special computer.

auditory trainers Type of amplification system used by children with hearing impairments in place of their hearing aids in educational settings.

augmentative or alternative communication (AAC) Symbols, aids, strategies, and techniques used as a supplement or alternative to oral language.

authentic assessment An evaluation of a student's ability by means of various work products, typically classroom assignments and other activities.

autism spectrum disorders A developmental disorder characterized by abnormal or impaired development in social interaction and communication and a markedly restricted repertoire of activity and interests.

autistic savant An individual with autism who possesses special skills in areas such as mathematical calculations, memory feats, artistic and musical abilities, or reading.

autosomal dominant A genetic form of inheritance involving the non-sex-linked chromosomes in which the individual has one normal and one abnormal gene in a gene pair.

autosomal recessive A genetic form of inheritance involving the non-sex-linked chromosomes in which both genes of a gene pair must be affected for the trait to be expressed.

behavioral curriculum model A curriculum approach based on learning principles derived from behavioral psychology.

behavioral inhibition A characteristic common in persons with ADHD; impacts executive functions. Typically affects the ability to (1) withhold a planned response; (2) interrupt an ongoing response; and (3) protect an ongoing response from distractions.

behavioral intervention plan A plan required by Public Law 105-17 for students withdisabilities who exhibit problematic behavior; a proactive intervention approach that includes a functional behavioral assessment and the use of positive behavioral supports.

bilingual education An educational approach whereby students whose first language is not English are instructed primarily through their native language while developing competency and proficiency in English.

bilingual special education Strategy whereby a pupil's home language and culture are used along with English in an individually designed program of special instruction.

biologically at-risk Young children with a history of pre-, peri-, or postnatal conditions and developmental events that heighten the potential for later atypical development.

birth trauma Difficulties associated with the delivery of the fetus.

blind An impairment in which an individual may have some light or form perception or be totally without sight.

bone-conduction audiometry A procedure for measuring hearing sensitivity at certain frequencies using pure tones presented through an oscillator placed on the forehead or mastoid bone of the listener. Sound is conducted to the inner ear through the bones of the skull.

Braille A communication system utilizing raised representation of written materials for tactual interpretation.

brain injury Actual or assumed trauma to the brain.

breech presentation Fetus exits the birth canal buttocks first rather than typical headfirst presentation.

cataracts Lenses that are opaque or cloudy due to trauma or age.

category Label assigned to individuals who share common characteristics and features.

central auditory nervous system Part of the hearing mechanism connecting the ear to the brain.

central auditory processing disorder (CAPD) A problem in the processing of sound not attributed to hearing loss or intellectual capacity, involving cognitive and linguistic functions that directly affect receptive communication skills.

central hearing disorder Difficulty in the reception and interpretation of auditory information in the absence of a hearing loss.

cerebral palsy Several nonprogressive disorders of voluntary movement or posture that are caused by damage to the developing brain.

CHARGE association A rare genetic disorder resulting in deaf-blindness, a syndrome representing a cluster of physical anomalies present at birth.

child-find A function of each state, mandated by federal law, to locate and refer individuals who might require special education.

child maltreatment The neglect and/or physical, emotional, or sexual abuse of a child.

childhood disintegrative disorder A marked regression in multiple areas of functioning following a period of at least two years of apparent normal development. After the first two years of life (but before

ten years), the child has a clinically significant loss of previously acquired skills in at least two of the following areas: expressive or receptive language, social skills or adaptive behavior, bowel or bladder control, play, or motor skills.

chorionic villus sampling A diagnostic medical procedure used to detect a variety of chromosomal abnormalities, usually conducted in the first trimester of pregnancy.

classroom ambience The feeling or sense a person experiences upon entering a classroom; the appeal of the room.

classroom arrangement The physical layout of the classroom and its décor; a proactive intervention technique designed to minimize disruptions while increasing pupil engagement.

cleft lip/cleft palate A congenital defect in which the upper lip is split or there is an opening in the roof of the mouth. Can often be surgically corrected. Hypernasality is common.

clinically derived classification system A system frequently used by mental health professionals to describe childhood, adolescent, and adult mental disorders.

cluster grouping The practice of placing five or more students who have similar needs and abilities with one teacher; promotes challenging cognitive development and positive social-emotional development.

cluttering Type of fluency disorder involving cognitive, linguistic, pragmatic, speech, and motor abilities.

cochlea Shell- or spiral-shaped structure in the inner ear that is responsible for hearing.

cohesion Within a family, the degree of freedom and independence experienced by each member.

collaboration How individuals work together; a style of interaction among professionals.

coloboma A congenital condition that results in a teardrop shape of the pupil, iris, lens, retina, choroids, or optic nerve; may involve loss of field vision as well as problems with glare and depth perception.

communication The sharing or exchange of ideas, information, thoughts, and feelings. Does not necessarily require speech or language.

communication breakdown Misunderstanding as to what is being communicated, especially as it relates to individuals who are using some form of augmentative communication.

community-based instruction A strategy for teaching functional skills in the environment in which they would naturally occur rather than in simulated settings.

comorbidity The simultaneous existence of two or more conditions within the same person.

complex partial seizure A type of epileptic seizure whereby the person exhibits purposeless motor activity for a brief period of time; consciousness is impaired

conduct disorders A common psychiatric disorder among children and youth characterized by disruptive and aggressive behavior as well as other actions that violate societal rules.

conductive hearing loss The loss of sound sensitivity produced by abnormalities of the outer ear and/or middle ear.

cone cells Light-sensitive cells located mainly in the central area of the retina that define color.

conflict resolution Program designed to teach problem-solving skills along with strategies for negotiation and mediation.

consultation A focused problem-solving process in which one individual offers support and expertise to another person.

content enhancements Instructional aids designed to assist pupils in understanding major concepts, ideas, and vocabulary in a way that aids the acquisition, organization, and recall of material.

contractures Shortened muscles that result in the inability to fully extend a joint.

cooperative learning Instructional process whereby heterogeneous groups of students work together on an assignment.

cooperative teaching An instructional approach in which a special education teacher and a general educator teach together in a general education classroom to a heterogeneous group of students.

cornea The transparent outer portion of the eyeball that transmits light to the retina.

creativity A term with multiple meanings, generally referring to the production of novel or original ideas or products.

crisis prevention and management programs Techniques taught to teachers on how to effectively and proactively deal with students' violent, aggressive, and/or self-injurious behaviors; a proactive preventative approach.

criterion-referenced assessment An assessment procedure in which a student's performance is compared to a particular level of mastery.

cultural pluralism The practice of appreciating and respecting ethnic and cultural differences.

cultural sensitivity A perspective adopted by professionals when working with families in which there is an awareness of and respect for the values, customs, and traditions of individuals and families.

culture The attitudes, values, belief systems, norms, and traditions shared by a particular group of people that collectively form their heritage.

curriculum-based measurement Evaluation technique for monitoring student progress in core academic areas such as reading, writing, and arithmetic.

curriculum compacting An instructional technique whereby the time spent on academic subjects is reduced so as to allow for enrichment activities; typically used with students who are gifted or talented.

cytomegalovirus Known as CMV, a common virus that is part of the herpes group; if initial exposure occurs during pregnancy, severe damage to the fetus often results.

deaf Limited or absent hearing for ordinary purposes of daily living.

deaf-blind A dual disability resulting in impaired hearing and vision.

decibel (dB) A unit of measure expressing the magnitude of a sound relative to the softest sound to which the normal human ear can respond.

deinstitutionalization A movement whereby persons with mental retardation are relocated from large institutions into smaller, community-based, group living settings.

developmental delay A term defined by individual states referring to children ages 3 to 9 who perform significantly below developmental norms.

developmental language delay Slowness in the development of adequate vocabulary and grammar, or when a child's language age does not correspond to the child's chronological age.

developmental/cognitive model A curriculum approach based on the work of Piaget; cognitive development seen as resulting from maturation coupled with active interaction and involvement with children's environment.

differentiation A modification of the curriculum that enables students who are gifted to learn at a level appropriate to their ability.

diplegia Paralysis (or spasticity) of the legs and partly the arms.

Direct Instruction A teacher-directed instructional technique used to produce gains in specific academic skills; emphasizes drill and practice along with immediate feedback and reward.

disability An inability or incapacity to perform a task or activity in a normative fashion.

discrepancy In regard to learning disabilities, the difference between the student's actual academic performance and his or her estimated ability.

distortions Articulation disorder in which a sound is said inaccurately, but resembles the intended sound (e.g., shlip for sip).

doctor's office effect The absence of symptoms of ADHD when the individual is evaluated in a structured environment such as a physician's office.

Down syndrome A chromosomal abnormality frequently resulting in mental retardation with accompanying distinctive physical features.

Duchenne muscular dystrophy An inherited disease that is characterized by progressive muscle weakness from the degeneration of the muscle fiber.

dyslexia A severe reading disability; difficulty in understanding the relationship between sounds and letters.

early childhood special education Provision of customized services uniquely crafted to meet the individual needs of youngsters with disabilities ages 3 to 5.

early intervention The delivery of a coordinated and comprehensive package of specialized services to infants and toddlers with developmental delays or at-risk conditions and their families.

educable mentally retarded Classification of a person with mild mental retardation who typically develops functional academic skills at a third- or fourth-grade level; IQ range generally between 50/55 and 70/75.

effective instructional cycle A teaching technique designed to enhance learning and student engagement.

emotional disturbance A term often used when referring to individuals with emotional or behavioral disorders.

emotional or behavioral disorders A chronic condition characterized by behaviors that significantly differ from age norms and community standards to such a degree that educational performance is adversely affected.

encephalitis An inflammation of the brain; may cause damage to the central nervous system.

enrichment An instructional approach typically used with pupils who are gifted and talented; providing additional learning opportunities and experiences not normally available in the curriculum.

environmental control unit A device that allows the user to control electric appliances, telephones, and other items that use electric outlets from a distance.

environmentally at-risk Youngsters who are biologically typical yet encounter life experiences or environmental circumstances that are so limiting that there is the possibility of future delayed development.

epilepsy A chronic condition in which the person has reoccurring seizures.

established risk Youngsters with a diagnosed medical disorder of known etiology and predictable prognosis or outcome.

ethnocentrism A perspective whereby a person views his or her cultural practices as correct and those of other groups as inferior, peculiar, or deviant.

etiology A term frequently used when describing the cause of a disability.

eugenics movement A campaign that sought to improve the quality of humankind through carefully controlled selective breeding.

evoked otoacoustic emissions Sounds produced by the inner ear in response to auditory stimulation and measured in the ear canal.

exceptional children Children who deviate from the norm to such an extent that special educational services are required.

exclusionary clause In regard to learning disabilities, the elimination of possible etiological factors to explain a pupil's difficulty in learning.

executive functions Internal regulation of one's behavior through control of emotions, inner speech, working memory, arousal levels, and motivation. Considered impaired in individuals with attention deficit hyperactivity disorder.

expressive language The formation and production of language, verbal and nonverbal, that is understood by and meaningful to others.

external locus of control The belief that the consequences or outcomes of a person's actions are the result of circumstances and

situations beyond one's control rather than a result of one's own efforts.

externalizing disorders A behavior disorder characterized by aggressive, disruptive, acting-out behavior.

familiality studies A method for assessing the degree to which a particular characteristic is inherited; the tendency for certain conditions to occur in a single family.

family characteristics One dimension of a family systems model; aspects include family size and form, cultural background, and socioeconomic status, as well as the type and severity of the disability.

family functions Interrelated activities found within a family systems model; functions range from affection to economics to socialization, among other variables.

family interactions One aspect of a family systems model; refers to the relationships and interactions occurring among and between various family subsystems.

family life cycle Developmental changes occurring within a family over time.

family systems model A model that considers a family as an interrelated social system with unique characteristics and needs.

family-centered early intervention (approach) A philosophy of working with families that stresses family strengths and capabilities, the enhancement of skills, and the development of mutual partnerships

between service providers and families.

family-directed assessment A form of assessment, useful for infants, toddlers, and preschool-age youngsters, that focuses on information that families choose to provide regarding needs, concerns, resources, and priorities.

fetal alcohol effect A less severe and more subtle form of fetal alcohol syndrome; caused by drinking alcohol while pregnant.

fetal alcohol syndrome Results from mother's consumption of alcohol while pregnant; mild to moderate mental retardation is common, along with physical deformities. A leading cause of mental retardation, although completely preventable.

field dependent/sensitive Students who approach learning intuitively rather than analytically and logically. These students tend to find success in cooperative learning situations and group work.

field independent Learners who are detail oriented and analytically inclined. These students tend to thrive in competitive settings.

field loss A restriction to the visual field within the quadrant regions to the right, left, up, and down while gazing straight ahead.

fingerspelling A form of manual communication; different positions or movements of the fingers indicate letters of the alphabet.

flexible grouping The combining or grouping of students according to needs and abilities matched to their level of achievement.

fluency disorders Disorders that involve the flow of speech, influencing the rate and smoothness of an individual's speech.

FM system A wireless system that allows the transmission of a signal from the teacher wearing a microphone to the student wearing a receiver, increasing the volume of the teacher's voice over the volume level of classroom noise.

formal supports Assistance provided by government social programs, habilitation services, or advocacy groups.

Fragile X syndrome A chromosomal abnormality leading to mental retardation along with physical anomalies; believed to be the most common form of inherited mental retardation.

frequency The number of vibrations per second of a given sound wave; typically measured as cycles per second (cps) or hertz (Hz).

full inclusion An interpretation of the principle of least restrictive environment advocating that all pupils with disabilities are to be educated in the general education classroom.

functional Etiologies of speech and language disorders that have no obvious physical basis (such as environmental stress).

functional academics The application of life skills as a means of teaching academic tasks; core of many instructional programs for students with mild or moderate mental retardation.

functional behavioral assessment A behavioral strategy that seeks to determine the purpose or function that a particular behavior serves—what is occasioning and maintaining the behavior.

functional curriculum A curriculum that emphasizes practical life skills rather than academic skills.

functional or nonorganic hearing loss A hearing loss that has no organic or biological basis.

functional vision How well students use the vision they have to complete a specific task.

functionally blind An educational description when the primary channel of learning is through tactile and auditory means.

galactosemia An inborn error of metabolism that makes infants unable to process galactose, resulting in a variety of physical problems in addition to mental retardation; dietary intervention reduces potential for problems.

generalizing The ability to transfer previously learned knowledge or skills acquired in one setting to another set of circumstances or situation.

gifted and talented Persons who possess abilities and talents that can be demonstrated, or have the potential for being developed, at exceptionally high levels.

glaucoma A disease caused by increased pressure inside the aqueous portion of the eye with loss in the visual field.

grade one Braille A beginning level of Braille in which a word is spelled out with a Braille letter corresponding to each printed letter.

grade two Braille A more complex level of Braille in which contractions are used to represent parts of words or whole words.

handicapism The unequal and differential treatment accorded individuals with a disability.

handicap Difficulties imposed by the environment on a person with a disability.

hard of hearing Refers to a person who has a hearing loss but uses the auditory channel as the primary avenue for oral communication, with or without a hearing aid.

hearing impairment Less than normal hearing (either sensitivity or speech understanding) resulting from auditory disorder(s).

hearing sensitivity loss Poorer than normal auditory sensitivity for sounds; usually measured in decibels using pure tones.

hemiplegia Paralysis (or spasticity) on the left or right side of the body.

heritability studies A method for assessing the degree to which a specific condition is inherited; a comparison of the prevalence of a characteristic in fraternal versus identical twins.

hertz (Hz) A unit of measurement for sound frequency, expressed as cycles per second (cps).

high-risk register A list of factors placing infants at increased risk for hearing impairment, including, but not limited to, low birth weight, congenital perinatal infections, a family history of childhood hearing impairment, severe asphyxia, and bacterial meningitis.

hydrocephalus A condition in which the head is unusually large due to accumulation of excessive cerebrospinal fluid; brain damage often minimized by surgically implanting a shunt to remove excess fluid.

hyperactive child syndrome A historical term commonly used to describe youngsters who exhibit impulsivity, inattention, and/or hyperactivity.

hypernasality Disorder of voice resonance, frequently observed as a result of cleft palate, in which too much air passes through the nasal cavities during the production of sounds, giving the speaker a distinctive nasal quality or "twang."

hyperopia Change in the shape of the eye, which shortens the light ray path and causes farsightedness.

hyponasality Disorder of voice resonance in which there is a restricted flow of air through the nostrils, often resulting in the speaker's sounding as if his or her nose is being held.

hypoxia Insufficient amount of oxygen to the brain; can result in brain damage.

incidence A rate of inception; number of new cases appearing in the population within a specific time period.

incus The second of the three middle ear bones for conducting sound to the inner ear, located between the malleus and the stapes; also called the anvil.

individualized transition plan (ITP) An individualized plan with identified goals and objectives used to prepare the student in making the transition from high school to work (or college).

individualized education program (IEP) A written detailed plan developed by a team for each pupil ages 3–21 who receives a special education; a management tool.

individualized family service plan (IFSP) A written plan developed by a team that coordinates services for infants and toddlers and their families.

infant stimulation Programs for infants with disabilities or those experiencing delays; emphasis usually on achieving developmental or cognitive milestones.

information technology Databases and computer-based information sources.

inner ear The snail-shaped part of the ear (cochlea) containing the organs of hearing and balance.

instructional technology Any apparatus or device that supports the teaching–learning process, such as computers or televisions; a tool for the delivery of instruction.

interdisciplinary A group of professionals from different disciplines who function as a team but work independently; recommendations, however, are the result of sharing information and joint planning.

interindividual differences Differences between two or more persons in a particular area.

internalizing disorders Behavior disorders characterized by anxiety, withdrawal, fearfulness, and other conditions reflecting an individual's internal state.

interpersonal problem solving Teaching pupils the cognitive skills needed to avoid and resolve interpersonal conflicts, peer pressure, and ways of coping with stress and their own feelings.

interpreter A professional who signs, gestures, and/or fingerspells a speaker's message as it is spoken to enable individuals with hearing impairments to understand spoken language.

intervener A person with specialized training and skills in dead-blindness who provides individualized assistance to students.

intraindividual differences Differences within the individual; unique patterns of strengths and weaknesses.

iris The colored, circular part of the eye in front of the lens that controls the size of the pupil.

job coach An individual who supervises a person with a disability for all or part of the day to provide training, assistance, or support to maintain a job.

juvenile rheumatoid arthritis A chronic arthritic condition affecting the joints that occurs before 16 years of age.

language A code used to communicate ideas via a conventional system of arbitrary signals.

language sample An observational evaluation that includes observing the speech and language characteristics of a child actively communicating.

lead poisoning An environmental toxin used at one time in the manufacture of gasoline and paint; ingestion of lead can cause seizures, brain damage, and impaired central nervous system functioning.

learned helplessness A lack of persistence at tasks that can be mastered; a tendency to expect failure.

learning disabilities A disability in which there is a discrepancy between a person's ability and academic achievement; individual possesses average intelligence.

learning medium The materials and methods a student uses in conjunction with the sensory channels in the process of learning.

learning strategies Instructional methodologies focusing on teaching students how to learn; designed to assist pupils in becoming more actively engaged and involved in their own learning.

least restrictive environment A relative concept individually determined for each student; principle that each pupil should be educated, to the maximum extent appropriate, with classmates who are typical.

legally blind A visual acuity of 20/200 or less in the better eye with correction or a visual field that is no greater than 20 degrees.

lens The transparent disc in the middle of the eye behind the pupil that brings rays of light into focus on the retina.

level of support A classification scheme for individuals with mental retardation that is based on the type and extent of assistance required to function in various areas.

limb deficiency Any number of skeletal abnormalities in which an arm(s) and/or leg(s) is partially or totally missing.

limited English proficient (LEP) A person with a reduced or diminished fluency in reading, writing, or speaking English.

literacy medium The student's preferred method of reading and writing.

low birth weight A term frequently used to describe babies who are born weighing less than 2,500 grams (5 lbs., 8 oz.)

low incidence A special education category representative of students with disabilities that occur relatively infrequently.

low vision A visual impairment that interferes with the ability to perform daily activities and in which the primary channel of learning is through the use of prescription and nonprescription devices.

macroculture The shared or national culture of a society.

macula The area of best central vision.

macular degeneration A common eye disease in adults, which may also occur in young people, involving damage to the central part of the retina cones, affecting central vision, light sensitivity, and color.

magnet high school A school with a strong instructional emphasis on a particular theme, such as performing arts or math and science; an option for secondary pupils who are gifted and talented.

mainstreaming An early term for the practice of integrating students with special needs into a general education classroom for all or part of the school day.

malleus The first and largest of the three middle ear bones for conducting sound to the inner ear. Also called the hammer, it is attached to the tympanic membrane.

manual communication Communication methods that utilize fingerspelling, signs, and gestures.

melting pot A metaphor describing the United States in the early decades of the twentieth century.

meningitis A neural or bacterial infection of the membranes covering the brain and spinal cord; associated with hearing loss and mental retardation.

mentally ill A generic term often used by professionals outside of the field of special education to refer to individuals with emotional or behavioral disorders.

mentor The role fulfilled by an older individual who is an expert in a particular field and who works with and guides a student in an area of mutual interest.

metacognition The ability to evaluate and monitor one's own performance.

microcephaly A condition in which the head is unusually small, leading to inadequate development of the brain and resulting in mental retardation.

microcultures Distinct subcultures within a larger culture; these groups maintain their own distinct values, norms, folkways, and identification.

middle ear The air-filled space behind the eardrum that contains three tiny bones (ossicles) that carry sound to the inner ear.

minimal brain injury A once popular term referring to individuals who exhibit behavioral signs of brain injury (such as distractibility or impulsivity) but with no neurological evidence.

minimal hearing loss (MHL) Technically not a hearing loss; however, individual experiences difficulty hearing spoken language at a distance or when background noise is present.

mixed cerebral palsy Cerebral palsy that consists of combinations of different types. A person who has both spastic and athetoid cerebral palsy would be considered to have mixed cerebral palsy.

mixed hearing loss Hearing losses resulting from both conductive and sensorineural hearing impairments.

mnemonic strategies A cognitive approach used to assist pupils in remembering material; the use of rhymes, pictures, acronyms, and similar aids to help in recall.

morphological disorder Difficulty learning and using morphological rules of language.

morphology Dictates how the smallest meaningful units of our language (morphemes) are combined to form words.

multiaxial system An assessment involving several axes, each of which refers to different domains of information, that may help a clinician plan treatment and predict outcome. Typically used by mental health professionals.

multicultural education An ambiguous concept that deals with issues of race, language, social class, and culture as well as disability and gender. Also viewed as an educational strategy wherein the cultural heritage of each pupil is valued.

multiculturalism Referring to more than one culture; acknowledges basic commonalities among groups of people while appreciating their differences.

multidisciplinary team A group of professionals from different disciplines who function as a team but perform their roles independent of one another.

multimodal interventions The use of concurrent treatment approaches with students who exhibit attention deficit hyperactivity disorder.

multiple disabilities Concomitant impairments that result in such severe educational needs that a student cannot be accommodated in a special education program solely on the basis of one of the impairments.

multiple intelligences An alternative perspective on intelligence suggesting that there are many different kinds of intelligence.

myopia Elongation of the eye that causes extreme nearsightedness and decreased visual acuity.

natural supports Assistance rendered by family members, friends, teachers, and coworkers.

neuromotor impairments Several types of impairments involving abnormality of, or damage to, the brain, spinal cord, or nerves that send impulses to the muscles of the body.

noncategorical Programs developed based on student needs and common instructional requirements rather than on disability.

nondiscriminatory testing Federal mandate that assessments be conducted in a culturally responsive fashion.

normalization A principle advocating that individuals with disabilities should be integrated, to the maximum extent possible, into all aspects of everyday living.

norm-referenced assessments Refers to standardized tests on which a pupil's performance is compared to that of his or her peers.

off-level testing The use of assessment instruments designed for older students when evaluating the academic ability of a child thought to be gifted.

omissions Articulation disorder that occurs when a sound is not pronounced in a word (e.g., han for hand).

optic nerve The nerve at the posterior of the eye that carries messages from the retina to the brain.

optic nerve atrophy Degeneration of the optic nerve, which may be congenital or hereditary, causing loss of central vision, color vision, and reduced visual acuity.

oral approaches Methods of instruction for children with hearing impairments that emphasize spoken language skills. Methodology attempts to use the child's residual hearing and employs auditory training and speechreading.

oral interpreter A professional who silently repeats a speaker's message as it is spoken so that a hearing-impaired person can lipread the message.

orbit A protective cone-shaped cavity in the skull, sometimes called the socket.

organ of Corti Organ of hearing found within the cochlea.

organic Etiologies of speech and language disorders that can be linked to a physiological deficit (such as cleft palate).

orientation and mobility Systematic techniques to plan routes and move from place to place for persons with visual impairments.

orthopedic impairments Physical disabilities that occur from congenital anomalies, diseases, or other causes that adversely affect a child's educational performance.

orthotics Various braces or splints that are used to help maintain alignment and decrease the development of contractures.

ossicular chain Three bones in the middle ear (malleus, incus, and stapes) that connect the eardrum to the inner ear and help to amplify sounds.

other health impairment A chronic or acute health problem that results in limited strength, vitality, or alertness and adversely affects educational performance.

otitis media Infection of the middle ear space, causing conductive hearing loss.

outer directedness A condition characterized by a loss of confidence in one's own capabilities and a reliance on others for cues and guidance.

outer ear The most visible (external) part of the ear, useful in funneling sound to the ear canal and in localizing the source of sound.

oval window The link between the inner ear and the middle ear.

overrepresentation A situation in which a greater number of students from minority groups are placed in special education programs than would be expected based on the proportion of pupils in the general school population.

paraplegia Paralysis (or spasticity) of the legs.

perinatal Events occurring at or immediately after birth.

person-centered planning Useful when developing a student's individualized education program; creates a vision for pupil's future based on an analysis of his or her strengths, needs, and preferences.

pervasive developmental disorder, not otherwise specified (PDD, NOS) Label applied when there is a severe and pervasive impairment in the development of reciprocal social interaction associated with impairment in either verbal or nonverbal communication skills or with the presence of stereotyped behavior, interests, and activities.

pervasive developmental disorders Disorders characterized by severe and pervasive impairment in several areas of development: reciprocal social interaction skills, communication skills, or the presence of stereotyped behavior, interests, and activities.

phenylketonuria (PKU) An inherited metabolic disorder resulting from the inability of the body to convert phenylalanine to tyrosine; can be detected at birth and controlled by diet; left untreated, consequences are often severe.

phonation Includes speech factors of pitch, loudness, and quality.

phonological awareness Possible explanation for the reading problems of some students with learning disabilities; difficulty in recognizing the correspondence between specific sounds and certain letters that make up words.

phonological disorder Abnormal organization of phonological system resulting in a significant deficit in speech production or perception.

phonology The sound system of a language, including the use of sounds to create meaningful syllables and words.

photophobic Sensitive to light.

play audiometry A method for measuring hearing sensitivity in young children by rewarding correct responses; turning the evaluation situation into a game in order to maintain interest and cooperation.

portfolio assessment A type of authentic assessment; samples of different work products gathered over time and across curriculum areas are evaluated.

positive behavioral support An alternative approach to punishment; a schoolwide, proactive way of addressing problematic behaviors.

postlingual Referring to the period of time after a child has developed language.

postnatal Events occurring after birth.

pragmatic difficulties Problems in understanding and using language in different social contexts.

pragmatics A sociolinguistic system involving the use of communication skills in social contexts.

preassessment An assessment of a pupil's previously acquired knowledge; allows teacher to provide differentiated learning experiences.

precipitous birth Birth that occurs in less than two hours.

prelingual Referring to the period of time prior to a child's development of language.

prelinguistic Communicative behaviors used by children before the formation of formal speech and language characteristics.

premature births Babies born prior to 37 weeks of gestation age.

prenatal Events occurring before birth.

prereferral intervention Instructional or behavioral strategies introduced by a general educator to assist students experiencing difficulty; designed to minimize inappropriate referrals for special education.

prevalence The total number of individuals in a given category during a particular period of time.

primary literacy medium An individual's most frequently used method of reading and writing.

primary prevention Activities aimed at eliminating a problem or condition prior to its onset; may also refer to reducing the number of new instances of problematic behavior.

problem-based learning Instructional approach in which authentic problems having multiple solutions are addressed through the application of critical thinking skills.

progress monitoring The frequent and systematic assessment of a pupil's academic progress.

proximity and movement management A classroom management strategy focusing on the effective use of classroom space and the arrangement of the physical environment as a means of minimizing disruptive behavior.

psychogenic theories Freudian perspective that if basic psychological bonds are not established between the parent and the child, the child will not be able to establish relationships with others and will fail to progress. Individual psychotherapy recommended as the treatment of choice.

psychostimulants Medications typically prescribed for persons with ADHD. These drugs activate or enhance specific aspects of neurological functioning that in turn affect executive functions.

pupil The circular opening at the center of the iris that controls the amount of light allowed into the eye.

pure-tone audiometry A procedure for measuring hearing sensitivity at certain frequencies using tones that are presented at various intensities.

quadriplegia Paralysis (or spasticity) of both legs and both arms.

rebound effect The behavioral deterioration sometimes observed in persons with ADHD as the effect of psychostimulant medication gradually wears off.

receptive language The ability to understand what is meant by spoken communication.

referral A formal request by a teacher or parent that a student be evaluated for special education services.

regular education initiative (REI) An approach that advocates that general educators assume greater responsibility for the education of students with disabilities.

related services Services defined by federal law whose purpose is to assist a student with exceptionalities derive benefit from a special education.

reliable means of response A consistent, reliable way of answering questions.

residual hearing Remaining usable hearing in a person with hearing loss.

residual vision An individual's usable vision.

resonance Sound quality of speech.

respite care Temporary or occasional care of an individual with disabilities by nonfamily members.

response to intervention (RTI) A strategy used for determining whether a pupil has a learning disability. Student is exposed to increasing levels of validated instructional intervention; responsiveness to the instruction is assessed; a lack of adequate progress typically leads to a referral for possible special education services.

retina The inner layer of the eye containing light-sensitive cells that connect with the brain through the optic nerve.

retinitis pigmentosa Pigmentation of the retina that can result in night blindness, photophobia, and eventual loss of vision in various parts of the periphery.

retinopathy of prematurity (ROP) An interruption in the vascular system of the eye, due to premature birth, in which veins and arteries begin to grow in an unorganized manner and cause bundles that pull together and detach the retina, resulting in loss of peripheral vision or total blindness.

Rett's disorder A pervasive developmental disorder occurring in females following a period of normal functioning after birth. Signs include characteristic hand-wringing or hand washing, severe or profound retardation, and delayed social development.

Rh incompatibility A condition that results when a woman who is Rh negative carries an Rh positive fetus. Mother's body will produce antibodies that can affect babies resulting from future pregnancies; often leads to mental retardation and other impairments if mother does not receive an injection of Rho immune globulin.

rod cells Light-sensitive cells located mainly in the peripheral areas of the retina that are responsible for shape and motion, function best in reduced illumination, and are not responsive to color.

rubella A viral disease also known as German measles; contact in first trimester of pregnancy often results in a variety of significant impairments.

scaffolding A cognitive teaching strategy in which teacher provides temporary support to student who is learning a new task; supports are gradually removed as pupil becomes increasingly competent with the activity.

schizophrenia A severe disorder characterized by psychotic symptoms, including hallucinations, delusions, disorganized thinking, and catatonic motor behaviors. These signs and symptoms are associated with marked social or occupational dysfunction.

secondary prevention Efforts focusing on minimizing or eliminating potential risk factors in regard to persons with emotional or behavioral disorders; refers to minimizing the possibility that maladaptive or inappropriate behaviors will occur.

seizure A sudden, temporary change in the normal functioning of the brain's electrical system due to excessive, uncontrolled electrical activity in the brain.

self-advocacy Speaking out for one's personal preferences; protecting one's own interests.

self-contained A separate classroom for children with disabilities, usually found in a public school.

self-determination Self-advocacy efforts by an individual with a disability; expression of desire to live one's life according to one's own wishes; assuming personal control over one's life.

self-instruction A cognitive strategy for changing behavior; pupils initially talk to themselves out loud while performing a task and verbally reward themselves for success.

self-monitoring strategies A behavioral self-control strategy; pupils compare their performance to a criterion, record their efforts, and obtain reinforcement if appropriate.

self-regulation The ability of an individual to manage or govern his or her own behavior.

semantic disorder Language difficulty associated with poor vocabulary development, inappropriate use of word meanings, and/or inability to comprehend word meanings.

semantics A psycholinguistic system that involves word meanings and word relationships and their use in communication.

sensorineural hearing loss The loss of sound sensitivity produced by abnormalities of the inner ear or nerve pathways beyond the inner ear to the brain.

sheltered workshop A structured work environment for persons with disabilities in which vocational and social skills are often the focus of attention; may be a temporary or permanent placement.

short-term memory The recall of information after a brief period of time.

signal-to-noise ratio The ratio of the signal level (in decibels) to the corresponding background noise level.

Snellen chart An eye chart of clinical measurement of the true amount of distance vision an individual has under certain conditions.

social skills training Using direct instruction to teach students appropriate social behaviors; goal is to increase individual's social competency and acceptance.

socially maladjusted Individuals whose social behaviors are atypical; often regarded as chronic social offenders.

sound field system A system to assist students with hearing impairments in which the teacher wears a microphone that transmits a signal to a speaker strategically placed in the classroom rather than to a body-worn receiver.

spastic cerebral palsy A type of cerebral palsy in which the person has very tight muscles occurring in one or more muscle groups, resulting in stiff, uncoordinated movements.

special education Specially designed instruction to meet the unique needs of an individual recognized as exceptional.

specialized instructional strategies Teaching techniques specifically designed for a particular

special education population to assist with learning specific material.

speech The expression of language via sounds; the oral modality for language.

speech audiometry A set of procedures for measuring auditory perception of speech, including syllables, words, and sentences.

speech recognition threshold (SRT) A measure of threshold sensitivity for speech. The SRT represents the softest sound level at which a listener can identify the stimuli 50 percent of the time.

spina bifida Failure of the neural tube to completely close during fetal development. In its most severe form, the baby is born with a sac on his or her back containing part of the spinal cord.

spread The practice of spreading inferences to other unrelated aspects of a disability, often resulting in stereotyping.

stage theory A hypothesized pattern of parental reaction to the news that their child has a disability.

standard deviation A descriptive statistic that expresses the variability and distribution of a set of scores relative to the mean.

stapes The third of the middle ear bones for conducting sound to the inner ear. It resembles a stirrup in shape and is sometimes called the stirrup. It is the smallest bone in the body.

statistically derived classification system A system developed to analyze patterns of behaviors

based on statistical procedures that characterize children and youth with emotional or behavioral disorders.

strength-based assessment An assessment model that looks at an individual's strengths, abilities, and accomplishments rather than focusing on his or her deficits.

Strauss syndrome A historical term applied to individuals with mental retardation who exhibit high levels of distractibility and hyperactivity.

stuttering Type of fluency disorder in which word sounds are repeated.

substitutions Articulation disorder that occurs when one sound is substituted for another in the pronunciation of a word (e.g., wabbit for rabbit).

supported (competitive) employment At a worksite for typical workers, individuals with disabilities are employed and work alongside their typical peers but receive ongoing assistance from a job coach.

syntactical deficits Difficulty in acquiring the rules that control word order and other aspects of grammar.

syntax A series of linguistic rules that determine word order and combinations to form sentences and how such word order is used in the communication process.

syphilis A venereal disease; infection of the mother in the last trimester of pregnancy can cause mental retardation in the child.

systems of care model Providing an individually tailored and coordinated system of services and care to students with emotional or behavioral disorders; developed by family members and service providers.

task analysis An instructional methodology whereby complex tasks are analyzed and broken down into sequential component parts; each part is taught separately and then as a whole.

technology productivity tools Computer software, hardware, and related systems designed to help people work effectively.

telecommunication device for the deaf (TDD) An instrument for sending typewritten messages over telephone lines to be received by a person who is deaf or severely hearing impaired as a printed message. Sometimes called TT, TTY, or TTD.

teratogen Infections, drugs, chemicals, or environmental agents that can produce fetal abnormalities.

tertiary prevention Efforts that attempt to limit the adverse consequences of an existing problem while maximizing a person's potential; in regard to persons with emotional or behavioral disorders, refers to an intense level of intervention using strategies and supports designed for individuals with chronic and intense behavior problems.

theory of mind A hypothesis that attempts to explain the inability of the individual with autism to realize that other people have their own unique point of view about the world—different thoughts, plans, and perspectives from their own.

therapeutic abortion Elective termination of a pregnancy due to the presence of a birth defect.

tiered assignments An instructional strategy that allows the teacher to offer variations of the same lesson to students with differing levels of ability.

time management A proactive intervention strategy that attempts to maximize student engagement time and appropriately schedule class activities in addition to instruction in time management skills.

tonic-clonic seizure A convulsive seizure whereby the individual loses consciousness, falls, and begins making rhythmic jerking motions, formerly known as grand mal seizures.

total communication A method of communication for students with hearing impairments, designed to provide equal emphasis on oral and signing skills to facilitate communication ability.

Tourette's syndrome A neurological disorder characterized by motor tics and uncontrollable verbal outbursts.

toxoplasmosis A maternal infection resulting from contact with parasites; especially devastating if exposure occurs during third trimester of pregnancy.

trainable mentally retarded Classification of a person with moderate mental retardation who is capable of learning self-care and social skills; IQ range generally between 35/40 and 50/55.

transdisciplinary A group of professionals from different disciplines who function as a team but

work independently; however, they share roles and a peer is identified as the primary interventionist.

transition A broad term used to describe the movement of an individual from one educational environment to another, from one class to another, or from one phase of life (high school) to another (independent adulthood).

transition management The regulating of students as they move from one assignment to another or from one activity to another; a proactive behavioral intervention strategy.

transition plan *See* individualized transition plan

transition services Individualized and coordinated services that assist the adolescent with a disability to successfully move from school to postschool activities.

transliteration Altering an interpreted message to facilitate understanding by a person who is hearing impaired.

traumatic brain injury An acquired injury to the brain caused by an external force that results in a disability or psychosocial impairment that adversely affects educational performance.

twice exceptional Students who are gifted and talented but also have a disability.

tympanic membrane A thin, membranous tissue between the ear canal and the middle ear that vibrates when struck by sound waves; also called the eardrum.

ultrasound The mapping or imaging of a fetus; useful in depicting a variety of defects.

underrepresentation A situation in which fewer children from minority groups are placed in special education programs than would be expected based on the proportion of pupils in the general school population.

universal design for learning The design of curriculum materials, instructional activities, and evaluation procedures that can meet the needs of learners with widely varying abilities and backgrounds.

Usher syndrome An inherited disorder resulting in deaf-blindness, deafness present at birth accompanied by progressive vision loss, sometimes associated with mental retardation.

vision screening A simple measure to determine possible vision loss.

visual acuity The ability to visually perceive details of near or distant objects.

visual efficiency How well an individual uses remaining visual acuity at a distance or close up.

visual field The amount of vision in the quadrant regions to the right, left, up, and down while gazing straight ahead.

visual impairment An impairment in vision that, even with correction, adversely affects an individual's educational performance. The term includes both partial sight and blindness.

vitreous body The thick, clear liquid gel that serves as a filter for light and helps maintain the shape of the eye.

vitreous humor A colorless mass of soft, gelatinlike material that fills the eyeball behind the lens.

voice disorders May result from disorders of the larynx or disorders in phonation.

voice output communication aid (VOCA) Device that can be programmed to produce speech.

walker A mobility aid for individuals requiring support when walking.

word prediction program A software program that provides a list of potential words that correspond to the letters the user is typing so that the user does not have to type out the entire word.

working memory The ability to retain information while also engaging in another cognitive activity.

wraparound plan A coordinated interagency effort at providing supports and services to a student and his or her family in the natural environment—school, home, or community.

X-linked A pattern of inheritance involving the X chromosome, one of an individual's two sex chromosomes.

References

Chapter 1

Ballard, J., Ramirez, B., & Weintraub, F. (1982). *Special education in America: Its legal and governmental foundations.* Reston, VA: Council for Exceptional Children.

Berryman, S. (1993). Learning in the workplace. In L. Darling-Hammond (Ed.), *Review of research in education* (pp. 343–404). Washington, DC: American Educational Research Association.

Bogdan, R., & Biklen, D. (1977). Handicapism. *Social Policy, 7*(5), 14–19.

Brown, L., Albright, K., Rogan, P., York, J., Solnar, A., Johnson, F., Van Deventer, P., & Loomis, R. (1988). An integrated curriculum model for transition. In B. Ludlow, A. Turnbull, & R. Luckasson (Eds.), *Transitions to adult life for people with mental retardation: Principles and practices* (pp. 67–84). Baltimore: Paul H. Brookes.

Bruder, M. (1994). Working with members of other disciplines: Collaboration for success. In M. Wolery & J. Wilbers (Eds.), *Including children with special needs in early childhood programs* (pp. 45–70). Washington, DC: National Association for the Education of Young Children.

Clark, G., & Knowlton, H. (1988). A closer look at transition issues for the 1990s: A response to Rusch and Menchetti. *Exceptional Children, 54*(4), 365–367.

Cook, B. (2001). A comparison of teachers' attitudes toward their included students with mild and severe disabilities. *Journal of Special Education, 34*(4), 203–213.

Crutchfield, M. (1997, August). Who's teaching our children with disabilities? *National Information Center for Children and Youth with Disabilities News Digest, 27,* 1–23.

Dunn, L. (1973). *Exceptional children in the schools* (2nd ed.). New York: Holt, Rhinehart & Winston.

Friend, M., & Cook, L. (2007). *Interactions: Collaboration skills for school professionals* (5th ed.). Needham Heights, MA: Allyn and Bacon.

Gargiulo, R., & Kilgo, J. (2005). *Young children with special needs* (2nd ed.). Clifton Park, NY: Delmar.

Giangreco, M., York, J., & Rainforth, B. (1989). Providing related services to learners with severe handicaps in educational settings: Pursuing the least restrictive option. *Pediatric Physical Therapy, 1*(2), 55–63.

Goodlad, J. (1984). *A place called school.* New York: McGraw-Hill.

Halpern, A. (1985). Transition: A look at the foundations. *Exceptional Children, 51*(6), 479–486.

Halpern, A. (1992). Transition: Old wine in new bottles. *Exceptional Children, 58*(3), 202–211.

Harris, L., and Associates. (2004). *National Organization on Disabilities/Harris Survey of Americans with Disabilities.* New York: Author.

Hitchcock, C., Meyer, A., Rose, D., & Jackson, R. (2002). Providing new access to the general curriculum: Universal design for learning. *Teaching Exceptional Children, 35*(2), 8–17.

Hobbs, N. (1975). *The futures of children.* San Francisco: Jossey-Bass.

Hobbs, T., & Westling, D. (1998). Promoting successful inclusion. *Teaching Exceptional Children, 31*(1), 10–14.

Hourcade, J., & Bauwens, J. (2003). *Cooperative teaching: Rebuilding and sharing the schoolhouse* (2nd ed.). Austin, TX: Pro-Ed.

Hughes, C., Eisenman, L., Hwang, B., Kim, J., Killian, D., & Scott, S. (1997). Transition from secondary special education to adult life: A review and analysis of empirical measures. *Education and Training in Mental Retardation and Developmental Disabilities, 32,* 85–104.

Keefe, E., Moore, V., & Duff, F. (2004). The four "knows" of collaborative teaching. *Teaching Exceptional Children, 36*(5), 36–41.

Kitchin, R. (1998). "Out of place," "knowing one's place": Space, power and the exclusion of disabled people. *Disability and Society, 13,* 343–356.

Kliewer, C., & Biklen, D. (1996). Labeling: Who wants to be called retarded? In W. Stainback & S. Stainback (Eds.), *Controversial issues confronting special education: Divergent perspectives* (pp. 83–95). Boston: Allyn and Bacon.

Koppelman, J. (1986). Reagan signs bills expanding services to handicapped preschoolers. *Report to Preschool Programs, 18,* 3–4.

Lane, H. (1979). *The wild boy of Aveyron.* Cambridge, MA: Harvard University Press.

Lipsky, D., & Gartner, A. (1996). Inclusive education and school restructuring. In W. Stainback & S. Stainback (Eds.), *Controversial issues confronting special education: Divergent perspectives* (pp. 3–15). Boston: Allyn and Bacon.

MacMillan, D. (1982). *Mental retardation in school and society* (2nd ed.). Boston: Little, Brown.

Maddux, R. (1988). *Team building: An exercise in leadership.* Los Altos, CA: Crisp.

McCormick, L. (2003). Policies and practices. In L. McCormick, D. F. Loeb, & R. Schiefelbusch (Eds.), *Supporting children with communication difficulties in inclusive settings* (2nd ed., pp. 155–187). Boston: Allyn and Bacon.

McDonnell, J., Hardman, M., & McDonnell, A. (2003). *Introduction to persons with moderate and severe disabilities* (2nd ed.). Needham Heights, MA: Allyn and Bacon.

McGoningel, M., Woodruff, C., & Roszmann-Millican, M. (1994). The transdisciplinary team: A model for family-centered early intervention. In L. Johnson, R. Gallagher, M. LaMontagne, J. Jordan, J. Gallagher, P. Hutinger, & M. Karnes (Eds.), *Meeting early intervention challenges* (pp. 95–131). Baltimore: Paul H. Brookes.

McLean, M., Wolery, M., & Bailey, D. (2004). *Assessing infants and preschoolers with special needs* (3rd ed.). Upper Saddle River, NJ: Pearson Education.

Meisels, S., & Shonkoff, J. (2000). Early childhood intervention: A continuing evolution. In J. Shonkoff & S. Meisels (Eds.), *Handbook of early childhood intervention* (2nd ed., pp. 3–31). Cambridge, England: Cambridge University Press.

Murawski, W., & Dieker, L. (2004). Tips and strategies for co-teaching at the secondary level. *Teaching Exceptional Children, 36*(5), 52–58.

National Commission on Excellence in Education. (1983). *A nation at risk: The imperative for educational reform.* Washington, DC: Author.

National Longitudinal Transition Study 2. (2005). *Parent/youth report of youth employment after secondary school.* Retrieved September 24, 2007 from http://www.nlts2.0rg/data_tables/tables/12/np3T7a_L7a_12bfrm.html

Ohio State University Partnership Grant. (2006). *Fast facts for faculty: Universal design for learning.* Retrieved June 29, 2007 from http://www.telr.osu.edu/dpg/fastfact/undesign.html

Orkwis, R., & McLane, K. (1998). *A curriculum every student can use: Design principles for student access.* Reston, VA: ERIC Clearinghouse on Disabilities and Gifted Education. (ED 423 654.)

Pugach, M., & Johnson, L. (2002). *Collaborative practitioners, collaborative schools* (2nd ed.). Denver: Love.

Reinhiller, N. (1996). Co-teaching: New variations on a not-so-new practice. *Teacher Education and Special Education, 19*(1), 34–48.

Reynolds, M., Wang, M., & Walberg, J. (1987). The necessary restructuring of special and regular education. *Exceptional Children, 53*(5), 391–398.

Rice, N., Drame, E., Owens, L., & Frattura, E. (2007). Co-instructing at the secondary level. *Teaching Exceptional Children, 39*(6), 12–18.

Scott, S., McGuire, J., & Shaw, S. (2003). Universal design for instruction: A new paradigm for adult instruction in secondary education. *Remedial and Special Education, 24,* 369–379.

Scruggs, T., Mastropieri, M., & McDuffie, K. (2007). Co-teaching in inclusive classrooms: A metasynthesis of qualitative research. *Exceptional Children, 73*(4), 392–416.

Stainback, S., Stainback, W., & Ayers, B. (1996). Schools as inclusive communities. In W. Stainback & S. Stainback (Eds.), *Controversial issues confronting special education: Divergent perspectives* (pp. 31–43). Boston: Allyn and Bacon.

Smith, R., Neisworth, J., & Hunt, F. (1983). *The exceptional child: A functional approach* (2nd ed.). New York: McGraw-Hill.

Smith, T., Polloway, E., Patton, J., & Dowdy, C. (2008). *Teaching students with special needs in inclusive settings* (5th ed.). Needham Heights, MA: Allyn and Bacon.

U.S. Department of Education. (1992). *Fourteenth annual report to Congress on the implementation of the Individuals with Disabilities Education Act.* Washington, DC: U.S. Government Printing Office.

U.S. Department of Education. (2006). *Twenty-sixth annual report to Congress on the implementation of the Individuals with Disabilities Education Act, 2004.* Washington, DC: U.S. Government Printing Office.

U.S. Department of Education. (2007). *IDEA data.* Available at https://www.ideadata.org/PartB Report.asp

U.S. Department of Education, Office for Civil Rights. (2002). *2002 elementary and secondary school survey.* Retrieved June 16, 2007 from http://vistademo.beyond2020.com/ocr2002r/

Walther-Thomas, C., Korinek, L., McLaughlin, V., & Williams, B. (2000). *Collaboration for inclusive education.* Needham Heights, MA: Allyn and Bacon.

Wehman, P. (1992). Transition for young people with disabilities: Challenges for the 1990s. *Education and Training in Mental Retardation, 27*(2), 112–118.

Wehmeyer, M., Lance, D., & Bashinski, S. (2002). Promoting access to the general curriculum for students with mental retardation. *Education and Training in Mental Retardation and Developmental Disabilities, 37*(3), 223–234.

Will, M. (1984). *OSERS programming for the transition of youth with disabilities: Bridges from school to working life.* Washington, DC: Office of Special Education and Rehabilitative Services.

Ysseldyke, J., Algozzine, B., & Thurlow, M. (1992). *Critical issues in special and remedial education* (2nd ed.). Boston: Houghton Mifflin.

Zigler, E. (2000). Foreword. In J. Shonkoff & S. Meisels (Eds.), *Handbook of early childhood intervention* (2nd ed., pp. xi–xv). Cambridge, England: Cambridge University Press.

Chapter 2

Bateman, B., & Linden, M. (1998). *Better IEPs* (3rd ed.). Longmont, CO: Sopris West.

Bennett, T., DeLuca, D., & Bruns, D. (1997). Putting inclusion into practice: Perspectives of teachers and parents. *Exceptional Children, 64*(1), 115–131.

Bronfenbrenner, U. (1979). *The ecology of human development: Experiments by nature and design.* Cambridge, MA: Harvard University Press.

Buck, G., Polloway, E., Smith-Thomas, A., & Cook, K. (2003). Prereferral intervention process: A survey of state practices. *Exceptional Children, 69*(3), 349–360.

CEC Today. (1997). What every teacher needs to know: A comparison of Section 504, ADA, and IDEA. 4(4), 1, 5, 15.

Center for Special Education Finance. (2004). *What are we spending on special education services in the United States, 1999–2000?* Retrieved March 28, 2007 from http://www.csef-air.org/index.php

Congress passes IDEA: President signed in early June. (1997). *AAMR News & Notes, 10*(3), 1, 6.

Council for Exceptional Children. (1994). *CEC policies for delivering services to exceptional children.* Reston, VA: Author.

Council for Exceptional Children. (2003). *No Child Left Behind Act of 2001: Reauthorization of the Elementary and Secondary Education Act* (technical assistance resource). Arlington, VA: Author.

Deno, E. (1970). Special education as developmental capital. *Exceptional Children, 37*(3), 229–237.

Dunn, L. (1968). Special education for the mildly retarded—Is much of it justifiable? *Exceptional Children, 35*(1), 5–22.

Dunst, C., & Trivette, C. (1989). An enablement and empowerment perspective of case management. *Topics in Early Childhood Special Education, 8*(4), 87–102.

Fox, N., & Ysseldyke, J. (1997). Implementing inclusion at the middle school level: Lessons from a negative example. *Exceptional Children, 64*(1), 81–98.

Gargiulo, R., & Kilgo, J. (2005). *Young children with special needs: An introduction to early childhood special education* (2nd ed.). Clifton Park, NY: Delmar.

Goodman, J., & Bond, L. (1993). The individualized education program: A retrospective critique. *Journal of Special Education, 26*(4), 408–422.

Henry, N., & Flynt, E. (1990). Rethinking special education referral: A procedural model. *Intervention in School and Clinic, 26*(1), 22–24.

Hoy, C., & Gregg, N. (1994). *Assessment: The special educator's role.* Pacific Grove, CA: Brooks/Cole.

Kauffman, J. (1995). Why we must celebrate a diversity of restrictive environments. *Learning Disabilities Research & Practice, 10*(4), 225–232.

Kennedy, C., & Horn, E. (Eds.). (2004). *Including students with severe disabilities.* Boston: Allyn and Bacon.

McLean, M., Wolery, M., & Bailey, D. (2004). *Assessing infants and preschoolers with special needs* (3rd ed.). Upper Saddle River, NJ: Pearson Education.

Meyen, E. (1995). Legislative and programmatic foundations of special education. In E. Meyen & T. Skrtic (Eds.), *Special education and student disability* (4th ed., pp. 35–95). Denver: Love.

Nolet, V., & McLaughlin, M. (2005). *Accessing the general curriculum* (2nd ed.). Thousand Oaks, CA: Corwin Press.

Osborne, A. (1996). *Legal issues in special education.* Needham Heights, MA: Allyn and Bacon.

Osborne, A., & DiMattia, P. (1995). Counterpoint: IDEA's LRE mandate: Another look. *Exceptional Children, 61*(6), 582–584.

Peterson, J., & Hittie, M. (2003). *Inclusive teaching: Creating effective schools for all learners.* Boston: Allyn and Bacon.

Polloway, E., Patton, J., & Serna, L. (2008). *Strategies for teaching learners with special needs* (9th ed.). Upper Saddle River, NJ: Pearson Education.

Pretti-Frontczak, K., & Bricker, D. (2004). *An activity-based approach to early intervention.* Baltimore: Paul H. Brookes.

Reynolds, M. (1962). A framework for considering some issues in special education. *Exceptional Children, 28*(7), 367–370.

Sailor, W. (Ed.). (2002). *Building partnerships for learning, achievement, and accountability.* New York: Teachers College Press.

Salend, S. (2008). *Creating inclusive classrooms* (6th ed.). Upper Saddle River, NJ: Pearson Education.

Skrtic, T. (1995). The special education knowledge tradition: Crisis and opportunity. In E. Meyen & T. Skrtic (Eds.), *Special education and student disability* (4th ed., pp. 609–672). Denver: Love.

Smith, T. (2002). Section 504: What teachers need to know. *Intervention in School and Clinic, 37*(5), 259–266.

Smith, T., & Patton, J. (1998). *Section 504 and public schools: A practical guide.* Austin, TX: Pro-Ed.

Stainback, S., & Stainback, W. (1992). Schools as inclusive communities. In W. Stainback & S. Stainback (Eds.), *Controversial issues confronting special education: Divergent perspectives* (pp. 29–43). Boston: Allyn and Bacon.

Stainback, S., & Stainback, W. (Eds.). (1996). *Inclusion: A guide for educators* (2nd ed.). Baltimore: Paul H. Brookes.

Trohanis, P. (1989). An introduction to PL 99-457 and the national policy agenda for serving young children with special needs and their families. In J. Gallagher, P. Trohanis, & R. Clifford (Eds.), *Policy implementation and PL 99-457: Planning for young children with special needs* (pp. 1–17). Baltimore: Paul H. Brookes.

Turnbull, A., Turnbull, H., Erwin, E., & Soodak, L. (2006). *Families, professionals, and exceptionality* (5th ed.). Upper Saddle River, NJ: Pearson Education.

Turnbull, H. (1993). *Free appropriate public education: The law and children with disabilities* (4th ed.). Denver: Love.

U.S. Department of Education. (1993). *Fifteenth annual report to Congress on the implementation of the Individuals with Disabilities Education Act.* Washington, DC: U.S. Government Printing Office.

U.S. Department of Education. (1995). *Seventeenth annual report to Congress on the implementation of the Individuals with Disabilities Education Act.* Washington, DC: U.S. Government Printing Office.

U.S. Department of Education (2002). *Twenty-fourth annual report to Congress on the implementation of the Individuals with Disabilities Education Act.* Washington, DC: U.S. Government Printing Office.

Weintraub, F., Abeson, A., Ballard, J., & LaVor, M. (Eds.). (1976). *Public policy and the education of exceptional children.* Reston, VA: Council for Exceptional Children.

Will, M. (1986a). Educating children with learning problems: A shared responsibility. *Exceptional Children, 52*(5), 411–415.

Will, M. (1986b). *Educating students with learning problems: A shared responsibility.* Washington, DC: U.S. Department of Education, Office of Special Education and Rehabilitative Services.

Yell, M. (1995). Least restrictive environment, inclusion, and students with disabilities: A legal analysis. *Journal of Special Education, 28*(4), 389–404.

Yell, M. (2006). *The law and special education* (2nd ed.). Upper Saddle River, NJ: Pearson Education.

Ysseldyke, J. (2001). Reflections on a research career: Generalization from 25 years of research on assessment and instructional decision making. *Exceptional Children, 67*(3), 295–309.

Chapter 3

Artiles, A., & Trent, S. (1994). Overrepresentation of minority students in special education: A continuing debate. *Journal of Special Education, 27*(4), 410–437.

Artiles, A., & Zamora-Durán, G. (1997). Disproportionate representation: A contentious and unresolved predicament. In A. Artiles & G. Zamora-Durán (Eds.), *Reducing disproportionate representation of culturally diverse students in special and gifted education* (pp. 1–6). Reston, VA: Council for Exceptional Children.

Baca, L., & Baca, E. (2004a). Bilingualism and bilingual education. In L. Baca & H. Cervantes (Eds.), *The bilingual special education interface* (4th ed., pp. 24–45). Upper Saddle River, NJ: Pearson Education.

Baca, L., & Baca, E. (2004b). Bilingual special education: A judicial perspective. In L. Baca & H. Cervantes (Eds.), *The bilingual special education interface* (4th ed., pp. 76–99). Upper Saddle River, NJ: Pearson Education.

Baca, L., Baca, E., & de Valenzuela, J. (2004). Background and rationale for bilingual special education. In L. Baca & H. Cervantes (Eds.), *The bilingual special education interface* (4th ed., pp. 1–23). Upper Saddle River, NJ: Pearson Education.

Banks, J. (2007). Multicultural education: Characteristics and goals. In J. Banks & C. Banks (Eds.), *Multicultural education issues and perspectives* (6th ed., pp. 3–30). Hoboken, NJ: Wiley.

Benner, S. (1998). *Special education issues within the context of American society.* Belmont, CA: Wadsworth.

Borland, J. (2004). *Issues and practices in the identification and education of gifted students from under-represented groups.* Storrs, CT: National Research Center on the Gifted and Talented.

Boyer, L., & Mainzer, R. (2003). Who's teaching students with disabilities? *Teaching Exceptional Children, 35*(6), 8–11.

CEC Today. (1997, October). *Making assessments of diverse students meaningful.* Reston, VA: Council for Exceptional Children.

Children's Defense Fund. (2005). *The state of children in America's union.* Washington, DC: Author.

Chinn, P., & Hughes, S. (1987). Representation of minority students in special education classes. *Remedial and Special Education 8*(4), 41–46.

Chinn, P. (2002). *Changing demographics in America.* Nashville, TN: Alliance Project, Vanderbilt University.

Clark, B. (2008). *Growing up gifted: Developing the potential of children at home and at school* (7th ed.). Upper Saddle River, NJ: Pearson Education.

Coutinho, M., & Oswald, D. (2000). Disproportionate representation in special education: A synthesis and recommendations. *Journal of Child and Family Studies, 9*(2), 135–156.

Crawford, J. (2004). Language legislation in the USA. Cited in L. Baca & H. Cervantes (Eds.), *The bilingual special education interface* (4th ed.). Upper Saddle River, NJ: Pearson Education.

Deshler, D., & Rodriguez-Walling, M. (2004). *Special education teaching conditions initiatives: Bright futures for exceptional learners.* Retrieved April 10, 2004 from www.cec.sped.org/spotlight/cond/bf_intro.html/

de Valenzuela, J., & Baca, L. (2004). Issues and theoretical considerations in the assessment of bilingual children. In L. Baca & H. Cervantes (Eds.), *The bilingual special education interface* (4th ed., pp. 162–183). Upper Saddle River, NJ: Pearson Education.

Donovan, S., & Cross, C. (Eds.). (2002). *Minority students in special and gifted education.* Washington, DC: National Research Council.

Figueroa, R. (1989). Psychological testing of linguistic-minority students: Knowledge gaps and regulations. *Exceptional Children, 56*(2), 145–152.

Ford, D. (1998). The underrepresentation of minority students in gifted education. *Journal of Special Education, 32*(1), 4–14.

Friend, M., & Bursuck, W. (2006). *Including students with special needs* (4th ed.). Boston: Allyn and Bacon.

Garcia, S., & Malkin, D. (1993). Toward defining programs and services for culturally and linguistically diverse learners in special education. *Teaching Exceptional Children, 26*(1), 52–58.

Garcia, S., & Ortiz, A. (2006). Preventing disproportionate representation: Culturally and linguistically responsive prereferral interventions. *Teaching Exceptional Children, 38*(4), 64–68.

Gardner, H. (1983). *Frames of mind: The theory of multiple intelligence.* New York: Basic Books.

Gardner, H. (1993). *Multiple intelligences: The theory in practice.* New York: Wiley.

Gargiulo, R., & Kilgo, J. (2005). *Young children with special needs* (2nd ed.) Clifton Park, NY: Delmar.

Gollnick, D., & Chinn, P. (2006). *Multicultural education in a pluralistic society* (7th ed.). Upper Saddle River, NJ: Pearson Education.

Gollnick, D., & Chinn, P. (2009). *Multicultural education in a pluralistic society* (8th ed.). Upper Saddle River, NJ: Pearson Education.

Harry, B. (1992a). *Cultural diversity, families, and the special education system: Communication and empowerment.* New York: Teachers College Press.

Harry, B. (1992b). Developing cultural self-awareness: The first step in values clarification for early interventionists. *Topics in Early Childhood Special Education, 12,* 333–350.

Hoover, J., & Collier, C. (2004). Methods and materials for bilingual special education. In L. Baca & H. Cervantes (Eds.), *The bilingual special education interface* (4th ed., pp. 274–297). Upper Saddle River, NJ: Pearson Education.

Hoover, J., & Patton, J. (2005). *Curriculum adaptation for students with learning and behavior problems: Principles and procedures* (3rd ed.). Austin, TX: Pro-Ed.

Janzen, R. (1994). Melting pot or mosaic? *Educational Leadership, 51*(8), 9–11.

Kaufman, A., & Kaufman, N. (2004). *Kaufman Assessment Battery for Children II.* Circle Pines, MN: American Guidance Service.

Ladson-Billings, G. (1994). What we can learn from multicultural education research. *Educational Leadership, 51*(8), 22–26.

Linn, R., & Miller, M. (2005). *Measurement and assessment in teaching* (9th ed.). Upper Saddle River, NJ: Pearson Education.

Lustig, M., & Koestner, J. (2006). *Intercultural competence: Interpersonal communication across cultures* (5th ed.). Boston: Allyn and Bacon.

MacMillan, D., & Reschly, D. (1998). Overrepresentation of minority students: The case for greater specificity or reconsideration of the variables examined. *Journal of Special Education, 32*(1), 15–24.

McLoughlin, J., & Lewis, R. (2005). *Assessing students with special needs* (6th ed.). Upper Saddle River, NJ: Pearson Education.

National Center for Education Statistics. (2006). *Characteristics of schools, districts, teachers, principals, and school libraries in the United States: 2003–04 schools and staffing survey.* Washington, DC: U.S. Government Printing Office.

National Center for Education Statistics. (2007). *The condition of education 2007.* Washington, DC: U.S. Government Printing Office.

National Collaborative on Diversity in the Teaching Force. (2004). *Assessment of diversity in America's teaching force.* Washington, DC: Author.

National Education Association. (2004). *NEA and teacher recruitment: An overview.* Retrieved April 5, 2004 from http://www.nea.org/student-program/about/overview.html

Ortiz, A., & Yates, J. (1988). Characteristics of learning disabled, mentally retarded and speech- language handicapped Hispanic students at initial evaluation and reevaluation. In A. Ortiz & B. Ramirez (Eds.), *Schools and the culturally diverse exceptional student* (pp. 51–62). Reston, VA: Council for Exceptional Children.

Patton, J. (1998). The disproportionate representation of African Americans in special education: Looking behind the curtain for understanding and solutions. *Journal of Special Education, 32*(1), 25–31.

Quality Education for Minorities Project. (1990). *Education that works: An action plan for the education of minorities.* Cambridge, MA: Massachusetts Institute of Technology.

Ryan, F. (1993). The perils of multiculturalism: Schooling for the group. *Educational Horizons, 71,* 134–138.

Salend, S., & Salinas, A. (2003). Language differences or learning difficulties. *Teaching Exceptional Children, 35*(4), 36–43.

Siccone, F. (1995). *Celebrating diversity: Building self-esteem in today's multicultural classrooms.* Boston: Allyn and Bacon.

Sleeter, C., & Grant, C. (2006). *Making choices for multicultural education* (5th ed.). New York: Wiley.

Smith, D., Smith-Davis, J., Clarke, C., & Mims, V. (2000). Technical assistance makes a difference: The Alliance 2000 story. *Teacher Education and Special Education, 23*(4), 302–310.

Tiedt, P., & Tiedt, I. (2005). *Multicultural teaching: A handbook of activities and resources* (7th ed.). Needham Heights, MA: Allyn and Bacon.

Tyler, N., Yzquierdo, Z., Lopez-Reyna, N., & Flippin, S. (2004). The relationship between cultural diversity and the special education workforce. *Journal of Special Education, 38*(1), 22–38.

U.S. Census Bureau. (2005). *American Indian and Alaska Native heritage month: November 2005.* Retrieved September 10, 2007 from http://www.census.gov/Press-release/www/releases/archives/ facts_for_features _special_editions/005684.html

U.S. Census Bureau. (2007). *Statistical abstract of the United States: 2008* (127th ed.). Washington, DC: Author.

U.S. Department of Education. (1997). *Nineteenth annual report to Congress on the implementation of the Individuals with Disabilities Education Act.* Washington, DC: U.S. Government Printing Office.

U.S. Department of Education. (2006). *Twenty-sixth annual report to Congress on the implementation of the Individuals with Disabilities Education Act, 2004* (Vol. 2). Washington, DC: U.S. Government Printing Office.

U.S. Department of Education, Office for Civil Rights. (1987). *Elementary and secondary school civil rights survey: National summaries.* Arlington, VA: DBS Corp. (ERIC Document Reproduction Service No. ED 304 485)

U.S. English. (2008). *About U.S. English.* Retrieved April 20, 2008 from http://www.us-english.org/inc/about/

Utley, C., & Obiakor, F. (2001). Learning problems or learning disabilities of multicultural learners: Contemporary perspectives. In C. Utley & F. Obiakor (Eds.), *Special education, multicultural education, and school reform: Components of quality education for learners with mild disabilities* (pp. 90–117). Springfield, IL: Charles C. Thomas.

Voltz, D. (1998). Cultural diversity and special education teacher preparation: Critical issues confronting the field. *Teacher Education and Special Education, 21*(1), 63–70.

Winzer, M., & Mazurek, K. (1998). *Special education in multicultural contexts.* Upper Saddle River, NJ: Prentice Hall.

Zelasko, N., & Antunez, B. (2000). *If your child learns in two languages.* Washington, DC: National Clearinghouse for Bilingual Education, George Washington University, Center for the Study of Language and Education.

Zirpoli, T. (1995). *Understanding and affecting the behavior of young children.* Englewood Cliffs, NJ: Prentice Hall.

Chapter 4

Banks, M. (2003). Disability in the family: A life span perspective. *Ethnic Minority Psychology, 9*(4), 367–384.

Bauer, A., & Shea, T. (2003). *Parents and schools: Creating a successful partnership for students with special needs.* Upper Saddle River, NJ: Pearson Education.

Berry, J., & Hardman, M. (1998). *Lifespan perspectives on the family and disability.* Needham Heights, MA: Allyn and Bacon.

Bettelheim, B. (1950). *Love is not enough.* Glencoe, NY: Free Press.

Bettelheim, B. (1967). *The empty fortress: Infantile autism and the birth of the self.* London: Collier-Macmillan.

Blacher, J. (1984). Sequential stages of parental adjustment to the birth of a child with handicaps: Fact or artifact? *Mental Retardation, 22*(2), 55–68.

Blue-Banning, M., Summers, J., Frankland, H., Nelson, L., & Beegle, G. (2004). Dimensions of family and professional partnerships: Constructive guidelines for collaboration. *Exceptional Children, 70*(2), 167–184.

Bronfenbrenner, U. (1977). Toward an experimental ecology of human development. *American Psychologist, 32*(7), 513–531.

Bronfenbrenner, U. (1979). *The ecology of human development: Experiments by nature and design.* Cambridge, MA: Harvard University Press.

Cook, R., Klein, M., & Tessier, A. (2008). *Adapting early childhood curricula for children in inclusive settings* (7th ed.). Upper Saddle River, NJ: Pearson Education.

D'Asaro, A. (1998). Caring for yourself is caring for your family: Methods of coping with the everyday stresses of care giving. *Exceptional Parent, 28*(6), 38–40.

Family Support Bulletin. (1991, Spring). Washington, DC: United Cerebral Palsy Association.

Flynn, L., & Wilson, P. (1998). Partnerships with family members: What about fathers? *Young Exceptional Children, 2*(1), 21–28.

Freidson, E. (1970). *Professional dominance.* Chicago: Aldine.

Gallagher, J., Beckman, P., & Cross, A. (1983). Families of handicapped children: Sources of stress and its amelioration. *Exceptional Children, 50*(1), 10–19.

Gallagher, P., Powell, T., & Rhodes, C. (2006). *Brothers and sisters: A special part of exceptional families* (3rd ed.). Baltimore: Paul H. Brookes.

Gargiulo, R. (1985). *Working with parents of exceptional children.* Boston: Houghton Mifflin.

Gargiulo, R., & Graves, S. (1991). Parental feelings: The forgotten component when working with parents of handicapped preschool children. *Childhood Education, 67,* 176–178.

Gargiulo, R., & Kilgo, J. (2005). *Young children with special needs* (2nd ed.). Clifton Park, NY: Delmar.

Gearheart, B., Mullen, R., & Gearheart, C. (1993). *Exceptional individuals.* Pacific Grove, CA: Brooks/ Cole.

Glidden, L., & Floyd, F. (1997). Disaggregating parental depression and family stress in assessing families of children with developmental delays: A multisample analysis. *American Journal on Mental Retardation, 102*(3), 250–266.

Graves, S., Gargiulo, R., & Sluder, L. (1996). *Young children: An introduction to early childhood education.* St. Paul, MN: West.

Grossman, F. (1972). *Brothers and sisters of retarded children.* Syracuse, NY: Syracuse University Press.

Hanson, M. (2004a). Ethnic, cultural, and language diversity in service settings. In E. Lynch & M. Hanson (Eds.), *Developing cross cultural competence* (3rd ed., pp. 3–18). Baltimore: Paul H. Brookes.

Hanson, M. (2004b). Families with Anglo-European roots. In E. Lynch & M. Hanson (Eds.), *Developing cross cultural competence* (3rd ed., pp. 81–104). Baltimore: Paul H. Brookes.

Hanson, M., Lynch, E., & Wayman, K. (1990). Honoring the cultural diversity of families when gathering data. *Topics in Early Childhood Special Education, 10*(1), 112–131.

Harry, B. (1992). *Cultural diversity, families, and the special education system: Communication and empowerment.* New York: Teachers College Press.

Harry, B. (1995). African American families. In B. Ford, F. Obiakor, & J. Patton (Eds.), *Effective education of African American exceptional learners* (pp. 211–233). Austin, TX: Pro-Ed.

Hayden, V. (1974). The other children. *Exceptional Parent, 4*(2), 26–29.

Hodapp, R., & Krasner, D. (1995). Families of children with disabilities: Findings from a national sample of eighth-grade students. *Exceptionality, 5*(2), 71–81.

Kalyanpur, M., & Harry, B. (1999). *Culture in special education.* Baltimore: Paul H. Brookes.

Kubler-Ross, E. (1969). *On death and dying.* New York: Macmillan.

Lamb, M., & Meyer, D. (1991). Fathers of children with special needs. In M. Seligman (Ed.), *The family with a handicapped child* (2nd ed., pp. 151–179). Boston: Allyn and Bacon.

Lambie, R. (2000). *Family systems within educational context* (2nd ed.). Denver: Love.

Linan-Thompson, S., & Jean, R. (1997). Completing the parent participation puzzle: Accepting diversity. *Teaching Exceptional Children, 30*(2), 46–50.

Lobato, D., Faust, D., & Spirito, A. (1988). Examining the effects of chronic disease and disability on children's sibling relationships. *Journal of Pediatric Psychology, 13,* 389–407.

Lynch, E., & Hanson, M. (Eds.). (2004). *Developing cross cultural competence* (3rd ed.). Baltimore: Paul H. Brookes.

Mason, E., Kruse, L., Farabaugh, A., Gershberg, R., & Kohler, M. (2000). Children with exceptionalities and their siblings: Opportunities for collaboration between family and school. In M. Fine & R. Simpson (Eds.), *Collaboration with parents and families of children and youth with exceptionalities* (2nd ed., pp. 69–88). Austin, TX: Pro-Ed.

Matuszny, R., Banda, D., & Coleman, T. (2007). A progressive plan for building collaborative relationships with parents from diverse backgrounds. *Teaching Exceptional Children, 39*(4), 24–33.

McHugh, M. (2003). *Special siblings: Growing up with someone with a disability.* Baltimore: Paul H. Brookes.

Meyer, D., & Vadasy, P. (1994). *Sibshops: Workshops for siblings of children with special needs.* Baltimore: Paul H. Brookes.

Misra, A. (1994). Partnerships with families. In S. Alper, P. Schloss, & C. Schloss (Eds.), *Families of students with disabilities* (pp. 143–179). Boston: Allyn and Bacon.

Olson, D. (1988). Family types, family stress, and family satisfaction: A family developmental perspective. In C. Folicov (Ed.), *Family transitions: Continuity and change over the life cycle* (pp. 55–79). New York: Guilford Press.

Olsson, M., & Hwang, C. (2001). Depression in mothers and fathers of children with intellectual disability. *Journal of Intellectual Disability Research, 45*(6), 535–543.

Parette, H., & Petch-Hogan, B. (2000). Approaching families: Facilitating culturally/linguistically diverse family involvement. *Teaching Exceptional Children, 33*(2), 4–10.

Perl, J. (1995). Improving relationship skills for parent conferences. *Teaching Exceptional Children, 28*(1), 29–31.

Power, P. (2004). *Families living with chronic illness and disability.* New York: Springer.

Robinson-Zañartu, C. (1996). Serving Native American children and families: Considering cultural variables. *Language, Speech, and Hearing Services in School, 27,* 373–384.

Rolland, J. (1994). *Families, illness, and disability: An integrative treatment model.* New York: Basic Books.

Roos, P. (1978). Parents of mentally retarded children—Misunderstood and mistreated. In A. Turnbull & H. Turnbull (Eds.), *Parents speak out* (pp. 12–27). Columbus, OH: Charles Merrill.

Rump, M. (2002). Involving fathers of young children with special needs. *Young Children, 57*(6), 18–20.

Russell, C., Russell, C., & Russell, M. (2003). We're here too! *Exceptional Parent, 33*(6), 36–39.

Salend, S., & Taylor, L. (1993). Working with families: A cross cultural perspective. *Remedial and Special Education, 14*(5), 25–32, 39.

Santelli, B., Turnbull, A., Marquis, J., & Lerner, J. (1997). Parent-to-parent programs: A resource for parents and professionals. *Journal of Early Intervention, 21*(1), 73–83.

Scorgie, K., & Sobsey, D. (2000). Transformational outcomes associated with parenting children who have disabilities. *Mental Retardation, 38*(3),195–206.

Scorgie, K., Wilgosh, L., & McDonald, L. (1998). Stress and coping in families of children with disabilities: An examination of recent literature. *Developmental Disabilities Bulletin, 26*(1), 22–42.

Seligman, M., & Darling, R. (2007). *Ordinary families, special children* (3rd ed.). New York: Guilford Press.

Seligman, M., Goodwin, G., Paschal, K., Applegate, A., & Lehman, A. (1997). Grandparents of children with disabilities: Perceived levels of support. *Education and Training in Mental Retardation and Developmental Disabilities, 32*(4), 293–303.

Sileo, T., Sileo, A., & Prater, M. (1996). Parent and professional partnership in special education. *Intervention in School and Clinic, 31*(3), 145–153.

Stewart, J. (1977). Unique problems of handicapped Native Americans. In *The White House Conference on Handicapped Individuals* (Vol. 1, pp. 438–444). Washington, DC: U.S. Government Printing Office.

Trachtenberg, S., Batshaw, K., & Batshaw, M. (2007). Caring and coping. In M. Batshaw, L. Pellegrino, & N. Roizen (Eds.), *Children with disabilities* (6th ed., pp. 601–612). Baltimore: Paul H. Brookes.

Turnbull, A., & Turnbull, H. (1990). *Families, professionals, and exceptionality: A special partnership* (2nd ed.). Columbus, OH: Merrill.

Turnbull, A., Turnbull, R., Erwin, E., & Soodak, L. (2006). *Families, professionals, and exceptionality* (5th ed.). Upper Saddle River, NJ: Pearson Education.

Voltz, D. (1995). Learning and cultural diversities in general and special education classes: Frameworks for success. *Multiple Voices for Ethnically Diverse Exceptional Learners, 1*(1), 1–11.

Voltz, D. (1998). Cultural diversity and special education teacher preparation: Critical issues confronting the field. *Teacher Education and Special Education, 21*(1), 63–70.

Young, D., & Roopnarnine, J. (1994). Father's child care involvement with children with and without disabilities. *Topics in Early Childhood Special Education, 14*(4), 488–502.

Ziskin, L. (1978). The story of Jennie. In A. Turnbull & H. Turnbull (Eds.), *Parents speak out* (pp. 70–80). Columbus, OH: Charles Merrill.

Chapter 5

Alberto, P., & Troutman, A. (2006). *Applied behavior analysis for teachers* (7th ed.). Upper Saddle River, NJ: Pearson Education.

Alexander, D. (1998). Prevention of mental retardation: Four decades of research. *Mental Retardation and Developmental Disabilities Research Reviews, 4,* 50–58.

Beirne-Smith, M., Patton, J., & Kim, S. (2006). *Mental retardation* (7th ed.). Upper Saddle River, NJ: Pearson Education.

Belmont, J. (1966). Long-term memory in mental retardation. *International Review of Research in Mental Retardation, 1,* 219–255.

Blatt, B., & Kaplan, F. (1966). *Christmas in purgatory.* Boston: Allyn and Bacon.

Browder, D., & Snell, M. (2000). Teaching functional academics. In M. Snell & F. Brown (Eds.), *Instruction of students with severe disabilities* (5th ed., pp. 493–542). Upper Saddle River, NJ: Prentice Hall.

Bush, A., & Beail, N. (2004). Risk factors for dementia in people with Down syndrome: Issues in assessment and diagnosis. *American Journal on Mental Retardation, 109,* 83–97.

Butterworth, J., & Strauch, J. (1994). The relationship between social competence and success in the competitive workplace for persons with mental retardation. *Education and Training in Mental Retardation and Developmental Disabilities, 29*(2), 118–133.

Bybee, J., & Zigler, E. (1998). Outer-directedness in individuals with and without mental retardation: A review. In J. Burack, R. Hodapp, & E. Zigler (Eds.), *Handbook of mental retardation and development* (pp. 434–460). Cambridge, England: Cambridge University Press.

Chadsey-Rusch, J. (1992). Toward defining and measuring social skills in employment settings. *American Journal on Mental Retardation, 96*(4), 405–418.

Channon, S., German, E., Cassina, C., & Lee, P. (2004). Executive functioning, memory, and learning in phenylketonuria. *Neuropsychology, 18,* 613–620.

Christenson, S., Ysseldyke, J., & Thurlow, M. (1989). Critical instructional factors for students with mild handicaps: An integrative review. *Remedial and Special Education, 10*(5), 21–31.

Conyers, C., Martin, T., Martin, G., & Yu, D. (2002). The 1983 AAMR manual, the 1992 AAMR manual, or the Developmental Disabilities Act: Which do researchers use? *Education and Training in Mental Retardation and Developmental Disabilities, 37*(3), 310–316.

Crawford, D., Acuna, J., & Sherman, S. (2001). FMRI and fragile X syndrome: Human genome epidemiology review. *Genetics in Medicine, 3,* 359–371.

Davidson, P., & Myers, G. (2007). Environmental toxins. In M. Batshaw, L. Pellegrino, & N. Roizen (Eds.), *Children with disabilities* (6th ed., pp. 61–70). Baltimore: Paul H. Brookes.

Denning, C., Chamberlain, J., & Polloway, E. (2000). An evaluation of state guidelines for mental retardation: Focus on definition and classification practices. *Education and Training in Mental Retardation and Developmental Disabilities, 35*(2), 135–144.

Drew, C., & Hardman, M. (2007). *Intellectual disabilities across the lifespan* (9th ed.). Upper Saddle River, NJ: Pearson Education.

Edgar, E. (1988). Employment as an outcome for mildly handicapped students: Current status and future directions. *Focus on Exceptional Children, 2*(1), 1–8.

Ellis, N. (1963). The stimulus trace and behavioral inadequacy. In N. Ellis (Ed.), *Handbook of mental deficiency* (pp. 134–158). New York: McGraw-Hill.

Fiscus, R., Schuster, J., Morse, T., & Collins, B. (2002). Teaching elementary students with cognitive disabilities food preparation skills while embedding instructive feedback in prompt and consequent events. *Education and Training in Mental Retardation and Developmental Disabilities, 37*(1), 55–69.

Friend, M., & Bursuck, W. (2006). *Including students with special needs* (4th ed.). Boston: Allyn and Bacon.

Gargiulo, R. (1985). *Working with parents of exceptional children.* Boston: Houghton Mifflin.

Gargiulo, R., & Kilgo, J. (2005). *Young children with special needs* (2nd ed.). Clifton Park, NY: Delmar.

Gelof, M. (1963). Comparison of systems of classification relating degree of retardation to measured intelligence. *American Journal of Mental Deficiency, 68,* 297–317.

Graham, M., & Scott, K. (1988). The impact of definitions of high risks on services to infants and toddlers. *Topics in Early Childhood Special Education, 8*(3), 23–28.

Greenspan, S., & Love, P. (1997). Social intelligence and developmental disorder: Mental retardation, learning disabilities, and autism. In W. MacLean (Ed.), *Ellis' handbook of mental deficiency, psychological theory and research* (3rd ed., pp. 311–342). Mahwah, NJ: Erlbaum.

Grossman, H. (1973). *Manual on terminology and classification in mental retardation*. Washington, DC: American Association on Mental Deficiency.

Grossman, H. (1983). *Classification in mental retardation*. Washington, DC: American Association on Mental Deficiency.

Harris, L., & Associates. (2004). *National Organization on Disabilities/Harris Survey of Americans with Disabilities*. New York: Author.

Heber, R. (1961). A manual on terminology and classification in mental retardation (Rev. ed.). *Monograph Supplement to the American Journal of Mental Deficiency, 64*.

Hickson, L., Blackman, L., & Reis, E. (1995). *Mental retardation: Foundations of educational programming*. Boston: Allyn and Bacon.

Hoover, J., & Patton, J. (2004). Differentiating standards-based education for students with diverse needs. *Remedial and Special Education, 25*(2), 74–78.

Johnson, D., Johnson, R., & Holubec, E. (1998). *Cooperation in the classroom* (7th ed.). Edina, MN: Interaction Book Co.

Johnson. L. (2005). First, do no harm: An argument against mandatory high-stakes testing for students with intellectual disabilities. *Mental Retardation, 43*, 292–298.

Jones, K., Smith, D., Ulleland, C., & Streissguth, A. (1973). Pattern of malformation in offspring of chronic alcoholic mothers. *Lancet, 1*(7815), 1267–1271.

Katims, D. (2000). Literacy instruction for people with mental retardation: Historical highlights and contemporary analysis. *Education and Training in Mental Retardation and Developmental Disabilities, 35*(1), 3–15.

Kaufman, A., & Kaufman, N. (2004). *Kaufman Assessment Battery for Children—Second Edition*. Circle Pines, MN: American Guidance Service.

Krauss, M., Seltzer, M., Gordon, R., & Friedman, D. (1996). Binding ties: The roles of adult siblings of persons with mental retardation. *Mental Retardation, 34*(2), 83–93.

Kregel, J. (2001). Promoting employment opportunities for individuals with mild cognitive limitations. In A. Tymchuk, K. Lakin, & R. Luckasson (Eds.), *The forgotten generation: The status and challenges of adults with mild cognitive limitations* (pp. 87–98). Baltimore: Paul H. Brookes.

Lambert, N., Nihira, K., & Leland, H. (1993). *AAMR Adaptive Behavior Scale* (2nd ed.). Austin, TX: Pro-Ed.

Langone, J., Clees, T., Oxford, M., Malone, M., & Ross, G. (1995). Acquisition and generalization of social skills by high school students with mild retardation. *Mental Retardation, 33*(3), 186–196.

Lejune, J., Gautier, M., & Turpin, R. (1959). Études des chromosomes somatiques de neuf enfants mongoliers. *Academie de Science, 248*, 1721–1722.

Lewis, R., & Doorlag, D. (2006). *Teaching special students in general education classrooms* (7th ed.). Upper Saddle River, NJ: Pearson Education.

Lindman, F., & McIntyre, K. (1961). *The mentally disabled and the law*. Chicago: University of Chicago Press.

Luckasson, R., Borthwick-Duffy, S., Buntinx, W., Coulter, D., Craig, E., Reeve, A., Schalock, R., Snell, M., Spitalnick, D., Spreat, S., & Tassé, M. (2002). *Mental retardation: Definition, support, and systems of supports* (10th ed.). Washington, DC: American Association on Mental Retardation.

Luckasson, R., Coulter, D., Polloway, E., Reiss, S., Schalock, R., Snell, M., Spitalnik, D., & Stark, J. (1992). *Mental retardation: Definition, classification, and systems of support*. Washington, DC: American Association on Mental Retardation.

MacMillan, D. (1989). Mild mental retardation: Emerging issues. In G. Robinson, J. Patton, E. Polloway, & L. Sargent (Eds.), *Best practices in mild mental retardation* (pp. 1–20). Reston, VA: Division on Mental Retardation of the Council for Exceptional Children.

Mank, D., Cioffi, A., & Yovanoff, P. (2003). Supported employment outcomes across a decade: Is there evidence of improvement in the quality of implementation? *Mental Retardation, 41*, 188–197.

March of Dimes. (2001). *Public health education information sheet: Rh disease*. White Plains, NY: Author.

March of Dimes. (2004). *Public health education information sheet: PKU*. White Plains, NY: Author.

March of Dimes. (2005). *Public health education information sheet: Drinking alcohol during pregnancy*. White Plains, NY: Author.

March of Dimes. (2007). *Public health education information sheet: Down syndrome*. White Plains, NY: Author.

Mazzocco, M. (2000). Advances in research on the Fragile X syndrome. *Mental Retardation and Developmental Disabilities Research Reviews, 6*, 96–106.

McDonnell, J., Hardman, M., & McDonnell, A. (2003). *An introduction to persons with moderate and severe disabilities* (2nd ed.). Boston: Allyn and Bacon.

McMaster, K., & Fuchs, D. (2002). Effects of cooperative learning on the academic achievement of students with learning disabilities. *Learning Disabilities Research and Practice, 17*, 107–117.

Meyer, G. (2007). X-linked syndromes causing intellectual disability. In M. Batshaw, L. Pellegrino, & N. Roizen (Eds.), *Children with disabilities* (6th ed., pp. 275–283). Baltimore: Paul H. Brookes.

Morrison, G., & Polloway, E. (1995). Mental retardation. In E. Meyen & T. Skirtic (Eds.), *Special education and student disability* (4th ed., pp. 213–269). Denver: Love.

Müller, E., & Markowitz, J. (2004). *Disability categories: State terminology, definitions, & eligibility criteria*. Alexandria, VA: National Association of State Directors of Special Education.

Murphy, S., Rogan, P., Handley, M., Kincaid, C., & Royce-Davis, J. (2002). People's situations and perspectives eight years after workshop conversion. *Mental Retardation, 40,* 30–40.

Nihira, K., Leland, H., & Lambert, N. (1993). *AAMR Adaptive Behavior Scale—Residential and Community* (2nd ed.). Austin, TX: Pro-Ed.

Nirje, B. (1969). The normalization principle and its human management implications. In R. Kugel & W. Wolfensberger (Eds.), *Changing patterns in residential services for the mentally retarded* (pp. 179–195). Washington, DC: President's Committee on Mental Retardation.

Oswald, D., Coutinho, M., Best, A., & Nguyen, N. (2001). Impact of sociodemographic characteristics on the identification rates of minority students as having mental retardation. *Mental Retardation, 39*(5), 351–367.

Owens, R. (2002). Mental retardation: Difference and delay. In D. Bernstein & E. Tiegerman-Farber (Eds.), *Language and communication disorders in children* (5th ed., pp. 436–509). Boston: Allyn and Bacon.

Polloway, E., Patton, J., & Serna, L. (2008). *Strategies for teaching learners with special needs* (9th ed.). Upper Saddle River, NJ: Pearson Education.

Polloway, E., Smith, J., Chamberlain, J., Denning, C., & Smith, T. (1999). Levels of deficits or supports in the classification of mental retardation: Implementation practices. *Education and Training in Mental Retardation and Developmental Disabilities, 34*(2), 200–206.

President's Committee for People with Intellectual Disabilities. (2007). *Fact sheet.* Retrieved March 28, 2007 from http://www.acf.hhs.gov/programs/pcpid/pcpid_fact.html

Reiss, S. (1994). Issues in defining mental retardation. *American Journal on Mental Retardation, 99,* 1–7.

Roid, G. (2003). *Stanford-Binet Intelligence Scale—Fifth Edition.* Itasca, IL: Riverside.

Roizen, N. (2007). Down syndrome. In M. Batshaw, L. Pellegrino, & N. Roizen (Eds.), *Children with disabilities* (6th ed., pp. 263–273). Baltimore: Paul H. Brookes.

Scheerenberger, R. (1983). *A history of mental retardation.* Baltimore: Paul H. Brookes.

Scheerenberger, R. (1987). *A history of mental retardation: A quarter century of concern.* Baltimore: Paul H. Brookes.

Schilit, J., & Caldwell, M. (1980). A word list of essential career/vocational words for mentally retarded students. *Education and Training of the Mentally Retarded, 15*(2), 113–117.

Seligman, M. (1992). *Helplessness: On depression, development, and death.* San Francisco: Freeman.

Simmons, T., & Whaley, B. (2008). Transition to employment. In R. Flexer, R. Baer, P. Luft, & T. Simmons (Eds.), *Transition planning for secondary students with disabilities* (3rd ed., pp. 230–257). Upper Saddle River: NJ: Pearson Education.

Sitlington, P., & Clark, G. (2006). *Transition education and services for students with disabilities* (4th ed.). Needham Heights, MA: Allyn and Bacon.

Smith, T., Polloway, E., Patton, J., & Dowdy, C. (2008). *Teaching students with special needs in inclusive settings* (5th ed.). Needham Heights, MA: Allyn and Bacon.

Taylor, P., Collins, B., Schuster, J., & Kleinert, H. (2002). Teaching laundry skills to high school students with disabilities: Generalization of targeted skills and nontargeted information. *Education and Training in Mental Retardation and Developmental Disabilities, 37*(2), 172–183.

Taylor, R., Richards, S., & Brady, M. (2005). *Mental retardation: Historical perspectives, current practices, and future directions.* Boston: Allyn and Bacon.

Test, D., Carver, T., Evers, L., Haddad, J., & Person, J. (2000). Longitudinal job satisfaction of persons in supported employment. *Education and Training in Mental Retardation and Developmental Disabilities, 35*(4), 365–373.

Thoma, C. (1999). Supporting student voice in transition planning. *Teaching Exceptional Children, 31*(5), 4–9.

Tomporowski, P., & Tinsley, V. (1997). Attention in mentally retarded persons. In W. MacLean (Ed.), *Ellis' handbook of mental deficiency, psychological theory and research* (3rd ed., pp. 219–244). Mahwah, NJ: Erlbaum.

Turnbull, A., Turnbull, R., Erwin, E., & Soodak, L. (2006). *Families, professionals, and exceptionality* (5th ed.). Upper Saddle River, NJ: Pearson Education.

U.S. Department of Education. (1991). *Thirteenth annual report to Congress on the implementation of the Individuals with Disabilities Education Act.* Washington, DC: U.S. Government Printing Office.

U.S. Department of Education. (1995). *Seventeenth annual report to Congress on the implementation of the Individuals with Disabilities Education Act.* Washington, DC: U.S. Government Printing Office.

U.S. Department of Education. (2006). *Twenty-sixth annual report to Congress on the implementation of the Individuals with Disabilities Education Act, 2004.* Washington, DC: U.S. Government Printing Office.

U.S. Department of Education. (2007). *IDEA data.* Available at https://www.ideadata.org/PartB Report.asp

Warren, S., & Yoder, P. (1997). Communication, language, and mental retardation. In W. MacLean (Ed.), *Ellis' handbook of mental deficiency, psychological theory and research* (3rd ed., pp. 379–403). Mahwah, NJ: Erlbaum.

Wechsler, D. (2003). *Wechsler Intelligence Scale for Children—Fourth Edition.* San Antonio, TX: Psychological Corp.

Wehmeyer, M. (2003). Defining mental retardation and ensuring access to the general curriculum. *Education and Training in Developmental Disabilities, 38*(3), 271–282.

Wehmeyer, M., & Sailor, W. (2004). High school. In C. Kennedy & E. Horns (Eds.), *Including students with severe disabilities* (pp. 259–281). Boston: Allyn and Bacon.

Westling, D., & Fox, L. (2004). *Teaching students with severe disabilities* (3rd ed.). Upper Saddle River, NJ: Pearson Education.

Wolfensberger, W. (1972). *Normalization: The principle of normalization in human services.* Toronto: National Institute on Mental Retardation.

Xin, J., & Holmdal, P. (2003). Snacks and skills: Teaching children functional counting skills. *Teaching Exceptional Children, 35*(5), 46–51.

Chapter 6

Aiken, L. (2006). *Psychological testing and assessment* (12th ed.). Boston: Allyn and Bacon.

Alley, G., & Deshler, D. (1979). *Teaching the learning disabled adolescent: Strategies and methods.* Denver: Love.

American Psychiatric Association. (2000). *Diagnostic and statistical manual of mental disorders—Text revision.* Washington, DC: Author.

Ariel, A. (1992). *Education of children and adolescents with learning disabilities.* New York: Macmillan.

Arnold, L., Christopher, J., Huestis, R., & Smeltzer, D. (1978). Megavitamins for minimal brain dysfunction: A placebo controlled study. *Journal of the American Medical Association, 240,* 2642–2643.

Ashbaker, M., & Swanson, H. (1996). Short-term memory and working memory operations and their contribution to reading in adolescents with and without learning disabilities. *Learning Disabilities Research and Practice, 11,* 206–213.

Association for Children with Learning Disabilities. (1986, September–October). ACLD definition: Specific learning disabilities. *ACLD Newsbrief,* pp. 15–16.

Bateman, B., & Linden, M. (1998). *Better IEPs* (3rd ed.). Longmont, CO: Sopris West.

Belson, S. (2003). *Technology for exceptional learners.* Boston: Houghton Mifflin.

Bender, W. (2008). *Learning disabilities: Characteristics, identification, and teaching strategies* (6th ed.). Needham Heights, MA: Allyn and Bacon.

Bereiter, C., & Engelmann, S. (1966). *Teaching disadvantaged children in the preschool.* Englewood Cliffs, NJ: Prentice Hall.

Blair, C., & Scott, K. (2002). Proportion of LD placements associated with low socioeconomic status: Evidence for a gradient? *Journal of Special Education, 36*(1), 14–22.

Bradley, R., Danielson, L., & Doolittle, J. (2007). Responsiveness to intervention: 1997–2007. *Teaching Exceptional Children, 39*(5), 8–12.

Brooks, M. (2002). A look at current practice. In R. Bradley, L. Danielson, & D. Hallahan (Eds.), *Identification of learning disabilities: Research to practice* (pp. 335–340). Mahwah, NJ: Erlbaum.

Bryant, D., & Bryant, B. (2003). *Assistive technology for people with disabilities.* Boston: Allyn and Bacon.

Butler, D. (1998). Metacognition and learning disabilities. In B. Wong (Ed.), *Learning about learning disabilities* (2nd ed., pp. 277–307). San Diego, CA: Academic Press.

CEC Today. (2003). Strategies + technology = solutions for reading challenges. *10*(1), 1, 5, 13, 15.

Clements, S. (1966). *Minimal brain dysfunction in children: Terminology and identification* (Public Health Services Publication No. 1415). Washington, DC: U.S. Department of Health, Education, and Welfare.

Cortiella, C. (2006). *Response-to-intervention: An emerging method for LD identification.* Retrieved April 30, 2007 from http://www.schwablelearning.org/articles.asp?r=840

Cott, A. (1972). Megavitamins: The orthomolecular approach to behavioral disorders and learning disabilities. *Academic Therapy, 7*(3), 245–258.

Council for Learning Disabilities. (1986). Use of discrepancy formulas in the identification of learning disabled individuals. *Learning Disabilities Quarterly, 9,* 245.

Crockett, J., & Kauffman, J. (2001). The concept of the least restrictive environment and learning disabilities: Least restrictive of what? Reflections on Cruickshank's 1997 guest editorial for the *Journal of Learning Disabilities.* In D. Hallahan & B. Keogh (Eds.), *Research and global perspectives in learning disabilities* (pp. 147–166). Mahwah, NJ: Erlbaum.

Cruickshank, W. (1972). Some issues facing the field of learning disabilities. *Journal of Learning Disabilities, 5*(5), 380–388.

Deiner, P. (1993). *Resources for teaching children with diverse abilities.* Fort Worth, TX: Harcourt Brace Jovanovich.

Deshler, D., Ellis, E., & Lenz, B. (1996). *Teaching adolescents with learning disabilities* (2nd ed.) Denver: Love.

Dyson, L. (1996). The experiences of families of children with learning disabilities: Parental stress, family functioning and sibling self-concept. *Journal of Learning Disabilities, 29*(3), 280–286.

Engelmann, S. (1977). Sequencing cognitive and academic tasks. In R. Kneedler & S. Tarver (Eds.), *Changing perspectives in special education* (pp. 46–61). Columbus, OH: Merrill.

Feingold, B. (1975). Hyperkinesis and learning disabilities linked to artificial food flavors and colors. *American Journal of Nursing, 75,* 797–803.

Feingold, B. (1976). Hyperkinesis and learning disabilities linked to ingestion of artificial food colors and flavorings. *Journal of Learning Disabilities, 9*(9), 551–559.

Forness, S., & Kavale, K. (2002). Impact of ADHD on school systems. In P. Jensen & J. Cooper (Eds.), *Attention deficit hyperactivity disorder* (pp. 24-1–24-20). Kingston, NJ: Civic Research Institute.

Friend, M., & Bursuck, W. (2006). *Including students with special needs* (4th ed.). Boston: Allyn and Bacon.

Fuchs, D., & Fuchs, L. (2005). Responsiveness-to-intervention: A blueprint for practitioners, policymakers, and parents. *Teaching Exceptional Children, 38*(1), 57–59.

Fuchs, D., Fuchs, L., Compton, D., Bouton, B., Caffrey, E., & Hill. L. (2007). Dynamic assessment as responsiveness to intervention. *Teaching Exceptional Children, 39*(5), 58–63.

Fuchs, D., Mock, D., Morgan, P., & Young, C. (2003). Responsiveness-to-intervention: Definitions, evidence, and implication for the learning disabilities construct. *Learning Disabilities Research and Practice, 18*(3), 157–171.

Fulk, B. (1996). The effects of combined strategy and attribution training on LD adolescents' spelling performance. *Exceptionality, 6,* 13–17.

Galaburda, A. (2005). Neurology of learning disabilities: What will the future bring? The answer comes from the successes of the recent past. *Learning Disabilities Quarterly, 28*(2), 107–110.

Gargiulo, R., & Kilgo, J. (2005). *Young children with special needs* (2nd ed.). Clifton Park, NY: Delmar.

Gersten, R., Carnine, D., & Woodward, J. (1987). Direct instruction research: The third decade. *Remedial and Special Education, 8*(6), 48–56.

Gollnick, D., & Chinn, P. (2009). *Multicultural education in a pluralistic society* (8th ed.). Upper Saddle River, NJ: Pearson Education.

Graham, S., Harris, K., & Larsen, L. (2001). Prevention and intervention of writing difficulties for students with learning disabilities. *Learning Disabilities Research and Practice, 16*(2), 74–84.

Hallahan, D., Kauffman, J., & Lloyd, J. (1999). *Introduction to learning disabilities* (2nd ed.). Needham Heights, MA: Allyn and Bacon.

Hallahan, D., Lloyd, J., Kauffman, J., Weiss, M., & Martinez, E. (2005). *Learning disabilities: Foundations, characteristics, and effective teaching* (3rd ed.). Boston: Allyn and Bacon.

Hallahan, D., & Mercer, C. (2002). Learning disabilities: Historical perspectives. In R. Bradley, L. Danielson, & D. Hallahan (Eds.), *Identification of learning disabilities: Research to practice* (pp. 1–67). Mahwah, NJ: Erlbaum.

Hammill, D. (1990). On defining learning disabilities: An emerging consensus. *Journal of Learning Disabilities, 23*(2), 74–84.

Hammill, D., & Larsen, S. (1974). The effectiveness of psycholinguistic training. *Exceptional Children, 41*(1), 5–15.

Hudson, B. (2006). Making and missing connections: Learning disabilities services and the transition from adolescence to adulthood. *Disability and Society, 21,* 47–60.

Jennings, J., Caldwell, J., & Lerner, J. (2006). *Reading problems: Assessment and teaching strategies* (5th ed.). Needham Heights, MA: Allyn and Bacon.

Kame'enui, E. (2007). A new paradigm: Responsiveness to intervention. *Teaching Exceptional Children, 39*(5), 6–7.

Kauffman, J. (1999). Commentary: Today's special education and its message for tomorrow. *Journal of Special Education, 32*(4), 244–254.

Kavale, K. (1990). Variances and verities in learning disability interventions. In T. Scruggs & B. Wong (Eds.), *Intervention research in learning disabilities* (pp. 3–33). New York: Springer-Verlag.

Kavale, K. (2002). Discrepancy models in the identification of learning disability. In R. Bradley, L. Danielson, & D. Hallahan (Eds.), *Identification of learning disabilities: Research to practice* (pp. 369–426). Mahwah, NJ: Erlbaum.

Kavale, K., & Forness, S. (1983). Hyperactivity and diet treatment: A meta-analysis of the Feingold hypothesis. *Journal of Learning Disabilities, 16*(6), 324–330.

Kavale, K., Holdnack, J., & Mostert, M. (2005). Responsiveness to intervention and the identification of specific learning disability: A critique and alternative proposal. *Learning Disability Quarterly, 28*(1), 2–16.

Kavale, K., & Mostert, M. (2004). Social skills interventions for individuals with learning disabilities. *Learning Disability Quarterly, 27*(1), 31–43.

Kirk, S. (1962). *Educating exceptional children.* Boston: Houghton Mifflin.

Klingner, J., & Edwards, P. (2006). Cultural considerations with response to intervention models. *Reading Research Quarterly, 41,* 108–117.

Klingner, J., Vaughn, S., Hughes, M., Schumm, J., & Elbaum, B. (1998). Outcomes for students with and without learning disabilities in inclusive classrooms. *Learning Disabilities Research and Practice, 13,* 153–161.

Kube, D., Peterson, M., & Palmer, F. (2002). Attention deficit hyperactivity disorder: Comorbidity and medication. *Clinical Pediatrics, 41*(7), 461–469.

Lenz, B., & Deshler, D. (2004). *Teaching content to all.* Boston: Allyn and Bacon

Lenz, B., Ellis, E., & Scanlon, D. (1996). *Teaching learning strategies to adolescents and adults with learning disabilities.* Austin, TX: Pro-Ed.

Lerner, J. (2003). *Learning disabilities* (9th ed.). Boston: Houghton Mifflin.

Lerner, J., & Kline, F. (2006). *Learning disabilities and related disorders* (10th ed.). Boston: Houghton Mifflin.

Lewis, B. (1992). Pedigree analysis of children with phonology disorders. *Journal of Learning Disabilities, 25*(9), 586–597.

Lovitt, T. (1978). The learning disabled. In N. Haring (Ed.), *Behavior of exceptional children* (2nd ed., pp. 155–191). Englewood Cliffs, NJ: Prentice Hall.

Lyon, G., Shaywitz, S., & Shaywitz, B. (2003). Defining dyslexia. *Annals of Dyslexia, 53,* 1–14.

MacArthur, C. (2000). New tools for writing: Assistive technology for students with writing difficulties. *Topics in Language Disorders, 20,* 85–100.

Marchand-Martella, N., Slocum, T., & Martella, R. (Eds.). (2004). *Introduction to direct instruction.* Boston: Allyn and Bacon.

Marston, D., Muyskens, P., Lau, M., & Canter, A. (2003). Problem-solving model for decision making with high incidence disabilities: The Minneapolis experience. *Learning Disabilities Research and Practice, 18*(3), 187–200.

Martin, E. (2002). Response to "Learning disabilities: Historical perspectives." In R. Bradley, L. Danielson, & D. Hallahan (Eds.), *Identification of learning disabilities: Research to practice* (pp. 81–87). Mahwah, NJ: Erlbaum.

McLesky, J., Hoppery, D., Williamson, P., & Rentz, T. (2004). Is inclusion an illusion? An examination of national and state trends toward the education of students with learning disabilities in the general education classroom. *Learning Disabilities Research and Practice, 19*(2), 109–115.

Meichenbaum, D. (1977). *Cognitive behavior modification*. New York: Plenum.

Meichenbaum, D., & Goodman, J. (1971). Training impulsive children to talk to themselves: A means of developing self-control. *Journal of Abnormal Psychology, 77,* 115–126.

Mercer, C. (1997). *Students with learning disabilities* (5th ed.). Upper Saddle River, NJ: Prentice Hall.

Mercer, C., Forgnone, C., & Wolking, W. (1976). Definitions of learning disabilities used in the United States. *Journal of Learning Disabilities, 9*(6), 376–386.

Mercer, C., & Pullen, P. (2005). *Students with learning disabilities* (6th ed.). Upper Saddle River, NJ: Pearson Education.

Mull, C., Sitlington, P., & Alper, S. (2001). Postsecondary education for students with learning disabilities: A synthesis of the literature. *Exceptional Children, 68*(1), 97–118.

National Joint Committee on Learning Disabilities. (2003). *A reaction to full inclusion: A reaffirmation of the right of students with learning disabilities to a continuum of services.* Retrieved August 27, 2007 from http://www.ldonline.org/about/partners/njcld

National Joint Committee on Learning Disabilities. (2006). *Learning disabilities and young children.* Retrieved August 29, 2007 from http://www.ldonline.org/about/partners/njcld/react_inclu.html

Osborne, A. (1997). *Legal issues in special education*. Boston: Allyn and Bacon.

Paulson, F., Paulson, P., & Meyer, C. (1991). What makes a portfolio a portfolio? *Educational Leadership, 48*(5), 60–63.

Pearl, R., & Donahue, M. (2004). Peer relationships and learning disabilities. In B. Wong (Ed.), *Learning about learning disabilities* (3rd ed., pp. 133–165). San Diego, CA: Elsevier/Academic Press.

Pennington, B. (1990). Annotation: The genetics of dyslexia. *Journal of Child Psychology and Child Psychiatry, 31*(2), 193–201.

Peterson, J., & Hittie, M. (2003). *Inclusive teaching*. Boston: Allyn and Bacon.

Plomin, R., & Kovas, Y. (2005). Generalist genes and learning disabilities. *Psychological Bulletin, 131,* 592–617.

Polloway, E., Patton, J., & Serna, L. (2008). *Strategies for teaching learners with special needs* (9th ed.). Upper Saddle River, NJ: Pearson Education.

Raskind, M., Goldberg, R., Higgins, E., & Herman, K. (2002). Teaching life success to students with learning disabilities: Lessons learned from a 20-year study. *Intervention in School and Clinic, 37*(4), 201–208.

Raskind, W. (2001). Current understanding of the genetic basis of reading and spelling disability. *Learning Disability Quarterly, 24*(2), 141–157.

Reynolds, C. (1992). Two key concepts in the diagnosis of learning disabilities and the habilitation of learning. *Learning Disability Quarterly, 15,* 2–12.

Reynolds, C., Hewitt, J., Erickson, M., Silberg, J., Rutter, M., Simonoff, E., Meyer, J., & Eaves, L. (1996). The genetics of children's oral reading performance. *Journal of Child Psychology and Psychiatry, 37,* 425–434.

Salend, S. (1998). Using portfolios to assess student performance. *Teaching Exceptional Children, 31*(2), 26–43.

Schumm, J., Moody, S., & Vaughn, S. (2000). Grouping for instruction: Does one size fit all? *Journal of Learning Disabilities, 33*(5), 477–488.

Seligman, M. (1992). *Helplessness: On depression, development and death*. San Francisco: W. H. Freeman.

Sexton, M., Harris, K., & Graham, S. (1998). Self-regulated strategy development and the writing process: Effects on essay writing and attributions. *Exceptional Children, 64*(3), 295–311.

Silver, L. (2004). *Attention-deficit/hyperactivity disorders* (3rd ed.). Washington, DC: American Psychiatric Press.

Smith, T., Polloway, E., Patton, J., & Dowdy, C. (2008). *Teaching children with special needs in inclusive settings* (5th ed.). Needham Heights, MA: Allyn and Bacon.

Speece, D., Case, L., & Molloy, D. (2003). Responsiveness to general education instruction as the first gate to learning disabilities instruction. *Learning Disabilities Research and Practice, 18*(3), 147–156.

Spivak, M. (1986). Advocacy and legislative action for head-injured children and their families. *Journal of Head Trauma Rehabilitation, 1,* 41–47.

Stecker, P. (2007). Tertiary intervention: Using progress monitoring with intensive services. *Teaching Exceptional Children, 39*(5), 50–57.

Sturomski, N. (1997, July). Teaching students with learning disabilities to use learning strategies. *NICHY News Digest, 25,* 2–12.

Swanson, H. (1989). Strategy instruction: Overview of principles and procedures for effective use. *Learning Disabilities Quarterly, 12,* 3–14.

Swanson, H. (1999). Cognition and learning disabilities. In W. Bender (Ed.), *Professional issues in learning disabilities* (pp. 415–460). Austin, TX: Pro-Ed.

Swanson, H. (2000). Issues facing the field of learning disabilities. *Learning Disability Quarterly, 23*(1), 37–50.

Swanson, H., & Sachse-Lee, C. (2001). A subgroup analysis of working memory in children with reading disabilities: Domain-general or domain-specific deficiency? *Journal of Learning Disabilities, 34*(3), 249–263.

Taylor, R. (2006). *Assessment of exceptional students: Educational and psychological procedures* (7th ed.). Boston: Allyn and Bacon.

Taylor, O., & Leonard, L. (Eds.). (1999). *Language acquisition across North America*. San Diego, CA: Singular.

Tur-Kaspa, H., & Bryan, T. (1995). Teacher's ratings of the social competence and school adjustment of students with LD in elementary and junior high school. *Journal of Learning Disabilities, 28*(1), 44–52.

Tymchuk, A., Lakin, K., & Luckasson, R. (2001). *The forgotten generation*. Baltimore: Paul H. Brookes.

U.S. Department of Education. (1994). *Sixteenth annual report to Congress on the implementation of the Individuals with Disabilities Education Act.* Washington, DC: U.S. Government Printing Office.

U.S. Department of Education. (2006). *Twenty-sixth annual report to Congress on the implementation of the Individuals with Disabilities Education Act, 2004.* Washington, DC: U.S. Government Printing Office.

U.S. Department of Education. (2007). *IDEA data.* Available at https://www.ideadata.org/PartB Report.asp

U.S. Office of Education. (1968). *First annual report of National Advisory Committee on Handicapped Children.* Washington, DC: U.S. Department of Health, Education, and Welfare.

U.S. Office of Education. (1977, December 29). Assistance to states for education of handicapped children: Procedures for evaluating specific learning disabilities. *Federal Register, 42*(250), 65082–65085.

Vaughn, R., & Hodges, L. (1973). A statistical survey into a definition of learning disabilities. *Journal of Learning Disabilities, 6*(10), 658–664.

Vaughn, S., Elbaum, B., & Boardman, A. (2001). The social function of students with learning disabilities: Implications for inclusion. *Exceptionality, 9,* 47–65.

Vaughn, S., & Fuchs, L. (2003). Redefining learning disabilities as inadequate response to instruction: The promise and potential problems. *Learning Disabilities Research and Practice, 18*(3), 137–146.

Vaughn, S., & Linan-Thompson, S. (2003). What is special about special education for students with learning disabilities? *Journal of Special Education, 37*(3), 140–147.

Vaughn, S., Sinagub, J., & Kim, A. (2004). Social competence/social skills of students with learning disabilities. In B. Wong (Ed.), *Learning about learning disabilities* (3rd ed., pp. 341–373). San Diego, CA: Elsevier/Academic Press.

Wagner, M., Newman, L., Cameto, R., Garza, N., & Levine, P. (2005). *After high school: A first look at the postschool experiences of youth with disabilities. A report from the National Longitudinal Transition Study-2.* Menlo Park, CA: SRI International. Available at http://www.nlts2.org/data_tables/tables/12/np3D4afrm.html

Walker, B., Shippen, M., Alberto, P., Houchins, D., & Cihak, D. (2005). Using the expressive writing program to improve the writing skills of high school students with learning disabilities. *Learning Disabilities Research and Practice, 20*(3), 175–183.

Wiener, J. (2004). Do peer relationships foster behavioral adjustment in children with learning disabilities? *Learning Disability Quarterly, 27*(1), 21–30.

Witte, R., Philips, L., & Kakela, M. (1998). Job satisfaction of college graduates with learning disabilities. *Journal of Learning Disabilities, 31*(3), 259–265.

Wood, F., & Grigorenko, E. (2001). Emerging issues in the genetics of dyslexia: A methodological preview. *Journal of Learning Disabilities, 34*(6), 503–511.

Yell, M. (2006). *The law and special education* (2nd ed.). Upper Saddle River, NJ: Pearson Education.

Zigmond, N. (2003). Where should students with disabilities receive special education services? *Journal of Special Education, 37*(3), 193–199.

Zigmond, N., & Baker, J. (1996). Full inclusion for students with learning disabilities: Too much of a good thing? *Theory into Practice, 35*(1), 26–34.

Chapter 7

Alberto, P., & Troutman, A. (2006). *Applied behavior analysis for teachers* (7th ed.). Upper Saddle River, NJ: Pearson Education.

American Academy of Pediatrics. (2000). Clinical practice guideline: Diagnosis and evaluation of the child with attention-deficit/hyperactivity disorder. *Pediatrics, 105*(5), 1158–1170.

American Psychiatric Association. (2000). *Diagnostic and statistical manual of mental disorders—Text revision.* Washington, DC: Author.

Barkley, R. (1998). *Attention deficit hyperactivity disorder* (2nd ed.). New York: Guilford.

Barkley, R. (1999–2000). *ADHD in children and adolescents.* Fairhope, AL: Institute for Continuing Education.

Barkley, R. (2000). *Taking charge of ADHD: The complete authoritative guide for parents* (Rev. ed.). New York: Guilford.

Barkley, R. (2006). *Attention deficit hyperactivity disorder* (3rd ed.). New York: Guilford.

Barkley, R., Fischer, M., Smallish, L., & Fletcher, K. (2006). Young adult outcome of hyperactive children: Adaptive functioning in major life activities. *Journal of the American Academy of Child & Adolescent Psychiatry, 45*(2), 192–202.

Bender, W. (2008). *Learning disabilities: Characteristics, identification, and teaching strategies* (6th ed.). Needham Heights, MA: Allyn and Bacon.

Bos, C., Nahmias, M., & Urban, M. (1999). Targeting home–school collaboration for students with ADHD. *Teaching Exceptional Children, 31*(6), 4–11.

Bradley, W. (1937). The behavior of children receiving benzedrine. *American Journal of Psychiatry, 94,* 577–585.

Brown, T. (2006). New understandings of AD/HD. In C. Dendy (Ed.), *CHADD educator's manual on attention-deficit/hyperactivity disorder* (pp. 3–12). Landover, MD: CHADD.

Cantwell, D. (1979). The "hyperactive child." *Hospital Practice, 14,* 65–73.

Castellanos, F. (1997). Toward a pathophysiology of attention-deficit/hyperactivity disorder. *Clinical Pediatrics 36,* 381–393.

Castellanos, F., Lee, P., Sharp, W., Jeffries, N., Greenstein, D., Classen, L., Blumenthal, J., James, R., Ebens, C., Walter, J., Zijdenbos, A., Evans, A., Giedd, J., & Rapoport, J. (2002). Developmental trajectories of brain volume abnormalities in children and adolescents with attention-deficit/hyperactivity disorder. *Journal of the American Medical Association, 288,* 1740–1748.

Chronis, A., Jones, H., & Raggi, V. (2006). Evidence-based psychosocial treatments for children and adolescents with attention-deficit/hyperactivity disorder. *Clinical Psychology Review, 26,* 486–502.

Cohen, D. (2006). Critiques of the "ADHD" enterprise. In G. Lloyd, J. Snead, & D. Cohen (Eds.), *Critical new perspectives on ADHD* (pp. 12–33). London: Routledge.

Conners, C. (1997). *Conners' Teachers Rating Scale—Revised.* North Tonawanda, NY: Multi-Health Systems.

Cruickshank, W., Bentzen, F., Ratzeburg, F., & Tannhauser, M. (1961). *A teaching method for brain-injured and hyperactive children.* Syracuse, NY: Syracuse University Press.

Crickshank, W., Bice, H., & Wallen, N. (1957). *Perception and cerebral palsy.* Syracuse, NY: Syracuse University Press.

Daley, D. (2006). Attention deficit hyperactivity disorder: A review of the essential facts. *Child: Care, Health and Development, 32,* 193–204.

Daly, P., & Ranalli, P. (2003). Using cartoons to teach self-monitoring skills. *Teaching Exceptional Children, 35*(5), 30–35.

Dodson, W. (2002). Attention deficit-hyperactivity disorder (AD/HD): The basics and the controversies. *Understanding Our Gifted, 14*(4), 17–21.

dos Reis, S., Owens, P., Puccia, K., & Leaf, P. (2004). Multimodal treatment for ADHD among youth in three Medicaid subgroups: Disabled, foster care, and low income. *Psychiatric Services, 55*(9), 1041–1048.

DuPaul, G. (2006). Academic achievement in children with ADHD. *Journal of the American Academy of Child & Adolescent Psychiatry, 45*(7), 766–767.

DuPaul, G., Power, T., Anastopoulos, A., & Reid, R. (1998). *ADHD Rating Scale–IV: Checklists, norms, and clinical interpretation.* New York: Guilford.

Evans, S., Timmins, B., Sibley, M., White, L., Serpell, Z., & Schultz, B. (2006). Developing coordinated, multimodal school-based treatment for young adolescents with ADHD. *Education and Treatment of Children, 29,* 359–378.

Friend, M., & Bursuck, W. (2006). *Including students with special needs* (4th ed.). Boston: Allyn and Bacon.

Gresham, F. (2002). Caveat emptor: Considerations before buying into the "new" medical model. *Behavioral Disorders, 27,* 158–167.

Glynn, E., Thomas, J., & Shee, S. (1973). Behavioral self-control of on-task behavior in an elementary classroom. *Journal of Applied Behavior Analysis, 6*(1), 105–113.

Gupta, V. (2000). A closer look at ADD/ADHD. *Exceptional Parent 30*(8), 74–81.

Hallahan, D., Lloyd, J., Kauffman, J., Weiss, M., & Martinez, E. (2005). *Learning disabilities: Foundations, characteristics, and effective teaching* (3rd ed.). Boston: Pearson Education.

Honos-Webb, L. (2005). *The gift of ADHD.* Oakland, CA: New Harbinger.

Imperio, W. (2003). Community forums: Bridging the cultural gap. *Attention!, 9*(5), 12–13, 40–41.

Johnson, L., & Johnson, C. (1999). Teaching students to regulate their own behavior. *Teaching Exceptional Children, 31*(4), 6–10.

Jones, C., & Teach, J. (2006). Impact of AD/HD on elementary students. In C. Dendy (Ed.), *CHADD educator's manual on attention-deficit/hyperactivity disorder* (pp. 61–72). Landover, MD: CHADD.

Kessler, R., Adler, L., Barkley, R., Biederman, J., Conners, C., Demler, O., Faraone, S., Greenhill, L., Howes, M., Secnik, K., Spencer, T., Ustun, T., Bedirthan, W., Walters, E., & Zaslavsky, A. (2006). The prevalence and correlates of adult ADHD in the United States: Results from the National Comorbidity Survey replication. *American Journal of Psychiatry, 163,* 716–723.

Larsson, J., Larsson, H., & Lichtenstein, P. (2004). Genetic and environmental contributions to stability and change of ADHD symptoms between 8 and 13 years of age. *Journal of the American Academy of Child & Adolescent Psychiatry, 43*(10), 1267–1275.

Lawrence, V., Houghton, S., Tannock, R., Douglas, G., Dunkin, K., & Whiting, K. (2002). ADHD outside the laboratory: Boys' executive function performance on tasks in video-game play and on a visit to the zoo. *Journal of Abnormal Child Psychology, 30,* 447–462.

Lerner, J., & Kline, F. (2006). *Learning disabilities and related disorders* (10th ed.). Boston: Houghton Mifflin.

Lerner, J., & Lowenthal, B. (1993). Attention deficit disorders: New responsibilities for the special educator. *Learning Disabilities: A Multidisciplinary Journal, 4*(1), 1–8.

Levy, F., Hay, D., & Bennett, K. (2006). Genetics of attention deficit hyperactivity disorder: A current review and future prospects. *International Journal of Disability, Development and Education, 53,* 5–20.

Martin, N., Levy, F., Pieka, J., & Hay, D. (2006). A genetic study of attention deficit hyperactivity disorder, conduct disorder, oppositional defiant disorder and reading disability: Aetiological overlaps and implications. *International Journal of Disability, Development and Education, 53,* 21–34.

Mercer, C., & Pullen, P. (2005). *Students with learning disabilities* (6th ed.). Upper Saddle River, NJ: Pearson Education.

Mill, J., Caspi, A., Williams, B., Craig, I., Taylor, A., Polo-Tomas, M., Beridge, C., Poulton, R., & Moffit, T. (2006). Prediction of heterogeneity in intelligence and adult prognosis by genetic polymorphisms in the dopamine system among children with attention-deficit/hyperactivity disorder. *Archives of General Psychiatry, 63,* 462–469.

Miranda, A., Jarque, S., & Tarraga, R. (2006). Intervention in school settings for students with ADHD. *Exceptionality, 14,* 35–52.

Moore, C., Biederman, J., Wozinak, J., Mick, E., Aleardi, M., Wardrop, M., Dougherty, M., Harpold, T., Hammerness, P., Randall, E., & Renshaw, P. (2006). Differences in brain chemistry in children and adolescents with attention deficit hyperactivity disorder with and without comorbid bipolar disorder: A proton magnetic resonance spectroscopy study. *American Journal of Psychiatry, 163,* 316–318.

MTA Cooperative Group. (1999a). A 14-month randomized clinical trial of treatment strategies for attention-deficit/hyperactivity disorder. *Archives of General Psychiatry, 56,* 1073–1086.

MTA Cooperative Group. (1999b). Moderators and mediators of treatment response for children with attention-deficit/hyperactivity disorder. *Archives of General Psychiatry, 56,* 1088–1096.

Murphy K., Barkley, R., & Bush, T. (2002). Young adults with attention deficit hyperactivity disorder: Subtype differences in educational and clinical history. *Journal of Nervous and Mental Disorders, 19,* 147–157.

National Dissemination Center for Children with Disabilities. (2004). *Fact Sheet No. 19: Attention deficit/hyperactivity disorder.* Washington, DC: Author.

National Institute of Mental Health. (2006). *Attention deficit hyperactivity disorder.* Retrieved April 3, 2007 from http://www.nimh.nih.gov/health/publications/adhd/summary.shtml

Northup, J., Gulley, V., Edwards, S., & Fountain, L. (2001). The effects of methylphenidate in the classroom: What dosage, for which children, for what problems? *School Psychology Quarterly, 16,* 303–323.

Olmeda, R., Thomas, A., & Davis, C. (2003). An analysis of sociocultural factors in social skills training studies with students with attention deficit hyperactivity disorder. *Multiple Voices, 6,* 58–72.

Pierce, K. (2003). Attention-deficit/hyperactivity disorder and comorbidity. *Primary Psychiatry, 10,* 69–70, 75–76.

Reid, R., Casat, C., Norton, H., Anastopoulos, A., & Temple, E. (2001). Using behavior rating scales for ADHD across ethnic groups: The IOWA Conners. *Journal of Emotional and Behavioral Disorders, 9*(4), 210–218.

Reid, R., Riccio, C., Kessler, R., DuPaul, G., Power, T., Anastopoulos, A., Rogers-Adkinson, D., & Noll, M. (2000). Gender and ethnic differences in ADHD as assessed by rating scales. *Journal of Emotional and Behavioral Disorders, 8*(1), 38–48.

Reis, E. (2002). Attention deficit hyperactivity disorder: Implications for the classroom teacher. *Journal of Instructional Psychology, 29,* 175–177.

Salend, S., & Rohena, E. (2003). Students with attention deficit disorders: An overview. *Intervention in School and Clinic, 38,* 259–266.

Silver, L. (1990). Attention deficit hyperactivity disorder: Is it a learning disability or a related disorder? *Journal of Learning Disabilities, 23,* 394–397.

Smith, T., Polloway, E., Patton, J., & Dowdy, C. (2008). *Teaching children with special needs in inclusive settings* (5th ed.). Needham Heights, MA: Allyn and Bacon.

Snider, V., Busch, T., & Arrowood, L. (2003). Teacher knowledge of stimulant medication. *Remedial and Special Education, 24*(1), 46–56.

Solanto, M. (2002). Dopamine dysfunction in AD/HD: Integrating clinical and basic neuroscience research. *Behavioral Brain Research, 130,* 65–71.

Still, G. (1902). Some abnormal psychical conditions in children. *Lancet, 1,* 1008–1012, 1077–1082, 1163–1168.

Strauss, A., & Werner, H. (1942). Disorders of conceptual thinking in the brain-injured child. *Journal of Nervous and Mental Disease, 98,* 153–172.

U.S. Department of Education. (2006a). *Identifying and treating attention deficit hyperactivity disorders: A resource for school and home.* Washington, DC: Author.

U.S. Department of Education. (2006b). *Teaching children with attention deficit hyperactivity disorders: Instructional strategies and practices.* Washington, DC: Author.

U.S. Department of Education. (2006c). *Twenty-sixth annual report to Congress on the implementation of the Individuals with Disabilities Education Act, 2004.* Washington, DC: U.S. Government Printing Office.

U.S. Department of Education. (2007). *IDEA data.* Available at https://www.ideadata.org/PartB Report.asp

Vaughn, S., Bos, C., & Schumm, J. (2007). *Teaching exceptional, diverse, and at-risk students in the general education classroom* (4th ed.). Boston: Allyn and Bacon.

Weiss, S., & Illes, T. (2006). Advanced strategies for challenging behaviors. In C. Dendy (Ed.), *CHADD educator's manual on attention-deficit/hyperactivity disorder* (pp. 73–79). Landover, MD: CHADD.

Werner, H., & Strauss. A. (1941). Pathology of figure–background relation in the child. *Journal of Abnormal and Social Psychology, 36,* 236–248.

Weyandt, L. (2001). *An ADHD primer.* Boston: Allyn and Bacon.

Weyandt, L. (2005). *The physiological bases of cognitive and behavioral disorders.* Mahwah, NJ: Erlbaum.

Wilens, T., Faraone, S., Biederman, J., & Gunawardene, S. (2003). Does stimulant therapy of attention deficit/hyperactivity disorder beget later substance abuse? *Pediatrics, 111*(1), 179–185.

Williams, L., Lerner, M., Wigal, T., & Swanson, J. (1995). Minority assessment of ADD: Issues in the development of new assessment techniques. *Attention!, 2*(1), 9–15.

Chapter 8

Achenbach, T. M., & Edelbrock, C. S. (1978). The classification of child psychopathology: A review and analysis of empirical efforts. *Psychological Bulletin, 85,* 1275–1301.

Achenbach, T. M., & Edelbrock, C. S. (1983). *Manual for the Child Behavior Checklist.* Burlington, VT: University of Vermont, Department of Psychiatry.

Allen, R. I., & Petr, C. G. (1997). Family-centered professional behavior: Frequency and importance to parents. *Journal of Emotional and Behavioral Disorders, 5*(4), 196–204.

Allen-DeBoer, R. A., Malmgren, K. W., & Glass, M. E. (2006). Reading instruction for youth with emotional and behavioral disorders in a juvenile correctional facility. *Behavioral Disorders, 32*(1), 18–28.

American Psychiatric Association. (2000). *Diagnostic and statistical manual of mental disorders—Text revision.* Washington, DC: Author.

Anderson, J. A., & Matthews, B. (2001). We care for students with emotional and behavioral disabilities and their families. *Teaching Exceptional Children, 33*(5), 34–39.

Barr, R., & Parrett, W. (2001). *Hope at last for at-risk youth* (2nd ed.). Needham Heights, MA: Allyn and Bacon.

Barton-Arwood, S. M., Wehby, J. H., & Falk, K. B. (2005). Reading instruction for elementary-age students with emotional and behavioral disorders: Academic and behavioral outcomes. *Exceptional Children, 72*(1), 7–27.

Beach Center on Families and Disabilities. (1999). *Information brief on behavior supports and functional assessment of behavior.* Lawrence: University of Kansas (available at http:www.lsi.ukans .edu/beach).

Beard, K. Y., & Sugai, G. (2004). First step to success: An early intervention for elementary children at risk for antisocial behavior. *Behavioral Disorders, 29*(4), 396–398.

Blanchard, L. T., Gurka, M. J., & Blackman, J. A. (2006). Emotional, developmental, and behavioral health of American children and their families: A report from the 2003 National Survey of Children's Health. *Pediatrics, 117,* 1202–1212.

Boe, E. E., & Cook, L. H. (2006). The chronic and increasing shortage of fully certified teachers in special and general education. *Exceptional Children, 72*(4), 443–460.

Bower, E. M. (1960). *Early identification of emotionally disturbed children in school.* Springfield, IL: Charles C. Thomas.

Bower, E. M. (1981). *Early identification of emotionally handicapped children in school* (3rd ed.). Springfield, IL: Charles C. Thomas.

Bower, E. M. (1982). Defining emotional disturbance: Public policy and research. *Psychology in the Schools, 19,* 55–60.

Chandler, L. K., & Dahlquist, C. M. (2006). *Functional assessment: Strategies to prevent and remediate challenging behavior in school settings* (2nd ed.). Upper Saddle River, NJ: Pearson Education.

Coleman, M. C., & Webber, J. (2002). *Emotional and behavioral disorders: Theory and practice* (4th ed.). Boston: Allyn and Bacon.

Collins, S. (2003, July 17). Mentally ill children face life without necessary services. *USA Today,* p. 13A.

Cooper, J. O., Heron, T. E., & Heward, W. M. (2007). *Applied behavior analysis* (2nd ed.). Upper Saddle River, NJ: Pearson Education.

Corbett, W. P., Clark, H. B., & Blank, W. (2002). Employment and social outcomes associated with vocational programming for youths with emotional or behavioral disorders. *Behavioral Disorders, 27*(4), 358–370.

CEC Today. (2001). New study of special education working conditions. 8(1), 9–12.

Council for Children with Behavioral Disorders. (1990). Position paper on the provision of service to children with conduct disorders. *Behavioral Disorders, 15*(3), 180–189.

Coutinho, M. J., Oswald, D. P., Best, A. M., & Forness, S. R. (2002). Gender and sociodemographic factors and the disproportionate identification of culturally and linguistically diverse students with emotional disturbance. *Behavioral Disorders, 27*(2), 109–125.

Crockenberg, S., & Leerkes, E. (2005). Infant social and emotional development in family context. In C. H. Zeanah, Jr. (Ed.), *Handbook of infant mental health* (2nd ed., pp. 60–90). New York: Guilford.

Cullinan, D. (2007). *Students with emotional and behavioral disorders* (2nd ed.). Upper Saddle River, NJ: Pearson Education.

Cullinan, D., Evans, C., Epstein, M. H., & Ryser, G. (2003). Characteristics of emotional disturbance of elementary school students. *Behavioral Disorders, 28*(2), 94–110.

Deno, S. L. (1998). Academic progress as incompatible behavior: Curriculum-based measurement (CBM) as intervention. *Beyond Behavior, 9*(3), 12–17.

Despert, J. L. (1965). *The emotionally disturbed child: Then and now.* New York: Brunner.

DeValenzuela, J. S., Copeland, S. R., Qi, C. H., & Park, M. (2006). Examining educational equity: Revising the disproportionate representation of minority students in special education. *Exceptional Children, 72*(4), 425–441.

DiGiulio, R. (2000). *Positive classroom management* (2nd ed.). Thousand Oaks, CA: Corwin Press.

Duckworth, S., Smith-Rex, S., Okey, S., Brookshire, M. A., Rawlinson, D., Rawlinson, R., Castillo, S., & Little, J. (2001). Wraparound services for young school children with emotional and behavioral disorders. *Exceptional Children, 33*(4), 54–60.

Dunlap, G., Strain, P. S., Fox, L., Carta, J. J., Conroy, M., Smith, B. J., Kern, L., Hemmeter, M. L., Timm, M. A., McCart, A., Sailor, W., Markey, U., Markey, D. J., Laridieri, S., & Sowell, C. (2006). Prevention and intervention with young children's challenging behavior: Perspectives regarding current knowledge. *Behavioral Disorders, 32*(1), 29–45.

Epstein, M. H. (2002). *Behavioral and Emotional Rating Scale* (2nd ed.). Austin, TX: Pro-Ed.

Epstein, M. H., Rudolph, S., & Epstein, A. A. (2000). Strength-based assessment. *Teaching Exceptional Children, 32*(6), 50–54.

Etscheidt, S. (2002). Psychotherapy services for students with emotional or behavioral disorders. *Behavioral Disorders, 27*(4), 386–399.

Forgan, J. W., & Gonzalez-DeHass, A. (2004). How to infuse social skills training into literacy instruction. *Teaching Exceptional Children, 36*(6), 24–30.

Forness, S. R. (2003). Parting reflections on education of children with emotional or behavioral disorders. *Behavioral Disorders, 28*(3), 198–201.

Forness, S. R., & Kavale, K. A. (2000). Emotional or behavioral disorders: Background and current status of E/BD terminology and definition. *Behavioral Disorders, 25*(3), 264–269.

Forness, S. R., Kavale, K. A., & Davanzo, P. A. (2002). The new medical model: Interdisciplinary treatment and the limits of behaviorism. *Behavioral Disorders, 27*(2), 168–178.

Forness, S. R., Walker, H. M., & Kavale, K. A. (2003). Psychiatric disorders and treatments: A primer for teachers. *Teaching Exceptional Children, 36*(2), 42–49.

Frey, A. (2002). Predictors of placement recommendations for children with behavioral or emotional disorders. *Behavioral Disorders, 27*(2), 126–136.

Gresham, F. M., Sugai, G., & Horner, R. H. (2001). Interpreting outcomes of social skills training for students with high-incidence disabilities. *Exceptional Children, 67*(3), 331–344.

Gumpel, T. P., & David, S. (2000). Exploring the efficacy of self-regulatory training as a possible alternative to social skills training. *Behavioral Disorders, 25*(2), 131–146.

Gunter, P. L., Shores, R. E., Jack, S. L., Rasmussen, S., & Flowers, J. (1995). Teacher/student proximity: A strategy for classroom control through teacher movement. *Teaching Exceptional Children, 28*(1), 12–14.

Haslam, R. H., & Valletutti, P. J. (2004). *Medical problems in the classroom: The teacher's role in diagnosis and management* (4th ed.). Austin, TX: Pro-Ed.

Hayman, M. (1939). The interrelations between mental defect and mental disorder. *Journal of Mental Science, 85*, 1183–1193.

Hocutt, A. M., McKinney, J. D., & Montague, M. (2002). The impact of managed care on efforts to prevent development of serious emotional disturbance in young children. *Journal of Disability Policy Studies, 13*(1), 51–60.

Hooper, S. R., Roberts, J. E., Zeisel, S. A., & Poe, M. (2003). Core language predictors of behavioral functioning in early elementary school children: Concurrent and longitudinal findings. *Behavioral Disorders, 29*(1), 10–24.

House, A. E. (2002). *DSM-IV diagnosis in the schools.* New York: Guilford.

Janas, M. (2002). Twenty ways to build resiliency. *Intervention in School and Clinic, 38*(2), 117–121.

Janney, R., & Snell, M. E. (2000). *Teacher's guide to inclusive practices: Behavioral support.* Baltimore: Paul H. Brookes.

Jensen, M. M. (2005). *Introduction to emotional and behavioral disorders.* Upper Saddle River, NJ: Pearson Education.

Johns, B., Mather, S., & McGrath, M. Z. (2003). Leadership necessary to promote a call to action. *Beyond Behavior, 13*(1), 20–22.

Jones, V., Dohrn, E., & Dunn, C. (2004). *Creating effective programs for students with emotional and behavior disorders.* Boston: Allyn and Bacon.

Kauffman, J. M. (1981). *Characteristics of children's behavioral disorders* (2nd ed.). Columbus, OH: Merrill.

Kauffman, J. M. (2005). *Characteristics of emotional and behavioral disorders of children and youth* (8th ed.). Upper Saddle River, NJ: Pearson Education.

Kerr, M. M., & Nelson, C. M. (2006). *Strategies for managing behavior problems in the classroom* (5th ed.). Upper Saddle River, NJ: Pearson Education.

Kline, F. M., Silver, L. B., & Russell, S. C. (2001). *The educator's guide to medical issues in the classroom.* Baltimore: Paul H. Brookes.

Kutash, K., Duchnowski, A. J., Sumi, W. C., Rudo, Z., & Harris, K. M. (2002). A school, family, and community collaborative program for children who have emotional disturbances. *Journal of Emotional and Behavioral Disorders, 10*(2), 99–107.

Landrum, T., Katsiyannis, A., & Archwamety, T. (2004). An analysis of placement and exit patterns of students with emotional or behavioral disorders. *Behavioral Disorders, 29*(2), 140–153.

Lane, K. L. (2003). Identifying young students at risk for antisocial behavior: The utility of "teachers as tests." *Behavioral Disorders, 28*(4), 360–369.

Lane, K. L., Little, M. A., Redding-Rhodes, J., Phillips, A., & Welsh, M. T. (2007). Outcomes of a teacher-led reading intervention for elementary students at risk for behavioral disorders. *Exceptional Children, 74*(1), 47–70.

Lane, K. L., Wehby, J., Menzies, H. M., Doukas, G. L., Munton, S. M., & Gregg, R. M. (2003). Social skills instruction for students at risk for antisocial behavior: The effects of small-group instruction. *Behavioral Disorders, 28*(3), 229–248.

Lane, K. L., Weisenbach, J. L., Phillips, A., & Wehby, J. H. (2007). Designing, implementing, and evaluating function-based interventions using a systematic, feasible approach. *Behavioral Disorders, 32*(2), 122–139.

Leedy, A., Bates, P., & Safran, S. (2004). Bridging the research-to-practice gap: Improving hallway behavior using positive behavior supports. *Behavioral Disorders, 29*(2), 130–139.

Leffert, J., & Siperstein, G. N. (2003). A focus on social skills instruction for students with learning disabilities. *Current Practice Alerts, 9*, 1–4.

Lewis, C. D. (1974). Introduction: Landmarks. In J. M. Kauffman & C. D. Lewis (Eds.), *Teaching exceptional children with behavior disorders: Personal perspectives* (pp. 2–23). Columbus, OH: Merrill.

Logan, K. R., & Stein, S. S. (2001). The research lead teacher model: Helping general education teachers deal with classroom behavior problems. *Teaching Exceptional Children, 33*(3), 10–15.

Luiselli, J. R., Putnam, R. F., & Sunderland, M. (2002). Longitudinal evaluation of behavior support intervention in a public middle school. *Journal of Positive Behavior Interventions, 4*(3), 182–188.

Maag, J. W. (2006). Social skills training for students with emotional and behavioral disorders: A review of reviews. *Behavioral Disorders, 32*(1), 5–17.

Mastropieri, M. A., & Scruggs, T. E. (2002). *Effective instruction for special education* (3rd ed.). Austin, TX: Pro-Ed.

McConnell, M. E., Cox, C. J., Thomas, D. D., & Hilvitz, P. B. (2001). *Functional behavioral assessment.* Denver, CO: Love.

McIntyre, T., & Forness, S. R. (1996). Is there a new definition yet or are our kids still seriously emotionally disturbed? *Beyond Behavior, 7*(3), 4–9.

Milstein, M. M., & Henry, D. A. (2000). *Spreading resiliency: Making it happen for schools and communities.* Thousand Oaks, CA: Corwin Press.

Moffitt, T. (1994). Adolescence-limited and life-course persistent antisocial behavior: A developmental taxonomy. *Psychological Review, 100,* 674–701.

National Dissemination Center for Children and Youth with Disabilities. (2003). *Interventions for chronic behavior problems.* Washington, DC: Author.

National Institute of Mental Health. (2006a). *The numbers count: Mental disorders in America.* Retrieved November 15, 2007 from http://www.nimh.nih.gov/publicat/numbers.cfm

National Institute of Mental Health. (2006b). *Depression in children and adolescents.* Retrieved November 15, 2007 from http://www.mentalhealth.gov/healthinformation/depchidmenu.cfm

Nelson, J. R., Babyak, A., Gonzalez, J., & Benner, G. J. (2003). An investigation of the problem behaviors exhibited by K-12 students with emotional or behavioral disorders in public school settings. *Behavioral Disorders, 28*(4), 348–359.

Nelson, J. R., Benner, G. J., & Rogers-Adkinson, D. L. (2003). An investigation of the characteristics of K–12 students with comorbid emotional disturbance and significant language deficits in public school settings. *Behavioral Disorders, 29*(1), 25–33.

Nelson, J. R., Benner, G., Lane, K. L., & Smith, B. W. (2004). An investigation of the academic achievement of K-12 students with emotional and behavioral disorders in public school settings. *Exceptional Children, 71*(1), 59–73.

New Freedom Commission on Mental Health. (2003). *Achieving the promise: Transforming mental health care in America.* Final report. DHHS Pub. No. SMA-03-3832. Rockville, MD: U.S. Department of Health and Human Services.

Newcomer, P. (2003). *Understanding and teaching emotionally disturbed children and adolescents* (3rd ed.). Austin, TX: Pro-Ed.

Obiakor, F. E., Utley, C. A., Smith, R., & Harris-Obiakor, P. (2002). The Comprehensive Support Model for culturally diverse exceptional learners: Intervention in an age of change. *Intervention in School and Clinic, 38*(1), 14–27.

Polloway, E. A., Patton, J. R., & Serna, L. (2008). *Strategies for teaching learners with special needs* (9th ed.). Upper Saddle River, NJ: Pearson Education.

Quay, H. C., & Peterson, D. R. (1975). *Manual for the Behavior Problem Checklist.* Coral Gables, FL: Author.

Quay, H. C., & Peterson, D. R. (1996). *Manual for the Revised Behavior Problem Checklist.* Odessa, FL: Psychological Assessment Resources.

Quinn, M. M., Rutherford, R. B., Leone, P. E., Osher, D. M., & Poirer, J. M. (2005). Youth with disabilities in juvenile corrections: A national survey. *Exceptional Children, 71*(3), 339–345.

Raiser, L., & Van Nagel, C. V. (1980). The loophole in Public Law 94-142. *Exceptional Children, 46,* 516–520.

Rie, H. E. (1971). Historical perspectives of concepts of child psychopathology. In H. E. Rie (Ed.), *Perspectives in child psychopathology* (pp. 3–50). New York: Aldine-Atherton.

Rinaldi, C. (2003). Language competence and social behavior of students with emotional or behavioral disorders. *Behavioral Disorders, 29*(1), 34–42.

Robinson, D. H., Funk, D. C., Beth, A., & Bush, A. M. (2005). Changing beliefs about corporal punishment: Increasing knowledge about ineffectiveness to build more consistent moral and informational beliefs. *Journal of Behavioral Education, 14*(2), 117–139.

Rodgers-Adkinson, D. (2003). Language processing in children with emotional disorders. *Behavioral Disorders, 29*(1), 43–47.

Rogers-Adkinson, D. L., & Hooper, S. R. (2003). The relationship of language and behavior: Introduction to the special issue. *Behavioral Disorders, 29*(1), 5–9.

Rosenberg, M. S., Wilson, R., Maheady, L., & Sindelar, P. T. (2004). *Educating students with behavior disorders* (3rd ed.). Needham Heights, MA: Allyn and Bacon.

Rosenshine, B., & Stevens, R. (1986). Teaching functions. In M. C. Wittrock (Ed.), *Handbook of research on teaching* (3rd ed., pp. 376–391). New York: Macmillan.

Rubin, R. A., & Balow, B. (1971). Learning and behavior disorders: A longitudinal study. *Exceptional Children, 38,* 293–299.

Ruef, M. B., Higgins, C., Glaeser, B., & Patnode, M. (1998). Positive behavioral support: Strategies for teachers. *Intervention in School and Clinic, 34*(1), 21–32.

Sabornie, E. J., & deBettencourt, L. U. (2004). *Teaching students with mild disabilities at the secondary level* (2nd ed.). Upper Saddle River, NJ: Pearson Education.

Safford, P. L., & Safford, E. J. (1996). *A history of childhood and disability.* New York: Teachers College Press.

Safran, S. P., & Oswald, K. (2003). Positive behavior supports: Can schools reshape disciplinary practices? *Exceptional Children, 69*(3), 361–373.

Salend, S. J. (2008). *Creating inclusive classrooms* (6th ed.). Upper Saddle River, NJ: Pearson Education.

Satcher, D. (1999). *Mental health: A report of the surgeon general.* Washington, DC: U.S. Department of Public Health Services.

Savage, T. V. (1999). *Teaching self-control through management and discipline* (2nd ed.). Needham Heights, MA: Allyn and Bacon.

Scheuermann, B. K., & Hall, J. A. (2008). *Positive behavioral supports for the classroom.* Upper Saddle River, NJ: Pearson Education.

Scott, T. M., Bucalos, A., Liaupsin, C., Nelson, C. M., Jolivette, K., & DeShea, L. (2004). Using functional behavior assessment in general education settings: Making a case for effectiveness and efficiency. *Behavioral Disorders, 29*(2), 189–201.

Scott, T. M., Payne, L. D., & Jolivette, K. (2003). Preventing predictable problem behaviors by using positive behavior support. *Beyond Behavior, 13*(1), 3–7.

Scruggs, T. E., & Mastropieri, M. A. (2000). Mnemonic strategies for students with behavior disorders: Memory for learning and behavior. *Beyond Behavior, 10*(1), 13–17.

Shaw, D. S., Gilliom, M., & Giovannelli, J. (2005). Aggressive behavior disorders. In C. H. Zeanah, Jr. (Ed.), *Handbook of infant mental health* (2nd ed., pp. 397–411). New York: Guilford.

Skiba, R. J., Poloni-Staudinger, L., Gallini, S., Simmons, A. B., & Feggins-Azziz, R. (2006). Disparate access: The disproportionality of African American students with disabilities across educational environments. *Exceptional Children, 72*(4), 411–424.

Stea, K., & Ristic, R. F. (2006). *Two peas in a pod: Integrating the Nonviolent Crisis Intervention training program and positive behavioral support strategies.* Brookfield, WI: Crisis Prevention Institute.

Stein, M., & Davis, C. A. (2000). Direct instruction as positive behavioral support. *Beyond Behavior, 10*(1), 7–12.

Sugai, G., Horner, R. H., Dunlap, G., Hieneman, M., Lewis, T. J., Nelson, C. M., Scott, T., Liaupsin, C., Sailor, W., Turnbull, A. P., Turnbull, R., III, Wickham, D., Ruef, M., & Wilcox, B. (1999). *Applying positive behavior support and functional assessment in schools.* Washington, DC: Office of Special Education Programs, Center on Positive Behavioral Interventions and Supports.

Taylor, P. B., Gunter, P. L., & Slate, J. R. (2001). Teachers' perceptions of inappropriate student behavior as a function of teachers' and students' gender and ethnic background. *Behavioral Disorders, 26*(2), 146–151.

Taylor-Richardson, K. D., Helflinger, C. A., & Brown, T. N. (2006). Experience of strain among of caregivers responsible for children with serious emotional and behavioral disorders. *Journal of Emotional and Behavioral Disorders, 14*(3), 157–168.

Umbreit, J., Ferro, J. B., Liaupsin, C. J., & Lane, K. L. (2007). *Functional behavioral assessment and function-based intervention.* Upper Saddle River, NJ: Pearson Education.

U.S. Department of Education. (1980). *Second annual report to Congress on the implementation of Public Law 94-142.* Washington, DC: Author.

U.S. Department of Education. (2000). *Safeguarding our children: An action guide.* Washington, DC: Author.

U.S. Department of Education. (2002). *Twenty-fourth annual report to Congress on the implementation of the Individuals with Disabilities Education Act.* Washington, DC: Author.

U.S. Department of Education. (2003). *Twenty-fifth annual report to Congress on the implementation of the Individuals with Disabilities Education Act.* Washington, DC: U.S. Government Printing Office.

U.S. Department of Education. (2006). *Twenty-sixth annual report to Congress on the implementation of the Individuals with Disabilities Education Act, 2004.* Washington, DC: U.S. Government Printing Office.

U.S. Department of Education. (2007). *IDEA data.* Available at https://www.ideadata.org/PartB Report.asp

Vaughn, S., Bos, C. S., & Schumm, J. S. (2007). *Teaching exceptional, diverse, and at-risk students in the general education classroom* (4th ed.). Needham Heights, MA: Allyn and Bacon.

Vaughn, S., & Lancelotta, G. X. (1990). Teaching interpersonal social skills to low accepted students: Peer-pairing versus no peer-pairing. *Journal of School Psychology, 28*(3), 181–188.

Vaughn, S., Levy, S., Coleman, M., & Bos, C. S. (2002). Reading instruction for students with LD and EBD: A synthesis of observation studies. *Journal of Special Education, 36*(1), 2–13.

Wacker, D. P., & Berg, W. K. (2002). PBS as a service delivery system. *Journal of Positive Behavior Interventions, 4*(1), 25–28.

Wagner, M., Cameto, R., & Newman, L. (2003). *Youth with disabilities: A changing population.* Retrieved November 11, 2007 from http://www.nlts2.0rg/reports/2003_04–1/nlts2_report_2003_04–1_complete.pdf

Wagner, M., & Davis, M. (2006). How are we preparing students with emotional disturbance in the transition to young adulthood? Findings from the National Longitudinal Transition Study-2. *Journal of Emotional and Behavioral Disorders, 14*(2), 86–98.

Wagner, M., Newman, L., Cameto, R., Garza, N. & Levine, P. (2005). *After high school: A first look at the post school experiences of youth with disabilities.* Available at www.nlts2.org/reports/2005_04/nlts2_report_2005_04_complete.pdf

Walker, H. M., Kavanagh, K., Stiller, B., Golly, A., Severson, H., & Feil, E. (1997). *First Steps to Success: An early intervention program for antisocial kindergartners.* Longmont, CO: Sopris West.

Walker, H. M., Ramsey, E., & Gresham, F. M. (2004). *Antisocial behavior in schools: Evidence-based practices* (2nd ed.). Belmont, CA: Wadsworth.

Warger, C. L. (2002). *Full-service schools' potential for special education.* ERIC Clearinghouse on Disabilities and Gifted Education. Available at http://eric.hoagiesgifted.org/osep/topical/ fullsvc.html

Webber, J., & Plotts, C. A. (2008). *Emotional and behavioral disorders: Theory and practice* (5th ed.). Boston: Allyn and Bacon.

Wehby, J., Symons, F., Canale, J., & Go, F. (1998). Teaching practices in classroom for students with emotional and behavioral disorders: Discrepancies between recommendations and observations. *Behavioral Disorders, 24,* 51–56.

Wehby, J. H., Falk, K. B., Barton-Arwood, S., Lane, K. L., & Cooley, C. (2003). The impact of comprehensive reading instruction on the academic and social behavior of students with emotional and behavioral disorders. *Journal of Emotional and Behavioral Disorders, 11*(4), 225–238.

White, C. R., Palmer, K., & Huffman, L. C. (2003). Technology instruction for students with emotional and behavioral disorders attending a therapeutic day school. *Beyond Behavior, 13*(1), 23–27.

Wicks-Nelson, R., & Israel, A. C. (2006). *Behavior disorders of childhood* (6th ed.). Upper Saddle River, NJ: Pearson Education.

Zigmond, N. (2006). Twenty-four months after high school: Paths taken by youth diagnosed with severe emotional and behavioral disorders. *Journal of Emotional and Behavioral Disorders, 14*(2), 91–107.

Chapter 9

Akshoomoff, N., Pierce, K., & Courchesne, E. (2002). The neurological basis of autism from a developmental perspective. *Development and Psychopathology, 14,* 613–634.

Alberto, P., & Troutman, A. (2006). *Applied behavior analysis for teachers* (7th ed.). Upper Saddle River, NJ: Pearson Education.

American Academy of Pediatrics. (2001). The pediatrician's role in the diagnosis and management of autistic spectrum disorders in children. *Pediatrics, 107*(5), 1221–1226.

American Psychiatric Association. (1994). *Diagnostic and statistical manual* (4th ed.). Washington, DC: Author.

American Psychiatric Association. (2000). *Diagnostic and statistical manual—text revision.* Washington, DC: Author.

Astington, J., & Barricult, T. (2001). Children's theory of mind: How young children come to understand that people have thoughts and feelings. *Infants and Young Children, 13*(1), 1–12.

Autism Society of America. (2000). *Early intervention package.* Bethesda, MD: Author.

Autism Society of America. (2007). *What is autism.* Retrieved December 11, 2007 from http://www .autism-society.org/site/PageServer?pagename=about_whatis_home

Bettleheim, B. (1967). *The empty fortress: Infantile autism and the birth of self.* New York: Free Press.

Blishak, D. M., & Schlosser, R. W. (2003). Use of technology to support spelling by students with autism. *Topics in Language Disorders, 23,* 293–304.

Bondy, A., & Frost, L. (1998). The picture exchange communication system. *Seminars in Speech & Language, 19*(4), 373–389.

Bowler, D. (2006). *Autism spectrum disorders.* Hoboken, NJ: Wiley.

Carter, A., Davis, N., Klin, A., & Volkmar, F. (2005). Social development in autism. In F. Volkmar, R. Paul, A. Klin, & D. Cohen (Eds.), *Handbook of autism and pervasive developmental disorders* (3rd ed., Vol. 1, pp. 312–334). Hoboken, NJ: Wiley.

Charlop-Christy, M. H., Carpenter, M., Le, L., LeBlanc, L. A., & Kellett, K. (2002). Using the picture exchange communication system (PECS) with children with autism: Assessment of PECS acquisition, speech, social communicative behavior, and problem behavior. *Journal of Applied Behavior Analysis, 35,* 213–231.

Courchesne, E. (2004). Brain development in autism: Early overgrowth followed by premature arrest of growth. *Mental Retardation and Developmental Disabilities Research Reviews, 10*(2), 106–111.

Dahle, K. B. (2003a). Services to include young children with autism in the general classroom. *Early Childhood Education Journal, 31*(1), 65–70.

Dahle, K. B. (2003b). The clinical and educational systems: Differences and similarities. *Focus on Autism and Other Developmental Disabilities, 18*(4), 238–246, 256.

Dahle, K. B., & Gargiulo, R. M. (2003). Understanding Asperger disorder: A primer for early childhood educators. *Early Childhood Education Journal, 32*(3), 199–203.

Dunn, W., Myles, B. S., & Orr, S. (2002). Sensory processing issues associated with Asperger syndrome: A preliminary investigation. *American Journal of Occupational Therapy, 56,* 97–102.

Edelson, M. (2006). Are the majority of children with autism mentally retarded? *Focus on Autism and Other Developmental Disabilities, 21*(2), 66–83.

Edelson, S. (2000). *Autistic savant.* Salem, OR: Center for Study of Autism.

Ehlers, S., Gillberg, C., & Wing, L. (1999). A screening questionnaire for Asperger's syndrome and other high-functioning autism spectrum disorders in school-age children. *Journal of Autism and Developmental Disorders, 29*(2), 129–141.

Freeman, B. (1999). *Diagnosis of the syndrome of autism: Questions parents ask.* Bethesda, MD: Autism Society of America.

Freeman, B., & Van Dyke, M. (2006). Are the majority of children with autism mentally retarded? *Focus on Autism and Other Developmental Disorders, 21*(2), 86–88.

Gallagher, P., Powell, T., & Rhodes, C. (2006). *Brothers & sisters* (3rd ed.). Baltimore: Paul H. Brookes.

Gargiulo, R., & Kilgo, J. (2005). *Young children with special needs* (2nd ed.). Clifton Park, NY: Delmar.

Gerhardt, P., & Holmes, D. (2005). Employment: Options and issues for adolescents and adults with autism spectrum disorders. In F. Volkmar, R. Paul, A. Klin, & D. Cohen (Eds.), *Handbook of autism and pervasive developmental disorders* (3rd ed., Vol. 2, pp. 1087–1101). Hoboken, NJ: Wiley.

Haist, F., Adamo, M., Westerfield, M., Courchesne, E., & Townsend, J. (2005). The functional neuroanatomy of spatial attention in autism spectrum disorder. *Developmental Psychology, 27*(3), 425–458.

Handelman, J., & Harris, S. (Eds.). (2008). *Preschool programs for children with autism* (3rd ed.). Austin, TX: Pro-Ed.

Harris, S., Handelman, J., & Jennett, H. (2005). Models of educational intervention for students with autism: Home, center, and school-based programming. In F. Volkmar, R. Paul, A. Klin, & D. Cohen (Eds.), *Handbook of autism and pervasive developmental disorders* (3rd ed., Vol. 2, pp. 1043–1054). Hoboken, NJ: Wiley.

Hume, K., Bellini, L., & Pratt, R. (2005). The usage and perceived outcomes of early intervention and early childhood programs for young children with autism. *Topics in Early Childhood Education, 25*(4), 195–207.

Hyman, S., & Towbin, K. (2007). Autism spectrum disorders. In M. Batshaw, L. Pellegrino, & N. Roizen (Eds.), *Children with disabilities* (6th ed., pp. 325–343). Baltimore: Paul H. Brookes.

Italia, C. (2007, April/May). One in 150. *Spectrum Magazine*, 26–30.

Johnson, C. (1994, November/December). Interview with Ivar Lovaas. *Advocate*, 2–12.

Johnson, C., & Myers, S. (2007). Identification and evaluation of children with autism spectrum disorders. *Pediatrics, 120*(5), 1183–1215.

Kanner, L. (1985). Autistic disturbance of affective contact. In A. Donnellan (Ed.), *Classic readings in autism* (pp. 11–50). New York: Teachers College Press. (Original work published 1943)

Klin, A., McPartland, J., & Volkmar, F. (2005). Asperger syndrome. In F. Volkmar, R. Paul, A. Klin, & D. Cohen (Eds.), *Handbook of autism and pervasive developmental disorders* (3rd ed., Vol. 1, pp. 88–125). Hoboken, NJ: Wiley.

Korvatska, E., Van de Water, J., Anders, T., & Gershwin, M. (2002). Genetic and immunologic considerations in autism. *Neurobiology of Disease, 9*(2), 107–125.

Kravits, T. R., Kamps, D. M., Kemmerer, K., & Potucck, J. (2002). Brief report: Increasing communication skills for an elementary-aged student with autism using picture exchange communication system. *Focus on Autism and Other Developmental Disabilities, 30*, 225–230.

Laramie, R. L. (2001). Asperger syndrome: Advice for school personnel. *Preventing School Failure, 45*, 148–152.

LaVigna, G. (1985). Commentary on positive reinforcement and behavioral deficits of autistic children by C. B. Fester. In A. Donnellan (Ed.), *Classic readings in autism* (pp. 53–73). New York: Teachers College Press.

Lord, C., Risi, S., DiLavore, P., Schulman, C., Thurm, A., & Pickles, A. (2006). Autism from 2 to 9 years of age. *Archives in General Psychiatry, 63*, 694–701.

Lord, C., Rutter, M., Goode, S., Heemsherbergen, J., Jordon, H., Mawhood, L., & Schopler, E. (1989). Autism diagnostic observation schedule: A standardized observation of communication and social behavior. *Journal of Autism and Developmental Disorders, 19*, 185–212.

Lord, C., Rutter, M., & LeCouteur, A. (1994). Autism diagnostic interview—revised: A revised version of a diagnostic interview for caregivers of individuals with possible pervasive developmental disorders. *Journal of Autism and Developmental Disorders, 24*, 659–685.

Lovaas, I. (1987). Behavioral treatment and normal educational and intellectual functioning in young autistic children. *Journal of Consulting and Clinical Psychology, 55*, 3–9.

Lovaas, I. (1993). The development of a treatment-research project for developmentally disabled and autistic children. *Journal of Applied Behavior Analysis, 26*(4), 617–630.

Marcus, L., Kunce, L., & Schopler, E. (2005). Working with families. In F. Volkmar, R. Paul, A. Klin, & D. Cohen (Eds.), *Handbook of autism and pervasive developmental disorders* (3rd ed., Vol. 2, pp. 1055–1086). Hoboken, NJ: Wiley.

Mesibov, G., Shea, V., & Schopler, E. (2005). *The TEACCH approach to autism spectrum disorders*. New York: Springer.

Millar, D., Light, J., & Schlosser, R. (2006). The impact of augmentative and alternative communication intervention on the speech production of individuals with developmental disabilities: A research review. *Journal of Speech, Language, & Hearing Research, 49*(2), 248–264.

Myers, S., & Johnson, C. (2007). Management of children with autism spectrum disorders. *Pediatrics, 120*(5), 1162–1182.

National Academy of Sciences. (2002). *Education and social issues*. Washington, DC: Author.

National Education Association. (2006). *The puzzle of autism*. Washington, DC: Author.

National Institute of Child Health and Human Development. (2005). *Autism overview: What we know*. Rockville, MD: National Institute of Child Health and Human Development Clearinghouse.

National Institute of Mental Health. (2007). *Autism spectrum disorders (pervasive developmental disorders)*. Retrieved December 22, 2007 from http://www.nimh.nih.gov/health/publications/autism/complete-publication.shtml

National Research Council. (2001). *Educating children with autism*. Washington, DC: National Academies Press.

Nordin, V., & Gillberg, C. (1998). The long-term course of autistic disorders: Update on follow-up studies. *Acta Psychiatrica Scandinavica, 97*(2), 99–108.

Paul, R., & Sutherland, D. (2005). Enhancing early language in children with autism spectrum disorders. In F. Volkmar, R. Paul, A. Klin, & D. Cohen (Eds.), *Handbook of autism and pervasive developmental disorders* (3rd ed., Vol. 2, pp. 946–976). Hoboken, NJ: Wiley.

Polleux, F., & Lauder, J. (2004). Toward a developmental neurobiology of autism. *Mental Retardation and Developmental Disabilities Research Reviews, 10*(4), 303–317.

Rank, B. (1949). Adaptation of the psychoanalytic technique for the treatment of young children with atypical development. *American Journal of Orthopsychiatry, 19*, 130–139.

Rimland, B. (1985). The etiology of infantile autism: The problem of biological versus psychological causation. In A. Donnellan (Ed.), *Classic readings in autism* (pp. 84–103). New York: Teachers College Press. (Original work published 1964)

Ronald, A., Happe, F., Bolton, P., Butcher, L., Price, T., Wheelwright, S., Baron-Cohen, S., & Plomin, R. (2006). Genetic heterogeneity between the three components of autism: A twin study. *Journal of the American Academy of Child & Adolescent Psychiatry, 45*(6), 691–699.

Rutter, M. (1978). Diagnosis and definition. In M. Rutter & E. Schopler (Eds.), *Autism: A reappraisal of concepts and treatment* (pp. 1–25). New York: Plenum.

Rutter, M. (1994). Psychiatric genetics: Research challenges and pathways forward. *American Journal of Medical Genetics (Neuropsychiatric Genetics), 54*, 185–198.

Rutter, M. (2005). Aetiology of autism: Findings and questions. *Journal of Intellectual Disability Research, 49*(4), 231–238.

Santos, M., Coelho, P., Maciel, P. (2006). Chromatin remodeling and neuronal functioning: Exciting links. *Genes, Brain and Behavior, 5* (Suppl. 2), 80–91.

Seligman, M., & Darling, R. (2007). *Ordinary families, special children* (3rd ed.). New York: Guilford.

Shea, V., & Mesibov, G. (2005). Adolescents and adults with autism. In F. Volkmar, R. Paul, A. Klin, & D. Cohen (Eds.), *Handbook of autism and pervasive developmental disorders* (3rd ed., Vol. 1, pp. 288–311). Hoboken, NJ: Wiley.

Smeeth, L., Cook, C., Fombonne, E., Heavey, L., Rodriques, L., Smith, P., & Hall, A. (2004). MMR vaccination and pervasive developmental disorders: A case-controlled study. *Lancet, 364***(9438)**, 963–969.

Smith, T., Polloway, E., Patton, J., & Dowdy, C. (2008). *Teaching students with special needs in inclusive settings* (5th ed.). Upper Saddle River, NJ: Pearson Education.

Sullivan, R. (2005). Community-integrated residential services for adults with autism: A working model. In F. Volkmar, R. Paul, A. Klin, & D. Cohen (Eds.), *Handbook of autism and pervasive developmental disorders* (3rd ed., Vol. 2, pp. 1255–1264). Hoboken, NJ: Wiley.

Trottier, G., Srivastava, L., & Walker, C. (1999). Etiology of infantile autism: A review of recent advances in genetic and neurobiological research. *Journal of Psychiatry and Neuroscience, 24*(2), 193–215.

Tsai, L. (2007). Asperger syndrome and medication treatment. *Focus on Autism and Other Developmental Disabilities, 22*(3), 138–148.

Tunali, B., & Powers, T. (2002). Coping by redefinition: Cognitive appraisals in mothers of children with autism and children without. *Journal of Autism and Developmental* Disorders, 32(1), 25–41.

U.S. Department of Education. (2006). *Twenty-sixth annual report to Congress on the implementation of the Individuals with Disabilities Education Act, 2004.* Washington, DC: U.S. Government Printing Office.

U.S. Department of Education. (2007). *IDEA data.* Available at https://www.ideadata.org

Volkmar, F. R., & Nelson, D. S. (1990). Seizure disorders in autism. *Journal of the American Academy of Child Psychiatry, 29,* 127–129.

Volkmar, F. R., & Pauls, D. (2003). Autism. *Lancet, 362*(9390), 1133–1141.

Williams, J., Scott, F., Stott, C., Allison, C., Bolton, P., Baron-Cohen, S., & Brayne, C. (2005). *Childhood Asperger Syndrome Test. Autism, 9*(1), 45–68.

Williams, L. (2001). Understanding the student with Asperger syndrome: Guidelines for teachers. *Intervention in School and Clinic, 36,* 287–292.

Chapter 10

American Speech-Language-Hearing Association. (1993). Definitions of communication disorders and variations. *ASHA, 35* (Suppl. 10), 40–41.

Bell, M. (2007). Infections and the fetus. In M. Batshaw, L. Pellegrino, & N. Roizen (Eds.), *Children with disabilities* (6th ed., pp. 71–82). Baltimore: Paul H. Brookes.

Bernthal, J., & Bankson, N. (2004). *Articulation and phonological disorders* (5th ed.). Boston: Allyn and Bacon.

Bos, C., & Vaughn, S. (2006). *Strategies for teaching students with learning and behavioral problems* (6th ed.). Needham Heights, MA: Allyn and Bacon.

Brigance, A. (2004). *Inventory of Early Development—Brigance Diagnostic II.* North Billerica, MA: Curriculum Associates.

Bryant, D., Smith, D., & Bryant, B. (2008). *Teaching students with special needs.* Boston: Pearson Education.

Bunce, B. (2003). Children with culturally diverse backgrounds. In L. McCormick, D. F. Loeb, & R. L. Schiefelbusch (Eds.), *Supporting children with communication difficulties in inclusive settings* (2nd ed., pp. 367–407). Boston: Allyn and Bacon.

Cohen, L., & Spenciner, L. (2007). *Assessment of children and youth with special needs* (3rd ed.). Boston: Allyn and Bacon.

DeThorne, L. S., & Watkins, R. V. (2001). Listeners' perceptions of language use in children. *Language, Speech, and Hearing Services in Schools, 32,* 142–148.

Friend, M., & Bursuck, W. (2006). *Including students with special needs: A practical guide for classroom teachers* (4th ed.). Needham Heights, MA: Allyn and Bacon.

Goldman, R., & Fristoe, M. (2000). *Goldman-Fristoe Test of Articulation-2.* Circle Pines, MN: American Guidance Service.

Guralnick, M., Connor, R., Neville, B., & Hammond, M. (2002). Mother's perspectives of the peer-related social development of young children with developmental delays and communication disorders. *Early Education and Development, 13*(1), 59–80.

Johnson, J. R., & Wong, M. A. (2002). Cultural differences in beliefs and practices concerning talk to children. *Journal of Speech, Language, and Hearing Research, 45,* 916–927.

Kangas, K., & Lloyd, L. (2006). Augmentative and alternative communication. In G. Shames & N. Anderson (Eds.), *Human communication disorders: An introduction* (7th ed., pp. 436–470). Boston: Allyn and Bacon.

Luterman, D. (2002). *Counseling persons with communication disorders and their families* (4th ed.). Austin, TX: Pro-Ed.

McCormick, L. (2003a). Introduction to language acquisition. In L. McCormick, D. F. Loeb, & R. L. Schiefelbusch (Eds.), *Supporting children with communication difficulties in inclusive settings* (2nd ed., pp. 1–42). Boston: Allyn and Bacon.

McCormick, L. (2003b). Language intervention in the inclusive preschool. In L. McCormick, D. F. Loeb, & R. L. Schiefelbusch (Eds.), *Supporting children with communication difficulties in inclusive settings* (2nd ed., pp. 333–366). Boston: Allyn and Bacon.

Millar, D., Light, J., & Schlosser, R. (2006). The impact of augmentative and alternative communication intervention on the speech production of individuals with developmental disabilities: A research review. *Journal of Speech, Language, and Hearing Research, 49,* 248–264.

National Dissemination Center for Children with Disabilities. (2004). *Fact sheet 11: Speech and language disorders.* Washington, DC: Author.

Owens, R. (2006). Development of communication, language, and speech. In G. Shames & N. Anderson (Eds.), *Human communication disorders: An introduction* (7th ed., pp. 22–58). Boston: Allyn and Bacon.

Owens, R., Metz, D., & Haas, A. (2007). *Introduction to communication disorders: A lifespan approach* (3rd ed.). Boston: Allyn and Bacon.

Piaget, J. (1952). *The origins of intelligence in children* (Margaret Cook, Trans.). New York: International Universities Press.

Quinones-Eatman, J. (2001). *Preschool second language acquisition: What we know and how we can effectively communicate with young second language learners* (CLAS Technical Report #5). Champaign: University of Illinois at Urbana-Champaign, Early Childhood Research Institute on Culturally and Linguistically Appropriate Services.

Ramig, P. R., & Shames, G. H. (2006). Stuttering and other disorders of fluency. In G. H. Shames & N. B. Anderson (Eds.), *Human communication disorders: An introduction* (7th ed., pp. 183–221). Boston: Allyn and Bacon.

Robinson, N. (2003). Families: The first communication partners. In L. McCormick, D. Loeb, & R. Schiefelbusch (Eds.), *Supporting children with communication difficulties in inclusive settings* (2nd ed., pp. 113–154). Boston: Allyn and Bacon.

Urban Institute. (2007). *Immigration studies.* Retrieved April 19, 2007 from http://www.urban.org/toolkit/issues/immigration.chm

U.S. Department of Education. (2007). *IDEA data.* Available at https://www.ideadata.org/PartB Report.asp

Van Hattum, R. (1969). *Clinical speech in the schools.* Springfield, IL: Charles C. Thomas.

Van Riper, C., & Emerick, L. (1996). *Speech correction: An introduction to speech pathology and audiology* (9th ed.). Boston: Allyn and Bacon.

Chapter 11

Allen, K., & Cowdery, G. (2009). *The exceptional child: Inclusion in early childhood special education* (5th ed.). Clifton Park, NY: Delmar/Cengage.

American Speech-Language-Hearing Association. (1993). Guidelines for audiology services in the schools. *ASHA, 35* (Suppl. 10), 24–32.

American Speech-Language-Hearing Association. (2004). *The prevalence and incidence of hearing loss in children.* Retrieved June 2, 2004 from http://www.asha.org/hearing/disorders/children

American Speech-Language-Hearing Association. (2006). *IDEA issue brief: Cochlear implants.* Retrieved December 1, 2007 from http://www.asha.org/NR/rdonlyres/71772E44-FCCE-4FCB-8A8C-0788D698B03C/% 200/CochlearImplantsBrief.pdf

American Speech-Language-Hearing Association. (2007a). *Hearing assessment.* Retrieved December 1, 2007 from http://www.asha.org/public/hearing/testing/assess.htm

American Speech-Language-Hearing Association. (2007b). *The prevalence and incidence of hearing loss in children.* Retrieved December 1, 2007 from http://www.asha.org/public/hearing/ disorders/children.htm

Berg, A., Ip, S., Hurst, M., & Herb, A. (2007). Cochlear implants in young children: Informed consent as a process and current practices. *American Journal of Audiology, 16*(1), 13–28.

Berk, L. E. (2006). *Child development* (7th ed.). Boston: Allyn and Bacon.

Bess, F. H., & Humes, L. E. (2003). *Audiology: The fundamentals* (3rd ed.). Baltimore: Williams and Wilkins.

Chin, S. B., Tsai, P. L., & Gao, S. (2003). Connected speech intelligibility of children with cochlear implants and children with normal hearing. *American Journal of Speech-Language Pathology, 12,* 440–451.

Chute, P. M. (2004). Cochlear implants: An evolving journey. *ASHA Leader, 9,* 7.

Clark, J., & Martin, F. (1994). *Effective counseling in audiology: Perspectives and practice.* Englewood Cliffs, NJ: Prentice Hall.

Early Hearing Campaign Honored. (2007, November 6). *The ASHA Leader, 12,* 3.

Easterbrooks, S., & Baker, S. (2001). Enter the matrix! Considering the communication needs of students who are deaf or hard of hearing. *Teaching Exceptional Children, 33*(3), 70–76.

Gallagher, P., Easterbrooks, S., Malone, D. (2006). Universal newborn hearing screening and intervention. *Infants & Young Children: An Interdisciplinary Journal of Special Care Practices, 19*(1), 59–71.

Gallaudet Research Institute. (2005, December). *Regional and national summary report of data from the 2004–2005 annual survey of deaf and hard of hearing children and youth.* Washington, DC: Gallaudet University.

Gallaudet Research Institute. (2007). *Literacy & deaf students.* Retrieved December 22, 2007 from http://gri.gallaudet.edu/Literacy/

Geers, A. (2006). Spoken language in children with cochlear implants. In P. Spencer & M. Marschark (Eds.), *Advances in spoken language development of deaf and hard-of-hearing children* (pp. 244–270). New York: Oxford University Press.

Herer, G., Knightly, C., & Steinberg, A. (2007). Hearing: Sounds and silences. In M. Batshaw, L. Pellegrino, & N. Roizen (Eds.), *Children with disabilities* (6th ed., pp. 157–183). Baltimore: Paul H. Brookes.

Hunt, N., & Marshall, K. (2006). *Exceptional children and youth* (4th ed.). Boston: Houghton Mifflin.

Iglehart, F. (2004). Speech perception by students with cochlear implants using sound-field systems in classrooms. *American Journal of Audiology, 13*(1), 62–72.

Innes, J. (1994). Full inclusion and the deaf student: A deaf consumer's issue. *American Annals of the Deaf, 139,* 152–156.

Johnson, C., & Danhauer, J. (1999). *Guidebook for support programs in aural rehabilitation.* San Diego, CA: Singular Publishing Group.

Johnson, C., Benson, P., & Seaton, J. (2001). *Educational audiology handbook* (2nd ed.). Albany, NY: Delmar.

Johnson, R. (2003, Fall). High stakes testing conference held at Gallaudet. *Research at Gallaudet,* 1–12.

Kaderavek J. N., & Pakulski, L A. (2002). Minimal hearing loss is not minimal. *Teaching Exceptional Children, 34*(6), 14–18.

Katz, L., & Schery, T. (2006). Including children with hearing loss in early childhood programs. *Young Children, 61*(1), 86–95.

Kaufman, A., & Kaufman, N. (2004). *Kaufman Assessment Battery for Children—Second Edition.* Circles Pines, MN: American Guidance Service.

King, S., De Caro, J., Karchmer, M., & Cole K. (2001). *College and career programs for deaf students* (11th ed.). Washington, DC: Gallaudet Research Institute.

Kuder, S. (2008). *Teaching students with language and communication disabilities* (3rd ed.). Boston: Allyn and Bacon.

Kuntze, M. (1998). Literacy and deaf children: The language question. *Topics in Language Disorders, 18*(4), 1–15.

Lederberg, A. (1993). The impact of deafness on mother–child and peer relationships. In M. Marschark & M. Clark (Eds.), *Psychological perspectives on deafness* (pp. 93–119). Hillsdale, NJ: Erlbaum.

Luckner, J., & Bowen, S. (2006). Assessment practices of professionals serving students who are deaf or hard of hearing: An initial investigation. *American Annals of the Deaf, 15*(4), 410–417.

Luterman, D. (2002). *Counseling persons with communication disorders and their families* (4th ed.). Austin, TX: Pro-Ed.

Marschark, M. (2006). Intellectual functioning of deaf adults and children: Answers and questions. *European Journal of Cognitive Psychology, 18*(1), 70–89.

Marschark, M. (Ed.). (2007). *Raising and educating a deaf child* (2nd ed.). New York: Oxford University Press.

Maxon, A. B., Brackett, D., & van den Berg, S. A. (1991). Self-perception of socialization: The effects of hearing status, age, and gender. *Volta Review, 93*(1), 15–17.

McLean, M., Wolery, M., & Bailey, D. B., (2004). *Assessing infants and preschoolers with special needs* (3rd ed.). Upper Saddle River, NJ: Pearson Education.

Meadows-Orlans, K. P. (1995). Source of stress for mothers and fathers of deaf and hard of hearing infants. *American Annals of the Deaf, 140,* 352–357.

Meadows-Orlans, K. P., Mertens, D. M., Sass-Lehrer, M. A., & Scott-Olson, K. (1997). Support services for parents and their children who are deaf or hard of hearing. *American Annals of the Deaf, 142,* 278–288.

Moores, D. E. (2001). *Educating the deaf: Psychology, principles, and practices* (5th ed.). Boston: Houghton Mifflin.

Moores, D. (2005). The No Child Left Behind Act and the Individuals with Disabilities Education Acts: The uneven impact of partially funded mandates on education of deaf and hard of hearing students. *American Annals of the Deaf, 150*(2), 75–80.

Paul, P. V., & Quigley, S. P. (1990). *Education and deafness.* White Plains, NY: Longman.

Petersen, M., & Willems, P. (2006). Non-syndromic, autosomal-recessive deafness. *Clinical Genetics, 69*(5), 371–392.

Picard, M. (2004). Children with permanent hearing loss and associated disabilities: Revisiting current epidemiological data and causes of deafness. *Volta Review, 104*(4), 221–236.

Psychological Corporation. (2002). *Stanford Achievement Test* (10th ed.). San Antonio, TX: Author.

Roeser, V., Valente, M., & Hosford-Dunn, H. (Eds.). (2007). *Audiology diagnosis* (2nd ed.). New York: Thieme.

Salvia, J., Ysseldyke, J., & Bolt, S. (2007). *Assessment* (10th ed.). Boston: Houghton Mifflin.

Sattler, J. M. (2006). *Assessment of children: Behavioral, social, and clinical foundations.* La Mesa, CA: Sattler.

Scheetz, N. A. (2001). *Orientation to deafness* (2nd ed.). Boston: Allyn and Bacon.

Schirmer, B. (2001). *Psychological, social, and educational dimensions of deafness.* Boston: Allyn and Bacon.

Schum, R. (2004). Psychological assessment of children with multiple handicaps who have hearing loss. *Volta Review, 104*(4), 237–255.

Scott, T. M. (2003). Auditory neuropathy in children, *AHSA Leader, 8,* 17–18.

Simeonsson, R., & Rosenthal, S. (Eds.). (2001). *Psychological and developmental assessment: Children with disabilities and chronic conditions.* New York: Guilford.

Stach, B. A. (1998). *Clinical audiology: An introduction.* San Diego, CA: Singular.

Strong, M., & Prinz, P. M. (1997). A study of the relationship between American Sign Language and English literacy. *Journal of Deaf Studies and Deaf Education, 2,* 37–46.

Toriello, H., Reardon, W., & Gorlin, R. (2004). *Hereditary hearing loss and its syndromes* (2nd ed.). New York: Oxford University Press.

Traxler, C. (2000). The Stanford Achievement Test, 9th Edition: National norming and performance standards for deaf and hard-of-hearing students. *Journal of Deaf Studies and Deaf Education, 5*(4), 337–348.

Ulrich, M., & Bauer, A. (2003). Levels of awareness: A closer look at communication between parents and professionals. *Teaching Exceptional Children, 35*(6), 20–23.

U.S. Department of Education. (2006). *Twenty-sixth annual report to Congress on the implementation of the Individuals with Disabilities Education Act, 2004.* Washington, DC: U.S. Government Printing Office.

U.S. Department of Education. (2007). *IDEA data.* Available at https://www.ideadata.org/PartB Report.asp

Van Hasselt, V., Strain, P. S., & Hersen, M. (1988). *Handbook of developmental and physical disabilities.* New York: Pergamon Press.

Wechsler, D. (2003). *Wechsler Intelligence Scale for Children* (4th ed.). San Antonio, TX: Psychological Corporation.

Williams, C., & Finnegan, M. (2003). From myth to reality: Sound information for teachers about students who are deaf. *Teaching Exceptional Children, 35*(3), 40–45.

Chapter 12

American Foundation for the Blind. (1993, March). *Educating students with visual impairments for inclusion in society.* Paper presented at the annual Josephine L. Taylor Leadership Institute, Washington, DC.

American Foundation for the Blind. (2007). *Transition happens, ready or not!* Retrieved November 12, 2007 from http://www.afb.org/Section.asp?SectionID=7&TopicID=269&DocumentID=3535

Barraga, N. C. (1973). Utilization of sensory-perceptual abilities. In B. Lowenfeld (Ed.), *The visually handicapped children in school* (pp. 117–151). New York: John Day.

Best, H. (1919). *The blind.* New York: Macmillan.

Council for Exceptional Children. (1996). Advocacy in action: CEC proves it makes a difference! *CEC Today, 2*(8), 4–5.

Council for Exceptional Children. (2000). *National plan for training personnel to serve children with blindness and low vision.* Reston, VA: Author.

Diderot, D. (1749). *Lettre sur les aveugles à l'usage de ceux qui voient.* London.

Ferrell, K. (2007). *Issues in the field of blindness and low vision.* National Center on Low-Incidence Disabilities, Retrieved November 14, 2007 from http://nclid.unco.edu/joomla/index.php?option=com_content&task=view&id=1497&Itemid=2

Goodman, S., & Wittenstein, S. (2003). *Collaborative assessment: Working with students who are blind or visually impaired, including those with additional disabilities.* New York: American Federation for the Blind Press.

Griffin, H., Williams, S., Davis, M., & Engleman, M. (2002). Using technology to enhance cues for children with low vision. *Teaching Exceptional Children, 35*(2), 36–42.

Huebner, K., Merk-Adam, B., Stryker, D., & Wolffe, K. (2004). *The national agenda for the education of children and youths with visual impairments, including those with multiple disabilities-revised.* New York: American Foundation for the Blind.

Koenig, A. (1992). A framework for understanding the literacy of individuals with visual impairments. *Journal of Visual Impairments and Blindness, 86*(7), 277–284.

Kuhn, F., Morris, R., Witherspoon, D., Mann, L., Mester, V., Modis, L., Berta, A., & Bearden W. (2000). Serious fireworks-related eye injuries. *Ophthalmic Epidemiology, 7*(2), 139–148.

Lang, M. A. (1992). Creating inclusive, nonstereotyping environments: The child with a disability. In R. M. Swallow & M. J. Sanspree (Eds.), *Project Video.* Los Angeles: California State University at Los Angeles.

Lash, J. P. (1980). *Helen and teacher: The story of Helen Keller and Anne Sullivan Macy.* New York: Delacorte Press.

Levack, N. (1994). *Low vision: A resource guide with adaptations for students with visual impairments.* Austin, TX: Texas School for the Blind and Visually Impaired.

Lewis, S., & Russo, R. (1998). Educational assessment for students who have visual impairments with other disabilities. In S. Sacks & R. Silberman (Eds.), *Educating students who have visual impairments with other disabilities* (pp. 39–71). Baltimore: Paul H. Brookes.

National Eye Institute. (2004). Retrieved April 8, 2004 from http://www.nei.nih.gov/

Optometric Extension Program Foundation. (2007). *Educator's guide to classroom vision problems.* Available at http://www.healthy.net/oep/educate.htm

Prevent Blindness America. (2007a). *Common eye problems in children.* Retrieved April 8, 2007 from http://www.preventblindness.org/children/ch_eye_problems.html

Prevent Blindness America. (2007b). *Eye safety.* Retrieved April 8, 2007 from http://www.preventblindness.org/safety

Pugh, G. S., & Erin, J. (Eds.). (1999). *Blind and visually impaired students: Educational service guidelines.* Watertown, MA: Perkins School for the Blind.

Scholl, G. T., Mulholland, M. E., & Lonergan, A. (1986). Education of the visually handicapped: A selective timeline. In G. T. Scholl (Ed.), *Foundations of education for blind and visually handicapped children and youth: Theory and practice* (Inside cover charts). New York: American Foundation for the Blind.

Texas School for the Blind. (2007). *Selected anomalies and diseases of the eye.* Retrieved April 8, 2007 from www.TSBVI.edu/education/anomalies/index.htm

U.S. Department of Education. (2007). *IDEA data.* Available at https://www.ideadata.org/PartB Report.asp

Chapter 13

Akman, C. I. (2000). Intrauterine subdural hemorrhage. *Developmental Medicine and Child Neurology, 42,* 843–846.

Alabama Institute for Deaf and Blind. (2007). *Information about deaf-blindness.* Retrieved January 5, 2007 from http://www.aidb.org/helenkeller/deafblind-info.asp

Alderman, N. (2003). Contemporary approaches to the management of irritability and aggression following traumatic brain injury. *Neuropsychological Rehabilitation, 13,* 211–240.

Alliance for Technology Access. (2004). *Computer resources for people with disabilities* (4th ed.). Alameda, CA: Hunter House.

American Lung Association. (2007). *Trends in asthma morbidity and mortality.* Retrieved May 12, 2007 from http://www.lungusa.org

Barakat, L. P., & Kazak, A. E. (1999). Family issues. In R. T. Brown (Ed.), *Cognitive aspects of chronic illness in children* (pp. 333–364). New York: Guilford Press.

Barraga, N., & Erin, J, (2001). *Visual impairments and learning* (4th ed.). Austin, TX: Pro-Ed.

Beattie v. Board of Education, 169 Wis. 231, 233, 172 N.W. 153, 154 (1919).

Becker, H., Schur, S., Paoletti-Schelp, M., & Hammer, E. (1983). *Functional Skills Screening Inventory.* Amarillo, TX: Functional Resources.

Beers, M. H., Porter, R. S., Jones, T. V., Kaplan, J. L., & Berkwits, M. (2006). *The Merck manual of diagnosis and therapy* (18th ed.). Whitehouse Station, NJ: Merck & Co.

Best, S., & Heller, K. W. (2009a). Acquired infections and AIDS. In K. W. Heller, P. E. Forney, P. A. Alberto, S. Best, & M. N. Schwartzman (Eds.), *Understanding physical, health, and multiple disabilities* (2nd ed., pp. 368–386). Upper Saddle River, NJ: Pearson Education.

Best, S., & Heller, K. W. (2009b). Congenital infections. In K. W. Heller, P. E. Forney, P. A. Alberto, S. Best, & M. N. Schwartzman (Eds.), *Understanding physical, health, and multiple disabilities* (2nd ed., pp. 387–398). Upper Saddle River, NJ: Pearson Education.

Best, S., Reed, P., & Bigge, J. (2005). Assistive technology. In S. Best, K. W. Heller, & J. Bigge (Eds.), *Teaching individuals with physical or multiple disabilities* (5th ed., pp. 179–225). Upper Saddle River, NJ: Pearson Education.

Blacher, J. (2001). Transition to adulthood: Mental retardation, families, and culture. *American Journal on Mental Retardation, 106,* 173–188.

Bowe, F. (2000). *Physical, sensory, and health disabilities: An introduction.* Upper Saddle River, NJ: Pearson Education.

Bowe, F. (2005). *Making inclusion work.* Upper Saddle River, NJ: Pearson Education.

Brown, D., & Bates, E. (2005). A personal view of changes in the deaf-blind population, philosophy, and needs. *Deaf-Blind Perspectives, 12*(3), 1–5.

Centers for Disease Control and Prevention. (2007a). *Basic statistics from the HIV/AIDS surveillance report.* Retrieved May 16, 2007 from http://www.cdc.gov/hiv/stats.htm

Centers for Disease Control and Prevention. (2007b). *Overview: TBI.* Retrieved May 18, 2007 from http://www.cdc.gov/ncipc/tbi/overview.htm

CHARGE Syndrome Foundation. (2007). *About CHARGE.* Retrieved January 14, 2007 from http://www.chargesyndrome.org/about-charge.asp

Clark G., & Bigge, J. (2005). Transition and self-determination. In S. Best, K. W. Heller, & J. Bigge (Eds.), *Teaching individuals with physical or multiple disabilities* (5th ed., pp. 367–398). Upper Saddle River, NJ: Pearson Education.

DB-Link. (2007). *Primary etiologies of deaf-blindness—alphabetical.* Retrieved January 14, 2007 from http://www.dblink.org/lib/topics/etiologies-alpha.htm

DPHD Critical Issues and Leadership Committee. (1999). Position statement on specialized health care procedures. *Physical Disabilities: Education and Related Services, 18*(1), 3–5.

Dunn, N. L., McCartan, K. W., & Fuqua, R. (1988). Young children with orthopedic handicaps: Self-knowledge about their disabilities. *Exceptional Children, 55,* 249–252.

Eberle, L. (1922, August). The maimed, the halt and the race. *Hospital Social Service, 5,* 59–63. Reprinted in R. H. Bremner (Ed.), *Children and youth in America, a documentary history: Vol. II. 1866–1932* (pp. 1026–1028). Cambridge, MA: Harvard University Press.

Effgen, S. (2005). *Meeting the physical therapy needs of children.* Philadelphia: F. A. Davis.

Engleman, M., Griffin, H., Griffin, L., & Maddox, J. (1999). A teacher's guide to communicating with students with deaf-blindness. *Teaching Exceptional Children, 31*(5), 64–70.

Epilepsy Foundation of America. (2007). *Answer place: Introduction.* Retrieved May 16, 2007 from www.epilepsyfoundation.org/about/statistics.cfm

Fadiman, A. (1997). *The spirit catches you and you fall down.* New York: Farrar, Straus & Giroux.

Gallaudet Research Institute. (2005). *Regional and national summary report of data from the 2004–2005 annual survey of deaf and hard of hearing children and youth.* Washington, DC: Gallaudet University.

Gargiulo, R. (1985). *Working with parents of exceptional children.* Boston: Houghton Mifflin.

Geenen, S., Powers, L. E., & Lopez-Vasquez, A. (2001). Multicultural aspects of involvement in transition planning. *Exceptional Children, 67,* 265–282.

Griffin, H. C., Fitch, C. L., & Griffin, L. W. (2002). Causes and interventions in the area of cerebral palsy. *Infants and Young Children, 14*(3), 18–23.

Heller, K. W. (2005a). Adaptations and instruction in literacy and language arts. In S. Best, K. W. Heller, & J. Bigge (Eds.), *Teaching individuals with physical or multiple disabilities* (5th ed., pp. 401–439). Upper Saddle River, NJ: Pearson Education.

Heller, K. W. (2005b). Adaptations and instruction in mathematics. In S. Best, K. W. Heller, & J. Bigge (Eds.), *Teaching individuals with physical or multiple disabilities* (5th ed., pp. 501–543). Upper Saddle River, NJ: Pearson Education.

Heller, K .W. (2009a). Learning and behavioral characteristics of students with physical, health, or multiple impairments. In K. W. Heller, P. E. Forney, P. A. Alberto, S. Best, & M. N. Schwartzman (Eds.), *Understanding physical, health, and multiple disabilities* (2nd ed., pp. 18–34). Upper Saddle River, NJ: Pearson Education.

Heller, K. W. (2009b). Monitoring health impairments and individualized healthcare plans. In K. W. Heller, P. E. Forney, P. A. Alberto, S. Best, & M. N. Schwartzman (Eds.), *Understanding physical, health, and multiple disabilities* (2nd ed., pp. 349–366). Upper Saddle River, NJ: Pearson Education.

Heller, K. W. (2009c). Traumatic spinal cord injury and spina bifida. In K. W. Heller, P. E. Forney, P. A. Alberto, S. Best, & M. N. Schwartzman (Eds.). *Understanding physical, health, and multiple disabilities* (2nd ed., pp. 94–117). Upper Saddle River, NJ: Pearson Education.

Heller, K. W., & Avant, J. (2009). Juvenile rheumatoid arthritis, arthrogryposis, and osteogenesis imperfecta. In K. W. Heller, P. E. Forney, P. A. Alberto, S. Best, & M. N. Schwartzman (Eds.), *Understanding physical, health, and multiple disabilities* (2nd ed., pp. 172–190). Upper Saddle River, NJ: Pearson Education.

Heller, K. W., & Bigge, J. (2005). Augmentative communication. In S. Best, K. W. Heller, & J. Bigge (Eds.), *Teaching individuals with physical or multiple disabilities* (5th ed., pp. 227–274). Upper Saddle River, NJ: Pearson Education.

Heller, K. W., Fredrick, L. D., Best, S., Dykes, M. K., & Cohen, E. T. (2000). Specialized health care procedures in the schools: Training and service delivery. *Exceptional Children, 66*, 173–186.

Heller, K. W., Fredrick, L. D., Tumlin, J., & Brineman, D. G. (2002). Teaching decoding for generalization using the nonverbal reading approach. *Journal of Physical and Developmental Disabilities, 14*, 19–35.

Heller, K. W., Mezei, P., & Schwartzman, M. (2009). Muscular dystrophies. In K. W. Heller, P. E. Forney, P. A. Alberto, S. Best, & M. N. Schwartzman (Eds.), *Understanding physical, health, and multiple disabilities* (2nd ed., pp. 232–248). Upper Saddle River, NJ: Pearson Education.

Heller, K. W., & Tumlin, J. (2004). Using expanded individualized healthcare plans to assist teachers of students with complex healthcare needs. *Journal of School Nursing, 20*(3), 150–160.

Heller, K. W., & Tumlin-Garrett, J. (2009). Cerebral palsy. In K. W. Heller, P. E. Forney, P. A. Alberto, S. Best, & M. N. Schwartzman (Eds.), *Understanding physical, health, and multiple disabilities* (2nd ed., pp. 72–93). Upper Saddle River, NJ: Pearson Education.

Herring, J. A. (2002). *Tachdjian's pediatric orthopaedics* (3rd ed.). Philadelphia: W. B. Saunders.

Hille, E., Weisglas-Kuperus, N., van Goudoever, J., Jacobusse, G., Ens-Dokkum, M., de Groot, L., Wit, J., Geven, W., Kok, J., de Kleine, M., Kollée, L., Mulder, A., van Straaten, H., de Vries, L., van Weissenbruch, M., & Verloove-Vanhorick, S. (2007). Functional outcomes and participation in young adulthood for very preterm and very low birth weight infants: The Dutch Project on preterm and small for gestational age infants at 19 years of age. *Pediatrics, 120*, 587–595.

Hsu, C., Lin, Y., Yang, Y., & Chiang, B. (2004). Factors affecting clinical and therapeutic outcomes of patients with juvenile rheumatoid arthritis. *Scandinavian Journal of Rheumatology, 33*, 312–317.

Hudson, L. (1997). *Classroom collaboration*. Watertown, MA: Perkins School for the Blind.

Iddon, J. L., Morgan, D., Loveday, C., Sahakian, B. J., & Pickard, J. D. (2006). Neuropsychological profile of young adults with spina bifida with or without hydrocephalus. *Journal of Neurology, Neurosurgery & Psychiatry, 75*, 1112–1118.

Jacobs, R., Northam, E., & Anderson, V. (2001). Cognitive outcome in children with myelomeningocele and perinatal hydrocephalus: A longitudinal perspective. *Journal of Developmental and Physical Disabilities, 13*, 389–405,

Kirshbaum, M. (2000). A disability culture perspective on early intervention with parents with physical or cognitive disabilities and their infants. *Infants and Young Children, 13*, 9–10.

Kliegman, R., Behrman, R., Jensen, H., & Stanton, B. (2007). *Nelson textbook of pediatrics* (18th ed.). Philadelphia: Elsevier.

Kuhtz-Buschbeck, J. P., Hoppe, B., Golge, M., Dreesmann, M., Damm-Stunitz, U., & Ritz, A. (2003). Sensorimotor recovery in children after traumatic brain injury: Analysis of gain, gross motor, and fine motor skills. *Developmental Medicine and Child Neurology, 45*, 821–828.

La Vor, M. L. (1976). Federal legislation for exceptional persons: A history. In F. J. Weintraub, A. Aberson, J. Balard, & M. L. La Vor (Eds.), *Public policy and the education of exceptional children* (pp. 96–111). Reston, VA: Council for Exceptional Children.

Lazzaretti, C., & Pearson, C. (2004). Myelodysplasia. In P. J. Allen & J. A. Vessey (Eds.), *Primary care of the child with a chronic condition* (4th ed., pp. 630–643). St. Louis, MO: Mosby.

Lin, S. (2000). Coping and adaptation in families of children with cerebral palsy. *Exceptional Children, 66*, 201–218.

Lindsey, L. D. (2008). *Technology and exceptional individuals* (4th ed.). Austin, TX: Pro-Ed.

Liptak, G. S. (2005). Complementary and alternative therapies for cerebral palsy. *Mental Retardation and Developmental Disabilities Research Reviews, 11*, 156–163.

Macmillan, D. L., & Hendrick, I. (1993). Evolution and legacy. In J. I. Goodlad & T. C. Lovitt (Eds.), *Integrating general and special education* (pp. 23–48). New York: Merrill.

Management of Myelomeningocele Study. (2007). *Overview of management of myelomeningocele.* Retrieved May 20, 2007 from http://www.spinabifidamoms.com/English/overview.html

Mavinkurve, G., Bagley, C., Pradilla, G., & Jallo, G. (2005). Advances in the management of hydrocephalus in pediatric patients with myelomeningocele. In M. Zesta (Ed.), *Trends in spina bifida research* (pp. 1–29). New York: Nova Biomedical Books.

Melancon, F. (2000). A group of students with Usher syndrome in south Louisiana. *Deaf-Blind Perspectives, 8*(1), 1–3.

Merrick, J., Merrick, E., Morad, M., & Kandel, I. (2006). Fetal alcohol syndrome and its long-term effects. *Minerva Pediatrica, 58*, 211–218.

Miles, B. (2005). *Overview on deaf-blindness.* Retrieved January 6, 2007 from http://www.dblink.org/ lib/overview.htm

Miller, F. (2005). *Cerebral palsy.* New York: Springer.

Mirenda, P. (2005). Augmentative and alternative communication techniques. In J. Downing (Ed.), *Teaching communication skills to students with severe disabilities* (2nd ed.). Baltimore: Paul H. Brookes.

Morgan, E. (1989). *INSITE Developmental Checklist: 0–6 Years.* Logan: Utah State University.

Murphy, N. A., Christian, B., Caplin, D. A., & Young, P. C. (2007). The health of caregivers for children with disabilities: Caregiver perspectives, *Child: Care, Health and Development, 33,* 180–187.

National Consortium on Deaf-Blindness. (2007). *The national deaf-blind child count.* Retrieved January 10, 2007 from http://www.tr.wou.edu/ntac/index.cfm?path=publications/publications_census.html

Nehring, W. M. (2004). Cerebral palsy. In P. J. Allen & J. A. Vessey (Eds.), *Primary care of the child with a chronic condition* (4th ed., pp. 327–346). St. Louis, MO: Mosby.

Prickett, J., & Welch, T. (1998). Educating students who are deaf-blind. In S. Sacks & R. Silberman (Eds.), *Educating students who have visual impairments with other disabilities* (pp. 137–159). Baltimore: Paul H. Brookes.

Rennie, J. M., Hagmann, C. F., & Robertson, N. (2007). Outcome after intrapartum hypoxic ischaemia at term. *Seminars in Fetal and Neonatal Medicine, 12,* 398–407.

Rydstrom, I., Englund, A., & Sandman, P. (1999). Being a child with asthma. *Pediatric Nursing, 25,* 589–596.

Sacks, S. Z., & Silberman, R. K. (2000). Social skills. In A. J. Koenig & M. C. Holbrook (Eds.), *Foundations of education: Instructional strategies for teaching children and youths with visual impairments* (2nd ed., Vol. 2, pp. 616–648). New York: American Foundation for the Blind Press.

Silberman, R., Bruce, S., & Nelson, C. (2004). Children with sensory impairments. In F. Orelove, D. Sobsey, & R. Silberman (Eds.), *Educating children with multiple disabilities* (4th ed., pp. 425–527). Baltimore: Paul H. Brookes.

Silverman, F. (1995). *Communication for the speechless* (3rd ed.). Boston: Allyn and Bacon.

Sitlington, P. L., & Clark, G. M., (2006). *Transition education and services for students with disabilities* (4th ed.). Needham Heights, MA: Allyn and Bacon.

Slomine, B. S., Gerring, J. P., Grados, M. A., Vasa, R., Brady, K. D., Christensen, J. R., & Denckla, M. B. (2002). Performance on measures of executive function following pediatric traumatic brain injury. *Brain Injury, 16,* 759–772.

Spina Bifida Association of America. (2004). *Facts about spina bifida.* Retrieved April 16, 2004 from http: //sbaa.org/html/sbaa_facts.html

Temkin, O. (1971). *The falling sickness: A history of epilepsy from the Greeks to the beginning of modern neurology* (2nd ed.). Baltimore: Johns Hopkins University Press.

Tovia, E., Goldberg-Stern, H., Shahar, E., & Kramer, U. (2005). Outcome of children with juvenile absence epilepsy. *Journal of Child Neurology, 21,* 766–768.

Tsai, J., Floyd, L., Green, P., & Boyle, C. (2007). Patterns and average volume of alcohol use among women of childbearing age. *Maternal and Child Health Journal, 11,* 437–445.

Tumlin, B. (2001, July). Personal communication.

Turnbull, A., Turnbull, R., Erwin, E., & Soodak, L. (2006). *Families, professionals, and exceptionality* (5th ed.). Upper Saddle River, NJ: Pearson Education.

United Cerebral Palsy Association. (2007). *Cerebral palsy: Facts and figures.* Retrieved May 16, 2007 from http://www.ucp.org/ucp_generaldoc.cfm/1/9/37/37–37/447

U.S. Department of Education. (2007). *IDEA data.* Available at https://www.ideadata.org/PartB Report.asp

Vachha, B., & Adams, R. (2003). Language differences in young children with myelomeningocele and shunted hydrocephalus. *Pediatric Neurosurgery, 39*(4), 184–189.

Valcamonico, A., Accorsi, P., Sanzeni, C., Martelli, P., La Boria, P., & Frusca, T. (2007). Mid- and long-term outcome of extremely low birth weight (ELBW) infants: An analysis of prognostic factors. *The Journal of Maternal-Fetal and Neonatal Medicine, 20,* 465–471.

Wehman, P. (2006). *Life beyond the classroom: Transition strategies for young people with disabilities* (4th ed.). Baltimore: Paul H. Brookes.

Wilfogn, A. A. (2002). Treatment considerations: Role of vagus nerve stimulator. *Epilepsy & Behavior, 3,* S41–44.

Ylvisaker, M., Jacobs, H., & Feeney, T. (2003). Positive supports for people who experience behavioral and cognitive disability after brain injury. *Journal of Head Trauma Rehabilitation, 18,* 7–32.

Ysseldyke, J. E., & Algozzine, B. (1982). *Critical issues in special and remedial education.* Boston: Houghton Mifflin.

Chapter 14

Archambault, F., Jr., Westberg, K., Brown, S., Hallmark, B., Zhang, W., & Emmons, C. (1993). Classroom practices used with gifted third and fourth grade students. *Journal for the Education of the Gifted, 16*(2), 103–119.

Baum, S. M., Rizza, M. G., & Renzulli, S. (2006). Twice-exceptional adolescents: Who are they? What do they need? In F. A. Dixon & S. M. Moon (Eds.), *The handbook of secondary gifted education* (pp. 137–164). Waco, TX: Prufrock Press.

Blackbourn, J., Patton, J., & Trainor, A. (2004). *Exceptional individuals in focus* (7th ed.). Upper Saddle River, NJ: Pearson Education.

Burns, D. E., Purcell, J. H., & Hertberg, H. (2006). Curriculum for gifted education students. In J. H. Purcell & R. D. Eckert (Eds.), *Designing services and programs for high-ability learners* (pp. 87–111). Thousand Oaks, CA: Corwin Press.

Clark, B. (2008). *Growing up gifted: Developing the potential of children at home and at school* (7th ed.). Upper Saddle River, NJ: Pearson Education.

Clasen, D., & Clasen, R. (2003). Mentoring the gifted and talented. In N. Colangelo & G. Davis (Eds.), *Handbook of gifted education* (3rd ed., pp. 254–267). Needham Heights, MA: Allyn and Bacon.

Colangelo, N., Assouline, S. G., & Gross, M. U. A. (2004). *A nation deceived: How schools hold back America's brightest students.* Iowa City: University of Iowa.

Cote, D. (2005). *Wicked: The grimmerie.* New York: Hyperion.

Csikszentmihalyi, M., Rathunde, K., & Whalen, S. (1997). *Talented teenagers: The roots of success and failure.* Cambridge, England: Cambridge University Press.

Davis, G., & Rimm, S. (2004). *Education of the gifted and talented* (5th ed.) Boston: Allyn and Bacon.

Evans, M. (2001). *Developing and testing an innovation component configuration map for gifted education in the elementary school.* Unpublished dissertation, University of Louisville and Western Kentucky University.

Flint, L. (2001). Challenges of identifying and serving gifted children with ADHD. *Teaching Exceptional Children, 33*(4), 62–69.

Ford, D. (1998). The underrepresentation of minority students in gifted education: Problems and promises in recruitment and retention. *Journal of Special Education 32*(1), 4–14.

Ford, D., Harris, J., Tyson, C., & Trotman, M. (2002). Beyond deficit thinking: Providing access for gifted African American students. *Roeper Review, 24,* 52–58.

Frasier, M., Hunsaker, S., Lee, J., Mitchell, S., Cramond, B., Krisel, S., Garcia, J., Martin, D., Frank, E., & Finley, S. (1995). *Core attributes of giftedness: A foundation for recognizing the gifted potential of minority and economically disadvantaged students.* National Research Center on the Gifted and Talented. Storrs: University of Connecticut.

Gallagher, J. (2003). Issues and challenges in the education of gifted students. In N. Colangelo & G. Davis (Eds.), *Handbook of gifted education* (3rd ed., pp. 11–23). Boston: Allyn and Bacon.

Gallagher, J., & Gallagher, S. (1994). *Teaching the gifted child* (4th ed.). Boston: Allyn and Bacon.

Gardner, H. (1983). *Frames of mind: The theory of multiple intelligences.* New York: Basic Books.

Gardner, H. (1993). *Multiple intelligences: The theory in practice.* New York: Basic Books.

Gibson, S., & Efinger, J. (2001). Revisiting the schoolwide enrichment model: An approach to gifted programming. *Teaching Exceptional Children, 33*(4), 48–53.

Gubbins, E. J. (2006). Constructing identification procedures. In J. H. Purcell & R. D. Eckert (Eds.), *Designing services and programs for high-ability learners* (pp. 49–61). Thousand Oaks, CA: Corwin Press.

Guilford, J. (1967). *The nature of human intelligence.* New York: McGraw-Hill.

Hollingworth, L. (1926). *Gifted children: Their nature and nurture.* New York: Macmillan.

Howley, C., Howley, A., & Pendarvis, E. (1995). *Out of our minds: Anti-intellectualism and talent development for American schooling.* New York: Teachers College Press.

Karnes, F., & Riley, T. (2005). *Competitions for talented kids.* Waco, TX: Prufrock Press.

Karnes, F. A., Stephens, K. R., & McHard, E. R. (2008). Legal issues in gifted education. In F. A. Karnes & K. R. Stephens (Eds.), *Achieving excellence: Educating the gifted and talented* (pp. 18–35). Upper Saddle River, NJ: Pearson Education.

King, E. (2005). Addressing the social and emotional needs of twice-exceptional students. *Teaching Exceptional Children, 38*(1), 16–20.

Kulik, J. (2003). Grouping and tracking. In N. Colangelo & G. Davis (Eds.), *Handbook of gifted education* (3rd ed., pp. 268–281). Boston: Allyn and Bacon.

Landrum, M., Callahan, C., & Shaklee, B. (Eds.). (2001). *Aiming for excellence: Gifted program standards.* Waco, TX: Prufrock Press.

Landrum, M., & Shaklee, B. (Eds.). (1998). *Pre-K–grade 12 gifted program standards.* Washington, DC: National Association for Gifted Children.

Marland, S. (1972). *Education of the gifted and the talented: Report to the Congress of the United States by the U.S. Commissioner of Education.* Washington, DC: U.S. Government Printing Office.

MENSA. (2007). Retrieved June 12, 2007 from http://www.usmensa.org/

National Association for Gifted Children. (2007). *Frequently asked questions.* Retrieved May 17, 2007 from http://www.nagc.org/index.aspx?id=548

National Center for Education Statistics. (1998). *Pursuing excellence: A study of U.S. twelfth-grade mathematics and science achievement in international context.* Washington, DC: U.S. Department of Education.

National Commission on Excellence in Education. (1983). *A nation at risk: The imperative for school reform.* Washington, DC: U.S. Government Printing Office.

National Council of Teachers of Mathematics. (1989). *Curriculum and evaluation standards for school mathematics.* Reston, VA: Author.

National Council of Teachers of Mathematics. (2000). *Principles and standards for school mathematics.* Reston, VA: Author.

National Education Commission on Time and Learning. (1994). *Prisoners of time.* Washington, DC: U.S. Government Printing Office.

Neal, D. A., & Schanzenbach, D. W. (2007, August). *Left behind by design: Proficiency counts and test-based accountability.* NBER Working Paper No. W13293. Retrieved November 18, 2007 from http://ssrn.com/abstract=1005606

Nielsen, M., & Higgins, L. (2005). The eye of the storm: Services and programs for twice-exceptional learners. *Teaching Exceptional Children, 38*(1), 8–15.

Noble, K., Subotnik, R., & Arnold, K. (1999). To thine own self be true: A new model of female talent development. *Gifted Child Quarterly, 43,* 140–149.

Pfeiffer, S., & Jarosewich, T. (2003). *Pfeiffer-Jarosewich Gifted Rating Scales.* San Antonio, TX: Psychological Corporation.

Piirto, J. (2007). *Talented children and adults: Their development and education* (3rd ed.). Waco, TX: Prufrock Press.

Plummer, D. (1995). Serving the needs of gifted children from a multicultural perspective. In J. Genshaft, M. Birely, & C. Hollinger (Eds.), *Serving gifted and talented students* (pp. 285–300). Austin, TX: Pro-Ed.

Reis, S. M. (2006). Gender, adolescence, and giftedness. In F. A. Dixon & S. M. Moon (Eds.), *The handbook of secondary gifted education* (pp. 87–111). Waco, TX: Prufrock Press.

Reis, S. M., Gubbins, E. J., Briggs, C., Schreiber, F. J., Richards, S., Jacobs, J., et al. (2003). *Reading instruction for talented readers: Case studies documenting few opportunities for continuous progress* (Research Monograph No. 03184). Storrs: National Research Center on the Gifted and Talented, University of Connecticut.

Reis, S. M., & Renzulli, J. S. (2005). *Curriculum compacting: An easy start to differentiating for high-potential students.* Waco, TX: Prufrock Press.

Renzulli, J. (1978). What makes giftedness? Reexamining a definition. *Phi Delta Kappan, 60,* 180–184, 261.

Renzulli, J. (1998). A rising tide lifts all ships: Developing the gifts and talents of all students. *Phi Delta Kappan, 80,* 104–111.

Renzulli, J., & Reis, S. (2003). The schoolwide enrichment model: Developing creative and productive giftedness. In N. Colangelo & G. Davis (Eds.), *Handbook of gifted education* (3rd ed., pp. 184–203). Boston: Allyn and Bacon.

Rimm, S. (2002). *How Jane won.* New York: Crown.

Roberts, J., & Roberts, R. (2005). Writing units that remove the learning ceiling. In F. Karnes & S. Bean (Eds.), *Methods and materials for teaching the gifted and talented* (2nd ed., pp. 179–210). Waco, TX: Prufrock Press.

Robinson, A., Shore, B. M., & Enersen, D. L. (2007). *Best practices in gifted education.* Waco, TX: Prufrock Press.

Roid, G. (2003). *Stanford-Binet Intelligence Test—Fifth Edition.* Itasca, IL: Riverside.

Ross, P. (Ed.). (1993). *National excellence: A case for developing America's talent.* Washington, DC: U.S. Department of Education, Office of Educational Research and Improvement.

Sanders, W. L. (1998). Value-added assessment. *School Administrator, 55,* 24–27.

Silverman, L. (1995a). Gifted and talented students. In E. Meyen & T. Skrtic (Eds.), *Special education and student disability* (4th ed., pp. 379–413). Denver: Love.

Silverman, L. (1995b). Highly gifted children. In J. Genshaft, M. Bireley, & C. Hollinger (Eds.), *Serving gifted and talented students: A resource for school personnel* (pp. 217–240). Austin, TX: Pro-Ed.

Smith, T., Polloway, E., Patton, J., & Dowdy, C. (2008). *Teaching students with special needs* (5th ed.). Upper Saddle River, NJ: Pearson Education.

Smutny, J. F., Walker, S. Y., & Meckstroth, E. A. (2007). *Acceleration for gifted learners, K–5.* Thousand Oaks, CA: Corwin Press.

Steinberg, L. (1996). *Beyond the classroom: Why school reform has failed and what parents need to do.* New York: Simon & Schuster.

Sternberg, R. (1985). *Beyond IQ: A triarchic theory of intelligence.* New York: Cambridge University Press.

Subotnik, R., Kassan, L., Summers, E., & Wasser, A. (1993). *Genius revisited: High IQ children grow up.* Norwood, NJ: Ablex.

Swiatek, M. (1993). A decade of longitudinal research on academic acceleration through the study of mathematically precocious youth. *Roeper Review, 15*(3), 120–123.

Terman, L. (1925). *Mental and physical traits of a thousand gifted children: Vol. 1, Genetic studies of genius.* Stanford. CA: Stanford University Press.658

Tomlinson, C. (1994). Gifted learners: The boomerang kids of middle school? *Roeper Review, 16*(3), 177–181.

Tomlinson, C. (1999). *The differentiated classroom: Responding to the needs of all learners.* Alexandria, VA: Association for Supervision and Curriculum Development.

Torrance, E. P. (1966; 1998). *Torrance Tests of Creative Thinking: Norms and technical manual.* Bensenville, IL: Scholastic Testing Service.

Torrance, E. P. (1969). Creative positives of disadvantaged children and youth. *Gifted Child Quarterly, 13,* 71–81.

Ward, V. (1961). *Educating the gifted: An axiomatic approach.* Columbus, OH: Charles Merrill.

Wechsler, D. (2003). *Wechsler Intelligence Scale for Children—Fourth Edition.* San Antonio, TX: Psychological Corporation.

Weinfeld, R., Barnes-Robinson, L., Jeweler, S., & Shevitz, B. (2005). What we learned: Experiences in providing adaptations and accommodations for gifted and talented students with learning disabilities. *Teaching Exceptional Children, 38*(1), 48–53.

Westberg, K., Archambault, F., Jr., Dobyns, S., & Salvin, T. (1993). The classroom practices observation study. *Journal for the Education of the Gifted, 16*(2), 120–146.

Westberg, K., & Daoust, M. (2003, Fall). The results of the replication of the classroom practices survey replication in two states. *The National Research Center on the Gifted and Talented Newsletter,* pp. 3–8.

Williams, F. (1993). *Creativity Assessment Packet.* Austin, TX: Pro-Ed.

Woodcock, R., McGrew, K., & Mather, N. (2001). *Woodcock-Johnson III Tests of Achievement.* Itasca, IL: Riverside.

Wyner, J. S., Bridgeland, J. M., & Diiulio, J. J. (2007). *Achievement trap: How America is failing millions of high-achieving students from lower-income families.* Retrieved October 15, 2007 from www.jackkentcookefoundation.org/jkcf_web/home.aspx?Page=Main

Photo Credits

Photo, First Person features. © Dmitriy Shironosov.
Photo, Making Inclusion Work features. © Elena Elisseeva.
Photo, Suggestions for the Classroom features. © Getty Images.

Part I

Photo, page 1. © JupiterImages.

Chapter 1

Photo, page 2. © Michael Newman/PhotoEdit.
Photo, page 5. © Cliff Parnell.
Photo, page 10. © Bill Aron/PhotoEdit.
Cartoon, page 11. © 1996 Joel Pett, Lexington Herald-Leader. All rights reserved.
Photo, page 19. © Hulton-Deutsch Collection/Corbis.
Photo, page 23. © Robin Nelson/PhotoEdit.
Photo, page 28. © Michael Newman/PhotoEdit.
Photo, page 33. © Wendy Shiao.
Photo, page 37. © James Shaffer/PhotoEdit.

Chapter 2

Photo, page 42. © Michael Newman/PhotoEdit.
Photo, page 49. Public Domain; State of Wyoming.
Photo, page 51. © LWA-Dann Tardif/Corbis.
Photo, page 55. © Andres Balcazar.
Photo, page 58. © Ed Kashi/Corbis.
Photo, page 64. © Nottingham Toddler Lab, University of Nottingham, UK. *Preschool Language Scale–Third Edition (PLS–3)*, Copyright © 1992 by NCS Pearson, Inc. Reproduced with permission. All rights reserved. "Preschool Language Scale" and "PLS" are trademarks, in the U.S. and/or other countries, of Pearson Education, Inc. or its affiliates.
Photo, page 69. © Spencer Grant/PhotoEdit.
Photo, page 75. © Nancy Sheehan/PhotoEdit.
Photo, page 77. © Richard Hutchings/PhotoEdit.

Chapter 3

Photo, page 84. © Gabe Palmer/Corbis.
Photo, page 89. © Thinkstock.
Photo, page 90. © Bonnie Jacobs.
Photo, page 96. © Robin Sachs/PhotoEdit.
Photo, page 100. © Catherine Karnow/Corbis.
Photo, page 103. © Corbis.

Chapter 4

Photo, page 112. © Laura Dwight/PhotoEdit.
Photo, page 117. © Michael Newman/PhotoEdit.
Photo, page 119. © Tony Freeman/PhotoEdit.
Photo, page 122. © Photodisc.
Photo, page 127. © Wendy Shiao.
Photo, page 130. © Michael Newman/PhotoEdit.

Part II

Photo, page 139. © Getty Images.

Chapter 5

Photo, page 140. © Richard Hutchings/PhotoEdit.
Photo, page 149. © Jeff Greenberg/PhotoEdit.
Photo, page 160. © Richard Hutchings/PhotoEdit.
Photo, page 164. © iStockphoto.
Photo, page 167. © Bob Daemmrich/PhotoEdit.
Photo, page 172. © Robin Nelson/PhotoEdit.
Photo, page 176. © Bonnie Jacobs.
Photo, page 183. © James L. Shaffer/PhotoEdit.
Photo, page 184. © James L. Shaffer/PhotoEdit.

Chapter 6

Photo, page 194. © Tom and Dee Ann McCarthy/Corbis.
Photo, page 198. © Bonnie Jacobs.
Photo, page 205. © Lajos Repasi.
Photo, page 212. © Cliff Parnell.
Photo, page 213. © Thinkstock.
Photo, page 224. © Bonnie Jacobs.
Photo, page 230. © Aldo Murillo.

Chapter 7

Photo, page 242. © O'Brien Productions/Corbis.
Photo, page 245. © Tatiana Mironenko.
Photo, page 248. © Mary Kate Denny/PhotoEdit.
Photo, page 250. © David Young-Wolff/PhotoEdit.
Photo, page 261. © Photodisc.
Photo, page 266. © Photoscom.

Chapter 8

Photo, page 274. © Stephanie Maze/Corbis.
Photo, page 279. © Spencer Grant/PhotoEdit.
Photo, page 289. © Nathan Benn/Corbis.
Photo, page 293. © David Young-Wolff/PhotoEdit.
Photo, page 304. © Kristina Buskirk.
Photo, page 311. © Dennis MacDonald/PhotoEdit.
Photo, page 312. © Dan Eckert.
Photo, page 314. © Forest Woodward.

Chapter 9

Photo, page 324. © Robin Nelson/PhotoEdit.
Photo, page 329. © Photodisc.
Photo, page 332. © Photodisc.
Photo, page 338. © Mary Kate Denny/PhotoEdit.
Photo, page 339. © David Young-Wolff/PhotoEdit.
Photo, page 351. © James Shaffer/PhotoEdit.

Chapter 10

Photo, page 360. © Christina Kennedy/PhotoEdit.
Photo, page 373. © Photodisc.
Photo, page 378. © BrandXPictures.
Photo, page 381. © Mary Kate Denny/PhotoEdit.
Photo, page 386. © BrandXPictures.
Photo, page 389. © Bob Daemmrich/Stock, Boston, Inc.

Chapter 11

Photo, page 394. © Gabe Palmer/Corbis.
Photo, page 400. © Mark Richards/PhotoEdit.
Photo, page 403. © Robin L. Sachs/PhotoEdit.
Photo, page 405. © Richard Lord/PhotoEdit.
Photo, page 411. © Robin Sachs/PhotoEdit.
Photo, page 423. © Will Hart/PhotoEdit.
Photo, page 424. © Michael Newman/PhotoEdit.
Photo, page 431. © Tony Freeman/PhotoEdit.
Photo, page 436. © David Young-Wolff/PhotoEdit.

Chapter 12

Photo, page 446. © Tony Freeman/PhotoEdit.
Photo, page 449. © Photodisc.
Photo, page 457. © Renee Lee.
Photo, page 460. © Robin Sachs/PhotoEdit.
Photo, page 463. © Carmen MartAnez Bana.
Photo, page 466. © Robin Sachs/PhotoEdit.
Photo, page 474. © Michael Newman/PhotoEdit.
Photo, page 478. © Michael Newman/PhotoEdit.

Chapter 13

Photo, page 486. © Ariel Skelley/Corbis.
Photo, page 489. © Courtesy of Kathryn Wolff Heller.
Photo, page 503. © Bob Daemmrich/Stock, Boston, Inc.
Photo, page 517. © Bob Daemmrich/PhotoEdit.
Photo, page 527. © Bob Daemmrich/PhotoEdit.
Photo, page 531. © Courtesy of Kathryn Wolff Heller.
Photo, page 532. © Courtesy of Kathryn Wolff Heller.
Photo, page 534. © Lon C. Diehl/PhotoEdit.

Chapter 14

Photo, page 540. © Ariel Skelley/Corbis.
Photo, page 545. © Courtesy of Julia L. Roberts.
Photo, page 551. © Courtesy of Julia L. Roberts.
Photo, page 554. © Courtesy of Julia L. Roberts.
Photo, page 562. © Courtesy of Julia L. Roberts.
Photo, page 568. © Courtesy of Julia L. Roberts.
Photo, page 574. © Courtesy of Julia L. Roberts.
Photo, page 581. © Courtesy of Julia L. Roberts.

Name Index

Larsson, J., 250
Lau, M., 216
Lauder, J., 335
LaVigna, G., 334
LaVor, M., 48
Lawrence, V., 252
Lazzaretti, C., 515
Le, L., 355
Leaf, P., 257
LeBlanc, L. A., 355
LeCouteur, A., 342
Lederberg, A., 411
Lee, J., 581
Lee, P., 161, 249
Leedy, A., 291
Leerkes, E., 288
Leffert, J., 310
Lehman, A., 127
Lejune, J., 158
Leland, H., 150
Lenz, B., 213, 224
Leonard, L., 234
Leone, P. E., 277, 294
Lerner, J., 124, 197, 202–204, 208–210, 214–215, 218–219, 222, 224, 230, 232, 235, 248, 264, 268
Lerner, M., 270
Levack, N., 463
Levine, P., 231, 312
Levy, F., 250, 293
Lewis, B., 206
Lewis, C. D., 283
Lewis, R., 105, 176, 188
Lewis, S., 465
Lewis, T. J., 291
Liaupsin, C., 291, 297
Liaupsin, C. J., 297
Lichtenstein, P., 250
Light, J., 355, 388
Lin, S., 529
Lin, Y., 502
Linan-Thompson, S., 131, 224
Linden, M., 67, 69, 220
Lindman, F., 154
Lindsey, L. D., 530
Linn, R., 103, 105
Lipsky, D., 12
Liptak, G. S., 499
Little, J., 319
Little, M. A., 303, 312
Lloyd, J., 201, 204–205, 207, 210–211, 222, 231, 236, 247, 250, 252, 255, 261, 267–268
Lloyd, L., 388
Lobato, D., 126
Logan, K. R., 299
Lonergan, A., 453
Loomis, R., 35

Lopez-Reyna, N., 87
Lopez-Vasquez, A., 529
Lord, C., 342
Lovaas, I., 334, 343
Love, P., 169
Loveday, C., 501
Lovitt, T., 207
Lowenthal, B., 264
Luckasson, R., 146–147, 150, 153, 158, 165, 231
Luckner, J., 413
Luiselli, J. R., 291
Lustig, M., 86
Luterman, D., 387, 431
Lynch, E., 128, 132
Lyon, G., 209

Maag, J. W., 310
MacArthur, C., 235
Maciel, P., 335
MacMillan, D., 11, 97, 99, 145
Macmillan, D. L., 493
Maddox, J., 511, 523–525
Maddux, R., 24
Maheady, L., 277, 280
Mainzer, R., 87
Malkin, D., 96
Malmgren, K. W., 303
Malone, D., 404
Malone, M., 168
Mank, D., 183
Mann, L., 457
Marchand-Martella, N., 224
Marcus, L., 353, 356
Markey, D. J., 294, 311–312
Markey, U., 294, 311–312
Marland, S., 545
Marquis, J., 124
Marschark, M., 410–411
Marshall, K., 439
Marston, D., 216
Martella, R., 224
Martelli, P., 497
Martin, D., 581
Martin, E., 236
Martin, F., 431
Martin, G., 147
Martin, N., 250
Martin, T., 147
Martinez, E., 205, 207, 210–211, 222, 231, 236, 247, 250, 252, 255, 261, 267–268
Mason, E., 126
Mastropieri, M., 26, 29
Mastropieri, M. A., 299, 305
Mather, N., 550
Mather, S., 291
Matthews, B., 313, 318

Subject Index

Braille and, 481
cochlear implants and, 438
comparison of features with section 504, 54 (table)
definitions and, 287
emotional or behavioral disorders and, 279, 313
full inclusion movement and, 236 (box)
hearing impairment and, 406, 428
health impairments and, 506
reauthorization of, 229
speech and language impairments and, 381
traumatic brain injury and, 505
2004 amendments to, 298
visual impairments and, 454, 466, 467
Individuals with Disabilities Education Improvement Act
    of 2004, 21 (box), 57–60
Industrial School for Crippled and Deformed Children, 492
Infants, with special needs, 33–34
Infant stimulation, 180
Infections
    hearing impairments and, 409
    mental retardation and, 163–164
Infectious diseases, 509
Ingals, Mary, 448
Inner ear, 397
INSITE Developmental Checklist, 511
Institutions (special education), establishment of, 16-18
Instruction, pacing, 563
Instructional approaches
    for autism spectrum disorders, 343
    for giftedness and talent, 562–567
    for learning disabilities, 221–225
    for mental retardation, 174–180
    for physical, health, and related low-incidence disabilities,
        518–522
    for visual impairments, 467–471
Instructional content, methods of presenting, 32 (table)
Instructional cycle, effective, 305
Instructional delivery, for students with emotional or behavioral
    disorders, 304–305
Instructional materials, guidelines for selecting and evaluating,
    107 (box)
Instructional modification, for ADHD, 264–265
Instructional practices, effective
    ADHD, managing students with, 262–263 (box)
    behavioral principles, 309 (box)
    differentiated instruction, 570 (box)
    language development for hearing impaired, 425 (box)
    language skills, teaching, 385 (box)
    social stories, 345 (box)
    teaching pupils with intellectual disabilities, 177 (box)
    teaching reading, 221 (box)
    teaching students with physical of health disabilities, 522 (box)
    visual impairments and, 469 (box)
Instructional programming
    appropriate placement and, 66–67
    designing individualized, 67–71

Instructional technology, 188, 191
INTASC. See Interstate New Teacher Assessment and Support
    Consortium
Intellectual ability, 148–150
Intellectual assessment, of autism spectrum disorders,
    340–341
Intellectual disabilities. See Mental retardation
Intellectual functioning, relationship with adaptive behavior,
    144 (figure)
Intelligence, 148, 190
    of individuals with hearing impairments, 410
    normal curve distribution, 145 (figure)
    theoretical distribution of, 552 (figure)
    See also Giftedness and talent
Interdisciplinary teams, 25
Interindividual differences, 61, 80
Internalizing disorders, 282, 319
Interpersonal problem solving, 310, 320
Interpreters, for individuals with hearing impairments,
    423–424
Interpreting technology, and hearing impairments, 436
Interstate New Teacher Assessment and Support Consortium
    (INTASC), Standards for General and Special Education
    Teachers
    principle 1, 604
    principle 2, 604
    principle 3, 605
    principle 4, 605
    principle 5, 606
    principle 6, 606
    principle 7, 607
    principle 8, 607
    principle 9, 608
    principle 10, 608
Interveners, 524
Intervention(s)
    academic and instructional, 302–305
    assistance team, 62
    behavioral and cognitive-behavioral, 305–308
    early. See Early intervention
    family-centered, 315
    instructional, for hearing impairments, 420–424
    physical environment, 299–301
    strategies, ladder of, 307 (figure)
Intervention assistance team, 62
Intoxicants, and mental retardation, 163–164
Intraindividual differences, 61, 80
Iris, 450, 451 (figure), 451 (table)
Itard, Jean Marc-Gaspard, 16, 17, 18 (table)
ITP. See Individualized transition plan

Jacob K. Javits Gifted and Talented Students Education Act, 555
James, William, 284
Job coach, 183, 353, 527
Jot-down sheet, 548, 549 (figure)
JRA. See Juvenile rheumatoid arthritis

About the Contributors

Carol Allison is an Instructor in the Program for the Visually Impaired, Department of Leadership, Special Education, and Foundations, University of Alabama at Birmingham (UAB). She has a dual assignment as the Project Coordinator for the Alabama Deafblind Program and as a consultant to local and state education agencies and individual families in the field of visual impairments. She received her M.A. from UAB and completed her postgraduate certification in the area of deafblind multihandicapped. She served as an adjunct faculty member at UAB from 1979 until she became a full-time member in 1999. Ms. Allison is a native of Louisiana, where she earned her undergraduate degree and worked with children with hearing impairments and emotional disabilities. She has worked in both the public and private sectors of general and special education for the past forty years.

Ms. Allison's special interests have included the development of a statewide program with an international foundation that serves as a coordinating agency for creating and promoting arts programs for individuals with disabilities. Other areas of interest include the development and creation of distance education teacher training programs in the field of visual impairments. Ms. Allison has made professional presentations to local, state, and international conferences and has served on advisory boards for many educational and civic organizations.

Karen Bowen Dahle has a doctorate in Special Education, Administration and Supervision; a master's in clinical psychology; and a bachelor's degree in behavior disorders and autism. With over 30 years' experience in the field of autism, she is a nationally certified school psychologist and a Nationally Board Certified Counselor with an endorsement in Clinical Mental Health Counseling, and she holds equivalent state and educational licenses and certifications.

Dr. Dahle is also trained in the administration of both the ADOS-R and ADI-R, with specialized booster training in the ADOS-R. With this background, she has participated in autism clinics for more than 30 years and does independent evaluations and advocacy work on behalf of parents and schools.

Dr. Dahle is recognized for her teaching excellence at both the public school and university level and for her work as an outstanding administrator in a private facility for individuals with autism spectrum disorders where she managed more than 10 programs for students ages 3 to 21. She has published extensively and is a field editor for *Focus on Autism and Other Developmental Disabilities*.

Kathryn Wolff Heller is a Professor of Special Education at Georgia State University, where she coordinates graduate level programs in orthopedic impairments and visual impairments. She created a specialist concentration in assistive technology, as well as a doctoral level concentration in physical disabilities. She also directs several projects, including a statewide bureau that provides technical assistance to school personnel in the area of physical and health impairments and an assistive technology grant that supports two classrooms assisting teachers who work with students with physical and multiple disabilities.

Dr. Heller, a registered nurse with experience in pediatric medicine, worked for five years in intensive care units and then went on to obtain master's and doctoral degrees in special education. She has worked as a classroom teacher of students with orthopedic impairments, mental retardation, traumatic brain injury, and visual impairments. She has coauthored three books, several book chapters, and numerous articles. She chairs and participates on several advisory boards and committees, and she makes frequent presentations. One of her primary interests is in providing effective educational instruction and health care for students with physical, sensory, and health impairments.

Betty Nelson, Ph.D., a faculty member at the University of Alabama at Birmingham, has taught in and administered programs ranging from early intervention programs for infants to secondary and postsecondary education for children with disabilities. Dr. Nelson has taught in the states of Louisiana, Texas, and Alabama, and by satellite connection to other states in Web-based instructional settings. Dr. Nelson currently teaches preservice undergraduate and graduate education majors in addition to administering numerous grants. Dr. Nelson has several years of classroom and administrative experience in addition to her years of university teaching. Her experience includes working with children in all areas of disabilities and within settings in universities, public schools, private institutions, home-based instruction, and hospital-based programming. Dr. Nelson serves as a consultant to many school districts serving children with a broad range of disabilities. Dr. Nelson has authored numerous books, monographs, videotapes, and teacher training modules. She has extensive expertise in the areas of applied and assistive technologies and has presented at many state, national, and international conferences in the areas of special education and educational technology, including assistive technology.

Julia Link Roberts, Ed.D., is Mahurin Professor of Gifted Studies at Western Kentucky University. She is also Executive Director of The Center for Gifted Studies and the Carol Martin Gatton Academy of Mathematics and Science in Kentucky. She was honored in 2001 as the first recipient of the National Association for Gifted Children David W. Belin Advocacy Award. Dr. Roberts serves on the boards of the National Association for Gifted Children, the Kentucky Association for Gifted Children, and the Governor's Advisory Council for Gifted and Talented Education; and she is one of three delegates from the United States to the World Council for Gifted and Talented Children. She has published books, chapters, and journal articles and is a frequent speaker at state, national, and international meetings. As the founding director of The Center for Gifted Studies, Dr. Roberts has initiated and implemented many programs and services for children and young people who are gifted and talented, educators, and parents. She earned a B.A. at the University of Missouri and an Ed.D. at Oklahoma State University.

Mary Jean Sanspree, Ph.D., is faculty in the School of Optometry and has an appointment as a Research Professor in the School of Education, University of Alabama at Birmingham (UAB), and as an Associate Scientist in the UAB Vision Science Research Center. She has served as president of the Division on Visual Impairments, Council for Exceptional Children, is a member of the National Institute of Health National Eye Institute Public Liaison Program Committee, and is chair of the Alabama Early Intervention Interagency Coordinating Personnel Preparation Committee, among other service responsibilities. She conducts vision research concerning rural eye care and access to eye care for persons with diabetes and glaucoma.

Dr. Sanspree has trained teachers in the field of visual impairments in underdeveloped countries and has published extensively on the topics of Braille literacy, distance education, multiple disabilities, and dual sensory impairment, as well as low vision habilitation. She has been associated with the Helen Keller Art Show of Alabama and the International Helen Keller Art Show since its inception in 1984.

Lou Anne Worthington received her Ph.D. from the University of Alabama. Her bachelor's and master's degrees are from Auburn University. She has been a special educator for thirty years. Her areas of expertise include assessment, special education law, behavioral interventions, functional assessment, cultural diversity, attention deficit hyperactivity disorder, and inclusion/collaboration. Dr. Worthington has taught children and youth with emotional and behavioral disorders in a variety of settings, including both public schools and private residential facilities. She has also served in a number of administrative special education positions in private residential schools.

Dr. Worthington is currently an Associate Professor and Chair, Department of Educational Leadership, Special Education, and Foundations, University of Alabama at Birmingham. She is an educational consultant to a number of school systems. Dr. Worthington has been the recipient of several teaching and service awards. She has presented at numerous international, national, regional, state, and local conferences and workshops. Areas in which she has published include autism, attention deficit hyperactivity disorder, cultural diversity, emotional and behavioral disorders, academic and behavioral interventions, prenatal cocaine exposure, and health care plans.